Directory of British Associations

& Associations in Ireland

trade associations, scientific & learned societies, professional institutes, research associations, chambers of trade & commerce, agricultural societies, trade unions, cultural, sports, welfare, hobby & interest organisations in the United Kingdom and in the Republic of Ireland

Over **7,000** important <u>national</u> organisations giving their:

- ★ Address
- ★ Telephone, Fax No. & Email Addresses
- ★ Abbreviations
- ★ Year of formation
- ★ Secretary/Chairman
- ★ Fields of interest
- ★ Membership statistics
- ★ Publications

★ ★ ★

Subject index – **4,500** headings
Index of **9,200** abbreviations & acronyms
Index of **3,000** publications

We welcome your enquiries

CBD Research Ltd

15 Wickham Road, Beckenham, Kent, BR3 5JS
Tel: 020 8650 7745 **Fax:** 020 8650 0768
E-mail: cbd@cbdresearch.com

www.cbdresearch.com

Councils, Committees & Boards

including
Government Agencies &
Authorities

A handbook of advisory, consultative, executive, regulatory & similar bodies in British public life

Edition 14

CBD Research Ltd

15 Wickham Rd, Beckenham, Kent, BR3 5JS, England
Tel: 020 8650 7745 Fax: 020 8650 0768
E-mail: cbd@cbdresearch.com
www.cbdresearch.com

First Published	1970
Edition 14	2011
Copyright ©	2011 CBD Research Ltd
Published by	CBD Research Ltd 15 Wickham Road, Beckenham, Kent, BR3 5JS, England. Telephone: 020 8650 7745 E-mail: cbd@cbdresearch.com Fax: 020 8650 0768 Internet: www.cbdresearch.com UK Registered Company No. 700855
ISBN	9780 9554514 4 7
Price	£195.00 US$325.00

No payment is either solicited or accepted for the inclusion of entries in this publication. Every possible precaution has been taken to ensure that the information it contains is accurate at the time of going to press and the publishers cannot accept any liability for errors or omissions however caused.

CBD Research Ltd founder members of the Data Publishers Association and the European Association of Directory Publishers, and are pledged to a strict code of professional practice designed to protect against fraudulent directory publishing and dubious selling methods.

CONTENTS

	Page
Introduction	v
Abbreviations & symbols used in main directory	x
Abbreviations used in indexes	xiii
Main directory	1
Abbreviations index	447
Index of names (Chairmen & all other personnel)	459
Subject index	505

*NOTE: the explanations of abbreviations are repeated inside
the front and back covers

© CBD Research Ltd . Beckenham. BR3 5JS . Tel 020 8650 7745 . Fax 020 8650 0768 . E-mail cbd@cbdresearch.com . www.cbdresearch.com

INTRODUCTION

The object of **Councils, Committees & Boards** (CCB) is to provide information on the various organisations whose common factor is that they bring together, by invitation or appointment, a group of experts or representatives of bodies concerned with a particular subject

- to advise a Government department or public authority
- to exercise certain regulatory or investigatory functions in the public interest
- to exercise certain administrative or executive functions in the public interest
- review a particular problem or problems of public concern, and recommend action to be taken
- to coordinate certain common interests of Government departments, public agencies, trade or professional associations, or interest groups.

On 14 October 2010 the Government published "Public Bodies Reform – Proposals for Change", popularly known as the Bonfire of the Quangos. Of 901 public bodies reviewed, it proposed the abolition of 192, the merger of 118 and the retention of 380, with the remainder subject to further review. This 14th edition of CCB incorporates the consequences as known at the time of going to press, in June 2011.

CCB is arranged in four sections

- The alphabetical directory, the alphabetisation of which ignores prepositions, articles and conjunctions
- An index of the abbreviations by which organisations are also known
- An index of the chairmen, chief executives and others named in the directory entries
- A subject index of the organisations' activities and fields of interest.

Each full entry in the main section includes wherever possible

- Name of organisation and its abbreviation
- Address, telephone and fax numbers and website
  Names of officials
- E When established, by what authority and composition of membership
- R Terms of reference, objects, duties and/or mission statement
- G Geographical area of competence
- ● Activities, branch offices, departments, divisions etc not specified in the terms of reference
- ¶ Publications
- X Former name if not mentioned in establishment
- ◢ Supplementary information

CCB contains information on the following bodies

- Three types of Non-Departmental Public Bodies (an NDPB has a distinct role in the processes of government but is not itself a government department)
  - Executive NDPBs are established by statute and carry out a wide range of operational and regulatory functions, various scientific and cultural activities and some commercial or semi-commercial activities. Each employs its own staff and is allocated its own budget.
  - Advisory NDPBs are usually composed of a group of experts in a particular sphere who advise Ministers on one narrow issue. They do not usually employ staff or incur expenditure on their own account; instead costs incurred are met within their sponsoring Department's expenditure.
  - Tribunals which, as the name suggests, have a judicial or quasi-judicial function.
- Government advisory committees, either statutory or non-statutory, which are composed wholly or partly by persons from outside Government.
- Departmental committees of enquiry which are composed wholly or partly of persons from outside Government and which are either active at the date of this 14th Edition or have reported since publication of our 13th Edition in 2004.
- Public boards, public authorities and statutory corporations.

- Consumer consultative committees and councils related to public undertakings.
- Non-governmental councils, committees and other organisations which include representatives or nominees of a number of separate organisations.
- Government Agencies and executive agencies of Government, each of which is established to undertake a particular executive function of Government, as distinct from policy advice.

The area covered is the United Kingdom (England, Wales, Scotland and Northern Ireland), but also includes a number of Commonwealth committees which have a secretariat or headquarters in the UK.

CCB contains information on UK national and regional bodies and does not include local government councils. It only includes local bodies if they form part of a national group. In such cases, where a substantial amount of common information applies to a whole group, there is a general descriptive note in the main directory under the group name.

CCB excludes, in addition to local bodies,
- Joint industrial councils, wages councils and similar bodies whose function is the negotiation of wages and conditions of employment in particular industries or occupations.
- Boards of public or private companies.
- Sub-committees or working parties appointed by a superior committee or council.
- Government committees which are composed solely of officials of one or more Government departments.

CCB includes information on bodies which have ceased to exist or have been superceded by other bodies since the 13th edition was published in 2004. It also includes information on bodies set up since the 13th edition and which have already closed. These entries are included to make successive editions of CCB as complete a record as possible within its field.

Entries of this kind include
- Committees of enquiry which have produced their report or otherwise fulfilled their function and have been wound up
- Bodies which have been wound up as a result of Government policy changes or administrative changes
- Bodies whose functions have been subsumed within the functions of another body
- Bodies that were set up as NDPBs but have not met for a number of years.

United Kingdom & England

The majority of the bodies listed in CCB have a UK-wide remit and are sponsored by the departments of the UK national Government in Westminster. Since 1999 England is the only nation without a devolved administration so bodies with an England only remit continue to be sponsored by the UK Government departments

- Cabinet Office
- Business, Innovation & Skills
- Communities & Local Government
- Culture, Media & Sport
- Defence
- Education
- Energy & Climate Change
- Environment, Food & Rural Affairs
- Equalities

- Foreign & Commonwealth
- Home Office
- Health
- International Development
- Justice
- Transport
- Treasury
- Work & Pensions

Scotland

Following a referendum in September 1997, the Scottish Government was established (as the Scottish Executive) on 1 July 1999. Established at the same time was the directly elected 129-member Scottish Parliament. The Government's six directorates are

- Office of the Permanent Secretary
- Enterprise & Environment

- Finance
- Governance & Communities

- Health & Social Care
- Learning & Justice

Wales
Following a referendum in September 1997, the Welsh Government was established (as the Welsh Assembly Government) on 1 July 1999. Established at the same time was the directly elected 60-member National Assembly for Wales. The Government's seven directorates are

- Children, Education, Lifelong Learning & Skills
- Economy & Transport
- Health & Social Services
- People, Places & Corporate Services
- Public Services & Local Government Delivery
- Strategic Planning, Finance & Performance
- Sustainable Futures

The equivalent in Wales of the NDPB is the Assembly Government Sponsored Body (AGSB).

Northern Ireland
Following the Good Friday Agreement, a referendum and elections in 1998, the 108-member Northern Ireland Assembly first met on 1 July of that year and assumed its full powers upon devolution on 2 December 1999. The Assembly elects the Northern Ireland Executive. The Government's twelve departments are

- Office of the First Minister & Deputy First Minister
- Agriculture & Rural Development
- Culture, Arts & Leisure
- Education
- Employment & Learning
- Enterprise, Trade & Investment
- Environment
- Finance & Personnel
- Health, Social Services & Public Safety
- Justice
- Regional Development
- Social Development

London & the English Regions
The nine regions of England were established in 1994.

- East of England
- East Midlands
- London
- North East
- North West
- South East
- South West
- West Midlands
- Yorkshire & the Humber

Indirectly elected Regional Assemblies were established in the eight outside London in 1998. In a test referendum in 2004, the North East Region rejected the proposal of an elected assembly and the project was dropped for all eight. Their Regional Assemblies were abolished on 31 March 2010.

However, a referendum in the London Region in 1998 led to the establishment in 2010 of a directly elected Mayor of London and 25-member London Assembly, which together make up the Greater London Authority.

CCB should not, in general, be regarded as an directory of sources for information and advice. The publishers would like to emphasise that many of the bodies listed – particularly Government advisory committees – have strictly limited functions which do not include answering enquiries about their own activities or on subjects within their field of interest. Some exceptions to this warning will be obvious; bodies such as the Health & Safety Executive are necessarily involved in informational activities

CCB's publishers will be glad to consider suggestions for inclusion in future editions. Our records are kept constantly under review and we are glad to assist any enquirer seeking relevant information which is not included in this edition. In making an enquiry, users are requested to provide the fullest information already available to them.

ABBREVIATIONS & SYMBOLS in MAIN ALPHABETICAL DIRECTORY

■	indicates an entry based, in whole or in part, on information supplied by the organisation concerned
E	prefixes information on the establishment, statutory or other authority, and membership of the organisation
R	prefixes terms of reference, objects, aims, duties and/or mission statement of the organisation
G	prefixes geographical area of competence
●	activities, branch offices, departments, divisions etc not specified in the terms of reference
P	publications
X	former name if not mentioned in establishment
≛	additional notes

CBI	Confederation of British Industry
CCB	'Councils, Committees and Boards'
Cllr	Councillor
Cm } Cmd } Cmnd}	Command papers (published by HMSO)
DHSSPS	Department of Health, Social Services & Public Safety
HMSO	Her Majesty's Stationery Office (now TSO)
LEC	Local Enterprise Company
NDPB	Non-Departmental Public Body
qv	quod vide - which see
SI	Statutory Instruments
SR&O	Statutory Rules & Orders
TSO	The Stationery Office
TUC	Trades Union Congress

ABBREVIATIONS in INDEXES

Advy	Advisory	**HM**	Her Majesty
Agricl	Agricultural	**HSS**	Health & Social Services
Assn	Association		
Auth	Authority	**Ind**	Industry
Bd	Board	**Indep**	Independent
Bldg	Building	**Indl**	Industrial
Capt	Captain	**Inf**	Information
C'ee	Committee	**Intl**	International
C'wealth	Commonwealth	**Jt**	Joint
Cllr	Councillor	**Maj**	Major
Cmsn	Commission	**Med**	Medical
Cmsnr	Commissioner	**Mgt**	Management
Conf	Conference	**Nat**	National
Conslt	Consultative	**NI**	Northern Ireland
Corpn	Corporation	**NTO**	National Training Organisation
Coun	Council		
Devt	Development	**Org**	Organisation
Educ	Education	**Prof**	Professor
Educl	Educational	**Res**	Research
Engg	Engineering	**Revd**	Reverend
Envt	Environment	**Stdg**	Standing
Envtl	Environmental	**Telecoms**	Telecommunications
Eqpt	Equipment	**Trg**	Training
Exec	Executive	**UK**	United Kingdom
GB	Great Britain	**Univ**	University
Gp	Group		

1st 4 Sport Qualifications

■ Chelsea Close, off Amberley Road, Armley, LEEDS, W Yorks, LS12 4HP.
 Tel 0113 290 7610   http://www.1st4sportqualifications.com
E 1st 4 Sport is a brand of Coachwise Ltd, the trading arm of the National Coaching Foundation (known as Sports Coach UK). It is an awarding body for courses and qualifications in the active learning and leisure industry.
G United Kingdom.
✍ See also **Federation of Awarding Bodies**.

1st Tier Tribunal   See **First Tier Tribunal**.

A

ABC Awards

■ Robins Wood House, Robins Wood Road, Aspley, NOTTINGHAM, NG8 3NH.
 Tel 0115 854 1616   **Fax** 0115 854 1617   http://www.abcawards.co.uk
 Executive Director: Nigel Florence
E Established in October 1998 by the merger of the Association of South East Colleges, CENTRA, the East Midlands Further Education Council and the South West Association for Further Education & Training which together formerly comprised the Awarding Bodies Consortium. It functions as a company limited by guarantee.
R To offer a coherent set of vocationally related qualifications that reflect the skills needs of learners.
G United Kingdom.
● A national awarding body offering vocational qualifications in a wide range of subjects, including engineering, construction, health and care, and business.
 In addition to the former EMFEC offices in Nottingham the merged company retains its former offices in Chorley (CENTRA) and Taunton (SWAFET).
✍ For more information on awarding bodies see **Federation of Awarding Bodies**.

Aberdeen Airport Consultative Committee   (AACC)

■ The Sidings, Burnett Park, BANCHORY, Aberdeenshire, AB31 4AE.
 Tel 01330 824101   http://www.aberdeenairport.com
 Chairman: Dr Peter Smart   Secretary: Alison Sharp
G Aberdeen.
✍ For further information see **Airport Consultative Committees**.

Aberdeen & Grampian Tourist Board
✍ Since 1 April 2005 an area office of **VisitScotland**.

Aberdeen Harbour Board

■ Harbour Office, 16 Regent Quay, ABERDEEN, AB11 5SS.
 Tel 01224 597000   **Fax** 01224 571507   http://www.aberdeen-harbour.co.uk
 Chief Executive: Colin Parker   Board Secretary: Ian Jessiman
E Established in 1960 under the Aberdeen Harbour Order Act 1960.
G Aberdeen.
✍ For further information see **Port & Harbour Authorities**.

Abertawe Bro Morgannwg Community Health Council

■ 2nd Floor, Derwen House, Court Road, BRIDGEND, CF31 1BN.
 Tel 01656 657909   **Fax** 01656 662749
 Suite B, Britannic House, Llandarcy, NEATH, SA10 6JQ.
 Tel 01792 324201   Fax 01792 324205
 Chairman: Mrs Gillian Davies

E   Established on 1 April 2010 by the merger of three former Community Health Councils. The full council comprises 36 volunteer members drawn from the three local committees (Bridgend, Neath Port Talbot and Swansea).
G   Bridgend, Neath Port Talbot, Swansea.
✍   For further information see **Community Health Councils** under **National Health Service - Wales**.

Abertawe Bro Morgannwg University Health Board   (ABM)

■   One Talbot Gateway, Baglan Energy Park, Baglan, PORT TALBOT, SA12 7BR.
     Tel 01639 683670   **Fax** 01639 687676
     Chairman: Mr Win Griffiths   Chief Executive: David Sissling
E   Established on 1 October 2009 by the merger of three former Local Health Boards (Bridgend, Neath Port Talbot and Swansea) and the Abertawe Bro Morgannwg University NHS Trust. The Board comprises eleven members including the Chairman.
G   Bridgend, Neath Port Talbot, Swansea.
✍   For further information see **NHS Wales - Local Health Boards**.
     Abertawe Bro Morgannwg University Health Board is the operational name of the Abebrtawe Bro Morgannwg University Local Health Board.

Accountancy & Actuarial Discipline Board   (AADB)

■   5th Floor, Aldwych House, 71-91 Aldwych, LONDON, WC2B 4HN.
     Tel 020 7492 2451   **Fax** 020 7492 2459   http://www.frc.org.uk/aadb
     Chairman: Timothy Walker
E   Established in 2002 as the Accountancy Investigation & Discipline Board, adopting its current name on 16 August 2007. AADB is part of the Financial Reporting Council (qv). The Board comprises eight members including the Chairman.
R   To safeguard the public interest by maintaining and enhancing the standards of conduct of members and member firms of the accountancy and actuarial professions.
G   United Kingdom.

Accountancy Investigation & Discipline Board
✍   Since 16 August 2007: **Accountancy & Actuarial Discipline Board**.

Accountant in Bankruptcy   (AiB)

■   1 Pennyburn Road, KILWINNING, Ayrshire, KA13 6SA.
     Tel 030 0200 2600   **Fax** 030 0200 2601   http://www.aib.gov.uk
     Chief Executive & Accountant in Bankruptcy: Rosemary Winter-Scott
E   Established in 1856, AiB derives its current authority from the Bankruptcy (Scotland) Act 1985 and the Bankruptcy (Scotland) Act 1993. AiB functions as an Executive Agency of the Scottish Executive Justice Department.
R   To generally supervise the process of sequestration in Scotland and to ensure that those involved in that process, principally trustees and commissioners, properly carry out their responsibilities, and to take appropriate action when they fail to do so.
     To maintain a public register of sequestrations, protected trust deeds and company insolvencies.
     To undertake the functions of commissioners in sequestrations where none may be, or are, elected.
     To act as interim and permanent trustees in sequestrations where no insolvency practitioner is appointed or elected to do so.
     To administer the Government's policies in respect of personal insolvency in Scotland and to monitor the implementation of these policies.
G   Scotland.
●   AiB maintains a register of all sequestrations awarded in the Scottish Courts and of protected trust deeds.

Accounting Standards Board   (ASB)

■   5th Floor, Aldwych House, 71-91 Aldwych, LONDON, WC2B 4HN.
     Tel 020 7492 2300   **Fax** 020 7492 2301   http://www.frc.org.uk/asb
     Chairman: Ian Mackintosh
E   Established on 1 August 1990, its authority derives from the Accounting Standards (Prescribed Body) Regulations SI 1990/1667. ASB is part of the Financial Reporting Council (qv). The Board comprises ten members including the Chairman.
R   To develop principles to guide the FRC in establishing standards and to provide a framework within which others can exercise judgement in resolving accounting issues.
     To issue new accounting standards, or amend existing ones, in response to evolving business practices, new economic developments and deficiencies being identified in current practice.
G   United Kingdom.

Accounts Commission

■ 110 George Street, EDINBURGH, EH2 4LH.
  Tel 0845 146 1010 **Fax** 0845 146 1009 http://www.audit-scotland.org.uk/about/ac/
  Chairman: Prof John Baillie

E Established 1 April 1975 under the Local Government (Scotland) Act 1973 as the Commission for Local Authority Accounts in Scotland. It is part of Audit Scotland (qv) and functions as an Executive NDPB of the Scottish Executive Finance & Central Services Department. The Commission comprises eleven members including the Chairman.

R To secure the audit of all local authorities, police and fire and rescue joint boards and similar public bodies.
  To report and make recommendations to Scottish Ministers and to the audited bodies.
  To hold hearings and apply sanctions to councillors and officers, where appropriate.

G Scotland.

Action of Churches Together in Scotland   (ACTS)

■ Inglewood House, ALLOA, Clackmannanshire, FK10 2HU.
  Tel 01259 216980 **Fax** 01259 215964 http://www.acts-scotland.org
  Convenor: Rt Revd Philip Kerr   General Secretary: Br Stephen Smyth

E Established in 1990 by agreement. ACTS functions as Scotland's national ecumenical instrument bringing together nine denominations in Scotland.

R To enable the Scottish churches in their common life through encouraging encounters between them in which each participant learns from the other, where difference is explored and respected and where division is healed.

G Scotland.

Action with Communities in Cumbria   (ACT)

■ The Old Stables, Redhills, PENRITH, Cumbria, CA11 0DT.
  Tel 01768 840827 **Fax** 01768 242134 http://www.cumbriaaction.org.uk
  Chief Executive: Roger Roberts

E Established in 1947. ACT functions as a registered charity and company limited by guarantee.

R To work with the people and communities of Cumbria to realise their potential.

G Cumbria.

✍ ACT is one of the 38 Rural Community Councils, represented at the national level by **Action with Communities in Rural England** (qv) and at the regional level by North West Rural Community Councils.

Action with Communities in Rural England   (ACRE)

■ Somerford Court, Somerford Road, CIRENCESTER, Glos, GL7 1TW.
  Tel 01285 653477 **Fax** 01285 654537 http://www.acre.org.uk
  Chairman: Sue Shaw   Chief Executive: Sylvia Brown, OBE

E Established in 1987. ACRE functions as a registered charity and company limited by guarantee. The Board comprises 16 Trustees including the Chairman and a representative from each of the eight Rural Community Action Network (RCAN) regions.

R To be the national umbrella body of the RCAN which operates at national, regional and local level in support of rural communities across the country.

G England.

● The Rural Community Action Network (RCAN) of 38 Rural Community Councils (RCCs) is organised into eight regions:
  North East Rural Community Councils
  North West Rural Community Councils
  Rural Action East
  Rural Community Action East Midlands
  South East Rural Community Councils
  SWAN - the South West ACRE Network
  West Midlands Rural Community Action Network, and
  Yorkshire & the Humber Rural Community Action Network.
  See those entries for a list of the RCCs in each.

Action with Communities in Rural Kent

■ The Old Granary, Penstock Hall Farm, Canterbury Road, EAST BRABOURNE, Kent, TN25 3LL.
  Tel 01303 813790 **Fax** 01303 814203 http://www.ruralkent.org.uk

E Action with Communities in Rural Kent, formerly known as Kent Rural Communities Council, functions as a registered charity and company limited by guarantee.

R To provide direct advice and support to community organisations.
  To stimulate community action, particularly voluntaty action, and encourage good practice.
  To develop and manage demonstration projects.

To provide professional support and advice to key service providers.
To raise awareness of rural issues and influence decision makers.

G   Kent.

✍   Action with Communities in Rural Kent is one of the 38 Rural Community Councils, represented at the national level by **Action with Communities in Rural England** (qv) and at the regional level by South East Rural Community Councils.

Action in rural Sussex

■   Sussex House, 212 High Street, LEWES, E Sussex, BN7 2NH.
     Tel 01273 473422   **Fax** 01273 485109   http://www.ruralsussex.org.uk
     Chairman: Patrick Shanahan   Chief Executive: Jeremy Leggett

E   Established in 1931 as Sussex Rural Community Council. It functions as a registered charity and company limited by guarantee. The board comprises 13 Trustees including the Chairman.

R   To provide practical help and support to villages in Sussex enabling them to be vibrant living and working places.
To identify needs and issues in rural Sussex and champion their needs with policy and decision makers, helping to ensure that there is a rural voice for Sussex.

G   East and West Sussex.

✍   Action in rural Sussex is one of the 38 Rural Community Councils, represented at the national level by **Action with Communities in Rural England** (qv) and at the regional level by South East Rural Community Councils.

Actis Capital LLP

■   2 More London Riverside, LONDON, SE1 2JT.
     Tel 020 7234 5000   **Fax** 020 7234 5010   http://www.act.is
     Chairman: Peter Smitham   Shareholder Executive contact: Mark Russell

E   Established in 2008. Actis Capital functions as a public-private partnership of the Department for International Development. The Supervisory Board comprises six members including the Chairman.

R   To promote the sustainable growth of the private sector in the emerging markets and to ensure that the capital raised and managed makes a lasting, tangible and profitable difference in the countries invested.

G   United Kingdom.

✍   One of the businesses managed by the **Shareholder Executive**.

Additional Support Needs Tribunals for Scotland   (ASNTS)

■   5th Floor, Highlander House, 58 Waterloo Street, GLASGOW, G2 7DA.
     Tel 0141 305 4116   http://www.asntscotland.gov.uk
     Chairman: Jessica Burns

E   Established on 14 November 2005 following commencement of the Education (Additional Support for Learning) (Scotland) Act 2004. ASNTS functions as a Tribunal NDPB of the Scottish Executive Education Department. The board comprises nine convenors including the Chairman, and 22 members.

R   To adjudicate where parents and the local education authority cannot agree on certain matters related to coordinated support plans.

G   Scotland.

Additives & Authenticity Methodology Working Group   (AAMWG)

■   Aviation House, 125 Kingsway, LONDON, WC2B 6NH.
     Tel 020 7276 8000   **Fax** 020 7276 8004

E   AAMWG functions as an advisory committee of the Food Standards Agency (qv). The Group comprises nine members.

R   To assess methods of analysis to be used to detect adulteration and misdescription of foods.

G   United Kingdom.

Adjudicator to HM Land Registry   (AHMLR)

■   7th Floor, Victory House, 34 Kingsway, LONDON, WC2B 6EX.
     Tel 020 3077 5800   **Fax** 020 3077 5836
     Adjudicator: Edward Cousins   Tribunal Manager: Gurvir Kaur

E   Established under the Land Registration Act 2002.

R   To help people who have a land registry dispute or who specialise in land registration issues.

G   England, Wales.

✍   Administrative support is provided by HM Courts & Tribunals Service (qv).

The Adjudicator's Office

■ 8th Floor, Euston Tower, 286 Euston Road, LONDON, NW1 3US.
Tel 0300 057 1111   Fax 0300 057 1212   http://www.adjudicatorsoffice.gov.uk
Adjudicator: Judy Clements, OBE

E Established on 5 May 1993 by the Inland Revenue, following an announcement by the then Chancellor of the Exchequer at the Citizen's Charter Conference in February 1993. The Organisation is governed by the Adjudicator's role and remit.

R To act as a fair and unbiased referee looking into complaints about HM Revenue & Customs, the Insolvency Service, the Public Guardianship Office, Office, the Tax Credit Office and the Valuation Office Agency (qqv).

G United Kingdom.

✍ The Adjudicator does not look at issues of:- law, tax liability, Government policy, complaints that have already been investigated by the Parliamentary Ombudsman, nor appeals against decisions made by the Secretary of State for Social Security about National Insurance liabilities.

Administration Estimate Audit Committee   See **United Kingdom Parliament: Committees**.

Administration of Radioactive Substances Advisory Committee   (ARSAC)

■ Radiation Protection Division, Health Protection Agency, Chilton, DIDCOT, Oxon, OX11 0RQ.
Tel 01235 822772   Fax 01235 834925   http://www.arsac.org.uk
Chairman: Dr John Rees

E Set up in January 1979 under provisions of the Medicines (Administration of Radioactive Substances) Regulations 1978. ARSAC functions as a Scientific Advisory Committee of the Department of Health. The Committee's members are nominated by professional bodies and UK Health Departments and appointed by the UK Health Ministers.

R To advise the UK Health Ministers on the granting of certificates to medical and dental practitioners wishing to administer radioactive medicinal products for diagnostic, therapeutic or research purposes.
In addition ARSAC acts as a source of informal advice to practitioners on the use of ionising radiation in clinical medicine and research.

G United Kingdom.

● ARSAC gives informal advice to practitioners on the use of ionising radiation in clinical medicine & research.

✍ For further information see **Scientific Advisory Committees**.

Administrative Justice & Tribunals Council   (AJTC)

■ 81 Chancery Lane, LONDON, WC2A 1BQ.
Tel 020 7855 5200   Fax 020 7855 5201   http://www.justice.gov.uk/ajtc/
George House, 126 George Street, EDINBURGH, EH2 4HH.
Tel 0131 271 4300   Fax 0131 271 4309
Chairman: Richard Thomas, CBE, LLD   Chairman of Welsh Committee: Prof Sir Adrian Webb   Chairman of Scottish Committee: Richard Henderson

E Established in 2007 under the Tribunals, Courts & Enforcement Act 2007, and formerly known as the Council on Tribunals. AJTC functions as an Advisory NDPB of the Ministry of Justice.

R To keep under review the administrative justice system as a whole with a view to making it accessible, fair and efficient.
To ensure that the relationships between the courts, tribunals, ombudsmen and alternative resolution providers satisfactorily reflect the needs of users.

G England, Scotland, Wales.

✍ The Council's Scottish Committee sits in Edinburgh.
AJTC and its functions are to be abolished on 31 December 2011.

Advantage West Midlands   (AWM)

■ 3 Priestley Wharf, Holt Street, Aston Science Park, BIRMINGHAM, B7 4BN.
Tel 0121 380 3500   Fax 0121 380 3501   http://www.advantagewm.co.uk
Chairman: Sir Roy McNulty, CBE   Chief Executive: Mick Laverty

E Established on 1 April 1999, one of the nine English Regional Development Agencies. AWM functions as an Executive NDPB of the Department for Business, Innovation & Skills. The board comprises 15 members including the Chairman.

G Herefordshire, Shropshire, Staffordshire, Warwickshire, West Midlands (Birmingham, Coventry, Dudley, Sandwell, Solihull, Walsall, Wolverhampton), Worcestershire.

● AWM, with strategic responsibility for tourism in the region, established Tourism West Midlands (qv) to deliver tourism policy, intelligence, marketing and communications.

✍ The Comprehensive Spending Review in October 2010 confirmed the Government's intention to abolish the RDAs and support the creation of Local Enterprise Partnerships (qv), to be in place by March 2012.

Adventure Activities Licensing Authority   (AALA)

■   44 Lambourne Crescent, Cardiff Business Park, Llanishen, CARDIFF, CF14 5GG.
    Tel 029 2075 5715   http://www.aala.org.uk
    Chief Executive: John Walsh-Heron
E   Established in 1996 under the Activity Centres Licensing Regulations. On 1 April 2007 it became an agency of the
     Health & Safety Executive (qv).
R   To inspect the safety management systems of those who provide certain adventure activities to young people
     under the age of 18 years and, where appropriate, issue a licence.
G   England, Scotland, Wales.
✍   In his report published on 15 October 2010, Lord Young of Graffham recommended that AALA be abolished and
     the statutory licensing regime be replaced by a code of practice.

Advertising Standards Authority   (ASA)

■   Mid City Place, 71 High Holborn, LONDON, WC1V 6QT.
    Tel 020 7492 2222   Fax 020 7492 3696   http://www.asa.org.uk
    Chairman: Lord Smith of Finsbury   Chief Executive: Guy Parker
E   Established in 1962 by the advertising industry. The Authority functions as an independent body, funded by a levy
     of 0.1% on display advertising and airtime and 0.2% on Royal Mail Mailsort contracts. The levies are collected
     by Asbof and Basbof (qqv). The Authority's council comprises 16 members including the Chairman.
R   To apply the advertising codes and uphold standards in all media by being a customer focussed, best practice
     regulator, where expertise is valued and shared.
G   United Kingdom.
●   The ASA is assisted in its work by the Committee of Advertising Practice [Broadcast & Non-Broadcast] (qv).
    It deals with complaints received direct from the public & industry on all aspects of advertising.
    The ASA's main sanction is the recommendation to media that such advertisements as it considers to be in
     breach of the Code should not be published.
    Regular reports are issued on the results of investigations, naming the companies involved, and regular
     monitoring is carried out on various categories of advertisements.
✍   Since November 2004 regulation of broadcast advertising has been delegated by Ofcom (qv) to Advertising
     Standards Authority (Broadcast) Ltd (ASAB).

Advertising Standards Board of Finance Ltd   (Asbof)

■   5th Floor, 21 Berners Street, LONDON, W1T 3LP.
    Tel 020 7580 7071   http://www.asbof.co.uk
    Chairman: Sir Chris Powell   Secretary: Stephen Hemsted
E   Established in January 1975. Asbof is an independent body set up by the main organisations involved in
     advertising. The Board consists of one representative from each of its 15 member bodies.
R   To operate a levy scheme in order to raise funding for the running of the Advertising Standards Authority (qv),
     thus assuring its operational independence.
G   United Kingdom.
●   Under the scheme advertisers pay a levy on display advertising, in the press, magazines, cinema, outdoor and,
     since August 2004, internet advertising.
    Since 1992 Asbof has also collected the Mailing Standards levy.
✍   See also **Basbof**.

Advisory Board on Naturalisation & Integration

✍   Established in November 2004, ABNI produced its final report in November 2008.

Advisory Board for Redundant Churches

✍   On 11 June 2008, with the Council for the Care of Churches, became the **Churches Building Council**.

Advisory Board on the Registration of Homoeopathic Products

✍   ABRH was an Advisory NDPB of MHRA, the Medicine & Healthcare Regulatory Agency (qv). On 14 October 2010
     the Government announced that it would be reconstituted as a committee of experts of MHRA.

Advisory Board on Restricted Patients

✍   ABRP ceased to function with effect from 16 September 2003.

© CBD Research Ltd · Beckenham · Kent BR3 5JS · Tel 020 8650 7745 · Fax 020 8650 0768 · E-mail cbd@cbdresearch.com · www.cbdresearch.com

Advisory Body for the Delivery of Official Controls
■   Aviation House, 125 Kingsway, LONDON, WC2B 6NH.
      Tel 020 7276 8000
      Chairman: Prof Patrick Wall
E   Established in December 2007 in response to the Tierney Review for the Delivery of Official Controls in Approved Meat Premises. It functions as an advisory committee of the Food Standards Agency (qv). The Committee consists of a Chairman and 16 members.
R   To involve those being regulated in decisions about how regulations are to be designed and implemented.
G   United Kingdom.

Advisory Committee on Advertising
✍   ACA was replaced in January 2008 by the Government Strategic Marketing Advisory Board (GSMAB) which was abolished in 2010.

Advisory Committee on Animal Feedingstuffs   (ACAF)
■   Room 3C, Aviation House, 125 Kingsway, LONDON, WC2B 6NH.
      Tel 020 7276 8468   Fax 020 7276 8910   http://www.acaf.food.gov.uk
      Chairman: Dr Ian Brown
E   Established in June 1999. ACAF functions as Scientific Advisory Committee and an Advisory NDPB of the Food Standards Agency (qv). The Committee consists of a Chairman and 13 members from various backgrounds including consumer affairs, farming, the feed industry and science.
R   To advise on the safety and use of animal feed in relation to human health.
G   United Kingdom.
✍   For further information see **Scientific Advisory Committees**.

Advisory Committee on Antimicrobial Resistance & Healthcare Associated Infection   (ARHAI)
■   Expert Advice Support Office, 61 Colindale Avenue, LONDON, NW9 5DF.
      Chairman: Prof Roger Finch
E   Established in April 2007, replacing the former Specialist Advisory Committee on Microbial Resistance. ARHAI functions as a Scientific Advisory Committee and an Advisory NDPB of the Department of Health. The committee comprises the Chairman and 15 members.
R   To provide practical and scientific advice to the Government on strategies to minimise the incidence of healthcare associated infections and to maintain the effectiveness of antimicrobial agents in the treatment and prevention of microbial infections in man and animals.
G   United Kingdom.
✍   On 14 October 2010 the Government announced that ARHAI would cease to function as a NDPB and be reconstituted as a committee of experts of the Department of Health and the new Public Health Service.

Advisory Committee on Borderline Substances   (ACBS)
■   80 Lightfoot Street, CHESTER, CH2 3AD.
      Chairman: Dr Ian R White
E   Established in 1971 by the Secretary of State for Health. ACBS functions as a Scientific Advisory Committee and an Advisory NDPB of the Department of Health. The Committee comprises eight persons including the Chairman.
R   To advise approved prescribers. Borderline substances are mainly foodstuffs, such as enteral feeds and foods that are specially formulated for people with medical conditions, but also include some toiletries, such as sun blocks for use by people with conditions such as photodermatosis.
G   United Kingdom.
✍   On 14 October 2010 the Government announced that ACBS would cease to function as a NDPB and be reconstituted as a committee of experts of the Department of Health and the new Public Health Service.

Advisory Committee on Business Appointments   (ACoBA)
■   3rd Floor, 35 Great Smith Street, LONDON, SW1P 3BQ.
      Tel 020 7276 2622   Fax 020 7276 2607   http://www.acoba.gov.uk
      Chairman: Lord Lang of Monkton, DL
E   Established by the Prime Minister in July 1975, following an announcement by him in a written answer to a Parliamentary question on 3 July 1975. The AcoBA functions as an Advisory NDPB of the Cabinet Office. The Committee comprises seven members including the Chairman.
R   To provide advice to the Prime Minister, the Foreign Secretary, or other Ministers if required, on applications from the most senior Crown servants who wish to take up outside appointments after they leave Crown service.
G   United Kingdom.

Advisory Committee on Business & the Environment
✍ No longer in existence.

Advisory Committee on Carbon Abatement Technologies
✍ Established in 2007 in response to the Government's report on the Energy Review, 'The Energy Challenge', which was released on 11 July 2006. ACCAT was abolished in July 2010.

Advisory Committee on Civil Costs
■ Post Point 4/19, 102 Petty France, LONDON, SW1H 9AJ.
   Chairman: Prof Stephen Nickell
E Established in 2007. The Committee functions as an Advisory NDPB of the Ministry of Justice.
R To provide independent advice on costs in civil claims.

Advisory Committee on Clinical Excellence Awards   (ACCEA)
■ Area 6A, Skipton House, 80 London Road, LONDON, SE1 6LH.
   Tel 020 7972 1448   **Fax** 020 7972 5390   http://www.dh.gov.uk/ab/ACCEA/
   Chairman: Prof Jonathan Montgomery   Secretary: Mrs Mary Holt
E Established in 1948 by minute of the then Minister of Health and known as the Advisory Committee on Distinction Awards until it changed to its current name in 2003. The ACCEA functions as an Advisory NDPB of the Department of Health. The Committee has 15 members including the Chairman.
R To advise the English and Welsh Health Departments as to which consultants and community physicians engaged in the National Health Service should receive awards for distinction or meritorious service.
G England, Wales.

Advisory Committee on Conscientious Objectors   (ACCO)
■ 07/C/19, MOD Main Building, Whitehall, LONDON, SW1A 2HB.
   Tel 020 7218 1231   **Fax** 020 7218 0844
   Vice Chairman: His Honour Judge Lawrence
E Established in December 1970 by administrative action. ACCO functions as an Advisory NDPB of the Ministry of Defence. The Committee consists of a legally qualified chairman and vice-chairman and four lay members. When the Committee is required to meet it must consist of the chairman or vice chairman and two of the lay members. The Committee was last required in July 1996.
R To provide advice on appeals by officers and other ranks of the Armed Forces whose applications for permission to retire or resign their commissions or for discharge, on grounds of conscience, have been refused by the Service authorities.
G United Kingdom.
● The Committee also interviews reservists of the Armed Forces who claim conscientious objection to their recall for full-time service and to express opinions regarding their claims.

Advisory Committee on Consumer Products & the Environment
✍ DEFRA run committee, disbanded in 2005.

Advisory Committee on Dangerous Pathogens   (ACDP)
■ Health Protection Agency, 61 Colindale Avenue, LONDON, NW9 5EQ.
   Tel 020 8327 7946   **Fax** 020 8327 6007
   Chairman: Prof George E Griffin
E Established in June 1981. ACDP functions as a Scientific Advisory Committee and an Advisory NDPB of the Department of Health. The Committee comprises the Chairman and up to 17 members.
R To advise the Health & Safety Executive (qv) and Health and Agriculture Ministers on all aspects of hazards and risks to workers and others from exposure to pathogens.
G United Kingdom.
✍ On 14 October 2010 the Government announced that ACDP would cease to function as a NDPB and be reconstituted as a committee of experts of the Department of Health and the new Public Health Service.

Advisory Committee on Dangerous Substances
✍ ACDS and its five subcommittees (Explosives, Flammable Substances, Gas, Major Hazards and Petroleum) closed in 2004.

Advisory Committee on Distinction Awards
✍ Since 2003 **Advisory Committee on Clinical Excellence Awards**.

Advisory Committee for England
■ Ofcom, Riverside House, 2A Southwark Bridge Road, LONDON, SE1 9HA.
   Tel 020 7783 4078
   Chairman: Prof William Dutton, PhD
E Established under the Communications Act 2003. The Committee functions as an Advisory NDPB of the Office of Communications (qv). The Committee consists of nine members including the Chairman.
R To advise Ofcom about the interests and opinions, in relation to communications matters, of persons living in England.
G England.
✍ For further information see **Advisory Committees for the Nations**.

Advisory Committee on Farm Plastics
✍ ACFP was established in 2006 as a subcommittee of the Advisory Committee on Packaging (ACP). On 14 October 2010 the Government announced that ACP was to be abolished as a NDPB and reconstituted as a panel of experts.

Advisory Committee on Genetic Modification   See **Scientific Advisory Committee on Genetically Organised Organisms (Contained Use)**.

Advisory Committee on the Government Art Collection   (GAC)
■ 2-4 Cockspur Street, LONDON, SW1Y 5DH.
   Tel 020 7211 9120   http://www.gac.culture.gov.uk
   Chairman: Julia Somerville
E Established in 1937 and known as the Advisory Committee on the Purchase of Works of Art, it was reconstituted in 1956. The Committee functions as an Advisory NDPB of the Department for Culture, Media & Sport. The GAC comprises ten members including the Chairman.
R To select and place works of art in Government buildings in the UK and abroad.
   To be responsible for the maintenance and care of works of art in the Collection.
   To develop the Collection through a programme of acquisition and research.
   To lend works of art to public exhibitions.
G United Kingdom.
✍ The Government announced on 14 October 2010 that GAC would be reconstituted as a committee of experts.

Advisory Committee on Hazardous Substances   (ACHS)
■ Area 2A, Nobel House, 17 Smith Square, LONDON, SW1P 3JR.
   Tel 020 7238 5400
   Chairman: Prof Stephen Holgate
E Established on 25 July 1991 under the Environmental Protection Act 1990. The ACHS functions as a Scientific Advisory Committee and an Advisory NDPB of the Department for Environment, Food & Rural Affairs. The Committee currently comprises 13 members including the Chairman.
R To provide expert advice on the science behind hazardous chemicals and the successful risk management of chemicals.
G United Kingdom.
✍ For further information see **Scientific Advisory Committees**.
   The Government announced on 14 October 2010 that ACHS would cease to function as a NDPB and be reconsitituted as a committee of experts.

Advisory Committee on Historic Wreck Sites   (ACHWS)
■ English Heritage, Fort Cumberland, Eastney, SOUTHSEA, Hants, PO4 9LD.
   Tel 023 9285 6735   **Fax** 023 9285 6701
   Chairman: Tom Hassall, OBE
E Established in July 1973 under the Protection of Wrecks Act 1973, it now derives its authority under the National Heritage Act 2002. It functions as an Advisory NDPB of the Department for Culture, Media & Sport.
   Responsibility for the administration of the ACHWS rests with English Heritage (qv). The Committee comprises 13 members including the Chairman.
R To advise the Secretary of State on the designation of sites for protection under the 1973 Act and the licensing of survey & excavation work on those sites.

G   United Kingdom.

✍   On 14 October 2010 the Government announced that the Committee would be abolished and its functions in relation to England transferred to English Heritage.

Advisory Committee on Mathematics Education   (ACME)

■   6-9 Carlton House Terrace, LONDON, SW1Y 5AG.
Tel 020 74511 2571   Fax 020 7451 2693   http://www.acme-uk.org
Chairman: Dame Julia Higgins, FRS

E   Established in January 2002 by the Royal Society and the Joint Mathematical Council of the UK (qv). ACME operates as an independent committee operating under the auspices of the Royal Society. The Committee comprises eight members including the Chairman.

R   To influence Government strategy and policies with a view to improving the outcomes of mathematics teaching and learning and so secure a mathematically enabled population.

G   England.

Advisory Committee on the Microbiological Safety of Blood, Tissues & Organs for Transplantation

✍   MSBTO, established in January 2001, held its last meeting in June 2007.

Advisory Committee on the Microbiological Safety of Food   (ACMSF)

■   Third Floor, Aviation House, 125 Kingsway, LONDON, WC2B 6NH.
Tel 020 7276 8947   http://www.acmsf.food.gov.uk
Chairman: Prof Sarah O'Brien

E   Established in 1990, the Committee now operates under the Food Standards Act 1999. The ACMSF functions as a Scientific Advisory Committee and an Advisory NDPB of the Food Standards Agency (qv). Its members are drawn from the microbiological, medical & veterinary professions and currently number 17 including the Chairman.

R   To assess the risk to humans of micro-organisms which are used or occur in or on food.
To advise the Food Standards Agency on any matters relating to the microbiological safety of food.

G   United Kingdom.

✍   For further information see **Scientific Advisory Committees**.

Advisory Committee on National Historic Ships   (ACNHS)

■   Park Row, Greenwich, LONDON, SE10 9NF.
Tel 020 8312 6574   Fax 020 8312 6632   http://www.nationalhistoricships.org
Head of National Historic Ships: Martyn Heighton

E   Established in 2006 as a successor to the National Historic Ships Register. ACNHS functions as an Advisory NDPB of the Department for Culture, Media & Sport. The Committee comprises eight members including the Chairman.

R   To advise Government on policy and funding priorities for historic ships.
To co-ordinate work within the sector to assist those directly engaged in preservation.
To maintain and develop the National Register of Historic Vessels and to develop and monitor an 'At Risk' register.

G   United Kingdom.

✍   On 20 February 2011, it was announced that ACNHS, though to be declassified as an NDPB, will continue in a new form.

Advisory Committee for Northern Ireland

■   Ofcom, 2nd Floor, Landmark House, Cromac Quay, Ormeau Road, BELFAST, BT7 2JD.
Tel 028 9041 7500   Fax 028 9071 7533
Chairman: Prof Wallace Ewart

E   Established under the Communications Act 2003. The Committee functions as an Advisory NDPB of the Office of Communications (qv).
The Committee consists of ten members including the Chairman.

R   To advise Ofcom about the interests and opinions, in relation to communications matters, of persons living in Northern Ireland.

✍   For further information see **Advisory Committees for the Nations**.

Advisory Committee on Novel Foods & Processes   (ACNFP)

■   Room 515b, Aviation House, 125 Kingsway, LONDON, WC2B 6NH.
Tel 020 7276 8595   Fax 020 7276 8564   http://www.acnfp.gov.uk
Chairman: Prof Peter Gregory

E   Established in October 1988 by ministers at the Department of Health and the Ministry of Agriculture, Fisheries & Food. The ACNFP now functions as a Scientific Advisory Committee and an Advisory NDPB of the Food Standards Agency (qv). The Committee comprises the Chairman and 14 members.
R   To advise the agency on matters relating to novel foods (including genetically modified foods) and novel food processes (including food irradiation).
G   United Kingdom.
●   The ACNFP evaluates applications for approval of novel foods under the EC Novel Food Regulations (258/97); it can also consider generic issues arising from individual applications.
✍   For further information see **Scientific Advisory Committees**.

Advisory Committee on Older & Disabled People   (ACOD)
■   Ofcom, Riverside House, 2A Southwark Bridge Road, LONDON, SE1 9HA.
     Tel 020 7981 3590
     Chairman: Jo Connell
E   Established under the Communications Act 2003. The Committee functions as an Advisory NDPB of the Office of Communications (qv). The Committee comprises the Chairman and ten members.
R   To represent within Ofcom the interests of older and disabled people on broadcasting, telecommunications and spectrum issues.
     To ensure that Ofcom's policies and practices take into consideration views expressed by older and disabled citizens and consumers.
G   United Kingdom.

Advisory Committee on Organic Standards
✍   ACOS was established in 2003, successor to the UK Register of Organic Food Standards. The Government announced on 14 October 2010 that the body will be abolished, as Defra is now the competent authority managing organic control bodies.

Advisory Committee on Packaging   (ACP)
■   Area 6/D, Ergon House, 17 Smith Square, LONDON, SW1P 3JR.
     Tel 020 7238 5878
     Chairman: Robert Lisney, OBE
E   Founded in 1998 under the Producer Responsibility Obligations (Packaging Waste) Regulations which came into force in March 1997. ACP functions as an Advisory NDPB of the Department for Environment, Food & Rural Affairs. The Committee comprises ten members including the Chairman.
R   To advise the Government on how to achieve its ambitions outlined in the UK's Packaging Strategy, entitled 'Making the Most of Packaging'.
G   United Kingdom.
✍   The Government announced on 14 October 2010 that ACP would cease to function as a NDPB and be reconsitituted as a committee of experts.

Advisory Committee on Pesticides   (ACP)
■   Mallard House, Kings Pool, 3 Peasholme Green, YORK, YO1 7PX.
     Tel 01904 455702   **Fax** 01904 455711   http://www.pesticides.gov.uk/acp_home.asp
     Chairman: Prof Jon Ayres
E   Set up by Ministers under the Food & Environment Protection Act 1985, the Committee is established by the Control of Pesticides (Advisory Committee on Pesticides) Order 1985. ACP functions as a Scientific Advisory Committee and an Advisory NDPB of the Department for Environment, Food & Rural Affairs, via the Chemicals Regulation Directorate (qv). The Committee comprises 16 members including the Chairman.
R   To advise Ministers on all matters relating to the control of pesticides.
G   United Kingdom.
●   The principal work undertaken by or under the auspices of the Committee consists of vetting applications for approval where the application involves a new pesticide product or a new use for products already on the market.
✍   For further information see **Scientific Advisory Committees**.
     The Government announced on 14 October 2010 that ACP would cease to function as a NDPB and be reconsitituted as a committee of experts.

Advisory Committee on Protection of the Sea   (ACOPS)
■   13-14 Trumpington Street, CAMBRIDGE, CB2 1QA.
     Tel 01223 748811   http://www.acops.org.uk
     President: Lord Hunt of Chesterton, CB, FRS   Chairman: Prof Laurence Mee

E   Established in 1952, and formerly known as the Advisory Committee on Oil Pollution of the Sea and then as the Advisory Committee on Pollution of the Sea. ACOPS functions as an international non-governmental organisation, a registered charity and a company limited by guarantee. The Committee comprises the Chairman and a council of 19 vice-presidents.

R   To promote strategies for sustainable development of the coastal and marine environment through scientific, legal and policy research, and advisory and public awareness activities.

G   International.

●   The Committee arranges global & regional conferences to promote its aims.

It also studies the seas and oceans both as indicators of pollution & as a threatened resource in their own right; ACOPS strives to identify cost-effective, long-term environmental solutions that can be effectively implemented across the globe.

The Committee also has representative offices in Colombia (for South America and the Caribbean), & New Zealand (for the Pacific Ocean and New Zealand).

Advisory Committee on Releases to the Environment   (ACRE)

■   Area 8A Millbank, Nobel House, 17 Smith Square, LONDON, SW1P 3JR.
Tel 0845 933 5577   http://www.defra.gov.uk/acre/
Chairman: Prof Christopher Pollock, CBE

E   Set up in 1990 under the Environmental Protection Act 1990. ACRE functions as a Scientific Advisory Committee and an Advisory NDPB of the Department for Environment, Food & Rural Affairs. It currently comprises 13 members including the Chairman.

R   To provide advice to Government regarding the release and marketing of genetically modified organisms.

G   United Kingdom.

●   The Committee has set up a number of sub-groups (currently seven) to examine and report on specific issues.

✍   For further information see **Scientific Advisory Committees**.

Advisory Committee on Research

✍   Now incorporated in the **General Advisory Committee on Science**.

Advisory Committee for Roofsafety   (ACR)

■   c/o Roofing House, 31 Worship Street, LONDON, EC2A 2DY.   http://www.roofworkadvice.info
Chairman: Ian Henning

E   Established in 1998 as the Advisory Committee for Roofwork. The Committee comprises the Chairman and 31 members who represent trade associations and organisations involved with roofwork.

R   To share its technical experience to make working on roofs safer.

G   United Kingdom.

Advisory Committee on the Safety of Blood, Tissues & Organs   (SaBTO)

■   Area 530, Wellington House, 133-155 Waterloo Road, LONDON, SE1 8UG.
Chairman: John Forsythe

E   The Committee comprises 20 members including the Chairman.

R   To advise Ministers of the UK Government and the Devolved Administrations on the most appropriate ways to ensure the safety of blood, tissues and organs for transfusion / transplantation.

G   United Kingdom.

✍   On 14 October 2010 the Government announced that SaBTO would cease to function as a NDPB and be reconstituted as a committee of experts of the Department of Health and the new Public Health Service.

Advisory Committee for Scotland

■   Ofcom, Sutherland House, 149 St Vincent Street, GLASGOW, G2 5NW.
Tel 0141 229 7400   Fax 0141 229 7433
Chairman: Prof Philip Schlesinger

E   Established under the Communications Act 2003, Section 20(1). The Committee functions as an Advisory NDPB of the Office of Communications (qv).

R   To advise Ofcom about the interests and opinions, in relation to communications matters, of persons living in Scotland.

G   Scotland

✍   For further information see **Advisory Committee for the Nations**.

Advisory Committee on Sites of Special Scientific Interest

✍   Under the Public Services Reform (Scotland) Act 2010, the functions of ACSSSI were transferred to **Scottish National Heritage**.

Advisory Committee on Toxic Substances (ACTS)

- ■ 5S1 Redgrave Court, Merton Road, BOOTLE, Merseyside, L20 7HS.
- E Established in January 1977 by the Health & Safety Executive (qv). The Committee has as its chairman a senior staff member of the HSE and up to 17 members.
- R To advise the HSE on matters relating to the prevention, control and management of hazards and risks to the health and safety of persons arising from the supply or use of toxic substances at work, with due regard to any related risks to consumers, the public and the environment.
- G United Kingdom.
- ● The ACTS is assisted in its work by six sub-committees:
  European Risk Management Advisory Group
  Occupational Exposure Limit Framework Review Working Group
  Standing Committee on Hazard Information & Packaging
  Working Group on Action to Control Chemicals (qv)
  Working Group on COSHH Essentials
  Working Group on European Exposure Limits.

Advisory Committee for Wales

- ■ Ofcom, 2 Caspian Way, Caspian Point, CARDIFF, CF10 4DQ.
  Tel 029 2046 7200   **Fax** 029 2046 7233
  Chairman: Prof Tony Davies
- E Established in 2003 under the Communications Act 2003. The Committee functions as an Advisory NDPB of the Office of Communications (qv). The Committee consists of nine members including the Chairman.
- R To advise Ofcom about the interests and opinions, in relation to communications matters, of persons living in Wales.
- G Wales.
- ✍ For further information see **Advisory Committees for the Nations**.

Advisory Committee on Works of Art   See **United Kingdom Parliament: Committees**.

Advisory Committee on Youth & Family Courts Lay Panel (Northern Ireland)
- ✍ Also known as the Lord Chancellor's Advisory Committee for the Appointment of Family Proceedings Courts & Youth Courts Lay Panel Members in Northern Ireland, the committee ceased to function early in 2005.

Advisory Committees on Justices of the Peace

- ■ Ministry of Justice, 102 Petty France, LONDON, SW1H 9AJ.
  Tel 020 3334 3272   **Fax** 020 3334 3300
- E Established in 1973. There are 101 committees and each functions as an Advisory NDPB of the Ministry of Justice.
- R To select for consideration candidates with the necessary judicial qualities for appointment as justices of the peace.
  To ensure that individual justices fulfil their obligations effectively.
- G United Kingdom.
- ✍ It was announced by the Government on 14 October 2010 that the number of committees would be reduced to 49 on the grounds of impartiality.

ADVISORY COMMITTEES for the NATIONS

- E Under the Communications Act 2003, the Office of Communications (qv) established separate advisory committees for the nations on the whole breadth of its communications responsibilities in the UK. Members of the advisory committee for each nation are appointed through an open public process.
  The national committees are:
  Advisory Committee for England
  Advisory Committee for Northern Ireland
  Advisory Committee for Scotland, and
  Advisory Committee for Wales (qqv).
- R The Committees are tasked to identify those aspects of Ofcom's current work and of communications in general which are of particular importance for their nation, to work with the Ofcom Executive to inform themselves on these topics and to offer advice to Ofcom accordingly.
  The Committees are also asked to be prepared to respond to specific consultation requests from Ofcom on matters where a non-metropolitan perspective will be valuable even though there may not be specific national issues.

Advisory Commonwealth Scholarship Commission in the UK   See **Commonwealth Scholarship Commission in the UK**.

Advisory, Conciliation & Arbitration Service   (ACAS)

■   Euston Tower, 286 Euston Road, LONDON, NW1 3JJ.
    Tel 020 7936 0022   **Fax** 020 7210 3708   http://www.acas.org.uk
    Chairman: Ed Sweeney   Chief Executive: John Taylor
E   Established in 1975 under the Employment Protection Act 1975, its current authority is derived from the Trade Union & Labout Relations (Consolidation) Act 1992. ACAS now functions as an Executive NDPB of the Department for Business, Innovation & Skills. The Council comprises 13 members including the Chairman.
R   To improve the performance & effectiveness of organisations by providing an independent & impartial service to prevent and resolve disputes and to build harmonious relationships at work.
G   England, Scotland, Wales.
●   ACAS provides up-to-date information, independent advice, high quality training and works with employers and employees to solve problems and improve performance.
✍   ACAS has offices in Cardiff, Glasgow and eleven English regions.

Advisory Council for the Education of Romany & other Travellers   (ACERT)

■   Moot House, The Stow, HARLOW, Essex, CM20 3AG.   http://www.acert.org.uk
E   Established in March 1973.
R   To campaign for equal access to education, health and other community services for Gypsies, Roma and Travellers (GRT) and safe and secure accommodation for GRT families.
G   United Kingdom.

Advisory Council on the Export of Works of Art   Advises and assists the **Reviewing Committee on the Export of Works of Art**.

Advisory Council on Historical Manuscripts
✍   Became in May 2010 the Forum on Historical Manuscripts and Academic Research. See **Advisory Council on National Records & Archives** of which it is a subcommittee.

Advisory Council on Infrastructure Investment
✍   Established in March 2004 as an Advisory NDPB of the Office of the First Minister & Deputy First Minister in Northern Ireland. The ACII ceased operating in January 2008.

Advisory Council on Libraries
✍   The Government announced on 1 July 2010 that ACL would be wound down. It was confirmed on 14 October 2010 that the NDPB and its functions would be abolished.

Advisory Council on the Misuse of Drugs   (ACMD)

■   Seacole 3, Marsham Street, LONDON, SW1P 4DP.
    Tel 020 7035 0454   http://www.homeoffice.gov.uk/drugs/acmd/
    Chairman: Prof Les Iverson
E   Established on 1 January 1972 under the Misuse of Drugs Act 1971. ACMD functions as a Scientific Advisory Committee and an Advisory NDPB of the Home Office. The Council comprises 25 members including the Chairman.
R   To consider any substance which is being or appears to be misused and of which is having or appears to be capable of having harmful effects sufficient to cause a social problem.
G   United Kingdom.
✍   For further information see **Scientific Advisory Committees**.

Advisory Council on National Records & Archives   (ACNRA)

■   The National Archives, Kew, RICHMOND, Surrey, TW9 4DU.
    Tel 020 8392 5377   http://www.nationalarchives.gov.uk/advisorycouncil/
    Chairman: Lord Neuberger of Abbotsbury, Master of the Rolls
E   Established on 1 April 2003 under the Freedom of Information Act 2000. ACNRA functions as an Advisory NDPB to the Lord Chancellor.
R   To advise the Lord Chancellor about public access to records and the care of archives and manuscripts.

G   United Kingdom.

✍   ACNRA encompasses the Advisory Council on Public Records which together act as a single advisory council. In May 2010 the Advisory Council on Historical Manuscripts became a subcommittee as the Forum on Historical Manuscripts & Academic Research. It was announced by the Government on 14 October 2010 that the three bodies would merge.

Advisory Council on Public Records   See **Advisory Council on National Records & Archives**.

Advisory Group on Enforcement Service Delivery

✍   AGESD was disbanded following publication of its fourth and final report in November 2003.

Advisory Group on Hepatitis   (AGH)

■   Expert Advice Support Office, 61 Colindale Avenue, LONDON, NW9 5DF.
        Chairman: Prof Will Irving

E   Established in 1998. AGH functions as a Scientific Advisory Committee and an Advisory NDPB of the Department of Health. The Group comprises the Chairman and 15 other members who are experts in virology, hepatology, occupational health, surgery, public health and infection control.

R   To advise the Chief Medical Officers of the Health Departments of the UK on appropriate policies for the prevention and control of viral hepatitis in the community and in healthcare settings, but excluding advice on the microbiological safety of blood and tissues for transplantation, and of health equipment.

G   United Kingdom.

✍   On 14 October 2010 the Government announced that AGH would cease to function as a NDPB and be reconstituted as a committee of experts of the Department of Health and the new Public Health Service.

Advisory Group on Medical Countermeasures

✍   In 2008 AGMC was replaced by the **Advisory Group on Military Medicine**.

Advisory Group on Military Medicine   (AGOMM)

■   06/E/03, MOD Main Building, Whitehall, LONDON, SW1A 2HB.
        Tel 020 7807 0449
        Chairman: Prof Peter Blain

E   Established in 2008, replacing the former Advisory Group on Medical Countermeasures. AGoMM functions as an Advisory NDPB of the Ministry of Defence.

R   To provide independent statements on the safety, efficacy and quality of medicines and medical devices that may be deployed and employed by the Armed Forces.

G   United Kingdom.

Advisory Group for National Specialised Services   (AGNSS)

■   2nd Floor, Southside, 105 Victoria Street, LONDON, SW1E 6QT.
        Tel 020 7932 3939   http://www.specialisedservices.nhs.uk/info/agnss/
        Chairman: Prof Michael Arthur

E   Established in April 1983 and formerly known as the National Specialised Commissioning Advisory Group. AGNSS functions as a Standing Committee of NHS Specialised Services (qv). The Group comprises 23 members including the Chairman.

R   To advise health Ministers on which services should be nationally commissioned and the centres that should provide them.

G   England.

Advisory Group on the Reform of the NHS (Pharmaceutical Services) Regulations 1992

✍   Established as an Advisory NDPB of the Department of Health, the Group has not met since March 2004.

Advisory Panel on Country Information   (APCI)

■   PO Box 1539, CROYDON, Surrey, CR9 3WR.
        Tel 020 8760 8108   http://www.apci.org.uk
        Chairman: Dr Khalid Koser

E   Established on 1 September 2003 under the National Asylum & Immigration Act 2002. The ASPCI functions as an Advisory NDPB of the Home Office. The Panel comprises twelve members including the Chairman.

R   To review and provide advice about the content of country information material produced by the Home Office, and to help ensure that this is as accurate, balanced, impartial and as up-to-date as possible.

G   United Kingdom.

Advisory Panel on Crown Copyright   Was renamed the **Advisory Panel on Public Sector Information** in April 2004.

Advisory Panel on Education for Sustainable Development
✍   A panel of the National Assembly for Wales, dormant since 2003.

Advisory Panel on Judicial Diversity   (APJD)
■   c/o Ministry of Justice, Constitution & Judiciary Division, 102 Petty France, LONDON, SW1H 9AJ.
Chairman: Dame Julia Neuberger, DBE
E   Established in April 2009. APJD functions as an Advisory NDPB of the Ministry of Justice. The Panel comprises six members including the Chairman.
R   To identify the barriers to progress on judicial diversity and make recommendations to the Lord Chancellor on how to make speedier and sustained progress to a more diverse judiciary at every level and in all courts in England and Wales.
G   England, Wales.

Advisory Panel on Public Sector Information   (APPSI)
■   Information Policy & Services Directorate, National Archives, Kew, RICHMOND, Surrey, KT9 4DU.
Tel 020 8392 5330 ext 2252   http://www.appsi.gov.uk
Chairman: Prof David Rhind, CBE
E   Established on 14 April 2003 following a recommendation of the Cross-Cutting Review of the Knowledge Economy (as part of the Spending Review 2000), and known as the Advisory Panel on Crown Copyright until April 2004. APPSI functions as an Advisory NDPB of the Ministry of Justice. The Panel comprises 19 members including the Chairman.
R   To advise Ministers on how to open up opportunities in the information industry for greater re-use of public information.
G   United Kingdom.
✍   The Ministry of Justice announced on 14 October 2010 that the future of APPSI was under consideration, subject to confirming its relationship with the new Public Sector Transparency Board (qv).

Advisory Panel on Standards for the Planning Inspectorate
✍   The Government announced on 14 October 2010 that it had abolished APOS. The Planning Inspectorate (qv) has an internal challenge process that offers quality assurance.

Advisory Panel on Substance Misuse   (APoSM)
■   Cathays Park, CARDIFF, CF10 3NQ.
Tel 029 2082 3799
Chairman: Joanna Jordan
E   Established in 2001 as an Advisory ASPB of the National Assembly for Wales.
R   To oversee the implementation of the Welsh Substance Misuse Strategy and to advise on its development.
To advise on substance misuse issues and operational arrangements.
To advise on the impact of policy developments in related fields.
G   Wales.

Advocacy Training Council   (ATC)
■   The Treasury Office, Lincoln's Inn, LONDON, WC2A 3TL.
Tel 020 7427 5797   http://www.advocacytrainingcouncil.org
Chairman: Charles Haddon-Cave, QC   Secretary: Sarah Perry
E   Established in 2004 in response to the Dutton reports on advocacy training.
R   To ensure that the highest standards of advocacy training are maintained.
To monitor carefully advocacy training at the Bar.
G   England.

Age Concern Cymru
✍   See **Age Cymru**.

Age Concern England
✍   See **Age UK**.

Age Concern Northern Ireland
✍ See **Age NI**.

Age Concern Scotland
✍ See **Age Scotland**.

Age Cymru

■ Tŷ John Pathy, 13-14 Neptune Court, Vanguard Way, CARDIFF, CF24 5PJ.
Tel 029 2043 1555   http://www.ageuk.org.uk/cymru
Chairman: Dr Bernadette Fuge
E Established on 1 April 2009 following the merger of Age Concern UK with Help the Aged and replacing Age
Concern Cymru. Age Cymru functions as a registered charity. The Board comprises eleven Trustees including
the Chairman.
R To campaign, research and fundraise to build a better life for all older people.
To ensure older people's voices are heard, challenge and change attitudes, fight discrimination and tackle elder
abuse in all its forms.
G Wales.

Age NI

■ 3 Lower Crescent, BELFAST, BT7 1NR.
Tel 028 9024 5729   **Fax** 028 9023 5497   http://www.ageuk.org.uk/northern-ireland/
Chairman: Prof Brendan McCormack   Chief Executive: Anne O'Reilly
E Established on 1 April 2009 following the merger of Age Concern UK with Help the Aged and replacing Age
Concern Northern Ireland. Age NI functions as a registered charity. The Board comprises 15 Trustees including
the Chairman.
R To deliver care services, provide advice and advocacy, fundraise, and influence decision makers to improve later
life for all.
To tackle ageism, fight for enough money for older people to live in dignity and demand the quality of care that
people in later life deserve.
G Northern Ireland.

Age Scotland

■ Causewayside House, 160 Causewayside, EDINBURGH, EH9 1PR.
Tel 0845 833 0200   **Fax** 0845 833 0759   http://www.agescotland.org.uk
Chairman: James Wright, CBE, DL   Chief Executive: David Manion
E Established on 1 April 2009 following the merger of Age Concern UK with Help the Aged and replacing Age
Concern Scotland. Age Scotland functions as a registered charity. The Board comprises ten Trustees including
the Chairman.
R To help all older people present a strong and effective voice and to reduce the challenges for those facing serious
and multiple disadvantages as they grow older.
G Scotland.
✍ The four national Age Concerns in the UK have joined together with Help the Aged to form new national charities
dedicated to improving the lives of older people.

Age UK

■ York House, 207-211 Pentonville Road, LONDON, N1 9UZ.
Tel 0800 107 8977   http://www.ageuk.org.uk
Astral House, 1268 London Road, LONDON, SW16 4ER.
Tel 020 8765 7200
Chairman: Dianne Jeffrey   Group Chief Executive: Tom Wright, CBE
E Established on 1 April 2009 following the merger of Age Concern UK with Help the Aged and replacing, in
England, Age Concern England. Age UK functions as a registered charity. The Board comprises 17 Trustees
including the Chairman.
R To improve later life for everyone through information and advice, campaigns, products, training and research.
G England.
● Age UK is a federation of more than 330 Age UKs and Age Concerns in England each of which is an independent
charity. The Age UK Group includes national partners Age Cymru, Age NI and Age Scotland (qqv).

Agri-Food & Biosciences Institute   (AFBI)
- ■ Newforge Lane, BELFAST, BT9 5PX.
    Tel 028 9025 5689   **Fax** 028 9025 5035   http://www.afbini.gov.uk
    Chairman: Seán Hogan   Chief Executive: Dr Seamus Kennedy
- E Established on 1 April 2006 under the Agriculture (Northern Ireland) Order 2004, the AFBI has absorbed the former Agricultural Research Institute of Northern Ireland and the Science Service. The Institute functions as an Executive NDPB of the Department of Agriculture & Rural Development Northern Ireland. The Board comprises twelve members including the Chairman.
- R To carry out high technology research and development, statutory, analytical and diagnostic testing functions for DARDNI and other Government departments, public bodies and commercial companies.
- G Northern Ireland.
- ✍ For further informtion see companion volume **Centres, Bureaux & Research Institutes**

Agricultural Dwelling House Advisory Committee
- ✍ On 22 July 2010 the Government announced its intention to abolish the 16 English regional ADHACs and the corresponding Agricultural Wages Committees.

Agricultural Land Tribunal (Wales)   (ALT)
- ■ Government Buildings, Spa Road East, LLANDRINDOD WELLS, Powys, LD1 5HA.
    Tel 01597 828281   **Fax** 01597 828385
    Secretary: Mrs C A Davies
- E Established under the Agriculture Act 1947.
- G Wales.
- ✍ For further information see **Agricultural Land Tribunals**.

AGRICULTURAL LAND TRIBUNALS   (ALTs)

- E Established under the Agriculture Act 1947 to hear appeals against decisions given by the Minister or County Agricultural Executive Committees; the Agriculture Act 1958 made them courts of first instance and amended the constitutional provisions in the 1947 Act; under the Agricultural Holdings Act 1986, ALTs play an important role in settling disputes and other issues which cannot be resolved between landlords and tenants; under the Land Drainage Act 1991 they have a role in settling drainage disputes between neighbours.
    Each Tribunal functions as a Tribunal NDPB and is an independent statutory authority with jurisdiction only within its own area; a separate Tribunal is constituted for each case and consists of a Chairman and two lay members.
- R To determine disputes between agricultural landlords and tenants (other than through the courts of arbitration) as provided for in the 1991 Act. The main issues considered by ALTs are:
    Applications by close relatives of a deceased or retiring tenant to succeed to the tenancy;
    Applications by landlords for consent to serve a notice to quit on the tenant;
    Applications by tenants for approval to carry out long-term improvements on the holding;
    Applications by landlords for a certificate of bad husbandry on the grounds that the tenant is not farming in accordance with the rules of good husbandry; and
    Applications for a direction to tend ditches or carry out drainage work on neighbouring land.
- G England, Wales.
- ● The Department for Environment, Food & Rural Affairs (Defra) provides a secretary in Crewe for:
    Midlands Agricultural Land Tribunal
    Northern Agricultural Land Tribunal
    Western Agricultural Land Tribunal
    Yorkshire & Humberside Agricultural Land Tribunal (qqv).
    and a secretary in Westbury-on-Trym (though this office is expected to relocate in 2011) for:
    Eastern Agricultural Land Tribunal
    South Eastern Agricultural Land Tribunal
    South Western Agricultural Land Tribunal (qqv).
    The Welsh Government provides the secretary for:
    Agricultural Land Tribunal (Wales) (qv).
- ✍ Defra was considering in 2010 its scope to transfer the ALTs' jurisdiction into the Tribunals Service (qv).

Agricultural Research Institute for Northern Ireland   See the **Agri-Food & Biosciences Institute**.

Agricultural Wages Board for England & Wales   (AWB)
- ■ Area 7E, 9 Millbank, c/o 17 Smith Square, LONDON, SW1P 3JR.
    Tel 020 7238 6523   **Fax** 020 7238 6553
    Chairman: Derek Evans, CBE

E   Established under the Agricultural Wages (Regulation) Act 1924, the Board's authority is now derived from the Agricultural Wages Act 1948, as extended by the Agriculture Act 1967, the Agriculture (Miscellaneous Provisions) Act 1968, and the Employment Protection Act 1975. Its constitution and proceedings are regulated by the 1948 Act and by the Agricultural Wages Board Regulations 1949 as amended 1983. AWB functions as an Executive NDPB of the Department for Environment, Food Rural Affairs. The Board comprises 21 members including the Chairman.

R   To fix minimum rates of pay for workers employed in agriculture on time work.
    To fix minimum rates of pay for piece work, define and fix rates for overtime, make directions regarding holidays and holiday pay, define and evaluate benefits and advantages which may be reckoned as payment of wages in lieu of payment in cash, and fix other terms and conditions of employment.

G   England, Wales.

✍ On 22 July 2010 the Defra announced that it would bring agricultural workers in England within scope of the National Minimum Wage Act 1998 and would agree with the Welsh Government the measures to bring about the abolition of AWB.

Agricultural Wages Board for Northern Ireland   (AWB(NI))

■   Dundonald House, Upper Newtownards Road, BELFAST, BT4 3SB.
    Tel 028 9052 4999   **Fax** 028 9052 4420   http://www.dardni.gov.uk/awb
    Chairman: Mrs Sarah Havlin

E   Established in February 1940 under the Agricultural Wages (Regulations) Act (Northern Ireland) 1939 and the Agricultural Wages Board (Terms & Conditions of Office of Members) Regulations (Northern Ireland) 1940; it is now constituted under the Agricultural Wages (Regulation) (Northern Ireland) Order 1977. AWB(NI) functions as an Executive NDPB of the Department for Agriculture & Rural Development Northern Ireland. The Board comprises 15 members including the Chairman.

R   To determine minimum gross wages payable to agricultural workers, and to set some conditions for holiday and sick pay entitlement.

G   Northern Ireland.

Agricultural Wages Committees

✍ On 22 July 2010 the Government announced its intention to abolish the 15 English regional AWCs and the corresponding Agricultural Dwelling House Committees. Permit of Exemption provisions was repealed before 1 October 2004, the employers' route for a craft certificate was withdrawn from 7 July 2003, and since 1995 there had been just seven applications to an AWC to fix the value of a house.

Agriculture & Environmental Biotechnology Commission

✍ Wound up on 30 April 2005.

Agriculture & Horticulture Development Board   (AHDB)

■   Stoneleigh Park, KENILWORTH, Warwickshire, CV8 2TL.
    Tel 024 7669 2051   http://www.ahdb.org.uk
    Chairman: John Bridge   Chief Executive: Kevin Roberts

E   Established on 1 April 2008, assuming and extending the functions of the former Meat & Livestock Commission. The AHDB functions as a Levy NDPB of the Department for Environment, Food & Rural Affairs (Defra).

R   To improve the efficiency and competitiveness of various agriculture sectors within the UK.
    Statutory functions encompass meat and livestock (cattle, sheep and pigs), in England; horticulture, milk and potatoes in Great Britain; cereals and oilseeds in the UK.

G   United Kingdom.

●   The responsibility for setting and delivering strategies to deploy AHDB levy is delegated to the executive boards of six sector divisions (qqv):
        British Pig Executive
        DairyCo
        English Beef & Lamb Executive
        Home-Grown Cereals Authority
        Horticulture Development Company
        Potato Council.

✍ Defra is debating (14 October 2010) with industry about the future of AHDB, including non-public sector options.

Agriculture Industry Advisory Committee   (AIAC)

■   Redgrave Court, Merton Road, BOOTLE, Merseyside, L20 7HS.
    Tel 0845 345 0055
    Chairman: Marcia Davies

E   Established in December 1976 by the Health & Safety Executive (qv). The AIAC functions as an Advisory NDPB of the HSE. The Committee comprises 17 members including the Chairman.

R   To consider and advise the HSE on the protection of people at work from hazards to health and safety arising from their occupation within agriculture and related industries.

G   United Kingdom.

●   The AIAC has set up project groups to address specific industry issues:
         Arboriculture & Forestry Advisory Group
         Gathering Intelligence about Behaviours, Attitudes & Cultures Project Group
         Training & Education Project Group
         Transport & Machinery Project Group
         Vulnerable Workers Project Group

Air Conditioning & Refrigeration Industry Board   (ACRIB)

■   Kelvin House, 76 Mill Lane, CARSHALTON, Surrey, SM5 2JR.
      Tel 020 8647 7033   **Fax** 020 8773 0165   http://www.acrib.org.uk

E   A membership representing manufacturers, distributors, contractors, consulting engineers, specifiers, end users, training providers, researchers and others with a direct interest in the environmentally friendly and cost effective provision and use of refrigeration, air conditioning and mechanical ventilation equipment.

R   To operate a widely recognised safe refrigerant handling certification scheme.
      To maintain active membership of the European Partnership for Energy & the Environment.
      To work closely with SummitSkills (qv) on the development of national qualifications.
      To repond to issues such as system efficiency and safety, performance standards, food safety and safety at work.
      To advise UK Government on the implementation of regulations and legislation.

G   United Kingdom.

Air Quality Expert Group   (AQEG)

■   Area 5C, Ergon House, 17 Smith Square, LONDON, SW1P 3JR.
      Tel 0845 933 5577   **Fax** 020 7238 2188
      Chairman: Prof Paul Monks

E   Established in 2001 as the Airborne Particles Expert Group. AQEG functions as a Scientific Advisory Committee and an Advisory NDPB of the Department for Environment, Food & Rural Affairs. The Group comprises 14 members including the Chairman.

R   To provide independent scientific advice on air quality, in particular the air pollutants contained in the Air Quality Strategy for England, Scotland, Northern Ireland & Wales, and those covered by the EU Directive on ambient air quality assessment and management (Air Quality Framework Directive).

G   United Kingdom.

✍   For further information see **Scientific Advisory Committees**.
      The Government announced on 14 October 2010 that AQEG would cease to function as a NDPB and be reconstituted as a committee of experts.

Air Transport Users Council

✍   When AUC ceased to exist on 9 March 2011, its complaints handling function transferred to the **Civil Aviation Authority**.

Air Travel Insolvency Protection Committee   (ATIPAC)

■   CAA House, 45-59 Kingsway, LONDON, WC2B 6TE.
      Tel 020 7453 6350   http://www.atipac.org.uk
      Chairman: John Cox, OBE

E   Established in 2000, replacing the former Air Travel Trust Committee. ATIPAC functions as an advisory committee to the Civil Aviation Authority (qv). The Committee comprises the Chairman and 14 other members.

R   To advise the CAA, the Secretary of State for Transport, and the Trustees of the Air Travel Trust (qv) on financial protection for air travellers and holidaymakers.

G   United Kingdom.

Air Travel Trust

✍   The ATT manages and applies the Air Travel Trust Fund, which is the primary source of funding when an ATOL holder fails. The Fund is administered on behalf of the Trust by the Consumer Protection Group of the **Civil Aviation Authority**.

Air Travel Trust Committee   Replaced by the **Air Travel Insolvency Protection Committee** in 2000.

Airborne Particles Expert Group   Former name of the **Air Quality Expert Group**.

Aircraft Noise Monitoring Advisory Committee   (ANMAC)
- ■ Great Minster House, 76 Marsham Street, LONDON, SW1P 4DR.
  Tel 0300 330 3000
  Chairman: Martin Capstick
- E Established as an Advisory NDPB of the Department for Transport.
- R To advise the Government on policy relating to aircraft noise at Heathrow, Gatwick & Stansted Airports.
- G United Kingdom.

Aircraft & Shipbuilding Industries Arbitration Tribunal
- ✍ It was announced by the Government on 14 October 2010 that the Tribunal, which was last convened in the early 1980s, will be abolished.

AIRPORT CONSULTATIVE COMMITTEES   (ACCs)

- E The Committees were established under the Civil Aviation Act 1982. Revised guidelines for ACCs were issued by the Department for Transport in December 2003. ACCs of British airports with an annual passenger throughput in excess of 600,000 are eligible for membership of the Liaison Group of UK Airport Consultative Committees (http://ukaccs.info).
- R Each Committee exists to enable aerodrome operators, communities in the vicinity of the aerodrome, local authorities, local business representatives, aerodrome users and other interested parties to exchange information and ideas.
- ✍ The 23 members of the Liaison Group can be found under **Airport consultative committees** in the Subject Index.

Airworthiness Requirements Board
- ✍ Part of the Civil Aviation Authority, abolished 16 February 2004.

Alcohol Advisory & Counselling Service
- ✍ Merged 24 October 2006 with the former Albyn House Association and now known as Alcohol Support Ltd.

Alcohol Education & Research Council   (AERC)
- ■ 4th Floor, Willow House, 17-23 Willow Place, LONDON, SW1P 1JH.
  Tel 020 7821 7880   http://www.aerc.org.uk
  Chairman: Prof Robin Davidson   Chief Executive: Dave Roberts
- E Set up in March 1982 under provisions of the Licensing (Alcohol Education & Research) Act 1981. AERC is a registered charity and functions as an Executive NDPB of the Department of Health. The Council comprises 16 members including the Chairman.
- R To generate and disseminate research based evidence to inform and influence policy and practice.
  To develop the capacity of people and organisations to address alcohol issues.
- G United Kingdom.
- ● AERC administers the Alcohol Education & Research Fund which finances projects within the UK for education and research on alcohol related issues.
- ✍ On 14 October 2010 the Goverment confirmed its earlier decision that AERC be abolished as a NDPB and remain as a charity.

Alderney Gambling Control Commission
- ■ St Anne's House, Queen Elizabeth II Street, ALDERNEY, Channel Islands, GY9 3TB.
  Tel 01481 825500   **Fax** 01481 823978   http://www.gamblingcontrol.org
  Chief Executive: André Wilsenach
- E The Commission comprises four members including the Chairman.
- R To ensure and maintain the integrity of the electronic gambling industry in Alderney.
- G Alderney.

All Wales Medicines Strategy Group   (AWMSG)

■   Welsh Medicines Partnership, Academic Centre University Hospital, Penlan Road, Llandough,
    VALE OF GLAMORGAN, CF64 2XX.
    Tel 029 2071 6900   **Fax** 029 2071 6783   http://www.wales.nhs.uk/awmsg/
    Chairman: Prof Philip Routledge, OBE   Contact: Mrs Ruth Lang

E   Established in 2003. AWMSG functions as a Scientific Advisory Committee and an Advisory NDPB of the National
    Assembly of Wales. There are 27 members of the Group including the Chairman.

R   To advise the Assembly of future developments in healthcare to assist in its strategic planning.
    To develop timely, independent and authoritative advice on new drugs, or on existing drugs with new indications,
    and on the cost implications of making these drugs routinely available on the NHS.
    To advise the Assembly on the development of a prescribing strategy for Wales.

G   Wales.

✍   For further information see **Scientific Advisory Committees**.

=   Grŵp Strategaeth Meddyginiaethau Cymru Gyfan

All Wales Prescribing Advisory Group   (AWPAG)

■   Welsh Medicines Partnership, Academic Centre University Hospital, Penlan Road, Llandough,
    VALE OF GLAMORGAN, CF64 2XX.
    Tel 029 2071 6900   **Fax** 029 2071 6783
    Chairman: Dr Tessa Lewis

E   Established in 2003 as a sub-group of the All Wales Medicines Strategy Group (qv).

R   To advise the AWMSG on strategic developments in prescribing within primary care; the impact of developments
    which involve the use of medicine; the development of a cost-effective prescribing strategy; interface
    prescribing issues; and documents and issues referred to it by the AWMSG.

G   Wales.

Alliance of Sector Skills Councils

■   Suite 12, Alpha House, 100 Borough High Street, LONDON, SE1 1LB.
    Tel 0845 072 5600   http://www.sscalliance.org
    Arthur House, 41 Arthur Street, BELFAST, BT1 4GB.
    Tel 0845 072 5670
    1 Caspian Point, Pierhead Street, CARDIFF, CF10 4DQ.
    Tel 029 2044 4135
    28 Castle Street, EDINBURGH, EH2 3HT.
    Tel 0131 226 7726   **Fax** 0131 220 6431
    Chief Executive: John McNamara

E   Established on 1 April 2008. The Alliance is owned by and responsible to the 24 Sector Skills Councils (SSCs)
    (qv); it functions as a company limited by guarantee and a registered charity.

R   To act as the collective voice of the SSCs.
    To promote understanding of the role of the SSCs within the skills system across England, Wales, Scotland and
    Northern Ireland.
    To coordinate policy positions and strategic work on skills with stakeholders across the four nations.
    To help build the performance capability of the SSCs to ensure they continue to work effectively on the employer-
    driven skills agenda.

G   United Kingdom.

●   The Alliance has offices in Edinburgh and London, each with a Director, and in Belfast and Cardiff, each with a
    Manager. England is divided into six regions, each with a Chairman.

Amgueddfa Cymru   See **National Museum Wales**.

Anabledd Cymru   See **Disability Wales**.

Ancient Monuments Advisory Board   (AMAB)

■   Plas Carew, Unit 5/7 Cefn Coed, Parc Nantgarw, CARDIFF, CF15 7QQ.
    Tel 01443 336000   **Fax** 01443 336001
    Chairman: Richard Brewer

E   Established on 1 April 2006 as successor to the Ancient Monuments Board for Wales which was set up in 1913.
    The AMAB functions as an Advisory Panel of the Welsh Government through Cadw (qv). The Board comprises
    19 members including the Chairman.

R   To advise the Welsh Government with respect to the exercise of its functions under the Ancient Monuments &
    Archaeological Areas Act 1979.

G   Wales.
✍   One of the four organisations which make up **Historic Wales**.
=   Bwrdd Ymghyngorol Henebion Cymru

Ancient Monuments Board for Wales
✍   See **Ancient Monuments Advisory Board**.

Aneurin Bevan Community Health Council
■   Raglan House, 6-8 William Brown Close, Llantarnam Business Park, CWMBRAN, NP44 3AB.
     Tel 01633 838516   Fax 01633 484623
     Chairman: Ralph James   Chief Officer: Mrs Catherine O'Sullivan
E   The Council comprises 60 members, twelve from each of Blaenau Gewnt, Caerphilly, Monmouthshire, Newport
     and Torfaen area committees.
G   Blaenau Gwent, Caerphilly, Monmouthshire, Newport, Torfaen.
✍   For further information see **Community Health Councils** under **National Health Service - Wales**.

Aneurin Bevan Health Board
■   Mamhilad House Block A, Mamhilad Park Estate, PONTYPOOL, Gwent, NP4 0YP.
     Tel 01873 732732
     Chairman: David Jenkins, OBE   Chief Executive: Dr Andrew Goodall
E   Established on 1 October 2009 by the merger of five former Local Health Boards (Blaenau Gwent, Caerphilly
     Teaching, Monmouthshire, Newport and Torfaen) and the Gwent Healthcare NHS Trust. The Board comprises
     eleven members including the Chairman.
G   Blaenau Gwent, Caerphilly, Monmouthshire, Newport, Torfaen.
✍   For further information see **NHS Wales - Local Health Boards**
     Aneurin Bevan Health Board is the operational name of the Aneurin Bevan Local Health Board.

Anglesey Local Health Board
✍   Merged on 1 October 2009 with the Conwy, Denbughshire, Flintshire, Gwynedd and Wrexham Local Health
     Boards to form **Betsi Cadawaladr University Health Board**.

Anglican Consultative Council   (ACC)
■   St Andrew's House, 16 Tavistock Crescent, LONDON, W11 1AP.
     Tel 020 7313 3900   Fax 020 7313 3999   http://www.anglicancommunion.org
     Chairman: Rt Revd James Tengatenga (Bishop of Southern Mamawi)   Secretary General: Revd Canon Kenneth
     Kearon
E   Established in 1969 following a resolution of the 1968 Lambeth Conference which discerned the need for more
     frequent and more representative contact among the churches than was possible through a once-a-decade
     conference of bishops; the constitution of the Council was accepted by the general synods and conventions of
     all the member churches of the Anglican Communion.
R   To encourage Anglicans to fulfil their common inter-Anglican and ecumenical responsibilities by promoting the
     unity, renewal and mission of the Church.
G   England.
●   Each self-governing church draws on advice and information from the ACC and makes decisions in the light of
     local needs and culture.

Angus & Dundee Tourist Board
✍   Since 1 April 2005 an area office of **VisitScotland**.

Animal Feed Law Enforcement Liaison Group   (AFLELG)
■   Aviation House, 125 Kingsway, LONDON, WC2B 6NH.
     Tel 020 7276 8000
     Chairman: Keith Millar
E   Established in 2005 in response to recommendations made by the Food & Veterinary Office (FVO) following a visit
     to the UK. It functions as an advisory committee of the Food Standards Agency (qv). The group comprises 25
     members including the Chairman.
R   To develop better liaison arrangements, coordination and information exchange between the various agencies
     responsible feed law enforcement in the UK.
G   United Kingdom.

Animal Health
✍ Established on 1 April 2007 by the merger of the Dairy Hygiene Inspectorate, Egg Marketing Inspectorate, State Veterinary Service and Wildlife Licensing Registration Service, Animal Health merged on 1 April 2011 with the Veterinary Laboratories Agency. See **Animal Health & Veterinary Laboratories**.

Animal Health & Veterinary Laboratories Agency   (AHVLA)
■ C3 Government Buildings, Whittington Road, WORCESTER, WR5 2LQ.
Tel 01905 763355   Fax 01905 768851   http://www.defra.gov.uk/animalhealth/
Woodham Lane, New Haw, ADDLESTONE, Surrey, KT15 3NB.
Tel 01932 341111   Fax 01932 347046
Chief Executive: Catherine Brown
E Established on 1 April 2011 by the merger of Animal Health and the Veterinary Laboratories Agency. AHVLA functions as an Executive Agency of the Department for Environment, Food & Rural Affairs.
R To safeguard public and animal health by detecting and diagnosing farm animal diseases.
To protect the welfare of farmed animals.
To maintain a disease emergency response capability for the Government.
G England, Scotland, Wales.
● AHVLA operates a network of 16 veterinary laboratories, including one in Scotland and two in Wales. In addition there are surveillance centres at Liverpool University and the Royal Veterinary College in North Mymms.

Animal Health & Welfare Strategy England Implementation Group
✍ AHWSEIG, established in 2005, has been dissolved (Defra, 14 October 2010).

Animal Medicines Training Regulatory Authority   (AMTRA)
■ 1c Woolpit Business Park, Windmill Avenue, Woolpit, BURY ST EDMUNDS, IP30 9UP.
Tel 01359 245801   Fax 01359 242569   http://www.amtra.org.uk
Chairman: Bob Stevenson
E Established in 1984. AMTRA functions as an independent regulatory body. The Board comprises eleven members including the Chairman.
R To ensure that the marketing and distribution of animal medicines in the UK is undertaken in a responsible manner by AMTRA qualified persons.
G United Kingdom.

Animal Procedures Committee   (APC)
■ 3rd Floor, Seacole SW Quarter, 2 Marsham Street, LONDON, SW1P 4DF.
Tel 020 7035 4776   Fax 020 7035 1135   http://www.homeoffice.gov.uk/agencies-public-bodies/apc/
Chairman: Sara Nathan, OBE
E Established under the Animal (Scientific Procedures) Act 1986. APC functions as a Scientific Advisory Committee and an Advisory NDPB of the Home Office. The Committee comprises the Chairman and twelve other members.
R To advise the Home Secretary on matters relating to any experimental or other scientific procedures applied to a protected animal which may have the effect of causing pain, suffering, distress or lasting harm.
G United Kingdom.
✍ For further information see **Scientific Advisory Committees**.

Animal Welfare Advisory Committee
✍ The Government announced on 21 July 2010 that AWAC, which had not met since 2007, was to be abolished.

Antarctic Act Tribunal
E Established under the Antarctic Regulations 1995 by the Foreign & Commonwealth Office.
R To decide any appeals against the Secretary of State in cases where permits granted under the Act have been revoked or suspended.
✍ The Tribunal is only constituted in the event of a claim, and to date no such claim has been made.

Anti-infectives, HIV & Hepatology Expert Advisory Group
■ 151 Buckingham Palace Road, LONDON, SW1W 9SZ.
Tel 020 3080 6000
Chairman: Dr Barbara Bannister, MSc, FRCP
E Established in 2005. The Group functions as an advisory body to the Commission on Human Medicines (CHM), qv. It comprises six members including the Chairman.

R   To advise CHM on the safety and efficacy of medicines for use in anti-infectives, HIV and hepatology.
G   United Kingdom.

The Appeals Service (Northern Ireland)   (TAS(NI))
■   Cleaver House, 3 Donegall Square North, BELFAST, BT1 5GA.
    Tel 028 9051 8518   Fax 028 9051 8516
    12-14 Dublin Road, OMAGH, Co Tyrone, BT78 1ES.
    Tel 028 8224 9595   Fax 028 8224 9956
E   The Service functions as a Tribunal NDPB of the Department for Social Development Northern Ireland.
R   To provide administrative support to the independent tribunals set up by legislation to hear appeals against decisions made by decision makers in the Social Security Agency, Northern Ireland Child Support Agency, Land & Property Services, Northern Ireland Housing Executive (qqv) and the Inland Revenue.
G   Northern Ireland.

Appointments Commission
■   Blenheim House, Duncombe Street, LEEDS, W Yorks, LS1 4PL.
    Tel 0870 240 3802   Fax 0113 394 2955   http://www.appointments.org.uk
    Chairman: Anne Watts, CBE   Chief Executive: Andrea Sutcliffe
E   Established in 2001 as the NHS Appointments Commission, adopting its current name in October 2006 when its powers were extended to provide recruitment and selection services for all Government Departments and NHS Foundation Trusts. It functions as an Executive NDPB. The Commission comprises nine members including the Chairman.
R   To provide independent recruitment and selection on behalf of ministers to boards of public bodies and advisory committees.
G   United Kingdom.
✍   The Secretary of State for Health announced on 26 July 2010 that the Appointments Commission will be abolished during 2012 in view of the very substantial reduction in the number of appointments required. Accountability for remaining public appointments will rest with Ministers.

Arboriculture & Forestry Advisory Group   A sub-committee of the Health & Safety Executive's **Agriculture Industry Advisory Committee**.

Archbishops' Council Board of Mission
✍   See the **Mission & Public Affairs** division of the Archbishops' Council.

Archbishops' Council of the Church of England
■   Church House, Great Smith Street, LONDON, SW1P 3NZ.
    Tel 020 7898 1000   Fax 020 7898 1369   http://www.cofe.anglican.org/
    Joint Presidents: The Archbishops of Canterbury & York
E   Established on 1 January 1999, under the National Institutions Measure 1998. The Council is the Church of England's national level executive policy and resource decision-making body. The Council comprises 19 members including the two Presidents.
R   To co-ordinate, promote, aid and further the work and mission of the Church of England.
G   England.

Architects Registration Board   (ARB)
■   8 Weymouth Street, LONDON, W1W 5BU.
    Tel 020 7580 5861   Fax 020 7436 5269   http://www.arb.org.uk
    Chairman: Beatrice Fraenkel   Chief Executive: Alison Carr
E   Established under the Architects Act 1997. The ARB is an independent body and NDPB of the Department of Communities & & Local Government. The Board comprises 15 members including the Chairman.
R   To maintain an up-to-date register of all architects.
    To promote good standards in both the education of architects and in professional practice.
    To provide consumers with an accessible service in cases of complaint.
    To investigate and prosecute unregistered individuals in business or practice who unlawfully call themselves architects.
G   United Kingdom.

Architecture & Design Scotland   (A+DS)
- ■   Bakehouse Close, 146 Canongate, EDINBURGH, EH8 8DD.
         Tel 0131 556 6699   **Fax** 0131 556 6633   http://www.ads.org.uk
         Chairman: Karen Anderson   Chief Executive: Jim MacDonald
- E   Established in April 2005 and replacing the former Royal Fine Art Commission. A+DS is a company limited by
         guarantee and functions as an Advisory NDPB of the Scottish Executive Environment & Rural Affairs
         department. The Board comprises 24 members including the Chairman.
- R   To champion high standards of architecture, landscape and urban design in Scotland, promoting wider
         understanding of the importance of good quality in the built environment, supporting skill building and
         encouraging sustainable development.
- G   Scotland
- ✍   One of four UK Commissions established to champion good design and a high quality built environment.

Archives Council Wales
- ✍   Since November 2004 **Archives & Records Council Wales**.

Archives & Records Council Wales   (ARCW)
- ■   National Library of Wales, Penglais, ABERYSTWYTH, Ceredigion, SY23 3BU.
         Tel 01970 632802   http://www.archiveswales.org.uk
         Chairman: Kim Collis
- E   Established in May 1995 as Archives Council Wales, it adopted its current name in November 2004. ARCW
         represents institutions and organisations from all parts of Wales involved with the administration of archives.
- R   To influence policy on archives and records management in Wales.
         To bring to the attention of the public, government or relevant institutions or organisations, matters of current
         concern in the field of archives and records management in Wales.
         To provide a focus for collaborative projects in the field of archives and records management in Wales.
         To bring together institutions and organisations involved with the administration of archives and records
         management in Wales and to provide a forum for the regular exchange of views between them.
- G   Wales.
- ✍   Also known as the Welsh Archives Council.
- =   Cyngor Archifau a Chofnodion Cymru

Argyll Fisheries Trust   See **Rivers & Fisheries Trusts of Scotland**.

Argyll & the Islands Enterprise
- ✍   See **Highlands & Islands Enterprise**.

Argyll, the Isles, Loch Lomond, Stirling & The Trossachs Tourist Board
- ✍   Since 1 April 2005 an area office of **VisitScotland**.

Armagh County Museum   See **National Museums Northern Ireland**.

Armagh Planetarium & Observatory
- ■   College Hill, ARMAGH, BT61 9DB.
         Tel 028 3752 4725   **Fax** 028 3752 6187   http://www.armaghplanet.com
         Chairman: The Most Revd Alan Harper, OBE, BA (Archbishop of Armagh)
         Observatory Director: Prof Mark Bailey   Planetarium Director: Dr Tom Mason, MBE
- E   The Armagh Observatory was established in 1791 under the Armagh Observatory & Museum Act of 1791, and the
         University & Collegiate & Scientific Institutions Act (NI) 1938. The Observatory is funded by grants from the
         Department of Culture, Arts & Leisure Northern Ireland.
         The Board of Governors comprises eleven members including the Chairman.
- R   To govern the Observatory and the Planetarium.

Armed Forces Chaplaincy Centre   See **Defence Academy Management Board**.

© CBD Research Ltd · Beckenham · Kent BR3 5JS · Tel 020 8650 7745 · Fax 020 8650 0768 · E-mail cbd@cbdresearch.com · www.cbdresearch.com

Armed Forces Committee   (AFC)
- BMA House, Tavistock Square, LONDON, WC1H 9JP.
  Tel 020 7383 6020   **Fax** 020 7383 6400   http://www.bma.org.uk
  Chairman: Dr Brendan McKeating
E   Established as a Branch of Practice committee of the British Medical Association. The Committee comprises up
    to 21 members including the Chairman.
R   To consider matters relating to medical branches of the armed forces and of the reserve armed forces and, so far
    as possible, ensure that their medical officers are not disadvantaged in relation to their civilian and military
    counterparts.
✍ See **British Medical Association** [Branch of Practice Committees] for further information.

Armed Forces Criminal Legal Aid Authority   (AFCLAA)
- Building 398c Room 10, Trenchard Lines, Upavon, PEWSEY, Wilts, SN9 6BE.
  Tel 01980 615973
E   Established on 1 April 2008 replacing the three separate single service legal aid departments. It is part of the
    Military Court Service (qv).
R   To effectively manage provision of civilian criminal legal representation for all elligible service personnel and
    civilians.
G   United Kingdom.

Armed Forces Pay Review Body   (AFPRB)
- 6th Floor, Kingsgate House, 66-74 Victoria Street, LONDON, SW1E 6SW.
  Tel 020 7215 8534   **Fax** 020 7215 4445
  Chairman: Prof Alasdair Smith
E   Established in 1971. AFPRB functions as an Advisory NDPB of the Ministry of Defence. The Review Body
    comprises eight members including the Chairman.
R   To advise the Government on the remuneration of and charges to members of the Naval, Military and Air Forces
    of the Crown.
G   United Kingdom.
✍ One of the Pay Review Bodies whose secretariat is provided by the **Office of Manpower Economics**.

Armed Forces Personnel Administration Agency
✍ On 1 April 2007 AFPAA merged with the Veterans Agency to form the **Service Personnel & Veterans Agency**.

Army Base Repair Organisation
✍ On 1 April 2008 ABRO merged with DARA to form the **Defence Support Group**.

Army Prosecuting Authority
✍ Ceased to exist on 31 October 2009. See **Service Prosecuting Authority**.

Army Sport Control Board   (ASCB)
- Clayton Barracks, Thornhill Road, ALDERSHOT, Hants, GU11 2BG.
  Tel 01252 348569   **Fax** 01252 348525
  Director: Major General C H Elliott, CVO, CBE
E   Established on 18 November 1918, by order of the Army Council.
R   To exercise control of sport in the Army in accordance with the strictest amateur principles.
G   United Kingdom.

Army Training & Recruitment Agency
✍ Now an integral part of the Army and no longer functions as an Executive Agency.

Arolygiaeth Ei Mawrhydi dros Addysg a Hyfforddiant yng Nghymru   See **Her Majesty's Inspectorate for
Education & Training in Wales**.

Arolygiaeth Gofal Iechyd Cymru   See **Healthcare Inspectorate Wales**.

Arts Council England   (ACE)

■   14 Great Peter Street, LONDON, SW1P 3NQ.
      Tel 0845 300 6200   **Fax** 020 7973 6564   http://www.artscouncil.org.uk
      Eden House, 48-49 Bateman Street, CAMBRIDGE, CB2 1LR.
      Fax 0870 242 1271
      St Nicholas Court, 25-27 Castle Gate, NOTTINGHAM, NG1 7AR.
      Fax 0115 950 2467
      Central Square, Forth Street, NEWCASTLE UPON TYNE, NE1 3PJ.
      Fax 0191 230 1020
      The Hive, 49 Lever Street, MANCHESTER, M1 1FN.
      Fax 0161 934 4426
      Sovereign House, Church Street, BRIGHTON, E Sussex, BN1 1RA.
      Fax 0870 242 1257
      Senate Court, Southernhay Gardens, EXETER, Devon, EX1 1UG.
      Fax 01392 498546
      82 Granville Street, BIRMINGHAM, B1 2LH.
      Fax 0121 643 7239
      21 Bond Street, DEWSBURY, W Yorks, WF13 1AX.
      Fax 01924 466522
      Chairman: Dame Liz Forgan   Chief Executive: Alan Davey
E   Established in 1945. ACE functions as an Executive NDPB of the Department for Culture, Media & Sport. The
      Council comprises 16 members including the Chairman.
R   To support a range of artistic activities, from theatre to music, literature to dance, photography to digital art,
      carnival to crafts.
      To foster the arts through the distribution of public money from central government and revenues generated by
      the National Lottery.
      When the Museums, Libraries & Archives Council (qv) closes in March 2012, Arts Council England will take over a
      number of its functions relating to museums and libraries.
G   England.
●   ACE has an office in each of the English regions.

Arts Council of Northern Ireland   (ACNI)

■   77 Malone Road, BELFAST, BT9 6AQ.
      Tel 028 9038 5200   **Fax** 028 9066 1715   http://www.artscouncil-ni.org
      Chairman: Rosemary Kelly   Chief Executive: Roisín McDonough
E   Established in 1943 as the Council for the Encouragement of Music & the Arts, the present name was adopted in
      1963 and the Council was reconstituted on 1 September 1995. It functions as an Executive NDPB of the
      Department of Culture, Arts & Leisure. The Council comprises the Chairman and 14 members.
R   To support the arts and arts organisations.
G   Northern Ireland.

Arts Council of Wales   (ACW)

■   Bute Place, CARDIFF, CF10 5AL.
      Tel 0845 873 4900   **Fax** 029 2044 1400   http://www.artswales.org
      Chairman: Prof Dai Smith   Chief Executive: Nick Capaldi
E   Established on 1 April 1994 under Royal Charter. ACW functions as an Executive NDPB and is funded by the
      National Assembly for Wales. The Council comprises twelve members including the Chairman.
R   To support the arts and arts organisations.
G   Wales.
●   The Council provides financial support, mainly in the form of grants and Lottery funding, to arts organisations and
      individual arts practitioners (across the whole spectrum) based in Wales.
      The Council also provides development, advisory and other specialist services in support of its objectives.
=   Cyngor Celfyddydau Cymru

Arts & Humanities Research Council   (AHRC)

■   Polaris House, North Star Avenue, SWINDON, Wilts, SN2 1FL.
      Tel 01793 416000   http://www.ahrc.ac.uk
      Chairman: Prof Sir Alan Wilson   Chief Executive: Prof Rick Rylance
E   Established in April 2005, replacing the Arts & Humanities Research Board established 1998. The AHRC functions
      as an independent NDPB accountable to the Department of Innovation, Universities & Skills. The Council
      currently comprises 15 members including the Chairman and the Chief Executive.
R   To promote and support the production of world-class research in the arts and humanities.
      To promote and support world-class postgraduate training designed to equip graduates for research and other
      professional careers.

© CBD Research Ltd · Beckenham · Kent BR3 5JS · Tel 020 8650 7745 · Fax 020 8650 0768 · E-mail cbd@cbdresearch.com · www.cbdresearch.com

To strengthen the impact of arts and humanities research by encouraging researchers to disseminate and transfer knowledge to other contexts where it makes a difference.

To raise the profile of arts and humanities research and to be an effective advocate for its social, cultural and economic significance.

G   United Kingdom.

✍   For further information see **Research Councils UK**.

Asbestos Liaison Group   (ALG)

■   Bedford House, 59 Bedford Road, EDINBURGH, EH4 3UE.
      Tel 0845 345 0055   **Fax** 0131 247 2121
      Chairman: Dr Paul Stollard

E   Established in 2000 by the Health & Safety Executive (qv). The Committee comprises 25 persons including the Chairman.

R   To share information and exchange views on asbestos issues, in particular those that impact upon the asbestos licensing regime.

G   United Kingdom.

Ascentis

■   West Lodge, Quernmore Road, LANCASTER, LA1 3JT.
      Tel 01524 845046   **Fax** 01524 388467   http://www.ascentis.co.uk
      Chief Executive: Phil Wilkinson

E   Established in 1975 as the Open College of the North West; it adopted its current name in 2009. Ascentis is an awarding body for courses and qualifications in a wide variety of subjects.

G   United Kingdom.

✍   See also **Federation of Awarding Bodies**.

Ashworth Hospital Authority

✍   Since April 2001 the hospital has been administered by the Mersey Care NHS Trust.

Asiantaeth yr Amgylchedd Cymru   See **Environment Agency Wales**.

Asiantaeth Ffilm Cymru   See **Film Agency for Wales**.

Asiantaeth Safonau Bwyd Cymru   See **Food Standards Agency Wales**.

Assembly Ombudsman for Northern Ireland   See **Northern Ireland Ombudsman**.

Assessment & Qualifications Alliance   (AQA)

■   Devas Street, MANCHESTER, M15 6EX.
      Tel 0161 953 1180   **Fax** 0161 273 7572   http://www.aqa.org.uk
      Chief Executive: Andrew Hall

E   Established on 30 September 1998. AQA is a registered charity and company limited by guarantee. The Executive Board comprises seven members including the Chief Executive.

R   To advance education for the benefit of young people and other learners, principally by providing high-quality qualifications.

G   United Kingdom.

✍   For more information see **Federation of Awarding Bodies**.
      A member of the **Joint Council for Qualifications** (qv).

Asset Management Group   A sub-group of the **United Kingdom Roads Board**.

Asset Protection Agency   (APA)

■   5th Floor, Eastcheap House, 11 Philpot Lane, LONDON, EC3M 8UD.
      Tel 020 7074 1824
      Chief Executive: Stephan Wilcke

E   Established in 2009. APA functions as an executive agency of HM Treasury.

R   To operate the Asset Protection Scheme (APS) whose objectives are to support the stability of the UK financial system, increase confidence and capacity to lend, and thus support the economy by protecting financial institutions participating in APS against exceptional credit losses on certain portfolios of assets.

G   United Kingdom.

Asset Skills

■   2 The Courtyard, 48 New North Road, EXETER, Devon, EX4 4EP.
      Tel 01392 423399   **Fax** 01392 423373   http://www.assetskills.org
      Chairman: Chris Cracknell   Chief Executive: Richard Beamish

E   Established on 6 September 2004. It is the recognised Sector Skills Council for the property, facilities management, housing, planning, cleaning and parking industries.

G   United Kingdom.

✍   For further information see **Sector Skills Councils**.

Assets Committee   A committee of the **Church Commissioners**.

Assets Recovery Agency

✍   Since 1 April 2008, the **Serious Organised Crime Agency** is responsible for civil recovery and tax investigation in England, Wales and Northern Ireland.

Assist UK

■   1 Portland Street, MANCHESTER, M1 3BE.
      Tel 0161 238 8776   http://www.assist-uk.org
      Chief Executive: Alan Norton

E   Successor to the Disabled Living Centres Council, established in 1978, Assist UK functions as a registered charity and a company limited by guarantee.

R   To promote and support the development of Disabled Living Centres to meet national quality standards for product information and advice.
      To provide a comprehensive range of services in support of Centres, including exhibitions, conferences, traing and consultancy.

G   United Kingdom.

●   The 60 member Centres each include a permanent exhibition of products and equipment that provide people with opportunities to see and try products and equipment and get information and advice from professional staff about what might suit them best of all.

Associated Board of the Royal Schools of Music   (ABRSM)

■   24 Portland Place, LONDON, W1B 1LU.
      Tel 020 7636 5400   **Fax** 020 7637 0234   http://www.abrsm.org
      Chairman: Lord Sutherland of Houndwood, KT   Chief Executive: Guy Perricone

E   Established in 1889 by Royal Patronage in accordance with an agreement between the Royal Academy of Music & the Royal College of Music; in 1947 they were joined by the Royal Northern College of Music, Manchester, & the Scottish Academy of Music & Drama, Glasgow. The ABRSM is a registered charity. Members of the Board are appointed by the music colleges and academies.

R   To improve the standard of musical education, and to conduct local music examinations.

G   United Kingdom.

●   Examinations are held in approximately 90 countries.

Association of North East Councils   (ANEC)

■   The Guildhall, Quayside, NEWCASTLE UPON TYNE, NE1 3AF.
      Tel 0845 076 0080   **Fax** 0191 232 4558   http://www.northeastcouncils.gov.uk
      Chairman: Cllr Paul Watson   Chief Executive: Melanie Laws

E   Established on 1 April 2009 following the abolition of the North East Assembly, ANEC is an independent membership organisation of the twelve local authorities in the region, represented by the nine council leaders and the elected mayors of Hartlepool, Middlesbrough and North Tyneside.

R   To be responsible, in conjunction with One North East (qv), for regional strategic planning and economic development.

G   County Durham, Northumberland, Teesside, Tyne & Wear.

Association of Salmon Fishery Boards   See **District Salmon Fishery Boards**.

Asylum & Immigration Tribunal

✍ Replaced on 15 February 2010 by Immigration & Asylum Chambers in the First-tier and Upper Tribunals of the **Tribunals Service**.

Atlantic Council of the United Kingdom

■ 130 City Road, LONDON, EC1V 2NW.
Tel 020 7251 6111   http://www.atlanticcounciluk.org
Chairman: Baroness Ramsay of Cartvale

E Established in 1994 following the merger of the British Atlantic Committee and Peace Through NATO. The Council is a non-governmental organisation and functions as a registered charity, it receives funding from the Government.

R To increase knowledge and interest in the North Atlantic Treaty Organisation in schools and universities, also in the general public.

G United Kingdom.

Audience Council England   (ACE)

■ BBC Trust England, The Mailbox, BIRMINGHAM, B1 1RF.   http://www.bbc.co.uk/england/ace/
Chairman: Alison Hastings

E Established on 1 January 2007 when the new BBC Royal Charter replaced the former Board of Governors with the BBC Trust and a formalised Executive Board. The ACE functions as part of the BBC Trust. In addition to the Chairman, the Council comprises the Chairmen of the twelve Regional Audience Councils (RACs) of England.

R To bring the diverse perspectives of licence fee payers in England to bear on the work of the BBC Trust, the governing body the British Broadcasting Corporation (qv), through its links with diverse communities, including geographically-based communities and other communities of interest.

G England.

Audience Council for Northern Ireland   (ACN)

■ Broadcasting House, Room G08, BELFAST, BT2 8HQ.
Tel 028 9033 8856   http://www.bbc.co.uk/northernireland/audiencecouncil/
Chairman: Rotha Johnston, CBE

E Established on 1 January 2007 when the new BBC Royal Charter replaced the former Board of Governors with the BBC Trust and a formalised Executive Board. The ACE is part of the BBC Trust. The Council comprises twelve members including the Chairman.

R To bring the diverse perspectives of licence fee payers in Northern Ireland to bear on the work of the BBC Trust, the governing body the British Broadcasting Corporation (qv), through its links with diverse communities, including geographically-based communities and other communities of interest.

G Northern Ireland.

● The Council also appoints members to serve on the Educational Broadcasting Council for Northern Ireland which provides the ACN with specialist advice on educational broadcasting issues.

✍ The ACN replaces the former Broadcasting Council for Northern Ireland.

Audience Council Scotland   (ACS)

■ Zone G11, 40 Pacific Quay, GLASGOW, G51 1DA.
Tel 0870 010 0212   http://www.bbc.co.uk/scotland/aboutus/acs/
Chairman: Bill Matthews

E Established on 1 January 2007 when the new BBC Royal Charter replaced the former Board of Governors with the BBC Trust and a formalised Executive Board. The ACE is part of the BBC Trust. The Council comprises twelve members including the Chairman.

R To bring the diverse perspectives of licence fee payers in Scotland to bear on the work of the BBC Trust, the governing body the British Corporation (qv), through its links with diverse communities, including geographically-based communities and other communities of interest.

G Scotland.

● The Council also appoints members to serve on the Educational Broadcasting Council for Scotland which provides the ACS with specialist advice on educational broadcasting issues.

✍ The ACS replaces the former Broadcasting Council for Scotland.

Audience Council Wales   (ACW)

■ Broadcasting House, Llandaff, CARDIFF, CF5 2YQ.   http://www.bbc.co.uk/wales/audiencecouncil/
Chairman: Elan Closs Stephens

E Established on 1 January 2007 when the new BBC Royal Charter replaced the former Board of Governors with the BBC Trust and a formalised Executive Board. The ACE is part of the BBC Trust. The Council comprises ten members including the Chairman.

R   To bring the diverse perspectives of licence fee payers in Wales to bear on the work of the BBC Trust, the governing body the British Corporation (qv), through its links with diverse communities, including geographically-based communities and other communities of interest.

G   Wales.

●   The Council also appoints members to serve on the Educational Broadcasting Council for Wales which provides the ACW with specialist advice on educational broadcasting issues.

Audit Advisory Committee Scotland

■   6th Floor, St Magnus House, 25 Guild Street, ABERDEEN, AB11 6NJ.
    Tel 01224 285100
    Chairman: Charlotte Maltin

E   The Committee functions as an advisory committee of the Food Standards Agency Scotland (qv). It comprises six members including the Chairman.

R   To provide advice to FSAS on matters relating to the process of audit of local authority food law enforcement and on the operation and effectiveness of the Framework Agreement on Local Authority Food Law Enforcement in Scotland.

G   Scotland.

Audit Commission for Local Authorities & the National Health Service in England

■   1st Floor, Millbank Tower, Millbank, LONDON, SW1P 4HQ.
    Tel 020 7828 1212   Fax 020 7166 2945   http://www.audit-commission.gov.uk
    Chairman: Michael O'Higgins   Chief Executive: Eugene Sullivan

E   Established on 1 April 1983 under the Local Government Finance Act 1982, as amended by the National Health Service & Community Care Act 1990 and the Local Government Act 1992. The Audit Commission functions as a Public Corporation accountable to the Department for Communities & Local Government. There are up to eleven Commissioners including the Chairman.

R   To ensure that public money is spent economically, efficiently and effectively in the areas of local government, housing, health, criminal justice and the fire and rescue services.
    The Commission's role is to secure the continued integrity of local government and the NHS by ensuring money is legally spent for the purposes intended, and to help local authorities and health authorities to ensure that the services they decide to provide are run as economically, efficiently and effectively as possible.

G   England.

●   The Audit Commission employs District Audit, which it operates as an arms-length agency.

✍   Under the Public Order (Wales) Act 2007 the Commission's functions in Wales were transferred to the Wales Audit Office (qv). The Government announced on 13 August 2010 that the Commission is to be disbanded and audit practice transferred into private ownership. The intention is to have new arrangements in place for auditing England's local public bodies by 31 December 2012.

Audit Committee   A committee of the **Church Commissioners**.

Audit Inspection Unit   See the **Professional Oversight Board**.

Audit Scotland

■   110 George Street, EDINBURGH, EH2 4LH.
    Tel 0845 146 1010   Fax 0845 146 1009   http://www.audit-scotland.gov.uk
    Chairman: Ronnie Cleland   Accountable Officer & Auditor General: Robert Black

E   Established on 1 April 2000 under provisions made in the Public Finance & Accountability (Scotland) Act 2000. The Audit Scotland board comprises the Chairman, the Auditor General, the the chairman of the Accounts Commission (qv), the Deputy Auditor General and an independent non-executive director.

R   To provide the Auditor General and the Accounts Commission with the services they need to check that public money is spent properly, efficiently and effectively.
    Public bodies that the Auditor General scrutinises include directorates, agencies and NDPBs of the Scottish Government, NHS bodies, further education colleges and Scottish Water (qv).

G   Scotland.

Auditing Practices Board   (APB)

■   5th Floor, Aldwych House, 71-91 Aldwych, LONDON, WC2B 4HN.
    Tel 020 7492 2300   Fax 020 7492 2301   http://www.frc.org.uk/apb
    Chairman: Richard Fleck, CBE

E   Established in April 2002 replacing a previous APB which had been in place since April 1991. APB is part of the Financial Reporting Council (qv). The Board comprises 15 members including the Chairman.

R   To set high quality standards for the performance of external audit and other activities undertaken by accountants that result in reports required by law or otherwise relied upon in the operation of the financial markets.

G   United Kingdom.

●   The Board is assisted in its work by three sub-committees:
        Investment Circulars Sub-Committee
        Public Sector Sub-Committee
        SME Audit Sub-Committee

Automotive Skills

✍   Merged in July 2007 with the **Institute of the Motor Industry** which in September 2007 was confirmed as the Sector Skills Council for the sector.

Avon, Gloucestershire & Wiltshire Strategic Health Authority

✍   On 1 July 2006 merged with the Dorset & Somerset and the South West Peninsular Strategic Health Authorities to form the **South West Strategic Health Authority**.

Avon & Somerset Police Authority

■   Valley Road, Portishead, BRISTOL, BS20 8JJ.
     Tel 01275 816377   http://www.aspola.org.uk
     Chairman: Dr Peter Heffer

E   Established in April 1995, the Authority is an independent body charged with ensuring that Avon & Somerset Constabulary provides an effective and efficient police service. It is made up of nine councillor members appointed by the local councils and eight independent members.

G   Somerset (including Bristol and Bath) and South Gloucestershire.

✍   For further information see **Police Authorities**.

Avon & Somerset Probation Trust

■   Queensway House, The Hedges, St Georges, WESTON-SUPER-MARE, BS22 7BB.
     Tel 01934 528740   Fax 01934 528797   http://www.aspa-online.org.uk
     Chairman: Joe Kuipers   Chief Officer: Sally Lewis

E   Established on 1 April 2001 under the Criminal Justice & Court Service Act 2000 as the Avon & Somerset Probation Area Board. It became a trust on 1 April 2010 under the Offender Management Act 2007. The Board comprises nine members including the Chairman.

G   Somerset (including Bristol and Bath) and South Gloucestershire.

✍   For further information see **Probation Trusts**.

Award Scheme Development & Accreditation Network   (ASDAN)

■   Wainbrook House, Hudds Vale Road, BRISTOL, BS5 7HY.
     Tel 0117 941 1126   Fax 0117 935 1112   http://www.asdan.co.uk
     Chairman: Bob Wolfson · Chief Executive: Marius Frank

E   Established in 1991 as a curriculum development organisation and awarding body. ASDAN functions as an educational charity. The Board of Trustees comprises five members including the Chairman.

R   To advance education by providing opportunities for all learners to develop their personal and social attributes and levels of achievement through ASDAN awards and resources.

G   United Kingdom.

✍   See also **Federation of Awarding Bodies**.

Awarding Body for the Built Environment   (ABBE)

■   Birmingham City University, Perry Barr, BIRMINGHAM, B42 2SU.
     Tel 0121 331 5174   Fax 0121 331 6883   http://www.abbeqa.co.uk
     Chief Executive: Roger Bishop

E   ABBE is an awarding body for courses and qualifications linked to the Energy Performance & Buildings Directive implemented by the Department for Communities & Local Government, Domestic Energy Assessment, On Construction Energy Assessment, Non Domestic Energy Assessment, Display Energy Certificates and Air Conditioning Energy Assessment.

R   To offer a full suite of energy awards, covering such disciplines as construction, surveying, plan and project management, home inspection, energy assessment and valuation.

G   United Kingdom.

✍   See also **Federation of Awarding Bodies**.

Awdurdod Heddlu De Cymru   See **South Wales Police Authority**.

Awdurdod Heddlu Gogledd Cymru   See **North Wales Police Authority**.

Awdurdod Parc Cenedlaethol Arfordir Penfro   See **Pembrokeshire Coast National Park Authority**.

Awdurdod Parc Cenedlaethol Bannau Brycheiniog   See **Brecon Beacons National Park Authority**.

Awdurdod Parc Cenedlaethol Eryri   See **Snowdonia National Park Authority**.

Ayrshire & Arran NHS Board
■   Eglinton House, Ailsa Hospital, Dalmellington Road, AYR, KA6 6AB.
    Tel 01292 513600   http://www.nhsayrshireandarran.com
    Chairman: Prof Bill Stevely, CBE   Chief Executive: Dr Wai-yin Hatton
G   Ayrshire and Arran.
✍   For further information see **NHS Scotland - Boards**.

Ayrshire & Arran Tourist Board
✍   Since 1 April 2005 an area office of **VisitScotland**.

Ayrshire Local Enterprise Company
✍   Now functions as the Kilmarnock office of **Scottish Enterprise**.

Ayrshire Rivers Trust   See **Rivers & Fisheries Trusts of Scotland**.

B

Bank of England
■   Threadneedle Street, LONDON, EC2R 8AH.
    Tel 020 7601 4444   **Fax** 020 7601 5460   http://www.bankofengland.co.uk
    Governor: Mervyn King
E   Founded in 1694, the Bank became a Public Corporation accountable to HM Treasury on 1 March 1946 and in
    1997 was granted operational independence over monetary policy. The Bank's Court of Directors comprises
    twelve members including the Governor.
G   United Kingdom.

Bank of England Monetary Policy Committee   **(MPC)**
■   Threadneedle Street, LONDON, EC2R 8AH.
    Tel 020 7601 4444   **Fax** 020 7601 5460   http://www.bankofengland.co.uk
    Governor: Mervyn King
E   Established under legislation on 1 June 1998, the Committee has been operating since 6 May 1997 when the
    Bank of England was given operational independence. The Committee comprises the Governor of the Bank of
    England, the two Deputy Governors, the Bank's Chief Economist, the Executive Director for Markets and four
    external members appointed by the Chancellor of the Exchequer.
R   To set an interest rate that it judges will enable the inflation target to be met.
G   United Kingdom.
●   The Committee meets monthly, its decisions are published as soon as practicable and minutes of its meetings
    must be published within six weeks.

Banking Code Standards Board

✍ BCSB changed its name to **Lending Standards Board** on 1 November 2009.

Banking Ombudsman   See **Financial Ombudsman Service**.

Bar Council   See the **General Council of the Bar** and the **General Council of the Bar of Northern Ireland**.

Bar Standards Board

■ 289-293 High Holborn, LONDON, WC1V 7HZ.
Tel 020 7611 1444   **Fax** 020 7831 9217   http://www.barstandardsboard.org.uk
Chairman: Baroness Ruth Deech   Director: Vanessa Davies

E Established in January 2006 as a result of the Bar Council separating its regulatory and representative functions. It functions as an independent regulatory board of the Bar Council. The Board comprises 15 members including the Chairman.

R To regulate barristers called to the Bar in England and Wales.
To promote and maintain excellence in the quality of legal services provided by barristers to support the rule of law.

G England, Wales.

● The Board runs its work through six committees, each of which reports to the board, namely:
Complaints; Education & training; Performance & best value; Qualifications; Quality assurance; Standards.

✍ One of the Approved Regulators overseen by the **Legal Services Board**.
See also the **General Council of the Bar**.

Barrantee Oaseirys Argidoil   See **Financial Supervision Commission**.

Barrow Regeneration

✍ A trading division of Furness West Cumbria New Vision Urban Regeneration Company which was wound up in April 2011.

BBC Alba   See **MG ALBA**.

BBC Trust

■ Room 211, 35 Marylebone High Street, LONDON, W1U 4AA.
Tel 0370 010 0222   http://www.bbc.co.uk/bbctrust/
Chairman: Sir Michael Lyons

E Established on 1 January 2007 under the BBC Royal Charter 2006, replacing the former Board of Governors. The Trust consists of twelve members including the Chairman, a vice-chairman, and a member for each of the nations of the United Kingdom.

R To set the overall strategic direction of the BBC.
To oversee the work of the BBC's Executive Board.
To perform these roles in the public interest, particularly the interest of licence fee payers.

G United Kingdom.

BBC World Service

■ Bush House, Strand, LONDON, WC2B 4PH.
Tel 020 7240 3456   **Fax** 020 7557 1254   http://www.bbc.co.uk/worldservice
Director: Peter Horrocks

E Established in 1932. Funded by the UK Government through Parliamentary Grant-in-Aid administered by the Foreign & Commonwealth Office (FCO). FCO is involved in the process of deciding which languages are broadcast, but all editorial control rests entirely with the BBC. The Management Board comprises 13 members including the Director and is accountable to the BBC Trust (qv).

R To provide programmes and content for radio, television, online and mobile phones in English and 31 other languages.
To produce impartial news reports, documentaries and analysis from its reporters and analysts from around the globe.

G United Kingdom.

The Beautiful South   Trading name of **Tourism South East**.

Bedfordshire & Hertfordshire Strategic Health Authority
✍ On 1 July 2006 merged with the Essex and the Norfolk, Suffolk & Cambridgeshire Strategic Health Authorities to
      form the **East of England Strategic Health Trust**.

Bedfordshire Police Authority
■ Bridgebury House, Woburn Road, Kempston, BEDFORD, MK43 9AX.
    Tel 01234 842066   **Fax** 01234 842068   http://www.bedfordshirepoliceauthority.co.uk
    Chairman: Peter Conniff
E Established in April 1995, the Authority is an independent body charged with ensuring that Bedfordshire Police
      provide an effective and efficient police service. It is made up of six County Councillors, three Luton Councillors
      and eight independent members.
G Bedfordshire and Luton.
✍ For further information see **Police Authorities**.

Bedfordshire Probation Trust
■ 3 St Peter's Street, BEDFORD, MK40 2PN.
    Tel 01234 213541   **Fax** 01234 327497   http://www.bedsprobation.org.uk
    Chairman: Adrian Heffernan   Chief Officer: Linda Hennigan
E Established on 1 April 2001 under the Criminal Justice & Court Service Act 2000 as the Berkshire Probation Area
      Board. It became a trust on 1 April 2010 under the Offender Management Act 2007. The Board comprises up to
      15 members including the Chairman.
G Bedfordshire and Luton.
✍ For further information see **Probation Trusts**.

Bedfordshire Rural Communities Charity   (BRCC)
■ The Old School, Cardington, BEDFORD, MK44 3SX.
    Tel 01234 838771   **Fax** 01234 838149   http://www.bedsrcc.org.uk
    Chairman: Mrs Judy Robinson   Chief Executive: Janet Ridge
E BRCC functions as a registered charity and company limited by guarantee. The board comprises 19 directors
      including the Chairman.
R To support local communities on the ground, and to work at a strategic level with the county's leading partners,
      to ensure that everyone has the best possible opportunity to be involved in a thriving community regardless of
      where they live.
G Bedfordshire.
✍ BRCC is one of the 38 Rural Community Councils, represented at the national level by **Action with Communities
      in Rural England** (qv) and at the regional level by Rural Action East.

Belfast City Airport Forum   See **George Best Belfast City Airport Forum**.

Belfast Education & Library Board   (BELB)
■ 40 Academy Street, BELFAST, BT1 2NQ.
    Tel 028 9056 4000   http://www.belb.org.uk
    Chief Executive: David Cargo
E Established in 1973. The Board functions as an Executive NDPB of the Department of Education Northern Ireland.
G Belfast.
✍ The ELBs and other legacy organisations will be dissolved when the Education & Skills Authority (qv) becomes
      fully operational.
    For further information see **Education & Library Boards (Northern Ireland)**.

Belfast Harbour Commissioners   (BHC)
■ Harbour Office, Corporation Square, BELFAST, BT1 3AL.
    Tel 028 9055 4422   **Fax** 028 9055 4420   http://www.belfast-harbour.co.uk
    Chairman: Leonard J P O'Hagan   Chief Executive: Roy Adair
E Established under the Belfast Harbour Act 1847. The board comprises up to 15 members including the Chairman
      and Chief Executive.
R To operate the Port of Belfast as a profitable organisation.
G Belfast.
✍ For further information see **Port & Harbour Authorities**.

© CBD Research Ltd · Beckenham · Kent BR3 5JS · Tel 020 8650 7745 · Fax 020 8650 0768 · E-mail cbd@cbdresearch.com · www.cbdresearch.com

Belfast Health & Social Care Trust

- Roe Villa, Knockbracken Healthcare Park, Saintfield Road, BELFAST, BT8 8BH.
  Tel 028 9096 0000   Fax 028 9096 0099   http://www.belfasttrust.hscni.net
  Chairman: Pat McCartan   Chief Executive: William McKee
- E   Established on 1 April 2007, the Trust brings together the former Belfast City Hospital, Green Park, Mater Hospital, North & West Belfast, Royal Hospitals and South & East Belfast Health & Social Services Trusts. The Board comprises 21 members including the Chairman and Chief Executive.
- G   Belfast and part of Castlereagh Borough.
- ✍   For further information see **Health & Social Care**.

Berwick-upon-Tweed Harbour Commission

- Harbour Master's Office, Tweed Dock, BERWICK-UPON-TWEED, Northumberland, TD15 2AB.
  Tel 01289 307404   Fax 01289 332854   http://www.portofberwick.co.uk
  Harbour Master: Brian Watson
- E   Established by the Berwick-upon-Tweed Harbour Act 1862. The Commission comprises ten members including the Harbour Master.
- G   Berwick-upon-Tweed.
- ✍   For further information see **Port & Harbour Authorities**.

Betsi Cadwaladr Community Health Council

- 4 Trinity Square, LLANDUDNO, Caernarfonshire, LL30 2PY.
  Tel 01492 878840   Fax 01492 860878
  Cartrelle, Cefn Road, WREXHAM, LL13 9NH.
  Tel 01978 356178   Fax 01978 346870
  4 Pepper Lane, CAERNARFON, LL55 1RG.
  Tel 01286 674961   Fax 01286 672253
  Arran House, Arran Road, DOLGELLAU, LL40 1HW.
  Tel 01341 422236   Fax 01341 422897
  Glanhwfa Road, LLANGEFNI, Ynys Môn, LL77 7EN.
  Tel 01248 723283   Fax 01248 750337
  Chairman: David Cooper   Chief Officer: Mrs Patricia Billingham
- E   Established on 1 April 2010 by the merger of six former Community Health Councils. The full Council comprises 72 volunteer members drawn from the six local committees (Caernarfonshire, Conwy, Denbighshire, Flintshire, Gwynedd and Ynys Môn).
- G   Conwy, Denbighshire, Flintshire, Gwynedd, Ynys Môn, Wrexham.
- ✍   For further information see **Community Health Councils** under **National Health Service - Wales**.

Betsi Cadwaladr University Health Board

- Ysbyty Gwynedd, Penrhosgarnedd, BANGOR, Caernarfonshire, LL57 2PW.
  Tel 01248 384384   http://www.bcu.wales.nhs.uk
  Chairman: Prof Merfyn Jones   Chief Executive: Mary Burrows
- E   Established on 1 October 2009 by the merger of six former Local Health Boards (Anglesey, Conwy, Denbighshire, Flintshire, Gwynedd and Wrexham) and the North Wales and North West Wales NHS Trusts. The Board comprises 19 members including the Chairman.
- G   Anglesey, Conwy, Denbighshire, Flintshire, Gwynedd, Wrexham.
- ✍   For further information see **NHS Wales - Local Health Boards**.
  Betsi Cadwaladr University Health Board is the operational name of the Betsi Cadwaladr University Local Health Board.

Better Regulation Advisory Group   (BRAG)

- Aviation House, 125 Kingsway, LONDON, WC2B 6NH.
  Tel 020 7276 8370   Fax 020 7276 8004
  Chairman: Chris Pomfret
- E   Established in 2006. BRAG functions as an Advisory NDPB of the Food Standards Agency (qv). The Group comprises 13 members including the Chairman.
- R   To undertake independent external scrutiny and challenge of the FSA's better regulation initiatives.
- G   United Kingdom.

Better Regulation Commission

- ✍   BRC produced its final report on 16 January 2008. The Risk & Regulation Advisory Council was established to oversee the implementation of the report's recommendations and completed its work in 2009.

Big Lottery Fund
- 1 Plough Place, LONDON, EC4A 1DE.
  Tel 0845 410 2030   **Fax** 020 7211 1750   http://www.biglotteryfund.co.uk
  Interim Chairman: Anna Southall   Chief Executive: Peter Wanless
- E Established on 1 December 2006, to assume the residual responsibilities of the Community Fund, Millennium Commission, National Lottery Charities Board and New Opportunities Fund. The Fund functions as an Executive NDPB of the Department for Culture, Media & Sport (policy responsibility is moving to the Cabinet Office). The Board comprises twelve members including the Chairman and the chairmen of the Fund's English, Scottish, Welsh and Northern Irish committees.
- R To be responsible for giving out half the money for good causes raised by the National Lottery to bring real improvements to communities and to the lives of people most in need.
- G United Kingdom.
- ✐ The Fund has a nine regional offices in England, one in Scotland, two in Wales and one in Northern Ireland.

Big Pit   See **National Museum Wales**.

Biocides Consultative Committee   (BCC)
- Redgrave Court, Merton Road, BOOTLE, Merseyside, L20 7HS.
  Tel 0845 345 0055
- E Established in 2001.
- R The advise the Health & Safety Executive (qv) on scientific and other associated issues in relation to the Biocidal Products Directive, the Biocidal Products Regulations 2001 and other general issues related to biocides.
- G United Kingdom.

Biologicals & Vaccines Expert Advisory Group   (BVEAG)
- 151 Buckingham Palace Road, LONDON, SW1W 9SZ.
  Tel 020 3080 6000
  Chairman: Dr Angela E Thomas, MB, BS, PhD, FRCP(E), FRCPath, FRCPCH
- E Established in 2005. BVEAG functions as an advisory body to the Commission on Human Medicines (CHM), qv. The Group consists of eleven members including the Chairman.
- R To advise CHM on the quality, safety and efficacy of medicinal products of biological or biotechnological origin including vaccines which are the subject of marketing authorisation applications, and to advise on such other matters as are referred to it.
- G United Kingdom.

Biotechnology & Biological Sciences Research Council   (BBSRC)
- Polaris House, North Star Avenue, SWINDON, Wilts, SN2 1UH.
  Tel 01793 413200   **Fax** 01793 413201   http://www.bbsrc.ac.uk
  Chairman: Prof Sir Tom Blundell, FRS   Chief Executive: Prof Douglas Kell
- E Established by Royal Charter in 1994 by the incorporation of the former Agricultural & Food Research Council with the biotechnology and biological sciences programmes of the former Science & Engineering Research Council. The BBSCR functions as an independent NDPB accountable to the Department for Business, Innovation & Skills. The Council comprises the Chairman, Chief Executive and 10-18 other members.
- R To promote and support, by any means, high quality basic, strategic and applied research and related postgraduate training relating to the understanding and exploitation of biological systems.
  To advance knowledge and technology and provide trained scientists and engineers which meet the needs of users and beneficiaries.
- G United Kingdom.
- ● The BBSRC sponsors various research institutes and funds research and training in universities and other higher education bodies involved in scientific research.
- ✐ For further information see **Research Councils UK**.

Birmingham & the Black Country Strategic Health Authority
- ✐ On 1 July 2006 merged with the Shropshire & Staffordshire and the West Midlands South Strategic Health Authorities to form the **West Midlands Strategic Health Authority**.

Birmingham International Airport Consultative Committee   (BIACC)
- Strategic Services Directorate, PO Box 18, Council House, SOLIHULL, B91 9QS.
  Tel 0121 704 6050   **Fax** 0121 704 6056   http://www.ukaccs.info/bham/
  Chairman: Mr Viv Astling, OBE   Secretary: Lee Stevenson

G   Birmingham.

✍   For further information see **Airport Consultative Committees**.

Bishoprics & Cathedrals Committee   A committee of the **Church Commissioners**.

Bishops' Conference of Scotland   (BCOS)

■   64 Aitken Street, AIRDRIE, Lanarks, ML6 6LT.
    Tel 01236 764061   **Fax** 01236 762489   http://www.bpsconfscot.com
    President: Cardinal Keith Patrick O'Brien   General Secretary: Revd Paul M Conroy

E   The Conference comprises all diocesan bishops and those equivalent to them in law; all coadjudicator bishops, auxiliary bishops and other titular bishops who exercise in Scotland a special office assigned to them by the Apostolic See or the Conference.

G   Scotland.

Blackpool Fylde & Wyre edc

■   The New Blackpool Enterprise Centre, Lytham Road, BLACKPOOL, Lancs, FY4 1EW.
    Tel 01253 478909   **Fax** 01253 408860   http://www.reblackpool.com
    Chairman: Mike Appleton   Chief Executive: Doug Garrett

E   Established in March 2003. Blackpool Flyde & Wyre edc is the Economic Development Company for the Fylde Coast. It replaced ReBlackpool, an Urban Regeneration Company.

G   Blackpool, Fylde and Wyre.

✍   For further information see **Economic Development Companies**.

Blaenau Gwent Local Health Board

✍   Merged on 1 October 2009 with the Caerphilly, Monmouthshire, Newport and Torfaen Local Health Boards to form **Aneurin Bevan Health Board**.

Blyth Harbour Commission

■   South Harbour, BLYTH, Northumberland, NE24 3PB.
    Tel 01670 352066   **Fax** 01670 355169   http://www.portofblyth.co.uk
    Chairman: Tom Dingwall

E   Trust established in 1882. The board comprises seven commissioners including the Chairman.

G   Blyth

✍   For further information see **Port & Harbour Authorities**.

Board for Actuarial Standards   (BAS)

■   5th Floor, Aldwych House, 71-91 Aldwych, LONDON, WC2B 4HN.
    Tel 020 7492 2328   **Fax** 020 7492 2301   http://www.frc.org.uk/bas/
    Chairman: Jim Sutcliffe   Director: Louise Pryor

E   Established in April 2006 following publication in March 2005 of the Morris Review of the Actuarial Profession, following which HM Treasury asked the Financial Reporting Council (qv) to take on responsibility for oversight of the UK actuarial profession. The Board comprises twelve members including the Chairman.

R   To support the FRC in achieving its strategic outcome that the users of actuarial information can place a high degree of reliance on its relevance, transparency of assumptions, completeness and comprehensibility.

G   United Kingdom.

Board of Community Health Councils in Wales

■   2nd Floor, 33-35 Cathedral Road, CARDIFF, CF11 9HB.
    Tel 029 2023 5558   **Fax** 029 2023 5574
    Director: Mrs Carol Lamyman-Jones

E   Established in 2004 under the Community Health Councils Regulations 2004. The Board is supported by a team of seven including the Director.

R   To represent the eight CHCs in Wales.

G   Wales.

✍   For further information see **Community Health Councils**.

=   Bwrdd Cynghorau Iechyd Cymuned Cymru

Board of Customs & Excise
✍ See **Her Majesty's Revenue & Customs**,

Board of Deputies of British Jews
■ 6 Bloomsbury Square, LONDON, WC1A 2LP.
  Tel 020 7543 5400   **Fax** 020 7543 0010   http://www.boardofdeputies.org.uk
  President: Vivian Wineman   Chief Executive: Jon Benjamin
E Established in 1760 as a joint committee of the Sephardi & Ashkenazi communities in London, the Board dates
    from 1835. It is an elected representative body of the British Jewish community. The Board comprises 300
    Deputies, each elected by a synagogue or institution.
R To protect, support and defend the interests and the religious rights and customs of Jews and the Jewish
    community in the United Kingdom.
  To promote the development of the British Jewish community.
G United Kingdom.

Board of Education of the Church of England   see **Church of England Board of Education**

Board of Inland Revenue
✍ See **Her Majesty's Revenue & Customs**.

Board of Mission
✍ See the **Mission & Public Affairs** division of the Archbishops' Council.

Board of Science   (BoS)
■ BMA House, Tavistock Square, LONDON, WC1H 9JP.
  Tel 020 7383 6755   **Fax** 020 7383 6400   http://www.bma.org.uk
  Chairman: Sir Kenneth Calman
E Established as a standing committee of the British Medical Association.
R To support and promote medical science on behalf of BMA members.
G United Kingdom.
✍ See **British Medical Association** [Boards & Committees] for further information.

Board for Social Responsibility
✍ See the **Mission & Public Affairs** division of the Archbishops' Council.

Board of Trustees of...   See specific institution, eg **British Museum**.

Boards of Visitors
✍ See **Independent Monitoring Boards**.

Bookmakers' Committee   (BMC)
■ Parnell House, 25 Wilton Road, LONDON, SW1V 1LW.
  Tel 020 7333 0043   **Fax** 020 7333 0041   http://www.hbib.org.uk
  Chairman: Will Roseff   General Secretary: Stuart McInroy, BSc, FCMI
E Established in 1961 by the Betting Levy Act 1961, the Committee is constituted under the Betting, Gaming &
    Lotteries Act 1963. The Committee comprises 15 members including the Chairman.
R To make recommendations annually to the Horserace Betting Levy Board (qv) on the categories, rates, conditions
    and definitions of the Levy Scheme for the following year and, if appropriate, to revise such recommendations
    in light of observations made by the Board.
G United Kingdom.

Booktrust
■ Book House, 45 East Hill, LONDON, SW18 2QZ.
  Tel 020 8516 2977   **Fax** 020 8516 2978   http://www.booktrust.org.uk
  Chairman: Sue Horner   Chief Executive: Viv Bird

E   Established in 1924 as the National Book Committee and subsequently known as the National Book League and the Book Trust before adopting its present name in 2001. It functions as a registered charity; its Board comprises nine Trustees including the Chairman.

R   To encourage people of all ages and cultures to enjoy books.

G   United Kingdom.

Tha Boord o Ulstèr-Scotch   See the **Ulster-Scots Agency**.

Bòrd na Gàidhlig

■   Darach House, Stoneyfield Business Park, INVERNESS, IV2 7PA.
    Tel 01463 225454 **Fax** 01463 716217 http://www.gaidhlig.org.uk
    Chairman: Arthur Cormack

E   Established on 13 February 2006 under the Gaelic Language (Scotland) Act 2005. It functions as an Executive NDPB of the Scottish Executive Education Department. The Bòrd comprises ten members including the Chairman.

R   To increase the number of Gaelic speakers and users of Gaelic.
    To strengthen Gaelic as a family and community language.
    To facilitate access to Gaelic language and culture throughout Scotland.
    To promote and celebrate Gaelic's contribution to Scottish cultural life.
    To extend and enhance the use of Gaelic in all aspects of life in Scotland.

G   Scotland

Borders Local Enterprise Company

✍   Now functions as the Galashiels office of **Scottish Enterprise**.

Borders NHS Board

■   Newstead, MELROSE, Roxburghshire, TD6 9DA.
    Tel 01896 826000 **Fax** 01896 825580 http://www.nhsborders.org.uk
    Chairman: Mary Wilson   Chief Executive: Calum Campbell

G   Scottish Borders.

✍   For further information see **NHS Scotland - Boards**.

Boundary Commission for England   (BCE)

■   2nd Floor, 35 Great Smith Street, LONDON, SW1P 3BQ.
    Tel 020 7276 1102 http://www.boundarycommissionforengland.org.uk
    Ex-Officio Chairman: The Speaker of the House of Commons   Deputy Chairman: The Hon Mr Justice Sales

E   Established in its current form under the Parliamentary Constituencies Act 1986 as amended, most recently by the Parliamentary Voting Systems & Constituencies Act 2011. BCE functions as an Advisory NDPB of the Cabinet Office. The Commission comprises the Chairman, his deputy and two other members.

R   To keep the parliamentary constituencies of England under continuous review and periodically, every eight to twelve years, conduct a general review of all English constituencies at the same time and submit to the Secretary of State a report showing the constituencies it recommends.

G   England.

✍   Also known as the Parliamentary Boundary Commission for England to distinguish it from the Local Government Boundary Commission for England (qv).

Boundary Commission for Northern Ireland   (BCNI)

■   Forestview, Purdy's Lane, Newtownbreda, BELFAST, BT8 7AR.
    Tel 028 9069 4800 **Fax** 028 9069 4801 http://www.boundarycommission.org.uk
    Ex-Officio Chairman: the Speaker of the House of Commons   Deputy Chairman: The Hon Mr Justice McLaughlin

E   Established in its current form under the Parliamentary Constituencies Act 1986 as amended, most recently by the Parliamentary Voting Systems & Constituencies Act 2011. BCNI functions as an Advisory NDPB of the Northern Ireland Office. The Commission comprises the Chairman, his deputy and two other members.

R   To keep under continuous review the number, names and boundaries of Northern Ireland's parliamentary constituencies and to make recommendations about these to the Secretary of State for Northern Ireland.

G   Northern Ireland.

●   The Northern Ireland Act 1998 provides that the parliamentary constituencies will also for the constituencies for elections to the Northern Ireland Assembly, with each returning six members.

✍   Also known as the Parliamentary Boundary Commission for Northern Ireland.

Boundary Commission for Scotland   (BCS)
- ■ Thistle House, 91 Haymarket Terrace, EDINBURGH, EH12 5HD.
  Tel 0131 538 7510   **Fax** 0131 538 7511   http://www.bcomm-scotland.gov.uk
  Ex-Officio Chairman: The Speaker of the House of Commons   Deputy Chairman: The Hon Lord Woolman
- E Established in its current form under the Parliamentary Constituencies Act 1986 as amended, most recently by
  the Parliamentary Voting Systems & Constituencies Act 2011. When determining boundaries of Scottish
  Parliament constituencies and regions, different legislation applies, namely the Scotland Act 1998 as amended
  by the Scottish Parliament (Constituencies) Act 2004. BCS functions as an Advisory NDPB of the Scotland
  Office. The Commission comprises the Chairman, his deputy and two other members.
- R To keep under under continuous review the constituencies in Scotland for the Westminster Parliament and the
  constituencies and regions for the Scottish Parliament, and periodically, every eight to twelve years, conduct a
  general review of all Westminster constituencies at the same time and submit to the Secretary of State for
  Scotland a report showing the constituencies it recommends.
- G Scotland.
- ✍ Also known as the Parliamentary Boundary Commission for Scotland to distinguish it from the Local Government
  Boundary Commission for Scotland (qv).

Boundary Commission for Wales   (BCW)
- ■ Caradog House, 1-6 St Andrews Place, CARDIFF, CF10 3BE.
  Tel 029 2039 5031   **Fax** 029 2039 5250   http://www.bcomm-wales.gov.uk
  Ex-Officio Chairman: The Speaker of the House of Commons   Deputy Chairman: The Hon Mr Justice Lloyd
  Jones
- E Established in its current form under the Parliamentary Constituencies Act 1986 as amended, most recently by
  the Parliamentary Voting Systems & Constituencies Act 2011. BCW functions as an Advisory NDPB of the
  Cabinet Office. The Commission comprises the Chairman, his deputy and two other members.
- R To keep the parliamentary constituencies in Wales under continuous review and periodically, every eight to twelve
  years, conduct a general review of all Welsh constituencies at the same time and submit to the Secretary of
  State a report showing the constituencies it recommends.
- G Wales.
- ✍ Also known as the Parliamentary Boundary Commission for Wales to distinguish it from the Local Government
  Boundary Commission for Wales (qv).
- = Comisiwn Ffiniau i Gymru

The Boundary Committee for England
- ✍ BCE was replaced on 1 April 2010 by the **Local Government Boundary Commission for England**.

Bournemouth Airport Consultative Committee   (BACC)
- ■ Bournemouth Airport, CHRISTCHURCH, Dorset, BH23 6SE.
  Tel 01202 364114   **Fax** 01202 364118   http://www.bournemouthairport.com
  Secretary: Ruth Osborn
- G Bournemouth.
- ✍ For further information see **Airport Consultative Committees**.

Bovine TB: TB Advisory Group
- ✍ Established in October 2006, the Group, under the chairmanship of Peter Jinman, published its final report on 8
  April 2009.

Bradford Centre Regeneration
- ✍ Established in February 2003, BCR was the Urban Regeneration Company for Bradford city centre. It was
  disbanded in 2010 and its functions transferred to Bradford Metropolitan Borough Council.

Branch of Practice Committees   See under **British Medical Association**.

BRB (Residuary) Ltd
- ■ 4th Floor, One Kemble Street, LONDON, WC2B 4AN.
  Tel 020 7904 5079   http://www.brbr.co.uk
- E The British Rail Board was originally established under the Transport Act 1962. BRB (Residuary) Ltd is owned by
  the Government and reports to the Department for Transport. The board of the company comprises the
  Chairman and three directors.

R   Following the transfer of all the Board's operational assets to successor companies under the Railways Act 1993, a variety of remaining functions, including obligations in respect of liabilities acquired by British Rail as a major employer over nearly half a century and as a direct result of the privatisation process, are now discharged by BRB (Residuary) Ltd.

G   United Kingdom.

✎   The Government announced on 14 October 2010 that the company will be wound up once a programme of asset disposals is complete.

BRE Trust

■   Bucknalls Lane, Garston, Watford, WD25 9XX.
Tel 01923 664743   http://www.bre.co.uk
Chairman: Sir Neville Simms, FREng

E   Established in April 1990 as the Building Research Establishment, an Executive Agency of the Department of the Environment. Since 1999 the Trust has functioned as a charitable company funded by its wholly owned subsidiary companies, BRE, BRE Global Ltd and FBE Management Ltd. There are twelve trustees including the Chairman.

R   To advance knowledge, innovation and communication in all matters concerning the built environment for public benefit.
To commission public benefit research from the BRE Group of companies and elsewhere.
To award scholarships and bursaries to PhD and MSc students.

G   United Kingdom.

Brecknock & Radnor Community Health Council

■   2nd Floor, 2 The Street, BRECON, Powys, LD3 7LH.
Tel 01874 624206   Fax 01874 611602
Chairman: Mrs Delcie Davies   Chief Officer: Bryn Williams

E   Established in 1974. The Council comprises twelve members including the Chairman.

G   South Powys.

✎   For further information see **Community Health Councils** under **National Health Service - Wales**.

Brecon Beacons National Park Authority   (BBNPA)

■   Plas y Ffynnon, Cambrian Way, BRECON, Powys, LD3 7HP.
Tel 01874 624437   Fax 01874 622574   http://www.breconbeacons.org
Chairman: Cllr Eric Saxon   Chief Executive: John Cook

E   The Brecon Beacons was designated a National Park in 1957. The present Authority was established on 1 April 1997 under the Environment Act 1995. It comprises 24 members including the Chairman.

G   Brecon Beacons.

✎   For further information see **National Park Authorities**.

=   Awdurdod Parc Cenedlaethol Bannau Brycheiniog

Bridgend Local Health Board

✎   Merged on 1 October 2009 with the Neath Port Talbot and Swansea Local Health Boards to form **Abertawe Bro Morgannwg University Health Board**.

Bridlington Harbour Commissioners

■   Gummers Wharf, West End, BRIDLINGTON, E Yorks, YO15 3AN.
Tel 01262 670148   Fax 01262 602041   http://www.bridlingtonharbour.com
Chairman: George Traves, MBE   Harbour Master & Chief Executive: Christopher Wright

G   Bridlington.

✎   For further information see **Port & Harbour Authorities**.

Brightlingsea Harbour Commissioners

■   Harbour Office, 4 Copperas Road, BRIGHTLINGSEA, Essex, CO7 0AP.
Tel 01206 302200   Fax 01206 308533   http://www.brightlingseaharbour.org
Chairman: Roger Robertson

E   Established in 1927.

G   Brightlingsea.

✎   For further information see **Port & Harbour Authorities**.

Bristol International Airport Consultative Committee
- c/o James Gore, Bristol International Airport, BRISTOL, BS48 3DY.
  Tel 01454 260781   http://www.bristolairport.co.uk
  Chairman: Peter Lacey   Secretary: Margaret Thornton
G   Bristol.
✍   For further information see **Airport Consultative Committees**.

Britain's Energy Coast West Cumbria
✍   A trading division of Furness West Cumbria New Vision Urban Regeneration Company which was wound up in
    April 2011.

British Accreditation Council for Independent Further & Higher Education   **(BAC)**
- 44 Bedford Row, LONDON, WC1R 4LL.
  Tel 020 7447 2584   **Fax** 020 7447 2585   http://www.the-bac.org
  Chairman: Tim Cox
E   Established in 1984, the BAC is a company limited by guarantee and a registered charity. The Council comprises
    individuals and representatives of stakeholder organisations who are closely involved in maintaining educational
    standards.
R   To define, monitor and improve standards in independent further and higher education institutions in the UK.
G   United Kingdom.
●   The Council accredits independent institutions which meet its required criteria - there are currently more than 450
    accredited institutions.

British Acupuncture Accreditation Board   **(BAAB)**
- 63 Jeddo Road, LONDON, W12 9HQ.
  Tel 020 8735 0466   http://www.baab.co.uk
  Chairman: Rita Lewis
E   Established in 1989 by agreement. The BAAB comprises representatives of the major schools, the British
    Acupuncture Council (qv), the medical & higher education fields and the public interests it seeks to serve. It
    functions as a company limited by guarantee.
R   To foster high standards of professional education through the development of appropriate criteria and
    guidelines.
G   United Kingdom.

British Acupuncture Council   **(BAcC)**
- 63 Jeddo Road, LONDON, W12 9HQ.
  Tel 020 8735 0400   **Fax** 020 8735 0404   http://www.acupuncture.org.uk
  Chief Executive: Nick Pahl
E   Established in 1995. BAcC is a membership organisation of around 3,000 professionally qualified acupuncturists
    and functions as a company limited by guarantee. The Executive Committee comprises 22 members.
R   To establish and maintain the highest professional standards of practice for acupuncture in the UK.
    To maintain a register of professional membership.
G   United Kingdom.

British American Security Information Council   **(BASIC)**
- 2nd Floor, The Grayston Centre, 28 Charles Square, LONDON, N1 6HT.
  Tel 020 7324 4680   **Fax** 020 7324 4681   http://www.basicint.org
  Suite 205, 110 Maryland Avenue NE, WASHINGTON, DC 20002, USA.
  Tel +1 202 546 8055   **Fax** +1 202 546 8056
  Chairman: Dr Trevor McCrisken   Executive Director: Paul Ingram
E   Established in 1987. BASIC functions as a registered charity. The Council comprises 14 members including the
    Chairman.
R   An independent research and advocacy organisation that works in the UK and USA to encourage sustainable
    transatlantic security policies and to develop the strategies that can achieve them.
    BASIC partners with other international NGOs which share its goals to promote public understanding of the
    danger of growing nuclear arsenals.
G   United Kingdom, United States of America.

British Approvals Board for Telecommunications (BABT)

■ Forsyth House, Churchfield Road, WALTON-ON-THAMES, Surrey, KT12 2TD.
   Tel 01932 251200 **Fax** 01932 251201 http://www.babt.com
   Managing Director: Jean-Louis Evans
E Established on 7 May 1982. BABT functions as a company limited by guarantee.
R To provide a comprehensive suite of compliance and certification services to help equipment suppliers bring their
   radio amd telecommunications terminal equipment to the market and network operators ensure their billing
   systems are accurate.
G United Kingdom.

British Approvals for Fire Equipment (BAFE)

■ Bridges 2, The Fire Service College, London Road, MORETON-IN-MARSH, Glos, GL56 0RH.
   Tel 0844 335 0897 **Fax** 01608 653359 http://www.bafe.org.uk
   General Manager: Stephen Adams
E Established in January 1985 by agreement of all parties concerned and consulted. Members are drawn from
   organisations concerned with fire protection including Government departments, manufacturers, certification
   bodies and test houses.
R To ensure the quality of all fire protection equipment, materials and related services.
G United Kingdom.

British Association for Central & Eastern Europe
✍ Closed on 29 January 2008.

British Board of Agrément (BBA)

■ Bucknalls Lane, Garston, WATFORD, Herts, WD25 9BA.
   Tel 01923 665300 **Fax** 01923 665301 http://www.bbacerts.co.uk
   Chairman: Digby Harper Chief Executive: Greg Cooper
E Established on 2 May 1966 by the Minister of Public Building & Works following the 1965 publication of the report
   'The Assessment of New Building Products' of the Gibson Committee. Previously known as the Agrément
   Board, its name was changed in December 1982 and it now functions as a company limited by guarantee.
R To assess and, if appropriate, issue certificates in respect of materials, products, systems and techniques of an
   innovative character for use in the construction industry.
G United Kingdom.
● The BBA assesses materials, products, systems & techniques by examination &testing.

British Board of Film Classification (BBFC)

■ 3 Soho Square, LONDON, W1D 3HD.
   Tel 020 7440 1570 **Fax** 020 7287 0141 http://www.bbfc.co.uk
   President: Sir Quentin Thomas, CB Chairman: Graham Lee Director: David Cooke
E Established in 1912 and known as the British Board of Film Censorship until 1 June 1985 when it was also
   designated by the Home Secretary as the authority responsible for classifying video works under the Video
   Recordings Act 1984. The BBFC is an independent body and is financed by fees charged for the examination
   cinema films and videos.
R To ensure that a proper national standard is maintained in films offered for cinema exhibition and in video works
   supplied to the public primarily for viewing in the home.
G United Kingdom.
● The Board at present grants certificates in the following categories: U (Universal), PG (Parental Guidance), 12A/12
   (Cinema/Video not suitable for children under 12), 15 (Not suitable for children under 15), 18 (Suitable for adults
   only) and R18 (Restricted: films to be shown only in licensed cinemas, and videos supplied only in licensed sex
   shops, and to adults only).

British Boxing Board of Control Ltd (BBBofC)

■ 14 North Road, CARDIFF, CF10 3DY.
   Tel 029 2036 7000 **Fax** 029 2036 7019 http://www.bbbofc.com
   Chairman: Charles Giles General Secretary: Robert Smith
E Established in 1929. The Board is incorporated as a limited liability company. It comprises eight administrative
   stewards and eight representative stewards; the membership consists of some 2,000 licence holders.
R To control, regulate and license professional boxing in Great Britain and Northern Ireland, and represent the
   interests of British licence holders internationally.
G United Kingdom.

British Broadcasting Corporation   (BBC)

■   Broadcasting House, Portland Place, LONDON, W1A 1AA.
     Tel 020 8743 8000   **Fax** 020 7580 7725   http://www.bbc.co.uk
     Director-General: Mark Thompson
E   Established on 20 December 1926 by Royal Charter, as a successor to the British Broadcasting Company Ltd;
         renewal Charters are granted every ten years. It functions as a Public Broadcasting Authority responsible to the
         Department for Culture, Media & Sport. The Corporation's activities are overseen by the BBC Trust (qv) which
         appoints the Director-General. The Executive Board comprises 17 members and is chaired by the Director-
         General.
R   The BBC operates two national television channels, five UK radio stations, separate radio stations for Scotland,
         Wales and Northern Ireland, and 40 local radio stations.
     It also operates six digital television channels, five digital radio stations, BBCi online and the BBC World Service.
G   United Kingdom.
✍   The BBC is a nominally autonomous corporation, independent from direct government intervention.
     See also the **Audience Councils** of England, Scotland, Wales and Northern Ireland.

British Cheese Board   (BCB)

■   Kindred, 90 Long Acre, LONDON, WC2E 9RA.
     Tel 020 7010 1864   http://www.britishcheese.com
     Secretary: Nigel White
E   Established in 1995 as a membership organisation for cheese producers, BCB currently has 27 members.
R   To educate the British public about the nutritional and health benefits of eating cheese as part of a balanced diet.
G   United Kingdom.

British Committee for the Reunification of the Parthenon Marbles   (BCRPM)

■   73 St Paul's Place, LONDON, N1 2LT.
     Tel 020 7226 6686   **Fax** 020 7704 8973   http://www.parthenonuk.com
     Chairman: Prof Anthony Snodgrass
E   Established in 1983 following a resolution passed in Mexico by the UNESCO Conference of Ministers of Culture in
         August 1982. The Committee comprises eleven members including the Chairman.
R   To secure the reunification of the Parthenon Marbles in Greece by presenting the case as fully as possible to the
         British public and to bring the most effective pressure on the Trustees of the British Museum and on the British
         Government.
G   United Kingdom.
●   The activities are those of a pressure group.
     The Committee organises lectures & seminars and answers a large number of queries on the subject of the return
         of the 'Parthenon Marbles'; it also offers help & information to students & academics doing research on this
         subject.

British Copyright Council   (BCC)

■   29-33 Berners Street, LONDON, W1T 3AB.
     Tel 01986 788122   **Fax** 01986 788847   http://www.britishcopyright.org
     Chairman: Paul Mitchell   Chief Executive: Janet Ibbotson
E   Established in 1965. BCC is a national consultative and advisory body representing organisations of copyright
         owners and performers and others interested in copyright in the UK. The Council comprises ten members
         including the Chairman.
R   To provide a forum where members can discuss matters of copyright interest.
     To act as a pressure group for changes in copyright law at UK, European and international level.
G   United Kingdom.

British Council   (BC)

■   Bridgewater House, 58 Whitworth Street, MANCHESTER, M1 6BB.
     Tel 0161 957 7000   **Fax** 0161 957 7111   http://www.britishcouncil.org
     10 Spring Gardens, LONDON, SW1A 2BN.
     Tel 020 7389 4385   **Fax** 020 7389 6347
     Chairman: Sir Vernon Ellis   Chief Executive: Martin Davidson, CMG
E   Established in 1934 by the Government, it was incorporated by Royal Charter in 1940 and granted a
         Supplemental Charter in 1993. The Council is a registered charity and functions as an Executive NDPB of the
         Foreign & Commonwealth Office. The Board of Trustees comprises twelve members including the Chairman.
R   To promote an enduring understanding and appreciation of Britain in other countries through cultural, educational
         and technical co-operation.
G   United Kingdom.
●   The Council has a network of offices in 110 countries worldwide.

© CBD Research Ltd · Beckenham · Kent BR3 5JS · Tel 020 8650 7745 · Fax 020 8650 0768 · E-mail cbd@cbdresearch.com · www.cbdresearch.com

British Council of Disabled People
✍ Now known as the **United Kingdom Disabled Person's Council**.

British Council for Prevention of Blindness   (BCPB)
- 4 Bloomsbury Square, LONDON, WC1A 2RP.
  Tel 020 7404 7114   http://www.bcpb.org
  Chairman: Dr Jeffrey Jay, CBE
E Established in 1976 by agreement between the leading organisations in Britain concerned with blindness, and
   known until 24 May 1983 as the British National Committee for the Prevention of Blindness. BCPB is a
   registered charity. The Board of Trustees comprises ten members including the Chairman.
R To provide training and research opportunities which help to prevent blindness worldwide, particularly in
   developing countries.
G United Kingdom.
✍ BCPB also uses the subtitle Save Eyes Everywhere (SEE).

British Crop Protection Council   (BCPC)
- 7 Omni Business Centre, Omega Park, ALTON, Hants, GU34 2QD.
  Tel 01420 593200   **Fax** 01420 593209   http://www.bcpc.org
  Chairman: Dr Colin Ruscoe   Manager: Chris Todd
E Established on 2 May 1978 by joint resolution of the British Weed Control Council and the British Insecticide &
   Fungicide Council. The Council is a membership body comprising approximately 20 organisations with an
   interest in crops, their protection and health. The Executive Board comprises nine members including the
   Chairman.
R To examine current and developing issues in the science and practice of crop production.
   To promote improved, environmentally sensitive crop production practices to produce wholesome food.
   To foster and support crop production science and practice through congresses, symposia and publications and
   through presentation of its views to government and other organisations.
   To present independent information to the general public on the place of crop production in agriculture and
   horticulture, and to encourage and contribute to education and training.
G United Kingdom.

British Dance Council   (BDC)
- Terpsichore House, 240 Merton Road, South Wimbledon, LONDON, SW19 1EQ.
  Tel 020 8545 0085   **Fax** 020 8545 0225   http://www.british-dance-council.org
  Chairman: Bryan Allen
E Established in 1929 as the Official Board of Ballroom Dancing; in November 1986 it became the British Council of
   Ballroom Dancing, and then assumed its present name in August 1996. Members of the Council are nominated
   by dance teacher organisations, professional and amateur dancers' organisations and public companies.
R To be the governing body for all matters pertaining to ballroom, latin american and disco freestyle dancing
   throughout England, Wales, Scotland, Northern Ireland and the Channel Islands.
G United Kingdom, Channel Islands.

British Educational Communications & Technology Agency
✍ Becta closed on 31 March 2011, its functions transferred to the Department for Education.

British Egg Industry Council   (BEIC)
- 2nd Floor, 89 Charterhouse Street, LONDON, EC1M 6HR.
  Tel 020 7608 3760   **Fax** 020 7608 3860   http://www.egginfo.co.uk/pages/ukeggs/
  Chief Executive: Mark Williams
E Established in July 1986. BEIC functions as an inter-professional organisation of eleven trade associations in the
   UK, which cover all aspects of the egg industry.
R To represent the interests of its members in discussions with Government, MPs, the European Commission, the
   European Parliament and other bodies.
   To finance research and development.
G United Kingdom.

British Electrotechnical Committee   (BEC)
- 389 Chiswick High Road, LONDON, W4 4AL.
  Tel 020 8996 9001   **Fax** 020 8996 7001   http://www.bsi-global.com
  President: Geoff Young
E Established in 1906.

R   To formulate the UK input to the International Electrotechnical Commission (IEC) and to the European Committee for Electrotechnical Standardisation (CENELEC).

G   United Kingdom.

British Fashion Council   (BFC)

■   5 Portland Place, LONDON, W1B 1PW.
Tel 020 7636 7788 **Fax** 020 7637 7515 http://www.britishfashioncouncil.com
Chairman: Harold Tillman

E   Established in 1983. The BFC is sponsored by various companies and organisations involved in the fashion industry.

R   To showcase British designers and develop London's position as a major player in the international fashion arena.

G   United Kingdom.

●   The BFC actively seeks to encourage the links throughout the fashion industry.

British Fenestration Rating Council   (BFRC)

■   54 Ayres Street, LONDON, SE1 1EU.
Tel 020 7403 9200 http://www.bfrc.org
Chief Executive: Graham Hinett

E   Set up in 1999 with assistance from Government and the major window industry trade associations, BFRC was established as a limited company in 2005. It operates with the support of the relevant trade associations and a broad range of other bodies, including research organisations, professional institutes and the Energy Saving Trust (qv).

R   To operate a uniform national rating system for the thermal performance of fenestration products.

G   United Kingdom.

●   Taking into account heat loss from the window through thermal transmittance and air leakage, together with heat gained from the sun, the scheme gives A to G ratings in a clear format.

British Film Commission

✍   In May 2003 BFC was absorbed by the former UK Film Council whose functions transferred in April 2011 the **British Film Institute** and **Film London**.

British Film Institute   (BFI)

■   21 Stephen Street, LONDON, W1T 1LN.
Tel 020 7255 1444 **Fax** 020 7436 7950
Chairman: Greg Dyke   Director: Amanda Nevill

E   Established in 1933 by Royal Charter, the BFI functions as an Executive NDPB of the Department for Culture, Media & Sport. In April 2011 it became the lead strategic body on film and the distributor of Lottery funds to UK film-makers. The Board comprises 15 Governors including the Chairman.

R   To promote understanding and appreciation of film and television heritage and culture.

G   United Kingdom.

✍   For further information see companion volume **Directory of British Associations**.

British Forces Post Office   (BFPO)

■   West End Road, RUISLIP, Middx, HA4 6DQ.
Tel 0845 769 7978 http://www.bpfo.org.uk

E   Established on 1 July 1992 as an Executive Agency of the Ministry of Defence and called the Defence Postal & Courier Service Agency until it was relaunched on 1 July 1999 as BFPO. It now functions as a Business Unit within the Defence & Equipment Support organisation (qv).

R   To provide an efficient and effective postal and courier service in order to sustain the fighting power of the UK armed forces worldwide.

G   United Kingdom.

British Greyhound Racing Board

✍   Merged with the National Greyhound Racing Club as the **Greyhound Board of Great Britain**, 1 January 2009.

British Hallmarking Council   (BHC)

■   1 Colmore Square, BIRMINGHAM, B4 6AA.
Tel 0870 763 1414 **Fax** 0870 763 1814 http://www.bis.gov.uk/britishhallmarkingcouncil/
Chairman: Tom Murray   Secretary: David Gwyther

E   Established on 1 January 1974 under the Hallmarking Act 1973 to perform the functions assigned to it under the Act from 1 January 1975. The BHC functions as an Executive NDPB and a Public Corporation accountable to the Department for Business, Innovation & Skills. The Council comprises 19 members including the Chairman. The Assay Masters of the Birmingham, Edinburgh, London and Sheffield Offices are entitled to attend Council meetings.
R   To ensure that adequate facilities for the assaying and hallmarking of articles of precious metal are available as from time to time required in the United Kingdom.
    To supervise the activities of assay offices.
    To take all steps to ensure enforcement of the law in respect of hallmarking.
    To advise the Secretary of State on all matters concerning the execution of the Act.
G   United Kingdom.

British Horseracing Authority   (BHA)

■   75 High Holborn, LONDON, WC1V 6LS.
    Tel 020 7152 0000   http://www.britishhorseracing.com
    Chairman: Paul Roy   Acting Chief Executive: Chris Brand
E   Established in July 2007 combining the governance functions of the British Horseracing Board with the regulatory functions of the Horseracing Regulatory Authority. The board comprises eight members including the Chairman.
R   To govern the sport of horseracing and regulate matters pertaining to it.
G   United Kingdom.

British Horseracing Board
✍   Merged with the Horseracing Regulatory Authority to form the **British Horseracing Authority** in July 2007.

British-Irish Council   (BIC)

■   6th Floor, Selborne House, 54-60 Victoria Street, LONDON, SW1E 6QW.
    Tel 020 7210 8500   Fax 020 7210 0647   http://www.british-irishcouncil.org
    Iveagh House, St Stephens Green, DUBLIN 2, Republic of Ireland.
E   Established under Strand Three of the Multi-Party Good Friday Agreement reached in Belfast on 10 April 1998, the BIC came into effect on 2 December 1999 with the devolution of power from Westminster to the Northern Ireland Assembly. Membership of the Council comprises representatives of the Governments of the United Kingdom, Ireland, Jersey, Guernsey and the Isle of Man, and of the devolved administrations of Northern Ireland, Scotland and Wales.
R   To promote positive, practical relationships among its members.
G   United Kingdom, Republic of Ireland, Channel Islands, Isle of Man.
●   The Council's secretariats are based at the Ministry of Justice in London and the Department of Foreign Affairs in Dublin.

British Judo Council   (BJC)

■   37 High Street, STALHAM, Norfolk, NR12 9AH.   http://www.britishjudocouncil.org
    President: Robin Otani
E   BJC is a membership organisation.
R   To promote and encourage Judo and Budo.
G   United Kingdom.

British Library

■   96 Euston Road, LONDON, NW1 2DB.
    Tel 0870 444 1500   http://www.bl.uk
    Chairman: Baroness Blackstone   Chief Executive: Dame Lynne Brindley, DBE
E   Established in July 1973 under provisions of the British Library Act 1972. The British Library Board functions as an Executive NDPB of the Department for Culture, Media and Sport. It comprises 14 members including the Chairman.
R   To provide, on a national scale, comprehensive reference, lending, bibliographic and other services.
G   United Kingdom.
●   The British Library holds 14,000,000 books, 920,000 journals and newspaper titles, 58,000,000 patents and 3,000,000 sound recordings.

British Library Advisory Council

■   96 Euston Road, LONDON, NW1 2DB.
    Tel 0870 444 1500   http://www.bl.uk
    Chairman: Sir David Arculus

E   The Council comprises 15 members including the Chairman.
R   To advise the British Library on the broad scope of its operations and policies for future developments.
      To help ensure that the Library's plans are formulated and implemented effectively.
G   United Kingdom.

BRITISH MEDICAL ASSOCIATION [Boards & Committees]   (BMA)

E   The BMA has numerous boards and committees each with a specific interest in one of the many aspects of medical practice.
G   United Kingdom.
●   See separate entries for:
        Board of Science
        Committee on Community Care
        Equality & Diversity Committee
        Medical Ethics Committee
        Medico-Legal Committee
        Ophthalmic Group Committee
        Pensions Committee
        Private Practice Committee
        Professional Fees Committee

BRITISH MEDICAL ASSOCIATION [Branch of Practice Committees]   (BMA)

E   BOP committees have been set up by the BMA to represent and act for all doctors in the various branches of practice, whether they are BMA members or not. The BOP structure is mirrored in Scotland, Wales and Northern Ireland.
R   Each committee is recognised by the health departments in national negotiations for pay and conditions of service and by the relevant pay review body at the Office of Manpower Economics (qv).
G   United Kingdom.
●   The eleven BOP committees are:
        Armed Forces Committee
        Central Consultants & Specialists Committee
        Civil & Public Services Committee
        Forensic Medicine Committee
        General Practitioners Committee
        Junior Doctors Committee
        Medical Academic Staff Committee
        Medical Students Committee
        Occupational Medicine Committee
        Public Health Medicine Committee
        Staff & Associate Specialists Committee (qqv).

British Museum
■   Great Russell Street, LONDON, WC1B 3DG.
      Tel 020 7323 8000   **Fax** 020 7323 8614   http://www.british-museum.ac.uk
      Chairman: Niall FitzGerald, KBE
E   The Museum, established by an Act of Parliament in 1753, is governed in accordance with the British Museum Act 1963 and the Museums & Galleries Act 1992. The Board of Trustees functions as an Executive NDPB of the Department for Culture, Media & Sport. It comprises 23 trustees including the Chairman.
R   To hold for the benefit and education of humanity a collection representative of world cultures.
      To ensure that the collection is housed in safety, conserved, curated, researched and exhibited.
G   United Kingdom.

British Music Writers Council
✍   Now the music writers' section of the Musicians' Union.

British-North American Committee   (BNAC)
■   St Clement's House, 27-28 Clement's Lane, LONDON, EC4N 7AE.
      Tel 020 3207 9432   **Fax** 020 3207 9134   http://www.bnac.org
      UK Chairman: Sir Paul Judge
E   Established in 1969, the Committee is sponsored in the UK by the British-North American Research Association. The three national chairmen are Sir Paul Judge (UK), Derek Oland (Canada) and Alan Griffith (USA). There are currently 98 members, leaders from business, industry and academia in the three countries.

R   To study and comment upon the developing relationships between Britain, the United States and Canada. To promote clearer understanding of the economic opportunities and problems facing the three countries.

G   United Kingdom, Canada, United States.

British Nuclear Fuels plc

✍   On 14 October 2010 the Government announced its intention to abolish BNFL, subject to transferring its remaining assets and liabilities. The transfer of its national facilities and their clean-up liabilities to the **Nuclear Decommissioning Authority** was completed in May 2009.

British Pharmacopoeia Commission   (BPC)

■   5th Floor, 151 Buckingham Palace Road, LONDON, SW1W 9SZ.
Tel 020 3080 6561   http://www.pharmacopoeia.gov.uk
Chairman: Prof David Woolfson

E   Established in 1928, following recommendations made in that year by a sub-committee of the Committee of Civil Research, it is now appointed under the Medicines Act 1968. BPC functions as an advisory body to the Medicines & Healthcare products Regulatory Agency (qv). It comprises 18 Commissioners including the Chairman.

R   To be responsible for the preparation under the Medicines Act 1968 of new editions of the British Pharmacopoeia and the British Pharmacopoeia (Veterinary), and for keeping them up to date.
To provide advice to the UK delegation to the European Pharmacopoeia Commission.

G   United Kingdom.

British Pig Executive   (BPEX)

■   AHDB, Stoneleigh Park, KENILWORTH, Warwickshire, CV8 2TL.
Tel 024 7669 2051   Fax 024 7647 8903   http://www.bpex.org.uk
Chairman: Stewart Houston, CBE   Chief Executive: Mick Sloyan

E   Established on 1 April 2008 via the Agriculture & Hortculture Development Board Order 2008. It functions as a subsidiary of the Agriculture & Horticulture Development Board (qv). The BPEX board comprises 11 members including the Chairman.

R   To enhance competitiveness, efficiency and profitability for pig levy payers and drive up demand for English pork and pig meat products in Britain and globally.

G   England.

✍   A subsidiary of the **Agriculture & Horticulture Development Board** and funded through an AHDB levy paid on all pigs slaughtered in or exported from England.

British Potato Council

✍   See **Potato Council**.

British Railways Board   See **BRB Residuary Ltd**.

British Safety Council

■   70 Chancellors Road, LONDON, W6 9RS.
Tel 020 8741 1231   Fax 020 8741 4555   http://www.britsafe.org
Chairman: Lynda Armstrong   Chief Executive: Julie Nerney

E   Founded in 1957 by agreement. The Council has 10,000 member companies and subscribers. It functions as an independent body and a registered charity. The Board of Trustees comprises twelve members including the Chairman.

R   To offer a complete range of health and safety qualifications, from entry level to Level 6 in the National Qualifications Framework.

G   United Kingdom.

British Screen Advisory Council   (BSAC)

■   73 Berwick Street, LONDON, W1F 8TE.
Tel 020 7287 1111   Fax 020 7287 1123   http://www.bsac.uk.com
Chairman: Adam Singer   Chief Executive: Fiona Clarke-Hackston

E   Established on 23 May 1985. BSAC functions as a non-statutory independent advisory body. The Council comprises 58 members including the Chairman.

R   To enhance the prosperity, effectiveness and reputation of the UK audiovisual industries.

G   United Kingdom.

- BSAC provides a unique forum for senior executives and specialists from diverse sectors to exchange ideas and information.
  It operates as an industry body, independent of government and individual corporate interests.
  It places priority on the collection and presentation of facts and views held by different sectors of the industry to inform business and public policy issues.
  It makes effective use of the broadest possible spectrum of knowledge and experience to convey informed independent and authoritative advice to the UK and European governments.
  It explores and assesses the impact of technological and commercial developments on the audiovisual industries.

British Shipbuilders
✎ On 14 October 2010 the Government announced the abolition of British Shipbuilders, its remaining functions already transferred to the Department for Business, Innovation & Skills.

British Shooting Sports Council   (BSSC)
■ PO Box 53608, LONDON, SE24 9YN.
  Tel 020 7095 8181   **Fax** 020 7095 8181   http://www.bssc.org.uk
  Chairman: Lord Glentoran, CBE   Secretary: David Penn
E Established in 1956 by agreement. BSSC is an umbrella organisation representing the major shooting associations in the UK.
R To promote and safeguard the lawful use of firearms and air weapons for sporting and recreational purposes in the UK amongst all sections of the community.
G United Kingdom.
- The Council acts as a conduit between the Home Office and other Government departments and agencies, the police service, etc, for the exchange of views and information across the spectrum of the sport of shooting.

British Sports Trust   See **Sports Leaders UK**.

British Tourism Development Committee   (BTDC)
■ 1 Palace Street, LONDON, SW1E 5HE.
  Tel 020 7578 1000
  Chairman: Tom Wright
E Established in 1995 by the British Tourist Authority (now VisitBritain). The Committee comprises approximately 50 members representing tourism organisations and companies.
R To provide a forum for discussion and representation to Government, VisitBritain (qv), other statutory tourist boards, and other public and private sector organisations on all matters affecting the British tourism industry.
G United Kingdom.

British Tourist Authority   See **VisitBritain**.

British Transport Police Authority   (BTPA)
■ 5th Floor North, The Forum, 74-80 Camden Street, LONDON, NW1 0EG.
  Tel 020 7383 0259   **Fax** 020 7383 2655   http://www.bt.police.uk
  Chairman: Millie Banerjee   Chief Executive: Andrew Figgures, CB, CBE
E Established on 1 July 2004 under the Railways, Transport & Safety Act 2003. The Authority functions as an Executive NDPB of the Department for Transport. The board comprises 13 members including the Chairman.
R To secure an efficient and effective police force for the railways.
G England, Wales, Scotland.

British Waterways
■ 64 Clarendon Road, WATFORD, Herts, WD17 1DA.
  Tel 01923 201120   **Fax** 01923 201304   http://www.britishwaterways.co.uk
  Chairman: Tony Hales, CBE   Chief Executive: Robin Evans, BSc, FRICS   Shareholder Executive contact: Peter Shortt
E Established on 1 January 1963 under the Transport Act 1962, taking over the inland waterway functions of the former British Transport Commission. Its powers and duties were extended under the Transport Act 1968. British Waterways functions as a Public Corporation accountable to the Department for Environment, Food & Rural Affairs, the Scottish Executive Enterprise, Transport & Lifelong Learning Department and the National Assembly for Wales. The Board comprises ten members including the Chairman.
R To manage and care for more than 2,200 miles of canals and rivers in England, Scotland and Wales on behalf of the British people.

G   England, Wales, Scotland.
✍   One of the businesses managed by the **Shareholder Executive**.
     On 14 October 2010 the Government announced that British Waterways will be abolished as a public corporation
     in England & Wales by April 2012 and will become a charitable body, similar to a National Trust for the
     waterways.

British Wool Marketing Board   (BWMB)

■   Wool House, Roydsdale Way, Euroway Trading Estate, BRADFORD, W Yorks, BD4 6SE.
     Tel 01274 688666   **Fax** 01274 652233   http://www.britishwool.org.uk
     Chairman: Frank Langrish   Chief Executive: Ian Hartley
E   Established in August 1950 by SI 1950/1326 (made under the provisions of the Agricultural Marketing Acts 1931
     to 1949, but now having effect under the Agricultural Marketing Act 1958); amendments to the original scheme
     have been made by subsequent Statutory Instruments. The BWMB is a non-profit making organisation and the
     only remaining agricultural commodity board in the UK. The Board comprises eleven members including the
     Chairman.
R   To operate a central marketing system for British fleece wool, with the aim of achieving the best possible return
     for producers.
G   United Kingdom.
●   The Board collects, grades, sells and promotes fleece wool.

British Youth Council   (BYC)

■   6th Floor, Hillgate House, 26 Old Bailey, LONDON, EC4M 7HW.
     Tel 0845 458 1489   **Fax** 0845 458 1847   http://www.byc.org.uk
     Chairman: Liam Preston   Chief Executive: James Cathcart
E   Established in 1948 as the British National Committee of the World Assembly of Youth (WAY). On 2 June 1966 the
     Council adopted its present title and increased the scope of its activities. BYC is a membership body with over
     130 local youth councils and other organisations. The Board of Trustees comprises 13 members including the
     Chairman.
R   To connect with member organisations to empower all aged 25 and under to get involved in the things that are
     important to them and to have a say in the decisions that affect their lives.
     To run training workshops, create volunteering opportunities and build inspiring campaigns which give everyone
     aged 25 and under the chance to make a positive contribution to society both in the UK and abroad.
G   United Kingdom.

Broadcast Advertising Standards Board of Finance Ltd   (Basbof)

■   5th Floor, 21 Berners Street, LONDON, W1T 3LP.
     Tel 020 7580 7071   http://www.basbof.co.uk
     Chairman: Sir Chris Powell   Secretary: Stephen Hemsted
E   Established in August 2004. Basbof is an independent body set up by the main organisations involved in
     advertising. The Board comprises representatives from eight major industry bodies.
R   To operate a levy scheme in order to raise funding for the running of the Advertising Standards Authority (qv),
     thus assuring its operational independence.
G   United Kingdom.
●   Under the scheme advertisers pay a levy on radio and television advertising on Ofcom (qv) licensed broadcasters.
✍   See also **Asbof**.

Broadcasters' Audience Research Board

✍   BARB, a private company limited by guarantee, is the sole provider of audience measurement for all television
     broadcasting across all channels (terrestrial, cable, satellite, analogue, digital) in the UK. It is funded by the
     major players in the industry it supports (BBC, ITV, IPA, Channel 4, BSkyB, Five).

Broadcasting Council for Northern Ireland

✍   Replaced 1 January 2007 by the **Audience Council for Northern Ireland**.

Broadcasting Council for Scotland

✍   Replaced 1 January 2007 by **Audience Council Scotland**.

Broadcasting Council for Wales

✍   Replaced 1 January 2007 by **Audience Council Wales**.

Broadmoor Hospital Authority
✍ Since April 2001 the hospital has been administered by the West London Mental Health NHS Trust.

Broads Authority
■ Dragonfly House, 2 Gilders Way, NORWICH, Norfolk, NR3 1UB.
   Tel 01603 610734   Fax 01603 765710   http://www.broads-authority.gov.uk
   Chairman: Dr Stephen Johnson
E The Authority was established under the Norfolk & Suffolk Broads Act 1988. Not in the strictest sense a National
   Park, it describes itself as a member of the National Park family. The Authority comprises 21 members including
   the Chairman.
R To conserve and enhance the natural beauty, wildlife and cultural heritage of the Broads.
   To promote opportunities for the understanding and enjoyment of the qualities of the Broads by the public.
   To protect the interests of navigation.
G Norfolk and Suffolk Broads.
✍ For further information see **National Park Authorities**.

Buckinghamshire Community Action
■ The Firs (Unit B), Aylesbury Road, Bierton, AYLESBURY, Bucks, HP22 5DX.
   Tel 01296 421036   Fax 01296 331464   http://www.bucks-comm-action.org.uk
   Chairman: Mike Moore   Executive Director: Michael Hunt
E Buckinghamshire Community Action functions as a registered charity and company limited by guarantee.
   The board comprises nine members including the Chairman.
R To offer help and support to local voluntary groups and community organisations working closely with both the
   voluntary and statutory sectors.
   To promote and enable true partnership working at strategic, operational and local levels, aiming to ensure that
   community development is understood by all.
G Buckinghamshire.
✍ Buckinghamshire Community Action is one of the 38 Rural Community Councils, represented at the national level
   by **Action with Communities in Rural England** (qv) and at the regional level by South East Rural Community
   Councils.

Budget Responsibility Committee   See **Office for Budget Responsibility**.

Building Regulations Advisory Committee   (BRAC)
■ Zone 5/E8, Eland House, Bressenden Place, LONDON, SW1E 3DU.
   Tel 0303 444 1819
   Chairman: Michael D Finn, MBE, FRICS, FBEng, FRSA, MCIArb
E Established in April 1962 under the Public Health Act 1961, its current authority is derived under the Building Act
   1984. BRAC functions as a Scientific Advisory Committee and an Advisory NDPB of the Department for
   Communities & Local Government. The Committee comprises 19 members including the Chairman.
R To advise the Secretary of State on the exercise of his powers to make building regulations, and on other
   subjects connected with building regulations.
G England, Wales.
✍ For further information see **Scientific Advisory Committees**.

Building Standards Advisory Committee
✍ Under the Public Services Reform (Scotland) Act 2010 and the Building (Scotland) Amendment Regulations 2010
   building standards are now the responsibility of Scottish Ministers and BSAC has been dissolved.

Built Environment Forum Scotland   (BEFS)
■ 9 Manor Place, EDINBURGH, EH3 7DN.
   Tel 0131 220 6241   Fax 0131 220 6241   http://www.befs.org.uk
   Chairman: Robin Burley
E Established in 2002. BEFS is a membership body functioning as a company limited by guarantee and registered
   charity. Members are non-governmental organisations and professional bodies in the built environment sector.
   The Board comprises seven members including the Chairman.
R To support organisations in pursuing excellence in place-making by providing a forum for understanding,
   promoting and influencing the dynamic relationship between the historic environment, new design and
   sustainable development.
G Scotland.

Burials & Cemeteries Advisory Group   (BCAG)
- ■ Selbourne House, 54 Victoria Street, LONDON, SW1E 6QW.
  Tel 020 3334 6390
- E Established in December 2001 following the report on cemeteries by the Environment, Transport & Regional Affairs Select Committee.
  The BCAG functions as an Advisory NDPB of the Ministry of Justice.
  The Panel comprises representatives of numerous associations of interested parties.
- R To provide good practice advice on the provision, management and maintenance of burial grounds, including such grounds closed to further burials.
  To produce advice on good burial practice and procedures, including exhumation.
  To make recommendations to the Ministry of Justice on appropriate policy and legislative change, including recommendations on future advisory arrangements.
- G England, Wales.

Bus Users Complaints Tribunal
- ✍ Superceded by the **Public Transport Users' Committee for Scotland** in 2007.

Business Development Service
- ✍ On 1 April 2006 BDS became part of the Delivery & Innovation Division, a directorate within the Department of Finance & Personnel Northern Ireland.

Business Services Organisation   (BSO)
- ■ 2 Franklin Street, BELFAST, BT2 8DQ.
  Tel 028 9032 4431   http://www.hscbusiness.hscni.net
- E Established on 1 April 2009 on the recommendation of the NI Review of Public Administration 2005, replacing the former Central Services Agency. BSO functions as Executive Agency of the Department of Health, Social Services & Public Safety Northern Ireland. The Board comprises 13 members including the Chairman.
- R To provide a broad range of regional business support functions and specialist professional services to the whole of the Health & Social Care sector in Northern Ireland (it is also known as the Health & Social Care Business Services Organisation).
- G Northern Ireland.

Buying Solutions
- ■ 3rd Floor, Royal Liver Building, Pier Head, LIVERPOOL, L3 1PE.
  Tel 0345 410 2222   Fax 0151 227 3315   http://www.buyingsolutions.gov.uk
- E OGCbuying.solutions was established on 2 April 2001, merging the procurement functions of the Buying Agency and the Central Computer & Telecommunications Agency; In 2009 it absorbed the procurement functions of NHS Purchasing & Supply Agency and adopted its current name. It functions as an Executive Agency of the Office of Government Commerce in HM Treasury. The Board comprises eight members and is chaired by the Chief Executive.
- R To maximise the value for money obtained by Government departments and other public bodies through the procurement and supply of goods and services.
- G United Kingdom.

Bwrdd Cynghorau Iechyd Cymuned Cymru   See the **Board of Community Health Councils in Wales**.

Bwrdd yr Iaith Gymraeg   See the **Welsh Language Board**.

Bwrdd Ymghyngorol Henebion Cymru   See **Ancient Monuments Advisory Board**.

C3HARGE

■ Redgrave Court, Merton Road, BOOTLE, Merseyside, L20 7HS.
Tel 0845 345 0055
E Established in December 1977 by the Health & Safety Executive (qv) as the Ceramics Industry Advisory
Committee, it adopted its current name when its remit was expanded to include other mineral industries. The
Board comprises eight members.
R To provide a forum to promote improved standards of health and safety within the brick, cement, ceramics,
concrete, glass, heavy clay and refractories industries.
G United Kingdom.
✍ The C3HARGE acronym is loosely derived from Cement, Ceramics, Concrete, Heavy Clay, Refractories & Glass
Manufacturing Industries Joint Health & Safety Advisory Committee.

Cadw

■ Plas Carew, Unit 5/7 Cefn Coed, Parc Nantgarw, CARDIFF, CF15 7QQ.
Tel 01443 336000   Fax 01443 336001   http://www.cadw.wales.gov.uk
E Established in 1984, replacing the former Historic Buildings Council for Wales, the word Cadw is pronounced
'cadoo' and means 'to keep'. Cadw is the Welsh Government's historic environment service.
R To protect the historic environment of Wales (historic buildings, ancient monuments, historic parks, gardens,
landscapes and underwater archaeology) by working with partners and private owners.
G Wales.
✍ One of the four organisations which make up **Historic Wales**.

Caernarfon Harbour Trust

■ Harbour Office, Slate Quay, CAERNARFON, LL55 2PB.
Tel 01286 672118   Fax 01286 678729   http://www.caernarfonharbour.co.uk
Harbour Master: Richard Jones
E Established under the Caernarfon Harbour Acts & Orders 1793 to 1989.
R To control navigation and to provide and maintain navigational aids in the area from Britannia Bridge to
Caernarfon Bay.
To provide pilotage throughout the Menai Strait.
G Caernarfon, Menai Strait.
✍ For further information see **Port & Harbour Authorities**.

Caerphilly Teaching Local Health Board

✍ Merged on 1 October 2009 with the Blaenau Gwent, Monmouthshire, Newport and Torfaue Local Health Boards
to form **Aneurin Bevan Health Board**.

Cairngorms National Park Authority   (CNPA)

■ 14 The Square, GRANTOWN-ON-SPEY, Moray, PH26 3HG.
Tel 01479 873535   Fax 01479 873527   http://www.cairngorms.co.uk
Convenor: David Green   Chief Executive: Mrs Jane Hope
E Established on 25 March 2003 under provisions made in the National Parks (Scotland) Act 2000. CNPA functions
as an Executive NDPB of the Scottish Executive Rural Affairs Department. The Authority comprises 23
members including the Convenor.
R To conserve and enhance the natural and cultural heritage of the area.
To promote the sustainable use of the natural resources of the area.
To promote understanding and enjoyment (including enjoyment in the form of recreation) of the special qualities
of the area by the public.
To promote sustainable economic and social development of the area's communities.
G Cairngorms.
✍ For further information see **National Park Authorities**.

Caithness & Sutherland Enterprise

✍ This former Local Enterprise Company is now an area office of **Highlands & Islands Enterprise**.

© CBD Research Ltd · Beckenham · Kent BR3 5JS · Tel 020 8650 7745 · Fax 020 8650 0768 · E-mail cbd@cbdresearch.com · www.cbdresearch.com

Caledonian MacBrayne Ltd
✍ See **David MacBrayne Limited**.

___

Caledonian Maritime Assets Ltd   (CMAL)
- Municipal Buildings, Fore Street, PORT GLASGOW, PA14 5EQ.
  Tel 01475 749920   http://www.cmassets.co.uk
  Chairman: Grenville Johnston, OBE   Managing Director: Guy Platten
- E   Established October 2006. CMAL functions as a Public Corporation, wholly owned by the Scottish Government. The board comprises three members including the Chairman.
- R   To provide, safeguard and develop the ferries and harbours serving the West Coast of Scotland and the Clyde Valley.
- G   Clyde and Hebrides.
- ● CMAL owns the vessels, harbours and equipment required for the operation of the Clyde & Hebrides Ferry Services. The vessels are leased to the operators of those services, currently CalMac Ferries Ltd.

___

Camborne, Pool & Redruth Urban Regeneration Company   See **CPR Regeneration**.

___

Cambridge ESOL
- 1 Hills Road, CAMBRIDGE, CB1 2EU.
  Tel 01223 553311   Fax 01223 460278   http://www.cambridgeesol.org
  Chief Executive: Dr Michael Milanovic
- E   An awarding body for courses and qualifications for learners and teachers of English.
- ✍   See also the **Federation of Awarding Bodies**.

___

Cambridgeshire ACRE
- 32 Main Street, Littleport, ELY, Cambs, CB6 1PJ.
  Tel 01353 860850   Fax 01353 862040   http://www.cambsacre.org.uk
  Chairman: John Yates   Chief Executive: Kirsten Bennett
- E   Established in 1924. Cambridgeshire ACRE functions as a registered charity and company limited by guarantee. The Board comprises nine Trustees including the Chairman.
- R   To deliver a wide range of advice, information and support to local communities in Cambridgeshire and Peterborough.
- G   Cambridgeshire.
- ✍   Cambridgeshire ACRE is one of the 38 Rural Community Councils, represented at the national level by **Action with Communities in Rural England** (qv) and at the regional level by Rural Action East.

___

Cambridgeshire & Peterborough Probation Trust
- 1 Brooklands Avenue, CAMBRIDGE, CB2 2BB.
  Tel 01223 712345   Fax 01234 568822   http://www.cambridgeshireprobation.gov.uk
  Chairman: Kevin Ellis   Chief Officer: John Budd
- E   Established on 1 April 2001 under the Criminal Justice & Court Service Act 2000 as the Cambridgeshire Probation Area Board. It became a trust on 1 April 2010 under the Offender Management Act 2007. The Board comprises ten members including the Chairman.
- G   Cambridgeshire.
- ✍   For further information see **Probation Trusts**.

___

Cambridgeshire Police Authority
- Room G038, Hinchingbrooke Park, HUNTINGDON, Cambs, PE29 6NP.
  Tel 0345 456 4564   Fax 01480 425748   http://www.cambs-pa.gov.uk
  Chairman: Ruth Rogers   Chief Executive: Dorothy Gregson
- E   Established in April 1995, the Authority is an independent body charged with ensuring that Cambridgeshire Constabulary provides an effective and efficient police service. It is made up of seven County Councillors, two Peterborough City Councillors and eight independent members.
- G   Cambridgeshire, including Peterborough.
- ✍   For further information on area police authorities see **Police Service**.

___

Campaign for National Parks   (CNP)
- 6-7 Barnard Mews, LONDON, SW11 1QU.
  Tel 020 7924 4077   Fax 020 7924 5761   http://www.cnp.org.uk
  President: Ben Fogle   Chairman: Anne Robinson   Chief Executive: Helen Jackson

E   Established in 1936 as the Standing Committee on National Parks, becoming the Council for National Parks in 1977 and adopting its present name in 2008. CNP is a registered charity and company limited by guarantee; it is an umbrella of nearly 40 environmental and amenity groups. The board of trustees comprises eleven members including the Chairman.
R   To ensure that national parks are protected and enhanced now and in the future.
     To promote good ideas and best practice for the benefit of the whole countryside which are relevant to urban lifestyles.
     To strengthen the capacity of the National Parks movement as a whole.
G   England, Wales
✍   For further information see **National Park Authorities**.
=   Ymgyrch y Parciau Cenedlaethol

Capacitybuilders
✍   An Executive NDPB of the Cabinet Office, established in April 2006 to ensure that charities, voluntary groups and social enterprises could access high quality advice and support, it closed on 31 March 2011.

Capital for Enterprise Limited   (CfEL)
■   1 Broadfield Close, SHEFFIELD, S Yorks, S8 0XN.
     Tel 0114 206 2131   **Fax** 0114 206 2146   http://www.capitalforenterprise.gov.uk
     Chairman: David Quysner, CBE   Chief Executive: Rory Earley
E   Established in April 2008. CfEL functions as a company limited by guarantee wholly owned by the Department for Business, Innovation & Skills. The Board comprises five non-executive members including the Chairman.
R   To be the Government's principal centre of knowledge, expertise and information on the design, implementation and management of finance measures to support small and medium size enterprises.
G   United Kingdom.

Carbon Trust
■   6th Floor, 5 New Street Square, LONDON, EC4A 3BF.
     Tel 0800 085 2005   http://www.carbontrust.co.uk
     PO Box 89, WITNEY, Oxon, OX29 4WB. (Postal address)
     Chairman: Sir Ian McAllister, CBE   Chief Executive: Tom Delay
E   Established in 2002. The Trust is a private company set up by Government. The board comprises eleven members including the Chairman.
R   To accelerate the move to a low carbon economy by working with business and the public sector to develop commercial low carbon technologies and help organisations reduce carbon emissions.
G   United Kingdom.

Cardiff Airport Consultative Committee
■   Cardiff Airport, VALE OF GLAMORGAN, CF62 3BD.
     Tel 01446 712532   http://www.tbicardiffairport.com
     Chairman: Cllr Jeff James
G   Cardiff.
✍   For further information see **Airport Consultative Committees**.

Cardiff Local Health Board
✍   Merged on 1 October 2009 with the Vale of Glamorgan Local Health Board to form **Cardiff & Vale University Health Board**.

Cardiff & Vale of Glamorgan Community Health Council   (CAVOG)
■   Ground Floor, Park House, Greyfriars Road, CARDIFF, CF10 3AF.
     Tel 029 2037 7407   **Fax** 029 2066 5470   http://www.thesprout.co.uk
     2 Stanwell Road, PENARTH, Vale of Glamorgan, CF64 3EA.
     Tel 029 2035 0614   **Fax** 029 2035 0609
     Chairman: Peter Arthur   Chief Officer: Phillip Williams
E   Established on 1 April 2010 by the merger of two former Community Health Councils. The full Council comprises 24 volunteer members drawn from the Cardiff and Vale of Glamorgan local committees.
G   Cardiff, Vale of Glamorgan.
✍   For further information see **Community Health Councils** under **National Health Service - Wales**.

Cardiff & Vale University Health Board

■ Whitchurch Hospital, Park Road, Whitchurch, CARDIFF, CF14 7XB.
  Tel 029 2074 7747
  Chairman: David Francis   Chief Executive: Jan Williams
E Established on 1 October 2009 by the merger of two former Local Health Boards (Cardiff and Vale of Glamorgan) and the Cardiff & Vale NHS Trust. The Board comprises 23 members including the Chairman.
G Cardiff, Vale of Glamorgan.
✍ For further information see **NHS Wales - Local Health Boards**.
  Cardiff & Vale University Health Board is the operational name of the Cardiff & Vale University Local Health Board.

Cardiovascular, Diabetes, Renal, Respiratory & Allergy Expert Advisory Group

■ 151 Buckingham Palace Road, LONDON, SW1W 9SZ.
  Tel 020 3080 6000
  Chairman: Dr J Colin Forfar, BSc(Hons), MBChB, PhD, MD, MA, FRCP
E Established in 2005. The Group functions as an advisory body to the Commission on Human Medicines (CHM), qv. It comprises eleven members including the Chairman.
R To advise CHM on the safety and efficacy of medicines for use in the treatment and prevention of cardiovascular, diabetes, renal, respiratory and allergy diseases.
G United Kingdom.

Care Commission   See **Scottish Commission for the Regulation of Care**.

Care Council for Wales   (CCW)

■ South Gate House, Wood Street, CARDIFF, CF10 1EW.
  Tel 029 2022 6257   Fax 029 2038 4764   http://www.ccwales.org.uk
  Chairman: Arwel Ellis Owen   Chief Executive: Rhian Huws Williams
E Established on 1 October 2001 under the Care Standards Act 2000. The CCW functions as an Assembly Government Sponsored Body of the National Assembly for Wales. The Council comprises 23 members including the Chairman.
R To promote high standards in the conduct and practice of social care and high standards in the training of social care workers.
  To improve safeguards for users of social care services.
G Wales.
● The Council maintains a Register of Social Care Workers.
✍ It is one of the six member alliance which makes up Skills for Care & Development (qv), the Sector Skills Council for social care, children, early years and young people's workforces in the UK.
  For further information see **Health & Social Care Regulators**.
= Cyngor Gofal Cymru

Care Quality Commission

■ Citygate, Gallowgate, NEWCASTLE UPON TYNE, NE1 4PA.
  Tel 0300 061 6161   Fax 0300 061 6171   http://www.cqc.org.uk
  Chairman: Jo Williams   Chief Executive: Cynthia Bower
E Established on 1 April 2009, merging the Healthcare Commission (the Commission for Healthcare Audit & Inspection), the Commission for Social Care Inspection and the Mental Health Act Commission, to be the independent regulator of health and adult social care in England.
G England.

Care Standards Inspectorate for Wales   Became the Care & Social Services Inspectorate for Wales in April 2007, a division of the National Assembly of Wales.

Care Standards Tribunal
✍ See the **First-tier Tribunal (Care Standards)**.

The Care Tribunal   (CT)

■ Courts & Tribunal Service, 3rd Floor, Bedford House, 16-22 Bedford Street, BELFAST, BT2 7TS.
  Tel 028 9072 8752   http://www.caretribunalni.gov.uk
  Secretary: Mark McClean

E   Established under the Health & Personal Social Services (Quality, Improvement & Regulation) (Northern Ireland) Order 2003. It functions as a Tribunal NDTB of the Department of Health, Social Services & Public Safety Northern Ireland.

R   To hear appeals against decisions prohibiting or restricting the employment of individuals teaching or working with children or working with vulnerable adults, or decisions concerning the registration of social workers.

G   Northern Ireland.

Careers Scotland   A service delivered by **Skills Development Scotland**.

Carmarthenshire Local Health Board

✍   Merged on 1 October 2009 with the Ceredigion and Pembrokeshire Local Health Boards to form **Hywel Dda Health Board**.

Castle Vale Housing Action Trust

✍   Wound up in 2005 upon completion of its programme.

Catalyst Corby Urban Regeneration Company   Merged in May 2006 with the North Northants Together Partnership as the **North Northants Development Company**.

Cathedrals Fabric Commission for England   **(CFCE)**

■   Church House, Great Smith Street, LONDON, SW1P 3NZ.
    Tel 020 7898 1866
    Chairman: Frank Field, MP, PC

E   Established on 1 March 1991 under the Care of Cathedrals Measure 1990. CFCE is a standing commission of the Church of England.

R   To help ensure that cathedrals are cared for and conserved to the highest possible standards, such that public confidence may be maintained in the Church of England's responsible stewardship of these buildings.

G   England.

Catholic Bishops Conference of England & Wales   **(CBCEW)**

■   39 Eccleston Square, LONDON, SW1V 1BX.
    Tel 020 7630 8220   **Fax** 020 7901 4821   http://www.catholic-ew.org.uk
    Chairman: Malcolm McMahon (Bishop of Nottingham)

E   Established on 1 January 1984 by decree of the Vatican Congregation of Bishops. CBCEW functions as a charitable trust. The Conference's members are all appointed by the Holy See.

R   To listen to the whole Church and the world.
    To discern with the Bishops the issues of the day and to engage with them.
    To work with the Bishops in the task of evangelisation.
    To promote the teaching of the Church for the common good.
    To serve the Dioceses, associated Conference bodies and Catholic networks and to assist the Bishops in representing the Catholic Church to Government and society as a whole.

G   England, Wales.

Catholic Bishops Conference of Scotland   See **Bishops' Conference of Scotland**.

Catholic Education Commission   **(CEC)**

■   75 Craig Park, GLASGOW, G31 2HD.
    Tel 0141 556 4727   **Fax** 0141 551 8467   http://www.catholiceducationcommission.org
    President: Bishop Joseph Devine

E   Established in 1972. The Commission, appointed by Bishops' Conference of Scotland (qv), comprises representatives from each diocese and other key stakeholders.

R   To advise the Bishops' Conference of Scotland on all matters pertaining to education and, on its behalf, to promote development in this field.

G   Scotland.

Catholic Youth Services for England & Wales

✍   Closed in 2008.

© CBD Research Ltd · Beckenham · Kent BR3 5JS · Tel 020 8650 7745 · Fax 020 8650 0768 · E-mail cbd@cbdresearch.com · www.cbdresearch.com

Cattewater Harbour Commissioners

- 2 The Barbican, PLYMOUTH, Devon, PL1 2LR.
  Tel 01752 665934   Fax 01752 253624   http://www.plymouthport.org.uk
  Chairman: Robin Love
- E The board comprises ten commissoners including the Chairman.
- R To be the competent harbour authority for the Port of Plymouth Pilotage Service.
- G Plymouth.
- ✍ For further information see **Port & Harbour Authorities**.

Cattle Compensation Advisory Group
✍ Established in 2006 by the Department for Environment, Food & Rural Affairs to help monitor the roll-out of the table of valuation based compensation arrangements, it has not convened since 2006 because of the long-running and ongoing legal challenge against the system. Defra has no plans to reconvene the Group.

CBAC   See **WJEC**.

CDC Group plc

- Cardinal Place, 80 Victoria Street, LONDON, SW1E 5JL.
  Tel 020 7963 4700   Fax 020 7963 4750   http://www.cdcgroup.com
  Chairman: Richard Gillingwater   Chief Executive: Richard Laing   Shareholder Executive contact: Roger Lowe
- E Established in 1948 as the Colonial Development Corporation, becoming the Commonwealth Development Corporation, and now known simply as CDC. The Group functions as a public-private partnership of the Department for International Development. The Board comprises six members including the Chairman.
- R To generate wealth, broadly shared, in emerging markets, particularly in poorer countries, by providing capital for investment in sustainable and responsibly managed private sector business.
- G United Kingdom.
- ✍ One of the businesses managed by the **Shareholder Executive**.

CDM 2007 Evaluation Working Group   A working group of the Health & Safety Executive's **Construction Industry Advisory Committee**. CDM 2007 refers to the Construction (Design & Management) Regulations 2007.

Central Advisory Committee of the Allied Health Professions   (ACAHP)

- Speech & Language Therapy, Altnagelvin Hospital, Glenshane Road, LONDONDERRY, BT47 6SB.
  Tel 028 7134 5171
  Chairman: Mrs Joan Skeffington
- E Established in 2004 under the Health & Personal Social Services (Northern Ireland Order) 1972. ACAHP functions as an Advisory Committee of the Department of Health, Social Services & Public Services Northern Ireland. The Committee comprises eight members including the Chairman.
- R To advise on various aspects connected with those working in the fields of the allied health professions - arts therapy, dietetics, occupational therapy, orthoptics, physiotherapy, podiatry, prosthetics/orthotics, radiography and speech/language therapy.
- G Northern Ireland.
- ✍ The Committee has close links with the Health Professions Council (qv).

Central Advisory Committee on Pensions & Compensation   (CAC)

- 6406 Tomlinson House, Norcross, THORNTON-CLEVELEYS, Lancs, FY5 3WP.
  Tel 01253 332886   Fax 01253 330437
  Chairman: Andrew Robathan, MP
- E Established in 1921 under the War Pensions Act 1921 and known as the Central Advisory Committee on War Pensions until 2008. CAC functions as an Advisory NDPB of the Ministry of Defence. It comprises twelve members including the Chairman.
- R To advise on policy issues and to act as a consultative mechanism for all the service pension and compensation schemes.
- G United Kingdom.

Central Advisory Committee for Scotland on Justices of the Peace
✍ See **Judicial Appointments Board for Scotland**.

Central Advisory Committee on War Pensions
✍ Since 2008 **Central Advisory Committee on Pensions & Compensation**.

Central Arbitration Committee   (CAC)
■   22nd Floor, Euston Tower, 286 Euston Road, LONDON, NW1 3JJ.
    Tel 020 7904 2300   **Fax** 020 7904 2301   http://www.cac.gov.uk
    Chairman: Sir Michael Burton   Chief Executive: Simon Gouldstone
E   Established on 1 February 1976, its current authority is derived from the Trade Union & Labour Relations
    Consolidation Act 1992 as inserted by the Employment Relations Act 1999. CAC functions as a Tribunal NDPB
    of the Department for Business, Innovation & Skills. The Committee comprises 67 members including the
    Chairman, approximately half the members have experience representing employers, half workers.
R   To adjudicate on applications relating to the statutory recognition and derecognition of trade unions for collective
    bargaining purposes, where such recognition or derecognition cannot be agreed voluntarily.
    To determine disputes between trade unions and employers over the disclosure of information for collective
    bargaining purposes, and in resolving applications and complaints under:
    the Information & Consulting Regulations, 2004,
    the European Public Limited-Liability Company Regulations, 2004, and
    the Transnational Information & Consultation of Employees Regulations, 1999.
G   England, Scotland, Wales
✍   It was announced by the Government on 14 October 2010 that CAC will merge with the Certification Office for
    Trade Unions & Employers' Associations (qv).

Central Consultants & Specialists Committee   (CCSC)
■   BMA House, Tavistock Square, LONDON, WC1H 9JP.
    Tel 020 7383 6056   **Fax** 020 7383 6400   http://www.bma.org.uk
    Chairman: Dr Mark Porter
E   Established as a Branch of Practice Committee of the British Medical Association. The Committee comprises 60
    voting members including the Chairman.
R   Recognised by the Department of Health as the body with sole negotiating rights on behalf of senior hospital
    doctors in the NHS.
G   United Kingdom.
✍   See **British Medical Association** [Branch of Practice Committees] for further information.

Central Council for Jewish Community Services   (CCJCS)
■   17 Highfield Road, LONDON, NW11 9LS.
    Tel 020 8458 1035
E   Established in 1972, the Council is a registered charity. It currently has 50 member organisations, each of which
    nominates its own member to the CCJCS Council.
R   To provide a forum for meeting and discussing issues concerning elderly people, children and youth, and people
    with physical and learning disabilities.
G   England, Scotland.

Central Council of Magistrates' Courts Committees   (CCMCC)
■   185 Marylebone Road, LONDON, NW1 5QB.
    Tel 020 7724 2906   **Fax** 020 7723 0951   http://www.ccmcc.co.uk
    Chairman: Dr Malcolm C Cohen   Chief Executive: Duncan Webster
E   Formed in 1952, the Council is a voluntary organisation set up after the establishment of Magistrates' Courts
    Committees (MCCs) by the Justices of the Peace Act 1949. The full Council comprises all 42 MCCs. The
    management committee comprises the Chairman and eight other members.
R   To improve the quality of the administration in Magistrates' Courts.
G   England, Wales.
●   MCCs are the managing bodies for each of the 42 courts areas of England and Wales. Each committee is a
    statutory body and comprised of magistrates selected for their expertise.

Central Council of Physical Recreation   **(CCPR)**
✍   CCPR has been renamed **Sport & Recreation Alliance**.

Central Nursing Advisory Committee   (CNAC)
■   Castle Buildings, Stormont Estate, BELFAST, BT4 3SQ.
    Tel 029 9052 0527   **Fax** 029 9052 0572
    Chairman: Angela McVeigh

E   Established in 1974 under the Health & Personal Social Services (Northern Ireland) Order 1972. CNAC functions as an Advisory NDPB of the Department of Health, Social Services & Public Safety Northern Ireland. The Committee comprises up to 18 members including the Chairman.
R   To provide nursing advice to the Department and the Chief Nursing Officer on matters concerning nursing and midwifery in Northern Ireland.
G   Northern Ireland.

Central Office of Information   (COI)
■   Hercules House, Hercules Road, LONDON, SE1 7DU.
     Tel 020 7928 2345   **Fax** 020 7928 5037   http://www.coi.gov.uk
     Chief Executive: Mark Lund
E   Established on 1 April 1946, formed mainly from the production division of the Ministry of Information. COI functions as an Executive Agency of the Cabinet Office.
R   To advise on information campaigns for its clients in Government departments and agencies.
G   United Kingdom.

Central Personal Social Services Advisory Committee   (CPSSAC)
■   Castle Buildings, Stormont, BELFAST, BT4 3SQ.
     Tel 028 9052 0500   **Fax** 028 9052 0572
E   Established in April 1975 under the Health & Personal Social Services (Northern Ireland) Order 1972. CPSSAD functions as an Advisory Committee of the Department of Health, Social Services & Public Safety Northern Ireland.
G   Northern Ireland.

Central Pharmaceutical Advisory Committee   (CPAC)
■   Castle Buildings, Stormont, BELFAST, BT4 3SQ.
     Tel 028 9052 0500   **Fax** 028 9052 0572
E   Established in July 1974 under the Health & Personal Social Services (Northern Ireland) Order 1972. CPAC functions as an Advisory Committee of the Department of Health, Social Service & Public Safety Northern Ireland.
G   Northern Ireland.

Central Police Training & Development Authority
✍   Centrex migrated into the **National Policing Improvement Agency**, established 1 April 2007.

Central Salford Urban Regeneration Company
✍   closed in February 2011

Central Science Laboratory
✍   On 1 April 2009 CSL became part of the **Food & Environment Research Agency**.

Central Scotland Joint Police Board
■   Municipal Buildings, FALKIRK, FK1 5RS.
     Convenor: Cllr George Matchett   Clerk: Rose Mary Glackin
E   The Joint Board is an independent body responsible for Central Scotland Police's budget and the management of its resources. It is made up of eleven councillor members.
G   Clackmannanshire, Falkirk and Stirling.
✍   For further information see **Police Authorities**.

Central Services Agency
✍   On 1 April 2009 CSA was replaced by the **Business Services Organisation**.

Centre for Environment, Fisheries & Aquaculture Science   (Cefas)
■   Pakefield Road, LOWESTOFT, Suffolk, NR33 0HT.
     Tel 01502 562244   **Fax** 01502 513865   http://www.cefas.co.uk
     The Nothe, Barrack Road, WEYMOUTH, Dorset, DT4 8UB.
     Tel 01305 206600   **Fax** 01305 206601
     Chief Executive: Dr Richard Judge

E Established on 1 April 1997. CEFAS functions as an Executive Agency of the Department for Environment, Food & Rural Affairs.
R To supply an efficient service of specialist scientific and technical support, consultancy and advice in the fields of fisheries' science and management, environmental assessment, aquaculture and fish health, to standards of objective enquiry agreed with its customers.
G England, Wales.
● CEFAS delivers specialised diagnostic, research and consultancy services and products as required by the Department in pursuit of the Department's statutory and policy objectives.
    In addition to Lowestoft, CEFAS has laboratories at Burnham-on-Crouch, Essex, and Weymouth, Dorset.

Centre for Maternal & Child Enquiries   (CMACE)

■ Lower Ground Floor, Chiltern Court, 188 Baker Street, LONDON, NW1 5SD.
    Tel 020 7486 1191   **Fax** 020 7486 6543   http://www.cmace.org.uk
    Chairman: Prof James Walker   Chief Executive: Richard Congdon
E Established in April 2003 as the Confidential Enquiry into Maternal & Child Health. It became a charitable company limited by guarantee and adopted its present name on 1 April 2009. The work of CMACE is commissioned and funded by the National Patient Safety Agency (qv). The Board of Trustees comprises eight members including the Chairman.
R To improve the health of mothers, babies and children by carrying out confidential enquiries on a nationwide basis and by widely disseminating the findings and recommendations.
G United Kingdom, Republic of Ireland, Isle of Man, Channel Islands.
● The London office also serves as a regional office for London and the South East. In addition CMACE has three regional and two subcontracted offices in England and affiliated offices in Northern Ireland, Scotland and the Republic of Ireland.

Centro

■ Centro House, 16 Summer Lane, BIRMINGHAM, B19 3SD.
    Tel 0121 200 2787   http://www.centro.org.uk
    Chief Executive: Geoff Inskip
E Established on 1 October 1969 under the Transport Act 1968 as the West Midlands Passenger Transport Executive. It operates under the brand name Centro. It is responsible to the West Midlands Integrated Transport Authority (qv). The board comprises seven members including the Chief Executive.
G West Midlands.
✍ For further information see **Passenger Transport Executives & Integrated Transport Authorities**.

Ceramic Heavy Clay Refractories & Glass Manufacturing Industries Joint Health & Safety Committee
✍ CHARGE, to include cement and concrete, is now **C3HARGE**.

Ceramics, Cement, Concrete, Heavy Clay, Refractories & Glass Manufacturing Industries Joint Health & Safety Advisory Board   See **C3HARGE**.

Ceredigion Community Health Council

■ 8 Portland Road, ABERYSTWYTH, Ceredigion, ST23 2NL.
    Tel 01970 624760   **Fax** 01970 627730
    Chairman: Jack Evershed
E The Council comprises 20 members including the Chairman.
G Ceredigion.
✍ For further information see **Community Health Councils** under **National Health Service - Wales**.

Ceredigion Local Health Board
✍ Merged on 1 October with the Carmarthenshire and Pembrokeshire Local Health Boards to form **Hywel Dda Health Board**.

Certification Office for Trade Unions & Employers' Associations

■ 22nd Floor, Euston Tower, 286 Euston Road, LONDON, NW1 3JJ.
    Tel 020 7210 3734   **Fax** 020 7210 3612   http://www.certoffice.org
    Certification Officer: David Cockburn
E Established in 1975 as an independent statutory authority, the functions of the Certification Office are contained in the Trade Union & Labour Relations (Consolidation) Act 1992 as amended. The Office is responsible to the Department for Business, Innovation & Skills.

R   To maintain a list of trade unions and employers' associations.

To receive and scrutinise annual returns from trade unions and employers' associations.

To determine complaints concerning trade union elections, certain other ballots and breaches of trade union rules.

To ensure observance of statutory requirements governing mergers between trade unions and employers'associations.

To oversee the political funds and finances of trade unions and employers' associations.

To certify the independence of trades unions.

G   United Kingdom.

✍   It was announced by the Government on 14 October 2010 that the Certification Office will merge with the Central Arbitration Committee (qv).

CfA - Business skills @ work   See **Council for Administration**.

Channel Four Television Corporation   (C4C)

■   124 Horseferry Road, LONDON, SW1P 2TX.

Tel 020 7396 4444 **Fax** 020 7306 8369 http://www.channel4.com

Chairman: Lord Burns   Chief Executive: David Abraham   Shareholder Executive contact: Emma Ward

E   Established in 1981, the Corporation derives its present authority under the Broadcasting Acts 1990 & 1996, and the Communications Act 2003. It functions as a Public Corporation accountable to the Department for Culture, Media & Sport.

R   To demonstrate innovation, experiment and creativity in the form and content of programmes.

To appeal to the tastes and interests of a culturally diverse society.

To make a significate contribution to meeting the need for the licensed public channels to include programmes of an educational nature and other programmes of educative value.

To exhibit a distinctive character.

G   England, Scotland, Northern Ireland.

✍   One of the businesses managed by the **Shareholder Executive**.

Wales is covered by the Welsh Fourth Channel, **S4C**, though Channel 4 broadcasts to some areas.

Channel Tunnel Safety Authority   (CTSA)

■   One Kemble Street, LONDON, WC2B 4AN.

Tel 020 7282 2000 **Fax** 020 7282 2040 http://www.hse.gsi.gov.uk

Contact: Terry Gates

E   Established 1987 under the Treaty of Canterbury (Cmnd 9745) Article 11, dated 12 February 1986, and the Channel Tunnel Act 1987. CTSA functions as an independent body which reports through the Channel Tunnel Intergovernmental Commission (IGC) to both the UK and French Governments. The UK secretariat is provided by the Office of Rail Regulation (qv).

R   To advise and assist the IGC on all matters relating to safety in the operation of the Channel Tunnel.

G   United Kingdom, France.

Charities Advisory Committee   (CAC)

■   Lighthouse Building, 1 Cromac Place, Gasworks Business Park, Ormeau Road, BELFAST, BT7 2JB.

Tel 028 9082 9425

E   The CAC functions as an Advisory NDPB of the Department for Social Development Northern Ireland.

R   To advise the Department on investment policy with regard to its management of the Northern Ireland Central Investment Fund for Charities.

G   Northern Ireland.

Charities Tribunal

✍   Since 1 September 2009 First-tier Tribunal (Charity).

Charity Commission

■   PO Box 1227, LIVERPOOL, L69 3UG.

Tel 0845 300 0218 http://www.charity-commission.gov.uk

Chairman: Dame Suzi Leather   Chief Executive: Sam Younger

E   Established in 1853 under the Charitable Trusts Act 1853, the Commission is now constituted under the Charities Act 2006. The Commission comprises nine members including the Chairman.

R   To promote the best possible regulation of charities in England and Wales, in order to increase charities' efficiency and effectiveness, their public confidence and trust.

G   England, Wales.

- Most charities in England and Wales are required to register with the Commission. The Register of Charities may be viewed on the website or at the Commission's offices.

Charity Commission for Northern Ireland   (CCNI)
■ 4th Floor, 24-26 Arthur Street, BELFAST, BT1 4GF.
    Tel 028 9051 5490
    Chairman (Chief Commissioner): Thomas McGrath   Chief Executive: Frances McCandless
E   Established on 27 March 2009 under the Charities Act (Northern Ireland) 2008. The CCNI functions as an Executive NDPB of the Department for Social Development Northern Ireland. The Commission comprises seven members including the Chairman.
R   To regulate, monitor and, where required, investigate charities in Northern Ireland.
G   Northern Ireland.

Chemical & Downstream Oil Industries Forum   (CDOIF)
■ 5S2 Redgrave Court, Merton Road, BOOTLE, Merseyside, L20 7HS.
    Tel 0845 345 0055
E   Established in 1997 as the Chemical Industries Forum. CDOIF functions as an Advisory NDPB of the Health & Safety Executive. The Forum comprises 21 members including the Chairman.
R   To protect people at work from hazards to health and safety arising from their occupation within the following industry sectors: chemical production, paints and coatings production, health product manufacture, compressed gas production, oil refining and associated industries, storage and road transport of chemicals. To protect the public from related hazards arising from such activities.
G   United Kingdom.

Chemical Industries Forum
✍ see **Chemical & Downstream Industries Forum**

Chemical Weapons Convention National Authority Advisory Committee   (NAAC)
■ 3 Whitehall Place, LONDON, SW1A 2AW.
    Tel 0300 060 4000
    Chairman: Dr Tony Bastock, OBE
E   Established in 1997 in response to the signing of the Chemical Weapons Convention (which came into force on 29 April 1997), the first international arms control treaty to seek to introduce a ban on an entire class of weapons. The Committee functions as an Advisory NDPB of the Department of Energy & Climate Change and comprises seven members including the Chairman.
R   To assist the Department with its task of ensuring that the Chemical Weapons Convention and the Chemical Weapons Act 1996 are implemented effectively in the UK, while taking into account cost and resource constraints and the need to avoid excessive regulation.
G   United Kingdom.
✍ It was annouced by the Government on 14 October 2010 that this body and its function are to be abolished, with options for retaining stakeholder input in this area being considered.

Chemicals Regulation Directorate   (CRD)
■ Mallard House, Kings Pool, 3 Peasholme Green, YORK, YO1 7PX.
    Tel 01904 640500   Fax 01904 455733   http://www.pesticides.gov.uk
    2-3 Redgrave Court, Merton Road, BOOTLE, Merseyside, L20 7HS.
    Director: Dr Kerr Wilson
E   Established on 1 April 2009 as a Directorate of the Health & Safety Executive (qv), merging the former Pesticides Safety Directorate and other relevant parts of the HSE, primarily the Chemicals Assessment Schemes Unit. The Directorate now functions as an Executive Agency of the Department for Environment, Food & Rural Affairs.
R   To ensure the safe use of biocides, industrial chemicals, pesticides and detergents to protect the health of people and the environment.
G   United Kingdom.

Chemistry, Pharmacy & Standards Expert Advisory Group   (CPSEAG)
■ 151 Buckingham Palace Road, LONDON, SW1W 9SZ.
    Tel 020 0080 6000
    Chairman: Prof Derek H Calam, OBE
E   Established in 2005. CPSEAG functions as an advisory body to the Commission on Human Medicines (CHM), qv. The Group comprises 14 members including the Chairman.

R   To advise CHM on the quality and quality in relation to safety and efficacy of medicinal products which are the subject of marketing authorisation applications, and to advise on such other matters as are referred to it.

G   United Kingdom.

Cheshire Community Action   (CCA)

■   96 Lower Bridge Road, CHESTER, CH1 1RU.
     Tel 01244 323602   Fax 01244 401036   http://www.cheshireaction.org.uk
     Chairman: Maureen Walmsley   Chief Executive: Alison Roylance-White

E   CCA functions as a registered charity and company limited by guarantee.

R   To promote, encourage and support self-help in the communities of Cheshire, Halton and Warrington by providing support, advice and access to funding for organisations and projects designed to protect and enhance the communities of Cheshire.

G   Cheshire.

✍   CCA is one of the 38 Rural Community Councils, represented at the national level by **Action with Communities in Rural England** (qv) and at the regional level by North West Rural Community Councils.

Cheshire & Merseyside Strategic Health Authority

✍   On 1 July 2006 merged with the Cumbria & Lancashire and the Greater Manchester Strategic Health Authorities to form the **North West Strategic Health Authority**.

Cheshire Police Authority

■   Clemonds Hey, Oakmere Road, WINSFORD, Cheshire, CW7 2UA.
     Tel 01244 614002   Fax 01244 614006   http://www.cheshirepa.police.uk
     Chairman: Mrs Margaret Ollerenshaw

E   Established in April 1995, the Authority is an independent body charged with ensuring that Cheshire Constabulary provides an effective and efficient police service. It is made up of nine councillor members and eight independent members.

G   Cheshire.

✍   For further information see **Police Authorities**.

Cheshire Probation Trust

■   Beech House, Park West, Sealand Road, CHESTER, CH1 4RJ.
     Tel 01244 394500   Fax 01244 394507   http://www.cheshireprobation.org.uk
     Chairman: Leslie Robinson, JP   Chief Officer: Steve Collett

E   Established on 1 April 2001 under the Criminal Justice & Court Service Act 2000 as the Cheshire Probation Area Board. It became a trust on 1 April 2010 under the Offender Management Act 2007. The Board comprises eleven members including the Chairman.

G   Cheshire.

✍   For further information see **Probation Trusts**.

Chichester Harbour Conservancy

■   Harbour Office, Itchenor, CHICHESTER, W Sussex, PO20 7AW.
     Tel 01243 512301   Fax 01243 513026   http://www.conservancy.co.uk
     Chairman: Mrs Louise Goldsmith

E   Established by the Chichester Harbour Conservancy Act 1974. The Conservancy consists of 15 members including the Chairman.

G   Chichester.

✍   For further information see **Port & Harbour Authorities**.

Chief Fire & Rescue Adviser   (CFRA)

■   Eland House, Bressenden Place, LONDON, SW1E 5DU.
     Tel 020 7944 4400
     Chief Adviser: Sir Ken Knight

E   Established in October 2007, replacing the former HM Fire Services Inspectorate. CFRA functions as an Advisory NDPB of the Department for Communities & Local Government.

R   To commission and publish quality assured operational guidance.
     To ensure that the Government is able to engage influentially in debate on Fire & Rescue Service issues and that the Service's interests are effectively represented by the Government both nationally and internationally.

G   England, Wales.

Chief Investigating Officer
✍ See the **Commission for Ethical Standards in Public Life in Scotland**.

Chiefs of Staff Committee
■ MOD Main Building, Whitehall, LONDON, SW1A 2HB.
  Tel 020 7218 9000
E A committee of the Ministry of Defence dating from 1923 comprising the Chief and Vice-Chief of the Defence Staff, the First Sea Lord, the Chief of the Air Staff and the Chief of the General Staff.

Child Maintenance & Enforcement Commission   (CMEC)
■ PO Box 239, Holbeck, LEEDS, W Yorks, LS1 1EB.
  Tel 0845 713 3133 (National Helpline) http://www.childmaintenance.org
  Chairmman: Janet Paraskeva   Commissioner: Stephen Geraghty
E The board comprises eleven members including the Chairman and Commissioner.
R To calculate and collect child maintenance from the parent who is not the main day-to-day carer of their child and make sure it is paid to the parent or person who is the day-to-day carer of the child.
G England, Wales, Scotland.
✍ CMEC was established as an Executive NDPB under the Child Maintenance & Other Payments Act 2008. The Government announced on 14 October 2010 that it will no longer function as a NDPB but become an executive agency of the Department for Work & Pensions which will have responsibility for its functions.

Child Support Agency
✍ Removed from the direct control of the Department for Work & Pensions and from 1 November 2008 managed by the **Child Maintenance & Enforcement Commission**.

Child Support Agency Northern Ireland
✍ Was replaced on 1 April 2008 by the Child Maintenance & Enforcement Division of the Department for Social Development Northern Ireland.

Child Support Commissioners
✍ On 3 November 2008 the **Upper Tribunal (Administrative Appeals Chamber)** took over the work of the Commissioners.

Children's Commissioner for England
■ 1 London Bridge, LONDON, SE1 9BG.
  Tel 0844 800 9113   **Fax** 020 7357 8329   http://www.childrenscommissioner.gov.uk
  Commissioner: Maggie Atkinson
E Established in July 2005 under the Children Act 2004. The Commissioner functions as an Executive NDPB of the Department for Education. The Management Board comprises four members.
R To be the independent voice for all children and young people and represent their views, opinions, interests and rights to the people who make decisions that affect them.
G England.
✍ The report of the independent review by Dr John Dunford of the Children's Commissioner for England was published in December 2010. It recommended that the Commissioner be given a stronger role to promote children's rights in order for the Government to meet its commitment to implement the United Nations Convention on the Rights of the Child (UNCRC).

Children's Commissioner for Wales
■ Oystermouth House, Phoenix Way, Llansamlet, SWANSEA, SA7 9FS.
  Tel 01792 765600   **Fax** 01792 765601   http://www.childcom.org.uk
  Penrhos Manor, Oak Drive, COLWYN BAY, Conwy, LL29 7YW.
  Tel 01492 523333   **Fax** 01492 523336
  Commissioner: Keith Towler
E Established in July 2005 under the Children's Act 2004.
R To be the independent voice for all children and young people and represent their views, opinions, interests and rights to the people who make decisions that effect them.
G Wales.
= Comisiynydd Plant Cymru

© CBD Research Ltd · Beckenham · Kent BR3 5JS · Tel 020 8650 7745 · Fax 020 8650 0768 · E-mail cbd@cbdresearch.com · www.cbdresearch.com

Children England

- Unit 25, Angel Gate, City Road, LONDON, EC1V 2PT.
  Tel 020 7833 3319   Fax 020 7833 8637   http://www.childrenengland.org.uk
  Chairman: Bob Reitemeier   Chief Executive: Maggie Jones
- E Established in 1942 and known as the National Council for Voluntary Child Care Organisations before adopting its current name in December 2008. Children England is an umbrella organisation whose members are all registered charities that work with children, young people and their families; it functions as a registered charity. The Board comprises 14 members including the Chairman.
- R To create a fairer world for children, young people and families by championing the voluntary organisations which work on their behalf.
- G England.

Children & Family Court Advisory Support Service   (Cafcass)

- 6th Floor, Sanctuary Buildings, Great Smith Street, LONDON, SW1P 3BT.
  Tel 0844 353 3350   Fax 0844 353 3351   http://www.cafcass.gov.uk
  Chairman: Baroness Howarth of Breckland, OBE   Chief Executive: Anthony Douglas, CBE
- E Established on 1 April 2001 under the Criminal Justice & Court Services Act 2001. Cafcass functions as an Executive NDPB of the Department for Education. The board comprises twelve members including the Chairman.
- R To safeguard and promote the welfare of children.
  To give advice to the family courts.
  To make provision for children to be represented.
  To provide information, advice and support to children and their families.
- G England.
- ● Cafcass has local offices throughout England.
- ✍ The future of Cafcass is being considered by the Family Justice Review Panel (qv) as part of a full review of the family justice system, reporting in 2011.

Children in Northern Ireland   (CiNI)

- Unit 9, 40 Montgomery Road, BELFAST, BT6 9HL.
  Tel 028 9040 1290   Fax 028 9070 9418   http://www.ci-ni.org
  Director: Pauline Leeson
- E CiNI is the umbrella organisation for the children's sector in Northern Ireland.
- R To enhance the lives of all children in Northern Ireland by promoting the work of the children's sector, and informing and influencing the policy agenda on the rights and needs of children and young people.
  CiNI membership includes large national and regional organisations, local voluntary and community groups, statutory agencies, independent organisations and individuals.
- G Northern Ireland.

Children's Panels

- CYPSCG, Area 2B South, Victoria Quay, EDINBURGH, EH6 6QQ.
  Tel 0131 244 7372   Fax 0131 244 3547   http://www.chscotland.gov.uk
  There are 32 Chairmen, each representing a local authority area (for contact details see the website).
- E Established in 1971 under the Social Work (Scotland) Act 1968 which was replaced by the Childrens (Scotland) Act 1995. Each Panel functions as a Tribunal NDPB of the Scottish Executive Education Department. There are approximately 2,500 panel members currently serving throughout Scotland.
- R Panel members sit on Children's Hearings, which make decisions in respect of children referred to a Hearing by the Principal Children's Reporter. These children are considered to be in need of compulsory measures of supervision because they are at risk or have offended.
- G Scotland.

Children in Scotland

- Princes House, 5 Shandwick Place, EDINBURGH, EH2 4RG.
  Tel 0131 228 8484   Fax 0131 228 8585   http://www.childreninscotland.org.uk
  Convenor: Lord Reed   Chief Executive: Dr Bronwen Cohen, OBE
- E Established in 1983 as Scottish Child & Family Alliance, adopting its current name in 1993. It is a membership organisation, a registered charity and a company limited by guarantee. The Board of Directors comprises ten members including the Convenor.
- R To enable and promote the exchange of information between children, young people and their families, practitioners, policy makers and politicians.
  To research, identify and promote the development of child, young person and family centred policies and practice which will improve the quality of life for Scotland's children, young people and their families.

To support through training, networking and information exchange the development of common understanding and sharing of values and experience between sectors, agencies and professional groups working with children, young people and their families.

G   Scotland.

✍   Children in Scotland works in partnership with the National Children's Bureau and Children in Wales (qqv).

=   Clann an Alba

Children in Wales

■   25 Windsor Place, CARDIFF, CF10 3BZ.
     Tel 029 2034 2434   **Fax** 029 2034 3134   http://www.childreninwales.org.uk
     Chairman: Dr Mike Shooter, CBE   Chief Executive: Catriona Williams

E   Established in 1992. Children in Wales is a membership body and registered charity which receives funding from the National Assembly for Wales. The Trustee Board comprises twelve members including the Chairman.

R   To advise, support and represent members.
     To disseminate information on policy, research and best practice.
     To promote Wales-based research about children and families.

G   Wales.

✍   Children in Wales works in partnership with the National Children's Bureau and Children in Scotland (qqv).

=   Plant yng Nghymru

Children's Workforce Development Council   (CWDC)

■   2nd Floor, City Exchange, 11 Albion Street, LEEDS, W Yorks, LS1 5ES.
     Tel 0113 244 6311   **Fax** 0113 390 7744   http://www.cwdcouncil.org.uk
     Chairman: Sir Paul Ennals   Chief Executive: Jane Haywood, MBE

E   Established in April 2005 following the Government's committment to workforce reform in its publication 'Every Child Matters'. CWDC functions as an Executive NDPB of the Department for Education. The Council comprises eight members including the Chairman.

R   To improve the lives of children, young people, their families and carers by ensuring that all people working with them have the best possible training, qualifications, support and advice.

G   England.

✍   It is one of the six member alliance which makes up Skills for Care & Development (qv), the Sector Skills Council for social care, children, early years and young people's workforces in the UK.
     The Government announced on 16 November 2010 that it would no longer fund workforce development activity through CWDC, would remove its NDPB status and transfer its ongoing key functions into the Department for Education.

China-Britain Business Council   (CBBC)

■   3rd Floor, Portland House, Bresenden Place, LONDON, SW1E 5BH.
     Tel 020 7802 2000   **Fax** 020 7802 2029   http://www.cbbc.org
     Chairman: Sir David Brewer, CMG   Chief Executive: Stephen Phillips

E   Formed on 1 January 1991 from the merger of the Sino-British Trade Council and the 48 Group of British Traders with China (each of which had been providing advice on China trade for more than 30 years), and known as the China-British Trade Group until it adopted its current name in 1998. The CBBC is a business-led partnership between government and industry and a membership organisation with some 900 British company and individual members.

R   To help British companies do business in China.

G   United Kingdom.

●   The Council organises missions to and from China and briefs British companies on the market through individual meetings and seminars; its services are open to all UK companies.
     The CBBC has offices in Glasgow and Newcastle as well as six in China. which are located in Beijing, Chengdu, Quindao, Shanghai, Shenzhen and Wuhan.

Church Buildings Council   (CBC)

■   Church House, Great Smith Street, LONDON, SW1P 3NZ.
     Tel 020 7898 1866   **Fax** 020 7898 1881
     Chairman: Anne Sloman

E   Established 11 June 2008 under the Diocesan Pastoral & Mission Measure 2007, the Council is successor to the former Council for the Care of Churches and the Advisory Board for Redundant Churches. CBC is a statutory body accountable to the General Synod of the Church of England.

R   To advise Chancellors, dioceses and parishes on faculty applications.
     To distribute grants for the conservation of church fabric and fittings
     To organise conferences and seminars and to publish books and other guidance on subjects relation to the care and use of church buildings, their contents and churchyards

To advise dioceses and the Church Commissioners on proposals for closing and closed churches.
G England.

Church Buildings (Uses & Disposals) Committee   A committee of the **Church Commissioners**.

Church Commissioners
- Church House, Great Smith Street, LONDON, SW1P 3AZ.
  Tel 020 7898 1000   http://www.churchcommissioners.org
E Established on 1 April 1948, by the union of Queen Anne's Bounty (1704) & the Ecclesiastical Commissioners (1836), under the Church Commissioners Measure 1947. The Commissioners are accountable to the General Synod and to Parliament. The 33 Commissioners are the Archbishops of Canterbury and York, three Church Estates Commissioners, two deans/provosts, eleven elected from the General Synod (four bishops, three clergy and four lay people), nine nominated by the Crown and the Archbishops, and six ex-officio commissioners (the Prime Minister, Lord President of the Council, Home Secretary, Secretary of State for Culture, Media & Sport, and the Speakers of the House of Lords and House of Commons).
R To obtain the best possible long term return from a diversified investment portfolio in order (1) to meet their pension commitments and (2) to provide the maximum sustainable funding for their other purposes such as support for the work of bishops, cathedrals and parish ministry.
  To pay particular regard to making additional provision for the cure of souls in parishes where such assistance is most required.
  To administer the legal framework for pastoral reorganisation and settle the future of redundant churches.
  To manage the national clergy payroll.
G England.
● The Commissioners are supported by six committees:
  Assets Committee: to direct asset management and investment policy,
  Bishoprics & Cathedrals Committee: responsible for bishops' staffing and working costs,
  Pastoral Committee: responsible for parsonages and glebe property,
  Church Buildings (Uses & Disposals) Committee: to decide the future of closed churches,
  Audit Committee, and
  Nominations & Governance Committee: to advise on appointments and governance matters.

Church of England Board of Education   (BOE)
- Church House, Great Smith Street, LONDON, SW1P 3AZ.
  Tel 020 7898 1000   http://www.cofe.anglican.org
  Chairman: Rt Revd John Pritchard, Bishop of Oxford
E Established in 1970 by resolution of the Church Assembly of the Church of England. The Board consists of the Chairman, twelve members and two observers.
R To advise the General Synod, the Archbishops' Council and the dioceses on all matters relating to education, specifically the Church's 4,700 schools and twelve higher education institutions, voluntary work in parishes with children, young people and adults, and chaplaincies in universities and colleges.
G England, Wales.
✍ The Board's sister organisation, the National Society, was established in 1811 as the Church's principal agent for the establishment of Anglican Schools and continues to have an important role supporting those schools and their teachers.

Church of England Board for Social Responsibility
✍ See the **Mission & Public Affairs** division of the Archbishops' Council.

Church of England Pensions Board   (CEPB)
- Church House, Great Smith Street, LONDON, SW1P 3AZ.
  Tel 020 7898 1800   **Fax** 020 7898 1802
  Chairman: Dr Jonathan Spencer, CB   Chief Executive: Bernadette Kenny
E Established in 1926 under the Clergy Pensions Measure 1926, its current authority is derived from the Clergy Pensions Measure 1961 as amended by the Pensions Measure 1997. CEPB is a registered charity. The Board comprises 20 members including the Chairman.
R To administer the clergy's pension scheme.
  To administer accommodation and discretionary benefits for retired clergy and their widow(er)s.
  To administer pension schemes for the Church's lay employees.
G England, Wales.

Church & Society Council

■ 121 George Street, EDINBURGH, EH2 4YN.
Tel 0131 225 5722   http://www.churchofscotland.org.uk/councils/churchsociety
Convenor: Revd Ian Galloway
E Established in 2005 by the Church of Scotland. The Council comprises 40 members including the Convenor.
R To continue the tradition of engaging, on behalf of the Church, in the national, political and social issues affecting Scotland and the world today.
G Scotland.

Churches' Committee on Hospital Chaplaincy   See **Hospital Chaplaincies Council**.

The Churches Conservation Trust   (TCCT)

■ 1 West Smithfield, LONDON, EC1A 9EE.
Tel 020 7213 0660   **Fax** 020 7213 0678   http://www.visitchurches.org.uk
Chairman: Loyd Grossman, OBE, FSA   Chief Executive: Crispin Truman
E Established in 1969 as the Redundant Churches Fund under the Pastoral Measure 1968. TCCT is a registered charity and functions as an Executive NDPB of the Department for Culture, Media & Sport. The Board of Trustees has seven members.
R To care for over 340 churches made redundant by the Church of England which are of exceptional historic, architectural or archaeological significance.
G England.

Churches' Legislation Advisory Service   (CLAS)

■ Church House, Great Smith Street, LONDON, SW1P 3AZ.
Tel 020 7222 1265   **Fax** 020 7222 1250   http://www.churcheslegislation.org.uk
Chairman: Rt Revd Michael Langrish
E Established in 1941 as the Churches' Main Committee, a Judaeo-Christian ecumenical body. It relaunched after a 2005 review as a Christian ecumenical body with its current name. CLAS functions as a registered charity. The Board of Governors comprises nine members including the Chairman.
R To convey to Government the views of Christia churches and the Jewish community on legislation and other matters (other than education) that affect them.
To provide information on the impact on Christian churches and the Jewish community of legislation and proposals for legislation.
G United Kingdom.

Churches' Main Committee
✎ Has now become the **Churches' Legislation Advisory Service**.

Churches Media Council
✎ Formerly the Churches Advisory Council for Local Broadcasting, CMC is now known as the Church + Media Network.

Churches Together in Britain & Ireland   (CTBI)

■ 3r Eccleston Square, LONDON, SW1V 1BX.
Tel 0845 680 6851   **Fax** 0845 680 6852   http://www.ctbi.org.uk
Moderator: Margaret Swinson   General Secretary: Revd Canon Bob Fyffe
E Established on 1 September 1990, following a decision of its 30 member churches during 1989 to amend the constitution of the former British Council of Churches. CTBI is a membership organisation and the coordinating body for the four National Ecumenical Instruments: Action of Churches Together in Scotland, Churches Together in England, Cytûn and the Irish Council of Churches (qqv). The Board of Trustees comprises 13 members including the Moderator.
R To take forward the churches' ecumenical agenda on a strategic Four Nations basis.
G United Kingdom, Republic of Ireland

Churches Together in England   (CTE)

■ 27 Tavistock Square, LONDON, WC1H 9HH.
Tel 020 7529 8131   http://www.cte.org.uk
General Secretary: David Cornick

© CBD Research Ltd · Beckenham · Kent BR3 5JS · Tel 020 8650 7745 · Fax 020 8650 0768 · E-mail cbd@cbdresearch.com · www.cbdresearch.com

E   Established in 1990 by agreement of member churches. CTE is a membership organisation comprising 30 Churches or Councils of Churches and 27 Bodies in Association. It functions as a registered charity and company limited by guarantee.

R   To seek a deepening of their communion with Christ and with one another, to proclaim the Gospel together by common witness and service.

G   England.

Churches Together in Wales   See **Cytr**

Chwaraeon Cymru (Sport Wales)   See **Sports Council for Wales**.

CILT, the National Centre for Languages   (CILT)

■   3rd Floor, 111 Westminster Bridge Road, LONDON, SE1 7HR.
Tel 0845 612 5885   **Fax** 0845 612 5995   http://www.cilt.org.uk
Chairman: Richard Bunker   Chief Executive: Kate Board

E   Established in 2003 through the merger of the Centre for Information on Language Teaching & Research & the Languages National Training Organisation. CILT is the UK standards-setting body for languages and provides advice, intelligence and other services to the UK Commission for Employment & Skills (qv). The Board of Governors comprises eleven members including the Chairman.

R   To improve the teaching and learning of languages and provide independent advice on all aspects of language teaching, learning and use.

G   United Kingdom.

✍   For further information see companion volume, **Centres, Bureaux & Research Institutes**.

CITB-ConstructionSkills

■   Bircham Newton, KING'S LYNN, Norfolk, PE31 6RH.
Tel 01485 577577   http://www.cskills.org
Chairman: James Wates   Chief Executive: Mark Farrar

E   Established on 25 September 2003. ConstructionSkills is recognised the Sector Skills Council for the construction industry. It incorporates the Construction Industry Training Board.

G   England, Wales, Scotland.

✍   For further information see **Sector Skills Councils**.

CITB-ConstructionSkills Northern Ireland   (CITB)

■   Nutts Corner Trading Centre, 17 Dundrod Road, CRUMLIN, Co Antrim, BT29 4SR.
Tel 028 9082 5466   **Fax** 028 9082 5693   http://www.citbni.org.uk
Chairman: Tony Doran, OBE

E   Established in September 1964 under the Industrial Training Act 1964 and the Industrial Training (Construction Industry Training Board) Order 1964, it derives its current authority from the Industrial Training Order 1984. Its current name derives from the recent merger of the Construction Industry Training Board and the Sector Skills Council for construction, ConstructionSkills in Northern Ireland. CITB is the construction industry's recognised Sector Training Council and functions as an Executive NDPB of the Department for Employment & Learning Northern Ireland. The Board comprises 15 members who represent employers, employees and the education field.

R   To encourage adequate training of persons employed or intending to be employed in the industry.

G   Northern Ireland.

✍   For further information see **Sector Training Councils**.

Citizenship Foundation

■   63 Gee Street, LONDON, EC1V 3RS.
Tel 020 7566 4141   **Fax** 020 7566 4131   http://www.citizenshipfoundation.org.uk
Chairman: Michael Maclay   Chief Executive: Andy Thornton

E   Established in 1989 following the Law in Education Project (1984) of the Law Society and the then National Curriculum Council. The Foundation is an independent education and participation charity. The Board of Trustees comprises 19 members including the Chairman.

R   To achieve a just, inclusive and cohesive society in which individuals have the knowledge, skills, confidence and motivation to engage effectively in their communities.

G   United Kingdom.

✍   The Council for Education in World Citizenship, established in 1939, merged with the Foundation in 2008.

City Disputes Panel   (CDP)
- 24 Angel Gate, City Road, LONDON, EC1V 2PT.
  Tel 020 7520 3817   **Fax** 020 7520 3004   http://www.citydisputespanel.org
- E Established in 1994 with the support of the Bank of England, the City of London Corporation, the CBI, the Financial Services Authority and Lloyd's of London.
- R To provide the financial services industry with a practical means of Alternative Dispute Resolution (ADR) away from the Law Courts.
- G United Kingdom.
- ✐ ADR is an umbrella term used to describe a range of alternatives to litigation - these include conciliation, mediation, evaluative mediation, expert determination, evaluation and arbitration.

City & Guilds   (C&G)
- 1 Giltspur Street, LONDON, EC1A 9DD.
  Tel 0844 543 0000   **Fax** 020 7294 2400   http://www.city-and-guilds.co.uk
  President: HRH The Prince Philip, Duke of Edinburgh, KG, KT   Chairman: Michael Howell, Hon FCGI
- E Established in 1878 and granted a Royal Charter by Queen Victoria in 1900. It functions as a Royal Chartered Institute and registered charity. The Council comprises 70 members.
- G United Kingdom.
- ● City & Guilds is an awarding body for 500 courses and qualifications across 28 industry sectors.
- ✐ See also **Federation of Awarding Bodies**.
  A member of the **Joint Council for Qualifications** (qv).

City of London Police Authority
- PO Box 270, Guildhall, LONDON, EC2P 2ET.
  Tel 020 7332 1406
  Chairman: Simon D'Olier Duckworth, MA, DL
- E The City of London Police Act 1839 established the City of London Corporation's Court of Common Council as the Police Authority, charged with ensuring that the City of London Police provide an effective and efficient police service. It is made up of 15 councillor members and two independent members.
- G City of London.
- ✐ For further information see **Police Authorities**.

Civil Aviation Authority   (CAA)
- CAA House, 45-59 Kingsway, LONDON, WC2B 6TE.
  Tel 020 7453 6350   http://www.caa.co.uk
  The Safety Regulation Group is at:
  CAA, Aviation House, GATWICK Airport South, W Sussex, RH6 0YR.
  Tel 01293 567171
  Chairman: Dame Deirdre Hutton   Chief Executive: Andrew Haines
- E Established in 1972 under the Civil Aviation Act 1971. The Authority functions as a Public Corporation accountable to the Department for Transport. The CAA Board comprises twelve persons including the Chairman.
- R The CAA is divided into four groups:
  To set certain national aviation standards, and to oversee the activities of the aviation community and it levels of compliance with national and European safety standards (the Safety Regulation Group).
  To regulate airports, air traffic services and airlines, and to provide advice on aviation policy from an economic standpoint (the Economic Regulation Group).
  To be responsible for the planning and regulation of all UK airspace including the navigation and communications infrastructure to support safe and efficient operations (the Directorate of Airspace Policy).
  To regulate UK tour operators and airlines and enforce European regulations, and to provide information and advice on consumer travel issues (the Consumer Protection Group).
- G United Kingdom.
- ● The CAA set up and supports the independent consumer watchdog for the airline industry, the Air Transport Users Council (qv).

Civil Justice Council   (CJC)
- Room E214, Royal Courts of Justice, Strand, LONDON, WC2A 2LL.
  Tel 020 7947 6670   **Fax** 020 7947 7475   http://www.civiljusticecouncil.gov.uk
  Chairman: Lord Neuberger of Abbotsbury
- E Established in February 1998 under the Civil Procedure Act 1997. CJC functions as an Advisory NDPB of the Ministry of Justice. The Council comprises 24 members and is chaired by the Master of the Rolls.
- R To keep the civil justice system under review.
  To consider how to make the civil justice system more accessible, fair and efficient.

© CBD Research Ltd · Beckenham · Kent BR3 5JS · Tel 020 8650 7745 · Fax 020 8650 0768 · E-mail cbd@cbdresearch.com · www.cbdresearch.com

To advise the Lord Chancellor and the judiciary on the development of the civil justice system.

To refer proposals for changes in the civil justice system to the Lord Chancellor and the Civil Procedure Rule Committee (qv).

To make proposals for research.

G England, Wales.

Civil Nuclear Police Authority   (CNPA)

■ H280 Hinton House, Birchwood Park Avenue, Risley, WARRINGTON, Cheshire, WA3 6AS.
Tel 01925 833300   Fax 01925 833301   http://www.cnpa.police.uk
Chairman: Sir Chris Fox, QPM   Executive Director: Tony Regan

E Established on 1 April 2005 under the Energy Act 2004. CNPA functions as an Executive NDPB of the Department of Energy & Climate Change. It has eight members including the Chairman.

R To ensure that the Civil Nuclear Constabulary polices effectively, efficiently and is responsive to the needs and priorities of the stakeholders they serve.

G United Kingdom.

✍ CNPA is is independent of the Civil Nuclear Constabulary. Unlike other police authorities (qv), CNPA is the employer of all Constabulary personnel.

Civil Procedure Rule Committee   (CPRC)

■ 4th Floor, 102 Petty France, LONDON, SW1H 9AJ.
Tel 020 3334 3184   Fax 020 3334 6457
Secretary: Mrs Jane Wright

E Established in 1997 under the Civil Procedure Act 1997. CPRC functions as an Advisory NDPB of the Ministry of Justice. The Committee comprises 16 members including, ex officio, the Head of the Civil Service (the Master of the Rolls) and the Deputy Head of Civil Justice.

R To make rules of court for the Civil Division of the Court of Appeal, the High Court and the county courts.

G England, Wales.

Civil & Public Services Committee   (CPSC)

■ BMA House, Tavistock Square, LONDON, WC1H 9JP.
Tel 020 7383 6158   Fax 020 7383 6400   http://www.bma.org.uk

E Established as a Branch of Practice Committee of the British Medical Association. The CPSC comprises up to ten members.

R To consider and act in matters affecting those employed by Government departments, their agencies or contractors, including those employed as full time or part time prison medical officers.

G United Kingdom.

✍ See **British Medical Association** [Branch of Practice Committees] for further information.

Civil Service Appeal Board   (CSAB)

■ Room G32, 22 Whitehall, LONDON, SW1A 2WH.
Tel 020 7276 3832   Fax 020 7276 3836   http://www.civilserviceappealboard.gov.uk
Chairman: John H Davies, OBE   Secretary: Keith Wright

E Established on 28 February 1972 by Ministers with the agreement of official and trade union sides of the Civil Service National Whitley Council. CSAB functions as an Advisory NDPB of the Cabinet Office. The Board comprises 21 members including the Chairman.

R To hear appeals against dismissal and early retirement, the non-payment of compensation paid to civil servants dismissed on inefficiency grounds, refusal to allow participation in political activities, and forfeiture of superannuation benefits.

G England, Wales, Scotland.

✍ On 14 October 2010 the Government announced that CSAB will close on 31 December 2011. Residual work will be accommodated elsewhere within the Civil Service.

Civil Service Appeal Board for Northern Ireland   (NICSAB)

■ Room 245, Rosepark House, Upper Newtownards Road, BELFAST, BT4 3NR.
Tel 028 9052 6617   Fax 028 9052 6132

E Established in January 1974. CSAB functions as an Advisory NDPB of the Department of Finance & Personnel Northern Ireland.

R To hear appeals from Northern Ireland civil servants against dismissal and early retirement.

G Northern Ireland.

✍ Also known as the Northern Ireland Civil Service Appeal Board.

Civil Service Commission
■ 3rd Floor, 35 Great Smith Street, LONDON, SW1P 3BQ.
  Tel 020 7276 2617   http://www.civilservicecommission.org.uk
  First Civil Service Commissioner: Sir David Normington   Chief Executive: Richard Jarvis
E Civil Service Commissioners, first appointed in 1855, were established as a body corporate on 11 November
    2010 under the Constitutional Reform & Governance Act 2010. There are eleven Commissioners of whom the
    First Commissioner is also the Commissioner for Public Appointments (qv).
R To uphold the principle that selection to appointments in the Civil Service must be on merit on the basis of fair
    and open competition.
  To hear and determine complaints made by civil servants under the Civil Service Code, the ethical code which
    forms part of the terms and conditions of every civil servant.
G England, Wales, Scotland.

Civil Service Commission
■ Goldie House, 1-4 Goldie Terrace, Upper Church Street, DOUGLAS, Isle of Man, IM1 1EF.
  Tel 01624 685000
  Chairman: John Houghton, MHK
E Currently constituted under the provisions of the Civil Service Act 1990. The Commission comprises up to five
    members including the Chairman.
R To make appointments to the Civil Service.
G Isle of Man.

Civil Service Commissioners for Northern Ireland   (CSCNI)
■ 5th Floor, Windsor House, Bedford Street, BELFAST, BT2 7SR.
  Tel 028 9054 9151   http://www.nicscommissioners.org
  Chairman: Brenda McLaughlin
E Established on 28 February 1923 by the Northern Ireland Governor's Order 1923, the Commissioners' current
    authority is derived from the Civil Service Commissioners (Northern Ireland) Order 1999. The six commissioners,
    including the Chairman, are accountable to the Department of Finance & Personnel Northern Ireland.
R To uphold the principle that selection to appointments in the Civil Service must be solely on merit and on the
    basis of fair and open competition.
G Northern Ireland.

Claims Management Services Tribunal
✍ Since 18 January 2010 **First-tier Tribunal (Claims Management Services)**.

Clann an Alba   see **Children in Scotland**.

Clergy Discipline Commission
■ Church House, Great Smith Street, LONDON, SW1P 3AZ.
  Tel 020 7898 1000
  Chairman: Rt Hon Sir John Mummery (Lord Justice Mummery)
E Established on 1 January 2006 under the Clergy Discipline Measure 2003.
R To advise disciplinary tribunals as to the penalties which are appropriate in connection with clergy discipline.
G England, Wales.

Cleveland Police Authority   (CPA)
■ Ladgate Lane, MIDDLESBROUGH, TS8 9EH.
  Tel 01642 301653   http://www.clevelandpa.org.uk
  Chairman: Cllr Dave McLuckie
E Established in April 1995, the Authority is an independent body charged with ensuring that Cleveland Police
    provide an effective and efficient police service. It is made up of nine councillor members and eight
    independent members.
G Hartlepool, Middlesbrough, Redcar-Cleveland and Stockton.
✍ For further information see **Police Authorities**.

Clinical Trials Expert Advisory Group
■ 151 Buckingham Palace Road, LONDON, SW1W 9SZ.
  Tel 020 3080 6000
  Chairman: Prof Robert Lechler, MB, ChB, PhD, FRCP, FRCPath, FMedSci

E   Established in 2005. It functions as an advisory body to the Commission on Human Medicines (CHM), qv. The Group comprises twelve members including the Chairman.
R   To advise CHM on First Time in Man (FTIM) studies of new compounds and other clinical trials.
G   United Kingdom.

Clusters Policy Steering Group
✍   Established in 2001, the Group was wound up in early 2003.

Clyde River Foundation   See **Rivers & Fisheries Trusts of Scotland**.

Co Durham & Tees Valley Strategic Health Authority
✍   On 1 July 2006 merged with the Northumberland, Tyne & Wear Strategic Health Authority to form the **North East Strategic Health Authority**.

The Coal Authority
■   200 Lichfield Lane, MANSFIELD, Notts, NG18 4RG.
    Tel 01623 637000   http://www.coal.gov.uk
    Chairman: Dr Helen Mounsey, BSc(Hons), PhD   Chief Executive: Philip Lawrence, ACA
E   Established on 19 September 1994 under the Coal Industry Act 1994 assuming the administrative functions of the former British Coal Corporation. The Authority functions as an Executive NDPB of the Department for Business, Innovation & Skills. The committee comprises seven members including the Chairman.
R   To license coal mining operations in Britain.
    To handle subsidence damage claims which are not the responsibility of licensed coal mine operators.
    To deal with property and historic liability issues, such as treatment of minewater discharges.
    To provide public access to information on past and present coal mining operations.
    To provide a 24 hour call-out service for reported surface hazards.
G   United Kingdom.

Coal Research Forum   (CRF)
■   PO Box 154, CHELTENHAM, Glos, GL52 5YL.
    Tel 01242 236973   Fax 01242 516672   http://www.coalresearchforum.org
    Chairmen: Greg Kelsall & Prof John Patrick   Secretary: Dr David McCaffrey
E   Established in March 1989. CRF is a membership body comprising corporate. industrial and academic (mostly university departments) members.
R   To provide a forum for the exchange of information between technology providers and key stakeholders.
    To support the utilisation of coal in the UK as a secure primary source of energy.
    To promote UK research and expertise on coal to a worldwide audience.
G   United Kingdom.

Coastguard Agency   See **Maritime & Coastguard Agency**.

Cogent
■   Unit 5, Mandarin Court, Centre Park, WARRINGTON, Cheshire, WA1 1GG.
    Tel 01925 515200   Fax 01925 515240   http://www.cogent-ssc.com
    Chairman: Dr John Beacham, CBE   Chief Executive: Joanna Woolf
E   Established on 1 February 2004. It is the recognised Sector Skills Council for the chemicals and petrochemicals, nuclear, oil and gas, petroleum and polymers industries.
G   United Kingdom.
✍   For further information see **Sector Skills Councils**.

Coleraine Harbour Commissioners
■   Harbour Office, 4 Riversdale Road, COLERAINE, Co Londonderry, BT52 1RY.
    Tel 028 7034 2012   Fax 028 7035 2000
E   Established in 1879 under the River Bann Navigation Act 1879. The Commission comprises 19 members.
G   Coleraine.
✍   For further information see **Port & Harbour Authorities**.

College of Management & Technology   See **Defence Academy Management Board**.

Comhairle na Gaelscolaíochta   (CnaG)
- 4 Queen Street, BELFAST, BT1 6ED.
  Tel 028 9032 1475   Fax 028 9032 4475   http://www.comhairle.org
  Chairman: Caoimhin Ó Peatáin
E   Established in 2000. CnaG functions as an Advisory NDPB of the Department of Education Northern Ireland. The
    board comprises 22 voluntary directors including the Chairman.
R   To promote, facilitate and encourage Irish-medium education and schools in the north of Ireland in a planned,
    educationally efficient and cost-effective way.
G   Northern Ireland.
✍   CnaG and other legacy organisations will be dissolved when the Education & Skills Authority (qv) becomes fully
    operational.

Comisiwn Brenhinol Henebion Cymru   See **Royal Commission on the Ancient & Historical Monuments of
Wales**.

Comisiwn Dylunio Cymru   See **Design Commission for Wales**.

Comisiwn Ffiniau i Gymru   See **Boundary Commission for Wales**.

Comisiwn Ffiniau Llywodraeth Leol i Gymru   See the **Local Government Boundary Commission for Wales**.

Comisiynydd Plant Cymru   See **Children's Commissioner for Wales**.

Comisiynydd Pobl Hŷn Cymru   See **Older People's Commissioner for Wales**.

Commission for Africa
✍   Established in Spring 2004, the Commission published its report in March 2005.

Commission for Architecture & the Built Environment   (CABE)
- 1 Kemble Street, LONDON, WC2B 4AN.
  Tel 020 7070 6700   Fax 020 7070 6777   http://www.cabe.org.uk
  Chairman: Paul Finch, OBE   Chief Executive: Richard Simmons
E   Established by Royal Warrant in May 1924, its terms of reference extended by Royal Warrants in August 1933
    and May 1946; it adopted its current name on 1 September 1999. CABE functions as an Executive NDPB of the
    Department for Culture, Media & Sport (DCMS). The Board comprises 16 Commissioners.
R   To encourage policy makers to create places that are safe, beautiful and efficient to run.
G   England.
✍   One of four UK Commissions established to champion good design and a high quality built environment.
    As a result of the government's Comprehensive Spending Review, DCMS announced on 14 October 2010 that it
    is withdrawing its funding from CABE and considering the options for reform.

Commission for the Compact
- 77 Paradise Circus, Queensway, BIRMINGHAM, B1 2DT.
  Tel 0121 237 5900   Fax 0121 233 2120   http://www.thecompact.org.uk
  Commissioner: Sir Bert Massie   Chief Executive: Richard Corden
E   Established in April 2007. The Commission functions as an NDPB of the Office for Civil Society. The Board
    comprises five members including the Chairman.
R   To promote good practice in partnership working between Government and the voluntary and community sector
    through the Compact, overseeing its operation.
G   England.
●   Local Compacts exist in many towns in the nine English Regions.
✍   The Compact was established in England in 1998 and is the agreement between the voluntary sector and the
    Government to ensure better working together. On 14 October 2010 the Government announced the abolition
    of the Commission. Its functions, to champion and promote the Compact, are to be carried out by Compact
    Voice (a membership body) and the Cabinet Office respectively.

Commission for Ethical Standards in Public Life in Scotland
■   39 Drumsheugh Gardens, EDINBURGH, EH3 7SW.
     Tel 0300 011 0550   http://www.ethicalstandards.org.uk
E   Established on 1 April 2011 under the Scottish Parliamentary Commission & Commissioners etc Act 2010. It
     brings together the offices of the former Scottish Parliamentary Standards Commissioner and Commissioner for
     Public Appointments in Scotland and incorporates the functions of the former Chief Investigating Officer. It was
     set up to support the offices the Public Appointments Commissioner for Scotland and the Public Standards
     Commissioner for Scotland (qv).
R   To make a visible, valued and lasting contribution to ethical standards in public life, thereby strengthening public
     trust and confidence in elected and appointed office-holders.
G   Scotland.

Commission on the Future of Multi-Ethnic Britain
✍   Established by the Runnymede Trust in 1997, it produced its final report. the Parekh Report, in October 2000.

Commission on the Future of Volunteering
✍   Established in 2005, the Commission produced its final report in January 2008.

Commission for Health Improvement
✍   With effect from 1 April 2004 the work of the CHI was taken over by the Commission for Healthcare Audit &
     Inspections, which itself ceased to exist on 31 March 2009. The new health and social care regulator is the
     Care Quality Commission.

Commission for Healthcare Audit & Inspection
✍   Better known as the Healthcare Commission, it ceased to exist on 31 March 2009. The new health and social
     care regulator is the **Care Quality Commission**.

Commission on Human Medicines
■   151 Buckingham Palace Road, LONDON, SW1W 9SZ.
     Tel 020 3080 6000
     Chairman: Prof Sir Gordon W Duff, MA, BM, BCh, PhD, FRCP, FRCPE, FMedSci
E   Established on 30 October 2005 following the merger of the former Committee on Safety of Medicines and the
     Medicines Commission, the Commission derives its authority under the Medicines Act 1968. CHM functions as
     a Scientific Advisory Committee and an advisory body to the Medicine & Healthcare products Regulatory
     Agency (qv). The Commission comprises 21 members including the Chairman.
R   To advise the Health Ministers and the Licensing Authority on matters relating to human medicinal products,
     including giving advice in relation to the safety, quality and efficacy of human medicinal products.
     To promote the collection and investigation of information relating to adverse reactions to human medicines.
G   United Kingdom.
●   The Commission is supported in its work by 16 Expert Advisory Groups (EAGs):
          Anti-infective HIV & AIDS Expert Advisory Group
          Biologicals & Vaccines Expert Advisory Group
          Cardiovascular/Diabetes/Renal Medicines Expert Advisory Group
          Chemistry, Pharmacy & Standards Expert Advisory Group
          Clinical Trials Expert Advisory Group
          Dermatology Expert Advisory Group
          Gastrointestinal & Hepatology Medicines Expert Advisory Group
          Neurology & Pain Relief Expert Advisory Group
          Oncology & Haematology Expert Advisory Group
          Paediatric Medicines Expert Advisory Group
          Patient Information Expert Advisory Group
          Pharmacovigilance Expert Advisory Group
          Psychiatry & Old Age Psychiatry Expert Advisory Group
          Respiratory & Allergy Medicines Expert Advisory Group
          Rheumatology & Immunology Expert Advisory Group
          Women's Health Expert Advisory Group (qqv).
✍   For further information see **Scientific Advisory Committees**.

Commission for Integrated Transport
✍   CfIT was abolished on 14 October 2010. The Government is seeking an arrangement that delivers external
     analysis and strategic advice on cross-modal transport policy at lower cost.

Commission on Integration & Cohesion
✍ Established in 2006, the Commission was disbanded after producing its final report, Our Shared Future, on 14 June 2007.

Commission for Local Administration in England
■ The Oaks No 2, Westwood Way, Westwood Business Park, COVENTRY, CV4 8JB.
Tel 024 7682 0000   http://www.lgo.org.uk
10th Floor, Millbank Tower, Millbank, LONDON, SW1P 4QP.
Tel 020 7217 4620
Beverley House, 17 Shipton Road, YORK, YO30 5FZ.
Tel 01904 380200
Local Government Ombudsmen: Jane Martin (Coventry office) and Anne Seex (York office). London vacant.
E Set up in 1974 under the Local Government Act 1974. The Commission runs the Local Government Ombudsman service and its members are the three Local Government Ombudsmen and the Parliamentary & Health Service Ombudsman (qv).
R To investigate complaints from members of the public about allegations of injustice caused by maladministration by local authorities and certain other bodies.
Local Government Ombudsmen will not investigate any complaint until it has been brought to the attention of the authority complained about, and until the authority has had a reasonable time in which to reply to the complaint.
A complaint can be sent direct to the Ombudsman or a complainant can ask a councillor to refer it.
G England.
● The Ombudsman in Coventry covers London Boroughs south of the River Thames (plus Harrow but excluding Lewisham and Richmond), Manchester, York, High Peak (Derbys), Trafford (Gtr Manchester), authorities in the south and west not covered from London and authorities in central England not covered from York.
The Ombudsman in London covers London Boroughs north of the River Thames (plus Richmond but excluding Harrow), Coventry City, Hambleton (N Yorks), Berkshire, Buckinghamshire, Essex, Hertfordshire, Kent, Surrey and Sussex.
The Ombudsman in York covers the London Borough of Lewisham, Birmingham and Solihull (W Midlands), Gloucestershire (but not South Gloucestershire), Derbyshire (excluding High Peak), Lincolnshire, Nottinghamshire, Warwickshire and the north (excluding Manchester, York and Trafford).

Commission for Local Administration in Scotland (Local Government Ombudsman)
✍ Abolished in 2002 with the establishing of the **Scottish Public Services Ombudsman**.

Commission for Local Administration in Wales
✍ Replaced on 1 April 2006 by the **Public Services Ombudsman for Wales**.

Commission for the New Towns
✍ CNT merged in 1999 with the Urban Regeneration Agency as English Partnerships, which became part of the **Homes & Communities Agency** in 2008.

Commission for Patient & Public Involvement in Health
✍ CPPIH, established on 1 January 2003 to support Patients' Forums, was abolished on 31 March 2008 when the Forums were replaced by **Local Involvement Networks (LINks)**.

Commission on the Powers & Electoral Arangements of the National Assembly of Wales (The Richard Commission)
✍ The Commission produced its final report in 2004.

Commission for Racial Equality
✍ On 1 October 2007 replaced by the **Equality & Human Rights Commission**.

Commission for Rural Communities   (CRC)
■ Unit 1, Sawmill End, Corinium Avenue, GLOUCESTER, GL4 3DE.   http://www.defra.gov.uk/crc/
Chairman: Dr Stuart Burgess, CBE
E Established in April 2005, it became an independent body on 1 October 2006 following enactment of the Natural Environment & Rural Communities Act 2006. CRC functions as an Executive NDPB of the Department for Environment, Food & Rural Affairs (Defra). The Commission comprises ten members including the Chairman.

R   To promote awareness of the social and economic needs of people who live and work in rural areas.
G   England.
✍   In June 2010, the Secretary of State announced that CRC was to be abolished and that Defra's internal rural policy capacity was to be expanded to create a Rural Communities Policy Unit (RCPU).

Commission for Social Care Inspection
✍   The Commission ceased to exist on 31 March 2009. The new health and social care regulator is the **Care Quality Commission**.

Commission on Taxation & Citizenship
✍   No longer in existence.

Commission for Victims & Witnesses
■   102 Petty France, LONDON, SW1H 9AJ.
      Tel 020 3334 3555   Fax 020 3334 4455
      Commissioner for Victims & Witnesses: Louise Casey
E   Established under the Domestic Violence, Crime & Victims Act 2004. The Victims' Commissioner functions as an Executive Agency of the Ministry of Justice.
R   To promote the interests of victims and witnesses, encourage good practice in their treatment, and regularly review the Code of Practice for Victims which sets out the services victims can expect to receive.
G   England, Wales.

Commissioner for Children & Young People for Northern Ireland   See **Northern Ireland Commissioner for Children & Young People**.

Commissioner for Judicial Appointments for Northern Ireland
✍   Office closed on 22 September 2006 with the establishment of the **Northern Ireland Judicial Appointments Ombudsman**.

Commissioner for Public Appointments   See the **Office of the Commissioner for Public Appointments** (Northern Ireland and England & Wales) and the **Public Appointments Commissioner for Scotland**.

Commissioners of HMRC   See **Her Majesty's Revenue & Customs**.

The Commissioners of Irish Lights
■   Harbour Road, DUN LAOGHAIRE, Co Dublin, Republic of Ireland.
      Tel +353 (0)1 271 5400   http://www.commissionersofirishlights.com
      Chairman: John Kidney   Chief Executive: Dr Stuart Ruttle
E   First established in 1786, Irish Lights' statutory authority is derived from the Merchant Shipping Act 1894. It functions the General Lighthouse Authority for the whole of Ireland. The Commission comprises 21 members including the Chairman.
R   To maintain aids to navigation around the coast of the whole island.
G   Northern Ireland, Republic of Ireland.

Commissioners of Northern Lighthouses   see **Northern Lighthouse Board**

Committee for the Accreditation of Medical Illustration Practitioners   (CAMIP)
■   Addenbrooke's Hospital, Hills Road, CAMBRIDGE, CB2 0QQ.   http://www.camip.org.uk
      Chairman: Jeremy Nayler, FIMI, FBIPP, RMIP
E   Established in January 1990. CAMIP functions as a limited company.
R   To promote and encourage the practice of medical illustration (in the form of photography, drawing, painting, film, television and sound broadcasting and recording and similar ilustrative arts and technologies).
G   United Kingdom.
●   CAMIP maintains a voluntary register of medical illustrators.

Committee on the Administration of Justice   (CAJ)

■   2nd Floor, Sturgen Building, 9-15 Queen Street, BELFAST, BT1 6EA.
        Tel 028 9031 6000   Fax 028 9031 4583   http://www.caj.org.uk
        Director: Mike Ritchie
E   Established in 1981. CAJ is an independent human rights organisation and membership is open to everyone.
R   To promote justice and protect rights.
G   Northern Ireland.
●   CAJ provides information, advice and, where appropriate, representation to victims (or potential victims) of human
        rights abuses in Northern Ireland, and monitors the handling of past human rights abuses.

Committee of Advertising Practice   (CAP)

■   Mid City Place, 71 High Holborn, LONDON, WC1V 6QT.
        Tel 020 7492 2200   Fax 020 7404 3404   http://www.cap.org.uk
        Chairman: Andrew Brown   Secretary: Shahriar Coupal
E   Established in 1961, it was formerly known as the Code of Advertising Practice Committee. There are two
        industry committees - Non-Broadcast (CAP) and Broadcast (BCAP). Each is independently administered by the
        Advertising Standards Authority (qv). Each consists of representatives of organisations linked to the relevant
        advertising media. The Committees share the same Chairman.
R   CAP - To write and enforce the British Code of Advertising, Sales Promotion & Direct Marketing (The Code), and
        covering sales promotions, direct marketing and mail order.BCAP - To write and enforce, on behalf of Ofcom
        (qv), the codes of practice that govern television and radio advertising.
G   United Kingdom.

Committee on Agricultural Valuation

✐   In March 2010 Defra announced its intention to abolish CAV, established under the Agricultural Holdings Act
        1986, which has been dormant for over a decade.

Committee on Analytical Requirements

✐   After its meeting on 16 May 2006 it was decided that CAR would continue as a correspondence group only.

Committee on Blood Pressure Monitoring in Clinical Practice

■   151 Buckingham Palace Road, LONDON, SW1W 9SZ.
        Tel 020 3080 6000
        Chairman: Prof Andrew Shennan
E   Established in 2003. The Committee functions as an advisory body to the Medicines & Healthcare products
        Regulatory Agency (qv). It comprises 13 members including the Chairman.
R   To evaluate whether mercury sphygmomanometers should continue to be used or removed from the clinical
        environment.
        To consider the alternatives to mercury devices and the evidence regarding their accuracy.
G   United Kingdom.
✐   The Committee last met on 10 March 2004.

Committee on Carcinogenicity of Chemicals in Food, Consumer Products & the Environment   (COC)

■   Centre for Radiation & Chemical Hazards, Chilton, DIDCOT, Oxon, OX11 0RQ.
        Tel 01235 841475   http://www.iacoc.org.uk
        Chairman: Prof David H Phillips   Administrative Secretary: Sue Kennedy
E   Established on 1 January 1978 by the Government's Chief Medical Officer, superseding the former Sub-
        Committee on Carcinogenicity of the Committee on Medical Aspects of Chemicals in Food & the Environment.
        COC now functions as a Scientific Advisory Committee and an Advisory NDPB of the Food Standards Agency
        (qv). The Committee comprises 13 members including the Chairman.
R   To provide advice to various Government departments and agencies on matters concerning the potential
        carcinogenicity of chemicals ranging from natural products to new synthetic chemicals used in pesticides or
        pharmaceuticals.
G   United Kingdom.
✐   On 14 October 2010 the Government announced that COC would cease to function as a NDPB and be
        reconstituted as a committee of experts of the Department of Health and the new Public Health Service.

Committee on Climate Change   (CCC)

■   4th Floor, Manning House, 22 Carlisle Place, LONDON, SW1P 1JA.
        Tel 020 7592 1553   http://www.theccc.org.uk
        Chairman: Lord Adair Turner   Chief Executive: David Kennedy

© CBD Research Ltd · Beckenham · Kent BR3 5JS · Tel 020 8650 7745 · Fax 020 8650 0768 · E-mail cbd@cbdresearch.com · www.cbdresearch.com

E   Established under the Climate Change Act (2008). CCC functions as an Advisory NDPB of the Department for Energy & Climate Change. The Committee comprises nine members including the Chairman.

R   To advise the Government on setting and meeting carbon budgets and on preparing for the impacts of climate change.

G   United Kingdom.

Committee on Community Care
■   BMA House, Tavistock Square, LONDON, WC1H 9JP.
Tel 0300 123 1233 Fax 020 7383 6400 http://www.bma.org.uk
Chairman: Dr Helena McKeown

E   Established as a professional committee of the British Medical Association.

R   To monitor policy and service trends in community care, and to advise on the resolution of problems at the interface of primary and secondary health care and social care.

G   United Kingdom.

✍   See **British Medical Association** [Boards & Committees] for further information.

Committee on the Ethical Aspects of Pandemic Influenza
✍   Established in 2006, CEAPI was disbanded after producing its report in 2007.

Committee of General Practice Education Directors   (COGPED)
■   14 Princes Gate, LONDON, SW7 1PU.
Tel 020 7344 3070 Fax 020 7225 3047 http://www.cogped.org.uk
Administrator: Sarah Robinson

E   COGPED offers a forum for Postgraduate GP Directors to meet and share good practice.

R   To encourage and maintain a consistent approach to GP training across the UK.

G   United Kingdom.

Committee of Heads of University Law Schools   (CHULS)
■   Christchurch House, Fern Barrow, POOLE, Dorset, BH12 5BB.
Tel 01202 965206 http://www.chuls.ac.uk
Chairman: Dr Elizabeth Mytton

E   Established in 1974, the Committee retained its name after merging with the Committee of Heads of Polytechnic Law Schools on 30 November 1992. The Executive Committee comprises twelve members including the Chairman.

R   To represent law schools and their management to the funding councils and other established committees in the legal sector.

      To promote mutual respect and active cooperation between law schools regionally, nationally and internationally.

G   United Kingdom.

Committee of Investigation for Great Britain
✍   Abolished by the Natural Environment & Rural Communites Act 2006 which established the **Commission for Rural Communities**.

Committee on Medical Aspects of Radiation in the Environment   (COMARE)
■   Centre for Radiation & Chemical Hazards, Chilton, DIDCOT, Oxon, OX11 0RQ.
Tel 01235 822629 Fax 01235 832447 http://www.comare.org.uk
Chairman: Prof Alex Elliott, BA, PhD, DSc

E   Established in November 1985 by the Minister for Health. COMARE functions as a Scientific Advisory Committee and an Advisory NDPB of the Department of Health. The Committee comprises the Chairman and 16 members who are appointed by the Chief Medical Officer on the basis of their medical and scientific expertise.

R   To provide advice to Government Departments and the Devolved Authorities on the health effects of natural and man-made radiation.

G   United Kingdom.

✍   On 14 October 2010 the Government announced that COMARE would cease to function as a NDPB and be reconstituted as a committee of experts of the Department of Health and the new Public Health Service.

Committee on Medical Effects of Air Pollutants   (COMEAP)
■   Centre for Radiation & Chemical Hazards, Chilton, DIDCOT, Oxon, OX11 0RQ.
Tel 01235 841475 Fax 01235 841478
Chairman: Prof Jon Ayres   Administrative Secretary: Sue Kennedy

E   Established in 1992. COMEAP functions as a Scientific Advisory Committee and an Advisory NDPB of the Department of Health. The Committee consists of 19 members (including the Chairman) who are appointed by the Chief Medical Officer of the Department of Health and the Government.
R   To provide advice to Government Departments and the Devolved Authorities on all matters concerning the potential toxicity and effects upon health of air pollutants.
G   United Kingdom.
✍   In 2007 the Committee absorbed the Expert Panel on Air Quality Standards.
     On 14 October 2010 the Government announced that COMEAP would cease to function as a NDPB and be reconstituted as a committee of experts of the Department of Health and the new Public Health Service.

Committee on Mutagenicity of Chemicals in Food, Consumer Products & the Environment   (COM)
■   Centre for Radiation & Chemical Hazards, Chilton, DIDCOT, Oxon, OX11 0RQ.
     Tel 01235 822836   **Fax** 01235 833891   http://www.iacom.org.uk
     Chairman: Prof Peter B Farmer   Administrative Secretary: Sue Kennedy
E   Set up on 1 January 1978 by the Government's Chief Medical Officer, superseding the former Sub-Committee on Mutagenicity of the Committee on Medical Aspects of Chemicals in Food & the Environment. COM functions as a Scientific Advisory Committee and an Advisory NDPB of the Department of Health and the Food Standards Agency (qv). The Committee comprises 13 members including the Chairman.
R   To provide advice to Government Departments and the Devolved Authorities on matters concerning the potential mutagenicity of chemicals ranging from natural products to new synthetic chemicals used in pesticides or pharmaceuticals.
G   United Kingdom.
✍   On 14 October 2010 the Government announced that COM would cease to function as a NDPB and be reconstituted as a committee of experts of the Department of Health and the new Public Health Service.

Committee of Postgraduate Dental Deans & Directors   (COPDEND)
■   Postgraduate Dental Education Office, Don Valley House, Savile Street East, SHEFFIELD, S4 7UQ.
     Tel 0114 226 4437   **Fax** 0114 226 4468   http://www.copdend.org.uk
     Chairman: Prof Chris Franklin
E   The Committee comprises 15 members including the Chairman.
R   To commission and manage the delivery of postgraduate dental and medical education and training for dental practitioners.
G   United Kingdom.

Committee on Products & Processes for use in Public Water Supply
✍   The Committee was disbanded in 2003.

Committee for Public Health Medicine & Community Health   See **Public Health Medicine Committee**.

Committee on Radioactive Waste Management   (CoRWM)
■   Area 3D, 3 Whitehall Place, LONDON, SW1A 2AW.
     Tel 0300 068 6109   http://www.corwm.decc.gov.uk
     Chairman: Prof Robert Pickard
E   Established on 17 November 2003 following the cessation of activities of the Radioactive Waste Management Advisory Committee. CoRWM functions as a Scientific Advisory Committee and an Advisory NDPB of the Department of Energy & Climate Change. The Committee comprises 15 members including the Chairman.
R   To provide independent scrutiny and advice to UK Governments on the long term management, including storage and disposal, of radioactive waste.
G   United Kingdom.
✍   For further information see **Scentific Advisory Committees**.

Committee on the Safety of Devices   (CSD)
■   151 Buckingham Palace Road, LONDON, SW1W 9SZ.
     Tel 020 3080 6000
     Chairman: Dr John Perrins, BSc, MD, FRCP, FACC
E   Established in April 2001. CSD functions as a Scientific Advisory Committee and an advisory body of the Medicines & Healthcare products Regulatory Authority (qv). The Committee comprises 25 members including the Chairman.
R   To take a strategic view of initiatives to make medical devices safer and more effective.
     To offer advice on the development of device related policies.

G   United Kingdom.

✍   On 14 October 2010 the Government announced that CSD would cease to function as a NDPB and be reconstituted as a committee of experts of the Medicines & Healthcare products Regulatory Agency (qv).

Committee on Safety of Medicines

✍   On 30 October 2005 the **Commission on Human Medicines** was established, combining the Committee's functions and those of the Medicines Commission.

Committee of Scottish Clearing Bankers   (CSCB)

■   38b Drumsheugh Gardens, EDINBURGH, EH3 7SW.
    Tel 0131 473 7770   **Fax** 0131 473 7799   http://www.scotbanks.org.uk

E   The Committee dates from 1764 and has operated under its present name since since 1970. CSCB is the representative body of the four Scottish clearing banks (Bank of Scotland, Royal Bank of Scotland, Clydesdale Bank & Lloyds TSB Scotland). The Committee comprises the Chief Executives of the four banks.

R   To represent Scottish clearing banking in the financial structure of Britain.
    To promote the industry by providing an authoritative voice on Scottish matters to ensure thay are adequately recognised and safeguarded.

G   Scotland.

Committee on Standards in Public Life   (CSPL)

■   35 Great Smith Street, LONDON, SW1P 3BQ.
    Tel 020 7276 2595   **Fax** 020 7276 2585   http://www.public-standards.gov.uk
    Chairman: Sir Christopher Kelly, KCB

E   Established on 25 October 1994 following an announcement by the Prime Minister, it became an independent statutory authority on 30 November 2000. CSPL functions as an Advisory NDPB of the Cabinet Office. The Committee comprises ten members including the Chairman.

R   To examine concerns about standards of conduct of all holders of public office, including arrangements relating to financial and commercial activities.
    To make recommendations as to any changes in present arrangements which might be required to ensure the highest standards of propriety in public life.

G   United Kingdom.

Committee on Toxicity of Chemicals in Food, Consumer Products & the Environment   (COT)

■   Aviation House, 125 Kingsway, LONDON, WC2B 6NH.
    Tel 020 7276 8522   **Fax** 020 7276 8513   http://www.cot.food.gov.uk
    Chairman: Prof David Coggon, OBE

E   Established on 1 January 1978 by the Government's Chief Medical Officer, superseding the former Sub-Committee on Toxicity of the Committee on Medical Aspects of Chemicals in Food & the Environment. COT functions as a Scientific Advisory Committee and an Advisory NDPB of the Food Standards Agency (qv). The Committee comprises the Chairman and 18 members.

R   To provide advice to Government Departments and the Devolved Authorities on all matters concerning the toxicity of chemicals.

G   United Kingdom.

✍   For further information see **Scientific Advisory Committees**.

Committee on Vocational Training for England & Wales [Dentistry]

✍   No longer in existence.

Common Services Agency for the National Health Service in Scotland

✍   See **NHS Scotland National Services**.

Commons Commissioners

✍   On 22 July 2010 Defra announced the abolition of the Commissioners who have concluded their work which was to adjudicate disputed applications to register common land and greens under the Commons Registration Act 1965.

Commons Select Committees   See **United Kingdom Parliament: Committees**.

Commonwealth Engineers' Council   (CEC)

- One Great George Street, LONDON, SW1P 3AA.
  Tel 020 7222 7722   http://www.cec.ice.org.uk
  President: Tom Foulkes, MBA, BSc, CEng, FICE, FIMechE, MIoD
- E Established in September 1946. The Council represents 45 engineering institutions in 44 Commonwealth countries.
- R To foster cooperation and exchange information among members.
  To present the views of the engineering profession to central Commonwealth bodies.
- G United Kingdom, Commonwealth.

Commonwealth Games Council for England   (CGCE)

- Jubilee Stand, Crystal Palace National Sports Centre, LONDON, SE19 2YY.
  Tel 020 8676 2543   Fax 020 8676 3604   http://www.weareengland.org
  Chairman: Sir Andrew Foster   Chief Executive: Ann Hogbin, CBE
- E Established in 1932.
- R To maintain the affiliation of England to the Commonwealth Games Federation.
  To encourage interest in the Commonwealth Games throughout England and to ensure that England is worthily represented at the Commonwealth Games, and that proper arrangements are made for the organisation of the Games whenever they are awarded to England by the Federaton.
  To work in close cooperation with the other Commonwealth Games organisations throughout the world and in particular within the British Isles.
- G England.

Commonwealth Games Council for Northern Ireland   (CGCNI)

- 22 Glencraig Park, CRAIGAVAD, Co Down, BT18 0BZ.
  Tel 028 9042 4009   http://www.cgcni.org.uk
  Chairman: Robert McVeigh   Hon Secretary: Ms Terry Crothers
- E To equip and send a Northern Ireland team to the Commonwealth Games.
- G Northern Ireland.

Commonwealth Games Council for Scotland   (CGCS)

- Gannochy Sports Centre, University of Stirling, STIRLING, FK9 4LA.
  Tel 01786 466480   Fax 01786 466481   http://www.cgcs.org.uk
  Chairman: Michael Cavanagh   Chief Executive: John Scott
- E Established in 1931. Membership of the Council comprises representatives of 26 sports in the Commonwealth Games programme.
- R To equip and send a Scottish team to the Commonwealth Games every four years and to the Commonwealth Youth Games every two years.
- G Scotland.

Commonwealth Games Council for Wales   (CGCW)

- Sport Wales, Sophia Gardens, CARDIFF, CF11 9SW.
  Tel 029 2033 4930   http://www.teamwales2010.co.uk
  Chaiman: Gareth John   Chef de Mission: Chris Jenkins
- R To equip and send a Welsh team to the Commonwealth Games.
- G Wales.

Commonwealth Institute

- ✍ The Commonwealth Institute building closed in 2002. The work of the Institute is carried out by the Commonwealth Education Trust, a charity established in 2007.

Commonwealth Scholarship Commission in the United Kingdom   (CSC)

- Woburn House, 20-24 Tavistock Square, LONDON, WC1H 9HF.
  Tel 020 7380 6700   Fax 020 7387 2655   http://www.cscuk.org.uk
  Chairman: Prof Tim Unwin   Executive Secretary: Dr John Kirkland, BSc, PhD
- E Established under the Commonwealth Scholarship Act 1959. CSC functions as an Executive NDPB of the Department for International Development. The Commission comprises 15 members including the Chairman.
- R To offer opportunities to Commonwealth citizens to study in the UK, and identify UK citizens to study overseas, as part of the UK's contribution to the international Commonwealth Scholarship & Fellowship Plan.
- G United Kingdom.

© CBD Research Ltd · Beckenham · Kent BR3 5JS · Tel 020 8650 7745 · Fax 020 8650 0768 · E-mail cbd@cbdresearch.com · www.cbdresearch.com

Commonwealth War Graves Commission   (CWGC)

■ 2 Marlow Road, MAIDENHEAD, Berks, SL6 7DX.
  Tel 01628 507200   Fax 01628 771208   http://www.cwgc.org
  Chairman: The Secretary of State for Defence (Rt Hon Liam Fox, MP)   Director-General & Secretary: Richard Kellaway, CBE

E Established on 21 May 1917 by Royal Charter as the Imperial War Graves Commission, it assumed its current functions and name by a supplemental charter in 1964. CWGC is a non-profit organisation. The Commission currently comprises 16 members including the Chairman.

R To pay tribute to the 1,700,000 men and women of the Commonwealth forces who died in the two World Wars.

G Worldwide.

● Since its inception, the Commission has constructed 2,500 war cemeteries and plots, erecting gravestones over graves and, in instances where the remains are missing, inscribing the names of the dead on permanent memorials.

The Commonwealth Youth Exchange Council   (CYEC)

■ 7 Lion Yard, Tremadoc Road, LONDON, SW4 7NQ.
  Tel 020 7498 6151   Fax 020 7622 4365   http://www.cyec.org.uk
  Chief Executive: Vic Craggs, OBE

E Established in 1970. CYEC is a membership body consisting of 134 local authorities and 88 voluntary organisations. It is registered as a UK educational charity. The members of the Board of Management act as trustees.

R To benefit young people by supporting the development of locally managed high quality exchange visits and programmes that promote skills for employability, global citizenship and inter-cultural understanding.

G The Commonwealth.

Communications for Business

✍ An Ofcom (qv) advisory committee which last met 2003.

Communications Commission

■ 2nd Floor, St Andrew's House, Finch Road, DOUGLAS, Isle of Man, IM1 2PX.
  Tel 01624 677022   Fax 01624 626499
  Chairman: Hon Adrian Earnshaw, MHK   Director: Dr Carmel McLaughlin

E Established in 1984 under the Telecommunications Act 1984 (of Tynwald), its powers extended under the Broadcasting Act 1993 and the Broadcasting (Amendment) Act 2007 (of Tynwald). The Commission functions as a Statutory Board of the Isle of Man Government.

R To promote the interests of consumers, purchasers and other users of telecommunications services in the Island.
  To license and regulate telecommunications and broadcasting in the Isle of Man.
  To further Manx interests in the whole broadcasting arena.

G Isle of Man.

✍ Also known as the Isle of Man Communications Commission.

Communications Consumer Panel

■ Riverside House, 2a Southwark Bridge Road, LONDON, SE1 9HA.
  Tel 020 7981 3798   http://www.communicationsconsumerpanel.org.uk
  Chairman: Anna Bradley   Chief Executive: Victor Olowe

E Established under the Communications Act 2003 as the independent policy advisory body on consumer interest in telecommunications, broadcasting and spectrum markets, excluding of content issues. The Panel consists of ten members including the Chairman.

R To advise the Office of Communications (qv), Government, the EU and others on how to achieve a communications marketplace in which the communications interests of all consumers and citizens are protcted and promoted.

G United Kingdom.

Communities Scotland

✍ Abolished on 1 April 2008, the work of its regulation and inspection division transferred to the **Scottish Housing Regulator**.

Community Action

■ Tunbridge Mill, Tunbridge Road, Chew Magna, BRISTOL, BS40 8SP.
  Tel 01275 333701   http://www.community-action.org.uk
  Chairman: Rosemary Todd   Chief Executive: Chris Head

E   Established in 1974. It functions as a registered charity and company limited by guarantee. The board comprises nine trustees including the Chairman.
R   To support community-led action and strong local governance.
    To increase long-term sustainability of local community life.
    To influence policies and services in order to achieve equity for rural communities.
G   Bath & North East Somerset, Bristol, North Somerset, and South Gloucestershire.
✍   Community Action is one of the 38 Rural Community Councils, represented at the national level by **Action with Communities in Rural England** (qv) and at the regional level by South West ACRE Network (SWAN).

Community Action Hampshire   (CAH)
■   Beaconsfield House, Andover Road, WINCHESTER, Hants, SO22 6AT.
    Tel 01962 854971   http://www.action.hants.org.uk
    Chairman: Paul Chamberlain   Chief Executive: Sue Dovey
E   CAH functions as a registered charity and company limited by guarantee. The Board comprises nine Trustees including the Chairman.
R   To be the independent county-wide support body for the voluntary and sector in Hampshire.
G   Hampshire.
✍   CAH is one of the 38 Rural Community Councils, represented at the national level by **Action with Communities in Rural England** (qv) and at the regional level by South East Rural Community Councils.

Community Action Northumberland   (CAN)
■   Tower Buildings, 9 Oldgate, MORPETH, Northumberland, NE61 1PY.
    Tel 01670 517178   **Fax** 01670 511400   http://www.ca-north.org.uk
    Chairman: George Scott   Director: David Francis
E   Established in 1951. CAN functions as a registered charity and company limited by guarantee. The Executive Committee comprises 14 members including the Chairman.
R   To develop the capacity of local voluntary and community groups to identify unmet need and to work to meet this need by building up the skills base of individuals within these organisations.
    To facilitate the development of new, and support existing networks of local voluntary and community groups, to enable them to be a mechanism for developing collaborative work across the sector.
    To enable the diverse views of the local voluntary and community sector to be voiced, and to be a conduit for them to be heard, within the decision making structures of other bodies, regionally and nationally.
G   Northumberland.
✍   CAN is one of the 38 Rural Community Councils, represented at the national level by **Action with Communities in Rural England** (qv) and at the regional level by North East Rural Community Councils.

Community Assessment Panel   See **Football Foundation**.

Community Council for Berkshire   (CCB)
■   27 Eldon Square, READING, Berks, RG1 7XG.
    Tel 0118 961 2000   http://www.actionforall.org.uk/ccb/
    Chairman: Prof Gavin Parker   Chief Executive: Elaine Cook
E   Established on 25 September 1973 as the Berkshire Community Service Council, adopting its current name in 1982. CCB functions as a registered charity and company limited by guarantee. The Board comprises six Trustees including the Chairman.
R   To provide community development support committed to tackling social exclusion and developing rural and urban communities.
G   Berkshire.
✍   CCB functions as one of the 38 Rural Community Councils, represented at the national level by **Action with Communities in Rural England** (qv) and at the regional level by South East Rural Community Councils.

Community Council of Devon   (CCD)
■   County Hall, Topsham Road, EXETER, Devon, EX2 4QB.
    Tel 01392 383443   **Fax** 01392 382062   http://www.devoncc.org.uk
    Chairman: David Baker   Chief Executive: Jay Talbot
E   Established in 1961. The Council functions as a registered charity and company limited by guarantee. The Board comprises 14 Trustees including the Chairman.
R   To engage with Devon's rural communities to actively shape their own futures with improved opportunities and quality of life for all.
G   Devon.
✍   CCD is one of the 38 Rural Community Councils, represented at the national level by **Action with Communities in Rural England** (qv) and at the regional level by South West ACRE Network (SWAN).

© CBD Research Ltd · Beckenham · Kent BR3 5JS · Tel 020 8650 7745 · Fax 020 8650 0768 · E-mail cbd@cbdresearch.com · www.cbdresearch.com

Community Council of Shropshire   (CCS)

- The Creative Quarter, Shrewsbury Business Park, SHREWSBURY, SY2 6LG.
  Tel 01743 360641   http://www.shropshire-rcc.org.uk
  Chairman: Mary Mantell   Chief Executive: Julia Baron
- E   Established in 1960. CCS functions as a registered charity and company limited by guarantee. The Board comprises eleven Trustees including the Chairman.
- R   To encourage, facilitate and enable voluntary effort and activity and work for productive partnerships between the statutory, voluntary and private sectors to maintain and improve the quality of life in Shropshire, particularly its rural communities.
- G   Shropshire.
- ✍   CCS is one of the 38 Rural Community Councils, represented at the national level by **Action with Communities in Rural England** (qv) and at the regional level by West Midlands Rural Community Action Network.

Community Council for Somerset

- Victoria House, Victoria Street, TAUNTON, Somerset, TA1 3JZ.
  Tel 01823 331222   **Fax** 01823 323652   http://www.somersetcc.org.uk
  Chairman: Mrs Philippa Hawkes, JP   Chief Executive: Katherine Armstrong
- E   The Council functions as a registered charity and company limited by guarantee. The Board comprises 18 Trustees including the Chairman.
- R   To enhance life throughout Somerset by equipping rural communities to effect positive change, using their inherent resources, abilities and commitment.
- G   Somerset.
- ✍   The Community Council for Somerset is one of the 38 Rural Community Councils, represented at the national level by **Action with Communities in Rural England** (qv) and at the regional level by South West ACRE Network (SWAN).

Community Council of Staffordshire   (CCS)

- Friars Mill, Friars Terrace, STAFFORD, ST17 4DX.
  Tel 01785 242525   **Fax** 01785 242176   http://www.staffs.org.uk
  Chief Executive: Chris Welch
- E   Established in 1954. CCS functions as a registered charity and company limited by guarantee. The Board comprises eight Trustees.
- R   To provide a wide range of advice, information and support for voluntary groups.
  To liaise between the statutory and voluntary sectors at all levels and across a wide range of subjects including environmental issues, affordable rural housing, health and community care, education, training, transport, village halls, shops, post offices, and all other rural issues.
  To assimilate information on such services and needs in order to react positively and appropriately to influence any remedial action that may be required.
- G   Staffordshire.
- ✍   CCS is one of the 38 Rural Community Councils, represented at the national level by **Action with Communities in Rural England** (qv) and at the regional level by West Midlands Rural Community Action Network.

Community Development Agency for Hertfordshire   (CDA)

- Birchwood Avenue, HATFIELD, Herts, AL10 0PS.
  Tel 01707 695504   http://www.cdaforherts.org.uk
  Chairman: Chris Tombs   Chief Executive: Kate Belinis
- E   Established in 1966. CDA for Herts functions as a registered charity and company limited by guarantee. The Board comprises eight Directors including the Chairman.
- R   To advocate on behalf of rural communities in Hertfordshire locally, regionally and nationally.
- G   Hertfordshire.
- ✍   CDA for Herts is one of the 38 Rural Community Councils, represented at the national level by **Action with Communities in Rural England** (qv) and at the regional level by Rural Action East.

Community Development Exchange   (CDX)

- Scotia Works, Leadmill Road, SHEFFIELD, S Yorks, S1 4SE.
  Tel 0114 241 2760   **Fax** 0114 241 2762   http://www.cdx.org.uk
  Chairman: Sue Shaw   Director: Amanda Greenwood

E   Established as the Standing Conference for Community Development, it became a company limited by guarantee and registered charity in 2001 when it adopted its current name. CDX receives the majority of its funding from the Office of the Third Sector in the Cabinet Office. It is a membership organisation comprising regional groups, local organisations and individual workers.

R   To bring about positive changes towards social justice and equality by using and promoting the values and approaches of community development.

G   United Kingdom.

Community Development Foundation   (CDF)
■   Unit 5, Angel Gate, 320-326 City Road, LONDON, EC1V 2PT.
     Tel 020 7833 1772   Fax 020 7837 6584   http://www.cdf.org.uk
     Chairman: Tom Levitt, MP   Chief Executive: Alison Seabrooke

E   Established in 1968. CDF is a registered charity and functions as an Executive NDPB of the Department for Communities & Local Government. The Foundation is governed by a Board of Trustees.

R   To lead community development analysis and strategy in order to empower people to influence decisions that affect their lives.

G   United Kingdom.

✍   CDF's Public Body status is to be removed. It will be supported by the Department for Communities & Local Government to develop as a social enterprise.

Community First
■   Wyndhams, St Joseph's Place, DEVIZES, Wilts, SN10 1DD.
     Tel 01380 722475   Fax 01380 728476   http://www.communityfirst.org.uk
     Chairman: Tom McCaw   Chief Executive: Philippa Read

E   Established in 1965. It functions as a registered charity and company limited by guarantee. The Board comprises twelve Trustees including the Chairman.

R   To provide technical advice, practical support and grant aid for a wide range of community-based projects meeting local needs locally with the aim of empowering people and strengtheninmg local communities.

G   Wiltshire.

✍   Community First is one of the 38 Rural Community Councils, represented at the national level by **Action with Communities in Rural England** (qv) and at the regional level by South West ACRE Network (SWAN).

Community First in Herefordshire & Worcestershire
■   Malvern View, Willow End Park, Blackmore Park Road, MALVERN, Worcs, WR13 6NN.
     Tel 01684 312730   Fax 01684 311278   http://www.comfirst.org.uk
     41a Bridge Street, HEREFORD, HR4 9DG.
     Tel 01432 267820   Fax 01432 269066
     Chief Executive: Richard Quallington

E   Established in 1975. Community First functions as a registered charity and company limited by guarantee.

R   To build the capacity of voluntary and community organisations to manage and grow in a sustainable way.
     To improve the quality and scope of services delivered by the voluntary and community sector.
     To build stronger, more inclusive communities, that provide a good quality of life for everyone.
     To raise the profile, value and resources of the sector and represent its interests in wider policy and strategic frameworks.
     To advance the governance, management and operations of the organisation, as a model of best practice.

G   Herefordshire, Worcestershire.

✍   Community First is one of the 38 Rural Community Councils, represented at the national level by **Action with Communities in Rural England** (qv) and at the regional level by West Midlands Rural Community Action Network.

Community Forum
✍   See **National Community Forum**.

Community Fund
✍   Responsibilities were transferred in 2006 to its successor body, the **Big Lottery Fund**.

Community Futures
■   15 Victoria Road, Fulwood, PRESTON, Lancs, PR2 8PS.
     Tel 01772 717461   Fax 01772 900250   http://www.communityfutures.org.uk
     Chairman: Ron Pickup   Chief Executive: Denise Partington

E Community Futures is the working name of the **Community Council of Lancashire**. The Council functions as a registered charity and company limited by guarantee. The Board comprises eight Trustees including the Chairman.

R To develop and support balanced and sustainable communities in Lancashire with our colleagues in the voluntary sector and in partnership with public and private organisations.

G Lancashire.

✍ Community Futures is one of the 38 Rural Community Councils, represented at the national level by **Action with Communities in Rural England** (qv) and at the regional level by North West Rural Community Councils.

COMMUNITY HEALTH COUNCILS   (CHCs)

E Initially set up in 1974, Community Health Councils are statutory bodies which exist to form a link between those who run the NHS and those who use it. The current organisational structure was introduced on 1 April 2010. There is one CHC for each Local Health Board, except for Powys which has two. With the exception of the Brecknock & Radnor and Montgomery CHCs of Powys, each CHC is made up of Local Committees, one for each Local Authority. The twelve members on each Local Committee are appointed by the Local Authority, local voluntary groups and organisations, and the Welsh Government.

R To provide help and advice with problems and complaints about NHS services, ensure that patients' views and needs influence the policies and plans put in place by health providers, monitor the quality of NHS services, and provide information about access to the NHS.

G Wales.

● The eight CHCs are:
  Abertawe Bro Morgannwg Community Health Council
  Aneurin Bevin Community Health Council
  Betsi Cadwaladr Community Health Council
  Brecnock & Radnor Community Health Council
  Cardiff & Vale of Glamorgan Community Health Council
  Cwm Taf Community Health Council
  Hywel Dda Community Health Council
  Montgomery Community Health Council (qqv).

✍ The eight CHCs are represented collectively by the Board of Community Health Councils in Wales (qv).

Community Lincs

■ The Old Mart, Church Lane, SLEAFORD, Lincs, NG34 7DF.
  Tel 01529 302466   **Fax** 01529 414267   http://www.communitylincs.com
  Chairman: James Epton   Chief Executive: Fiona White

E Established in 1927. Community Lincs functions as a registered charity and company limited by guarantee. The Board comprises twelve Trustees including the Chairman.

R To support communities and individuals across Lincolnshire, helping them to identify their needs and aspirations through the parish planning process and other consultation techniques.

G Lincolnshire.

✍ Community Lincs is one of the 38 Rural Community Councils, represented at the national level by **Action with Communities in Rural England** (qv) and at the regional level by Rural Community Action East Midlands.

Community Pharmacy Scotland

■ 42 Queen Street, EDINBURGH, EH2 3NH.
  Tel 0131 467 7766   **Fax** 0131 467 7767   http://www.communitypharmacyscotland.org.uk
  Chairman: Martin Green   Chief Executive: Harry McQuillan

E Established as the Pharmaceutical General Council (Scotland) and latterly known as the Scottish Pharmaceutical General Council. Community Pharmacy Scotland comprises representatives of the 42 Area Pharmacy Contractor Committees which were established for the former NHS health board areas, together with representatives from the Company Chemists' Association Ltd and the Co-operative Pharmacy. The Board comprises 16 members including the Chairman.

R To negotiate with the Scottish Executive on behalf of Scottish community pharmacists the terms and conditions of service and their remuneration and reimbursement for the provision of NHS pharmaceutical services.

G Scotland.

Community Pharmacy Wales   (CPW)

■ 2 Caspian Point, Caspian Way, CARDIFF, CF10 4DQ.
  Tel 029 2044 2070   **Fax** 029 2044 2071   http://www.cpwales.org.uk
  Chairman: Ian Cowan   Chief Executive: Russell Goodway

E Established in 1977 as the Welsh Central Pharmaceutical Committee, it adopted its current name in November 2001 to reflect its role more clearly. CPW is independent of but functions as the Welsh arm of the Pharmaceutical Services Negotiating Committee (qv) and represents the interests of over 700 community pharmacies in Wales. The Committee comprises 13 members including the Chairman.

R To secure for pharmacy contractors proper remuneration and other contractual terms in respect of the services provided under the NHS by those contractors.

G Wales.

● The CPW is supported by three regional committees covering Mid & West Wales, North Wales and South East Wales.

Community Relations Council   (CRC)

■ 6 Murray Street, BELFAST, BT1 6DN.
Tel 028 9022 7500   Fax 028 9022 7551   http://www.community-relations.org.uk
Chairman: Tony McCusker   Chief Executive: Duncan Morrow

E Established in January 1990. CRC is a registered charity and a company limited by guarantee. The Council comprises 15 members including the Chairman.

R To encourage other organisations, both voluntary and statutory, to develop a community relations aspect to their policies and practices.
To work with churches and groups which have a primary community relations focus.
To encourage greater acceptance of and respect for cultural diversity.

G Northern Ireland.

Compact   See **Commission for the Compact**.

Compact Voice

■ 8 Regents Wharf, LONDON, N1 9RL.
Tel 020 7713 6161   http://www.compactvoice.org.uk
Chairman: Simon Blake

G England.

Companies House

■ Crown Way, Maindy, CARDIFF, CF14 3UZ.
Tel 0303 123 4500   Fax 029 2038 0900   http://www.companieshouse.gov.uk
4th Floor, Edinburgh Quay 2, 139 Fountainbridge, EDINBURGH, EH3 9FF.
Chairman: Andrew Summers, CMG   Chief Executive: Gareth Jones   Registrar of Companies for Scotland: Dorothy Blair

E Established on 3 October 1988. Companies House is a Trading Fund and an Executive Agency of the Department for Business, Innovation & Skills. The Steering Board comprises between eight and 14 members including the Chairman.

R To incorporate and dissolve limited companies.
To examine and store company information delivered under the Companies Acts and related legislation.
To make this information available to the public.

G England, Wales, Scotland.

● There are more than two million limited companies registered in Great Britain.

✍ The Registrar of Companies for England & Wales is the Chief Executive.
The Registrar of Companies for Scotland is based at the Edinburgh address.

Company Law Review Consultative Committee

✍ The Committee was wound up in 2001.

The Compensation Agency   (CA)

■ Royston House, 34 Upper Queen Street, BELFAST, BT1 6FD.
Tel 028 9054 7417   http://www.compensationni.gov.uk
Chief Executive: Marcella McKnight

E Established on 1 April 1992. It functions as an Executive Agency of the Department of Justice Northern Ireland.

R To support the victims of violent crime by administrating the criminal injuries, criminal damage and Justice & Security Act compensation schemes.

G Northern Ireland.

© CBD Research Ltd · Beckenham · Kent BR3 5JS · Tel 020 8650 7745 · Fax 020 8650 0768 · E-mail cbd@cbdresearch.com · www.cbdresearch.com

Competition Appeal Tribunal   (CAT)

■ Victoria House, Bloomsbury Place, LONDON, WC1A 2EB.
Tel 020 7979 7979   Fax 020 7979 7978   http://www.catribunal.org.uk
President: Hon Mr Justice Barling   Registrar: Charles Dhanowa, OBE

E Established in 2002 by the Enterprise Act 2002. CAT functions as a Tribunal NDPB of the Department for Business, Innovation & Skills. The Tribunal is headed by the President and consists of two panels: a panel of chairmen and a panel of ordinary members.

R To hear and decide appeals and other applications or claims involving competition of economic regulatory issues.

G United Kingdom.

Competition Commission

■ Victoria House, Southampton Row, LONDON, WC1B 4AD.
Tel 020 7271 0100   Fax 020 7271 0367   http://www.competition-commission.gov.uk
Chairman: Peter Freeman, CBE, QC   Chief Executive: David Saunders

E Established in 1998 under the Competition Act 1998. The Competition Commission functions as an Executive NDPB of the Department for Business, Innovation & Skills. There are six council members including the Chairman, and around 50 Commissioners who sit on various advisory panels.

R To conduct in-depth inquiries into mergers, markets and the regulation of the major regulated industries.

G United Kingdom.

✍ It was announced by the Government on 14 October 2010 that it will consult in 2011 on a merger of the Commission with the competition functions of the Office of Fair Trading (qv).

Competition Service

✍ Established in 2002 to provide support services to the Competition Appeal Tribunal (qv). It was abolished in 2011 and its functions transferred to HM Courts & Tribunals Service (qv).

Complementary & Natural Health Council   (CNHC)

■ 83 Victoria Street, LONDON, SW1H 0HW.
Tel 020 3178 2199   http://www.cnhc.org.uk
Co-Chairmen: Maggie Dunn & Maggie Wallace

E Established in April 2008, the CNHC is the national voluntary regulator for complementary healthcare practitioners in the UK.

R To support the use of complementary and natural healthcare as a uniquely positive, safe and effective experience.
To protect the public by means of regulating practitioners on a voluntary register for complementary and natural practitioners.

G United Kingdom.

Conference of Drama Schools   (CDS)

■ PO Box 34252, LONDON, NW5 1XJ.   http://www.drama.ac.uk
Chairman: Peter Barlow   Executive Secretary: Saul Hyman

E Established in 1969. CDS is a membership body of Britain's 22 leading drama schools. The Conference comprises the directors or principals of the member schools.

R To strengthen the voice of member schools.
To set and maintain the highest standards of training within the vocational drama sector.
To make it easier for prospective students to understand the range of courses on offer and the application process.

G United Kingdom.

Conference of Postgraduate Medical Deans of the United Kingdom   (COPMeD)

■ 4th Floor, Thistle House, 91 Haymarket Terrace, EDINBURGH, EH12 5HE.
Tel 0131 313 8044   Fax 0131 313 8001   http://www.copmed.org.uk
Chairman: Dr Mike Watson

E Established as a medical education forum within the NHS.

R To provide a forum in which Postgraduate Deans meet to discuss current issues and agree a consistent and equitable approach to medical training in all deaneries across the UK.

G United Kingdom.

Confidential Enquiry into Maternal & Child Health

✍ On 1 July 2009 CEMACH became the **Centre for Maternal & Child Health**.

Construction Industry Advisory Committee   (CONIAC)
- Floor 5SW, Rose Court, 2 Southwark Bridge, LONDON, SE1 9HS.
  Tel 020 7556 2191   **Fax** 020 7556 2209
  Chairman: Philip White
- E   Established in February 1978 by the Health & Safety Executive (qv), the Committee was reconstituted in 2004. CONIAC functions as an Advisory NDPB of the HSE. The Committee is chaired by the Chief Inspector of Construction and comprises representatives of key industry stakeholders (including SMEs) and a local authority representative.
- R   To advise the HSE on the protection of people at work from hazards to health and safety within the building, civil engineering and engineering construction industries.
  To protect the public from related hazards arising from such activities.
- G   United Kingdom.
- The Committee is assisted in its work by four working groups:
  CDM 2007 Evaluation Working Group
  Health Risks Working Group
  Safety Working Group
  Working Well Together Steering Group

Construction Industry Council   (CIC)
- 26 Store Street, LONDON, WC1E 7BT.
  Tel 020 7399 7400   **Fax** 020 7399 7425   http://www.cic.org.uk
  Chairman: Gordon Masterton, OBE   Chief Executive: Graham Watts, OBE
- E   Established in 1988. CIC is a membership body whose members represent over 500,000 professionals for, and in association with, the construction industry and more than 25,000 construction firms. It is a non-profit making company limited by guarantee. The Council comprises up to 24 representatives.
- R   To serve society by promoting quality and sustainability in the built environment.
- G   United Kingdom.
- The construction industry Sector Skills Council (qv) is ConstructionSkills (qv), a partnership between CIC and the Construction Industry Training Board (qv).

Construction Industry Training Board   See **CITB-ConstructionSkills**.

Construction Project Information Committee   (CPIC)
- c/o NBS, The Old Post Office, St Nicholas Street, NEWCASTLE UPON TYNE, NE1 1RH.
  Tel 01420 560068   **Fax** 01420 562842   http://www.cpic.org.uk
  Secretary: Sarah Delany
- E   Established as an independent body, the CPIC is formed from representatives of the major industry institutions. The Committee comprises 13 members.
- R   To provide best practice guidance on the content, form and preparation of construction production information.
- G   United Kingdom.

ConstructionSkills   See **CITB-ConstructionSkills**.

Consultative Committee of Accountancy Bodies   (CCAB)
- PO Box 433, Moorgate Place, LONDON, EC2P 2BJ.
  Tel 020 7920 8405   http://www.ccab.org.uk
  Chairman: Gerald Russell, FCA
- E   Established in 1974 by joint authority of its six member bodies. Each is represented on the Committee by a senior member, usually its president.
- R   To promote the advancement of the standing and effectiveness of the accountancy profession at home and internationally.
- G   United Kingdom, Republic of Ireland.
- CCAB members:
  Association of Chartered Certified Accountants
  Chartered Institute of Management Accountants
  Chartered Institute of Public Finance & Accountancy
  Institute of Chartered Accountants in England & Wales
  Institute of Chartered Accountants in Ireland
  Institute of Chartered Accountants of Scotland

© CBD Research Ltd · Beckenham · Kent BR3 5JS · Tel 020 8650 7745 · Fax 020 8650 0768 · E-mail cbd@cbdresearch.com · www.cbdresearch.com

Consultative Committee on Construction Industry Statistics   (CCCIS)

- 1 Victoria Street, LONDON, SW1H 0ET.
  Tel 020 7215 1248
  Chairman: Keith Folwell
- E CCCIS functions as an Advisory NDPB of the Department for Business, Innovation & Skills. The Committee comprises representatives from Government, the construction industry and independent analysts.
- R To discuss issues relating to the collection and dissemination of the UK construction statistics.
- G United Kingdom.

Consultative Group on Campylobacter & Salmonella in Chickens

- ✍ CGCSC met on 19 July 2001 (inaugural) and 2 December 2002. Its report was published by the Food Standards Agency (qv) on 27 February 2003.

Consumer Communications for England

- ✍ Superceded by the Ofcom **Advisory Committee for England**.

The Consumer Council for Northern Ireland   (CC)

- 116 Holywood Road, BELFAST, BT4 1NY.
  Tel 028 9067 2488   Fax 028 9065 7701   http://www.consumercouncil.org.uk
  Chairman: Rick Hill   Chief Executive: Antoinette McKeown
- E Established on 1 April 1985 under the General Consumer Council (Northern Ireland) Order 1984. The CC functions as an Executive NDPB of the Department of Enterprise, Trade & Investment Northern Ireland. The Council comprises eleven members including the Chairman.
- R To promote and safeguard the interests of consumers and to campaign for the best possible standards of service and protection.
- G Northern Ireland.

Consumer Council for Postal Services

- ✍ On 1 October 2008 the Consumer Council for Postal Services (Postwatch), with others, was replaced by **Consumer Focus**.

Consumer Council for Water   (CCWater)

- Victoria Square House, Victoria Square, BIRMINGHAM, B2 4AJ.
  Tel 0121 345 1000   http://www.ccwater.org.uk
  Chairman: Dame Yve Buckland   Chief Executive: Tony Smith
- E Established on 1 October 2005, replacing the former WaterVoice Council. CCWater functions as an Executive NDPB of the Department for Environment, Food & Rural Affairs. The Council comprises 13 members including the Chairman.
- R To represent water and sewerage consumers in England and Wales and to handle complaints about water and sewerage companies.
- G England, Wales.
- ✍ A decision on the future of CCWater is to be taken as part of the Ofwat review launched on 26 August 2010. The outcome of the review will be set out in the Water White Paper due for publication in June 2011. Like Consumer Focus (qv) its functions may transfer to Citizens Advice.

Consumer Financial Education Body   (CFEB)

- 25 The North Colonnade, Canary Wharf, LONDON, E14 5HS.
  Tel 020 7943 0500   http://www.cfebuk.org.uk
  Chairman: Gerard Lemos, CMG   Chief Executive: Tony Hobman
- E Established in April 2010 by the Financial Services Authority (qv) under the Financial Services Act 2010. The Body is funded through public funds, dormant accounts and from levies paid by consumer credit firms to the Office of Fair Trading (qv). The board comprises eight members including the Chairman.
- R To offer free, impartial information and resources to help those working with people who need help with financial matters.
- G United Kingdom.

Consumer Focus

- Fleetbank House, Salisbury Square, LONDON, EC4Y 8JX.
  Tel 020 7799 7900   Fax 020 7799 7901   http://www.consumerfocus.org.uk
  Chairman: Christine Farnish   Chief Executive: Mike O'Connor

E   Established on 1 October 2008 under the Consumers, Estate Agents & Redress Act 2007, through the merger of energywatch, Postwatch and the National Consumer Council (including the Welsh and Scottish Consumer Councils). It functions as an Executive NDPB of the Department for Business, Innovation & Skills. The Focus board comprises 13 members including the Chairman.

R   To campaign for a fair deal for consumers in England, Wales and Scotland and, for postal services, Northern Ireland.

G   United Kingdom.

●   Consumer Focus has strong legislative powers. These include the right to investigate any consumer complaint if it is of wider interest, the right to open up information from providers, the power to conduct research, and the ability to make an official 'super-complaint' about failing services.
    Consumer Focus Scotland and Consumer Focus Wales have offices in Glasgow and Cardiff respectively. Consumer Focus Post (Northern Ireland) has an office in Belfast.

✍   The Government announced on 14 October 2010 its intention to abolish Consumer Focus and transfer its functions to the charity, Citizens Advice. It is likely to be at least 1 April 2012 before Consumer Focus ceases to exist.

Consumer Protection & Markets Authority   (CPMA)

Chief Executive: Martin Wheatley (unconfirmed)

E   One of the successor organisations of the Financial Services Authority (qv).

R   To regulate financial firms providing services to consumers and to maintain the integrity of the UK financial markets.

G   United Kingdom.

✍   No further information available at time of going to press.

Consumers' Committee for Great Britain under the Agricultural Marketing Act 1958

■   Room 247, Nobel House, 17 Smith Square, LONDON, SW1P 3JR.
    Tel 020 7238 3185   Fax 020 7238 3198
    Chief Executive: John O'Rourke

E   Functions as an Advisory NDPB of the Department for the Environment, Food & Rural Affairs.

R   To report to the Secretary of State on the effect of any product marketing scheme approved by the Secretary of State, which is for the time being in force, on consumers of the regulated product.

G   United Kingdom.

Continuing Care Conference   (CCC)

■   c/o Counsel & Care, Twyman House, 16 Bonny Street, LONDON, NW1 9PG.
    Tel 020 7241 8521   http://www.ccc-ltc.org.uk
    Chairman: Dr Clive Bowman

E   Established in 1992, the CCC is a membership body of 29 commercial, charitable and public service organisations with a mutual interest in providing better care for current and future generations of older people. The Steering Group comprises 20 members including the Chairman.

R   CCC's mission statement:
    We believe that all older people in Britain should live their lives in dignity, comfort and a place of their choosing. We want all elements of society to make the necessary individual and social investment to ensure that happens. Our task is to ensure that policy-makers pursue this goal and to encourage the public to join with the us in our mission to persuade them to do so.

G   United Kingdom.

Conwy Local Health Board

✍   Merged on 1 October 2009 with the Anglesey, Denbighshire, Flintshire, Gwynedd and Wrexham Local Health Boards to form **Betsi Cadwaladr University Health Board**.

Copyright Licensing Agency Ltd   (CLA)

■   Saffron House, 6-10 Kirby Street, LONDON, EC1N 8TS.
    Tel 020 7400 3100   Fax 020 7400 3101   http://www.cla.co.uk
    CBC House, 24 Canning Street, EDINBURGH, EH3 8EG.
    Tel 0131 272 2711   Fax 0131 272 2811

E   Established in 1982 by agreement, the CLA is a non-profit making company limited by guarantee. It is owned by its members who are the Authors' Licensing & Collecting Society (ALCS) and the Publishers Licensing Society (PLS). ALCS and PLS establish the Agency's Board by nominating six members each.

R   To encourage respect for copyright.
    To license users for the copying of extracts from books, journals and periodicals.
    To collect fees from licensed users for such copying.

© CBD Research Ltd · Beckenham · Kent BR3 5JS · Tel 020 8650 7745 · Fax 020 8650 0768 · E-mail cbd@cbdresearch.com · www.cbdresearch.com

To pay authors and publishers (via ALCS and PLS) their shares of the copying fees collected.
To institute legal proceedings, if necessary, for the enforcement of the rights entrusted to the CLA.
G United Kingdom.

The Copyright Tribunal

■ 21 Bloomsbury Street, LONDON, WC1B 3HF.
 Tel 020 7034 2836 **Fax** 020 7034 2826 http://www.ipo.gov.uk/ctribunal.htm
 Chairman: His Honour Judge Birss, QC
E Established in 1989 under the Copyright, Designs & Patents Act 1988. It functions as a Tribunal NDPB of the Department for Business, Innovation & Skills. The Tribunal comprises the Chairman, two deputy chairmen, and between two and eight ordinary members.
R To provide impartial settlement of disputes over copyright licences, usually those offered by collecting societies.
G United Kingdom.
✍ The Government has announced its intention to move the Copyright Tribunal into HM Courts & Tribunals Service (qv). A timetable for the move has not been set.

Cornwall Rural Community Council (CRCC)

■ 2 Princes Street, TRURO, Cornwall, TR1 2ES.
 Tel 01872 273952 **Fax** 01872 241511 http://www.cornwallcc.co.uk
 Chairman: Paul Parkin Chief Executive: Peter Jefferson
E Established in 1946. The Council functions as a registered charity and company limited by guarantee.
R To enable Cornish communities to be vibrant, sustainable and inclusive.
G Cornwall.
✍ CRCC is one of the 38 Rural Community Councils, represented at the national level by **Action with Communities in Rural England** (qv) and at the regional level by South West ACRE Network (SWAN).

Corporate Governance Committee

■ 5th Floor, Aldwych House, 71-91 Aldwych, LONDON, WC2B 4HN.
 Tel 020 7492 2300 **Fax** 020 7492 2301 http://www.frc.org.uk/corporate.corpgovcommittee.cfm
 Chairman: Sir John Sunderland
E Established in 2004 by the Financial Reporting Council (qv). The Committee comprises eight members including the Chairman.
R To keep under review developments in corporate governance generally, reflecting the FRC's objective of fostering high standards of corporate governance.
G United Kingdom.

The Corporation of Trinity House of Deptford Strond

■ Trinity House, Tower Hill, LONDON, EC3N 4DH.
 Tel 020 7481 6900 http://www.trinityhouse.co.uk
 Master: HRH Princess Anne, the Princess Royal Executive Chairman: Captain Ian McNaught
E Established on 20 May 1514 by Royal Charter, it derives most of its present functions and powers from the Merchant Shipping Act 1895. Commonly known as **Trinity House**, the Corporation functions as an Executive NDPB of the Department for Transport. Trinity House is led by a court of Elder Brethren under the Master. The Lighthouse Board comprises Elder Brethren, senior staff and outside representatives.
R As the General Lighthouse Authority for England, Wales, the Channel Islands and Gibraltar, to be responsible for a range of general aids to navigation, from lighthouses to radar beacons.
 As a Deep Sea Pilotage Authority, to deal with wrecks which are dangerous to navigation, other than those within ports or HM ships.
 As a marine charitable organisation, to continue its dedication to the safety, welfare and training of mariners.
G England, Wales, Channel Islands, Gibraltar.
● The Corporation controls and maintains 69 lighthouses, ten light vessels/floats, 412 buoys, 19 beacons, 48 radar beacons and seven DGPS reference stations.

Correctional Services Accreditation Panel (CSAP)

■ 102 Petty France, LONDON, SW1H 9AJ.
 Tel 020 7217 5714
 Chairman: David Griffiths
E Established in July 1999. CSAP functions as an Advisory NDPB of the Ministry of Justice. The Panel comprises a pool of up to 20 experts including the Chairman.
R To accredit programmes for offenders which are designed to reduce re-offending.
G England, Wales.

Council for Administration   (CfA)

- 6 Graphite Square, Vauxhall Walk, LONDON, SE11 5EE.
  Tel 020 7091 9620   Fax 020 7091 7340   http://www.cfa.uk.com
  Chief Executive: Jenny Hewell   Director of Operations: Andrew Young
- E Established in 1987. CfA is an independent registered charity and the national standards setting body for business and administration skills.
- R To help learners enter employment and advance their careers with competitive skills.
  To develop and promote training and qualifications that enable employers and learners to make a difference.
  To build knowledge and remain the acknowledged expert in business and administration skills.
  To help employers and government understand the critical importance of business and administration skills to the UK economy.
- G United Kingdom.
- ✍ Now going by the name of **CfA - Business skills @ work**.

Council for the Advancement of Arab-British Understanding   (CAABU)

- 1 Gough Square, LONDON, EC4A 3DE.
  Tel 020 7832 1321   Fax 020 7832 1329   http://www.caabu.org
  Director: Chris Doyle
- E Established in July 1967. The Council is a non-governmental organisation. Its Executive Committee comprises ten members.
- R To promote an enlightened and positive approach to Arab-British relations in Government, Parliament, the media, education and amongst the wider public.
- G United Kingdom.
- ✍ Also known as the **Council for Arab-British Understanding**.

Council for the Advancement of Communication with Deaf People
- ✍ Since January 2009 **Signature**.

Council for Arab-British Understanding   See **Council for the Advancement of Arab-British Understanding**.

Council for Assisting Refugee Academics   (CARA)

- London South Bank University, Technopark, 90 London Road, LONDON, SE1 6LN.
  Tel 020 7021 0880   Fax 020 7021 0881   http://www.academic-refeguees.org
  Executive Secretary: John Akker
- E Established in 1933 as the Academic Assistance Council. It functions as a registered charity and company limited by guarantee. CARA's Council of Management comprises 25 members.
- R To make grants to enable refugee academics achieve employment in the UK.
- G United Kingdom.

Council for Awards in Care, Health & Education   (CACHE)

- Apex House, 81 Camp Road, ST ALBANS, Herts, AL1 5GB.
  Tel 01727 818616   http://www.cache.org.uk
  Chief Executive: Dr Richard C Dorrance, BSc, PhD, FRSC
- E Established on 1 April 1994 following the merger of the Council for Early Years Awards and the National Nursery Examination Board. CACHE is a registered charity. It is the awarding body for courses and qualifications in the care and education of children and young people.
- G United Kingdom, Republic of Ireland.

Council on Bioethics   See the **Nuffield Council on Bioethics**.

Council of British Geography   (COBRIG)

- 1 Kensington Gore, LONDON, SW7 2AR.
  Tel 020 7591 3000   Fax 020 7591 3001
- E Established in 1988. COBRIG is a membership body of British geographical societies.
- R To coordinate the policies of member societies and to take initiatives in educational, academic, research and policy matters.
- G United Kingdom.

© CBD Research Ltd · Beckenham · Kent BR3 5JS · Tel 020 8650 7745 · Fax 020 8650 0768 · E-mail cbd@cbdresearch.com · www.cbdresearch.com

Council of Bureaux
✍ The Council, which manages the international motor insurance ('Green Card') system, moved its secretariat to Brussels in 2006.

Council for the Care of Churches
On 11 June 2008, with the Advisory Board for Redundant Churches, became the **Church Buildings Council**.

Council for Catholic Maintained Schools (CCMS)
■ 160 High Street, HOLYWOOD, Co Down, BT18 9HT.
Tel 028 9042 6972 Fax 028 9042 4255 http://www.onlineccms.com
Chairman: The Most Revd John McAreavey, Bishop of Dromore
E Established on 1 April 1990 under the Education Reform (Northern Ireland) Order 1989. CCMS functions as an Executive NDPB of the Department of Education Northern Ireland. The Board comprises 36 members including the Chairman.
R To represent trustees, schools and governors on issues such as raising and maintaining standards, the school estate and teacher employment.
G Northern Ireland.
✍ CCMS and other legacy organisations will be dissolved when the Education & Skills Authority (qv) becomes fully operational.

Council for the Central Laboratory of the Research Councils
✍ See **Science & Technology Facilities Council**.

Council for Christian Unity (CCU)
■ Church House, Great Smith Street, LONDON, SW1P 3AZ.
Tel 020 7898 1481 Fax 020 7898 1483
Chairman: The Rt Revd Christopher Hill, Bishop of Guildford
E Established in April 1991 by the General Synod of the Church of England as one of two successor bodies to the former Board for Mission & Unity, the other being the Mission & Public Affairs division of the Archbishops' Council. CCU forms part of the Church & World Division of the Archbishops' Council through which it reports to the General Synod. The Council comprises 15 members including the Chairman.
R To support the Church of England in seeking the unity of the Christian Church through ecumenical conversations, local unity initiatives, theological research and reflection.
G United Kingdom.

Council of Christians & Jews (CCJ)
■ Godliman House, 21 Godliman Street, LONDON, EC4V 5BD.
Tel 020 7015 5160 Fax 020 7015 5161 http://www.ccj.org.uk
Chairman: Rt Revd Nigel McCulloch Chief Executive: David Gifford, MA
E Established in October 1942. The Council is a membership organisation and functions as a registered charity. The Board comprises twelve Trustees including the Chairman.
R To promote religious and cultural understanding between Christian and Jewish communities.
To work for the elimination of religious and racial prejudice, hatred and discrimination.
To promote religious and racial harmony on the basis of the ethical and social teachings common to Judaism and Christianity.
G United Kingdom.
● CCJ has 36 local branches across the UK.

Council for the Curriculum, Examinations & Assessment (CCEA)
■ 29 Clarendon Road, Clarendon Dock, BELFAST, BT1 3BG.
Tel 028 9026 1200 Fax 028 9026 1234 http://www.ccea.org.uk
Interim Chief Executive: Gavin Boyd
E Established on 1 April 1994, its authority is derived from the Education Reform (Northern Ireland) Order 1989, the Education & Libraries (Northern Ireland) Order 1993 and the Education (Northern Ireland) Order 1998. CCEA functions as an Executive NDPB of the Department of Education Northern Ireland. The Council comprises the Chairman and between nine and 17 members.
R To keep under review all aspects of the curriculum, examinations and assessment for grant aided schools and colleges of further education, and to undertake statutory consultations on proposals relating to legislation.
G Northern Ireland.
✍ CCEA and other legacy organisations will be dissolved when the Education & Skills Authority (qv) becomes fully operational.
A member of the **Joint Council for Qualifications** (qv).

Council of Deans of Dental Schools
✍ CDDS became the Council of Heads & Deans of Dental Schools in 2005 and, in 2008, the **Dental Schools Council**.

Council for Disabled Children   (CDC)
■ 8 Wakley Street, LONDON, EC1V 7QE.
Tel 020 7843 1900   **Fax** 020 7278 6313   http://www.ncb.org.uk/cdc
Director: Christine Lenehan, OBE
E Established in 1974 as the Voluntary Council for Handicapped Children, adopting its current name in 1995/6. The CDC is a semi-independent council of the National Children's Bureau. The Council comprises a wide range of professional, voluntary and statutory organisations, including parent representatives and representatives of disabled people.
R CDC is the umbrella body for the disabled children's sector in England, with links to the other UK nations.
It works to influence national policy that impacts upon disabled children, children with special educational needs and their families.
It aims to promote the active participation of disabled children and young people, making sure that their voices and success stories are heard.
G England.

Council for Education in the Commonwealth   (CEC)
■ Commonwealth House, 7 Lion Yard, Tremadoc Road, LONDON, SW4 7NQ.
Tel 01277 212357   http://www.cecomm.org.uk
Joint Parliamentary Chairmen: Simon Hughes, MP, David Lammy, MP and Gavin Williamson, MP
Executive Chairman: Sally Keeble
E Established in 1959. CEC is a parliament-based non-governmental organisation with over 200 members.
The Council's Governing Board comprises 26 members, including the three Parliamentary Chairmen and the Executive Chairman.
R To provide a forum where Members of Parliament and others with an interest in education in the Commonwealth can exchange information and views.To initiate action to foster educational co-operation and the sharing of experience among the countries and governments of the Commonwealth.
G The Commonwealth.
● To achieve its aims the Council holds public meetings, often in the Houses of Parliament, and briefs Commonwealth High Commissions.

Council for Education in World Citizenship
✍ Merged in 2008 with the **Citizenship Foundation**.

Council for Education in World Citizenship - Cymru   (CEWC Cymru)
■ Temple of Peace, Cathays Park, CARDIFF, CF10 3AP.
Tel 029 2022 8549   **Fax** 029 2064 0333   http://www.cewc-cymru.org.uk
Chairman: Gareth Price
E CEWC Cymru is the schools arm of the Welsh Centre for International Affairs, operating as an independent registered charity. It is governed by the 26 WCIA trustees.
R To help young citizens develop the skills, knowledge and self-belief that will enable them to contribute to the future of Wales and the world.
G Wales.

Council for Environmental Education
✍ An American organisation based in Houston, TX.

Council of Ethnic Minority Voluntary Sector Organisations   (CEMVO)
■ Boardman House, 64 Broadway, LONDON, E15 1NG.
Tel 020 8432 0200   **Fax** 020 8432 0318   http://www.emf-cemvo.co.uk
Director: Dr Zelalem Kebede
E Established in 1999. CEMVO is a national registered charity and company limited by guarantee.
R To extend opportunities to people from the most disadvantaged communities in the UK.
G United Kingdom.
● CEMVO has offices in London, the South West, North West, Wales and Scotland.

© CBD Research Ltd · Beckenham · Kent BR3 5JS · Tel 020 8650 7745 · Fax 020 8650 0768 · E-mail cbd@cbdresearch.com · www.cbdresearch.com

Council of Ex-Muslims of Britain   (CEMB)

■ BM Box 1919, LONDON, WC1N 3XX.
Tel 07719 166731   http://www.ex-muslim.org.uk
Spokesman: Maryam Namazie

E Established on 21 June 2007 following similar councils in Germany, Finland, Denmark, Norway and Sweden. CEMB is a membership body for former Muslims who have renounced Islam. The executive Committee comprises nine members including the Spokesman.

R The Council has adopted the ten-point manifesto agreed by the Council of Ex-Muslims of Germany, demanding freedom of religion and atheism and the prohibition religious customs, rules, ceremonies and activities that are incompatible with or infringe people's rights and freedoms.

G United Kingdom.

Council of Food Policy Advisors

■ Eastbury House, 30-34 Albert Embankment, LONDON, SE1 7TL.
Tel 0845 933 5577   Fax 020 7238 2188

E Established on 6 October 2008. CFPA functions as an Advisory NDPB of the Department for Environment, Food and Rural Affairs. The Council comprises 15 members including the Chairman.

R To advise on how to achieve sustainable production, distribution and consumption of food.

G United Kingdom.

✍ CFPA produced its second report on 15 March 2010. The term of appointment of the Council's members ended on 31 December 2010 and the future of the body was under review.

Council for Healthcare Regulatory Excellence   (CHRE)

■ 151-197 Buckingham Palace Road, LONDON, SW1W 9SP.
Tel 020 7389 8030   Fax 020 7389 8040   http://www.chre.org.uk
Chairman: Baroness Pitkeathley, OBE   Chief Executive: Harry Cayton

E Established in April 2003 as the Council for the Regulation of Healthcare Professionals under the NHS Reform & Health Care Professions Act 2002. CRHE functions as an Executive NDPB of the Department of Health. The Council comprises seven members including the Chairman.

R To scrutinise and oversee the nine health professions regulators in the UK, working with them in identifying and promoting good practice in regulation, carrying out research, developing policy and giving advice.

G United Kingdom.

● The nine regulators are:
General Chiropractic Council
General Dental Council
General Medical Council
General Optical Council
General Osteopathic Council
General Pharmaceutical Council
Health Professions Council
Nursing & Midwifery Council
Pharmaceutical Society of Northern Ireland (qqv)

✍ The Secretary of State for Health announced on 26 July 2010 that CHRE will be abolished as a NDPB and made a self-funding body, its role extended to cover quality assurance of voluntary registers.

Council of Her Majesty's Circuit Judges   (CoCJ)

■ 11th Floor, Thomas More Building, Royal Courts of Justice, Strand, LONDON, WC2A 2LL.
President: Charles Harris, QC

E Established after the formation of the Crown Court in 1972. Members are elected by serving judges to represent each of the Circuits in England and Wales. The President serves for one year.

G England, Wales.

Council for the Homeless Northern Ireland   (CHNI)

■ 4th Floor, Andras House, 60 Great Victoria Street, BELFAST, BT2 7BB.
Tel 028 9024 6440   Fax 028 9024 1266   http://www.chni.org.uk
Director: Ricky Rowledge

E Established in 1983 by Act of Parliament. CHNI is a membership organisation and functions as a company limited by guarantee.

R To improve the quality of life of homeless people throughout Northern Ireland by providing information, training, support, technical support and networking opportunities to homelessness and related organisations.

G Northern Ireland.

● CHNI membership comprises over 100 organisations from the community/voluntary, statutory and private sectors which between them offer some 2,000 accommodation places for homeless people.

Council for Hospitality Management Education   (CHME)
- ■ University of Bournemouth, Fern Barrow, Talbot Campus, POOLE, Dorset, BH12 5BB.
  Tel 01202 961480   http://www.chme.co.uk
  Co-Chairmen: Dr Angela Roper & Prof Isabell Hodgson   Hon Secretary: Ina Grebliunaite
- E Established in 1979. CHME is a voluntary non-profit making body which represents 40 UK universities and colleges offering courses in the management of hotel and catering business.
- R To promote high quality and internationally relevant hospitality management education.
- G United Kingdom.

The Council for Industry & Higher Education   (CIHE)
- ■ Studio 11, Tiger House, Burton Street, LONDON, WC1H 9BY.
  Tel 020 7383 7667   Fax 020 7383 3433   http://www.cihe-uk.com
  Chairman: Richard Greenhalgh   Chief Executive: Dr David Docherty
- E Established in 1986. CIHE functions as a company limited by guarantee and registered charity. Its Board of Trustees comprises seven members including the Chairman.
- R To develop and promote an agreed agenda on the higher education talent and research issues that affect the UK's global competitiveness and social well being as well as individual development.
  To build and publish an evidence base so that policy and behaviour changes can be better based on fact.
  To change policy and behaviour to reflect strategic educational and research needs.
  To create strategic task forces on issues of national significance where business and university collaboration can effect real strategic change.
- G United Kingdom.

Council of the Inns of Court   (COIC)
- ■ The Treasury Office, Lincoln's Inn, LONDON, WC2A 3TL.
  Tel 020 7405 1393   Fax 020 7831 1839
  Chairman: The Rt Hon Lady Justice Smith, DBE   Secretary: Colonel David Hills, MBE
- E Established on 1 January 1981 by an agreement made on 11 November 1968 replacing, in some measure, the Senate of the Inns of Court and the Bar.
- R To be the representative body of the Inns with power to bind the Inns by its decision on any matter referred to it by the Bar Council (qv) or any one or more of the Inns.
  To formulate policies for the Inns and to consolidate the policies of the Inns.
  To serve as a channel of communication between the Inns themselves and between the Inns and the Bar Council.
  To procure the implementation or acceptance by the Inns of such general policies laid down by the Bar Council from time to time.
  To keep under review and amend as necessary, in consultation with the Bar Council, the Consolidated Regulations of the Inns.
- G England.
- ✍ Also known as the Inns' Council.

Council for Learning Outside the Classroom   (CLOtC)
- ■ 6 Breams Buildings, LONDON, EC4A 1QL.   http://www.lotc.org.uk
  Chairman: Anthony Thomas   Chief Executive: Beth Gardner
- E Established on 1 April 2009 to assume responsibility for the Learning Outside the Classroom Manifesto launched by the Secretary of State in November 2006. The Council functions as a registered charity. The Board of Trustees comprises nine members including the Chairman.
- R To promote and suport learning outside the classroom.
- G United Kingdom.
- ● The LOtC Advisory Group (LOtCAG) comprises a range of independent LOtC experts, representing a diverse range of users and providers from subject associations to school workforce unions.

Council for Learning Resources in Colleges   (CoLRiC)
- ■ PO Box 51156, LONDON, SE13 9AN.
  Tel 07505 434069   Fax 020 3137 1546   http://www.colric.org.uk
  Chairman: Nicola Scott, BA(Hons), MA, MCLIP
- E Established in 1993. CoLRiC is a membership body consisting of over 250 college learning resources services in the UK and Republic of Ireland. The Executive Committee comprises 13 members including the Chairman.
- R To act as an independent support agency to enable learning resources services to provide quality services throughout the further education sector (including sixth form colleges).
- G United Kingdom, Republic of Ireland.
- ● CoLRiC defines a learning resources service as a discrete service that is recognised by the college to contain any or all of the following (listed in order of importance):
  library or learning resource centre (or similar name)

© CBD Research Ltd · Beckenham · Kent BR3 5JS · Tel 020 8650 7745 · Fax 020 8650 0768 · E-mail cbd@cbdresearch.com · www.cbdresearch.com

resource-based learning
flexible learning and similar learning workshop
information technology and computer centre
study centre
audio-visual and reprographic facilities
and similar cross-college centres to enable learning.

Council for Licensed Conveyancers   (CLC)
■   16 Glebe Road, CHELMSFORD, Essex, CM1 6QG.
Tel 01245 349599   Fax 01245 341300   http://www.conveyancer.org.uk
Chairman: Anna Bradley
E   Established in 1987 under the Administration of Justice Act 1985. CLC is the regulatory body for licensed
conveyancers. The Council comprises 15 members including the Chairman.
R   To ensure that the standards of competence and professional conduct among persons who practise as licensed
conveyancers are sufficient to secure adequate protection for consumers and that the conveyancing services
provided by such persons are provided both economically and efficiently.
G   United Kingdom.
✍   One of the Approved Regulators overseen by the **Legal Services Board**.

Council of Museums in Wales
✍   Abolished on 1 April 2004. See **CyMAL: Museums Archives & Libraries in Wales**.

Council for National Parks
✍   Since 2008 **Campaign for National Parks**.

Council for Nature Conservation & the Countryside   (CNCC)
■   1st Floor, Calvert House, 23 Castle Place, BELFAST, BT1 1FY.
Tel 028 9025 4835   Fax 028 9025 4856   http://www.cnccni.gov.uk
Chairman: Patrick Casement
E   Established on 16 May 1989 under the Nature Conservation & Amenity Lands (Amendment) Order 1989, its
statutory role further covered by the provisions of the Environment (Northern Ireland) Order 2002. CNCC
functions as an Advisory NDPB of the Department of the Environment Northern Ireland. The Council comprises
20 members including the Chairman.
R   To advise the Department on issues relating to nature conservation and the protection of the countryside.
G   Northern Ireland.

Council of Photographic News Agencies Ltd   (CPNA)
■   c/o UPP, 29-31 Saffron Hill, LONDON, EC1N 8SW.
Tel 020 7421 6002   Fax 020 7421 6006
Contact: Peter Dare
E   Originally established in 1951, the Council became a company limited by guarantee without share capital on 12
March 1990. It consists of five members nominated by the Board of Directors.
R   To promote the reputation of the photographic industry by fostering and enhancing the mutual cooperation of
major photographic news agencies in the distribution and reproduction of photographs.
To obtain passes for its members to attend events for the purposes of taking photographs where access is
restricted basis, such as Royal, sporting and political events.
G   United Kingdom.

Council for the Registration of Forensic Practitioners
✍   CRFP ceased trading on 31 March 2009.

Council for the Regulation of Healthcare Professionals
✍   See the **Council for Healthcare Regulatory Excellence**.

Council for Science & Technology   (CST)
■   2nd Floor, 1 Victoria Street, LONDON, SW1H 0ET.
Tel 020 7215 1092   http://www.bis.gov.uk/cst/
Co-Chairmen: Prof Dame Janet Finch, DBE,   Prof Sir John Beddington, CMG

E   Established in October 1993 following an announcement in the White Paper 'Realising Our Potential' (Cmnd 2250) in May 1993, and replacing the former Advisory Council on Science & Technology; the Council was relaunched in 2004. CST functions as a Scientific Advisory Committee and an Advisory NDPB of the Department for Business, Innovation & Skills. The Council comprises 15 members including the Co-Chairmen.

R   To advise the Prime Minister on the strategic policies and framework for sustaining and developing science, engineering and technology (SET) in the UK, and promoting international cooperation in SET.

G   United Kingdom.

✍   For further information see **Scientific Advisory Committees**.

Council on Tribunals

✍   See the **Administrative Justice & Tribunals Council** (2007).

Council of Validating Universities   (CVU)

■   Academic Quality Unit - Clough 10, Edge Hill University, St Helens Road, ORMSKIRK, Lancs, L39 4QP.
    Tel 01695 657167   http://www.cvu.ac.uk

E   Established in 1982, the CVU was registered as a charity in 1996 and became a company in 2005. CVU is a non-statutory body comprising representatives from higher education institutions and related organisations.

R   To validate programmes of study by universities and colleges ('awarding institutions') for delivery by other colleges and organisations ('partner institutions').

G   United Kingdom.

Council of Voluntary Welfare Work

✍   The umbrella body for a dozen church organisations and Christian associations that support the work of the UK armed forces worldwide. operation of Forces clubs and/or canteens.

Council for World Mission

✍   An international body beyond the scope of this volume.

Councillors Commission

✍   Established in February 2007 to develop recommendations to encourage a more diverse range of people to become councillors. It published its report on 10 December 2007.

COUNCILS for VOLUNTARY SERVICE   (CVS)

E   The CVS network consists of 56 Councils operating across Scotland which provide a range of development and support services to voluntary organisations.
    Through its Thrive programme, the network provides start-up support, including advice on legal structures, governance and recruitment, as well as on securing funding and ongoing developmental support.
    Under its Connect agenda, the network represents the interests of community and voluntary organisations on a wide range of forums.
    The CVS network is supported by the CVS team within the **Scottish Council for Voluntary Organisations** (qv).

G   Scotland.

Counselling & Psychotherapy Central Awarding Body   (CPCAB)

■   PO Box 1768, GLASTONBURY, Somerset, BA6 8YP.
    Tel 01458 850350   **Fax** 01458 852055   http://www.cpcab.co.uk
    Chief Executive: Dr Anthony Crouch

E   Established in 1993. CPCAB is the awarding body for courses and qualifications in the counselling profession.

G   United Kingdom.

✍   For more information see the **Federation of Awarding Bodies** and the **Office of the Qualifications & Examinations Regulator**.

Counter Fraud & Security Management Service

✍   Since 2006, the NHS Counter Fraud and Security Management Services are divisions of the **NHS Business Services Authority**.

Countryside Access & Activities Network   (CAAN)

■ The Stableyard, Barnett's Demesne, Malone Road, BELFAST, BT9 5PB.
  Tel 028 9030 3930   Fax 028 9062 6248   http://www.countrysiderecreation.com
  Network Director: Dr Caro-lynne Ferris

E Established in 1999 in response to the publication in November 1998 of Northern Ireland's first Countryside Recreation Strategy. Subsidiary company, Countryside Recreation Northern Ireland, functions as a company limited by guarantee and registered charity and is responsible for securing funding to enable CAAN to undertake practical outdoor recreation projects.

R To develop, manage and promote outdoor recreation across Northern Ireland.

G Northern Ireland.

Countryside Agency

✍ On 1 October 2006 its landscape, access and recreation functions passed to the newly established **Natural England**.

Countryside Council for Wales   (CCW)

■ Maes-y-Ffynnon, Penrhosgarnedd, BANGOR, Caernarfonshire, LL57 2DW.
  Tel 0845 130 6229   http://www.ccw.gov.uk
  Chairman: Morgan Parry   Chief Executive: Roger Thomas

E Established on 1 April 1991 under the Environmental Protection Act 1990. CCW functions as an Executive NDPB of the National Assembly for Wales. The Council comprises twelve members including the Chairman.

R To champion the environment and landscapes of Wales and its coastal waters as sources of natural and cultural riches, as a foundation for economic and social activity, and as a place for leisure and learning opportunities.
  To make the environment a valued part of everyone's life in Wales.

G Wales.

= Cyngor Cefn Gwlad Cymru

Countryside Recreation Network   (CRN)

■ Sheffield Hallam University, Unit 1 Sheffield Science Park, SHEFFIELD, S1 2LX.
  Tel 0114 225 4494   Fax 0114 225 6319   http://www.countrysiderecreation.org.uk
  Chairman: Geoff Hughes   Network Manager: Magali Fleurot   Network Assistant: Sian Griffiths

E Established in October 1992 to replace the former Countryside Recreation Research Advisory Group (established January 1968). CRN is funded by a range of Government departments, agencies and other bodies which share an interest in countryside recreation issues. various bodies who share an interest in countryside recreation issues.

R To encourage cooperation between members in identifying and promoting the need for research related to countryside recreation, to encourage joint ventures, and to disseminate information about members' recreation programmes.
  To promote information exchange relating to countryside recreation, and to foster general debate about relevant trends and issues.
  To share information to develop best practice through training and professional development in provision for and management of countryside recreation.

G United Kingdom, Republic of Ireland.

Court Funds Office   (CFO)

■ 22 Kingsway, LONDON, WC2B 6LE.
  Tel 0845 223 8500   Fax 020 7947 7967   http://www.courtfunds.gov.uk

E Established on 1 April 2001 as the Strategic Investment Board. On 1 April 2007 it left HM Courts Service (qv) and joined with the Official Solicitor & Public Trustee, then demerged on 1 April 2009. The work of the Office is governed by the Civil Procedure Rules and Court Funds Rules. It is an associated office of the Ministry of Justice.

R To provide a banking and administration service for the courts, accounting for money being paid into and out of court, and looking after any investments made with that money.

G England, Wales.

✍ The Government announced on 14 October 2010 that CFO would be retained on the grounds of performing a function which requires political impartiality, but that its investment activity would be outsourced.

Court of Session Rules Council

■ The Lord President's Private Office, Parliament House, EDINBURGH, EH1 1RQ.
  Chairman: Rt Hon Lord Hamilton (as Lord President)

E Established in its current form under the Court of Session Act 1988. The Council comprises the Chairman and twelve other members.

R   To frame rules regarding any matters which the Court could regulate by act of sederunt and submit those rules to the Court for approval.

G   Scotland.

Courts Boards

✍ 21 Boards were established under the Courts Act 2003 to work in partnership with HM Courts Service (qv) to scrutinise, review and make recommendations about the way in which the courts were being run in their areas. Their abolition was announced in the Budget Statement on 24 March 2010.

Covent Garden Market Authority   (CGMA)

■   Covent House, New Covent Garden Market, LONDON, SW8 5NX.
    Tel 020 7720 2211   Fax 020 7622 5307   http://www.newcoventgardenmarket.com
    Chairman: Baroness Dean of Thornton-le-Fylde   Chief Executive: Jan Lloyd
    Shareholder Executive contact: Peter Shortt

E   Established on 30 October 1961 under the Covent Garden Market Act 1961; the Authority is now constituted under the Covent Garden Market Acts 1966 and 1969. CGMA functions as a Public Corporation accountable to the Department for Environment, Food & Rural Affairs. The board comprises eight members including the Chairman.

R   To provide facilities for a wholesale market at Nine Elms, London.

G   United Kingdom.

●   CGMA owns and operates the 56 acre New Covent Garden Market which has been trading at Nine Elms since 1974.

✍ One of the businesses managed by the **Shareholder Executive**.

Cowes Harbour Commission   (CHC)

■   Harbour Office, Town Quay, COWES, Isle of Wight, PO31 7AS.
    Tel 01983 293952   Fax 01983 299357   http://www.cowes.co.uk
    Chairman: Jeremy Preston   Chief Executive & Harbour Master: Stuart McIntosh

E   Established in 1897 by Act of Parliament. The Commission comprises 19 members including the Chairman.

G   Cowes.

✍ For further information see **Port & Harbour Authorities**.

CPR Regeneration

■   The Berlewen Building, Trevenson Road, POOL, Cornwall, TR15 3PL.
    Tel 01209 722099   Fax 01209 722090   http://www.cprregeneration.co.uk
    Chairman: David Brewer   Chief Executive: Nigel Tipple

E   Established in September 2002 as an Urban Regeneration Company. Since April 2010 CPR Regeneration has functioned as an Economic Development Company, a subsidiary of the Cornwall Development Company Ltd which is wholly owned by Cornwall Council. The Board comprises nine members including the Chairman.

R   To bring prosperity back to Camborne, Pool and Redruth.

G   Camborne, Pool, Redruth.

✍ For further information see **Economic Development Companies**.

Crafts Council

■   44a Pentonville Road, LONDON, N1 9BY.
    Tel 020 7278 7700   Fax 020 7837 6891   http://www.craftscouncil.org.uk
    Chairman: Joanna Foster, CBE   Executive Director: Rosy Greenlees

E   Set up in 1971 (first meeting 6 October 1971) as the Crafts Advisory Committee, by the Paymaster General who was then Minister responsible for the Arts; its present title was adopted in 1979 and it was incorporated under Royal Charter in July 1982. It is funded by Arts Council England, with grants from the Scottish Arts Council and the Arts Council of Wales (qqv). The Board comprises 13 members including the Chairman.

R   To make contemporary craft exciting and relevant to the widest possible audience.
    To nurture and support makers and craft professionals throughout their careers.
    To promote the teaching and studying of craft within schools.

G   United Kingdom.

●   The Council administers the Government grant which has been allocated to the crafts and seeks ways of spending it which will be of most benefit to crafts people; grants are offered to help crafts people equip their first workshop and support themselves during their first year of business.
    The Council also runs the national centre for crafts at its headquarters in London; this houses Britain's largest gallery of contemporary crafts exhibitions, plus the specialist picture library and reference library, which are open to the public.

The Council also runs the Chelsea Crafts Fair, and co-ordinates British groups at overseas trade fairs; it tours its own exhibitions.

Creative & Cultural Skills
- Lafone House, The Leathermarket, Weston Street, LONDON, SE1 3HN.
  Tel 020 7015 1800   Fax 020 7015 1847   http://www.ccskills.org.uk
  Chairman: David Worthington   Joint Chief Executives: Catherine Large, Pauline Tambling
- E Established on 1 June 2005. It is the recognised Sector Skills Council for craft, cultural heritage, design, literature, music, performing and visual arts. The board comprises the Chairman, Chief Executive and 13 trustees.
- G United Kingdom.
- ✍ For further information see **Sector Skills Councils**.

Creative England
  Chairman: John Newbigin
- E On 29 November 2010 the Minister for Culture, Communications & Creative Industries announced the proposal to set up Creative England. It will replace the network of Regional Screen Agencies (RSAs), qv, which will reform into a new network based on three key hubs: Creative North (Manchester), Creative Central (Birmingham) and Creative South (Bristol). It will function as a joint venture company of existing agencies and will be fully operational from October 2011.
- R Creative England will support the content industries of film, television, games, and digital and creative services. It will operate in cooperation with the British Film Institute and Film London (qqv). It will also work with bodies such as Arts Council England, Skillset, the Design Council, National Endowment for Science, Technology & the Arts, and the Technology Strategy Board (qqv).
- G England.

Creative Scotland
- Waverley Gate, 2-4 Waterloo Place, EDINBURGH, EH1 3EG.
  Tel 0330 333 2000   http://www.creativescotland.org.uk
  249 West George Street, GLASGOW, G2 4QE.
  Chairman: Sir Sandy Crombie   Chief Executive: Andrew Dixon
- E Established on 1 July 2010 under the Public Services Reform (Scotland) Act 2010, combining the functions of the Scottish Arts Council and Scottish Screen. The Board comprises nine members including the Chairman.
- R To invest in and develop the arts, screen and creative industries in Scotland and play a lead role in promoting the value and importance of these to everyone.
- G Scotland.

Creativesheffield
- First Floor, The Fountain Precinct, Balm Green, SHEFFIELD, S Yorks, S1 2JA.
  Tel 0114 223 2345   Fax 0114 223 2346   http://www.creativesheffield.co.uk
  Chairman: Sir Peter Middleton, GCB   Chief Executive: Paul Firth
- E Established in 1 April 2006, replacing Sheffield One as the regeneration vehicle for Sheffield. Creativesheffield is incorporated as a company limited by guarantee and functions as a Economic Development Company. It has a fixed life of seven years. The Board comprises twelve members including the Chairman.
- G Sheffield.
- ✍ For further information see **Economic Development Companies**.

Criminal Cases Review Commission   (CCRC)
- Alpha Tower, Suffolk Street Queensway, BIRMINGHAM, B1 1TT.
  Tel 0121 633 1800   Fax 0121 633 1823   http://www.ccrc.gov.uk
  Chairman: Richard Foster, CBE   Chief Executive: Claire Bassett
- E Established in March 1997 under the Criminal Appeal Act 1995. The Commission functions as an Executive NDPB of the Ministry of Justice. It comprises eleven Commissioners including the Chairman.
- R To review possible miscarriages of justice in the criminal courts of England, Wales and Northern Ireland and refer appropriate cases to the appeal courts.
- G England, Wales, Northern Ireland.

Criminal Courts Rules Council   (CCRC)
- The Lord President's Private Office, Parliament House, EDINBURGH, EH1 1RQ.
  Chairman: Rt Hon Lord Hamilton (as Lord Justice General)
- E Established in 1995 under the Criminal Procedure (Scotland) Act 1995. The Council comprises 18 members under the chairmanship of the Lord Justice General.

R   To keep under general review the procedures and practices of the courts exercising criminal jurisdiction in Scotland.
     To consider and comment on any draft Act of Adjournal submitted to it by the High Court.
G   Scotland.

Criminal Injuries Compensation Appeals Panel
✍ Since 2008, **First-tier Tribunal (Criminal Injuries Compensation)**.

Criminal Injuries Compensation Appeals Panel for Northern Ireland   (CICAPNI)
■   2nd Floor, The Corn Exchange Building, 31 Gordon Street, BELFAST, BT1 2LG.
     Tel 028 9092 4400   **Fax** 028 9092 4420   http://www.cicapni.org.uk
     Chairman: Oliver Loughran, BA
E   Established on 1 May 2002 under the Criminal Injuries Compensation (Northern Ireland) Order 2002 (which also introduced the Northern Ireland Criminal Injuries Compensation Scheme 2002). The Panel functions as a Tribunal NDPB of the Department of Justice Northern Ireland. It comprises 23 members including the Chairman.
R   To determine appeals against reviewed decisions made by the Compensation Agency (qv) arising from claims for criminal injuries compensation for incidents that occurred on or after 1 May 2002.
G   Northern Ireland.
✍   Appeals against outstanding claims for compensation made before 1 May 2002 are dealt with by the County Court.

Criminal Injuries Compensation Authority   (CICA)
■   Tay House, 300 Bath Street, GLASGOW, G2 4LN.
     Tel 0800 358 3601   **Fax** 0141 331 2287   http://www.cica.gov.uk
     Chief Executive: Carole Oatway
E   Established on 1 April 1996 under the Criminal Injuries Compensation Act 1995. CICA functions as an Executive NDPB of the Ministry of Justice. The Board comprises five directors, including the Chief Executive, and three non-executive advisors.
R   To administer the Criminal Injuries Compensation Scheme.
     To pay compensation to any eligible applicant who has been the victim of a violent crime.
G   England, Scotland, Wales.

Criminal Justice Inspection Northern Ireland   (CJI)
■   14 Great Victoria Street, BELFAST, BT2 7BA.
     Tel 028 9025 8000   **Fax** 028 9025 8011   http://www.cjini.org
     Chief Inspector: Dr Michael Maguire
E   Established on 1 October 2004 under the Justice (Northern Ireland) Act 2002. CJINI functions as an independent statutory inspectorate and NDPB (in the person of the Chief Inspector) of the Department of Justice Northern Ireland. The Management Team comprises the Chief Inspector and three other members.
R   To conduct inspections on all aspects of the criminal justice system in in Northern Ireland apart from the judiciary.
G   Northern Ireland.

Criminal Law Revision Committee
✍   The Committee was established in 1959 to examine aspects of the law and consider whether any revision was necessary. It produced 18 reports and, although never formally abolished, has had no matters referred to it since 1986.

Criminal Procedure Rule Committee   (CPRC)
■   7/36, 102 Petty France, LONDON, SW1H 9AJ.
     Tel 020 3334 4032   **Fax** 020 3334 3001
     Chairman: Rt Hon Lord Judge
E   Established in June 2004 under the Courts Act 2003, combining the functions of the Crown Court Rule Committee and the Magistrates' Courts Rule Committee. CPRC functions as an Advisory NDPB of the Ministry of Justice. The Committee comprises 17 members and is chaired by the Lord Chief Justice of England & Wales.
R   To streamline and modernise the practice and procedure to be followed in the criminal trials of England and Wales.
G   England, Wales.

© CBD Research Ltd · Beckenham · Kent BR3 5JS · Tel 020 8650 7745 · Fax 020 8650 0768 · E-mail cbd@cbdresearch.com · www.cbdresearch.com

Criminal Records Bureau (CRB)

- ■ PO Box 110, LIVERPOOL, L69 3EF.
  Tel 0870 909 0811   http://www.crb.gov.uk
  Chief Executive: Steve Long
- E Established in 1997 under the Police Act 1997. CRB functions as an Executive Agency of the Home Office.
- R To operate its Disclosure Service enabling organisations in the public and voluntary sectors to make safer recruitment decisions by identifying candidates who may be unsuitable for certain work, especially that involve children and young adults.
- G England, Wales.
- ✍ On 11 February 2011 the Government published the findings of its Review into the Vetting & Barring Scheme of the Independent Safeguarding Authority (ISA), qv. Among its recommendations was the merger of CRB and ISA.

Croeso Cymro   See **Visit Wales**.

Crofters Commission

- ■ Great Glen House, Leachkin Road, INVERNESS, IV3 8NW.
  Tel 01463 663450   Fax 01463 725067   http://www.crofterscommission.org.uk
  Convener: Drew Ratter   Chief Executive: Nick Reiter
- E Established in 1955 under the Crofters (Scotland) Act 1955, the Commission's current authority is derived from the Crofters (Scotland) Act 1993. It functions as an Executive NDPB of the Scottish Executive Rural Affairs Department. The Commission comprises seven members including the Convenor.
- R To reorganise, develop and regulate crofting and promote the interests of the crofters.
- G The Highlands & Islands of Scotland.
- = Ughdarras nan Croitearan

Cromarty Firth Fisheries Trust   See **Rivers & Fisheries Trusts of Scotland**.

Cromarty Firth Port Authority (CFPA)

- ■ Shore Road, INVERGORDON, Ross-shire, IV18 0HD.
  Tel 01349 852308   http://www.cfpa.co.uk
  Chairman: Neil McArthur
- E Established in 1975 under Cromarty Firth Port Authority Order Confirmation Act 1973.
- G Cromarty Firth.
- ✍ For further information see **Port & Harbour Authorities**.

Crouch Harbour Authority

- ■ The Quay, BURNHAM-ON-CROUCH, Essex, CM0 8AS.
  Tel 01621 783602   http://www.crouchharbour.org
  Chairman: Cllr John P F Archer
- E Established under the Crouch Harbour Act 1974. The Authority comprises twelve members including the Chairman.
- G Burnham-on-Crouch.
- ✍ For further information see **Port & Harbour Authorities**.

Crown Agents Holding & Realisation Board

- ✍ The Board was disbanded on 28 March 2008, its property, rights, liabilities and obligations transferred to the Secretary of State for International Development.

The Crown Agents for Oversea Governments & Administrations Ltd (Crown Agents)

- ■ St Nicholas House, St Nicholas Road, SUTTON, Surrey, SM1 1EL.
  Tel 020 8643 3311   Fax 020 8643 8232   http://www.crownagents.com
  Chairman: Paul Batchelor   Chief Executive: Terence Jagger, CBE
- E Joint Agents General of the Crown Colonies were established on 26 March 1833 by a Treasury Mandate; from 1863 they were known as the Crown Agents for the Colonies, adopting the current name in April 1954. Under the Crown Agents Act 1995 Crown Agents functions as an international development company owned by the Crown Agents Foundation, a company limited by guarantee with a social and developmental purpose. The management board comprises twelve members including the Chairman.
- R To help governments raise revenue, manage debt and plan expenditure more effectively through its expertise in public financial management.

To help ensure that wealth generated is spent or invested for the good of all, through its procurement and supply chain services, and banking and asset management services.

To help reduce poverty, improve health and increase prosperity through technical assistance, consultancy and training.

G   United Kingdom.

●   Crown Agents delivers specialist and multidisciplinary services in international trade, procurement, finance and institutional development. Projects are often in joint venture or partnership with other companies or organisations, frequently in the private sector and, increasingly, with local firms in client countries. Crown Agents works for the public and private sector in 130 countries, as well as for multilateral and bilateral donors. It is independent of any commercial interest, in Britain or elsewhere.

Crown Appointments Commission

✍   Since 2003 **Crown Nominations Commission**.

Crown Court Rule Committee   See **Criminal Procedure Rule Committee**.

The Crown Estate

■   16 New Burlington Place, LONDON, W1S 2HX.
Tel 020 7851 5000   http://www.thecrownestate.co.uk
Chairman (First Commissioner): Sir Stuart Hampson
Chief Executive (Second Commissioner): Roger Bright, CB, MA

E   The Commissioners of Crown Lands (constituted under the Crown Lands Acts 1829 to 1943 as successors to the Commissioners of Woods), were reconstituted as the Crown Estate Commissioners by the Crown Estate Act 1956; it is now constituted under the Crown Estate Act 1961. The Crown Estate functions as a non-ministerial government department. The Estate's board comprises eight Commissioners.

R   To benefit the taxpayer by paying the revenue from the Crown Estate's assets directly to HM Treasury.
To enhance the value of the Estate and the income it generates.

G   United Kingdom.

●   The Crown Estate property portfolio encompasses many of the UK's cityscapes, ancient forests, farms, parkland, coastline and communities.

Crown Nominations Commission   (CNC)

■   Church House, Great Smith Street, LONDON, SW1P 3AZ.
Tel 020 7898 1000
Archbishops' Appointments Secretary: Caroline Boddington

E   Established in 1977 as the Crown Appointments Commission by Act of the General Synod of the Church of England, adopting its current name in 2003. The Commission consists of the Archbishops of Canterbury and York, three elected members of each of the Synod's Houses of Clergy and Laity, and six members of the Vacancy-in-See Committee of the diocese whose bishopric is to become, or has become, vacant.

R   To consider individuals for a vacant Episcopal See and nominate two, in order of preference, to the Prime Minister who decides upon a single candidate to recommend to HM the Queen.

G   England.

Crown Prosecution Service   (CPS)

■   Rose Court, 2 Southwark Bridge, LONDON, SE1 9HS.
Tel 020 3357 0000   http://www.www.cps.gov.uk
United House, Piccadilly, YORK, YO1 9PQ.
Tel 01904 545400
Director of Public Prosecutions: Keir Starmer, QC Chief Executive: Peter Lewis

E   Established in 1986 under the Prosecution of Offences Act 1985. On 1 January 2010 it incorporated the former Serious Fraud Office and the Revenue & Customs Prosecution Service. CPS functions as a non-ministerial government department. The board comprises nine members and is chaired by the Director of Public Prosecutions who is superintended by the Attorney General.

R   To determine the charge and prosecute criminal cases investigated by the police in England and Wales.

G   England, Wales.

●   CPS operates under a structure of 42 geographical areas in England and Wales which correspond with the boundaries of the 43 police forces (the City of London Police and the Metropolitan Police areas being treated as one CPS area). Each is headed by a Chief Crown Prosecutor.

Cultural Strategy Group for London
✍ Since 2004 **London Cultural Strategy Group**.

Culture East Midlands
✍ One of the eight Regional Cultural Consortiums established for England in 1999, it closed on 31 March 2009, its functions returned to the Department for Culture, Media & Sport.

Culture North East
✍ One of the eight Regional Cultural Consortiums established for England in 1999, it closed on 31 March 2009, its functions returned to the Department for Culture, Media & Sport.

Culture Northwest, or Culture North West, formerly the North West Cultural Consortium
✍ One of the eight Regional Cultural Consortiums established for England in 1999, it closed on 31 March 2009, its functions returned to the Department for Culture, Media & Sport.

Culture South East
✍ One of the eight Regional Cultural Consortiums established for England in 1999, it closed on 31 March 2009, its functions returned to the Department for Culture, Media & Sport.

Culture South West
✍ One of the eight Regional Cultural Consortiums established for England in 1999, it closed on 31 March 2009, its functions returned to the Department for Culture, Media & Sport.

Culture West Midlands
✍ One of the eight Regional Cultural Consortiums established for England in 1999, it closed on 31 March 2009, its functions returned to the Department for Culture, Media & Sport.

Cumbria & Lancashire Strategic Health Authority
✍ On 1 July 2006 merged with the Cheshire & Merseyside and the Greater Manchester Strategic Health Authorities to form the **North West Strategic Health Authority**.

Cumbria Police Authority
■ Carleton Hall, PENRITH, Cumbria, CA10 2AU.
Tel 01768 217734   http://www.cumbriapoliceauthority.org.uk
Chairman: Cllr Ray Cole
E Established in April 1995, the Authority is an independent body charged with ensuring that Cumbria Constabulary provides an effective and efficient police service. It is made up of nine councillor members and eight independent members.
G Cumbria.
✍ For further information see **Police Authorities**.

Cumbria Probation Trust
■ Lime House, The Green, Wetheral, CARLISLE, Cumbria, CA4 8EW.
Tel 01228 560057   Fax 01228 561164   http://www.cumbriaprobation.org.uk
Chairman: Richard Rhodes, JP   Chief Officer: Annette Hennessy
E Established on 1 April 2001 under the Criminal Justice & Court Service Act 2000 as the Cumbria Probation Area Board. It became a trust on 1 April 2010 under the Offender Management Act 2007. The Board comprises ten members including the Chairman.
G Cumbria.
✍ For further information see **Probation Trusts**.

Cumbria Tourism
■ Windermere Road, Staveley, KENDAL, Cumbria, LA8 9PL.
Tel 01539 822222   Fax 01539 825079   http://www.cumbriatourism.org
Chairman: Eric Robson   Chief Executive: Ian Stephens
R To create a world class visitor experience.

G   Cumbria.
✍   Cumbria Tourism is the trading name of the Cumbria Tourist Board, one of the five tourist boards supported by the Northwest Regional Development Agency (qv).

Current & Future Meat Controls Stakeholder Group   Alternative name of the **Stakeholder Group on Current & Future Meat Controls**.

Cwm Taf Community Health Council
■   3rd Floor, Hollies Health Centre, Swan Street, MERTHYR TYDFIL, CF47 8ET.
Tel 01685 384023   Fax 01685 382644
10 Maritime Offices, Woodland Terrace, Maesycoed, PONTYPRIDD, CF37 1DZ.
Tel 01443 405830
Chairman: Jeff Moore   Chief Officer: Gordon Harrop
E   The Council comprises 20 members including the Chairman.
G   Merthyr Tydfil, Rhondda Cynon Taff.
✍   For further information see **Community Health Councils** under **National Health Service - Wales**.

Cwm Taf Health Board
■   Ynysmeurig House, Navigation Park, ABERCYNON, Glamorgan, CF45 4SN.
Tel 01443 744800   http://www.cwntafhb.wales.nhs.uk
Chairman: Dr Chris Jones, CBE   Chief Executive: Mrs Allison Williams
E   Established on 1 October 2009 by the merger of two former Local Health Boards (Merthyr Tydfil and Rhonddha Cynon Taff) and the Cwm Taff NHS Trust. The Board comprises 25 members including the Chairman.
G   Merthyr Tydfil, Rhondda Cynon Taff.
✍   For further information see **NHS Wales - Local Health Boards**.
Cwm Taf Health Board is the operational name of the Cwm Taf Local Health Board.

Cycling England
■   PO Box 54810, LONDON, SW1P 4XX.
Tel 020 7260 2782   http://www.dft.gov.uk/cyclingengland/
Chairman: Phillip Darnton
E   Established in March 2005 by the Department for Transport, replacing the earlier National Cycling Strategy Board. Cycling England is the national body which coordinates the development of cycling across England; it functions as a cross-government group which includes representatives from Sport England (qv) and six Government departments. The Board comprises nine members including the Chairman.
R   To create the conditions which will result in more people cycling, more safely and more often.
G   England.
✍   The Government announced on 14 October 2010 that the body, which is funded to 2011, will be abolished. The Department for Transport has announced a Local Sustainable Transport Fund and will explore ways of marshalling expert input on cycling issues including to support the Fund.

Cyd-Bwyllgor Addysg Cymru   Now known as CBAC, the Welsh version of **WJEC**, the former Welsh Joint Education Committee.

CyMAL: Museums Archives & Libraries in Wales
■   Unit 10, The Science Park, ABERYSTWYTH, Ceredigion, SY23 3AH.
Tel 01970 610224   http://www.cymal.wales.gov.uk
Chairman: Rt Hon Alun Ffred Jones
E   Established on 1 April 2004 replacing the Council of Museums in Wales. It functions as a division of the National Assembly of Wales. The Advisory Council comprises twelve members, chaired by the Heritage Minister.
R   To support the development of local museums, archives and library services.
G   Wales.

Cyngor Addysgu Cyffredinol Cymru   See the **General Teaching Council for Wales**.

Cyngor Archifau a Chofnodion Cymru   See **Archives & Records Council Wales**.

Cyngor Cefn Gwlad Cymru   See **Countryside Council for Wales**.

Cyngor Celfyddydau Cymru   See **Arts Council of Wales**.

Cyngor Chwaraeon Cymru   See **Sports Council for Wales**.

Cyngor Cyllido Addysg Uwch Cymru   See **Higher Education Funding Council for Wales**.

Cyngor Cymru i Bobl Fyddar   See **Wales Council for Deaf People**.

Cyngor Cymru i'r Deillion   See **Wales Council for the Blind**.

Cyngor Defnyddwyr Cymru
✍   On 1 October 2008 Cyngor Defnyddwyr Cymru (Welsh Consumer Council), with others, was replaced by **Consumer Focus**.

Cyngor Ffoaduriaid Cymru   See **Welsh Refugee Council**.

Cyngor Gofal Cymru   See **Care Council for Wales**.

Cyngor Gweithredu Gwirfoddol Cymru   See **Wales Council for Voluntary Action**.

Cyngor Llyfrau Cymru   See **Welsh Books Council**.

Cyngor Rheolaeth Cymru   See **Wales Management Council**.

Cyngor Ymghyngorol Adeiladau Hanesyddol Cymru   See **Historic Buildings Advisory Council for Wales**.

Cytûn - Churches Together in Wales / Eglwysi Ynghyd yng Nghymru
■   58 Richmond Road, CARDIFF, CF24 3UR.
    Tel 029 2046 4375   http://www.cytun.org.uk
    Chief Executive: Revd Aled Edwards, OBE
E   Established on 1 September 1990 as successor to the former Welsh Council of Churches. Cytûn is a membership organisation of Churches in Wales.
R   To challenge and enable the 13 member Christian denominations to witness, work, reflect and pray together more effectively.
G   Wales.

D

DA-Notice Committee   See **Defence, Press & Broadcasting Advisory Committee**.

The Dairy Council
■   93 Baker Street, LONDON, W1U 6QQ.
    Tel 020 7467 2629   Fax 020 7935 3920   http://www.milk.co.uk
    Chairman: Sandy Wilkie   Director: Dr Judith Bryans

E   Established in 1920 as the National Milk Publicity Council. The Council is a non-profit making organisation funded by farmers and processors via Dairy UK.
R   To provide science-based information to health professionals, the media, industry and consumers on the role of dairy foods as part of a healthy balanced diet and lifestyle.
G   United Kingdom.

DairyCo
■   AHDB, Stoneleigh Park, KENILWORTH, Warwicks, CV8 2TL.
     Tel 024 7669 2051   **Fax** 024 7647 8904   http://www.dairyco.org.uk
     Chairman: Tim Bennett
E   Established on 1 April 2008 via the Agriculture & Horticulture Development Board Order 2008. It replaces the former Milk Development Council. The Board comprises twelve members including the Chairman.
R   To promote world-class knowledge to British dairy farmers so they can profit from a sustainable future.
G   England, Wales, Scotland.
✍   A subsidiary of the **Agriculture & Horticulture Development Board** and funded through an AHDB levy paid on all milk sold off-farm.

Dart Harbour & Navigation Authority   (DHNA)
■   6 Oxford Street, DARTMOUTH, Devon, TQ6 9AL.
     Tel 01803 832337   **Fax** 01803 833631   http://www.dartharbour.org.uk
     Chairman: Neil Hockaday
E   Established in 1976 under the Dart Harbour & Navigation Authority Act 1975. The Authority comprises nine members including the Chairman.
G   Dartmouth.
✍   For further information see **Port & Harbour Authorities**.

Dartmoor National Park Authority   (DNPA)
■   Parke, Bovey Tracey, NEWTON ABBOT, Devon, TQ13 9JQ.
     Tel 01626 832093   **Fax** 01626 834684   http://www.dartmoor-npa.gov.uk
     Chairman: Cllr Bill Hitchins   Chief Executive: Dr Kevin Bishop
E   Dartmoor was designated a National Park in 1951. The present Authority was established on 1 April 1997 under the Environment Act 1995. It comprises 22 members including the Chairman.
G   Dartmoor.
✍   For further information see **National Park Authorities**.

Dartmoor Steering Group   (DSG)
■   Parke, Bovey Tracey, NEWTON ABBOT, Devon, TQ13 9JQ.
     Tel 01626 832093   **Fax** 01626 834684   http://www.dartmoor-npa.gov.uk
     Chairman: Dr Kevin Bishop
E   Established in 1978 following the recommendations of an enquiry in 1975 into the military use of Dartmoor. DSG functions as an Advisory NDPB of the Ministry of Defence. The Group comprises twelve members and the Chairmanship alternates between the Chief Executive of Dartmoor National Park Authority (qv) and the Commander Defence Training Estate South West.
R   To reconcile the competing demands made upon Dartmoor by the military, conservation and public access.
G   Dartmoor.

Darwin Advisory Committee
✍   Reconstituted as a committee of experts on 24 January 2011. See **Darwin Expert Committee**.

Darwin Expert Committee   (DEC)
■   Defra, Nobel House, 17 Smith Square, LONDON, SW1P 3JR.
     Tel 0845 933 5577
     Chairman: Prof David Macdonald
E   Established on 24 January 2011 as a scientific expert committee of the Department for Environment, Food & Rural Affairs. DEC replaced the Darwin Advisory Committee, DAC, an Defra Advisory NDPB. The DEC Committee retains DAC's twelve members, including Chairman.
R   To provide independent advice to the Secretary of State via Defra officials on applications for funding under the Darwin Initiative.
     To monitor the progress of the Initiative and evaluate the achievement of its objectives.
G   United Kingdom.

© CBD Research Ltd · Beckenham · Kent BR3 5JS · Tel 020 8650 7745 · Fax 020 8650 0768 · E-mail cbd@cbdresearch.com · www.cbdresearch.com

- The Darwin Initiative assists countries that are rich in biodiversity but poor in financial resources to meet their objectives under the Convention on Biological Diversity (CBD, 1992), the Convention on International Trade in Endangered Species (CITES, 1973) or the Convention on the Conservation of Migratory Species (CMS, 1979), through the funding of collaborative projects which draw on UK biodiversity expertise.

The Darwin Initiative   See the **Darwin Advisory Committee**.

David MacBrayne Limited
■　The Ferry Terminal, GOUROCK, PA19 1QP.
　　Tel 01475 650100　**Fax** 01475 650336
　　Chairman: Peter Timms, CBE　Chief Executive: Archie Robertson, OBE
E　The Company was formerly dormant but was reactivated in 2006 as a group holding company to prepare for the tendering of the Clyde and Hebridean Ferry Services. It functions as a Public Corporation. The board comprises six members including the Chairman.
R　To operate ferry services serving the West Coast of Scotland and the Clyde Valley.
G　Clyde and Hebrides.

Dean Gallery　See **National Galleries of Scotland**.

Debt Management Office　See the **United Kingdom Debt Management Office**.

Deer Commission for Scotland
✍　On 1 August 2010 DCS was dissolved and its functions transferred to **Scottish Natural Heritage**.

Defence Academy Management Board
■　Greenhill House, Shrivenham, SWINDON, Wilts, SN6 8LA.
　　Tel 01793 785615　http://www.da.mod.uk
　　Director General: Lieutenant General Andrew Graham, CBE
E　Established on 1 April 2002. The Academy functions as a national and international centre of excellence of the Ministry of Defence; it brings together the Armed Forces Chaplaincy Centre, College of Management & Technology, Joint Services Command & Staff College and Royal College of Defence Studies. The Board comprises nine members including the Director General.
R　To oversee the Academy's aim of providing civilian and military personnel with a high quality education primarily at postgraduate level, and conducting research in fields related to defence.
G　United Kingdom.

Defence Analytical Services & Advice　　(DASA)
■　03/K/22, MOD Main Building, Whitehall, LONDON, SW1A 2HB.
　　Tel 020 7807 8792　http://www.dasa.mod.uk
　　Contact: Mark Towers
E　Established on 1 July 1992 as the Defence Analytical Services Agency. DASA functions as an Executive Agency of the Ministry of Defence.
R　To provide professional analytical, economic and statistical services and advice to the Ministry of Defence, and defence-related statistics to Parliament, other Government Departments and the public.
G　United Kingdom.

Defence Aviation Repair Agency
✍　On 1 April 2008 DARA merged with ABRO to form the **Defence Support Group**.

Defence Bills Agency
✍　Since April 2007 has operated as the Financial Management Shared Services Centre based in Liverpool and Bath.

Defence Board
■　MOD Main Building, Whitehall, LONDON, SW1A 2HB.
　　Tel 020 7218 9000
　　Chairman: Mrs Ursula Brennan

E   Known as the Defence Management Board until 2008, the Defence Board is the highest non-Ministerial
    committee in the Ministry of Defence. The Board comprises 13 members including the Chairman who is the
    Permanent Under-Secretary of State for Defence.
R   To help define and articulate the Ministry's strategic direction, and provide a clear vision and set of values for
    defence.
    To establish the key priorities and defence capabilities needed to deliver the strategy.
    To ensure that defence priorities and tasks are appropriately resourced.
    To manage corporate performance and resources in-year to deliver the required results.
G   United Kingdom.

Defence Communication Services Agency
✍   The DCSA ceased operating on 31 March 2007 when it was replaced by the Information Systems & Services
    cluster of **Defence Equipment & Support**.

Defence Council
■   MOD Main Building, Whitehall, LONDON, SW1A 2HB.
    Tel 020 7218 9000
    Chairman: Rt Hon Dr Liam Fox, MP
E   Established on 1 April 1964 under the Defence (Transfer of Functions) Act 1964. It is the senior Departmental
    committee of the Ministry of Defence. The Council comprises 15 members including the its Chairman, the
    Secretary of State for Defence.
R   To provide the formal legal basis for the conduct of defence in the UK through a range of powers vested in it by
    statute and Letters Patent.
G   United Kingdom.

Defence Equipment & Support   (DE&S)
■   Maple 0a, #2043, MOD Abbey Wood, BRISTOL, BS34 8JH.
    Tel 0117 913 0010
    Chief of Defence Materiel: Bernard Gray   Chief Operating Officer: Dr Andrew Tyler
E   Established on 1 April 2007 by the merger of the Defence Logistics Organisation (DLO) and the Defence
    Procurement Agency (DPA). It also incorporates the former Defence Communication Services Agency (DCSA)
    and Defence Transport & Movement Agency (DTMA). DE&S functions as an Executive Agency of the Ministry of
    Defence.
R   To equip and support the UK's armed forces for current and future operations.
G   United Kingdom.
●   It acquires and supports through-life, including disposal, equipment and services ranging from ships, aircraft,
    vehicles and weapons, to electronic systems and information systems.

Defence Estates   (DE)
■   Kingston Road, SUTTON COLDFIELD, W Midlands, B75 7RL.
    Tel 0121 311 2140   http://www.defence-estates.mod.uk
    Chief Executive: Andrew Manley
E   Established on 17 March 1997 as the Defence Estates Organisation, adopting its current name on 1 April 1999. It
    relaunched on 1 April 2003 with changed responsibilities. It absorbed the former Defence Housing Executive on
    1 April 2004. DE functions as an Executive Agency of the Ministry of Defence.
R   To manage the defence estate as a corporate whole and in a sustainable manner.
    To develop new methods of procurement that provide for an improved intelligent interface between the Ministry
    and its suppliers.
    To develop and promulgate best practice and be a centre of excellence on estate matters.
G   United Kingdom.

Defence Housing Executive
✍   On 1 April 2004 the DHE merged with **Defence Estates**.

Defence Industries Council   (DIC)
■   Salamanca Square, 9 Albert Embankment, LONDON, SE1 7SP.
    Tel 020 7091 4531   **Fax** 020 7091 4545   http://www.intellectuk.org
    Chairman: Ian King   Secretary: Rees Ward
E   DIC is a forum for senior executives from defence companies and trade associations. The Council comprises 15
    members including the Chairman.

R   To discuss issues of strategic importance to the UK defence industry and to help prepare the positions adopted by industry at meetings of the National Defence Industries Council (qv).

G   United Kingdom.

✍   The National Defence Industries Council is co-chaired by the Chairman of the Defence Industries Council and the Secretary of State for Defence.

Defence Intelligence & Security Centre
✍   DISC ceased to hold government agency status on 1 April 2005.

Defence Logistics Organisation
✍   On 1 April 2007 the DLO was merged with the Defence Procurement Agency to form **Defence Equipment & Support**.

Defence Management Board
✍   See **Defence Board**.

Defence Medical Education & Training Agency
✍   On 1 April 2008, DMETA was incorporated in the new **Joint Medical Command**.

Defence Nuclear Safety Committee   (DNSC)
■   01/L/02, MOD Main Building, Whitehall, LONDON, SW1A 2HB.
      Tel 020 7218 2442   **Fax** 020 7218 1769
      Chairman: Rear Admiral Paul Thomas, CB, FREng

E   Established in October 1998 through the merger of the Nuclear Powered Warships Safety Committee and the Nuclear Weapons Safety Committee. DNSC functions as a Scientific Advisory Committee and an Advisory NDPB of the Ministry of Defence. The Committee comprises the Chairman and eleven members.

R   To advise the Secretary for State for Defence, the Services and other Ministry of Defence authorities on all safety matters pertaining to the construction, operation and maintanance of nuclear powered warships, and the design, manufacture, transport, storage, handling and operational training relating to nuclear weapon systems.

G   United Kingdom.

✍   For further information see **Scientific Advisory Committees**.

Defence, Press & Broadcasting Advisory Committee   (DA-Notice Committee)   (DPBAC)
■   MOD Main Building, Whitehall, LONDON, SW1A 2HB.
      Tel 020 7218 9000   http://www.dnotice.org.uk
      Chairman: Mrs Ursula Brennan

E   Established in 1912 as the Admiralty, War Office & Press Committee, it became the Admiralty, War Office, Air Ministry & Press Committee in 1919, the Services, Press & Broadcasting Committee in 1967 and adopted its current name in 1993 in which year D-Notices were renamed DA-Notices. It functions as an Advisory NDPB of the Ministry of Defence. The Committee comprises 16 members representing press and broadcasting, four representing Government departments (Home Office, Ministry of Defence, Foreign & Commonwealth Office and Cabinet Office) and is chaired by the Permanent Under-Secretary of State for Defence.

R   To oversee the voluntary code which operates between those Government departments which have responsibilities for national security and the media, using as its vehicle the DA-Notice system.

G   United Kingdom.

●   The five standing DA-Notices (Defence Advisory Notices) provide national and provincial newspaper editors, periodical editors, radio and television organisations and relevant book publishers with general guidance on which areas of national security the Government considers it has a duty to protect. The five are
      Military operations, plans and capabilities
      Nuclear and non-nuclear weapons and equipment
      Ciphers and secure communications
      Sensitive installations and home addresses
      UK security and intelligence services and special services

---

Defence Procurement Agency
✍   On 1 April 2007 the DPA was merged with the Defence Logistics Organisation to form **Defence Equipment & Support**.

Defence Science & Technology Laboratory   (Dstl)

- Porton Down, SALISBURY, Wilts, SP4 0JQ.
  Tel 01980 613000   Fax 01980 613004   http://www.dstl.gov.uk
  Chairman: Sir Richard Mottram   Chief Executive: Dr Frances Saunders
  Shareholder Executive contact: Peter Shortt
- E   Established on 1 July 2001. Dstl functions as an Agency and Training Fund of the Ministry of Defence.
- R   To supply the very best, impartial, scientific and technical research and advice to the Ministry of Defence and other Government departments.
- G   United Kingdom.
- ● Dstl has three other sites: Alverstoke (near Gosport, Hampshire), Fort Halstead (near Sevenoaks, Kent) and Portsdown West (near Fareham, Hampshire).
- ✍ One of the businesses managed by the **Shareholder Executive**.

Defence Scientific Advisory Council   (DSAC)

- 01/M/14, MOD Main Building, Whitehall, LONDON, SW1A 2HB.
  Tel 020 7218 7996   Fax 020 7218 9678
  Chairman: Prof Ian Poll, OBE, FREng
- E   Established in April 1969 by the Secretary of State for Defence. DSAC functions as a Scientific Advisory Committee and Advisory NDPB of the Ministry of Defence. The Council comprises 17 members including the Chairman.
- R   To provide independent advice to the Secretary of State for Defence on matters of concern to the MOD in the fields of non-nuclear science, engineering, technology and analysis.
- G   United Kingdom.
- ✍ For further information see **Scientific Advisory Committees**.

Defence Storage & Distribution Agency   (DSDA)

- Building C16, C Site, Lower Arncott, BICESTER, Oxon, OX25 1LP.
  Tel 01869 256128   Fax 01869 256389
- E   Established on 5 April 1995 by the Secretary of State for Defence as the Army Base Storage & Distribution Agency, adopting its current name on 1 April 1999. DSDA functions as an Enhanced Executive Agency of the Ministry of Defence and is the storage and distribution arm of Defence Equipment & Support (qv).
- R   To store, maintain, issue, process and distribute materiel for the MOD and other designated users.
- G   United Kingdom.
- ● DSDA operates from eleven major storage and munitions sites in the UK and one in Germany.

Defence Support Group   (DSG)

- Building 203, Monxton Road, ANDOVER, Hants, SP11 8HT.
  Tel 01264 383295   Fax 01264 383280
  email info@dsg.mod.uk   http://www.dsg.mod.uk
  Chairman: Jamie Pike, MBA, MIMechE   Chief Executive: Archie Hughes
  Shareholder Executive contact: Peter Shortt
- E   Established on 1 April 2008 following the merger of the Army Base Repair Organisation (ABRO) and the Defence Aviation Repair Agency (DARA).
- R   To provide expert in-house maintenance, repair, overhaul and upgrade services for the through life support of the UK Armed Forces.
- G   United Kingdom.
- ● In addition to its Head Office in Andover, DSG has a network of 16 sites around the UK.
  Its services cover Armour; Artillery & engineer systems support; Armoured vehicle overhaul; Calibration equipment support; Electronic / Optronic repair; Engine & transmission testing; Medical & dental equipment support; Weapons systems support; & Whole fleet management.
- ✍ One of the businesses managed by the **Shareholder Executive**.

Defence Transport & Movements Agency

- ✍ Ceased to hold agency status on 1 April 2007, now functions as the Defence Supply Chain Operations & Movements (DSCOM) division of **Defence Equipment & Support**.

Defence Vetting Agency   (DVA)

- Imphal Barracks, Fulford Road, YORK, YO10 4AS.
  Tel 01904 662644   http://www.mod.uk/dva
  Chief Executive: Mrs Jacky Ridley
- E   Established on 1 April 1997. DVA functions as an Executive Agency of the Ministry of Defence.
- R   To provide National Security Vetting (NSV) to the armed services, the MOD civil service and defence contractors.

© CBD Research Ltd · Beckenham · Kent BR3 5JS · Tel 020 8650 7745 · Fax 020 8650 0768 · E-mail cbd@cbdresearch.com · www.cbdresearch.com

G   United Kingdom.
●   The DVA also delivers a range of NSV services on a commercial basis to customers across the public sector.

Denbighshire Local Health Board
✍   Merged on 1 October 2009 with the Anglesey, Conwy, Flintshire, Gwynedd and Wrexham Local Health Boards to form **Betsi Cadwaladr University Health Board**.

Dental Practice Board
✍   Since 2006, the Dental Services division of the **NHS Business Services Authority**.

Dental Schools Council   (DSC)
■   Woburn House, 20 Tavistock Square, LONDON, WC1H 9HD.
     Tel 020 7419 5494   Fax 020 7380 1482   http://www.dentalschoolscouncil.ac.uk
     Chairman: Prof William P Saunders
E   Established on 31 January 1931 as the Education Consultative Committee of the Dental Schools of Great Britain, it adopted it current name in 2008. The council comprises the dean (or equivalent) of each dental school in the UK.
R   To represent the interests and ambitions of UK dental schools as they relate to the generation of national health, wealth and knowledge acquisition through research and the profession of dentistry.
G   United Kingdom.
●   The DSC set up the UK Dental Schools Senior Officers Group in 2007. Membership comprises the most senior administrative staff member of each dental school.

Dental Vocational Training Authority
✍   On 31 March 2006 the DVTA was dissolved, its principal functions transferred to the **NHS Business Services Authority**.

Derby Cityscape
✍   Established on 15 July 2003 as the Urban Regeneration Company for Derby city centre. It was wound up on 1 July 2010, its functions transferred to Derby City Council.

Derbyshire Police Authority
■   Butterley Hall, RIPLEY, Derbys, DE5 3RS.
     Tel 01773 733771   http://www.derbyshire.police.co.uk/policeauthority/
     Chairman: Cllr Philip Hickson   Chief Executive: Simon Bate, OBE
E   Established in April 1995, the Authority is an independent body charged with ensuring that Derbyshire Constabulary provides an effective and efficient police service. It is made up of seven county councillors, two city councillors and eight independent members.
G   Derbyshire.
✍   For further information see **Police Authorities**.

Derbyshire Probation Trust
■   18 Brunswood Road, MATLOCK BATH, Derbys, DE4 3PA.
     Tel 01629 55422   Fax 01629 580838   http://www.dpsonline.org.uk
     Chairman: Gillian Wilmot   Chief Officer: Denise White
E   Established on 1 April 2001 under the Criminal Justice & Court Service Act 2000 as the Derbyshire Probation Area Board. It became a trust on 1 April 2010 under the Offender Management Act 2007. The Board comprises ten members including the Chairman.
G   Derbyshire.
✍   For further information see **Probation Trusts**.

Design Commission for Wales   (DCfW)
■   4th Floor Building 2, Caspian Point, Caspian Way, CARDIFF BAY, CF10 4DQ.
     Tel 029 2045 1964   Fax 029 2045 1958   http://www.dcfw.org
     Chairman: Alan Francis   Chief Executive: Carole-Anne Davies
E   Established in 2002. DCfW functions as a NDPB of the National Assembly for Wales. It comprises six Commissioners including the Chairman.

R   To champion high standards of architecture, landscape and urban design in Wales, promoting wider understanding of the importance of good quality in the built environment, supporting skill building, encouraging social inclusion and sustainable development.

G   Wales.

✍   One of four UK Commissions established to champion good design and a high quality built environment.

=   Comisiwn Dylunio Cymru

Design Council

■   34 Bow Street, LONDON, WC2E 7DL.
Tel 020 7420 5200   **Fax** 020 7420 5300   http://www.designcouncil.org.uk
Chairman: Lord Bichard   Chief Executive: David Kester

E   Established by the Government in 1944 as the Council of Industrial Design, a a grant-aided body sponsored by the then Board of Trade; the Council adopted its present title on 1 April 1972 and was incorporated by Royal Charter on 19 May 1976. It now functions as an Executive NDPB of the Department for Business, Innovation & Skills. The Council comprises eleven members including the Chairman.

R   To promote the use of design throughout the UK's businesses and public services.

G   United Kingdom.

✍   On 14 October 2010 the Government announced that the Design Council should cease to function as a NDPB and will seek to establish it as an independent charity, subject to Privy Council agreement.

Deveron, Bogie & Isla Rivers Charitable Trust   See **Rivers & Fisheries Trusts of Scotland**.

Devon & Cornwall Police Authority

■   PO Box 229, EXETER, Devon, EX2 5YT.
Tel 01392 268333   **Fax** 01392 268330   http://www.dcpa.police.uk
Chairman: Mike Bull   Chief Executive: Sue Howl

E   Established in April 1995, the Authority is an independent body charged with ensuring that Devon & Cornwall Constabulary provides an effective and efficient police service. It is made up of ten councillor members (from Devon and Cornwall County Councils, Plymouth City Council, Torbay Council and the Council for the Isles of Scilly) and nine independent members.

G   Cornwall (including the Isles of Scilly) and Devon (including Plymouth and Torbay).

✍   For further information see **Police Authorities**.

Devon & Cornwall Probation Trust

■   Queen's House, Little Queen Street, EXETER, Devon, EX4 3LJ.
Tel 01392 474100   **Fax** 01392 413563   http://www.dcpa.co.uk
Chairman: Alan Wooderson   Chief Officer: Rob Menary

E   Established on 1 April 2001 under the Criminal Justice & Court Service Act 2000 as the Devon & Cornwall Probation Area Board. It became a trust on 1 April 2010 under the Offender Management Act 2007. The Board comprises up to 15 members including the Chairman.

G   Cornwall (including the Isles of Scilly) and Devon (including Plymouth and Torbay).

✍   For further information see **Probation Trusts**.

Diplomatic Service Appeal Board   (DSAB)

■   Old Admiralty Building, LONDON, SW1A 2PA.
Tel 020 7008 1500

E   Established in 1996. DSAB functions as an Advisory NDPB of the Foreign & Commonwealth Office. The Board comprises eight members including the Chairman.

R   To advise the Secretary of State in the event of appeals from Diplomatic Service officers against premature retirement, termination of an appointment on the grounds of failed probation, or dismissal on any grounds.

G   United Kingdom.

✍   The Foreign & Commonwealth Office announced on 14 October 2010 that it was reviewing and exploring options on the future of DSAB.

Directly Operated Railways Ltd   (DOR)

■   4th Floor, One Kemble Street, LONDON, WC2B 4AN.
Tel 020 7904 5043   http://www.directlyoperatedrailways.co.uk
Chief Executive: Elaine Holt

E   Established in July 2009 under the Railways Act 1993 as amended by the Transport Act 2000 and the Railways Act 2005. DOR functions as holding company set up by the Department for Transport. East Coast Main Line Company Limited is its wholly owned subsidiary.

R   To secure the continued provision of passenger railway services should an existing franchise not be able to complete its full term.
G   United Kingdom.
●   To operate, through its subsidiary East Coast Main Line Company Ltd, the East Coast rail franchise after default of the previous private franchise holder.

Director of Public Prosecutions   See **Crown Prosecution Service**.

Disability & Carers Service
✍   Merged in 2008 with the Pension Service to form the **Pension, Disability & Carers Service**.

Disability Employment Advisory Committee
✍   DEAC closed on 30 November 2010 as part of the Government's commitment to increase the transparency and accountability of public services. **Equality 2025** (qv) has a remit to advise on issues affecting disabled people and is available to provide Government with advice on disability employment issues.

Disability Living Allowance Advisory Board   (DLAAB)
■   1st Floor Zone C, Caxton House, 6-12 Tothill Street, LONDON, SW1H 9NA.
     Tel 020 7449 5288   **Fax** 020 7449 5467
     Chairman: Mrs Anne Spaight, MBE, MA, MCSP
E   Established on 6 April 1992 under the Disability Living Allowance & Disability Working Allowance Act 1991. DLAAB functions as a Scientific Advisory Council and an Advisory NDPB of the Department for Work & Pensions. The Board comprises the Chairman and between eleven and 20 other members.
R   To give advice to the Secretary of State on such matters as he may refer to them for consideration.
     To give medical advice to Medical Services doctors, on any case or question which they refer to the Board.
G   England, Scotland, Wales.
✍   The Government announced on 14 October 2010 that DLAAB will be disbanded. Its functions will be shared between the Department for Work & Pensions, with external specialist advice if required, and **Equality 2025** (qv).

Disability Living Allowance Advisory Board for Northern Ireland   (DLAAB)
■   Castle Court, Royal Avenue, BELFAST, BT1 1DS.
     Tel 028 9033 6916
     Chairman: Stanley Millar, MBE, JP   Secretary: Dr Martin Donnelly
E   Established on 21 October 1991 under the Disability Living Allowance & Disability Working Allowance (Northern Ireland) Order 1991. DLAAB functions as an Advisory NDPB of the Department for Social Development Northern Ireland. The Board comprises 14 members including the Chairman.
R   To give advice to the Department of Social Development on matters as it may refer.
     To give advice to Medical Officers of the Department dealing with Disability Living Allowance or Attendance Allowance on any cases or questions which they refer to the Board.
G   Northern Ireland.

Disability Rights Commission
✍   On 1 October replaced by the **Equality & Human Rights Commission**.

Disability Wales
■   Bridge House, Caerphilly Business Park, Van Road, CAERPHILLY, CF83 3GW.
     Tel 029 2088 7325   **Fax** 029 2088 8702   http://www.disabilitywales.org
     Chairman: Wendy Ashton   Chief Executive: Rhian Davies
E   Founded in 1972 as part of the Council of Social Service for Wales, it became an autonomous registered charity in April 1977. It is a membership organisation of disabled groups and allies across Wales. The Board of Directors comprises 13 members including the Chairman.
R   To influence policy development at local, national and international level on various policy initiatives which affect the lives of disabled people, for example, employment and skills, health and social care, transport, and housing.
G   Wales.
=   Anabledd Cymru

Disabled Living Centres Council
✍ See **Assist UK**.

Disabled Persons Transport Advisory Committee   (DPTAC)
■ 2/23 Great Minster House, 76 Marsham Street, LONDON, SW1P 4DR.
   Tel 020 7944 8011   **Fax** 020 7944 6998   http://www.dptac.independent.gov.uk
   Chairman: Dai Powell, OBE
E Established in 1986 under the Transport Act 1985. DPTAC functions as a Scientific Advisory Committee and an
   Executive NDPB of the Department for Transport. The Committee comprises 19 members including the
   Chairman.
R To advise the Government on the transport needs of disabled people.
G United Kingdom.
✍ The Government announced on 14 October 2010 that DPTAC will be disbanded. The Department for Transport is
   exploring options for continuing to gain the disability advice it needs through a more flexible, accountable
   structure.

Disasters Emergency Committee   (DEC)
■ 1st Floor, 43 Chalton Street, LONDON, NW1 1DU.
   Tel 020 7387 0200   **Fax** 020 7387 2050   http://www.dec.org.uk
   Chairman: Mike Walsh
E Established in 1963. The DEC is the umbrella organisation for 13 humanitarian aid agencies and functions as a
   registered charity and company limited by guarantee. The board of trustees comprises the chief executive of
   each member agency plus up to four independent trustees, an honorary treasurer and the Chairman.
R To bring together, at times of overseas emergencies, a unique alliance of the UK's aid, corporate, public and
   broadcasting sectors to rally the nation's compassion.
   To ensure that funds raised go to DEC agencies best placed to deliver effective and timely relief to people most
   in need.
G United Kingdom.
● The 13 member agencies are:
   ActionAid, British Red Cross, CAFOD, CARE International UK, Christian Aid, Concern Worldwide, Help the Aged,
   Islamic Relief, Merlin, Oxfam, Save the Children, Tearfund and Worldvision.

Disposal Services Agency   (DSA)
■ H Site Building 9 Room 16, Ploughley Lane, Lower Arncott, BICESTER, Oxon, OX25 2LD.
   Tel 01869 256866   **Fax** 01869 258606   http://www.edisposals.com
   Head of Disposal Services: Commodore Paul Cunningham, RN
E Established on 3 October 1994 as the Disposal Sales Agency. On 1 April 2005 it became part of the former
   Defence Logistics Organisation and since 1 April 2007 is part of Defence Equipment & Supplies (qv).
R To secure the best return to the UK taxpayer from the sale of surplus equipment and stores held by the Ministry
   of Defence and other Government departments.
G United Kingdom.

Distilling Industry Training Committee
■ 20 Atholl Crescent, EDINBURGH, EH3 8HF.
   Tel 0131 222 9200   **Fax** 0131 222 9210
   Chairman: Peter Nelson
E Established in 1991.
R To be the awarding body for the Spirits Industry Vocational Qualification (SIVQ).
G United Kingdom.

Distinction & Meritorious Service Awards Committee   (DMSAC)
■ Room D1/17, Castle Buildings, Stormont Estate, BELFAST, BT4 3SJ.
   Tel 028 9052 0500
E Established in 1949 under the Health Services (Northern Ireland) Act 1948 by the then Northern Ireland Hospitals
   Authority. DMSAC functions as an Advisory NDPB of the Department of Health, Social Services & Public Safety
   Northern Ireland.
R To advise the DHSSPS as to which consultants employed by the Health and Social Services should receive
   awards for professional distinction having regard to the number of awards available for allocation.
G Northern Ireland.

Distributed Generation Co-ordination Group
✍ The DCGC was succeeded by the **Electricity Networks Strategy Group** in July 2008.

District Audit   see **Audit Commission for Local Authorities in England & Wales**

DISTRICT SALMON FISHERY BOARDS   (DSFBs)

E   Scotland is divided into 54 statutory salmon fishery districts, each comprising the catchment area of a river or group of rivers.

District Salmon Fishery Boards were established in the mid 1800s under various Acts now consolidated in the Salmon & Freshwater Fisheries (Consolidation) (Scotland) Act 2003. The Boards finance the cost of local administration, protection and improvement of the fisheries by levying a rate on the salmon fishery owners in the district.

The core membership of a DSFB is the elected representatives of the owners. In 1986 membership was extended to include representatives of salmon anglers and salmon netsmen. In 1999 membership was further extended to representatives of the Scottish Environment Protection Agency, Scottish Natural Heritage (qqv) and other bodies such as local angling clubs.

The Association of Salmon Fishery Boards was established in 1932 to represent the interests of the DSFBs. It can be contacted at:

CBC House, 24 Canning Street, EDINBURGH, EH3 8EG.
Tel 0131 272 2797   **Fax** 0131 272 2800

Dorset Community Action

■   Community House, The Barracks, Bridport Road, DORCHESTER, Dorset, DT1 1YG.
Tel 01305 250921   **Fax** 01305 216420   http://www.dorsetcommunityaction.org.uk
Chairman: Sam Field   Chief Executive: Steve Place

E   Dorset Community Action functions as a registered charity and company limited by guarantee. The Board comprises up to 15 Trustees including the Chairman.

R   To encourage and support the interests of local communities, in consultation, transport, community facilities, regeneration, sustainable living and social issues.

G   Dorset.

✍   Dorset Community Action is one of the 38 Rural Community Councils, represented at the national level by **Action with Communities in Rural England** (qv) and at the regional level by South West ACRE Network (SWAN).

Dorset Police Authority   (DPA)

■   Winfrith, DORCHESTER, Dorset, DT2 8DZ.
Tel 01305 223966   **Fax** 01305 223967   http://www.dpa.police.uk
Chairman: Michael Taylor, CBE, DL

E   Established in April 1995, the Authority is an independent body charged with ensuring that Dorset Police provide an effective and efficient police service. It is made up of nine councillor members and eight independent members.

G   Dorset

✍   For further information see **Police Authorities**.

Dorset Probation Trust

■   Forelle House, Marshes End, Upton Road, POOLE, Dorset, BH17 7AG.
Tel 01202 664060   **Fax** 01202 664061   http://www.dorset-probation.gov.uk
Chairman: Mary Fielding   Chief Officer: John Wiseman

E   Established on 1 April 2001 under the Criminal Justice & Court Service Act 2000 as the Dorset Probation Area Board. It became a trust on 1 April 2010 under the Offender Management Act 2007. The Board comprises six members including the Chairman.

G   Dorset.

✍   For further information see **Probation Trusts**.

Dorset & Somerset Strategic Health Authority
✍   On 1 July 2006 merged with the Avon, Gloucestershire & Wiltshire and the South West Peninsular Strategic Health Authorities to form the **South West Strategic Health Authority**.

Dover Harbour Board

- Harbour House, Marine Parade, DOVER, Kent, CT17 9BU.
  Tel 01304 240400   Fax 01304 240465   http://www.doverport.co.uk
  Chairman: Roger Mountford   Chief Executive: Dr Bob Goldfield
E   Established in 1606 by Royal Charter. The Board comprises nine members including the Chairman.
G   Dover.
✍   For further information see **Port & Harbour Authorities**.

Drainage Council for Northern Ireland   (DCNI)

- c/o Rivers Agency, Hydebank, 4 Hospital Road, BELFAST, BT8 8JP.
  Tel 028 9025 3355   Fax 028 9025 3455
  Chairman: Gerald Crawford
E   Established on 31 March 1947 under the Drainage (Northern Ireland) Act, the Council is now constituted under the Drainage (Northern Ireland) Order 1973. It functions as an Advisory NDPB of the Department of Agriculture & Rural Development Northern Ireland.
R   To advise the Rivers Agency (qv) in relation to flood defences, drainage schemes or variations to schemes.
  To decide which watercourses and sea defences should be designated for maintenance by the Rivers Agency at public expense.
G   Northern Ireland.
●   The Council also acts in a consultative capacity on the environmental assessment of proposed drainage works.
✍   Alternatively known as the Northern Ireland Drainage Council.

Dribiwlys Adolygu Iechyd Meddwi Cymru   See the **Mental Health Review Tribunal for Wales**.

Drinking Water Inspectorate   (DWI)

- Room M03, 55 Whitehall, LONDON, SW1A 2EY.
  Tel 0300 068 6400   Fax 0300 068 6401   http://www.dwi.gov.uk
  Chief Inspector: Prof Jeni Colbourne, MBE
E   Established in 1990. DWI is responsible to the Department for Environment, Food & Rural Affairs and the National Assembly for Wales.
R   To assess the quality of drinking water, taking enforcement action if standards are not being met, and appropriate action when water is unfit for human consumption.
G   England, Wales.

Drinking Water Inspectorate

- Klondyke Building, Gasworks Business Park, Lower Ormeau Road, BELFAST, BT7 2JA.
  Tel 028 9056 9291
  Chief Inspector: Margaret Herron
E   Established in April 2007 under the Water Supply (Water Quality) Regulations (Northern Ireland) 2007. The Inspectorate is part of the Northern Ireland Environment Agency (qv) and acts on behalf of the Department for Regional Development Northern Ireland for public water supplied by Northern Ireland Water (qv) and of the Department of the Environment Northern Ireland in respect of private water supplies.
R   To assess the quality of drinking water, taking enforcement action if standards are not being met, and appropriate action when water is unfit for human consumption.
G   Northern Ireland.

Drinking Water Quality Regulator for Scotland   (DWQR)

- PO Box 23598, EDINBURGH, EH6 6WW.
  Tel 0131 244 0224   Fax 0131 244 0259   http://www.dwqr.org.uk
  Regulator: Colin McLaren
E   Established under the Water Industry (Scotland) Act 2002. DWQR is responsible to the Scottish Government.
R   To enure that Scottish Water (qv) complies with its duties in respect of the quality of public drinking water supplies in Scotland.
G   Scotland.

Driver & Vehicle Agency   (DVA)

- County Hall, Castlerock Road, COLERAINE, BT51 3HS.
  Tel 028 7034 1469   Fax 028 7034 1351   http://www.dvani.gov.uk
  Chief Executive: Stanley Duncan

E   Established on 1 April 2007 through the merger of Driver & Vehicle Licencing Northern Ireland (DVLNI) and the
        Driver & Vehicle Testing Agency (DVTA). DVA functions as an Executive Agency of the Department of the
        Environment Northern Ireland.
R   To exercise overall responsibility for licensing and testing all vehicles and drivers in Northern Ireland.
G   Northern Ireland.

Driver & Vehicle Licensing Agency   (DVLA)
■   SWANSEA, SA6 7JL.
        Tel 0300 790 6801/2/6/7   http://www.dft.gov.uk/dvla
        Chief Executive: Simon Tse
E   Established on 2 April 1990. DVLA functions as an Executive Agency of the Department for Transport. The Board
        comprises the Chief Executive, five executive members and two non-executive members.
R   To facilitate road safety and general law enforcement by maintaining registers of drivers and vehicles.
        To collect vehicle excise duty (car tax).
G   England, Wales, Scotland.
●   DVLA also hosts six medical advisory panels. See **Secretary of State for Transport's Honorary Medical
        Advisory Panels** for further information.
✍   DVLA is part of the DfT's Motoring & Freight Services Group, along with the Driving Standards Agency, the
        Government Car & Despatch Agency, the Vehicle Certification Agency and the Vehicle & Operator Services
        Agency (qqv).

Driver & Vehicle Licensing Northern Ireland
✍   Merged 1 April 2007 with the Driver & Vehicle Testing Agency to form the **Driver & Vehicle Agency**.

Driver & Vehicle Testing Agency
✍   Merged 1 April 2007 with Driver & Vehicle Licensing Northern Ireland to form the **Driver & Vehicle Agency**.

Driving Standards Agency   (DSA)
■   The Axis Building, 112 Upper Parliament Street, NOTTINGHAM, NG1 6LP.
        Tel 0115 936 6666   http://www.dft.gov.uk/dsa
        Chief Executive: Rosemary Thew
E   Established on 1 April 1990. DSA functions as an Executive Agency of the Department for Transport. The board
        comprises the Chief Executive, nine executive members and two non-executive members.
R   To set the standards for pre-driver education and driver trainers.
        To register and supervise quality assured Approved Driving Instructors.
        To carry out theory and practical driving and riding tests.
        To assure the quality of all testing activity.
        To investigate cases of suspected theory test and practical test impersonations and identity fraud.
        To develop the future education and testing environment through the DSA Learning to Drive programme.
G   England, Scotland, Wales.
✍   DSA is part of the DfT's Motoring & Freight Services Group, along with the Driver & Vehicle Licensing Agency, the
        Government Car & Despatch Agency, the Vehicle Certification Agency and the Vehicle & Operator Services
        Agency (qqv).

The Duke of York's Royal Military School
✍   In September 2010 DYRMS became an Academy with military traditions responsible to the Department for
        Education.

Dumfries & Galloway Local Enterprise Company
✍   Now functions as the Dumfries office of **Scottish Enterprise**.

Dumfries & Galloway NHS Board
■   Mid North, Crichton Hall, DUMFRIES, DG1 4TG.
        Tel 01387 272702   http://www.nhsdg.scot.nhs.uk
        Chairman: Michael Keggans   Chief Executive: John Burns
G   Dumfries & Galloway.
✍   For further information see **NHS Scotland - Boards**.

Dumfries & Galloway Police Authority
✍ Six of the eight Scottish police forces are administered a police authority or joint board. Dumfries & Galloway Constabulary is directly administered by Dumfries & Galloway Council.

Dumfries & Galloway Tourist Board
✍ Since 1 April 2005 an area office pf **VisitScotland**.

Dunbartonshire Local Enterprise Company
✍ Now functions as the Clydebank office of **Scottish Enterprise**.

Durham Police Authority
■ County Hall, DURHAM, DH1 5UL.
   Tel 0191 383 3941   **Fax** 0191 383 4206   http://www.durham-pa.gov.uk
   Chairman: Peter Thompson   Chief Executive: Lesley Davies
E Established in April 1995, the Authority is an independent body charged with ensuring that Durham Constabulary provides an effective and efficient police service. It is made up of nine councillor members and eight independent members.
G County Durham.
✍ For further information see **Police Authorities**.

Durham Rural Community Council   (DRCC)
■ Park House, Station Road, LANCHESTER, Co Durham, DH7 0EX.
   Tel 01207 529621   **Fax** 01207 529619   http://www.durhamrcc.org.uk
   Chairman: Jenny Flynn, MBE   Executive Director: Jo Laverick
E Established in 1935. DRCC functions as a registered charity and company limited by guarantee. The Executive Committee comprises 14 members including the Chairman.
R To support the rural communities of County Durham.
G County Durham.
✍ DRCC is one of the 38 Rural Community Councils, represented at the national level by **Action with Communities in Rural England** (qv) and at the regional level by North East Rural Community Councils.

Durham Tees Valley Airport Consultative Committee   (DTVACC)
■ Chief Executive's Department, Hartlepool Borough Council, Civic Centre, HARTLEPOOL, TS24 8AY.
   Tel 01429 523019   **Fax** 01429 284009   http://www.durhamteesvalleyairport.com
   Secretary: David Cosgrove
G County Durham.
✍ For further information see **Airport Consultative Committees**.

Durham Tees Valley Probation Trust
■ Centre North East, 6th Floor, 73-75 Albert Road, MIDDLESBROUGH, TS1 2RU.
   Tel 01642 230533   **Fax** 01642 220083   http://www.dtvprobation.org.uk
   Chairman: Sebert Cox   Chief Officer: Russell Bruce
E Established on 1 April 2010 under the Offender Management Act 2007, merging two area boards (Durham and Teeside) which had been set up on 1 April 2001 under the Criminal Justice & Court Service Act 2000. The Board comprises nine members including the Chairman.
G County Durham, Hartlepool, Middlesbrough, Redcar-Cleveland and Stockton.
✍ For further information see **Probation Trusts**.

Dyfed-Powys Police Authority
■ PO Box 99, Llangunnor, CARMARTHEN, SA31 2PF.
   Tel 01267 226440   **Fax** 01267 226448   http://www.dyfedpowyspoliceauthority.co.uk
   Chairman: Mrs Delyth Humfryes   Chief Executive: Keith B Reeves, LLB(Hons), LLM
E Established in April 1995, the Authority is an independent body charged with ensuring that Dyfed-Powys Police provide an effective and efficient police service. It is made up of ten County Council members and nine independent members.
G Carmarthenshire, Ceredigion, Pembrokeshire and Powys.
✍ For further information see **Police Authorities**.

Dyfed Powys Probation Trust

- Llangunnor Road, CARMARTHEN, SA31 2PD.
  Tel 01267 221567 **Fax** 01267 221566 http://www.dyfedpowysprobation.org
  Chairman: Keith Turner, OstJ, QPM Chief Executive: Caroline Morgan
- E Established on 1 April 2001 under the Criminal Justice & Court Service Act 2000 as Dyfed Powys Probation Area Board, on 1 April 2008 it became a Trust under the Offender Management Act 2007. The Board comprises ten members including the Chairman.
- G Carmarthenshire, Ceredigion, Pembrokeshire and Powys.
- ✍ For further information see **Probation Area Boards**.

E

e-skills UK

- 1 Castle Lane, LONDON, SW1E 6DR.
  Tel 020 7963 8920 http://www.e-skills.com
  Chairman: Larry Hirst Chief Executive: Karen Price
- E Established on 1 April 2003. It is the recognised Sector Skills Council for information technology and telecommunications.
- G United Kingdom.
- ✍ For further information see **Sector Skills Councils**.

East of England Development Agency   (EEDA)

- Victory House, Vision Park, Chivers Way, Histon, CAMBRIDGE, CB24 9ZR.
  Tel 01223 713900 **Fax** 01223 713940 http://www.eeda.org.uk
  Chairman: Will Pope Chief Executive: Deborah Cadman, OBE
- E Established on 1 April 1999, one of the nine English Regional Development Agencies. EEDA functions as an Executive NDPB of the Department for Business, Innovation & Skills. The board comprises 15 members including the Chairman.
- G Bedfordshire, Cambridgeshire, Essex, Hertfordshire, Norfolk, Suffolk.
- ✍ The Comprehensive Spending Review in October 2010 confirmed the Government's intention to abolish the RDAs and support the creation of Local Enterprise Partnerships (qv), to be in place by March 2012.

East of England Industrial Development Board
- ✍ See note under **Industrial Development Boards**.

East of England Local Government Association

- Flempton House, Flempton, BURY ST EDMUNDS, Suffolk, IP28 6EG.
  Tel 01284 728151 **Fax** 01284 729429 http://www.eelga.gov.uk
  Chairman: Cllr Robert Gordon Lead Chief Executive: Caroline Tapster
- E Established 1 April 2010 following the abolition of the East of England Regional Assembly, EELGA is an independent membership organisation of the 52 local authorities in the region, represented by the 50 council leaders and the two elected mayors (Bedford and Watford). The Management Committee comprises five members including the Chairman.
- R To be responsible, in conjunction with the East of England Development Agency (qv), for regional strategic planning and economic development.
- G Bedfordshire, Cambridgeshire, Essex, Hertfordshire, Norfolk, Suffolk.

East of England Regional Assembly
- ✍ EERA was dissolved on 31 March 2010 (see Regional Assemblies). The region's local authority leaders cooperate as the **East of England Local Government Association**.

East of England Regional Select Committee and East of England Grand Committee See **United Kingdom Parliament: Committees**.

East of England Strategic Health Authority

- ■ Victoria House, Capital Park, Fulbourn, CAMBRIDGE, CB21 5XB.
  Tel 01223 597500   **Fax** 01223 597555   http://www.eoe.nhs.uk
  Chairman: Keith Pearson   Chief Executive: Sir Neil McKay, CBE
- E Established on 1 July 2006 replacing three former Strategic Health Authorities: the Bedfordshire & Hertfordshire, the Essex and the Norfolk, Suffolk & Cambridgeshire.
  The board comprises six non-executive directors including the Chairman, and ten executive directors including the Chief Executive.
- R To relay and explain national policy, set direction and support and develop NHS Trust bodies (Primary Care Trusts and NHS Trusts providing acute, mental health and ambulance services).
  To ensure that local health systems operate effectively and efficiently, and that national standards and priorities are met.
- G Bedfordshire, Cambridgeshire, Essex, Hertfordshire, Norfolk, Suffolk.
- ✍ One of the ten regional Strategic Health Authorities of England - see **NHS - England** in the Subject Index.

East of England Tourism   Trading name of the **East of England Tourist Board**.

East of England Tourist Board   (EETB)

- ■ Dettingen House, Dettingen Way, BURY ST EDMUNDS, Suffolk, IP33 3TU.
  Tel 01473 822922   **Fax** 01473 823063   http://www.eet.org.uk
  Chairman: Dr Derek Langslow, CBE   Chief Executive: Keith Brown
- E Established in 1971 as the East Anglia Tourist Board, before adopting its current name; it trades as **East of England Tourism** and uses the **visiteastofengland.com** brand. The Board comprises eleven members including the Chairman.
- R To promote sustainable tourism in partnership with the East of England Development Agency (qv).
- G Bedfordshire, Cambridgeshire, Essex, Hertfordshire, Norfolk, Suffolk.
- ✍ For further information see **English Regional Tourist Boards**.

East Midlands Airport Independent Consultative Committee

- ■ East Midlands Airport, Building 34, Castle Donington, DERBY, DE74 2SA.
  Tel 01332 852990   **Fax** 01332 810045   http://www.eastmidlandsairport.com
  Chairman: Barrie Whyman   Secretary: Anthea Hartshorne
- G Derbyshire, Leicestershire, Nottinghamshire.
- ✍ For further information see **Airport Consultative Committees**.

East Midlands Counties   (EMC)

- ■ Phoenix House, Nottingham Road, MELTON MOWBRAY, Leics, LE13 0UL.
  Tel 01664 502620   **Fax** 01664 502659   http://www.emcouncils.gov.uk
  Chairman: Cllr David Parsons
- E Established on 1 April 2010 following abolition of the East Midlands Regional Assembly, EMC is an independent membership organisation of the 92 local authorities in the region, represented by the 91 council leaders and the one elected mayor (Mansfield).
- R To be responsible, in conjunction with the East Midlands Development Agency (qv), for regional strategic planning and economic development.
- G Derbyshire, Leicestershire, Lincolnshire, Northamptonshire, Nottinghamshire, Rutland.

East Midlands Development Agency   (EMDA)

- ■ Apex Court, City Link, NOTTINGHAM, NG2 4LA.
  Tel 0115 988 8300   **Fax** 0115 853 3666   http://www.emda.org.uk
  Chairman: Dr Bryan Jackson, OBE   Chief Executive: Jeff Moore
- E Established on 1 April 1999, one of the nine English Regional Development Agencies. EMDA functions as an Executive NDPB of the Department for Business, Innovation & Skills. The board comprises 15 members including the Chairman.
- G Derbyshire, Leicestershire, Lincolnshire, Northamptonshire, Nottinghamshire, Rutland.
- ✍ The Comprehensive Spending Review in October 2010 confirmed the Government's intention to abolish the RDAs and support the creation of Local Enterprise Partnerships (qv), to be in place by March 2012.

East Midlands Industrial Development Board
- ✍ See note under **Industrial Development Boards**.

    © CBD Research Ltd · Beckenham · Kent BR3 5JS · Tel 020 8650 7745 · Fax 020 8650 0768 · E-mail cbd@cbdresearch.com · www.cbdresearch.com

East Midlands Regional Assembly
✐ EMRA was abolished on 31 March 2010 (see Regional Assemblies). The region's local authority leaders
    cooperate as **East Midlands Councils**.

East Midlands Regional Select Committee and East Midlands Grand Committee   See **United Kingdom
Parliament: Committees**.

East Midlands Screen Commission   See **EM-Media**.

East Midlands Strategic Health Authority

■ Octavia House, Bostocks Lane, Sandiacre, NOTTINGHAM, NG10 5QG.
   Tel 0115 968 4444   **Fax** 0115 968 4400   http://www.eastmidlands.nhs.uk
   Chairman: Sir John Brigstocke, KCB   Chief Executive: Dame Barbara Hakin
E Established on 1 July 2006 replacing two former Strategic Health Authorities: the Leicestershire,
    Northamptonshire & Rutland and the Trent.
    The board comprises six non-executive directors including the Chairman, and ten executive directors including
    the Chief Executive.
R To relay and explain national policy, set direction and support and develop NHS Trust bodies (Primary Care
    Trusts and NHS Trusts providing acute, mental health and ambulance services).
    To ensure that local health systems operate effectively and efficiently, and that national standards and priorities
    are met.
G Derbyshire, Leicestershire, Lincolnshire, Northamptonshire, Nottinghamshire, Rutland.
✐ One of the ten regional Strategic Health Authorities of England - see **NHS - England** in the Subject Index.

East Midlands Tourism

■ Apex Court, City Link, NOTTINGHAM, NG2 4LA.
   Tel 0115 988 8546   **Fax** 0115 853 3657   http://www.eastmidlandstourism.co.uk
   Chairman: Chas Bishop   Tourism Director: Ruth Hyde
E Established in 2004 following a government decision that England's Regional Development Agencies (qv) should
    take over responsibility for tourism.
    The Council comprises eleven members including the Chairman.
R To oversee the delivery of 'Destination East Midlands', the tourism strategy of the East Midlands Development
    Agency (qv), to allocate funding, and to measure the successful delivery of key targets.
G Derbyshire, Leicestershire, Lincolnshire, Northamptonshire, Nottinghamshire, Rutland.

Eastern Agricultural Land Tribunal

■ Government Buildings (Block 3), Burghill Road, Westbury-on-Trym, BRISTOL, BS10 6NJ.
   Tel 0117 959 8648   **Fax** 0117 959 8605
   Secretary: Tony Collins
G Bedfordshire, Cambridgeshire, Essex, Hertfordshire, Lincolnshire, Norfolk, Northamptonshire, Suffolk, London
    Boroughs north of the River Thames (except Richmond upon Thames).
✐ For further information see **Agricultural Land Tribunals**. The office is expected to relocate in 2011.

Eastern Health & Social Services Board
✐ On 1 April 2009 the four regional boards were replaced by a single **Health & Social Care Board** for Northern
    Ireland.

Eastern Health & Social Services Council
✐ On 1 April 2009 the four regional councils were replaced by a single **Patient & Client Council** for Northern
    Ireland.

Eastern Rent Assessment Panel   (ERAP)

■ Unit 4C Queen House, Mill Court, Great Shelford, CAMBRIDGE, CB22 5LD.
   Tel 01223 841524   **Fax** 01223 843224
   Secretary: Ann Oates
G Bedfordshire, Buckinghamshire, Cambridgeshire, Essex, Hertfordshire, Norfolk, Northamptonshire, Oxfordshire,
    Suffolk.
✐ For further information on the five regional panels see **Rent Assessment Panels** [England].

Eastern Traffic Commissioner   See **Traffic Commissioners**.

Ecclesiastical Committee   See **United Kingdom Parliament: Committees**.

ECONOMIC DEVELOPMENT COMPANIES   (EDCs)

E   Promoted by the Government in 2007, initially as City Development Companies, EDCs are local authority wide or cover a group of local authorities within a local area or sub region. They are not limited, as were Urban Regeneration Companies (qv), to certain sites or zones, nor to regeneration programmes. EDCs are not established or mandated by Government, have no statutory powers and bring with them no additional resources or tools for intervention. The companies are driven and shaped by Local Authorities in conjunction with other partners which may include the Homes & Communities (qv), and the Government.

R   To drive economic growth and regeneration within a determined urban, rural or coastal area or sub region, focusing on areas of deprivation.

G   England.

●   Several EDCs (see Subject Index for list) were formerly established as Urban Redevelopment Companies.

✍   The 2010 Coalition Government's proposed model to bring together local authorities and businesses to promote local economic development is the Local Enterprise Partnership (qv).

Economic Research Council   (ERC)

■   Baker Tilly, 65 Kingsway, LONDON, WC2B 6TD.
      Tel 020 7439 0271   http://www.ercouncil.org
      Chairman: Damon de Laszlo   Chief Executive: Dan Lewis

E   Established in 1943 as the Joint Council for Economic & Monetary Research. ERC is a registered charity. The Executive Committee comprises twelve members including the Chairman.

R   To be the UK's leading independent think tank and hub institution promoting high quality economic ideas and debate.

Economic Research Institute of Northern Ireland   (ERINI)

■   Floral Buildings, 2-14 East Bridge Street, BELFAST, BT1 5HB.
      Tel 028 9072 7350   **Fax** 028 9031 9003   http://www.erini.ac.uk
      Chairman: Prof John Beath

E   Established on 12 January 2004 following the merger of the Northern Economic Council & the Northern Ireland Economic Research Centre. ERINI functions as an Executive NDPB of the Office of the First Minister & Deputy First Minister in Northern Ireland. The Board comprises the Chairman & 13 other members.

R   To provide, for the public benefit, good quality, independent economic research and analyses and advice aimed at challenging and developing public policy making and strategic thinking on the issues facing Northern Ireland society.

G   Northern Ireland.

✍   For further information see companion volume**Centres, Bureaux and Research Institutes**.

Economic & Social Research Council   (ESRC)

■   Polaris House, North Star Avenue, SWINDON, Wilts, SN2 1UJ.
      Tel 01793 413000   **Fax** 01793 413001   http://www.esrc.ac.uk
      Chairman: Dr Alan Gillespie   Chief Executive: Prof Paul Boyle

E   Established by Royal Charter on 1 December 1965 as the Social Science Research Council, under the Science & Technology Act 1965; it adopted its present title on 3 January 1984. ESRC functions as an independent NDPB accountable to the Department for Business, Innovation & Skills. The Council comprises 14 members including the Chairman.

R   To promote and support, by any means, high-quality basic, strategic and applied research and related postgraduate training in the social sciences.

G   United Kingdom.

✍   For further information see **Research Councils UK**.

Edexcel

■   190 High Holborn, LONDON, WC1V 7BH.
      Tel 0844 844 0655   http://www.edexcel.com
      Chairman: Martin Cross, MA, FCIS, FCIPD, MCMI, FRSA   Managing Director: Ziggy Liaquat

E   Established in 1996 as a result of a merger between the Business & Technology Education Council (BTEC) and the University of London Examinations & Assessment Council (ULEAC). The Board comprises seven members including the Chairman.

R   To promote, develop and encourage the advancement of education and to be the UK's leading provider of qualifications and support across the national framework, thereby stimulating and recognising individual achievement.

G   United Kingdom.

●   Edexcel is an awarding body for courses and qualifications in a wide variety of subjects.

✍   A member of the **Joint Council for Qualifications** (qv).

EDI plc

■   International House, Siskin Parkway East, Middlemarch Business Park, COVENTRY, CV3 4PE.
     Tel 024 7651 6500   **Fax** 024 7651 6505   http://www.ediplc.com
     Chairman: Richard Price   Chief Executive: Nigel Snook

E   Established in April 2000 as GOAL plc, becoming Education Development International plc in December 2002 through merger with the London Chamber of Commerce & Industry Examinations Board. It acquired Qualifications for Industry Ltd in 2005 and the Joint Examining Board in 2006. EDI is an accredited awarding body of a wide range of vocational and professional courses and qualifications. The Board of Directors comprises six members including the Chairman.

R   To produce a wide range of products and services including vocational and professional qualifications both within the UK and internationally through the London Chamber of Commerce & Industry, GOAL online asessments for schools, approved training programmes for employers, an electronic assessment delivery system, electronic portfolio package and specialist business broadband package.

G   United Kingdom.

✍   For more information of awarding bodies see the Federation of Awarding Bodies.

Edinburgh Airport Consultative Committee   (EACC)

■   BAA Edinburgh Airport, EDINBURGH, EH12 9DN.
     Tel 0131 344 3151   **Fax** 0131 344 4108   http://www.ukaccs.info/edinburgh
     Chairman: Alastair O'Neil   Secretary: Tom Wright

G   Edinburgh.

✍   For further information see **UK Airport Consultative Committees**.

Edinburgh & Lothian Local Enterprise Company

✍   Now functions as the Edinburgh office of **Scottish Enterprise**.

Edinburgh & Lothians Tourist Board

✍   Since 1 April 2005 an area office of **VisitScotland**.

Education & Learning Wales

✍   ELWa was the umbrella body for the **Higher Education Funding Council for Wales** and the National Council for Education & Training in Wales. The functions of the latter and ELWa have been transfreed to the Welsh Government.

EDUCATION & LIBRARY BOARDS

E   Education & Library Boards were established in 1973 under the Education & Libraries (Northern Ireland) Order 1973.

R   Each Board is the Local Education Authority and Library Authority. Their role is one of establishing general systems, both practical and advisory, to support schools and colleges. Their duties include ensuring that there are sufficient schools of all kinds to meet the educational needs of their areas and they are wholly responsible for the schools under their management. They are also required to deliver a comprehensive and efficient library service for their areas.

●   The five boards are the Belfast, North Eastern, South Eastern, Southern and Western Education & Library Boards (qqv).

✍   The ELBs and other legacy organisations will be dissolved when the Education & Skills Authority (qv) becomes fully operational.

Education Otherwise

■   PO Box 7420, LONDON, N9 9SG.
     Tel 0870 730 0074   http://www.education-otherwise.org

E   Established as a UK-based membership organisation.

R   To provide support for parents whose children are being educated outside school, & for those who wish to uphold proper responsibility for the education of their children.

Education & Skills Authority   (ESA)

■   Forestview, Purdy's Lane, BELFAST, BT8 7AR.
    Tel 028 9069 4964   **Fax** 028 9069 4979   http://www.esani.org.uk
    Chairman: Seán Hogan   Chief Executive Designate: Gavin Boyd

E   Was to have been established on 1 April 2009; the organisations it is to merge are still 'converging''. The ESA Implementation Team, set up in summer 2006, functions as an Executive NDPB of the Department of Education Northern Ireland.

R   To monitor school performance and raise standards.
    To provide high quality services for children and young people.
    To develop the school curriculum and assessment methodologies; to set, moderate and mark examinations and award qualifications.
    To be responsible for the strategic planning of schools and youth services; to develop a new service for the procurement, delivery and maintenance of the education estate.
    To deliver a range of operational services to schools, including transport, meals, cleaning and caretaking; and a range of services to support students/pupils such as awards, grants and benefits.

G   Northern Ireland.

✍   The Authority will absorb the functions of:
        Comhairle na Gaelscolaíochta
        Council for Catholic Maintained Schools
        Council for the Curriculum, Examinations & Assessment
        Education & Library Boards
        Northern Ireland Council for Integrated Education
        Staff Commission for Education & Library Boards
        Youth Council for Northern Ireland

Education & Training Inspectorate   (ETI)

■   Rathgael House, 43 Balloo Road, BANGOR, Co Down, BT19 7PR.
    Tel 028 9127 9726   **Fax** 028 9127 9721   http://www.etini.gov.uk
    Chief Inspector: Stanley J Goudie

E   Established in 1832, the Inspectorate's work was extended to include the training service in Northern Ireland in January 1989. ETI is responsible to the Northern Ireland Departments of Culture, Arts & Leisure, of Education, and of Employment & Learning.

R   To inspect and report on the quality of education and training.

G   Northern Ireland.

Egg Marketing Inspectorate

✍   Egg Margeting Inspectors are now fully integrated into the **Animal Health & Veterinary Laboratories Agency**.

Eglwysi Ynghyd yng Nghymru   See **Cytûn**.

The Electoral Commission

■   Trevelyan House, 30 Great Peter Street, LONDON, SW1P 2HW.
    Tel 020 7271 0500   **Fax** 020 7271 0505   http://www.electoralcommission.org.uk
    Chairman: Jenny Watson   Chief Executive: Peter Wardle

E   Established on 1 November 2000 by the UK Parliament, the Commission's functions and powers are set out in the Political Parties, Elections & Referendums Act, 2000. It functions as an independent body. The Commission comprises ten members including the Chairman.

R   To register political parties.
    To make sure people understand and follow the rules on party and election finance.
    To publish details of where parties and candidates get money from and how they spend it.
    To set the standards for running elections and report on how well this is done.
    To make sure people understand it is important to register to vote, and know how to vote.
    To make sure boundary arrangements for local government in England are fair.

G   United Kingdom.

✍   The Commission has a further four regional offices in England, and one each in Scotland, Wales and Northern Ireland.
    See also **Boundary Committee for England**.

© CBD Research Ltd · Beckenham · Kent BR3 5JS · Tel 020 8650 7745 · Fax 020 8650 0768 · E-mail cbd@cbdresearch.com · www.cbdresearch.com

Electrical & Electronics Servicing Training Council   (EESTC)

- ■   Retra House, 1 Ampthill Street, BEDFORD, MK42 9EY.
      Tel 01234 269110   http://www.eestc.co.uk
- E   Established in 1991
- R   To develop national occupational standards for the consumer electronics and domestic electrical appliance
      servicing industries.
- G   United Kingdom.

Electrical Training Trust   (ETT)

- ■   57-59 Ballymena Business Centre, 62 Fenaghy Road, BALLYMENA, Co Antrim, BT42 1FL.
      Tel 028 2565 0750   **Fax** 028 2563 0725   http://www.ett-ni.org
      Chief Executive: Derek Thompson
- E   Established in 1994. ETT is a recognised Sector Training Council for the electrical contracting industry.
- R   To provide an adequate and cost effective training organisation and respond quickly and effectively to any
      training need.
- G   Northern Ireland.
- ✎   For further information see **Sector Training Councils**.

Electricity Training Association

- ✎   See note under **Sector Skills Councils**.

Electronics Examination Board

- ✎   EEB was wound up in 2005.

EM Media

- ■   Antenna Media Centre, Beck Street, NOTTINGHAM, NG1 1EQ.
      Tel 0115 993 2333   http://www.em-media.org.uk
      Chairman: Lisa Opie   Chief Executive: Debbie Williams
- E   Established in 2002 as the East Midlands Screen Commission. The Board comprises eleven members including
      the Chairman.
- G   Derbyshire, Leicestershire, Lincolnshire, Northamptonshire, Nottinghamshire, Rutland.
- ✎   For further information see **Creative England** and **Regional Screen Agencies**.

Employers' Organisation for Local Government   (EOLG)

- ■   Local Government House, Smith Square, LONDON, SW1P 3HZ.
      Tel 020 7664 3000   **Fax** 020 7664 3030   http://www.lge.gov.uk
      Chairman: Sir Steve Bullock
- E   Established on 1 April 1999 by the Local Government Associaton. EOLG operates under the business name
      Local Government Employers (LGE). The Board comprises eleven members including the Chairman.
- R   To provide national support to local authorities, as employers, in relation to national negotiations on the pay and
      conditions of local government employees.
- G   England, Wales.

Employment Appeal Tribunal   (EAT)

- ■   Audit House, 58 Victoria Embankment, LONDON, EC4Y 0DS.
      Tel 020 7273 1041   **Fax** 020 7273 1045
      52 Melville Street, EDINBURGH, EH3 7HF.
      Tel 0131 225 3963   **Fax** 0131 220 6694
      President: The Hon Mr Justice Underhill   Registrar: Pauline Dunleavy
- E   Established in 1996 under the Employment Tribunals Act 1996 and the Employment Appeal Tribunal Rules 1993
      (as amended). EAT functions as a Tribunal NDPB of the Department for Business, Innovation & Skills.
- R   To hear appeals on decisions made by the Employment Tribunals (qv), also on those made by the Certification
      Officer and the Central Arbitration Committee (qv).
- G   England, Wales, Scotland.
- ✎   Administrative support is provided by HM Courts & Tribunal Service (qv).

Employment Medical Advisory Service   (EMAS)

- ■   Rose Court, 2 Southwark Bridge, LONDON, SE1 9HS.
      Tel 020 7556 2100   **Fax** 020 7556 2102

E   Established in 1974 under the Employment Medical Advisory Service Act 1972. EMAS is an advisory body within the Health & Safety Executive (qv).

R   To provide an expert, independent and consistent service to a wide range of organisations and people by investigating complaints and concerns of ill health raised by employers under the Reporting of Injuries, Diseases & Dangerous Occurrences Regulations 1985.

     To help other HSA inspectors and local authorities make sure that people comply with health and safety law.

     To provide expert advice to other doctors and nurses, in general health care and occupational health.

G   England, Scotland, Wales.

●   The service has 17 offices in England, three in Scotland and two in Wales.

Employment Tribunals

■   102 Petty France, LONDON, SW1H 9AJ.
     Tel 0845 747 4747

E   Established in 1996 under the Industrial Tribunals Act 1996 and until 1998 known as Industrial Tribunals.

R   To deal with matters of employment law, redundancy, dismissal, contract disputes, discrimination on the grounds of sex, race and disability and related areas of dispute which may arise in the workplace.

G   England, Scotland, Wales.

●   England is covered by 20 hearing centres, Scotland by four and Wales by one.

✍   Administrative support is provided by HM Courts & Tribunals Service (qv).

EMTA Awards Ltd   (EAL)

■   14 Upton Road, WATFORD, Herts, WD18 0JT.
     Tel 01923 652400   **Fax** 01923 652401   http://www.eal.org.uk
     Chairman: Stephen Tilsley

E   Established in 1964 as the Engineering Industry Training Board. EAL is an awarding body for courses and qualifications in engineering and technology. It supports Sector Skills Councils: Semta, ConstructionSkills and SummitSkills (qqv).

G   United Kingdom.

✍   For further information on awarding bodies see the **Federation of Awarding Bodies**.

Energy Action Scotland   (EAS)

■   Suite 4a, Ingram House, 227 Ingram Street, GLASGOW, G1 1DA.
     Tel 0141 226 3064   **Fax** 0141 221 2788   http://www.eas.org.uk
     Director: Norman Kerr

E   Established in 1983, EAS functions as a charity, grant-aided by the Scottish Government.

R   To raise awareness of fuel poverty, particularly as it affects low income households.

     To identify effective solutions which can transform cold, damp homes into warm, dry homes.

G   Scotland.

Energy Networks Strategy Group   (ENSG)

■   9 Millbank, LONDON, SW1P 3GE.   http://www.ensg.gov.uk
     Joint Chairmen: Jonathan Brearley (DECC) and Stuart Cook (Ofgem)

E   Established in July 2008 as a joint working group of the Department of Energy & Climate Change and Ofgem. The Group comprises 17 members including the Chairmen.

R   To bring together key stakeholders in electricity networks that work together to support government in meeting the long-term energy challenges of tackling climate change and ensuring secure, clean and affordable energy.

G   United Kingdom.

Energy Ombudsman

■   PO Box 966, WARRINGTON, Cheshire, WA4 9DF.
     Tel 01925 530263   **Fax** 01925 530264   http://www.enso.org.uk
     Acting Chairman: Julian Anderton   Ombudsman with lead responsibility for energy complaints: Dr Richard Sills

E   Established on 1 July 2006 as the Energy Supply Ombudsman, adopting its current name on 1 April 2008. It is the sole provider of redress in the energy industry under the Consumer, Estate Agents and Redress Act 2007. The Council comprises nine members including the Chairman.

R   To resolve disagreements between gas and electricity companies and their domestic and small business customers.

G   United Kingdom.

✍   The Energy Ombudsman is run by Ombudsman Services (qv).

Energy Saving Trust

- 21 Dartmouth Street, LONDON, SW1H 9BP.
  Tel 020 7222 0101   Fax 020 7654 2460   http://www.energysavingtrust.org.uk
  Chairman: Edward Hyams   Chief Executive: Philip Sellwood
- E   Established in 1993 by the Government. The Trust functions as a non-profit organisation funded by both the private sector and Government. The board of Directors comprises 13 members including the Chairman.
- R   To cut carbon emissions by promoting the sustainable and efficient use of energy, water conservation and waste reduction.
- G   United Kingdom.
- ●   The Trust also has offices in Belfast, Cardiff and Edinburgh, and advice centres in many parts of the UK (Tel 0800 512012).

Energy & Utility Skills

- Friars Gate, 1011 Stratford Road, Shirley, SOLIHULL, W Midlands, B90 4BN.
  Tel 0845 077 9922   Fax 0845 077 9933   http://www.euskills.co.uk
  Chairman: Jack Carnell, PhD   Chief Executive: Tim Balcon
- E   Established on 1 December 2003. It is the recognised Sector Skills Council for the gas, power, waste management and water industries. The board comprises 16 members including the Chairman.
- G   United Kingdom.
- ✍   For further information see **Sector Skills Councils**.

energywatch

- ✍   On 1 October 2008 energywatch (the Gas & Electricity Consumer Council), with others, was replaced by **Consumer Focus**.

Enforcement Liaison Group   (ELG)

- Aviation House, 125 Kingsway, LONDON, WC2B 6NH.
  Tel 020 7276 8000
  Chairman: Sarah Appleby
- E   Established in May 1999 as the Local Authority Enforcement Liaison Group, it adopted its present name in November 2001. It functions as an advisory committee of the Food Standards Agency (qv). The Group comprises 28 members including the Chairman.
- R   To strengthen and develop the FSA's links with local authority food law enforcement.
- G   United Kingdom.

Engineering Construction Industry Training Board   (ECITB)

- Blue Court, Church Lane, KINGS LANGLEY, Bucks, WD4 8JP.
  Tel 01923 260000   Fax 01923 270969   http://www.ecitb.org.uk
  Chairman: Terry Lazenby, MBE
  Chief Executive: David Edwards
- E   Established in 1991. ECITB functions as an Executive NDPB of the Department for Business, Innovation & Skills. The Management Board comprises seven members including the Chairman.
- R   To help employers by ensuring that there are, and will be in the future, enough trained people to meet the needs of the construction industry.
- G   England, Wales, Scotland.
- ●   The Board provides training opportunities and grants for training to new entrants and experienced people across a wide range of disciplines.

Engineering Council

- Weston House, 246 High Holborn, LONDON, WC1V 7EX.
  Tel 020 3206 0500   Fax 020 3206 0501   http://www.engc.org.uk
  Director: Prof Kel Fidler, FREng   Chief Executive: Jon Prichard
- E   Established in January 2002 from the separation of the regulatory and promotional functions of the former Engineering Council established in 1982 (see EngineeringUK). The Board of Trustees comprises 22 members including the Chairman.
- R   To set and maintain internationally recognised standards of professional competence and ethics for the engineering profession.
  To maintain the national registers of Chartered Engineers, Incorporated Engineers, Engineering Technicians and Information & Communication Technology Technicians.
- G   United Kingdom.

Engineering & Physical Sciences Research Council   (EPSRC)

■   Polaris House, North Star Avenue, SWINDON, Wilts, SN2 1ET.
     Tel 01793 444000   http://www.eprsc.ac.uk
     Chairman: John Armitt, CBE, FREng, FICE   Chief Executive: Prof David Delpy, FRS
E   Established under the Science & Technology Act 1995 and by Royal Charter, replacing the former Science &
     Engineering Research Council. EPSRC functions as an independent NDPB accountable to the Department for
     Business, Innovation & Skills. The Council comprises 17 members including the Chairman.
R   To promote and support, by any means, high quality basic, strategic and applied research and related
     postgraduate training in engineering and the physical sciences.
     To advance knowledge and technology, and provide trained scientists and engineers, which meet the needs of
     users and beneficiaries, thereby contributing to the economic competitiveness of the UK and the quality of life.
G   United Kingdom.
✍   For further information see **Research Councils UK**.

Engineering & Technology Board   See **EngineeringUK**.

Engineering Training Council NI   (ETC NI)

■   Interpoint, 20-24 York Street, BELFAST, BT15 1AQ.
     Tel 028 9032 9878   http://www.etcni.org.uk
     Chairman: John Cochrane   Chief Executive: Bill Brown
E   Established in July 1990. ETC NI is a recognised Sector Training Council for the engineering industry.
R   To identify skill requirements and training needs of the industry.
     To represent the industry's training interest to the Government.
     To promote initiatives such as National Vocational Qualifications, Investors in People and Modern
     Apprenticeships.
     To promote engineering as a career to young people by providing information and advice to schools, career
     advisors and directly to young people and their parents.
G   Northern Ireland.
✍   For further information see **Sector Training Councils**.

EngineeringUK

■   Weston House, 246 High Holborn, LONDON, WC1V 7EX.
     Tel 020 3206 0400   Fax 020 3206 0401   http://www.engineeringuk.com
     Chairman: Sir Anthony Cleaver   Chief Executive: Paul Jackson
E   Established in January 2002 from the separation of the regulatory and promotional functions of the former
     Engineering Council established in 1982 (see the current Engineering Council). EngineeringUK is the working
     name of the **Engineering & Technology Board**. It functions as a company limited by guarantee and a
     registered charity. The Board comprises 17 members including the Chairman.
R   To promote the vital role of engineers, engineering and technology in our society and to inspire people to pursue
     careers at all levels in engineering and technology.
G   United Kingdom.

England Implementation Group (Animal Health & Welfare Strategy)
✍   AHWSEIG, established in 2005, has been dissolved (Defra, 14 October 2010).

England Marketing Advisory Board
✍   For its successor organisation see **VisitEngland**.

England's North Country   see **North West Tourist Board**

England Volunteering Development Council   See **Volunteering England**.

England & Wales Cricket Board   (ECB)

■   Lord's Cricket Ground, LONDON, NW8 8QZ.
     Tel 020 7432 1200   Fax 020 7286 5583   http://www.ecb.co.uk
     Chairman: Giles Clarke   Chief Executive: David Collier

E   Established on 1 January 1997, replacing the duties and functions of the Test & Cricket Board, the Cricket Council and the National Cricket Association all of which were wound up on 31 December 1996. ECB is the single national governing body for cricket in England and Wales. The board comprises twelve members including the Chairman.
R   To provide support for the game of cricket at all levels.
G   England, Wales.

English Beef & Lamb Executive   (EBLEX)

■   AHDB, Stoneleigh Park, KENILWORTH, Warwickshire, CV8 2TL.
    Tel 024 7669 2051   http://www.eblex.org.uk
    Chairman: John Cross
E   Established on 1 April 2008 via the Agriculture & Horticulture Development Board Order 2008. The Board comprises 15 members including the Chairman.
R   To deliver a wide range of technology transfer, marketing and promotional programmes to farmers, consumers and businesses in the beef and lamb supply chain.
G   England.
✍   A subsidiary of the **Agriculture & Horticulture Development Board** and funded through an AHDB levy paid on all cattle and sheep slaughtered in or exported from England.

English Heritage

■   Kemble Drive, SWINDON, Wilts, SN2 7YP.
    Tel 01793 414700   Fax 01793 414707   http://www.english-heritage.org.uk
    1 Waterhouse Square, 138-142 Holborn, LONDON, EC1N 2ST.
    Tel 020 7973 3000   Fax 020 7973 3001
    Chairman: Baroness Andrews, OBE   Chief Executive: Dr Simon Thurley
E   Established under the National Heritage Act 1983. English Heritage, officially known as the Historic Buildings & Monuments Commission for England, functions as an Executive NDPB of the Department for Culture, Media & Sport. It is governed by a board of 13 Commissioners including the Chairman.
R   To protect and promote England's historic environment and ensure that its past is researched and understood. To provide statutory advice to government on historic buildings, ancient monuments and conservation areas and to give grants for their repair.
G   England.
●   English Heritage maintains the National Monuments Record, the central database containing records of over one million historic sites and buildings and more than 12 million photographs, drawings, maps and reports.

English National Board for Nursing, Midwifery & Health Visiting
✍   See the **Nursing & Midwifery Council**.

English Nature   (Nature Conservancy Council)
✍   Since 1 October 2006 **Natural England**.

English Partnerships
✍   On 1 December 2008 merged the the Housing Corporation as the **Homes & Communities Agency**.

English Regional Tourist Boards
✍   Under a government decision in 2003, responsibility for tourism in the English regions was passed to the Regional Development Agencies (qv).

English Speaking Board   (ESB)

■   9 Hattersley Court, Burscough Road, ORMSKIRK, Lancs, L39 2AY.
    Tel 01695 573439   Fax 01695 228003   http://www.esbuk.org
    Chief Executive: Lesley Cook
E   Established in 1953.
R   To promote clear, effective oral communication at all levels by providing high quality assessments, training and services in the UK and overseas, recognising and encouraging the potential of all.
G   United Kingdom.
●   The ESB is the awarding body for courses and qualifications in spoken English.
✍   See also the **Federation of Awarding Bodies**.

Enterprise Ulster
✍ Dissolved on 2 April 2007 under the Review of Public Administration. See the **RPA Strategic Review Group** for
further information.

ENTRUST
■ 60 Holly Walk, LEAMINGTON SPA, Warwickshire, CV32 4JE.
Tel 01926 488300   **Fax** 01926 488388   http://www.entrust.org.uk
Chairman: Philip Smith   Chief Executive: Christopher Welford
E Established in 1996 under terms contained in the Landfill Tax Regulations 1996. ENTRUST functions as a not-for-
profit company appointed as the Regulator of the Landfill Communities Fund (LCF); it is not a Government
Agency. The Board of Directors comprises the Chairman and four other members.
R To regulate the LCF under agreement with HM Revenue & Customs.
G United Kingdom.

Environment Agency
■ Chairman & Secretariat, Press & Parliamentary Offices:
25th Floor, Millbank Tower, 21/24 Millbank, LONDON, SW1P 4XL.
Tel 0870 850 6506 (all offices)   http://www.environment-agency.gov.uk
Water Management Communications, Resources, Operations, Finance, Environment Protection, Legal, Chief
Executive Office:
Horizon House, Deanery Road, BRISTOL, BS1 5AH.
Chairman: Lord Chris Smith   Chief Executive: Paul Leinster
E Established on 1 April 1996 under the Environment Act 1995. The Agency functions as an Executive NDPB of the
Department for the Environment, Food & Rural Affairs and as an Assembly Sponsored Public Body of the Welsh
Government. Its Board comprises 14 members including the Chairman.
R To act to reduce climate change and its consequences.
To protect and improve air, land and water quality.
To put people and communities at the heart of what the Agency does.
To work with businesses and the public sector to use resources wisely.
G England, Wales.
● The Agency is divided into eight regions.
In each region, statutory committees advise on the Agency's operational performance, regional issues of concern
and regional implications of national policy proposals.
For further information see
Regional Environmental Protection Advisory Committees
Regional Fisheries, Ecology & Recreational Advisory Committees
Regional Flood Defence Committees
✍ The Government announced on 14 October 2010 that the Agency in England would be reformed through
structural, process and cultural change, with its accountabilities clarified, to become a more efficient and
customer focused organisation. The Agency in Wales may move to form part of an environmental body of the
Welsh Government.

Environment Agency [Anglian Region]
■ Kingfisher House, Goldhay Way, Orton Goldhay, PETERBOROUGH, PE2 5ZR.
Tel 0870 850 6506 (all offices)
Northern Area Office:
Waterside House, Waterside North, LINCOLN, LN2 5HA.
Eastern Area Office:
Cobham Road, IPSWICH, Suffolk, IP3 9JE.
Central Area Office:
Bromholme Lane, Brampton, HUNTINGDON, Cambs, PE28 4NE.
Anglian Regional Director: Paul Woodcock
Committee Chairmen: Alan Woods (REPAC), David Moore (RFERAC), Robert Caudwell (Northern RFDC), Stephen
Wheatley (Central RFDC), Anthony Coe (Eastern RFDC)
G Cambridgeshire, Essex, Lincolnshire, Norfolk, Northamptonshire and Suffolk.
● The Anglian Region has five statutory committees:
Regional Environment Protection Advisory Committee (REPAC)
Regional Fisheries, Ecology & Recreation Advisory Committee (RFERAC)
Anglian (Northern) Regional Flood Defence Committee (RFDC)
Anglian (Central) Regional Flood Defence Committee (RFDC)
Anglian (Eastern) Regional Flood Defence Committee (RFDC)

Environment Agency [Midlands Region]

- Sapphire East, 550 Streetsbrook Road, SOLIHULL, W Midlands, B91 1QT.
  Tel 0870 850 6506 (all offices)
  Central Area Office:
  Sentinel House, 9 Wellington Crescent, Fradley Park, LICHFIELD, Staffs, WS13 8RR.
  East Area Office:
  Trentside Offices, Scarrington Road, West Bridgford, NOTTINGHAM, NG2 5FA.
  West Area Office:
  Riversmeet House, Northway Lane, TEWKESBURY, Glos, GL20 8JG.
  Midlands Regional Director: Mark Sitton-Kent
  Committee Chairmen: John Turner (REPAC), Geoff Nickolds (RFERAC), Tim Farr (RFDC)
- G Derbyshire, Herefordshire, Nottinghamshire, Shropshire, Staffordshire, Warwickshire, West Midlands and Worcestershire.
- The Midlands Region has three statutory committees:
  Regional Environment Protection Advisory Committee (REPAC)
  Regional Fisheries, Ecology & Recreation Advisory Committee (RFERAC)
  Regional Flood Defence Committee (RFDC)

Environment Agency [North East Region]

- Rivers House, 21 Park Square South, LEEDS, W Yorks, LS1 2QG.
  Tel 0870 850 6506 (all offices)
  North East Area Office:
  Tyneside House, Skinnerburn Road, Newcastle Business Park, NEWCASTLE UPON TYNE, NE4 7AR.
  Yorkshire & Humber Area Office:
  Phoenix House, Global Avenue, Millshaw, Beeston Ring Road, LEEDS, W Yorks, LS11 8PG.
  North East Regional Director: Toby Willison
  Committee Chairmen: Dr Ian Brown (REPAC), David Stewart (RFERAC), Arthur Barker (Yorkshire RFDC), Frank Major (Northumbria RFDC)
- G County Durham, Northumberland, Tyne & Wear, Yorkshire.
- The North East Region has four statutory committees:
  Regional Environment Protection Advisory Committee (REPAC)
  Regional Fisheries, Ecology & Recreation Advisory Committee (RFERAC)
  Yorkshire Regional Flood Defence Committee (RFDC)
  Northumbria Regional Flood Defence Committee (RFDC)

Environment Agency [North West Region]

- PO Box 12, Richard Fairclough House, Knutsford Road, Latchford, WARRINGTON, Cheshire, WA4 1HT.
  Tel 0870 850 6506 (all offices)
  Central Area Office:
  Lutra House, Dodd Way, Walton Summit, Bamber Bridge, PRESTON, Lancs, PR5 8BX.
  Northern Area Office:
  Ghyll Mount, Gilian Way, Penrith 40 Business Park, PENRITH, Cumbria, CA11 9BP.
  Southern Area Office:
  Appleton House, 430 Birchwood Boulevard, WARRINGTON, Cheshire, WA3 7WD.
  North West Regional Director: Tony Dean
  Committee Chairmen: Derek Norman (REPAC), Judith Clark (RFERAC), Derek Antrobus (RFDC)
- G Cheshire, Cumbria, Lancashire, Greater Manchester and Merseyside.
- The North West Region has three statutory committees:
  Regional Environment Protection Advisory Committee (REPAC)
  Regional Fisheries, Ecology & Recreation Advisory Committee (RFERAC)
  Regional Flood Defence Committee (RFDC)

Environment Agency [South East Region]
- Kings Meadow House, Kings Meadow Road, READING, Berks, RG1 8DQ.
  Tel 0870 850 6506 (all offices)
  Kent & South London Area Office:
  Orchard House, Endeavour Park, London Road, Addington, WEST MALLING, Kent, ME19 5SH.
  North East Thames Area Office:
  Apollo Court 2, Bishops Square Business Park, St Albans Road West, HATFIELD, Herts, AL10 9EX.
  Solent & South Downs Area Office:
  Guildbourne House, Chatsworth Road, WORTHING, W Sussex, BN11 1LD.
  West Thames Area Office:
  Howbery Park, Crowmarsh Gifford, WALLINGFORD, Oxon, OX10 8BD.
  South East Regional Director: Howard Davidson
  Former Southern Region Committee Chairmen: Susan Pyper (REPAC),   Ivor Llewelyn (RFERAC),   Dr Mike
    Bateman (RFDC),   Richard Bezant (HORAC)
  Former Thames Region Committee Chairmen: Valerie Owen (REPAC),   Chris Poupard (RFERAC),   Amanda
    Nobbs (RFDC)
- G   Bedfordshire, Berkshire, Buckinghamshire, Hampshire, Hertfordshire, Kent, Greater London, Oxfordshire, Surrey
    and Sussex.
- ● The former Southern Region has four statutory committees:
    Regional Environment Protection Advisory Committee (REPAC)
    Regional Fisheries, Ecology & Recreation Advisory Committee (RFERAC)
    Regional Flood Defence Committee (RFDC)
    Harbour of Rye Advisory Committee (HORAC)
  The former Thames Region has three statutory committees:
    Regional Environment Protection Advisory Committee (REPAC)
    Regional Fisheries, Ecology & Recreation Advisory Committee (RFERAC)
    Regional Flood Defence Committee (RFDC)
- ✍ The South East Region was formed on 1 April 2011 by the merger of the Southern and Thames regions.

Environment Agency [South West Region]
- Manley House, Kestrel Way, EXETER, Devon, EX2 7LQ.
  Tel 0870 850 6506 (all offices)
  Cornwall Area Office:
  Sir John Moore House, Victoria Square, BODMIN, Cornwall, PL31 1EB.
  North Wessex Area Office:
  Rivers House, East Quay, BRIDGWATER, Somerset, TA6 4YS.
  South Wessex Area Office:
  Rivers House, Sunrise Business Park, Higher Shaftesbury Road, BLANDFORD, Dorset, DT11 8ST.
  Devon Area Office:
  Exminster House, Miller Way, EXMINSTER, Devon, EX6 8AS.
  South West Regional Director: Richard Cresswell
  Committee Chairmen: Elaine Hayes (REPAC), Chris Klee (RFERAC), James Morrish (South West RFDC)
- G   Cornwall, Devon, Dorset, Gloucestershire, Somerset and Wiltshire.
- ● The South West Region has four statutory committees:
    Regional Environment Protection Advisory Committee (REPAC)
    Regional Fisheries, Ecology & Recreation Advisory Committee (RFERAC)
    South West Regional Flood Defence Committee (RFDC)
    Wessex Regional Flood Defence Committee (RFDC)

Environment Agency Wales
- Cambria House, 29 Newport Road, CARDIFF, CF24 0TP.
  Tel 0870 850 6506 (all offices)
  Northern Area Office:
  Ffordd Pentan, Parc Menai, BANGOR, Gwynedd, LL57 4DE.
  South East Area Office:
  Rivers House, St Mellons Business Park, St Mellons, CARDIFF, CF3 0EY.
  South West Area Office:
  Maes Newydd, Llandarcy, NEATH, Glamorgan, SA10 6JQ.
  Director Wales: Chris Mills
  Committee Chairmen: Prof Tom Pritchard (EPAC Wales), Dr Graeme Harris (FERAC Wales), Deep Sagar (FRMW)
- E   Environment Agency Wales is both an Assembly Government Sponsored Body and part of the national
    Environment Agency (qv).
- G   Wales.
- ● Environment Agency Wales has three statutory committees:
    Environment Protection Advisory Committee (EPAC) Wales

Fisheries, Ecology & Recreation Advisory Committee (FERAC) Wales
Flood Risk Management Wales (FRMW) Committee
✍ The Welsh Government is considering moving Environment Agency Wales and Forestry Commission Wales (qv) to form part of a Welsh Government environmental body.
= Asiantaeth yr Amgylchedd Cymru

The Environment Council   (TEC)
■ 212 High Holborn, LONDON, WC1V 7BF.
Tel 020 7836 2626   Fax 020 7242 1180   http://www.the-environment-council.org.uk
Chief Executive: Winsome MacLaurin
E Established on 25 November 1969 following the Royal Society of Arts 'Future of the Countryside' events, the Council for Environmental Conservation adopted its current name in November 1988. The Council functions as a registered charity and a company limited by guarantee.
R To transform conventional decision-making to make the environment as important as economics and politics.
G United Kingdom.
● The Council seeks to facilitate cooperation on environmental issues by producing a range of publications and holding training workshops and seminars.

Environment & Heritage Service
✍ Since 1 July 2008 **Northern Ireland Environment Agency**.

Environment Protection Advisory Committees   See **Regional Environment Protection Advisory Committees**.

Environmental Investigation Agency   (EIA)
■ 62/63 Upper Street, LONDON, N1 0NY.
Tel 020 7354 7960   Fax 020 7354 7961   http://www.eia-international.org
PO Box 53343, WASHINGTON, DC 20009, USA.Tel +1 202 483 6621   Fax +1 202 986 8626
E Established in 1984. EIA is an independent international non-government organisation and functions as a registered charity and company limited by guarantee.
R To investigate and expose the illegal trade in wildlife and the destruction of the natural environment.
G Worldwide.
● The EIA carries out detailed scientific research and undercover investigations. It works closely with other NGOs and presents its evidence to governments and decision makers around the world in order to bring about legislative change to protect wildlife and the environment.

Equal Opportunities Commission
✍ Replaced on 1 October 2007 by the **Equality & Human Rights Commission**.

Equality 2025
■ Office for Disability Issues, Caxton House, 6-12 Tothill Street, LONDON, SW1H 9NA.
http://www.dwp.gov.uk/equality-2025/
E Established on 7 December 2006. Equality 2025 functions as an Advisory NDPB of the Department for Work & Pensions. The group comprises the Chairman and nine members.
R To help Government understand the needs and wishes of disabled people when developing policies and designing service delivery.
G United Kingdom.

Equality Commission for Northern Ireland   (ECNI)
■ Equality House, 7-9 Shaftesbury Square, BELFAST, BT2 7DP.
Tel 028 9050 0600   Fax 028 9024 8687   http://www.equalityni.org
Chief Commissioner: Bob Collins   Chief Executive: Evelyn Collins, CBE
E Established in March 1999 under the Northern Ireland Act 1998. It functions as an independent public body. The Commission comprises twelve members including the Chief Commissioner.
R To promote awareness of and enforce anti-discrimination law on the following grounds: age, disability, race, sex (including marital and civil partner status), sexual orientation, religious belief and political opinion.
G Northern Ireland.
= Also known as the Northern Ireland Equality Commission

Equality & Diversity Committee   (EDC)

- ■ BMA House, Tavistock Square, LONDON, WC1H 9JP.
  Tel 0300 123 1233   **Fax** 020 7383 6400   http://www.bma.org.uk
  Chairman: Prof Bhupinder Sandhu
- E Established as a standing committee of the British Medical Association. Formerly known as the Equal Opportunities Committee, it adopted its current name in January 2010.
- R To promote equal opportunities for the medical workforce.
- G United Kingdom.
- ✍ See **British Medical Association** [Boards & Committees] for further information.

Equality & Human Rights Commission   (EHRC)

- ■ 3 More London, Riverside Tooley Street, LONDON, SE1 2RG.
  Tel 020 3117 0235   **Fax** 020 3117 0237   http://www.equalityhumanrights.com
  3rd Floor, 3 Callaghan Square, CARDIFF, CF10 5BT.
  Tel 029 2044 7713   **Fax** 029 2044 7712
  The Optima Building, 58 Robertson Road, GLASGOW, G2 8BU.
  Tel 0141 228 5910   **Fax** 0141 228 5912
  Chairman: Trevor Phillips
- E Established on 1 October 2007 under the Equality Act 2006, and replacing the former Commission for Racial Equality, the Disability Rights Commission, and the Equal Opportunities Commission. EHRC functions as an Executive NDPB of the Home Office. The Commission comprises 15 members including the Chairman.
- R To eliminate descrimination, reduce inequality, protect human rights and to build good relations, ensuring that everyone has a fair chance to participate in society.
- G United Kingdom.
- ✍ The Government announced on 14 October 2010 that EHRC would be substantially reformed, with better focus on its core regulatory functions and improved use of taxpayers' money.

Escape & Rescue Operations in Mines Working Group   A working group of the **Mining Industry Committee**.

Esks Rivers & Rivers Fisheries Trust   See **Rivers & Fisheries Trusts of Scotland**.

Essex Police Authority

- ■ 3 Hoffmanns Way, CHELMSFORD, Essex, CM1 1GU.
  Tel 01245 291600   http://www.essex.police.uk/authority/
  Chairman: Cllr Robert Chambers
- E Established in April 1995, the Authority is an independent body charged with ensuring that Essex Police provide an effective and efficient police service.
  It is made up of nine councillor members and eight independent members.
- G Essex.
- ✍ For further information see **Police Authorities**.

Essex Probation Trust

- ■ Cullen Mill, 49 Braintree Road, WITHAM, Essex, CM8 2DD.
  Tel 01376 501626   **Fax** 01376 501174   http://www.essexprobation.org.uk
  Chairman: Bill Puddicombe   Chief Officer: Mary Archer
- E Established on 1 April 2001 under the Criminal Justice & Court Service Act 2000 as the Essex Probation Area Board. It became a trust on 1 April 2010 under the Offender Management Act 2007. The Board comprises 14 members including the Chairman.
- G Essex.
- ✍ For further information see **Probation Trusts**.

Essex Strategic Health Authority
- ✍ On 1 July 2006 merged with the Bedfordshire & Hertfordshire and the Norfolk, Suffolk & Cambridgeshire Strategic Health Authorities to form the **East of England Strategic Health Authority**.

Estyn (extend)   See **Her Majesty's Inspectorate for Education & Training in Wales**.

Ethnic Minority Business Forum

✍ The Forum ceased to exist in March 2007. Its successor organisation, the Ethnic Minority Business Task Force, completed its work on 16 July 2009.

European Risk Management Advisory Group   A sub-committee of the Health & Safety Executive's **Advisory Committee on Toxic Substances**.

European Union Select Committee   See **United Kingdom Parliament: Committees**.

Examinations Appeals Board   (EAB)

■ Spring Place, Coventry Business Park, Herald Avenue, COVENTRY, CV5 6UB.
Tel 024 7667 1848   http://www.theeab.org.uk
Chairman: Prof Jeff Thompson

E Established in 1999 by Ministers to replace the Independent Appeals Authority for School Examinations (IAASE). EAB functions as an independent body and is part of the Qualifications & Curriculum Authority (qv). The Board comprises the Chairman and two deputies.

R To ensure, in the very few cases where disputes cannot be resolved between centres or private candidates and the awarding bodies, that there is a fully independent avenue of appeal to review the correct application of procedures governing the setting, marking and grading of qualifications.

G England, Wales, Northern Ireland.

● The EAB hears final appeals on GCSE and GCE examinations, also on Principal Learning and Project components of the Diploma.

Executive Council of the Inn of Court of Northern Ireland

■ 91 Chichester Street, BELFAST, BTI 3JQ.
Tel 028 9056 2349   Fax 028 9056 2350   http://www.barlibrary.com

E The Council comprises 18 members including the Chairman.

R To consider Memorials submitted by applicants for admission as students of the Inn and by Bar students of the Inn for admission to the degree of Barrister-at-Law and making recommendations to the Benchers.

G Northern Ireland.

Exmoor National Park Authority   (ENPA)

■ Exmoor House, DULVERTON, Somerset, TA22 9HL.
Tel 01398 323665   Fax 01398 323150   http://www.exmoor-nationalpark.gov.uk
Chairman: John Dyke   Chief Executive: Dr Nigel Stone

E Exmoor was designated a National Park in 1954. The present Authority was established on 1 April 1997 under the Environment Act 1995. It comprises 26 members including the Chairman.

G Exmoor.

✍ For further information see **National Park Authorities**.

Expert Advisory Group on AIDS   (EAGA)

■ Expert Advice Support Office, 61 Colindale Avenue, LONDON, NW9 5EQ.
Chairman: Prof Brian Gazzard

E Established in January 1985 by decision of UK Health Ministers. EAGA functions as a Scientific Advisory Committee and an Advisory NDPB of the Department of Health. The Committee comprises 17 members including the Chairman.

R To provide advice on such matters relating to HIV/AIDS as may be referred to it by the Chief Medical Officers of the United Kingdom.

G United Kingdom.

✍ On 14 October 2010 the Government announced that EAGA would cease to function as a NDPB and be reconstituted as a committee of experts of the Department of Health and the new Public Health Service.

Expert Advisory Group on Infertility Services

✍ Established in January 1998, EAGISS published its report in February 2000.

Expert Group on Cryptosporidium in Water Supplies

✍ The Group is currently dormant.

Expert Panel on Air Quality Standards
✍ EPAQS was merged into the **Committee on the Medical Effects of Air Pollutants** in 2009.

Explosives Inspectorate
■ 1/2 Redgrave Court, Merton Road, BOOTLE, Merseyside, L20 7HS.
  Tel 0151 951 4025
E The Inspectorate is part of the Health & Safety Executive (qv).
R To license manufacturing and larger storage sites as well as enforcing legislation for these sites and for the classification and transport of explosives.
G England, Wales, Scotland.

Explosives Subcommittee
✍ A subcommittee of the Advisory Committee on Dangerous Substances which closed in 2004.

Export Control Organisation   (ECO)
■ 3rd Floor, 1 Victoria Street, LONDON, SW1H 0ET.
  Tel 020 7215 4594   Fax 020 7215 2635
  Director: Glyn Williams
E ECO is part of the Europe & World Trade Directorate and functions as an Advisory NDPB of the Department for Business, Innovation & Skills.
R To process applications for licences to export strategic goods, technology and software from the UK.
G United Kingdom.

Export Credits Guarantee Department   (ECGD)
■ PO Box 2200, 2 Exchange Tower, Harbour Exchange Square, LONDON, E14 9GS.
  Tel 020 7512 7000   Fax 020 7512 7649   http://www.ecgd.gov.uk
  Chairman: Guy Beringer, QC   Chief Executive: Patrick Crawford   Shareholder Executive contact: Oliver Griffiths
E Established in 1939, its statutory powers are set out in the Export & Investment Guarantees Act 1991. ECGD functions as a public-private partnership of the Department for Business, Innovation & Skills. The Management Board comprises ten members including the Chairman.
R To benefit the UK economy by helping exporters of UK goods and services to win business, and UK firms to invest overseas, by providing guarantees, insurance and reinsurance against loss, taking into account the Government's international policies.
G United Kingdom.
● The ECGD is advised by the Export Guarantees Advisory Council (qv).
✍ One of the businesses managed by the **Shareholder Executive**.

Export Guarantees Advisory Council   (EGAC)
■ PO Box 2200, 2 Exchange Tower, Harbour Exchange Square, LONDON, E14 9GS.
  Tel 020 7512 7000   Fax 020 7512 7649   http://www.ecgd.gov.uk
  Chairman: Andrew Wiseman
E Established in 1939 under the Export Guarantees Act 1939, the Council is now constituted under the Export & Investment Guarantees Act 1991. EGAC functions as an Advisory NDPB to Export Credits Guarantee Department (qv). The Council comprises nine members including the Chairman.
R To advise the Export Credits Guarantee Department (qv), the UK's official export credit insurer, in providing guarantees to exporters and financing banks for the purpose of encouraging the UK export trade.
G United Kingdom.

F

Facilities Advisory Panel   See **Football Foundation**.

The Faculty Office

■ 1 The Sanctuary, Westminster, LONDON, SW1P 3JT.
 Tel 020 7222 5381 **Fax** 020 7222 7502 http://www.facultyoffice.org.uk
 Master of the Faculties: Charles George, QC

E Established under the Ecclesiastical Licences Act 1533, its jurisdiction over notaries confirmed and enhanced by the Courts & Legal Services Act 1990. The Master of the Faculties is the Dean of Arches who is appointed jointly by the Archbishops of Canterbury and York.

R To regulate the notarial profession. (Also to issue marriage licences and regulate the awarding of Archbishop of Lambeth degrees.)

G England, Wales.

✍ One of the Approved Regulators overseen by the **Legal Services Board**.

Fáilte Ireland

■ 88-95 Amiens Street, DUBLIN 1, Republic of Ireland.
 Tel +353 (0)1 884 7700 **Fax** +353 (0)1 855 6821 http://www.failteireland.ie
 Chairman: Redmond O'Donoghue

E Established under the National Tourism Development Authority Act 2003 replacing the former Bord Fáilte. Fáilte Ireland Authority's board comprises 13 members including the Chairman.

R To provide practical and strategic support to develop and sustain the Republic as a high quality and competitive tourist destination.

G Republic of Ireland.

● Fáilte Ireland has offices in the Republic in Cork, Galway, Mullingar, Sligo and Waterford, and in Belfast and Derry in Northern Ireland.

✍ Fáilte Ireland works in partnership with Tourism Ireland (qv) which promotes Ireland as a holiday destination to overseas markets, and the Northern Ireland Tourist Board (qv) which is responsible for tourism development and marketing in the north.

Fair Employment Tribunal [Northern Ireland] See **Industrial Tribunals & the Fair Employment Tribunal**.

Faith Communities Consultative Council   (FCCC)

■ Eland House, Bressenden Place, LONDON, SW1E 5DU.
 Tel 0303 444 0000
 Chairman: Parmjit Dhanda

E Established in April 2006 replacing the Inner Cities Religious Council and the Working Together Steering Group. FCCC functions as a Advisory NDPB of the Department for Communities & Local Government.

R To provide a forum chiefly concerned with issues related to cohesion, integration, the development of sustainable communities, neighbourhood renewal and social inclusion.

G United Kingdom.

Falmouth Harbour Commissioners

■ 44 Arwenack Street, FALMOUTH, Cornwall, TR11 3JQ.
 Tel 01326 312285 **Fax** 01326 211352 http://www.falmouthport.co.uk
 Chairman: David Ellis   Chief Executive & Harbour Master: Captain Mark Sansom

E Established under the Falmouth Harbour Order 1870. The Commission comprises nine members including the Chairman.

✍ For further information see **Special Health Authorities**.

Family Health Services Appeal Authority

✍ Since 18 January 2010 **First-tier Tribunal (Primary Health Lists)**.

Family Justice Council   (FJC)

■ E201 East Block, Royal Courts of Justice, Strand, LONDON, WC2A 2LL.
 Tel 020 7947 7333 **Fax** 020 7947 7875 http://www.family-justice-council.org.uk
 Chairman: Sir Nicholas Wall

E Established on 27 January 2004. FJC functions as an Advisory NDPB of the Ministry of Justice. The Council, which currently comprises 18 members, is chaired by the President of the Family Division.

R To promote an inter-disciplinary approach to the needs of family justice,
 To monitor the effectiveness of the system and advise on reforms necessary for continuous improvement.

G United Kingdom

Family Justice Review Panel

■ 102 Petty France, LONDON, SW1H 9AJ.
  Tel 020 3334 3555   **Fax** 020 3334 4455
  Chairman: David Norgrove
E Established in January by the Ministry of Justice. The Panel comprises five members including the Chairman.
R To examine reform of the current family justice system so that it better supports children and parents.
G England, Wales.

Family Procedure Rule Committee   (FPRC)

■ 4th Floor, 102 Petty France, LONDON, SW1H 9AJ.
  Tel 020 3334 3181   **Fax** 020 3334 6457
  Chairman: Sir Nicholas Wall
E Established under the Courts Act 2003. FPRC functions as an Advisory NDPB of the Ministry of Justice. The Committee, which comprises 16 members, is chaired by the President of the Family Division.
R To produce a single, coherent and simply expressed set of rules governing practice and procedure in family proceedings in the High Court, county courts and magistrates' courts.
G England, Wales.

Farm Animal Welfare Council   (FAWC)

■ 9 Millbank Area 8B, c/o 17 Smith Square, LONDON, SW1P 3JR.
  Tel 020 7238 5016   **Fax** 020 7238 3169   http://www.fawc.org.uk
  Chairman: Prof Christopher Wathes
E Established on 25 July 1979 by the Agriculture Departments. FAWC functions as a Scientific Advisory Committee of the Department for Environment, Food & Rural Affairs. The Council comprises 18 members including the Chairman.
R To keep under review the welfare of farm animals on agricultural land, at market, in transit and at the place of slaughter.
  To advise the Government of any legislative or other change that may be necessary.
G England, Wales, Scotland.
✍ For further information see **Scientific Advisory Committees**.
  The Government announced on 14 October 2010 that FAWC would cease to function as a NDPB and be reconstituted as a committee of experts.

Farming & Wildlife Advisory Group   (FWAG)

■ Stoneleigh Park, KENILWORTH, Warks, CV8 2RX.
  Tel 024 7669 6699   **Fax** 024 7669 6760   http://www.fwag.org.uk
  Chairman: Henry Lucas   Managing Director: Andy Ormiston
E Established in 1969. FWAG is a membership organisation and an independent registered charity. The Board of Trustees comprises nine members including the Chairman.
R To provide environmental and conservation advice to farmers and others who manage the countryside.
G United Kingdom.
● FWAG has offices in Wales (Anglesey and Llandrindod Wells), Scotland (Perth) Northern Ireland (Magherafelt) and in Exeter.

Farriers Registration Council

■ Sefton House, Adam Court, Newark Road, PETERBOROUGH, PE1 5PP.
  Tel 01733 319911   **Fax** 01733 319910   http://www.farrier-reg.gov.uk
  Chairman: Prof Ron Jones, OBE, JP, DVSc, FRCA, FRCVS
E Established in 1975 under the Farriers (Registration) Act 1975 as amended. The Council comprises 16 members including the Chairman.
R To maintain and develop the highest standards of equine foot welfare in Great Britain by ensuring that only suitably qualified persons shoe horses, that farriers maintain and improve their professional standards and that the public are aware of the regulatory processes.
G United Kingdom (excluding the Highlands & Islands of Scotland)
● The Council's Investigating Committee, a statutory committee established under the 1975 Act, investigates complaints against Registered Farriers, fraudulent registrations and convictions for offences involving cruelty to animals.
  The Disciplinary Committee, also established under the 1975 Act, is a properly constituted judicial tribunal with the power to remove a farrier's name from the Register of Farriers.

Federation of Awarding Bodies   (FAB)

■   1 Giltspur Street, LONDON, EC1A 9DD.
     Tel 020 7294 8023   **Fax** 020 7294 2414   http://www.www.awarding.org.uk
     Chairman: Isabel Sutcliffe   Chief Executive: Jill Lanning
E   Established in 2000 by the four largest vocational awarding bodies, City & Guilds, Edexcel, Oxford & Cambridge &
     RSA Examinations Board, and the London Chamber of Commerce & Industry Examinations Board (qqv). FAB is
     a membership organisation representing bodies which award vocational qualifications in the UK. The Executive
     Committee comprises 14 members including the Chairman.
R   To provide a forum for awarding bodies to collectively consider developments in vocational qualifications.
G   United Kingdom.
●   Many of the Federation's members are listed in the Subject Index under **Awarding bodies**.

Fife Local Enterprise Company

✍   Now functions as the Glenrothes office of **Scottish Enterprise**.

Fife NHS Board

■   Hayfield House, Hayfield Road, KIRKCALDY, Fife, KY2 5AH.
     Tel 01592 643355   **Fax** 01592 648142   http://www.nhsfife.scot.nhs.uk
     Chairman: Prof James McGoldrick   Chief Executive: George Brechin
G   Fife.
✍   For further information see **NHS Scotland - Boards**.

Fife Police Authority

✍   Six of the eight Scottish police forces are administered a police authority or joint board. Fife Constabulary is
     directly administered by Fife Council.

Fife Tourist Board

✍   Since 1 April 2005 an area office of **VisitScotland**.

Film Agency for Wales

■   Suite 7, 33-35 West Bute Street, CARDIFF, CF10 5LH.
     Tel 029 2046 7480   **Fax** 029 2046 7481   http://www.filmagencywales.com
     Chairman: Peter Edwards   Chief Executive: Pauline Burt
E   Established in July 2006. The Agency's board comprises seven members including the Chairman.
R   To accelerate the development of a dynamic and sustainable screen industry for Wales.
     To promote Wales as a major production location.
G   Wales.
=   Asiantaeth Ffilm Cymro

Film London

■   Suite 6/10, The Tea Building, 56 Shoreditch High Street, LONDON, E1 6JJ.
     Tel 020 7613 7676   **Fax** 020 7613 7677   http://www.filmlondon.org.uk
     Chairman: David Parfitt   Chief Executive: Adrian Wootton
E   Established on 17 March 2003 replacing the former London Film Commission and London Film & Video
     Development Agency.
R   To sustain, promote and develop London as a major international film-making and film cultural capital.
     To develop and manage a national strategy to generate inward investment through film production via a public-
     private partnership with key industry bodies following the closure of the UK Film Council.
G   United Kingdom and London.
✍   For further information see **Creative England** and **Regional Screen Agencies**.

Financial Ombudsman Service   (FOS)

■   South Quay Plaza, 183 Marsh Wall, LONDON, E14 9SR.
     Tel 020 7964 1000   **Fax** 020 7964 1001   http://www.financial-ombudsman.org.uk
     Chairman: Sir Christopher Kelly, KCB   Chief Ombudsman: Natalie Ceeney, CBE
E   Established on 1 April 2000 under the Financial Services & Markets Act 2000. FOS brings together various
     complaints-handling schemes within the financial sector including the Banking Ombudsman, the Insurance
     Ombudsman, the Investment Ombudsman and the Personal Investment Authority Ombudsman. The Board
     comprises nine members includng the Chairman.
R   To help settle individual disputes between businesses providing financial services and their customers.

G   United Kingdom
- The FOS can look into complaints about most financial matters, including:
  Banking; Insurance; Mortgages; Pensions; Savings & investments; Credit cards & store cards; Loans & credit;
  Hire purchase & pawnbroking; Financial advice; Stocks, shares, unit trusts & bonds.
  The Ombudsman works closely with the Financial Services Authority (qv), the Office of Fair Trading and the
  Pensions Ombudsman (qv).

Financial Policy Committee
■   Bank of England, Threadneedle Street, LONDON, EC2R 8AH.
E   A committee of the Bank of England (qv). One of the successor organisations of the Financial Services Authority
    (qv).
R   To ensure that the City as a whole does not take excessive risks.
G   United Kingdom.

Financial Reporting Advisory Board   (FRAB)
■   1/W1, 1 Horse Guards Parade, LONDON, SW1A 2HQ.
    Chairman: Kathryn Cearns
E   Established in June 1996 and given statutory footing by the Government Resources & Accounts Act 2000. FRAB
    functions as an independent NDPB of HM Treasury. The Board comprises 14 members including the Chairman.
R   To advise HM Treasury, the Scottish Ministers and the Department of Finance & Personnel Northern Ireland on
    the application of financial reporting standards and procedures.
G   United Kingdom.

Financial Reporting Council   (FRC)
■   5th Floor, Aldwych House, 71-91 Aldwych, LONDON, WC2B 4HN.
    Tel 020 7492 2300 **Fax** 020 7492 2301 http://www.frc.org.uk
    Chairman: Baroness Hogg   Chief Executive: Stephen Haddrill
E   Established in 1990. The Council functions as a company limited by guarantee. The FRC board comprises 16
    members of whom the Chairman and his deputy are appointed by the Department for Business, Innovation &
    Skills.
R   To support investor, market and public confidence in the financial and governance stewardship of listed and
    other entities by establishing and improving standards of financial accounting and reporting.
G   United Kingdom.
- The functions of the FRC are exercised principally by its six operating bodies:
  Accountancy & Actuarial Discipline Board
  Accounting Standards Board
  Auditing Practices Board
  Board for Actuarial Standards
  Financial Reporting Review Panel
  Professional Oversight Board (qqv)
  In addition, in March 2004 the FRC set up a new committee to lead its work on corporate governance:
  Corporate Governance Committee (qv).
✍   The Government announced on 14 October 2010 its intention to retain but substantially reform FRC, removing its
    reliance on Government funding.

Financial Reporting Review Panel   (FRRP)
■   5th Floor, Aldwych House, 71-91 Aldwych, LONDON, WC2B 4HN.
    Tel 020 7492 2300 **Fax** 020 7492 2479 http://www.frc.org.uk/frrp
    Chairman: Bill Knight
E   Established in 1990, its authority derives from the Company (Defective Accounts) (Authorised Person) Order 1991.
    FRRP is part of the Financial Reporting Council (qv). The Board comprises 29 members including the Chairman.
R   To ensure that the annual accounts of public and large private companies comply with the requirements of the
    Companies Act 2006 and applicable accounting standards.
G   United Kingdom.

Financial Services Authority   (FSA)
■   25 The North Colonnade, Canary Wharf, LONDON, E14 5HS.
    Tel 020 7066 1000 **Fax** 020 7066 9706 http://www.fsa.gov.uk
    Chairman: Lord Adair Turner   Chief Executive: Hector Sants

E   Established in October 1997 when the Securities & Investments Board was renamed the Financial Services Authority. In June 1998 banking supervision transferred to the FSA from the Bank of England. In May 2000 it took over role of UK Listing Authority from the London Stock Exchange. Under the Financial Services & Markets Act 2000 it assumed the regulatory functions of the Building Societies Commission, Friendly Societies Commission, Investment Management Regulatory Organisation, Personal Investment Authority, Register of Friendly Societies and the Securities & Futures Authority. In October 2004 and January 2005 it took on responsibility for the regulation of mortgage and general insurance business respectively. It functions as an independent non-governmental body with statutory powers, a company limited by guarantee and is financed by the financial services industry. The Board is appointed by HM Treasury and currently comprises 14 members including the Chairman.

R   To maintain confidence in the financial system.
     To promote public understanding of the financial system.
     To secure an appropriate degree of protection for consumers.
     To reduce financial crime.

G   United Kingdom.

●   In May 2002 the FSA acquired responsibility from the London Stock Exchange for acting as the competent authority for listing companies in the UK
     A single Financial Ombudsman Service (qv) & a new single Financial Services Compensation Scheme have also been set up.

✍   FSA is to be abolished in 2012. The Bank of England will set up a Financial Policy Committee to ensure the City as a whole is not taking excessive risks; a Prudential Regulatory Authority, also operated by the Bank, will regulate banks and other financial institutions; and a new Consumer Protection & Markets Authority will be created.

Financial Services & Markets Tribunal
✍   FINSMAT has been replaced by the **Upper Tribunal (Tax & Chancery)**.

Financial Services Skills Council   (FSSC)
■   51 Gresham Street, LONDON, EC2V 7HQ.
     Tel 0845 257 3772   **Fax** 0845 257 3770   http://www.fssc.org.uk
     Chairman: Trevor Matthews   Chief Executive: Paul Boyle

E   Established on 1 April 2004. It is the recognised Sector Skills Council for the financial services, accountancy and finance sector. The board comprises 16 members including the Chairman and Chief Executive.

G   United Kingdom.

✍   For further information see **Sector Skills Councils**.

Financial Supervision Commission   (FSC)
■   PO Box 58, Finch Hill House, DOUGLAS, Isle of Man, IM99 1DT.
     Tel 01624 689300   **Fax** 01624 689399   http://www.fsc.gov.im
     Chairman: Rosemary Penn, MBE   Chief Executive: John Aspden

E   Established in 1983. FSC functions as an independent statutory body. The Commission comprises seven members including the Chairman, all of whom are appointed by the Treasury.

R   To supervise effectively the private financial and commercial sector in the Island.

G   Isle of Man.

●   The Commission licenses and supervises banks, building societies, investment business, collective investment schemes, and corporate and trust service providers.
     It is also responsible for the Companies Registry.

✍   The insurance is supervised by a separate body, the Insurance & Pensions Authority (qv).

=   Barrantee Oaseirys Argidoil

Findhorn, Nairn & Lossie Trust   See **Rivers & Fisheries Trusts of Scotland**.

Fire Authority for Northern Ireland
✍   Replaced in 2006 by the Board of the **Northern Ireland Fire & Rescue Service**.

FIRE SERVICE

E   Every part of the UK is covered by a local authority Fire Service.
     Each authority must by law make provision for firefighting and maintain an effective Fire Service to meet normal firefighting requirements in its area.

✍   Numerous fire bodies are in existence and they can be found in the subject index under the appropriate headings.

Fire Service College
- London Road, MORETON-IN-MARSH, Glos, GL56 0RH.
  Tel 01608 650831   **Fax** 01608 651788   http://www.fireservicecollege.ac.uk
  Chief Executive: Kim Robinson
- E Established in 1968 as the Fire Service Technical College, it adopted its its current name upon merger with the Fire Service Staff College in 1981. The College functions as an Executive Agency of the Department for Communities & Local Government.
- R To be the central training establishment for the UK fire service.
- G United Kingdom.
- ● It also provides a wide range of specialist fire related services.

Fire Services Examinations Board
- ✍ Ceased to exist on 31 July 2006.

Firearms Consultative Committee
- ✍ Ceased to exist on 31 January 2004.

Firebuy Limited
- ✍ Established in 2006 to deliver English Fire & Rescue Service procurement at a national level. In 2010 it was being abolished, its procurement functions transferred to alternative suppliers and its residual functions to the Department for Communities & Local Government.

First East (1st East)
- ✍ Established in 2006, 1st East was the Urban Regeneration Company (qv) for Lowestoft and Great Yarmouth. It ceased trading on 31 March 2011.

First for Sport Qualifications   See **1st 4 Sport Qualifications** (at the beginning of this section).

FIRST-TIER TRIBUNAL

- E The Tribunals, Courts & Enforcement Act 2007 created a new two-tier tribunal system, First-tier and Upper, both of which are organised into Chambers. Each Chamber comprises similar jurisdictions or jurisdictions which bring together similar types of experts to hear appeals. The Upper Tribunal primarily, but not exclusively, reviews and decides appeals arising from a First-tier Tribunal.
- ● The Chambers of the First-tier Tribunal are:
  General Regulatory Chamber
     First-tier Tribunal (Charity)
     First-tier Tribunal (Claims Management Services)
     First-tier Tribunal (Consumer Credit)
     First-tier Tribunal (Environment)
     First-tier Tribunal (Estate Agents)
     First-tier Tribunal (Gambling)
     First-tier Tribunal (Immigration Services)
     First-tier Tribunal (Information Rights)
     First-tier Tribunal (Local Government Standards in England)
     First-tier Tribunal (Transport)
  Health, Education & Social Care Chamber
     First-tier Tribunal (Care Standards)
     First-tier Tribunal (Mental Health)
     First-tier Tribunal (Special Educational Needs & Disability)
     First-tier Tribunal (Primary Health Lists)
  Immigration & Asylum Chamber
     First-tier Tribunal (Immigration & Asylum Chamber)
  Social Entitlement Chamber
     First-tier Tribunal (Asylum Support)
     First-tier Tribunal (Social Security & Child Support)
     First-tier Tribunal (Criminal Injuries Compensation)
  Tax Chamber
     First-tier Tribunal (Tax)
  War Pensions & Armed Forces Compensation Chamber
     First-tier Tribunal (War Pensions & Armed Forces Compensation)

First-tier Tribunal (Asylum Support)   (AS)

■ Anchorage House 2nd Floor, 2 Clove Crescent, East India Dock, LONDON, E14 2BE.
   Tel 020 7538 6171   Fax 020 7538 6200
E Appointed on 3 April 2000 by the Secretary of State under the Immigration & Asylum Act 1999, and formerly
   known as the Asylum Support Adjudicator. AS sits in the Social Entitlement Chamber of the First-tier Tribunal
   and is administered by HM Courts & Tribunals Service (qv). The Tribunal numbers 25 Tribunal Judges.
R To consider appeals from decisions made by the UK Border Agency (qv).
G United Kingdom.
✍ Onward appeal from this Tribunal is to the Upper Tribunal (Administrative Appeals) (qv).

First-tier Tribunal (Care Standards)

■ Mowden Hall, Staindrop Road, DARLINGTON, Co Durham, DL3 9BG.
   Tel 01325 392712   Fax 01325 391045
E Established on 2 October 2000 under the Protection of Children Act 1999 and known as the Protection of
   Children Act Tribunal until April 2002 and the Care Standards Tribunal until 2008. It incorporates the former
   Registered Homes Tribunal. It sits in the Health, Education & Social Care Chamber of the First-tier Tribunal and
   is administered by HM Courts & Tribunals Service (qv).
R To consider appeals against a decision made by the Secretary of State to restrict or bar an individual from
   working with children or vulnerable adults and decisions to cancel, vary or refuse registration of certain health,
   childcare and social care provision.
G United Kingdom.
✍ Onward appeal from this Tribunal is to the Upper Tribunal (Administrative Appeals) (qv).

First-tier Tribunal (Charity)

■ PO Box 9300, LEICESTER, LE1 8DJ.
   Tel 0300 123 4504   Fax 0116 249 4253
   Principal Judge: Alison McKenna
E Established under the Charities Act 2006 and known as the Charities Tribunal until 1 September 2009. It sits in
   the General Regulatory Chamber of the First-tier Tribunal and is administered by HM Courts & Tribunals Service
   (qv). The Tribunal comprises five judges and seven other members.
R To hear appeals against the decisions of the Charity Commission (qv).
   To hear applications for review of the Commission's decisions.
G England, Wales.
✍ Onward appeal from this Tribunal is to the Upper Tribunal (Tax & Chancery) (qv).

First-tier Tribunal (Claims Management Services)

■ PO Box 9300, LEICESTER, LE1 8DJ.
   Tel 0300 123 4504   Fax 0116 249 4253
   Principal Judge: Sir Stephen Oliver, QC
E Established in 2006 under the Compensation Act 2006 and known as the Claims Management Services Tribunal
   until 18 January 2010. It sits in the General Regulatory Chamber of the First-tier Tribunal and is administered by
   HM Courts & Tribunals Service (qv). The Tribunal comprises five judges and 16 other members.
R To hear appeals from businesses and individuals providing claims management services in areas including
   personal injury, criminal injuries compensation, employment matters, housing disrepair, financial products and
   services, and industrial injury disablement benefits. The Tribunal considers cases where the Claims
   Management Regulator has refused them authorisation or has imposed sanctions on them.
G United Kingdom.
✍ Onward appeal from this Tribunal is to the Upper Tribunal (Administrative Appeals) (qv).

First-tier Tribunal (Consumer Credit)

■ PO Box 9300, LEICESTER, LE1 8DJ.
   Tel 0300 123 4504
   Principal Judge: His Hon Judge Peter Wulwik
E Established in 2009 replacing the Department for Business, Innovation & Skills' panel of Persons Hearing
   Consumer Credit Licensing Appeals. It sits in the General Regulatory Chamber of the First-tier Tribunal and is
   administered by HM Courts & Tribunals Service (qv).
R To hear and decide appeals against decisions of the Office of Fair Trading relating to
   licensing decisions of the OFT made under the Consumer Credit Act 1974,
   the imposition of requirements or a civil penalty on licensees under the 1974 Act, and
   the refusal to register, cancellation of registration or imposition of a penalty under the Money Laundering
   Regulations 2007.
G England, Scotland, Wales.
✍ Onward appeal from this Tribunal is to the Upper Tribunal (Administrative Appeals) (qv).

First-tier Tribunal (Criminal Injuries Compensation)

■ 5th Floor, Fox Court, 14 Gray's Inn Road, LONDON, WC1X 8HN.
   Tel 020 3206 0664   **Fax** 020 3206 0652
   Wellington House, 134-136 Wellington Street, GLASGOW, G2 2XL.
   Tel 0141 354 8555   **Fax** 0141 354 8556

E   Established on 1 April 1996 under the Criminal Injuries Compensation Act 1995, and formerly known as the Criminal Injuries Compensation Appeals Panel. It sits in the Social Entitlement Chamber of the First-tier Tribunal and is administered by HM Courts & Tribunals Service (qv).

R   To deal with appeals against review decisions of the Criminal Injuries Compensation Authority (qv) on claims for compensation made on or after 1 April 1996 under the Criminal Injuries Compensation Scheme.

G   United Kingdom.

✍   Onward appeal from this Tribunal is to the Upper Tribunal (Administrative Appeals) (qv).

First-tier Tribunal (Environment)

■ PO Box 9300, LEICESTER, LE1 8DJ.
   Tel 0300 123 4504   **Fax** 0116 249 4253
   Principal Judge: Professor John Angel

E   Established in 2010. It sits in the General Regulatory Chamber of the First-tier Tribunal and is administered by HM Courts & Tribunals Service (qv).

R   To hear appeals from civil sanctions made available for certain offences for use by the regulators Natural England and the Environment Agency (qqv).

G   England.

✍   Onward appeal from this Tribunal is to the Upper Tribunal (Administrative Appeals) (qv).

First-tier Tribunal (Estate Agents)

■ PO Box 9300, LEICESTER, LE1 8DJ.
   Tel 0300 123 4504   **Fax** 0116 249 4253   http://www.estateagentappeals.tribunals.gov.uk
   Principal Judge: His Hon Judge Peter Wulwik

E   Established in 2009 replacing the Department for Business, Innovation & Skills' panel of Persons Hearing Estate Agents Appeals. It sits in the General Regulatory Chamber of the First-tier Tribunal and is administered by HM Courts & Tribunals Service (qv).

R   To hear and decide appeals under the Estate Agents Act 1979 against decisions made by the Office of Fair Trading (qv) relating to
   an order prohibiting a person from acting as an estate agent where for example a person has been convicted of an offence involving fraud or other dishonesty,
   an order warning a person where for example that person has not met his duties under the 1979 Act, and
   a decision to revoke or vary a prohibition order or warning order made under the 1979 Act.

G   England, Scotland, Wales.

✍   Onward appeal from this Tribunal is to the Upper Tribunal (Administrative Appeals) (qv).

First-tier Tribunal (Gambling)

■ PO Box 9300, LEICESTER, LE1 8DJ.
   Tel 0300 123 4504   **Fax** 0116 249 4253
   Principal Judge: Nicholas John Warren

E   Established in 2007 under the Gambling Act 2005 and known as the Gambling Appeals Tribunal until 18 January 2010. It sits in the General Regulatory Chamber of the First-tier Tribunal and is administered by HM Courts & Tribunals Service (qv). The Tribunal comprises twelve judges.

R   To hear appeals against the decisions of the Gambling Commission (qv) relating to their existing licence or licence application.

G   United Kingdom.

✍   Onward appeal from this Tribunal is to the Upper Tribunal (Administrative Appeals) (qv).

First-tier Tribunal (Immigration & Asylum)   (FTTIAC)

■ PO Box 7866, LOUGHBOROUGH, Leics, LE11 2ZX.
   Tel 0845 600 0877   **Fax** 01509 221403

E   Established on 15 February 2010 in place of the Asylum & Immigration Tribunal which on 4 April 2005 had merged the former Immigration Appeal Tribunal and Immigration Appellate Authority. FTTIAC forms a chamber of and is administered by HM Courts & Tribunals Service (qv). The Tribunal comprises Immigration Judges and non-legal members.

R   To hear and decide appeals against decisions made by the Home Secretary and his officials in immigration, asylum and nationality matters, mainly against decisions to
   refuse a person asylum in the UK
   refuse a person entry to, or leave to remain in, the UK, or

© CBD Research Ltd · Beckenham · Kent BR3 5JS · Tel 020 8650 7745 · Fax 020 8650 0768 · E-mail cbd@cbdresearch.com · www.cbdresearch.com

deport someone already in the UK.

G   United Kingdom.

✍   Onward appeal from this Tribunal is to the Upper Tribunal (Immigration & Asylum Chamber) (qv).

First-tier Tribunal (Immigration Services)

■   7th Floor, Victory House, 30-34 Kingsway, LONDON, WC2B 6EX.
     Tel 020 3077 5860   **Fax** 020 3077 5836
     Judicial Head: Judge D Hunter, QC

E   Established on 30 October 2000 under the Immigration & Asylum Act 1999 and known as the Immigration
     Services Tribunal until 18 January 2010. It sits in the General Regulatory Chamber of the First-tier Tribunal and
     is administered by HM Courts & Tribunals Service (qv). The Tribunal comprises judicial members who are legally
     qualified and lay members with experience in immigration services or in the law nad procedure relating to
     immigration.

R   To hear appeals against decisions made by the Office of the Immigration Services Commissioner (qv) and to
     consider disciplinary charges brought against immigration advisers by the Commissioner.

G   United Kingdom.

✍   Onward appeal from this Tribunal is to the Upper Tribunal (Administrative Appeals) (qv).

First-tier Tribunal (Information Rights)

■   PO Box 9300, LEICESTER, LE1 8DJ.
     Tel 0300 123 4504   **Fax** 0116 249 4253
     Principal Judge: Prof John Angel

E   Established in 1984 as the Data Protection Tribunal, it was renamed the Information Tribunal under the Freedom
     of Information Act 2000 and adopted its current name on 18 January 2010. It sits in the General Regulatory
     Chamber of the First-tier Tribunal and is administered by HM Courts & Tribunals Service (qv). The Tribunal
     comprises 16 judges and 34 lay members.

R   To hear appeals from notices issued by the Information Commissioner (qv) under the
     Freedom of Information Act 2000
     Data Protection Act 1998
     Privacy & Electronic Communications Regulation 2003, and
     Environmental Information Regulations 2004
     except when a Minister of the Crown issues a certificate on the grounds of national security, in which case the
     appeal is automatically transferred to the Upper Tribunal (Administrative Appeals Chamber) (qv).

G   United Kingdom.

✍   Onward appeal from this Tribunal is to the Upper Tribunal (Administrative Appeals) (qv).

First-tier Tribunal (Local Government Standards in England)

■   York House, 31-36 York Place, LEEDS, W Yorks, LS1 2ED.
     Tel 0113 389 6086   **Fax** 0113 389 6002

E   The Tribunal replaces a judicial tribunal established under the Local Government Act 2000. Since 18 January
     2010 it sits in the General Regulatory Chamber of the First-tier Tribunal and is administered by HM Courts &
     Tribunals Service (qv). The Tribunal comprises eight judges and 19 lay members.

R   To determine references and appeals about the conduct of members of local authorities.
     To consider appeals made by councillors against a decision of a Standards Committee of a local authority.

G   England.

✍   Onward appeal from this Tribunal is to the Upper Tribunal (Administrative Appeals) (qv).

First-tier Tribunal (Mental Health)

■   PO Box 8793, 5th Floor, LEICESTER, LE1 8BN.
     Tel 0845 223 2022
     Principal Judge: Judge John Wright

E   Established in 1983 under the Mental Health Act 1983, and formerly known as the Mental Health Review Tribunal.
     It sits in the Health, Education & Social Care Chamber of the First-Tier Tribunal and is administered by HM
     Courts & Tribunals Service (qv).

R   To hear applications and references for people detained under the 1983 Act, as amended by the Mental Health
     Act 2007. statutory criteria for discharge have been satisfied.

G   England.

✍   Onward appeal from this Tribunal is to the Upper Tribunal (Administrative Appeals) (qv).

First-tier Tribunal (Primary Health Lists)   (FHSAA)

■   Mowden Hall, Staindrop Road, DARLINGTON, Co Durham, DL3 9BG.
    Tel 01325 391130
    Deputy Chamber President: Judge John Aitken
E   Established on 1 December 2001 under the Health & Social Care Act 2001 and known as the Family Health
    Services Appeal Authority until 18 January 2010. It sits in the Health, Education & Social Care Chamber of the
    First-tier Tribunal and is administered by HM Courts & Tribunals Service (qv).
R   To hear appeals and applications resulting from decisions made by Primary Care Trusts in respect of permitting
    general practitioners, dentists, optometrists and some pharmacists to provide NHS services within the Trust
    area.
G   United Kingdom.
✍   Onward appeal from this Tribunal is to the Upper Tribunal (Administrative Appeals) (qv).

First-tier Tribunal (Social Security & Child Support)   (SSCS)

■   Administrative Support Centre, PO Box 14620, BIRMINGHAM, B16 6RF.
    Tel 0845 408 3500   Fax 0121 634 7201   http://www.appeals-service.gov.uk
    Eastgate House, Newport Road, CARDIFF, CF24 0YP.
    Tel 0300 123 1142   Fax 029 2044 0596
    Wellington House, 134-136 Wellington Street, GLASGOW, G2 2XL.
    Tel 0141 354 8400   Fax 0141 354 8463
    York House, York Place, LEEDS, W Yorks, LS1 2ED.
    Tel 0113 389 6000   Fax 0113 389 6001
    36 Dale Street, LIVERPOOL, L2 5UZ.
    Tel 0151 243 1400   Fax 0151 243 1401
    Manorview House, Kings Manor, NEWCASTLE UPON TYNE, NE1 6PA.
    Tel 0191 201 2300   Fax 0191 201 2357
    Copthall House, 9 The Pavement, Grove Road, SUTTON, Surrey, SM1 1DA.
    Tel 020 8652 2300   Fax 020 8652 2381
E   Established on 3 April 2000 under the Social Security Act 1998, and formerly known as the Social Security &
    Child Support Appeals Tribunal. SSCS sits in the Social Entitlement Chamber of the First-tier Tribunal and is
    administered by HM Courts & Tribunals Service (qv). It functions as a Tribunal NDPB of the Ministry of Justice
    and is headed by the Social Entitlement Chapter President.
R   To deal with disputes about Income Support, Jobseeker's Allowance, Incapacity Benefit, Employment Support
    Allowance, Disability Living Allowance, Attendance Allowance and Retirement Pensions. Also Child Support,
    Tax Credits, Statutory Sick Pay, Statutory Maternity Pay, Compensation Recovery Scheme/Road Traffic (NHS)
    charges, Vaccine Damage, Housing Benefit and Council Tax Benefit.
G   United Kingdom.
✍   Onward appeal from this Tribunal is to the Upper Tribunal (Administrative Appeals) (qv).

First-tier Tribunal (Special Educational Needs & Disability)

■   Mowden Hall, Staindrop Road, DARLINGTON, Co Durham, DL3 9BG.
    Tel 01325 392760   Fax 01325 391310   http://www.sendist.gov.uk
E   Established on 3 November 2008 replacing the former Special Educational Needs & Disability Tribunal. It sits in
    the Health, Education & Social Care Chamber of the First-tier Tribunal and is administered by HM Courts &
    Tribunals Service (qv).
R   To consider appeals from parents whose children have special educational needs against decisions made by
    Local Education Authorities in England about their children's education.
G   England.
✍   Onward appeal from this Tribunal is to the Upper Tribunal (Administrative Appeals) (qv).

First-tier Tribunal (Tax)

■   2nd Floor, 54 Hagley Road, BIRMINGHAM, B16 8PE.
    Tel 0845 223 8080
E   Established on 1 April 2009 under the Tribunals, Courts & Enforcement Act 2007, replacing the General
    Commissioners of Income Tax, Special Commissioners of Income Tax, VAT & Duties Trubunals and the Section
    706 Tribunal. It sits in the General Regulatory Chamber of the First-tier Tribunal and is administered by HM
    Courts & Tribunals Service (qv). The Tribunal comprises legally qualified Judges and non-legally qualified expert
    members.
R   To hear appeals against decisions made by HM Revenue & Customs relating to Income Tax, Corporation Tax,
    Capital Gains Tax, Inheritance Tax, Stamp Duty Land Tax, PAYE coding notices, National Insurance
    contributions, Statutory payments, VAT or duties such as custom duties, excise duties or landfill tax,
    aggregates or climate change levies.
G   England, Scotland, Wales.
✍   Onward appeal from this Tribunal is to the Upper Tribunal (Tax & Chancery) (qv).

© CBD Research Ltd · Beckenham · Kent BR3 5JS · Tel 020 8650 7745 · Fax 020 8650 0768 · E-mail cbd@cbdresearch.com · www.cbdresearch.com

First-tier Tribunal (Transport)
- ■ 7th Floor, Victory House, 30-34 Kingsway, LONDON, WC2B 6EX.
  Tel 020 3077 5860   Fax 020 3077 5836   http://www.transporttribunal.gov.uk
- E Established in 1985 under the Transport Act 1985 and known as the Transport Tribunal until 2010. Since 18 January 2010 it sits in the General Regulatory Chamber of the First-tier Tribunal and is administered by HM Courts & Tribunals Service (qv). The Tribunal comprises four judges and non-legal members who have experience in transport operations and its law and procedure.
- R To hear and decide appeals against decisions of the Registrar of Approved Driving Instructors.
  To hear appeals for London service permits against decisions of Transport for London (qv).
  To resolve disputes over postal charges between universal service providers and carriers under the Postal Services Act 2000.
- G England, Wales, Scotland.
- ✍ Onward appeal from this Tribunal is to the Upper Tribunal (Administrative Appeals) (qv).

First-tier Tribunal (War Pensions & Armed Forces Compensation)   (WPAFC)
- ■ 5th Floor, Fox Court, 14 Gray's Inn Road, LONDON, WC1X 8HN.
  Tel 020 3206 0701   Fax 020 3206 0702
- E Established in 1919 under the War Pensions Act 1919 and known as the Pensions Appeal Tribunal until 3 Nov 2008. WPAFC forms a chamber of and is administered by HM Courts & Tribunals Service (qv).
- R To hear appeals from ex-servicemen and women who have had their claims for a War Pension or Armed Forces Compensation rejected by the Secretary of State for Defence.
- G England, Wales.
- ● The War Pensions Scheme started in 1918 and continues in respect of injuries that occurred before 5 April 2005. For injuries after 5 April 2005 a new Scheme, the Armed Forces Compensation Scheme applies.
- ✍ Onward appeal from this Tribunal is to the Upper Tribunal (Administrative Appeals) (qv).

Fish Health Inspectorate   (FHI)
- ■ The Nothe, Barrack Road, WEYMOUTH, Dorset, DT4 8UB.
  Tel 01305 206700   Fax 01305 206602   http://www.cefas.co.uk/fish-health-inspectorate.aspx
- E Established in 1937 under the Fish Disease Act. FHI is part of the Centre for Environment, Fisheries & Aquaculture Science (qv) and reports to the Department for Environment, Food & Rural Affairs and the National Assembly for Wales.
- R To act for Defra and the National Assembly for Wales in undertaking statutory and inspection duties resulting from the EU Fish Health regime and other national legislation in the area of fish and shellfish health in England and Wales.
  To license and monitor imports of shellfish from other countries, and to run an enforcement programme aimed at preventing the illegal importation of these animals.
- G England, Wales.

Fisheries Conservancy Board for Northern Ireland
- ✍ On 1 June 2009 the Board was abolished, its functions transferred to the Department of Culture, Arts & Leisure Northern Ireland.

Fisheries, Ecology & Recreation Advisory Committees   See **Regional Fisheries, Ecology & Recreation Advisory Committees**.

Fisheries (Electricity) Committee
- ■ R408A Pentland House, 47 Robb's Loan, EDINBURGH, EH14 1TY.
  Tel 0131 244 5245   Fax 0131 244 6313
  Chairman: James Cockburn
- E Established in 1943 under the Hydro-Electric Development (Scotland) Act 1943, its current authority is derived from the Electricity Act 1989. The Committee functions as an Advisory NDPB of the Scottish Executive Rural Affairs Department. It comprises four members including the Chairman.
- R To advise and assist Scottish Ministers and any person engaged in, or proposing to engage in, the generation of hydro-electric power on questions relating to the effect on fisheries or stocks of fish.
  To advise on intakes and outfalls at some other types of power station, particularly the large coastal and estuarine fossil-fuelled and nuclear stations that use very large quantities of seawater for cooling purposes.
- G Scotland.

Fisheries Research Services
✍ On 1 April 2009 FRS and the Scottish Fisheries Protection Agency merged with the Scottish Government Marine Directorate to form **Marine Scotland**.

Flammable Substances Subcommittee
✍ A subcommittee of the Advisory Committee on Dangerous Substances which closed in 2004.

Fleet Air Arm Museum   See the **National Museum of the Royal Navy**.

Flight Safety Committee   See **United Kingdom Flight Safety Committee**.

Flintshire Local Health Board
✍ Merged on 1 October 2010 with the Anglesey, Conwy, Denbighshire, Gwynedd and Wrexham Local Health Boards to form **Betsi Cadwaladr University Health Board**.

Flood Risk Management Committees   See **Environment Agency**.

Food from Britain
✍ Wound up on 31 March 2009.

The Food Commission (UK) Ltd
■ 94 White Lion Street, LONDON, N1 9PF.
Tel 020 7837 2250   Fax 020 7837 1141   http://www.foodmagazine.org.uk
E Established in 1990 in place of the former London Food Commission. The Commission functions as a not-for-profit company limited by guarantee and an independent consumer watchdog on food issues. It is funded by donations and by subscriptions to the Food Magazine.
R To campaign for safer, healthier food and report on such issues as genetically modified food, food irradiation, animal growth hormones, additives, pesticides, food labelling and advertising, as well as health issues such as functional foods, fat, sugar and salt.
G United Kingdom.

Food & Drink Qualifications Ltd   The awarding body for the **Meat Training Council**.

Food & Drink Sector Skills   (FDSS)
■ 2nd Floor, Belfast Mills, 71-75 Percy Street, BELFAST, BT13 2HW.
Tel 028 9032 9269   http://www.foodanddrinksectorskills.co.uk
E Established in 1994, formerly known as the Food & Drink Training Council. FDSS is an employer led body which exists to champion the skills agenda on behalf of the Northern Ireland agri-food manufacturing sector. The Board comprises nine members.
R To ensure that the supply of skills training is matched to employer demand.
G Northern Ireland.
✍ For further information see **Sector Training Councils**.

Food & Drink Training Council
✍ See **Food & Drink Sector Skills**.

Food & Environment Research Agency   (FERA)
■ Sand Hutton, YORK, YO41 1LZ.
Tel 01904 462000   Fax 01904 462111   http://www.fera.defra.gov.uk
Chief Executive: Adrian Belton
E Established on 1 April 2009, bringing together the Central Science Laboratory, the UK Government Decontamination Service, Defra's Plant Health Division (includes Bee Health and the Plant Health & Seeds Inspectorate) and the Plant Variety Rights Office & Seeds Division. FERA functions as an Executive Agency of the Department for Environment, Food & Rural Affairs.
R To support and develop a sustainable food chain, a healthy natural environment, and to protect the global community from biological and chemical risks.

© CBD Research Ltd · Beckenham · Kent BR3 5JS · Tel 020 8650 7745 · Fax 020 8650 0768 · E-mail cbd@cbdresearch.com · www.cbdresearch.com

G   United Kingdom.
- FERA's work is carried out for government departments and for private and pubic sector organisations - both nationally and internationally.

Food Ethics Council   (FEC)
- 39-41 Surrey Street, BRIGHTON, E Sussex, BN1 3PB.
 Tel 01273 766654   Fax 01273 766653   http://www.foodethicscouncil.org
 Chairman: Helen Browning, OBE
E   Established in 1998 with support from the Joseph Rowntree Charitable Trust and the Farm & Food Society. FEC functions as a company limited by guarantee and a registered charity. The Council comprises 14 members including the Chairman.
R   To provide independent advice on the ethics of food and farming.
G   United Kingdom.

Food Incidents Task Force
- Aviation House, 125 Kingsway, LONDON, WC2B 6NH.
 Tel 020 7276 8000
E   The Task Force functions as an advisory committee of the Food Standards Agency (qv).
R   To reduce the possibility of contamination incidents in the food chain and to improve the management of such incidents should they occur.
G   United Kingdom.

Food Safety Promotion Board   (FSPB)
- 7 Eastgate Avenue, Eastgate, Little Island, CORK, Republic of Ireland.
 Tel +353 (0)21 230 4100   Fax +353 (0)21 230 4111   http://www.safefood.eu
 Block B, Abbey Court, Lower Abbey Street, DUBLIN 1, Republic of Ireland.
 Tel +353 (0)1 448 0600   Fax +353 (0)1 448 0699
 Chairman of Advisory Board: John Dardis   Chairman of Scientific Advisory Committee: Dr Ken Baird
 Chief Executive: Martin Higgins
E   Established on 2 December 1999, the Board is one of the North/South Implementation Bodies set up under the British-Irish Agreement of 8 March 1999. Operating under the name **SafeFood**, it is responsible to the North South Ministerial Council (qv), the Department of Culture, Arts & Leisure Northern Ireland and the Irish Government. The Advisory Board comprises eleven members including the Chairman.
R   To promote food safety; To research into food safety; To communicate any food alerts; To conduct surveillance of foodborne disease; To promote scientific co-operation and laboratory linkages; To develop cost-effective facilities for specialised laboratory testing.
G   Northern Ireland, Republic of Ireland.
✍   For further information see the **North South Ministerial Council**.

Food Standards Agency   (FSA)
- Aviation House, 125 Kingsway, LONDON, WC2B 6NH.
 Tel 020 7276 8000   http://www.food.gov.uk
 Foss House, Kings Pool, 1-2 Peasholme Green, YORK, YO1 7PR.
 Chairman: Jeff Rooker
 Chief Executive: Tim Smith
E   Established on 1 April 2000 under the Food Standards Act 1999. FSA functions as a non-ministerial government department. It is accountable to Parliament through Health Ministers and to the devolved administrations for its activities within their areas. The board comprises 13 members including the Chairman.
R   To protect the health of the public, and the interests of consumers, in relation to food.
G   United Kingdom.
- The Agency is assisted in its work by numerous committees.
✍   The Agency has national offices in Scotland, Wales and Northern Ireland (see below).

Food Standards Agency Northern Ireland   (FSA)
- 10c Clarendon Road, BELFAST, BT1 3BG.
 Tel 028 9041 7700   http://www.foodstandards.gov.uk/northernireland/
 Director: Gerry McCurdy
E   Established on 3 April 2000 under the Food Standards Act 1999.
G   Northern Ireland.
✍   See the Food Standards Agency's main entry for further information.

Food Standards Agency Scotland (FSA)

■ 6th Floor, St Magnus House, 25 Guild Street, ABERDEEN, AB11 6NJ.
Tel 01224 285100 http://www.foodstandards.gov.uk/scotland/
Director: Prof Charles Milne

E Established on 3 April 2000 under the Food Standards Act 1999.
G Scotland.
✍ See the Food Standards Agency's main entry for further information.

Food Standards Agency Wales (FSA)

■ 11th Floor, Southgate House, Wood Street, CARDIFF, CF10 1EW.
Tel 029 2067 8999 http://www.food.gov.uk/wales/
= Asiantaeth Safonau Bwyd Cymru
Director: Steve Wearne

E Established on 3 April 2000 under the Food Standards Act 1999.
G Wales.
✍ See the Food Standards Agency's main entry for further information.

Food Standards Sampling Co-ordination Working Group

■ Aviation House, 125 Kingsway, LONDON, WC2B 6NH.
Tel 020 7276 8000
Chairman: Gwyneth Beddoe

E Established in May 2003 jointly by the Food Standards Agency (FSA) and Local Authorities Coordinators of Regulatory Services (LACORS) (qqv). The working group, which functions as an advisory committee of FSA and LACORS, comprises 24 members including the Chairman.
R To encourage better coordination of foods standards sampling across local authorities and the FSA and to promote focussed sampling programmes.
G United Kingdom.

Football Foundation

■ Whittington House, 19-30 Alfred Place, LONDON, WC1E 7EA.
Tel 0845 345 4555 Fax 0845 345 7057 http://www.footballfoundation.org.uk
Chairman: Clive Sherling Chief Executive: Paul Thorogood

E Established in July 2000. The Foundation is a registered charity and is funded by the Football Association, the Premier League and, through Sport England (qv), the Department for Culture, Media & Sport. The Board of Trustees comprises seven members including the Chairman.
R To improve facilities, create opportunities and build communities by providing a combined investment programme for grass roots football community and education projects.
G England.
● The Foundation is assisted by three panels:
    Community Assessment Panel
    Facilities Advisory Panel
    FSIF Safety Improvement Panel

Football Licensing Authority (FLA)

■ Floor 6, Oceanic House, 1a Cockspur Street, LONDON, SW1Y 5BG.
Tel 020 7930 6693 http://www.flaweb.org.uk
Chairman: Paul Darling, QC Chief Executive: Ruth Shaw

E Established in 1989 under the Football Spectators Act 1989. FLA functions as an Executive NDPB of the Department for Culture, Media & Sport. Its board comprises nine members including the Chairman.
R To ensure that all spectators, regardless of age, gender, ethnic origin, disability or the team that they support, are able to attend football grounds in safety, comfort and security.
G England, Wales.
✍ The Government announced on 14 October 2010 that FLA would continue as a separate body until after 2012 when its expertise and functions would be transferred to another body. Meanwhile, the Government is supporting a private member's bill which would see FLA renamed the Sports Grounds Safety Authority and its remit extended.

Footway & Cycle Track Management Group A sub-group of the **United Kingdom Roads Board**.

Foras Na Gaeilge

■ 7 Merrion Square, DUBLIN 2, Republic of Ireland.
   Tel +353 (0)1 639 8400   http://www.forasnagaeilge.ie
   Chairman: Liam Ó Maoilmhichíl   Chief Executive: Ferdie Mac an Fhailigh
E Established on 2 December 1999. The Foras functions as an agency responsible to the North/South Language
   Body (qv). The Board comprises 15 members including the Chairman.
R To promote the Irish language throughout the whole island of Ireland.
G Republic of Ireland, Northern Ireland.
✍ For further information see the **North/South Language Body**.

Foreign Compensation Commission   (FCC)

■ Old Admiralty Building, LONDON, SW1A 2PA.
   Tel 020 7008 5000
   Chairman: Dr John Barker   Secretary: Barrie England
E Established in 1950 under the Foreign Compensation Act 1950. It functions as a Tribunal NDPB of the Foreign &
   Commonwealth Office.
R To take stock of British property losses abroad arising from the actions of foreign governments.
   To judicially determine the entitlement of claimants when compensation is secured through diplomatic or other
   means.
G United Kingdom.
✍ The Foreign & Commonwealth Office announced on 14 October 2010 that the future of FCC was under
   consideration.

Forensic Medicine Committee   (FMC)

■ BMA House, Tavistock Square, LONDON, WC1H 9JP.
   Tel 020 7383 6180   **Fax** 020 7383 6400   http://www.bma.org.uk
   President: Dr George Fernie
E Established as a Branch of Practice Committee of the British Medical Association. The Committee comprises nine
   members including the President.
R To represent members of the BMA engaged in forensic medicine and to advise the BMA on matters affecting
   forensic medicine.
G United Kingdom.
✍ See **British Medical Association** [Branch of Practice Committees] for further information.

Forensic Science Advisory Council   (FSAC)

■ 3rd Floor, SW Quarter, Seacole Building, 2 Marsham Street, LONDON, SW1P 4DF.
   Tel 020 7035 4848
   Forensic Science Regulator: Andrew Rennison
E Established in 2007. FSAC functions as an Advisory NDPB of the Home Office. The Council comprises 16
   members and is chaired by the Forensic Science Regulator.
R To advise and support the Regulator across a wide range of issues relevant to quality standards in forensic
   science.
G United Kingdom.
● The Forensic Science Regulator is a public appointee whose function is to ensure that the provision of forensic
   science services across the criminal justice system is subject to an appropriate regime of scientific quality
   standards.

Forensic Science Northern Ireland   (FSNI)

■ 151 Belfast Road, CARRICKFERGUS, Co Antrim, BT38 8PL.
   Tel 028 9036 1888   **Fax** 028 9036 1900   http://www.fsni.gov.uk
   Chief Executive: Stan Browm
E Established on 1 September 1995. FSNI functions as an Executive Agency of the Department of Justice Northern
   Ireland. The Executive Board comprises nine members including the Chief Executive.
R To provide effective impartial forensic science to support justice.
G Northern Ireland.

Forensic Science Service   (FSS)

■ Trident Court, 2920 Solihull Parkway, Birmingham Business Park, BIRMINGHAM, B37 7YN.
   Tel 0300 123 1232   http://www.forensic.gov.uk
   Chairman: Bill Griffiths   Chief Executive: Simon Bennett   Shareholder Executive contact: Antony Stimpson
E Established on 1 April 1991. FSS functions as a Government owned company of the Home Office.
R To meet the needs of specific police investigations into all types of crime.

G   England and Wales.
- The service has eleven regional facilities.
  FSS also carries out day-to-day running of the National DNA Database (NDNAD) under contract to the Home Office.
- ✍ One of the businesses managed by the **Shareholder Executive**.
  The Government announced on 14 December 2010 that the loss-making FSS will be gradually broken up and close completely by March 2012.

Forest Research
- Alice Holt Lodge, FARNHAM, Surrey, GU10 4LH.
  Tel 01420 22255   **Fax** 01420 23653   http://www.forestresearch.gov.uk
  Chief Executive: James Pendlebury
E   Established on 1 April 1997. Forest Research functions as an Executive Agency of the Forestry Commission (qv). The executive board comprises ten persons.
R   To provide research services relevant to UK and international forestry interests and inform and support forestry's contribution to governmental policies.
G   England, Scotland, Wales.
- Forest Research has a Northern Research Station at Roslin, Midlothian, and numerous field stations.

Forest Service
- Dundonald House, Upper Newtownards Road, BELFAST, BT4 3SB.
  Tel 028 9052 4480   **Fax** 028 9052 4570   http://www.forestserviceni.org.uk
  Chief Executive: David Small
E   Established on 1 April 1998. The Service functions as an Executive Agency of the Department of Agriculture & Rural Development Northern Ireland. The board comprises six members including the Chief Executive.
R   To contribute to the economic development of the entire forestry sector in Northern Ireland, whilst at the same time promoting the sustainable management of forests for multiple use and conserving and enhancing the rural environment.
G   Northern Ireland.

Forestry Commission
- Silvan House, 231 Corstorphine Road, EDINBURGH, EH12 7AT.
  Tel 0131 334 0303   **Fax** 0131 334 3047   http://www.forestry.gov.uk
  Chairman: Mrs Pamela Warhurst, CBE   Director General: Tim Rollinson
E   Established in 1919 under the Forestry Act 1919, its responsibilities and powers are derived mainly from the Forestry Act 1967 and the Plant Health Act 1967. The Commission functions as a non-ministerial government department. Its Board comprises the Chairman and ten other Commissioners.
R   To prevent loss of tree cover and ensure that new forests and related operations do not harm the environment.
  To protect Britain's forests from pests and disease by managing plant health legislation for trees and inspecting imported timber.
  To provide assurance of the source of tree seeds, cones, cuttings and other planting stock.
G   England, Wales, Scotland.
- On 1 April 2003 the current devolved structure of separate Forestry Commissions for England, Wales and Scotland (qqv) was established.
  Forest Research (qv) is a Great Britain-wide agency of the Commission.
- ✍ The Forestry Commission manages 7,720 square kilometres of land and disburses government funding in support of private forests and woodlands.
  The Government announced on 14 October 2010 that the Commission is to be substantially reformed in England and Wales.

Forestry Commission England
- Great Eastern House, Tenison Road, CAMBRIDGE, CB1 2DU.
  Tel 01223 314546   **Fax** 01223 460699
  Director: Paul Hill-Tout
E   Established on 1 April 2003. Forestry Commission England is overseen by the National Committee for England of the Forestry Commission (qv).
R   To deliver the Great Britain-wide policies of the Forestry Commission in England and the forestry policies for England of the Department for Environment, Food & Rural Affairs.
G   England.
- ✍ The Government announced on 14 October 2010 that Forestry Commission England will be substantially reformed.

Forestry Commission Scotland

- ■ Silvan House, 231 Corstophine Road, EDINBURGH, EH12 7AT.
  Tel 0131 334 0303   Fax 0131 314 6152   http://www.forestry.gov.uk/scotland
  Chairman: Hamish Macleod   Forestry Commissioner Scotland: Dr Bob McIntosh
- E Established on 1 April 2003. The Commission is funded by the Scottish Parliament and directed by Scottish Ministers through the national Board of Commissioners and the National Committee for Scotland. The National Committee for Scotland comprises eight members including the Chairman and the Forestry Commissioner Scotland.
- R To protect and expand Scotland's forests and woodlands and increase their value to society and the environment.
- G Scotland.
- ✍ See also **Forest Enterprise Scotland**.

Forestry Commission Wales

- ■ Rhodfa Padarn, Llanbadarn Fawr, ABERYSTWYTH, Ceredigion, SY23 3UR.
  Tel 0300 068 0300   Fax 0300 068 0301
  Chairman: Jon Owen Jones   Director: Trefor Owen
- E Established on 1 April 2003. Forestry Commission Wales acts as the Department of Forestry of the Welsh Asembly Government. The National Committee comprises seven members including the Chairman.
- R To advise on the development and implementation of the forestry policy of the Welsh Government.
  To encourage sustainable woodland management within the private sector.
  To administer grants and regulatory work, including licensing for felling and replanting.
- G Wales.
- ✍ The Welsh Government is considering moving Forestry Commission Wales and Environment Agency Wales (qv) to form part of a Welsh Government environmental body.

Forestry Enterprise Scotland

- ■ 1 Highlander Way, INVERNESS, IV2 7GB.
  Tel 01463 232811   Fax 01463 243846
  Chief Executive: Simon Hodge
- E Established on 1 April 2003. Forest Enterprise Scotland functions as an Executive Agency of Forestry Commission Scotland (qv).
- R To protect, manage and maintain Scotland's woodlands and forests and recreation and access facilities for the general public.
- G Scotland.

Forth Fisheries Trust   See **Rivers & Fisheries Trusts of Scotland**.

Forth Valley Local Enterprise Company
- ✍ Now functions as the Stirling office of **Scottish Enterprise**.

Forth Valley NHS Board

- ■ Carseview House, Castle Business Park, STIRLING, FK9 4SW.
  Tel 01786 463031   http://www.nhsforthvalley.com
  Chairman: Ian Mullen, OBE, DL   Chief Executive: Prof Fiona Mackenzie
- G Clackmannanshire, Falkirk and Stirling.
- ✍ For further information see **NHS Scotland - Boards**.

Forum on Historical Manuscripts & Academic Research   See **Advisory Council on National Records & Archives**.

Forward Swindon

- ■ Wiltshire Court, Farnsby Street, SWINDON, Wilts, SN1 5AH.
  Tel 01793 429250   Fax 01793 619299   http://www.forwardswindon.co.uk
  Chief Executive: Ian Piper
- E Established in 2002 as the New Swindon Company Ltd, an Urban Regeneration Company, on 1 April 2010 it became Economic Development Company and adopted the Forward Swindon trading name.
- R To promote cultural development, economic development, inward investment, place marketing and regeneration in Swindon.

G   Swindon.
✍   For further information see **Economic Development Companies**.

Foundries Industry Advisory Committee   (FIAC)
■   Arden House, Regent Centre, Gosforth, NEWCASTLE UPON TYNE, NE3 3JN.
     Tel 0191 202 6272
E   Established on 17 July 1979 by the Health & Safety Executive (qv) under the Health & Safety at Work etc Act
     1974. The Committee comprises the chairman & 18 other members.
R   To provide a forum for member industries to promote improved standards of health and safety and the
     'Revitalising Agenda' within the foundries industry.
G   United Kingdom
●   The FIAC is assisted in its work by two sub-committees:
         Noise & Vibration Sub-Committee
         Occupational Health & Hygiene Sub-Committee.

Fourth Plinth Commissioning Group
■   City Hall, The Queen's Walk, More London, LONDON, SE1 2AA.
     Tel 020 7983 4100   http://www.london.gov.uk/fourthplinth/
     Chairman: Ekow Eshun   Director: Justine Simons
E   Established in 1999 by the Mayor of London following the success of a series of three works commissioned by
     the Royal Society for the Encouragement of the Arts, Manufactures & Commerce (RSA) in 1998. The Group
     comprises nine members including the Chairman.
R   To guide and monitor a programme of contemporary art commissions from leading national and international
     artists for the Fourth Plinth in Trafalgar Square.
G   United Kingdom.

Fowey Harbour Commissioners
■   Harbour Office, Albert Quay, FOWEY, Cornwall, PL23 1AJ.
     Tel 01726 832471   **Fax** 01726 833738   http://www.foweyharbour.co.uk
     Chairman: Max Pemberton   Chief Executive & Harbour Master: Captain Mike Sutherland, MBE
E   Established in 1869 under the Fowey Harbour Order Act 1869. The Commission comprises ten members
     including the Chairman.
G   Fowey.
✍   For further information see **Port & Harbour Authorities**. Executive NDPB of the Department of Agriculture &
     Rural Development. as 1 of the 6 North/South Implementation Bodies, while functioning as an provisions made
     in the Good Friday Agreement which also established the FCILC kniown as the Foyle Fisheries Commission; it
     adopted its new name under Republic of Ireland) & the Foyle Fisheries Act (Northern Ireland) 1952, & Executive
     NDPB of the Department of Agriculture & Rural Development. as 1 of the 6 North/South Implementation Bodies,
     while functioning as an provisions made in the Good Friday Agreement which also established the FCILC
     kniown as the Foyle Fisheries Commission; it adopted its new name under Republic of Ireland) & the Foyle
     Fisheries Act (Northern Ireland) 1952, &

Foyle, Carlingford & Irish Lights Commission   (FCILC)
■   Joint Secretariat, 39 Abbey Street, ARMAGH, BT61 7EB.
     Tel 028 3751 8068   **Fax** 028 3751 1874   http://www.loughs-agency.org
     Chairman: Tarlach O Crosain
E   Established on 2 December 1999 under the North/South Co-operation (Implementation Bodies) (NI) Order 1999
     and the British-Irish Agreement of 8 March 1999. It functions as an Executive NDPB of the Department of
     Agriculture & Rural Development Northern Ireland and of the Department of Communications, Marine & Natural
     Resources (Republic of Ireland). The Commission comprises twelve members appointed by the North/South
     Ministerial Council.
R   FCILC was intended to oversee two agencies, the Loughs Agency (qv) and the Lights Agency, but it was
     announced in April 2011 that the latter would not be established and that the Commissioners of Irish Lights (qv)
     would continue as the General Lighthouse Authority for Ireland.
G   Northern Ireland, Republic of Ireland.
✍   For further information see the **North South Ministerial Council**.

Fraserburgh Harbour Commissioners
■   Shore Street, FRASERBURGH, AB43 5BR.
     Tel 01346 515858   **Fax** 01346 516641   http://www.fraserburghharbour.co.uk
     Convenor: Peter Bruce

G   Fraserburgh.
✍   For further information see **Port & Harbour Authorities**.

FSIF Safety Improvement Panel   See **Football Foundation**.

Fuel Cells Advisory Panel
✍   The Panel was disbanded in 2003-04.

Fuel Poverty Advisory Group   (FPAG)
■   3 Whitehall Place, LONDON, SW1A 2AW.
    Tel 0300 060 4000
    Chairman: Derek Lickorish
E   Established in 2002. FPAG functions as an Advisory NDPB of the Department of Energy & Climate Change. The Group comprises the Chairman and senior representatives from the energy industry, charities and consumer bodies.
R   To consider and report on the effectiveness of current policies aiming to reduce fuel poverty.
    To consider and report on the case for greater coordination.
    To identify barriers to reducing fuel poverty and to developing effective partnerships, and to propose solutions.
    To consider and report on any additional policies needed to achieve the Government's targets.
    To encourage key organisations to tackle fuel poverty.
    To consider and report on the results of work to monitor fuel poverty.
G   United Kingdom.

Fulbright Commission   See **US-UK Educational Commission**.

Fundraising Standards Board   (FRSB)
■   1st Floor, 89 Albert Embankment, LONDON, SE1 7TP.
    Tel 0845 402 5442   Fax 0845 402 5443   http://www.frsb.org.uk
    Chairman: Colin Lloyd   Chief Executive: Alistair McLean
E   Established in February 2006. FRSB functions as a not for profit, community interest company, supported by the Office of the Third Sector, the Scottish Government and the Welsh Government. The Board comprises the Chairman, representatives from the major voluntary sector bodies in the UK, a representative from the Consumers' Association, and five lay board members.
R   To ensure that the general public can give with confidence to charities and fundraisers displaying the FRSB tick logo.
G   England, Wales, Scotland.

Funeral Planning Authority   (FPA)
■   Knellstone House, Udimore, RYE, E Sussex, TN31 6AR.
    Tel 0845 601 9619   http://www.funeralplanningauthority.com
    Chairman: Sandy MacDonald   Chief Executive: Stuart Harland
E   Established on 1 January 2002 by the Funeral Planning Council and the National Association for Pre-Paid Funeral Plans following the introduction of regulation by HM Treasury under the Financial Services & Markets Act 2000. The Authority is a company limited by guarantee whose shareholders are the FPC and the NAPFP. FPA has six directors including the Chairman.
R   To ensure that funeral plan providers that are regulated by the Authority maintain high standards of professional conduct.
    To ensure that the money that customers pay to a plan provider for a funeral plan is safeguarded so that, when the time comes, their funeral will be provided in accordance with that plan.
G   United Kingdom.
●   The Authority operates a conciliation service to resolve any complaints or or disputes.
✍   The FPA also performs duties previously undertaken by the former Funeral Ombudsman Scheme Council, Funeral Planning Council and Funeral Standards Council.

Furness West Cumbria New Vision Urban Regeneration Company Ltd
✍   An Urban Regeneration Company (qv) established in 2003, it traded as West Lakes Renaisance until 2009, then as two trading divisions, Barrow Regeneration and Britain's Energy Coast West Cumbria. The company was wound up in April 2011 following the withdrawal of funding from the Northwest Regional Development Agency (qv).

Future (Awards & Qualifications) Ltd

- ■ EMP House, Telford Way, COALVILLE, Leics, LE67 3HE.
  Tel 01530 836662   Fax 01530 836668   http://www.futurequals.com
- E Future is an awarding body offering a range courses and qualifications that are transferable across many industries.
- ✍ For more information on awarding bodies see the **Federation of Awarding Bodies**.

Futurebuilders Advisory Panel
- ✍ The Advisory Panel was abolished in 2010.

G

Gaelic Media Service   See **MG ALBA**.

Galloway Fisheries Trust   See **Rivers & Fisheries Trusts of Scotland**.

Gambling Appeals Tribunal
- ✍ Since 18 January 2010 **First-tier Tribunal (Gambling)**.

Gambling Commission

- ■ Victoria Square House, Victoria Square, BIRMINGHAM, B2 4BP.
  Tel 0121 230 6666   Fax 0121 230 6720   http://www.gamblingcommission.gov.uk
  Chairman: Brian Pomeroy, CBE   Chief Executive: Jenny Williams
- E Established in October 2005 under the Gambling Act 2005, the Commission has taken over the role previously played by the Gaming Board of Great Britain. It functions as an Executive NDPB of the the Department for Culture, Media & Sport. The Board of Commissioners comprises nine members including the Chairman.
- R To regulate all commercial gambling, except spread betting and the National Lottery.
- G United Kingdom.
- ✍ It was confirmed by the Government on 14 October 2010 that the Gambling Commission will merge with the National Lottery Commission (qv).

Gambling Supervision Commission

- ■ Government Office, Buck's Road, DOUGLAS, Isle of Man, IM1 3PZ.
  Tel 01624 694331   http://www.im.gov/gambling
  Chairman: Claire Milne
- E Established in 1962. It functions as a fully independent corporate body, its secretariat provided by the Treasury. The Commission comprises five members including the Chairman.
- R To keep gambling crime free.
  To protect the young and vulnerable.
  To ensure that the services offered by licensees are fair and that players receive their true winnings.
- G Isle of Man.
- ● The Commission licences coin operated amusements, betting offices, the Casino and online gambling and maintains an unobtrusive but vigilant stance on the many charity draws and raffles that are collectively known as society lotteries.

Gaming Board for Great Britain
- ✍ The Board produced its 34th and final Report in Summer 2005. The relevant body is now the **Gambling Commission**.

Gangmasters Licensing Authority   (GLA)

- ■ PO Box 8538, NOTTINGHAM, NG8 9AF.
  Tel 0845 602 5020   http://www.gla.gov.uk
  Chairman: Paul Whitehouse

E   Established on 1 April 2005 under the Gangmasters (Licensing) Act 2004, with subsequent legislation enacted in 2005 and 2006 concerning licensing, appeals and exclusions. GLA functions as an Executive NDPB of the Department for Environment, Food & Rural Affairs. The Board comprises 30 members including the Chairman.

R   To protect workers from exploitation in agriculture, forestry, horticulture, shellfish gathering and food processing and packaging.
To ensure labour providers operate within the law.

G   United Kingdom.

Gas & Electricity Consumer Council

✍   On 1 October 2008 the Gas & Electricity Consumer Council (energywatch), with others, was replaced by **Consumer Focus**.

Gas & Electricity Markets Authority   (GEMA)

■   9 Millbank, LONDON, SW1P 3GE.
Tel 020 7901 7000 Fax 020 7901 7066 http://www.ofgem.gov.uk
3rd Floor, Cornerstone, 107 West Regent Street, GLASGOW, G2 2BA.
Tel 0141 331 2678   Fax 0141 331 2777
Chairman: Lord Mogg, KCMG Chief Executive, Ofgem: Alistair Buchanan, CBE

E   Established in 1999, the Authority's powers are provided for under the Gas Act 1986, the Electricity Act 1989, the Competition Act 1998, the Utilities Act 2000 and the Enterprise Act 2002. The Authority comprises 16 members including the Chairman and two advisers.

R   To govern the Office of Gas & Electricity Markets (Ofgem).
To determine strategy, set policy priorities and take decisions on a range of matters including price controls and enforcement.

G   England, Wales, Scotland.

✍   Consumers are represented by Consumer Focus (qv).

Gas Safety Subcommittee

✍   A subcommittee of the Advisory Committee on Dangerous Substances which closed in 2004.

Gastrointestinal, Rheumatology, Immunology & Dermatology Expert Advisory Group

■   151 Buckingham Palace Road, LONDON, SW1W 9SZ.
Tel 020 3080 6000
Chairman: Prof Stuart Ralston, MD, FRCP, FMedSci, FRSE

E   Established in 2005. The Group functions as an advisory body to the Commission on Human Medicines (qv). It comprises five members including the Chairman.

R   To advise the CHM on the safety and efficacy of medicines for use in gastroenterological, rheumatological, immunological and dermatological diseases.

G   United Kingdom.

Gatwick Airport Consultative Committee   (GATCOM)

■   GATCOM, County Hall, CHICHESTER, W Sussex, PO19 1RQ.
Tel 01243 752703 Fax 01243 530439 http://www.ukaccs.info/gatwick
Chairman: Dr John Godfrey Assistant Secretary: Paula Street

G   Surrey, East and West Sussex.

✍   For further information see **Airport Consultative Committees**.

Geffrye Museum

■   Kingsland Road, LONDON, E2 8EA.
Tel 020 7739 9893 Fax 020 7729 5647 http://www.geffrye-museum.org.uk
Chairman: Penny Egan Director: David Dewing

E   Originally opened in 1914. The museum functions as an Executive NDPB of the Department for Culture, Media & Sport. The Board of Trustees comprises eleven members including the Chairman.

R   To encourage people to learn from and enjoy the museum's collections, buildings and gardens, and to promote the study of English domestic interiors.

G   England.

Gender Recognition Panel   (GRP)

- ■ PO Box 9300, LEICESTER, LE1 8DJ.
  Tel 0845 355 5155
  President: Jeremy Bennett
- E Established in 2007 under the Gender Recognition Act 2004. The Panel comprises eleven members including the President.
- R To assess applications from transsexual people for legal recognition of their acquired gender.
- G United Kingdom.
- ✍ Administrative support is provided by HM Courts & Tribunals Service (qv).

Gene Therapy Advisory Committee   (GTAC)

- ■ Area 604, Wellington House, 135-155 Waterloo Road, LONDON, SE1 8UG.
  Tel 020 7972 3057   **Fax** 020 7972 4300
  Chairman: Prof Martin Gore
- E Established in 1993. GTAC functions as a Scientific Advisory Committee and an Advisory NDPB of the Department of Health. The Committee comprises 18 members including the Chairman.
- R To assess and improve classical trials of gene therapy products according to the definition given in Part IV of Directive 2003/63/EC.
- G United Kingdom.
- ✍ On 14 October 2010 the Government announced that GTAC will be abolished. Some of its functions will transfer to a new research regulator.

General Advisory Committee on Science   (GACR)

- ■ Area 3B, Aviation House, 21 Kingsway, LONDON, WC2B 6NH.
  Tel 020 7276 8277   **Fax** 020 7276 8910   http://www.gacs.food.gov.uk
  Chairman: Prof Colin Blakemore, FMedSci, Hon FSB, Hon FRCP, FRS   Secretary: Patrick Miller
- E Established in December 2007, the Committee has absorbed the functions formerly carried out by the Advisory Committee on Research. GACS functions as a Scientific Advisory Committee and an Advisory NDPB of the Food Standards Agency (qv). The Committee comprises an independent Chairman, four independent expert members, two lay members and the Chairmen of the FSA's Scientific Advisory Councils.
- R To provide independent advice on the FSA's governance and use of science.
- G United Kingdom.
- ✍ For further information see **Scientific Advisory Committees**.

General Aviation Awareness Council   (GAAC)

- ■ RAeS House, 4 Hamilton Place, LONDON, W1J 7BQ.
  Tel 020 7670 4501   **Fax** 020 7670 4309   http://www.gaac.org.uk
  Chairman: Charles Henry, FRAeS   Secretary: Michael Powell
- E The GAAC is a membership body supported by commercial and professional organisations. The Board comprises eleven members including the Chairman.
- R To ensure that general aviation activity in the UK does not decline.
- G United Kingdom.

General Aviation Safety Council   (GASCo)

- ■ Rochester Airport, CHATHAM, Kent, ME5 9SD.
  Tel 01634 200203   **Fax** 01634 200203   http://www.gasco.org.uk
  Chairman: Gerald Hackemer   Chief Executive: Mike O'Donoghue
- E Established on 4 September 1964 at a meeting of the Conference of General Aviation Organisations as the General Aviation Safety Committee; it adopted its present title on 31 March 1994. GASCo is a membership body of organisations which participate in general aviation; it functions as a non-profit making charitable limited company. The Board of Directors comprises nine members including the Chairman.
- R To collect, collate and disseminate flight safety information among users of UK general aviation aircraft.
  To study all matters affecting, or which might affect, flight safety in UK general aviation and to make recommendations to interested parties as necessary.
- G United Kingdom.

General Chiropractic Council   (GCC)

- ■ 44 Wicklow Street, LONDON, WC1X 9HL.
  Tel 020 7713 5155   **Fax** 020 7713 5844   http://www.gcc-uk.org
  Chairman: Peter Dixon   Chief Executive: Margaret Coats
- E Established on 14 Aug 1998 under Chiropractors Act 1994. The Council comprises 20 members including the Chairman.

© CBD Research Ltd · Beckenham · Kent BR3 5JS · Tel 020 8650 7745 · Fax 020 8650 0768 · E-mail cbd@cbdresearch.com · www.cbdresearch.com

R   To regulate and develop the chiropractic profession.
G   United Kingdom.
✍   For further information see **Health & Social Care Regulators**.

General Commissioners of Income Tax
✍   Merged with others on 1 April 2009 to be replaced by the **First-tier Tribunal (Tax)**.

General Consumer Council for Northern Ireland   See the **Consumer Council for Northern Ireland**.

General Council of the Bar
■   289-293 High Holborn, LONDON, WC1V 7HZ.
    Tel 020 7242 0082   **Fax** 020 7831 9217   http://www.barcouncil.org.uk
    Chairman: Nicholas Green, QC   Chief Executive: David Hobart
E   Established in 1894. Known as the **Bar Council**, its membership comprises approximately 115 barristers who represent the Inns, Circuits and other interest groups.
R   To promote and improve the services and functions of the Bar on all matters relating to the profession, whether trade union, disciplinary, public interest or in any way affecting the administration of justice.
G   England, Wales.
●   The Bar Council has a number of different committees each covering a specific subject.
✍   In January 2006 the Bar Council transferred its regulatory duties to the Bar Standards Board (qv) while retaining its representative functions.

General Council of the Bar of Northern Ireland
■   The Bar Library, 91 Chichester Street, BELFAST, BT1 3JQ.
    Tel 028 9056 2349   **Fax** 028 9056 2350   http://www.barlibrary.com
    Chairman: Adrian Colton, QC
E   Established on 20 January 1922. Known as the **Bar Council**, membership comprises 22 members including the Chairman.
R   To maintain the standards, honour and independence of the Bar and, through its Professional Conduct Committee, receive and investigate complaints against members of the Bar in their professional capacity.
G   Northern Ireland.

General Dental Council   (GDC)
■   37 Wimpole Street, LONDON, W1G 8DQ.
    Tel 020 7887 3800   **Fax** 020 7224 3294   http://www.gdc-uk.org
    Chairman: Alison Lockyer   Chief Executive & Registrar: Evlynne Gilvarry
E   Established on 4 July 1956 under the Dentists Act 1956; its current authority derives from the Dentists Act 1984 as amended. The Council comprises 24 members including the Chairman.
R   To protect the public by regulating the dental team; all dentists, clinical dental technicians, dental hygienists, dental nurses, dental technicians, dental therapists and orthodontic therapists must be registered with the GDC to work in the UK.
    To set standards in dental practice and conduct, to assure the quality of dental education and to ensure that professionals keep up-to-date.
    To help patients with complaints about a dentist or dental care practitioner and to work to strengthen patient protection.
G   United Kingdom.
✍   For further information see **Health & Social Care Regulators**.

General Hypnotherapy Standards Council   (GHSC)
■   PO Box 204, LYMINGTON, Hants, SO41 6WP.   http://www.ghsc.co.uk
    Registrar: William Broom, SQHP, FNCP
E   GHSC is a membership organisation comprising professional bodies and hypnotherapy training schools. The Committee of Management comprises eight persons.
R   To act as a link between the hypnotherapy industry and the Department of Health to achieve eventually the status of Voluntary Self-regulation (VSR) for the hypnotherapy profession.
G   United Kingdom.

General Insurance Standards Council
✍   GISC's functions were taken over on 14 January 2005 by the **Financial Services Authority**.

General Lighthouse Authorities   (GLAs)
England, Wales, Channel Islands and Gibraltar: **Corporation of Trinity House**.
Scotland and Isle of Man: **Northern Lighthouse Board**.
Northern Ireland and Republic of Ireland: **Commissioners of Irish Lights**.

General Medical Council   (GMC)
- Regent's Place, 350 Euston Road, LONDON, NW1 3JN.
  Tel 0845 357 8001   http://www.gmc-uk.org
  Chairman: Prof Sir Peter Rubin, BM, BCh, MA, DM, FRCP   Chief Executive: Niall Dickson
E Established in 1858 by the Medical Act 1858; the Medical Act 1983 as amended defines the Council's current
   powers and responsibilities. The Postgraduate Medical Education & Training Board merged with GMC on 1
   April 2010. The Council comprises 24 members including the Chairman.
R To keep up to date registers of qualified doctors.
   To foster good medical practice.
   To promote high standards of medical education and training.
   To deal firmly and fairly with doctors whose fitness to practise is in doubt.
G United Kingdom.
✍ For further information see **Health & Social Care Regulators**.

General Optical Council   (GOC)
- 41 Harley Street, LONDON, W1G 8DJ.
  Tel 020 7580 3898   Fax 020 7307 3939   http://www.optical.org
  Chairman: Anna Bradley   Chief Executive & Registrar: Samantha Peters
E Established on 1 January 1959 under the Opticians Act 1958, and now consolidated in the Opticians Act 1989 as
   amended in 2005. The Council comprises twelve members including the Chairman.
R To set standards for optical education and training, performance and conduct.
   To approve qualifications leading to registration.
   To maintain a register of individuals who are qualified and fit to practise, train or carry on business as
   optometrists and dispensing opticians.
   To investigate and act where registrants' fitness to practise, train or carry on business is impaired.
G United Kingdom.
✍ For further information see **Health & Social Care Regulators**.

General Osteopathic Council   (GOsC)
- 176 Tower Bridge Road, LONDON, SE1 3LU.
  Tel 020 7357 6655   Fax 020 7357 0011   http://www.osteopathy.org.uk
  Chairman: Prof Adrian Eddleston   Chief Executive & Registrar: Tim Walker
E Established in January 1997 under the Osteopaths Act 1993. The Council comprises 14 members including the
   Chairman.
R To maintain the register of all those permitted to practise osteopathy in the UK.
   To set, maintain and develop standards of osteopathic practice and conduct.
   To assure the quality of osteopathic education and training.
   To help pateints with any concerns or complaints about an osteopath.
G United Kingdom.
✍ For further information see **Health & Social Care Regulators**.

General Pharmaceutical Council   (GPhC)
- 129 Lambeth Road, LONDON, SE1 7BT.
  Tel 020 3365 3400   http://www.pharmacyregulation.org
  Chairman: Bob Nicholls, CBE
E Established in 2010 to assume the regulatory functions of the Royal Pharmaceutical Society of Great Britain. The
   Council comprises 14 members including the Chairman.
R To regulate pharmacists, pharmacy technicians and pharmacy premises.
G England, Wales, Scotland.
✍ For further information see **Health & Social Care Regulators**.

General Practitioners Committee   (GPCC)
- BMA House, Tavistock Square, LONDON, WC1H 9JP.
  Tel 020 7383 6014   Fax 020 7383 6400   http://www.bma.org.uk
  Chairman: Dr Laurence Buckman
E Established as a Branch of Practice Committee of the British Medical Association. The Committee comprises up
   to 27 members.

© CBD Research Ltd · Beckenham · Kent BR3 5JS · Tel 020 8650 7745 · Fax 020 8650 0768 · E-mail cbd@cbdresearch.com · www.cbdresearch.com

R   To represent general practitioners throughout the UK whether or not they are members of the BMA.
G   United Kingdom.
✍   See **British Medical Association** [Branch of Practice Committees] for further information.

General Register Office   GRO became part of the **Identity & Passport Service** on 1 April 2008.

General Regulatory Council for Complementary Therapies   (GRCCT)
■   Swift House, High Street, Staveley, CHESTERFIELD, S43 3UX.
     Tel 0870 314 4031   **Fax** 0870 879 4045   http://www.grcct.org
E   Established in 2007 following the publication in February of the Government report 'Trust, Assurance & Safety -
     The Regulation of Health Professionals in the 21st Century'.
R   To establish a national register of complementary therapists and protect the public by validating the status of all
     registered therapists.
G   United Kingdom.

General Social Care Council   (GSCC)
■   Goldings House, 2 Hay's Lane, LONDON, SE1 2HB.
     Tel 020 7397 5100   **Fax** 020 7397 5101   http://www.gscc.org.uk
     Chairman: Rosie Varley, OBE   Chief Executive: Penny Thompson
E   Established on 1 October 2001 under Care Standards Act 2000. GSCC functions as an Executive NDPB of the
     Department of Health. The Council comprises ten members including the Chairman.
R   To set standards of conduct and practice for social care workers and their employers, for regulating the
     workforce, and regulating social work education and training.
G   England.
✍   It is one of the six member alliance which makes up Skills for Care & Development (qv), the Sector Skills Council
     for social care, children, early years and young people's workforces in the UK.
     For further information see **Health & Social Care Regulators**.
     The Secretary of State for Health announced on 26 July 2010 that GSCC's functions will be transferred to the
     Health Professions Council (qv) which will be renamed to reflect its new remit.

General Teaching Council for England   (GTCE)
■   Whittington House, 19-30 Alfred Place, LONDON, WC1E 7EA.
     Tel 0370 001 0308   **Fax** 020 7023 3909   http://www.gtce.org.uk
     Chairman: Gail Mortimer   Chief Executive: Keith Bartley
E   Established on 1 September 2000 under the Teaching & Higher Education Act 1998. GTCE functions as a Public
     Corporation of the Department for Education. The Council comprises 64 members (25 teacher members, nine
     nominated by teaching trade unions and associations, 17 nominated by other organisations connected with
     teaching and 13 appointed through the public appointments procedure).
R   To contribute to improving standards of teaching and the quality of learning, and to maintain and improve
     standards of professional conduct among teachers, in the interests of the public.
     To support teachers' professional efforts to offer children and young people high quality teaching that meets their
     needs and enables them to learn and thrive.
G   England.
●   The Council maintains a Register of qualified teachers in England and regulates the teaching profession in the
     public interest.
✍   On 2 June 2010 DfE announced its intention to abolish GTCE and is working towards a closure date of 31 March
     2012.

General Teaching Council for Northern Ireland   (GTCNI)
■   3rd Floor, Albany House, 73-75 Victoria Street, BELFAST, BT2 7AF.
     Tel 028 9033 3390   **Fax** 028 9034 8787   http://www.gtcni.org.uk
     Chairman: Ivan Arbuthnot
E   Established in 1998 under the Education (Northern Ireland) Order 1998. GTCNI functions as an Executive NDPB
     of the Department of Education Northern Ireland. The Council comprises 33 members including the Chairman.
R   To enhance the status of teaching.
     To promote the highest standards of professional conduct and practice.
G   Northern Ireland.

General Teaching Council for Scotland   (GTCS)
- ■ Clerwood House, 96 Clermiston Road, EDINBURGH, EH12 6UT.
  Tel 0131 314 6000   Fax 0131 314 6001   http://www.gtcs.org.uk
  Convener: David Drever   Chief Executive: Anthony Finn
- E Established on 1 November 1965, under the Teaching Council (Scotland) Act 1965; the constitution later
  amended by SI 1970/523 (S 34). GTCS functions as an Advisory NDPB of the Scottish Executive Education
  Department. The Council comprises 50 members who serve as teachers of various age groups or represent
  educational organisations.
- R To maintain a register of qualified teachers.
  To keep under review the standards of entry to the teaching profession.
  To make recommendations to the Scottish Ministers on standards of education, training, career development and
  fitness to teach of teachers.
  To advise Ministers on supply of teachers.
- G Scotland.

General Teaching Council for Wales   (GTCW)
- ■ 9th Floor, Eastgate House, 35-43 Newport Road, CARDIFF, CF24 0AB.
  Tel 029 2055 0350   Fax 029 2055 0360   http://www.gtcw.org.uk
  Chairman: Mrs Angela Jardine
- E Established on 1 September 2000 under the Teaching & Higher Education Act 1998, as amended by the
  Education Act 2002. GCTW functions as an Executive NDPB of the National Assembly for Wales. The Council
  comprises 24 members including the Chairman.
- R To contribute to improving the standards of teaching and the quality of learning, and to maintain and improve
  standards of professional conduct amongst teachers, in the interests of the people.
- G Wales.
- = Cyngor Addysgu Cyffredinol Cymru

Genetics & Insurance Committee   (GAIC)
- ■ Area 604, Wellington House, 135-155 Waterloo Road, LONDON, SE1 8UG.   Fax 020 7972 4300
  Chairman: Prof David Johns
- E Established 12 April 1999. GAIC functions as a Scientific Advisory Committee and an Advisory NDPB of the
  Department of Health. The Committee comprises eight members including the Chairman.
- R To develop and publish criteria for the evaluation of specific genetic tests, their application to particular
  conditions and their reliability to particular types of insurance.
- G United Kingdom.
- ✍ The Government announced on 14 October 2010 that GAIC will be abolished. Its functions have been transferred
  to other bodies.

General Synod's Board of Mission
- ✍ See the **Mission & Public Affairs** division of the Archbishops' Council.

George Best Belfast City Airport Forum   (GBBCA Forum)
- ■ George Best Belfast City Airport, BELFAST, BT3 9JH.
  Tel 028 9093 5013   Fax 028 9093 9094   http://www.belfastcityairport.com
  Chairman: Alan Crowe
- G Belfast.
- ✍ For further information see **Airport Consultative Committees**.

Gingerbread
- ■ 255 Kentish Town Road, LONDON, NW5 2LX.
  Tel 020 7428 5400   Fax 020 7482 4851   http://www.gingerbread.org.uk
  Chief Executive: Fiona Weir
- E Established in June 2007 by the merger of Gingerbread (established in 1970) and the National Council for One
  Parent Families (established in 1918). Gingerbread is registered in England & Wales as the **National Council for
  One Parent Families**, a company limited by guarantee and a charity.
- R To improve the lives of single parent families by championing their voices and needs and providing support
  services.
- G England, Wales.

GLA Group Collective name for the four administrative bodies created for London at the same time as the **Greater London Authority**.

Glasgow Airport Consultative Committee (GACC)
- 32 Lochhead Avenue, LOCHWINNOCH, Renfrewshire, PA12 4AW.
  Tel 01505 843193
  Chairman: John Richmond
- G Glasgow.
- ✍ For further information see **Airport Consultative Committees**.

Glasgow Local Enterprise Company
- ✍ Now functions as the Glasgow office of **Scottish Enterprise**.

Glasgow Prestwick Airport Consultative Committee (GPACC)
- Ayrshire Joint Planning Unit, 15 Links Road, PRESTWICK, Ayrshire, KA9 1QG.
  Tel 01292 673762   Fax 01292 671455   http://www.ukaccs.info/prestwick/
  Chairman: Prof Dugald Cameron   Secretary: Nigel Wallace
- G Ayrshire.
- ✍ For further information see **Airport Consultative Committees**.

Glass Qualifications Authority Ltd (GQA)
- Provincial House, Solly Street, SHEFFIELD, S Yorks, S1 4BA.
  Tel 0114 272 0033   Fax 0114 272 0060   http://www.glassqualificationsauthority.com
  Chief Executive: Allan Murray
- E The awarding body for courses and qualifications in the glass industries.
- R To achieve a world class qualified workforce in glass and glass related occupations.
- G United Kingdom.
- ✍ See also the **Federation of Awarding Bodies**.

Gloucester Harbour Trustees (GHT)
- Navigation House, The Docks, Sharpness, BERKELEY, Glos, GL13 9UD.
  Tel 01453 811913   Fax 01453 810381   http://www.gloucesterharbourtrustees.org.uk
  Chairman: Edmund Dorman
- E Established in 1890 under The Pier & Harbour Orders Confirmation (No 3) Act 1889, the Trustees derive their current authority under The Pilotage Act 1987. The board comprises ten Trustees including the Chairman.
- G Gloucester.
- ✍ For further information see **Port & Harbour Authorities**.

Gloucester Heritage (GHURC)
- 15 Ladybellegate Street, GLOUCESTER, GL1 2HN.
  Tel 01452 782990   Fax 01452 306702   http://www.glouesterurc.co.uk
  Chairman: Greg Smith   Chief Executive: Chris Oldershaw
- E Established on 5 February 2004. GHURC is the Urban Regeneration Company for Gloucester.
- G Gloucester.
- ✍ For further information see **Urban Regeneration Companies**.

Gloucestershire Police Authority
- Pate Court, North Place, CHELTENHAM, Glos, GL50 4DY.
  Tel 01242 268916   Fax 01242 262521   http://www.gloucestershirepoliceauthority.co.uk
  Chairman: Cllr Rob Garnham
- E Established in April 1995, the Authority is an independent body charged with ensuring that Gloucestershire Constabulary provides an effective and efficient police service. It is made up of nine councillor members and eight independent members.
- G Gloucestershire (excluding South Gloucestershire).
- ✍ For further information see **Police Authorities**.

Gloucestershire Probation Trust

- Bewick House, 1 Denmark Road, GLOUCESTER, GL1 3HW.
  Tel 01452 389200 **Fax** 01452 541155 http://www.glosprobation.org.uk
  Chairman: Tony FitzSimons Chief Officer: John Bensted
- E Established on 1 April 2001 under the Criminal Justice & Court Service Act 2000 as the Gloucestershire Probation Area Board. It became a trust on 1 April 2010 under the Offender Management Act 2007. The Board comprises nine members including the Chairman.
- G Gloucestershire (excluding South Gloucestershire).
- ✍ For further information see **Probation Trusts**.

Gloucestershire Rural Community Council   (GRCC)

- Community House, 15 College Green, GLOUCESTER, GL1 2LZ.
  Tel 01452 528491 **Fax** 01452 528493 http://www.grcc.org.uk
  Chairman: John Hazelwood Chief Executive: Lesley Archer
- E Established in 1923. The Council functions as a registered charity and company limited by guarantee. The Board comprises 22 Trustees including the Chairman.
- R To engage with Gloucestershire's rural communities to enable sustainable community development and empower community groups.
- G Gloucestershire.
- ✍ GRCC is one of the 38 Rural Community Councils, represented at the national level by **Action with Communities in Rural England** (qv) and at the regional level by South West ACRE Network (SWAN).

GM Inspectorate [England & Wales]

- FERA, Sand Hutton, YORK, YO41 1LZ.
  Tel 01904 462000 **Fax** 01904 462111
- E The Inspectorate was established under the Environmental Protection Act 1990. It functions in England & Wales as part of the Food & Environment Research Agency (qv).
- R To undertake inspections and enforcement, if necessary, concerning releases and marketing of genetically modified organisms (GMOs) in England and Wales.
- G England, Wales.

GM Inspectorate [Scotland]

- SASA, Roddinglaw Road, EDINBURGH, EH12 9FJ.
  Tel 0131 244 8837
- E The Inspectorate was established under the Environmental Protection Act 1990. It functions in Scotland as part of Science & Advice for Scottish Agriculture (qv).
- R To undertake inspections and enforcement, if necessary, concerning releases and marketing of genetically modified organisms (GMOs) in Scotland.
- G Scotland.

GoSkills

- Concorde House, Trinity Park, BIRMINGHAM, B37 7UQ.
  Tel 0121 635 5520 **Fax** 0121 635 5521 http://www.goskills.org
  Chairman: Nick Mitchell Chief Executive: Neil Stokell
- E Established on 1 November 2004. It is the recognised Sector Skills Council for the passenger transport sector. The board comprises twelve members including the Chairman.
- G United Kingdom.
- ✍ For further information see **Sector Skills Councils**.

Government Actuary's Department   (GAD)

- Finlaison House, 15-17 Furnival Street, LONDON, EC4A 1AB.
  Tel 020 7211 2601 http://www.gad.gov.uk
  Abbey Business Centre, 83 Princes Street, EDINBURGH, EH2 2ER.
  Tel 0131 247 7510
  Government Actuary: Trevor Llanwarne
- E The post of Government Actuary dates from 1912 and the Department from 1919. GAD has functioned as a non-ministerial government department since 1989. The management board comprises six members including the Government Actuary and there are ten Chief Actuaries.
- R To provide actuarial analysis to the public sector from the public sector.
- G United Kingdom.

© CBD Research Ltd · Beckenham · Kent BR3 5JS · Tel 020 8650 7745 · Fax 020 8650 0768 · E-mail cbd@cbdresearch.com · www.cbdresearch.com

Government Car & Despatch Agency   (GCDA)

■   46 Ponton Road, LONDON, SW8 5AX.
Tel 020 7217 3849   Fax 020 7217 3840   http://www.dft.gov.uk/gcda/
Interim Chief Executive: Paul Markwick

E   Established on 1 April 1997. GCDA functions as an Executive Agency of the Department for Transport and is split into two businesses: Government Car and Government Mail.

R   To provide long and short term chauffeur and care hire, a taxi-style booking service, protected security cars and specially-trained VIP drivers; and fleet management and maintenance services to other public sector bodies.
To provide secure mail services within Government and the wider public sector, and offer mail screening services for Government departments and secure waste disposal.

G   United Kingdom.

✍   GCDA is part of the DfT's Motoring & Freight Services Group, along with the Driving Standards Agency, the Driver & Vehicle Licencing Agency, the Vehicle Certification Agency and the Vehicle & Operator Services Agency (qqv).

Government Hospitality Advisory Committee for the Purchase of Wine

✍   GHACPW was abolished in 2010.

Government Mail   See **Government Car & Despatch Agency**.

Government Offices for the English Regions

✍   The closure of the London Office was announced in May 2010. The Comprehensive Spending Review in October 2010 confirmed the closure of the remaining eight Offices at the end of March 2011.

Government Skills

■   2nd Floor, 1 Victoria Street, LONDON, SW1H 0ET.
Tel 020 7215 1424   http://www.government-skills.gov.uk
Chairman: Sir John Elvidge, KCB   Chief Executive: Gill Hammond

E   Established on 1 January 2006. For operational purposes and resourcing, it became part of the Department for Innovation, Universities & Skills on 1 April 2008. It is the recognised Sector Skills Council for people working in government departments, NDPBs and the armed forces. The board comprises eight members including the Chairman.

G   United Kingdom.

✍   For further information see **Sector Skills Councils**.

Government Statistical Service   See **UK Statistics Authority**.

Grampian Joint Police Board

■   Town House, Broad Street, ABERDEEN, AB10 1AU.
Tel 01224 523811   Fax 01224 522937
Convenor: Cllr Martin Greig, JP   Clerk: Mrs Jane MacEachran

E   The Joint Board is an independent body responsible for Grampian Police's budget and the management of its resources. The Board is made up of six councillor members from Aberdeenshire, six from Aberdeen City and three from Moray.

G   Aberdeenshire, Aberdeen City and Moray.

✍   For further information see **Police Authorities**.

Grampian Local Enterprise Company

✍   Now functions as the Aberdeen office of **Scottish Enterprise**.

Grampian NHS Board

■   Room 16, Ashgrove House, Foresthill, ABERDEEN, AB25 2ZA.
Tel 01224 554400   http://www.nhsgrampian.org
Chairman: Dr David Cameron   Chief Executive: Richard Carey

G   Aberdeenshire, Aberdeen City and Moray.

✍   For further information see **NHS Scotland - Boards**.

Great Britain-China Centre   (GBCC)

- 15 Belgrave Square, LONDON, SW1X 8PS.
  Tel 020 7235 6696   **Fax** 020 7245 6885   http://www.gbcc.org.uk
  Chairman: Peter Batey, OBE   Director: Katie Lee, OBE
- E Established in 1974. GBCC is a centre of excellence and functions as an Executive NDPB of the Foreign & Commonwealth Office. The Executive Committee comprises 26 members including the Chairman.
- R To promote closer understanding between Britain and China particularly in the areas of legal and judicial reform, and labour reform.
- G United Kingdom.
- ✍ The Foreign & Commonwealth Office announced on 14 October 2010 that the future of GBCC was under consideration. For further information see companion volume **Centres, Bureaux & Research Institutes**.

Great Yarmouth Port Authority

- ✍ Since May 2007 the port is privately owned and operated by EastPort UK.

Greater Glasgow & Clyde NHS Board

- J B Russell House, Gartnavel Royal Hospital Campus, 1055 Great Western Road, GLASGOW, G12 0XH.
  Tel 0141 201 4444   **Fax** 0141 201 4400   http://www.nhsggc.org.uk
  Chairman: Andrew Robertson, OBE   Chief Executive: Richard Calderwood
- G Glasgow City, East and West Dunbartonshire, Inverclyde, Renfrewshire and East Renfrewshire.
- ✍ For further information see **NHS Scotland - Boards**.

Greater Glasgow & Clyde Valley Tourist Board

- ✍ Since 1 April 2005 an area office of **VisitScotland**.

Greater London Authority   (GLA)

- City Hall, The Queen's Walk, More London, LONDON, SE1 2AA.
  Tel 020 7983 4000   **Fax** 020 7983 4057   http://www.london.gov.uk
  Chairman (Mayor of London): Boris Johnson
- E Established on 3 July 2000 under the Greater London Authority Act 1999. GLA consists of the directly elected mayor and a separately elected 25-member body, the London Assembly. The GLA Corporate Management Team comprises six directors and two mayoral appointees.
- R To be responsibe for eight London-wide issues:
  Culture, Economic development, Environment, Fire & emergency planning, Health, Police, Strategic planning, and Transport.
- G Greater London.
- ● The GLA is supported by four administrative bodies, known collectively as the GLA Group, which were created at the same time:
  London Development Agency
  London Fire & Emergency Planning Authority
  Metropolitan Police Authority, and
  Transport for London Authority (qqv).

Greater Manchester Integrated Transport Authority   (GMITA)

- PO Box 532, Town Hall, MANCHESTER, M60 2LA.
  Tel 0161 234 4619   http://www.gmita.gov.uk
  Chairman: Cllr Ian Macdonald
- E Established on 15 September 1985 under the Local Government Act 1985 and known as the Greater Manchester Passenger Transport Authority until renamed on 9 February 2009 under the Local Transport Act 2008. The Authority comprises 33 Councillors who are appointed by the ten Metropolitan District Councils that make up Greater Manchester.
- G Greater Manchester.
- ✍ For further information see **Passenger Transport Executives & Integrated Transport Authorities**.

Greater Manchester Passenger Transport Authority

- ✍ Since 2008 **Greater Manchester Integrated Transport Authority**.

© CBD Research Ltd · Beckenham · Kent BR3 5JS · Tel 020 8650 7745 · Fax 020 8650 0768 · E-mail cbd@cbdresearch.com · www.cbdresearch.com

Greater Manchester Passenger Transport Executive   (GMPTE)

■   2 Piccadilly Place, MANCHESTER, M1 3BG.
Tel 0161 244 1000   http://www.gmpte.com
Chief Executive: David Leather
E   Established in 1985. The Executive is responsible to the Greater Manchester Integrated Transport Authority (qv).
G   Greater Manchester.
✍   For further information see **Passenger Transport Executives & Integrated Transport Authorities**.

Greater Manchester Police Authority   (GMPA)

■   Salford Civic Centre, Chorley Road, Swinton, SALFORD, Lancs, M27 5DA.
Tel 0161 793 3127   Fax 0161 793 2019   http://www.gmpa.gov.uk
Chairman: Cllr Paul Murphy
E   Established in April 1995, the Authority is an independent body charged with ensuring that Greater Manchester Police provide an effective and efficient police service. It is made up of ten councillor members and nine independent members.
G   Greater Manchester.
✍   For further information see **Police Authorities**.

Greater Manchester Probation Trust

■   6th Floor, Oakland House, Talbot Road, MANCHESTER, M16 0PQ.
Tel 0161 872 4802   Fax 0161 872 3483   http://www.gm-probation.org.uk
Chairman: Hilary Tucker   Chief Executive: John Crawforth
E   Established on 1 April 2001 under the Criminal Justice & Court Service Act 2000 as the Greater Manchester Probation Area Board. It became a trust on 1 April 2009 under the Offender Management Act 2007. The Board comprises twelve members including the Chairman.
G   Greater Manchester.
✍   For further information see **Probation Trusts**.

Greater Manchester Strategic Health Authority
✍   On 1 July 2006 merged with the Cheshire & Merseyside and the Cumberland & Lancashire Strategic Health Authorities to form the **North West Strategic Health Authority**.

Green Fiscal Commission
✍   Established on 14 November 2007 to examine the whole range of issues surrounding green taxes and environmental tax reform, the Commission presented its report on 26 October 2009.

Greyhound Board of Great Britain   (GBGB)

■   Procter House, 1 Procter Street, LONDON, WC1V 6DW.
Tel 020 7421 3770   Fax 020 7421 3777   http://www.thedogs.co.uk
GBGB Chairman: Maurice Watkins   Chief Executive: Barry Faulkner   GRB Chairman: Steve Winfield
E   Established on 1 January 2009 by the merger of the British Greyhound Racing Board and the National Greyhound Racing Club, following the publication of the Lord Donoughue's Independent Review of the Greyhound Industry in Great Britain, published November 2007. The Board comprises the Chairman, Chief Executive and four independent directors.
R   To be responsible for the governance, regulation and management of the sport of greyhound racing in England, Scotland and Wales.
G   England, Scotland, Wales.
●   Incorporated within the GBGB but with independent status is the Greyhound Regulatory Roard (GRB). The GRB's key function is to implement and manage the rules of racing.

Greyhound Regulatory Board
✍   An independent board incorporated within the **Greyhound Board of Great Britain**.

Grŵp Strategaeth Meddyginiaethau Cymru Gyfan   See **All Wales Medicines Strategy Group**.

Guernsey Financial Services Commission   (GFSC)

■   PO Box 128, Glategny Court, Glategny Esplanade, ST PETER PORT, Guernsey, GY1 3HQ.
Tel 01481 712706   Fax 01481 712010   http://www.gfsc.gg
Chairman: Peter Harwood, LLB   Director General: Nik van Leuven, QC

E   Established in 1987 under the Financial Services Commission (Bailiwick of Guernsey) Law 1987 as amended. There are five Commissioners including the Chairman.

R   To regulate and supervise financial services in Guernsey with integrity and efficiency and in so doing help to uphold the international reputation of Guernsey as a finance centre.

G   Guernsey.

Guernsey Tourism Board

✍   See **Visit Guernsey**.

Guidance Council

✍   Wound up 1 November 2006.

GuildHE

■   Woburn House, 20 Tavistock Square, LONDON, WC1H 9HB.
    Tel 020 7387 7711   **Fax** 020 7387 7712   http://www.guildhe.ac.uk
    Chief Executive: Alice Hynes

E   Established in 1978 and known as the Standing Conference of Principals, it adopted its current name in 2006 to reflect its more diversified membership. GuildHE is a membership body of heads of higher educational institutions and their staff. There are currently 21 full members and ten associate members.

R   To highlight the interests and strengths of its member higher education institutions to government, national and international agencies, employers, potential students and the wider community.

G   United Kingdom.

Gwasanaeth Gwaed Cymru   See **Welsh Blood Service**.

Gwasanaeth Gwybodeg GIG Cymru   See **NHS Wales Informatics Service**.

Gwent Police Authority   (GPA)

■   Croesyceiliog, CWMBRAN, Gwent, NP44 2XJ.
    Tel 01633 642200   **Fax** 01633 643095   http://www.gwentpa.police.uk
    Chairman: Mrs Cilla Davies, OBE, JP   Chief Executive: Shelley Bosson

E   Established in April 1995, the Authority is an independent body charged with ensuring that Gwent Police provide an effective and efficient police service. It is made up of nine local councillor members and eight independent members.

G   Blaenau Gwent, Caerphilly, Cwmbran, Monmouthshire, Newport and Torfaen.

✍   For further information see **Police Authorities**.

Gwynedd Local Health Board

✍   Merged on 1 October with the Anglesey, Conwy, Denbighshire, Flintshire and Wrexham Local Health Boards to form **Betsi Cadwadalr University Health Board**.

H

Habia

■   Oxford House, Sixth Avenue, Sky Business Park, Robin Hood Airport, DONCASTER, DN9 3GG.
    Tel 01302 774928   **Fax** 01302 774949   http://www.habia.org
    Chairman: Michael Thornhill

E   Established in 1986 as the Hair Training Board, it merged in 1997 with the Beauty Industry Authority to become the Hairdressing & Beauty Industry Authority (HABIA). Following the addition of nail services and spa therapy, the name was officially changed to Habia in 2004. Habia is a membership body and functions as a company limited by guarantee. It is the standards setting body for the hair, beauty, nails and spa industries.

R   To create the standards that form the basis of all qualifications in the industries including NVQs, SVQs, Apprenticeships, Diplomas and Foundation degrees, as well as industry codes of practice.

G   United Kingdom.

© CBD Research Ltd · Beckenham · Kent BR3 5JS · Tel 020 8650 7745 · Fax 020 8650 0768 · E-mail cbd@cbdresearch.com · www.cbdresearch.com

Hairdressing & Beauty Industry Authority
✍ In 2004 HABIA was renamed **Habia**.

Hairdressing Council
■ 30 Sydenham Road, CROYDON, Surrey, CR0 2EF.
Tel 020 8760 7010   http://www.haircouncil.org.uk
E Established in 1964 under the Hairdressers (Registration) Act 1964. The Council comprises 17 members.
R To establish and maintain a register of hairdressers qualified under the provisions of the Act.
To approve training courses, training institutions and qualificiations.
G United Kingdom.

Halal Food Authority   (HFA)
■ 109 Fulham Palace Road, LONDON, W6 8JA.
Tel 020 8563 1994   Fax 020 8563 1993   http://www.halalfoodauthority.co.uk
President: Masood Khawaja
E Established in July 1994. HFA functions as a non-profit making organisation.
R To monitor, audit and regulate red meat and poultry in the United Kingdom to ensure it meets halal standards.
G United Kingdom.
● The HFA licences slaughterhouses, distribution centres, retailers and providers of halal meat and poultry for human consumption.
It further regulates, endorses and authenticates foodstuffs, pharmaceuticals, confectionery, toiletries, flavourings, emulsifiers and colourings for Muslim usage.
✍ HFA's rules for slaughter are based on Islamic Sharia. The animal should be conscious at the time of slaughter and all flowing blood should be drained out.

Hampshire & Isle of Wight Strategic Health Authority
✍ See the **South Central Strategic Health Authority**.

Hampshire Police Authority
■ Westgate Chambers, Staple Gardens, WINCHESTER, Hants, SO23 8AW.
Tel 01962 871595   Fax 01962 851697   http://www.hampshirepoliceauthority.org
Chairman: Cllr Jacqui Rayment   Chief Executive: Jennifer Douglas-Todd
E Established in April 1995, the Authority is an independent body charged with ensuring that Hampshire Constabulary provides an effective and efficient police service.
It is made up of nine councillor members and eight independent members.
G Hampshire (including Portsmouth and Southampton), Isle of Wight.
✍ For further information see **Police Authorities**.

Hampshire Probation Trust
■ Friary House, Middle Brook Street, WINCHESTER, Hants, SO23 8DQ.
Tel 01962 842202   Fax 01962 865278   http://www.hampshire-probation.gov.uk
Chairman: Mike Fisher   Chief Officer: Barrie Crook
E Established on 1 April 2001 under the Criminal Justice & Court Service Act 2000 as the Hampshire Probation Area Board. It became a trust on 1 April 2010 under the Offender Management Act 2007. The Board comprises ten members including the Chairman.
G Hampshire and the Isle of Wight.
✍ For further information see **Probation Trusts**.

Hannah Research Institute
■ Hannah Research Park, AYR, KA6 5HL.
Tel 01292 674000   Fax 01292 674003   http://www.hannahresearch.org.uk
Chief Executive: Keith McKellar
E Established in 1928 as the Hannah Dairy Research Institute. The Institute is a company limited by guarantee and functions as an Executive NDPB of the Scottish Executive Rural Affairs Department.
R Following changes in core Government research funding in 2005, the Institute is no longer able to conduct its own research, but will become a research trust, awarding research grants, fellowships and studentships.
G Scotland.
✍ For further information see companion volume **Centres, Bureaux & Research Institutes**.

Harbour Authorities   See **Port & Harbour Authorities**.

Harbour of Rye Advisory Committee   See **Environment Agency** [Southern Region].

Harris Tweed Authority   (HTA)
■   6 Garden Road, STORNOWAY, Isle of Lewis, HS1 2QJ.
   Tel 01851 702269   **Fax** 01851 702600   http://www.harristweed.org
   Chairman: Donald Martin
E   The Harris Tweed Association was established in 1909 under the provisions of the Trade Marks Act 1905. It
      became the Harris Tweed Authority under the Harris Tweed Act 1993. The Authority comprises ten members
      including the Chairman.
R   To promote and maintain the authenticity, standard and reputation of Harris Tweed.
G   Outer Hebrides.

Harwich Haven Authority   (HHA)
■   Harbour House, The Quay, HARWICH, Essex, CO12 3HH.
   Tel 01255 243030   **Fax** 01255 241302   http://www.hha.co.uk
   Chairman: Tim Clarke, BA(Hons), FCILT   Chief Executive: Stephen Bracewell
E   Established in 1863 by Act of Parliament. The Board comprises ten members including the Chairman.
G   Harwich.
✍   For further information see **Port & Harbour Authorities**.

Hawk Board
■   Le Moulin de l'Age, 86390 LATHUS ST REMY, France.
   Tel +33 (0)5 49 91 79 30   http://www.hawkboard-cff.org.uk
   Chairman: Terry Large   Treasurer: Mike Clowes
E   Established in July 1979. The Board is a voluntary organisation.
R   To represent all falconers and bird of prey keepers in the UK.
G   United Kingdom.

Health Commission Wales
✍   Established in 2003, HCW ceased to exist on 31 March 2010. Much of its work has transferred to the NHS where
      it is being undertaken by the **Welsh Health Specialised Services Committee**.

Health Development Agency
✍   On 1 April 2005 the HDA joined with the National Institute for Clinical Excellence to form the **National Institute
      for Health & Clinical Excellence**.

Health Education Board for Scotland
✍   Merged 31 March 2003 with Public Health Institute of Scotland as **NHS Health Scotland**.

Health Estates   See **Northern Ireland Health & Social Services Estates Agency**.

Health Professions Council   (HPC)
■   Park House, 184 Kennington Park Road, LONDON, SE11 4BU.
   Tel 020 7582 0866   **Fax** 020 7820 9684   http://www.hpc-uk.org
   Chairman: Dr Anna van der Gaag
E   Established in 2001 under the Health Professions Order 2001. The Council comprises 20 members, made up of
      ten registrant and ten lay members.
R   To maintain and publish a public register of properly qualified members of the professions.
   To approve and uphold high standards of education and training, and continuing good practice.
   To investigate complaints and take appropriate action.
G   United Kingdom.
●   The 2001 Order specifies that four statutory committees be set up:
      Education & Training Committee to ensure that registrants have the education and training needed to do their
   job safely
      Investigation Committee look to at complaints about registrants

© CBD Research Ltd · Beckenham · Kent BR3 5JS · Tel 020 8650 7745 · Fax 020 8650 0768 · E-mail cbd@cbdresearch.com · www.cbdresearch.com

Conduct & Competence Committee to advise the HPC on what constitutes appropriate conduct, performance and ethics of all registrants

Health Committee to deal with allegations of a registrant's ill health.

✍ The 15 health professions regulated are:

Arts therapists
Biomedical scientists
Chiropodists, Podiatrists
Clinical scientists
Dietitians
Hearing aid dispensers
Occupational therapists
Operating department practitioners
Orthoptists
Paramedics
Physiotherapists
Practitioner psychologists
Prosthetists, orthotists
Radiographers
Speech and language therapists.

For further information see **Health & Social Care Regulators**.

Health Professions Wales
✍ Abolished 1 April 2006.

Health Promotion Agency for Northern Ireland   **(HPANI)**
✍ On 1 April 2009 all HPANI responsibilities were transferred to the **Public Health Agency**.

Health Protection Agency   **(HPA)**
■ 151 Buckingham Palace Road, LONDON, SW1W 9SZ.
Tel 020 7811 7000   **Fax** 020 7811 7750   http://www.hpa.org.uk
Chairman: Dr David Heymann   Chief Executive: Justin McCracken
E   Established on 1 April 2003 as a Special Health Authority, incorporating the former Public Health Laboratory Service. On 1 April 2005 it absorbed the National Radiological Protection Board and in 2007 the National Biological Standards Board. HPA functions now functions as an Executive NDPB of the Department of Health. The Board comprises 15 members including the Chairman.
R   To provide an integrated approach to the protection of public health through the provision of support and advice to the NHS, local authorities, emergency services, other bodies, the Department of Health and the devolved administrations.
G   United Kingdom.
●   HPA operates four centres:
Centre for Emergency Preparedness & Response
    Porton Down, SALISBURY, Wilts, SP4 0JG.
Centre for Infections
    61 Colindale Avenue, LONDON, NW9 5EQ.
Centre for Radiation, Chemical & Environmental Hazards
    Chilton, DIDCOT, Oxon, OX11 0RQ.
National Institute of Biological Standards & Control
    Blanche Lane, South Mimms, POTTERS BAR, Herts, EN6 3GQ.
✍ HPA provides the secretariat for numerous Advisory Committees, Groups and Panels.
The Secretary of State for Health announced on 26 July 2010 that HPA would be abolished as a NDPB and its functions transferred to the new Public Health Service.

Health Risks Working Group   A working group of the Health & Safety Executive's **Construction Industry Advisory Committee**.

Health & Safety Commission
✍ Merged with the **Health & Safety Executive** on 1 April 2008.

Health & Safety Executive   (HSE)

■ Redgrave Court, Merton Road, BOOTLE, Merseyside, L20 7HS.
Tel 0845 345 0055   http://www.hse.gov.uk
Chairman: Judith Hackitt, CBE   Chief Executive: Geoffrey Podger

E The Health & Safety Commission was established on 31 July 1974 and the Health & Safety Executive on 1 January 1975, both under the Health & Safety at Work etc Act 1974. The two merged as the Health & Safety Executive on 1 April 2008. HSE functions as an Executive NDPB of the Department for Work & Pensions. Its Board comprises ten members including the Chairman.

R To secure the health, safety and welfare of people at work and protect others from risks to health and safety from work activity.

G England, Wales, Scotland.

● The HSE is assisted in its work by numerous industry and topic advisory groups. It also operates the following agencies:
    Adventure Activities Licensing Authority
    Health & Safety Laboratory (qqv).

Health & Safety Executive Local Authorities Enforcement Liaison Committee   (HELA)

■ 1/3 Redgrave Court, Merton Road, BOOTLE, Merseyside, L20 7HS.
Tel 0151 951 3114   Fax 0151 951 3984
Joint Chairmen: Kevin Myers, Paul Unsworth

E Established as an advisory committee of the Health & Safety Executive (qv). HELA membership comprises senior local authority officers, HSE officials and representatives of the Chartered Institute of Environmental Health and Royal Environmental Health Institute of Scotland. It is jointly chaired by the HSE Deputy Chief Executive and the Chairman of the Health & Safety Policy Forum of the Local Authority Co-ordinators of Regulatory Services (LACoRS, qv).

R To provide effective liaison between local authorities and the HSE to ensure that health and safety legislation is enforced in a consistent way.

G England, Wales, Scotland.

Health & Safety Executive for Northern Ireland   (HSENI)

■ 83 Ladas Drive, BELFAST, BT6 9FR.
Tel 028 9024 3249   Fax 028 9023 5383   http://www.hseni.gov.uk
Chairman: Prof Peter McKie, CBE   Chief Executive: Jim Keyes

E Established on 1 April 1999. HSENI functions as an Executive NDPB of the Department of Enterprise, Trade & Investment Northern Ireland.

R To ensure that risks to people's health and safety arising from work activities are effectively controlled.
    To promote key workplace health and safety messages and themes to targeted sectors and groups.

G Northern Ireland.

Health & Safety Laboratory   (HSL)

■ Harpur Hill, BUXTON, Derbys, SK17 9JN.
Tel 01298 218000   Fax 01298 218986   http://www.hsl.gov.uk
Chief Executive: Eddie Morland

E Established in 1996. HSL functions as an Executive Agency of the Health & Safety Executive (qv). The Board comprises nine members including the Chief Executive.

R To protect people's health and safety by ensuring that risks in the changing workplace are properly controlled.

G United Kingdom.

Health Scotland   See **NHS Health Scotland**.

Health Service Commissioner for Scotland   See the **Scottish Public Services Ombudsman**.

Health Service Commissioners [England & Wales]   see **Office of the Parliamentary Commissioner for Administration & the Health Service Commissioners**

Health Service Ombudsman   See **Parliamentary & Health Service Ombudsman**.

© CBD Research Ltd · Beckenham · Kent BR3 5JS · Tel 020 8650 7745 · Fax 020 8650 0768 · E-mail cbd@cbdresearch.com · www.cbdresearch.com

Health Services Advisory Committee (HSAC)

■ Rose Court, 2 Southwark Bridge, LONDON, SE1 9HS.
   Tel 0845 345 0055
E Established in 1980 by the Health & Safety Executive (qv) and last reconstituted in June 2003. HSAC functions as an Advisory NDPB of the HSE.
R To improve occupational health and safety in the health services by promoting good management and control measures at a national and strategic level, particularly with regard to delivering Government programmes.
G United Kingdom.

HEALTH & SOCIAL CARE (HSC)

E In Northern Ireland the NHS is referred to as Health & Social Care (HSC) which, in addition to health services, provides social care services such as home care services, family and children's services, day care services and social work services.
   HSC is responsible to the Department of Health, Social Services & Public Safety Northern Ireland.
R Services are commissioned by the Health & Social Care Board (qv) and provided by five regional HSC Trusts, with ambulance services provided by the Northern Ireland Ambulance Service HSC Trust (qv).
G Northern Ireland.
● The five regional HSC Trusts are:
   Belfast Health & Social Care Trust
   Northern Health & Social Care Trust
   South Eastern Health & Social Care Trust
   Southern Health & Social Care Trust
   Western Health & Social Care Trust (qqv).

Health & Social Care Board (HSC)

■ 12-22 Linenhall Street, BELFAST, BT2 8BS.
   Tel 028 9032 1313   http://www.hscboard.hscni.net
   Chairman: Dr Ian Clements   Chief Executive: John Compton
E Established on 1 April 2009 on the recommendation of the NI Review of Public Administration 2005, centralising four regional Health & Social Care Boards (Eastern, Northern, Southern and Western). The Board comprises 13 members including the Chairman.
R To ensure effective commissioning to secure the provision of health and social services that address the needs of the people.
   Five Local Commissioning Groups (LCGs), aligned to the boundaries of the Health & Social Care Trusts (qv), plan and commission health and social care to meet the needs of the people of their area.
G Northern Ireland.

Health & Social Care Business Services Organisation   See **Business Services Organisation**.

Health & Social Care Information Centre   See the **NHS Information Centre** for Health & Scoial Care.

HEALTH & SOCIAL CARE REGULATORS (HSCs)

E Currently there are 13 bodies classed as Health & Social Care Regulators.
   Practitioners from any of the professions listed below must, by law, register with the relevant Regulator, whose Registers are made up of only those professionals who have demonstrated high standards of safety and competency.
   The healthcare scheme is overseen by the Council for Healthcare Regulatory Excellence (qv).
● The nine healthcare regulators are:
   General Chiropractic Council
   General Dental Council
   General Medical Council
   General Optical Council
   General Osteopathic Council
   Health Professions Council
   Nursing & Midwifery Council
   Pharmaceutical Society of Northern Ireland
   Royal Pharmaceutical Society of Great Britain (qqv).
   The regulatory functions of the last named were scheduled to transfer to the newly established General Pharmaceutical Council (qv) in 2010.

In addition there are four national social care regulators:
Care Council for Wales
General Social Care Council
Northern Ireland Social Care Council
Scottish Social Services Council (qqv).

Health Solutions Wales
✍ HSW became part of the **NHS Wales Informatics Service** on 1 April 2010.

Healthcare-Associated Infection Surveillance Centre (HISC)
■ Kelvin Buildings, Royal Victory Hospital, Grosvenor Road, BELFAST, BT12 6BA.
  Tel 028 9063 4119   **Fax** 028 9031 4043   http://www.hisc.n-i.nhs.uk
  Director: Dr Edward Smyth   General Manager: Gerard McIlvenny
E Established in September 2001. HISC functions as a Health & Personal Social Services NDPB of the Department
  of Health, Social Services & Public Safety Northern Ireland.
R To conduct surveillance programmes in elective orthopoedics and surgical sites.
G Northern Ireland.

Healthcare Commission
✍ The Commission for Healthcare Audit & Inspection ceased to exist on 31 March 2009. The new health and social
  care regulator is the **Care Quality Commission**.

Healthcare Industries Task Force
✍ HITF was a year long initiative which disbanded in November 2004 following publication of its report.

Healthcare Inspectorate Wales (HIW)
■ Bevan House, Caerphilly Business Park, Van Road, CAERPHILLY, CF83 3ED.
  Tel 029 2092 8850   http://www.hiw.org.uk
  = Arolygiaeth Gofal Iechyd Cymru
  Chief Executive: Peter Higson
E Established in 2004 under the Health & Social Care (Community Health & Standards) Act 2003. HIW is
  responsible to the National Assembly for Wales.
R To review, investigate and regulate the provision of healthcare commissioned and provided by healthcare
  organisations in Wales, and to regulate the private and voluntary healthcare sector.
  To act as the Local Supervising Authority (LSA) for midwives.
G Wales.
● HIW has also entered into an agreement with the Nursing & Midwifery Council (qv) to conduct annual monitoring
  of higher education institutions in Wales which offer NMC programmes.

Hearing Aid Council
✍ HAC's functions were transferred to the **Health Professions Council** on 1 April 2010 and HAC abolished on 31
  July 2010.

Heathrow Airport Consultative Committee (HACC)
■ Ground Floor Heathrow Academy, Building 1154 Newall Road, HOUNSLOW, Middx, TW6 2RQ.
  Tel 020 8745 7589   **Fax** 020 8745 0580   http://www.lhr-acc.org
  Chairman: Sam Jones, CBE, DL   Secretary: Carole Havercroft
G Berkshire, West London.
✍ For further information see **Airport Consultative Committees**.

Heating & Hotwater Industry Council (HHIC)
■ Camden House, Warwick Road, KENILWORTH, Warwicks, CV8 1TH.
  Tel 0845 600 2200   http://www.centralheating.co.uk
E HHIC is a membership organisation.
R To support and promote the sustained growth of the UK domestic heating and hot water industry by providing
  quality information, activities and services to a range of audiences including members, government, installers,
  consumers and other associations.
G United Kingdom.

© CBD Research Ltd · Beckenham · Kent BR3 5JS · Tel 020 8650 7745 · Fax 020 8650 0768 · E-mail cbd@cbdresearch.com · www.cbdresearch.com

Helideck Certification Agency   (HCA)
■   Enterprise Business Centre, Admiral Court, Poynernook Road, ABERDEEN, AB11 5QX.
    Tel 01224 289729   http://www.helidecks.org
    General Manager: Alex Knight
R   To conduct surveys of helicopter landing sites, onshore, offshore and afloat, to ensure full compliance with
    international regulations, applying operational limitations or restrictions where appropriate.
G   United Kingdom, Norway.
●   The HCA is responsible for the inspection and certification of all helidecks on offshore vessels and inatallations
    operating in UK and Norwegian waters.
    The Agency has an office in Norwich and Norwegian offices in Bergen and Stavanger.

Her Majesty's Courts Service   (HMCS)
■   Zone C, First Floor, 102 Petty France, LONDON, SW1H 9AJ.
    Tel 0845 456 8770   Fax 020 3334 4087   http://www.hmcourts-service.org.uk
    Chairman: Sir Duncan Nichol, CBE   Chief Executive: Peter Handcock, CBE
E   Established on 2 April 2005 as an Executive Agency of the Ministry of Justice. The Board comprises eleven
    members including the Chairman.
R   To provide administrative support for the Court of Appeal, High Court, Crown Court, County Courts, Magistrates'
    Courts and the Probation Service.
G   England, Wales.
✍   On 1 April 2011, HMCS and the Tribunals Service became a single, unified organisation, **HM Courts & Tribunals
    Service**.

Her Majesty's Courts & Tribunals Service   (HMCTS)
■   102 Petty France, LONDON, SW1H 9AJ.
    Tel 0845 456 8771;   020 3334 6510
    Chairman: Bob Ayling   Chief Executive: Peter Handcock, CBE
E   Established on 1 April 2011, bringing together Her Majesty's Courts Service and the Tribunals Service. HMCTS
    functions as an Executive Agency of the Ministry of Justice and operates as a partnership between the Lord
    Chancellor, the Lord Chief Justice and the Senior President of Tribunals. The Service's work is overseen by a
    board of ten, comprising non-executive, executive and judicial members and an independent chairman.
R   To be responsible for the administration of the criminal, civil and family courts and tribunals in England and
    Wales, and non-devolved tribunals in Scotland and Northern Ireland.
    To ensure that all citizens receive timely access to justice according to their different needs, whether as victims or
    witnesses of crime, defendants accused of crimes, consumers in debt, children at risk of harm, businesses
    involved in commercial disputes or as individuals asserting their employment rights or challenging the decisions
    of government bodies.
G   United Kingdom.
●   The Service employs 21,000 staff and operates from around 650 locations.
✍   The Tribunals, Courts & Enforcement Act 2007 created a new two-tier system of First-tier Tribunals and Upper
    Tribunals (qqv).

Her Majesty's Crown Prosecution Service Inspectorate   (HMCPSI)
■   26-28 Old Queen Street, LONDON, SW1H 9HP.
    Tel 020 7210 1197   http://www.hmcpsi.gov.uk
    Chief Inspector: Michael Fuller, QPM, BA, MBA, HonLLD
E   Established in October 2000 under the Crown Prosecution Service Inspectorate Act 2000. HMCPSI is responsible
    to the Ministry of Justice. The board comprises seven members including the HMCI.
R   To promote continuous improvement in the efficiency, effectiveness and fairness of the prosecution services with
    a joined-up criminal justice system through the process of inspection, evaluation and identification of good
    practice.
G   England, Wales.

Her Majesty's Inspectorate of Constabulary   (HMIC)
■   6th Floor, Globe House, 89 Eccleston Square, LONDON, SW1V 1PN.
    Tel 020 3513 0500   Fax 020 3513 0650   http://www.hmic.gov.uk
    Chief Inspector: Sir Denis O'Connor, QPM, CBE
E   Established in 1856 under the provisions of the County & Borough Police Act 1856. HMIC is responsible to the
    Home Office.

R   To promote the efficiency and effectiveness of policing and law enforcement in England, Wales and Northern Ireland through assessment and inspection of organisaton and functions for which it has responsibility, to ensure performance is improved, good practice is spread, and standards are agreed, achieved and maintained.

G   England, Wales, Northern Ireland.

Her Majesty's Inspectorate of Constabulary for Scotland   (HMICS)

■   1st Floor West, St Andrew's House, Regent Road, EDINBURGH, EH1 3DG.
     Tel 0131 244 5614   **Fax** 0131 244 5616
     Chief Inspector: Bill Skelly, MBA

E   Established under the Police (Scotland) Act 1857. HMICS is responsible to the Scottish Executive Justice Department.

R   To monitor, inspect, advise and improve the eight Scottish police forces and the five organisations that make up the Scottish Police Services Authority (qv).

G   Scotland.

Her Majesty's Inspectorate of Court Administration

✍   Established on 1 April 2005, HMICA was abolished on 31 December 2010.

Her Majesty's Inspectorate of Education   (HMIE)

■   Denholm House, Almondvale Business Park, Almondvale Way, LIVINGSTON, W Lothian, EH54 6GA.
     Tel 01506 600200   http://www.hmie.gov.uk
     HM Senior Chief Inspector: Dr Bill Maxwell

E   Established on 1 April 2001 under the Scotland Act 1998. HMIE functions as an Executive Agency of the Scottish Executive Education Department. The board comprises the HMSCI, seven chief inspectors, the Corporate Services Director and three non-executive members.

R   To inspect, evaluate and report on pre-school education, primary and secondary schools, teacher education, community learning and development, further education and local authorities.

G   Scotland.

Her Majesty's Inspectorate for Education & Training in Wales

■   Anchor Court, Keen Road, CARDIFF, CF24 5JW.
     Tel 029 2044 6446   **Fax** 029 2044 6448   http://www.estyn.gov.uk
     Chief Inspector: Ann Keane

E   Established in 1998 under Government of Wales Act 1998. Known as **Estyn**, the Inspectorate functions as an Executive NDPB of the Welsh Government.

R   To inspect and report on nursery schools and settings that are maintained by, or receive funding from, local education authorities, primary, secondary, independent and special schools, pupil referral units, further education, adult community-based learning, youth support services, Local Education Authorities (LEAs), teacher education and training, youth and community work training, work-based learning, offender learning, careers companies, and the education, guidance and training elements of the Department for Work & Pensions funded programmes.

G   Wales.

=   Arolygiaeth Ei Mawrhydi dros Addysg a Hyfforddiant yng Nghymru

Her Majesty's Inspectorate of Mines   (HMIM)

■   Foundry House, 3 Millsands, Riverside Exchange, SHEFFIELD, S Yorks, S3 8NH.
     Tel 0114 291 2390   **Fax** 0114 291 2399

E   Commonly known as the Mines Inspectorate, HMIM is part of the Health & Safety Executive (qv).

R   To inspect, regulate and advise on health and safety matters in UK mining operations.

G   United Kingdom.

Her Majesty's Inspectorate of Prisons   (HMI Prisons)

■   First Floor, Ashley House, 2 Monck Street, LONDON, SW1P 2BQ.
     Tel 020 7035 2136   **Fax** 020 7035 2141
     Chief Inspector: Nick Hardwick

E   Established in 1961 under the Prisons Act 1952. HMI Prisons is an independent inspectorate responsible to the Ministry of Justice.

R   To provide independent scrutiny in England & Wales of the conditions for and treatment of prisoners and other detainees, promoting the concept of 'healthy prisons' in which staff work effectively to support prisoners and detainees to reduce re-offending or achieve other agreed outcomes.
     To inspect all immigration removal centres, holding facilities and youth offender institutions.

To inspect, by invitation, the Military Corrective Training Centre in Colchester and prisons in Northern Ireland, the Channel Islands and the Isle of Man.

G   England, Wales, Northern Ireland, Channel Islands, Isle of Man.

Her Majesty's Inspectorate of Prisons for Scotland   (HMIP)

■   Saughton House, Broomhouse Drive, EDINBURGH, EH11 3XD.
Tel 0131 244 8481   **Fax** 0131 244 8446
Chief Inspector: Brigadier Hugh Munro, CBE

E   Established on 1 January 1981, the HMCIP is appointed by the Crown under the Prisons (Scotland) Act 1989. The Inspectorate is responsible to the Scottish Executive Justice Department.

R   To carry out a full inspection of each of the 16 prison establishments within the Scottish Prison Service (qv).

G   Scotland.

=   Also frequently referred to as Her Majesty's Prison Inspectorate for Scotland.

Her Majesty's Inspectorate of Probation   (HMI Probation)

■   South Wing (6th Floor), Trafford House, Chester Road, Stretford, MANCHESTER, M32 0RS.
Tel 0161 869 1300   **Fax** 0161 869 1350
Second Floor, Ashley House, 2 Monck Street, LONDON, SW1P 2BQ.
Chief Inspector: Andrew Bridges

E   Established in 1936. HMI Probation is an independent inspectorate responsible to the Ministry of Justice.

R   To inspect and report to the Secretary of State for Justice on the effectiveness of work with individual offenders, children and young people aimed at reducing re-offending and protecting the public.

G   England, Wales.

Her Majesty's Inspectorate of Schools   For England see **Office for Standards in Education, Children's Services & Skills**; For Wales see **Her Majesty's Inspectorate for Education & Training in Wales**; For Scotland see **Her Majesty's Inspectorate of Education**.

Her Majesty's Land Registry   See **Land Registry**.

Her Majesty's Prison Inspectorate for Scotland   See **Her Majesty's Inspectorate of Prisons for Scotland**.

Her Majesty's Prison Service
✍   Functions as part of the **National Offender Management Service** since 1 April 2008.

Her Majesty's Revenue & Customs   (HMRC)

■   100 Parliament Street, LONDON, SW1A 2BQ.
Tel 020 7620 1313   http://www.hmrc.gov.uk
Chairman: Mike Clasper, CBE   Chief Executive: Lesley Strathie

E   Established on 18 April 2005 under the Commissioners for Revenue & Customs Act 2005 which merged Inland Revenue and HM Customs & Excise. HMRC functions as a non-ministerial government department. The Board comprises 16 members including the Chairman.

R   To collect and administer direct and indirect taxes.
To pay and administer tax credits, child benefit and child trust funds.
To enforce and administer border protection, environmental taxes, the national minimum wage and the recovery of student loans.

G   United Kingdom.

●   The Queen appoints **Commissioners of HMRC**. Currently six in number, they are responsible for handling individual taxpayers' affairs impartially. They are also responsible for providing leadership to HMRC and managing its resources efficiently and effectively and for delivering the objectives and targets set by the Chancellor of the Exchequer.

Herbal Medicine Regulatory Working Group
✍   Established in Summer 2006, the Working Group published its report on 16 June 2008.

Herbal Medicines Advisory Committee
✍   HMAC was an Advisory NDPB of MHRA, the Medicine & Healthcare Regulatory Agency (qv). On 14 October 2010 the Government announced that it would be reconstituted as a committee of experts of MHRA.

Heritage Lottery Fund   See **National Heritage Memorial Fund**.

Heritage Memorial Fund   See **National Heritage Memorial Fund**.

Hertfordshire Police Authority
- ■ Leahoe House, Pegs Lane, HERTFORD, SG13 8DE.
  Tel 01992 556600   **Fax** 01992 555625   http://www.hertspa.org
  Chairman: Stuart Nagler, JP, DL   Chief Executive: Andrew White
- E Established in April 1995, the Authority is an independent body charged with ensuring that Hertfordshire Constabulary provides an effective and efficient police service. It is made up of nine county councillors and eight independent members.
- G Hertfordshire.
- ✍ For further information see **Police Authorities**.

Hertfordshire Probation Trust
- ■ Graham House, Yeoman's Court, Ware Road, HERTFORD, SG13 7HJ.
  Tel 01992 504444   **Fax** 01992 504544   http://www.hertfordshireprobation.gov.uk
  Chairman: Delbert Sandiford   Chief Officer: Tessa Webb
- E Established on 1 April 2001 under the Criminal Justice & Court Service Act 2000 as the Hertfordshire Probation Area Board. It became a trust on 1 April 2010 under the Offender Management Act 2007. The Board comprises twelve members including the Chairman.
- G Hertfordshire.
- ✍ For further information see **Probation Trusts**.

Higher Education Funding Council for England   (HEFCE)
- ■ Northavon House, Coldharbour Lane, BRISTOL, BS16 1QD.
  Tel 0117 931 7317   **Fax** 0117 931 7203   http://www.hefce.ac.uk
  Chairman: Tim Melville-Ross, CBE   Chief Executive: Sir Alan Langlands, FRSE
- E Established on 31 March 1993 under the Further & Higher Education Act 1992, the Council replaced the Polytechnics & Colleges Funding Council & the Universities Funding Council. HEFCE functions as an Executive NDPB of the Department for Business, Innovation & Skills. The Board comprises 14 members including the Chairman.
- R To distribute public money for teaching and research to universities and colleges with the aim of producing high quality education and research within a financially healthy sector.
- G England.

Higher Education Funding Council for Wales   (HEFCW)
- ■ Linden Court, Ilex Close, Llanishen, CARDIFF, CF14 5DZ.
  Tel 029 2076 1861   **Fax** 029 2076 3163   http://www.hefcw.ac.uk
  Chairman: Roger Thomas   Chief Executive: Prof Philip Gummett
- E Established on 6 May 1992 under the Further & Higher Education Act 1992. HEFCW functions as an Executive NDPB of the National Assembly for Wales. The Council comprises twelve members including the Chairman.
- R To promote internationally excellent higher education in Wales, for the benefit of individuals, society and the economy, in Wales and more widely.
- G Wales.
- = Cyngor Cyllido Addysg Uwch Cymru

Higher Education Statistics Agency   (HESA)
- ■ 95 Promenade, CHELTENHAM, Glos, GL50 1HZ.
  Tel 01242 255577   **Fax** 01242 211122   http://www.hesa.ac.uk
  Chairman: Prof Gordon Marshall, CBE   Chief Executive: Alison Allden
- E Established in 1993 following a Government White Paper 'Higher Education: a new framework', which called for more coherence in higher education statistics. HESA functions as a company limited by guarantee and registered charity. The Board comprises nine members including the Chairman.
- R To collect, analyse and disseminate quantitative information about higher education.
- G United Kingdom.

Higher & Further Education Advisory Committee   (HIFEAC)
- ■ Wren House, Hedgerows Business Park, Colchester Road, CHELMSFORD, CM2 5PF.
  Tel 0845 345 0055

E   Established in 1981 by the Health & Safety Executive (qv). HIFEAC functions as an Advisory NDPB of the HSE.
R   To advise the HSE on the protection of people at work and others (including students and members of the public) from hazards to health and safety arising within the field of education.
G   United Kingdom.

Highland NHS Board
■   Assynt House, Beechwood Park, INVERNESS, IV2 3BW.
Tel 01463 717123 http://www.nhshighland.scot.nhs.uk
Chairman: Garry Coutts   Chief Executive: Elaine Mead
G   Highland, Argyll & Bute
✍   For further information see **NHS Scotland - Boards**.

Highlands & Islands Airports   (HIA)
■   Inverness Airport, INVERNESS, IV2 7JB.
Tel 01667 464000 Fax 01667 462041 http://www.hial.co.uk
Chairman: Grenville Johnston, OBE   Managing Director: Inglis Lyon
E   Established in 1986 as a wholly owned subsidiary company of the Civil Aviation Authority (qv); in 1995 ownership was transferred to the Scottish Office. HIA now fuctions as a Public Corporation accountable to the Scottish Executive Enterprise, Transport & Lifelong Learning Department. The Board of Directors comprises six members including the Chairman.
R   To be responsible for the management and operation of eleven airports serving the Highlands & Islands of Scotland - Barra, Benbecula, Campbeltown, Dundee, Inverness, Islay, Kirkwall, Stornoway, Sumburgh, Tiree and Wick.
G   Scotland - Highlands & Islands.

Highlands & Islands Enterprise   (HIE)
■   Cowan House, Inverness Retail & Business Park, INVERNESS, IV2 7GF.
Tel 01463 234171 Fax 01463 244469 http://www.hie.co.uk
Chairman: William Roe   Chief Executive: Alex Paterson
E   Established on 1 April 1991 under the Enterprise & New Towns (Scotland) Act 1990. HIE functions as an Executive NDPB of the Scottish Executive Enterprise & Lifelong Learning Department. The Board comprises eleven members including the Chairman.
R   To support high growth businesses and sectors.
To create the infrastructure and conditions to improve regional competitiveness.
To strengthen communities, especially in the fragile parts of the region.
G   Scotland - Highlands & Islands.
●   HIE aims to build sustainable growth in all parts of the Highlands and delivers its services through its local teams. It has area offices in Dingwall, Forres, Fort William, Golspie, Kirkwall, Lerwick, Lochgilphead, Portree, Stornoway and Skye, with administrative offices in Auchtertyre, Benbecula, Dingwall and Inverness.

Highlands & Islands Transport Partnership   (HITRANS)
■   Building 25, Inverness Airport, INVERNESS, IV2 7JB.
Tel 01667 460464 http://www.hitrans.org.uk
Chairman: Cllr Duncan MacIntyre
E   Established on 1 December 2005. The Partnership Board comprises eight Councillor members and five appointed members.
G   Argyll & Bute, Highland, Moray, Orkney, Shetland, Western Isles.
✍   For further information see **Regional Transport Partnerships**.

Highlands of Scotland Tourist Board
✍   Since 1 April 2005 an area office of **VisitScotland**.

Highways Agency
■   123 Buckingham Palace Road, LONDON, SW1W 9HA.
Tel 0845 955 6575 http://www.highways.gov.uk
Chief Executive: Graham Dalton
E   Established on 1 April 1994. It functions as an Executive Agency of the Department for Transport. The Agency's Board comprises ten members including the Chief Executive.
R   To be responsible for operating, maintaining and improving the strategic road network in England.
G   England.

- The Agency has offices in Bedford, Birmingham, Bristol, Dorking, Exeter, Leeds and Manchester in addition to London.

Hill Farming Advisory Committee for England
✍ Replaced in 2002 by the **Uplands Land Management Advisory Panel**.

Hill Farming Advisory Committee for Scotland
✍ Abolished under the Natural Environment & Rural Communities Act 2006, having last met in 2000.

Hill Farming Advisory Sub-Committee for Wales
✍ Replaced in 2005 by the **Upland Forum**.

Historic Buildings Advisory Council for Wales (HBAC)

■ Plas Carew, Unit 5/7 Cefn Coed, Parc Nantgarw, CARDIFF, CF15 7QQ.
  Tel 01443 336000   **Fax** 01443 336001
  Chairman: Richard Keen
E Established on 1 April 2006 as a successor to the Historic Buildings Council which was set up in 1953. HBAC functions as an Advisory Panel of the Welsh Government through Cadw (qv). The Council comprises ten members including the Chairman.
R To advise the Welsh Government on matters concerning historic buildings in Wales and, particularly, assessing whether buildings which are the subject of grant applications to Cadw meet the eligibility criteria.
G Wales.
✍ One of the four organisations which make up **Historic Wales**.
= Cyngor Ymghyngorol Adeiladau Hanesyddol Cymru

Historic Buildings Council (HBC)

■ 4th Floor, Clarence Court, 10-18 Adelaide Street, BELFAST, BT2 8GB.
  Tel 028 9054 1071   http://www.hbcni.gov.uk
  Chairman: Frank Robinson
E Established in 1974 under the Planning (Northern Ireland) Order 1972, its current authority is derived from the Planning (Northern Ireland) Order 1991. HBC functions as an Advisory NDPB of the Department of the Environment Northern Ireland. The Council comprises 18 members including the Chairman.
R To advise the Department on the listing and delisting of buildings, listed building consent, buildings preservation notices, urgent works to preserve buildings, Conservation Areas, and matters of the industrial and defence heritage.
G Northern Ireland.

Historic Buildings & Monuments Commission for England   Official name of **English Heritage**.

Historic Environment Advisory Council for Scotland
✍ HEACS, which last met on 31 May 2009, was dissolved under the Public Services Reform (Scotland) Act 2010.

Historic Monuments Council (HMC)

■ 4th Floor, Clarence Court, 10-18 Adelaide Street, BELFAST, BT2 8GB.
  Tel 028 9054 1071   http://www.hmcni.gov.uk
  Chairman: Prof Gabriel Cooney
E Established on 1 October 1971 under the Historic Monuments Act (Northern Ireland) 1971, it derives its current authority under the Historic Monuments & Archaeological Objects (Northern Ireland) Order 1995. HMC functions as an Advisory NDPB of the Department of the Environment Northern Ireland. The Council comprises 15 members including the Chairman.
R To advise the Department on the scheduling of monuments, conservation of monuments in state care, maritime archaeology, industrial and defence heritage, and Areas of Significant Archaeological Interest within Development Plans.
G Northern Ireland.

© CBD Research Ltd · Beckenham · Kent BR3 5JS · Tel 020 8650 7745 · Fax 020 8650 0768 · E-mail cbd@cbdresearch.com · www.cbdresearch.com

Historic Royal Palaces   (HRP)

■ Apartment 39A, HAMPTON COURT PALACE, Surrey, KT8 9AU.
Tel 020 3166 6610   http://www.hrp.org.uk
Chairman: Charles Mackay   Chief Executive: Michael Day

E Established on 1 October 1989, HRP has functioned as an independent charity since 1998. The Board comprises twelve members including the Chairman and is accountable to the Department for Culture, Media & Sport for the management of the palaces on the Queen's behalf.

R To help everyone explore the story of how monarchs and people have shaped society in the five unoccupied royal palaces in its care: the Banqueting House, Hampton Court Palace, the state rooms only of Kensington Palace, Kew Palace and the Tower of London.

G United Kingdom.

Historic Scotland

■ Longmore House, Salisbury Place, EDINBURGH, EH9 1SH.
Tel 0131 668 8600   http://www.historic-scotland.gov.uk
Chief Executive: Ruth Parsons

E Established on 1 April 1991. It functions as an Executive Agency of the Scottish Executive Education Department. The Board comprises 14 members including the Chief Executive.

R To safeguard the nation's built heritage and to promote its understanding and enjoyment.

G Scotland.

Historic Wales   Historic Wales is an umbrella name for the **Ancient Monuments Advisory Board**, **Cadw**, the **Historic Buildings Advisory Council for Wales** and the **Royal Commission on the Ancient & Historic Monuments of Wales**.

Historical Manuscripts Commission   See **National Archives**.

HM . . .   See **Her Majesty's . . .**

HM Customs & Excise
✍ See **Her Majesty's Revenue & Customs**.

Home-Grown Cereals Authority   (HGCA)

■ AHDB, Stoneleigh Park, KENILWORTH, Warwicks, CV8 2TL.
Tel 024 7669 2051   http://www.hgca.com
Chairman: Jonathan Tipples

E Established on 1 April 2008 via the Agriculture & Horticulture Development Board Order 2008. HGCA functions as a Levy Board and NDPB of the Department for Environment, Food & Rural Affairs. The board comprises 14 members including the Chairman.

R To continuously improve the production, wholesomeness and marketing of UK cereals and oilseeds so as to increase their competitiveness in UK and overseas markets in a sustainable manner.

G United Kingdom.

✍ A subsidiary of the **Agriculture & Horticulture Development Board** and funded through an AHDB levy collected from growers, dealers, processors and intermediaries.

Home Grown Timber Advisory Committee
✍ HGTAC last met in September 2005 and was abolished in October 2010.

Homes & Communities Agency   (HCA)

■ 110 Buckingham Palace Road, LONDON, SW1W 9SA.
Tel 0300 123 4500   http://www.homesandcommunities.co.uk
Arpley House, 110 Birchwood Boulevard, Birchwood, WARRINGTON, WA3 7QH.
Chairman: Robert Napier   Chief Executive: Pat Ritchie

E Established on 1 December 2008 under the Housing & Regeneration Act 2008, combining the functions and assets of English Partnerships and the investment functions of the Housing Corporation. The former Academy for Sustainable Communities has become the HCA Academy, the skills arm of the HCA. HCA functions as a NDPB of the Department for Communities & Local Government. The Agency's board comprises eleven members including the Chairman.

R To improve the supply and quality of housing in England.

To secure the regeneration or development of land or infrastructure in England.

To support in other ways the creation, regeneration or development of communities in England or their continued well-being.

To contribute to the achievement of sustainable and good design in England, with a view to meeting the needs of people living in England.

G England.

✍ The Government announced on 14 October 2010 its intention to retain but substantially reform HCA, creating a smaller enabling and investment body working for local communities and taking on responsibility for the regulation of social housing. Its London functions will be devolved to the Greater London Authority (qv).

Honours Scrutiny Committee

✍ In April 2005 the functions of the Committee were taken over by the **House of Lords Appointments Commission**.

Horniman Public Museum & Public Park Trust

■ 100 London Road, Forest Hill, LONDON, SE23 3PQ.
Tel 020 8699 1872 **Fax** 020 8291 5506 http://www.horniman.ac.uk
Chairman: Timothy Hornsby Chief Executive: Janet Vitmayer

E The Museum opened in 1901. It functions as an Executive NDPB of the Department for Culture, Media & Sport. The Museum is governed by a board of twelve trustees including the Chairman.

R To manage the Horniman Museum and Gardens and to this end seek to encourage a wider appreciation of the world, its peoples and their cultures, and its environments.

G United Kingdom.

Horserace Betting Levy Appeal Tribunal for England & Wales

■ AJTC, 81 Chancery Lane, LONDON, WC2A 1BQ.
Tel 020 7855 5200 **Fax** 020 7855 5201

E Established in May 1963 under the Betting, Gaming & Lotteries Act 1963. It functions as a Tribunal NDPB of the Department for Culture, Media & Sport.

R To hear appeals from bookmakers regarding the amount of levy payable to the Horserace Betting Levy Board (qv).

G England, Wales.

✍ The Tribunal has not had a hearing since 2001.

Horserace Betting Levy Board   (HBLB)

■ Parnell House, 25 Wilton Road, LONDON, SW1V 1LW.
Tel 020 7333 0043 **Fax** 020 7333 0041 http://www.hblb.org.uk
Chairman: Paul Lee Chief Executive: Douglas Erskine-Crum

E Established in 1961 by the Betting Levy Act 1961 and now operating in accordance with the provisions of the Betting, Gaming & Lotteries Act 1963 (as amended). HBLB functions as an Executive NDPB of the Department for Culture, Media & Sport. The Board comprises eight members including the Chairman.

R To assess and collect monetary contributions from bookmakers and the Tote (Horserace Totalisator Board, qv) via a levy.

To apply the funds so raised to one or more of the following:
  the improvement of horseracing
  the improvement of breeds of horses
  the advancement of veterinary science and education.

G England, Scotland, Wales.

Horserace Totalisator Board   (The Tote)

■ Douglas House, Tote Park, Chapel Lane, WIGAN, Lancs, WN3 4HS.
Tel 01942 617500 http://www.corporate.totesport.com
Chairman: Mike Smith Chief Executive: Trevor Beaumont Shareholder Executive contact: Mark Boyle

E Established in 1929 under the Racehorse Betting Act 1928, with subsequent legislation regulating its operation, notably the Betting Levy Act 1961 and the Horserace Betting & Olympic Lottery Act 2004. The Tote functions as a Public Corporation and its board is accountable to the Department for Culture, Media & Sport. The Board comprises nine members including the Chairman.

R To conduct cash betting on horseracing and a wide range of sporting and non-sporting events.

G United Kingdom.

✍ One of the businesses managed by the **Shareholder Executive**.

The Government announced on 14 October 2010 that it would proceed with plans, shelved in 2008, to sell the Tote.

© CBD Research Ltd · Beckenham · Kent BR3 5JS · Tel 020 8650 7745 · Fax 020 8650 0768 · E-mail cbd@cbdresearch.com · www.cbdresearch.com

Horseracing Regulatory Authority
✍ Merged with the British Horseracing Board to form the **British Horseracing Authority** in July 2007.

Horticultural Development Company   (HDC)
■ AHDB, Stoneleigh Park, KENILWORTH, Warwicks, CV8 2TL.
Tel 024 7669 2051   http://www.hdc.org.uk
Chairman: Neil Bragg
E Established on 1 April 2008 via the Agriculture & Horticulture Development Board Order 2008. It replaces the former Horticultural Development Council. The board comprises 15 members including the Chairman.
R To serve British growers by being a top class, efficient and progressive facilitator of near-market horticultural research and development and the associated technology transfer.
To provide clear value for money and be respected as making a major contribution to the profitability of the British horticulural industry.
G England, Wales, Scotland.
✍ A subsidiary of the **Agriculture & Horticulture Development Board** and funded through an AHDB levy collected for most crops.

Hospital Chaplaincies Council   (HCC)
■ Church House, Great Smith Street, LONDON, SW1P 3NZ.
Tel 020 7898 1892   Fax 020 7898 1891   http://www.nhs-chaplaincy-spiritualcare.org.uk
Chairman: Rt Revd Michael Perham, Bishop of Gloucester
E Established in 1948 by resolution of the Church Assembly of the Church of England; reconstitued in 1971 by the General Synod of the Church. The Council currently comprises 14 members including the Chairman.
R To enable and coordinate the ministry and mission of the Church of England in the care of the sick.
G England, Wales.
● In 1964 the Council set up, in conjunction with the Roman Catholic Church and the Free Churches, the Churches' Committee on Hospital Chaplaincy.

Hospitality Awarding Body   (HAB)
■ c/o City & Guilds, 1 Giltspur Street, LONDON, EC1A 9DD.
Tel 0844 543 0000   http://www.hab.org.uk
E The HAB is part of the City & Guilds group (qv). It is an awarding body for courses and qualifications in the hospitality industry.
G United Kingdom.
✍ See also **Federation of Awarding Bodies**.

House of Commons Commission
■ Committee Office, House of Commons, LONDON, SW1A 0AA.
Tel 020 7219 3299   Fax 020 7219 2622
Secretary: Dorian Gerhold
E Established in 1978 under the House of Commons (Administration) Act 1978. The Commission comprises six Members of Parliament including the Speaker of the House of Commons who acts as Chairman.
R To appoint staff of the House.
To prepare and lay before the House the Estimates for the House of Commons Service.
To allocate functions to House departments.
To keep staff pay and conditions broadly in line with those of the Civil Service.
G United Kingdom.

House of Lords Appointments Commission   (HoLAC)
■ 35 Great Smith Street, LONDON, SW1P 3BQ.
Tel 020 7276 2005   Fax 020 7276 2602   http://www.lordsappointments.independent.gov.uk
Chairman: Lord Jay of Ewelme, GCMG
E Established in May 2000 as set out in the Government's white paper 'Modernising Parliament, Reforming the House of Lords'. In April 2005 it absorbed the former Honours Scrutiny Committee. HoLAC functions as an Executive NDPB of the Cabinet Office. The Commission comprises seven members including the Chairman.
R To select new independent members of the House of Lords, on merit and on their commitment to the work of the House in scrutinising legislation, and to vet party-political nominations put forward by the political parties.
G United Kingdom

House of Lords Audit Committee   See **United Kingdom Parliament: Committees**.

Housing Action Trusts (Castle Vale, Liverpool, Stonebridge & Tower Hamlets)
✍   Wound up in 2005 upon completion of their programmes.

Housing Association Ombudsman for Scotland
✍   See the **Scottish Public Services Ombudsman**.

Housing Corporation
✍   On 1 December 2008 the Corporation's investment functions were transferred to the **Homes & Communities Agency**. Its regulatory functions were transferred to the **Tenant Services Authority** but on 14 October 2010 the Government announced that these too would pass to HCA.

Housing Council   (NIHC)
■   The Housing Centre, 2 Adelaide Street, BELFAST, BT2 8PB.
     Tel 028 9024 0588   http://www.nihousingcouncil.org
     Chairman: Gerry Gallagher
E   Established on 25 February 1971 under the Housing Executive Act (Northern Ireland) 1971. The Council comprises one representative from each of the 26 District Councils in Northern Ireland.
R   To consider any matter affecting housing which is referred to it by the Department for Social Development Northern Ireland or the Northern Ireland Housing Executive (qv) or any matter that appears to the Housing Council to be a matter pertinent to housing on the wider front.
G   Northern Ireland.

Housing Ombudsman Service   (HOS)
■   81 Aldwych, LONDON, WC2B 4HN.
     Tel 0300 111 3000   **Fax** 020 7831 1942   http://www.housing-ombudsman.org.uk
     Ombudsman: Dr Mike Biles
E   Established, as the Independent Housing Ombudsman Scheme, on 1 April 1997 under the Housing Act 1996. It operates under the name Housing Ombudsman Service and functions as an Executive NDPB of the Department for Communities & Local Government.
R   To deal with any complaints about shortcomings from residents in homes managed by a member of the Service.
G   United Kingdom.
●   The Act, amended by the Housing & Regeneration Act 2008, requires all social housing providers to belong to the Service. The Service also covers non-social housing providers who have joined it voluntarily.
✍   Complaints about public housing (councils or local authorities) have to be made to the Local Government Ombudsman (qv).

Hull Citybuild
✍   Operated from 2002 until 2008 when **Hull Forward** was established.

Hull Forward
✍   An Economic Development Company established on 1 April 2008 when it replaced Hull Citybuild, an Urban Regeneration Company. Hull Forward closed on 30 September 2010.

Human Fertilisation & Embryology Authority   (HFEA)
■   21 Bloomsbury Street, LONDON, WC1B 3HF.
     Tel 020 7291 8200   **Fax** 020 7291 8201   http://www.hfea.gov.uk
     Chairman: Prof Lisa Jardine, CBE   Chief Executive: Alan Doran
E   Established in August 1991 under the Human Fertilisation & Embryology Act 1990. HFEA functions as an Executive NDPB of the Department of Health. The Board has 18 members including the Chairman.
R   To license and monitor clinics that carry out in vitro fertilisation (IVF), artificial insemination (AI) and human embryo research.
     To regulate the storage of gametes (eggs and sperm) and embryos.
G   United Kingdom.
✍   The Government intends to introduce legislation to transfer HFEA's regulatory functions to the Care Quality Commission and the NHS Information Centre (qqv).

Human Genetics Commission   (HGC)

■   605 Wellington House, 133-155 Waterloo Road, LONDON, SE1 8UG.
    Tel 020 7972 4351   **Fax** 020 7972 4300   http://www.hgc.gov.uk
    Chairman: Prof Jonathan Montgomery
E   Established in December 1996 as the Human Genetics Advisory Commission, it adopted its shorter name in 1999.
    HGC functions as a Scientific Advisory Committee and an Advisory NDPB of the Department of Health. The
    Commission comprises 21 members including the Chairman.
R   To analyse current and potential developments in human genetics and advise Ministers on their likely impact on
    human health and healthcare, and their social, ethical, legal and economic implications.
G   United Kingdom.
✍   The Government announced on 14 October 2010 that HGC would cease to function as a NDPB and be
    reconstituted as a committee of experts of the Department of Health.
    For further information see **Scientific Advisory Committees**.

Human Tissue Authority   (HTA)

■   151 Buckingham Palace Road, LONDON, SW1W 9SZ.
    Tel 020 7269 1900   http://www.hta.gov.uk
    Chairman: Baroness Diana Warwick   Chief Executive: Craig Muir
E   Established on 1 April 2005 under the Human Tissue Act 2004. On 1 September 2006 it absorbed the functions
    formerly carried out by Unrelated Live Transplant Regulatory Authority. HTA functions as an Executive NDPB of
    the Department of Health. The Authority comprises 13 members including the Chairman.
R   To license and inspect organisations that store and use human tissue for purposes such as research, patient
    treatment, post-mortem examination, teaching and public exhibitions.
    To approve organ and bone marrow transplants from living people.
G   England, Wales, Northern Ireland.
✍   The Secretary of State for Health announced on 26 July 2010 that HTA would be abolished before 2015 and was
    examining the practicalities and legal implications of dividing its statutory functions between a new research
    regulator, the Care Quality Commission (qv) and the Health & Social Care Information Centre (qv).

Humber & Wolds Rural Community Council   (HWRCC)

■   14 Market Place, HOWDEN, E Yorks, DN14 7BJ.
    Tel 01430 430904   **Fax** 01430 432037   http://www.hwrcc.org.uk
    Chairman: Tony Cooper   Chief Executive: Penny Brown
E   Established in 1975. HWRCC functions as a registered charity and company limited by guarantee. The Board
    comprises 22 Trustees including the Chairman.
R   To improve the sustainability and vibrancy of rural communities across the sub-region.
G   East Riding of Yorkshire, North and North East Lincolnshire.
✍   HWRCC is one of the 38 Rural Community Councils, represented at the national level by **Action with
    Communities in Rural England** (qv) and at the regional level by the Yorkshire & the Humber Rural Community
    Action Network.

Humberside Police Authority   (HPA)

■   Pacific Exchange, 40 High Street, HULL, HU1 1PS.
    Tel 01482 334818   **Fax** 01482 334822   http://www.humberside-pa.org.uk
    Chairman: Cllr Chris Matthews   Chief Executive: Kevin Sharp
E   Established in April 1995, the Authority is an independent body charged with ensuring that Humberside Police
    provide an effective and efficient police service. It is made up of nine councillor members and eight
    independent members.
G   East Riding of Yorkshire, North and North East Lincolnshire.
✍   For further information see **Police Authorities**.

Humberside Probation Trust

■   21 Flemingate, BEVERLEY, E Yorks, HU17 0NP.
    Tel 01482 867271   **Fax** 01482 864928   http://www.humberside-probation.org.uk
    Chairman: Jonathan Carruthers   Chief Executive: Steve Hemming
E   Established on 1 April 2001 under the Criminal Justice & Court Service Act 2000 as the Humberside Probation
    Area Board. It became a trust on 1 April 2008 under the Offender Management Act 2007. The Board comprises
    eleven members including the Chairman.
G   East Riding of Yorkshire, North and North East Lincolnshire.
✍   For further information see **Probation Trusts**.

Hybu Cig Cymru   See **Meat Promotion Wales**.

Hydrographic Office   See **United Kingdom Hydrographic Office**.

Hywel Dda Community Health Council
■   Suite 1, Cedar Court, Haven's Head, MILFORD HAVEN, Pembs, SA73 3LS.
    Tel 01646 697610   **Fax** 01646 697256
    8 Portland Road, ABERYSTWYTH, SY23 2NL.
    Tel 01970 624760   **Fax** 01970 62730
    103 Lammas Street, CARMARTHEN, SA31 3AP.
    Tel 01267 231384   **Fax** 01267 230443
    Chairman: David Thomson   Chief Officer: Ashley Warlow
E   The Executive Committee comprises eight members including the Chairman. The full Council comprises 36
    volunteer members drawn from the three local committees (Carmarthenshire, Ceredigion and Pembrokeshire).
G   Carmarthenshire, Ceredigion, Pembrokeshire.
✍   For further information see **Community Health Councils** under **National Health Service - Wales**.

Hywel Dda Health Board
■   Merlin's Court, Winch Lane, HAVERFORDWEST, Pembs, SA61 1SB.
    Tel 01437 771220   http://www.hywelddalhb.wales.nhs.uk
    Chairman: Chris Martin   Chief Executive: Trevor Purt
E   Established on 1 October 2009 by the merger of three former Local Health Boards (Carmarthenshire, Ceredigion
    and Pembrokeshire) and three NHS Trusts (Carmarthenshire, Ceredigion & Mid Wales and Pembrokeshire &
    Derwen). The Board comprises twelve members including the Chairman.
G   Carmarthenshire, Ceredigion, Pembrokeshire.
✍   For further information see **NHS Wales - Local Health Boards**
    Hywel Dda Health Board is the operational name of the Hywel Dda Local Health Board.

I

Identity & Passport Service   (IPS)
■   Globe House, 89 Ecclestone Square, LONDON, SW1V 1PN.
    Tel 0300 222 0000   http://www.ips.gov.uk
    Regional passport offices:
    Law Society House, 90-106 Victoria Street, BELFAST, BT1 3GN.
    Millburngate House, DURHAM, DH97 1PA.
    3 Northgate, 96 Milton Street, Cowcaddens, GLASGOW, G4 0BT.
    101 Old Hall Street, LIVERPOOL, L3 9BD.
    Olympia House, Upper Dock Street, NEWPORT, Gwent, NP20 1XA.
    Aragon Court, Northminster Road, PETERBOROUGH, PE1 1QG.
    Chief Executive: Sarah Rapson
E   Established on 1 April 2006 as the successor to the UK Passport Service. Since 1 April 2008 it incorporates the
    General Register Office. IPS functions as an Executive Agency of the Home Office. The Board comprises 15
    members including the Chief Executive.
R   To issue passports and provide passport verification services.
    To issue, through the General Register Office, certificates of birth, marriage, civil partnership and death.
G   United Kingdom.

Iechyd Cyhoeddus Cymru   See **Public Health Wales**.

IFS School of Finance   (IFS)
■   4-9 Burgate Lane, CANTERBURY, Kent, CT1 2XJ.
    Tel 01227 818609   **Fax** 01227 784331   http://www.ifslearning.ac.uk
    Chairman: Dr Paul Fisher   Principal: Gavin Shreeve

© CBD Research Ltd · Beckenham · Kent BR3 5JS · Tel 020 8650 7745 · Fax 020 8650 0768 · E-mail cbd@cbdresearch.com · www.cbdresearch.com

E Established by Royal Charter on 10 May 1987. The School functions as a registered charity. The Board of
   Governors comprises 14 members including the Chairman.
R An awarding body for courses and qualifications in the financial services industry.
✍ See also the **Federation of Awarding Bodies**.

Ilex

■ Exchange House, Queen's Quay, DERRY-LONDONDERRY, BT48 7AS.
  Tel 028 7126 9226 **Fax** 028 7127 9669 http://www.ilex-urc.com
  Chairman: Sir Roy McNulty, CBE Chief Executive: Aideen McGinley
E Established in 2003 by the Office of the First Minister & the Deputy First Minister and the Department for Social
   Development Northern Ireland. Ilex is the only Urban Regeneration Company in Northern Ireland. It functions as
   an Executive NDPB of the Office of the First Minister & Deputy First Minister in Northern Ireland.
R To plan, develop and sustain the economic, physical and social regeneration of the Derry City Council area and
   the North West region.
   To develop two former security bases, Ebrington and Fort George.
G Derry-Londonderry.
✍ For further information see **Urban Regeneration Companies**.

ILEX Professional Standards Ltd   (IPS)

■ Kempston Manor, Kempston, BEDFORD, MK42 7AB.
  Tel 01234 845770 **Fax** 01234 840989 http://www.ilex.org.uk/ips/ips_home.aspx
  Chairman: Alan Kershaw Chief Executive: Ian Watson
E Established in October 2008 under the Legal Services Act 2007. IPS is accountable to the Institute of Legal
   Executives (ILEX), ILEX members and the Legal Services Board (qv). The IPS Board comprises seven members
   including the Chairman.
R To ensure that the Institute of Legal Executives (ILEX) complies with its responsibilities as an approved regulator
   of lawyers.
G United Kingdom.
✍ One of the Approved Regulators overseen by the **Legal Services Board**.

IMB National Council   See **Independent Monitoring Boards** (England & Wales).

IMI Awards Ltd   See the **Institute of the Motor Industry**.

Immigration Advisory Service   (IAS)

■ 3rd Floor, County House, 190 Great Dover Street, LONDON, SE1 4YB.
  Tel 020 7967 1200 **Fax** 020 7403 5875 http://www.iasuk.org
  Chairman: John Scampion, CBE Chief Executive: Lynn McDougall
E Established in 1993 under the Immigration Act 1971, replacing the former United Kingdom Immigrants Advisory
   Service. UKIAS functions as a registered charity and company limited by guarantee. The Board of Trustees
   comprises eight members including the Chairman.
R To give free advice and assistance on all immigration, asylum and nationality issues to persons in the UK and
   abroad eligible for Legal Help & Controlled Legal Representation.
   To present appeals against refusal decisions for all who have a right of appeal.
G United Kingdom.
● The Service has 38 offices in Britain, three in Pakistan, two in Nigeria and one in Bangladesh.

Immigration Appeal Tribunal
✍ Merged with the Immigration Apellate Authority. See **First-tier Tribunal (Immigration & Asylum)**.

Immigration Appellate Authority
✍ Merged with the Immigration Appeal Tribunal. See **First-tier Tribunal (Immigration & Asylum)**.

Immigration Services Commissioner   See **Office of the Immigration Services Commissioner**.

Immigration Services Tribunal
✍ Since 18 January 2010 **First-tier Tribunal (Immigration Services)**.

Imperial War Museum   (IWM)

- Lambeth Road, LONDON, SE1 6HZ.
  Tel 020 7416 5320   **Fax** 020 7416 5374   http://www.iwm.org.uk
  Chairman: Air Chief Marshal Sir Peter Squire, GCB, DFC, AFC, DL, DSc, FRAeS   Director General: Diane Lees
- E Established in 1917 by decision of the War Cabinet to record the story of the Great War and the contributions
     made by the peoples of the Empire to it. The Museum functions as an Executive NDPB of the Department for
     Culture, Media & Sport. The Board of Trustees comprises 22 members including the Chairman and, ex officio,
     the High Commissioners of Australia, Canada, India, New Zealand, Pakistan, South Africa and Sri Lanka.
- R To provide for and to encourage the study and understanding of the history of modern war and the 'wartime
     experience'.
- G United Kingdom.
- The five branches of the Museum are:
     Churchill Museum & Cabinet War Rooms, Imperial Ward Museum Duxford, Imperial War Museum London,
     Imperial War Museum North (Manchester) and HMS Belfast.

Improve Ltd

- Ground Floor, Providence House, 2 Innovation Close, Heslington, YORK, YO10 5ZF.
  Tel 0845 644 0448   **Fax** 0845 644 0449   http://www.improveltd.co.uk
  Chairman: Paul Wilkinson   Chief Executive: Jack Matthews
- E Established on 1 June 2004. It is the recognised Sector Skills Council for the food and drink manufacturing and
     processing industry. The board comprises twelve members including the Chairman.
- R To achieve world class skills for the food and drink industry.
- G United Kingdom.
- ✍ For further information see **Sector Skills Councils**.

Improvement & Development Agency for local government

- ✍ Since 2010 **Local Government Improvement & Development**.

In Vitro Diagnostic Advisory Committee   (IVDAC)

- 151 Buckingham Palace Road, LONDON, SW1W 9SZ.
  Tel 020 3080 6000   http://www.mhra.gov.uk
- E IVDAC functions as an advisory body of the Medicines & Healthcare products Regulatory Authority (qv).
- R To advise the MHRA on matters relating to the use of in vitro diagnostic medical devices (IVDs).
- G United Kingdom.

Incorporated Council of Law Reporting for England & Wales   (ICLR)

- Megarry House, 119 Chancery Lane, LONDON, WC2A 1PP.
  Tel 020 7242 6471   **Fax** 020 7831 5247   http://www.iclr.co.uk
  Chairman: His Honour Judge N M Chambers, QC
- E Established in 1865 by members of the legal profession. ICLR is a company limited by guarantee and registered
     as a charity. The Council comprises 21 members including the Chairman.
- R To prepare and publish, in a convenient form, at a moderate price, and under gratuitous professional control, [The
     Law] Reports of Judicial Directions of the Superior & Appelate Courts in England & Wales.
- G England, Wales.

Independent Advisory Group on Sexual Health & HIV   (IAG)

- 133-155 Waterloo Road, LONDON, SE1 8UJ.
  Tel 020 7972 3981   **Fax** 020 7972 4700
  Chairman: Baroness Joyce Gould
- E Established in March 2003. IAG functions as an Advisory NDPB of the Department of Health. The Group
     comprises 25 members including the Chairman.
- R To provide advice to the Government and monitor progress on the implementation of the National Strategy for
     Sexual Health & HIV, including any further action necessary to achieve the Strategy's aims of
     reducing the transmission of HIV and STIs
     reducing unwanted pregnancy rates
     improving the health and social care for people living with HIV and STIs
     and reducing the stigma associated with HIV and STIs.
- G United Kingdom.
- ✍ Following the Department of Health's review of its Advisory NDPBs in 2010, IAG is to be abolished and replaced
     by a stakeholder advisory group on sexual health.

Independent Advisory Panel on Deaths in Custody   (IAP)

- ■ 4th Floor, Clive House, 70 Petty France, LONDON, SW1H 9EX.
  Tel 0300 047 5728   Fax 0300 047 6857   http://www.iapdeathsincustody.independent.gov.uk
  Chairman: Lord Toby Harris
- E Established in April 2009 following publication of the Review of the Forum for Preventing Deaths in Custody (the Fulton Report) in February 2008. The Panel comprises seven members including the Chairman.
- R To provide independent advice and expertise to the Ministerial Board on Deaths in Custody, which brings together the Department of Health, the Home Office and the Ministry of Justice.
- G England, Wales.
- ● IAP, the Ministerial Board on Deaths in Custody, and the Practitioner & Stakeholder Group together form the three-tier Ministerial Council on Deaths in Custody.
  IAP's remit covers deaths which occur in prisons, in or following police custody, immigration detention, the deaths of residents of approved premises and the deaths of those detained under the Mental Health Act in hospital.

Independent Agricultural Appeals Panel

- ■ 621 Kings House, Kings Road, READING, Berks, RG1 3BU.
  Tel 0118 953 1907   Fax 0118 939 3817
- E Established on 1 April 2002, the Panel absorbed the functions of the former Dairy Produce Quota Tribunal. It functions as an Advisory NDPB for the Department for Environment, Food & Rural Affairs. The Panel comprises three members including the Chairman.
- R To consider appeals against decisions by the Rural Payments Agency (qv).
- G United Kingdom.
- ✍ A Panel was last convened in April 2002.

Independent Betting Adjudication Service   (IBAS)

- ■ PO Box 62639, LONDON, EC3P 3AS.
  Tel 020 7347 5883   Fax 020 7347 5882   http://www.ibas-uk.com
  Chief Executive: Chris O'Keeffe
- E Established in 1998 as the Independent Betting Arbitration Service, it adopted its current name in 2007 to better reflect its role under the Gambling Act 2005.
- R To act as an impartial adjudicator in disputes that arise between betting/gambling operators and their customers.
- G United Kingdom.

Independent Board of Visitors to the Military Corrective Training Centre Colchester   See **Independent Monitoring Board (Military Corrective Training Centre)**.

Independent Chief Inspector of the UK Border Agency

- ■ 5th Floor, Globe House, 89 Eccleston Square, LONDON, SW1V 1PN.
  Tel 020 3513 0487   http://www.icinspector.gov.uk
  Chief Inspector: John Vine, CBE, QPM
- E Established on 1 April 2008 under the UK Borders Act 2007. He functions as an independent inspectorate of the Home Office. The Executive Team comprises the Chief Inspector and three Assistant Chief Inspectors.
- R To ensure independent scrutiny of the UK Border Agency (qv), providing confidence and assurance as to its effectiveness and efficiency.
- G United Kingdom.

Independent Committee for the Supervision of Standards of Telephone Information Services
- ✍ Now known as **PhonepayPlus**.

Independent Housing Ombudsman Scheme   IHO Ltd, a company limited by guarantee not trading for profit, provides the financial and administrative support for the Scheme which operates under the name **Housing Ombudsman Service**.

Independent International Commission on Decommissioning
- ✍ The IICD's mandate terminated on 9 February 2010 in the British jurisdiction and, in the jurisdiction of the Republic of Ireland, on 25 February on which day it published its last operational report.

Independent Living Fund   (ILF)

■ Equinox House, Island Business Quarter, City Link, NOTTINGHAM, NG2 4LA.
  Tel 0115 945 0700   **Fax** 0115 945 0945   http://www.dwp.gov.uk/ilf/
  Chairman: Stephen Jack   Chief Executive: Patrick Boyle

E The original ILF operated from 1988 to 1993 when replaced by the 1993 Fund and the Extension Fund; the current ILF was established on 1 October 2007 by the Independent Living Fund (2006) Trust Deed which reunited the former funds. ILF functions as an Executive NDPB of the Department for Work & Pensions. The Board of Trustees comprises nine members including the Chairman.

R To provide discretionary cash payments directly to disabled people so they can purchase care from an agency or pay the wages of a privately employed personal assistant, so enabling them to live in the community rather than in residential care.

G United Kingdom.

✍ The Fund was closed to new applicants in 2010. Payments to existing users will continue to 2015 only.

Independent Monitoring Board (Military Corrective Training Centre)

■ Berechurch Hall Road, COLCHESTER, Essex, CO2 9NU.
  Tel 01206 816757

E The Board functions as an Advisory NDPB of the Ministry of Defence.

R To inspect relevant military premises in order to ensure that the state of the premises, their administration and the treatment of detainees is satisfactory.

G United Kingdom.

Independent Monitoring Boards   (IMBs)

■ 2nd Floor, Ashley House, 2 Monck Street, LONDON, SW1P 2BQ.
  Tel 020 7035 2254   **Fax** 020 7035 2250   http://www.imb.gov.uk
  President: Dr Peter Selby   Head of Secretariat: Mick Robins

E Boards of Visitors (for prisons) were established under the Prison Act 1952 and Visiting Committees (for immigration removal centres) under the Immigration & Asylum Act 1999. They adopted their present name in April 2003. There is an Independent Monitoring Board attached to each prison and immigration removal centre and at some short term holding facilities at airports. Each functions as an Advisory NDPB of the Ministry of Justice and is served by a national secretariat. The IMB National Council comprises eight area representatives for prison boards and one for immigration removal centres, and is chaired by a non-executive President. There are also two co-opted members looking at diversity and training.

R Each IMB, which comprises members of the public, is specifically charged to monitor the day-to-day life in their local prison or removal centre and ensure that proper standards of care and decency are maintained.

G England, Wales.

Independent Monitoring Boards for Northern Ireland   (IMBs)

■ 22nd Floor, Windsor House, Bedford Street, BELFAST, BT2 7FT.
  Tel 028 9044 3998   **Fax** 028 9044 3993   http://www.imb-ni.org.uk
  IMB Chairmen: Brian Collins (Magilligan), James McAllister (Maghaberry) and Jimmy McClean (Hydebank Wood)

E Established under the Prison Act (Northern Ireland) 1953 and known as Boards of Visitors until 20 August 2005 when they became IMBs under provisions of the Criminal Justice (Northern Ireland) Order 2005 (SI 2005/1965 (Northern Ireland 15)). Maghberry Prison, Magilligan Prison and Hydebank Wood Prison & Young Offenders Centre each has a Board, and each Board functions as an Advisory NDPB of the Department of Justice Northern Ireland.

R Each IMB comprises members of the community in which the prison or centre is situated, and is specifically charged to visit prisons weekly to satisfy themselves as to the proper treatment of prisoners and the cleanliness and adequacy of the prison facilities.

G Northern Ireland.

Independent Parliamentary Standards Authority   (IPSA)

■ 7th Floor, Portland House, Bressenden Place, LONDON, SW1E 5BH.
  Tel 020 7811 6400   http://www.ipsa-home.org.uk
  Chairman: Prof Sir Ian Kennedy   Chief Executive: Andrew McDonald

E Established on 12 April 2010 under the Parliamentary Standards Act 2009. The Authority comprises five members including the Chairman.

R To establish clear guidelines setting out what Members of Parliament can and cannot claim for.
  To process, validate and pay or reject MPs' claims for expenses and publish on its website every claim made by every MP.

G United Kingdom.

     © CBD Research Ltd · Beckenham · Kent BR3 5JS · Tel 020 8650 7745 · Fax 020 8650 0768 · E-mail cbd@cbdresearch.com · www.cbdresearch.com

Independent Police Complaints Commission   (IPCC)

- ■ 5th Floor, 90 High Holborn, LONDON, WC1V 6BH.
  Tel 0845 300 2002   http://www.ipcc.gov.uk
  Interim Chairman: Len Jackson   Chief Executive: Jane Furniss
- E Established on 1 April 2004 under the Police Reform Act 2002. IPCC functions as an Executive NDPB of the Home Office. The Commission comprises the Chairman, two deputies and 11 operational commissioners, each responsible for specific forces, who work from the regional offices.
- R To ensure that complaints against the police are dealt with effectively.
  To set standards for the way the police handle complaints and, when something has gone wrong, help the police learn lessons and improve the way they work.
- G England, Wales.
- ● The Commission has offices in Cardiff (Wales & South West), Coalville (Central), Sale (North West) and Wakefield (North East) in addition to London (London & South East).

Independent Reconfiguration Panel   (IRP)

- ■ 6th Floor, 157-197 Buckingham Palace Road, LONDON, SW1W 9SP.
  Tel 020 7389 8046   http://www.irpanel.org.uk
  Chairman: Dr Peter Barrett   Chief Executive: Richard Jeavons
- E Established on 1 April 2003. IRP functions as an Advisory NDPB of the Department of Health. The Panel comprises 16 members including the chairman.
- R To advise ministers on proposals for NHS service change in England that have been contested locally and referred to the Secretary of State for Health.
  To offer support and generic advice to the NHS, local authorities and other interested bodies involved in NHS reconfiguration.
- G England.

Independent Regulator of NHS Foundation Trusts   See **Monitor**.

Independent Review Panel on the Advertising of Medicines
- ✍ The Panel was an Advisory NDPB of MHRA, the Medicine & Healthcare Regulatory Agency (qv). On 14 October 2010 the Government announced that it would be reconstituted as a committee of experts of MHRA.

Independent Review Panel on the Classification of Borderline Products
- ✍ The Panel was an Advisory NDPB of MHRA, the Medicine & Healthcare Regulatory Agency (qv). On 14 October 2010 the Government announced that it would be reconstituted as a committee of experts of MHRA.

Independent Review Service for the Social Fund   (IRS)

- ■ 4th Floor, Centre City Podium, 5 Hill Street, BIRMINGHAM, B5 4UB.
  Tel 0800 096 1926   http://www.irs-review.org.uk
  Scottish Amicable Building, 11 Donegal Square South, BELFAST, BT1 5JE.
  Tel 028 9023 0921
  Social Fund Commissioner: Karamajit Singh, CBE
- E Established on 11 April 1998 by Act of Parliament. The Secretary of State for Work & Pensions appoints the Social Fund Commissioner who in turn appoints Social Fund Inspectors.
- R To deliver an independent review of discretionary Social Fund decisions made in Jobcentre Plus offices.
  To share information and expertise with those who have an interest in the discretionary Social Fund and its review.
  To participate in social police research that contributes to the wider debate about the Social Fund and related issues.
- G United Kingdom.
- ● The Service is based in Birmingham and serves England, Wales and Scotland. The Belfast office serves Northern Ireland.

Independent Safeguarding Authority   (ISA)

- ■ PO Box 181, DARLINGTON, Co Durham, DL1 9FA.
  Tel 0300 123 1111   http://www.isa-gov.org.uk
  Chairman: Sir Roger Singleton, CBE   Chief Executive: Adrian McAllister
- E Established in 2009 under the Safeguarding Vulnerable Groups Act 2006. The board comprises twelve members including the Chairman.
- R To help prevent unsuitable people from working with children and vulnerable adults.

G   England, Wales, Northern Ireland.

✍   On 11 February 2011 the Government published the findings of its Review into the Vetting & Barring Scheme. Key recommendations included merging ISA and the Criminal Records Bureau (qv) and a large reduction in the number of positions requiring checks.

Independent Schools Council   (ISC)

■   St Vincent House, 30 Orange Street, LONDON, WC2H 7HH.
    Tel 020 7766 7070   **Fax** 020 7766 7071   http://www.isc.co.uk
    Chairman: Dame Judith Mayhew Jonas   Chief Executive: David Lyscom

E   Established in 1974. ISC is a politically independent, not-for-profit organisation representing 1,280 independent schools educating more than 500,000 children. The Governing Council comprises 16 members including the Chairman.

R   To promote and preserve the quality, diversity and excellence of UK independent education both at home and abroad.

G   United Kingdom.

Independent Schools Examinations Board   (ISEB)

■   The Pumo House, 16 Queen's Avenue, CHRISTCHURCH, Dorset, BH23 1BZ.
    Tel 01202 487538   **Fax** 01202 473728   http://www.iseb.co.uk
    General Secretary: Mrs Jennie Williams, BA

E   ISEB is an independent body.

R   To offer examinations to pupils transferring from junior to independent senior school at the ages of 11+ and 13+.

G   United Kingdom.

●   The main examination is Common Entrance, established in 1904.

Independent Schools Inspectorate   (ISI)

■   CAP House, 9-12 Long Lane, LONDON, EC1A 9HA.
    Tel 020 7600 0100   **Fax** 020 7776 8849   http://www.isi.net

E   Established in 2000, ISI operates under the Education Act 2005. The Inspectorate reports to the Department for Education.

R   To inspect all schools in membership of the Independent Schools Council (qv).

G   England, Wales.

Independent Scientific Advisory Committee for MHRA database research   (ISAC)

■   151 Buckingham Palace Road, LONDON, SW1W 9SZ.
    Tel 020 3080 6000   http://www.mhra.gov.uk
    Chairman: Prof Jennifer Adgey, CBE

E   Established in 2006. ISAC functions as an advisory body to the Medicines & Healthcare products Regulatory Agency (qv). The Committee comprises 15 members including the Chairman.

R   To provide advice on research related requests to access data from the Yellow Card Scheme and the General Practice Research Database.

G   United Kingdom.

✍   The MHRA and the Commission on Human Medicines (qqv) run the Yellow Card Scheme, which is the UK's spontaneous adverse drug reaction (ADR) reporting scheme - the scheme receives reports of suspected ADRs from healthcare professionals.

Independent Scientific Committee on Drugs   (ISCD)

■   Centre for Crime & Justice Studies, King's College London, Strand, LONDON, WC2R 2LS.
    Tel 020 7848 1688   **Fax** 020 7848 1689
    Chairman: Prof David Nutt

E   Established in January 2010 by Prof David Nutt following his enforced resignation in October 2009 from the Home Office's Advisory Committee on the Misuse of Drugs (qv). The Committee comprises about 20 members including the Chairman.

R   To provide independent advice on the scientific risk of drugs.

G   United Kingdom.

Independent Scientific Group on Cattle TB

✍   The Group was dissolved on 30 June 2007 following publication of its final report.

Industrial Court

- Room 203, Adelaide House, 39-49 Adelaide Street, BELFAST, BT2 8FD.
  Tel 028 9025 7599   Fax 028 9025 7555   http://www.industrialcourt.gov.uk
  Acting Chairman: Barry Fitzpatrick   Secretary: Dr Alan Scott
- E Established in 1919, the Court derives its authority under provisions made in the Employment Relations (Northern Ireland) Order 1999.
  It functions as a Tribunal NDPB of the Department for Employment & Learning Northern Ireland.
  The Court comprises the Chairman, his deputy, three members experienced as representatives of employers and four as representatives of workers.
- R To adjudicate on applications relating to statutory recognition and derecognition of trade unions for collective bargaining purposes, where such recognition or derecognition cannot be agreed voluntarily.
  To determine disputes between trade unions and employers over the disclosure of information for collective bargaining purposes.
  To deal with complaints under a range of legislation deriving from European Directives.
- G Northern Ireland.
- ● The Industrial Court is a close equivalent to the Central Arbitration Committee (qv).

Industrial Development Advisory Board   (IDAB)

- Room 1130, 1 Victoria Street, LONDON, SW1H 0ET.
  Tel 020 7215 6392   Fax 020 7215 5579
  Chairman: Mark Seligman
- E Established in October 1972 under the Industry Act 1972 and continued under the Industrial Development Act 1982. IDAB now functions as an Advisory NDPB of the Department for Business, Innovation & Skills. The Board comprises twelve members plus the Chairman.
- R To advise the Ministers on applications from companies who are proposing to undertake capital investment projects in the Assisted Areas of England and have applied for regional selective assistance under the Grant for Business Investment (GBI) scheme or the Regional Growth Fund.
- G England.

Industrial Development Boards

- ✍ IDBs for the English regions were appointed by the Government Offices for the regions to administer the Grant for Business Investment (GBI). GBI is now administered by the **Regional Development Agencies**. There were seven IDBs (for the nine regions) as the East Midlands and Yorkshire & the Humber was a single IDB, as was London and the South East.

Industrial Injuries Advisory Council   (IIAC)

- 2nd Floor, Caxton House, Tothill Street, LONDON, SW1H 9NA.
  Tel 020 7749 5618   http://www.iiac.org.uk
  Chairman: Prof Keith Palmer
- E Established on 4 July 1948 under the National Insurance (Industrial Injuries) Act 1946, the Council's authority is now derived from the Social Security Act 1992. IIAC functions as a Scientific Advisory Committee and an Advisory NDPB of the Department for Work & Pensions. The Council comprises 17 members including the Chairman.
- R To provide independent scientific advice to the Secretary of State for Work & Pensions and the Department of Social Development Northern Ireland on matters relating to the Industrial Injury Disablement Benefit Scheme.
- G United Kingdom.
- ✍ For further information see **Scientific Advisory Committees**.

Industrial Pollution & Radiochemical Inspectorate   (IPRI)

- Klondyke Building, Cromac Avenue, Lower Ormeau Road, BELFAST, BT7 2JA.
  Tel 028 9056 9296   Fax 028 9056 9263
- E Established in 1996, IPRI derives its authority under the Radioactive Substances Act 1993. The Inspectorate is part of the Environment & Heritage Service (qv).
- R To control the keeping and use of radioactive material and the disposal of radioactive waste.
- G Northern Ireland.

Industrial Tribunals   See **Employment Tribunals**.

Industrial Tribunals & the Fair Employment Tribunal

- Killymeal House, 2 Cromac Quay, Ormeau Road, BELFAST, BT7 2JD.
  Tel 028 9032 7666   Fax 028 9025 0100   http://www.employmenttribunalsni.co.uk

E   Industrial Tribunals were established in 1999 under the Fair Employment & Treatment (Northern Ireland) Order 1998. The Fair Employment Tribunal was established in 2005 under the Fair Employment Tribunal (Rules of Procedure) Regulations (Northern Ireland) 2005. They were brought together under a single secretariat on 15 April 2009.

R   The tribunals are independent judicial bodies that hear and determine claims to do with employment matters. Industrial Tribunals deal with a range of claims which include unfair dismissal, breach of contract, wages/other payments, as well as discrimination on the grounds of race, disability, sexual orientation, age, part time working and equal pay.
     The Fair Employment Trubunal deals with claims of discrimination on the grounds of religious belief or political opinion.

G   Northern Ireland.

Information Assurance Advisory Council (IAAC)
■   1st Floor Block D, North Star House, North Star Avenue, SWINDON, Wilts, SN2 1FA.
     Tel 01793 417453   http://www.iaac.org.uk
     Chairman: Sir Edmund Burton

E   Established on 21 March 2000. IAAC is an independent membership body of UK-based companies and central and local government departments.

R   To advance information assurance to ensure that the UK's information society can count on a robust, resilient and secure foundation.

G   United Kingdom.

Information Centre for Health & Social Care, aka the **Information Centre**   See the **NHS Information Centre** for Health & Social Care.

Information Commissioner's Office (ICO)
■   Wycliffe House, Water Lane, WILMSLOW, Cheshire, SK9 5AF.
     Tel 0303 123 1113   **Fax** 01625 524510   http://www.ico.gov.uk
     Information Commissioner: Christopher Graham

E   Established under the Data Protection Act 1984 as the (Office of the) Data Protection Registrar, it changed to its current name under the Freedom of Information Act 2000. The Office functions as an Executive NDPB of the Ministry of Justice. The management board comprises ten members including the Commissioner.

R   To promote access to official information.
     To protect personal information.

G   United Kingdom.

●   The ICO's three regional offices in Cardiff, Edinburgh and Belfast were established in 2003 as a direct response to the devolution process in Wales, Scotland and Northern Ireland.

Information Systems Examinations Board (ISEB)
■   1st Floor Block D, North Star House, North Star Avenue, SWINDON, Wilts, SN2 1FA.
     Tel 0845 300 4417   **Fax** 01793 417444   http://www.bcs.org.uk/iseb

E   Established in 1967 as the Systems Analysis Examinations Board which was a joint venture of the BCS the Chartered Institute for IT and the National Computing Centre; it adopted its present name in 1990. ISEB, part of BSC, functions as a company limited by guarantee.

R   To establish, maintain and encourage standards of learning and experience in computing.
     To supervise education and training, and conduct examinations.

G   United Kingdom.

Information Technology Working Party
■   BMA House, Tavistock Square, LONDON, WC1H 9JP.
     Tel 0300 123 1233   **Fax** 020 7383 6400   http://www.bma.org.uk

E   Established in 2005 as a standing committee of the British Medical Association.

R   To ensure that the BMA has a collective policy position on UK information technology issues and is in a position to influence future developments in the area.

G   United Kingdom.

✍   See **British Medical Association** [Boards & Committees] for further information.

Information Tribunal
✍   Since 18 January 2010 **First-tier Tribunal (Information Rights)**.

Infrastructure Planning Commission (IPC)

■ Temple Quay House, Temple Quay, BRISTOL, BS1 6PN.
Tel 0303 444 5000   http://www.infrastructure.independent.gov.uk
Chairman: Sir Michael Pitt   Chief Executive: John Saunders, OBE

E Established on 1 October 2009 under the Planning Act 2008. IPC functions as an independent NDPB of the Department for Communities & Local Government. The Commission comprises 39 members including the Chairman.

R To make decisions on applications for nationally significant infrastructure projects, including major roads, high-speed rail, large wind farms, power stations, reservoirs, harbours, airports and sewage treatment works.

G England, Wales.

✍ Under the Government's Decentralisation & Localism Bill 2010/11, IPC will cease to function as a Public Body and become a Major Infrastructure Unit with its own special character, within a revised departmental structure that includes the Planning Inspectorate (qv).

Inland Revenue
✍ See **Her Majesty's Revenue & Customs**.

Inland Waterways Advisory Council (IWAC)

■ City Road Lock, 38 Graham Street, LONDON, N1 8JX.
Tel 020 7253 1745   http://www.iwac.org.uk
Chairman: John Edmonds

E Established on 1 April 2007 under the Natural Environment & Rural Communities (NERC) Act 2006. IWAC functions as an independent statutory body sponsored by the Department for Environment, Food and Rural Affairs and the Scottish Government. The Council comprises 13 members including the Chairman.

R To advise Government, navigation authorities and others about the use and development of Britain's inland waterways.

G England, Wales, Scotland.

✍ Defra announced on 22 July 2010 that IWAC would be abolished and the Department take on a stronger role in developing policy for inland waterways.

Inner Cities Religious Council
✍ Replaced in April 2006 by the **Faith Communities Consultative Council**.

Inns' Council   See the **Council of the Inns of Court**.

Insight East   See **Regional Observatories**.

Insolvency Practitioners Tribunal

■ Area 5/1, 21 Bloomsbury Street, LONDON, WC1B 3QW.
Tel 020 7291 6896   http://www.insolvency.gov.uk

E Established in 1986 under the Insolvency Act 1986. It functions as a Tribunal NDPB of the Department for Business, Innovation & Skills. When the Tribunal is required to sit it comprises a chairman with a general qualification and two other members with experience in insolvency matters.

R To deal with cases referred by the Secretary of State at the request of individuals in respect of a refusal to grant, or intention to withdraw, authorisation to act as an insolvency practitioner under the Insolvency Act 1986.

G England, Wales.

Insolvency Rules Committee (IRC)

■ 21 Bloomsbury Street, LONDON, WC1B 3QW.
Tel 020 7674 6902   Fax 020 7291 6773   http://www.insolvency.gov.uk
Chairman: His Honour Mr Justice Richards

E Established under the Insolvency Act 1986. IRC functions as an Advisory NDPB of the Ministry of Justice. The Committee comprises ten members and its secretariat by provided by the Insolvency Service (qv).

R To consider amendments to the rules arising out of a review of secondary insolvency legislation to consolidate and modernise its provisions.

G England, Wales.

Insolvency Service

■ 21 Bloomsbury Street, LONDON, WC1B 3QW.
Tel 0845 602 9848   http://www.insolvency.gov.uk
Chairman: Philip Wallace   Chief Executive: Stephen Speed

E Established on 21 March 1990, the Service derives most of its authority from the Insolvency Acts 1986 and 2000, the Company Directors Disqualifications Act 1986 and the Employment Rights Act 1996. The Service functions as an Executive Agency of the Department for Business, Innovation & Skills. The Steering Board comprises ten members including the Chairman.

R To administer and investigate the affairs of bankrupts, of companies and partnerships wound up by the court, and establish why they became bankrupt.
To act as trustee/liquidator where no private sector insolvency practitioner is appointed.
To act as nominee and supervisor in fast-track individual voluntary agreements.
To take forward reports of bankrupts' and directors' misconduct.
To deal with the disqualification of unfit directors in all corporate failures.
To deal with bankruptcy restrictions orders and undertakings.
To authorise and regulate the insolvency professon.
To assess and pay statutory entitlement to redundancy payments whenever an employer cannot or will not pay its employees.
To provide banking and investment services for bankruptcy and liquidation estate funds.
To advise Department ministers and other Government Departments and agencies on insolvency, redundancy and related issues.
To provide information to the public on insolvency and redundancy matters via its website, leaflets, Insolvency Enquiry Line and Redundancy Payments Helpline.
To conduct confidential fact-finding investigations into companies where it is in the public interest to do so.

G England, Wales.

● The Service has 38 Official Receiver offices throughout England and Wales.

Insolvency Service of Northern Ireland

■ Fermanagh House, Ormeau Avenue, BELFAST, BT2 8NJ.
Tel 028 9025 1441

E The legislation under which most formal insolvency procedures are administered are the Insolvency (Northern Ireland) Order 1989 and the Company Directors Disqualification (Northern Ireland) Order 2002. The Service functions as an Executive Agency of the Department of Enterprise, Trade & Investment Northern Ireland.

R To administer and investigate the affairs of bankrupts and companies in compulsory liquidation.
To establish the reasons for the insolvency.
To handle the disqualification of directors in all corporate insolvencies.
To deal with any fraudulent activity in the management of insolvent businesses.
To regulate the insolvency profession.
To operate the Insolvency Account.
To formulate Northern Ireland specific insolvency legislation and policy.

G Northern Ireland.

Institute of Customer Service   (ICS)

■ 2 Castle Court, St Peter's Street, COLCHESTER, Essex, CO1 1EW.
Tel 01206 571716   Fax 01206 546688   http://www.instituteofcustomerservice.com
Chairman: Mary Chapman   Chief Executive: Jo Causon

E Established in 1996. ICS is an independent membership body and functions as a company limited by guarantee. The Board comprises five members including the Chairman.

R To be the first port of call for every aspect of customer service, delivering high quality, tangible benefits to organisations, individuals and other stakeholders, so that members can improve their customers' experiences and their business performance.
To raise the passive profile of effective customer service through the provision of benchmarking and accreditation services.

G United Kingdom.

✍ For further information see **Sector Skills Councils & standards setting bodies**.

The Institute of the Motor Industry   (IMI)

■ Fanshaws, Brickendon, HERTFORD, SG13 8PQ.
Tel 01992 511521   Fax 01992 511548   http://www.motor.org.uk

E Automotive Skills, the Sector Skills Council for the retail motor industry, was established on 1 December 2003. In July 2007 it merged with the IMI which, in September 2007, was formally designated a Sector Skills Council.

G United Kingdom.

● Subsidiary IMI Awards Ltd is an awarding body for courses and qualifications in the motor industry.

✍ For further information see **Sector Skills Councils** and the **Federation of Awarding Bodies**.

Institutional Shareholders' Committee   (ISC)

■   51 Gresham Street, LONDON, EC2V 7HQ.
    Tel 020 7216 7541   http://www.institutionalshareholderscommittee.org.uk
    Secretary: Marc Jobling
E   Established in 1988. ISC is a membership body comprising the Association of British Insurers, Association of Investment Companies, Investment Management Association and the National Association of Pension Funds.
R   To provide a forum through which its member organisations may inform each other about their views on issues of concern to institutional shareholders.
G   United Kingdom.

Insurance Ombudsman   See **Financial Ombudsman Service**.

Insurance & Pensions Authority   (IPA)

■   4th Floor, HSBC House, Ridgeway Street, DOUGLAS, Isle of Man, IM1 1ER.
    Tel 01624 646000 **Fax** 01624 646001 http://www.gov.im/ipa/
    Chairman: Donald Gelling, CBE, CP Chief Executive: David Vick, ACII
E   Established in 1986 under the Insurance Act 1986 as the Insurance Authority, it adopted its present name in January 1997. The board comprises five members including the Chairman.
R   To maintain and develop an effective regulatory framework for insurance and pension business in the Island.
G   Isle of Man.
=   Lught-reill Urryssaght as Penshynyn

Integrated Transport Authorities   See **Passenger Transport Executives & Integrated Transport Authorities**.

Intellectual Property Advisory Committee
✍   No longer in existence.

Intellectual Property Office   (IPO)

■   Concept House, Cardiff Road, NEWPORT, Gwent, NP10 8QQ.
    Tel 0300 300 2000 **Fax** 01633 817777 http://www.ipo.gov.uk
    Chairman: Bob Gilbert Chief Executive: John Alty
E   Established in 1852 and known as the **Patent Office** until 2 April 2007 when it adopted its current operating name. IPO functions as an Executive Agency of the Department for Business, Innovation and Skills. The Steering Board comprises seven members including the Chairman.
R   To grant intellectual property rights in the United Kingdom, including patents, designs, trade marks and copyright.
G   United Kingdom.
●   The Office administers the Patent Acts, Registered Design Act and Trade Mark Act. It also deals with questions relating to the Copyright Designs & Patents Act 1988.

Intellectual Property Regulation Board   (IPReg)

■   3rd Floor, 95 Chancery Lane, LONDON, WC2A 1DT.
    Tel 020 7440 9371 **Fax** 020 7440 9374 http://www.ipreg.org.uk
    Chairman: Michael Heap
E   Established by the Chartered Institute of Patent Attorneys (CIPA) and the Institute of Trade Mark Attorneys (ITMA). The Board comprises ten members including the Chairman.
R   To regulate the patent attorney and trade mark attorney professions on behalf of CIPA and ITMA.
G   United Kingdom.
✍   One of the Approved Regulators overseen by the **Legal Services Board**.

Intelligence & Security Committee   (ISC)

■   35 Great Smith Street, LONDON, SW1P 3BQ. http://www.isc.independent.gov.uk
    Chairman: Rt Hon Sir Michael Rifkind, QC, MP
E   Established in 1994 under the Intelligence & Security Act, 1994. ISC functions as an Advisory NDPB of the Cabinet Office. The Committee comprises nine members including the Chairman.
R   To examine the policy, administration and expenditure of the Security Service, Secret Intelligence Service, Government Communications Headquarters, Joint Intelligence Committee (qv), Intelligence & Security Secretariat and parts of the Ministry of Defence.
G   United Kingdom.

Intelligence Services Commissioner

- 22 Whitehall, LONDON, SW1A 2WH.
  Tel 020 7273 4514   http://www.intelligence.gov.uk
  Commissioner: The Rt Hon Sir Peter Gibson
- E Established in 2000, the Commissioner's duties are specified in the Regulation of Investigatory Powers Act 2000. The Commissioner is appointed by the Prime Minister.
- R To keep under review the issue of warrants by the Secretaries of State as detailed under the 2000 Act.
- G United Kingdom.

INTend

- ✍ Former trading name of **Tendring Regeneration Ltd**.

Inter-Agency Committee on Marine Science & Technology

- ✍ In 2008 became the Marine Science Coordination Committee of the Ministerial Marine Science Group, coordinating the Marine Assessment & Reporting Group (MARG), Marine Environmental Data & Information Network (MEDIN), Underwater Sound Forum, and Marine Industries Liaison Group.

Interception of Communications Commissioner

- 22 Whitehall, LONDON, SW1A 2WH.
  Tel 020 7273 4514
  Commissioner: Rt Hon Sir Paul Kennedy
- E Established on 10 April 1986 under the Interception of Communications Act 1985, his current role defined under the Regulation of Investigatory Powers Act 2000.
  The Commissioner, who must hold or have held high judicial office, is appointed by the Prime Minister.
- R To review the Secretary of State's power to issue, renew or cancel warrants to intercept communications in the course of their transmission by post or on a public communication system.
- G United Kingdom.

INTERNAL DRAINAGE BOARDS   (IDBs)

- E Dating from 1252, most current IDBs were established under the Land Drainage Act 1930 and now operate under the Land Drainage Act 1991. Each board operates in a water catchment area irrespective of local government boundaries. There are 154 Boards, concentrated in the Broads, Fens, Somerset Levels, Lincolnshire and Yorkshire. IDBs are responsible to the Department for Environment, Food and Rural Affairs and work closely with the Environment Agency (qv).
- R To maintain rivers, drainage channels, ordinary watercourses, pumping stations and other critical infrastructure to secure clean water drainage and water level management.
- G England & Wales.
- ✍ All IDBs are members of the Association of Drainage Authorities - see companion volume, the Directory of British Associations, for details.
  The Government announced on 14 October 2010 that IDBs would be reformed to improve efficiency and accountability and increase the involvement of local communities.

International Curriculum & Assessment Agency   (ICAA)

- Bighton, ALRESFORD, Hants, SO24 9RE.
  Tel 01962 735801   **Fax** 01962 735597   http://www.icaa.com
- E Established in 1989. ICAA is an awarding body for courses and qualifications in communications technology, handling data and information, systems and control registration, and business Chinese.
- G United Kingdom.
- ✍ For more information on awarding bodies see the **Federation of Awarding Bodies**.

International Slavery Museum   See **National Museums Liverpool**.

InterTradeIreland   See **Trade & Business Development Business Body**.

Inverness Airport Consultative Committee   (IACC)

- Ar Dachaidh, 4 Muirfield Park, INVERNESS, IV2 4HA.
  Tel 01463 236969
  Chairman: Pat Hayden

© CBD Research Ltd · Beckenham · Kent BR3 5JS · Tel 020 8650 7745 · Fax 020 8650 0768 · E-mail cbd@cbdresearch.com · www.cbdresearch.com

G   Inverness.

✍   For further information see **Airport Consultative Committees**.

Invest in Britain Bureau
✍   Since October 2003 known as **United Kingdom Trade & Investment**.

Invest Northern Ireland   (INI)
■   Bedford Square, Bedford Street, BELFAST, BT2 7ES.
     Tel 028 9069 8000   **Fax** 028 9043 6536   http://www.investni.com
     Chairman: Stephen Kingon, CBE   Chief Executive: Alastair Hamilton
E   Established on 1 April 2002. Invest Northern Ireland functions as an Executive NDPB of the Department
     Enterprise, Trade & Investment Northern Ireland. The Board comprises twelve members including the Chairman.
R   To grow the Northern Ireland economy by helping new and existing businesses to compete internationally, and by
     attracting new investment into Northern Ireland.
G   Northern Ireland.

Investigatory Powers Tribunal   (IPT)
■   PO Box 33220, LONDON, SW1H 9ZQ.
     Tel 020 7035 3711   http://www.ipt-uk.com
     President: Lord Justice Mummery
E   Established in 2000 under the Regulation of Investigationary Powers Act 2000. IPT functions as a Tribunal NDPB
     of the Home Office. The Tribunal comprises ten members including the President.
R   To investigate complaints about any alleged conduct by or on behalf of the Intelligence Services - the Security
     Service (MI5), the Secret Intelligence Agency (MI6) and the Government Communications Headquarters
     (GCHQ).
G   United Kingdom.

Investment Ombudsman   See **Financial Ombudsman Service**.

Investors in People   (IIP)
■   28-30 Grosvenor Gardens, LONDON, SW1W 0TT.
     Tel 020 7467 1900   http://www.investorsinpeople.co.uk
     Chief Executive: Simon Jones
E   Established in 1993. On 1 April 2010 strategic ownership of Investors in People was transferred to the UK
     Commission for Employment & Skills (qv).
R   To increase the productivity of the UK economy by improving the way in which organisations manage and
     develop their people, leading to business improvement and better public services.
G   United Kingdom.
●   There are Investment in People Centres in Wales, Scotland, Northern Ireland and in each of the nine English
     Regions.

Ionising Radiation Health & Safety Forum   (IRHSF)
■   7NW Rose Court, 2 Southwark Bridge, LONDON, SE1 9HS.
     Tel 020 7717 6854
     Chairman: Dr Penny Allisy-Roberts, OBE
E   Established in 1987 and known as the Ionising Radiations Advisory Committee until a change of name in 2003.
     The Forum comprises representatives of a wide range of organisations with an interest in radiation protection.
R   To provide a liaison mechanism between the Health & Safety Executive (qv) and stakeholders on matters
     concerning protection against exposure to ionising radiations that are relevant to the work of the HSE, and to
     identify significant issues for future action.
G   United Kingdom.

Irish Council of Churches   (ICC)
■   Inter-Church Centre, 48 Elmwood Avenue, BELFAST, BT9 6AZ.
     Tel 028 9066 3145   **Fax** 028 9066 4160   http://www.irishchurches.com
     President: Revd Tony Davidson   General Secretary: Michael Earle
E   Established in 1922 as the United Council of Christian Churches & Religious Communities in Ireland, its current
     mandate derives from its 1966 Constitution as amended in 1995. ICC is a membership organisation comprising
     15 member Churches. The Executive Committee comprises four members.
R   To create spaces where Irish churches from all traditions may pray, dialogue and act together.
G   Northern Ireland, Republic of Ireland.

Irish Lights   See the **Commissioners of Irish Lights**.

Irish Lights Commission   See note under the **Foyle, Carlingford & Irish Lights Commission**.

Isle of Man Arts Council
- St Andrew's House, Finch Road, DOUGLAS, Isle of Man, IM1 2PX.
  Tel 01624 694598   Fax 01624 686860
  email www.gov.im/artscouncil/
  Chairman: Juan Turner, MLC
- E   Established in 1978. The Council comprises ten members including the Chairman.
- R   To support the work of local amateurs and professionals as well as visiting artists.
- G   Isle of Man.

Isle of Man Civil Service Commission   See **Civil Service Commission**.

Isle of Man Communications Commission   See **Communications Commission**.

Isle of Man Film
- Hamilton House, Peel Road, DOUGLAS, Isle of Man, IM1 5EP.
  Tel 01624 687173   Fax 01624 687171   http://www.gov.im/ded/iomfilm
- E   Established in 1995 as the Isle of Man Film Commission.
- R   To raise the profile of the Island's film industry and to actively market the Isle of Man as a film location at major film industry events.
- G   Isle of Man.

Isle of Man Financial Supervision Commission   See **Financial Supervision Commission**.

Isle of Man Gambling Supervision Commission   See **Gambling Supervision Commission**.

Isle of Man Office of Fair Trading
- Government Building, Lord Street, DOUGLAS, Isle of Man, IM1 1LE.
  Tel 01624 686500   Fax 01624 686504   http://www.gov.im/oft
  Chairman: Bill Henderson, MHK
- E   Established as a statutory board.
- R   To provide the appropriate legislation, advice and compliance services to benefit and protect the Island's consumers and businesses from unfair trading practices.
- G   Isle of Man.
- =   Oik Dellal Cair Ellan Vannin

Isle of Man Post Office
- Postal Headquarters, DOUGLAS, Isle of Man, IM2 1AA.
  Tel 01624 698400   Fax 01624 698406   http://www.iompost.com
  Chairman: E Alan Crowe, MLC   Acting Chief Executive: Mike Kelly
- E   Constituted under the Post Office Act 1993 as a statutory board of Tynwald. The Board comprises six members including the Chairman.
- R   To be a successful, innovative and socially responsible postal services provider, achieving excellence in all that it does.
- G   Isle of Man.
- =   Oik Postagh Ellan Vannin

Isle of Man Tourism Board
- St Andrew's House, Finch Road, DOUGLAS, Isle of Man, IM1 2PX.
  Tel 01624 686801   http://www.gov.im/tourism
- G   Isle of Man.

© CBD Research Ltd · Beckenham · Kent BR3 5JS · Tel 020 8650 7745 · Fax 020 8650 0768 · E-mail cbd@cbdresearch.com · www.cbdresearch.com

Isle of Man War Pensions Committee

- ■ Government Office, Bucks Road, DOUGLAS, Isle of Man, IM1 3PG.
  Chairman: Brigadier Norman Butler
- E The Committee comprises twelve members including the Chairman.
- R To supervise the War Pensions Welfare Service and coordinate the efforts of the providers of welfare support to war pensioners and war widows.
  To administer the Manx War Disablement Fund and the Manx Ex-Services' Fund 2002.
- G Isle of Man.

Isle of Wight Rural Community Council   (IWRCC)

- ■ 3 Langley Court, Pyle Street, NEWPORT, Isle of Wight, PO30 1LA.
  Tel 01983 524058   Fax 01983 526905   http://www.iwrcc.org.uk
  Chairman: Richard Priest   Chief Executive: Michael Bullpitt
- E IWRCC functions as a registered charity and company limited by guarantee. The Board comprises ten Trustees including the Chairman.
- R To promote, develop and support voluntary and community organisations.
  To support and empower Island communities to address their local concerns, especially with regard to disadvantage and inequality.
- G Isle of Wight.
- ✍ IWRCC is one of the 38 Rural Community Councils, represented at the national level by **Action with Communities in Rural England** (qv) and at the regional level by South East Rural Community Councils.

Isles of Scilly Tourist Board

- ■ Hugh Street, ST MARY'S, Isles of Scilly, TR21 0LL.
  Tel 01720 424031   http://www.simplyscilly.co.uk
- E Established on 1 May 1992.
- G Isles of Scilly.

J

The James Hutton Institute

- ■ Craigiebuckler, ABERDEEN, AB15 8QH.
  Tel 0844 928 5428   Fax 0844 928 5429   http://www.hutton.ac.uk
  Invergowrie, DUNDEE, DD2 5DA.
  Chairman: Ray Perman   Chief Executive: Prof Iain Gordon
- E Established on 1 April 2011 by the merger of the Macaulay Land Use Research Institute and the Scottish Crop Research Institute. It functions as an Executive NDPB of the Scottish Executive Rural Affairs Affairs Department. The Institute's Board of Directors comprises eleven members including the Chairman.
- R To conduct research into achieving sustainable land use for the good of both society and the environment.
  To conduct excellent research in plant and environment sciences (particularly in managed ecosystems) and to study the impact of climate change on Scotland and the wider world.
- G United Kingdom.
- ✍ For further information see companion volume **Centres, Bureaux & Research Institutes**.

Jersey Financial Services Commission   (JFSC)

- ■ PO Box 267, 14-18 Castle Street, ST HELIER, Jersey, JE4 8TP.
  Tel 01534 822000   Fax 01534 822001   http://www.jerseyfsc.org
  Chairman: Clive Jones   Director General: John Harris
- E There are ten Commissioners including the Chairman.
- R To regulate and supervise financial services in Jersey with integrity and efficiency and in so doing help to uphold the international reputation of Jersey as a financial centre.
- G Jersey.

Jersey Legal Information Board   (JLIB)

- Morier House, ST HELIER, Jersey, JE1 1DD.
  Tel 01534 441361   Fax 01534 441399   http://www.jerseylaw.je
  Chairman: Michael Birt
- E   Established in August 1998. The Board is chaired by the Bailiff and comprises nine other members.
- R   To see Jersey's legal system recognised as the global best for a small jurisdiction.
- G   Jersey.

Jersey Tourist Board

- Liberation Place, ST HELIER, Jersey, JE1 1BB.
  Tel 01534 448800   Fax 01534 448898   http://www.jersey.com
  Chairman: Deputy Lyndon Farnham
- G   Jersey.

Jobcentre Plus

- Level One, Steel City House, West Street, SHEFFIELD, S1 2GQ.
  Tel 0845 606 0234
  Chief Executive: Dara Singh, OBE
- E   Established in 2003 following the merger of the Employment Service's job centres with the social security payments function of the Benefits Agency. Jobcentre Plus functions as an Executive Agency of the Department for Work & Pensions.
- R   To support people of working age from welfare into work, and to help employers fill their vacancies.
- G   England.

Joint Committee of the Assay Offices of Great Britain

- PO Box 151, The Assay Office, Newhall Street, BIRMINGHAM, B3 1SB.
  Tel 0871 871 6020   Fax 0121 236 9032   http://www.theassayoffice.co.uk
- E   Established in 1970. The Committee has twelve members comprising three nominees from each of the four Assay Offices in Great Britain.
- R   To coordinate the work of the Assay Offices, and to formulate policy concerning interpretation, reform and practice of law, technical matters concerning procedures for assay and hallmarking, negotiating with Government departments, trade associations and other similar bodies.
- G   United Kingdom.

Joint Committee on Mobility of Blind & Partially Sighted People   (JCMBPS)

- Hillfields, Burghfield Common, READING, Berks, RG7 3YG.
  Tel 0118 983 8359   Fax 0118 983 8206   http://www.jcmbps.org.uk
  Chairman: Alan Brooks
- E   JCMBPS is an independent body consisting of representatives from the principal organisations of blind, deafblind and partially sighted people, with a specific interest in access and mobility.
- R   To consider how best to improve the built environment, allowing visually impaired people to move around independently, safely and without restriction, as pedestrians, public transport users and public building occupants.
- G   United Kingdom.
- ✍   The secretariat is provided by the Guide Dogs for the Blind Association.

Joint Committee on Mobility for Disabled People   (JCMD)

- 11 Rothesay Court, Le May Avenue, LONDON, SE12 0BA.
  Tel 020 8857 8640   http://www.jcmd.org.uk
  Chairman: Joe Hennessy, OBE
- E   Established in December 1961. JCMD functions as a joint committee of representatives from national organisations.
- R   To achieve equal accessibility and mobility for disabled people throughout the built and natural environment and transport systems within the United Kingdom.
- G   United Kingdom.

Joint Committee on Vaccination & Immunisation   (JCVI)

- Skipton House, 80 London Road, LONDON, SE1 6LH.
  Tel 020 7972 1522   Fax 020 7972 5758
  Chairman: Prof Andrew Hall, MB, BS, MSc, PhD, FRCP, FFPH, FMedSci

E   Established in 1962, the Committee was granted the status of a Standing Advisory Committee in 1981 under the National Health Service Act 1977 as amended by the Health Services Act 1980. JCVI functions as a Scientific Advisory Committee and an Advisory NDPB of the Department of Health. The Committee comprises 20 members including the Chairman and four persons ex-officio.

R   To advise Health Ministers on matters relating to communicable diseases, preventable and potentially preventable through immunisation.

G   United Kingdom.

✍   On 14 October 2010 the Government announced that JCVI would cease to function as a NDPB and be reconstituted as a committee of experts of the Department of Health and the new Public Health Service.

Joint Committees   See **UK Parliament: Committees**.

Joint Council for Qualifications   (JCQ)

■   Sixth Floor, 29 Great Peter Street, LONDON, SW1P 3LW.
     Tel 020 7638 4132   Fax 020 734 4343   http://www.jcq.org.uk
     Director: Dr Jim Sinclair

E   Established in January 2004, superceding the former Joint Council for General Qualifications. JCG is a membership body, its members being the seven largest providers of qualifications in the UK, offering GCSE, GCE, AEA, Scottish Highers, Entry Level, Vocational and vocationally-related qualifications.

R   To provide to members, wherever possible, common administrative arrangements for the schools and colleges and other providers which offer their qualifications.
     To deal with regulators in responding to proposals and initiatives on assessment and the curriculum.
     To deal with the media on issues affecting member bodies.

G   United Kingdom.

Joint Council for the Welfare of Immigrants   (JCWI)

■   115 Old Street, LONDON, EC1V 9RT.
     Tel 020 7251 8708   Fax 020 7251 8707   http://www.jcwi.org.uk
     Chair: Eric Fripp   Chief Executive: Habib Rahman

E   Established in 1967. JCWI is an independent voluntary organisation. The Executive Committee comprises twelve members including the Chairman.

R   To provide free legal advice on immigration, nationality and asylum matters to immigration law professionals and private individuals.

G   United Kingdom.

Joint Examining Board
✍   Acquired in 2006 by **EDI**.

Joint Industry Board for the Electrical Contracting Industry   (JIBECI)

■   Kingswood House, 47-51 Sidcup Hill, SIDCUP, Kent, DA14 6HP.
     Tel 020 8302 0031   Fax 020 8309 1103   http://www.jib.org.uk
     Chairman: Sir Michael Latham

E   JEBICI is a partnership between the Electrical Contractors Association and Unite the Union. The Board comprises the Chairman, eleven ECA representatives and ten Unite representatives.

R   To enhance the image, capability and profitability of the industry through the creation of a safe working environment and the utilisation of the required range operative skills, up to the highest level and in the most efficient manner, within a regulated structure, to ensure stable and quality employment.

G   United Kingdom.

Joint Industry Board for Plumbing Mechanical Engineering Services in England & Wales   (JIBPMES)

■   PO Box 267, ST NEOTS, Cambs, PE19 9DN.
     Tel 01480 476925   Fax 01480 403081   http://www.jib-pmes.org.uk

E   Established in 1972. JIBPMES comprises representatives from the Association of Plumbing & Heating Contractors, the Construction Confederation and Unite the Union.

R   To set the terms and conditions of employment of operatives working for participant employers.
     To be part of the awarding body for plumbing qualifications.

G   England, Wales.

Joint Information Systems Committee   (JISC)
- Brettenham House, 5 Lancaster Place, LONDON, WC2E 7EN.
  Tel 020 3006 6099   Fax 020 7240 5377   http://www.jisc.ac.uk
  Chairman: Prof Sir Timothy O'Shea
- E Established on 1 April 1993 under the provisions of the Further & Higher Education Act 1992. JISC receives its
  core funding from the UK's higher and further education funding bodies. The JISC Board comprises 24
  members including the Chairman.
- R To provide world-class leadership in the innovative use of information and communications technology (ICT) to
  support education and research.
- G United Kingdom.
- JISC currently manages and funds 191 projects within 28 programmes and supports 49 services.

Joint Intelligence Committee   (JIC)
- 22 Whitehall, LONDON, SW1A 2WH.
  Tel 020 7276 3000
  Chairman: Alex Allan
- E Established in 1936. JIC is part of the Cabinet Office. The Committee draws its membership from senior officials
  in the Foreign & Commonwealth Office, Home Office, Department for Business, Innovation & Skills, HM
  Treasury, Ministry of Defence, Department for International Development and the Cabinet Office; also the heads
  of the Secret Intelligence Service, Security Service and GCHQ, and the Chief of the Assessments staff. The
  Chairman is a senior civil servant.
- R To advise ministers on intelligence collection and analysis priorities in support of national objectives.
  To direct the collection and analysis effort of the intelligence services and the Ministry of Defence.
  To assure the professional standards of civilian intelligence analysis staff.
- G United Kingdom.

Joint Mathematical Council of the United Kingdom   (JMC)
- Faculty of Engineering & Computing, Coventry University, Priory Street, COVENTRY, CV1 5FB./l/
  http://www.jmcuk.org.uk
  Chairman: Prof Duncan Lawson   Secretary: Dr David Martin
- E Established in 1963 by agreement of the constituent societies, currently 13 in number, involved with mathematics
  at all levels - from primary to higher education. The Council consists of one representative from each of its
  constituent bodies.
- R To provide coordination between the constituent societies to promote the advancement of mathematics and the
  improvement of the teaching of mathematics.
- G United Kingdom.

Joint Medical Command   (JMC)
- Coltman House, DMS Whittington, LICHFIELD, Staffs, WS14 9PY.
  Tel 01543 434634
  Commander: Air Vice Marshal C P A Evans
- E Established on 1 April 2008 incorporating the former Defence Medical Education & Training Agency. JMC
  functions as an Executive Agency of the Ministry of Defence.
- R To make a real and sustained improvement to the delivery of operational medical capability and the provision of
  secondary healthcare to service personnel.
- G United Kingdom.
- The JMC operates from ten principal sites across the UK.
- ✍ The JMC will move to new headquarters in Whittington Barracks, Lichfield, in 2010.

Joint Nature Conservation Committee   (JNCC)
- Monkstone House, City Road, PETERBOROUGH, PE1 1JY.
  Tel 01733 562626   Fax 01733 555948   http://www.jncc.gov.uk
  Chairman: Dr Peter Bridgewater   Managing Director: Marcus Yeo
- E Established in 1990 under the Environmental Protection Act 1990 and reconstituted by the Natural Environment &
  Rural Communities Act 2006. JNCC functions as an Executive NDPB of the Department for Environment, Food
  & Rural Affairs. The Committee comprises the Chairman and five independent members appointed by the
  Secretary of State, and two representatives from each of the four national organisations involved in nature
  conservation (below).
- R To deliver the UK and international responsibilities of
      Council for Nature Conservation & the Countryside,
      Countryside Council for Wales,
      Natural England, and
      Scottish Natural Heritage (qqv).

© CBD Research Ltd · Beckenham · Kent BR3 5JS · Tel 020 8650 7745 · Fax 020 8650 0768 · E-mail cbd@cbdresearch.com · www.cbdresearch.com

The functions that arise from these responsibilities are:

To advise Government on the development and implementation of policies for, or affecting, nature conservation in the UK

To provide advice and disseminate knowledge on nature conservation issues affecting the UK and internationally

To establish common standards throughout the UK for nature conservation, including monitoring, research and the analysis of results

To commission and support research which it deems relevant to these functions.

G   United Kingdom.

Joint Security Industry Council   (JSIC)

■   c/o IPSA, Northumberland House, 11 Popes Lane, LONDON, W5 4NG.
Tel 020 8832 7417   Fax 020 8832 7418   http://www.jsic.org.uk
Chairman: Patrick J Somerville, QPM

E   Incorporated as a company limited by guarantee on 16 July 1996. JSIC functions as an umbrella organisation of associations, businesses, inspectorates and other organisations with an interest in or responsibility for security.

R   To enhance awareness of and professionalism in security in all sectors of industry and commerce.

To extend the role and influence of the security industry in all aspects of commercial, industrial and community safety activities.

To provide a single, representational and powerful line of communication with Government departments, European agencies, the UK parliamentary bodies and assemblies and the print and broadcast media.

G   United Kingdom.

Joint Services Command & Staff College   See **Defence Academy Management Board**.

Joint University Council   (JUC)

■   Room 517, Victoria House, Nottingham Trent University, NOTTINGHAM, NG1 4BU.
Tel 0115 848 8117   Fax 0115 848 6808   http://www.jac.org.uk
Hon Chairman: Jim Goddard   Secretary: Sandra Odell

E   Established in 1918 to promote the interests of the universities in the fields of public administration and social policy. Social work education was added to its brief in the 1970s.

R   To promote, develop and coordinate the work of higher education institutions in the pursuit of education, training and research in public administration, social policy and social work.

G   United Kingdom.

●   JUC is a federal body and works mainly through its three standing committees:
        Public Administration Committee (PAC)
        Social Policy Committee (SPC)
        Social Work Education Committee (SWEC).

Judicial Appointments Board for Scotland

■   38-39 Drumsheugh Gardens, EDINBURGH, EH3 7SW.
Tel 0131 528 5101   Fax 0131 528 5105   http://www.judicialappointmentsscotland.org.uk
Chairman: Sir Muir Russell, KCB, FRSE   Chief Executive: Trevor Lodge

E   Established on 1 June 2009 under the Judiciary & Courts (Scotland) Act 2008. The Board comprises ten members including the Chairman.

R   To recommend to Scottish Ministers individuals for appointment to judicial offices within the Board's remit and to provide advice to Scottish Ministers in connection with such appointments.

To approve procedures for the appointment of Justices of the Peace.

G   Scotland.

●   Judicial offices within the Board's remit:
        Judges of the Court of Session and Chairman of the Scottish Land Court
        Sheriffs Principal, Sheriffs and Part-Time Sheriffs
        Temporary judges except in cases where the individual to be appointed already holds or has held the office of judge of the European Court, judge of the European Court of Human Rights, Chair of the Scottish Land Court, Sheriff Principal, or Sheriff.

Judicial Appointments Commission   (JAC)

■   Steel House, 11 Tothill Street, LONDON, SW1H 9LJ.
Tel 020 3334 0453   Fax 020 3334 0124   http://www.judicialappointments.gov.uk
Vice Chairman: Lord Justice Toulson

E   Established in 3 April 2006 under the Constitutional Reform Act 2005. JAC functions as an Executive NDPB of the Ministry of Justice. The Commission comprises 15 members including the Chairman.

R   To select candidates for judicial office in courts and tribunals in England and Wales, and for some tribunals whose jurisdiction extends to Scotland and Northern Ireland.

G   United Kingdom.

✍   The Ministry of Justice announced on 14 October 2010 that the future of JAC was under consideration, subject to Judicial Appointments Review.

Judicial Appointments & Conduct Ombudsman

■   9/53 The Tower, 102 Petty France, LONDON, SW1H 9AJ.
Tel 020 3334 2900   Fax 020 3334 2913   http://www.judicialombudsman.gov.uk
Ombudsman: Sir John Brigstocke, KCB

E   Established on 3 April 2006 under the Constitutional Reform Act 2005. The Ombudsman functions as an independent statutory office of the Ministry of Justice.

R   To seek redress in the event of maladministration.
To improve standards and practices, through recommendations and constructive feedback, in the authorities or departments concerned.

G   England, Wales.

✍   The Ministry of Justice announced on 14 October 2010 that the future of the Ombudsman was under consideration, subject to Judicial Appointments Review.

Judicial Committee of the Privy Council   (JCPC)

■   Parliament Square, LONDON, SW1P 3BD.
Tel 020 7960 1500   Fax 020 7960 1501   http://www.jcpc.gov.uk
Acting Registrar of the Privy Council: Louise di Mambro

E   Established under the Judicial Committee Act 1833.

R   JPCC is the court of final appeal for many current and former Commonwealth countries, UK overseas territories, crown dependencies and military sovereign base areas.
Five judges normally sit to hear Commonwealth cases.
JCPC shares a building, and many administrative functions, with the Supreme Court where it usually sits in Court Three.

G   United Kingdom, Commonwealth.

Judicial Office for England & Wales   (JO)

■   11th Floor, Thomas More Building, Royal Courts of Justice, Strand, LONDON,
WC2A 2LL.   http://www.judiciary.gov.uk

E   Established in April 2006 under the Constitutional Reform Act 2005. The Office functions, with the Judicial Studies Board (qv) and the Judicial Communications Office, as part of an independent directorate of the Ministry of Justice.

R   To represent the views of the judiciary of England & Wales to Parliament, the Lord Chancellor and ministers generally.
To maintain arrangements for the welfare, training and guidance of the judiciary within the resources made available by the Lord Chancellor.
To maintain arrangements for the deployment of judges and the allocation of work within the courts.

G   England, Wales.

Judicial Office for Scotland

■   Saughton House, Broomhouse Drive, EDINBURGH, EH11 3XD.
Tel 0131 444 3352
Director: Steve Humphreys

E   Established on 1 April 2010 under the Judiciary & Courts (Scotland) Act 2008. The Office operates within the Scottish Court Service (qv) to provide support to its Chairman, the Lord President.

R   To be responsible for the efficient disposal of business in Scottish courts.
To represent the views of the Scottish judiciary to the Scottish Parliament and to the Scottish Ministers.

G   Scotland.

Judicial Studies Board   (JSB)

■   Steel House, 11 Tothill Street, LONDON, SW1H 9LJ.
Tel 020 3334 0700   Fax 020 3334 0789   http://www.jsboard.co.uk
Chairman: Lady Justice Hallett

E   Established on 1 April 1979 by the Lord Chancellor, the Board derives its authority under a Memorandum of Understanding made with the Lord Chancellor's Department in June 1996. It functions as an independent judicial body responsible to the Lord Chief Justice. The Executive Board comprises 13 members including the Chairman.

R   To ensure the delivery of high quality training to enable judicial office holders to discharge their duties effectively in a way that preserves judicial independence and supports public confidence in the judiciary.

G   England, Wales.

●   The JSB is directly responsible for the development and delivery of training to judges in the Crown, county and higher courts.

It also provides advice and support to those providing training in the magistrates' courts and tribunals communities.

The training requirements of the different jurisdictions are the responsibility of five committees:

      Equal Treatment Advisory Committee
      Judicial Training Committee
      Magisterial Committee
      Senior Judiciary Committee
      Tribunals Committee.

Judicial Studies Board for Northern Ireland   (JSBNI)

■   Royal Courts of Justice, Chichester Street, BELFAST, BT1 3JF.
Tel 028 9072 5908 Fax 028 9072 5900 http://www.jsbni.com
Chairman: Lord Justice Higgins

E   Established in 1994. The Board comprises twelve members including the Chairman.

R   To provide suitable and effective programmes of practical studies for full- and part-time members of the judiciary, and to improve upon the system of disseminating information to them.

G   Northern Ireland.

Judicial Studies Committee   (JSC)

■   Bearford House, 39 Hanover Street, EDINBURGH, EH2 2PJ.
Tel 0131 220 9320 Fax 0131 220 9321 http://www.judicialstudies-scotland.org.uk
Chairman: The Hon Lord Brodie

E   Established in 1997 following a statement by the Secretary of State for Scotland on 14 January 1997. The Committee comprises twelve members including the Chairman.

R   To promote training for the judiciary, both in the Supreme Courts (the Court of Session and the High Court of Judiciary) and the sheriff court.

To decide priorities for judicial training and co-ordinating the practical arrangements for delivering it.

G   Scotland.

Junior Doctors Committee   (JDC)

■   BMA House, Tavistock Square, LONDON, WC1H 9JP.
Tel 020 7383 6252 Fax 020 7383 6400 http://www.bma.org.uk
Chairman: Dr Shreelata Datta

E   Established as a Branch of Practice Committee of the British Medical Association. The Committee comprises 78 members including the Chairman.

R   To represent junior doctors throughout the UK.

G   United Kingdom.

✍   See **British Medical Association** [Branch of Practice Committees] for further information,

---

Justices of the Peace Advisory Committees

■   St Andrew's House, Regent Road, EDINBURGH, EH1 3DG.
Tel 0845 774 1741

E   Established in 1949 on the recommendations of the Royal Commission on Justices of the Peace whose report was published in 1948. The Committees function an Advisory NDPB of the Scottish Executive Justice Department.

R   To advise on the appointment of new Justices of the Peace.

G   Scotland.

●   There are six Committees corresponding to the six Sheriffdoms:

      Glasgow & Strathkelvin
      Grampian, Highlands & Islands
      Lothian & Borders
      North Strathclyde
      South Strathclyde, Dumfries & Galloway
      Tayside, Central & Fife.

✍   The Committees are administered by the relevant Local Authorities.

Kent & Medway Strategic Health Authority
✍ On 1 July 2006 merged with the Surrey & Sussex Strategic Health Authority to form **NHS South East Coast**.

K

Kent Police Authority
■ First Floor, Gail House, Lower Stone Street, MAIDSTONE, Kent, ME15 6NB.
Tel 01622 677055 Fax 01622 604489 http://www.kentpoliceauthority.gov.uk
Chairman: Mrs Ann Barnes, JP
E Established in April 1995, the Authority is an independent body charged with ensuring that Kent Police provide an
effective and efficient police service. Membership comprises seven Kent County Councillors, two Medway
Councillors and eight independent members.
G Kent.
✍ For further information see **Police Authorities**.

Kent Probation Trust
■ Chaucer House, 25 Knightrider Street, MAIDSTONE, Kent, ME15 6ND.
Tel 01622 350820 Fax 01622 750333 http://www.kentprobation.org
Chairman: Janardan Sofat Chief Executive: Sarah Billiald
E Established on 1 April 2001 under the Criminal Justice & Court Service Act 2000 as the Kent Probation Area
Board. It became a trust on 1 April 2010 under the Offender Management Act 2007. The Board comprises
seven members including the Chairman.
G Kent.
✍ For further information see **Probation Trusts**.

Kew Gardens   See **Royal Botanic Gardens Kew**.

King's Lynn Conservancy Board
■ Harbour Office, Common Staith, KING'S LYNN, Norfolk, PE30 1LL.
Tel 01553 773411 Fax 01553 763431 http://www.portauthoritykingslynn.fsnet.co.uk
Chairman: Roger Ward
R To provide the pilotage and towage for the Port of King's Lynn which is owned and operated by Associated
British Ports
G King's Lynn.
✍ For further information see **Port & Harbour Authorities**.

Kyle of Sutherland Fisheries Trust   See **Rivers & Fisheries Trusts of Scotland**.

L

Labour Relations Agency   (LRA)
■ 2-8 Gordon Street, BELFAST, BT1 2LG.
Tel 028 9032 1442 Fax 028 9033 0827 http://www.lra.org.uk
Chairman: Jim McCusker Chief Executive: Bill Patterson
E Established on 1 October 1976 under the Industrial Relations (Northern Ireland) Order 1976. LRA functions as an
Executive NDPB of the Department of Employment & Learning Northern Ireland. The board comprises ten
members including the Chairman.
R To promote the improvement of employment relations in Northern Ireland.
G Northern Ireland.

Lady Lever Art Gallery   See **National Museums Liverpool**.

Laganside Corporation
✍ An Urban Development Corporation to regenerate the waterfront area of Belfast between 1989 and 2007.

Lake District National Park Authority   (LDNPA)
■ Murley Moss, Oxenholme Road, KENDAL, Cumbria, LA9 7RL.
Tel 01539 724555   Fax 01539 740822   http://www.lake-district.gov.uk
Chairman: William Jefferson, OBE   Chief Executive: Richard Leafe
E The Lake District was designated a National Park on 15 August 1951. The present Authority was established on 1 April 1997 under the Environment Act 1995. It comprises 22 members including the Chairman.
G Lake District.
✍ For further information see **National Park Authorities**.

Lanarkshire Local Enterprise Company
✍ Now functions as the Bellshill office of **Scottish Enterprise**.

Lanarkshire NHS Board
■ 14 Beckford Street, HAMILTON, Lanarks, ML3 0BR.
Tel 01698 281313
Chairman: Ken Corsar   Chief Executive: Tim Davison
G North and South Lanarkshire.
✍ For further information see **NHS Scotland - Boards**.

Lancashire & Blackpool Tourist Board
■ St George's House, St George's Street, CHORLEY, Lancs, PR7 2AA.
Tel 01257 226600   Fax 01257 469016   http://www.lancashireandblackpool.com
Chairman: Lesley Lloyd   Chief Executive: Mike Wilkinson
E Established in April 2004. LBTB functions as a company limited by guarantee, under the control of Blackpool and Blackburn Borough Councils and Lancashire County Council.
R To support tourism business in the Lancashire and Blackpool sub-region by representing their interests regionally and nationally, by coordinating marketing activity, managing and developing the tourism product and working in partnership with industry.
G Lancashire, Blackpool.
✍ One of the five tourist boards supported by the Northwest Regional Development Board (qv).

Lancashire Police Authority
■ PO Box 653, PRESTON, Lancs, PR2 2WB.
Tel 01772 533587   Fax 01772 768870   http://www.lancspa.gov.uk
Chairman: Cllr Malcolm Doherty   Chief Executive: Miranda Carruthers-Watt
E Established in April 1995, the Authority is an independent body charged with ensuring that Lancashire Constabulary provides an effective and efficient police service. It is made up of nine councillor members and eight independent members.
G Lancashire.
✍ For further information see **Police Authorities**.

Lancashire Probation Trust
■ 99-101 Garstang Road, PRESTON, Lancs, PR1 1LD.
Tel 01772 201209   Fax 01772 884399   http://www.probation-lancashire.org.uk
Chairman: Roy Male, CBE, MA   Chief Executive: Bob Mathers
E Established on 1 April 2001 under the Criminal Justice & Court Service Act 2000 as the Lancashire Probation Area Board. It became a trust on 1 April 2009 under the Offender Management Act 2007. The Board comprises eleven members including the Chairman.
G Lancashire.
✍ For further information see **Probation Trusts**.

Lancaster Port Commission
■ West Quay, Glasson Dock, LANCASTER, LA2 0DB.
Tel 01524 751724

E   Established in 1750.
G   Lancaster.
✍   For further information see **Port & Harbour Authorities**.

Land & Property Services   (LPS)
■   4th Floor, Queens Court, 56-66 Upper Queen Street, BELFAST, BT1 6FD.
     Tel 028 9054 3929   **Fax** 028 9054 3806   http://www.lpsni.gov.uk
     Chief Executive: John Wilkinson
E   Established on 1 April 2007, replacing the former Rate Collection and Valuation & Lands Agencies, absorbing
     Land Registers of Northern Ireland and Ordnance Survey of Northern Ireland on 1 April 2008. LPS functions as
     an Executive Agency of the Department of Finance & Personnel Northern Ireland. The board comprises six
     members including the Chief Executive.
R   To value properties and collect rates throughout Northern Ireland.
     To administer the Housing Benefit and Disabled Person's Allowance Schemes.
     To maintain the Title Register and provide up to date and accurate Land Information Services.
     To supply mapping information for Northern Ireland.
G   Northern Ireland.

Land Registers of Northern Ireland
✍   Since 1 April 2008 part of the **Land & Property Services** agency.

Land Registration Rule Committee   (LRRC)
■   Land Registry, 32 Lincoln's Inn Fields, LONDON, WC2A 3PH.
     Tel 020 7166 4869   **Fax** 020 7166 4842
     Chairman: Mr Justice Blackburne
E   Established in December 2002 under the Land Registration Act 2002. LRRC functions as an Advisory NDPB of
     the Ministry of Justice. The Committee comprises eight members including the Chairman.
R   To give advice and assistance on land registration rules and fee orders.
G   England, Wales.

Land Registry
■   32 Lincoln's Inn Fields, LONDON, WC2A 3PH.
     Tel 020 7166 4543   http://www.landregistry.gov.uk
     Chief Executive & Chief Land Registrar: Marco Pierleoni
E   Established in 1862 under the Land Registry Act 1862 as a separate Government department. Formerly known as
     Her Majesty's Land Registry, it now functions as an Executive Agency and Trading Fund of the Ministry of
     Justice. The Board comprises ten members including the Chief Land Registrar.
R   To maintain and develop a stable and effective land registration system throughout England and Wales.
     To guarantee title to registered estates and interests in land for the whole of England and Wales.
     To provide ready access to up-to-date and guaranteed land information, so enabling confident dealings in
     property and security of title.
G   England, Wales.
●   The Registry has 21 local offices in England and Wales.
✍   It was announced on 14 October 2010 that the Land Registry would be retained on the grounds of transparency
     but that the Government will undertake a feasibility study to scope out the opportunities presented by private
     sector investment.

Lands Tribunal   See the **Upper Tribunal (Lands Chamber)**.

Lands Tribunal for Northern Ireland   (LTNI)
■   Royal Courts of Justice, Chichester Street, BELFAST, BT1 3JJ.
     Tel 028 9032 7703   **Fax** 028 9054 6187   http://www.landstribunalni.org
     President: Mr Justice Coghlin
E   Established in 1964 under the Lands Tribunal & Compensation Act (Northern Ireland) 1964, its rules of procedure
     are laid down in the Lands Tribunal Rules (Northern Ireland) 1976, as amended. LTNI functions as a judicial
     body and Tribunal NDPB of the Department of Finance & Personnel Northern Ireland. The Tribunal comprises
     the President and a chartered surveyor.
R   To resolve disputes over the amount of compensation to be paid for the compulsory acquisition of land or for the
     injury of land by, for instance, the making of roads.
     To hear appeals and references concerning the valuation of land for rate relief purposes.
G   Northern Ireland.

Lands Tribunal for Scotland   (LTS)

- George House, 126 George Street, EDINBURGH, EH2 4HH.
  Tel 0131 271 4350   Fax 0131 271 4399   http://www.lands-tribunal-scotland.org.uk
  President: The Hon Lord McGhie, QC   Clerk: Neil Tainsh
- E   Established on 1 March 1971 under the Lands Tribunal Act 1949, the Tribunal's jurisdiction has been extended by various subsequent legislation. LTS functions as a Tribunal NDPB of the Scottish Executive Justice Department. The Tribunal comprises four members including the President.
- R   To determine a wide range of questions relating to land, including disputed valuations, the discharge of restrictive title conditions, disputes during council house purchase under tenents' rights legislation, appeals against Registers of Scotland (qv), and voluntary or joint references of consent.
- G   Scotland.
- ●   The President of the Lands Tribunal is also Chairman of the Scottish Land Court (qv); the two organisations share the same premises.

Langstone Harbour Board

- Harbour Office, Ferry Road, HAYLING ISLAND, Hants, PO11 0DG.
  Tel 023 9246 3419   Fax 023 9246 7144   http://www.langstoneharbour.org.uk
  Chairman: Cllr Lee Mason
- E   Established in 1962 under the Pier & Harbour Order (Langstone Harbour) Confirmation) Act 1962.
- G   Langstone (Portsmouth).
- ✍   For further information see **Port & Harbour Authorities**.

Lantra

- Lantra House, STONELEIGH PARK, Warks, CV8 2LG.
  Tel 024 7669 6996   http://www.lantra.co.uk
  Chairman: Dr Gordon McGlone, OBE   Chief Executive: Peter Martin
- E   Established on 1 April 2004. It is the recognised Sector Skills Council for environmental and land-based industries. Its subsidiary, Lantra Awards, is the awarding body for training and assessment for the environmental and land-based sector. The council comprises 17 members including the Chairman.
- G   United Kingdom.
- ●   Lantra also has national offices in Wales (Llanelwedd), Scotland (Scone) and Northern Ireland (Magherafelt).
- ✍   For further information see **Sector Skills Councils** and the **Federation of Awarding Bodies**.

Law Commission

- Steel House, 11 Tothill Street, LONDON, SW1H 9LJ.
  Tel 020 3334 0200   Fax 020 3334 0201   http://www.lawcom.gov.uk
  Chairman: Rt Hon Lord Justice Munby (Sir James Munby)   Chief Executive: Mark Ormerod, CB
- E   Established in 1965 under the Law Commissions Act 1965. The Commission functions as an Advisory NDPB of the Ministry of Justice. There are five Commissioners including the Chairman.
- R   To ensure that the law is as fair, modern, simple and cost-effective as possible.
  To conduct research and consultations in order to make systematic recommendations for consideration by Parliament.
  To codify the law, eliminate anomalies, repeal obsolete and unnecessary enactments and reduce the number of separate statutes.
- G   England, Wales.

Law Reform Advisory Committee for Northern Ireland
- ✍   Ceased to exist with the establishment in 2007 of the **Northern Ireland Law Commission**.

learndirect   See **Ufi Ltd**.

Learning & Skills Council
- ✍   LSC was replaced on 1 April 2010 by the **Skills Funding Agency**.

Learning & Skills Development Agency
- ✍   Established in 1995 and renamed in 2000, LSDA in 2006 split into the **Learning & Skills Network**, which operates in Northern Ireland as the **Learning Skills & Development Agency Northern Ireland**, and the Quality Improvement Agency. In 2008 the latter merged with the Centre for Excellence in Leadership as the **Learning & Skills Improvement Service**.

Learning & Skills Development Agency Northern Ireland   (LSDANI)

■   2nd Floor, Alfred House, 19-21 Alfred Street, BELFAST, BT2 8ED.
    Tel 028 9044 7700   Fax 028 9031 9077   http://www.lsdani.org.uk
    Director: Trevor Carson
E   Established in 2003 as part of the Learning & Skills Network (qv).
R   To make a difference to education and training by delivering quality improvement and staff development
    programmes that support specific government iniatives through research, training and consultancy and by
    supplying services direct to schools, colleges and training organisations.
G   Northern Ireland.

Learning & Skills Improvement Service   (LSIS)

■   Friars House, Manor House Drive, COVENTRY, CV1 2TE.
    Tel 024 7662 7900   http://www.lsis.org.uk
    Chairman: Dame Ruth Silver, DBE   Chief Executive: Rob Wye
E   Established in 2008 by the merger of the Quality Improvement Agency and the Centre for Excellence in
    Leadership. The former dated from April 2006 when the Learning & Skills Development Agency devolved into
    two separate organisations. LSIS is sector-owned NDPB, owned, directed and governed by further education
    and skills colleges and providers. It is governed and advised by a member council made up of 30 members
    including the Chairman.
R   To accelerate the drive for excellence in the learning and skills sector, building the sector's own capacity to
    design, commission and deliver improvement and strategic change.
G   England.

Learning & Skills Network   (LSN)

■   Fifth Floor, Holborn Centre, 120 Holborn, LONDON, EC1N 2AD.
    Tel 020 7492 5000   Fax 020 7492 5001   http://www.lsnlearning.org.uk
    Chairman: Chris Hughes, CBE   Chief Executive: John Stone
E   Established in April 2006 following the devolvement of the former Learning & Skills Development Agency into two
    separate organisations. LSN is an independent not-for-profit organisation. The board comprises ten members
    including the Chairman.
R   To deliver quality improvement and staff development programmes that support specific Government initiatives,
    through research, training and consultancy.
    To supply services directly to schools, colleges and training organisations.
G   England, Northern Ireland.
✍   LSN operates in Northern Ireland as Learning & Skills Development Agency Northern Ireland (qv).

Learning & Teaching Scotland   (LTS)

■   The Optima, 58 Robertson Street, GLASGOW, G2 8DU.
    Tel 0141 282 5000   Fax 0141 383 5050   http://www.ltscotland.com
    Deputy Chairman: Graeme Ogilvy
E   Established on 1 July 2000 following the merger of the former Scottish Council for Educational Technology and
    the Scottish Consultative Council on the Curriculum. It functions as an Executive NDPB of the Scottish
    Executive Education Department. The Board of Directors comprises eight members (nine including Chairman).
R   To actively promote a climate of innovation and ambition throughout the Scottish education system.
    To support teachers, schools and local authorities in improving the quality of education and raising levels of
    achievement of all learners.
    To ensure that the curriculum and approaches to learning and teaching, including the use of ICT, assist children
    and young people in Scotland to develop their full potential.
    To work in close partnership with the Scottish Government and other key stakeholders to build capacity and
    support the delivery of a first class education that is recognised as such nationally and internationally.
G   Scotland.

Leasehold Advisory Service   (LEASE)

■   Maple House, 149 Tottenham Court Road, LONDON, W1T 7BN.
    Tel 020 7383 9800   Fax 020 7383 9849   http://www.lease-advice.org
    Chairman: Deep Sagar   Chief Executive: Anthony Essien
E   Established in 1994. LEASE functions as an Executive NDPB of the Department for Communities and Local
    Government and the Welsh Government. The board comprises six members including the Chairman.
R   To provide free legal advice to leaseholders, landlords, professional advisers, managers and others on the law
    affecting residential leasehold and commonhold.
G   England, Wales.
✍   T LEASE with a specialist advice service. A decision was expected by April 2011.

© CBD Research Ltd · Beckenham · Kent BR3 5JS · Tel 020 8650 7745 · Fax 020 8650 0768 · E-mail cbd@cbdresearch.com · www.cbdresearch.com

Leasehold Valuation Tribunals   See **Rent Assessment Panels**.

Lee Valley Regional Park Authority   (LVRPA)

■ Myddelton House, Bulls Cross, ENFIELD, Middx, EN2 9HG.
 Tel 0845 677 0600   http://www.leevalleypark.org.uk
 Chairman: Derrick Ashley   Chief Executive: Shaun Dawson
E Established on 1 January 1967 under the Lee Valley Regional Park Act 1966. The Board comprises 28 members including the Chairman. 20 represent the two county, three district and six London borough councils of the Lee Valley; a further eight represent the remaining London boroughs.
R To manage and develop the 26 mile long, 10,000 acre linear regional park for leisure, recreation, nature conservation and sports development, and to preserve its natural heritage.
G Lee Valley.

Leeds Bradford International Airport Consultative Committee

■ Business Support Unit, Leeds Bradford International Airport, LEEDS, W Yorks, LS19 7TU.
 Tel 0871 288 2288   Fax 0113 250 5426   http://www.leedsbradfordairport.co.uk
 Chairman: Michael Goodman   Secretary: Abigail Houlden
G Yorkshire.
✍ For further information see **Airport Consultative Committees**.

Legal Aid Advisory Committee

■ 3rd Floor, Windsor House, 9-15 Bedford Street, BELFAST, BT2 7LT.
 Tel 028 9041 2236   Fax 028 9032 1758
E Established in 1967 under the Legal Aid & Advice Act (Northern Ireland) 1965; the Committee is now constituted under the Legal Aid, Advice & Assistance (Northern Ireland) Order 1981. It functions as an Advisory NDPB of the Northern Ireland Court Service.
R To consider the Law Society of Northern Ireland's annual report on the operation and finance of the civil legal aid scheme in Northern Ireland.
G Northern Ireland.
✍ Also known as the Lord Chancellor's Legal Aid Advisory Committee (Northern Ireland).

Legal Complaints Service
✍ LCS closed on 6 October 2010, its functions transferred to the **Office for Legal Complaints**.

Legal Deposit Advisory Panel   (LDAP)

■ Libraries Branch, 2-4 Cockspur Street, LONDON, SW1Y 5DH.
 Tel 020 7211 6174
 Chairman: Dr Ann Limb
E Established in September 2005 following the passing of the Legal Deposit Libraries Act 2003. The Panel functions as an Advisory NDPB of the Department for Culture, Media & Sport. The Panel comprises eleven members including the Chairman.
R To advise the Secretary of State on the implementation of the Act, including both non-regulatory and regulatory options for the deposit of non-print publications.
G United Kingdom.
✍ The Government confirmed on 14 October 2010 that LDAP and it functions would be abolished.

Legal Ombudsman   The Legal Ombudsman service is administered by the **Office for Legal Complaints**.

Legal Services Board   (LSB)

■ Victoria House, Southampton Row, LONDON, WC1B 4AD.
 Tel 020 7271 0050   Fax 020 7271 0051   http://www.legalservicesboard.org.uk
 Chairman: David Edmonds, CBE   Chief Executive: Chris Kenny
E Established on 1 January 2009 under the Legal Services Act 2007. LSB functions as an Executive NDPB of the Ministry of Justice. The Board comprises eight members including the Chairman.
R To oversee the bodies named as Approved Regulators in the 2007 Act.
 To oversee the Office for Legal Complaints (qv).
G England, Wales.
● The Board is the oversight regulator of:
     Association of Law Costs Draftsmen
     Bar Standards Board (qv) (barristers)

Council for Licensed Conveyancers (qv)
Faculty Office (qv) (notaries)
ILEX Professional Standards Ltd (qv) (legal executives)
Intellectual Property Regulation Board (qv) (patent and trade mark attorneys)
Solicitors Regulation Authority (qv).
and, in relation to reserved probate activities only, of
Association of Chartered Certified Accountants
Institute of Chartered Accountants in Scotland.

Legal Services Commission   (LSC)

■   4 Abbey Orchard Street, LONDON, SW1P 2BS.
    Tel 020 7783 7000   **Fax** 020 7783 7633   http://www.legalservices.gov.uk
    Chairman: Sir Bill Callaghan...Chief Executive: Carolyn Downs
E   Established on 1 April 2000 under the Access to Justice Act 1999, replacing the former Legal Aid Board. LSC
    functions as an Executive NDPB of the Ministry of Justice. (It was announced by the Government on 14
    October 2010 that it will be abolished as an NDPB and become an Executive Agency.) The Commission
    comprises the Chairman and up to eleven members.
R   To run the Legal Aid Scheme.
    To make sure that people get the information, advice and legal help they need to deal with a wide range of
    problems.
G   England, Wales.
●   The Commission has 13 other offices in England and Wales.

Legal Services Consultative Panel
✍   LSCOP ceased to exist on 1 January 2010.

Legal Services Ombudsman
✍   See replacement organisations, the **Office for Legal Complaints** (England and Wales) and the **Scottish Legal
    Complaints Committee**.

Legionella Committee

■   Redgrave Court, Merton Road, BOOTLE, Merseyside, L20 7HS.
    Tel 0845 345 0055
E   A working group of the Health & Safety Executive (qv).
R   To share information and engage all interested parties on issues, initiatives and research concerning the control
    of legionella.
    To provide advice and an operational steer on control of legionella issues to HSE policy units and to support
    operational activity in the HSE directorates and divisions.
    To promote and monitor an overall coherent and consistent approach to inspection and investigation of control of
    legionella issues within HSE and with Local Authorities and to review the outcomes of these interventions.
G   United Kingdom.

Leicester, Northamptonshire & Rutland Strategic Health Authority
✍   On 1 July 2006 merged with the Trent Strategic Health Authority to form the **East Midlands Strategic Health
    Authority**.

Leicester Regeneration Company
✍   Established in April 2001, LRC was the Urban Regeneration Company for central Leicester. In April 2009 it was
    merged by the City and County Councils with the latter's Leicester Shire Economic Partnership to form
    Prospect Leicestershire.

Leicestershire Police Authority

■   St John's, Enderby, LEICESTER, LE19 2BX.
    Tel 0116 229 8980   **Fax** 0116 229 8985   http://www.leics-pa.police.uk
    Chairman: Cllr Barrie Roper
E   Established in April 1995, the Authority is an independent body charged with ensuring that Leicestershire
    Constabulary provides an effective and efficient police service. It is made up of seven councillor members
    appointed by the local councils and eight independent members.
G   Leicester, Leicestershire and Rutland.
✍   For further information see **Police Authorities**.

© CBD Research Ltd · Beckenham · Kent BR3 5JS · Tel 020 8650 7745 · Fax 020 8650 0768 · E-mail cbd@cbdresearch.com · www.cbdresearch.com

Leicestershire & Rutland Probation Trust

■ 2 St John Street, LEICESTER, LE1 3WL.
Tel 0116 251 6008   Fax 0116 242 3250   http://www.leicsprobation.co.uk
Chairman: Jane Wilson   Chief Executive: Helen West

E Established on 1 April 2001 under the Criminal Justice & Court Service Act 2000 as the Leicestershire & Rutland Probation Area Board. It became a trust on 1 April 2008 under the Offender Management Act 2007. The Board comprises nine members including the Chairman.

G Leicester, Leicestershire and Rutland.

✍ For further information see **Probation Trusts**.

Lending Standards Board   (LSB)

■ Level 17, City Tower, 40 Basinghall Street, LONDON, EC2V 5DE.
Tel 020 7012 0085   Fax 020 7374 4414   http://www.lendingstandardsboard.org.uk
Chairman: Gerard Lemos, CMG   Chief Executive: Robert Skinner

E Established in 1999 and known as the Banking Code Standards Board until adopting its current name on 2 November 2009. LSB is a membership organisation which works closely with other regulators, particularly the FSA, Office of Fair Trading and Financial Ombudsman Service (qqv). The Board comprises eight members including the Chairman.

R To assist firms to interpret and meet the requirements of the Lending Code.
To monitor and enforce compliance with the Code and take enforcement action for material breaches.
To identify any gaps and deficiencies in the Code that could lead to consumer detriment and to advocate change.

G United Kingdom.

● The Lending Code replaced the Banking Codes following the transfer of responsibilities for the conduct of business regulation for deposit and payment products to the Financial Services Authority (qv) on 1 November 2009.

Lerwick Port Authority   (LPA)

■ Albert Building, LERWICK, Shetland Islands, ZE1 0LL.
Tel 01595 692991   Fax 01595 693452   http://www.lerwick-harbour.co.uk
Chief Executive: Sandra Laurenson

E Established in 1877 by Act of Parliament. The board comprises eleven members.

G Shetland Islands.

✍ For further information see **Port & Harbour Authorities**.

Liaison Group of UK Airport Consultative Committees   See **Airport Consultative Committees**.

Liberty   See **National Council for Civil Liberties**.

Libraries NI   See the **Northern Ireland Library Authority**.

Library & Information Services Council (Northern Ireland)   (LISC)

■ Craigantlet Buildings, Stoney Road, BELFAST, BT4 3SX.
Tel 028 9052 7423   Fax 028 9040 1180   http://www.liscni.co.uk
Chairman: Kirby Porter   Director: Linda Houston

E Established in 1978 and known as the Library Advisory Council until 1982 when it changed to its current name. The Council functions as an Executive NDPB of the Department of Culture, Arts & Leisure Northern Ireland.

R To maintain and enhance the standard of library and information services in Northern Ireland.

G Northern Ireland.

Library & Information Services Council for Wales
✍ Abolished 1 April 2004 (see **CyMAL**).

Life Sentence Review Commissioners
✍ Superceded in 2008 by the **Parole Commissioners of Northern Ireland**.

Lifelong Learning UK   (LLUK)

■   8th Floor, Centurion House, 24 Monument Street, LONDON, EC3R 8AQ.
     Tel 0300 303 8077   **Fax** 020 7375 9301   http://www.lluk.org
     Chairman: Pat Bacon   Chief Executive: Sue Dutton
E   Established on 1 January 2005. It is the recognised Sector Skills Council for careers guidance, community
     learning and development, further and higher education, libraries, archives, and information services, and work-
     based learning and development. The council comprises 17 members including the Chairman.
G   United Kingdom.
✍   For further information see **Sector Skills Councils**.

Lincolnshire Police Authority

■   Deepdale Lane, Nettleham, LINCOLN, LN2 2LT.
     Tel 01522 558022   **Fax** 01522 558739   http://www.lincolnshire-pa.gov.uk
     Chairman: Cllr Barry Young
E   Established in April 1995, the Authority is an independent body charged with ensuring that Lincolnshire Police
     provide an effective and efficient police service.
     It is made up of nine County Councillors and eight independent members.
G   Lincolnshire (excluding North and North East Lincolnshire).
✍   For further information on area see **Police Authorities**.

Lincolnshire Probation Trust

■   7 Lindum Terrace, LINCOLN, LN2 5RP.
     Tel 01522 520776   **Fax** 01522 527685
     Chairman: Christopher Cook   Chief Officer: Graham Nicholls
E   Established on 1 April 2001 under the Criminal Justice & Court Service Act 2000 as the Lincolnshire Probation
     Area Board. It became a trust on 1 April 2010 under the Offender Management Act 2007. The Board comprises
     up to 15 members including the Chairman.
G   Kent.
✍   For further information see **Probation Trusts**.

Littlehampton Harbour Board

■   Harbour Office, Pier Road, LITTLEHAMPTON, W Sussex, BN17 5LR.
     Tel 01903 721215   **Fax** 01903 739472   http://www.littlehampton.org.uk
     Chairman: Cllr Graham Tyler
E   The board comprises eleven members including the Chairman.
G   Littlehampton.
✍   For further information see **Port & Harbour Authorities**.

Liverpool Housing Action Trust

✍   Wound up in 2005 upon completion of its programme.

Liverpool John Lennon Airport Consultative Committee   (LJLACC)

■   Democratic Services, Room 251, County Hall, CHESTER, CH1 1SF.
     Tel 01244 975996   **Fax** 01244 972632   http://www.ljlacc.org.uk
     Chairman: Cllr Denis Knowles   Assistant Secretary; Mike A Jones
G   Cheshire, Merseyside.
✍   For further information see **Airport Consultative Committees**.

Liverpool Vision

■   10th Floor, The Capital, 29 Old Hall Street, LIVERPOOL, L3 9PP.
     Tel 0151 600 2900   http://www.liverpoolvision.co.uk
     Chairman: Mike Parker   Chief Executive: Max Steinberg
E   Established on 1 May 2008. Liverpool Vision is an Economic Development Company, bringing together the
     activities of Liverpool Vision (the Urban Regeneration Company established in 1999), Liverpool Land
     Development Company and Business Liverpool.
G   Liverpool.
✍   For further information see **Economic Development Companies**.

© CBD Research Ltd · Beckenham · Kent BR3 5JS · Tel 020 8650 7745 · Fax 020 8650 0768 · E-mail cbd@cbdresearch.com · www.cbdresearch.com

Livestock & Meat Commission for Northern Ireland   (LMC)
- ■   Lissue House, 31 Ballinderry Road, LISBURN, Co Antrim, BT28 2SL.
  Tel 028 9263 3000   Fax 028 9263 3001   http://www.lmcni.com
  Chairman: Pat O'Rourke   Chief Executive: David Rutledge
- E   Established in 1967 under the Livestock Marketing Commission Act (Northern Ireland) 1967. LMC functions as an Executive NDPB of the Department of Agriculture & Rural Development Northern Ireland. The Board comprises seven members including the Chairman.
- R   To serve the beef and sheepmeat industry in Northern Ireland.
- G   Northern Ireland.

Living East
- ✍   One of the eight Regional Cultural Consortiums established for England in 1999, it closed on 31 March 2009, its functions returned to the Department for Culture, Media & Sport.

Llyfrgell Genedlaethol Cymru   See National Library of Wales.

Local Authorities Coordinators of Regulatory Services
- ✍   LACORS is now **Local Government Regulation**.

Local Authority Forum   (LAF)
- ■   Redgrave Court, Merton Road, BOOTLE, Merseyside, L20 7HS.
  Tel 0845 345 0055
- E   Established in 2002 by the Health & Safety Executive (qv). The Forum comprises the Chairman and 15 persons from the HSE, local authority employer representatives and trade unions.
- R   To engender an approach in the way that local authorities manage health and safety, and to influence and guide the factors that will bring about that change.
- G   United Kingdom.
- ✍   LAF last met formally met on 22 February 2007. HSE is working towards creating a new, high level, strategic body with revised terms of reference and governance.

Local Authority Leaders' Boards   (LALBs)
- ✍   Established under the Local Democracy, Economic Development & Construction Act 2009 following the abolition of the eight English Regional Assemblies, 2008-2010, and principally responsibile for scrutiny of the Regional Development Agencies (qv). Each comprised local authority leaders representive of key sub-regions, upper and lower tier authorities and the political balance of the region. Their abolition was announced by the incoming Coalition Government in June 2010.

Local Authority Recycling Advisory Committee   (LARAC)
- ■   PO Box 28, KNIGHTON, Powys, LD8 2WA.
  Tel 01544 267860   http://www.larac.org.uk
  Chairman: Joy Blizzard   Executive Officer: Colin Kirkby
- E   Established in 1985, LARAC is a membership organization of district, county and unitary local authority recycling and waste professionals. The Executive Committee comprises 20 local authority waste management officers.
- R   To provide quality representation for local authority officers on recycling and waste management issues.
- G   United Kingdom.

Local Better Regulation Office   (LBRO)
- ■   The Axis, 10 Holliday Street, BIRMINGHAM, B1 1TG.
  Tel 0121 226 4000   http://www.lbro.org.uk
  Chairman: Clive Grace   Chief Executive: Graham Russell
- E   Established in May 2007 as a government-owned limited company. Under the Regulatory Enforcement & Sanctions Act 2008, LBRO functions as an Executive NDPB of the Department for Business, Innovation & Skills. The Board comprises six members including the Chairman.
- R   To reduce unnecessary red tape for law-abiding businesses to allow greater focus on targeting the rogue traders who harm vulnerable people and damage communities.
  To encourage the provision of local authority regulatory services in a way that accords with the better regulation principles.
- G   United Kingdom.

LOCAL ENTERPRISE PARTNERSHIPS   (LEPs)

E   Following the decision to close the Government Offices for the Regions and the Regional Development Agencies, the Government devised Local Enterprise Partnerships as the means of offering local areas the opportunity to take control of their future economic development. LEPs are locally owned partnerships between local authorities and businesses.

R   To play a central in determining local economic priorities and undertaking activities to drive economic growth and create local jobs.
To be a key vehicle in delivering Government objectives for growth and decentralisation, while also providing a means for local authorities to work together with business in order to quicken the economic recovery.
To play a role in coordinating across areas and communities in bidding for the Regional Growth Fund.

G   England.

●   On 28 October 2010 the Government announced 24 partnerships that were ready to move forward and establish their LEP boards.

Local Government Boundaries Commissioner for Northern Ireland
✍   The 2008/9 review concluded on 22 June 2009 and the office closed.

Local Government Boundary Commission for England   (LGBCE)
■   Layden House, 76-86 Turnmill Street, LONDON, EC1M 5LG.
Tel 020 7664 8534   Fax 020 7296 6227   http://www.lgbce.org.uk
Chairman: Max Caller, CBE   Chief Executive: Alan Cogbill

E   Established on 1 April 2010, taking over the functions of the Boundary Committee for England. LGBCE is independent of Government and political parties and is directly accountable to Parliament through a committee chaired by the Speaker of the House of Commons. The Commission comprises the Chairman, a Deputy Chairman and four other commissioners.

R   To conduct thorough, consultative, and robust reviews of local government areas in England, and to make recommendations that are evidence-based, accurate and accepted.

G   England.

Local Government Boundary Commission for Scotland   (LGBCS)
■   Thistle House, 91 Haymarket Terrace, EDINBURGH, EH12 5HD.
Tel 0131 538 7510   Fax 0131 538 7511   http://www.lgbc-scotland.gov.uk
Chairman: Peter Mackay, CB

E   Established on 1 January 1974 under the Local Government (Scotland) Act 1973. LGBCS functions as an Advisory NDPB of the Scottish Executive Finance & Central Services Department. The Commission comprises the Chairman, his deputy and three other members.

R   To carry out reviews of the boundaries of the local authority areas of Scotland, and of electoral arrangements for the local authorities.

G   Scotland.

Local Government Boundary Commission for Wales   (LGBCW)
■   Caradog House, 1-6 St Andrews Place, CARDIFF, CF10 3BE.
Tel 029 2039 5031   Fax 029 2039 5250   http://www.lgbc-wales.gov.uk
Chairman: Paul Wood

E   Established in June 1974 under provisions of the Local Government Act 1972. LGBCW functions as an Advisory NDPB sponsored by the National Assembly for Wales. The Commission comprises the Chairman, his deputy and one other member.

R   To keep under review all local government areas in Wales, and the electoral arrangements for the principal areas, and to make such proposals to the Welsh Government as seem desirable in the interests of effective and convenient local government.

G   Wales.

=   Comisiwn Ffiniau Llywodraeth Leol i Gymru

Local Government Employers   The business name of **Employers' Organisation for Local Government**.

Local Government Improvement & Development
■   Layden House, 76-86 Turnmill Street, LONDON, EC1M 5LG.
Tel 020 7296 6600   Fax 020 7296 6666   http://www.idea.gov.uk
Chairman: Cllr Ian Swithenbank, CBE   Managing Director: Rob Whiteman

---

© CBD Research Ltd · Beckenham · Kent BR3 5JS · Tel 020 8650 7745 · Fax 020 8650 0768 · E-mail cbd@cbdresearch.com · www.cbdresearch.com

E Established on 1 April 1999. LG Improvement & Development (formerly IDeA, Improvement & Development Agency for local government) is wholly owned by the Local Government Association and is a registered company. The Board of Directors comprises 14 members including the Chairman.

R To support improvement and innovation in local government, focusing on the issues that are important to councils and using tried and tested ways of working.

G England, Wales.

Local Government Ombudsman

For England, see the **Commission for Local Administration in England**;
For Northern Ireland, see the **Northern Ireland Ombudsman**;
For Scotland, see the **Scottish Public Services Ombudsman**;
For Wales, see the **Public Services Ombudsman for Wales**.

Local Government Regulation

■ Local Government House, Smith Square, LONDON, SW1P 3HZ.
Tel 020 7664 3000 **Fax** 020 7664 3030 http://www.lacors.gov.uk
Chairman: Cllr Paul Bettison

E Established in 1978 by its current members, the four UK local authority associations, and known as the Local Authorities Coordinators of Regulatory Services (LACORS) until a recent change of name. It is accountable to its members - Convention of Scottish Local Authorities, Local Government Association, Northern Ireland Local Government Association and Welsh Local Government Association. The Board comprises ten members including the Chairman.

R To be responsible for overseeing local authority regulatory and related services.

G United Kingdom.

Local Government Staff Commission for Northern Ireland   (LGSC)

■ Commission House, 18-22 Gordon Street, BELFAST, BT1 2LG.
Tel 028 9031 3200 **Fax** 028 9031 3151 http://www.lgsc.org.uk
Chairman: Brian Hanna, CBE   Chief Executive: Adrian E Kerr, MBE

E Established on 1 September 1974 under the Local Government Act (Northern Ireland) Act 1972. LGSC functions as an Executive NDPB of the Department of the Environment Northern Ireland.

R To provide professional services and advice on human resource issues to councils and the Northern Ireland Housing Executive (qv).

G Northern Ireland.

Local Government Yorkshire & Humber   (LGYH)

■ 18 King Street, WAKEFIELD, W Yorks, WF1 2SQ.
Tel 01924 331631 **Fax** 01924 331559 http://www.lgyh.gov.uk
Chairman: Cllr Roger Stone

E Established on 1 April 2009 following abolition of the Yorkshire & Humber Assembly, LGYH is an independent membership organisation of the 22 local authorities in the region, represented by the 21 council leaders and the one elected mayor (Doncaster).

R To be responsible, in conjunction with Yorkshire Forward (qv), for regional strategic planning and economic development.

G Yorkshire (North, South, East and West), Lincolnshire (North and North East).

Local Health Boards   See **National Health Service - Wales**.

LOCAL INVOLVEMENT NETWORKS   (LINks)

E Established under the Local Government & Public Involvement Act 2007. Every local authority (that provides social services) has been given funding and is under a legal duty to make contractual arrangements that enable LINk activities to take place. It is up to each community to decide how it wants its LINk to be run and on which issues they it should focus.

R To give citizens a stronger voice in how their health and social care services are delivered.

G England.

✍ The former Patient & Public Involvement Forums, based on NHS Trusts, were abolished on 31 March 2008.

Local Supervising Authority for Midwives   See **Healthcare Inspectorate Wales**.

Loch Lomond Fisheries Trust   See **Rivers & Fisheries Trusts of Scotland**.

Loch Lomond & the Trossachs National Park Authority   (LLTNPA)
- Carrochan, Carrochan Road, BALLOCH, Dunbartonshire, G83 8EG.
  Tel 01389 722600   Fax 01389 722633   http://www.lochlomond-trossachs.org
  Convener: Dr Mike Cantlay   Chief Executive: Fiona Logan
- E   Established in 2002 under provisions made in the National Parks (Scotland) Act 2000. LLTNPA functions as an Executive NDPB of the Scottish Executive Rural Affairs Department. The Authority's board comprises 25 members including the Convener.
- R   To conserve and enhance the natural and cultural heritage of the area.
  To promote the sustainable use of the natural resources of the area.
  To promote understanding and enjoyment (including enjoyment in the form of recreation) of the special qualities of the area by the public.
  To promote sustainable economic and social development of the area's communities.
- G   Loch Lomond and the Trossachs.
- ✍ For further information see **National Park Authorities**.

Lochaber Enterprise
- ✍ See **Highlands & Islands Enterprise**.

Lochaber Fisheries Trust   See **Rivers & Fisheries Trusts of Scotland**.

London Academy of Professional Training   (LAPT)
- 29 Harley Street, LONDON, W1G 9QR.
  Tel 020 7612 4401   Fax 020 7182 6826   http://www.lapt.org
  Chairman: Dr Desmond Adair
- E   LAPT is an awarding body for courses and qualifications in English communication, office administration, computerised accounting and management studies.
- G   United Kingdom.
- ✍ For further information on awarding bodies see the **Federation of Awarding Bodies**.

London Assembly   See **Greater London Authority**.

London Chamber of Commerce and Industry Examinations Board
- ✍ Now LCCI International Qualifications, part of **EDI**.

London City Airport Consultative Committee   (LCACC)
- London City Airport, PO Box 66353, LONDON, E16 9BA.
  Tel 01487 842623   http://www.lcacc.org
  Chairman: John Adshead   Secretary: Stuart Innes
- G   East London.
- ✍ For further information see **Airport Consultative Committees**.

London Conference on Overseas Students   (LCOS)
- 229 Great Portland Street, LONDON, W1W 5PN.
  Tel 020 7631 8300   Fax 020 7631 8307   http://www.lcos.org.uk
  Chairman: David Anderson-Evans
- E   Established in 1950 as the Conference of Voluntary Societies on the Welfare of Colonial Students; in 1955 the responsibilities of the Conference were widened to include students of all nationalities and in 1959 the current name was adopted.
- R   To publish a directory of hostels in London for international students.
- G   London.
- ●   The Conference provides a forum for London organisations concerned with overseas student housing issues.

London & Continental Railways   (LCR)
- 3rd Floor, 183 Eversholt Street, LONDON, NW1 1AY.
  Tel 020 7391 4300   Fax 020 7391 4400   http://www.lcrhq.co.uk
  Chairman: Sir David Cooksey, GBE   Chief Executive: Mark Bayley

E   In 1996 the company won the the contract to build and operate the Channel Tunnel and high speed rail link. The Department for Transport announced in June 2009 that the UK Government would takeover sole ownership of LCR.

London Councils Grants Committee

■   59½ Southwark Street, LONDON, SE1 0AL.
    Tel 020 7934 9999   http://www.londoncouncils.gov.uk
    Chairman: Cllr Lynne Hillan
E   The London Borough Grants Scheme was established in 1986 under the Local Government Act 1985; the Grants Committee was set up by all the London Councils to administer it.
    The Committee comprises 33 members, one from the Executive of each of the 33 London Boroughs.
R   To invest £28 million annually in voluntary organisations on behalf of all the London Councils.
G   London.
✍   London Councils (formerly the Association of London Government) lobbies for more resources for London and a fair deal for its councils. It develops policies in many key areas and runs a range of services designed to make life better for Londoners.

London Councils Transport & Environment Committee   (TEC)

■   59½ Southwark Street, LONDON, SE1 0AL.
    Tel 020 7934 9999   http://www.londoncouncils.gov.uk
    Chairman: Cllr Catherine West
E   Established in 1986 under the Local Government Act 1972. The Committee comprises 33 members, one from the Executive of each of the 33 London Boroughs.
R   To provide a range of high-quality operational services such as parking and traffic appeals, the London night-time and weekend lorry ban, the Freedom Pass and Taxicard schemes.
    To ensure that the London boroughs' concerns and best practice are taken into account in the development and implementation of the whole range of transport and environment policies generated by Government departments, the European Union, and the Mayor of London.
G   London.
●   The scheme, commonly known as the 'London Lorry Ban', restricts heavy goods vehicles over 16.5 tonnes entering the capital at night & weekends.

London Cultural Strategy Group   (LCSG)

■   PP25, City Hall, The Queen's Walk, LONDON, SE1 2AA.
    Tel 020 7983 4000   http://www.london.gov.uk
    Chairman: Iwona Blazwick, OBE
E   Established in 2000 as the Cultural Strategy Group for London under the Greater London Act 1999, adopting its current name in 2004. LCSG functions as a special advisory group to the Mayor of London via the Greater London Authority (qv). The Group comprises 24 members including the Chairman.
R   To advise and help the Mayor deliver a strategy to promote and develop London as a world-class city of culture.
    To represent the key agencies that support culture in London.
G   London.

London Development Agency   (LDA)

■   Palestra, 197 Blackfriars Road, LONDON, SE1 8AA.
    Tel 020 7593 8000   http://www.lda.gov.uk
    Chairman: Harvey McGrath   Chief Executive: Peter Rogers
E   Established on 3 July 2000 following the formation of the Greater London Authority (qv). One of the nine English Regional Development Agencies, it is directly responsible to the Mayor of London at the GLA and functions as an Executive NDPB of the Department for Business, Innovation & Skills.
G   Greater London.
✍   The Comprehensive Spending Review in October 2010 confirmed the Government's intention to abolish the RDAs and support the creation of Local Enterprise Partnerships (qv), to be in place by March 2012.

London Emergency Services Liaison Panel   (LESLP)

■   Emergency Preparedness Operational Command Unit, New Scotland Yard, Broadway, LONDON,
    SW1H 0BG.   http://www.leslp.gov.uk
E   Established in 1973. LESLP consists of representatives from the Metropolitan Police Service, the London Fire Brigade, the City of London Police, the British Transport Police, the London Ambulance Service and local authorities.
R   To ensure a partnership approach between the relevant agencies in the planning for, and the response to, a major incident of whatever kind.
G   London.

London Film Commission   Replaced by **Film London**.

London Film & Video Development Agency   Replaced by **Film London**.

London Fire & Emergency Planning Authority   (LFEPA)
■   169 Union Street, LONDON, SE1 0LL.
　　Tel 020 8555 1200   http://www.london-fire.gov.uk
　　Chairman: Cllr Brian Coleman, AM, FRSA
E   Established on 3 July 2000 following the formation of the Greater London Authority (qv). LFEPA is directly
　　accountable to the Mayor of London at the GLA. The Authority comprises 17 members including the Chairman.
R   To set the strategy for the provision of fire services in London.
　　To ensure the London Fire Brigade can meet all normal firefighting requirements efficiently.
　　To ensure members of the London Fire Brigade are properly trained and equipped.
G   London.
✍   Part of the GLA Group - see **Greater London Authority** for more details.

London Gatwick Airport Consultative Committee   See **Gatwick Airport Consultative Committee**.

London Heathrow Airport Consultative Committee   See **Heathrow Airport Consultative Committee**.

London Luton Airport Consultative Committee   (LLACC)
■   Navigation House, Airport Way, LUTON, Beds, LU2 9LY.
　　Tel 01582 395049   http://www.llacc.com
　　Chairman: Martin Routledge   Administrator: Tricia Harris
G   Bedfordshire, Buckinghamshire, Hertfordshire.
✍   For further information see **Airport Consultative Committees**.

London Organising Committee of the Olympic & Paralympic Games   (LOCOG)
■   One Churchill Place, Canary Wharf, LONDON, E14 5LN.
　　Tel 020 3201 2000   http://www.london2012.com
　　Chairman: Lord Coe   Chief Executive: Paul Deighton
E   Established in July 2005. LOCOG is a company registered in England & Wales. The Board comprises 18
　　members including the Chairman.
R   To be responsible for preparing and staging the 2012 Games.
G   United Kingdom.
✍   The Committee works with the Olympic Delivery Authority (qv).

London Pensions Fund Authority   (LPFA)
■   Dexter House, 2 Royal Mint Court, LONDON, EC3N 4LP.
　　Tel 020 7369 6118   http://www.lpfa.org.uk
　　Chairman: Anthony Mayer   Chief Executive: Mike Taylor
E   Established on 31 October 1989 under the London Government Reorganisation (Pensions etc) Order 1989. LFPA
　　functions as an NDPB of the Greater London Authority (qv). The board comprises eleven members including the
　　Chairman.
R   To administer the former GLC Superannuation Scheme with over 65,000 members.
G   London.

London Probation Trust
■   71/73 Great Peter Street, LONDON, SW1P 2BN.
　　Tel 020 7222 5656   **Fax** 020 7960 1188   http://www.london-probation.org.uk
　　Chairman: Julie Dent, CBE   Chief Officer: Paul Wilson, CBE
E   Established on 1 April 2001 under the Criminal Justice & Court Service Act 2000 as the London Probation Area
　　Board. It became a trust on 1 April 2010 under the Offender Management Act 2007. The Board comprises nine
　　members including the Chairman.
G   Greater London.
✍   For further information see **Probation Trusts**.

London Rent Assessment Panel (LRAP)

■ 10 Alfred Place, LONDON, WC1E 7LR.
   Tel 020 7446 7700   Fax 020 7637 1250
G Greater London.
✍ For further information on the five regional panels see **Rent Assessment Panels** [England].

London & South East Industrial Development Board
✍ See note under **Industrial Development Boards**.

London Stansted Airport Consultative Committee   See **Stansted Airport Consultative Committee**.

London Strategic Health Authority

■ Southside, 105 Victoria Street, LONDON, SW1E 6QT.
   Tel 020 7932 3700   http://www.london.nhs.uk
   Chairman: Prof Mike Spyer   Chief Executive: Ruth Carnall, CBE
E Established on 1 July 2006 replacing five former London Strategic Health Authorities: The North Central, the North East, the North West, the South East and the South West.
   The board comprises six non-executive directors including the Chairman, and eleven executive directors including the Chief Executive.
R To relay and explain national policy, set direction and support and develop NHS Trust bodies (Primary Care Trusts and NHS Trusts providing acute, mental health and ambulance services).
   To ensure that local health systems operate effectively and efficiently, and that national standards and priorities are met.
G Greater London.
✍ One of the ten regional Strategic Health Authorities of England - see **NHS - England** in the Subject Index.

London Thames Gateway Development Corporation
✍ LTGDC was established in 2004 to be the Government's lead regeneration agency for the Lower Lea Valley and London Riverside. On 14 October 2010 the Government announced that it would abolish the body and devolve its functions to local government or other London bodies.

London Transport Users Committee (LTUC)

■ 6 Middle Street, LONDON, EC1A 7JA.
   Tel 020 7505 9000   Fax 020 7505 9003   http://www.londontravelwatch.org.uk
   Chairman: Sharon Grant   Chief Executive: Janet Cooke
E Established on 3 July 2000 under the Greater London Authority Act 1999, it operates under the name **London TravelWatch**. The Committee is sponsored and funded by the London Assembly which is part of the Greater London Authority (qv). The Board comprises the Chairman and twelve other members.
R To promote integrated transport policies.
   To press for better public transport, with higher standards of quality, performance and accessibility.
G An area bounded by Bedford, Dartford, Gatwick and Slough.

London TravelWatch   Operating name of the **London Transport Users Committee**.

London Voluntary Service Council (LVSC)

■ 4th Floor, 88 Old Street, LONDON, EC1V 9HU.
   Tel 020 3349 8900   Fax 020 7253 0065   http://www.lvsc.org.uk
   Chairman: Paul Butler   Chief Executive: Peter Lewis
E Established in 1910. LVSC functions as a registered charity and company limited by guarantee. The Board of Trustees comprises 13 members including the Chairman, three representatives of LVSC member organisations and seven co-optees.
R To bring London voluntary and community sector organisations together to learn and share best practice and to create a coordinated voice to influence policy makers.
G London.

London Waste & Recycling Board (LWARB)

■ 3rd Floor, City Hall, The Queen's Walk, LONDON, SE1 2AA.
   Tel 020 7983 4970   http://www.lwarb.gov.uk
   Chairman: James Cleverly, AM

E Established in 2008 under the Greater London Authority Act 2007. LWARB has an investment fund comprising money from the Department for Environment, Food & Rural Affairs and the London Development Agency (qv). The Board comprises eight members including the Chairman.
R To promote and encourage the production of less waste, an increase in the proportion of waste that is re-used or recycled and the use of methods of collection, treatment and disposal of waste which are more beneficial to the environment.
G London.

Londonderry Port & Harbour Commissioners   (LPHC)
■ Harbour Office, Port Road, Lisahally, LONDONDERRY, BT47 1FL.
   Tel 028 7186 0555   Fax 028 7186 1168   http://www.londonderryport.com
   Chairman: Garvan O'Doherty   Chief Executive: Brian McGrath
E Established in 1854 under the Londonderry Port & Harbour Act 1854.
G Londonderry.
✍ For further information see **Port & Harbour Authorities**.

Looe Harbour Commissioners
■ Harbour, EAST LOOE, Cornwall, PL13 1DX.
   Tel 01503 262839
   Harbour Master: Capt Jeff Penhaligon
E The Commission comprises nine members including the Chairman.
G Looe.
✍ For further information see **Port & Harbour Authorities**.

Lord Chancellor's Legal Aid Advisory Committee (Northern Ireland)   See **Legal Aid Advisory Committee**.

Lord Chancellor's Standing Conference on Legal Education see **Standing Conference on Legal Education**.

Lords Select Committees   See **United Kingdom Parliament: Committees**.

Lothian & Borders Police Board
■ City Chambers, High Street, EDINBURGH, EH1 1YJ.   http://www.edinburgh.gov.uk/lbpb/
   Chief Executive & Clerk: Cllr Tom Aitchison
E The Board is an independent body responsible for Lothian & Borders Police's budget and the management of its resources. It comprises 18 councillor members.
G East Lothian, Midlothian (including the City of Edinburgh), West Lothian and the Scottish Borders.
✍ For further information see **Police Authorities**.

Lothian NHS Board
■ Waverley Gate, 2-4 Waterloo Place, EDINBURGH, EH1 3EG.
   Tel 0131 536 9000   Fax 0131 536 9164   http://www.nhslothian.scot.nhs.uk
   Chairman: Dr Charles Winstanley   Chief Executive: Prof James Barbour, OBE
G City of Edinburgh, East, Mid- and West Lothian.
✍ For further information see **NHS Scotland - Boards**.

Loughs Agency
■ 22 Victoria Road, LONDONDERRY, BT47 2AB.
   Tel 028 7134 2100   Fax 028 7134 2720
   email www.loughs-agency.org
   Chief Executive: Derick Anderson
E Established on 2 December 1999, successor to the Foyle Fisheries Commission. The Agency is responsible to the Foyle, Carlingford & Irish Lights Commission (qv).
R To provide sustainable social, economic and environmental benefits through the effective conservation, protection, management, promotion and development of the fisheries and marine resources of the Foyle and Carlingford catchments.
G Northern Ireland.

© CBD Research Ltd · Beckenham · Kent BR3 5JS · Tel 020 8650 7745 · Fax 020 8650 0768 · E-mail cbd@cbdresearch.com · www.cbdresearch.com

Low Carbon Vehicle Partnership

- 83 Victoria Street, LONDON, SW1W 0HW.
  Tel 020 3178 7859   Fax 020 3008 6180   http://www.lowcvp.org.uk
  Chairman: Prof Neville Jackson
- E Established in 2003 following publication of the Government's Powering Future Vehicles Strategy in 2002. The Partnership is an action and advisory group which brings together a wide range of organisations with a stake in the move to cleaner vehicles and fuels and is part funded by the Department for Transport and the Department for Business, Innovation & Skills. It became a not-for-profit company limited by guarantee in April 2009. The board comprises the Chairman and 20 directors drawn from across LowCVP's principal stakeholder groups.
- R To take a lead in accelerating the shift to low carbon road vehicles and fuels in the UK and to help ensure that UK business can benefit from that shift.
- G United Kingdom.

Low Pay Commission   (LPC)

- 1st Floor, Kingsgate House, 66-74 Victoria Street, LONDON, SW1E 6SW.
  Tel 020 7515 8459   http://www.lowpay.gov.uk
  Chairman: David Norgrove
- E Established under the National Minimum Wage Act 1998. LPC functions as an Advisory NDPB of the Department for Business, Innovation & Skills. The Commission comprises nine members including the Chairman.
- R To monitor and evaluate the National Minimum Wage and to make recommendations to Government.
- G United Kingdom.

Lught-reill Urryssaght as Penshynyn   See **Insurance & Pensions Authority**.

Luton Airport Consultative Committee   See **London Luton Airport Consultative Committee**.

Lymington Harbour Commissioners

- Harbour Office, Bath Road, LYMINGTON, Hants, SO41 3SE.
  Tel 01590 672014   Fax 01590 671823   http://www.lymingtonharbour.co.uk
  Chairman: Peter Griffiths   Chief Executive & Harbour Master: Ryan Willegers
- E Established under the Pier & Harbour Order (Lymington) Confirmation Act 1951. The Commission comprises ten members including the Chairman.
- G Lymington.
- ✍ For further information see **Port & Harbour Authorities**.

M

Macaulay Land Use Research Institute
- ✍ Merged on 1 April 2011 with the Scottish Crop Research Institute to form the **James Hutton Institute**.

Magistrates' Courts Committees   See **Central Council of Magistrates' Courts Committees**.

Magistrates' Courts Rule Committee   See **Criminal Procedure Rule Committee**.

Main Honours Advisory Committee
- ✍ In the Government's Spending Review of October 2010, MHAC (established 2005) was abolished as an Advisory NDPB. It survives as an advisory group administered from within the Cabinet Office.

Major Energy Users' Council   (MEUC)

- PO Box 30, LONDON, W5 3ZT.
  Tel 020 8997 3854   Fax 020 8566 7073   http://www.meuc.co.uk
  Director General: Andrew Bainbridge, FIoD

E   Established in 1987. MEUC is a company limited by guarantee and membership is open to all professional buyers of utilities, energy and environmental managers. It compromises over 200 energy, water and telecoms users from the private and public sectors.
R   To provide professional guidance and support to utility buyers and energy managers.
G   United Kingdom, Republic of Ireland.
●   The Council conducts buyers' meetings, holds special interest workshops, has conferences with government and regulatory speakers, and conducts training courses.

Major Hazards Subcommittee
✍   A subcommittee of the Advisory Committee on Dangerous Substances which closed in 2004.

Mallaig Harbour Authority
■   Harbour Offices, MALLAIG, Inverness-shire, PH41 4QB.
    Tel 01687 462154   Fax 01687 462172
G   Mallaig.
✍   For further information see **Port & Harbour Authorities**.

Manchester Airport Consultative Committee   (MACC)
■   Cheshire East Democratic Services, Westfields, Middlewich Road, SANDBACH, CW11 1HZ.
    Tel 01270 529743   http://www.ukaccs.info/manchester/
    Chairman: Stephen Wilkinson   Assistant Secretary: Rachel Graves
G   Cheshire, Greater Manchester.
✍   For further information see **Airport Consultative Committees**.

Manx Electricity Authority   (MEA)
■   PO Box 177, DOUGLAS, Isle of Man, IM99 1PS.
    Tel 01624 687687   Fax 01624 687612   http://www.gov.im/mea/
    Chairman: Eddie Lowey, MLC   Chief Executive: Ashton Lewis, CEng, FIET
E   Established under the Electricity Act 1996. MEA is constituted as a Statutory Board of Tynwald. The Board comprises seven members including the Chairman.
R   To provide the people of the Isle of Man with a safe, reliable and economic electricity supply.
G   Isle of Man.

Manx National Heritage   (MNH)
■   Kingswood Grove, DOUGLAS, Isle of Man, IM1 3LY.
    Tel 01624 648000   Fax 01624 648001   http://www.gov.im/mnh/
E   Established in 1992.
R   To combine heritage responsibilities on behalf of the Government and the people of the Isle of Man, including the National Archive, the National Monuments Service, the National Museum Service and the National Trust Service.
G   Isle of Man.

Marine & Fisheries Agency
✍   Closed on 31 March 2010 when its functions were transferred to the **Marine Management Organisation**.

Marine Information Council   See **United Kingdom Marine Information Council**.

Marine Management Organisation   (MMO)
■   PO Box 1275, NEWCASTLE UPON TYNE, NE99 5BN.
    Tel 0300 123 1302   Fax 0191 376 2681   http://www.marinemanagement.org.uk
    Interim Chairman: Dr Derek Langslow   Acting Chief Executive: James Cross
E   Established on 1 April 2010 under the Marine & Coastal Access Act 2009, it incorporates the work of the Marine & Fisheries Agency. MMO functions as an Executive NDPB of the Department for Environment, Food & Rural Affairs. The Board comprises nine members including the Chairman.
R   To implement a new marine planning system and a new marine licensing scheme.
    To manage UK fishing fleet capacity and UK fisheries quotas.
    To work with Natural England and the Joint Nature Conservation Committee (qqv) to create and manage a network of marine protected areas.
    To respond to marine emergencies alongside other agencies.
G   United Kingdom.

© CBD Research Ltd · Beckenham · Kent BR3 5JS · Tel 020 8650 7745 · Fax 020 8650 0768 · E-mail cbd@cbdresearch.com · www.cbdresearch.com

Marine Scotland

■ 1st Floor, Victoria Quay, EDINBURGH, EH6 6QQ.   http://www.scotland.gov.uk/marinescotland
   Acting Director: Linda Rosborough
E Established on 1 April 2009 by the merger of Fisheries Research Services and the Scottish Fisheries Protection
   Agency with the Scottish Government Marine Directorate. Marine Scotland functions as a Directorate of the
   Scottish Government.
R To manage Scotland's seas for prosperity and environmental sustainability.
G Scotland.

Marine Stewardship Council   (MSC)

■ 3rd Floor, Mountbarrow House, 6-20 Elizabeth Street, LONDON, SW1W 9RB.
   Tel 020 7811 3300   **Fax** 020 7811 3301   http://www.msc.org
   Chairman: Will Martin   Chief Executive: Rupert Howes
E Established in 1997 by Unilever and the World Wide Fund for Nature, the MSC has been independent since 1999.
   It functions as an independent, global, non-profit making organisation in more than 20 countries. The Board of
   Trustees comprises a maximum of 15 members.
R To harness consumer purchasing power to generate change and promote environmentally responsible
   stewardship of the world's most important renewable food source.
G International.
● The Council has regional offices in New South Wales and Seattle and a number of local offices.

Maritime & Coastguard Agency   (MCA)

■ Spring Place, 105 Commercial Road, SOUTHAMPTON, Hants, SO15 1EG.
   Tel 023 8032 9102   **Fax** 023 8032 9105   http://www.mcga.gov.uk
   Chief Executive: Alan Massey
E Established on 1 April 1998 by the merger of the Coastguard Agency and the Marine Safety Agency. MCA
   functions as an Executive Agency of the Department for Transport. The Agency's board comprises three
   executive and three non-executive directors.
R To provide a 24-hour maritime Search & Rescue service.
   To prevent pollution from ships and minimise the effects of pollution incidents.
   To maintain the safety, security and environmental standards of commercial vessels flying the UK flag, and the
   safety of seafarers serving on those vessels.
G United Kingdom.

Marshall Aid Commemoration Commission

■ Woburn House, 20-24 Tavistock Square, LONDON, WC1H 9HF.
   Tel 020 7380 6700   http://www.marshallscholarship.org
   Chairman: Dr Frances Dow   Executive Secretary: Dr John Kirkland, BSc, PhD
E Established in 1953 under the Marshall Aid Commemoration Act 1953, extended by the Marshall Scholarships Act
   1959. It functions as an Executive NDPB of the Foreign & Commonwealth Office. The Commission comprises
   ten members including the Chairman.
R To oversee the Marshall Scholarships which finance young Americans of high ability to study for a degree in the
   United Kingdom; up to 40 Scholars are selected each year, the Scholarships mainly funded by the Foreign &
   Commonwealth Office.
G United Kingdom.
✍ The Scholarships commemorate the humane ideals of the Marshall Plan and express the continuing gratitude of
   the British people to their American counterparts.

Martial Arts Development Commission   (MADeC)

■ PO Box 416, WEMBLEY, Middx, HA0 3WD.
   Tel 0870 770 0461   **Fax** 0870 770 0462   http://www.madec.org
   Chairman: Richard Thomas
E MADeC is the governing body for martial arts in the UK.
G United Kingdom.

Mathematics in Education & Industry   (MEI)

■ Monckton House, Epsom Centre, White Horse Business Park, TROWBRIDGE, BA14 0XG.
   Tel 01225 776776   **Fax** 01225 775755   http://www.mei.org.uk
   Chairman: Peter Mitchell
   Chief Executive: Roger Porkess
E Established in the early 1960s. MEI is a membership body, an independent curriculum body and a registered
   charity. The board comprises ten members including the Chairman.

R   To promote inspirational teaching, train and motivate teachers, and support and improve mathematics in the workplace.
     To innovate, develop and publish teaching and learning resources.
     To create specifications and schemes of assessment.
G   United Kingdom.

Measurement Advisory Committee
✍   The Committee published its final report in February 2007.

Meat Hygiene Policy Forum   (MHPF)
■   Aviation House, 125 Kingsway, LONDON, WC2B 6NH.
     Tel 020 7276 8000
E   Established on 16 April 2002. MHPF functions as an advisory committee of the Food Standards Agency (qv).
R   To provide those with an interest in meat hygiene issues - consumers, enforcers, retailers and the meat industry - with the opportunity to discuss meat hygiene issues with the FSA officials responsible for policy development and implementation.
G   United Kingdom.

Meat Hygiene Service
✍   MHS merged with the **Food Standards Agency**, of which it had been an Executive Agency, on 1 April 2010.

Meat & Livestock Commission
✍   Wound up on 31 March 2008 as part of a re-organisation of levy boards. The new body is the **Agriculture & Horticulture Development Board**.

Meat Promotion Wales   (HCC)
■   Ty Rheidol, Parc Merlin, ABERYSTWYTH, Ceredigion, SY23 3FF.
     Tel 01970 625050   Fax 01970 615148
     email www.hccmpw.org.uk
     Chairman: Dai Davies   Chief Executive: Gwyn Howells
E   Established in 2003 by the former Meat & Livestock Commission. Since 1 April 2007 HCC is responsible to the Welsh Government. The Board comprises eight members including the Chairman.
R   To improve quality, increase cost-effectiveness and add value to red meat products across the whole supply chain in Wales.
G   Wales.
=   Hybu Cig Cymru

Meat Training Council   (MTC)
■   PO Box 141, Winterhill House, Snowdon Drive, MILTON KEYNES, Bucks, MK6 1YY.
     Tel 01908 231062   Fax 01908 231063   http://www.meattraining.org.uk
     Chairman: Bill Jermey
E   The MTC is a registered charity limited by guarantee. Through its subsidiary, Food & Drink Qualifications Ltd (a company limited by guarantee), the MTC is the awarding body for courses and qualifications in the meat and poultry sector.
G   United Kingdom.
✍   See also the **Federation of Awarding Bodies**.

Medical Academic Staff Committee   (MASC)
■   BMA House, Tavistock Square, LONDON, WC1H 9JP.
     Tel 020 7383 6615   Fax 020 7383 6400   http://www.bma.org.uk
     Co-Chairmen: Prof Michael Rees and Dr Peter Dangerfield
E   Established as a Branch of Practice Committee of the British Medical Association. The Committee comprises up to 36 members including the Chairmen.
R   To represent all doctors who are full time personnel with contracts of employment from a university, medical school, the Medical Research Council (qv), or other institution engaged in medical research.
G   United Kingdom.
✍   See **British Medical Association** [Branch of Practice Committees] for further information.

Medical Advisory Panels on Driving   See **Secretary of State for Transport's Honorary Medical Advisory Panels**.

Medical Council on Alcohol   (MCA)

■   5 St Andrew's Place, LONDON, NW1 4LB.
    Tel 020 7487 4445   **Fax** 020 7935 4479   http://www.m-c-a.org.uk

E   Established in 1967. MCA is a membership organisation of 370 members, either medical professionals with an interest in alcoholism or alcohol professionals with interest in the effects of alcohol on health. It functions as a registered charity and company limited by guarantee.

R   To improve medical understanding of alcohol related problems.

G   United Kingdom.

✍   MCA seeks to ensure that medical students are suitably aware of the risks associated with alcohol both on their practice and on their own health. As well as educating doctors and medical students, MCA gives advice to certain other bodies as well as being a link for doctors concerned about their own use of alcohol.

Medical Devices Agency

✍   Merged on 1 April 2003 with the Medicines Control Agency to form the **Medicines & Healthcare products Regulatory Agency**.

Medical Education England   (MEE)

■   Room 531B, Skipton House, 80 London Road, LONDON, SE1 6LH.
    Tel 020 7972 5894   http://www.mee.nhs.org.uk
    Chairman: Prof Sir Christopher Edwards   Managing Director: Christine Outram

E   Established in 2009. MEE functions as an Advisory NDPD of the Department of Health. The Board comprises 29 members including the Chairman.

R   To provide independent expert advice to Ministers and input into the policy-making process on the content and structure of professional education and training as it relates to dental teams, doctors, healthcare scientists and technologists, and pharmacy teams, and on the quality of workforce planning for these groups at a national level.

G   England.

Medical Ethics Committee   (MEC)

■   BMA House, Tavistock Square, LONDON, WC1H 9JP.
    Tel 020 7383 6286   **Fax** 020 7383 6400   http://www.bma.org.uk
    Chairman: Dr Anthony Calland

E   Established as a professional committee of the British Medical Association. The committee comprises 18 members.

R   To consider the ethical implications of all matters to do with the practice of medicine and relations between doctors their patients.
    To produce ethical advice and guidance on specific issues.

G   United Kingdom.

✍   See **British Medical Association** [Boards & Committees] for further information.

Medical Research Council   (MRC)

■   2nd Floor David Phillips Building, Polaris House, North Star Avenue, SWINDON, Wilts, SN2 1FL.
    Tel 01793 416200   http://www.mrc.ac.uk
    14th Floor, One Kemble Street, LONDON, WC2B 4AN.
    Chairman: Sir John Chisholm   Chief Executive: Sir John Savill

E   Established in 1913 as the Medical Research Committee to administer funds provided for medical research under the terms of the National Insurance Act 1911; the Council was incorporated under its present title by Royal Charter in 1920. MRC functions as an independent NDPB accountable to the Department for Business, Innovation & Skills. The Council currently comprises 14 members including the Chairman.

R   To support research across the biomedical spectrum, from fundamental lab-based science to clinical trials, and in all major disease areas, with the aim of improving human health.

G   United Kingdom.

✍   For further information see **Research Councils UK**.

Medical Research Scotland   The operational name of the **Scottish Hospital Endowments Research Trust**.

Medical Schools Council   (MSC)

- ■ Woburn House, 20 Tavistock Square, LONDON, WC1H 9HD.
  Tel 020 7419 5494   **Fax** 020 7380 1482   http://www.medschools.ac.uk
  Chairman: Prof Sir John Tooke
- E Established in January 1992 as the Council of Heads of Medical Schools, adopting its current name in 2006. The Council comprises 31 members including the Chairman.
- R To represent the interests and ambitions of UK medical schools as they relate to the generation of national health, wealth and knowledge, through biomedical research and the profession of medicine.
- G United Kingdom.

Medical Students Committee   (MSC)

- ■ BMA House, Tavistock Square, LONDON, WC1H 9JP.
  Tel 020 7383 6274   **Fax** 020 7383 6400   http://www.bma.org.uk
  Co-Chairmen: Nick Deakin and Tom Foley
- E Established as a Branch of Practice Committee of the British Medical Association. The Committee comprises an elected representative from each UK medical school.
- R To represent the views of BMA medical student members, to facilitate co-operation between student members and the medical profession, and to discuss with the Department of Health pay and conditions of service for medical students working in the NHS.
- G United Kingdom.
- ✍ See **British Medical Association** [Branch of Practice Committees] for further information.

Medical Supplies Agency

- ✍ Ceased 1 April 2005, its functions transferred to the **Defence Equipment & Support** agency.

Medicines Commission

- ✍ On 30 October 2005 the **Commission on Human Medicines** was established, combining the functions of this and the Committee on Safety of Medicines.

Medicines Control Agency

- ✍ Merged on 1 April 2003 with the Medical Devices Agency to form the **Medicines & Healthcare products Regulatory Agency**.

Medicines & Healthcare products Regulatory Agency   (MHRA)

- ■ 151 Buckingham Palace Road, LONDON, SW1W 9SZ.
  Tel 020 3080 6000   http://www.mhra.gov.uk
  Chairman: Prof Sir Alasdair Breckenridge, CBE   Chief Executive: Prof Kent Woods
- E Established on 1 April 2003 following the merger of the Medical Devices Agency and the Medicines Control Agency. MHRA functions as an Executive Agency of the Department of Health. The board comprises eight members including the Chairman.
- R To ensure that medicines and medical devices work and are acceptably safe.
- G United Kingdom.
- ● The Agency is assisted in its work by the following statutory bodies:
  British Pharmacopoeia Commission
  Commission on Human Medicines, and its 16 Expert Advisory Groups
  In Vitro Diagnostic Advisory Committee (qqv).
  The following former NDPBs have been reconstituted as committees of experts:
  Advisory Board on the Registration of Homoeopathic Products
  Herbal Medicines Advisory Committee
  Independent Review Panel on the Advertising of Medicines
  Independent Review Panel on the Classification of Borderline Products.

Medicines for Women's Health Expert Advisory Group

- ■ 151 Buckingham Palace Road, LONDON, SW1W 9SZ.
  Tel 020 3080 6000
  Chairman: Dr Mary Armitage, BSc, MB, ChB(Hons), DM, FRCP, FRCPE
- E Established in 2005. The Group functions as an advisory body to the Commission on Human Medicines (qv). It comprises 14 members including the Chairman.

R   To advise the CHM on the safety and efficacy of medicines related to endocrinology and women's reproductive health from menarche to menopause and conditions related to the menopause, such as osteoporosis. The medicines include medicines for contraception, emergency contraception and termination of pregnancy, medicines for infertility and assisted conception, hormone replacement therapy and non-hormonal treatments for osteoporosis.

G   United Kingdom.

Medico-Legal Committee   (MLC)

■   BMA House, Tavistock Square, LONDON, WC1H 9JP.
Tel 020 7383 6611   Fax 020 7383 6400   http://www.bma.org.uk
Chairman: Dr Jan Wise

E   Established as a standing committee of the British Medical Association.

R   To consider and report on medico-legal issues of direct concern to the profession, including those referred to the committee by the BMA Council, Political Board, other BMA committees and external bodies.

G   United Kingdom.

✍   See **British Medical Association** [Boards & Committees] for further information.

Members Estimate Committee   See **United Kingdom Parliament: Committees**.

Mental Health Act Commission
✍   The Commission ceased to exist on 31 March 2009. The new health and social care regulator is the **Care Quality Commission**.

Mental Health Commission for Northern Ireland
✍   Under the Health & Social Care (Reform) Act (Northern Ireland) 2009, the Commission's duties were transferred to the **Regulation & Quality Improvement Authority**.

Mental Health Media
✍   Merged in 2008 with the mental health charity Mind.

Mental Health Review Tribunal for Northern Ireland   (MHRT)

■   3rd Floor, Bedford House, 16-22 Bedford Street, BELFAST, BT2 7FD.
Tel 028 9072 4843   Fax 028 9031 3510

E   Established in 1986 under the Mental Health (Northern Ireland) Order 1986. The tribunal functions as an Advisory NDPB of the Department of Health, Social Services & Public Safety Northern Ireland.

R   To review the cases of patients who are detained or subject to guardianship under the 1986 Order.

G   Northern Ireland.

Mental Health Review Tribunal for Wales   (MHRT)

■   Crown Buildings, Cathays Park, CARDIFF, CF10 3NQ.
Tel 029 2082 5328   http://www.mhrt.org.uk
Clerk: Antonia Castello

E   Established in 1983 under the Mental Health Act 1983. MHRT for Wales is an independent judicial body and functions as a Tribunal NDPB of the National Assembly for Wales.

R   To review the cases of patients detained under provisions made in the Mental Health Act 1983, and to direct the discharge of any patients where the statutory criteria for discharge have been satisfied.

G   Wales.

=   Dribiwlys Adolygu Iechyd Meddwi Cymru

Mental Health Review Tribunals   [England]
✍   See **First-tier Tribunal (Mental Health)**.

Mental Health Tribunal for Scotland   (MHTS)

■   First Floor, Bothwell House, Hamilton Business Park, Caird Park, HAMILTON, ML3 0QA.
Tel 01698 390000   Fax 01698 390010   http://www.mhtscot.org
President: Dr Joe Morrow   Chief Executive: Patricia Lewis

E   Established on 5 October 2005 under the Mental Health Care (Care & Treatment) (Scotland) Act 2003. MHTS functions as a Tribunal NDPB of the Scottish Executive Health Department. Each Tribunal comprises a Legal Member (a solicitor or advocate) who acts as Convenor, a Medical Member (a psychiatrist experienced in the diagnosis and treatment of mental disorders) and a General Member (people with experience or qualifications in social care facilities); The three members are selected from a pool of approximately 350.

R   To make decisions and issue orders regarding the long-term compulsory care and treatment of people with mental disorders.

G   Scotland.

Mental Welfare Commission for Scotland   (MWC)
■   Thistle House, 91 Haymarket Terrace, EDINBURGH, EH12 5HE.
    Tel 0131 313 8777   http://www.mwcscot.org.uk
    Chairman: Very Revd Dr Graham Forbes, CBE
E   Established in 1960, under the Mental Health (Scotland) Act 1960, its role extended by the Adults with Incapacity (Scotland) Act 2000. MWC functions as an NHS body of the Scottish Executive Health Department. The Commission comprises eight members including the Chairman.
R   To protect people who may, by reason of mental disorder, are incapable of protecting themselves or their interests adequately.
G   Scotland.
●   The Commission investigates alleged deficiencies for care and treatment by patients in hospitals and in the community, and reports as appropriate to the relevant authorities.

Merchant Navy Training Board   (MNTB)
■   Carthusian Court, 12 Carthusian Street, LONDON, EC1M 6EZ.
    Tel 020 7417 8400   **Fax** 020 7726 2080   http://www.mntb.org.uk
    Chairman: Captain Nigel Palmer, OBE
E   Established in 1937. MNTB is a voluntary body. The Board comprises the Chairmen and 17 members drawn from employer companies, seafarer organisations and educational bodies.
R   To be the authoritative centre of expertise and information on careers, qualifications, education and training, and skill needs in the industry.
G   United Kingdom.

Merchant Navy Welfare Board   (MNWB)
■   30 Palmerston Road, SOUTHAMPTON, Hants, SO14 1LL.
    Tel 023 8033 7799   **Fax** 023 8063 4444   http://www.mnwb.org
    Chief Executive: David Parsons
E   Established on 31 March 1948. The Board has over 40 constituent member charities; it functions as a registered charity and company limited by guarantee. The Council of Management has 24 members.
R   To assess the welfare needs of merchant seafarers and their dependents.
    To coordinate the work of the societies and charitable organisations concerned with the provision of welfare services.
G   United Kingdom.

Merseyside Integrated Transport Authority   (MITA)
■   24 Hatton Garden, LIVERPOOL, L3 2AN.
    Tel 0151 227 5181   **Fax** 0151 236 2457
    Chairman: Cllr Mark Dowd
E   Established on 15 September 1985 under the Local Government Act 1985 and known as the Merseyside Passenger Transport Authority until renamed on 9 February 2009 under the Local Transport Act 2008. The Authority comprises 18 Councillors who are appointed by the five Metropolitan District Councils that make up Merseyside.
G   Merseyside.
✍   For further information see **Passenger Transport Executives & Integrated Transport Authorities**.

Merseyside Maritime Museum   See **National Museums Liverpool**.

The Merseyside Partnership   (TMP)
■   12 Princes Parade, LIVERPOOL, L3 1BG.
    Tel 0151 227 2727   **Fax** 0151 227 2325   http://www.most.merseyside.org.uk
    Chief Executive: Lorraine Rogers

G Merseyside (Halton, Knowsley, Liverpool, Sefton, St Helens and Wirral Boroughs).
✍ One of the five tourist boards supported by the Northwest Region Development Board (qv).

Merseyside Passenger Transport Executive Operates under the brand name **Merseytravel**.

Merseyside Police Authority   (MPA)
■ West House, Mercury Court, Tithebarn Street, LIVERPOOL, L69 2NU.
   Tel 0151 236 4748 Fax 0151 236 4527 http://www.merseysidepoliceauthority.gov.uk
   Chairman: Cllr Bill Weightman
E Established in April 1995, the Authority is an independent body charged with ensuring that Merseyside Police
   provide an effective and efficient police service.
   It is made up of eight councillor members and eight independent members.
G Merseyside.
✍ For further information see **Police Authorities**.

Merseyside Probation Trust
■ Burlington House, Crosby Road North, Waterloo, LIVERPOOL, L22 0PJ.
   Tel 0151 920 9201 Fax 0151 949 0528 http://www.merseysideprobationtrust.org
   Chairman: Linda Bloomfield Chief Executive: John Stafford
E Established on 1 April 2001 under the Criminal Justice & Court Service Act 2000 as the Merseyside Probation
   Area Board. It became a trust on 1 April 2008 under the Offender Management Act 2007. The Board comprises
   eight members including the Chairman.
G Merseyside.
✍ For further information see **Probation Trusts**.

Merseytravel
■ 24 Hatton Garden, LIVERPOOL, L3 2AN.
   Tel 0151 227 5181 Fax 0151 236 2457 http://www.merseytravel.gov.uk
   Chief Executive: Neil Scales, OBE
E Established on 1 December 1969 under the Transport Act 1968, the Merseyside Passenger Transport Executive
   has operated as Merseytravel since October 1986. Merseytravel is responsible to the Merseyside Integrated
   Transport Authority (qv).
G Merseyside.
✍ Since 1988 the Merseyside Integrated Transport Authority, a separate entity, has operated with the Executive
   under the Merseytravel corporate brand.For further information see **Passenger Transport Executives &
   Integrated Transport Authorities**.

Merthyr Tydfil Local Health Board
✍ Merged on 1 October 2009 with the Rhondda Cynon Taff Local Health Board to form **Cwm Taf Health Board**.

Met Office
■ FitzRoy Road, EXETER, Devon, EX1 3PB.
   Tel 01392 885680 Fax 01392 885681 http://www.metoffice.com
   Chairman: Robert Napier Chief Executive: John Hirst Shareholder Executive contact: Peter Shortt
E Established on 2 April 1990. It now functions as an Executive Agency of the Ministry of Defence. The board
   comprises twelve members including the Chairman.
R To provide meteorological services, including climate advice, to Government departments, the Armed Forces, the
   public, civil aviation, shipping, industry and commerce.
G United Kingdom.
✍ One of the businesses managed by the **Shareholder Executive**.

Meteorological Office See **Met Office**.

Metro
■ Wellington House, 40-50 Wellington Street, LEEDS, W Yorks, LS1 2DE.
   Tel 0113 251 7272 Fax 0113 251 7333 http://www.wymetro.com
   Chairman: Cllr Chris Greaves Director General: Kieran Preston

---

E   Established in 1986 under the Local Government Act 1985 as the West Yorkshire Passenger Transport Executive. It operates under the brand name Metro. Metro is responsible to the West Yorkshire Integrated Transport Authority (qv).

G   West Yorkshire.

✍   For further information see **Passenger Transport Executives & Integrated Transport Authorities**.

Metropolitan Police Authority   (MPA)

■   10 Dean Farrar Street, LONDON, SW1H 0NY.
Tel 020 7202 0202   **Fax** 020 7202 0200   http://www.mpa.gov.uk
Chairman: Kit Malthouse   Chief Executive: Catherine Crawford

E   Established on 3 July 2000 following the formation of the Greater London Authority (qv). MPA is directly responsible to the Mayor of London at the GLA. The Authority comprises 23 members including the Chairman.

R   To make sure that the Metropolitan Police Service is accountable for the services it provides to the people in the capital.

G   Greater London.

✍   Part of the GLA Group - see **Greater London Authority** for more details.
See also **Police Authorities** for further information.

Mevagissey Harbour

■   Harbour Office, Mevagissey, ST AUSTELL, Cornwall, PL26 6QU.
Tel 01726 843305   **Fax** 01726 842535   http://www.mevagisseyharbour.co.uk
Harbour Master: Captain Hugh Bowles

E   A trust port and registered charity, established by the Mevagissey Harbour Act 1774.

G   Mevagissey.

✍   For further information see **Port & Harbour Authorities**.

MG ALBA

■   Seaforth Road, STORNOWAY, Isle of Lewis, HS1 2SO.
Tel 01851 705550   **Fax** 01851 706432   http://www.mgalba.com
Chairman: Alasdair Morrison   Chief Executive: Donald Campbell

E   Established under the Communications Act 2003. MG ALBA is the operating name of the **Gaelic Media Service (Seirbheis nam Meadhanan Gàidhlig)**. The Board comprises the Chairman and up to eleven other members.

R   To ensure a wide and diverse range of high quality Gaelic programmes is made available to persons in Scotland.

G   Scotland.

✍   MG ALBA formed a partnership with the BBC to broadcast BBC Alba, Scotland's Gaelic television channel, which was launched on 19 September 2008.

Microbiological Research Authority

✍   No longer in existence.

Microbiology Advisory Committee   (MAC)

■   151 Buckingham Palace Road, LONDON, SW1W 9SZ.
Tel 020 3080 7306
Secretariat: Ian Smith

E   MAC functions as an ad-hoc advisory group to the Medicines and Healthcare products Regulatory Agency (MHRA), qv.

R   To advise the Department of Health, through MHRA, on disinfection and sterilisation practices for medical devices applicable in and appropriate to the health service.

G   United Kingdom.

Midlands Agricultural Land Tribunal

■   Defra Building, Electra Way, CREWE, Cheshire, CW1 6GJ.
Tel 01270 754156   **Fax** 01270 754260
Secretary: Mr M Baker

E   Established under the Agriculture Act 1947 (Section 73).

G   Derbyshire, Herefordshire, Leicestershire, Nottinghamshire, Warwickshire, West Midlands, Worcestershire.

✍   For further information see **Agricultural Land Tribunals**.

Midlands Regional Flood Defence Committee   Also known as the Severn-Trent Flood Defence Committee; see **Environment Agency** [Midlands Region].

Midlands Rent Assessment Panel   (MRAP)
■   2nd Floor, Louisa House, 92-93 Edward Street, BIRMINGHAM, B1 2RA.
       Tel 0121 236 7837   Fax 0121 236 9337
G   Derbyshire, Leicestershire, Nottinghamshire, Rutland, Shropshire, Staffordshire, Warwickshire, West Midlands, Worcestershire.
✍   For further information on the five regional panels see **Rent Assessment Panels** [England].

Migration Advisory Committee   (MAC)
■   1st Floor, Green Park House, 29 Wellesley Road, CROYDON, Surrey, CR0 2AJ.
       Tel 020 8760 2812
       Chairman: Prof David Metcalf, CBE
E   Established on 7 December 2007. MAC functions as an Advisory NDPB of the UK Border Agency (qv). The Committee comproses the Chairman and four other independent economists.
R   To provide transparent, independent and evidence-based advice to Government on where skilled labour market shortages exist that can sensibly be filled by migration.
G   United Kingdom.

Milford Haven Port Authority
■   Gorsewood Drive, Hakin, MILFORD HAVEN, Pembrokeshire, SA73 3ER.
       Tel 01646 696100   Fax 01646 696125   http://www.mhpa.co.uk
       Chairman: David Benson   Chief Executive: Ted Sangster
E   Established under the Milford Haven Conservancy Act 1958, as amended by the Milford Haven Port Authority Acts & Orders 1983 to 2002.
       The board comprises up to ten non-executive members, including the Chairman, and up to three executive members, including the Chief Executive.
G   Milford Haven.
✍   For further information see **Port & Harbour Authorities**.

Military Aviation Authority   (MAA)
■   Spur 10, Block E, MOD Ensleigh, Granville Road, BATH, BA1 9BE.
       Director General: Air Marshal Timo Anderson
E   Established on 1 April 2010 following recommendations made in the Nimrod Review Report published in October 2009. MAA brings together the regulatory functions of the Directorate of Aviation Regulation & Safety, Defence Aerospace & Air Traffic Management, the Air Systems Group and the Military Flight Test Regulator.
R   To execute on behalf of the Secretary of State for Defence an integrated suite of regulatory, surveillance, inspection and assurance functions across the defence air operating and technical domains, to underpin the safe design and use of military systems within the defence operating context.
G   United Kingdom.
●   MAA comprises:
       Operations Group
       Technical Group
       Military Air Accident Investigation Branch.

Military Corrective Training Centre   See **Independent Board of Visitors to the Military Corrective Training Centre Colchester**.

Military Court Service   (MCS)
■   Building 398, Trenchard Lines, Upavon, PEWSEY, Wilts, SN9 6BE.
       Tel 01980 618058   Fax 01980 618060
E   Formed in January 2004 by the merger of the Army and Royal Air Force court staffs, joined by the Royal Navy in 2007. MCS is headed by a civil servant (Director MCS), appointed by the Defence Council (qv).
R   To provide a criminal court service for the Royal Navy, Army and Royal Air Force in the Court Martial, Summary Appeal Court and Service Civilian Court.
G   United Kingdom.
●   There are five permanently manned Military Court Centres in the UK at Aldergrove, Bulford, Catterick, Colchester and Portsmouth, and one in Germany at Sennelager.

Milk Development Council
✍ On 1 April 2008 was replaced by **DairyCo**.

Millennium Commission
✍ Responsibilities were transferred in 2006 to its successor body, the **Big Lottery Fund**.

Milton Keynes Partnership Committee (MKPC)
■ Central Business Exchange II, 414-428 Midsummer Boulevard, MILTON KEYNES, Bucks, MK9 2EA.
   Tel 01908 353636 **Fax** 01908 353963 http://www.miltonkeynespartnership.info
   Chairman: Dr Ann Limb
E Established in June 2004. MKPC functions as a committee of the Homes & Communities Agency (qv) and
   operates as Milton Keynes Partnership (MKP). The Committee comprises 16 members including the Chairman.
R To coordinate and implement the delivery of growth and development in the new city.
G Milton Keynes.
✍ For further information see **Urban Development Corporations**.

Mineral Products Qualifications Council (MPQC)
■ 7 Regent Street, NOTTINGHAM, NG1 5BS.
   Tel 0115 964 4926 http://www.epicltd.com
E Established in August 2008, replacing EMP Awarding Body Ltd and EPIC Training & Consulting Services Ltd.
   MPQC is the awarding body for courses and qualifications in the extractive and mineral processing industries.
G United Kingdom.
✍ For further information on awarding bodies see the **Federation of Awarding Bodies**.

Mines Inspectorate   See **Her Majesty's Inspectorate of Mines**.

Mining Industry Committee (MIC)
■ 1/2 Redgrave Court, Merton Road, BOOTLE, Merseyside, L20 7HS.
   Tel 0845 345 0055
E Established in 1995. MIC functions as an Advisory NDPB of the Health & Safety Commission (qv).
R To provide a forum for the mining industry to maintain and improve major hazard controls and standards of health
   and safety.
G United Kingdom.
● MIC is assisted in its work by three sub-committees:
      Escape & Rescue Operations in Mines Working Group
      National Technical Liaison Committee for Safe Manriding in Mines
      Safety & Health in Mines Research Advisory Board.

Mining Qualifications Board (MQB)
■ Foundry House, 3 Millsands, Riverside Exchange, SHEFFIELD, S Yorks, S3 8NH.
   Tel 0845 345 0055
E The current Board was established by the Management & Administration of Safety & Health at Mines Regulations
   1993 which came into operation on 1 October 1993.
R To advise the Health & Safety Executive (qv) on the setting of standards for the approval of qualifications under
   Regulation 17 of the 1993 regulations.
G United Kingdom.

Ministerial Advisory Group (MAG)
■ DCAL, Causeway Exchange, 1-7 Bedford Street, BELFAST, BT2 7FB.
   Tel 028 9025 8825 **Fax** 028 9082 3450
   Chairman: Arthur Acheson
E Established in September 2007. MAG functions as an Advisory NDPD of the Department for Culture, Arts &
   Leisure Northern Ireland. The Group comprises nine members including the Chairman.
R To be the Ministerial Design Champion on the implementation and development of policy on architecture and the
   built environment in Northern Ireland.
G Northern Ireland.
✍ One of four UK Commissions established to champion good design and a high quality built environment.

Ministerial Board on Deaths in Custody   See **Independent Advisory Panel on Deaths in Custody**.

Ministerial Council on Deaths in Custody   See **Independent Advisory Panel on Deaths in Custody**.

Ministry of Defence Police & Guarding Agency   (MDPGA)
■   HQ Wethersfield, BRAINTREE, Essex, CM7 4AZ.
    Tel 01371 854008
    Chief Executive: Steve Love
E   Established on 1 April 2004 by the merger of Ministry of Defence Police, formed in 1971, and the Ministry of
    Defence Guard Service, formed in 1992. MDPGA functions as an Executive Agency of the Ministry of Defence.
R   To counter various crime and security risks, including terrorist attacks and the threat of such attacks, disruption
    and disorder caused by protesters, theft of key assets, major financial fraud, and unauthorised intrusion onto
    the Defence Estate.
G   United Kingdom.

Mission & Public Affairs
■   Church House, Great Smith Street, LONDON, SW1P 3AZ.
    Tel 020 7898 1000
    Director: Malcolm Brown
E   Established on 1 April 2003 following the merger of the former Archbishops' Council Board of Mission and the
    Church of England Board of Social Responsibility. It functions as a division of the Archbishops' Council.
R   To coordinate, promote and further the national work of the Church of England in the fields of
        Mission and evangelism,
        Community and public affairs, and
        Healthcare chaplaincy.
G   England.

Misuse of Drugs Advisory Council   See **Advisory Council on the Misuse of Drugs**.

Misuse of Drugs Professional Panel
✍   No longer in existence.

Mobile Telecommunications & Health Research Programme Committee   (MHTR)
■   Radiation Protection Division, Chilton, DIDCOT, Oxon, OX11 0RQ.
    Tel 01235 822887   **Fax** 01235 834925   http://www.mthr.org.uk
    Chairman: Prof David Coggon, OBE
E   Established in 2001 on the recommendation of the Independent Expert Group on Mobile Phones (Stewart
    Committee). MTHR is part of the Health Protection Agency (qv). The Committee comprises twelve members
    including the Chairman.
R   To coordinate and scientifically manage a research programme into the possible impact on health of mobile
    telecommunications.
G   United Kingdom.

Mobility & Access Committee for Scotland   (MACS)
■   Area 2D Dockside, Victoria Quay, EDINBURGH, EH6 6QQ.
    Tel 0131 244 0869   http://www.macs-mobility.org
    Convener: Anne MacLean, OBE
E   Established on 22 March 2002 under the Transport (Scotland) Act 2001. MACS functions as an Advisory NDPB of
    the Scottish Executive Enterprise, Transport & Lifelong Learning Department. The Committee comprises eleven
    members including the Convenor.
R   To advise Scottish Ministers on the travel needs of disabled people.
G   Scotland.

Momentum
■   NiSoft House, Ravenhill Business Park, Ravenhill Road, BELFAST, BT6 8AW.
    Tel 028 9045 0101   **Fax** 028 9045 2123   http://www.momentumni.org
    Chairman: Ed Brown
E   Established in 1994. Momentum is a membership organisation and is a recognised Sector Training Council
    representing the information, communications and technology industry.

R   To design and deliver a range of innovative member services which support the development of a globally competitive ICT industry in Northern Ireland, in particular developing skills in both quantity and quality.

G   Northern Ireland.

✍   For further information see **Sector Training Councils**.

Monetary Policy Committee   See **Bank of England Monetary Policy Committee**.

Monitor - Independent Regulator of NHS Foundation Trusts

■   4 Matthew Parker Street, LONDON, SW1H 9NP.
Tel 020 7340 2400   **Fax** 020 7340 2401   http://www.monitor-nhsft.gov.uk
Chairman & Interim Chief Executive: Dr David Bennett

E   Established in January 2004, its functions and powers are detailed in the National Health Service Act 2006. Monitor functions as an Executive NDPB of the Department of Health. The Board comprises five members including the Chairman.

R   To determine if NHS trusts are ready to become NHS foundation trusts.
To ensure that NHS foundation trusts comply with the conditions they signed up to, and that they are well managed and financially robust.
To support NHS foundation trust development.

G   United Kingdom.

Monmouthshire Local Health Board

✍   Merged on 1 October with the Blaenau Gwent, Caerphilly, Newport and Torfaen Local Health Boards to form **Aneurin Bevan Health Board**.

Montgomery Community Health Council

■   Room 203, Ladywell House, NEWTOWN, Powys, SY16 1JB.
Tel 01686 627632   **Fax** 01686 629091
Chairman: Dave Morrell   Chief Officer: John Howard

E   Established in 1974 The Council comprises twelve members including the Chairman.

G   North Powys.

✍   For further information see **Community Health Councils** under **National Health Service - Wales**.

Montrose Port Authority

■   Harbour Office, South Quay, Ferryden, MONTROSE, DD10 9SL.
Tel 01674 672302   **Fax** 01674 675530   http://www.montroseport.co.uk
Chief Executive: John M Paterson

G   Montrose.

✍   For further information see **Port & Harbour Authorities**.

Moredun Research Institute   **(MRI)**

■   Pentlands Science Park, Bush Loan, PENICUICK, Midlothian, EH26 0PZ.
Tel 0131 445 5111   **Fax** 0131 445 6111   http://www.mri.sari.ac.uk
Chairman: John Jeffrey   Director: Prof Julie Fitzpatrick

E   Established in 1920. MRI is a company limited by guarantee and a registered charity; it also functions as an Executive NDPB of the Scottish Executive Environment & Rural Affairs Department. The Board of Directors comprises nine members including the Chairman.

R   To carry out innovative basic and strategic multidisciplinary research on diseases of sheep and other ruminants which undermine biological efficiency, impair animal welfare or threaten public health.

G   United Kingdom.

✍   For further information see the companion volume **Centres, Bureaux & Research Institutes**.

Motor Vehicle Repair Health & Safety Forum   **(MVR)**

■   Edgar Allen House, 241 Glossop Road, SHEFFIELD, S Yorks, S10 2GW.
Tel 0114 291 2398
Chairman: Peter Woolgar

E   Established in January 1999 by the Health & Safety Executive (qv). The Forum comprises members of the HSE and representatives of trade associations and other bodies with an interest in the automotive repair industry.

R   To consider and advise on the protection of people at work from hazards to health and safety arising out of their work activities connected with any aspect of the repair, maintenance or servicing of all types of motor vehicle.

G   United Kingdom.

Mountain Leader Training   (MLT)

- Siabod Cottage, CAPEL CURIG, Caernarfonshire, LL24 OES.
  Tel 01690 720272   Fax 01690 720248   http://www.mltuk.org
  Chief Officer: Steve Long
- E   Established in 1965 as the Scottish Mountain Leader Training Board, since 1991 it is a national organisation with four home nation boards. MLT is a company limited by guarantee and a registered charity.
- R   To advance education and training in the skills required for leadership and instruction of safe hill, mountain and moorland walking, mountaineering, rock and ice climbing, and other associated activities practised in cliff and mountain environments, and to offer advice on matters of training and safety.
- G   United Kingdom.

Museum of Liverpool   See **National Museums Liverpool**.

The Museum of London

- 150 London Wall, LONDON, EC2Y 5HN.
  Tel 020 7001 9844   http://www.museumoflondon.org.uk
  Chairman: Michael Cassidy, CBE   Director: Prof Jack Lohman
- E   Established on 1 June 1975 by the merger of the London Museum and the Guildhall Museum; it is governed by the Museum of London Acts 1965 and 1986. It functions as an Executive NDPB of the Department of Culture, Media & Sport. The board comprises 20 governers, appointed by the Prime Minister and the City of London.
- R   To communicate London's history, archaeology and contemporary cultures to a wider world.
  To reach all of London's communities through playing a role in the debate about London.
  To facilitate and contribute to London-wide cultural and educational networks.
- G   London.
- ● The Museum of London group comprises:
    The Museum of London
    The Museum of London Docklands
    The Museum of London Archaeology Service
    The London Archaeological Archive & Research Centre.

Museum of Science & Industry   (MOSI)

- Liverpool Road, Castlefield, MANCHESTER, M3 4FP.
  Tel 0161 832 2244   Fax 0161 833 1471   http://www.mosi.org.uk
  Director/Chief Executive: Tony Hill
- E   Originally established in 1969, the Museum opened at its current site on 15 September 1983. MUSI functions as an Executive NDPB of the Department for Culture, Media & Sport. The Board of Trustees comprises 13 members including the Chairman.
- R   To advance the education of the public by securing the preservation, restoration, improvement, enhancement and maintenance of features and objects of industrial, scientific and historical interest in Greater Manchester and surrounding areas.
- G   North West England.
- ● The Museum occupies 5 large listed industrial buildings including the world's oldest railway station.
  The first stages of a £15 million expansion programme opened in 2000, including education, collection storage, exhibition, retail and restaurant facilities.

Museums Archives & Libraries in Wales   See **CyMAL**.

Museums Galleries Scotland   (MGS)

- 1 Papermill Wynd, McDonald Road, EDINBURGH, EH7 4QL.
  Tel 0131 550 4100   Fax 0131 550 4139   http://www.museumsgalleriesscotland.org.uk
  Chairman: Fiona Ballantyne   Chief Executive: Joanne Orr
- E   Established in 1964 as the Scottish Museums Council; it adopted its current name in 2008. MGS is a membership organisation and functions as a company limited by guarantee and a registered charity. The Board comprises 13 members including the Chairman.
- R   To advocate and communicate the contribution museums and galleries make to people's lives.
  To support the development of museums and galleries.
  To promote and provide excellent customer services.
  To build an evidence base to inform policy and support decision making.
  To build partnerships and sustainable relationships at national and regional levels.
- G   Scotland.
- ● MGS has over 350 member museums and galleries.

Museums, Libraries & Archives Council (MLA)

■ Grosvenor House, 14 Bennetts Hill, BIRMINGHAM, B2 5RS.
Tel 0121 345 7300 Fax 0121 345 7303 http://www.mla.gov.uk
Wellcome Wolfson Building, 165 Queen's Gate, LONDON, SW7 5HD.
Tel 020 7273 1444   Fax 020 7273 1404
Chairman: Sir Andrew Motion   Chief Executive: Roy Clare, CBE

E Launched in April 2000, replacing the Museums & Galleries Commission and the Library & Information Commission. MLA functions as an Executive NDPB of the Department for Culture, Media & Sport. Its board comprises eleven members including the Chairman.

R To work with and for the museums, archives and libraries sector to raise professional standards and champion better services for users and readers of all ages and backgrounds, whether residents or visitors.

G England.

● The MLA has 9 regional offices:
MLA East of England, MLA East Midlands, MLA London, MLA North East, MLA North West, MLA South East, MLA South West, MLA West Midlands and MLA Yorkshire.

✎ The Government announced on 26 July 2010 that MLAC would close by March 2012. On 9 December 2010, Arts Council England (qv) announced its agreement to take over a number of MLAC's functions relating to museums and libraries.

Muslim Council of Britain (MCB)

■ PO Box 57330, LONDON, E1 2WJ.
Tel 0845 262 6786 Fax 020 7247 7079 http://www.mcb.org.uk
Secretary General: Dr Muhammad Abdul Bari

E Established on 23 November 1997 by agreement. MCB is a national representative membership body comprising 500 affiliated national, regional and local organisations, mosques, charities and schools.

R To promote cooperation, consensus and unity on Muslim affairs in the UK, and to work for a more enlightened appreciation of Islam and Muslims in the wider society.
To encourage and strengthen all existing efforts being made for the benefit of the Muslim community, and to work for the eradication of disadvantages and forms of discrimination faced by Muslims.
To establish a position for the Muslim community within British society that is fair and based on due rights, and to foster better community relations and work for the good of society as whole.

G United Kingdom.

N

National Advisory Group for the Professional Development of the Children's Workforce in Schools (NAS)

■ City Tower, Piccadilly Plaza, MANCHESTER, M1 4TD.
Tel 0845 600 0991
Chairman: Graham Holley

E Set up in Autumn 2008 replacing the National Reference Group and the School Workforce Development Board. NAG is chaired by the Chief Executive of the Training & Development Agency for Schools (qv) and comprises 27 members.

R To advise the TDA on the professional development of teachers and support staff.

G England.

National Air Traffic Management Advisory Committee (NATMAC)

■ K6 G7, CAA House, 45-59 Kingsway, LONDON, WC2B 6TE.
Tel 020 7453 6523 Fax 020 7453 6565 http://www.caa.co.uk
Chairman: Mark Swan

E Established on 1 January 1977. NATMAC is a non-statutory body but the Civil Aviation Act 1982 as amended required the CAA's Directorate of Airspace Policy to consult with the aviation industry. The Committee comprises 28 representatives from the whole spectrum of the UK aviation community and is chaired by the Director of Airspace Policy.

R To assist the the CAA's Directorate of Airspace Policy in the development of airspace policies, configurations and procedures in order that due attention may be given to the various requirements of all the national users of UK airspace, both civil & military.

G United Kingdom.

National Air Traffic Services   See **NATS**.

National Apprenticeship Service   (NAS)
■   Cheylesmore House, Quinton Road, COVENTRY, CV1 2WT.
    Tel 024 7682 3703   http://www.apprenticeships.org.uk
    Chief Executive: Simon Waugh
E   Established on 27 April 2009. NAS works with the Department for Education and the Department for Business,
    Innovation & Skills to drive forward the Government's ambition for apprenticeships.
R   To deliver and fund apprenticeship places across England, to make it as easy as possible for employers to take
    on apprentices, and provide support and help to both employer and learner.
G   England.

The National Archives
■   Ruskin Avenue, Kew, RICHMOND, Surrey, TW9 4DU.
    Tel 020 8876 3444   **Fax** 020 8878 8905   http://www.nationalarchives.gov.uk
    Chief Executive: Oliver Morley
E   Established on 1 April 2003, bringing together the Public Record Office, Historical Manuscripts Commission, Her
    Majesty's Stationery Office and, in 2006, the Office of Public Sector Information. The National Archives
    functions as an Executive NDPB of the Ministry of Justice. The Management Board comprises seven executive
    and four non-executive directors and is chaired by the Chief Executive.
R   The National Archives is the UK government's official archive, containing almost 1,000 years of history, with
    records ranging from parchment and paper scrolls through to digital files and archived websites.
    It gives detailed advice to government departments and the public sector on information management, in order to
    ensure the survival of records, and advises others throughout the public and private sectors about the care of
    historical archives.
    It also publishes all UK legislation and encourages the re-use of public sector information.
G   United Kingdom.
●   The National Archives administers the Manorial Documents Register (MDR) which notes all changes in the
    ownership of manorial documents. It maintains the National Register of Archives (NRA), which was set up by
    the Historical Manuscripts Commission in 1945 to collect information on the nature and location of manuscripts
    and historical records that relate to British history and is searchable on the National Archives website.
✍   The Advisory Council on National Records & Archives (qv) advises the Lord Chancellor, who is responsible for the
    National Archives, on general archival practice and policy and questions relating to access to public records.

The National Archives of Scotland   (NAS)
■   HM General Register House, 2 Princes Street, EDINBURGH, EH1 3YY.
    Tel 0131 535 1314   **Fax** 0131 535 1360   http://www.nas.gov.uk
    Keeper of the Records of Scotland: George MacKenzie
E   Established on 1 April 1993. NAS functions as an Executive Agency of the Scottish Executive.
R   To select, preserve and make available the national archives of Scotland in whatever medium and to the highest
    standards.
    To promote the growth and maintenance of proper archive provision throughout the country.
    To lead the development of archival practice in Scotland.
G   Scotland.
●   NAS keeps the administrative records of pre-Union Scotland, the public registers of property rights and legal
    documents, the registers of central and local courts of law, and substantial collections of local and church
    records and private archives.

National Army Museum   (NAM)
■   Royal Hospital Road, LONDON, SW3 4HT.
    Tel 020 7730 0717   **Fax** 020 7823 6573   http://www.national-army-museum.ac.uk
    Chairman: General Sir Jack Deverell, KCB, OBE   Director: Mrs Janice Murray, BA, AMA, FRSA
E   Established on 8 April 1960 by Royal Charter. The Museum is a registered charity and functions as an Executive
    NDPB of the Ministry of Defence. The Council comprises eight members including the Chairman.
R   To use objects in its collection as tools to deliver the ongoing story of the Army and not as an end in themselves.
G   United Kingdom, and wherever the British Army has served or been stationed.

National Assembly for Wales   See **Welsh Government**.

National Audit Office (NAO)

■ 157-197 Buckingham Palace Road, LONDON, SW1W 9SP.
Tel 020 7798 7000 Fax 020 7798 7070 http://www.nao.gov.uk
Chairman: Sir Andrew Likierman Comptroller & Auditor General: Amyas Morse

E Established in 1983 under the National Audit Act 1983 which created the Public Accounts Commission (qv) to oversee the work of the NAO. The NAO Board comprises five non-executive members including the Chairman, plus the Comptroller & Auditor General, the Chief Operating Officer and two Assistant Auditors General.

R To audit the accounts of all government departments and agencies as well as a wide range of other public bodies.
To report to Parliament on the economy, efficiency and effectiveness with which these bodies have used public money.

G United Kingdom.

National Biological Standards Board

✍ The Board was abolished in 2007 and its functions transferred to the **Health Protection Agency**.

National Blood Service

✍ Since October 2005 the service is part of **NHS Blood & Transplant**.

National Board for Nursing, Midwifery & Health Visiting (Northern Ireland/Scotland)

✍ For both see **Nursing & Midwifery Council**.

National Board of Registration of Medical Illustrators NBRMI is regulated by the **Committee for the Accreditation of Medical Illustration Practitioners**.

National Broadcasting Councils

✍ In 2007 the Councils were replaced by four **Audience Councils**.

National Care Standards Commission

✍ On 1 April 2004 the NCSC's functions were split between the Commissions for Healthcare Audit & Inspection and for Social Care Inspection, which on 1 1 April 2009 were merged with the Mental Health Act Commission to form the **Care Quality Commission**.

National Care Standards Committee

✍ Convened in 1999 and 2002, this Scottish committee has completed its work.

National Centre for Languages See **CILT, the National Centre for Languages**.

National Children's Bureau (NCB)

■ 8 Wakley Street, LONDON, WC1V 7QE.
Tel 020 7843 6000 Fax 020 7278 9512 http://www.ncb.org.uk
Chairman: Dame Gillian Pugh Chief Executive: Sir Paul Ennals

E Established in 1963 as the National Bureau for Cooperation in Child Care, adopting its current name in 1970. NCB is a membership and infrastructure agency, and a registered charity. The Board of Trustees comprises 13-14 members including the Chairman.

R To reduce inequalities in childhood.
To ensure children and young people have a strong voice in all matters that affect their lives. To promote positive images of children and young people.
To enhance the health and wellbeing of all children and young people.
To encourage positive and supportive family and other environments.

G United Kingdom.

✍ NCB works in partnership with Children in Scotland and Children in Wales (qqv).

National Clinical Assessment Authority

✍ NCAA, renamed the National Clinical Assessment Service, is now operated by the **National Patient Safety Agency**.

© CBD Research Ltd · Beckenham · Kent BR3 5JS · Tel 020 8650 7745 · Fax 020 8650 0768 · E-mail cbd@cbdresearch.com · www.cbdresearch.com

National Coal Museum   See **National Museum Wales**.

National College for Leadership of Schools & Children's Services
- Triumph Road, NOTTINGHAM, NG8 1DH.
  Tel 0845 609 0009   Fax 0115 872 2001   http://www.nationalcollege.org.uk
  Chairman: Vanni Treves   Chief Executive: Steve Munby
E Established in 2000 as the National College for School Leadership, adopting its current name on 15 September 2009 upon extension of its remit. The National College functions as an Executive Agency of the Department for Education. The Governing Council comprises eleven members including the Chairman, plus three ex-officio appointees and two observers.
R To develop and oversee a coherent national training and development framework for heads, deputies and others in leadership positions in schools, offering them high-quality practical and professional support at all stages of their careers.
  To provide training and support for directors of children's services and those who aspire to the role.
G England.

National College for School Leadership
✍ Since 15 September 2009 **National College for Leadership of Schools & Children's Services**.

National Commissioning Advisory Board   (NCAB)
- Unit 3a, Caerphilly Business Park, CAERPHILLY, Glamorgan, CF83 3ED.
  Tel 029 2080 7575   Fax 029 2080 7599
  Chairman: Dr David Salter
E Established in April 2003. NCAB functions as an Advisory NDPB of Health Commission Wales (qv).
R To consider and sign off the National Specialised and Tertiary services commissioning plan.
G Wales.

National Community Forum   (NCF)
- 6th Floor, Eland House, Bressenden Place, LONDON, SW1E 5DU.
  Tel 020 7944 8306
  Chairman: Graham Brownlee
E Established in 2002. The Forum functions as an Advisory NDPB of the Department for Communities & Local Government. It comprises 25 members.
R To advise on how communities' priorities and needs can be met in neighbourhood renewal by improving community participation.
  To act as a sounding board and refining tool for policy ideas and a source of information and experience about developments in neighbourhood renewal.
G United Kingdom.

National Confidential Enquiry into Patient Outcome and Death   (NCEPOD)
- 4-8 Maple Street, LONDON, W1T 5HD.
  Tel 020 7631 3444   Fax 020 7631 4443   http://www.ncepod.org.uk
  Chairman: Bertie Leigh   Chief Executive: Dr Marisa Mason
E Established in 1988. NCEPOD is a registered charity and company limited by guarantee. It reports to the National Patient Survey Agency (qv).
  It has six trustees including the Chairman, 13 administrative staff including the Chief Executive, and a Steering Group comprising representatives nominated by the relevant Royal Colleges, faculties and associations which have made a corporate commitment to NCEPOD.
R To assist in maintaining and improving standards of medical and surgical care for the benefit of the public by reviewing the management of patients, undertaking confidential surveys and research, maintaining and improving the quality of patient care, and publishing and generally making available the results of such activities.
G England, Wales, Northern Ireland.

National Confidential Inquiry into Suicide & Homicide by People with Mental Illness   (NCISH)
- Centre for Suicide Prevention, 2nd Floor, Jean McFarlane Building, Oxford Road, MANCHESTER, M13 9PL.
  Tel 0161 275 0700   http://www.medicine-manchester.ac.uk
  Director: Prof Louis Appleby   Senior Project Manager: Kirsten Windfuhr
E Established in April 1996. The Inquiry is carried out by the Centre for Suicide Prevention at the University of Manchester and reports to the National Patient Safety Agency.
R To examine all incidences of suicide and homicide by people in contact with mental health services in the UK.

To examine cases of sudden death in the psychiatric in-patient population.

To improve mental health services and to help reduce the risk of these tragedies happening again in the future.

G   United Kingdom.

✍   NCISH is funded by the National Patient Safety Agency (qv), the Scottish Government and the Northern Ireland Department for Health, Social Services & Public Safety.

National Conservation Centre   See **National Museums Liverpool**.

National Consumer Council

✍   On 1 October 2008 NCC, with others, was replaced by **Consumer Focus**.

National Council on Archives   (NCA)

■   Ruskin Avenue, Kew, RICHMOND, Surrey, TW9 4DU.
     Tel 020 8392 5376   http://www.nca.org.uk
     Chairman: Geoff Pick

E   Established in 1988 by agreement between eleven organisations closely concerned with the care and use of archives. The Council comprises eight members including the Chairman.

R   To bring to the attention of the public, government and relevant institutions and organisations, matters of current concern in the field of archives.

     To assist the work of the National Archives and the Museums, Libraries & Archives Council (qqv).

G   United Kingdom.

National Council for Civil Liberties

■   21 Tabard Street, LONDON, SE1 4LA.
     Tel 020 7403 3888   http://www.liberty-human-rights.org.uk
     Director: Shami Chakrabarti

E   Established in 1934. Usually known as **Liberty**, NCCL is a cross party, non-party membership organisation, a registered charity and company limited by guarantee. The Liberty Council comprises 30 NCCL members.

R   To protect civil liberties and promote human rights for everyone.

G   England, Wales.

National Council for Drama Training   (NCDT)

■   249 Tooley Street, LONDON, SE1 2JX.
     Tel 020 7407 3686   http://www.ncdt.co.uk
     Chairman: Sir Brian Fender   Director: Hilary Strong

E   Set up in June 1976 following recommendations in the 1975 Gulbenkian Foundation report 'Going on the Stage'. NCDT is an independent body and registered charity functioning as a partnership of employers in the theatre, broadcast and media industries, employee representatives and training providers. The Council comprises ten members including the Chairman.

R   To accredit vocational courses, act as a champion for the industry and optimise support for professional drama training and education.

G   United Kingdom.

National Council for Education and Training in Wales

✍   The functions of the Council have been transferred to the Welsh Government Assembly.

National Council for Hospice & Specialist Palliative Care Services

✍   Since 3 November 2004 **National Council for Palliative Care**.

National Council for Housing & Planning

✍   Merged in 2003 with the Royal Town Planning Institute.

National Council for Hypnotherapy   (NCH)

■   PO Box 14542, STUDLEY, Warks, B97 9HH.
     Tel 0845 544 0788   http://www.hypnotherapists.org.uk
     Chairman: Paul White, NCH(Lic)

E   Established in 1973. NCH is a membership body. The Executive comprises eleven members including the Chairman.

    © CBD Research Ltd · Beckenham · Kent BR3 5JS · Tel 020 8650 7745 · Fax 020 8650 0768 · E-mail cbd@cbdresearch.com · www.cbdresearch.com

R   To raise the standards of hypnotherapy in the UK in every possible way.
G   United Kingdom.

National Council for Metal Detecting   (NCMD)

■   51 Hilltop Gardens, Denaby, DONCASTER, S Yorks, DN12 4SA.
     Tel 01709 868521   http://www.ncmd.co.uk
     General Secretary: Trevor Austin
E   Established in 1981.
R   To provide a democratic forum where responsible metal detectors can meet to discuss problems affecting the hobby.

     To be an authoritative voice to counter ill-informed and frequently misleading criticism of the hobby.
G   United Kingdom.

National Council for One Parent Families   Established in 1918 as the National Council for the Unmarried Mother & her Child, it adopted the above name in 1970. It merged in June 2007 with the charity **Gingerbread**.

National Council for Osteopathic Research   (NCOR)

■   Aldro Building, University of Brighton, 49 Darley Road, EASTBOURNE, BN20 7UR.
     Tel 01273 643766   Fax 01273 643944   http://www.brighton.ac.uk/ncor/
     Chairman: Prof Ann Moore
E   Established in 2003 by the General Osteopathic Council (qv), the British Osteopathic Association and all the osteopathic education institutions in the UK.
R   To establish and develop a comprehensive information resource for osteopathic research in order to promote a mutual research dialogue within the osteopathic profession and with related professions.
G   United Kingdom.

National Council for Palliative Care   (NCPC)

■   The Fitzpatrick Building, 188-194 York Way, LONDON, N7 9AS.
     Tel 020 7697 1520   Fax 020 7697 1530   http://www.ncpc.org.uk
     Chairman: Prof Mayur Lakhani, CBE   Chief Executive: Eve Richardson
E   Established in November 1991 as the National Council for Hospice & Specialist Palliative Care Services, it adopted its current name on 3 November 2004. NCPC is the umbrella organisation for all those involved in providing, commissioning and using palliative care and hospice services; it is a registered charity. The Board of Trustees comprises twelve members including the Chairman.
R   To promote improvement in the quality and availablity of palliative care to patients, their families and carers.
     To promote palliative care in health and social care settings across all sectors to government, national and local policy makers.
G   England, Wales, Northern Ireland.

National Council for Social Concern   (NCSC)

■   3 Vinson Road, LISS, Hants, GU33 7NE.
     Tel 01730 300974
E   Established in 1862 as the Church of England Temperance Society. NCSC is a grant support agency and registered Church of England charity. The Council comprises four Trustees and the Chairman.
R   To support and further all or any charitable activities carried out in connection with the Church of England and in particular those relating to (1) the promotion of temperance and of higher standards of moral life in the individual, family and community, (2) the restoration of the intemperate or delinquent and of those addicted to drugs, alcohol or gambling or otherwise in need of help, and (3) the relief of distress and suffering arising from delinquency, intemperance or addiction.
G   England.

National Council for the Training of Journalists   (NCTJ)

■   The New Granary, Station Road, Newport, SAFFRON WALDEN, CB11 3PL.
     Tel 01799 544014   Fax 01799 544015   http://www.nctj.com
     Chairman: Kim Fletcher   Chief Executive: Joanne Butcher
E   Established in 1951 following the findings of a Royal Commission on the Press. The Council functions as an independent registered charity and its trading subsidiary, NCTJ Training Ltd, as a company limited by guarantee. The Board comprises 13 members including the Chairman.
R   To provide a world-class education and training system that develops current and future journalists for the demands of the 21st century.
G   United Kingdom.

National Council of Voluntary Child Care Organisations
✍ Since December 2008 **Children England**.

National Council for Voluntary Organisations (NCVO)
■ Regent's Wharf, 8 All Saints Street, LONDON, N1 9RL.
   Tel 020 7713 6161   **Fax** 020 7713 6300   http://www.ncvo-vol.org.uk
   Chairman: Sir Graham Melmoth   Chief Executive: Stuart Etherington
E Established in 1919 as the National Council of Social Services. NCVO is a membership based body representing over 7,000 voluntary organisations and functions as a registered charity and company limited by guarantee. The Trustee Board comprises 26 members including the Chairman.
R To extend the involvement of voluntary organisations in responding to social social issues.
   To be a resource centre for voluntary organisations and protect their interests and independence.
G England.

National Council for Voluntary Youth Services (NCVYS)
■ Third Floor, Lancaster House, 33 Islington High Street, LONDON, N1 9LH.
   Tel 020 7278 1041   **Fax** 020 7833 2491   http://www.ncvys.org.uk
   Chairman: Kanchan Jadeja   Chief Executive: Susanne Rauprich
E Established in 1936. NCVYS is a membership body of over 170 national organisations and regional and local networks; it functions as a registered charity. The Board of Trustees comprises 15 members including the Chairman.
R To work with its members from voluntary and community organisations to build thriving communities and sustainable networks that help all young people achieve their potential.
G England.

National Council of Women of Great Britain (NCW)
■ 72 Victoria Road, DARLINGTON, Co Durham, DL1 5JG.
   Tel 01325 367375   **Fax** 01325 367378   http://www.ncwgb.org
   London Policy Centre: 36 Danbury Street, LONDON, N1 8JU.
   President: Sheila Eaton
E Established in 1895 as the Union of Women Workers, it adopted its current name in 1918.
   NCW is an independent educational charity open to all women.
   The Management Committee comprises 15 members including the President.
R To monitor legislation, represent women's opinions and concerns to Parliament and systematically follow them up.
G United Kingdom.
● 10 specialist committees meet regularly at headquarters; working parties & study days are held in London & regionally.
   Representations are made to Government and outside bodies on matters including legislation both pending and proposed.

National Crime Agency
✍ A new agency, due to launch in 2013, which will incorporate the **Serious Organised Crime Agency**.

National Crime Squad
✍ Merged with the National Criminal Intelligence Service and parts of HM Revenue & Customs and the Immigration Service becoming, from 1 April 2006, the **Serious Organised Crime Agency**.

National Criminal Intelligence Service
✍ Merged with the National Crime Squad and parts of HM Revenue & Customs and the Immigration Service becoming, from 1 April 2006, the **Serious Organised Crime Agency**.

National Cycling Strategy Board
✍ Organisation replaced in March 2005 by **Cycling England**.

National Dairy Council   See the **Dairy Council**.

© CBD Research Ltd · Beckenham · Kent BR3 5JS · Tel 020 8650 7745 · Fax 020 8650 0768 · E-mail cbd@cbdresearch.com · www.cbdresearch.com

National Defence Industries Council   (NDIC)

- ◼ MOD Main Building, Whitehall, LONDON, SW1A 2HB.
  Tel 020 7218 7909
  Co-chairmen: The Secretary of State for Defence and the Chairman of the Defence Industries Council (qv).
- E Established in 1969 by the Secretary of State for Defence. NDIC is the most senior forum for consultation between the Government and industry on defence matters. The Government members are Ministers and senior officials from relevant Government Departments. The industry members are individuals from defence companies or trade association representatives nominated by the Defence Industries Council.
- R To provide a focus for regular consultation between the Ministry of Defence & industry on questions of defence supply and procurement of mutual concern,
  To define areas of profitable consultation and study and the appropriate machinery to be used in each case.
- G United Kingdom.

National DNA Database Ethics Committee

- ◼ 3rd Floor, SW Quarter, Seacole Building, 2 Marsham Street, LONDON, SW1P 4DF.
  Tel 020 7035 3049
  Chairman: Christopher Hughes, OBE
- E Established on 25 July 2007. NDNAD Ethics Committee functions as an Advisory NDPB of the Home Office. The Group comprises eleven members including the Chairman.
- R To provide Ministers with independent ethical advice on the operation and practice of the National DNA Database (NDNAD) and related issues.
- G United Kingdom.

National Employer Advisory Board   (NEAB)

- ◼ Holderness House, Clifton Street, LONDON, EC2A 4EY.
  Tel 0800 389 5459   Fax 020 7426 8390   http://www.sabre.mod.uk
  Chairman: Richard Boggis-Rolfe
- E Established in 1986 as the National Employers' Liaison Committee, it was renamed with the launch of SaBRE in September 2002. NEAB functions as an Advisory NDPB of the Ministry of Defence. The Board comprises 15 members including the Chairman.
- R To advise the Secretary of State for Defence on issues surrounding the employment of members of the volunteer reserve forces.
  To advise the MoD's SaBRE (Supporting Britain's Reservists & Employers) campaign, on its strategy, focus and effectiveness.
- G United Kingdom.
- ✍ The Government announced on 14 October 2010 that the future of NEAB was under consideration, including looking at how its functions could be provided by a committee of experts.

National Employment Panel

- ✍ On 31 March 2008 the NEP merged with the Sector Skills Development Agency and together were succeeded by the **United Kingdom Commission for Employment & Skills**.
  The Panel supported the network of **Employment Coalitions**.

National Employment Savings Trust   See **NEST Trust**.

National Endowment for Science, Technology & the Arts   (NESTA)

- ◼ 1 Plough Place, LONDON, EC4A 1DE.
  Tel 020 7438 2500   Fax 020 7438 2501   http://www.nesta.org.uk
  Chairman: Sir John Chisholm   Interim Chief Executive: Daniel Oppenheimer
- E Established on 2 July 1998 under the National Lottery Act 1998 as an Executive NDPB of the Department for Culture, Media & Sport. The Board comprises eleven Trustees including the Chairman.
- R To support and promote talent, innovation and creativity in the fields of science, technology and the arts.
- G United Kingdom.
- ● NESTA invests in early stage companies, informs innovation policy and encourages a culture that helps innovation to flourish.
- ✍ On 14 October 2010 the Government announced that NESTA has been granted full independence, moving from the public to the voluntary sector to become a charitable company.

National Energy Action (NEA)

- West 1, Forth Banks, NEWCASTLE UPON TYNE, NE1 3PA.
  Tel 0191 261 5677 Fax 0191 261 6496 http://www.nea.org.uk
  Chairman: Ruth Thompson, OBE Chief Executive: Jenny Saunders
- E NEA is a membership body whose members include local authorities, housing associations, health agencies, charities and community groups, and contracted installers through Warm Front or energy provider schemes. The Board of Trustees comprises 15 members including the Chairman.
- R To develop and promote energy efficiency services to tackle the heating and insulation problems of low-income households.
- G England, Wales, Northern Ireland.
- ● NEA operates 20 demonstration projects at ten offices in England and Wales. It has a separate office in Belfast which works throughout Northern Ireland. It works closely with its sister organisation, Energy Action Scotland (qv).

National Equality Panel (NEP)

- 9th Floor, Eland House, Bressenden Place, LONDON, SW1E 5DU.
  Tel 0303 444 1204 Fax 0303 444 3303
  Chairman: Prof John Hills
- E Established in October 2008. NEP is an Advisory NDPB of the Government Equalities Office. The Panel comprises ten members including the Chairman.
- R To investigate relationships between the distribution of various kinds of economic outcome on the one hand and people's characteristics and circumstances on the other.
- G United Kingdom.

National Examination Board in Occupational Safety & Health (NEBOSH)

- Dominus Way, Meridian Business Park, LEICESTER, LE19 1QW.
  Tel 0116 263 4700 Fax 0116 282 4000 http://www.nebosh.org.uk
  Chairman: David Morris Chief Executive: Teresa Budworth
- E Established in 1979 by the Institution of Occupational Safety & Health and colleges teaching that discipline. NEBOSH is a registered charity and a company limited by guarantee. The Board of Trustees comprises eleven members including the Chairman.
- R To preserve health by the study and promotion of high standards of health and safety at work.
- G United Kingdom.
- ● It is also the awarding body for courses and qualifications in health and safety for managers, supervisors and people starting out in a career in health and safety.
- ✍ For further information see the **Federation of Awarding Bodies**.

National Examining Board for Dental Nurses (NEBDN)

- 110 London Street, FLEETWOOD, Lancs, FY7 6EU.
  Tel 01253 778417 Fax 01253 777268 http://www.nebdn.org
  Chairman: Beverley Coker Chief Executive: Phil Hughes
- E Established in 1943. NEBDN functions as a registered charity and company limited by guarantee. The Board of Directors comprises eight members including the Chairman.
- R To advance the education of dental nurses for the benefit of the public.
- G United Kingdom.

National Expert Group on Transboundary Air Pollution

- ✍ Established in 2000, it produced its report in 2001.

National Expert Panel on New & Emerging Infections (NEPNEI)

- Emerging Infections & Zoonoses, 61 Colindale Avenue, LONDON, NW9 5EQ.
  Chairman: Prof Christopher Whitty
- E Established on 25 November 2003 following the publication of the Chief Medical Officer's Infectious Disease Strategy 'Getting Ahead of the Curve'. NEPNEI is a Scientific Advisory Committee and an Advisory NDPB of the Department of Health. The Panel comprises 17 members inclicding the Chairman.
- R To identify emerging and potential infectious threats to public health, both nationally and internationally.
- G United Kingdom.
- ✍ For further information see **Scientific Advisory Committees**.

The National Forest Company   (NFC)

- Enterprise Glade, Bath Yard, Moira, SWADLINCOTE, Derbys, DE12 6BA.
  Tel 01283 551211   Fax 01283 552844   http://www.nationalforest.org
  Chairman: Dinah Nichols   Chief Executive: Sophie Churchill
- E   Established in April 1995. The Company functions as an Executive NDPB of the Department for Environment, Food & Rural Affairs.
- R   To lead the creation of The National Forest, a new woodland landscape for the nation across 200 square miles of central England.
  To attract and use resources for ambitious and imaginative forest creation that is sensitive to the landscape and environment.
  To provide the setting for new businesses, recreation, tourism and an improved quality of life.
  To enhance wildlife and biodiversity.
- G   Central England.

National Foundation for Educational Research in England & Wales   (NFER)

- The Mere, Upton Park, SLOUGH, Berks, SL1 2DQ.
  Tel 01753 574123   Fax 01753 691632   http://www.nfer.ac.uk
  Chairman: Richard Bunker   Chief Executive: Sue Rossiter
- E   Established in 1946, NFER functions as a registered charity and company limited by guarantee. The Board comprises twelve members including the Chairman.
- R   To provide research, assessment and information services for education, training and children's services, to enable policy makers and practitioners to make better, more informed decisions, drawing on sound evidence and accurate information.
- G   England, Wales.

National Fraud Authority   (NFA)

- PO Box 64170, LONDON, WC1A 9BP.
  Tel 020 3356 1000   Fax 020 3356 1001   http://www.attorneygeneral.gov.uk/nfa/
  Chief Executive: Dr Bernard Herdan, CB
- E   Established in October 2008. NFA functions as an executive agency of the Attorney General's Office.
- R   To work with private, public and third sector organisations to increase protection for the UK economy from the harm caused by fraud, and to create a more hostile environment for fraudsters, both home and abroad.
- G   United Kingdom.

National Galleries of Scotland

- The Dean Gallery, 73 Belford Road, EDINBURGH, EH4 3DS.
  Tel 0131 624 6200   Fax 0131 623 7126   http://www.nationalgalleries.org
  Chairman: Ben Thomson   Director General: John Leighton
- E   Established under the National Galleries of Scotland Act 1906 as amended by the National Heritage (Scotland) Act 1985. The Galleries function as an Executive NDPB of the Scottish Executive Education Department. The Board of Trustees comprises twelve members including the Chairman.
- R   To care for, preserve and add to the objects in their collections.
  To ensure objects are exhibited to the public.
  To promote generally the public's enjoyment and understanding of fine arts.
- G   Scotland.
- The National Galleries of Scotland are:
  Dean Gallery
  National Gallery of Scotland
  Royal Scottish Academy Building
  Scottish National Gallery of Modern Art
  Scottish National Portrait Gallery

The National Gallery

- Trafalgar Square, LONDON, WC2N 5DN.
  Tel 020 7747 2885   Fax 020 7747 2423   http://www.nationalgallery.org.uk
  Chairman: Mark Getty   Director: Nicholas Penny
- E   Established by Treasury Minute in 1824, the Gallery's Board of Trustees is now constituted under the Museums & Galleries Act 1992. The National Gallery functions as an Executive NDPB of the Department for Culture, Media & Sport. The Board comprises 13 Trustees including the Chairman.
- R   To keep the pictures in the nation's collection safe for future generations.
  To acquire great pictures across the whole range of European painting to maintain and enhance the collection.
  To encourage all aspects of scholarship on the collection.

To display the pictures well and allow the public to use the collection as their own by maintaining free admission and convenient opening hours.

G   United Kingdom.

● The National Gallery houses the national collection of West European painting from the 13th to the 20th centuries; almost all of the collection is on show, 360 days of the year, free of charge.

National Health Service

✍ See **NHS** - all bodies whose names begin with NHS or National Health Service are printed and filed as NHS to avoid any confusion generated by two separate sequences.

National Heritage Memorial Fund   (NHMF)

■ 7 Holbein Place, LONDON, SW1W 8NR.
   Tel 020 7591 6000   **Fax** 020 7591 6001   http://www.hlf.org.uk
   Chairman: Dame Jenny Abramsky   Chief Executive: Carole Souter

E   Established on 1 April 1980 under the National Heritage Act 1980. NHMF functions as an Executive NDPB of the Department for Culture, Media & Sport. The Board comprises 15 Trustees including the Chairman.

R   To make grants to help acquire, maintain or preserve any land, building or structure, or any object or collection which is of outstanding scenic, historic, aesthetic, architectural, scientific or artistic interest.

G   United Kingdom.

● NHMF administers the Heritage Lottery Fund.

National History Museum (St Fagans)   See **National Museum Wales**.

National House-Building Council   (NHBC)

■ NHBC House, Davy Avenue, Knowlhill, MILTON KEYNES, Bucks, MK5 8FP.
   Tel 0844 633 1000   http://www.nhbc.co.uk
   Chairman: Sir John Carter   Chief Executive: Imtiaz Farookhi

E   Established in 1936 as the Housing Improvement Association, which later became the National House-Builders Registration Council; NHBC assumed its present title in 1973. NHBC functions as an independent, non-political, non-profit-making body, made up of nominees of all the interests concerned with private housing. The Council comprises 16 members including the Chairman.

R   To serve the building industry and its customers by the setting of standards, the promotion of good building practices, the prevention of defects, and the provision of technical and insurance services.

G   United Kingdom.

● The Council offers a wide range of insurance products for house-builders, housing associations & their customers, including the Buildmark ten year warranty, which is currently issued on approximately 90% of all new houses built in the UK.
   The Council also has branch offices in other parts of the UK.

National Illumination Committee of Great Britain   (CIE-UK)

■ 222 Balham High Road, LONDON, SW12 9BS.
   Tel 020 8675 5211   **Fax** 020 8673 3302   http://www.cie-uk.org.uk
   Chairman: Nigel Pollard

E   Established in 1913. The Board of Trustees comprises five members including the Chairman.

R   To be the member body for Great Britain on the Commission Internationale de l'Eclairage.

G   United Kingdom.

● CIE is the international organisation that is active in all professional matters relating to light, lighting and image technology.

National Information Governance Board for Health & Social Care   (NIGB)

■ Floor 7, New Kings Beam House, 22 Upper Ground, LONDON, SE1 9BW.
   Tel 020 7633 7052   http://www.nigb.nhs.uk
   Chairman: Harry Cayton, OBE

E   Established on 1 January 2009 under the Health & Social Care Act 2008, the Board replaces the former Patient Information Advisory Group. NIGB functions as an Advisory NDPB of the Department of Health. The Board comprises 20 members including the Chairman.

R   To consider ethical issues, the interpretation and application of the law and policies, and to advise on information governance matters at a national level.
   To consider under section 251 of the NHS Act 2006 which allows the common law duty of confidentiality to be set aside in specific circumstances.

G   England.

✍   The Government announced on 14 October 2010 that NIGB would be abolished with its statutory functions transferred to the Care Quality Commission (qv). Advice currently provided by NIGB will be obtainable from within the Department of Health or other bodies.

National Inspection Council for Electrical Installation Contracting   (NICEIC)

■   Warwick House, Houghton Hall Park, Houghton Regis, DUNSTABLE, LU5 5ZX.
Tel 0870 013 0382   Fax 01582 539090   http://www.niciec.org.uk
Executive Chairman: Jim Speirs

E   Established in 1986. NICIEC is a non-profit making registered charity. The Council comprises representatives from organisations concerned with electricity supply, the professions, consumer interest bodies, trade and industry associations and other regulators. The Executive Management Team comprises the Executive Chairman, Group Finance Director and Chief Operating Officer.

R   To protect the user of electricity from unsafe electrical installations.

G   United Kingdom.

●   NICEIC maintains maintains a Roll of Approved Contractors and a Register of Domestic Installers.

National Institute for Biological Standards & Controls

✍   On 1 April 2008 the NIBSC became part of the **Health Protection Agency**.

National Institute for Clinical Excellence

✍   On 1 April 2005 NICE joined with the Health Development Agency to form the **National Institute for Health & Clinical Excellence**.

National Institute for Health & Clinical Excellence   (NICE)

■   MidCity Place, 71 High Holborn, LONDON, WC1V 6NA.
Tel 0845 003 7780   Fax 0845 003 7784   http://www.nice.org.uk
Chairman: Prof Sir Michael Rawlins   Chief Executive: Andrew Dillon

E   Established on 1 April 1999 as the National Institute for Clinical Excellence; on 1 April 2005 it took over the functions of the former Health Development Agency and adopted its current name. NICE functions as a Special Health Authority of the Department of Health. The Board comprises 14 members including the Chairman.

R   To provide guidance on the promotion of good health and the prevention of ill health for those working in the NHS, local authorities and the wider public and voluntary sector.
To provide guidance on the use of new and existing medicines, treatments and procedures within the NHS.
To provide guidance on the appropriate treatment and care of people with specific diseases and conditions within the NHS.

G   United Kingdom.

●   NICE issues guidelines based on clinical and cost effectiveness, and aims to ensure that they reach all parts of the NHS.

National Joint Pitch Council

✍   Established in October 1988 by the Horserace Betting Levy Board (qv) to promulgate and enforce its new pitch rules, the NJPC ceased to exist on 1 September 2007.

National Joint Registry Steering Committee

✍   An Advisory NDPB responsible for the work of NJR which was established in 2002 to assure care quality of recipients of hip, knee and ankle replacement surgery. The Government announced on 14 October 2010 that the Steering Committee will be reconstituted as a committee of experts of the Department of Health.

National Library of Scotland

■   George IV Bridge, EDINBURGH, EH1 1EW.
Tel 0131 623 3700   Fax 0131 623 3701   http://www.nls.uk
Chairman: Prof Michael Anderson, OBE, MA, PhD, FBA, FRSE
National Librarian & Chief Executive: Martyn Wade

E   Established in 1689 as the Library of the Faculty of Advocates, the National Library Scotland came into being in 1925 under the National Library of Scotland Act 1925. The Library functions as an Executive NDPB of the Scottish Executive Education Department. The Board of Trustees comprises 31 members including the Chairman.

R   To have general management & control of the National Library of Scotland.

G   Scotland.

- The Library has large collections of printed books, manuscripts and maps and has an unrivalled collection of Scottish material. It is a library of legal deposit, entitled to claim works published in the United Kingdom and Ireland.

National Library of Wales   (NLW)
■ Penglais, ABERYSTWYTH, Ceredigion, SY23 3BU.
  Tel 01970 632800   **Fax** 01970 615709   http://www.llgc.org.uk
  President: Dafydd Wigley   Librarian & Chief Executive: Andrew Green
E Established by Royal Charter in 1907, with Supplemental Charters in 1911 and 1978. A Supplemental Charter granted by HM the Queen on 19 July 2006 dissolved the 1978 Charter and significantly amended the Museum's constitution and governance. The Library functions as an Executive NDPB of the National Assembly for Wales via its sponsoring division CyMAL (qv). The Board comprises 15 Trustees, eight of whom are appointed by the National Assembly and seven by the Library.
R To have general management and control of the National Library of Wales and its buildings.
G Wales.
● NLW acquires and preserves the printed and manuscript record of the culture of Wales.
  It contains approximately four million books & pamphlets, 40,000 manuscripts, many deeds and documents, and many pre-1858 Welsh probate records.
= Llyfrgell Genedlaethol Cymru

National Lottery Charities Board
✍ Responsibilities were transferred in 2006 to its successor body, the **Big Lottery Fund**.

National Lottery Commission   (NLC)
■ 101 Wigmore Street, LONDON, W1U 1QU.
  Tel 020 7016 3400   **Fax** 020 7016 3401   http://www.natlotcomm.gov.uk
  Chairman: Dr Anne Wright, CBE   Chief Executive: Mark Harris
E Established on 25 October 1993 under the National Lottery (etc) Act 1993. NLC functions as an Executive NDPB of the Department for Culture, Media & Sport. The Commission comprises seven members including the Chairman.
R To license and regulate the National Lottery.
  To protect the integrity of the Lottery, to protect players and to maximise the funds for good causes.
G United Kingdom.
✍ It was confirmed by the Government on 14 October 2010 that the National Lottery Commission will merge with the Gambling Commission (qv).

National Maritime Museum
■ Romney Road, Greenwich, LONDON, SE10 9NF.
  Tel 020 8858 4422   http://www.nmm.ac.uk
  Chairman: Lord Sterling of Plaistow, GCVO, CBE   Director: Kevin Fewster, AM, FRSA
E Established in 1934 by Act of Parliament. The Museum functions an Executive NDPB of the Department of Culture, Media & Sport. The Board of Trustees comprises 14 members including the Chairman.
R To illustrate for everyone the importance of the sea, ships, time and the stars and their relationship with people.
G United Kingdom.
● The National Maritime Museum includes the Royal Observatory and the Queen's House in Greenwich.

National Measurement Office   (NMO)
■ Stanton Avenue, TEDDINGTON, Middx, TW11 0JZ.
  Tel 020 8943 7272   **Fax** 020 8943 7270   http://www.nmo.bis.gov.uk
  Chairman: Noel Hunter   Chief Executive: Peter Mason
E Established on 18 April 1989 and known as the National Weights & Measures Laboratory until April 2008. NMO functions as an Executive Agency of the Department for Business, Innovation & Skills. The steering board comprises seven members including the Chairman.
R To provide world class fair, legal, accurate, sustainable measurement and enforcement services, driving forward innovation to promote trade and protecting consumers, health and the environment.
G United Kingdom.

National Media Museum   See **National Museum of Science & Industry**.

National Monuments Record

✍ The National Monuments Records are the responsibility of **English Heritage** and the **Royal Commissions on the Ancient & Historical Monuments of Scotland** and **Wales**.

National Museum Cardiff   See **National Museum Wales**.

National Museum of Costume   See **National Museums Scotland**.

National Museum of Flight   See **National Museums Scotland**.

National Museum of the Royal Navy   (NMRN)

■   HM Naval Base, PORTSMOUTH, Hants, PO1 3LR.
Tel 023 9272 7562   **Fax** 023 9272 7575
Chairman: Admiral Sir Peter Abbott, GBE, KCB
E   Established in September 2009. The Museum functions as an Executive NDPB of the Ministry of Defence.
R   To preserve the past and promote the future of the Royal Navy's activities either on the sea, under the sea, in the air or on the land.
G   United Kingdom.
●   The National Museum comprises, in addition to HMS Victory, the Royal Navy's four service museums:
Fleet Air Arm Museum, Yeovilton, Somerset
Royal Marines Museum, Southsea, Hants
Royal Naval Museum, Portsmouth Historical Dockyard
Royal Navy Submarine Museum, Gosport, Hants.

National Museum of Rural Life   See **National Museums Scotland**.

National Museum of Science & Industry   (NMSI)

■   Exhibition Road, South Kensington, LONDON, SW7 2DD.
Tel 0870 870 4771   http://www.nmsi.ac.uk
Chairman: Lord Waldegrave of North Hill   Director: Martin J Earwicker, FREng
E   Established on 1 April 1984 under the National Heritage Act 1983 (the **Science Museum** itself was founded in 1857). NMSI functions as an Executive NDPB of the Department for Culture, Media & Sport. The Board comprises 17 Trustees including the Chairman.
R   To be the nation's leading centre for the public understanding of science by caring for, presenting and interpreting the national collections of science, technology & medicine.
G   United Kingdom.
●   The National Museum of Science & Industry comprises:
National Media Museum, Bradford
National Railway Museum, Shildon and York
Science Museum, London and Wroughton (Swindon).

National Museum of Scotland   See **National Museums Scotland**.

National Museum Wales

■   Cathays Park, CARDIFF, CF10 3NP.
Tel 029 2039 7951   **Fax** 029 2037 3219   http://www.museumwales.ac.uk
President of the Trustees: Paul Loveluck, CBE, JP   Director General: Michael Houlihan
E   Established on 19 March 1907 by Royal Charter, the Museum opened in 1927. It functions as an Executive NDPB of the National Assembly for Wales via its sponsoring division CyMAL (qv).
R   To have general control and management of its museums to preserve, present and promote the heritage and culture of Wales in a world-wide context.
G   Wales.
●   National Museum Wales comprises:
National Museum Cardiff
National Coal Museum (Big Pit), Blaenavon
National History Museum (St Fagans)
National Roman Legion Museum, Caerleon
National Slate Museum, Llanberis
National Waterfront Museum, Swansea

National Wool Museum, Llandysul
Rhagor (the website for the national collections and the stories behind them).
= Amgueddfa Cymru

National Museums Collection Centre   See **National Museums Scotland**.

National Museums & Galleries of Northern Ireland
✍ Since 2005 **National Museums Northern Ireland**.

National Museums Liverpool
■   127 Dale Street, LIVERPOOL, L1 2JH.
     Tel 0151 207 0001   **Fax** 0151 478 4321   http://www.liverpoolmuseums.org.uk
     Chairman: Prof Phil Redmond, CBE   Director: David Fleming, OBE
E   Originally founded in 1851 as the Liverpool Museum, National Museums Liverpool was established in 1986. It
     functions as an Executive NDPB of the Department for Culture, Media & Sport. The Board comprises twelve
     Trustees including the Chairman.
R   To promote the public enjoyment and understanding of art, history and science.
G   United Kingdom.
●   National Museums Liverpool are:
          International Slavery Museum
          Lady Lever Art Gallery
          Merseyside Maritime Museum
          Museum of Liverpool
          National Conservation Centre
          Sudley House
          Walker Art Gallery
          World Museum.
✍   Seized! Revenue & Customs Uncovered, known as the Customs & Excise Museum until May 2008, is a gallery at
     Merseyside Maritime Museum.

National Museums Northern Ireland   (NMNI)
■   Cultra, HOLYWOOD, Co Down, BT18 0EU.
     Tel 0845 608 0000   **Fax** 028 9042 8728   http://www.nmni.com
     Chairman: Dan Harvey, OBE   Chief Executive: Tim Cooke
E   Established on 1 April 1998, as National Museums & Galleries of Northern Ireland, by the merger of the four
     museums; It rebranded as National Museums Northern Ireland in 2005. NMNI functions as an Executive NDPB
     of the Department of Culture, Arts & Leisure Northern Ireland. The Board of Trustees comprises 14 members
     including the Chairman.
R   To have general control and management of Northern Ireland's four nationally funded museums and W5, the
     interactive science centre.To preserve, present and promote the heritage and culture of Northern Ireland in a
     world-wide context.
G   Northern Ireland.
●   National Museums Northern Ireland are:
          Armagh County Museum
          Ulster American Folk Park
          Ulster Folk & Transport Museum
          Ulster Museum
          W5 (whowhatwhenwherewhy)

National Museums Scotland   (NMS)
■   Chambers Street, EDINBURGH, EH1 1JF.
     Tel 0131 247 4260   **Fax** 0131 247 4308   http://www.nms.ac.uk
     Chairman: Sir Angus Grossart, CBE   Director: Dr Gordon Rintoul
E   Established on 1 October 1985, under the National Heritage (Scotland) Act 1985, when the Royal Scottish
     Museum & the National Museum of Antiquities of Scotland were amalgamated under one Board of Trustees. It
     functions as an Executive NDPB of the Scottish Executive Education Department. The Board comprises 14
     Trustees including the Chairman.
R   To care for, preserve and add to the objects in their collections.
     To ensure that the objects are exhibited to the public.
     To make the collections available through research, exhibitions, education and other activities.
G   Scotland.

© CBD Research Ltd · Beckenham · Kent BR3 5JS · Tel 020 8650 7745 · Fax 020 8650 0768 · E-mail cbd@cbdresearch.com · www.cbdresearch.com

- National Museums Scotland are:
    National Museum of Costume
    National Museum of Flight
    National Museum of Rural Life
    National Museum of Scotland
    National Museums Collection Centre
    National War Museum

National Muslim Women's Advisory Group   (NMWAG)
- ■ Eland House, Bressenden Place, LONDON, SW1E 5DU.
    Tel 0303 444 0000
- E   Established in January 2008. NMWAG functions as an advisory NDPB of the Department for Communities & Local Government. The Group comprises 19 members.
- R   To act as ambassadors for Muslim women at grass roots and represent their views and concerns to Parliament.
    To empower Muslim women to engage more with the media on a wide range of issues and help dispel myths around the role of Muslim women in society.
- G   United Kingdom.

National Nuclear Laboratory
- ■ Sellafield, SEASCALE, Cumbria, CA20 1PG.
    Tel 01925 289800   http://www.nnl.co.uk
    Managing Director: Mike Lawrence   Shareholder Executive contact: Richard Ramsay
- E   Established in 2008. NNL functions as a private limited company in which the Secretary of State for Energy & Climate Change holds all the shares through a holding company, NNL Holdings Ltd. The Board comprises nine members including the Managing Director.
- R   To profitably deploy nuclear technology to a broad range of national and international markets.
    To provide independent, authoritative advice on nuclear issues.
    To be the employer of choice for nuclear scientists and engineers, with a highly motivated and empowered workforce working in state-of-the-art facilities.
- G   United Kingdom.
- ✍ One of the businesses managed by the **Shareholder Executive**.

National Offender Management Service   (NOMS)
- ■ Cleland House, Page Street, LONDON, SW1P 4LN.
    Tel 0300 047 6325   http://www.justice.gov.uk/about/noms.htm
    Chief Executive: Michael Spurr
- E   Established on 1 June 2004, integrating HM Prison Service and the National Probation Service under a single headquarters structure since 1 April 2008. NOMS functions as an Executive Agency of the Ministry of Justice. The Board comprises nine directors and three non-executive directors.
- R   To commission and deliver adult offender management services, in custody and the community.
    To keep the public safe by ensuring that around 260,000 offenders each year safely and securely undertake the punishment of the courts through custodial (prison) or community sentences provided through the prison and probation services.
- G   England, Wales.
- ● There are currently 137 prisons in England and Wales of which 126 are run by the public sector through HM Prison Service and 11 by private sector partners.
    Probation services are provided by 35 Probation Trusts (qv) across England and Wales.

National Open College Network   (NOCN)
- ■ The Quadrant, Parkway Business Park, 99 Parkway Avenue, SHEFFIELD, S9 4WG.
    Tel 0114 227 0500   **Fax** 0114 227 0501   http://www.nocn.org.uk
    Chairman: David Knight
- E   Established in 1975. NOCN functions as a registered and a company limited by guarantee. The Board of Trustees comprises 14 members including the Chairman.
- R   NOCN is the awarding body for courses and qualifications in a wide variety of subjects.
- G   United Kingdom.
- ✍ For further information see the **Federation of Awarding Bodies**.

E The UK's first ten National Parks were established in England and Wales under the National Parks & Access to the Countryside Act 1949. The Environment Act 1995 established new National Park Authorities. There are currently 15.

The broad purpose of each Authority is to conserve and enhance the natural beauty, wildlife and cultural heritage of the park area and to promote opportunities for the understanding and enjoyment of the special qualities of the area by the public.

In pursuing these purposes each Authority seeks to foster the social and economic well-being of local communities and sympathetic employment opportunities in the Park.

R The Authorities are brought together by the UK Association of National Park Authorities, and those in England by the English National Parks Authorities Association, where they aim to raise the profile of the parks and promote joint working.

The Campaign for National Parks (qv) campaigns for the English and Welsh parks, while the Scottish Council for National Parks (qv) performs similar functions for the two in Scotland.

G England, Scotland, Wales.

● National Parks (with date established):

England:
>   The Broads (1988)
>   Dartmoor (1951)
>   Exmoor (1954)
>   Lake District (1951)
>   New Forest (2005)
>   North York Moors (1952)
>   Northumberland (1956)
>   Peak District (1951)
>   South Downs (2011)
>   Yorkshire Dales (1954)

Scotland:
>   Cairngorms (2003)
>   Loch Lomand & the Trossachs (2002)

Wales:
>   Brecon Beacons (1957)
>   Pembrokeshire Coast (1952)
>   Snowdonia (1951).

✍ For further information see individual Authorities.

National Park Homes Council   (NPHC)

■ Catherine House, Victoria Road, ALDERSHOT, Hants, GU11 1SS.
Tel 01252 313251   Fax 01252 322596   http://www.theparkhome.net
E Established in 1983. NPHC is a specialist division of the National Caravan Council.
R To represent the interests of the residential park home industry.
G United Kingdom.
✍ For details of the National Caravan Council see **Directory of British Associations**.

National Patient Safety Agency   (NPSA)

■ 4-8 Maple Street, LONDON, W1T 5HD.
Tel 020 7927 9500   Fax 020 7927 9501   http://www.npsa.nhs.uk
Chairman: Sir Liam Donaldson   Acting Chief Executive: Sarndrah Horsfall
E Established in July 2001. NPSA functions as a Special Health Authority of the Department of Health. There are 13 members of the NPSA Board including the Chairman.
R To reduce risks to patients receiving NHS care and to improve safety (the National Reporting & Learning Service).

To resolve concerns about the performance of individual clinical practitioners to help ensure their practice is safe and valued (the National Clinical Assessment Service).

To protect the rights, safety, dignity and well-being of research participants that are part of clinical trials and other research within the NHS (the National Research Ethics Service).

G England, Wales.

● NPSA commissions and monitors:
>   Confidential Enquiry into Maternal & Child Health
>   National Confidential Enquiry into Patient Outcome & Death
>   National Confidential Inquiry into Suicide & Homicide by People with Mental Illness (qqv).

The NPSA also operates the National Clinical Assessment Service, formerly the National Clinical Assessment Authority.

✍ The Secretary of State for Health announced on 26 July 2010 that NPSA will be abolished:
the National Reporting & Learning Service's functions will transfer to the new NHS Commissioning Board;

the National Clinical Assessment Service will become self-funding within two to three years; and
the National Research Ethics Service's functions will transfer to a single research regulator.

National Policing Improvement Agency (NPIA)

- Fry Building, 2 Marsham Street, LONDON, SW1P 4DF.
  Tel 020 3113 6000   http://www.npia.police.uk
  Chairman: Peter Holland, CBE, DL   Chief Executive: Nick Gargan
- E Established on 1 April 2007 under the Police & Justice Act 2006. NPIA functions as an Executive NDPB of the Home Office.
- R To support the police service by providing expertise in information and communications technology, support to information and intelligence sharing, core police processes, managing change and recruiting, developing and deploying people.
- G United Kingdom.
- ✍ NPIA is to be phased out by March 2012. The Home Office is looking at which functions are still needed and how they might best be delivered in a new, streamlined landscape.

National Portrait Gallery (NPG)

- St Martin's Place, LONDON, WC2H 0HE.
  Tel 020 7306 0055   http://www.npg.org.uk
  Chairman: Prof Sir David Cannadine, FBA, FRSL   Director: Sandy Nairne
- E Established in 1856 by Act of Parliament. The Gallery functions as an Executive NDPB of the Department for Culture, Media & Sport. The Board comprises 16 Trustees including the Chairman.
- R To have general control & management of the National Portrait Gallery.
- G United Kingdom.

National Probation Service

- ✍ Since 1 April 2008, NPS functions as part of the **National Offender Management Service**.

National Proficiency Tests Council (NPTC)

- Building 500, Abbey Park, STARETON, Warwickshire, CV8 2LY.
  Tel 024 7685 7300   Fax 024 7669 6128   http://www.nptc.org.uk
  Chief Executive: Jack Ward
- E Established in 1971 as a result of a National Federation of Young Farmers' Clubs' Annual General Meeting Minute of 18 May 1961. NPTC is a financially independent registered charity and part of City & Guilds group (qv). It is also the awarding body for courses and qualifications in agriculture and various land-based industries.
- R To promote competence and professionalism in the workforce of the land-based industries by the encouragement of continuous learning and the recognition of skill.
- G United Kingdom.
- ✍ For further information see the **Federation of Awarding Bodies**.

National Radiological Protection Board

- ✍ On 1 April 2005 the NRPB merged with the **Health Protection Agency**, forming its new Radiation Protection Division.

National Railway Museum   See **National Museum of Science & Industry**.

National Roman Legion Museum   See **National Museum Wales**.

National Savings & Investments (NS&I)

- GLASGOW, G58 1SB.
  Tel 0845 964 5000   http://www.nsandi.com
  Chairman: Martin Gray   Chief Executive: Jane Platt
- E Established in 1861 as the Post Office Savings Bank, becoming National Savings in 1969, and adopting its current name on 1 July 1996. NS&I functions as an Executive Agency of HM Treasury. The Board comprises 14 members including the Chairman.
- R To provide a totally safe place for people to save, backed by Government.
  To provide the Exchequer with a source of funding.
- G United Kingdom.

National School of Government

- Sunningdale Park, Larch Avenue, ASCOT, Berks, SL5 OQE.
  Tel 01344 634000   Fax 01344 634233   http://www.nationalschool.gov.uk
  Principal & Chief Executive: Rod Clark
- E   Established on 6 June 1989 and known as the Civil Service College prior to its merger with the Centre for Management & Policy Studies on 1 April 2000. The School functions as a non-ministerial government department.
- R   To provide a centre of excellence for developing the managerial and professional skills of civil servants.
- G   United Kingdom.

National Screening Committee   See **United Kingdom National Screening Committee**.

National Security Appeals Panel

- ✍   Formerly a special panel of the Information Tribunal, its functions were transferred on 18 January 2010 to the **Upper Tribunal (Administrative Appeals Chamber)**.

National Security Council   (NSC)

- 70 Whitehall, LONDON, SW1A 2AS.
  Tel 020 7276 3000
- E   Established on 12 May 2010 by the Prime Minister, NSC is the main forum for collective discussion of the Government's objectives for national security. The Council comprises eleven Government Ministers, chaired by the Prime Minister.
- R   To ensure that Ministers consider national security in the round and in a strategic way.
- G   United Kingdom.

National Security Inspectorate   (NSI)

- Sentinel House, 5 Reform Road, MAIDENHEAD, Berks, SL6 8BY.
  Tel 01628 637512   http://www.nsi.org.uk
- E   Established in 2001 following the merger of the National Approval Council for Security Systems (NACOSS) and the Inspectorate of the Security Industry (ISI). NSI functions as an independent not-for-profit approvals body.
- R   To inspect companies that provide home security, business security and fire protection services.
- G   United Kingdom.

National Services Division   (NSD)

- Gyle Square, 1 South Gyle Crescent, EDINBURGH, EH12 9EB.
  Tel 0131 275 5555   http://www.nsd.scot.nhs.uk
  Director: Deirdre Evans
- E   NSD is a division within NHS National Services Scotland (qv).
- R   To ensure provision of high quality, effective, specialised health and screening services to meet the needs of the population of Scotland.
- G   Scotland.

National Slate Museum   See **National Museum Wales**.

National Specialised Commissioning Advisory Group

- ✍   See the **Advisory Group for National Specialised Services**.

National Specialised Commissioning Group   (NSCG)

- 2nd Floor, Southside, 105 Victoria Street, LONDON, SW1E 6QT.
  Tel 020 7932 3939   http://www.specialisedservices.nhs.uk
  Chairman: Ruth Carnall, CBE
- E   Established on 1 April 2007 following the Review of Commissioning Specialised Services (the Carter Review). NSCG functions as part of NHS Specialised Services.
  The Group comprises 20 members, including a representative from each of the ten Specialised Commissioning Groups (SCGs) of England, observers from Wales, Scotland and Northern Ireland, and the Chairman.
- R   To oversee and coordinate the work of the ten regional SCGs where the specialised service has a catchment or planning population which is bigger than that of a single SCG.
  To encourage collaborative working between the SCGs and promote the sharing of best practice.
- G   England.

© CBD Research Ltd · Beckenham · Kent BR3 5JS · Tel 020 8650 7745 · Fax 020 8650 0768 · E-mail cbd@cbdresearch.com · www.cbdresearch.com

National Standing Committee on Farm Animal Genetic Resources   (NSC FAnGR)

- ■ 9 Millbank Area 5A, c/o 17 Smith Square, LONDON, SW1P 3JR.
  Tel 020 7238 4946
  Chairman: Prof Geoff Simm
- E Established in 2008. NSC FAnGR functions as an Advisory NDPB of the Department for Environment, Food & Rural Affairs with participation from the devolved administrations. The Committee comprises 15 members including the Chairman.
- R To provide advice to Government and interested parties on issues relating to farm animal genetic resources (FAnGR) and to oversee implementation of the UK's 2006 National Action Plan on FAnGR.
- G United Kingdom.
- ● The UK's FAnGR - its farm animal breeds, strains and varieties, and the variability within them - are of great economic, social and cultural importance. For these reasons alone it is important that we care for them. Additionally, we have national and international obligations to do so.
- ✍ The Government announced on 14 October 2010 that NSC FAnGR would cease to function as a NDPB and be reconsitituted as a committee of experts.

National Technical Liaison Committee for Safe Manriding in Mine Shafts
- ✍ NTLC SMIM is a sub-committee of the **Mining Industry Committee**.

National Toy Council   (NTC)

- ■ 80 Camberwell Road, LONDON, SE5 0EG.
  Tel 020 7701 7271   Fax 020 7708 2437   http://www.btha.co.uk
  Chairman: Prof Jeffrey Goldstein
- E Established in 1989. NTC is a forum which was set up by the British Toy & Hobby Association. The Council consists of the Chairman and 15 other members who represent represent various institutions and professions.
- R To ensure that a responsible and well-informed dialogue is maintained between the toy industry and the public, particularly in regard to the safety of its products and the manner in which they are marketed.
  To encourage the exchange of ideas on toy-related issues affecting children and their parents.
  To provide a forum in which such issues can be identified and examined in an environment where both commercial and social interests are represented.
- G United Kingdom.

National Training Inspectorate for Professional Dog Users   (NTIPDU)

- ■ New House, Cefn Vaynor, Berriew, WELSHPOOL, SY21 8PP.
  Tel 01686 640781   Fax 01686 640781   http://www.ntipdu.org
- E Established on 23 October 2002 after the Private Security Industry Act 2001 failed to identify dog handling as a licensable activity. NTIPDU is a membership organisation and functions as company limited by guarantee.
- R To promote the professionalism and training of security dog users and to regulate them in their operational duties.
  To promote, regulate and maintain the training of security dogs and ensure their safety and welfare.
  To formalise a suitable policy for training security dogs, detail strict licensing conditions and maintain set standards.
- G United Kingdom.

National Treatment Agency for Substance Misuse   (NTA)

- ■ 6th Floor, Skipton House, 80 London Road, LONDON, SE1 6LH.
  Tel 020 7972 1999   Fax 020 7972 1997   http://www.nta.nhs.uk
  Chairman: Baroness Massey of Darwen   Chief Executive: Paul Hayes
- E Established in 2001. NTA functions as a Special Health Authority of the Department of Health. The Board comprises 17 members including the Chairman.
- R To improve the availability, capacity and effectiveness of treatment for drug misuse in England.
- G England.
- ✍ The Secretary of State for Health announced on 26 July 2010 that NTA will be abolished as a Special Health Authority (qv) and its functions transferred to the new Public Health England.

National War Museum   See **National Museums Scotland**.

National Water Safety Forum   (NWSF)

- ■ RoSPA House, Edgbaston Park, Bristol Road, BIRMINGHAM, B5 7ST.
  Tel 0121 248 2000   Fax 0121 248 2001   http://www.nationalwatersafety.org.uk
  Chairman: Michael Vlasto

E	Established in 1961 as the National Water Safety Committee, adopting its current name following the publication in August 2002 of Inland Water Safety: Final Report of Scoping Study: Present Roles & Responsibilities. The Forum is sponsored by the Departments for Transport and for Environment, Food & Rural Affairs and the Royal Society for the Prevention of Accidents provides the secretariat. The Coordinating Group comprises eleven members including the Chairman.

R	To be the natural body in which organisations involved in water safety will participate in order to have a strong voice with Government on water safety issues.

G	United Kingdom.

●	The Forum has advisory groups on:
Beach Safety
Sea Safety
Swimming Pool Safety
Water Sports Safety
Water Safety at Home.

National Waterfront Museum   See **National Museum Wales**.

National Weights & Measures Laboratory
✍	Since April 2008 known as the **National Measurement Office**.

National Wool Museum   See **National Museum Wales**.

National Youth Agency   (NYA)

■	Eastgate House, 19-23 Humberstone Road, LEICESTER, LE1 2GJ
Tel 0116 242 7350   **Fax** 0116 242 7444   http://www.nya.org.uk
Chairman: Janice Shiner   Chief Executive: Fiona Blacke

E	Established on 1 April 1991 following an announcement by the Secretary of State for Education on 5 April 1990. NYA functions as an independent public agency and a registered charity. The board of trustees comprises 16 members including the Chairman.

R	To support those involved in young people's personal and social development and to work to enable all young people to fulfil their potential within a just society.

G	United Kingdom.

NATS

■	4000 Parkway, Whiteley, FAREHAM, Hants, PO15 7FL.
Tel 01489 616001   http://www.nats.co.uk
Chairman: John Devaney   Chief Executive: Richard Deakin   Shareholder Executive contact: Roger Lowe

E	Established in July 2001 under Transport Act 2000. NATS operates under licence from the Civil Aviation Authority (qv) and functions as a public-private partnership of the Department for Transport. The board comprises 14 members including the Chairman.

R	To provide air traffic control services at 15 of the UK's biggest airports, and 'en route' air traffic services for aircraft flying through UK airspace.

G	United Kingdom.

✍	One of the businesses managed by the **Shareholder Executive**.
NATS = National Air Traffic Services

Natural England

■	1 East Parade, SHEFFIELD, S Yorks, S1 2ET.
Tel 0300 060 6000   **Fax** 0300 060 1622   http://www.naturalengland.org.uk
Chairman: Poul Christensen, CBE   Chief Executive: Dr Helen Phillips

E	Established on 1 October 2006 under the Natural Environment & Rural Communities Act 2006. Natural England brings together the former English Nature, the landscape, access and recreation elements of the former Countryside Agency, and the environmental land management functions of the Rural Development Service. It functions as an Executive NDPB of the Department for Environment, Food & Rural Affairs. The Board comprises 16 members including the Chairman.

R	To provide practical advice, grounded in science, to Government on how best to safeguard England's natural wealth for the benefit of everyone.
To ensure sustainable stewardship of the land and sea so that people and nature can thrive, and to see that England's rich natural environment can adapt and survive intact for future generations to enjoy.
To work with farmers and land managers, business and industry, planners and developers, national, regional and local government, interest groups and local communities to help them improve their local environment.

G   England.
*   Natural England has offices in the nine English regions.
✍   The Government announced on 14 October 2010 that Natural England would be reformed through structural, process and cultural change to become a more efficient and customer focused organisation, and its accountabilities would be clarified.

Natural Environment Research Council   (NERC)

■   Polaris House, North Star Avenue, SWINDON, Wilts, SN2 1EU.
    Tel 01793 411500   **Fax** 01793 411501   http://www.nerc.ac.uk
    Chairman: Edmund Wallis   Chief Executive: Prof Alan Thorpe
E   Established by Royal Charter on 1 June 1965, under the Science & Technology Act 1965, and granted a Supplemental Charter on 16 December 1993. NERC functions as an independent NDPB accountable to the Department for Business, Innovation & Skills. The Council currently comprises 17 members including the Chairman.
R   To promote and support, by any means, high-quality basic, strategic and applied research and related postgraduate training in the environmental sciences.
G   United Kingdom.

Natural History Museum

■   Cromwell Road, LONDON, SW7 5BD.
    Tel 020 7942 5000   http://www.nhm.ac.uk
    Chairman: Oliver Stocken   Director: Dr Michael Dixon
E   Established under the British Museum Act 1963 as the British Museum (Natural History); it became the Natural History Museum through the Museums & Galleries Act 1992. The Museum functions as an Executive NDPB of the Department for Culture, Media & Sport. The governing Board of Trustees comprises twelve members including the Chairman.
R   To maintain and develop the museum's collections and use them to promote the discovery, understanding, responsible use and enjoyment of the natural world.
G   United Kingdom.

Naval Manning Agency

✍   NMA, established on 1 July 1996, was dissolved on 1 April 2004.

Naval Recruiting & Training Agency

✍   Now an integral part of the Royal Navy and no longer functions as an Executive Agency.

Navy, Army & Air Force Institutes   (NAAFI)

■   6 The Beehive, Lingfield Point, McMullen Road, DARLINGTON, Co Durham, DL1 1YN.
    Tel 01325 343880   http://www.naafi.co.uk
    Chairman: Sir Ian Prosser   Chief Executive: Reg Curtis
E   Established in 1921. NAAFI functions as a Public Corporation of the Ministry of Defence. The Board of Directors comprises seven members including the Chairman.
R   To provide a wide range of services, including catering, retail, leisure and facilities management, for members of HM Armed Forces and their families.
    To add value in terms of military effectiveness by assisting in improving morale, welfare, recruitment and retention within the Armed Forces.
    To offer the best value for money to the Treasury, the Ministry of Defence, HM Armed Forces and particularly the customer.
G   United Kingdom.

Navy Prosecution Authority

✍   Ceased to exist on 31 October 2009. See **Service Prosecuting Authority**.

NCFE

■   Citygate, St James' Boulevard, NEWCASTLE UPON TYNE, NE1 4JE.
    Tel 0191 239 8000   **Fax** 0191 239 8001   http://www.ncfe.org.uk
    Chairman: Chris Hughes, CBE

E The Northern Union of Mechanics' Institutes, established in 1848, was replaced in 1920 by the Northern Counties Technical Examinations Council. In 1981 it merged with the Northern Advisory Council for Further Education, established in 1947, taking the name Northern Council for Further Education. The name became NCFE in the early 1990s to reflect the company's national focus. NCFE functions as a registered charity and company limited by guarantee. The Board comprises nine members including the Chairman.

R To promote and advance the education and training of young persons and adults.

G England, Wales, Northern Ireland.

● NCFE is the awarding body for courses and qualifications in a wide variety of subjects.
   NCFE qualifications are offered by over 500 further education sector colleges, adult education centres, training providers, schools and businesses.

✍ For further information see the **Federation of Awarding Bodies**.

Neath Harbour Commissioners

■ Bank Side, NEATH, SA11 1RY.
   Tel 01639 633486   **Fax** 01639 631040

E Established in 1800 by Act of Parliament.

G Neath.

✍ For further information see **Port & Harbour Authorities**.

Neath Port Talbot Local Health Board

✍ Merged on 1 October 2009 with the Bridgend and Swansea Local Health Boards to form **Abertawe Bro Morgannwg University Health Board**.

Ness & Beauly Fisheries Trust   See **Rivers & Fisheries Trusts of Scotland**.

NEST Corporation

■ St Dunstan's House, 201-211 Borough High Street, LONDON, SE1 1JA.
   Tel 020 7940 8519   http://www.nestpensions.org.uk
   Chairman: Lawrence Churchill, CBE   Chief Executive: Tim Jones

E Established on 5 July 2010 when it took over the former Personal Accounts Delivery Authority which was set up under the Pensions Act 2007. The Corporation functions as an Executive NDPB of the Department for Work & Pensions. The board comprises a Chairman and up to 14 trustees.

R To administer NEST, the National Employment Savings Trust.

G United Kingdom.

● NEST is the new low cost pension scheme any employer can use to meet new legal requirements that start to be introduced from October 2102. NEST is being designed specifically to meet the needs of people who are largely new to pension saving and their employers.

Nestrans

■ Archibald Simpson House, 27-29 King Street, ABERDEEN, AB24 5AA.
   Tel 01224 625524   **Fax** 01224 626596   http://www.nestrans.org.uk
   Chairman: Cllr Kevin Stewart

E Established on 1 December 2005 as the North-East of Scotland Transport Partnership. The Partnership Board comprises eight Councillor members and four appointed members.

G Aberdeen City and Shire.

✍ For further information see **Regional Transport Partnerships**.

Neurology, Pain & Psychiatry Expert Advisory Group

■ 151 Buckingham Palace Road, LONDON, SW1W 9SZ.
   Tel 020 3080 6000
   Chairman: Dr Michael J Donaghy, DPhil(Oxon), FRCP

E Established in 2005. The Group functions as an advisory body to the Commission on Human Medicines (CHM), qv. It comprises 16 members including the Chairman.

R To advise CHM on the safety and efficacy of medicines for use in neurology, pain management, psychiatry and old age psychiatry.

G United Kingdom.

New Covent Garden Market   See **Covent Garden Market Authority**.

© CBD Research Ltd · Beckenham · Kent BR3 5JS · Tel 020 8650 7745 · Fax 020 8650 0768 · E-mail cbd@cbdresearch.com · www.cbdresearch.com

New East Manchester

■ 187 Grey Mare Lane, Beswick, MANCHESTER, M11 3ND.
   Tel 0161 223 1155   http://www.east-manchester.com
   Chairman: Simon Bate   Chief Executive: Eddie Smith

E Established in October 1999. New East Manchester is the Urban Regeneration Company for east Manchester and functions as a wholly-owned subsidiary company of and controlled by Manchester City Council.

R To transform an area covering almost 2,000 hectares immediately east of Manchester City Centre into an attractive and vibrant destination, home to a proud and growing community of investors, businesses and residents.

G East Manchester

✍ For further information see **Urban Regeneration Companies**

New Forest National Park Authority   (NFNPA)

■ South Efford House, Milford Road, Everton, LYMINGTON, Hants, SO41 0JD.
   Tel 01590 646600   Fax 01590 646666   http://www.newforestnpa.gov.uk
   Chairman: Julian Johnson   Chief Executive: Alison Barnes

E The New Forest was designated a National Park on 1 March 2005 and the Authority established in 1 April 2005. The Authority comprises 22 members including the Chairman.

G New Forest.

✍ For further information see **National Park Authorities**.

New Homes Marketing Board   (NHMB)

■ 1st Floor, Byron House, 7-9 St James's Street, LONDON, SW1A 1DW.
   Tel 020 7960 1600   Fax 020 7960 1601   http://www.nhmb.co.uk
   Chairman: David Pretty

E Established in 1982 by the Home Builders Federation.

R To promote the benefits of buying newly built homes.
   To promote the need for new housing amongst the general public and key opinion formers.

G United Kingdom

● In 2002 NHMB and the Home Builders Federation established an online database of new housing developments at www.new-homes.co.uk.

New Millennium Experience Company Ltd

✍ Established in February 1997 to build and operate the Millennium Dome, the company was liquidated in 2001.

New Opportunities Fund

✍ Responsibilities were transferred in 2006 to its successor body, the **Big Lottery Fund**.

New Swindon Company

✍ The former Urban Regeneration Company became an Economic Development Company on 1 April 2010 and adopted the trading name **Forward Swindon**.

Newcastle Airport Consultative Committee   (NACT)

■ Newcastle International Airport, Woolsington, NEWCASTLE UPON TYNE, NE13 8BZ.
   Tel 0191 214 3279   Fax 0191 214 3563   http://www.newcastleairport.com
   Hon Secretary: Graeme Mason

G County Durham, Northumberland, Tyneside.

✍ For further information see **Airport Consultative Committees**.

Newlyn Pier & Harbour Commissioners

■ Harbour Office, Newlyn, PENZANCE, Cornwall, TR18 5HW.
   Tel 01736 362523   Fax 01736 351614   http://www.newlynharbour.co.uk
   Harbour Master: Andrew Munson

E Established in 1884 by Act of Parliament.

G Newlyn.

✍ For further information see **Port & Harbour Authorities**.

Newport Harbour Commissioners
- 24 Bridge Street, NEWPORT, Gwent, NP20 4SF.
  Tel 01633 265702   Fax 01633 258431   http://www.newportharbourcommissioners.org.uk
  Chairman: Colin P Crick
- E   Established under the Newport (South Wales) Harbour Acts & Orders 1836 to 2003. The board comprises eight
     members.
- G   Newport, Gwent.
- ✍   For further information see **Port & Harbour Authorities**.

Newport Local Health Board
- ✍   Merged on 1 October 2009 with the Blaenau Gwent, Caerphilly, Monmouthshire, and Torfaen Local Health
     Boards to form **Aneurin Bevan Health Board**.

Newport Unlimited
- One Gold Tops, NEWPORT, Gwent, NP20 4PG.
  Tel 01633 844141   Fax 01633 844144   http://www.newportunlimited.co.uk
  Chairman: Grant Watson   Chief Executive: Gareth Beer
- E   Established in March 2003 as Newport Urban Regeneration Company Ltd. Trading as Newport Unlimited, it is a
     partnership of the Welsh Government and Newport City Council working with the private sector to promote
     investment and regeneration in Newport.
- G   Newport, South Wales (Gwent).
- ✍   For further information see **Urban Regeneration Companies**.

Newspaper Licensing Agency   (NLA)
- Wellington Gate, Church Road, TUNBRIDGE WELLS, Kent, TN1 1NL.
  Tel 01892 525273   Fax 01892 525275   http://www.nla.co.uk
  Chairman: Dominic Young   Managing Director: David Pugh
- E   Established in 1996 by the UK national newspapers to manage newspaper copyright collection.
- R   To license organisations to copy from the UK's national and regional newspapers in both paper and digital
     formats.
     To collect fees from licensed users for this copying and to distribute the fees to the publishers.
- G   United Kingdom.

Nexus
- Nexus House, St James' Boulevard, NEWCASTLE UPON TYNE, NE1 4AX.
  Tel 0191 203 3333   Fax 0191 203 3180   http://www.nexus.org.uk
  Director General: Bernard Garner
- E   Established on 1 January 1970 under the Transport Act 1968 as the Tyneside Passenger Transport Executive,
     becoming the Tyne & Wear Passenger Transport Executive under the Local Government Act 1972. It operates
     under the brand name Nexus. Nexus is responsible to the Tyne & Wear Integrated Transport Authority (qv).
- R   In addition to its responsibilities as a Passenger Transport Executive, Nexus operates the Tyne & Wear Metro and
     the Shields Ferry.
- G   Tyne & Wear.
- ✍   For further information see **Passenger Transport Executives & Integrated Transport Authorities**.

NHS - NATIONAL HEALTH SERVICE

E   The National Health Service officially came into being on 5 July 1948; its statutory basis lies in a series of Acts of
    Parliament starting with the National Health Service Act 1946 (these acts are consolidated in the National Health
    Service Act 1977, as amended by the Health Services Act 1980).

There are four health departments in the UK and each is responsible for national strategic planning and
administration in its own area:

ENGLAND - Department of Health
Richmond House, 79 Whitehall, LONDON, SW1A 2NL.
Tel 020 7210 4850   http://www.dh.gov.uk
Chief Medical Officer: Prof Dame Sally Davies

SCOTLAND - Department of Health & Community Care
St Andrew's House, Regent Road, EDINBURGH, EH1 3DG.
Tel 0131 556 8400   http://www.scotland.gov.uk
Chief Medical Officer: Dr Harry Burns

WALES - Department for Public Health & Health Professions
Second Floor, Cathays Park (1), CARDIFF, CF10 3NQ.
Tel 029 2037 0011   http://www.wales.gov.uk
Chief Medical Officer: Dr Tony Jewell

NORTHERN IRELAND - Department of Health, Social Services & Public Safety
Castle Buildings, Stormont, BELFAST, BT4 3SJ.
Tel 028 9052 0500   http://www.dhsspsni.gov.uk
Chief Medical Officer: Dr Michael McBride

The many and various national and local bodies that contribute to the running of the NHS in each country are listed in the Subject Index under **NHS: ENGLAND**, etc.

NHS 24

■ Caledonia House, Fifty Pitches Road, Cardonald Park, GLASGOW, G51 4EB.
Tel 0141 337 4501   **Fax** 0141 882 6764   http://www.nhs24.com
Chairman: Allan Watson   Chief Executive: John Turner

E Established under the NHS 24 (Scotland) Order 2001. It functions as an NHS Body of the Scottish Executive Health Department. The Board comprises 14 members including the Chairman.

R To establish, implement and manage a confidential 24-hour nurse consultation and health information telephone advice service across Scotland.
NHS 24 Helpline: 0845 424 2424.

G Scotland.

● NHS 24 has operates from three main centres in the East, North and West of Scotland, and from six local centres.

✍ One of the seven Special NHS Boards in Scotland.

NHS Appointments Commission
✍ Since 2006 the **Appointments Commission**.

NHS Blood & Transplant   (NHSBY)

■ Oak House, Reeds Crescent, WATFORD, Herts, WD24 4QN.
Tel 01923 486800   **Fax** 01923 486801   http://www.nhsbt.nhs.uk
Chairman: Bill Fullagar   Chief Executive: Lynda Hamlyn

E Established in October 2005 through the merger of the National Blood Service, UK Transplant and the Bio Products Laboratory. NHSBT functions as a Special Health Authority of the Department of Health. The Board comprises nine members including the Chairman.

R To encourage people to donate organs, blood and tissues.
To optimise the safety and supply of organs, blood and tissues.
To help raise the quality, effectiveness and clinical outcomes of blood and transplant services.
To provide expert advice to other HNS organisations, the Department of Health and the devolved administrations.
To provide advice and support to health services in other countries.
To commission and conduct research and development.
To implement EU statutory frameworks and guidance.

G United Kingdom.

✍ For further information see **Special Health Authorities**.

NHS Business Services Authority   (NHSBSA)

■ Bridge House, 152 Pilgrim Street, NEWCASTLE UPON TYNE, NE1 6SN.
Tel 0191 232 5371   **Fax** 0191 232 2480   http://www.nhsbsa.nhs.uk
Chairman: Paul Rich   Chief Executive: Nick Scholte

E Established on 1 October 2005, bringing together the former Counter Fraud & Security Management Service Authority, Dental Practice Board, NHS Logistics Authority, NHS Pensions Agency and Prescription Pricing Authority. NHSBSA functions as a Special Health Authority of the Department of Health. The board comprises eleven members including the Chairman.

R To provide a wide range of services to support the NHS frontline and directly to the public.

G United Kingdom.

● The NHS Counter Fraud Service is responsible for policy and operational matters relating to the prevention, detection and investigation of fraud in the NHS.
Dental Services pay dentists promptly and accurately. They also provide dental statistics and key information to national, regional and local NHS bodies.
Help with Health Costs provides exemption certificates to those entitled and sells Prescription Pre-payment Certificates.

The NHS Injury Benefits Scheme provides an annual allowance for staff who suffered a permanent loss of earning ability as the result of an illness or injury, wholly or mainly, attributable to their NHS employment.

NHS Pensions administers the NHS Pension Scheme.

NHS Supply Chain provides customer-focused healthcare products and supply chain services to the NHS.

NHS Prescription Services remunerate and reimburse dispensing chemists across England. They also provide the NHS with a range of financial, prescribing and drug information.

The NHS Security Management Service is responsible for the security of people and property across the NHS in England.

NHSBSA administers the NHS Bursary Scheme for eligible NHS students which covers everyday living costs, including childcare. NHSBSA also administers the social work and postgraduate bursaries.

NHS Commissioning Board

- ■ Department of Health, Richmond House, 79 Whitehall, LONDON, SW1A 2NS.
- E Due to be established in April 2012. It will incorporate elements of the National Patient Safety Agency, the NHS Institute for Innovation & Improvement, and the Specialised Commissioning Groups (qqv). The proposed Board will have the responsibility for holding GP consortia to account and for allocating and accounting for NHS resources.
- R To control and support GP consortia; to hold them to account in terms of outcomes, financial performance and operating in a fair and transparent manner when commissioning.
  To commission specialised services for people with rare conditions.
- G England.

NHS Direct

- ■ 207 Old Street, LONDON, EC1V 9NR.
  Tel 0845 4647   http://www.nhsdirect.nhs.uk
  Chairman: Joanne Shaw   Chief Executive: Nick Chapman
- E Established in 1997. It now functions as a Special Health Authority of the Department of Health. The Board comprises eleven directors including the Chairman.
- R To be the national healthline, providing expert health advice, information and reassurance, using its world class telephone service and website, and to be the NHS's provider of choice for telephone and digitally delivered health services.
- G England.
- ✍ For further information see **Special Health Authorities**

NHS Direct Wales

- ■ Thanet House, 10 Phoenix Way, Enterprise Park, SWANSEA, Glamorgan, SA7 9EH.
  Tel 0845 4647   http://www.nhsdirect.wales.nhs.uk
- E NHS Direct was established in England and Wales in 1997. As NHS Direct Wales, it became part of the Welsh Ambulance Services NHS Trust (qv) on 1 April 2007. The Board comprises eleven directors including the Chairman.
- R To be the national healthline, providing expert health advice, information and reassurance, using its world class telephone service and website, and to be the NHS's provider of choice for telephone and digitally delivered health services.
- G Wales.

NHS East of England   See **East of England Strategic Health Authority**.

NHS East Midlands   See **East Midlands Strategic Health Authority**.

NHS Education for Scotland   (NES)

- ■ Thistle House, 91 Haymarket Terrace, EDINBURGH, EH12 5HD.
  Tel 0131 313 8000   **Fax** 0131 313 8001   http://www.nes.scot.nhs.uk
  2nd Floor, Hanover Buildings, 66 Rose Street, EDINBURGH, EH2 2NN.
  Tel 0131 225 4365   **Fax** 0131 225 5891
  Chairman: Dr Lindsay Burley, CBE   Chief Executive: Malcolm Wright, OBE
- E Established on 1 April 2002 under NHS Education for Scotland Order 2002. NES functions as a Special Health Board of the Scottish Executive Health Department. The Board comprises 15 members including the Chairman.
- R To contribute to the delivery of highest quality healthcare by promoting best practice in the education and lifelong learning of NHS Scotland staff, particularly through multi-disciplinary working and learning.
- G Scotland.

© CBD Research Ltd · Beckenham · Kent BR3 5JS · Tel 020 8650 7745 · Fax 020 8650 0768 · E-mail cbd@cbdresearch.com · www.cbdresearch.com

- In addition to its central offices, NES has regional centres in Aberdeen, Dundee, Edinburgh, Glasgow and Inverness.
- ✍ One of the seven Special NHS Boards in Scotland.

NHS ENGLAND - STRATEGIC HEALTH AUTHORITIES   (SHAs)

E   In 2002, 28 Strategic Health Authorities were established to replace the 95 Health Authorities into which the NHS in England had been organised in 1996. On 1 July 2006 the number of SHAs was further reduced to ten, based on the standard regions of England with the South East split into South Central and South East Coast.
     The Chairmen and non-executive directors of the SHAs are appointed by the Appointments Commission (qv).
R   To enact the directives and implement the fiscal policy of the Department of Health in their regions.
     To be responsible for the NHS Trusts (Primary Care Trusts, Hospital Trusts, Ambulance Services Trusts, Mental Health Services Trusts and Care Trusts) which are responsible for running and commissioning local NHS services.
G   England.
●   The current SHAs are:
        East of England SHA
        East Midlands SHA
        London SHA
        North East SHA
        North West SHA
        South Central SHA
        South East Coast SHA
        South West SHA
        West Midlands SHA
        Yorkshire & the Humber SHA (qqv).
✍   See also the **Office of the Strategic Health Authorities**.

NHS Estates Management & Health Building Agency
✍   The Agency closed on 30 September 2005.

NHS Health Scotland
■   Woodburn House, Canaan Lane, EDINBURGH, EH10 4SG.
     Tel 0131 536 5500   Fax 0131 536 5501   http://www.healthscotland.com
     Chairman: Margaret Burns, CBE   Chief Executive: Gerald McLaughlin
E   Established on 1 April 2003 (when the Health Education Board for Scotland merged with the Public Health Institute of Scotland) under the National Health Service & Community Care Act 1990, the Health Education Board for Scotland Order 1990 and the Health Education Board for Scotland Amendment Order 2003. It functions as an NHS Body of the Scottish Executive Health Department. The Board comprises 15 members including the Chairman.
R   To provide a national focus for improving health and to work with the Scottish Government and other key partners to take action to improve health and reduce health inequalities in Scotland.
G   Scotland.
✍   One of the seven Special NHS Boards in Scotland.

NHS Information Authority
✍   Ceased operation on 1 April 2005.

NHS Information Centre   (IC)
■   1 Trevelyan Square, Boar Lane, LEEDS, W Yorks, LS1 6AE.
     Tel 0845 300 6016   http://www.ic.nhs.uk
     7th Floor, New Kings Beam House, 22 Upper Ground, LONDON, SE1 9BW.
     Smedley Hydro, Trafalgar Road, Birkdale, SOUTHPORT, Lancs, PR8 2HH.
     Chairman: Mike Ramsden   Chief Executive: Tim Straughan
E   Established in 2005. IC functions as a Special Health Authority of the Department of Health. The Board comprises 13 members including the Chairman.
R   To drive the use of information to improve decision making and deliver better care.
     To provide accessible, high quality and timely information to help frontline health and social care deliver better care.
G   England.

NHS Institute for Innovation & Improvement   (NHSIII)

■ Coventry House, University of Warwick Campus, COVENTRY, CV4 7AL.
   Tel 024 7647 5800   http://www.institute.nhs.uk
   Chairman: Dame Yve Buckland   Chief Executive: Prof Bernard Crump
E Established in July 2005 under Section 11 of the NHS Act 1977. The Institute functions as a Special Health
   Authority of the Department of Health. The Board comprises eleven members including the Chairman.
R To support the NHS in its efforts to transform healthcare for patients and the public by rapidly developing and
   spreading new ways of working, new technology and world class leadership.
G United Kingdom.
✍ The Secretary of State for Health announced on 26 July 2010 that NHSIII will be abolished as a Special Health
   Authority (qv). Its functions which will support the new NHS Commissioning Board in leading for quality
   improvement will be transferred to the Board. The Department of Health is reviewing the potential for its
   remaining functions to be delivered through alternative commercial delivery models.

NHS Litigation Authority   (NHSLA)

■ 2nd Floor, 151 Buckingham Place Road, LONDON, SW1W 9SZ.
   Tel 020 7811 2700   Fax 020 7821 0029   http://www.nhsia.com
   1 Trevelyan Square, Boar Lane, LEEDS, W Yorks, LS1 6AE.
   Tel 0113 866 5500
   Chairman: Prof Dame Joan Higgins, DBE   Chief Executive: Stephen Walker, CBE
E Established in 1995. NHSLA functions as a Special Health Authority of the Department of Health. The Board
   consists of the Chairman, four non-executive directors, the Chief Executive and the Director of Finance.
R To handle negligence claims and work to improve risk management practices in the NHS.
   To be responsible for resolving disputes between practitioners and primary care trusts, giving advice to the NHS
   on human rights case law, and handling equal pay claims on behalf of the NHS.
G England.
✍ For further information see **Special Health Authorities**.

NHS Logistics Authority
✍ Replaced in 2006 by **NHS Supply Chain**.

NHS London   See **London Strategic Health Authority**.

NHS Medical Education England   See **Medical Education England**.

NHS National Services Scotland   (NSS)

■ Gyle Square, 1 South Gyle Crescent, EDINBURGH, EH12 9EB.
   Tel 0131 275 6250   Fax 0131 275 7500   http://www.nhsnss.org
   Chairman: Bill Matthews   Chief Executive: Ian Crichton
E Established on 1 April 1974 under provisions of the National Health Service (Scotland) Act 1972 & the National
   Health Service (Common Services Agency Membership & Procedure) (Scotland) Regulations, SI 1975/76 (S15).
   It functions as an Executive NDPB of the Scottish Executive Health Department. The Board comprises 13
   members including the Chairman.
R To provide national strategic support services and expert advice to NHS Scotland.
G Scotland.
● Core services are delivered through NSS divisions, which are grouped into Health Support and Business Support:
   Health Support:
         Health Facilities Scotland (operational advice on all facilities topics)
         Health Protection Scotland (coordinating health protection)
         Information Services (health statistics and analysis)
         National Services (screening and specialist health services)
         Scottish National Blood Transfusion Service
   Business Support:
         Central Legal Office (specialist legal services)
         Counter Fraud Service (deterring, detecting and investigating fraud)
         National Information Systems Group (supports the delivery of IM&T)
         National Procurement (acquiring, storing and delivering goods and services)
         Practitioner Services (family health service payments and patient registration)
         Scottish Health Service Centre (conference facilities and event organising)
✍ Formerly known as the Common Services Agency for the Scottish Health Service.

NHS National Waiting Times Centre Board
- ■ Golden Jubilee National Hospital, Agamemnon Street, CLYDEBANK, G81 4DY.
  Tel 0141 951 5000   http://www.nhsgoldenjubilee.co.uk
  Chairman: Jeane Freeman, OBE   Chief Executive: Jill Young
- E Established on 27 June 2002 under the National Waiting Times Centre Board (Scotland) Order 2002 (Nr 305). It functions as an NHS Body of the Scottish Executive Health Department. The Board comprises 14 members including the Chairman.
- R To manage the former HCI facility (the Golden Jubilee National Hospital, Clydebank) as a national centre to address waiting time priorities.
- G Scotland.
- ✍ One of the Special NHS Boards in Scotland.

NHS North East   See **North East Strategic Health Authority**.

NHS North West   See the **North West Strategic Health Authority**.

NHS Northern Ireland   See **Health & Social Care**.

NHS Pay Review Body   (NHSPRB)
- ■ 6th Floor, Kingsgate House, 66-74 Victoria Street, LONDON, SW1E 6SW.
  Tel 020 7215 8559   Fax 020 7215 4445
  Chairman: Prof Gillian Morris
- E Established in 1983 as the Review Body for Nurses & Allied Professionals, subsequently the Review Body for Nursing & Other Health Professions, it adopted its current name in 2007. NHSPRB functions as an Advisory NDPB of the Department of Health. The Review Body comprises eight members including the Chairman.
- R To advise the Government on the pay of all staff taking part in the National Health Service (with the exception of doctors, dentists and very senior managers).
- G United Kingdom.
- ✍ One of the Pay Review Bodies whose secretariat is provided by the **Office of Manpower Economics**.

NHS Pensions Agency
- ✍ In 2006 the NHS Pensions Agency became a division of the **NHS Business Services Authority**.

NHS Professionals
- ■ Richmond House, 79 Whitehall, LONDON, SW1A 2NS.
  Tel 020 7210 4850   http://www.nhsprofessionals.nhs.uk
  Chairman: Richard Martin   Chief Executive: Neil Lloyd
- E Established on 1 January 2004. NHS Professionals functions as a Special Health Authority of the Department of Health.
- R To help NHS Trusts meet their overall cost saving objectives and give them greater understanding and control of their flexible staffing.
  To give staff the opportunity to work flexibly in the NHS, enabling them to achieve a better balance of work and life.
  To lead on the development of higher standards of clinical governance in the provision of flexible workers to the NHS.
- G England.

NHS Purchasing & Supply Agency
- ✍ In 2009 PASA's purchasing functions were transferred to **Buying Solutions** and its supply functions to **NHS Supply Chain**.

NHS Quality Improvement Scotland   (NHS QIS)
- ■ Elliott House, 8-10 Hillside Crescent, EDINBURGH, EH7 5EA.
  Tel 0131 623 4300   Fax 0131 623 4299   http://www.nhshealthquality.org
  Delta House, 50 West Nile Street, GLASGOW, G1 2NP.Tel 0141 225 6999   Fax 0141 248 3778
  Chairman: Prof Sir Graham Teasdale   Chief Executive: Dr Frances Elliot
- E Established on 1 January 2003 under SSI 2002 No 534 (Scotland) Order 2002.
  NHS QIS functions as an NHS Body of the Scottish Executive Health Department.
  The Board comprises 15 members including the Chairman.

R   To support, ensure and monitor the quality of healthcare provided by NHS Scotland.
G   Scotland.
✍ One of the seven Special NHS Trusts in Scotland.

NHS SCOTLAND - BOARDS

E   On 1 April 2004 14 geographically-based Boards replaced NHS Trusts.
    Each board comprises non-executive members (including the Chairman and Local Authority elected members)
        and executive members.
R   To provide strategic leadership and performance management for the entire local NHS system in their areas and
        ensure that services are delivered effectively and efficiently.
G   Scotland.
✍ For a full list of the 14 Boards, see the Subject Index under **NHS Scotland (Regional)**.

NHS South Central   See the **South Central Strategic Health Authority**.

NHS South East Coast   See the **South East Coast Strategic Health Authority**.

NHS South West   See the **South West Strategic Health Authority**.

NHS Specialised Services
■   2nd Floor, Southside, 105 Victoria Street, LONDON, SW1E 6QT.
    Tel 020 7932 3939   http://www.specialisedservices.nhs.uk
E   Established on 1 April 2007 following the Review of Commissioning Specialised Services (the Carter Review).
        NHS Specialised Services is the national organisation resonsible for the commissioning of about 60 specialised
        services that help improve the lives of children and adults with rare diseases or disorders.
R   In England there are ten Specialised Commissioning Groups (SCGs) that commission specialised services for
        their regional population. The National Specialised Commissioning Group (NSCG), qv, facilitates working across
        the SCGs. The Advisory Group for National Specialised Services (AGNSS), qv, advises health Ministers on
        which services should be nationally commissioned.
G   England.

NHS Supply Chain
■   West Way, Coles Park Industrial Estate, ALFRETON, Derbys, DE55 4QJ.
    Tel 01773 724000   **Fax** 01773 724225   http://www.supplychain.nhs.uk
E   NHS Supply Chain is under a ten-year contract operated by DHL on behalf of the NHS Business Services
        Authority (qv); It replaces the former NHS Logistics Authority.
R   To provide end-to-end supply chain services, incorporating procurement, logistics, e-commerce and customer
        end supplier support, to more than 600 NHS trusts, hospitals and other healthcare organisations.
G   United Kingdom.

NHS Wales Informatics Service   (NWIS)
■   12th Floor, Brunel House, 2 Fitzalan Road, CARDIFF, CF24 0HA.
    Tel 029 2050 0500   http://www.hsw.wales.nhs.uk
    Director: Andrew Griffiths
E   Established on 1 April 2010 by merging Informing Healthcare, Health Solutions Wales, Business Services Centre
        Information Management & Technology element, Corporate Health Information Programme and Primary Care
        Informatics Programme. NWIS is under the overall direction of the Chief Information Officer of the Welsh
        Government.
R   To support NHS Wales and make better use of scarce skills and resources by bringing together the strategic
        development of Information Communications Technology (ICT), the delivery of operational ICT services and
        information management.
G   Wales.
=   Gwasanaeth Gwybodeg GIG Cymru

E   The National Health Service in Wales was part of NHS England & Wales from its foundation in 1946 until 1969 when it came under the Secretary of State for Wales. After devolution in 1999 jurisdiction passed to the Welsh Government.

Local Health Boards were introduced for primary care in 2003, one for each of the 22 Unitary Authorities. In addition there were nine regional NHS Trusts providing hospitals, community care and mental health functions.

On 1 October 2009 this was simplified to seven LHBs, each responsible for the provision of all NHS services within its group of Unitary Authorities. Each has dropped the word 'local' from its operational name. For the full list, see the Subject Index under NHS Wales (Regional).

The boards' chairmen and non-executive directors are appointed by the Minister for Health & Social Services.

R   To plan, secure and deliver healthcare services in their areas.

G   Wales.

●   In addition to LHBs, NHS Wales operates four nationwide services: NHS Wales Informatics Service, Public Health Wales, Welsh Ambulance Services NHS Trust and Velindre NHS Trust (qqv).

✍   LHBs are monitored by Community Health Councils (qv).

NHS West Midlands   See the **West Midlands Strategic Health Authority**.

NHS-Wide Clearing Service Security & Confidentiality Advisory Group
✍   NWCS closed in 2006.

NHS Yorkshire & the Humber   See **Yorkshire & the Humber Strategic Health Authority**.

Noise & Vibration Sub-Committee   A sub-committee of the Health & Safety Executive's **Foundries Industry Advisory Committee**.

Nominations & Governance Committee   A committee of the **Church Commissioners**.

Norfolk Police Authority
■   Jubilee House, Falconers Chase, WYMONDHAM, Norfolk, NR18 0WW.
      Tel 01953 424455   Fax 01953 424462   http://www.norfolk-pa.gov.uk
      Chairman: Cllr Stephen Bett   Chief Executive: Chris Harding
E   Established in April 1995, the Authority is an independent body charged with ensuring that Norfolk Constabulary provides an effective and efficient police service. It is made up of nine county councillors and eight independent members.
G   Norfolk.
✍   For further information see **Police Authorities**.

Norfolk Rural Community Council   **(NRCC)**
■   Signpost House, Ambassador Way, Greens Road, DEREHAM, Norfolk, NR20 3TL.
      Tel 01362 698216   Fax 01362 851083   http://www.norfolkrcc.org.uk
      Chief Executive: Jon Clemo
E   Established in 1986. NRCC functions as a registered charity and company limited by guarantee.
R   To help communities all the way from identifying needs to delivering solutions with friendly support and genuine expertise.
      To provide a voice to rural communities to ensure that decisions on services, policies and strategies do not discriminate against them and adequately serve and reflect their needs.
      To research, consult and develop initiatives to solve the problems faced by communities in Norfolk.
G   Norfolk.
✍   Norfolk RCC is one of the 38 Rural Community Councils, represented at the national level by **Action with Communities in Rural England** (qv) and at the regional level by Rural Action East.

Norfolk, Suffolk & Cambridgeshire Strategic Health Authority
✍   On 1 July 2006 merged with the Bedfordshire & Hertfordshire and the Essex Strategic Health Authorities to form the **East of England Strategic Health Authority**.

Norfolk & Suffolk Probation Trust
- ■ Centenary House, 19 Palace Street, NORWICH, Norfolk, NR3 1RT.
  Tel 01603 724000   Fax 01603 768270   http://www.nsprobation.org.uk
  Chairman: Gill Lewis   Chief Officer: Martin Graham
- E Established on 1 April 2010 under the Offender Management Act 2007, merging two area boards (Norfolk and Suffolk) which had been set up on 1 April 2001 under the Criminal Justice & Court Service Act 2000. The Board comprises eight members including the Chairman.
- G Norfolk, Suffolk.
- ✍ For further information see **Probation Trusts**.

North Central London Strategic Health Authority
- ✍ On 1 July 2006 merged with the North East, North West, South East and South West London Strategic Health Authorities to form a single **London Strategic Health Authority**.

North East Assembly
- ✍ Abolished in March 2009 (see Regional Assemblies). The region's local authority leaders cooperate as the **Association of North East Councils**.

North East England Regional Select Committee and North East England Grand Committee   See **United Kingdom Parliament: Committees**.

North East Industrial Development Board
- ✍ See note under **Industrial Development Boards**.

North East London Strategic Health Authority
- ✍ On 1 July 2006 merged with the North Central, North West, South East and South West London Strategic Health Authorities to form a single **London Strategic Health Authority**.

North East Regional Development Agency   The Agency operates as **One North East**.

North East Regional Information Partnership   See **Regional Observatories**.

North East Rural Community Councils   RuCANNE represents **Community Action Northumberland, Durham Rural Community Council** and **Tees Valley Rural Community Council**; it operates under the umbrella of **Action with Communities in Rural England**.

North-East of Scotland Transport Partnership   See **Nestrans**.

North East Strategic Health Authority
- ■ Waterfront 4, Goldcrest Way, NEWCASTLE UPON TYNE, Tyne & Wesr, NE15 8NY.
  Tel 0191 210 6400   Fax 0191 210 6401   http://www.northeast.nhs.uk
  Chairman: Sir Peter Carr   Chief Executive: Ian Dalton
- E Established on 1 July 2006 replacing two former Strategic Health Authorities: the Northumberland, Tyne & Wear, and the Co Durham & Tees Valley.
  The board comprises six non-executive directors including the Chairman, and five executive directors including the Chief Executive.
- R To relay and explain national policy, set direction and support and develop NHS Trust bodies (Primary Care Trusts and NHS Trusts providing acute, mental health and ambulance services).
  To ensure that local health systems operate effectively and efficiently, and that national standards and priorities are met.
- G County Durham, Northumberland, Teesside, Tyne & Wear.
- ✍ One of the ten regional Strategic Health Authorities of England - see **NHS - England** in the Subject Index.

North & East Yorkshire & Northern Lincolnshire Strategic Health Authority
- ✍ On 1 July 2006 merged with the South and West Yorkshire Strategic Health Authorities to form **Yorkshire & the Humber Strategic Health Authority**.

© CBD Research Ltd · Beckenham · Kent BR3 5JS · Tel 020 8650 7745 · Fax 020 8650 0768 · E-mail cbd@cbdresearch.com · www.cbdresearch.com

North Eastern Education & Library Board   (NEELB)

- County Hall, 182 Galgorm Road, BALLYMENA, Co Antrim, BT42 1HN.
  Tel 028 2565 3333   http://www.neelb.org.uk
  Chief Executive: Shane McCurdy
- E Established in 1973. NEELB functions as an Executive NDPB of the Department of Education Northern Ireland. The Board comprises 23 members.
- G Local Government Districts Antrim, Ballymena, Ballymoney, Carrickfergus, Coleraine, Larne, Magherafelt, Moyle and Newtownabbey.
- ✍ The ELBs and other legacy organisations will be dissolved when the Education & Skills Authority becomes fully operational.
  For further information see **Education & Library Boards (Northern Ireland)**.

North Eastern Traffic Commissioner   See **Traffic Commissioners**.

North Northants Development Company   (NNDC)

- 1 Exchange Court, Cottingham Road, CORBY, Northants, NN17 1TY.
  Tel 01536 274979   Fax 01536 443951   http://www.nndev.co.uk
  Chairman: David Reynolds   Chief Executive: Simon Evans
- E Established in May 2006 by the merger of Corby Catalyst (Urban Regeneration Company) and the North Northants Together partnership. NNDC is the Local Delivery Vehicle (similar to an Urban Regenaration Company, qv) for North Northamptonshire. The Board comprises twelve members including the Chairman.
- R To bring forward the necessary infrastructure improvements to in turn create the right environment for investment, new jobs and significant housing growth.
- G North Northamptonshire (Corby, Kettering and Wellingborough).
- ✍ For further information see **Urban Regeneration Companies**.

North of Scotland Electricity Consumers Committee
- ✍ The work of NSECC was taken over by energywatch which was replaced in 2008 by **Consumer Focus**.

North South Language Body

- Joint Secretariat, 58 Upper English Street, ARMAGH, BT61 7LG.
  Tel 028 3751 8068   Fax 028 3751 1874   http://www.ulsterscotsagency.com
  Joint chairmen: Liam Ó Maoilmhichil and Tom Scott, OBE
- E Established on 2 December 1999, one of the six North South Implementation Bodies set up under the British-Irish Agreement of 8 March 1999. It is responsible to the North South Ministerial Council (qv), the Department of Culture, Arts & Leisure Northern Ireland and to the Irish Government. The Body is jointly chaired by the Chairmen of Foras Na Gaeilge (the Irish language agency) and the Ulster-Scots Agency (qqv).
- R To oversee the operation of the two agencies.
- G Northern Ireland, Republic of Ireland.
- ✍ For further information see the **North South Ministerial Council**.

North South Ministerial Council   (NSMC)

- Joint Secretariat, 39 Abbey Street, ARMAGH, BT61 7EB.
  Tel 028 3751 8068   Fax 028 3751 1874   http://www.northsouthministerialcouncil.org
  Joint Secretaries: Mary Bunting (Northern Ireland)   Tom Hanney (Republic of Ireland)
- E Established on 2 December 1999 under the Belfast/Good Friday Agreement 1998. NSMC comprises ministers of the Northern Ireland Executive and the Irish Government.
- R To develop consultation, cooperation and action within the island of Ireland, including through implementation on an all-island and cross-border basis, on matters of mutual interest and within the competence of the Administrations, North and South.
- G Northern Ireland, Republic of Ireland
- ● In five Areas of Cooperation common policies and approaches are agreed in the NSMC but implemented separately in each jurisdiction:
  Agriculture (Common Agricultural Policy issues; Animal and plant health policy and research; Rural development)
  Education (Education for children with special needs; Educational under-achievement; Teacher qualifications; School, youth and teacher exchanges)
  Environment (Environmental protection, pollution, water quality management and waste management in a cross-border context)
  Health (Accident and emergency planning; Cooperation on high technology equipment, cancer research and health promotion)

Transport (Cooperation on strategic transport planning, including road and rail infrastructure and public transport services; Road and rail safety).
✍ Seven North South Implementation Bodies operate on an all-island basis under the overall direction of the NSMC:
Food Safety Promotion Board
Foyle, Carlingford & Irish Lights Commission
North South Language Body
Special EU Programmes Body
Tourism Ireland
Trade & Business Development Body
Waterways Ireland (qqv)

North Wales Police Authority
■ Glan-y-Don, COLWYN BAY, Conwy, LL28 9AW.
 Tel 01492 805486   **Fax** 01492 805489   http://www.nwalespa.org
 Chairman: Cllr Ian Roberts
E Established in April 1995, the Authority is an independent body charged with ensuring that North Wales Police provide an effective and efficient police service.
 It is made up of nine local councillor members and eight independent members.
G Anglesey, Conwy, Denbighshire, Flintshire, Gwynedd and Wrexham.
✍ For further information see **Police Authorities**.
= Awdurdod Heddlu Gogledd Cymru

North West England Regional Select Committee and North West England Grand Committee   See **United Kingdom Parliament: Committees**.

North West Industrial Development Board
✍ See note under **Industrial Development Boards**.

North West London Strategic Health Authority
✍ On 1 July 2006 merged with the North Central, North East, South East and South West London Strategic Health Authorities to form a single **London Strategic Health Authority**.

North West Regional Assembly
✍ Abolished in July 2008 (see Regional Assemblies). The region's local authority leaders cooperate as **4NW**.

North West Regional Flood Defence Committee   See **Environment Agency** (North West Region).

North West Regional Leaders Board   (4NW)
■ c/o Town Hall, Victoria Square, ST HELENS, Merseyside, WA10 1HP.   http://www.4nw.org.uk
 Chairman: Cllr Sir Richard Leese
E Established on 15 July 2008 following the abolition of the North West Assembly, 4NW is the Leaders Board for the North West of England. Membership comprises the leaders of 15 councils, the Chairman of the Lake District National Park Authority (qv) and representatives of seven Social, Economic & Environmental Partners (SEEPS). The current Chairman is the Leader of Manchester City Council.
R To be responsible, in conjunction with the Northwest Regional Development Agency (qv), for regional strategic planning and economic development.
G Cheshire, Cumbria, Greater Manchester, Lancashire, Merseyside.

North West Rural Community Councils   NWRCC represents **Action with Communities in Cumbria**, **Cheshire Community Action** and **Community Futures** (Lancashire); it operates under the umbrella of **Action with Communities in Rural England**.

North West Strategic Health Authority
■ 7th Floor, Gateway House, Station Approach, Piccadilly South, MANCHESTER, M60 7LP.
 Tel 0845 050 0194   http://www.northwest.nhs.uk
 Chairman: Sir David Henshaw   Chief Executive: Mike Farrar, CBE

E Established on 1 July 2006 replacing three former Strategic Health Authorities: the Cheshire & Merseyside, the Cumbria & Lancashire and the Greater Manchester. The board comprises six non-executive directors including the Chairman, and eight executive directors including the Chief Executive.

R To relay and explain national policy, set direction and support and develop NHS Trust bodies (Primary Care Trusts and NHS Trusts providing acute, mental health and ambulance services).
To ensure that local health systems operate effectively and efficiently, and that national standards and priorities are met.

G Cheshire, Cumbria, Greater Manchester, Lancashire, Merseyside.

✍ One of the ten regional Strategic Health Authorities of England - see **NHS - England** in the Subject Index.

North West Tourist Board

✍ NWTB has been replaced by the Visitor Economy Commission of the **Northwest Regional Development Agency** which supports five sub-regional tourist boards.

North West Vision

✍ Merged in May 2007 with Media Training Northwest as **Vision+Media**.

North Western Traffic Commissioner   See **Traffic Commissioners**.

North York Moors National Park Authority   (NYMNPA)

■ The Old Vicarage, Bondgate, Helmsley, YORK, YO62 5BP.
Tel 01439 770657   Fax 01439 770691   http://www.northyorkmoors.org.uk
Chairman: John Fletcher   Chief Executive: Andy Wilson

E The North York Moors were designated a National Park in 1952. The present Authority was established on 1 April 1997 under the Environment Act 1995. It consists of 26 members including the Chairman.

G North York Moors.

✍ For further information see **National Park Authorities**.

North Yorkshire Police Authority   (NYPA)

■ BBP House, Keld Close, Melmerby, RIPON, N Yorks, HG4 5NB.
Tel 01765 641839   Fax 01765 641844   http://www.nypa.gov.uk
PO Box 106, RIPON, N Yorks, HG4 5WA.
Chairman: Cllr Jane Kenyon

E Established in April 1995, the Authority is an independent body charged with ensuring that North Yorkshire Police provide an effective and efficient police service. It is made up of seven North Yorkshire County Councillors, two City of York Councillors and eight independent members.

G North Yorkshire.

✍ For further information see **Police Authorities**.

Northamptonshire ACRE

■ The Hunsbury Hill Centre, Harksome Hill, NORTHAMPTON, NN4 9QX.
Tel 01604 765888   Fax 01604 708571   http://www.northantsacre.org.uk
Chief Executive: David Quayle

E Northamptonshire ACRE functions as a registered charity and company limited by guarantee.

R To help enhance the quality of life for people living in the rural areas of the county, particularly those disadvantaged through lack of access to services, and to support and advise rural communities and rural community groups on rural and community development issues.

G Northamptonshire.

✍ Northamptonshire ACRE is one of the 38 Rural Community Councils, represented at the national level by **Action with Communities in Rural England** (qv) and at the regional level by Rural Community Action East Midlands.

Northamptonshire Police Authority

■ 36 Billing Road, NORTHAMPTON, NN1 5DQ.
Tel 01604 887430   http://www.northantspoliceauthority.org.uk
Chairman: Mrs Deirdre Newham, JP

E Established in April 1995, the Authority is an independent body charged with ensuring that Northamptonshire Police provide an effective and efficient police service. It is made up of nine councillor members, three magistrate members and five independent members.

G Northamptonshire.

✍ For further information see **Police Authorities**.

Northamptonshire Probation Trust

■ Walter Tull House, 43-47 Bridge Street, NORTHAMPTON, NN1 1NS.
Tel 01604 658000   **Fax** 01604 658089   http://www.northants-probation.org.uk
Chairman: David Moir, JP   Chief Officer: Beverley Thompson

E   Established on 1 April 2001 under the Criminal Justice & Court Service Act 2000 as the Northamptonshire
Probation Area Board. It became a trust on 1 April 2010 under the Offender Management Act 2007. The Board
comprises eleven members including the Chairman.

G   Northamptonshire.

✍ For further information see **Probation Trusts**.

Northeast Tourism Advisory Board

■ Stella House, Goldcrest Way, Newburn Riverside, NEWCASTLE UPON TYNE, NE15 8NY.
Tel 0191 229 6200   **Fax** 0191 229 6201   http://www.onenortheast.co.uk
Chairman: Geoff Hodgson

E   Established by One North East (qv) when it assumed responsibility for tourism development from the former
Northumbria Tourist Board in March 2004. The Board comprises twelve members including the Chairman.

G   County Durham, Northumberland, Teesside, Tyne & Wear.

Northern Agricultural Land Tribunal

■ Defra Building, Electra Way, CREWE, Cheshire, CW1 6GJ.
Tel 01270 754156   **Fax** 01270 754260
Secretary: Mr M Baker

E   Established under the Agriculture Act 1947 (Section 73).

G   Cumbria, Durham, Northumberland, Tyne & Wear, Tees Valley.

✍ For further information see **Agricultural Land Tribunals** [England & Wales].

Northern Council for Further Education   See **NCFE**.

Northern Film & Media

■ Studio 3, The Kiln, Hoults Yard, NEWCASTLE UPON TYNE, NE6 1AB.
Tel 0191 275 5930   **Fax** 0191 275 5931   http://www.northernmedia.org
Chairman: Sir Les Elton   Chief Executive: Tom Harvey

E   Established in October 2002.

G   County Durham, Northumberland, Teesside, Tyne & Wear.

✍ For further information see **Creative England** and **Regional Screen Agencies**.

Northern Health & Social Care Trust

■ The Cottage, 5 Greenmount Avenue, BALLYMENA, Co Antrim, BT43 6DA.
Tel 0845 601 2333   **Fax** 028 2563 3733   http://www.northerntrust.hscni.net
Chairman: Jim Stewart   Chief Executive: Norma Evans

E   Established on 1 April 2007, the Trust brings together the former Causeway, Homefirst Community and United
Hospitals Health & Social Services Trusts. The Board comprises 13 members including the Chairman.

G   Antrim, Ballymena, Ballymoney, Carrickfergus, Coleraine, Cookstown, Larne, Magherafelt, Moyne and
Newtownabbey.

✍ For further information see **Health & Social Care**.

Northern Health & Social Services Board

✍ On 1 April 2009 the four regional boards were replaced by a single **Health & Social Care Board** for Northern
Ireland.

Northern Health & Social Services Council

✍ On 1 April 2009 the four regional councils were replaced by a single **Patient & Client Council** for Northern
Ireland.

Northern Ireland Advisory Committee on Telecommunications   Superceded by Ofcom's **Advisory Committee
for Northern Ireland**.

Northern Ireland Ambulance Service HSC Trust   (NIAS)

- ■ Site 30, Knockbracken Healthcare Park, Saintfield Road, BELFAST, BT8 8SG.
  Tel 028 9040 0999   **Fax** 028 9040 0900   http://www.niamb.co.uk
  Chairman: Paul Archer   Chief Executive: Liam McIvor
- E Established on 1 April 1995 under the Health & Personal Social Services (Northern Ireland) Order 1991 and the Establishment Order (Northern Ireland) 1995. NIAS functions as a Health & Personal Social Services NDPB of the Department of Health, Social Services & Public Safety Northern Ireland. The Board comprises ten members including the Chairman.
- R To manage ambulance, patient transport and communication services provided from ambulance control centres.
- G Northern Ireland.
- ✍ See also **Health & Social Care**.

NORTHERN IRELAND ASSEMBLY: Committees

- E There are three types of committee established by the Northern Ireland Assembly:
  Departmental Committees - There is one Committee for each of the eleven Northern Ireland Government Departments. Each advises and assists the Minister on matters within his responsibility, undertakes a scrutiny, policy development and consultation role with respect to the Department, and plays a key role in the consideration and development of legislation.
  Standing Committees - There are currently six:
  Assembly & Executive Review Committee
  Audit Committee
  Business Committee
  Committee on Procedures
  Public Accounts Committee
  Committee on Standards & Privileges
  Ad Hoc Committees - These Committees are established from time to time to deal with specific time-bounded terms of reference that the Assembly may set.
- ✍ See also Introduction.

Northern Ireland Authority for Utility Regulation   (NIAUR)

- ■ Queens House, 14 Queen Street, BELFAST, BT1 6ER.
  Tel 028 9031 1575   **Fax** 028 9031 1740   http://www.niaur.gov.uk
  Chairman: Prof Peter Matthews   Chief Executive: Iain Osborne
- E Established in 2003 under the Energy (Northern Ireland) Order 2003 as amended by the Water & Sewerage Services (Northern Ireland) Order 2006; the Authority was formerly the Office for the Regulation of Electricity & Gas before taking on the additional regulation of water and sewerage. NIAUR functions as an independent public body. The Authority comprises eight members including the Chairman.
- R To ensure the effective regulation of the electricity, gas and water and sewerage industries in Northern Ireland.
- G Northern Ireland.

Northern Ireland Blood Transfusion Service   (NIBTS)

- ■ Lisburn Road, BELFAST, BT9 7TS.
  Tel 028 9032 1414   **Fax** 028 9043 9017   http://www.nibts.org
  Chairman: Jim Lennon   Acting Chief Executive: Dr K Morris
- E Established in 1946, the Service now derives its authority under the Northern Ireland Blood Transfusion (Special Agency) (Establishment & Consitution) Order (Northern Ireland) 1994. NIBTS functions as a Special Agency of the Department of Health, Social Services & Public Safety Northern Ireland. The Board comprises four members including the Chairman.
- R To fully supply the needs of all hospitals and clinical units in the Province with safe and effective blood and blood products and other related services.
- G Northern Ireland.
- ✍ The service collects, tests and distributes over 75,000 blood donations each year.

Northern Ireland Building Regulations Advisory Committee   (NIBRAC)

- ■ Level 5, Causeway Exchange, 1-7 Bedford Street, BELFAST, BT2 7EG.
  Tel 028 9051 2704   **Fax** 028 9028 3282
  Chairman: Kenneth Hunter
- E Established in June 1973 under the Building Regulations (Northern Ireland) Order 1972 and continuing under the Building Regulations (Northern Ireland) Order 1979. NIBRAC functions as an Advisory NDPB of the Department of Finance & Personnel Northern Ireland. The Committee comprises 18 members including the Chairman.
- R To advise the Department on matters relating to building regulations.
- G Northern Ireland.

Northern Ireland Central Investment Fund for Charities' Advisory Committee　(CIFC)

- 1 Cromac Place, Gasworks Business Park, Ormeau Road, BELFAST, BT7 2JB.
  Tel 028 9082 9459　Fax 028 9082 9516
- E　Established on 1 March 1965 under the Charities Act (Northern Ireland) 1964.
- R　To advise the Department for Social Development with respect to the investments of the Northern Ireland Central Investments Fund for Charities.
- G　Northern Ireland.
- ●　The Fund aims to give charity trustees the opportunity to invest all or part of their assets with the benefit of expert supervision.

Northern Ireland Child Support Agency

- ✍　On 1 April 2008 NICSA was replaced by the **Child Maintenance & Enforcement Division** of the Department for Social Development Northern Ireland.

Northern Ireland Civil Service Appeal Board　See **Civil Service Appeal Board**.

Northern Ireland Clinical Excellence Awards Committee　(NICEAC)

- Castle Buildings, Stormont, BELFAST, BT4 3SJ.
  Tel 028 9052 0500
  Chairman: Pat Carvill
- E　NICEAC functions as an Advisory NDPB of the Department of Health, Social Services & Public Safety Northern Ireland. The Committee comprises nine members including the Chairman.
- R　To make recommendations to the Department on which health and social care consultants should receive the higher value Clinical Excellence Awards.
- G　Northern Ireland.

Northern Ireland Commissioner for Children & Young People　(NICCY)

- Millennium House, 17-25 Great Victoria Street, BELFAST, BT2 7BA.
  Tel 028 9031 1616　Fax 028 9031 4545　http://www.niccy.org
  Commissioner: Patricia Lewsley　Chief Executive: Gerard Campbell
- E　Established on 27 February 2003 under the Commissioner for Children & Young People (Northern Ireland) Order 2003. The Commissioner functions as an Executive NDPB of the Office of the First Minister & Deputy First Minister.
- R　To promote and safeguard the rights and best interests of children and young people.
- G　Northern Ireland.

Northern Ireland Commissioner for Complaints　See **Northern Ireland Ombudsman**.

Northern Ireland Community Relations Council　See **Community Relations Council**.

Northern Ireland Construction Industry Training Board　See **CITB-ConstructionSkills Northern Ireland**.

Northern Ireland Consumer Committee for Electricity

- ✍　Now part of the **Consumer Council for Northern Ireland**.

Northern Ireland Council for the Curriculum, Examinations & Assessment　See **Council for the Curriculum, Examinations & Assessment**.

Northern Ireland Council for Ethnic Minorities　(NICEM)

- 3rd Floor, Ascot House, 24-31 Shaftesbury Square, BELFAST, BT2 7DB.
  Tel 028 9023 8645　Fax 028 9031 9485　http://www.nicem.org.uk
  Executive Director: Patrick Yu
- E　Established on 8 June 1994. NICEM is an independent non-governmental organisation which acts as an umbrella for its 28 member groups.
- R　To promote good race ralations and to endeavour to achieve the elimination of racial discrimination and the promotion of racial equality.
- G　Northern Ireland.

© CBD Research Ltd · Beckenham · Kent BR3 5JS · Tel 020 8650 7745 · Fax 020 8650 0768 · E-mail cbd@cbdresearch.com · www.cbdresearch.com

- NICEM's services: Legislation & campaigning; Capacity building; Support to migrants; Support to victims of racial harrassment; Anti-racism training.

Northern Ireland Council for Integrated Education   (NICIE)
- ◼ Aldersgate House, 13-19 University Road, BELFAST, BT7 1NA.
  Tel 028 9023 6200   Fax 028 9023 6237   http://www.nicie.org
  Chairman: Colm Cavanagh   Chief Executive: Noreen Campbell
- E Established in March 1989 under the Education Reform Order (Northern Ireland) 1989. NICIE functions as a company limited by guarantee, registered charity and Advisory NDPB of the Department of Education Northern Ireland. The Board comprises 16 members including the Chairman.
- R To develop, support and promote integrated education in Northern Ireland.
- G Northern Ireland.
- ✍ NICIE and other legacy organisations will be dissolved when the Education & Skills Authority (qv) becomes fully operational.

Northern Ireland Council for Postgraduate Medical & Dental Education
- ✍ In 2004 was replaced by the **Northern Ireland Medical & Dental Training Agency**.

Northern Ireland Council for Voluntary Action   (NICVA)
- ◼ 61 Duncairn Gardens, BELFAST, BT15 2GB.
  Tel 028 9087 7777   Fax 028 9087 7799   http://www.nicva.org
  Chairman: Bob Stronge   Chief Executive: Seamus McAleavey
- E Established in 1938. NICVA is an umbrella membership body, registered charity and company limited by guarantee. The Executive Committee comprises 15 members including the Chairman.
- R To work for justice, equality and dignity throughout society by promoting opportunities for community participation in the essential decisions that affect the lives of people in Northern Ireland.
- G Northern Ireland.

Northern Ireland Courts & Tribunals Service   (NICTS)
- ◼ Laganside House, 23-27 Oxford Street, BELFAST, BT1 3LA.
  Tel 028 9032 8594   Fax 028 9031 0227   http://www.courtsni.gov.uk
  Director: David A Lavery
- E Established in 1979 under the Judicature (Northern Ireland) Act 1978. NICTS functions as an Executive Agency of the Department of Justice Northern Ireland. The Agency Board comprises ten members including the Director.
- R To provide administrative support for Northern Ireland Courts, Judiciary and Tribunals.
  To enforce civil court judgments through a centralised enforcement service provided by the Enforcement of Judgments Office.
  To support the Lord Chancellor in discharging his ministerial responsibilities in Northern Ireland, including responsibility for judicial appointments and legal aid.
- G Northern Ireland.

Northern Ireland Drainage Council   See **Drainage Council Northern Ireland**.

Northern Ireland Environment Agency   (NIEA)
- ◼ Klondyke Building, Cromac Avenue, Gasworks Business Park, BELFAST, BT7 2JA.
  Tel 0845 302 0008   http://www.doeni.gov.uk/niea/
  Chief Executive: John McMillen
- E Established on 1 April 1996 as the Environment Service, adopting its current name on 1 July 2008. NIEA functions as an Executive Agency of the Department of the Environment Northern Ireland.
- R To protect, conserve and promote the natural environment and built heritage for the benefit of present and future generations.
- G Northern Ireland.

Northern Ireland Equality Commission   See **Equality Commission for Northern Ireland**.

Northern Ireland Film & Television Commission
- ✍ See **Northern Ireland Screen**.

Northern Ireland Fire & Rescue Service   (NIFRS)

■ 1 Seymour Street, LISBURN, Co Antrim, BT27 4SX.
    Tel 028 9266 4221   **Fax** 028 9267 7402   http://www.nifrs.org
    Chairman: Dr Joe McKee   Chief Executive & Chief Fire Officer: Peter Craig
E   Established on 1 July 2006 under the Fire & Rescue Services (Northern Ireland) Order 2006, the NIFRS Board
    replaces the former Fire Authority of Northern Ireland. It functions as an Executive NDPB of the Department of
    Health, Social Services & Public Safety Northern Ireland. The Board comprises twelve members including the
    Chairman.
R   To be responsible for providing fire and rescue services across the Province.
G   Northern Ireland.

Northern Ireland Fishery Harbour Authority   (NIFHA)

■ 3 St Patrick's Avenue, DOWNPATRICK, Co Down, BT30 6DW.
    Tel 028 4461 3844   **Fax** 028 4461 7128   http://www.nifha.co.uk
    Chairman: Margaret Andrews   Chief Executive: Chris Warnock, BSc, CDipFA, MIE
E   Established 31 May 1973, under the Harbours Act (Northern Ireland) 1970 and the Northern Ireland Fishery
    Harbour Authority Order (Northern Ireland) 1973. NIFHA functions as an Executive NDFPB of the Department of
    Agriculture & Rural Development. The board comprises six members including the Chairman.
R   To improve, manage and maintain the harbours of Ardglass, Kilkeel and Portavogie.
G   County Down (Ardglass, Kilkeel and Portavogie).
✍ For further information see **Port & Harbour Authorities**.

Northern Ireland Food Advisory Committee   (NIFAC)

■ 10a Clarendon Road, BELFAST, BT1 3BG.
    Tel 028 9041 7700
    Chairman: Dr Henrietta Campbell
E   Established in 2000. NIFAAC acts as an independent advisory body to the Food Standards Agency (qv). The
    Committee comprises nine members including the Chairman.
R   To advise the Agency of food safety and standards issues, with particular emphasis to Northern Ireland.
G   Northern Ireland.

Northern Ireland Grand Committee   See **United Kingdom Parliament: Committees**.

Northern Ireland Guardian Ad Litem Agency   (NIGALA)

■ Centre House, 79 Chichester Street, BELFAST, BT1 4JE.
    Tel 028 9031 6550   **Fax** 028 9031 9811   http://www.nigala.hscni.net
    Chairman: Jim Currie   Chief Executive: Ronnie Williamson
E   Established in 1995 under the Children (Northern Ireland) Order 1995. NIGALA functions as a Health & Personal
    Social Services NDPB of the Department of Health, Social Services & Public Safety Northern Ireland. The Board
    comprises five members including the Chairman.
R   To recruit and manage a panel of persons from whom courts in Northern Ireland shall appoint Guardians ad litem
    for the purposes of specified proceedings under the Children (Northern Ireland) Order 1995 and adoption
    proceedings under the Adoption (Northern Ireland) Order 1987.
G   Northern Ireland.

Northern Ireland Health & Social Services Estates Agency

■ HEIG, Annex 6, Castle Buildings, BELFAST, BT4 3SQ.
    Tel 028 9052 3741   **Fax** 028 9052 3900
    Chief Executive: John Cole
E   Established on 2 October 1995. **Health Estates** functions as an Executive Agency of the Department of Health,
    Social Services & Public Safety Northern Ireland.
R   To support the mission statement of the Department by providing a centre of specialist professional and technical
    estate expertise which supports the development and maintenance of an efficient and effective HSS estate for
    the delivery of health and personal social services.
G   Northern Ireland.

Northern Ireland Healthcare-Associated Infection Surveillance Centre   See **Healthcare-Associated Infection
    Surveillance Centre**.

Northern Ireland Higher Education Council   (NIHEC)

- Adelaide House, 39-49 Adelaide Street, BELFAST, BT2 8FD.
  Tel 028 9025 7777   **Fax** 028 9025 7778
  Chairman: Tony Hopkins, CBE
- E   Established on 1 April 1993. NIHEC functions as an Advisory NDPB of the Department of Employment & Learning Northern Ireland. The Council comprises 14 members including the Chairman.
- R   To advise DELNI on issues pertaining to strategic priorities, strategic funding issues and policy and planning for all aspects of higher education in Northern Ireland.
- G   Northern Ireland.

Northern Ireland Horse Board   (NIHB)

- 23 Ballykeigle Road, COMBER, Co Down, BT23 5SD.
  Tel 028 9752 8324   **Fax** 028 9752 8500   http://www.nihorseboard.org
- E   Established in 1996. NIHB functions as a non-profit making membership organisation and registered co-operative society. The Board comprises twelve members.
- R   To maintain and promote the Irish Horse Register in Northern Ireland, providing registration at affordable prices.
  To improve the quality of stock bred in Northern Ireland.
  To identify and publicise successful Northern Ireland bred horses.
- G   Northern Ireland.
- ● The NIHB encourages and implements marketing initiatives and works closely with the Irish Horse Board in areas of mutual benefit.

Northern Ireland Housing Council   See **Housing Council**.

Northern Ireland Housing Executive   (NIHE)

- The Housing Centre, 2 Adelaide Street, BELFAST, BT2 8PB.
  Tel 028 9024 0588   http://www.nihe.gov.uk
  Chairman: Brian Rowntree   Chief Executive: Paddy McIntyre
- E   Established in 1971 under the Housing Executive Act (Northern Ireland) 1971; it is now constituted under the Housing (Northern Ireland) Order 1981. NIHE functions as an Executive NDPB of the Department for Social Development Northern Ireland. The Board comprises ten members including the Chairman.
- R   To promote affordable housing, independent living, urban and rural regeneration, stronger communities and improved public services.
- G   Northern Ireland.

Northern Ireland Human Rights Commission   (NIHRC)

- Temple Court, 30 North Street, BELFAST, BT1 1NA.
  Tel 028 9024 3987   **Fax** 028 9024 7844   http://www.nihrc.org
  Chief Commissioner: Prof Monica McWilliams
- E   Established on 1 March 1999 under the Northern Ireland Act 1998. NIHRC functions as an Executive NDPB funded by the Northern Ireland Office. It comprises eight commissioners including the Chief Commissioner.
- R   To promote awareness of the importance of human rights in Northern Ireland.
  To review existing law and practice.
  To advise the Secretary of State for Northern Ireland and the Executive of the Northern Ireland Assembly on what legislative or other measures ought to be taken to protect human rights in Northern Ireland.
- G   Northern Ireland.

Northern Ireland Industrial Court   See **Industrial Court**.

Northern Ireland Industrial Tribunals   See **Industrial Tribunals & the Fair Employment Tribunal**.

Northern Ireland Judicial Appointments Commission   (NIJAC)

- Headline Building, 10-14 Victoria Street, BELFAST, BT1 3GG.
  Tel 028 9056 9100   **Fax** 028 9056 9101   http://www.nijac.org
  Chairman: Sir Declan Morgan   Chief Executive: Edward Gorringe
- E   Established on 15 June 2005 under the Justice (Northern Ireland) Acts 2002 and 2004. NIJAC functions as an Executive NDPB of the Department of Justice Northern Ireland. The Commission comprises 13 members including the Chairman, the Lord Chief Justice for Northern Ireland.
- R   To select and recommend candidates for judicial service in Northern Ireland, on merit, through a fair and open competition and by selecting from the widest possible range of eligible candidates.
- G   Northern Ireland.

Northern Ireland Judicial Appointments Ombudsman   (NIJAO)
- ■   6th Floor, Bedford House, Bedford Street, BELFAST, BT2 7DS.
       Tel 028 9072 8930   **Fax** 028 9072 8936   http://www.nijao.gov.uk
       Ombudsman: Karamjit Singh, CBE
- E   Established on 25 September 2006, the NIJAO replaces the former Office of the Commissioner for Judicial
       Appointments in Northern Ireland.
- R   To investigate complaints from applicants for judicial appointments where maladministration or unfairness is
       alleged to have occurred in the process by the Northern Ireland Judicial Appointments Commission (qv), the
       Northern Ireland Court Service (qv), or the Lord Chancellor.
- G   Northern Ireland.

Northern Ireland Law Commission   (NILC)
- ■   Linum Chambers, 8th Floor, 2 Bedford Square, BELFAST, BT2 7ES.
       Tel 028 9054 4860   http://www.nilawcommission.gov.uk
       Chairman: The Hon Mr Justice McCloskey   Chief Executive: Judena Goldring
- E   Established in 2007 under the Justice (Northern Ireland) Act 2002 following the recommendations of the Criminal
       Justice Review Group 2000.
       NILC functions as an Advisory NDPB of the Office of the First Minister & Deputy First Minister.
       The Commission comprises five members including the Chairman.
- R   To keep the law of Northern Ireland under review and make recommendations for its systematic development and
       reform.
- G   Northern Ireland.

Northern Ireland Legal Services Commission   (LSC)
- ■   2nd Floor, Waterfront Plaza, 8 Laganbank Road, Mays Meadow, BELFAST, BT1 3BN.
       Tel 028 9040 8888   **Fax** 028 9040 8990   http://www.nilsc.org.uk
       Chairman: Ronnie Spence
- E   Established on 1 November 2003 under the Access to Justice (Northern Ireland) Order 2003. LSC functions as an
       Executive NDPB of the Department of Justice Northern Ireland. The Board comprises ten members including
       the Chairman.
- R   To promote fair and equal access to justice in Northern Ireland in its provision of publicly funded legal services.
- G   Northern Ireland.

Northern Ireland Library Authority   (NILA)
- ■   Unit 3A, The Sidings Office Park, Antrim Road, LISBURN, Co Antrim, BT28 3RG.
       Tel 028 9263 5322   http://www.librariesni.org.uk
       Chairman: Dr David Elliott   Chief Executive: Irene Knox
- E   Established on 1 April 2009 under the Libraries Act (Northern Ireland) 2008. Known as **Libraries NI**, the Authority
       functions as an Executive NDPB of the Department of Culture, Leisure & Arts Northern Ireland. The Board
       comprises up to 19 members including the Chairman.
- R   To develop the best quality library service within the budget and policy guidelines provided by the Department.
       To ensure equity of provision across Northern Ireland.
- G   Northern Ireland.

Northern Ireland Local Government Officers' Superannuation Committee   (NILGOSC)
- ■   411 Holywood Road, BELFAST, BT4 2LP.
       Tel 0845 308 7345   **Fax** 0845 308 7344   http://www.nilgosc.org.uk
       Chairman: Trevor Salmon, OBE
- E   Established on 1 April 1950 under the Local Government (Superannuation) Act (Northern Ireland) 1950, the
       Committee's present authority is derived from the Local Government Pension Scheme (Administration)
       Regulations (Northern Ireland) 2009. NILGOSC functions as an Executive NDPB of the Department for
       Employment & Learning Northern Ireland. The Committee comprises 13 members including the Chairman.
- R   To administer the Local Government Pension Scheme for Northern Ireland, membership of which is open to
       employees working in local government and employees in the public sector who are not eligible to join another
       scheme, such as the Teachers', Lecturers' or Firefighters' schemes.
- G   Northern Ireland.

Northern Ireland Medical & Dental Training Agency   (NIMDTA)
- ■   Beechill House, 42 Beechill Road, BELFAST, BT8 7RL.
       Tel 028 9040 0000   **Fax** 028 9079 8312   http://www.nimdta.gov.uk
       Chief Executive: Dr Terry McMurray

© CBD Research Ltd · Beckenham · Kent BR3 5JS · Tel 020 8650 7745 · Fax 020 8650 0768 · E-mail cbd@cbdresearch.com · www.cbdresearch.com

E   Established in April 2004 replacing the former Northern Ireland Council for Postgraduate Medical & Dental Education. NIMDTA functions as a Special Agency of the Department of Health, Social Services & Public Safety Northern Ireland. The Board comprises six members including the Chief Executive.
R   To fund, manage and support postgraduate medical and dental education within the Northern Ireland Deanery.
G   Northern Ireland.

Northern Ireland Museums Council   (NIMC)
■   6 Crescent Gardens, BELFAST, BT7 1NS.
    Tel 028 9055 0215   Fax 028 9055 0216   http://www.nimc.org.uk
    Chairman: Mr Lexie Scott
E   Established in 1993 by order of the Minister for Education in Northern Ireland. NIMC functions both as a compnay limited by guarantee with charitable status and as an Executive NDPB of the Department of Culture, Arts & Leisure Northern Ireland. The Board comprises 14 Directors including the Chairman.
R   To support local museums in Northern Ireland in maintaining and improving their standards of collections care and services to the public.
    To promote a coherent framework of museum provision.
G   Northern Ireland.

Northern Ireland Ombudsman
■   Progressive House, 33 Wellington Place, BELFAST, BT1 6HN.
    Tel 028 9023 3821   Fax 028 9023 4912   http://www.ni-ombudsman.org.uk
    Ombudsman: Tom Frawley
E   Northern Ireland Ombudsman is a popular name for two offices, the **Assembly Ombudsman for Northern Ireland** and the **Northern Ireland Commissioner for Complaints**. They were established in 1969 under the Parliamentary Commissioner Act (Northern Ireland) 1969 and the Commissioner for Complaints Act (Northern Ireland) 1969. Their current powers and responsibilities are laid down in the Ombudsman (Northern Ireland) Order 1996 and the Commissioner for Complaints (Northern Ireland) Order 1996, extended by the Commissioner for Complaints (Amendment) (Northern Ireland) Order 1997.
R   To deal with complaints from people who believe they have suffered injustice as a result of maladministration by government departments and public bodies in Northern Ireland.
G   Northern Ireland.

Northern Ireland Parades Commission   See the **Parades Commission**.

Northern Ireland Policing Board   (NIPB)
■   Waterside Tower, 31 Clarendon Road, Clarendon Dock, BELFAST, BT1 3BG.
    Tel 028 9040 8500   Fax 028 9040 8540   http://www.nipolicingboard.org.uk
    Chairman: Barry Gilligan
E   Set up on 4 November 2001 under the Police (Northern Ireland) Act 2000, as extended by the Police (Northern Ireland) Act 2003. NIPB functions as an Executive NDPB funded by the Department of Justice Northern Ireland. The Board comprises ten political and nine independent members.
R   To secure an effective and efficient force.
G   Northern Ireland.
✍   For further information see **Police Authorities**.
    On 14 October 2010 the Home Office announced that it had launched a review of police remuneration and conditions of service and how these are determined. The future roles of NIPB, the Police Advisory Boards for Scotland, England & Wales, Police Arbitration Tribunal and Police Negotiating Board are all under consideration.

Northern Ireland Polymers Association   (NIPA)
■   c/o Canyon Europe Ltd, 4 Mallusk Road, NEWTOWNABBEY, Co Antrim, BT36 4PR.
    Tel 028 9084 1917   Fax 028 9084 4528   http://www.nipa.net
    Chairman: Hugh Ross
E   NIPA is the recognised Sector Training Council for the plastics and rubber industries.
G   Northern Ireland.
✍   For further information see **Sector Training Councils**.

Northern Ireland Practice & Education Council for Nursing & Midwifery   (NIPEC)
■   Centre House, 79 Chichester Street, BELFAST, BT1 4JE.
    Tel 028 9023 8152   Fax 028 9033 3298   http://www.nipec.hscni.net
    Chairman: Maureen Griffith   Chief Executive: Frances McMurray

E   Established in 2002 under the Health & Personal Social Services Act (Northern Ireland) 2001. NIPEC functions as an Executive NDPB of the Department of Health, Social Services & Public Safety Northern Ireland. The Council comprises 15 members including the Chairman.
R   To improve the quality of health and care by supporting the practice, education and performance of nurses and midwives.
G   Northern Ireland.

Northern Ireland Prison Service

■   Dundonald House, Upper Newtownards Road, BELFAST, BT4 3SU.
      Tel 028 9052 5065   http://www.niprisonservice.gov.uk
      Director General: Colin McConnell
E   Established on 1 April 1995, its statutory duties are set out in the Prison Act (Northern Ireland) 1953. The Service functions as an Executive Agency of the Department of Justice Northern Ireland.
R   To provide prison services for Northern Ireland.
G   Northern Ireland.
●   The Service's three prison establishments:
      Hydebank Wood Prison & Young Offenders' Centre (Belfast), Maghaberry Prison (Lisburn) and Magilligan Prison (Limavady).

Northern Ireland Regional Medical Physics Agency
✍   NIRMPA transferred to the **Belfast Health & Social Care Trust** on 1 April 2009.

Northern Ireland Screen

■   Alfred House, 21 Alfred Street, BELFAST, BT2 8ED.
      Tel 028 9023 2444   Fax 028 9023 9918   http://www.northernirelandscreen.co.uk
      Chairman: Rick Hill   Chief Executive: Richard Williams
E   Established on 26 February 1997 as the Northern Ireland Film Council, adopting its current name circa 2002. It functions as a company limited by guarantee and an Executive NDPB of the Department of Culture, Arts & Leisure Northern Ireland; it is also the Sector Training Council for the film industry. The board comprises seven members including the Chairman.
R   To accelerate the development of a dynamic and sustainable screen industry for Northern Ireland.
      To promote Northern Ireland as a major production location.
G   Northern Ireland.
●   Northern Ireland Screen is funded by Invest Northern Ireland (qv) and part financed by the European Regional Development Fund and the Department for Media, Culture & Sport. It is delegated by the Arts Council of Northern Ireland (qv) to administer Lottery funding for film in Northern Ireland.
✍   For further information see **Sector Training Councils**.

Northern Ireland Social Care Council   (NISCC)

■   7th Floor, Millennium House, 19-25 Great Victoria Street, BELFAST, BT2 7AQ.
      Tel 028 9041 7600   Fax 028 9041 7601   http://www.niscc.info
      Chairman: Dr Jeremy Harbison, CB   Chief Executive: Brendan Johnston
E   Established on 1 October 2001 under the Health & Personal Social Services Act (Northern Ireland) 2001. NISCC functions as an Executive NDPB of the Department Health, Social Services & Public Safety Northern Ireland. The Council comprises twelve members and the Chairman.
R   To raise the quality of social care practice through workforce education and training.
      To put in place better safeguards for the protection of people using social care services.
      To increase public confidence in the workforce.
G   Northern Ireland.
✍   It is one of the six member alliance which makes up Skills for Care & Development (qv), the Sector Skills Council for social care, children, early years and young people's workforces in the UK.
      For further information see **Health & Social Care Regulators** and **Sector Skills Councils in Northern Ireland**.

Northern Ireland Statistics & Research Agency   (NISRA)

■   McAuley House, 2-14 Castle Street, BELFAST, BT1 1SA.
      Tel 028 9034 8100   Fax 028 9034 8106   http://www.nisra.gov.uk
      Chief Executive: Dr Norman Caven
E   Established on 1 April 1996. NISRA functions as an Executive Agency of the Department of Finance & Personnel Northern Ireland.
R   To produce statistics which inform policy process within Government, academic research and contribute to debate in the wider community.

To provide a civil registration service to the public and produce summary statistics relating to life events which inform annual population estimates.

G　　Northern Ireland.

Northern Ireland Teachers' Council　　(NITC)

■　　23 College Gardens, BELFAST, BT9 6BS.
　　　Tel 028 9038 1455　Fax 028 9066 2803　http://www.into.ie
　　　Hon Secretary: Frank Bunting
E　　NITC comprises comprises three teachers' unions and functions as a representative body.
G　　Northern Ireland.
●　　The three unions represented by the Council are:
　　　　Irish National Teachers Organisation
　　　　National Association of Head Teachers
　　　　Ulster Teachers' Union.

Northern Ireland Tourist Board　　(NITB)

■　　St Anne's Court, 59 North Street, BELFAST, BT1 1NB.
　　　Tel 028 9023 1221　Fax 028 9024 0960　http://www.nitb.com
　　　Chairman: Howard Hastings　Chief Executive: Alan Clarke
E　　Established on 4 February 1948 under the Development of Tourist Traffic Act (Northern Ireland) 1948; the Board derives its current authority from the Tourism (Northern Ireland) Order 1992. NITB functions as an Executive NDPB of the Department of Enterprise, Trade & Investment Northern Ireland. The Board comprises nine members including the Chairman.
R　　To promote, market and develop Northern Ireland's tourism industry.
G　　Northern Ireland.
✍　　The Board works in partnership with Tourism Ireland (qv) which promotes Ireland as a holiday destination to overseas markets, and Fáilte Ireland (qv) which is responsible for tourism development and marketing in the Republic.

Northern Ireland Transport Holding Company　　(NITHC)

■　　Central Station, BELFAST, BT1 3PB.
　　　Tel 028 9089 9400　Fax 028 9089 9401　http://www.translink.co.uk
　　　Chairman: Veronica Palmer, OBE　Chief Executive: Catherine Mason
E　　Established on 1 April 1968 under the Transport Act (Northern Ireland) 1967, taking over the railway and bus activities of the former Ulster Transport Authority; in 1973 it incorporated Citybus (now Metro) from the Belfast Corporation Transport Department. NITHC functions as a Public Corporation of the Department for Regional Development Northern Ireland.
R　　To approve the strategic direction of the operating companies and ensure their property governance.
G　　Northern Ireland.
●　　**Translink** is the brand name, introduced in 1996, of the three operating companies: Metro (formerly Citybus), Northern Ireland Railways and Ulsterbus.

Northern Ireland Water

■　　PO Box 1026, BELFAST, BT1 9DJ.
　　　Tel 0845 744 0088　Fax 028 9035 4798　http://www.niwater.com
　　　Chairman: Chris Mellor　Chief Executive: Laurence MacKenzie　Shareholder Executive contact: Tim Martin
E　　Established on 1 April 2007 under the Water & Sewerage Services (Northern Ireland) Order 2006. Northern Ireland Water Ltd functions as a Public Corporation accountable to the Department of Finance & Personnel Northern Ireland. The board comprises nine members including the Chairman.
R　　To provide water and sewerage services in Northern Ireland.
G　　Northern Ireland.
✍　　One of the business managed by the **Shareholder Executive**.

Northern Joint Police Board

■　　Council Headquarters, Glenurquhart Road, INVERNESS, IV3 5NX.
　　　Tel 01463 702845
　　　Convenor: Cllr Norman Macleod
E　　The Joint Board is an independent body responsible for Northern Constabulary's budget and the management of its resources. The Board is made up of councillor members from each of the district councils.
G　　Highland, Western Isles, Orkney Islands, Shetland Islands.
✍　　For further information see **Police Authorities**.

Northern Lighthouse Board   (NLB)
- 84 George Street, EDINBURGH, EH2 3DA.
  Tel 0131 473 3100   Fax 0131 220 2093   http://www.nlb.org.uk
  Chairman: Sir Andrew Cubie, CBE   Chief Executive: Roger Lockwood
- E   Established in 1786, the Board is now constituted under the Merchant Shipping Act 1995 and the Merchant Shipping & Maritime Security Act 1997. NLB functions as an Executive NDPB of the Department for Transport. There are 19 Commissioners including the Chairman.
- R   To deliver a reliable, efficient and cost effective network of aids to navigation for the benefit and safety of all mariners.
- G   Scotland, Isle of Man.
- ● The Board is responsible for Scotland and the Isle of Man and controls and maintains 208 lighthouses, 166 buoys, 34 beacons, 27 Racons, nine AIS stations, four DGPS stations and one GLA Loran station.

Northern Rent Assessment Panel   (NRAP)
- First Floor, 5 New York Street, MANCHESTER, M1 4JB.
  Tel 0845 100 2614   Fax 0161 237 3656
- G   Cheshire, County Durham, Cumbria, Greater Manchester, Lancashire, Lincolnshire, Merseyside, Northumberland, Teesside, Tyne & Wear, Yorkshire.
- ✍ For further information on the five regional panels see **Rent Assessment Panels** [England].

Northumberland National Park Authority   (NNPA)
- Eastburn, South Park, HEXHAM, Northumberland, NE46 1BS.
  Tel 01434 605555   Fax 01434 611675   http://www.northumberlandnationalpark.org.uk
  Chairman: Cllr John Riddle   Chief Executive: Tony Gates
- E   Northumberland was designated a National Park on 6 April 1956. The present Authority was established on 1 April 1997 under the Environment Act 1995. It consists of 22 members including the Chairman.
- G   Northumberland.
- ✍ For further information see **National Park Authorities**.

Northumberland, Tyne & Wear Strategic Health Authority
- ✍ On 1 July 2006 merged with the Co Durham & Tees Valley Strategic Health Authority to form the **North East Strategic Health Authority**.

Northumbria Police Authority
- Public Relations Office, Civic Centre, GATESHEAD, Tyne & Wear, NE8 1HH.
  Tel 0191 433 3000   Fax 0191 477 5154   http://www.northumbria-police-authority.org
  Chairman: Cllr Mick Henry, CBE
- E   Established in April 1995, the Authority is an independent body charged with ensuring that Northumbria Police provide an effective and efficient police service. It is made up of nine councillor members and eight independent members.
- G   Northumberland and Tyne & Wear.
- ✍ For further information see **Police Authorities**.

Northumbria Probation Trust
- Lifton House, Eslington Road, Jesmond, NEWCASTLE UPON TYNE, NE2 4SP.
  Tel 0191 281 5721   Fax 0191 281 3548   http://www.northumbria-probation.co.uk
  Chairman: Lesley Bessant   Chief Officer: Pauline Williamson
- E   Established on 1 April 2001 under the Criminal Justice & Court Service Act 2000 as the Northumberland Probation Area Board. It became a trust on 1 April 2010 under the Offender Management Act 2007. The Board comprises eight members including the Chairman.
- G   Northumberland and Tyne & Wear.
- ✍ For further information see **Probation Trusts**.

Northumbria Regional Flood Defence Committee   See **Environment Agency** [North East Region].

Northumbria Tourist Board
- ✍ In March 2004 NTB was transferred to the regional development agency, One North East, which set up a **Northeast Tourism Advisory Board**.

© CBD Research Ltd · Beckenham · Kent BR3 5JS · Tel 020 8650 7745 · Fax 020 8650 0768 · E-mail cbd@cbdresearch.com · www.cbdresearch.com

Northwest Regional Development Agency   (NWDA)

■ Renaissance House, Centre Park, WARRINGTON, Cheshire, WA1 1XB.
  Tel 01925 400100   Fax 01925 400400   http://www.nwda.co.uk
  Chairman: Robert Hough   Chief Executive: Mark Hughes

E Established on 1 April 1999, one of the nine English Regional Development Agencies. NWDA functions as an Executive NDPB of the Department for Business, Innovation & Skills. The board comprises 14 members including the Chairman.

G Cheshire, Cumbria, Greater Manchester, Lancashire, Merseyside.

● The Agency and its Visitor Economy Commission has the leading strategic role for tourism and is responsible for setting direction, allocating resources, managing relationships with and supporting the regions five tourist boards:
  Cumbria Tourism
  Lancashire & Blackpool Tourist Board
  Merseyside Partnership
  Visit Chester & Cheshire
  Visit Manchester (qqv).

✍ The Comprehensive Spending Review in October 2010 confirmed the Government's intention to abolish the RDAs and support the creation of Local Enterprise Partnerships (qv), to be in place by March 2012.

Nottingham Regeneration Limited   (NRL)

■ LH Box 24, Loxley House, Station Street, NOTTINGHAM, NG2 3NG.
  Tel 0115 876 4504   Fax 0115 876 3238   http://www.nottinghamregeneration.ltd.uk
  Joint Deputy Chairmen: Ken Grundy & Mich Stevenson, OBE   Director of Regeneration: Mike Taylor

E Established in 1998. NRL's partners include Nottingham City Council, East Midlands Development Agency (qv) and the Homes & Communities Agency (qv). The Board comprises 15 members.

R To deliver regeneration of the city's three Regeneration Zones.
  To work with partners in the surrounding districts to identify opportunities in the wider conurbation.

G Nottingham.

Nottinghamshire Police Authority

■ County Hall, West Bridgford, NOTTINGHAM, NG2 7QP.
  Tel 0115 977 3078   Fax 0115 977 2451   http://www.nottinghamshire.police.uk/npa/
  Chairman: Cllr John Clarke

E Established in April 1995, the Authority is an independent body charged with ensuring that Nottinghamshire Police provide an effective and efficient police service. It is made up of seven Nottinghamshire County Councillors, two Nottingham City Councillors and eight independent members.

G Nottinghamshire.
✍ For further information see **Police Authorities**.

Nottinghamshire Probation Trust

■ Marina Road, NOTTINGHAM, NG7 1TP.
  Tel 0115 840 6500   Fax 0115 840 6502   http://www.nottinghamshire-probation.co.uk
  Chairman: Christine Goldstraw   Chief Officer: Jane Geraghty

E Established on 1 April 2001 under the Criminal Justice & Court Service Act 2000 as the Nottinghamshire Probation Area Board. It became a trust on 1 April 2010 under the Offender Management Act 2007. The Board comprises eight members including the Chairman.

G Nottinghamshire.
✍ For further information see **Probation Trusts**.

Nuclear Decommissioning Authority   (NDA)

■ Herdus House, Westlakes Science & Technology Park, MOOR ROW, Cumbria, CA24 3HU.
  Tel 01925 802001   Fax 01925 802003   http://www.nda.gov.uk
  Chairman: Stephen Henwood   Chief Executive: Tony Fountain   Shareholder Executive contact: Craig Lester

E Established in 2005 under the Energy Act 2004. NDA functions as an Executive NDPB of the Department for Energy & Climate Change. The board comprises twelve members including the Chairman.

R To ensure the safe, accelerated and affordable clean-up of the UK's civil nuclear legacy.

G United Kingdom.
✍ One of the businesses managed by the **Shareholder Executive**.

Nuclear Liabilities Fund   (NLF)

■ c/o PKF (UK) LLP, Farringdon Place, 20 Farringdon Road, LONDON, EC1M 3AP.
 Tel 020 7065 0000   http://www.nlf.uk.net
 Chairman: Lady Balfour of Burleigh, CBE
E Established on 28 March 1996. NLF functions as a company limited by guarantee. The Chairman and two
   directors are appointed by HM Government, the remaining two directors by British Energy.
R To provide funding for the eventual decommissioning of eight nuclear power stations operated by British Energy.
G United Kingdom.
● NLF is wholly owned by the Nuclear Trust of which it is the only asset. The Trust's five trustees act as the
   directors of NLF.

Nuclear Research Advisory Council   (NRAC)

■ Level 1 Zone L, MOD Main Building, Whitehall, LONDON, SW1A 2HB.
 Tel 020 7218 7606   Fax 020 7218 1769
 Chairman: Sir David Davies, CBE, FREng, FRS
E Established as a Scientific Advisory Committee and an Advisory NDPB of the Ministry of Defence. NRAC
   comprises seven members including the Chairman.
R To review the Atomic Weapons Establishment (AWE) nuclear warhead research and capability maintenance
   programme, including the requirement for above ground experiments and other facilities and techniques
   necessary to develop and maintain a UK nuclear weapon capability in the absence of underground testing.
   To examine AWE's programme of international cooperation.
G United Kingdom.
✍ For further information see **Scientific Advisory Committees**.

Nuclear Safety Advisory Committee

✍ NuSAC's term of office expired on 31 October 2008. The Health & Safety Executive (qv) is considering what
   arrangements to make for a successor body.

Nuffield Council on Bioethics

■ 28 Bedford Square, LONDON, WC1B 3JS.
 Tel 020 7681 9619   Fax 020 7323 6203   http://www.nuffieldbioethics.org
 Chairman: Prof Albert Weale, FBA
E Established in July 1991 by the Nuffield Foundation. The Council functions as an independent body funded jointly
   by the Medical Research Council (qv), the Nuffield Foundation and the Wellcome Trust. The Council comprises
   18 members including the Chairman.
R To identify, examine and report on the ethical questions raised by recent advances in biological and medical
   research.
G United Kingdom.

Nursing Council on Alcohol   (NCA)

■ c/o Lyn McIver, Liverpool DAAT, 14 Tapton Way, Wavertree Technology Park, LIVERPOOL,
 L13 1DA.   http://www.nursingcouncilonalcohol.org
 Chairman: Dr Lynn Owens   Treasurer: Prof Hazel Watson
E Established on 30 November 2000 at a conference attended by over 300 senior nurses, chief executives and
   nurse specialists throughout the UK. NCA is a membership body and functions as a registered charity.
R To provide support, advice, guidance and information to nurses, midwives and health visitors relating to
   prevention and management of harmful alcohol use.
G United Kingdom.

Nursing & Midwifery Council   (NMC)

■ 23 Portland Place, LONDON, W1B 1PZ.
 Tel 020 7637 7181   Fax 020 7436 2024   http://www.nmc-uk.org
 Chairman: Prof Tony Hazell   Chief Executive: Sarah Thewlis
E Established on 1 April 2002 under the Nursing & Midwifery Order 2001, replacing the UK Central Council and the
   four national boards for nursing, midwifery and health visiting. NMC is the UK-wide regulatory body for the
   nursing and midwifery professions. Within the Governing Council of 25, the NMC has a voting body of 23
   members, of whom twelve are registrant members and eleven are appointed lay members.
R To protect the public by ensuring that nurses, midwives and specialist community public health nurses provide
   high standards of care.
G United Kingdom.
● The Council also offers various services including free and confidential advice for nurses, midwives and health
   visitors.
✍ For further information see **Health & Social Care Regulators**.

© CBD Research Ltd · Beckenham · Kent BR3 5JS · Tel 020 8650 7745 · Fax 020 8650 0768 · E-mail cbd@cbdresearch.com · www.cbdresearch.com

Nutrition Forum

- Aviation House, 125 Kingsway, LONDON, WC2B 6NH.
  Tel 020 7276 8000   **Fax** 020 7276 8004
- E Established in 2002, the Forum functions as an Advisory NDPB of the Department of Health. Members of the Forum are drawn from consumer & voluntary organisations, health bodies, industry & Government.
- R To improve health through improvements in diets and changes in dietary habits through the assistance in the development and implementation of nutrition policies and the support of an effective, co-ordinated nutrition strategy.
- G United Kingdom.
- ✍ The Forum has not met since June 2004.

O

Occupational Exposure Limit Framework Review Working Group   A working group of the **Advisory Committee on Toxic Substances**.

Occupational Health & Hygiene Sub-Committee   A sub-committee of the Health & Safety Executive's **Foundries Industry Advisory Committee**.

Occupational Health Reference Group
✍ At the end of 2003 it was decided not to reconstitute the Group which had held its last meeting on 17 July 2003.

Occupational Medicine Committee   (OMC)

- BMA House, Tavistock Square, LONDON, WC1H 9JP.
  Tel 020 7383 6158   **Fax** 020 7383 6400   http://www.bma.org.uk
  Chairman: Paul Nicholson
- E Established as a Branch of Practice Committee of the British Medical Association. The Committee comprises ten members including the Chairman.
- R To represent specialists and non-specialists working in the specialty of occupational medicine both inside and outside the NHS.
- G United Kingdom.
- ✍ See **British Medical Association** [Branch of Practice Committees] for further information.

Occupational Pensions Advisory Service
✍ Formerly operating as OPAS Ltd, it was renamed the **Pensions Advisory Service** in 2004.

Occupational Pensions Regulatory Authority
✍ Replaced in 2004 by the **Pensions Regulator**.

Ofcom   See **Office of Communications**.

Ofcom Spectrum Advisory Board   (OSAB)

- 05/146, Riverside House, 2a Southwark Bridge Road, LONDON, SE1 9HA.   http://www.osab.org.uk
  Chairman: Sir David Brown   Secretary: Paul Rogers
- E Established in May 2004 to provide independent advice to the Office of Communications (qv) on strategic spectrum management issues. The Board comprises 13 members including the Chairman.
- R To advise on:
  The UK Spectrum Strategy, major Ofcom allocation decisions, spectrum management, and the application of spectrum pricing/trading;
  The spectrum policy objectives to be pursued in relevant international fora;
  New technologies or means of managing the radio spectrum and their implications for Ofcom;
  The high-level strategic direction for Ofcom's research programme, including key areas of market and technical research required for new spectrum allocation and analysis of gaps in industry/academia research programmes;

The extent to which spectrum policy objectives create a climate for innovation;

The need to safeguard the interests of citizen-consumers, e.g. protection of vulnerable users, change management, etc.

G   United Kingdom.

Office of the Accountant in Bankruptcy   See **Accountant in Bankruptcy**.

Office for Budget Responsibility   (OBR)
- 20 Victoria Street, LONDON, SW1H 0NF.
  Tel 020 7271 2442   http://www.budgetresponsibility.independent.gov.uk
  Chairman: Robert Chote
E   Established in May 2010. The Budget Responsibility Committee comprises the Chairman and two other members.
R   To make an independent assessment of the public finances and the economy for each Budget and Pre-Budget Report.
G   United Kingdom.

Office of the Civil Service Commissioners
✍   In 2010 replaced by the **Civil Service Commission**.

Office of the Civil Service Commissioners for Northern Ireland   See **Civil Service Commissioners for Northern Ireland**.

Office for Civil Society Advisory Body
✍   The Office for Civil Society replaced the Office for the Third Sector in May 2001, taking responsibility for charities, social enterprises and voluntary organisations in the Cabinet Office. The Advisory Body was abolished when its members' terms of office came to an end on 31 March 2011.

Office of the Commissioner for Judicial Appointments for Northern Ireland
✍   Closed on 22 September 2006 with the establishing of the Office of the **Northern Ireland Judicial Appointments Ombudsman**.

Office of the Commissioner for Public Appointments   (OCPA)
- 3rd Floor, 35 Great Smith Street, LONDON, SW1P 3BQ.
  Tel 020 7276 2625   **Fax** 020 7276 2633   http://www.publicappointscommissioner.org
  Commissioner for Public Appointments: Sir David Normington, GCB
E   Established on 23 November 1995 by the Public Appointments Order in Council 1995. The Commissioner is independent of Government.
R   To regulate, monitor, report and advise on appointments made by UK Ministers to the boards of English and UK public bodies and by the Welsh Government to Welsh public bodies.
G   England, Wales.
●   The Commissioner is assisted by Independent Public Appointments Assessors.

Office of the Commissioner for Public Appointments for Northern Ireland   (OCPANI)
- Dundonald House, Annexe B, Upper Newtownards Road, BELFAST, BT4 3SR.
  Tel 028 9052 4820   **Fax** 028 9052 5534   http://www.publicappointmentsni.org
  Commissioner: Mrs Felicity Huston
E   Established in 1995 in response to the First Report of the Committee on Standards in Public Life (qv), and the application of the Code of Practice for Public Appointments Procedures which has been in force since 1 July 1996. The Commissioner is independent of Government.
R   To regulate, monitor, report and advise on appointments made by Northern Ireland Ministers to the boards of around 75 national and regional public bodies in Northern Ireland.
G   Northern Ireland.

Office of Communications
- Riverside House, 2a Southwark Bridge Road, LONDON, SE1 9HA.
  Tel 020 7981 3000   **Fax** 020 7981 3333   http://www.ofcom.org.uk
  Chairman: Collette Bowe   Chief Executive: Ed Richards

E Established in July 2002 under the Office of Communications Act 2002 and universally known as **Ofcom**, its statutory duties are contained in the Communications Act 2003. Ofcom functions as a Public Corporation responsible to the Department for Business, Innovation & Skills. The Ofcom board comprises ten members including the Chairman.

R To ensure the optimal use of the radio spectrum.

To ensure that a wide range of electronic communications services - including high speed data services - is available throughout the UK.

To ensure that a wide range of TV and radio services of high quality and wide appeal and to maintain plurality in the provision of broadcasting.

To apply adequate protection for audiences against offensive and harmful material.

To apply adequate protection for audiences against unfairness or the infringement of privacy.

G United Kingdom

● Ofcom is the regulator for the UK communications industries, with responsibilities across television, radio, telecommunications and wireless communications services.

✍ It was announced by the Government on 14 October 2010 that Postcomm (qv) will be merged into Ofcom and that several Ofcom duties will be removed or modified.

Office for Fair Access   (OFFA)

■ Northavon House, Coldharbour Lane, BRISTOL, BS16 1QD.
Tel 0117 931 7171   **Fax** 0117 931 7083   http://www.offa.org.uk
Director of Fair Access: Sir Martin Harris

E Established under the Higher Education Act 2004. OFFA functions as an independent NDPB which reports to the Department for Business, Innovation & Skills. The OFFA team comprises the Director, three full-time and one part-time staff.

R To ensure that the introduction of higher tuition fees does not deter people from entering higher education for financial reasons.

To ensure that universities and colleges are explicitly committed to increase participation in higher education among under-represented groups.

G England.

Office of Fair Trading   (OFT)

■ Fleetbank House, 2-6 Salisbury Square, LONDON, EC4Y 8JX.
Tel 020 7211 8000   http://www.oft.gov.uk
Chairman: Philip Collins   Chief Executive: John Fingleton

E Established under the Fair Trading Act 1973, on 1 April 2003 its role and powers were modified by the Enterprise Act 2002. The OFT functions as a Non-Ministerial Government Department. The Board comprises eleven members including the Chairmen.

R To encourage business to comply with competition and cunsumer law and to improve their trading practices through self-regulation.

To act decisively to stop hardcore or flagrant offenders.

To study markets and recommend action where required.

To empower consumers with the knowledge and skills to make informed choices and get the best value from markets, and to help them resolve problems with suppliers through Consumer Direct.

G United Kingdom.

● Consumer Direct
Tel 0845 404 0506
http://www.consumerdirect.gov.uk

✍ It was announced by the Government on 14 October 2010 that it will consult in 2011 on a merger of OFT's competition functions with the Competition Commission (qv) and the transfer of its consumer and enforcement functions.

Office of Fair Trading (Isle of Man)   See **Isle of Man Office of Fair Trading**.

Office of Gas & Electricity Markets   Ofgem is governed by the **Gas & Electricity Markets Authority**.

Office of the Immigration Services Commissioner   (OISC)

■ 5th Floor, Counting House, 53 Tooley Street, LONDON, SE1 2QN.
Tel 020 7211 1500   **Fax** 020 7211 1553   http://www.oisc.gov.uk
Immigration Services Commissioner: Suzanne McCarthy

E Established in 2000 under the Immigration & Asylum Act 1999. OISC functions as an Executive NDPB of the Home Office.

R   To regulate those who provide immigration advice and services by promoting good practice and investigating complaints.
G   United Kingdom
✍   The Government announced on 14 October 2010 that it was considering future options for OISC including possible merger.

Office of the Information Commissioner
✍   See **Information Commissioner's Office**.

Office of the Judge Advocate General   (OJAG)
■   9th Floor, Thomas More Building, Royal Courts of Justice, Strand, LONDON, WC2A 2LL.
      Tel 020 7218 8095   **Fax** 020 7218 8094
E   OJAG functions as an independent body within the Ministry of Justice.
R   To support the Judge Advocates in the exercise of their judicial functions.
G   United Kingdom.
✍   OJAG deals with criminal trials of service men and women for serious offences (or where the defendent chooses not to be dealt with by the Commanding Officer) which are heard in a standing court known as the Court Martial. Judges who sit in the Court Martial are known as Judge Advocates and are appointed by the Lord Chancellor.

Office of the Judicial Committee   See **Judicial Committee of the Privy Council**.

Office for Judicial Complaints   (OJC)
■   10th Floor Tower 10/52, 102 Petty France, LONDON, SW1H 9AJ.
      Tel 020 3334 2555   **Fax** 020 3334 2541   http://www.judicialcomplaints.gov.uk
      Head: Sheridan Greenland, OBE
E   Established under the Concordat of January 2004 between the Lord Chancellor and the Lord Chief Justice with regard to their responsibilityes under the Constitutional Reform Act 2005 and the Judicial Discipline (Prescribed Procedures) Regulations 2006. It is an associated office of the Ministry of Justice.
R   To provide advice and assistance to the Lord Chancellor and the Lord Chief Justice in the performance of their joint role of considering and determining complaints about the personal conduct of all judicial office holders in England and Wales, and some in Scotland and Northern Ireland who sit in Tribunals.
G   United Kingdom.

Office for Legal Complaints   (OLC)
■   PO Box 15870, BIRMINGHAM, B30 9EB.
      Tel 0300 555 0333   http://www.legalombudsman.org.uk
      Chairman: Elizabeth France, CBE   Chief Ombudsman: Adam Sampson
E   Established on 1 July 2009 under the Legal Services Act 2007 to assume the functions of the Office of the Legal Services Ombudsman, the Office of Legal Services Complaints Commissioner and the Law Society's Legal Complaints Service. OLC functions as an Executive NDPB of the Ministry of Justice. The board comprises seven members including the Chairman and is appointed by the Legal Services Board (qv).
R   To develop and administer an independent **Legal Ombudsman** scheme to deal with complaints by consumers about legal services.
G   England, Wales.

Office of the Legal Services Complaints Commissioner
✍   OLSCC closed on 31 March 2010, its functions transferred to the **Office for for Legal Complaints**.

Office of the Legal Services Ombudsman
✍   See replacement organisations, the **Office for Legal Complaints** (England and Wales) and the **Scottish Legal Complaints Committee**.

Office of Manpower Economics   (OME)
■   6th Floor, Kingsgate House, 66-74 Victoria Street, LONDON, SW1E 6SW.
      Tel 020 7215 8253   **Fax** 020 7215 4445   http://www.ome.uk.com
      Director: Geoff Dart
E   Established in April 1971. OME functions as an independent non-statutory NDPB.

© CBD Research Ltd · Beckenham · Kent BR3 5JS · Tel 020 8650 7745 · Fax 020 8650 0768 · E-mail cbd@cbdresearch.com · www.cbdresearch.com

R   To provide the secretariat for six Pay Review Bodies:
        Armed Forces Pay Review Body
        NHS Pay Review Body
        Prison Service Pay Review Body
        Review Body on Doctors' & Dentists' Remuneration
        School Teachers' Review Body
        Senior Salaries Review Body (qqv).

G   United Kingdom.

●   OME also provides the secretariat for:
        School Support Staff Negotiating Body
    and two Police Boards:
        Police Advisory Board for England & Wales
        Police Negotiating Board (qqv).

Office for National Statistics   ONS is under the governance of the **UK Statistics Authority**.

Office of the Official Solicitor & Public Trustee

■   81 Chancery Lane, LONDON, WC2A 1DD.
    Tel 020 7911 7127   Fax 020 7911 7105   http://www.courtfunds.gov.uk

E   The Official Solicitor to the Senior Courts is part of the judicial system of England & Wales and is appointed by the Lord Chancellor under the Supreme Court Act 1981.
    The Public Trustee is an officer appointed by the Lord Chancellor under Public Trustee Act 1906 and is a corporation sole under that name.

R   The Official Solicitor represents children and adults who lack mental capacity to act for themselves in legal proceedings.
    The Public Trustee administers trusts and estates where he has accepted appointment to do so.

G   England, Wales.

Office of the Public Guardian

■   PO Box 15118, BIRMINGHAM, B16 6GX.
    Tel 0300 456 0300   Fax 0870 739 5780   http://www.publicguardian.gov.uk
    Chairman: Rose Varley, OBE   Public Guardian & Chief Executive: Martin John

E   Established in October 2007 under the Mental Capacity Act 2005, replacing the former Public Guardianship Office. OPG functions as an Executive NDPB of the Ministry of Justice. The board comprises seven members including the Chairman.

R   To support and promote decision making for those who lack capacity and would like to plan for their future.

G   England, Wales.

✍   It was announced by the Government on 14 October 2010 that the Public Guardian Board, which was set up to monitor the work of the Public Guardian, is to be abolished.

Office of the Public Guardian

■   Hadrian House, Callendar Business Park, Callendar Road, FALKIRK, FK1 1XR.
    Tel 01324 678300   Fax 01324 678301   http://www.publicguardian-scotland.gov.uk
    Public Guardian: Sandra McDonald

E   Established in April 2001 under Adults with Incapacity (Scotland) Act 2000. The management team comprises four members including the Public Guardian.

R   To supervise those individuals who have been appointed to manage the financial or property affairs of an adult who lacks the capacity to do so for themselves.

G   Scotland.

Office of the Qualifications & Examinations Regulator

■   Spring Place, Coventry Business Park, Herald Avenue, COVENTRY, CV5 6UB.
    Tel 0300 303 3344   Fax 0300 303 3348   http://www.ofqual.gov.uk
    Deputy Chairman: Dame Sandra Burslem, DBE   Chief Executive: Isabel Nisbet

E   **Ofqual** began its interim work on 8 April 2008, operating within and assuming the regulatory functions of the Qualifications & Curriculum Authority (qv); it was formally established on 1 April 2010 under the Apprenticeships, Skills, Children & Learning Act 2009.
    The Ofqual Committee comprises seven members including the Chairman.

R   To regulate qualifications, examinations and assessments in England and vocational qualifications in Northern Ireland.
    To ensure that learners get the results they deserve and that the qualifications they receive count, both now and in the future.

G   England, Northern Ireland.

Office of Rail Regulation (ORR)

■ One Kemble Street, LONDON, WC2B 4AN.
Tel 020 7282 2000 **Fax** 020 7282 2040 http://www.rail-reg.gov.uk
Chairman: Anna Walker Chief Executive: Bill Emery

E Established on 5 July 2004 under the Railways & Transport Safety Act 2003, replacing the former Rail Regulator. ORR functions as an independent statutory body. The board comprises twelve members including the Chairman.

R To ensure that Network Rail manages the national railway infrastructure (track and signalling) effectively.
To encourage continuous improvement in health and safety performance.
To secure compliance with relevant health and safety law, including taking enforcement action when necessary.
To license operators of railway assets.

G United Kingdom.

● On 1 April 2006, and in addition to its role as economic regulator, the Office became the health and safety regulator for the rail industry when responsibility was transferred from the Health & Safety Executive (qv).

Office for the Regulation of Electricity & Gas In 2003 OFREG was replaced by the **Northern Ireland Authority for Energy Regulation**.

Office of the Scottish Charity Regulator (OSCR)

■ 2nd Floor, Quadrant House, 9 Riverside Drive, DUNDEE, DD1 4NY.
Tel 01382 220446email oscr.org.uk
Chairman: John Naylor Chief Executive: Jane Ryder

E Established in July 2005 under the Charities & Trustee Investment (Scotland) Act 2005. OSCR functions as a Non-Ministerial Department of the Scottish Executive. The Board comprises eight members including the Chairman.

R To increase public confidence in charities through effective regulation.

G Scotland.

Office of the Social Security & Child Support Commissioners

■ 3rd Floor, Bedford House, 16-22 Bedford Street, BELFAST, BT2 7FD.
Tel 028 9033 2344 **Fax** 028 9031 3510
Chief Commissioner: His Hon Judge Martin

E Established in 1991 under the Child Support Act 1991. The Commissioners are specialised members of the judiciary.

R To determine appeals on points of law from Appeal Tribunals under the Social Security and Child Support legislation.

G Northern Ireland.

Office of the Social Security & Child Support Commissioners [England, Wales & Scotland]

✍ On 3 November 2008 the **Upper Tribunal (Administrative Appeals Chamber)** took over the work of the Commissioners.

Office of Social Services (OSS)

■ C4, Castle Buildings, Stormont Estate, BELFAST, BT4 3SQ.
Tel 028 9052 0517
Chief Social Services Officer: Sean Holland

E The OSS functions as a professional grouping within the Social Policy Group of the Department of Health, Social Services & Public Safety Northern Ireland (DHSSPS).

R To work with Ministers, the DHSSPS, other Government Departments, Agencies and organisations working in the field to ensure that the social work and social care services are responsive to the needs of the people living and working in Northern Ireland and are of the highest possible standard in keeping with the resources available.

G Northern Ireland.

● The OSS sponsors and holds to account the Northern Ireland Social Care Council (qv).

Office for Standards in Education, Children's Services & Skills (Ofsted)

■ Royal Exchange Buildings, St Ann's Square, MANCHESTER, M2 7LA.
Tel 0300 123 4234 http://www.ofsted.gov.uk
HM Chief Inspector: Christine Gilbert Chairman: Baroness Sally Morgan

E Established in September 1992 under the Education (Schools) Act 1992, the new Ofsted came into being on 1 April 2007 under the Education & Inspections Act 2006 which widened the Inspector's remit. Ofsted functions as a non-ministerial Government department. The Board comprises nine members including HMCI and the Chairman.

© CBD Research Ltd · Beckenham · Kent BR3 5JS · Tel 020 8650 7745 · Fax 020 8650 0768 · E-mail cbd@cbdresearch.com · www.cbdresearch.com

R   To inspect and regulate care for children and young people.
     To inspect education and training for learners of all ages.
G   England.
●   Ofsted has offices in Bristol, London and Nottingham.

Office of the Strategic Health Authorities   (OSHA)
■   Southside, 105 Victoria Street, LONDON, SW1E 6QT.
     Tel 020 7932 3900   **Fax** 020 7932 3800   http://www.osha.nhs.uk
E   Established in 2003 by the ten Strategic Health Authorities (SHAs) in England.
R   To facilitate collaboration between and with SHA Chief Executives and Chairmen in delivering their collective
     responsibilities.
     To provide a focal point for their relationships with the Department of Health and other national bodies.
G   England.

Office of the Subsidence Adviser
✍   Established in October 1994, the office was wound up on 9 October 2004.

Office of Surveillance Commissioners   (OSC)
■   PO Box 29105, LONDON, SW1V 1ZU.
     Tel 020 7592 1774   http://www.surveillancecommissioners.gov.uk
     Chief Commissioner: Rt Hon Sir Christopher Rose
E   Established under the Police Act 1997, the Regulation of Investigatory Powers Act 2000 and the Regulation of
     Investigatory Powers (Scotland) Act 2000. OSC functions as a NDPB of the Home Office.
R   To provide effective and efficient oversight of those who authorise and conduct covert surveillance and use
     covert human intelligence sources (i.e. informants and undercover officers).
G   United Kingdom.

Office for Tax Simplification   (OTS)
■   2/W1, 1 Horse Guards Road, LONDON, SW1A 2HQ.
     Tel 020 7270 4558   **Fax** 020 7270 4861
     Chairman: Rt Hon Michael Jack   Tax Director: John Whiting, OBE
E   Established on 20 July 2010 as an independent office of HM Treasury for the life of the Parliament (2010-2005). It
     draws together expertise from across the tax and legal professions, the business community and other
     interested parties.
R   To streamline the 400 tax reliefs, allowances and exemptions.
     To simplify the tax system for small businesses.
G   United Kingdom.

Office of the Telecommunications Ombudsman   (Otelo)
■   PO Box 730, WARRINGTON, Cheshire, WA4 6WU.
     Tel 01925 430049   **Fax** 01925 430049   http://www.otelo.org.uk
     Chairman: Chris Holland   Ombudsman with lead responsibility for Otelo complaints: Andrew Walker
E   Established in January 2006. The service is an approved scheme under the Communications Act 2003. The
     Member Board comprises six members including the Chairman.
R   To resolve disagreements between public communication providers and their domestic and small business
     customers.
G   United Kingdom.
✍   Otelo is run by Ombudsman Services (qv).

Office of Water Services
✍   See the **Water Services Regulation Authority**.

Offices of Court Funds, Official Solicitor & Public Trustee
✍   Demerged on 1 April 2009. See **Court Funds Office** and the Offices of the Official Solicitor & Public Trustee.

Official Receiver   See **Insolvency Service**.

Official Solicitor   See **Office of the Official Solicitor & Public Trustee**.

Offshore Industry Advisory Committee   (OIAC)
- 5S/2 Redgrave Court, Merton Road, BOOTLE, Merseyside, L20 7HS.
  Tel 0845 345 0055   Fax 0845 408 9566
  Chairman: Steve Walker
- E   Established in August 1978 by the Health & Safety Executive (qv) and previously known as the Oil Industry Advisory Committee. The Committee's members represent employers, employees, unions, trade associations and government departments.
- R   To discuss health and safety matters in the offshore industry.
- G   United Kingdom.
- ● OIAC has two permanent subgroups:
    Helicopter Liaison Group
    Workforce Involvement Group.

Ofgem   See **Gas & Electricity Markets Authority**.

Ofqual   See **Office of the Qualifications & Examinations Regulator**.

Ofsted   See **Office for Standards in Education, Children's Services & Skills**.

Ofwat   See the **Water Services Regulation Authority**.

OGCbuying.solutions
- ✍ Re-branded, circa 2009 **Buying Solutions**.

Oik Dellal Cair Ellan Vannin   See **Isle of Man Office of Fair Trading**.

Oik Postagh Ellan Vannin   See **Isle of Man Post Office**.

Oil Industry Advisory Committee
- ✍ See **Offshore Industry Advisory Committee**.

Oil & Pipelines Agency   (OPA)
- York House, 23 Kingsway, LONDON, WC2B 6UJ.
  Tel 020 7420 1670   Fax 020 7379 0500
  Chairman: Francis Dobbyn   Chief Executive: Tony Nicholls
- E   Established on 1 December 1985 under the Oil & Pipelines Act 1985. OPA functions as an Executive NDPB and Public Corporation accountable to the Ministry of Defence.
- R   To provide for the safe, efficient, economic and effective management of the Government Pipeline & Storage System (GPSS).
- G   United Kingdom.

Older People's Commissioner
- Block E3 18, Castle Buildings, Stormont Estate, BELFAST, BT4 3SR.
  Tel 028 9052 8273   Fax 028 9052 3323
- E   To be established early in 2011 under the Commissioner for Older People Act (Northern Ireland) which received Royal Assent on 25 January 2011. The Commissioner will function as a corporation sole, independent of Government.
- R   To safeguard and promote the interests of people aged over 60.
- G   Northern Ireland.

Older People's Commissioner for Wales
- Cambrian Buildings, Mount Stuart Square, Butetown, CARDIFF, CF10 5FL.
  Tel 029 2044 5030 Fax 0844 264 0680 http://www.olderpeoplewales.com
  Commissioner: Ruth Marks
- E Established on 21 April 2008 under the Commission for Older People (Wales) Act 2006. The Commissioner is independent of government and functions as a corporation sole.
- R To promote awareness of the interests of older people.
  To promote the end of age discrimination.
  To encourage good practice in the treatment of older people.
  To review the law affecting the interests of old people.
- G Wales.
- = Comisiynydd Pobl Hŷn Cymru

Olympic Delivery Authority   (ODA)
- One Churchill Place, Canary Wharf, LONDON, E14 5LN.
  Tel 020 3201 2000 http://www.london2012.com
  Chairman: John Armitt, CBE, FREng, FICE   Chief Executive: David Higgins
- E Established in 2006 by the London Olympic Games & Paralympic Games Act 2006. ODA functions as an Executive NDPB of the Department for Culture, Media & Sport. The Board comprises 14 members including the Chairman.
- R To develop and build the new venues and infrastructure for the Games and for their use after 2012.
- G United Kingdom.
- ✍ The Authority works with the London Organising Committee of the Olympic & Paralympic Games (qv).

Olympic Lottery Distributor   (OLD)
- 1 Plough Place, LONDON, EC4A 1DE.
  Tel 020 7880 2012 http://www.olympiclotterydistributor.org.uk
  Chairman: Rt Hon Dame Janet Paraskeva, DBE   Chief Executive: Ian Brack
- E Established on 28 September 2005. The Distributor functions as an Executive NDPB of the Department for Culture, Media & Sport. The Board comprises seven members including the Chairman.
- R To fund the delivery of the infrastructure for the London 2012 Olympic and Paralympic Games and their legacy.
- G United Kingdom.

Olympic Park Legacy Company
- ✍ OPLC was established in 2009 as the body responsible for the long-term planning, development, management and maintenance of the Olympic Park and its facilities after the London 2012 Games. The Government announced on 14 October 2010 that its functions would be devolved to the Mayor of London, there reconstituted as a Mayoral Development Corporation.

Ombudsman for Estate Agents
- ✍ Since 1 May 2009 known as the **Property Ombudsman**.

Ombudsman Services   (tOSI)
- Wilderspool Park, Greenall's Avenue, WARRINGTON, Cheshire, WA4 6HL.
  Tel 01925 430870 http://www.tosl.org.uk
  Chairman: Prof Dame Janet Finch, DBE   Chief Ombudsman: Lewis Shand Smith
- E Established in 2006. The Ombudsman Service Ltd (tOSI) functions as a not-for-profit private limited company. The Council comprises nine members including the Chairman.
- R To provide services to help its members provide independent dispute resolution to their customers.
- G United Kingdom.
- ● tOSI runs four high profile national, private sector ombudsman schemes, each of which is entirely funded by its members. The four are:
  Energy Ombudsman
  Office of the Telecommunications Ombudsman
  Ombudsman Services: Property
  PRS for Music Ombudsman (qqv).

Ombudsman Services Property
- PO Box 1021, WARRINGTON, Cheshire, WA4 9FE.
  Tel 01925 530270 Fax 01925 530271 http://www.surveyors-ombudsman.org.uk
  Chairman: Baroness Maggie Jones   Ombudsman with lead responsbility for property complaints: Gillian Fleming

E   Established on 1 June 2007 by the Royal Institution of Chartered Surveyors and known as the Surveyors Ombudsman Service until April 2010. It is an approved estate agent redress scheme under the Consumer, Estate Agents & Redress Act 2007, and is the ombudsman scheme recommended by the Association of Residential Managing Agents. The Member Board comprises seven independent members including the Chairman.

R   To resolve complaints about chartered surveying firms, surveyors, estate agents, residential managing agents and other property professionals from consumers using their services.

G   United Kingdom.

✍   Ombudsman Service: Property is run by Ombudsman Services (qv).

Ombudsman Services: PRS for Music

■   PO Box 1124, WARRINGTON, Cheshire, WA4 9GH.
Tel 01925 532111   Fax 01925 532112   http://www.surveyors-ombudsman.org
Chairman: Prof Dame Janet Finch, DBE   Chief Ombudsman: Lewis Shand Smith

E   Established on 1 August 2009. The Board comprises nine members including the Chairman.

R   To resolve disagreements between PRS for Music, which licenses the use of copyright music in the UK, and those who may require or have obtained a licence for the public performance of copyright music.

G   United Kingdom.

✍   Ombudsman Services: PRS for Music is run by Ombudsman Services (qv).

Ombwdsmon Gwasanaethau Cyhoeddus Cymru   See **Public Services Ombudsman for Wales**.

Oncology & Haematology Expert Advisory Group

■   151 Buckingham Palace Road, LONDON, SW1W 9SZ.
Tel 020 3080 6000
Chairman: Prof John F Smyth, MD, FRCP, FRCS, FRCR, FRS

E   Established in 2005. The Group functions as an advisory body to the Commission on Human Medicines (CHM), qv. It comprises ten members including the Chairman.

R   To advise CHM on the safety, quality and efficacy of medicines for use in the treatment of malignant disease or blood disorders.

G   United Kingdom.

One NG   (1NG)

■   9th Floor, Baltic Place East, South Shore Road, GATESHEAD, Tyne & Wear, NE8 3AE.
Tel 0191 441 4570   Fax 0191 441 4598   http://www.1ng.org.uk
Chairman: Lord Charles Falconer   Chief Executive: Jim McIntyre

E   Established in March 2009. 1NG is the Economic Development Company for Newcastle upon Tyne and Gateshead, incorporated as a company limited by guarantee, its members being Gateshead Council, Newcastle City Council and the regional development agency, One North East (qv). The Board comprises twelve members including the Chairman.

R   To drive forward economic development and improvement in Newcastle/Gateshead.

G   Gateshead, Newcastle upon Tyne.

✍   For further Information see **Economic Development Companies**.

One North East   (ONE)

■   Stella House, Goldcrest Way, Newburn Riverside, NEWCASTLE UPON TYNE, NE15 8NY.
Tel 0191 229 6200   Fax 0191 229 6201   http://www.onenortheast.co.uk
Chairman: Paul Callaghan   Chief Executive: Alan Clarke

E   Established on 1 April 1999, one of the nine English Regional Development Agencies. ONE functions as an Executive NDPB of the Department for Business, Innovation & Skills. The board comprises 15 members including the Chairman.

G   County Durham, Northumberland, Teesside, Tyne & Wear.

●   In March 2004 the former Northumbria Tourist was transferred to One North East which appointed a Northeast Tourism Advisory Board (qv).

✍   The Comprehensive Spending Review in October 2010 confirmed the Government's intention to abolish the RDAs and support the creation of Local Enterprise Partnerships (qv), to be in place by March 2012.

OPAS Ltd

✍   The Occupational Pensions Advisory Service was renamed the **Pensions Advisory Service** in 2004.

© CBD Research Ltd · Beckenham · Kent BR3 5JS · Tel 020 8650 7745 · Fax 020 8650 0768 · E-mail cbd@cbdresearch.com · www.cbdresearch.com

Open College of the North West
✍ Established in 1975, OCNW in 2009 changed its name to **Ascentis**.

Open & Distance Learning Quality Council   (ODLQC)
■ 16 Park Crescent, LONDON, W1B 1AH.
Tel 020 7612 7090   **Fax** 020 7612 7092   http://www.odlqc.org.uk
Chairman: John Ainsworth   Chief Executive: Dr David Morley
E Established by Government on 24 July 1969 as the Council for the Accreditation of Correspondence Colleges, the
Council adopted its current name in 1995. ODLQC functions as an independent body and registered charity.
The Council comprises eleven members including the Chairman.
R To identify and enhance quality in education and training, and to protect the interests of learners.
G United Kingdom.

Ophthalmic Group Committee
■ BMA House, Tavistock Square, LONDON, WC1H 9JP.
Tel 0300 123 1233   **Fax** 020 7383 6400   http://www.bma.org.uk
E Established as a standing committee of the British Medical Association.
R To consider matters arising out of ophthalmology service provision within the NHS in the community (primary
care/ophthalmic medical practice) or the Hospital Eye Service (HES) (secondary care) or the Independent
Sector Treatment Centres.
G United Kingdom.
✍ See **British Medical Association** [Boards & Committees] for further information.

Opportunity Peterborough
■ Stuart House, St John's Street, PETERBOROUGH, PE1 5DD.
Tel 01733 317417   **Fax** 01733 317400   http://www.peterboroughurc.co.uk
Chairman: John Bridge, OBE   Chief Executive: Steve Compton
E Established on 2 March 2005 as an Urban Regeneration Company, Opportunity Peterborough now functions as
an Economic Development Company.
G Peterborough.
✍ For further information see **Economic Development Companies**.

Ordnance Survey   (OS)
■ Adanac Drive, SOUTHAMPTON, Hants, SO16 0AS.
Tel 0845 605 0505   **Fax** 023 8079 2906   http://www.ordnancesurvey.co.uk
Chairman: Sir Rob Margetts, CBE, FREng, FIChemE   Chief Executive: Vanessa Lawrence, CB
Shareholder Executive contact: Emma Ward
E Established in 1791. OS functions as a Government Department and Executive Agency with trading fund status
responsible to the Department for Communities & Local Government.
R To collect, portray and distribute the definitive record of Great Britain's natural, built and planned environment.
G England, Wales, Scotland.
● The Ordnance Survey makes topographic data and maps of Britain available to users.
✍ One of the businesses managed by the **Shareholder Executive**.

Ordnance Survey of Northern Ireland
✍ Since 1 April 2008 part of the **Land & Property Services** agency.

Orkney Enterprise
✍ This former Local Enterprise Company is now an area office of **Highlands & Islands Enterprise**.

Orkney NHS Board
■ Balfour Hospital, New Scapa Road, KIRKWALL, Orkney, KW15 1BH.
Tel 01856 888000   http://www.ohb.scot.nhs.uk
Chairman: John Ross Scott   Chief Executive: Cathie Cowan
G Orkney Islands.
✍ For further information see **NHS Scotland - Boards**.

Orkney Tourist Board
✎ Since 1 April 2005 an area office of **VisitScotland**.

Outer Hebrides Fisheries Trust See **Rivers & Fisheries Trusts of Scotland**.

Oxford, Cambridge & RSA Examinations   (OCR)
■ 1 Hills Road, CAMBRIDGE, CB1 2EU.
Tel 01223 553998 **Fax** 01223 552627 http://www.ocr.org.uk
Chief Executive: Mark Dawe
E Established on 6 January 1998 when the University of Cambridge Local Examinations Syndicate was joined by the RSA Examinations Board. OCR is a company limited by guarantee. The Executive Team comprises the Chief Executive and six Directors.
R To provide qualifications that engage learners of all ages, at school, college, in work or through part-time learning programmes, to achieve their full potential.
G United Kingdom.
✎ For more information on awarding bodies see the **Federation of Awarding Bodies**.

Oxfordshire Rural Community Council   (ORCC)
■ Jericho Farm, Worton, WITNEY, Oxon, OX29 4SZ.
Tel 01865 883488 **Fax** 01865 883191 http://www.oxonrcc.org.uk
Chairman: Dr John Sharp   Chief Executive: Linda Watson
E Established in 1920. ORCC functions as a registered charity and company limited by guarantee. The Board comprises 23 members including the Chairman.
R To promote thriving, sustainable rural communities and to alleviate the disadvantage experienced by many people who live in them.
G Oxfordshire.
✎ ORCC is one of the 38 Rural Community Councils, represented at the national level by **Action with Communities in Rural England** (qv) and at the regional level by South East Rural Community Councils.

P

PAA/VQ-SET
■ Brooke House, 24 Dam Street, LICHFIELD, Staffs, WS13 6AA.
Tel 01543 254223 **Fax** 01543 257848 http://www.paa-uk.org
Chief Executive: Ann Randall
E Established in July 2002 when Process Awards Authority Ltd acquired, from the Chemical Industries Association, the awarding body Vocational Qualifications for Science, Engineering & Technology (VQSET).
R It is the awarding body for courses and qualifications in processing and manufacturing, refining, science and technology, engineering, warehousing, and learning and development.
✎ For further information see the **Federation of Awarding Bodies**.

Padstow Harbour Commissioners   (PHC)
■ Harbour Office, PADSTOW, Cornwall, PL28 8AQ.
Tel 01841 532239 **Fax** 01841 533346 http://www.padstow-harbour.co.uk
E Established under the Padstow Harbour Revision Order 1987.
G Padstow.
✎ For further information see **Port & Harbour Authorities**.

Paediatric Medicines Expert Advisory Group
■ 151 Buckingham Palace Road, LONDON, SW1W 9SZ.
Tel 020 3080 6000
Chairman: Prof Rosalind L Smyth, MA, MBBS, MD, FRCPCH, FMedSci
E Established in 2005. The Group functions as an advisory body to the Commission on Human Medicines (CHM), qv. It comprises 19 members including the Chairman.

R To advise CHM on the safety, quality and efficacy of medicines for paediatric use, and on the implementation of the paediatric strategy of the Department of Health and the Medicines & Healthcare products Regulatory Agency (qv), the recently implemented EU paediatric worksharing project, and the European regulation on medicines for paediatric use.

G United Kingdom.

Panel on Takeovers & Mergers   (The Takeover Panel)

■ 10 Paternoster Square, LONDON, EC4M 7DY.
Tel 020 7382 9026   **Fax** 020 7236 7005   http://www.thetakeoverpanel.org.uk
Chairman: Sir Gordon Langley, QC

E Established in 1968, its statutory functions are set out in the Companies Act 2006. It has been designated as the supervisory authority to carry out certain regulatory functions under the EC Directive on Takeover Bids 2004. The Panel comprises up to 35 members including the Chairman.

R To issue and administer the City Code on Takeovers & Mergers and to supervise and regulate takeovers and other matters to which the Code applies, with the central objective of ensuring fair treatment for all shareholders in takeover bids.

G United Kingdom.

Paper & Board Industry Advisory Committee   (PABIAC)

■ Marshalls Mill, Marshall Street, LEEDS, W Yorks, LS11 9YJ.
Tel 0845 345 0055
Chairman: Geoff Cox

E Established in 2001 by the Health & Safety Executive (qv). The Committee comprises the Chairman and 19 members who are drawn from the HSE, relevant trade associations, unions and professional bodies.

R The advise the HSE on the protection of people at work and others from hazards to health and safety arising in the paper and board industry.

G United Kingdom.

Parades Commission   (PC)

■ Windsor House, 9-15 Bedford Street, BELFAST, BT2 7EL.
Tel 028 9089 5900   **Fax** 028 9032 2988   http://www.paradescommission.org
Chairman: Peter Osborne

E Established as a statutory body on 16 February 1998 under the Public Processions (Northern Ireland) Act 1998. PC functions as an Executive NDPB of the Northern Ireland Office. The Commission comprises seven members including the Chairman.

R To promote greater understanding by the general public of issues concerning public processions.
To promote and facilitate mediation as a means of resolving disputes concerning public processions.

G Northern Ireland.

✍ Also referred to as the Northern Ireland Parades Commission.

Parliamentary Advisory Council for Transport Safety   (PACTS)

■ Clutha House, 10 Storey's Gate, LONDON, SW1P 3AY.
Tel 020 7222 7732   **Fax** 020 7222 7106   http://www.pacts.org.uk
Chairmen: Barry Sherman, MP

E PACTS functions as a registered charity and a company limited by guarantee. It was established in 1982 as an associate Parliamentary Group to advise the House of Commons and the House of Lords on air, rail and road safety issues. The Board of Directors comprises politicians, academics, retired public and private sector leaders and consultants.

R To protect human life through the promotion of transport safety for the public benefit.

G United Kingdom.

Parliamentary Boundary Commission   See **Boundary Commission**.

Parliamentary Commissioner for Standards

■ House of Commons, LONDON, SW1A 0AA.
Tel 020 7219 0311   **Fax** 020 7219 0490
Commissioner: John Lyon, CB

E Established in 1995 as a result of recommendations made by the Committee on Standards in Public Life (qv). The Commissioner is an officer of the House, his office wholly funded by the House of Commons.

R To oversee the maintenance and to monitor the operation of the Register of Members' Financial Interests.

To provide advice on the interpretation of the Code of Conduct and Guide to the Rules relating to the Conduct of Members (of the House of Commons).

To receive and investigate complaints about Members who are allegedly in breach of the Code of Conduct and Guide to the Rules.

G   United Kingdom.

● The Commissioner is also responsible for maintaining and monotoring the operation of the following registers and lists, providing advice about them, and receiving and investigating complaints about them:

Approved List of All-Party Parliamentary Groups & Associate Parliamentary Groups

Register of All-Party Groups

Register of Interests of Members' Secretaries & Research Assistants

Register of Journalists' Interests.

Parliamentary & Health Service Ombudsman   (PHSO)

■   Millbank Tower, Millbank, LONDON, SW1P 4QP.

Tel 0345 015 4033   Fax 0300 061 4000   http://www.ombudsman.org.uk

Ombudsman: Ann Abraham

E   Established in 1967 under the Parliamentary Commissioner Act 1967 and the Parliamentary & Health Service Commissioners Act 1987. The Ombudsman is solely accountable to Parliament for the decisions and operation of his office. The Executive Board comprises the Ombudsman and three others.

R   To carry out independent investigations into complaints about UK Government departments and their agencies, and the NHS in England, and help improve services as as result.

G   United Kingdom.

Parliamentary & Scientific Committee   (P&SC)

■   3 Birdcage Walk, LONDON, SW1H 9JJ.

Tel 020 7222 7085   Fax 020 7222 7189   http://www.scienceinparliament.org.uk

Chairman: Ian Taylor, MBE, MP   Secretary: Annabel Lloyd

E   Established in 1939. Membership of the Committee is open to Members of any party and either House, to Members of the European Parliament, and to nominated representatives of affiliated scientific and technological organisations and some science-based companies. There are 20 Officers of the Committee including the Chairman.

R   To provide long-term liaison on scientific and technological issues between Parliamentarians and scientific bodies, science-based industry and the academic world.

G   United Kingdom.

Parole Board for England & Wales

■   Grenadier House, 99-105 Horseferry Road, LONDON, SW1P 2DX.

Tel 0845 251 2220   Fax 0845 251 2221   http://www.paroleboard.gov.uk

Chairman: Sir David Latham   Chief Executive: Linda Lennon, CBE

E   Established in 1968 under the Criminal Justice Act 1967, it became an independent Executive NDPB of the Ministry of Justice under the Criminal Justice & Public Order Act 1994. The Board comprises over 200 judicial, psychiatrist, psychologist, probation and independent. The senior management team is headed by the Chairman.

R   To protect the public by making risk assessments about prisoners to decide who may safely be released into the community and who must be retained in or return to custody.

G   England, Wales.

✍   It was announced on 14 October 2010 that the Board would be retained on the grounds of performing a technical function which should remain independent of Government but that its future status would be reviewed.

Parole Board for Scotland

■   Saughton House, Broomhouse Drive, EDINBURGH, EH11 3XD.

Tel 0131 244 8373   Fax 0131 244 6794   http://www.scottishparoleboard.gov.uk

Chairman: Prof Sandy Cameron, CBE

E   Established on 1 January 1968 under the Criminal Justice Act 1967; the PBS now operates under the terms of the Prisoners and Criminal Proceedings (Scotland) Act 1993 (as amended). It functions as an Tribunal NDPB of the Scottish Executive Justice Department. The Board comprises 23 members including the Chairman.

R   To consider whether prisoners should be granted parole.

G   Scotland.

Parole Commissioners for Northern Ireland

- Linum Chambers, 2 Bedford Square, Bedford Street, BELFAST, BT2 7ES.
  Tel 028 9054 5900   Fax 028 9054 5915   http://www.parolecomni.org.uk
  Chief Commissioner: Peter Smith, CBE, QC

E Established on 8 October 2001 as Life Sentence Review Commissioners, they were renamed Parole Commissioners on 6 November following enactment of the Criminal Justice (Northern Ireland) Order 2008. The Commissioners are accountable to the Northern Ireland Office. There are 25 Commissioners including the Chief Commissioner.

R To advise the Secretary of State for Northern Ireland on any matter referred to them by him connected with the release or recall of life sentence prisoners and of prisoners sentenced to indeterminate custodial and extended custodial sentences, and the recall of prisoners sentenced to determinate sentences.

G Northern Ireland.

Particle Physics & Astronomy Research Council

✍ See **Science & Technology Facilities Council**.

Partnership for Action against Wildlife Crime   (PAW)

- Zone 1/11, 2 The Square, Temple Quay, BRISTOL, BS1 6EB.
  Tel 0117 372 8551   Fax 0117 372 8393   http://www.defra.gov.uk/paw/
  Joint Chairmen: Richard Brunstrom;   Francis Marlow

E Established in 2001. PAW is a multi-agency body and NDPB of the Department for Environment, Food & Rural Affairs.

R To support the networks of Police Wildlife Crime Officers (PWCOs) and HM Revenue & Customs officers in enforcing wildlife law.
   To draw attention to the growing problem of wildlife crime and to raise awareness of the need for tough enforcement action.

G England, Wales.

Partnership Fund Assessment Panel   (PFAP)

✍ NFAP closed in December 2003.

Partnerships for Schools   (PfS)

- 33 Greycoat Street, LONDON, SW1P 2QF.
  Tel 020 3301 7000   Fax 020 3301 7199   http://www.partnershipsforschools.org.uk
  Chairman: Michael Grabiner   Chief Executive: Tim Byles

E Established in March 2004. PfS functions as a company limited by guarantee and an Executive NDPB of the Department for Education. The Board comprises eight members including the Chairman.

R To work with local authorities and the private sector, organised as Local Education Partnerships (LEPs), to rebuild or renew every one of England's 3,500 state secondary schools during the 15-year lifetime of the programme, with funding from Building Schools for the Future (BSF).

G England.

✍ The PfS programme was cancelled in July 2010 at which time 33 LEPs had been set up and 135 schools had received BSF funding. The Chairman's current appointment has been extended by twelve months to 1 January 2012.

Partnerships UK

✍ PUK has embarked on a process of disposing of its various businesses and is expecting to close down in 2011.

Passenger Focus

- 7th Floor, Piccadilly Gate, Store Street, MANCHESTER, M1 2WD.
  Tel 0300 123 2140   Fax 0161 236 1574   http://www.passengerfocus.org.uk
  2nd Floor, One Drummond Gate, LONDON, SW1V 2QY.
  Tel 0300 123 0860   Fax 020 7630 7355
  Chairman: Colin Foxall, CBE   Chief Executive: Anthony Smith

E Established in 2005 under the Railways Act 2005 which abolished the national Rail Passengers Council and the eight regional Rail Passengers Committees. Passenger Focus functions as an Executive NDPB of the Department for Transport. The Board comprises 13 members including the Chairman.

R To get the best deal for Britain's rail and bus passengers.

G United Kingdom.
✍ The Government announced on 14 October 2010 that Passenger Focus would be retained on the grounds of performing a function which requires impartiality. However it will be substantially reformed to focus on its core role of protecting passengers while reducing its cost to taxpayers.

Passenger Transport Executive Group   (PTEG)

■ Wellington House, 40-50 Wellington Street, LEEDS, W Yorks, LS1 2DE.
   Tel 0113 251 7204 **Fax** 0113 251 7333 http://www.pteg.net
   Chairman: Neil Scales
E Established by agreement. PTEG comprises (as full members) the six Passenger Transport Executives, and (as associate members) Strathclyde Partnership for Transport, Transport for London (qqv) and Nottingham City Council. The Group's Board includes the Director General of each of the full members.
R To promote efficiencies and the exchange of knowledge and good practice within the PTE network.
   To raise awareness nationally about the key transport challenges which face the city regions and the public transport solutions which PTEs are implementing.
G England, Scotland.

PASSENGER TRANSPORT EXECUTIVES & INTEGRATED TRANSPORT AUTHORITIES   (PTEs & ITAs)

E Passenger Transport Authorities (PTAs) and Passenger Transport Executives (PTEs) were established under the Transport Act 1968. The Metropolitan County Councils of England, established and abolished under the Local Government Acts of 1972 and 1985, assumed the functions of the PTAs while in existence. Reconstituted in 1986, the PTAs were renamed Integrated Transport Authorities (ITAs) on 9 February 2009 under the Local Transport Act 2008.
   The six ITAs are Greater Manchester, Merseyside, South Yorkshire, Tyne & Wear, West Midlands and West Yorkshire (qqv).
   The six PTEs are:
       Centro (West Midlands PTE)
       Greater Manchester Passenger Transport Executive
       Merseytravel (Merseyside PTE)
       Metro (West Yorkshire PTE)
       Nexus (Tyne & Wear PTE)
       South Yorkshire Passenger Transport Executive (qqv).
   The six are members of the Passenger Transport Executive Group (qv) of which
       Strathclyde Partnership for Transport, and
       Transport for London Authority (qqv) are associate members.
R The function of an ITA is to lay down the general policy to be followed for passenger transport in the area concerned. It appoints the professional PTE to be responsible for securing subsidised bus services, reaching agreements with train operating companies for local rail services, providing stations and bus shelters, planning and funding new public transport facilities, funding free passes and 'Dial-a-Ride'' services for the elderly and disabled, and giving out travel information about transport services.
G England.

Passengers' View Scotland   The name under which **Public Transport Users' Committee for Scotland** operates.

Passport & Records Agency   see **United Kingdon Passport Service**

Passport Service   See **Identity & Passport Service**.

Pastoral Committee   A committee of the **Church Commissioners**.

Patent Office   Since 2 April 2007 the Patent Office operates as the **Intellectual Property Office**.

Patient & Client Council   (PCC)

■ 1st Floor, Lesley House, 25-27 Wellington Place, BELFAST, BT1 6GD.
   Tel 0800 917 0222 http://www.patientclientcouncil.hscni.net
   Chairman: John Keanie, MBA   Chief Executive: Mrs Maeve Hully

E   Established on 1 April 2009 on the recommendation of the NI Review of Public Administration 2005, replacing four regional Health & Social Services Councils (Eastern, Northern, Southern and Western). The Board comprises 17 members including the Chairman.
R   To provide a strong voice for patients, clients and carers.
G   Northern Ireland.

Patient Information Advisory Group
✍   PIAG was wound up on 31 December 2008 and replaced by the **National Information Governance Board for Health & Social Care**.

Patient Information Expert Advisory Group
■   151 Buckingham Palace Road, LONDON, SW1W 9SZ.
Tel 020 3080 6000
E   Established in 2005. The Group functions as an advisory body to the Commission on Human Medicines (CHM), qv.
R   To advise CHM on communication with patients and the public about risk: benefit of medicines.
G   United Kingdom.
✍   The Group last met on 28 February 2008.

Patient & Public Involvement (PPI) Forums
✍   These were replaced on 1 April 2008 by **Local Involvement Networks (LINks)**.

Pavement Condition Management Group   A sub-group of the **UK Roads Board**.

Pay & Personnel Agency
✍   Renamed in April 2006 **People, Pay & Pensions Agency**.

PAY REVIEW BODIES

E   In 1971 three review bodies were set up by the then Prime Minister to advise on the remuneration of certain groups in the public sector for which the normal procedures for negotiation of collective agreements were not appropriate. Other review bodies were subsequently established.
The Office of Manpower Economics (qv) provides the secretariat for these and other similar bodies.

Peak District National Park Authority
■   Aldern House, Baslow Road, BAKEWELL, Derbys, DE45 1AE.
Tel 01629 816200   Fax 01629 816310   http://www.peakdistrict-npa.org.uk
Chairman: Narendra Bajaria, CBE   Chief Executive: Jim Dixon
E   The Peak District was designated a National Park on 20 August 1951. The present Authority was established on 1 April 1997 under the Environment Act 1995. It comprises 30 members including the Chairman.
G   Peak District.
✍   For further information see **National Park Authorities**.

Pembrokeshire Coast National Park Authority   (PCNPA)
■   Llanion Park, PEMBROKE DOCK, Pembrokeshire, SA72 6DY.
Tel 0845 345 7275   Fax 01646 689076   http://www.pcpna.org.uk
Chairman: Richard Howells   Chief Executive: Tegryn Jones
E   Pembrokeshire Coast was designated a National Park in 1952. The present Authority was established on 1 April 1997 under the Environment Act 1995. It comprises 18 members including the Chairman.
G   Pembrokeshire Coast.
✍   For further information see **National Park Authorities**.
=   Awdurdod Parc Cenedlaethol Arfordir Penfro

Pembrokeshire Local Health Board
✍   Merged on 1 October with the Carmarthenshire and Ceredigion Local Health Boards to form **Hywel Dda Health Board**.

Pension, Disability & Carers Service   (PDCS)

■ 3rd Floor, Caxton House, Tothill Street, LONDON, SW1H 9NA.
   Tel 020 7712 2171   http://www.the pensionservice.gov.uk
   Chairman: John de Trafford   Chief Executive: Terry Moran, CB
E Established in 2008 by the merger of the Pension Service and the Disability & Carers Service. PDCS functions as an Executive Agency of the Department for Work & Pensions. The Board comprises twelve members including the Chairman.
R To provide its customers with pensions, benefits and retirement information.
   To provide financial support for customers claiming disability benefits and their carers.
G England, Wales, Scotland.

Pension Protection Fund   (PPF)

■ Knollys Tower, 17 Addiscombe Road, CROYDON, Surrey, CR0 6SR.
   Tel 0845 600 2541   **Fax** 020 8633 4910   http://www.pensionprotectionfund.org.uk
   Chairman: Lady Barbara Judge   Chief Executive: Alan Rubenstein
E Established in 2004 under the Pensions Act 2004 in place of the Fraud Compensation Fund of the former Pensions Compensation Board. PPF functions as an Executive NDPB of the Department for Work & Pensions. The Board of Trustees comprises eleven members including the Chairman.
R To assume responsibility for a pension scheme when an insolvency event has occurred in relation to the scheme's employer and there are insufficient assets in the scheme to secure benefits on wind up that are at least equal to the compensation that the PPF would pay.
G United Kingdom.

Pension Protection Fund Ombudsman   See **Pensions Ombudsman**.

Pension Service
✍ Merged in 2008 with the Disability & Carers Service to form the **Pension, Disability & Carers Service**.

The Pensions Advisory Service   (TPAS)

■ 11 Belgrave Road, LONDON, SW1V 1RB.
   Tel 020 7630 2250   **Fax** 020 7592 7000   http://www.pensionsadvisoryservice.org.uk
   Chairman: Partha Dasgupta   Chief Executive: Marta Phillips, OBE
E Established in 1983 as the Occupational Pensions Advisory Service or OPAS Ltd before it changed to its current name in 2004. TPAS is an independent voluntary organisation, a company limited by guarantee and registered charity; it functions as an Executive NDPB of the Department for Work & Pensions. The board comprises eight members including the Chairman.
R To provide information and advice to members of the public on all pensions matters, covering state, company, personal and stakeholder schemes.
   To help any member of the public who has a problem, complaint or dispute with their occupational or private pension arrangement.
G United Kingdom.
● The service is free and is provided by a nationwide network of volunteer advisers who are supported and augmented by technical and administrative staff based in London.

Pensions Appeal Tribunals
✍ Since 3 November 2008 **First-tier Tribunal (War Pensions & Armed Forces Compensation)**.

Pensions Appeal Tribunals Scotland   (PAT)

■ George House, 126 George Street, EDINBURGH, EH2 4HH.
   Tel 0131 271 4340   **Fax** 0131 271 4398   http://www.patscotland.org.uk
   President: Colin M McEachran, QC
E Established in their present form under the Pensions Appeal Tribunals Act 1943. PAT Scotland functions as a Tribunal NDPB of the Scottish Executive Justice Department. The Tribunals are headed by the President, who is legally qualified, and supported by a panel of part-time legal chairmen, medical members and Service members.
R To hear appeals from ex-servicemen and women and widows who have had their claims for a war pension rejected by the Secretary of State for Defence.
G Scotland.

Pensions Commission

✍ Established in 2002, the Commission finished its review of the UK private pension system and was disbanded after making its report in November 2005.

Pensions Committee

■ BMA House, Tavistock Square, LONDON, WC1H 9JP.
   Tel 0300 123 1233   Fax 020 7383 6400   http://www.bma.org.uk
E Established as a standing committee of the British Medical Association. The Committee comprises 19 members.
R To consider all questions of superannuation and compensation not specifically referred to other BMA committees.
G United Kingdom.
✍ See **British Medical Association** [Boards & Committees] for further information.

Pensions Compensation Board

✍ See **Pension Protection Fund**.

Pensions Ombudsman

■ The Office of the Pensions Ombudsman, 11 Belgrave Road, LONDON, SW1V 1RB.
   Tel 020 7630 2200   Fax 020 7821 0065   http://www.pensions-ombudsman.org.uk
   Ombudsman: Tony King   Deputy Ombudsman: Jane Irvine
E Established in April 1991, the Ombudsman's present authority is derived from the Pension Schemes Act 1993. The Ombudsman functions as an Advisory NDPB of the Department for Work & Pensions. He is appointed by the Secretary of State who may also appoint a Deputy.
R To investigate and decide pension complaints between members of pension schemes (including personal pensions) or their beneficiaries, employers, trustees, managers and scheme administrators.
G United Kingdom.
✍ The Pensions Ombudsman is also the Pension Protection Fund Ombudsman. However, the Government announced on 14 October 2010 that the two were to be merged as a single Tribunal NDPB.

The Pensions Regulator

■ Napier House, Trafalgar Place, BRIGHTON, BN1 4DW.
   Tel 0870 606 3636   Fax 0870 241 1144   http://www.thepensionsregulator.gov.uk
   Chairman: Michael O'Higgins   Chief Executive: Bill Galvin
E Established in 2004 under the Pensions Act 2004 and replacing the former Occupational Pensions Regulatory Authority. The Regulator functions as an Executive NDPB of the Department for Work & Pensions. The Board comprises twelve members including the Chairman.
R To protect members of work-based pension schemes.
   To promote good administration of work-based pension schemes.
   To reduce the risk of situations arising that may lead to claims for compensation from the Pension Protection Fund (qv).
G United Kingdom.

Pensions Regulator Tribunal

✍ Now **Upper Tribunal (Tax & Chancery)**.

People 1st

■ 2nd Floor, Armstrong House, 38 Market Square, UXBRIDGE, Middx, UB8 1LH.
   Tel 01895 817000   http://www.people1st.co.uk
   Chairman: David Fairhurst   Chief Executive: Brian Wisdom
E Established on 1 April 2004. It is the recognised Sector Skills Council for the hospitality, leisure, travel and tourism industries. The board of trustees consists of nine members including the Chairman.
G United Kingdom.
✍ For further information see **Sector Skills Councils**.

People, Pay & Pensions Agency   (PPPA)

■ J Block Foxhill, Combe Down, BATH, Somerset, BA1 5AB.
   Tel 01225 829572
   Chief Executive: Mark Hutchinson
E Established in April 1991 as the Defence Accounts Agency, became the Pay & Personnel Agency on 1 February 1996 and adopted its current name in April 2006. PPPA functions as an Executive Agency of the Ministry of Defence. The Management Board comprises six members.

R   To provide a comprehensive and integrated personnel service for Ministry of Defence civilian staff and their managers, which is also available in whole or in part commercially to other customers
G   United Kingdom.
●   The Agency also has offices in Bath.

Personal Accounts Delivery Authority
✍   See **NEST Corporation**.

Personal Investment Authority Ombudsman   See the **Financial Ombudsman Service**.

Persons Hearing Consumer Credit Licensing Appeals
✍   Since 2009 part of HM Courts & Tribunals Service as the **First-tier Tribunal (Consumer Credit)**.

Persons Hearing Estate Agents Appeals
✍   Since 2009 part of HM Courts & Tribunals Service as the **First-tier Tribunal (Estate Agents)**.

Perthshire Tourist Board
✍   Since 1 April 2005 an area office of **VisitScotland**.

Pesticide Residues Committee   (PRC)
■   Mallard House, Kings Pool, 3 Peasholme Green, YORK, YO1 7PX.
     Tel 01904 455980   **Fax** 01904 455733   http://www.pesticides.gov.uk/prc_home.asp
     Chairman: Dr Ian Brown, OBE
E   Set up in 2000 and reconstituted in 2001, the Committee is part of the Chemicals Regulation Directorate (qv). PRC functions as a Scientific Advisory Committee and an Advisory NDPB of the Department for Environment, Food & Rural Affairs. The Committee has nine members who are drawn from the industry and various organisations.
R   To advise Ministers and the Chief Executives of the Chemicals Regulation Directorate and the Food Standards Agency (qqv) on:
     the planning of surveillance programmes for pesticides residues in the UK food supply and the evaluation of the results, and
     the procedures for sampling, sample processing and new methods of analysis.
G   United Kingdom.
✍   For further information see **Scientific Advisory Committees**.
     The Government announced on 14 October 2010 that PRC would cease to function as a NDPB and be reconstituted as a committee of experts.

Pesticides Forum
■   Mallard House, Kings Pool, 3 Peasholme Green, YORK, YO1 7PX.
     Tel 01904 455723   **Fax** 01904 455733   http://www.pesticides.gov.uk/pesticides_forum_home.asp
     Chairman: James Clarke
E   Set up in May 1996, the Forum is part of the Chemicals Regulation Directorate (qv). It functions as a Stakeholder Group of the Department for Environment, Food & Rural Affairs. The Forum has 24 members drawn from industry and various organisations.
R   To advise Government and industry on ways of encouraging and promoting responsible pesticide use.
G   United Kingdom.

Pesticides Safety Directorate
✍   Merged with parts of the Health & Safety Executive on 1 April 2009 to form the **Chemicals Regulation Directorate**.

Pet Advisory Committee   (PAC)
■   198 High Holborn, LONDON, WC1V 7BD.
     Tel 020 7025 2341   http://www.petadvisory.org.uk
     President: Lord Soulsby of Swaffham Prior   Chairman: Andrew Stunell, MP
E   Established voluntarily in February 1974 as the Joint Advisory Committee on Pets in Society, it adopted its present title on 1 March 1992. The Committee comprises the President, Chairman, five vice-presidents and representatives from 15 animal welfare organisations and veterinary bodies.

R   To examine the role of companion animals in society and to make recommendations to central and local government as to how pets can best fit into the environment, in the interests of the animal, its owner and the wider community.

G   United Kingdom.

Pet Health Council   (PHC)

■   4th Floor, 6 Catherine Street, LONDON, WC2B 5JJ.
Tel 020 7379 6545 http://www.pethealthcouncil.co.uk

E   Established in 1969. PHC comprises representatives from ten dedicated associate organisations from all aspects of the pet world.

R   To promote, inform and advise on the health and welfare of pet animals in the interests of both pets and people.

G   United Kingdom.

Peterhead Port Authority

■   Harbour Office, West Pier, PETERHEAD, AB42 1DW.
Tel 01779 483600 **Fax** 01779 475715 http://www.peterheadport.co.uk
Chief Executive: John Wallace

E   Established in 1983 under the Peterhead Bay Harbour Trust & Transfer Order 1983. Peterhead Bay Authority and Peterhead Harbour Trustees merged to form the present Authority on 1 January 2006.

G   Peterhead.

✍   For further information see **Port & Harbour Authorities**.

Petroleum Working Group

✍   A working group of the Advisory Committee on Dangerous Substances which closed in 2004.

Pharmaceutical Services Negotiating Committee   (PSNC)

■   59 Buckingham Street, AYLESBURY, Bucks, HP20 2PJ.
Tel 01296 432823 **Fax** 01296 438427 http://www.psnc.org.uk
Chairman: Dr Christopher Hodges Chief Executive: Sue Sharpe

E   Established in 1946 as the Central NHS (Chemist Contractors) Committee, it adopted its present title in January 1976. PSNC is financed by Local Pharmaceutical Committees. Its main committee comprises 32 members including the Chairman.

R   To secure the best possible NHS service opportunities, remuneration, terms and conditions for NHS pharmacy contractors in England and Wales.

G   England, Wales.

●   PSNC operates the National Prescription Research Centre.
The Committee's representation in Wales is run by Community Pharmacy Wales (qv).

Pharmaceutical Society of Northern Ireland   (PSNI)

■   73 University Street, BELFAST, BT7 1HL.
Tel 028 9032 6927 http://www.psni.org.uk
President: Ann Bowen, MPSNI Chief Executive: Trevor Patterson

E   Established under the Pharmacy & Poisons Act (Northern Ireland) 1925; its current powers and responsibilities derive from the Pharmacy (Northern Ireland) Order 1976. The PSNI Council comprises 22 members including the President.

R   To maintain a publicly accessible register of pharmacists and pharmaceutical premises in Northern Ireland.
To set and promote standards for pharmacists' admission to the register and for remaining on the register.
To ensure high standards of education and training for pharmacists in Northern Ireland.
To handle concerns about the Fitness to Practise of registrants.

G   Northern Ireland.

✍   For further information see **Health & Social Care Regulators**.

Pharmacists' Review Panel

✍   Abolished on 31 March 2005.

Pharmacovigilance Expert Advisory Group   (PvEAG)

■   151 Buckingham Palace Road, LONDON, SW1W 9SZ.
Tel 020 3800 6000
Chairman: Prof Munir Pirmohamed, PhD, FRCP

E   Established in 2005. The Group functions as an advisory body to the Commission on Human Medicines (CHM), qv. It comprises eleven members including the Chairman.
R   To advise the HMC on the following in relation to human medicines including herbal medicines:
         the public health importance of potential new signals,
         the confirmation and quantification of risks identified,
         appropriate risk minimisation measures including communications,
         design and progress of pharmacovigilance plans, and
         methodologies for pharmacovigilance.
G   United Kingdom.

PhonepayPlus
■   Clove Building, 4 Maguire Street, LONDON, SE1 2NQ.
     Tel 020 7940 7474   http://www.phonepayplus.org.uk
     Chairman: Sir Alistair Graham   Chief Executive: Paul Whiteing
E   Established in September 1986 and known as the Independent Commission for the Supervision of Standards of Telephone Information Services until it changed to its current name. PhonepayPlus is the non-profit making industry-funded regulatory body for all premium rate charged telecommunication services. The Board comprises ten members including the Chairman.
R   To regulate the content and promotion of telecommunication services.
     To investigate complaints.
     To offer advice and guidance to both existing and new service providers.
G   United Kingdom.

Pig Production Development Committee
✍   The Committee was wound up on 31 March 2008.

Planning Appeals Commission   (PAC)
■   Park House, 87-91 Great Victoria Street, BELFAST, BT2 7AG.
     Tel 028 9024 4710   **Fax** 028 9031 2536   http://www.pacni.gov.uk
     Chief Commissioner: Maire Campbell
E   Established on 1 October 1973 under the Planning (Northern Ireland) Order 1972 and continued under the Planning (Northern Ireland) Order 1991. PAC now functions as a Tribunal NDPB of the Office of the First Minister & Deputy First Minister in Northern Ireland.
R   To make decisions on all appeals against Departmental decisions on a wide range of planning and environmental matters.
G   Northern Ireland.

The Planning Inspectorate
■   Room 3/05 Kite Wing, Temple Quay House, 2 The Square, Temple Quay, BRISTOL, BS1 6PN.
     Tel 0117 372 6372   http://www.planning-inspectorate.gov.uk
     Crown Buildings, Cathays Park, CARDIFF, CF10 3NQ.
     Tel 029 2082 3866   **Fax** 029 2082 5150
     Chief Executive: Katrine Sporle, CBE
E   Established in 1909. The Inspectorate functions as an Executive Agency of the Department for Communities & Local Government and for the National Assembly for Wales. The strategic management board comprises eight persons including the Chief Executive.
R   To process planning and enforcement appeals and hold examinations into regional spatial strategies and local development plans.
     To deal with a wide variety of other planning related casework.
G   England, Wales.

The Planning Service
■   Millennium House, 17-25 Great Victoria Street, BELFAST, BT2 7BN.
     Tel 028 9041 6700   **Fax** 028 9041 6802   http://www.planningni.gov.uk
     Chief Executive: Cynthia Smith
E   Established on 1 April 1996; the Service derives its authority from the Planning (Northern Ireland) Order 1991. It functions as an Executive Agency of the Department of the Environment Northern Ireland.
R   To provide operational planning policy, development plans and high quality professional planning decisions.
     To improve delivery of services, having regard to the effective use of available resources, Section 75 of and Schedule 9 to the Northern Ireland Act 1998 and associated human rights and equality policies.
     To provide an accurate and speedy land and property information service to the conveyancing community.
G   Northern Ireland.

- The Agency's two main business areas are Development Planning and Development Control; it also interacts with a number of agencies and public services in order to deliver its services.

Plant yng Nghymru   See **Children in Wales**.

Plant Varieties & Seeds Tribunal
■ FERA (Varieties & Seeds), Whitehouse Lane, CAMBRIDGE, CB3 0LF.
   Tel 01223 342322   Fax 01223 342386
E Established under the Plant Varieties & Seeds Act 1964. It functions as a Tribunal NDPB of the Department for Environment, Food & Rural Affairs (Defra).
R To consider decisions made by:
   the Controller of Plant Breeders' Rights (if the decision is about UK Plant Breeders' Rights),
   ministers (if the decision is about additions to the UK National List),
   ministers (if the decision is about certain seed certification matters), and
   Forestry Commissioners under the Forest Reproductive Materials Regulations.
G United Kingdom.
✍ Defra was considering in 2010 its scope to transfer the Tribunal's jurisdiction into HM Courts & Tribunals Service (qv).

Plymouth City Development Company
✍ Established as an Economic Development Company in February 2008, it announced in August 2010 that it would cease trading due to cuts in its funding.

Plymouth Pilotage Service   See **Cattewater Harbour Commissioners**.

Police Advisory Board for England & Wales   (PABEW)
■ 6th Floor, Kingsgate House, 66-74 Victoria Street, LONDON, SW1E 6SW.
   Tel 020 7215 8101   Fax 020 7215 4445
   Chairman: John Randall   Deputy Chairman: Prof Gillian Morris
E Established in 1965 under the Police Act 1964 in succession to the former statutory Police Council for England & Wales, the Board's current authority is derived from the Police Act 1996. PABEW functions as an Advisory NDPB of the Home Office. Its members are the Association of Police Authorities, the Association of Chief Police Officers, the Chief Police Officers' Staff Association, the Police Superintendents' Association of England & Wales and the Police Federation, plus members nominated by the Home Secretary. The Board's independent Chairman and Deputy Chairman are appointed by the Prime Minister.
R To advise the Home Secretary on general questions affecting the police in England and Wales.
G England, Wales.
✍ One of the bodies whose secretariat is provided by the **Office of Manpower Economics**. On 14 October 2010 the Home Office announced that it had launched a review of police remuneration and conditions of service and how these are determined. The future roles of PABEW, the Police Advisory Board for Scotland, Northern Ireland Policing Board, Police Arbitration Tribunal and Police Negotiating Board are all under consideration.

Police Advisory Board for Scotland   (PABS)
■ St Andrew's House, Regent Road, EDINBURGH, EH1 3DG.
   Tel 0845 774 1741
E Established on 23 June 1965 under Section 46 of the Police Act 1964 (now Section 63 of the Police Act 1996). PABS functions as an Advisory NDPB of the Scottish Executive Justice Department.
R To advise the Scottish Ministers on general matters affecting the police in Scotland.
G Scotland.
✍ On 14 October 2010 the Home Office announced that it had launched a review of police remuneration and conditions of service and how these are determined. The future roles of PABS, the Police Advisory Board for England & Wales, Northern Ireland Policing Board, Police Arbitration Tribunal and Police Negotiating Board are all under consideration.

Police Arbitration Tribunal   (PAT)
■ Euston Tower, 286 Euston Road, LONDON, NW1 3JJ.
   Tel 020 7936 0022   Fax 020 7210 3708
   Chairman: Prof John Goodman, CBE

E   Established in 1979. PAT functions as a Tribunal NDPB of the Home Office and operates under the auspices of the Advisory, Conciliation & Arbitration Service (qv). The Tribunal comprises three arbiters including the Chairman.

R   To decide on any dispute that has previously been unresolved by the Police Negotiating Board (qv), and where any attempt at reconciliation has not resulted in an agreed recommendation between the Staff Side and the Official Side.

G   United Kingdom.

✍   On 14 October 2010 the Home Office announced that it had launched a review of police remuneration and conditions of service and how these are determined. The future roles of PAT, the Police Advisory Boards for Scotland, England & Wales, Northern Ireland Policing Board and Police Negotiating Board are all under consideration.

POLICE AUTHORITIES

E   There are 50 police authorities in the United Kingdom, each of which oversees the work of its local police force. They were established on 1 April 1995 under the Police & Magistrates Act 1994, their statutory role contained in the Police Act 1996.

Each authority comprises councillor members nominated by local government (usually nine in number) and independent members (usually eight in number). At least one member must be a magistrate.

Two police forces in Scotland (Fife and Dumfries & Galloway) have no police authority but are administered directly by their local council.

In 2010 the Coalition Government proposed to replace police authorities with directly elected individuals (commissioners).

R   Police authorities make sure the local police force is efficient and effective and seek to improve policing performance and standards.

It is their job to make sure that local people have a say in how they are policed and to hold the chief police officer to account for the services delivered.

Police authorities also set the force budget and decide how much money to raise towards the cost of policing through the local council tax.

✍   The full list of Police Authorities can be found in the Subject Index.

Police Authority for Northern Ireland

✍   PANI was dissolved on 4 November 2001 and replaced by the **Northern Ireland Policing Board**.

Police Complaints Commissioner for Scotland   (PCCS)

■   Hamilton House, Hamilton Business Park, Caird Park, HAMILTON, ML3 0QA.
    Tel 0808 178 5577   **Fax** 01698 542901   http://www.pcc-scotland.org
    Commissioner: John McNeill   Director: Ian Todd

E   Established on 1 April 2007 under the Police, Public Order & Criminal Justice (Scotland) Act 2006. PCCS functions as an Executive NDPB of the Scottish Executive Justice Department.

R   To scrutinise independently the manner in which police forces, police authorities and policing agencies deal with complaints.

G   Scotland.

Police Discipline Appeals Tribunal

■   2 Marsham Street, LONDON, SW1P 4DF.
    Tel 020 7035 4848   **Fax** 020 7035 4745

E   A Tribunal NDPB of the Home Office.

R   To enquire into and report on any appeal referred by Home Secretary in respect of police discipline against an officer.

G   United Kingdom.

Police Information Technology Organisation

✍   PITO migrated into the **National Policing Improvement Agency**, established 1 April 2007.

Police Negotiating Board   (PNB)

■   6th Floor, Kingsgate House, 66-74 Victoria Street, LONDON, SW1E 6SW.
    Tel 020 7215 8101   **Fax** 020 7215 4445
    Chairman: John Randall   Deputy Chairman: Prof Gillian Morris

E   Established under the Police Negotiating Board Act 1980. PNB functions as an Advisory NDPB of the Home Office. The staff side of the Board is provided by the Employers' Organisation for Local Government (qv), the staff side by the Police Federation, the Superindendents' Association and the Chief Police Officers' Staff Association. The full Board comprises 22 members on each side. The independent Chairman and his deputy are appointed by the Prime Minister.

R   To negotiate agreements on the pay and conditions of all UK police officers.

G   United Kingdom.

✍   One of the bodies whose secretariat is provided by the **Office of Manpower Economics**.

On 14 October 2010 the Home Office announced that it had launched a review of police remuneration and conditions of service and how these are determined. The future roles of PNB, the Police Advisory Boards for Scotland, England & Wales, Northern Ireland Policing Board and Police Arbitration Tribunal are all under consideration.

Police Ombudsman for Northern Ireland

■   New Cathedral Buildings, St Anne's Square, BELFAST, BT1 1PG.
Tel 028 9082 8600   **Fax** 028 9082 8659   http://www.policeombudsman.org
Ombudsman: Al Hutchinson   Chief Executive: Sam Pollock

E   Established in September 2000 under the Police (Northern Ireland) Act 1998, replacing the former Independent Commission for Police Complaints for Northern Ireland. The Ombudsman functions as a corporation sole and his office as an Executive NDPB of the Northern Ireland Office. The Police Ombudsman for Northern Ireland is appointed by Her Majesty.

R   To provide an independent and impartial police complaints service in which both the public and the police have confidence.

G   Northern Ireland.

Police Service of Northern Ireland   For the police authority for the PSNI see **Northern Ireland Policing Board**.

Pool Water Treatment Advisory Group   (PWTAG)

■   Field House, Thrandeston, DISS, Norfolk, IP21 4BU.
Tel 01379 783678   **Fax** 01379 783865   http://www.pwtag.org
Chairman: Janice Calvert

E   Established on 4 December 1984 in place of the former Department of the Environment Sub-Committee on the Treatment of Water in Swimming Pools. PWTAG is a membership body comprising 22 organisations.

R   To monitor and advise on swimming and spa pool water treatment.
To review existing advice and initiate and carry out research projects.
To develop standards and legislation.

G   United Kingdom.

Poole Harbour Commissioners   (PHC)

■   20 New Quay Road, Hamworthy, POOLE, Dorset, BH15 4AF.
Tel 01202 440200   **Fax** 01202 440212   http://www.phc.co.uk
Chairman: Richard Lacey   Chief Executive: Jim Stewart

E   Established in 1895 under the Poole Harbour Act 1895. The board comprises twelve commissioners including the Chairman.

R   To be responsible for the conservation, regulation & improvement of Poole Harbour.

G   Poole.

✍   For further information see **Port & Harbour Authorities**.

Population Investigation Committee   (PIC)

■   Room PS201, London School of Economics, Houghton Street, LONDON, WC2A 2AE.
Tel 020 7955 7666
General Secretary: Anne Shepherd

E   Established in 1936. PIC is registered as a charity. The Committee consists of individuals who have expertise in the field of population, and representatives appointed by the London School of Economics.

R   To promote the study of demography.
To offer scholarships to students following a one year masters course with a high demographic content.

G   United Kingdom.

Port Authorities   See **Port & Harbour Authorities**.

E   Organisations responsible for the management of the many ports and harbours in the United Kingdom vary widely; they can be local councils, companies, harbour authorities, commissions, commissioners, etc.
Each body runs the port or harbour under local statutory provisions and is regulated by the appropriate Government department in England, Scotland, Wales or Northern Ireland.

R   Each body's main duty is the maintenance, development, management, conservation and improvement of its port or harbour.

✍   Individual authorities are listed under **Ports & harbours** in the subject index.

Port of London Authority   (PLA)

■   Baker's Hall, 7 Harp Lane, LONDON, EC3R 6LB.
Tel 020 7743 7900 **Fax** 020 7743 7999 http://www.pla.co.uk
London River House, Royal Pier Road, GRAVESEND, Kent, DA12 1BG.
Tel 01474 562200   **Fax** 01474 562281
Chairman: Helen Alexander, CBE   Chief Executive: Richard Everitt

E   Established in 1908, its current authority is derived under the Port of London Act 1968, Harbour Revision Orders of 1975 and 1992, and the Pilotage Act 1987. PLA functions as a self-financing public sector trust of the Department for Transport. The Authority's board comprises ten members including the Chairman.

R   To keep commercial and leisure users safe over 95 miles of River.
To protect the unique habitats on the Thames.
To promote the use of the tidal Thames.

G   London, Thames Estuary.

●   PLA is responsible for the conservancy of 150km of the tidal River Thames and owns much of the riverbed and foreshore to the high water mark.
It provides navigational services for ships using the Port, including maintenance of shipping channels and moorings.
It registers craft and licenses watermen, lightermen, river works and structures.

✍   For further information see **Port & Harbour Authorities**.

Port of Sunderland Authority

✍   Commissioners established in 1717, a municipal port since 1972.

Port of Tyne Authority

■   Maritime House, Tyne Dock, SOUTH SHIELDS, Tyne & Wear, NE34 9PT.
Tel 0191 455 2671 **Fax** 0191 454 1460 http://www.portoftyne.co.uk
Chairman: Sir Ian Wrigglesworth   Chief Executive: Andrew Moffat

E   Established in 1850, the PTA's current authority is derived from the Port of Tyne Reorganisation Scheme 1967.

G   Newcastle upon Tyne, Gateshead, Tynemouth, South Shields.

✍   For further information see **Port & Harbour Authorities**.

Post Office   See **Royal Mail Group plc**.

Postal Services Commission   See **Postcomm**.

Postcomm - The Postal Services Commission

■   Hercules House, 6 Hercules Road, LONDON, SE1 7DB.
Tel 020 7593 2100 **Fax** 020 7593 2142 http://www.psc.gov.uk
Chairman: Nigel Stapleton   Chief Executive: Tim Brown

E   Established on 1 April 2000 under the Postal Services Act 2000. Postcomm functions as an independent regulator and is classified as a non-ministerial Government department. There are eight Commissioners including the Chairman.

R   To make sure licensed postal operators, including Royal Mail, meet the needs of their customers throughout the UK.

G   United Kingdom.

✍   It was announced by the Government on 14 October 2010 that Postcomm will be merged into the Office of Communications (qv).

Postgraduate Medical Education & Training Board
✍ PMETB merged on 1 April 2010 with the **General Medical Council**.

Postwatch
✍ On 1 October 2008 Postwatch (the Consumer Council for Postal Services), with others, was replaced by **Consumer Focus**.

Potato Council
■ AHDB, Stoneleigh Park, KENILWORTH, Warwicks, CV8 2TL.
Tel 024 7669 2051   http://www.potato.org.uk
Chairman: Allan Stevenson
E Established on 1 April 2008 via the Agriculture & Horticulture Development Board Order 2008, it replaced the former British Potato Council. Since December 2009 it has functioned as a division of AHDB. The board comprises 15 members including the Chairman.
R To make the British potato industry more competitive.
To stimulate the use of the British potato crop in home and export markets.
G England, Wales, Scotland.
✍ A subsidiary of the **Agriculture & Horticulture Development Board** and funded through an AHDB levy collected from growers and buyers.

Powys Local Health Board
✍ Since 1 October 2009: **Powys Teaching Health Board**.

Powys Teaching Health Board   (THB)
■ Mansion House, Bronllys, BRECON, Powys, LD3 0LS.
Tel 01874 711661   http://www.powysthb.wales.nhs.uk
Chairman: Chris Mann   Chief Executive: Andrew Cottom
E Established on 1 October 2009 by the merger of the former Powys Local Health Board and Powys Healthcare NHS Trust.
G Powys.
✍ For further information see **NHS Wales - Local Health Boards**.
Powys Teaching Health Board is the operational name of the Powys Teaching Local Health Board.

Practitioner & Stakeholder Group   See **Independent Advisory Panel on Deaths in Custody**.

Prescription Medicines Code of Practice Authority   (PMCPA)
■ 12 Whitehall, LONDON, SW1A 2DY.
Tel 020 7747 8880   **Fax** 020 7747 8881   http://www.pmcpa.org.uk
Chairman: William Harbage, QC   Director: Heather Simmonds
E Established on 1 January 1993 by the Association of the British Pharmaceutical Industry (ABPI). The Board comprises the Chairman, eight independent members and seven industry members.
R To be responsible for all matters relating to the ABPI's Code of Practice for the Pharmaceutical Industry.
G United Kingdom.

Prescription Pricing Authority
✍ Since 2006, the Prescription Services division of the **NHS Business Services Authority**.

Press Complaints Commission   (PCC)
■ Halton House, 20/23 Holborn, LONDON, EC1N 2JD.
Tel 020 7831 0022   **Fax** 020 7831 0025   http://www.pcc.org.uk
Chairman: Baroness Buscombe
E Established in January 1991 following recommendations made to Parliament by the Calcutt Committee, and replacing the former Press Council. PCC is an independent regulatory body. The Commission comprises 16 members including the Chairman.
R To deal with complaints by members of the public about the editorial content of newspapers and magazines.
G United Kingdom.
● The Commission is charged with enforcing a Code of Practice which was framed by the newspaper and periodical industry and was ratified by the PCC on 1 August 2007.

Press Standards Board of Finance   (PressBof)

■ 12 Lansdowne Crescent, EDINBURGH, EH12 5EH.
Tel 0131 240 3270   Fax 0131 220 4344   http://www.pcc.org.uk
Chairman: Guy Black   Secretary & Treasurer: Jim Raeburn, OBE
E Established in 1992. Pressbof is an independent set up by the main organisations involved in the newspaper and periodical industries. The Board comprises nine members including the Chairman.
R To operate a levy scheme in order to raise funding for the running of the Press Complaints Commission (qv), thus ensuring its operational independence.
G United Kingdom.

Prestwick Airport Consultative Committee   See **Glasgow Prestwick Airport Consultative Committee**.

Primary Health Lists   See **First-tier Tribunal (Primary Health Lists)**.

Prince's Trust Council

■ 18 Park Square East, LONDON, NW1 4LH.
Tel 020 7543 1234   Fax 020 7543 1200   http://www.princes-trust.org.uk
Chairman: Charles Dunstone   Chief Executive: Martina Milburn
E Founded in 1976 by HRH the Prince of Wales. The Trust functions as a registered charity. The Council comprises 14 members including the Chairman. It sets the strategy and agrees the Trust's business plan and budget and has authority to take all decisions and set all policy.
R To improve the lives of disadvantaged young people in the UK by offering a range of opportunities including training, personal development, business start up support, mentoring and advice.
G United Kingdom.
● Wales, Scotland, Northern Ireland and each of the English regions has its own fully accountable Director and Council.

Printing Industry Advisory Committee   (PIAC)

■ 1st Floor, City Gate West, Toll House Hill, NOTTINGHAM, NG1 5AT.
Tel 0845 345 0055   Fax 0845 408 9566
Chairman: Geoff Cox
E Established in August 1979 by the Health & Safety Executive (qv). PIAC functions as an Advisory NDPB of the HSE.
R To advise the HSE on the protection of people at work and others from hazards to health and safety arising within the printing industry.
G United Kingdom.

Printing & Packaging Training Committee

✍ A Northern Ireland Sector Training Council established in 1990, PPTC is currently dormant.

Prisoner Ombudsman for Northern Ireland

■ 22nd Floor, Windsor House, Bedford Street, BELFAST, BT2 7FT.
Tel 028 9044 3982   Fax 028 9044 3993   http://www.niprisonerombudsman.gov.uk
Ombudsman: Pauline McCabe
E The Ombudsman is appointed by the Secretary of State for Northern Ireland.
R To investigate complaints from prisoners held in Northern Ireland who remain unhappy with the answer received from the Northern Ireland Prison Service (qv).
To investigate all deaths in prison custody in Northern Ireland.
G Northern Ireland.

Prisons & Probation Ombudsman for England & Wales   (PPO)

■ Ashley House, 2 Monck Street, LONDON, SW1P 2BQ.
Tel 020 7035 2876   Fax 020 7035 2860   http://www.ppo.gov.uk
Acting Ombudsman: Jane Webb
E Established on 1 October 1994 by the Home Secretary. The Ombudsman is completely independent of the Prison and Probation Services and functions as an Executive NDPB of the Ministry of Justice. Her duties are achieved with the help of three deputies and nine assistants.
R To provide prisoners and those under community supervision with an accessible, independent and effective means to resolve their complaints, and to contribute to a just and humane penal system.
G England, Wales.

© CBD Research Ltd · Beckenham · Kent BR3 5JS · Tel 020 8650 7745 · Fax 020 8650 0768 · E-mail cbd@cbdresearch.com · www.cbdresearch.com

Private Practice Committee   (PPC)

- BMA House, Tavistock Square, LONDON, WC1H 9JP.
  Tel 020 7387 4499   Fax 020 7383 6400   http://www.bma.org.uk
  Chairman: Derek Machin
- E   Established as a committee of the British Medical Association.
- R   To represent doctors engaged in private general and consultant practice (whether whole or part time).
- G   United Kingdom.
- ✍   See **British Medical Association** [Boards & Committees] for further information.

Private Rented Housing Panel   (PRHP)

- 3rd Floor, 140 West Campbell Street, GLASGOW, G2 4TZ.
  Tel 0141 572 1170   Fax 0141 572 1171   http://www.prhpscotland.gov.uk
  President: Mrs Aileen Devanny, LLB, Dip LP
- E   Established in 1965 under the Rent Act 1965, the Panel derives its current authority under the Rent (Scotland) Act 1984. PRHP functions as a Tribunal NDPB of the Scottish Executive Development Department.
- R   To provide members of Rent Assessment Committees which consider objections to fair rents and assess the market rent when landlord and tenant cannot agree.
  To provide the means by which private rented sector tenants can enforce the Repairing Standard provisions introduced through the Housing (Scotland) Act 2006 which extend the statutory obligations of a private landlord to repair a house or flat.
- G   Scotland.

Probation Board for Northern Ireland   (PBNI)

- 80-90 North Street, BELFAST, BT1 1LD.
  Tel 028 9026 2400   Fax 028 9026 2470   http://www.pbni.org.uk
  Chairman: Ronnie Spence, CB   Director: Brian McCaughey
- E   Established in December 1982 under the Probation Board (Northern Ireland) Order 1982. PBNI functions as an Executive NDPB of the Department of Justice Northern Ireland. The Board comprises 13 members including the Chairman.
- R   To protect the public by working with the courts, other agencies and partners to reduce re-offending and integrate offenders back into the community.
- G   Northern Ireland.

PROBATION TRUSTS

- E   Established under the Offender Management Act 2007 and phased in to replace the Probation Boards which came into existence in 2001. The Trusts operate within the National Offender Management Service (qv). Each Trust comprises a minimum of five members including the Chairman.
- R   To prepare pre-sentence reports to court to help judges and magistrates choose the most appropriate sentence.
  To manage community sentences ordered by the courts, including community payback projects and projects to help offenders change their behaviour.
  To run hostels for people who have served a prison sentence and need a place to stay where they can get support and an environment with firm rules that reduce the liklihood of their returning to a life of crime.
  To work with victims of crime by keeping them informed about the offender's sentence and ensuring their views are considered at the times of sentence and release.
- G   England, Wales.
- ●   In general, the Trusts operate within the same geographical boundaries as the police forces, the exceptions being:
  Wales Probation Trust combines the Dyfed-Powys, Gwent, North Wales and South Wales police areas.
  Norfolk & Suffolk, Staffordshire & West Midlands and Surrey & Sussex Probation Trusts each cover two police areas.
- ✍   The full list of the Trusts can be found in the Subject Index.

Professional Conduct Committee   See the **General Council of the Bar of Northern Ireland**.

Professional Fees Committee   (PFC)

- BMA House, Tavistock Square, LONDON, WC1H 9JP.
  Tel 020 7387 4499   Fax 020 7387 6400   http://www.bma.org.uk
  Chairman: Dr John Canning
- E   Established as a committee of the British Medical Association.
- R   To negotiate fees for a range of non-NHS services.
- G   United Kingdom.
- ✍   See **British Medical Association** [Boards & Committees] for further information.

Professional & Linguisitic Assessments Board   (PLAB)

■   Regent's Place, 350 Euston Road, LONDON, NW1 3JN.
       Tel 0845 357 3456   http://www.gmc-uk.org
E   Established in 1999. PLAB operates as part of the General Medical Council (qv).
R   To supervise the English language testing of foreign medical personnel practising in the United Kingdom.
G   United Kingdom.

Professional Oversight Board   (POB)

■   5th Floor, Aldwych House, 71-91 Aldwych, LONDON, WC2B 4HN.
       Tel 020 7492 2300   **Fax** 020 7492 2301   http://www.frc.org.uk/poba
       Chairman: Dame Barbara Mills, DBE, QC
E   Established in 2002 as the Professional Board for Accountancy, adopting its current name on 5 May 2006. POB is
       part of the Financial Reporting Council (qv). The Board comprises 13 members including the Chairman.
R   To provide independent oversight of the regulation of the auditing, accounting and actuarial professions by the
       recognised supervisory and qualifying bodies, and to monitor the quality of the auditing function in relation to
       economically significant entities.
G   United Kingdom.
●   The POB's Audit Inspection Unit (AIU) was set up following the Government's post-Enron review of the regulation
       of the UK accountancy profession which reported in January 2003. It is responsible for the monitoring of the
       audits of all listed and other major public interest entities.

The Property Ombudsman   (TPO)

■   Beckett House, 4 Bridge Street, SALISBURY, Wilts, SP1 2LX.
       Tel 01722 333306   **Fax** 01722 332296   http://www.tpos.co.uk
       Ombudsman: Christopher J Hamer   TPO Council Chairman: Lord Best, OBE
       TPO Board Chairman: Bill McClintock
E   Established on 12 September 1990 under authority derived from the Companies Act 1985; known firstly as the
       Ombudsman for Corporate Estate Agents and latterly as the Ombudsman for Estate Agents, it adopted its
       current name on 1 May 2009. With effect from 1 October 2008 all estate agents are required to register with an
       Estate Agents Redress Scheme that has been approved by the Office of Fair Trading (qv) and which
       investigates complaints against estate agents. The TPO Scheme, established on 1 January 1998 as the
       Ombudsman for Estate Agents Scheme, is one of the schemes approved by the OFT. The TPO Council
       comprises eight members including its Chairman. The TPO Board comprises 13 members including its
       Chairman.
R   To provide a free, fair and independent service for dealing with unresolved disputes between TPO member sales
       and letting agents and consumers who are actual or potential buyers, sellers, landlords or tenants of residential
       property in the UK.
       To report to the TPO Council whose function is the ensure the Ombudsman's independence and funding, to act
       as an advisory body to the Ombudsman and to refer matters of consideration to the TPO Board.
       To administer membership of the TPO Scheme on behalf of the TPO Board whose function is to manage the
       business of the company, to raise sufficient funds from members to administer the Scheme and to represent
       member agents.
G   United Kingdom.

Proscribed Organisations Appeals Commission   (POAC)

■   PO Box 6987, LEICESTER, LE1 6ZX.
       Tel 0845 600 0877
E   Established on 5 July 2007 under the provisions of the Terrorism Act 2000. POAC functions as a Tribunal NDPB
       of the Ministry of Justice.
R   To deal with appeals in cases where the Secretary of State for the Home Department refuses to de-proscribe
       organisations believed to be involved in terrorism.
G   United Kingdom.
✍   Administrative support is provided by HM Courts & Tribunals Service (qv).

Proskills UK

■   Centurion Court, 85B Milton Park, ABINGDON, Oxon, OX14 4RY.
       Tel 01235 833844   http://www.proskills.co.uk
       Chief Executive: Terry Watts
E   Established on 1 August 2005. It is the recognised Sector Skills Council for process and manufacturing in the
       building products, coatings, glass, printing, extractive and mineral processing industries.
G   United Kingdom.
✍   For further information see **Sector Skills Councils**.

Prospect Leicestershire

- Two Cotton Square, LEICESTER, LE1 1QH.
  Tel 0116 222 3322   Fax 0116 248 8129   http://www.prospectleicestershire.co.uk
  Chairman: Nick Carter   Chief Executive: David Hughes
- E Established in April 2009 by Leicester City Council and Leicestershire County Council. It is an Economic
  Development Company, bringing together the activities of Leicester Regeneration Company (the Urban
  Regeneration Company established in 2001) and Leicester Shire Economic Partnership. The Board comprises
  twelve members including the Chairman.
- R To deliver physical regeneration and growth, business innovation and support and inward investment across
  Leicester and Leicestershire.
- G Leicestershire.
- ✍ For further information see **Economic Development Companies**.

PRS for Music Ombudsman   See **Ombudsman Services: PRS for Music**.

Prsion Service Pay Review Body   (PSPRB)

- 6th Floor, Kingsgate House, 66-74 Victoria Street, LONDON, SW1E 6SW.
  Tel 020 7215 8252   Fax 020 7215 4445
  Chairman: Jerry Cope
- E Established in February 2001. PSRPRB functions as an Advisory NDPB of the Home Office. The Review Body
  consists of eight members including the Chairman.
- R To advise the Government on the remuneration of governing governors and operational managers, prison officers
  and support grades in the England & Wales Prison Service.
- G England, Wales.
- ✍ One of the Pay Review Bodies whose secretariat is provided by the Office of Manpower Economics.

Prudential Regulatory Authority   (PRA)

- Bank of England, Threadneedle Street, LONDON, EC2R 8AH.
  Chief Executive: Hector Sants (from the Financial Services Authority)   Deputy Chief Executive: Andrew Bailey
  (Chief Cashier, Bank of England)
- E To be established in 2012.
- R To supervise the banking sector.
- G United Kingdom.

Public Accounts Commission

- Committee Office, House of Commons, LONDON, SW1A 0AA.
  Tel 020 7219 3270
  Secretary: Dorian Gerhold
- E Established in 1984, the role of the Commission is defined by the National Audit Act 1983. The Commission
  comprises six Members of Parliament including the Leader of the House.
- R To examine the National Audit Office Estimates, to consider reports from the appointed auditor of the National
  Audit Office (qv), and to report from time to time.
- G United Kingdom.
- ✍ For further information see **United Kingdom Parliament: Committees**.

Public Administration Committee   A standing committee of the **Joint University Council**.

Public Appointments Commissioner for Scotland

- 39 Drumsheugh Gardens, EDINBURGH, EH3 7SW.
  Tel 0131 226 8138   http://www.publicappointments.org
  Commissioner: Karen Carlton
- E Established in June 2004 under the Public Appointments & Public Bodies (Scotland) Act 2003 as (the Office of)
  the Commissioner for Public Appointments in Scotland, it adopted its current name on 1 April 2011 under the
  Scottish Parliamentary Commission & Commissioners etc Act 2010. The Commissioner is one of the two
  comprising the Commission for Ethical Standards in Public Life in Scotland (qv). The Commissioner is
  independent of the Government.
- R To publish a code of practice to be followed when making non-executive appointments to the boards of public
  bodies.
  To examine practices used during appointment rounds to ensure they comply with the code of practice.
  To investigate complaints about the public appointments process.

To ensure that appointments are made fairly and openly and that everyone who may be interested in an appointment has the opportunity to apply.

G   Scotland.

Public Corporations   See **Shareholder Executive**.

Public Guardian   See **Office of the Public Guardian**.

Public Guardianship Office

✍   See the **Court Funds Office** and the **Office of the Public Guardian**.

Public Health Agency

■   18 Ormeau Avenue, BELFAST, BT2 8HS.
    Tel 028 9031 1611   **Fax** 028 9031 1711   http://www.publichealth.hscni.net
    Chairman: Mary McMahon   Chief Executive: Dr Eddie Rooney

E   Established on 1 April 2009, on the recommendation of the NI Review of Public Administration 2005, in place of the former Health Promotion Agency for Northern Ireland. The Board comprises twelve members including the Chairman.

R   To provide an renewed and enhanced focus on public health and wellbeing by bringing together a wide range of public health functions under one prganisation.

G   Northern Ireland.

Public Health England

✍   Its establishment was announced in a Government White Paper published on 30 November 2010. Power over public health issues in England will be devolved from NHS Trusts to local authorities, while PHE will keep 'a firm national grip on crucial population-wide issues such as flu pandemics'.

Public Health Laboratory Service

✍   In 2003 became part of the newly established Health Protection Agency.

Public Health Medicine Committee   (PHMC)

■   BMA House, Tavistock Square, LONDON, WC1H 9JP.
    Tel 020 7383 6158   **Fax** 020 7383 6400   http://www.bma.org.uk
    Co-Chairmen: Dr Richard Jarvis and Dr Keith Reid

E   Established as a Branch of Practice Committee of the British Medical Association. The Committee comprises around 30 members including the Chairman.

R   To represent public and community health doctors.

G   England, Wales, Northern Ireland.

✍   See**British Medical Association** [Branch of Practice Committees] for for further information.

Public Health Wales

■   14 Cathedral Road, CARDIFF, CF11 9LJ.
    Tel 029 2022 7744   **Fax** 029 2022 6749   http://www.publichealthwales.wales.nhs.uk
    Chairman: Prof Sir Mansel Aylward, CB   Chief Executive: Bob Hudson

E   Established on 1 October 2009 as an NHS Trust under the Public Health Wales NHS Trust (Establishment) Order 2009. It incorporates the functions of the Wales Centre for Health which was established on 1 April 2005 under the Health (Wales) Act 2003. The Board comprises 13 members including the Chairman.

R   To provide and manage a range of public health, healthcare protection, health improvement, health advisory, child protection and microbiological laboratory services; and services relating to the surveillance, prevention and control of communicable diseases.

    To develop and maintain arrangements for making information about matters related to the protection and improvement of health available to the public in Wales; to undertake and commission research into such matters; and to contribute to the development and provision of training in such matters.

    To undertake the systematic collection, analysis and dissemination of information about the health of the people of Wales in particular including cancer incidence, mortality and survival; and prevalence of congenital anomalies.

    To provide, manage, monitor, evaluate and conduct research into screening of health conditions and screening of health related matters.

© CBD Research Ltd · Beckenham · Kent BR3 5JS · Tel 020 8650 7745 · Fax 020 8650 0768 · E-mail cbd@cbdresearch.com · www.cbdresearch.com

G   Wales.
=   Iechyd Cyhoeddus Cymru

Public Lending Right   (PLR)

■   Richard House, Sorbonne Close, STOCKTON-ON-TEES, TS17 6DA.
    Tel 01642 604699   **Fax** 01642 615641   http://www.plr.uk.com
    Registrar: Jim Parker
E   Established in 1982 under the Public Lending Right Act 1979. The Registrar of PLR functions as a Corporation
    Sole responsible to the Secretary of State for Culture, Media & Sport. The Registrar is advised by a
    Management Board comprising six members which he chairs.
R   To administer the Public Lending Right Scheme.
G   United Kingdom.
●   The 1979 Act gives British authors a legal right to receive payment for the free lending of their books in public
    libraries.
✍   The Government announced on 14 October 2010 that the present NDPB is to be abolished its function
    transferred to another body.

Public Record Office   See **National Archives**.

Public Record Office of Northern Ireland   (PRONI)

■   66 Balmoral Avenue, BELFAST, BT9 6NY.
    Tel 028 9025 5905   **Fax** 028 9025 5999   http://www.proni.gov.uk
    Director: Mrs Aileen McClintock
E   Established in 1923 under the Public Records Act (Northern Ireland) 1923. PRONI functions as an Executive
    NDPB of the Department of Culture, Arts & Leisure Northern Ireland. The management board comprises seven
    members including the Director.
R   To identity, preserve and make available Northern Ireland's unique archival heritage and community memory.
G   Northern Ireland.

Public Sector Transparency Board

■   70 Whitehall, LONDON, SW1A 2AS.
    Tel 020 7276 3000
    Chairman: Rt Hon Francis Maude, MP
E   Established in May 2010 by the Prime Minister. The Board comprises five members including the Chairman.
R   To drive forward the Government's transparency agenda.
G   United Kingdom.

Public Services Commission   (PSC)

■   2nd Floor, 10 Cromac Place, Cromac Wood, BELFAST, BT7 2JB.
    Tel 028 9026 6279   **Fax** 028 9026 2797   http://www.pscni.gov.uk
    Chairman: Sid McDowell, CBE   Chief Executive: Patricia Stringer
E   Established on 8 March 2006. The Commission comprises seven members including the Chairman.
R   To make recommendations to Government on the guiding principles and steps necessary to safeguard the
    interests of staff and to ensure their smooth transfer to new organisations established as a consequence of
    Government decisions on the review of public administration, taking into account statutory obligations,
    including those arising from Section 75 of the Northern Ireland Act 1998.
G   Northern Ireland.

Public Services Ombudsman for Wales

■   1 Fford yr Hen Gae, PENCOED, CF35 5LJ.
    Tel 01656 641150   **Fax** 01656 641199   http://www.ombudsman-wales.org
    Ombudsman: Peter Tyndall
E   Established on 1 April 2006, the Ombudsman combines the duties carried out by the former Health Services
    Ombudsman for Wales, the Commission for Local Administration in Wales (Local Government Ombudsman for
    Wales), the Social Housing Ombudsman for Wales, and the Welsh Administration Ombudsman. His role and
    powers are defined by the Public Services Ombudsman (Wales) Act 2005.
R   To investigate complaints made to him by members of the public that they have suffered hardship or injustice
    through maladministration or service failure on the part of a body within his jurisdiction.
G   Wales.
=   Ombwdsmon Gwasanaethau Cyhoeddus Cymru

Public Services Productivity Panel
✍ PSPP drew to a close in 2006.

Public Standards Commissioner for Scotland
■ 39 Drumsheugh Gardens, EDINBURGH, EH3 7SW.
Tel 0300 011 0550 **Fax** 0131 220 5149 http://www.publicstandardscommissioner.org.uk
Commissioner: Stuart Allan
E The Scottish Parliamentary Standards Commissioner and the Chief Investigating Officer were established under the Scottish Parliamentary Standards Commissioner Act 2002. The Scottish Parliamentary Commission & Commissioners etc Act 2010 created the Commission for Ethical Standards in Public Life in Scotland (qv) which brings together the offices of the above and of the Commissioner for Public Appointments in Scotland.
R To investigate complaints that a Councillor or a Member of the Scottish Parliament or a member of a devolved Public Body has contravened the relevant Code of Conduct.
G Scotland.

Public Transport Users' Committee for Scotland (PTUCS)
■ Area 2D, Dockside, Victoria Quay, EDINBURGH, EH6 6QQ.
Tel 0131 244 0849
Convenor: James King
E Established on 1 January 2007 under the Public Transport Users' Committee for Scotland Order 2006; it operates under the name **Passengers' View Scotland**. PTUCS functions as an Advisory NDPB of the Scottish Executive Enterprise, Transport & Lifelong Learning Department. The Committee comprises twelve members including the Convenor.
R To represent effectively the interests of public transport users.
To consider and make recommendations to Scottish Ministers relating to public transport services in, from and to Scotland.
G Scotland.

Public Trustee See **Offices of Court Funds, Official Solicitor & Public Trustee**.

Public Works Loan Board (PWLB)
■ Eastcheap Court, 11 Philpot Lane, LONDON, EC3M 8UD.
Tel 0845 357 6610 **Fax** 0845 357 6509 http://www.dmo.gov.uk
Chairman: John Parkes, CBE, DL Secretary: Mark Frankel
E Originated in 1793, its functions are derived chiefly from the Public Works Loan Act 1875 and the National Loans Act 1968. PWLB is an independent statutory body and has operated within the UK Debt Management Management Office (qv) since July 2002. The Board comprises twelve Commissioners including the Chairman.
R To consider applications from local authorities and other prescribed bodies for loans from the National Loans Fund and, where loans are made, to collect the repayments.
G United Kingdom.

Q

QinetiQ plc
✍ Founded in 2001 by the partition of the former Defence Evaluation & Research Agency, it was floated on the London stock market in February 2006. The Ministry of Defence sold its shareholding in 2009.

Qualifications, Curriculum & Assessment Authority for Wales
✍ On 1 April 2006 the Authority merged with the Welsh Government Department for Education, Lifelong Learning & Skills.

Qualifications & Curriculum Authority
✍ See the **Qualifications & Curriculum Development Authority** (closing in2011/2012) and the **Office of the Qualifications & Examinations Regulator**.

Qualifications & Curriculum Development Authority   (QCDA)
- ■ 53-55 Butts Road, Earlsdon Park, COVENTRY, CV1 3BH.
  Tel 0300 303 3010   Fax 0300 303 3014   http://www.qcda.gov.uk
  Chairman: Christopher Trinick, DL   Acting Chief Executive: Lin Hinnigan
- E Established on 1 April 2010 under the Apprenticeships, Skills, Children & Learning Act 2009 to carry out the non-regulatory functions of the former Qualifications & Curriculum Authority. It functions as an Executive NDPB of the Department for Education. The Board comprises 13 members including the Chairman.
- R To develop the curriculum, improve and deliver assessments, and review and reform qualifications, to ensure that everyone can get the knowledge, skills and qualifications they need for life in the 21st century.
- G England.
- ✍ Until legislation, expected in early 2012, is passed to abolish QCDA, the Authority will continue to fulfil its statutory responsibilities. It will continue to support schools and colleges in national curriculum assessment and examinations delivery until autumn 2011 when these functions will transfer to the Department for Education.

Qualifications for Industry Ltd
- ✍ Acquired in 2005 by **EDI**.

Quality Assurance Agency for Higher Education   (QAA)
- ■ Southgate House, Southgate Street, GLOUCESTER, GL1 1UB.
  Tel 01452 557000   Fax 01452 557070   http://www.qaa.ac.uk
  183 St Vincent Street, GLASGOW, G2 5QD.
  Tel 0141 572 3420   Fax 0141 572 3421
  Chairman: Sir Rodney Brookes, CBE   Chief Executive: Anthony McClaran
- E Established on 1 August 1997 to provide an integrated quality assurance service for UK higher education institutions. QAA is an independent body funded by subscriptions from universities and colleges and through contacts with the higher education funding bodies. The Board of Directors comprises 15 members including the Chairman.
- R To safeguard the public interest in sound standards of higher education qualifications.
  To inform and encourage continuous improvement in the management of the quality of higher education.
- G United Kingdom.

Quality Meat Scotland   (QMS)
- ■ Rural Centre, West Mains, Ingliston, NEWBRIDGE, EH28 8NZ.
  Tel 0131 472 4040   Fax 0131 472 4038   http://www.qmscotland.co.uk
  Chairman: Donald Biggar   Chief Executive: Uel Morton
- E Established on 1 April 2008 under the Natural Environment & Rural Communities Act 2006 and the Quality Meat Scotland Order 2008. QMS functions as an Executive NDPB of the Scottish Executive Rural Affairs Department. The board comprises twelve members including the Chairman.
- R To work with the Scottish red meat industry to improve its efficiency and profitability and to maximise its contribution to Scotland's economy.
- G Scotland.
- ✍ Prior to its establishment as an NDPB, Quality Meat Scotland was a private company withing the former Meat & Livestock Commission.

Quarries National Joint Advisory Committee   (QNJAC)
- ■ Lyme Vale Court, Newcastle Road, Trent Vale, STOKE-ON-TRENT, ST4 6NW.
  Tel 01782 602337
  Chairman: Geoff Cox
- E Established in 2000 by the Health & Safety Executive (qv). The Committee comprises the Chairman and 21 members who are drawn from the HSE, relevant trade associations, unions and professional bodies.
- R To promote health and safety in all sectors of the quarrying and associated industries and raise health and safety concerns.
- G United Kingdom.
- ● QNJAC is assisted in its work by ten sub-committees.

The Queen Elizabeth II Conference Centre   (QEIICC)
- ■ Broad Sanctuary, Westminster, LONDON, SW1P 3EE.
  Tel 020 7222 5000   Fax 020 7798 4200   http://www.qeiicc.co.uk
  Chief Executive: Ernest Vincent   Shareholder Executive contact: Robert Heskett
- E Opened in 1986. The Centre functions as an Executive Agency of the Department for Communities & Local Government. The Board comprises seven members and is chaired by the Chief Executive.

R   To provide and manage fully secure conference facilities for national and international meetings up to the highest level, and to market its facilities as a high quality venue for both Government and private sector use.

G   United Kingdom.

✍   One of the businesses managed by the **Shareholder Executive**.

Queen Victoria School   (QVS)

■   DUNBLANE, Perthshire, FK15 0JY.
    Tel 01786 822288   **Fax** 0131 310 2926   http://www.qvs.org.uk
    Head: Mrs Wendy Bellars

E   Established on 28 September 1908 when officially opened by HM King Edward VII. Since 1 April 1992 the School has functioned as an Executive Agency of the Ministry of Defence. The Board of HM Commissioners is responsible to the Secretary of State for Defence through the Adjutant General for the government of the school.

R   To provide stable, uninterrupted and high quality education for the children of Scottish service personnel, or of service personnel who are serving or have served in Scotland.

G   Scotland.

R

Radio Authority   see **Office of Communications**

Radio Joint Audience Research Ltd

✍   RAJAR, a private company jointly owned by RadioCentre (the trade body representing commercial radio stations) and the BBC, is the sole provider of audience measurement for all the radio broadcasting in the UK.

Radioactive Waste Management Advisory Committee   See **Committee on Radioactive Waste Management**.

Radiocommunications Agency   see **Office of Communications**

The Radon Council

■   PO Box 39, SHEPPERTON, Middx, TW17 8AD.
    Tel 01932 221212   http://www.radoncouncil.org
    Chairman: Brian Ahern, CEng, FIEECompany Secretary: Diane V Pead

E   Established on 12 October 1990 in response to the interim report of the Parliamentary Select Committee on Indoor Pollution. It functions as an independent non-profit making regulatory body. The Council comprises eight directors including the Chairman.

R   To regulate the UK radon industry.

G   United Kingdom.

RAF   See **Royal Air Force**.

Rail Passengers Council

✍   A network of eight regional committees abolished under the Railways Act 2005 which established **Passenger Focus**.

Rail Safety & Standards Board   (RSSB)

■   Block 2, Angel Square, 1 Torrens Street, LONDON, EC1V 1NY.
    Tel 020 3142 5300   http://www.rssb.co.uk
    Chairman: Paul Thomas, CB, FREng   Chief Executive: Len Porter

E   Established on 1 April 2003. RSSB functions as a not-for-profit company owned by major industry stakeholders. The Board comprises ten members including the Chairman.

R   To lead and facilitate the rail industry's work to achieve continuous improvement in the health and safety performance of the railways in Great Britain and thus to facilitate the reduction of risk to passengers, employees and the affected public.

G   England, Wales, Scotland.

The Railway Heritage Committee   (RHC)

■   Zone 4/13, Temple Quay House, 2 The Square, Temple Quay, BRISTOL, BS1 6EB.
Tel 0117 372 8545   Fax 0117 372 8193   http://www.dft.gov.uk/rhc/
Company Secretary (and Acting Chairman): Peter Ovenstone

E   Established in 1997 under the Railway Heritage Act 1996 as amended by the Railways Act 2005. RHC functions as an Executive NDPB of the Department for Transport. The Committees has 14 members including the Chairman.

R   To designate railway records or artefacts (or classes of record or artefact) which are historically significant and should be permanently preserved.

     To agree which institution shall hold those records or artefacts so designated when no longer required by the rail business that owns them and the terms under which they shall be offered to such institutions.

G   United Kingdom.

✍   The Government announced on 14 October 2010 that RHC and its functions will be abolished.

Railway Industry Advisory Committee   (RIAC)

■   One Kemble Street, LONDON, WC2B 4AN.
Tel 020 7282 2000   Fax 020 7282 2040
Interim Chairman: Ian Prosser

E   Established in February 1978 by the Health & Safety Executive (qv) under the Health and Safety at Work Act 1974. Since 1 April 2006 RIAC functions as an Advisory of the Office of Rail Regulation (qv). The Committee comprises 20 members including the Chairman.

R   To provide advice to the ORR on railway health and safety, exchange information, comment on proposed new legislation and guidance, and work to progress health and safety issues and other related developments in the industry.

G   England, Scotland, Wales.

Rampton Hospital Authority

✍   Since April 2001 the hospital has been administered by Nottinghamshire Healthcare NHS Trust.

Rate Collection Agency

✍   Since 1 April 2007 part of the **Land & Property Services** agency.

ReBlackpool

✍   See **Blackpool Fylde & Wyre edc.**

Refugee Council

■   240-250 Ferndale Road, LONDON, SW9 8BB.
Tel 020 7346 6700   Fax 020 7346 6701   http://www.refugeecouncil.org.uk
Chairman: Douglas Board   Chief Executive: Donna Covey

E   Established in December 1981. The Council is a registered charity and membership organisation. The Board of Trustees comprises 15 members including the Chairman.

R   To provide practical help to asylum seekers and refugees in the UK and to campaign for their rights in the UK and abroad.

G   United Kingdom.

●   The Council has offices in Birmingham, Hounslow, Ipswich and Leeds.

Regenco

✍   The Urban Regeneration Company for Sandwell which ceased trading in December 2009.

RegenWM

■   Level 4, Millennium Point, Curzon Street, BIRMINGHAM, B4 7XG.
Tel 0121 202 3260   Fax 0121 202 3261   http://www.regenwm.org
Chairman: Gerard Coyne   Chief Executive: Adrian Passmore

E Established in 2003. RegenWM functions an operating unit of Advantage West Midlands (qv). The Board comprises comprises 15 members including the Chairman.
R To promote and develop regeneration excellence in the West Midlands.
G West Midlands.

Regional Advisory Committee on Communicable Disease Control   (RACCDC)
■ McBrien Building, Belfast City Hospital, Lisburn Road, BELFAST, BT9 7AB.
   Tel 028 9026 3765   **Fax** 028 9026 3511
E Established as a Scientific Advisory Committee and an Advisory NDPB of the Department of Health, Social Services & Public Safety Northern Ireland.
R To advise the Department on matters relating to communicable disease control.
G Northern Ireland.
✍ For further information see **Scientific Advisory Committees**.

Regional Assemblies
✍ Established under the Regional Development Agencies Act 1998, they were abolished on 31 March 2010, with executive responsibility for developing the Single Regional Plans being transferred to the eight **Regional Development Agencies**.

Regional Audience Councils   See **Audience Councils**.

Regional Cultural Consortiums
✍ Established in 1999, they were closed on 31 March 2009 and their functions returned to the Department for Culture, Media & Sport. They were:
   Culture East Midlands/North East/Northwest/South East/South West/West Midlands, Living East, and Yorkshire Culture.

REGIONAL DEVELOPMENT AGENCIES   (RDAs)

E Eight RDAs were established on 1 April 1999 under the Regional Development Agencies Act 1998, with the London Development Agency (qv) following in 2000. Each functions as an Executive NDPB of the Department for Business, Innovation & Skills. The board of an RDA comprises 16 members, made up of experienced leaders from business, local government, the voluntary sector and trade unions.
R To further economic development and regeneration.
   To promote business efficiency and competitiveness.
   To promote employment.
   To enhance the development and application of skills relevant to employment.
   To contribute to sustainable development.
G England.
● The nine RDAs are:
   Advantage West Midlands
   East of England Development Agency
   East Midlands Development Agency
   London Development Agency
   Northwest Regional Development Agency
   One North East
   South East England Development Agency
   South West Regional Development Agency
   Yorkshire Forward (qqv)
✍ The Comprehensive Spending Review in October 2010 confirmed the Government's intention to abolish the RDAs and support the creation of Local Enterprise Partnerships (qv) to be in place by March 2012.

REGIONAL ENVIRONMENT PROTECTION ADVISORY COMMITTEES   (REPACs)

E REPACs were established under the Environment Act 1995, one for each operational region of the Environment Agency (qqv).
   Under the Act, the Agency is required to consult REPACs about proposals relating to the way in which it carries out its functions in the regions, and must also consider representations they make to it.
   Each Committee has around 20 members who are appointed by the Agency and comprise representatives of local authorities, organisations regulated by the Agency, non-government organisations, scientists, and the Chairmen of the Agency's Regional Fisheries and Flood Defence Committees (qqv).

Each REPAC can be contacted through the relevant Environment Agency regional office, or via its Secretariat based in London.

R   To advise on regional implications of national policy proposals (concentrating specifically on pollution control, water resources, air quality, control of complex processes and disposal of controlled wastes).

To advise on issues related to agriculture, climate change and sustainable communities.

G   England, Wales.

REGIONAL FISHERIES ECOLOGY & RECREATION ADVISORY COMMITTEES (RFERACs)

E   RFERACs were established under the Environment Act 1995, one for each operational region of the Environment Agency (qqv).

Under the Act, the Agency is required to consult RFERACs about proposals relating to the way in which it carries out its functions in the regions, and must also consider representations they make to it.

Each Committee has around 20 members who are appointed by the Agency and comprise representatives of local authorities and other organisations interested in the subject.

Each RFERAC can be contacted through the relevant Environment Agency regional office, or via its Secretariat based in London.

R   To advise the Agency on issues of regional concern in relation to fisheries, recreation, navigation and related conservation issues.

G   England, Wales.

REGIONAL FLOOD DEFENCE COMMITTEES (RFDCs)

E   RFDCs were established under the Environment Act 1995, in each operational region of the Environment Agency (qqv).

Under the Act, the Agency is required to consult RFDCs about proposals relating to the way in which it carries out its functions in the regions, and must also consider representations they make to it.

Each Committee has around 20 members who are appointed by the Agency and comprise representatives of local authorities, organisations regulated by the Agency, non-government organisations, scientists, and others with an interest in land drainage and flood defence.

Each RFDC can be contacted through the relevant Environment Agency regional office, or via its Secretariat based in London.

R   To maintain and improve any watercourses which are designated as main rivers.

To maintain and improve any tidal defences.

To install and operate flood warning systems.

To control actions by riparian owners and occupiers which might interefere with the free flow of watercourses.

To supervise the Internal Drainage Boards (qv).

G   England.

REGIONAL OBSERVATORIES

E   Regional Observatories exist in each of the English regions except London and the South East.

R   To enable access to a wide range of data and intelligence in economic, social and environmental issues.

To support better decision making by providing better evidence to underpin policy making.

G   England.

●   The Regional Observatories, and the Regional Development Agencies they are sponsored by, are:

        East Midlands Development Agency (the same)
        Insight East (East of England Development Agency)
        North East Regional Information Partnership (One North East)
        Research & Intelligence Unit (Northwest Regional Development Agency)
        South West Observatory (South West Regional Development Agency)
        West Midlands Regional Observatory (Advantage West Midlands)
        Yorkshire Futures (Yorkshire Forward).

✍   All are members of the Association of Regional Observatories (see companion volume, the **Directory of British Associations**).

REGIONAL SCREEN AGENCIES

E   Established in 2002 by the former UK Film Council, one in each of the English regions.

They are funded by the Department for Culture, Media & Sport via the British Film Institute (qv).

R   To develop and promote the screen industries (film, television, video, commercials and new interactive media) in their region.

G   England.

- The Agencies are:
  - EM Media (East Midlands)
  - Film London
  - Northern Film & Media
  - Screen South
  - Screen WM (West Midlands)
  - Screen Yorkshire
  - South West Screen
  - Vision+Media (North West) (qqv)
  - (Screen East ceased trading on 7 September 2010)
- ✍ Following the decision to abolish the UK Film Board, the RSA network will be reorganised as Creative England (qv).

REGIONAL TRANSPORT PARTNERSHIPS   (RTPs)

E   Regional Transport Partnerships were established on 1 December 2005 under the Transport (Scotland) Act 2005 to prepare a regional transport strategy so as to strengthen the delivery of regional transport in Scotland for the benefit of people and businesses.

RTPs are independent bodies corporate defined in the Act and function in a similar way to joint boards, bringing councils together to perform local government functions collective and strategically over a larger area.

All local authorities in Scotland are members of RTPs and councillors make up around two-thirds of the membership, the other third being non-council members who fulfill a role similar to that of non-executive members.

R   The Scottish Executive Transport Group and Transport Scotland (qv) work to ensure close liaison with the RTPs and local authorities so that transport policy in Scotland is properly co-ordinated.

G   Scotland.

- The seven RTPs are:
  - Highlands & Islands Transport Partnership
  - Nestrans (North-East of Scotland Transport Partnership)
  - Shetland Transport Partnership
  - South East of Scotland Transport Partnership
  - South West of Scotland Transport Partnership
  - Strathclyde Partnership for Transport
  - Tayside & Central Scotland Transport Partnership (qqv).

Registered Homes Tribunal

✍ Now part of the **First-tier Tribunal (Care Standards)**.

Registered Inspectors of Schools Appeal Tribunal

✍ Closed on 1 September 2005.

Registers of Scotland

■   Erskine House, 68 Queen Street, EDINBURGH, EH2 4NF.
Tel 0845 607 0161   **Fax** 0131 200 3932   http://www.ros.gov.uk
9 George Square, GLASGOW, G2 1DY.
Tel 0845 607 0164   **Fax** 0141 306 1721
Keeper & Chief Executive: Sheenagh Adams

E   Established on 6 April 1990. Registers of Scotland functions as an Executive Agency of the Scottish Executive Justice Department.

R   To compile and maintain registers relating to property and other legal documents.
To record and safeguard rights whilst providing open and efficient access to important information.

G   Scotland.

- There are 16 registers of which the largest are the two property registers, the General Register of Sasines and the Property Register. The smaller registers are grouped under the collective name of the Chancery & Judicial Registers.

Registrar of Public Lending Right   See **Public Lending Right**.

© CBD Research Ltd · Beckenham · Kent BR3 5JS · Tel 020 8650 7745 · Fax 020 8650 0768 · E-mail cbd@cbdresearch.com · www.cbdresearch.com

Registration Council for Clinical Physiologists   (RCCP)

■   c/o EBS, City Wharf, Davidson Road, LICHFIELD, Staffs, WS14 9DZ.
     Tel 0845 226 3064   Fax 0121 355 2420   http://www.rccp.co.uk
     Chairman: Mrs Anne Burge   Registrar: Mrs Jacqui Howard
E   The Council comprises the Chairman and 13 members who represent the fields of audiology, cardiology, GI
        physiology, hearing therapy, neurophysiology and respiratory physiology.
R   To promote and advance, and to encourage the study and practice of, the application of clinical physiology in the
        prevention, diagnosis, treatment and management of disease and disability.
G   United Kingdom.
●   RCCP is compiling the voluntary register for individuals practising in the disciplines of clinical physiology.

Regulation & Quality Improvement Authority   (RQIA)

■   9th Floor, Riverside Tower, 5 Lanyon Place, BELFAST, BT1 3BT.
     Tel 028 9051 7500   Fax 028 9051 7501   http://www.rqia.org.uk
     Chairman: Dr Ian Carson   Chief Executive: Glenn Houston
E   Established in April 2005 under the Health & Personal Social Services (Quality, Improvement & Regulation)
        (Northern Ireland) Order 2003. Its remit was extended under the Health & Social Care (Reform) Act (Northern
        Ireland) 2009. RQIA functions as an Executive NDPB of the Department of Health, Social Services & Public
        Safety Northern Ireland. The Board comprises 13 members including the Chairman.
R   To ensure that the quality of services provided by the Health & Social Care Services (HSC) bodies in Northern
        Ireland reaches the standards laid down by the DHSSPS and expected by the public.
     To inspect and regulate nursing and residential care homes, children's homes, independent hospitals and clinics,
        and nursing agencies.
     To regulate the care and treatment of people with a mental illness and those with a learning disability.
G   Northern Ireland.

Religious Education Council of England & Wales   (REC)

■   CAN Mezzanine, 1 London Bridge, LONDON, SE1 9BG.
     Tel 020 7022 1833   http://www.religiouseducationcouncil.org
     Chairman: Prof Brian Gates
E   Established in November 1973. REC draws its membership from the national bodies of a variety of faiths and
        beliefs, as well as national bodies representing Religious Education professionals. The Executive Committee
        comprises 17 members including the Chairman.
R   To provide a multi-faith forum where national organisations with an interest in supporting and promoting religious
        education in schools and colleges can share matters of common concern.
G   England, Wales.
●   REC works in partnership with the Department for Education.

Removals Industry Ombudsman Scheme

■   PO Box 3862, GERRARDS CROSS, Bucks, SL9 7WG.
     Tel 01753 888206   http://www.removalsombudsman.org.uk
     Ombudsman: Matti Alderson
E   Established in 2002 by the industry. Members of the Scheme are members of the National Guild of Removers &
        Storers. The Scheme is managed by an independent Committee which appoints the Ombudsman.
R   To provide the removals industry with an independent service to resolve disputes between member companies
        and their clients.
G   United Kingdom.

Remploy Ltd

■   18c Meridian East, Meridian Business Park, LEICESTER, LE19 1WZ.
     Tel 0845 155 2700   Fax 0845 155 2701   http://www.remploy.co.uk
     Chairman: Ian Russell, CBE   Chief Executive: Tim Matthews
E   Established in April 1945 under the Disabled Persons (Employment) Act 1944. Remploy functions as an Executive
        NDPB and Public Corporation accountable to the Department for Work & Pensions. The board comprises
        eleven members including the Chairman and seven non-executive members.
R   To enable thousands of disabled people, people with a health condition and those who face complex barriers to
        employment to gain sustainable and rewarding employment by giving them the specialist support they need.
G   United Kingdom.
●   Remploy has 27 branch offices in England, Wales and Scotland.
         Banbury (recruitment)
         Leicester (return to work and vocational rehabilitation)
✍   The Government announced on 14 October 2010 that the future of Remploy was under consideration.

Renaissance Southend

✍ An Urban Regeneration Company established on 18 March 2005, it closed on 31 December 2010. (For further information see **Urban Regeneration Companies**).

Renewable Fuels Agency (RFA)

■ Ashdown House, Sedlescombe Road North, ST LEONARDS-ON-SEA, E Sussex, TN37 7GA.
Tel 020 7944 8555   http://www.renewablefuelsagency.gov.uk
Chief Executive: Prof Ed Gallagher

E Established in October 2007. RFA is a NDPB sponsored by the Cleaner Fuels & Vehicles Division of the Department for Transport. The Board comprises six members including the Chief Executive.

R To allocate Renewable Transport Fuel Certificates (RTFCs) to suppliers of biofuels, to ensure obligated companies meet their annual obligation, and to report to Parliament and the public on the impacts of fuel supplied under the Renewable Transport Fuel Obligation (RTFO).

G United Kingdom.

● RTFO requires suppliers of fossil fuels to ensure that a specified percentage of the road fuels they supply is made up of renewable fuels, and to report on the carbon and sustainability of the biofuels supplied.

✍ The Government announced on 14 October 2010 that RFA will be abolished and its functions transferred to the Cleaner Fuels & Vehicles Division.

Renewables Advisory Board (RAB)

■ DECC, 3 Whitehall Place, LONDON, SW1A 2AW.
Tel 0300 068 5844

E Established on 1 April 2002. RAB functions as an Advisory NDPB of the Department of Energy & Climate Change. The Board comprises twelve members and is chaired by the Secretary of State.

R To provide advice to the Government on the key issues and barriers to delivering the UK's share of the EU target for 20 percent renewable energy by 2020.

G United Kingdom.

✍ On 14 December 2010 the Government announced that RAB would be abolished.

Renfrewshire Local Enterprise Company

✍ Now functions as the Paisley office of **Scottish Enterprise**.

RENT ASSESSMENT COMMITTEES

E Rent Assessment Committees are appointed by the Private Rented Housing Panel (qv) and convene throughout Scotland.

R Their remit is to consider objections to fair rents set by the Rent Officers under the Rent (Scotland) Act 1984.
They also assess the market rent for assured and short assured tenancies created under the Housing (Scotland) Act 1988 when the landlord and tenant cannot agree on an appropriate rent.

G Scotland.

Rent Assessment Committees   For England, see **Rent Assessment Panels**.

Rent Assessment Panel (RAP)

■ Cleaver House, 3 Donegall Square North, BELFAST, BT1 5GA.
Tel 028 9051 8518   Fax 028 9051 8516

E Established as a Tribunal NDPB of the Department for Social Development Northern Ireland.

R To determine appropriate rents for properties in the private rented sector.

G Northern Ireland.

Rent Assessment Panel [Scotland]   See **Private Rented Housing Panel**.

Rent Assessment Panel [Wales]

✍ See **Residential Property Tribunal for Wales**.

E   Established in 1965.
Five regional Panels cover the whole of England, each functioning as a Tribunal NDPB with quasi-judicial powers. RAPs receive administrative support from the Residential Property Tribunal Service (qv).

R   The Panels provide an independent, fair and accessible tribunal service in England for settling disputes involving private rented and leasehold property through:
Leasehold Valuation Tribunals - for disputes involving leasehold property
Rent Assessment Committees - for disputes about fair and market rents
Residential Property Tribunals - for certain appeals against denial of the right to buy.

G   England.

●   Each RAP covers an area of England, contact details can be found under:
Eastern Rent Assessment Panel
London Rent Assessment Panel
Midlands Rent Assessment Panel
Northern Rent Assessment Panel
Southern Rent Assessment Panel.

✍   On 14 October 2010 the Government announced that Residential Property Tribunal Service (qv) is to be abolished and jurisdiction of the RAPs transferred to HM Courts & Tribunals Service (qv).

The Rent Service

✍   On 1 April 2009 the functions of TRS transferred to the **Valuation Office Agency**.

Research Council for Complementary Medicine   (RCCM)

■   Royal London Homoeopathic Hospital, 6 Great Ormond Street, LONDON, WC1N 3HR.   http://www.rccm.org.uk
Chairman: Prof Nicola Robinson

E   Established in July 1983 as a registered charitable trust. The Council comprises eight Trustees including the Chairman.

R   To develop and extend the evidence base for complementary medicine in order to provide practitioners and their patients with information about the effectiveness of individual therapies and the treatment of specific conditions.

G   United Kingdom.

Research Councils UK   (RCUK)

■   Polaris House, North Star Avenue, SWINDON, Wilts, SN2 1ET.
Tel 01793 444420   **Fax** 01793 444409   http://www.rcuk.ac.uk
Chairman: Prof Alan Thorpe

E   Established in May 2002 following the Quinquennial Review of the Research Councils on 2001. RCUK receives support from the seven Research Councils and functions as the coordinating body for cross-Council activities. The RCUK Executive Group comprises the seven Chief Executives, one of whom is Chairman, selected annually.

R   To develop and implement RCUK strategies - eg science vision, external relations, knowledge transfer and science in society.

G   United Kingdom.

●   The seven Research Councils are:
Arts & Humanities Research Council
Biotechnology & Biological Sciences Research Council
Economic & Social Research Council
Engineering & Physical Sciences Research Council
Medical Research Council
Natural Environent Research Council
Science & Technology Facilities Council (qqv).

Research & Education Advisory Panel

✍   The Panel was established in November 2004 by the Department of Agriculture & Rural Development Northern Ireland. Following an independent review commissioned in July 2008, the Minister stood down REAP while considering the report's recommendations.

Research & Intelligence Unit   See **Regional Observatories**.

Research Regulator
✍ Not yet established. It will regulate the research activities currently regulated by:
Gene Therapy Advisory Committee
Human Fertilisation & Embryology Authority
Human Tissue Authority
National Patient Safety Agency

Reserve Forces Appeal Tribunals (RFAT)
■ Alexandra House, 14-22 The Parsonage, MANCHESTER, M3 2JA.
 Tel 0161 833 6100 **Fax** 0161 832 0249
E Established under the Reserve Forces Act 1996.
R To re-hear applications by members of the Reserve Forces and their civilian employers, including Reservists who are self-employed, against the decisions or determinations of Ministry of Defence Adjudication Officers in respect of callout and disputed claims for financial assistance.
G United Kingdom.
✍ Administrative support is provided by HM Courts & Tribunals Service (qv).

Residential Property Tribunal Service (RPTS)
■ 10 Alfred Place, LONDON, WC1E 7LR.
 Tel 020 7446 7740 **Fax** 020 7580 5684 http://www.rpts.gov.uk
E RPTS is the umbrella organisation of the five regional Rent Assessment Panels (qv).
R To provide members to sit on Rent Assessment Panels.
G England.
✍ On 14 October 2010 the Government announced that RPTS is to be abolished and jurisdiction of the five regional Rent Assessment Panels (qv) of England transferred to HM Courts & Tribunals Service (qv).

Residential Property Tribunal for Wales
■ 1st Floor, West Wing, Southgate House, Wood Street, CARDIFF, CF10 1EW.
 Tel 029 2023 1687 **Fax** 029 2023 6146
 President: Gareth Morgan
E Established in 1965 under the Rent Act 1965 and formerly known as the Rent Assessment Panel for Wales. It functions as a Tribunal NDPB of the National Assembly for Wales.
R To set up Rent Assessmant Committees and Rent Tribunals to consider appeals over rent levels and to fix an appropriate rent where there are disputes between landlords and tenants.
 To set up Leasehold Valuation Tribunals to settle certain disputes between leaseholders and freeholders.
G Wales.
✍ For further information see **Rent Assessment Panels** [England]

Restraint Accreditation Board (RAB)
■ 4th Floor, 102 Petty France, LONDON, SW1H 9AJ.
 Tel 020 3334 2443
 Chairman: Prof Susan Bailey
E Established in July 2010. RAB functions as an Advisory NDPB of the Ministry of Justice.
 The Board is made up of child forensic psychiatrists, behaviour management specialists, physiotherapists, paediatricians, pathologists, academics and operational experts.
R To accredit restraint techniques and packages of techniques used in the under-18 secure estate.
G England, Wales.

Resuscitation Council (UK)
■ 5th Floor, Tavistock House North, Tavistock Square, LONDON, WC1H 9HR.
 Tel 020 7388 4678 **Fax** 020 7383 0773 http://www.resus.org.uk
 Chairman: Dr Jasmeet Soar Director: Sarah Mitchell
E Established in August 1981 by Trust Deed. The Council is registered charity. Its Executive Committee comprises 24 members including the Chairman.
R To save life by educating the public and by improving the education of medical practitioners, nursing, ambulance and other healthcare professionals.
 To encourage and conduct research into methods of resuscitation and to disseminate the useful results of such research.
G United Kingdom.

Retail Prices Index Advisory Committee
✍ The Committee has met periodically since 1946 and is still convened from time to time to advise the Chancellor of the Exchequer on the construction and coverage of the Retail Prices Index. It consists of representatives of employers' and employees' organisations, consumer interests, academic experts and Government departments.

Revenue & Customs Prosecution Service
✍ RCPS was incorporated into the **Crown Prosecution Service** on 1 January 2010.

Review Board for Government Contracts
■ Athene Place, 66 Shoe Lane, LONDON, EC4A 3BQ.
Tel 020 7438 3000   **Fax** 020 7489 6291
Chairman: John Price
E Set up in 1969 following the establishment, by agreement between Government and industry in 1968, of the Profit Formula for Non-Competitive Government Contracts. The Board functions as an Advisory NDPB of the Ministry of Defence. It comprises five members including the Chairman.
R To oversee the profit formula and its associated arrangements.
G United Kingdom.

Review Board for Overseas Qualified Practitioners
✍ Abolished in 2005.

Review Body on Armed Forces Pay   See **Armed Forces Pay Review Body**.

Review Body on Doctors' & Dentists' Remuneration   (DDRB)
■ 6th Floor, Kingsgate House, 66-74 Victoria Street, LONDON, SW1E 6SW.
Tel 020 7215 8407   **Fax** 020 7215 4445
Chairman: Ron Amy, OBE
E Established in July 1971. DDRB functions as an Advisory NDPB of the Department of Health. The Review Body comprises eight members including the Chairman.
R To advise on the remuneration of doctors and dentists taking any part in the National Health Service.
G United Kingdom.
✍ One of the Pay Review Bodies whose secretariat is provided by **Office of Manpower Economics.**
Also known as the Doctors' & Dentists' Review Body.

Review Body for Nursing & Other Health Professions
✍ Established in 1983 and known as the Review Body for Nurses & Allied Health Professions until 2004, it became the **NHS Pay Review Body** in 2007.

Review Body on School Teachers' Pay & Conditions of Service   See **School Teachers' Review Body**.

Review Body on Senior Salaries   See **Senior Salaries Review Body**.

Reviewing Committee on the Export of Works of Art & Objects of Cultural Interest   (RCEWA)
■ Grosvenor House, 14 Bennetts Hill, BIRMINGHAM, B2 5RS.
Tel 0121 345 7300   **Fax** 0121 345 7303
Chairman: Lord Inglewood
E Established in 1952 following the recommendations of the Waverley Committee's Report. RCEWA functions as an Advisory NDPB of the Department for Culture, Media & Media & Sport. The Committee comprises eight members including the Chairman.
R To advise the Department on the export of those cultural objects which are considered to be of national importance.
G United Kingdom.
● RCEWA is advised by the Advisory Council on the Export of Works of Art (ACEWA) which is chaired by the RCEWA Chairman and comprises, in addition to RCEWA members, representatives of government departments, museums and galleries, and arts organisations.

Rhagor   See **National Museum Wales**.

Rhondda Cynon Taff Teaching Local Health Board
✍ Merged on 1 October 2009 with the Merthyr Tydfil Local Health Board to form **Cwm Taf Health Board**.

RIPA Technical Advisory Board   See **Technical Advisory Board**.

Risk Management Authority   (RMA)
■   St James House, 25 St James Street, PAISLEY, Renfrewshire, PA3 2HQ.
    Tel 0141 567 3112   **Fax** 0141 567 3111   http://www.rmascotland.gov.uk
    Convenor: Peter Johnston   Chief Executive: Yvonne Gailey
E   Established on 27 June 2003 under the Criminal Justice (Scotland) Act 2003. RMA functions as an Executive
    NDPB of the Scottish Executive Justice Department. The board comprises eight members including the
    Convenor.
R   To be responsible for overseeing arrangements for the risk assessment of offenders whose liberty presents a risk
    to the public at large.
    To minimise risk in respect of a small number of serious violent and sexual offenders who may be or have been
    sentenced to the Order of Lifelong Restriction (OLR).
G   Scotland.

Risk & Regulation Advisory Council
✍ RRAC completed its work programme in 2009.

River Dee Trust   See **Rivers & Fisheries Trusts of Scotland**.

River Don Trust   See **Rivers & Fisheries Trusts of Scotland**.

Rivers Agency
■   Hydebank, 4 Hospital Road, BELFAST, BT8 8JP.
    Tel 028 9025 3355   **Fax** 028 9025 3455   http://www.riversagencyni.gov.uk
    Chief Executive: John Clarke
E   Established on 1 October 1996 as the statutory drainage and flood defence authority, originally derived from the
    Drainage (Northern Ireland) Order 1973 as amended. The Agency functions as an Executive Agency of the
    Department of Agriculture & Rural Development Northern Ireland. The Management Board comprises the Chief
    Executive and three functional directors.
R   To reduce risk to life and damage to property from flooding from rivers and the sea.
    To preserve the productive potential of agricultural land.
G   Northern Ireland.
●   The Rivers Agency is assisted in its work by the Drainage Council for Northern Ireland (qv).

Rivers & Fisheries Trusts of Scotland   (RAFTS)
■   Capital Business Centre, 24 Canning Street, EDINBURGH, EH3 8EG.
    Tel 0131 272 2797   **Fax** 0131 272 2800   http://www.rafts.org.uk
    Chairman: Roger Brook   Managing Director: Andrew Wallace
E   Established in 2005. RAFTS functions as a Scottish Charity and an unincorporated association. The Executive
    Committee comprises nine members including the Chairman.
R   To conserve and enhance native freshwater fish and their environments in Scotland.
G   Scotland.
●   The 17 members of RAFTS are:Argyll Fisheries Trust; Ayrshire Rivers Trust; Clyde River Foundation; Cromarty
    Firth Fisheries Trust; River Dee Trust; Deveron, Bogie & Isla Rivers Charitable Trust; River Don Trust; Esks
    Rivers & Rivers Fisheries Trust; Findhorn, Nairn & Lossie Trust; Forth Fisheries Trust; Galloway Fisheries Trust;
    Kyle of Sutherland Fisheries Trust; Loch Lomond Fisheries Trust; Lochaber Fisheries Trust; Ness & Beauly
    Fisheries Trust; Outer Hebrides Fisheries Trust; Skye Fisheries Trust; Spey Research Trust; Tay Foundation;
    Tweed Foundation; West Sutherland Fisheries Trust; Wester Ross Fisheries Trust.

Road Operators' Safety Council   (ROSCO)

- Osborn House, 20 High Street South, OLNEY, Bucks, MK46 4AA.
  Tel 01234 714420   **Fax** 01234 714420   http://www.rosco.org.uk
  Chairman: Peter Shipp
- E   Established in 1955 by associations representing road transport employers and by trade unions. The Council consists of 12 members.
- R   To promote among owners and operators of road transport vehicles and their employees measures to prevent accidents and encourage safety on the roads.
- G   United Kingdom.

Road Safety Advisory Panel   (RSAP)

- Great Minster House, 76 Marsham Street, LONDON, SW1P 4DR.
  Tel 020 7944 8300   **Fax** 020 7944 9643
  Chairman: Stephen Ladyman, MP
- E   Established in 2000. RSAP functions as an Advisory NDPB of the Department for Transport. It comprises the Chairman and representatives of road user groups, road safety organisations, government departments, local authorities, police and motor manufacturers
- R   To review all aspects of road safety.
- G   United Kingdom.

Road Safety Council of Northern Ireland   (RSCNI)

- Unit 1A, Boucher Business Centre, Apollo Road, BELFAST, BT12 6HP.
  Tel 028 9066 5757   **Fax** 028 9066 5353   http://www.roadsafetycouncil.com
  Executive Officer: Barry Griffin
- E   Established in September 1963. RSCNI functions as a registered charity and company limited by guarantee. It receives support from the Department of the Environment Northern Ireland.
- R   To reduce the incidence of death and serious injuries sustained by Northern Ireland road users.
- G   Northern Ireland.

Roads Service

- Clarence Court, 10-18 Adelaide Street, BELFAST, BT2 8GB.
  Tel 028 9054 0540   **Fax** 028 9054 0024   http://www.roadsni.gov.uk
  Chief Executive: Geoff Allister
- E   Established on 1 April 1996. The Service functions as an Executive Agency of the Department for Regional Development Northern Ireland.
- R   To implement the roads related elements of the Regional Transportation Strategy for Northern Ireland 2002-2012. To ensure that the public road network is managed, maintained and developed.
- G   Northern Ireland.

Robin Hood Airport Consultative Committee

- South Yorkshire Joint Secretariat, 18 Regent Street, BARNSLEY, S Yorks, S70 2HG.
  Tel 01226 772848   http://www.rhacc.org.uk
  Chairman: Alan Tolhurst, OBE   Secretary: Len Cooksey
- G   Lincolnshire, Nottinghamshire, South Yorkshire.
- ✍   For further information see **Airport Consultative Committees**.

Ross & Cromarty Enterprise Ltd

- ✍   A former Local Enterprise Company, now an area office of **Highlands & Islands Enterprise**.

Rowett Institute of Nutrition & Health   (RINH)

- Greenburn Road, Bucksburn, ABERDEEN, AB21 9SB.
  Tel 01224 712751   **Fax** 01224 715349   http://www.rowett.ac.uk
  Director: Prof Peter Morgan
- E   Established in on 1 July 2008 by the merger of the Rowett Research Institute (established 1913) and the University of Aberdeen where it now forms part of the College of Life Sciences & Medicine. RINH is a Major Research Provider for the Scottish Government.
- R   To conduct research at the forefront of nutrition.
  To define how nutrition can prevent disease, improve health and enhance the quality of food production in agriculture.
- G   Scotland.

Royal Air Force Museum

■ Grahame Park Way, Hendon, LONDON, NW9 5LL.
Tel 020 8205 2266   http://www.rafmuseum.org.uk
Chairman: Air Chief Marshal Sir John Day, KCB, OBE

E Established on 6 August 1965 by Deed of Trust. The Museum is a registered charity and functions as an Executive NDPB of the Ministry of Defence. The Board of Trustees comprises 17 members including the Chairman.

R To educate and inform present and future generations about the history and traditions of the RAF, air power and defence, aviation links with the RAF, and to promote the RAF.

G United Kingdom.

● The collections are held at Hendon, North London, and at Cosford, Shropshire.

Royal Air Force Personnel Management Agency
✍ Relinquished Executive Agency status on 1 April 2004.

Royal Air Force Prosecuting Authority
✍ Ceased to exist on 31 October 2009. See **Service Prosecuting Authority**.

Royal Air Force Sports Board   (RAFSB)

■ Room 43, Kermode Hall, RAF Halton, AYLESBURY, Bucks, HP22 5PG.
Tel 01296 657137   Fax 01296 657138   http://www.raf.mod.uk/rafsportsboard/
Director: Air Commodore Barry Dogget

E Established on 1 November 1921 by the Air Council of the RAF. The Board's secretariat comprises nine members including the Director.

R To decide matters of sports policy and funding, provide guidance to volunteer sporting committees throughout the RAF, and administer funding for sport.

G United Kingdom.

Royal Air Force Training Group Defence Agency
✍ Formerly an Executive Agency, it is now an integral part of the RAF.

Royal Armouries

■ Armouries Drive, LEEDS, W Yorks, LS10 1LT.
Tel 0113 220 1999   Fax 0113 220 1916   http://www.royalarmouries.org
Chairman: Ann Green, CBE, FMCI, FRSA   Master & Director General: Lt-Gen Jonathon Riley, CB, DSO, PhD, MA

E Established on 1 April 1984 under the National Heritage Act 1983. Royal Armouries functions as an Executive NDPB of the Department for Culture, Media & Sport. The Board of Trustees comprises ten members including the Chairman.

R To care for the national collections of arms and armour including artillery, to keep them, study them and increase our knowledge of them, so that this be passed on to future generations along with the objects themselves.

G United Kingdom.

● Royal Armouries is Britain's oldest national museum and one of the oldest in the world.
The whole collection was originally housed in the Tower of London. There are now three further museums at: Leeds, Fort Nelson near Portsmouth, and Louisville, Kentucky, USA.

Royal Botanic Garden Edinburgh   (RBGE)

■ 20A Inverleith Row, EDINBURGH, EH3 5LR.
Tel 0131 552 7171   Fax 0131 248 2901   http://www.rbge.org.uk
Chairman: Sir George Mathewson, CBE, LLD, FRSE   Regius Keeper (Chief Executive): Prof Stephen Blackmore, CBE

E Established in 1670, the Garden statutorily came into being on 1 April 1986 under the National Heritage (Scotland) Act 1985. RGBE functions as an Executive NDPB of the Scottish Executive Rural Affairs Department. The Board of Trustees comprises nine members including the Chairman.

R To explore and explain the world of plants.
To maintain and develop the living and preserved collections.
To project science into society both at home and internationally.

G Scotland.

● Founded as a physic garden, it now extends over four gardens:
Royal Botanic Garden Edinburgh
Benmore Botanic Garden, near Dunoon, Argyll
Dawyck Botanic Garden, near Peebles, and
Logan Botanic Garden, near Stranraer, Dumfries & Galloway.

Royal Botanic Gardens Kew   (RBG)

■   Kew, RICHMOND, Surrey, TW9 3AB.
    Tel 020 8332 5000   **Fax** 020 8332 5197   http://www.kew.org
    Chairman: Marcus Agius   Director: Prof Stephen D Hopper

E   Established by Princess Augusta as a botanic garden in 1759 and transferred to state control by the Treasury in 1841; the Gardens were officially established on 1 April 1984 under the National Heritage Act 1983. RGG functions as an Executive NDPB of the Department for Environment, Food & Rural Affairs. The Board of Trustees comprises twelve members including the Chairman.

R   To carry out investigation and research into the science of plants and related subjects, and disseminate the results.

G   United Kingdom.

●   The Board of Trustees is responsible for both the Royal Botanic Gardens, Kew (Richmond, Surrey) and Wakehurst Place, home of the Millennium Seed Bank (Ardingly, West Sussex).

Royal College of Defence Studies   See **Defence Academy Management Board**.

Royal Commission on the Ancient & Historical Monuments of Scotland   (RCAHMS)

■   John Sinclair House, 16 Bernard Terrace, EDINBURGH, EH8 9NX.
    Tel 0131 662 1456   **Fax** 0131 662 1477   http://www.rcahms.gov.uk
    Chairman: Prof John R Hume, OBE, BSc ARCST, Hon FRIAS, FSA Scot   Secretary (Chief Executive): Mrs Diana Murray, MA, FSA, FSA Scot, MIFA

E   Established in 1908 by Royal Warrant, the Commission's terms of reference were extended by a Royal Warrant dated 21 April 1992. The National Buildings Record of Scotland was transferred to the Commission in 1966 and reconstituted as the National Monuments Record of Scotland. RCAHMS functions as an Executive NDPB of the Scottish Executive Education Department. The Commission comprises ten members including the Chairman.

R   To collect, record and interpret information on the architectural, industrial, archaeological and maritime heritage of Scotland.

    To gather information on the built environment of the nation, to safeguard the resulting archive to the highest standards and to make this information as widely available as possible.

G   Scotland.

●   The Commission National Monuments Record is an extensive collection of pictorial and documentary material relating to Scotland's ancient monuments and historic buildings and is open daily for public reference.

Royal Commission on the Ancient & Historical Monuments of Wales   (RCAHMW)

■   Plas Crug, ABERYSTWYTH, Ceredigion, SY23 1NJ.
    Tel 01970 621200   **Fax** 01970 627701   http://www.rcahmw.org.uk
    Chairman: Dr Eurwyn Wiliam, MA, PhD, FSA   Secretary: Peter Wakelin

E   Established in 1908 by Royal Warrant, last renewed in 2000. RCAHMW now functions as an Executive NDPB of the Welsh Government. The Commission comprises nine members including the Chairman.

R   To manage the archaeological, built and maritime heritage of Wales.

    To compile information by surveying, recording and interpreting terrestrial and maritime archaeological and historical sites, structures and landscapes, particularly those of national and local importance which are threatened with destruction.

G   Wales.

●   The Royal Commission maintains a comprehensive archive in the form of the National Monuments Record of Wales, a national index to regional sites and monuments records.

✍   One of the four organisations which make up **Historic Wales**.

=   Comisiwn Brenhinol Henebion Cymru

Royal Commission on Environmental Pollution

✍   RCEP closed at the end of March 2011 following publication of its report 'The Environmental Impact of Demographic Change'.

Royal Commission for the Exhibition of 1851

■   453 Sherfield Building, Imperial College, LONDON, SW7 2AZ.
    Tel 020 7594 8790   **Fax** 020 7594 8794   http://www.royalcommission1851.org.uk
    Chairman: Sir Alan Rudge, CBE, FREng, FRS

E   Originally established in 1850 to organise the Great Exhibition, the Commission was enjoined by a Supplemental Charter dated 2 December 1851 to administer the Exhibition's profits for charitable purposes. There are nine Commissioners including the Chairman.

R   To support the development of science and technology and its profitable exploitation by British industry, by giving fellowships and grants to pure research in science and engineering, applied research in industry, industrial design and other projects.
G   United Kingdom.

Royal Commission on Historical Manuscripts   See the **National Archives**.

Royal Fine Art Commission for Scotland
✍   Since April 2005 **Architecture & Design Scotland**.

Royal Hospital Chelsea
■   Royal Hospital Road, LONDON, SW3 4SR.
    Tel 020 7881 5200   **Fax** 020 7881 5463   http://www.chelsea-pensioners.co.uk
E   The building of the Hospital was authorised by Royal Warrant dated 22 December 1681 and its independent Board of Commissioners created by Letters Patent in 1702. It functions as an Executive NDPB of the Ministry of Defence. The Board comprises 19 Commissioners and is chaired by HM Paymaster General.
R   To provide a fitting home and community for ageing or infirm veteran soldiers.
G   United Kingdom.

Royal Mail Group plc
■   100 Victoria Embankment, LONDON, EC4Y 0HQ.
    Tel 020 7250 2888   **Fax** 020 7250 2729   http://www.royalmail.com
    Chairman: Donald Brydon, CBE   Chief Executive: Moya Greene
    Shareholder Executive contact: Jo Shanmugalingam
E   Established on 1 October 1969 under provisions of the Post Office Act 1969, having previously been a Government department. Royal Mail functions as a Public Corporation of the Department for Business, Innovation & Skills. The Board comprises eleven members including the Chairman.
G   United Kingdom.
✍   One of the businesses managed by the **Shareholder Executive**.

Royal Mail Stamp Advisory Committee   See **Stamp Advisory Committee**.

Royal Marines Museum   See **National Museum of the Royal Navy**.

The Royal Mint   (RM)
■   Llantrisant, PONTYCLUN, CF72 8YT.
    Tel 01443 222111   http://www.royalmint.com
    Chairman: Mike Davies   Chief Executive: Andrew Stafford   Shareholder Executive contact: Tim Martin
E   Established on 2 April 1990. The Royal Mint functions as an Executive Agency of HM Treasury. The Board comprises the Chairman and nine other members.
R   To issue coins, medals, seals and decorations.
G   United Kingdom.
●   The Royal Mint is advised on its work by the Royal Mint Advisory Committee (qv).
✍   One of the businesses managed by the **Shareholder Executive**.

Royal Mint Advisory Committee on the Design of Coins, Medals, Seals & Decorations   (RMAC)
■   Llantrisant, PONTYCLUN, CF72 8YT.
    Tel 01443 623005   http://www.royalmint.com
    Chairman: Prof Sir Christopher Frayling
E   Established in June 1922 with the personal approval of King George V. RMAC functions as an Advisory NDPB of HM Treasury, through the Royal Mint (qv). The Committee comprises up to twelve members.
R   To advise and recommend designs of coins, medals, seals and decorations for UK issues.
G   United Kingdom.

Royal National Theatre
■   Upper Ground, South Bank, LONDON, SE1 9PX.
    Tel 020 7452 3333   **Fax** 020 7452 3344   http://www.nationaltheatre.org.uk
    Chairman: Sir Hayden Phillips, GCB, DL

E The National Theatre was formed on 8 February 1963 and moved to its present site in 1976. It was granted the title 'Royal' in 1988. The Theatre functions as a company limited by guarantee and a registered charity. The Board comprises 14 members including the Chairman.

R To maintain and re-energise the great traditions of the British stage and to expand the horizons of audiences and artists alike.

G United Kingdom.

Royal Naval Museum   See **National Museum of the Royal Navy**.

Royal Navy Submarine Museum   See **National Museum of the Royal Navy**.

The Royal Parks

■ The Old Police House, Hyde Park, LONDON, W2 2UH.
Tel 020 7298 2000   **Fax** 020 7298 2005   http://www.royalparks.org.uk
Chief Executive: Mark Camley

E Established on 1 April 1993. Royal Parks functions as an Executive Agency of the Department for Culture, Media & Sport.

R To manage, maintain, develop and protect the eight Royal Parks - Bushy Park, Green Park, Greenwich Park, Hyde Park, Kensington Gardens, Regent's Park (with Primrose Hill), Richmond Park and St James's Park.

G London.

Royal Pharmaceutical Society of Great Britain   (RPSGB)

■ 1 Lambeth High Street, LONDON, SE1 7JN.
Tel 020 7735 9141   **Fax** 020 7735 7629   http://www.rpsgb.org
President: Steve Churton   Chief Executive: Helen Gordon

E Established on 15 April 1841. The RPSGB Council comprises 30 members including the President.

R To lead, develop and represent the profession of pharmacy.

G England, Wales, Scotland.

✍ For further information see **Health & Social Care Regulators**.

Royal Scottish Academy Building   See **National Galleries of Scotland**.

Rubber Industry Advisory Committee   (RUBIAC)

■ Marshalls Mill, Marshall Street, LEEDS, W Yorks, LS11 9YJ.
Tel 0845 345 0055
Chairman: Terry Aston

E Established in February 1983 by the Health & Safety Executive (qv) under the Health & Safety at Work etc Act 1974. The Committee consists of the Chairman and 22 members who are nominated by the CBI and the TUC.

R To advise the HSE on the protection of people at work and others from hazards to health and safety arising within the rubber industry.

G United Kingdom.

Rules of Golf Committee

■ R&A Rules Ltd, The Royal & Ancient Golf Club, ST ANDREWS, Fife, KY16 9JD.
Tel 01334 472112   **Fax** 01334 477580   http://www.randa.org
Chairman representing the R&A: W Michael B Brown
Chairman representing the USGA: James T Bunch

E The R&A, a group of companies formed in 2004 which includes the Royal & Ancient Golf Club of St Andrews, is the ruling authority of golf everywhere except the USA and Mexico, where responsibility rests with the United States Golf Association (USGA).

R The R&A cooperates with the USGA to produce and regularly revise 'The Rules of Golf' and to publish 'Decisions on the Rules of Golf'.

G International.

Rural Action Derbyshire   (RAD)

■ Church Street, Wirksworth, MATLOCK, Derbys, DE4 4EY.
Tel 01629 824797   **Fax** 01629 826053   http://www.derbyshirercc.org.uk
Chief Executive: Sylvia Green

E Established in 1924. RAD functions as a registered charity and company limited by guarantee.

R   To support people in rural communities, villages and market towns, to help them tackle the challenges and opportunities they face, both now and in the future.

G   Derbyshire.

✍   RAD is one of the 38 Rural Community Councils, represented at the national level by **Action with Communities in Rural England** (qv) and at the regional level by Rural Community Action East Midlands.

Rural Action East

✍   Rural Action East represents **Bedfordshire Rural Communities Charity, Cambridgeshire ACRE, Community Development Agency for Hertfordshire, Norfolk Rural Community Council, Rural Community Council of Essex** and **Suffolk ACRE**; it operates under the umbrella of **Action with Communities in Rural England**.

Rural Action Yorkshire

■   Unit A, Tower House, Askham Fields Lane, Askham Bryan, YORK, YO23 3NU.
     Tel 0845 313 0270   **Fax** 0845 313 0271   http://www.ruralyorkshire.org.uk
     Chairman: Linda Lloyd   Chief Executive: Bill Cross

E   Established in 1929 as Yorkshire Rural Community Council; it adopted its current name on 1 October 2008. It functions as a registered charity and company limited by guarantee. The Board comprises twelve Trustees including the Chairman.

R   To enable communities to improve the quality of life for all people living and working in rural Yorkshire.

G   North, West and South Yorkshire.

✍   Rural Action Yorkshire is one of the 38 Rural Community Councils, represented at the national level by **Action with Communities in Rural England** (qv) and at the regional level by the Yorkshire & the Humber Rural Community Action Network.

Rural Climate Change Forum   (RCCF)

■   Eastbury House, 30-34 Albert Embankment, LONDON, SE1 7TL.
     Tel 0845 933 5577
     Chairman: John Gilliland, OBE

E   Established in March 2005. RCCF functions as a NDPB of the Department for Environment, Food & Rural Affairs. The Forum comprises representatives of the key organisations with an interest in the agriculture, forestry and land management sector.

R   To help raise awareness of climate change among farmers and land managers.
     To act as a catalyst and coordinator of work on climate change in the rural sector.
     To advise Defra on policies to ensure the sector plays a full part in mitigating and adapting to climate change.
     To advise on research priorities to build a stronger evidence base on reducing greenhouse emissions from agriculture and managing the impacts of a changing climate.
     To engage with international counterparts in the agriculture, forestry and land management sector.

G   United Kingdom.

Rural Community Action East Midlands

✍   RCAEM represents **Community Lincs, Northamptonshire ACRE, Rural Action Derbyshire, Rural Community Action Nottinghamshire** and **Rural Community Council (Leicestershire & Rutland)**; it operates under the umbrella of **Action with Communities in Rural England**.

Rural Community Action Network

✍   RCAN is the collective name for the 38 Rural Community Councils throughout England, their eight regional bodies and their national umbrella, **Action with Communities in Rural England** (qv).

Rural Community Action Nottinghamshire   (RCAN)

■   The Newstead Centre, Tilford Road, Newstead Village, NOTTINGHAM, NG15 0BS.
     Tel 01623 727600   **Fax** 01623 720148   http://www.rcan.org.uk
     Chairman: Cllr Liz Jefferies   Chief Executive: Robert Crowder

E   Established in 1924. RCAN functions as a registered charity and company limited by guarantee. The Board comprises 15 Trustees including the Chairman.

R   To support thriving, sustainable and cohesive rural communities in Nottinghamshire.

G   Nottinghamshire.

✍   RCAN is one of the 38 Rural Community Councils, represented at the national level by **Action with Communities in Rural England** (qv) and at the regional level by Rural Community Action East Midlands.

Rural Community Council of Essex   (RCCE)

■ Threshelfords Business Park, Inworth Road, FEERING, Essex, CO5 9SE.
  Tel 0844 477 3938   Fax 01376 573524   http://www.essexrcc.org.uk
  Chairman: Canon John Brown   Executive Director: Nick Shuttleworth

E Established in 1929. RCCE functions as a registered charity and company limited by guarantee. The Board comprises twelve Trustees including the Chairman.

R To provide local communities with the skills, resources and expertise necessary to achieve a thriving and sustainable future.
  To provide a voice for rural communities, representing their interests to government at local, regional and national level.

G Essex.

✍ RCCE is one of the 38 Rural Community Councils, represented at the national level by **Action with Communities in Rural England** (qv) and at the regional level by Rural Action East.

Rural Community Council (Leicestershire & Rutland)   (RCC)

■ 133 Loughborough Road, LEICESTER, LE4 5LQ.
  Tel 0116 266 2905   http://www.ruralcc.org.uk
  Director: Jeremy Prescott

E Established in 1924. RCC functions as a registered charity and company limited by guarantee.

R To help those who live and work in rural Leicestershire and Rutland.

G Leicestershire, Rutland.

✍ RCC is one of the 38 Rural Community Councils, represented at the national level by **Action with Communities in Rural England** (qv) and at the regional level by Rural Community Action East Midlands.

Rural Community Councils

✍ The 38 RCCs are charitable local development agencies, largely county-based, which provide a comprehensive range of support to enable rural communities across England to enhance their quality of life and improve access to services. Known collectively as the Rural Community Action Network, their national umbrella body is **Action with Communities in Rural England**.

Rural Development Council   (RDC)

■ 17 Loy Street, COOKSTOWN, Co Tyrone, BT80 8PZ.
  Tel 028 8676 6980   Fax 028 8676 6922   http://www.rdc.org.uk
  Chairman: Dr Arthur Mitchell, MBE   Chief Executive: Martin McDonald

E Established on 31 July 1991 as a special rural development division within the Department of Agriculture Northern Ireland. RDC is an independent organisation and functions as a council of rural stakeholders. The Council comprises ten members including the Chairman.

R To promote positive and sustainable change helping to develop and regenerate rural areas of Northern Ireland for the better.

G Northern Ireland.

Rural Housing Advisory Group   (RHAG)

■ 110 Buckingham Palace Road, LONDON, SW1W 9SA.
  Tel 0300 123 4500   http://www.homesandcommunities.co.uk
  Chairman: Candy Atherton

E Established in April 2007 at the request of the Department for Communities & Local Government. RHAG is a group of the Homes & Communities Agency (qv). The Group comprises 21 members.

R To advise Government on and seek ways to improve delivery of affordable rural housing, promoting joint working between key stakeholders through the provision of a forum for sharing good practice and encouraging innovation.

G England.

Rural Payments Agency   (RPA)

■ Kings House, 33 Kings Road, READING, Berks, RG1 3BU.
  Tel 0118 958 3626   http://www.rpa.gov.uk
  Chief Executive: Mark Grimshaw

E Established on 16 October 2001 replacing the former Intervention Board Executive Agency (established on 22 November 1972). RPA functions as an Executive Agency of the Department for Environment, Food & Rural Affairs. The Management Board comprises eight members including the Chief Executive.

R To be responsible for the European Union's Common Agricultural Policy payment functions.

G England.

● RPA also has offices in Carlisle, Exeter, Newcastle upon Tyne, Northallerton and Workington.

S4C Authority

- Parc Tŷ Glas, Llanishen, CARDIFF, CF14 5DU.
  Tel 0870 600 4141   Fax 029 2075 4444   http://www.s4c.co.uk
  Vice Chairman: Rheon Tomos   Interim Chief Executive: Arwel Ellis Owen
- E Established in 1982 under the Broadcasting Acts of 1980 and 1981. S4C functions as a Public Broadcast
  Authority of the Department for Culture, Media & Sport. The Authority's board comprises eight members
  including the Chairman.
- R To broadcast Welsh language programmes across a range of platforms, including television and broadband.
- G Wales.
- ✍ S4C is Sianel Pedwar Cymru, the Welsh Fourth Channel.

SafeFood   See **Food Safety Promotion Board**.

Safety & Health in Mines Research Advisory Board   A sub-committee of the **Mining Industry Committee**.

Safety Working Group   A working group of the Health & Safety Executive's **Construction Industry Advisory Committee**.

Saint Fagans - National History Museum   See **National Museum Wales**.

Sandwich Port & Haven Commissioners

- 21 Potter Street, SANDWICH, Kent, CT14 9DR.
  Tel 01304 612162
- E Established in 1925 under Sandwich Port & Haven Act, 1925.
- G Sandwich.
- ✍ For further information see **Port & Harbour Authorities**.

Save Eyes Everywhere   An alternative name of the **British Council for Prevention of Blindness**.

School Food Trust   (SFT)

- 3rd Floor, 2 St Paul's Place, 125 Norfolk Street, SHEFFIELD, S Yorks, S1 2JF.
  Tel 0114 274 2318   http://www.schoolfoodtrust.org.uk
  Chairman: Rob Rees, MBE
- E Established in September 2005, SFT was an Advisory NDPB of the Department for Education until April 2011. It
  continues to function as a charity, registered in April 2007, trading its services as a community interest
  company. The Trust's Board comprises twelve members including the Chairman.
- R To advise Government on school food and related skills.
  To provide expert support services to schools, local health partnerships, local authorities and others working to
  improve children's health through food.
- G United Kingdom.

School Support Staff Negotiating Body   (SSSNB)

- 6th Floor, Kingsgate House, 66-74 Victoria Street, LONDON, SW1E 6SW.
  Tel 020 7215 8461   Fax 020 7215 4445
  Chairman: Philip Ashmore
- E Established on 7 July 2009 under the Apprenticeships, Skills & Learning Act 2009. SSSNB functions as an
  Advisory NDPB of the Department for Education. The Review Body comprises nine members including the
  Chairman.
- R To negotiate school support staff pay and conditions of employment.
- G England, Wales.
- ✍ One of the bodies whose secretariat is provided by the **Office of Manpower Economics**.
  Legislation to abolish SSSNB is included in the Education Bill which was introduced into the House of Commons
  on 26 January 2011.

School Teachers' Review Body   (STRB)

■   6th Floor, Kingsgate House, 66-74 Victoria Street, LONDON, SW1E 6SW.
     Tel 020 7215 8314   **Fax** 020 7215 4445
     Chairman: Dr Anne Wright, CBE
E   Established in September 1991. STRB functions as an Advisory NDPB of the Department for Business, Innovation
     & Skills. The Review Body comprises nine members including the Chairman.
R   To examine and report on such matters relating to the statutory conditions of employment of school teachers in
     England and Wales as may from time to time be referred to it by the Secretary of State.
G   England, Wales.
✍   One of the Pay Review Bodies whose secretariat is provided by the **Office of Manpower Economics**.

School Workforce Development Board

✍   Set up in autumn 2004, SWDB was dissolved in autumn 2008. See its successor, the **National Advisory Group
     for the Professional Development of the Children's Workforce in Schools**.

Schools Education Advisory Committee   (SEAC)

■   Wren House, Hedgerows Business Park, Colchester Road, CHELMSFORD, CM2 5PF.
E   Established in 1981 by the Health & Safety Executive (qv).
R   To advise the HSE on the protection of people at work and others from hazards to health and safety arising within
     the field of education.
G   United Kingdom.

Science & Advice for Scottish Agriculture   (SASA)

■   Roddinglaw Road, EDINBURGH, EH12 9FJ.
     Tel 0131 244 8890   **Fax** 0131 244 8940   http://www.sasa.gov.uk
E   Established on 1 April 1992 as the Scottish Agricultural Science Agency, it adopted its current name in 2008.
     Formerly an Executive Agency, SASA now functions as a department of the Scottish Executive Environment &
     Rural Affairs Department.
R   To provide the appropriate scientific input (tests, diagnoses and analyses) for the implementation and
     enforcement of legislation and regulations in the areas of crops and environmental protection, and to provide
     SEERAD with information and advice to support policy in these areas.
G   Scotland.

Science Advisory Council   (SAC)

■   Area 1A, Nobel House, 17 Smith Square, LONDON, SW1P 3JR.
     Tel 020 7238 6357   **Fax** 020 7238 1504   http://www.sac.defra.gov.uk
     Chairman: Prof Chris Gaskell
E   Established in February 2004. SAC functions as a Scientific Advisory Committee and an Advisory NDPB of the
     Department for Environment, Food & Rural Affairs. The Council comprises 15 independent members.
R   To provide Defra with expert, independent and published advice on science policy and strategy.
G   United Kingdom.
✍   For further information see **Scientific Advisory Committees**.
     Following a review, it was announced on 2 February 2011 that SAC will be reconstituted as a smaller and more
     agile body of six individuals and an independent Chairman.

The Science Council

■   32-36 Loman Street, LONDON, SE1 0EH.
     Tel 020 7922 7888   **Fax** 020 7922 7879   http://www.sciencecouncil.co.uk
     President: Sir Tom McKillop   Chief Executive: Diana Garnham
E   Established in 2003 by Royal Charter. The Science Council is a membership body representing 30 learned
     societies and professional institutions; it is a company limited by guarantee. The Board comprises the President
     and a representative of each member organisation.
R   To advance science and its applications for the public benefit.
     To promote the profession of scientist through the Chartered Scientist designation and the development of codes
     of practice.
     To promote awareness of the contribution of professional scientists to science and society.
G   United Kingdom.

Science Museum   See **National Museum of Science & Industry**.

Science & Technology Facilities Council   (STFC)

■ Polaris House, North Star Avenue, SWINDON, Wilts, SN2 1SZ.
Tel 01793 442000   Fax 01793 442002   http://www.scitech.ac.uk
Chairman: Prof Michael Sterling, FREng   Chief Executive: Prof Keith Mason

E Established in April 2007 following the merger of the former Particle Physics & Astronomy Research Council and the Council for the Central Laboratory of of the Research Councils. The Council currently comprises ten members including the Chairman.

R To promote and support, by any means, high-quality basic, strategic and applied research.

G United Kingdom.

✍ For further information see **Research Councils UK**.

Scientific Advisory Committee on Genetic Modification (Contained Use)   (SACGM(CU))

■ 1/2 Redgrave Court, Merton Road, BOOTLE, Merseyside, L20 7HS.
Tel 0845 345 0055
Chairman: Prof Janet Bainbridge, OBE

E Established on 1 January 2004 replacing the former Advisory Committee on Genetic Modification. SACGM functions as a Scientific Advisory Committee of the Health & Safety Executive (qv). The Committee comprises twelve members including the Chairman.

R To provide technical and scientific advice to the UK competent authorities on all aspects of the human and environmental risks of the contained use of genetically modified organisms.

G United Kingdom.

✍ For further information see **Scientific Advisory Committees**.

Scientific Advisory Committee on the Medical Implications of Less Lethal Weapons   (SACMILL)

■ 01/M/14, MOD Main Building, Whitehall, LONDON, SW1A 2HB.
Tel 020 7218 7996   Fax 020 7218 9678

E Established in 2009 in place of the Defence Science Advisory Council sub-committee on the Medical Implications of Less Lethal Weapons (DOMILL). SACMILL functions as an Advisory NDPB of the Ministry of Defence.

R To provide valuable, authoritative and independent advice to MOD and other government departments on medical aspects of less lethal weapons.

G United Kingdom.

Scientific Advisory Committee on Nutrition   (SACN)

■ 6th Floor, Wellington House, 133-155 Waterloo Road, LONDON, SE1 8UG.
Tel 020 7972 4018   http://www.sacn.gov.uk
Chairman: Dr Ann Prentice, OBE, PhD

E Established in 1963 as the Committee on Medical Aspects of Food & Nutrition Policy, changing to its present name on 1 April 2000. SACN functions as a Scientific Advisory Committee and an Advisory NDPB of the Food Standards Agency (qv) and the Department of Health. The Committee comprises the Chairman and 15 members who are independent scientific experts.

R To advise the Food Standards Agency, the Department of Health and other Government agencies and departments on matters concerning the nutrition content of individual foods, diet and the nutritional status of people.

G United Kingdom.

✍ The Government announced on 14 October 2010 that SACN would cease to function as a NDPB and be reconstituted as a committee of experts of the Department of Health.

SCIENTIFIC ADVISORY COMMITTEES   (SACs)

E Numerous bodies follow the Government's Code of Practice for Scientific Advisory Committees, the latest edition of which was published on 14 December 2007. It addresses all aspects of a committee's work including its role and remit, responsibilities of members, chairmen and secretariats, working practices, publication of documents and public consultation. The Code ensures that high levels of openness and transparency are maintained throughout the vast network of relationships between SACs and Government.

✍ A list of SACs can be found in the Subject Index under **Scientific Advisory Committees**.

Scientific Committee on Antarctic Research   (SCAR)

■ Scott Polar Research Institute, Lensfield Road, CAMBRIDGE, CB2 1ER.
Tel 01223 336550   Fax 01223 336549   http://www.scar.org
President: Prof Mahlon C Kennecutt II (Texas A&M University)   Executive Director: Dr Mike Sparrow

E   Established in 1958 by the Board of the International Council of Scientific Unions (ISCU). Membership of SCAR is open to national academies of science undertaking scientific research in Antarctica; at present there are 31 full members, four associate members and nine ICSU scientific unions. The Executive Committee comprises the President, four Vice-Presidents, the Executive Director and the Immediate Past President.

R   To initiate, promote and coordinate scientific research in the Antarctic and to provide international, independent scientific advice to the Antarctic Treaty system.

G   Antarctica.

Scientific Committee on Tobacco & Health   (SCOTH)

■   Room 708, Wellington House, 135-155 Waterloo Road, LONDON, SE1 8UG.
Tel 020 7972 4191
Chairman: Prof James Friend   Scientific Secretary: Dr Rob Shayer

E   Established in 1994 replacing the former Independent Scientific Committee on Smoking & Health. SCOTH functions as an Advisory NDPB of the Department of Health. The Committee comprised 14 members including the Chairman in July 2003.

R   To provide advice to the Chief Medical Officers of the UK on scientific matters concerning tobacco and health, in particular to review scientific and medical evidence and to advise on research priorities.

G   United Kingdom.

✍   The Committee has not met since publication of a report on secondhand smoking on 16 November 2004.

Scientific Diving Supervisory Committee   (SDSC)

■   School of Ocean & Earth Science, Southampton Oceanography Centre, SOUTHAMPTON, SO14 3ZH.
Tel 023 8059 6010   Fax 023 8059 6010   http://www.uk-sdsc.com
Chairman: Bobby Forbes   Secretary: Dr Ken Collins

E   Established on 1 April 1991, SDSC receives its current authority under the Diving at Work Regulations 1997. The Committee is funded by and reports to the Natural Environment Research Council (qv). Membership is open to self-employed divers and employers of divers who dive at work in support of research, development or education in any field of science or archaeology.

R   To advise its members on all matters of diving safety policy.
To review the adequacy of training supervision and the supply of information, and to use its best endeavours to ensure that equipment and practices are up to best international standards.

G   United Kingdom.

✍   Also known as the UK Scientific Diving Supervisory Committee.

Scientific Pandemic Influenza Advisory Committee   (SPI)

■   Area 452C, Skipton House, 80 London Road, LONDON, SE1 6LH.
Tel 020 7972 5599
Chairman: Prof Sir Gordon W Duff

E   Established in 2005 as the Scientific Advisory Group on Pandemic Influenza, it adopted its current in January 2008. SPI functions as a Scientific Advisory Committee and an Advisory NDPB of the Department of Health. The Committee comprises 37 members including the Chairman.

R   To advise the UK Government on scientific matters relating to the health response to an influenza pandemic.

G   United Kingdom.

✍   For further information see **Scientific Advisory Committees**.

Scotland's Colleges

■   Argyll Court, Castle Business Park, STIRLING, FK9 4TY.
Tel 01786 892000   Fax 01786 892001   http://www.scotlandscolleges.ac.uk
Chairman: Brian Keegan   Chief Executive: John Henderson

E   Established in June 2009 as the trading name of the Scottish Further Education Unit (SFEU) and the Association of Scotland's Colleges (ASC). Both SFEU and ASC are companies limited by guarantee and registered charities. The board comprises 15 directors including the Chairman.

R   To seek to prepare and assist the Scottish college sector deliver its vital contribution to the economic and social needs of Scotland.
To serve the ambitions of Scotland's learners and the demands of Scotland's employers.
To enhance the sector's national and international reputation.

G   Scotland.

●   ASC has a membership of 42 colleges of further and higher education.

Scotland's Commissioner for Children & Young People   (SCCYP)

■   85 Holyrood Road, EDINBURGH, EH8 8AU.
     Tel 0131 558 3733   Fax 0131 556 3378   http://www.sccyp.org.uk
     Commissioner: Tam Baillie
E   Established in April 2004 under the Commissioner for Children & Young People (Scotland) Act 2003.
R   To promote and safeguard the rights of children and young people living in Scotland.
G   Scotland.

ScotStat

■   Room 4ER, St Andrew's House, Regent Road, EDINBURGH, EH1 3OG.
     Tel 0131 556 8400
     Chief Statistician: Rob Wishart
E   ScotStat is a network for users and providers of Scottish Official Statistics. The Board comprises 16 members
         and is chaired by the Chief Statistician.
R   To improve communication amongst those interested in particular statistics and to facilitate the setting up of
         working groups on specific statistical issues.
G   Scotland.

Scottish Accident Prevention Council   (SAPC)

■   43 Discovery Terrace, Heriot-Watt University Research Park, EDINBURGH, EH14 4AP.
     Tel 0131 449 9379   Fax 0131 449 9380   http://www.sapc.org.uk
     President: Brian Topping
E   Established in 1931. SAPC is a membership body comprising representatives from local authorities (including
         police, fire services, education, social work and road departments), health boards, housing associations and
         voluntary and professional organisations; it functions as a registered charity. The Executive Committee
         comprises the President, Vice-President and Treasurer, and the Chairmen and Vice-Chairmen of the three
         Principal Committees.
R   To promote good practice in accident and injury prevention.
     To provide support for members in their accident and injury prevention work.
     To influence policies in relation to accident and injury prevention.
     To sponsor and undertake research into accident and injury prevention.
G   Scotland.
●   SAPC's three principal committees are:
         Home Safety Committee
         Road Safety Committee
         Water & Leisure Safety Committee.

Scottish Advisory Committee on Alcohol Misuse

✍   Superceded in 2004 by the **Scottish Ministerial Advisory Committee on Alcohol Problems**.

Scottish Advisory Committee on Credit & Access   (SACCA)

■   183 St Vincent Street, GLASGOW, G2 5QD.
     Tel 0141 572 3420   Fax 0141 572 3421   http://www.qaa.ac.uk
E   Established as a joint committee of the Scottish office of the Quality Assurance Agency for Higher Education (qv)
         and Universities Scotland. Members are drawn from universities and colleges in Scotland.
R   To advise universities and colleges on a wide range of matters relating to widening participation in lifelong
         learning and matters relating to credit and qualifications.
     To undertake development work in areas related to its remit.
G   Scotland.

Scottish Advisory Committee on Distinction Awards   (SACDA)

■   Scottish Health Service Centre, Crewe Road South, EDINBURGH, EH4 2LF.
     Tel 0131 275 7738   Fax 0131 315 2369   http://www.sacda.scot.nhs.uk
     Chairman: Kenneth Thomson
E   Established in 1998. SACDA functions as an Advisory NDPB of the Scottish Executive Health Department. The
         Committee comprises 14 members including the Chairman.
R   To advise the Minister for Health & Community Care and Scottish Ministers on which specialists engaged in the
         NHS in Scotland should receive awards for professional distinction.
G   Scotland.

© CBD Research Ltd · Beckenham · Kent BR3 5JS · Tel 020 8650 7745 · Fax 020 8650 0768 · E-mail cbd@cbdresearch.com · www.cbdresearch.com

Scottish Advisory Committee on Drug Misuse   (SACDM)

- 1st Floor, Gyle Square, 1 South Gyle Crescent, EDINBURGH, EH12 9EB.
  Tel 0131 275 6050   Fax 0131 275 7511   http://www.drugmisuse.isdscotland.org
  Chairman: Bridget Campbell
- E Established in 1994 and reconstituted in 2006. SACDM functions as an Advisory NDPB of the Scottish Executive Health Department. The Committee comprises representatives from various organisations involved in drug prevention and misuse.
- R To advise Scottish Ministers on the further development of the national strategy for tackling drug misuse and the future direction and priorities of the strategy.
  To provide an early warning system to Scottish Ministers about emerging drugs issues.
  To identify, take part in and/or oversee any short-life project groups tasked with taking forward specific tasks as directed by Scottish ministers.
- G Scotland.

Scottish Advisory Committee on the Medical Workforce

- ✍ SACMW's roles were remitted in 2008 to local NHS Boards.

Scottish Advisory Committee on Telecommunications

- ✍ Superceded in 2003 by Ofcom's **Advisory Committee for Scotland**.

Scottish Agricultural Science Agency

- ✍ Since 2008 **Science & Advice for Scottish Agriculture**.

Scottish Agricultural Wages Board   (SAWB)

- Pentland House, 47 Robb's Loan, EDINBURGH, EH14 1TY.
  Tel 0131 244 6397   Fax 0131 244 6551
  Chairman: John Menzies
- E Established in 1949 under the Agricultural Wages (Scotland) Act 1949. SAWB functions as an Executive NDPB of the Scottish Executive Rural Affairs Department. The Board comprises 17 members.
- R To make Orders fixing minimum wage rates, holiday entitlements and other conditions for workers employed in agriculture in Scotland. The Board's Orders have the force of law, subject to any overriding pay legislation that might be in force.
- G Scotland.

Scottish Ambulance Service   (SAS)

- Tipperlinn Road, EDINBURGH, EH10 5UU.
  Tel 0131 446 7000   Fax 0131 446 7001   http://www.scottishambulance.com
  Chairman: David Garbutt   Chief Executive: Pauline Howie
- E Established in 1999. The Board comprises 14 members including the Chairman.
- R To provide an emergency ambulance service and a patient transport service to all of the nation's mainland and island communities.
- G Scotland.
- ✍ One of the seven Special NHS Boards in Scotland.

Scottish Arts Council

- ✍ The Scottish Arts Council and Scottish Screen were replaced by a single organisation, **Creative Scotland**, on 1 July 2010.

Scottish Borders Tourist Board

- ✍ Since 1 April 2005 an area office of **VisitScotland**.

Scottish Broadcasting Commission

- ✍ Established on 8 August 2007 to conduct an independent investigation into the television production and broadcasting industry in Scotland, it published its final report on 8 September 2008.

Scottish Building Apprenticeship & Education Council   (SBATC)
- Crichton House, 4 Crichton's Close, Holyrood, EDINBURGH, EH8 8DT.
  Tel 0131 556 8866   Fax 0131 558 5247   http://www.sbatc.co.uk
  Chairman: David Smith
- E   Established in 1936.
- R   To regulate the working conditions, wages, recruitment and training of apprenticeships within the building
  industry in Scotland.
- G   Scotland.

Scottish Building Contract Committee   (SBCC)
- 7 Manor Place, EDINBURGH, EH3 7DN.
  Tel 0131 240 0832   Fax 0131 240 0830   http://www.sbcconline.com
  Chairman: Iain Fergusson   Secretary: Mrs Jasmine Sneddon, MCIArb
- E   Established in April 1964. SBCC is registered as a limited company; its shareholders are the Association of
  Consulting Engineers, National Specialist Contractors Council, RICS Scotland, Royal Incorporation of Architects
  in Scotland, Scottish Building Federation and the Scottish Confederation of Associations of Specialist
  Engineering Contractors. The Board comprises the Chairman and ten members, including the Chairmen of
  SBCC's Consultative and Drafting Committees.
- R   To amend, draft and publish forms of building contracts for use in Scotland.
  To promote best practice in building contracts in Scotland.
- G   Scotland.

Scottish Building Standards Agency
- ✍ Established on 21 June 2004 to write the Scottish building regulations, SBSA was disbanded on 1 April 2008.

Scottish Care
- 54A Holmston Road, AYR, KA7 3BE.
  Tel 01292 270240   http://www.scottishcare.org
  Chief Executive: Ranald Mair
- E   Established in January 2000. Scottish Care functions as an independent body, a not-for-profit limited company
  and represents the large majority of all care homes in Scotland, including some from the charity and voluntary
  sectors. The Executive Committee comprises care home owners and corporate providers.
- R   To represent residential care homes and care providers in Scotland.
- G   Scotland.

Scottish Central Fire Brigades Advisory Council
- ✍ Abolished in 2005.

Scottish Charity Appeals Panel   (SCAP)
- 2W St Andrew's House, Regent Road, EDINBURGH, EH1 3DG.
  Tel 0131 244 3311   http://www.scap.gov.uk
  Chairman: Saria Akhter
- E   Established on 1 October 2006, under the Charities & Trustee Investment (Scotland) Act 2005. The Panel
  functions as a Tribunal NDPB of the Scottish Executive Finance & Central Services Department. SCAP
  comprises a pool of eight chairmen, who are qualified solicitors, and 16 members; each Panel will comprise a
  chairman and two members.
- R   To provide fair, independent and informed adjudication of appeals against decisions made by the Office of the
  Scottish Charity Regulator (qv).
- G   Scotland.

Scottish Charity Law Commission
- ✍ Established in April 2000, the Commission reported its recommendations in in May 2001. It was chaired by Joan
  McFadden and known as the McFadden Commission.

Scottish Charity Regulator   See **Office of the Scottish Charity Regulator**.

© CBD Research Ltd · Beckenham · Kent BR3 5JS · Tel 020 8650 7745 · Fax 020 8650 0768 · E-mail cbd@cbdresearch.com · www.cbdresearch.com

Scottish Children's Reporter Administration (SCRA)

- Ochil House, Springkerse Business Park, STIRLING, FK7 7XE.
  Tel 0300 200 1555 Fax 01786 459532 http://www.scra.gov.uk
  Chairman: Carole Wilkinson Chief Executive: Netta MacIver, OBE
- E Established on 1 April 1995 under the Local Government, etc (Scotland) Act 1994, becoming operational on 1 April 1996. SCRA functions as an Executive NDPB of the Scottish Executive Education Department. The board comprises six members including the Chairman.
- R To facilitate the performance by the Principal Reporter (Chief Executive) in her statutory functions in relation to children and young people who may be in need of compulsory measures of care.
  To deploy and manage staff to carry out that work and to provide suitable facilities for Children's Hearings (see Children's Panels).
- G Scotland.
- ● SCRA has approximately 220 Children's Reporters, located throughout Scotland in every local authority area.

Scottish Commission for Public Audit (SCPA)

- The Scottish Parliament, EDINBURGH, EH99 1SP.
  Tel 0131 348 5000
  Convenor: Angela Constance, MSP
- E Established in 2000 under the Public Finance & Accountability (Scotland) Act 2000. The Commission comprises five MSPs including the Convenor.
- R To examine proposals by Audit Scotland (qv) for the use of resources and expenditure and to report on them to the Parliament.
  To appoint a qualified person to audit the accounts of Audit Scotland.
- G Scotland.

Scottish Commission for the Regulation of Care (The Care Commission) (SCRC)

- Compass House, 11 Riverside Drive, DUNDEE, DD1 4NY.
  Tel 01382 207100 Fax 01382 207289 http://www.carecommission.com
  Convenor: Prof Frank Clark, CBE Chief Executive: Jacquie Roberts
- E Established on 1 April 2002 under the Regulation of Care (Scotland) Act 2001. The SCRC functions as an Executive NDPB of the Scottish Executive Health Department. The Commission comprises twelve members including the Convenor.
- R To regulate for the improvement of care in Scotland through improved consistency in the application of standards and regulations.
- G Scotland.
- ● The Commission operates throughout Scotland, with regional offices in Aberdeen, Dundee, Hamilton, Musselburgh and Paisley.

Scottish Committee of the Council on Tribunals
- ✍ See the **Administrative Justice & Tribunals Council** (2007).

Scottish Committee of Optometrists (SCO)

- 5 St Vincent Street, EDINBURGH, EH3 6SW.
  Tel 0131 220 4542 Fax 0131 220 4542 http://www.sco-online.org
  Chairman: Neil Leslie Vice Chairman: Ian Rough Office Manager: Lorna Cameron
- E SCO is a non-profit making organisation run by optometrists for optometrists and is recognised by the Scottish Executive and Optometry Scotland as the optometric training organisation for the country's 1,100+ practitioners. The Executive Committee comprises the Chairman, Vice Chairman and Office Manager.
- R To improve the clinical skills of every optometrist in Scotland.
- G Scotland.

Scottish Consumer Council
- ✍ On 1 October 2008 the Scottish Consumer Council, with others, was replaced by **Consumer Focus**.

Scottish Council for Development & Industry (SCDI)

- Campsie House, 17 Park Circus Place, GLASGOW, G3 6AH.
  Tel 0141 332 9119 Fax 0141 333 0039 http://www.scdi.org.uk
  Chairmant: Robert Armour, OBE Chief Executive: Dr Lesley Sawers
- E Established in 1931. SCDI is an independent membership-driven economic development organisation supported by 1,200 members drawn from business, trade unions, public agencies, educational institutions, local authorities and the voluntary sector. The Board comprises 21 members including the Chairman.

R   To strengthen Scotland's competitiveness by influencing Government policies to encourage sustainable
        economic prosperity.
G   Scotland.
●   SCDI has offices in Aberdeen (North East Scotland) and Inverness (Highlands and Islands).

Scottish Council of Independent Schools   (SCIS)
■   21 Melville Street, EDINBURGH, EH3 7PE.
     Tel 0131 220 2106   Fax 0131 225 8594   http://www.scis.org.uk
     Chairman: Prof Sir David Edward   Director: Judith Sischy
E   Established in 1978. SCIS is a membership organisation of over 70 schools and functions as a company limited
        by guarantee and registered charity.
R   To provide information, advice and guidance to parents.
     To advance education through curriculum development and the training of teachers.
     To advise member schools and their governors on educational developments and legislation affecting
        independent schools.
     To communicate and negotiate with the Scottish Parliament, the Government, and public and private bodies on
        behalf of the independent sector.
G   Scotland.

Scottish Council for International Arbitration   (SCIA)
■   Excel House, 30 Semple Street, EDINBURGH, EH3 8BL.
     Tel 0131 220 4776   Fax 0131 229 0849
     Chairman: Lord Dervaird (Prof John Murray, QC)   Director & Secretary: James M Arnott, WS
E   Established as an Advisory body. It comprises the Chairman and 12 commissioners.
R   To promote international arbitration and alternative dispute resolution facilities in Scotland.
G   Scotland.

Scottish Council of Law Reporting   (SCLR)
■   Darkfaulds Cottage, BLAIRGOWRIE, Perthshire, PH10 6PY.
     Tel 01250 873487   Fax 01250 870920   http://www.scottishlawreports.org.uk
     Chairman: Andrew Gibb, SSC
E   Established on 10 December 1957. SCLR functions as a not-for-profit charitable company limited by guarantee.
        The Council consists of four members including the Chairman.
R   To manage publication of Session Cases and other materials intended to help promote the best practice of Scots
        law, and to make its publications available to the widest possible audience at as economic a price as possible.
G   Scotland.

Scottish Council for National Parks   (SCNP)
■   The Barony, 2 Glebe Road, KILBIRNIE, Ayrshire, KA25 6HX.
     Tel 01505 682447   http://www.scnp.saltire.org
     Chairman: Robert G Maund
E   Established in 1943. SCNP is a registered charity. The Council comprises ten members including the Chairman.
R   To protect and enhance the existing national parks (Cairngorms and Loch Lomond & the Trossachs) and to
        promote the case for new ones.
G   Scotland.
✍   For further information see **National Park Authorities**.

Scottish Council for Research in Education
✍   SCRE now forms part of the Faculty of Education of Glasgow University.

Scottish Council for Single Homeless   (SCSH)
■   Wellgate House, 200 Cowgate, EDINBURGH, EH1 1NQ.
     Tel 0131 226 4382   Fax 0131 225 4382   http://www.scsh.co.uk
     Chief Executive: Robert Aldridge
E   Established in 1974. SCSH is the national membership body for organisations and individuals tackling
        homelessness. It is a company limited by guarantee and a registered charity.
R   To highlight the needs of homeless people and offer practical ideas and information to tackle homelessness.
G   Scotland.

Scottish Council for Voluntary Organisations   (SCVO)

■ Mansfield Traquair Centre, 15 Mansfield Place, EDINBURGH, EH3 6BB.
   Tel 0131 556 3882   http://www.scvo.org.uk
   Convenor: Dr Alison Elliot   Chief Executive: Martin Sime

E Established in 1946. SCVO is a membership based body representing voluntary organisations in Scotland and
   functions as a charitable company limited by guarantee. The Management Board comprises ten persons
   including the Convenor.

R To build voluntary sector capacity and strengthen governance.
   To increase the effectiveness of the voluntary sector's infrastructure.
   To promote citizen action and civic engagement.
   To improve the voluntary sector's contribution to better Scottish public services.
   To promote civil society interaction locally, nationally and globally.

G Scotland.

✍ See also **Councils for Voluntary Service**.

Scottish Court Service   (SCS)

■ Saughton House, Broomhouse Drive, EDINBURGH, EH11 3XD.
   Tel 0131 444 3352   http://www.scotcourts.gov.uk
   Chief Executive: Eleanor Emberson

E Established on 3 April 1995; on 1 April 2010 it became an independent body under the Judiciary & Courts
   (Scotland) Act 2008. The Corporate Board is chaired by the Lord President, the most senior judge in Scotland,
   and comprises twelve other persons.

R To provide the people, buildings and technology to support the operation of the Courts, the work of the
   independent judiciary, the courts' Rules Councils and of the Office of the Public Guardian (qv).

G Scotland.

Scottish Crime & Drug Enforcement Agency   (SCDEA)

■ Osprey House, Inchinnan Road, PAISLEY, PA3 2RE.
   Tel 0141 302 1000   Fax 0141 302 1130   http://www.scdea.police.uk
   Director General: Deputy Chief Constable Gordon Meldrum

E Established on 1 April 2001 and known as the Scottish Drug Enforcement Agency until it adopted its current
   name under the Police, Public Order & Criminal Justice (Scotland) Act 2006. The Agency is part of the Scottish
   Police Services Authority (qv) and functions as an Executive NDPB of the Scottish Executive Justice
   Department.

R To protect Scotland's communities from organised crime.

G Scotland.

Scottish Criminal Cases Review Commission   (SCCRC)

■ Portland House, 17 Renfield Street, GLASGOW, G2 5AH.
   Tel 0141 270 7030   Fax 0141 270 7040   http://www.sccrc.org.uk
   Chairman: Mrs Jean Couper, CBE   Chief Executive: Gerard Sinclair, LLB, DipLP, NP

E Established on 1 April 1999 under the Criminal Procedure (Scotland) Act 1995. SCCRC functions as an Executive
   NDPB of the Scottish Executive Justice Department. Members of the SCCRC are appointed by HM The Queen
   following recommendations of the First Minister; senior staff are appointed by the Commission.

R To consider alleged miscarriages of justice and to refer deserving cases to the High Court for determination.

G Scotland.

Scottish Crop Research Institute

✍ Merged on 1 April 2011 with the Macaulay Land Use Research to form the **James Hutton Institute**.

Scottish Dental Practice Board   (SDPB)

■ Scottish Health Service Centre, Crewe Road South, EDINBURGH, EH4 2LF.
   Tel 0131 275 7740   http://www.sdpb.scot.nhs.uk
   Chairman: Dr Donald B McNicol

E Established on 5 July 1948 as the Scottish Dental Practice Board; it assumed its present title on 1 April 1989 and
   is currently constituted under the National Health Service (General Dental Services) (Scotland) Regulations
   1974. The Board comprises eight members including the Chairman.

R To authorise payments to dentists working in the National Health Service under General Dental Service
   regulations and to monitor all aspects of the Service.

G Scotland.

Scottish Enterprise (SE)

- Atrium Court, 50 Waterloo Street, GLASGOW, G2 6HQ.
  Tel 0141 248 2700
  http://www2.scottish-enterprise.com
  Chairman: Crawford Gillies   Chief Executive: Lena C Wilson
- E Established on 1 April 1991 under the Enterprise & New Towns (Scotland) Act Act 1990. Scottish Enterprise functions as an Executive NDPB of the Scottish Executive Enterprise & Lifelong Learning Department. The Board comprises twelve members including the Chairman.
- R To improve Scotland's economic performance, to help the businesses and people of Scotland succeed and, in so doing, build a world-class Scottish Economy.
- G Scotland, excluding area covered by Highlands & Islands Enterprise (qv).
- ● Five Regional Advisory Boards ensure that the private sector and key stakeholders in specific regions continue to have an influential role in Scottish Enterprise's future strategy.
  Each board comprises up to 15 members including the Chairman.
  The Regional Boards and their chairmen are:
  Aberdeen City & Shire: Tom Smith
  East of Scotland: Colin Stewart
  South of Scotland: Gareth Baird
  Tayside: Jim McPhillimy
  West of Scotland: Graeme Waddell.
  In addition to the headquarters in Glasgow, there are local offices in Aberdeen, Bellshill, Clydebank, Dumfries, Dundee, Edinburgh, Galashiels, Glenrothes, Kilmarnock, Paisley and Stirling.

Scottish Environment Protection Agency (SEPA)

- Erskine Court, Castle Business Park, STIRLING, FK9 4TR.
  Tel 01786 457700   Fax 01786 446885   http://www.sepa.org.uk
  Chairman: Prof David Sigsworth   Chief Executive: Dr Campbell Gemmell
- E Established on 1 April 1996, under the Environment Act 1995. SEPA functions as an Executive NDPB of the Scottish Executive Rural Affairs Department. The board comprises twelve members including the Chairman.
- R To provide an efficient and integrated environmental protection system for Scotland which will both improve the environment and contribute to the Scottish Ministers' goal of sustainable development.
- G Scotland.
- ● SEPA's activities are concentrated on the control of pollution to land, air and water.

Scottish Fire & Rescue Advisory Unit (SFRAU)

- Area 1R, St Andrew's House, Regent Road, EDINBURGH, EH1 3DG.
  Tel 0131 244 3275   Fax 0131 244 2564
  Chief Adviser: Brian Fraser, QFSM
- E Established on 1 January 2008 replacing the former HM Fire Service Inspectorate for Scotland. The Unit is responsible to the Scottish Executive.
- R To provide independent advice to Scottish Ministers and government officials on fire and rescue related matters and on the operational preparedness of Fire & Rescue Service in Scotland.
  To appoint the Chief Inspector of Fire & Rescue Authorities as specified in the Fire (Scotland) Act 2005.
- G Scotland.

Scottish Fisheries Protection Agency

- ✍ On 1 April 2009 SFPA and Fisheries Research Services merged with the Scottish Government Marine Directorate to form **Marine Scotland**.

Scottish Food Advisory Committee (SFAC)

- 6th Floor, St Magnus House, 25 Guild Street, ABERDEEN, AB11 6NJ.
  Tel 01224 285100
  Chairman: Prof Graeme Millar, CBE
- E Established in 2000. SFAC functions as an Advisory NDPB of the Food Standards Agency Scotland (qv). There are currently eleven members including the Chairman.
- R To give advice to the Agency on food safety and standards issues effecting Scotland.
- G Scotland.

Scottish Food Enforcement Liaison Committee (SFELC)

- 6th Floor, St Magnus House, 25 Guild Street, ABERDEEN, AB11 6NJ.
  Tel 01224 285100
  Secretariat: Neil Douglas

E Established in 2006. SFELC functions as an advisory committee of the Food Standards Agency Scotland (qv). The Committee comprises 20 members drawn from industry, enforcement, professional and consumer backgrounds.
R To coordinate the food law enforcement and the sampling and surveillance activities of Scottish local authorities.
G Scotland.

Scottish Funding Council   Familiar name of the **Scottish Further & Higher Education Funding Council**.

Scottish Further Education Funding Council
✍ Dissolved on 3 October 2005 upon the establishment of the **Scottish Further & Higher Education Funding Council**.

Scottish Further Education Unit
✍ SFEU, established in 1985 as the Curriculum Advice & Support Team, adopted in June 2009, with the Association of Scotland's Colleges, the trading name **Scotland's Colleges**.

Scottish Further & Higher Education Funding Council   (SFC)

■ Donaldson House, 97 Haymarket Terrace, EDINBURGH, EH12 5HD.
   Tel 0131 313 6500 **Fax** 0131 313 6501   http://www.sfc.ac.uk
   Chairman: John McClelland, CBE   Chief Executive: Mark Batho
E Established on 3 October 2005 under the Further & Higher Education (Scotland) Act 2005, which dissolved the Scottish Further Education Funding Council and the Scottish Higher Education Funding Council. SFC functions as an Executive NDPB of the Scottish Executive Enterprise, Transport & Lifelong Learning Department. The Council comprises 16 members including the Chairman.
R To fund teaching and learning provision, research and other activities in Scotland's 43 colleges and 20 higher education institutions.
G Scotland.
✍ More commonly known as the Scottish Funding Council.

Scottish Futures Trust   (SFT)

■ 1st Floor, 11-15 Thistle Street, EDINBURGH, EH2 1DF.
   Tel 0131 510 0800 **Fax** 0131 510 0801   http://www.scottishfuturestrust.org.uk
   Chairman: Sir Angus Grossart, CBE   Chief Executive: Barry White
E Established 2008. The Trust functions as a Public Corporation of the Scottish Executive.
R To support the efficiency and effectiveness of public infrastructure, planning, funding and delivery, leading to real improved value for money solutions.

Scottish Grand Committee   See **United Kingdom Parliament: Committees**.

Scottish Health Council   (SHC)

■ Delta House, 50 West Nile Street, GLASGOW, G1 2NP.
   Tel 0141 241 6308 **Fax** 0141 221 2529   http://www.scottishhealthcouncil.org
   Chairman: Brian Beacom, MBE
E Established on 1 April 2005. SHC is part of NHS Quality Improvement Scotland (qv). The Council comprises eight members including the Chairman.
R To help improve the way that people are involved in decisions about health services.
   To scrutinise local NHS Boards to ensure that they are working with, and listening to, people in their community.
G Scotland.

Scottish Higher Education Funding Council
✍ Dissolved on 3 October 2005 upon the establishment of the **Scottish Further & Higher Education Funding Council**.

Scottish Highlands & Islands Film Commission   (SHIFC)

■ Inverness Castle, Castle Hill, INVERNESS, IV2 3EG.
   Tel 01463 710121 **Fax** 01463 710848   http://www.scotfilm.org
E Established on 10th November 1997 and known as the Highlands of Scotland Film Commission before adopting its current title; the Commission is run by a partnership of five Scottish Councils.

R   To encourage film- and television-related activity in the Highlands and Islands by making it as simple and efficient as possible for film and television companies from around the world to operate in the area.

G   Argyll & Bute, Highland, Moray, Orkney Islands, Shetland Islands.

Scottish Hospital Endowments Research Trust

■   Princes Exchange, 1 Earl Grey Street, EDINBURGH, EH3 9EE.
    Tel 0131 659 8800   **Fax** 0131 228 8118   http://www.medicalresearchscotland.org
    Chairman: Prof David J Harrison

E   Constituted under the Hospital Endowments (Scotland) Act 1953, the Trust is currently empowered by the National Health Service & Community Care Act 1990, and operates under the name **Medical Research Scotland**. It functions as an Executive NDPB of the Scottish Executive Health Department and a registered charity. The Trust's board comprises 13 members including the Chairman.

R   To improve health by funding high-quality research into the cause, diagnosis, treatment and prevention of human disease, and into the advancement of medical technology.

G   Scotland.

Scottish Hospital Trust

✍   SHT was abolished in May 2004 under the Public Appointments & Public Bodies (Scotland) Act 2003.

The Scottish Housing Regulator   (SHR)

■   Highlander House, 58 Waterloo Street, GLASGOW, G2 7DA.
    Tel 0141 271 3810   **Fax** 0141 221 0117   http://www.scottishhousingregulator.gov.uk
    Acting Chief Executive: Michael Cameron

E   Established on 1 April 2008 under the Housing (Scotland) Act 2001. SHR functions as an Executive Agency of the Scottish Executive.

R   To regulate all social landlords in Scotland.
    To protect the interests of tenants, as well as people who face homelessness or who have bought their house from a council or housing association.

G   Scotland.

●   The main work of Communities Scotland involves regenerating neighbourhoods, improving the effectiveness of investment and empowering communities.
    It also has offices in Aberdeen, Ayr, Dundee, Edinburgh, Glasgow, Hamilton, Inverness and Paisley.

Scottish Industrial Development Advisory Board

✍   Since 1 October 2009 the Regional Selective Assistance (RSA) grant scheme has been operated by **Scottish Enterprise** under its own powers. The Board was dissolved under the Public Services Reform (Scotland) Act 2010.

Scottish Information Commissioner

■   Kinburn Castle, Doubledykes Road, ST ANDREWS, Fife, KY16 9DS.
    Tel 01334 464610   **Fax** 01334 464611   http://www.itspublicknowledge.info
    Commissioner: Kevin Dunion

E   Established in 2005 under the Freedom of Information (Scotland) Act 2002 and the Environmental Information (Scotland) Regulations 2004, both of which came into force on 1 January 2005. The Commissioner functions as a Scottish public authority.

R   To enforce and promote the right to access information held by public authorities.

G   Scotland.

●   The Act and Regulations give anyone, anywhere in the world, the right to access information held by more than 10,000 public authorities in Scotland.

Scottish Inter Faith Council   (SIFC)

■   523 Shields Road, GLASGOW, G41 2RF.
    Tel 0141 420 6982   http://www.scottishinterfaithcouncil.org
    Convenor: Farkhanda Chaudhry   Chief Executive: Pramila Kaur

E   The Council comprises representatives from the major faith traditions, local inter faith groups, educationalists, a youth representative, treasurer, accountant and an HR consultant.

R   To promote mutual understanding and good relationships between people of different religious faiths in Scotland.

G   Scotland.

© CBD Research Ltd · Beckenham · Kent BR3 5JS · Tel 020 8650 7745 · Fax 020 8650 0768 · E-mail cbd@cbdresearch.com · www.cbdresearch.com

Scottish Joint Committee on Religious & Moral Education   (SJCRME)

- 6 Clairmont Gardens, GLASGOW, G3 7LW.
  Tel 0141 353 3595   Fax 0141 332 2778
  Contact: Lachlan Bradley
- R   To promote religious education, religious studies and moral education in schools and in further and higher education.
  To give advice and to receive and make submissions on the curricula for these subjects.
  To engage in dialogue with groups which have an interest in this field.
- G   Scotland.

Scottish Land Court

- George House, 126 George Street, EDINBURGH, EH2 4HH.
  Tel 0131 271 4360   Fax 0131 271 4399   http://www.scottish-land-court.org.uk
  Chairman: The Hon Lord McGhie, QC
- E   Established in 1911. The Scottish Land Court functions as a Court of Law, its Chairman having the same status as a Court of Session judge.
- R   To resolve disputes arising in connection with:
    agricultural holdings
    crofts landholders
    holdings.
- G   Scotland.
- ●   The Chairman of the Scottish Land Court is also President of the Lands Tribunal for Scotland (qv); the two organisations share the same premises.

Scottish Law Commission   (SLC)

- 140 Causewayside, EDINBURGH, EH9 1PR.
  Tel 0131 668 2131   Fax 0131 662 4900   http://www.scotlawcom.gov.uk
  Chairman: The Hon Lord Drummond Young   Chief Executive: Malcolm McMillan
- E   Established on 16 June 1965 under the Law Commissions Act 1965. SLC functions as an Advisory NDPB of the Scottish Executive Justice Department. It comprises five Commissioners including the Chairman.
- R   To recommend reforms to improve, simplify and update the law of Scotland.
- G   Scotland.

Scottish Legal Aid Board   (SLAB)

- 44 Drumsheugh Gardens, EDINBURGH, EH3 7SW.
  Tel 0131 226 7061   Fax 0131 220 4878   http://www.slab.org.uk
  Chairman: Iain Robertson, CBE   Chief Executive: Lindsay Montgomery, CBE
- E   Established on 1 April 1987 under the Legal Aid (Scotland) Act 1986. SLAB functions as an Executive NDPB of the Scottish Executive Justice Department. The board comprises 11-15 members including the Chairman.
- R   To assess applications for and, where appropriate, grant legal aid.
  To scrutinise and pay legal aid accounts submitted by solicitors and advocates.
  To advise Scottish Ministers on legal aid matters.
- G   Scotland.

Scottish Legal Complaints Committee   (SLCC)

- The Stamp Office, 10-14 Waterloo Place, EDINBURGH, EH1 3DG.
  Tel 0131 528 5111   Fax 0131 528 5110   http://www.scottishlegalcomplaints.com
  Chairman: Mrs Jane Irvine   Chief Executive: Rosemary Agnew
- E   Established on 1 October 2008 under the Legal Profession & Legal Aid (Scotland) Act 2007. SLCC functions as an Executive NDPB of the Scottish Executive Justice Department. The board comprises 4-8 lay members including the Chairman, and 3-7 lawyer members.
- R   To investigate complaints made by members of the public about services provided by legal practitioners in Scotland.
- G   Scotland.

Scottish Legal Services Ombudsman
- ✍   Ceased to exist when the **Scottish Legal Complaints Committee** was established on 1 October 2008.

Scottish Library & Information Council   (SLIC)

■   Building C (1st Floor), Brandon Gate, Leechlee Road, HAMILTON, ML3 6AU.
    Tel 01698 458888   Fax 01698 283170   http://www.slainte.org.uk
    Chairman: Christine May
E   Established in 1991. SLIC is an independent national advisory body and a company limited by guarantee; it is funded by organisational membership subscriptions and the Scottish Executive. The Management Board comprises 20 members including the Chairman.
R   To advise the Scottish Government and Scottish Ministers on library and information matters.
    To coordinate and develop library and information services.
G   Scotland.
●   The Council works in close partnership with the Chartered Institute of Library & Information Professionals in Scotland (CILIPS).

Scottish Local Authorities Remuneration Committee   (SLARC)

■   Area 3J North, Victoria Quay, EDINBURGH, EH6 6QQ.
    Tel 0131 244 0801   Fax 0131 244 7020
    Chairman: Ian Livingstone, CBE, BL, NP
E   Established in February 2005 under the Local Governance (Scotland) Act 2004. SLARC functions as an Advisory NDPB of the Scottish Executive Enterprise, Transport & Lifelong Learning Department. The Committee comprises seven members including the Chairman.
R   To prepare and submit to Scottish Ministers advice in relation to the payment by local authorities of remuneration (including pensions) and allowances and reimbursement of expenses incurred by members of local authorities, and the payment of severance payments in relation to members of local authorities.
G   Scotland.

Scottish Medicines Consortium   (SMC)

■   8th Floor, Delta House, 50 West Nile Street, GLASGOW, G1 2NP.
    Tel 0141 225 6989   Fax 0141 248 3839   http://www.scottishmedicines.org.uk
    Chairman: Prof Kenneth R Paterson
E   Established in January 2002. SMC functions as an Executive NDPB of the Scottish Executive Health Department. The Executive comprises seven members including the Chairman.
R   To provide advice to NHS boards and their Area Drug and Therapeutic Committees about the status of all newly licensed medicines, all new formulations of existing medicines and new indications for established products licensed since January 2002.
G   Scotland.

Scottish Ministerial Advisory Committee on Alcohol Problems   (SMACAP)

■   St Andrew's House, Regent Road, EDINBURGH, EH1 3DG.
    Tel 0131 556 8400   Fax 0131 242 2162
    Chairman: Tom McCabe, MSP
E   Established in 2004. SMACAP functions as an Advisory NDPB of the Scottish Executive Health Department. The Committee comprises 22 members including the Chairman.
R   To advise the Scottish Executive on policy, priorities and strategic planning in relation to tackling alcohol misuse in Scotland.
G   Scotland.

Scottish Museums Council

✍   Since 2008 **Museums Galleries Scotland**.

Scottish National Blood Transfusion Service   (SNBTS)

■   21 Ellen's Glen Road, EDINBURGH, EH17 7QT.
    Tel 0131 536 5700   Fax 0131 315 2369   http://www.scotblood.co.uk
    Director: Keith Thompson
E   Established in 1940.
R   To supply high quality blood, tissues, products and services to all hospitals and other clinical units in Scotland.
G   Scotland.
●   SNBTS has donor centres in Aberdeen, Dundee, Edinburgh, Glasgow and Inverness.

Scottish National Gallery of Modern Art   See **National Galleries of Scotland**.

Scottish National Portrait Gallery   See **National Galleries of Scotland**.

Scottish National War Memorial   (SNWM)

■   The Castle, EDINBURGH, EH1 2YT.
   Tel 0131 226 7393   **Fax** 0131 225 8920   http://www.snwm.org
   Secretary: Lt Colonel Ian Shepherd

E   Established in 1927 and incorporated by Royal Charter dated 28 October 1947, amended by supplementary
   Royal Charter dated 6 August 1975. The Memorial is a registered charity. The Board of Trustees comprises up
   to 18 members.

R   The Trustees to administer and maintain the Memorial.
   To compile and correct existing and future Rolls of Honour of Scottish casualities.
   To hold regular services of commemoration.
   To collect subscriptions, donations and bequests for these purposes and expend any surpluses if desired for the
   benefit of service charities.

G   Scotland.

●   The Memorial is situated in Crown Square, Edinburgh Castle, and commemorates the casualities of the two World
   Wars and of campaigns since 1945, whose names are contained in the volumes of the Roll of Honour on
   permanent display.

Scottish Natural Heritage   (SNH)

■   Great Glen House, Leachkin Road, INVERNESS, IV3 8TG.
   Tel 01463 725000   **Fax** 01463 725067   http://www.snh.org.uk
   Chairman: Andrew Thin   Chief Executive: Ian Jardine

E   Established in April 1992 under the Natural Heritage (Scotland) Act 1991. The functions of the Deer Commission
   for Scotland were transferred to SNH on 1 August 2010. SNH functions as an Executive NDPB of the Scottish
   Executive Rural Affairs Department. The board comprises twelve members including the Chairman.

R   To secure the conservation and enhancement of Scotland's natural heritage and to foster understanding and
   facilitate enjoyment of it.

G   Scotland.

●   SNH has many local offices throughout Scotland.

Scottish Official Board of Highland Dancing   (SOBHD)

■   Heritage House, 32 Grange Loan, EDINBURGH, EH9 2NR.
   Tel 0131 668 3965   **Fax** 0131 662 0404   http://www.sobhd.net
   Chairman: Miss Christine Lacey

E   Established in November 1950. The Board is a membership body comprising representatives of highland dance
   organisations and associations, delegates from dance examining bodies and from affiliated organisations
   abroad (in Australia, Canada, New Zealand, South Africa and the United States), competition organisations and
   independent members.

R   To standardise dance steps for competition purposes, establish rules for competitions and attire, and to certify
   competitions and instructors.

G   Worldwide.

Scottish Parent Teacher Council   (SPTC)

■   53 George Street, EDINBURGH, EH2 2HT.
   Tel 0131 226 4378   **Fax** 0131 226 4378   http://www.sptc.info

E   Established in 1947, SPTC is a membership body for parents' groups in schools and functions as a company
   limited by guarantee and a registered charity. The Council's Board comprises 18 elected Directors including the
   Convenor.

R   To improve the working partnership between parents, teachers and all involved in education thereby supporting
   the education of children in Scotland.

G   Scotland.

SCOTTISH PARLIAMENT: Committees

E   Committees play a central part in the work of the Scottish Parliament, taking evidence from witnesses,
   scrutinising legislation and conducting enquiries.
   There are currently seven **Mandatory Committees**: Equal Opportunities; European & External Relations; Finance;
   Public Audit; Standards, Procedures & Public Appointments; and Subordinate Legislation.
   Subject Committees are usually established at the beginning of each parliamentary session and cover:
   Economy, Energy & Tourism; Education, Lifelong Learning & Culture; Health & Sport; Justice; Local Government
   & Communities; Rural Affairs & Environment; and Transport, Infrastructure & Climate Change.

A third category comprises committees which conduct detailed examination of Bills before Parliament and other parliamentary business.

R   Further information can be found on the Parliament's website: http://www.scottish.parliament.uk

✍   See also Introduction.

Scottish Parliamentary Commissioner for Administration

✍   Abolished in 2002 with the establishing of the **Scottish Public Services Ombudsman**.

Scottish Parliamentary Standards Commissioner

✍   On 1 April 2011 became the **Public Standards Commissioner**.

Scottish Partnership for Palliative Care   (SPPC)

■   1A Cambridge Street, EDINBURGH, EH1 2DY.
    Tel 0131 229 0538   **Fax** 0131 228 2967   http://www.palliativecarescotland.org.uk
    Chairman: Maria McGill

E   Established in 1991, its Memorandum & Articles adopted on 7 May 1991. SPPC is the national umbrella and representative body for palliative care; it functions as a company limited by guarantee and a registered charity. The Council comprises 14 members including the Chairman.

R   To promote, enhance, improve and extend the provision of palliative care services to patients suffering from life-threatening progressive conditions, for the benefit of such people and their families.

G   Scotland.

●   Member organisations of the Partnership comprise NHS Boards, voluntary hospices, national charities and support organisations, and professional associations.

Scottish Pharmaceutical General Council

✍   Now known as **Community Pharmacy Scotland**.

Scottish Police Services Authority   (SPSA)

■   Elphinstone House, 65 West Regent Street, GLASGOW, G2 2AF.
    Tel 0141 585 8300   **Fax** 0141 331 1596   http://www.spsa.police.uk
    Convenor: Vic Emery   Chief Executive: Andrea Quinn

E   Established on 4 July 2006 under the Police, Public Order & Criminal Justice (Scotland) Act 2006. SPSA functions as an Executive NDPB of the Scottish Executive Justice Department. The board comprises six members including the Convenor.

R   To work closely with partners and stakeholders to provide expert policing and support services to Scotland's eight police forces and criminal justice community, and bring about relevant changes within policing support functions necessary to make this support more efficient.

G   Scotland.

●   SPSA comprises five divisions:
    Scottish Crime & Drug Enforcement Agency (qv)
    Scottish Police College
    SPSA Corporate Services
    SPSA Forensic Services
    SPSA Information Services.

Scottish Pre-Retirement Council   (SPRC)

■   204 Bath Street, GLASGOW, G2 4JP.
    Tel 0141 332 9427   **Fax** 0141 333 1327   http://www.sprc.org.uk
    Director: Angela Fowlis

E   Established in 1958 as the Glasgow Retirement Council, becoming the Scottish Retirement Council, it adopted its present title on 1 October 1993. SPRC is a membership body and functions as a registered charity.

R   To provide pre-retirement education to facilitate the change from working life to retirement.

G   Scotland.

●   SPRC provides its courses in various Colleges of Further Education in and around Glasgow.

Scottish Prison Complaints Commission   (SPCC)

■   Saughton House, Broomhouse Drive, EDINBURGH, EH11 3XD.
    Tel 0131 244 8423   **Fax** 0131 244 8430
    Commissioner: Vaughan Barrett

E   Established in 1994.
R   To provide thorough reviews to complaints it receives from prisoners who remain dissatisfied after they have processed their complaints through the system.
G   Scotland.

Scottish Prison Service   (SPS)

■   Calton House, 5 Redheughs Rigg, EDINBURGH, EH12 9HW.
Tel 0131 244 8745   http://www.sps.gov.uk
Chief Executive: Willie Pretswell
E   Established on 1 April 1993, SPS functions as an Executive Agency of the Scottish Executive Justice Department.
R   To provide prison services in Scotland.
G   Scotland.

Scottish Public Pensions Agency   (SPPA)

■   7 Tweedside Park, Tweedbank, GALASHIELS, TD1 3TE.
Tel 01896 893000   **Fax** 01896 893214   http://www.sppa.gov.uk
Chief Executive: Neville Mackay
E   Established on 1 April 1993 as the Scottish Office Pension Agency before adopting its current name in 1999. SPPA now functions as an Agency of the Scottish Government Directorate General Economy.
R   To administer, on behalf of Scottish Ministers, the public service pensions, premature retirement compansation and injury benefit schemes for which the Scottish Ministers have administrative responsibility so as to provide an efficient and effective service for those who use the schemes, at an economic cost to the public purse.
G   Scotland.

Scottish Public Services Ombudsman   (SPSO)

■   4 Melville Street, EDINBURGH, EH3 7NS.
Tel 0800 377 7330   **Fax** 0800 377 7331   http://www.spso.org.uk
Ombudsman: Jim Martin
E   Established in 2002 under the Scottish Public Services Ombudsman Act 2002, the Ombudsman combines the duties carried out by the former Housing Association Ombudsman for Scotland, Local Government Ombudsman for Scotland, and Scottish Parliamentary & Health Service Ombudsman.
R   To investigate complaints about most organisations providing public services in Scotland, including councils, the National Health Service, housing associations, the Scottish Government and its agencies and departments, universities and colleges and most Scottish public authorities.
G   Scotland.
●   Complaints considered by the Ombudsman can be about poor service, failure to provide a service and administrative failure.
The public bodies which can be investigated are outlined in the 2002 Act.

Scottish Qualifications Authority   (SQA)

■   The Optima Building, 58 Robertson Street, GLASGOW, G2 8DQ.
Tel 0845 279 1000   **Fax** 0845 213 5000   http://www.sqa.org.uk
Ironmills Road, DALKEITH, Midlothian, EH22 1LE.
Chairman: Graham Houston   Chief Executive: Dr Janet Brown
E   Established on 1 April 1997 under the Education (Scotland) Act 1996 as amended by the Scottish Qualifications Act 2002. SQA functions as an Executive NDPB of the Scottish Executive Education Department. The Board of Management comprises ten members including the Chairman.
R   To manage the qualifications system below degree level to allow students to fulfil their potential to participate in the economy, society and communities of Scotland.
G   Scotland.
●   SQA develops and awards qualifications in the national education system in Scotland, and also qualifications for work. It is also Scotland's national accrediting body for work based SVQ qualifications. SQA qualifications are available in schools, colleges, training centres and the workplace.
✍   For more information on awarding bodies see **Federation of Awarding Bodies**.
A member of the **Joint Council for Qualifications** (qv).

Scottish Records Advisory Council

✍   The Council held its final meeting on 27 February 2008. Its closure was confirmed in the Public Services Reform (Scotland) Act 2010.

Scottish Refugee Council   (SRC)

- 170 Blythswood Court, 5 Cadogan Square, GLASGOW, G2 7PH.
  Tel 0141 248 9799   Fax 0141 243 2499   http://www.scottishrefugeecouncil.org.uk
  Chairman: David Fraser   Chief Executive: John Wilkes
- E Established in 1985, SRC is a Scottish registered charity. The Board comprises twelve Directors including the Chairman.
- R To increase understanding of refugees and campaign for an end to discrimination, racism and prejudice.
  To advocate for the rights of refugees and people seeking asylum and for fair and just legislation and policies.
  To support refugees' integration and inclusion ensuring refugee voices are heeded.
  To ensure that refugees and people seeking asylum have access to quality advice services, information and support.
- G Scotland.

Scottish Science Advisory Council   (SSAC)

- Room 1N:01, St Andrews House, Regent Road, EDINBURGH, EH1 3DG.
  Tel 0131 244 3252   http://www.scottishscience.org.uk
  Chief Scientific Adviser for Scotland: Prof Anne Glover, CBE, FRSE, FAAM
  Co-Chairman: Ian Ritchie, CBE, FREng, FRSE, FBCS
- E Established in May 2002 as the Scottish Science Advisory Committee following following the publication of 'A Science Strategy for Scotland', and renamed Council in February 2008. SSAC operates as a semi-formal advisory body reporting to the Scottish Government's Chief Scientific Adviser for Scotland (CSA). The Council is chaired by the CSA and an independent co-chairman and comprises 16 other members.
- R To provide independent advice and recommendations on science strategy, policy and priorities to the CSA and to the Scottish Government.
- G Scotland.

Scottish Screen

- ✍ Scottish Screen and the Scottish Arts Council were replaced by a single organisation, **Creative Scotland**, on 1 July 2010.

Scottish Social Services Council   (SSSC)

- Compass House, 11 Riverside Drive, DUNDEE, DD1 4NY.
  Tel 01382 207101   Fax 01382 207215   http://www.sssc.uk.com
  Convener: Garry Coutts   Chief Executive: Anna Fowlie
- E Established on 1 October 2001 under the Regulation of Care (Scotland) Act 2001. SSSC functions as an Executive NDPB of the Scottish Executive Health Department. The Council comprises twelve members including the Chairman.
- R To promote high standards of practice among social care workers, high standards in their training, and to improve safeguards for users of social care services.
- G Scotland.
- ● The Council maintains a Register of Social Care Workers which opened on 1 April 2003.
- ✍ It is one of the six member alliance which makes up Skills for Care & Development (qv), the Sector Skills Council for social care, children, early years and young people's workforces in the UK.
  For further information see **Health & Social Care Regulators**.

Scottish Solicitors' Discipline Tribunal   (SSDT)

- Unit 3/5, The Granary Business Centre, Coal Road, CUPAR, Fife, KY15 5YQ.   http://www.ssdt.org.uk
  Chairman: A M Cockburn
- E Established under the Solicitors (Scotland) Act 1980, the Tribunal is now governed under the Scottish Solicitors' Discipline Tribunal Procedure Rules 2005. The Tribunal is an independent statutory body, with a panel of 18 members who are appointed by the Lord President of the Court of Session.
- R To consider complaints of professional misconduct and inadequate professional service against solicitors in Scotland.
  To hear appeals by solicitors against findings of inadequate professional service by the Law Society of Scotland and applications for restoration to the Roll of Solicitors.
  To decide on applications to enforce orders made by the Law Society of Scotland.
- G Scotland.

Scottish Tourist Board   See **VisitScotland**.

© CBD Research Ltd · Beckenham · Kent BR3 5JS · Tel 020 8650 7745 · Fax 020 8650 0768 · E-mail cbd@cbdresearch.com · www.cbdresearch.com

Scottish Traffic Commissioner   See **Traffic Commissioners**.

Scottish Water

■   Castle House, 6 Castle Drive, Carnegie Campus, DUNFERMLINE, Fife, KY11 8GG.
    Tel 0845 601 8855   **Fax** 01383 622090   http://www.scottishwater.co.uk
    Chairman: Ronnie Mercer   Chief Executive: Richard K Ackroyd   Shareholder Executive contact: Tim Martin
E   Established on 1 April 2002 under Water Industry (Scotland) Act 2002. Scottish Water functions as a Public
    Corporation accountable to the Scottish Executive Rural Affairs Department. The Board comprises eleven
    members including the Chairman.
R   To provide water and waste water services to households and businesses across Scotland.
G   Scotland.
✍   One of the businesses managed by the **Shareholder Executive**.

Scrabster Harbour Trust

■   Harbour Office, SCRABSTER, Caithness, KW14 7UJ.
    Tel 01847 892779   **Fax** 01847 892353   http://www.scrabster.co.uk
    Chairman: William Calder
E   Established 1856.
G   Scrabster.
✍   For further information see **Port & Harbour Authorities**.

Screen East
✍   Ceased trading on 7 September 2010.

Screen South

■   The Wedge, 75-81 Tontine Street, FOLKESTONE, Kent, CT20 1JR.
    Tel 01303 259777   **Fax** 01303 259786   http://www.screensouth.org
    Chairman: Graham Benson   Chief Executive: Jo Nolan
E   Established in 2002 replacing the former Southern Screen Commission.
G   Berkshire, Buckinghamshire, Hampshire, Isle of Wight, Kent, Oxfordshire, Surrey, East and West Sussex.
✍   For further information see **Creative England** and **Regional Screen Agencies**.

Screen WM

■   9 Regent Place, BIRMINGHAM, B1 3NJ.
    Tel 0121 265 7120   **Fax** 0121 265 7180   http://www.screenwm.co.uk
    Chairman: Dr Samir Shah, OBE   Chief Executive: Suzie Norton
E   Established in 2002 replacing the former Central England Screen Commission.
G   Herefordshire, Shropshire, Staffordshire, Warwickshire, West Midlands (Birmingham, Coventry, Dudley, Sandwell,
    Solihull, Walsall, Wolverhampton), Worcestershire.
✍   For further information see **Creative England** and **Regional Screen Agencies**.

Screen Yorkshire

■   Studio 22, 46 The Calls, LEEDS, W Yorks, LS2 7EY.
    Tel 0113 294 4410   **Fax** 0113 294 4989   http://www.screenyorkshire.co.uk
    Chairman: Steve Abbott   Chief Exec: Sally Joynson
E   Established in 2002 replacing the former Yorkshire Screen Commission.
G   Yorkshire (North, South, East and West), Lincolnshire (North and North East).
✍   For further information see **Creative England** and **Regional Screen Agencies**.

Sea Fish Industry Authority

■   18 Logie Mill, Logie Green Road, EDINBURGH, EH7 4HG.
    Tel 0131 558 3331   **Fax** 0131 558 1442   http://www.seafish.org
    Origin Way, Europort, GRIMSBY, Lincs, DN37 9TZ.
    Tel 01472 252300   **Fax** 01472 268792
    Chairman: John Whitehead, OBE   Chief Executive: Paul Williams
E   Established on 1 October 1981 under the Fisheries Act 1981; it is now commonly known as **Seafish**. The
    Authority functions as a Levy Board and NDPB of the Department for Environment, Food & Rural Affairs and the
    devolved administrations. The Board comprises twelve members including the Chairman.
R   To work with fishermen, processors, wholesalers, seafood farmers, fish friers, caterers, retailers and the import/
    export trade to promote good quality, sustainable seafood.

To carry out and give advice on research and development in respect of any matters relating to the seafish industry.

G   United Kingdom.

●   The Authority is split into two distinct directorates, with Business Development in Edinburgh and the majority of the Research directorate in Grimsby.

Sea Fish Licence Tribunal

✍   The Department for Environment, Food & Rural Affairs was considering in 2010 its scope to transfer the Tribunal's jurisdiction into HM Courts & Tribunals Service (qv). It was established under the Sea Fish (Conservation) Act 1967 to hear appeals from fishermen against their 'days at sea' allocations. However, as the 'days at sea' programme was never commenced, the Tribunal has never been convened.

Seafish   The commonly used name of the **Sea Fish Industry Authority**.

SECRETARY of STATE for TRANSPORT'S HONORARY MEDICAL ADVISORY PANELS

E   Under the Road Traffic Act 1988 and the Motor Vehicles (Driving Licences) Regulations 1999, responsibility rests with the medical advisers at the Driver & Vehicle Licensing Agency (qv) to apply medical standards and decide whether a person is fit to drive.

The Secretary of State for Transport has appointed six advisory panels to provide expert advice on the medical standards required for safe driving.

There are separate panels for

Alcohol, drugs and substance misuse and driving

Cardiovascular system and driving

Diabetes mellitus and driving

Disorders of the nervous system and driving

Psychiatric disorders and driving

Visual disorders and driving.

Each panel functions as a Scientific Advisory Committee and an Advisory NDPB of the Department for Transport.

✍   For further information see **Scientific Advisory Committees**.

Section 706 Tribunal

✍   Merged with others on 1 April 2009 to be replaced by the **First-tier Tribunal (Tax)**.

SECTOR SKILLS COUNCILS   (SSCs)

E   The 25 SSCs, collectively known as the Skills for Business Network, are regulated by the UK Commission for Employment & Skills (qv).

The SSCs jointly own the Alliance of Sector Skills Councils (qv) which acts as their collective voice.

R   To reduce skills gaps and shortages.

To improve productivity, business and public service.

To increase opportunities to boost skills and productivity of everyone in the sector's workforce.

To improve learning supply for Apprenticeships, Higher Education and National Occupational Standards.

G   United Kingdom.

●   The fully licensed SSCs are:

Asset Skills (property, facilities management, housing and cleaning)

CITB-ConstructionSkills

CITB-ConstructionSkills Northern Ireland

Cogent (chemicals, pharmaceuticals, nuclear, oil & gas, petroleum and polymers)

Creative & Cultural Skills (advertising, crafts, music, performing, heritage, design and arts)

e-skills UK (information technology and telecommunications)

Energy & Utility Skills (energy, waste and utilities)

Financial Services Skills Council (financial services, accountancy and finance)

GoSkills (passenger transport)

Government Skills (central government)

Improve Ltd (food and drinks manufacturing and processing)

The Institute of the Motor Industry (retail motor industry)

Lantra (environmental and land-based sector)

Lifelong Learning UK (community learning, education, FE, HE, libraries, work-based learning and training providers)

People 1st (hospitality, leisure travel and tourism)

Proskills UK (building products, coatings, extractive & mineral processing, furniture, furnishings & interiors, glass & glazing, glazed ceramics, paper & pulp and printing)

Semta (science, engineering and manufacturing technologies)
SkillsActive (sports & recreation, health & fitness, outdoors, playwork and caravanning industry)
Skills for Care & Development (social care, children, early years and young people)
Skills for Health
Skills for Justice (policing & law enforcement, youth justice, custodial care, community justice, courts service, prosecution services and forensic science)
Skills for Logistics (freight logistics and wholesaling industry)
Skillset (broadcasting, photo imaging, audio visual, publishing, fashion and textiles)
Skillsmart Retail
SummitSkills (building services engineering)

Sector Skills Development Agency
✍ On 31 March 2008 SSDA merged with the National Employment Panel and together were succeeded by the **United Kingdom Commission for Employment & Skills**.

SECTOR TRAINING COUNCILS   (STCs)

E   Following the reorganisation of training in Northern Ireland in 1990, the former statutory Industrial Training Boards were replaced by Sector Training Councils (STCs) in 1994.
STCs function as independent employer representative bodies.
R   To articulate the skills, education and training needs of their sectors in the short and longer term.
To advise on the training standards required for those sectors.
To work with the Department for Employment & Learning Northern Ireland and corresponding Sector Skills Councils (qv) to ensure that those training needs and standards are met.
G   Northern Ireland.
●   Seven organisations currently enjoy STC status:
CITB-ConstructionSkills Northern Ireland
Electrical Training Trust
Engineering Training Council NI
Food & Drink Sector Skills
Momentum (information, communication and technology)
Northern Ireland Polymers Association
Northern Ireland Screen (qqv).

Security Commission
✍ The Government announced on 14 October 2010, as part of its Spending Review, that the Commission had been abolished. For any future breach of security the Government itself will consider the need for an enquiry and how it chould be conducted.

Security Industry Authority   (SIA)
■   PO Box 1293, LIVERPOOL, L69 1AX.
Tel 0844 892 1025   **Fax** 0844 892 0975   http://www.the-sia.org.uk
Chairman: Baroness Ruth Henig, CBE   Chief Executive: Bill Butler
E   Established in 2003 under the Private Security Industry Act 2001. The Authority functions as an Executive NDPB of the Home Office. The SIA Board comprises six members including the Chairman.
R   To help protect society by colloboratively developing and achieving high standards within the private security industry.
To conduct compulsory licensing of individuals working in specific sectors of the private security industry.
To manage the Approved Contractor Scheme which measures private security companies against a set of independently assessed criteria.
G   United Kingdom.
✍ The Government announced on 14 October 2010 that SIA will be abolished as part of a phased transition to a new regulatory regime.

Security Industry Training Council
✍ Established in 1994, SITC was one of Northern Ireland's Sector Training Councils.

Security Systems & Alarms Inspection Board   (SSAIB)
■   The Smoke Houses, Cliffords Fort, NORTH SHIELDS, Tyne & Wear, NE30 1JE.
Tel 0191 296 3242   **Fax** 0191 296 2667   http://www.ssaib.co.uk
Chief Executive: Geoff Tate

E   Established in 1994. SSAIB functions as a not-for-profit organisation and company limited by guarantee. The Governing Board comprises representatives of the police, fire services and insurance industry, and from various government departments, trade associations, professional bodies, practitioners and relevant consumer organisations.

R   To ensure high standards of service and business ethics within the community of electronic security, guarding and fire system providers in the interests of end users.

G   United Kingdom.

Security Vetting Appeals Panel   (SVAP)

■   Room 2/42, Ripley Building, 26 Whitehall, LONDON, SW1A 2WH.
    Tel 020 7276 5645
    Chairman: Sir George Newman

E   Established in 1997. SVAP functions as an Advisory NDPB of the Cabinet Office.

R   To hear appeals against the withdrawal or refusal of national security vetting clearance.

G   United Kingdom.

Seirbheis nam Meadhanan Gàidhlig   See **MG ALBA**.

Seized! Revenue & Customs Uncovered   Known until May 2008 as the Customs & Excise Museum, the collection is now a gallery at Merseyside Maritime Museum. See **National Museums Liverpool**.

Semta

■   14 Upton Road, WATFORD, Herts, WD19 0JT.
    Tel 01923 238441   **Fax** 01923 256086   http://www.semta.org.uk
    Chairman: Allan Cook, CBE

E   Established on 1 April 2003. It is the recognised Sector Skills Council for science, engineering and manufacturing technologies. The board comprises 13 members including the Chairman.

G   United Kingdom.

✍   For further information see **Sector Skills Council**.

Senior Salaries Review Body   (SSRB)

■   6th Floor, Kingsgate House, 66-74 Victoria Street, LONDON, SW1E 6SW.
    Tel 020 7215 8276   **Fax** 020 7215 4445
    Chairman: Bill Cockburn, CBE, TD

E   Established in September 1991. SSRB functions as an Advisory NDPB of the Cabinet Office. The Review Body comprises ten members including the Chairman.

R   To advise the Prime Minister, the Lord Chancellor and the Secretary of State for Defence on the remuneration of holders of judicial office, senior civil servants, senior officers of the armed forces, and other such public appointments as may from time to time be specified.

G   United Kingdom.

✍   One of the Pay Review Bodies whose secretariat is provided by the **Office of Manpower Economics**.

Sentence Review Commissioners

■   Linum Chambers, 9th Floor, 2 Bedford Square, BELFAST, BT2 7ES.
    Tel 028 9054 5900   **Fax** 028 9054 5915   http://www.sentencereview.org.uk
    Joint Chairmen: Sir John Blelloch, Brian Currin

E   Established in 1998 under provisions made in the Northern Ireland (Sentences) Act 1996. There are ten Commissioners including the Chairmen.

R   To consider applications from prisoners serving sentences in Northern Ireland for declaration that they are entitled to release in accordance with the provisions of the Act.

G   Northern Ireland.

Sentencing Advisory Panel
✍   The Panel, together with the Sentencing Guidance Council it advised, was replaced in 2010 by the **Sentencing Council**.

© CBD Research Ltd · Beckenham · Kent BR3 5JS · Tel 020 8650 7745 · Fax 020 8650 0768 · E-mail cbd@cbdresearch.com · www.cbdresearch.com

Sentencing Council

- Steel House (2nd Floor), 11 Tothill Street, LONDON, SW1H 0LJ.
  Tel 020 3334 0634 Fax 020 3334 0406 http://www.sentencingcouncil.org
  Chairman: Lord Justice Levenson
- E Established in April 2010 under the Coroners & Justice Act 2009, replacing the Sentencing Guidelines Council and the Sentencing Advisory Panel. It function as an independent NDPB of the Ministry of Justice. The Council comprises 14 members including the Chairman.
- R To promote greater transparency and consistency in sentencing, whilst maintaining the independence of the judiciary.
  To issue guidelines on sentencing which the courts must follow unless it is in the interest of justice not to do so.
- G England, Wales.

Sentencing Guidance Council

- ✍ The Council, together with its Sentencing Advisory Panel, was replaced in 2010 by the **Sentencing Council**.

Serious Fraud Office

- ✍ SFO was incorporated into the **Crown Prosecution Service** on 1 January 2010.

Serious Organised Crime Agency   (SOCA)

- PO Box 8000, LONDON, SE11 5EN.
  Tel 0370 496 7622 http://www.soca.gov.uk
  Chairman: Sir Ian Andrews   Interim Director General: Trevor Pearce
- E Established in 2006 under the Serious Organised Crime & Police Act 2005, it was formed from the amalgamation of the National Crime Squad, the National Criminal Intelligence Service, a part of HM Revenue & Customs and a part of UK Immigration. On 1 April 2008 the Assets Recovery Agency merged with SOCA. SOCA functions as an Executive NDPB of the Home Office. Its Board comprises eleven members including the Chairman and Director General.
- R To build knowledge and understanding of serious organised crime, the harm it causes, and of the effectiveness of different responses.
  To increase the amount of criminal assets recovered and increase the proportion of cases in which the proceeds of crime are pursued.
  To increase the risk to serious organised criminals operating in the UK, through proven investigation capabilities and in new ways.
  To collaborate with partners in the UK and internationally to maximise efforts to reduce harm.
  To provide agreed levels of high quality support to SOCA's operational partners and, as appropriate, seek their support in return.
- G United Kingdom.
- ✍ In 2013 SOCA will become part of a new National Crime Agency which will include a new specialised border policing unit and the Child Exploitation & Online Protection Centre.

Service Children's Education   (SCE)

- JHQ, BFPO 40.
  Tel +49 (0)2161 472 2975
- E Established on 1 April 1996 following the merger of Service Children's Schools (North West Europe) and the Service Children's Education Authority. SCE functions as an Executive Agency of the Ministry of Defence.
- R To provide an effective and efficient education service, from foundation stage through to sixth form, for the children of HM Armed Forces, MoD personnel and sponsored organisations stationed overseas.
- G United Kingdom.

Service Complaints Commissioner for the Armed Forces

- PO Box 61755, LONDON, SW1A 2WA.
  Tel 020 3178 7634 http://www.armedforcescomplaints.independent.gov.uk
  Commissioner: Dr Susan Atkins
- E Established on 1 January 2008 under the Armed Forces Act 2006.
- R To provide a rigorous and independent oversight of how the complaints system is working and to report back to Ministers and to Parliament.
- G United Kingdom.

Service Personnel & Veterans Agency   (SPVA)

■　Norcross, THORNTON-CLEVELEYS, Lancs, FY5 3WP.
　　Tel 0800 169 2277　http://www.veterans-uk.info
　　Chief Executive: Kathy Barnes
E　Established on 2 April 2007 following a merger between the Armed Forces Personnel Administration Agency and the Veterans Agency. SPVA functions as an Executive Agency of the Ministry of Defence.
R　To improve personnel, pensions, welfare and support services to serving members of the Armed Forces and veterans.
G　United Kingdom.

Service Prosecuting Authority   (SPA)

■　RAF Northolt, West End Road, RUISLIP, Middx, HA4 6NG.　http://www.spa.independent.gov.uk
　　Director Service Prosecutions: Bruce Houlder, QC
E　Established on 1 January 2009 under the Armed Forces Act 2006 by the merger of the separate Navy, Army and Royal Air Force Prosecuting Authorities. SPA comes under the general superintendance of the Attorney General.
R　To review cases referred to it by the Service Police or Chain of Command and prosecute that case at Court Martial or Service Civilian Court where appropriate.
G　United Kingdom.

Severn-Trent Flood Defence Committee　Alternative name of the Regional Flood Defence Committee of the **Environment Agency** [Midlands Region].

Shareholder Executive   (ShEx)

■　1 Victoria Street, LONDON, SW1H 0ET.
　　Tel 020 7215 3909　**Fax** 020 7215 5336　http://www.bis.gov.uk/shareholderexecutive/
　　Chairman: Philip Remnant　Chief Executive: Stephen Lovegrove
E　Established in September 2003 to improve the Government's performance as a shareholder in businesses. ShEx is based at the offices of the Department for Business, Innovation & Skills. The Executive team comprises 13 members including the Chairman.
R　To work with Government departments and management teams to help these businesses perform better.
　　To advise Ministers and officials on a wide range of shareholder issues, including objectives, governance, strategy, performance monitoring, board appointments and remuneration.
G　United Kingdom.
●　The Executive currently has a portfolio of 26 Government-owned businesses with a combined turnover of around £24 billion.
✍　For a list of the businesses see **Public Companies** in the Subject Index.

Sheffield One
✍　Ceased to trade 31 March 2006. The regeneration vehicle in Sheffield is now **Creativesheffield**.

Sheriff Court Rules Council   (SCRC)

■　Saughton House, Spur N1, Broomhouse Drive, EDINBURGH, EH11 3XD.
　　Tel 0131 444 3461
　　Chairman: Sir Stephen S T Young, Bt, QC
E　Established in its current form under the Sheriff Courts (Scotland) Act 1971.
　　The Council comprises 15 members, including the Chairman, appointed by the Lord President and one by the Minister for Justice.
R　To review the procedure and practice in civil proceedings in the Sheriff Court.
G　Scotland.

Shetland Enterprise
✍　This former Local Enterprise Company is now an area office of **Highlands & Islands Enterprise**.

Shetland Islands Tourist Board
✍　Since 1 April 2005 an area office of **VisitScotland**.

Shetland NHS Board
- ■ Brevik House, South Road, LERWICK, Shetland, ZE1 0TG.
  Tel 01595 743060   Fax 01595 696727   http://www.shb.scot.nhs.uk
  Chairman: Ian Kinniburgh   Chief Executive: Miss Sandra Laurenson
- G Shetland Islands.
- ✍ For further information see **NHS Scotland - Boards**.

Shetland Transport Partnership
- ■ Grantfield, LERWICK, Shetland, ZE1 0NT.
  Tel 01595 744868   Fax 01595 744880   http://www.zettrans.org.uk
  Chairman: Cllr Allan Wishart
- E Established on 1 December 2005 and commonly known as **ZetTrans**. The Partnership Board comprises four
  Councillor members and two appointed members.
- G Shetland.
- ✍ For further information see **Regional Transport Partnerships**.

Shoreham Port Authority
- ■ Nautilus House, 90-100 Albion Street, SOUTHWICK, W Sussex, BN42 4ED.
  Tel 01273 598100   Fax 01273 592492   http://www.portshoreham.co.uk
  Chairman: Dennis Scard   Chief Executive: Rodney Lunn
- G Shoreham.
- ✍ For further information see **Port & Harbour Authorities**.

Shropshire & Staffordshire Strategic Health Authority
- ✍ On 1 July 2006 merged with the Birmingham & the Black Country and the West Midlands South Strategic Health
  Authorities to form the **West Midlands Strategic Health Authority**.

Sianel Pedwar Cymru   See **S4C Authority**.

Signature
- ■ Mersey House, Mandale Business Park, DURHAM, DH1 1TH.
  Tel 0191 383 1155   Fax 0191 383 7914   http://www.signature.org.uk
  Chief Executive: Jim Edwards
- E Established in December 1980 as the Council for the Advancement of Communication with Deaf People, it
  adpoted its current name in January 2009. Signature operates as the UK's only awarding body offering
  nationally accredited qualifications in British Sign Language and other accessible communication methods used
  by deaf people. The senior management team comprises the Chief Executive and three Directors.
- R To improve communication between deaf and hearing people and thus advance the welfare, status and
  opportunities of those who are deaf in a hearing world.
- G United Kingdom.
- ● Signature also administers the recognised professional registers for communication professionals working with
  deaf and deafblind people.
- ✍ For more information on awarding bodies see the **Federation of Awarding Bodies**.

Sir John Soane's Museum
- ■ 13 Lincoln's Inn Fields, LONDON, WC2A 3BP.
  Tel 020 7495 2107   Fax 020 7831 3957   http://www.soane.org
  Chairman: Richard Griffiths   Director: Tim Knox, FSA
- E Originally opened in 1823, the Museum was vested in a Board of Trustees under an 1833 Act of Parliament which
  came into force after the death of Sir John in 1837. The Board functions as an Executive NDPB of the
  Department for Culture, Media & Sport.
- R To preserve the house and collection for the benefit of 'amateurs and students' of architecture, painting and
  sculpture.
- G United Kingdom.
- ✍ Sir John Soane (1753-1837) was a distinguished architect.

SITPRO Ltd
- ✍ Abolished at the end of September 2010, its remaining functions transferred to the Department for Business,
  Innovation & Skills.

Skillfast-UK
✍ Since 1 April 2010 the fashion and textiles sector has been covered by **Skillset**.

Skills for Business Network   See **Sector Skills Councils**.

Skills for Care
■ Albion Court, 5 Albion Place, LEEDS, W Yorks, LS1 6JL.
Tel 0113 245 1716   **Fax** 0113 243 6417   http://www.skillsforcare.org.uk
Chairman: Prof David Croisdale-Appleby, OBE   Chief Executive: Andrea Rowe
E Established in 2000. It is the employer led authority on the training standards and development needs of social
care staff in England. The board comprises 24 members including the Chairman and the chairs of the nine
regional committees.
R To work with social care employers and training providers both regionally and nationally to establish the
necessary standards and qualifications that equip social care workers with the skills needed to deliver an
improved standard of care.
G England.
✍ It is one of the six member alliance which makes up Skills for Care & Development (qv), the Sector Skills Council
for social care, children, early years and young people's workforces in the UK.

Skills for Care & Development   (SfC&D)
■ 2nd Floor, City Exchange, 11 Albion Place, LEEDS, W Yorks, LS1 5ES.
Tel 0113 390 7666   **Fax** 0113 246 8066   http://www.skillsforcareanddevelopment.org.uk
Chairman: Prof David Croisdale-Appleby, OBE
E Established on 1 February 2005. SfC&D is an alliance of six organisations and is the recognised Sector Skills
Council for social care, children, early years and young people's workforces in the UK. The board comprise
twelve members including the Chairman.
G United Kingdom
● The six organisations making up the SfC&D alliance are:
Care Council for Wales
Children's Workforce Development Council [England]
General Social Care Council [England]
Northern Ireland Social Care Council
Scottish Social Services Council
Skills for Care [England] (qqv).
✍ For further information see **Sector Skills Councils**.

Skills Development Scotland   (SDS)
■ 150 Broomielaw, Atlantic Quay, GLASGOW, G2 8LU.
Tel 0141 225 6710   **Fax** 0141 225 6711   http://www.skillsdevelopmentscotland.co.uk
Chairman: William Roe   Chief Executive: Damien Yeates
E Established 1 April 2008, replacing the former Scottish University for Industry, incorporating Careers Scotland,
and assuming the skills functions of Scottish Enterprise and Highlands & Islands Enterprise (qqv). SDS functions
as public company of the Scottish Executive Education & Lifelong Learning Department. The board comprises
seven members including the Chairman.
R To help individuals to realise their full potential.
To help employers be more successful through skills development.
G Scotland.
● The ten services delivered by SDS cover three areas:
Advice
Careers Scotland
learndirect scotland
learndirect scotland for business
Partnership Action for Continuing Employment (PACE)
The Big Plus
Funding
ILA Scotland
Skills and training
Modern Apprenticeships
Get Ready for Work
Skillseekers
Training for Work.

© CBD Research Ltd · Beckenham · Kent BR3 5JS · Tel 020 8650 7745 · Fax 020 8650 0768 · E-mail cbd@cbdresearch.com · www.cbdresearch.com

Skills Funding Agency

- Cheylesmore House, Quinton Road, COVENTRY, CV1 2WT.
  Tel 0845 377 5000   http://www.skillsfundingagency.bis.gov.uk
  Chief Executive: Geoff Russell
- E   Established on 1 April 2010, replacing the former Learning & Skills Council. It functions as an Executive Agency of the Department for Business, Innovation & Skills. The Council comprises 15 members including the Chairman.
- R   To fund and regulate adult further education and skills training.
  To ensure that people and businesses can access the skills training they need to succeed in playing their part in society and in growing England's economy.
- G   England.
- ●   The Agency has an office in each of the nine English Regions.

Skills for Health

- 2nd Floor, Goldsmiths House, Broad Plain, BRISTOL, BS2 0JP.
  Tel 0117 922 1155   Fax 0117 925 1800   http://www.skillsforhealth.org.uk
  Chairman: Chris Hannah   Chief Executive: John Rogers
- E   Established on 1 April 2004. It is the recognised Skills Sector Council for the health sector across the UK. The Board comprises 15 members including the Chairman.
- G   United Kingdom.
- ✍   For further information see **Sector Skills Councils**.

Skills for Justice

- Centre Court, Atlas Way, SHEFFIELD, S Yorks, S4 7QQ.
  Tel 0114 261 1499   http://www.skillsforjustice.com
  Chairman: Sir Duncan Nichol, CBE   Chief Executive: Alan Woods, OBE
- E   Established on 1 April 2004.
  It is the recognised Sector Skills Council for policing and law enforcement, custodial care, community justice, courts service, prosecution service and forensic science.
- G   United Kingdom.
- ✍   For further information see **Sector Skills Councils**.

Skills for Logistics

- 12 Warren Yard, Warren Farm Office Village, MILTON KEYNES, Bucks, MK12 5NW.
  Tel 01908 313360   Fax 01908 313006   http://www.skillsforlogistics.org
  Chairman: Paul Brooks
- E   Established on 1 February 2004. It is the recognised Sector Skills Council for the freight logistics industries.
- G   United Kingdom.
- ✍   For further information see **Sector Skills Councils**.

SkillsActive

- Castlewood House, 77-91 New Oxford Street, LONDON, WC1A 1PX.
  Tel 020 7632 2000   Fax 020 7632 2001   http://www.skillsactive.com
  Chairman: Elaine Clowes
- E   Established on 1 October 2003. It is the recognised Sector Skills Council for sport and recreation, health and fitness, the outdoors, playwork, and the caravan industry. The board of trustees comprises 12 members including the Chairman.
- G   United Kingdom.
- ✍   For further information see **Sector Skills Councils**.

Skillset

- Focus Point, 21 Caledonian Road, LONDON, N1 9GB.
  Tel 020 7713 9800   Fax 020 7713 9801   http://www.skillset.org
  Chairman: Clive Jones, CBE   Chief Executive: Dinah Caine
- E   Established on 1 April 2004.
  It is the recognised Sector Skills Council for the creative media industry and, since 1 April 2010, the fashion and textiles sector formerly covered by Skillfast-UK.
  The Skillset board comprises twelve members including the Chairman.
- G   United Kingdom.
- ●   Skillset subdivides the creative media industry into ten sectors:
  Animation
  Computer games

Facilities (which includes post production, studio and equipment hire, special physical effects, outside broadcast, processing laboratories, transmission, manufacture of AV equipment and other services for film and television)
Film
Interactive media
Other content creation (pop promos, corporate and commercials production)
Photo imaging
Publishing (books, journals, magazines, newspapers, directories and databases, news agencies, and electronic information services)
Radio, and
Television
✍ For further information see **Sector Skills Councils**.

Skillsmart Retail
■ 4th Floor, 93 Newman Street, LONDON, W1T 3EZ.
  Tel 020 7462 5060   **Fax** 020 7462 5061   http://www.skillsmartretail.com
  Chairman: Martin Beaumont   Chief Executive: Anne Seaman
E Established on 1 September 2004. It is the recognised Sector Skills Council for retail. The board comprises eleven members including the Chairman.
G United Kingdom.
✍ For further information see **Sector Skills Councils**.

Skye Fisheries Trust   See **Rivers & Fisheries Trusts of Scotland**.

Small Business Council
✍ Established in May 2000 by the Department for Trade & Industry, SBC was closed in 2007 to be replaced by a less formal Small Business Forum.

Small Business Investment Taskforce
✍ This organisation is no longer in existence.

Small Business Service
✍ Renamed Enterprise & Business Support and integrated into the Department for Business, Innovation & Skills.

Small Business Trade Association Forum   (SBTAF)
■ Redgrave Court, Merton Road, BOOTLE, Merseyside, L20 7HS.
  Tel 0151 951 3746
  Chairman: Frances Outram
E Established in 2004. The Forum comprises representatives of 54 trade associations and is chaired by a non-executive member of the HSE board.
R To make sure that HSE hears the concerns of small businesses.
  To improve the way HSE communicates with small businesses.
  To consult small businesses on new initiatives and proposed changes in health and safety law.
G United Kingdom.

Small & Medium-sized Enterprises Working Group   A working group of the Health & Safety Executive's **Construction Industry Advisory Committee**.

Snowdonia National Park Authority
■ National Park Office, PENRHYNDEUDRAETH, Gwynedd, LL48 6LS.
  Tel 01766 770274   **Fax** 01766 771211   http://www.snowdonia-npa.gov.uk
  Chairman: Cllr Caerwyn Roberts, MBE, JP, FRAgS   Chief Executive: Aneurin Phillips
E Snowdonia was designated a National Park on 18 October 1951. The present Authority was established on 1 April 1997 under the Environment Act 1995. It comprises 18 members including the Chairman.
✍ For further information see **National Park Authorities**.
= Awdurdod Parc Cenedlaethol Eryri

Social Care Tribunal
✍ Since 2005, the **Care Tribunal**.

Social Fund Commissioner   See the **Independent Review Service for the Social Fund**.

Social Housing Ombudsman for Wales
✍ Replaced on 1 April 2006 by the **Public Services Ombudsman for Wales**.

Social Policy Committee   A standing committee of the **Joint University Council**.

Social Science Research Committee   **(SSRC)**
- Area 3B, Aviation House, 125 Kingsway, LONDON, WC2B 6NH.
  Tel 020 7276 8761   Fax 020 7276 8289   http://www.ssrc.food.gov.uk
  Acting Chairman: Prof Peter Jackson
E Established in April 2008. SSRC functions as a Scientific Advisory Committee and an Advisory NDPB of the Food
   Standards Agency (qv). The Committee comprises twelve members including the Chairman.
R To advise and critically assess how FSA gathers and uses social science evidence and advice.
G United Kingdom.
✍ For further information see **Scientific Advisory Committees**.

Social Security Advisory Committee   **(SSAC)**
- Level 3 North East Spur, The Adelphi Building, 1-11 John Adam Street, LONDON, WC2N 6HT.
  Tel 020 7962 8345   Fax 020 7962 8916   http://www.ssac.org.uk
  Chairman: Sir Richard Tilt
E Established on 24 November 1980 under the Social Security Act 1980. SSAC functions as an Advisory NDPB of
   the Department for Work & Pensions. The Committee comprises 14 members including the Chairman.
R To advise the Secretary of State for Work & Pensions and the Department of Social Development Northern
   Ireland on social security matters.
G United Kingdom.

Social Security Agency   **(SSA)**
- Castle Court, Royal Avenue, BELFAST, BT1 1SB.
  Chief Executive: Bryan Davis
E Established on 1 July 1991. SSA functions as an Executive Agency of the Department for Social Development
   Northern Ireland.
R To assess and pay social security benefits and give advice and information about the schemes.
G Northern Ireland.
● SSA provides services through a network of 50 Social Security offices.

Social Security Benefits Agency   See **Jobcentre Plus** and the **Pension Service**.

Social Security & Child Support Appeals Tribunal
✍ See the **First-tier Tribunal (Social Security & Child Support)**.

Social Security & Child Support Commission   See **Office of the Social Security & Child Support
Commissioners** [Northern Ireland].

Social Security Commissioners
✍ On 3 November 2008 the **Upper Tribunal (Administrative Appeals Chamber)** took over the work of the
   Commissioners.

Social Work Education Committee   A standing committee of the **Joint University Council**.

Social Work Inspection Agency   (SWIA)

■ Ladywell House, Ladywell Road, EDINBURGH, EH12 7TB.
   Tel 0131 244 4735   Fax 0131 244 5496   http://www.swia.gov.uk
   Chief Social Work Inspector: Alexis Jay
E Established in April 2005; it derives its powers under the Children (Scotland) Act 1995, the Regulation of Care (Scotland) Act 2001 and the Joint Inspection of Children's Services & Inspection of Social Care Services (Scotland) Act 2006. SWIA functions as an Executive Agency of the Scottish Executive Health Department. The Management Board comprises seven members. The Chief Inspector is the Agency's Chief Executive.
R To evaluate the quality of social work services in Scotland through inspection or review and to advise the First Minister about social work services.
   To work with others to continually improve social work services by identifying areas for improvement and disseminating best practice.
G Scotland.

Society of College, National & University Libraries

✍ SCONUL, the former Standing Conference of National & University Libraries, is a membership organisation. For details see our companion volume, the Directory of British Associations.

Solicitors' Disciplinary Tribunal

■ 3rd Floor, Gate House, 1 Farringdon Street, LONDON, EC4M 7NS.
   Tel 020 7329 4808   Fax 020 7329 4833   http://www.solicitorstribunal.org.uk
   President: Jeremy Barnecutt   Clerk: Mrs Susan Elson, MBE
E Established on 1 May 1975 under the Solicitors Act 1974. SDT functions as a Tribunal NDPB of Ministry of Justice. It comprises about 60 members of which two thirds are solicitor members and one third lay members.
R To hear and determine applications in respect of solicitors relating to allegations of professional misconduct or breaches of the Rules and/or Code relating to professional practice; jurisdiction extends to Registered Foreign and Registered EU Lawyers and the legal entities through which they practise, and to persons, not qualified solicitors, that solicitors employ or remunerate.
G England, Wales.

Solicitors Regulation Authority   (SRA)

■ Ipsley Court, Berrington Close, REDDITCH, Worcs, B98 0TD.
   Tel 01527 504450   Fax 01527 510213   http://www.sra.org.uk
   Chairman: Charles Plant   Chief Executive: Antony Townsend
E Established under the Legal Services Act 2007. SRA functions as an independent regulatory body of the Law Society of England & Wales. The board comprises 16 members including the Chairman.
R To set, promote and secure in the public interest standards of behaviour and professional performance necessary to ensure that clients receive a good service and that the rule of law is upheld.
G England, Wales.
✍ One of the Approved Regulators overseen by the **Legal Services Board**.

South Central Strategic Health Authority

■ Newbury Business Park, London Road, NEWBURY, Berks, RG14 2PZ.
   Tel 01635 275500   Fax 01635 33983   http://www.southcentral.nhs.uk
   Chairman: Dr Geoffrey Harris   Chief Executive: Andrea Young
E Established on 1 July 2006 replacing two former Strategic Health Authorities: the Hampshire & Isle of Wight and the Thames Valley. The board comprises eight non-executive directors including the Chairman, and seven executive directors including the Chief Executive.
R To relay and explain national policy, set direction and support and develop NHS Trust bodies (Primary Care Trusts and NHS Trusts providing acute, mental health and ambulance services).
   To ensure that local health systems operate effectively and efficiently, and that national standards and priorities are met.
G Berkshire, Buckinghamshire, Hampshire, Isle of Wight, Oxfordshire,
✍ One of the ten regional Strategic Health Authorities of England - see **NHS - England** in the Subject Index.

South Downs Joint Committee

✍ SDJC, which merged the Sussex Downs Conservation Board and the East Hampshire Area of Outstanding Natural Beauty Advisory Committee, was superceded on 1 April 2010 by a Shadow Authority which became the **South Downs National Park Authority** on 1 April 2011.

South Downs National Park Authority

■ Rosemary's Parlour, North Street, MIDHURST, W Sussex, GU29 9SB.
Tel 0300 303 1053   http://www.southdowns.gov.uk
Chairman: Margaret Paren   Chief Executive: Richard Shaw

E Established on 1 April 2011 under the South Downs National Park Authority (Establishment) Order 2010, it supercedes a Shadow Authority, established on 1 April 2010, and the former South Downs Joint Committee. The Authority comprises 27 members including the Chairman.

R To conserve and enhance the natural beauty, wildlife and cultural heritage of the area.
To promote opportunities for the understanding and enjoyment of the Park's special qualities by the public.

G South Downs.

✍ For further information see **National Park Authorities**.

South East Coast Strategic Health Authority

■ York House, 18-20 Massetts Road, HORLEY, Surrey, RH6 7DE.
Tel 01293 778899   Fax 01293 778888   http://www.southeastcoast.nhs.uk
Chairman: Kate Lampard   Chief Executive: Candy Morris, CBE

E Established on 1 July 2006 replacing two former Strategic Health Authorities: the Kent & Medway and the Surrey & Sussex.
The board comprises six non-executive directors including the Chairman, and eight executive directors including the Chief Executive.

R To relay and explain national policy, set direction and support and develop NHS Trust bodies (Primary Care Trusts and NHS Trusts providing acute, mental health and ambulance services).
To ensure that local health systems operate effectively and efficiently, and that national standards and priorities are met.

G Kent, Surrey, East and West Sussex.

✍ One of the ten regional Strategic Health Authorities of England - see **NHS - England** in the Subject Index.

South East England Councils   (SEEC)

■ Dover District Council, White Cliffs Business Park, DOVER, Kent, CT16 3PJ.
Tel 01304 872090   Fax 01304 872377   http://www.secouncils.gov.uk
Chairman: Cllr Paul Carter

E Established on 1 April 2009 following abolition of the South East England Regional Assembly, SEEC is an independent membership organisation of almost all of the 74 local authorities in the region, represented by their council leaders. The SEEC Executive comprises up to 22 members including the Chairman.

R To be responsible, in conjunction with South East England Development Agency (qv), for the regional strategic planning and economic development.

G Berkshire, Buckinghamshire, Hampshire, Isle of Wight, Kent, Oxfordshire, Surrey, East and West Sussex.

South East England Development Agency   (SEEDA)

■ Cross Lanes, GUILDFORD, Surrey, GU1 1YA.
Tel 01483 484200   Fax 01483 484247   http://www.seeda.co.uk
Chairman: Rob Douglas, CBE   Chief Executive: Pam Alexander

E Established on 1 April 1999, one of the nine English Regional Development Agencies.
SEEDA functions as an Executive NDPB of the Department for Business, Innovation & Skills.
The board comprises 15 members including the Chairman.

G Berkshire, Buckinghamshire, Hampshire, Isle of Wight, Kent, Oxfordshire, Surrey, East and West Sussex.

✍ The Comprehensive Spending Review in October 2010 confirmed the Government's intention to abolish the RDAs and support the creation of Local Enterprise Partnerships (qv), to be in place by March 2012.

South East England Regional Assembly

✍ Abolished on 31 March 2009 (see Regional Assemblies). The region's local authority leaders cooperate as **South East England Councils**.

South East England Regional Select Committee and South East England Grand Committee   See **United Kingdom Parliament: Committees**.

South East London Strategic Health Authority

✍ On 1 July 2006 merged with the North Central, North East, North West and South West London Strategic Health Authorities to form a single **London Strategic Health Authority**.

South East Rural Community Councils   SERCC represents **Action with Communities in Rural Kent, Action in rural Sussex, Buckinghamshire Community Action, Community Action Hampshire, Community Council for Berkshire, Isle of Wight Rural Community Council, Oxfordshire Rural Community Council** and **Surrey Community Action**; it operates under the umbrella of **Action with Communities in Rural England**.

South East of Scotland Transport Partnership   (SEStran)
■　First Floor, Hopetoun Gate, 8b McDonald Road, EDINBURGH, EH7 4LZ.
　　Tel 0131 524 5150   Fax 0131 524 5151   http://www.sestran.gov.uk
　　Chairman: Cllr Russell Imrie
E　Established on 1 December 2005. The Partnership Board comprises 20 Councillor members and eight appointed members.
G　Clackmannanshire, Edinburgh, Falkirk, Fife, East, Mid- & West Lothian, and Scottish Borders.
✍　For further information see **Regional Transport Partnerships**.

South Eastern Agricultural Land Tribunal
■　Government Buildings (Block 3), Burghill Road, Westbury-on-Trym, BRISTOL, BS10 6NJ.
　　Tel 0117 959 8648   Fax 0117 959 8605
　　Secretary: Tony Collins
E　Established under the Agriculture Act 1947 (Section 73).
G　Berkshire, Buckinghamshire, East Sussex, Hampshire, Isle of Wight, Kent, Oxfordshire, Surrey, West Sussex, London Boroughs south of River Thames (including Richmond upon Thames).
✍　For further information see **Agricultural Land Tribunals**. The office is expected to relocate in 2011.

South Eastern Education & Library Board   (SEELB)
■　Grahamsbridge Road, Dundonald, BELFAST, BT16 2HS.
　　Tel 028 9056 6200   Fax 028 9056 6266   http://www.seelb.org.uk
　　Chief Executive: Stanton Sloan, BSc, DASE, MA(Ed), CBiol, MIBiol
E　Established in 1973. SEELB functions as an Executive NDPB of the Department of Education Northern Ireland.
G　Ards, Castlereagh, Down, North Down and Lisburn.
✍　The ELBs and other legacy organisations will be dissolved when the Education & Skills Authority (qv) becomes fully operational.
　　For further information see **Education & Library Boards (Northern Ireland)**.

South Eastern Health & Social Care Trust
■　Ulster Hospital, Upper Newtownards Road, Dundonald, BELFAST, BT16 1RH.
　　Tel 028 9055 3100   http://www.setrust.hscni.net
　　Chairman: Colm McKenna   Chief Executive: Hugh McCaughey
E　Established on 1 April 2007, the Trust brings together the former Down Lisburn Trust and Ulster Community & Hospitals Trust. The Board comprises 17 members including the Chairman and Chief Executive.
G　Newtownards, Down, North Down and Lisburn.
✍　For further information see **Health & Social Care**.

South Eastern & Metropolitan Traffic Commissioner   See **Traffic Commissioners**.

South Wales Police Authority
■　Tŷ Morgannwg, BRIDGEND, CF31 3SU.
　　Tel 01656 869366   Fax 01656 869407   http://www.southwalespoliceauthority.org.uk
　　Chairman: Cllr Russell Roberts
E　Established in April 1995, the Authority is an independent body charged with ensuring that South Wales Police provide an effective and efficient police service.
　　It is made up of ten local authority councillors and nine independent members.
G　Bridgend, Cardiff, Merthyr Tydfil, Neath Port Talbot, Rhondda Cynon Taff, Swansea and Vale of Glamorgan.
✍　For further information see **Police Authorities**.
=　Awdurdod Heddlu De Cymru

South West ACRE Network   SWAN represents **Community Action** (Avon), **Community Council of Devon, Community Council for Somerset, Community First** (Wiltshire), **Cornwall Rural Communuty Council, Dorset Community Action** and **Gloucestershire Rural Community Council**; it operates under the umbrella of **Action with Communities in Rural England**.

South West Councils (SWC)

- Dennett House, 11 Middle Street, TAUNTON, Somerset, TA1 1SH.
  Tel 01823 270101   Fax 01823 425200   http://www.swcouncils.gov.uk
  Chairman: Cllr Alan Connett   Chief Executive: Bryony Houlden
- E   Established in May 2009 following abolition of the South West Regional Assembly, SWC is an independent membership organisation of the 41 local authorities in the region, represented by the 40 council leaders and the one elected mayor (Torbay).
- R   To be responsible, in conjunction with the South West of England Regional Development Agency (qv), for regional strategic planning and economic development.
- G   Bristol, Cornwall, Devon, Dorset, Gloucestershire, Isles of Scilly, Somerset, Wiltshire.

South West England Regional Select Committee and South West England Grand Committee   See **United Kingdom Parliament: Committees**.

South West Industrial Development Board
- ✍   See note under **Industrial Development Boards**.

South West London Strategic Health Authority
- ✍   On 1 July 2006 merged with the North Central, North East, North West and South East London Strategic Health Authorities to form a single **London Strategic Health Authority**.

South West Observatory   See **Regional Observatories**.

South West Peninsular Strategic Health Authority
- ✍   On 1 July 2006 merged with the Avon, Gloucestershire & Wiltshire and the Dorset & Somerset Strategic Health Authorities to form the **South West Strategic Health Authority**.

South West Regional Assembly
- ✍   Abolished in May 2009 (see Regional Assemblies). The region's local authority leaders cooperate as **South West Councils**.

South West Regional Development Agency

- Sterling House, Dix's Field, EXETER, Devon, EX1 1QA.
  Tel 01392 214747   Fax 01392 214848   http://www.southwestrda.org.uk
  Chairman: Sir Harry Studholme   Chief Executive: Jane Henderson
- E   Established on 1 April 1999, one of the nine English Regional Development Agencies. South West RDA functions as an Executive NDPB of the Department for Business, Innovation & Skills. The board comprises 15 members including the Chairman.
- G   Cornwall, Devon, Dorset, Gloucestershire, Isles of Scilly, Somerset, Wiltshire.
- ✍   The Comprehensive Spending Review in October 2010 confirmed the Government's intention to abolish the RDAs and support the creation of Local Enterprise Partnerships (qv), to be in place by March 2012.

South West Regional Flood Defence Committee   See **Environment Agency** [South West Region].

South West of Scotland Transport Partnership (SWestrans)

- Militia House, English Street, DUMFRIES, DG1 2HR.
  Tel 01387 260141   Fax 01387 260092   http://www.swestrans.org.uk
  Chairman: Cllr Brian Collins
- E   Established on 1 December 2005. The Partnership Board comprises five Councillor members and one appointed member.
- G   Dumfries & Galloway.
- ✍   For further information see **Regional Transport Partnerships**.

South West Screen

- St Bartholomews Court, Lewins Mead, BRISTOL, BS1 5BT.
  Tel 0117 952 9977   Fax 0117 952 9988   http://www.swscreen.co.uk
  Chairman: Kip Meek   Chief Executive: Caroline Norbury

E Established in 2002 replacing the former South West Film Commission.
G Cornwall, Devon, Dorset, Gloucestershire, Isles of Scilly, Somerset, Wiltshire.
✍ For further information see **Creative England** and **Regional Screen Agencies**.

South West Strategic Health Authority
■ South West House, Blackbrook Park Avenue, TAUNTON, Somerset, TA1 2PX.
   Tel 01823 361000   http://www.southwest.nhs.uk
   Chairman: Charles Howeson   Chief Executive: Sir Ian Carruthers, OBE
E Established on 1 July replacing three former Strategic Health Authorities: the Avon, Gloucestershire & Wiltshire,
   the Dorset & Somerset and the South West Peninsular. The board comprises five non-executive directors
   including the Chairman, and eight executive directors including the Chief Executive.
R To relay and explain national policy, set direction and support and develop NHS Trust bodies (Primary Care
   Trusts and NHS Trusts providing acute, mental health and ambulance services).
   To ensure that local health systems operate effectively and efficiently, and that national standards and priorities
   are met.
G Cornwall, Devon, Dorset, Gloucestershire, Isles of Scilly, Somerset, Wiltshire.
✍ One of the ten regional Strategic Health Authorities of England - see **NHS - England** in the Subject Index.

South West Tourism
■ Sterling House, Dix's Field, EXETER, Devon, EX1 1QA.
   Tel 01392 229618   http://www.swtourism.org.uk
   Chairman: Alistair Handyside   Director of Tourism: Maureen McAllister
E Established in March 2004 by the South West of England Regional Development Agency (qv) replacing the former
   West Country Tourist Board which had been operating under the same name, South West Tourism. The Board
   comprises eight members including the Chairman.
R To encourage the development of tourism in the south west.
G Cornwall, Devon, Dorset, Somerset, Gloucestershire, Wiltshire.

South Western Agricultural Land Tribunal
■ Government Buildings (Block 3), Burghill Road, Westbury-on-Trym, BRISTOL, BS10 6NJ.
   Tel 0117 959 8648   **Fax** 0117 959 8605
   Secretary: Tony Collins
E Established under the Agriculture Act 1947 (Section 73).
G Cornwall & the Isles of Scilly, Devon, Dorset, Gloucestershire, Somerset, Wiltshire.
✍ For further information see **Agricultural Land Tribunals**. The office is expected to relocate in 2011.

South Western Region Electricity Consumers Committee
✍ The work of SWECC was taken over by energywatch which in turn was replaced by **Consumer Focus** in 2008.

South Yorkshire Integrated Transport Authority
■ 18 Regent Street, BARNSLEY, S Yorks, S70 2HG.
   Tel 01226 772800   **Fax** 01226 772899   http://www.southyorks.org.uk
   Chairman: Cllr Mick Jameson
E Established in 1986 under the Local Government Act 1985 and known as the South Yorkshire Passenger
   Transport Authority until renamed on 9 February 2009 under the Transport Act 2008. The Authority comprises
   12 Councillors who are appointed by the four Metropolitan District Councils that make up South Yorkshire.
G South Yorkshire.
✍ For further information see **Passenger Transport Executives & Integrated Transport Authorities**.

South Yorkshire Passenger Transport Executive   (SYPTE)
■ 11 Broad Street West, SHEFFIELD, S Yorks, S1 2BQ.
   Tel 0114 276 7575   **Fax** 0114 275 9908   http://www.sypte.co.uk
   Director General: David Brown, BA (Hons)
E Established in 1986 under the Local Government Act 1985. The Executive is responsible to the South Yorkshire
   Integrated Transport Authority (qv). The board comprises seven members.
G South Yorkshire.
✍ For further information see **Passenger Transport Executives & Integrated Transport Authorities**.

South Yorkshire Police Authority

■ 18 Regent Street, BARNSLEY, S Yorks, S70 2HG.
Tel 01226 772800   Fax 01226 772899
Chairman: Charles Perryman, JP

E Established in April 1995, the Authority is an independent body charged with ensuring that South Yorkshire Police provide an effective and efficient police service.
It is made up of nine councillor members and eight independent members.

G South Yorkshire.

✍ For further information see **Police Authorities**.

South Yorkshire Probation Trust

■ 45 Division Street, SHEFFIELD, S Yorks, S1 4GE.
Tel 0114 276 6911   Fax 0114 276 1967   http://www.syps.org.uk
Chairman: Peter Smith, JP   Chief Officer: Roz Brown

E Established on 1 April 2001 under the Criminal Justice & Court Service Act 2000 as the South Yorkshire Probation Area Board. It became a trust on 1 April 2010 under the Offender Management Act 2007. The Board comprises eleven members including the Chairman.

G South Yorkshire.

✍ For further information see **Probation Trusts**.

South Yorkshire Strategic Health Authority

✍ On 1 July 2006 merged with the North & East Yorkshire & Northern Lincolnshire and the West Yorkshire Strategic Health Authorities to form **Yorkshire & the Humber Strategic Health Authority**.

Southampton Airport Consultative Committee   (SACC)

■ Civic Offices, Leigh Road, EASTLEIGH, Hants, SO5 4YN.
Tel 023 8068 8113   http://www.southamptonairport.com
Chairman: Tony Balcombe   Secretary: Richard Ward

G Hampshire.

✍ For further information see **Airport Consultative Committees**.

Southern Education & Library Board   (SELB)

■ 3 Charlemont Place, ARMAGH, BT61 9AX.
Tel 028 3751 2200   Fax 028 3751 2490   http://www.selb.org.uk
Chief Executive: Tony Murphy

E Estalished in 1973. The Board functions as an Executive NDPB of the Department of Education Northern Ireland.

G Armagh, Banbridge, Cookstown, Craigavon, Dungannon & South Tyrone, Newry & Mourne.

✍ The ELBs and other legacy organisations will be dissolved when the Education & Skills Authority (qv) becomes fully operational.
For further information see **Education & Library Boards (Northern Ireland)**.

Southern Health & Social Care Trust

■ College of Nursing, Craigavon Area Hospital, 68 Lurgan Road, PORTADOWN, BT63 5QQ.
Tel 028 3833 4444   Fax 028 3833 5496   http://www.southerntrust.hscni.net
Chairman: Mrs Anne Balmer, LLB, BL   Chief Executive: Colm Donaghy

E Established on 1 April 2007, the Trust brings together the former Armagh & Dungannon, Craigavon & Area Hospital Group, Craigavon & Banbridge Community and the Newry & Mourne Health & Social Services Trusts. The Board comprises 13 members including the Chairman.

G Armagh, Banbridge, Craigavon, Dungarvon and Newry & Mourne.

✍ For further information see **Health & Social Care Trusts**.

Southern Health & Social Services Board

✍ On 1 April 2009 the four regional boards were replaced by a single **Health & Social Care Board** for Northern Ireland.

Southern Health & Social Services Council

✍ On 1 April 2009 the four regional councils were replaced by a single **Patient & Client Council** for Northern Ireland.

Southern Rent Assessment Panel   (SRAP)

- ■ 1st Floor, 1 Market Avenue, CHICHESTER, W Sussex, PO19 1JU.
   Tel 01243 779394   Fax 01243 779389
- G Cornwall, Devon, Dorset, Gloucestershire, Hampshire, Isle of Wight, Isles of Scilly, Kent, Somerset, Surrey, East and West Sussex, Wiltshire.
- ✍ For further information on the five regional panels see **Rent Assessment Panels** [England].

Southern & South East England Tourist Board   See **Tourism South East**.

Space Advisory Council
- ✍ SAC was established in 2005 following the demise of the Space Strategy Council. In March 2010 it was itself replaced by the **Space Leadership Council**.

Space Leadership Council

- ■ Polaris House, North Star Avenue, SWINDON, Wilts, SN2 1SZ.
   Tel 020 7215 5000
   Co-chairmen: David Willetts, MP & Andy Green
- E Established in March 2010. The Council comprises 25 senior representatives from across industry, the research community and government. The current Chairmen are the Minister of State for Universities & Science the Chief Executive of Logica.
- R To provide advice to the UK Space Agency (qv) on its work plan and future opportunities.
   To offer advice on the areas of space activity in which the UK should seek to develop and maintain global leadership.
   To promote the UK's space industry and scientific excellence in space research, technology and applications and oversee the implementation of agreed recommendations of the Innovation & Growth Strategy.
- G United Kingdom.

Speaker's Committee on the Electoral Commission   See **United Kingdom Parliament: Committees**.

Speaker's Committee for the Independent Parliamentary Standards Authority   See **United Kingdom Parliament: Committees**.

Special Commissioners of Income Tax
- ✍ Merged with others on 1 April 2009 to be replaced by the **First-tier Tribunal (Tax)**.

Special Educational Needs and Disablility Tribunal
- ✍ See the **First-tier Tribunal (Special Educational Needs & Disability)**.

Special Educational Needs Tribunal for Wales   (SENTW)

- ■ Unit 32, Ddole Road Enterprise Park, LLANDRINDOD WELLS, Powys, LD1 6PF.
   Tel 01597 829800   Fax 01597 829801   http://www.wales.gov.uk/sentwsub/home/?lang=en
   President: Rhiannon Ellis Walker   Secretary: Sian Mills
- E Established in 2003 under the Special Educational Needs & Disability Act 2001. The Tribunal's members are appointed by the Secretary for Education in the National Assembly for Wales.
- R To consider appeals from parents whose children have special educational needs against decisions made by Welsh Local Education Authorities about their children's education.
- G Wales.
- ● The Tribunal holds its hearings in locations throughout Wales.

Special EU Programmes Body   (SEUPB)

- ■ 7th Floor, Clarence West Building, 2 Clarence Street West, BELFAST, BT2 7GP.
   Tel 028 9026 6660   Fax 028 9026 6661   http://www.seupb.org
   M:Tek II Building, Armagh Road, MONAGHAN, Republic of Ireland.
   Tel +353 (0)477 7003   Fax +353 (0)477 1258
   EU House, 11 Kevlin Road, OMAGH, Co Tyrone, BT78 1LB.
   Tel 028 8225 5750   Fax 028 8224 8427
   Chief Executive: Pat Colgan

E Established on 2 December 1999, the SEUPB is one of the six North/South Implementation Bodies set up under the British-Irish Agreement of 8 March 1999. It is responsible to the North South Ministerial Council (qv), the Department of Culture, Arts & Leisure Northern Ireland and to the Irish Government.

R To manage the European Structural Funds programmes PEACE III (Peace & Reconciliation) and INTERREG IVA (Cross-Border Territorial Cooperation) in Northern Ireland, the Border Region of Ireland and parts of Western Scotland.
   To oversee the closure of programmes PEACE II and INTERREG IIIA.

G Northern Ireland, Republic of Ireland.

✍ For further information see **North/South Ministerial Council**.

Special Immigration Appeals Commission   (SIAC)

■ PO Box 6987, LEICESTER, LE1 6ZX.
   Tel 0845 600 0877   **Fax** 0116 249 4130   http://www.siac.tribunals.gov.uk

E Established in 1998 under the Special Immigration Appeals Commission Act 1997. The Commission functions as a Tribunal NDPB of the Ministry of Justice. The Panel consists of three members, one of whom must have held high judicial office.

R To consider appeals against decisions made by the Home Office to deport or exclude someone from the UK on national security grounds or for other public interest reasons.

G United Kingdom.

✍ Administrative support is provided by HM Courts & Tribunals Service (qv).

Specialised Commissioning Group   Ten SCGs cover the same regions as the ten English Strategic Health Authorities. Their work is coordinated by the **National Specialised Commissioning Group**.

Specialist Advisory Committee on Antimicrobial Resistance

✍ SACAR has been officially stood down and replaced by the **Advisory Committee on Antimicrobial Resistance & Healthcare Associated Infection** (qv).

Spectrum Management Advisory Committee

✍ SMAC was disbanded in 2003-04.

Spey Research Trust   See **Rivers & Fisheries Trusts of Scotland**.

Spoliation Advisory Panel   (SAP)

■ 2-4 Cockspur Street, LONDON, SW1Y 5DH.
   Tel 020 7211 6102   **Fax** 020 7211 6130
   Chairman: Rt Hon Sir David Hirst

E Established on 30 April 2000. SAP functions as an Advisory NDPB of the Department for Culture, Media & Sport. The Panel comprises eleven members including the Chairman.

R To help resolve claims from people, or their heirs, who lost cultural property during the Nazi era and which is now held by UK national collections.

G United Kingdom.

Spongiform Encephalopathy Advisory Committee   (SEAC)

■ Area 5A, 9 Millbank, c/o 17 Smith Square, LONDON, SW1P 3JR.
   Tel 020 7238 4946   http://www.seac.gov.uk
   Chairman: Prof Chris Higgins

E Established in April 1990. SEAC functions as a Scientific Advisory Committee and an Advisory NDPB of the Food Standards Agency (qv). The Committee comprises 16 members including the Chairman.

R To advise the Department of Health, the Department for Environment, Food & Rural Affairs and the devolved administrations on Transmissable Spongiform Encephalopathies (TSEs).

G United Kingdom.

✍ For further information see **Scientific Advisory Committees**.
   Defra announced on 14 October 2010 that SEAC will be abolished and its functions transferred to the Department of Health to ensure closer working with the relevant committees on public health.

Sport England
■ 3rd Floor, Victoria House, Bloomsbury Square, LONDON, WC1B 4SE.
   Tel 0845 850 8508   Fax 020 7383 5740   http://www.sportengland.org
   Chairman: Richard Lewis   Chief Executive: Jennie Price
E Established on 1 January 1997 as the English Sports Council, it adopted its current name on 1 March 1999. Sport
   England functions as an Executive NDPB of the Department for Culture, Media & Sport. The Board comprises
   eight members including the Chairman.
R To grow and sustain the numbers of people taking part in sport and improving talent development to help more
   people excel.
G England.
✍ It was confirmed by the Government on 14 October 2010 that Sport England will merge with UK Sport (qv) after
   2012.

Sport Northern Ireland   See **Sports Council for Northern Ireland**.

Sport & Recreation Alliance
■ Burwood House, 14-16 Caxton Street, LONDON, SW1H 0QT.
   Tel 020 7976 3900   Fax 020 7976 3901   http://www.sportandrecreation.org.uk
   Chairman: Brigid Simmonds, OBE   Chief Executive: Tim Lamb
E Established in 1935 as the umbrella organisation organisation for the governing and representative bodies of
   sport and recreation. It was known as the Central Council of Physical Recreation until a recent change of name.
   It has more than 320 member organisations. The board comprises nine members including the Chairman.
R To represent members' views to people who make decisions, promote the interests of sport and recreation so
   that as many people as possible know about members' work, and campaign on issues affecting the members.
G United Kingdom.

Sport Scotland   (sportscotland)
■ Doges, Templeton on the Green, 62 Templeton Street, GLASGOW, G40 1DA.
   Tel 0141 534 6500   Fax 0141 534 6501   http://www.sportscotland.org.uk
   Chairman: Louise Martin, CBE   Chief Executive: Stewart Harris
E Established in 1972 by Royal Charter. sportscotland functions as an Executive NDPB of the Scottish Executive
   Education Department. The board comprises eleven members including the Chairman.
R To promote sporting opportunities for all Scots at all levels, whatever their interest and ability.
   To be the National Lottery distributor body for the Lottery Sports Fund in Scotland.
G Scotland.

Sport Wales   See **Sports Council for Wales**.

Sports Council for Northern Ireland
■ House of Sport, 2a Upper Malone Road, BELFAST, BT9 5LA.
   Tel 028 9038 1222   Fax 028 9068 2757   http://www.sportni.net
   Chairman: Dominic Walsh   Chief Executive: Eamonn McCartan
E Established on 1 April 1974. It functions as an Executive NDPB of the Department of Culture, Arts & Leisure
   Northern Ireland, operating under the name **Sport Northern Ireland**. The Council comprises 13 members
   including the Chairman.
R To increase participation in sport and physical recreation.
   To improve sporting performances.
   To improve efficiency and effectiveness in the administartion of sport.
G Northern Ireland.

Sports Council for Wales
■ Sophia Gardens, CARDIFF, CF11 9SW.
   Tel 0845 045 0904   Fax 0845 846 0014   http://www.sports-council-wales.org.uk
   Chairman: Prof Laura McAllister   Chief Executive: Dr Huw Jones
E Established on 1 April 1972 by Royal Charter. It functions as an Executive NDPB of the National Assembly for
   Wales, operating under the name **Sport Wales** (**Chwaraeon Cymru**). The Council comprises eleven members
   including the Chairman.
R To develop and promote sport and active lifestyles.
G Wales.
● The Council distributes funds from the National Lottery to sport in Wales.
= Cyngor Chwaraeon Cymru

© CBD Research Ltd · Beckenham · Kent BR3 5JS · Tel 020 8650 7745 · Fax 020 8650 0768 · E-mail cbd@cbdresearch.com · www.cbdresearch.com

Sports Councils (national) See **Sport England**, **Sport Northern Ireland**, **Sports Council for Wales** and **sportscotland**.

Sports Grounds Safety Authority See **Football Licensing Authority**.

Sports Leaders UK

- 23-25 Linford Forum, Rockingham Drive, Linford Wood, MILTON KEYNES, MK14 6LY.
  Tel 01908 689180 Fax 01908 393744 http://www.sportsleaders.org
  Chairman: Margaret Peggie, BEd(Hons), MA, OBE
- E Established in 1982. Sports Leaders UK is the operating name of the **British Sports Trust** which functions as an independent charity. It is the awarding body for courses and qualifications in leadership in sport. The Board of Trustees/Directors comprises seven members including the Chairman.
- G United Kingdom.
- ✍ For more information on awarding bodies see the **Federation of Awarding Bodies**.

Staff & Associate Specialists Committee   (SASC)

- BMA House, Tavistock Square, LONDON, WC1H 9JP.
  Tel 020 7383 6040 Fax 020 7383 6400 http://www.bma.org.uk
  Chairman: Dr Radhakrishna Shanbhag
- E Established in July 2002 as a Branch of Practice Committee of the British Medical Association. The Committee comprises around 40 members including the Chairman.
- R To represent staff grades, associate specialists, clinical assistants, hospital practitioners and other non-standard non-training 'trust' grades.
- G United Kingdom.
- ✍ See **British Medical Association** [Branch of Practice Committees] for further information.

Staff Commission for Education & Library Boards   (SCELB)

- Forestview, Purdy's Lane, BELFAST, BT8 7AR.
  Tel 028 9049 1461 Fax 028 9040 1744 http://www.staffcom.org.uk
  Chairman: Prof Bernard Cullen   Chief Executive: Mrs Patricia Weir
- E Established in 1972 under the Education & Libraries (Northern Ireland) Order 1972, now consoludated in the Education & Libraries (Northern Ireland) Order 1986. SCELB functions as an Executive NDPB of the Department of Education Northern Ireland. The Board comprises 13 members including the Chairman.
- R To exercise general oversight of matters connected with the recruitment, training and terms and conditions of employment of officers of Education & Library Boards, and to make recommendations to Boards on such matters.
- G Northern Ireland.
- ✍ SCELB and other legacy organisations will be dissolved when the Education & Skills Authority (qv) becomes fully operational.

Staffordshire Police Authority

- Police Headquarters, Weston Road, STAFFORD, ST18 0YY.
  Tel 01785 232245 http://www.staffordshirepoliceauthority.org.uk
  Chairman: David Pearsall   Chief Executive: Alan Wallis
- E Established in April 1995, the Authority is an independent body charged with ensuring that Staffordshire Police provide an effective and efficient police service. It is made up of nine councillor members and eight independent members.
- G Staffordshire including Stoke-on-Trent
- ✍ For further information see **Police Authorities**.

Staffordshire & West Midlands Probation Trust

- 1 Victoria Square, BIRMINGHAM, B1 1BD.
  Tel 0121 248 6666 Fax 0121 248 6667 http://www.swmprobation.gov.uk
  Chairman: Dr Alan Harrison   Chief Officer: Mike Maiden
- E Established on 1 April 2010 under the Offender Management Act 2007, merging two area boards (Staffordshire and West Midlands) which had been set up on 1 April 2001 under the Criminal Justice & Court Service Act 2000. The Board comprises nine members including the Chairman.
- G Staffordshire, West Midlands (Birmingham, Coventry, Dudley, Sandwell, Solihull, Walsall and Wolverhampton).
- ✍ For further information see **Probation Trusts**.

Stakeholder Group on Current & Future Meat Controls (CFMC)

- Aviation House, 125 Kingsway, LONDON, WC2B 6NH.
  Tel 020 7276 8000
  Chairman: Liz Redmond
E The Group first met on 25 June 1910. CFMC functions as an advisory committee of the Food Standards Agency (qv).
R To inform FSA's work in developing proposals for more risk-based and proportionate meat hygiene and TSE/SRM (transmissible spongiform encephalopathy, specified risk material) requirements and the official controls relating to those requirements.
G United Kingdom.

Stamp Advisory Committee (SAC)

- Royal Mail Stamps, 148 Old Street, LONDON, EC1V 9HQ. http://www.royalmail.com
E Set up on 21 February 1968 by the Postmaster General. The Committee comprises about twelve members including Royal Mail's Design Director, a Government representative, designers and members of the general public. It is chaired by the General Manager of Royal Mail.
R To advise the Royal Mail on postage stamp design.
G United Kingdom.

Standards Commission for Scotland

- 23 Walker Street, EDINBURGH, EH3 7HX.
  Tel 0131 260 5368   Fax 0131 220 5941   http://www.standardscommissionscotland.org.uk
  Convenor: Ian Gordon, OBE, QPM, LLB (Hons)
E Established in 2000 under the Ethical Standards in Public Life etc (Scotland) 2000. It functions as an Executive NDPB of the Scottish Executive. The Commission comprises five members including the Convenor.
R To ensure that standards of ethical conduct are maintained across local authorities and public bodies.
  To deal with complaints against individual members submitted to it by the Chief Investigating Officer (CIO).
G Scotland.
● The CIO is appointed by the Scottish Ministers to investigate and report on complaints alleging a breach of the Commission's codes of contact. If the CIO concludes that there was a breach the matter is then referred to the Commission.
  The Commission works with 32 local authorities and 129 public bodies.

Standards Council for Community Learning & Development (CLD)

- 5th Floor, 5 Atlantic Quay, 150 Broomielaw, GLASGOW, G2 8LU.
  Tel 0300 244 1369   http://www.cldstandardscouncil.org.uk
  Chairman: Duncan Simpson
E Established in 2007. The Executive Committee comprises 21 members including the Chairman.
R To establish and maintain high standards of practice in Community Learning & Development.
G Scotland.
● Community & Development Learning (CLD) embraces adult learning, youth work and community development.

Standards for England (SfE)

- 4th Floor, Griffin House, 40 Lever Street, MANCHESTER, M1 1BB.
  Tel 0161 817 5300   Fax 0161 817 5499   http://www.standardsforengland.gov.uk
  Chairman: Dr Robert Chilton
E Established in March 2001 under the Local Government Act 2000. CfE functions as an Executive NDPB of the Department for Communities & Local Government. The Board comprises nine members including the Chairman.
R To promote and maintain high ethical standards of conduct by the councillors, members and co-opted members of 351 local authorities, 8,350 parish councils, 31 fire and rescue authorities, 38 police authorities, six integrated transport authorities, nine national park authorities, the Greater London Authority, the City of London Corporation, the Broads Authority and the Council of the Isles of Scilly.
  To investigate allegations that members' behaviour may have fallen short of the standards required by the Code of Conduct which came into force on 3 May 2007.
G England.
✍ SfE and its functions are being abolished. It is likely that it will cease to investigate complaints in late 2011 and formally close in early 2012.

Standards Verification UK (SVUK)

- 4th Floor, 36 Park Row, LEEDS, W Yorks, LS1 5JL.
  Tel 0113 241 0427   Fax 0113 242 5897   http://www.standardsverificationuk.org
  Chief Officer: Susan Edge

E   A wholly owned subsidiary of Lifelong Learning UK (qv).

R   Responsible for the verification of initial teacher training for FE/skills plus other forms of workforce training and development for the lifelong learning sector.

G   United Kingdom.

Standing Advisory Committee on Trunk Road Assessment   (SACTRA)

■   Great Minster House, 76 Marsham Street, LONDON, SW1P 4DR.
    Tel 0300 330 3000   **Fax** 020 7944 9643

E   Established on 7 June 1978 by the Secretary of State for Transport.

✍   The Committee has been dormant since 1999.

STANDING ADVISORY COUNCILS for RELIGIOUS EDUCATION   (SACREs)

E   Established on a voluntary basis under the Education Act 1944, the Education Act 1988 placed a statutory duty on each Local Education Authority (LEA) to establish its own SACRE.

R   To advise the LEA in matters concerning the teaching of religious education and collective acts of worship, and to have a monitoring role in this subject.

    To decide on applications for determinations of cases in which requirements for Christian collective worship is not to apply.

    To require the LEA to review its Agreed Syllabus from time to time.

Standing Committee on Hazard Information & Packaging   A sub-committee of the Health & Safety Executive's **Advisory Committee on Toxic Substances**.

Standing Committee on Structural Safety   (SCOSS)

■   11 Upper Belgrave Street, LONDON, SW1X 8BH.
    Tel 020 7235 4535   **Fax** 020 7235 4294   http://www.scoss.org.uk
    Chairman: Gordon Masterton, OBE

E   Established on 22 March 1976 by the Institution of Civil Engineers, the the Institution of Structural Engineers and the Health & Safety Executive (qv). SCOSS is an independent body. The Committee comprises 16 members including the Chairman.

R   To identify in advance those trends and developments which might contribute to an increasing risk to structural safety and, to that end, interact with the professions, industry and government on all matters concerned with design, construction and use of building and civil engineering structures.

G   United Kingdom.

Standing Conference on Academic Practice   (SCAP)

■   North Wing, University House, Kirby Corner Road, COVENTRY, CV4 8UW.
    Tel 024 7652 4766
    http://www2.warwick.ac.uk

E   Established in 1996.

R   The national body for leaders in staff development in research-intensive institutions.

G   United Kingdom.

Standing Conference on Archives & Museums   (SCAM)

■   Victoria & Albert Museum, South Kensington, LONDON, SW7 2RL.
    Tel 020 7602 5349   **Fax** 020 7602 0980   http://www.archivesandmuseums.org.uk
    Chairman: Christopher Marsden

E   Established in 1989. SCAM is a membership body comprising representatives from the Museum Association, the Society of Archivists and the Association of Independent Museums.

R   To benefit the care of archives and their public use by giving practical advice and sharing problems common amongst museum curators and archivists.

G   United Kingdom.

Standing Conference of East Anglian Local Authorities

✍   SCEALA's functions have devolved to the **East of England Local Government Association**.

Standing Conference of Heads of European Studies   (SCHES)
- c/o UACES, UCL School of Public Policy, 29/30 Tavistock Square, LONDON, WC1H 9QU.
  Tel 020 7679 4975   Fax 020 7679 4973   http://www.uaces.org
  Chairman: Dr Susan Milner   Administrator: Mrs Sue Davis
- E   Established in 1992. SCHES is a membership body comprising over 40 educational institutions and other bodies offering European Studies programmes in the UK. The Executive Committee comprises eight members including the Chairman.
- R   To lobby for and promote the interests of European Studies as a subject area.
- G   United Kingdom.

Standing Conference of Heads of Modern Languages in Universities
✍   In July 2008 SCHM amalgamated with the **University Council of Modern Languages**.

Standing Conference on Legal Education   SCLE advises the **Legal Services Consultative Panel**.

Standing Conference on Library Materials on Africa   (SCOLMA)
- Bodleian Library at Rhodes House, South Parks Road, OXFORD, OX1 3RG.
  Tel 01865 270908   Fax 01865 270911   http://www.lse.ac.uk/library/scolma/
  Chairman: Barbara Spina   Secretary: Lucy McCann
- E   Established in 1962. SCOLMA is a membership body open to libraries and institutions concerned with library materials on Africa. The committe comprises 15 members including the Chairman.
- R   To provide a forum for librarians and others concerned with the provision of materials for African studies in libraries in the UK.
  To monitor, coordinate and improve the acquisition of library materials on Africa.
- G   United Kingdom.

Standing Conference on London Archaeology
✍   SCOLA, established in 1992, was dissolved in April 2009 and replaced by CBA London, a branch of the membership organisation, the Council for British Archaeology (see our companion volume, the Directory of British Associations for further information).

Standing Conference of National & University Libraries
✍   SCONUL changed its name in 2001 to the Society of College, National & University Libraries. For further information see our companion volume, the Directory of British Associations.

Standing Conference of Physics Professors   (SCPP)
- Institute of Physics, 76 Portland Place, LONDON, W1B 1NT.
  Tel 020 7470 4800   Fax 020 7470 4848
  Chairman: Prof John Chapman
- E   Established in 1994. SCPP is a membership body comprising all the heads of physics departments at UK and Irish universities.
- R   To discuss policy issues which are considered important to their research and teaching.
- G   United Kingdom, Republic of Ireland.

Standing Conference of Principals
✍   Renamed in 2006 **GuildHE**.

Standing Conference on Problems Associated with the Coastline   (SCOPAC)
- Democratic Services, Civic Centre, HAVANT, Hants, PO9 2AX.
  Tel 023 9244 6230   http://www.scopac.org.uk
  Chairman: Cllr Roger Elkins   Secretary: Tristan Fieldsend
- E   Established in October 1986.
- R   To promote sustainable shoreline management.
  To facilitate the duties and responsibilities of local authorities and other organisations managing the coastal zone of central southern England.
- G   Dorset, Hampshire, Isle of Wight, West Sussex.

Standing Conference of University Drama Departments   (SCUDD)

- University of Worcester, Henwick Grove, WORCESTER, WR2 6AJ.
  Tel 01905 855000   http://www.scudd.org.uk
  Chairman: Tom Maguire   Secretary: Claire Cochrane
- E   SCUDD represents the interests of drama, theatre and performing arts in the higher education sector in the UK.
- R   To promote the multi-disciplined areas of drama, theatre and performance.
  To mediate with organisations such as funding councils, the Arts & Humanities Research Council and the Arts
      Councils (qqv) and to consult with such organisations when matters of future policy are discussed and decided.
- G   United Kingdom.

Standing Conference on University Teaching & Research in the Education of Adults   (SCUTREA)

- Centre for Community Engagement, Mantell Building, University of Sussex, Falmer, BRIGHTON, BN1 9RH.
  Tel 01273 872534   Fax 01273 877534   http://www.scutrea.ac.uk
  Chairman: Pam Coare
- E   Established in 1971. SCUTREA is a membership organisation.
- R   To provide a focus and meeting place for institutions, departments and individuals engaged in the education and
      training of adults and/or in research in the broad field of continuing education.
- G   United Kingdom.

Standing Council of the Baronetage

- Forestside, Martin's Corner, HAMBLEDON, Hants, PO7 4RA.
  Tel 023 9263 2672   Fax 023 9263 2672   http://www.baronetage.org
  Chairman: Sir Ian Lowson, Bt, OStJ   Secretary: Commander Perry Abbott, OBE, RN (Retd)
- E   Established in January 1898 as the Honourable Society of the Baronetage, and reconstituted in July 1903 under
      its present name.
- R   To take such action in the interests of the Baronetage, or of any individual baronet or members of their families,
      as may be appropriate.
  To publish the Official Roll of the Baronetage at regular intervals.
  To advise Heirs Apparent seeking to prove their succession to enable them to be added to the Roll and
      addressed and received as baronets.
- G   United Kingdom.

Standing Council of Scottish Chiefs   (SCSC)

- Hope Chambers, 52 Leith Walk, EDINBURGH, EH6 5HW.   http://www.clanchiefs.org
  Convenor: The Earl of Caithness
- E   Established on 25 March 1952 by the then Lord High Constable of Scotland. The Executive Committee comprises
      nine members including the Convenor.
- R   To consider matters affecting Scottish Chiefs and the Clans and Names which they represent and to submit their
      views and interests to Government, Departments of State, local authorities, press and public, and to
      associations connected with Clan and Family in Britain and overseas.
  To educate the general public in matters connected with the rights, functions and historical position of the Chiefs
      and the Clans and Names which they represent.
  To protect the titles, armorial bearings and other insignia of the Chiefs from exploitation or misuse in trade or
      otherwise.
- G   Scotland.

Standing Dental Advisory Committee

- ✍   SDAC was abolished on 2 May 2005 under the National Health Service (Standing Advisory Committee)
  Amendment Order 2005.

Standing Medical Advisory Committee

- ✍   SMAC was abolished on 2 May 2005 under the National Health Service (Standing Advisory Committee)
  Amendment Order 2005.

Standing Nursing & Midwifery Advisory Committee

- ✍   SNMAC was abolished on 2 May 2005 under the National Health Service (Standing Advisory Committee)
  Amendment Order 2005.

Standing Orders Committee   See **United Kingdom Parliament: Committees**.

Standing Pharmaceutical Advisory Committee
✍ SPAC was abolished on 2 May 2005 under the National Health Service (Standing Advisory Committee) Amendment Order 2005.

Stansted Airport Consultative Committee (STACC)
■ c/o Governance Team, County Hall, CHELMSFORD, Essex, CM1 1LX.
Tel 01245 430360 **Fax** 01245 290180 http://www.stacc.info
Chairman: Stewart Ashurst Secretary: Graham Redgwell
G Essex, Hertfordshire.
✍ For further information see **Airport Consultative Committees**.

The State Hospitals Board for Scotland
■ The State Hospital, Carstairs, LANARK, ML11 8RP.
Tel 01555 840293 **Fax** 01555 840024 http://www.tsh.scot.nhs.uk
Chairman: Gordon Craig Chief Executive: Andreana Adamson
E Established in April 1995 under the State Hospital (Scotland) Act 1994. The Board functions as a Special Health Board of the Scottish Executive Health Department. The Board comprises 14 members including the Chairman.
R To ensure provision of high quality, secure and clinically effective services to meet the needs of those with mental disorder who, because of their dangerous, violent or criminal propensities, cannot be cared for in any other setting.
G Scotland.
✍ One of the seven Special NHS Boards in Scotland.

Statistics Advisory Committee (SAC)
■ McAuley House, 2-14 Castle Street, BELFAST, BT1 1SA.
Tel 028 9034 8100 http://www.nisra.gov.uk
Chairman: Mike Stevenson
E Established on 25 September 1989 under the Statistics of Trade & Employment (Northern Ireland) Order 1988. The SAC functions as an Advisory NDPB of the Department of Finance & Personnel Northern Ireland. The Committee comprises 16 members including the Chairman.
R To advise Northern Ireland departments on all matters relating to the collection and disclosure of statistical information from businesses and to advise on issues such as quality assurance, National Statistics, Codes of Practice and such matters as may be referred to it by departments.
G Northern Ireland.

Statistics Authority See **United Kingdom Statistics Authority**.

Statistics Commission
✍ Abolished on 31 March 2008, its responsibilities transferred to the **United Kingdom Statistics Authority**.

Statute Law Committee for Northern Ireland
■ 2nd Floor, The Arches Centre, 11-13 Bloomfield Avenue, BELFAST, BT5 5HD.
Tel 028 9052 6961 **Fax** 028 9052 6952
Contact: Lyn McCulloch
E The Committee functions as an Advisory NDPB of the Office of the First Minister & the Deputy First Minister. It comprises the Lord Chief Justice of Northern Ireland as Chairman and a maximum of 18 other members.
R To exercise a general supervision over the publication of the annual volumes and indices of the Statutes of Northern Ireland and of Statutory Rules within the meaning of the Statutory Rules (Northern Ireland) Order 1979.
To make recommendations with respect to the publication, revision or consolidation of the Statute Law of Northern Ireland and of such Statutory Rules.
G Northern Ireland.

Steering Committee on Pharmacy Postgraduate Education
✍ No longer in existence.

Stonebridge Housing Action Trust
✍ Wound up in 2005 upon completion of its programme.

Stornoway Pier & Harbour Commission
✍ Since 1 May 2004 **Stornoway Port Authority**.

Stornoway Port Authority
■ Amity House, Esplanade Road, STORNOWAY, Isle of Lewis, HS1 2XS.
  Tel 01851 702688   Fax 01851 705714   http://www.stornoway-portauthority.com
  Chairman: Iain A Macleod   Chief Executive: Jane Maciver
E Under the Stornoway Harbour Revision (Constitution) Order 2003, Stornoway Pier & Harbour Commission was re-
  constituted as Stornoway Port Authority. The board comprises nine members including the Chairman.
G Stornoway.
✍ For further information see **Port & Harbour Authorities**.

Strangford Lough Management Advisory Committee   (SLMAC)
■ No 1 The Square, PORTAFERRY, Co Down, BT22 1LW.
  Tel 028 4272 8886   Fax 028 4772 9588   http://www.strangfordlough.org
  Chairman: Cllr Jim McBriar   Strangford Lough Officer: Caroline Nolan, MSc, HDipEd
E Established in 1992 under provisions made in a 1985 Northern Ireland Order, SLMAC functions as an NDPB of
  the Department of the Environment Northern Ireland. The Committee consists of 27 members who are
  appointed by the Northern Ireland Environment Minister.
R To represent local and specialist interests in the development, interpretation and adaptation of legislation.
  To promote strategic, coordinated management designed to protect the environmental resource while
  encouraging appropriate economic and recreational activity.
G Northern Ireland.

Strategic Advisory Body for Intellectual Property Policy
✍ Established on 2 June 2008, Sabip's closure was announced on 19 July 2010. Some of its functions have
  transferred to the **Intellectual Property Office**.

Strategic Health Aauthorities   See under **NHS - England**.

Strategic Implementation Group   **(SIG)**
✍ Formed to oversee the implementation of the output of the Healthcare Industries Taskforce in November 2004,
  SIG closed after its report on 6 March 2007.

Strategic Investment Board
✍ The UK SIB was abolished at the end of June 2008.

Strategic Investment Board   (SIB)
■ Clare House, 303 Airport Road West, BELFAST, BT3 9ED.
  Tel 028 9081 6181   Fax 028 9081 6968   http://www.sibni.org
  Chairman: Dr David Dobbin, CBE
E Established on 1 April 2003. SIB functions as an Executive NDPB of the Office of the First Minister & Deputy First
  Minister in Northern Ireland. The Board comprises six members including the Chairman.
R To work with Northern Ireland departments and agencies to help them accelerate the delivery of major public
  infrastructure projects.
G Northern Ireland.

Strategic Rail Authority
✍ Wound up 1 December 2006 and its functions transferred to the Department for Transport's Rail Group.

Strathclyde Partnership for Transport   (SPT)
■ Consort House, 12 West George Street, GLASGOW, G2 1HN.
  Tel 0141 332 6811   http://www.spt.co.uk
  Chairman: Cllr Jonathan Findlay

E   Established on 1 December 2005 under the Transport (Scotland) Act 2005, SPT was formed following a merger between the Strathclyde Passenger Authority & Executive and the WESTRANS voluntary partnership. SPT functions as an Executive Agency of the Scottish Executive Enterprise, Transport & Lifelong Learning Department. The Partnership Board comprises 20 Councillors representing the twelve Unitary Authorities that make up the Strathclyde region, and between seven and nine appointed members.

R   To plan and deliver transport solutions for all modes of transport across the region, in conjunction with member councils and industry partners.
     To consult with private bus operators on the registration of bus services and the provision of passenger information.

G   Argyll & Bute, Ayrshire, Dunbartonshire, Glasgow, Inverclyde, Lanarkshire and Renfrewshire.

●   The Partnership owns and runs the Glasgow Subway and the Renfrew-Yoker Ferry. It subsidises other ferry and bus services, provides services for people mobility problems, and works with other organisations to provide free and discounted travel to those who are eligible.

✍   For further information see **Regional Transport Partnerships**.

Strathclyde Police Authority

■   City Chambers, George Square, GLASGOW, G2 1DU.
     Tel 0141 287 4167   http://www.strathclydepoliceauthority.gov.uk
     Convenor: Cllr Stephen Curran   Chief Executive: Keith Mannings, MBA, BA(Hons)

E   The Authority is an independent body responsible for Strathclyde Police's budget and the management of its resources. The Board is made up of eight councillors from Glasgow, four each from North and South Lanarkshire, and two from each of the other nine district councils in the Force's area.

G   Argyll & Bute; East, North & South Ayrshire; East & West Dunbartonshire; Glasgow; Inverclyde; North & South Lanarkshire; Renfrewshire & East Renfrewshire.

✍   For further information see **Police Authorities**.

Student Awards Agency for Scotland   (SAAS)

■   Gyleview House, 3 Redheughs Rigg, EDINBURGH, EH12 9HH.
     Tel 0845 111 1711   **Fax** 0131 244 5887   http://www.saas.gov.uk
     Chief Executive: Tracey Slaven

E   Established on 5 April 1994. SAAS functions as an Executive Agency of the Scottish Executive Education Department. The Management Board comprises eight members.

R   To provide financial support to full-time students in higher education by administering the Students' Allowance Scheme, Postgraduate Students' Allowance Scheme, Nursing & Midwifery Burseries Scheme and applications for student loans, and by making arrangements for the collection of the Graduate Endowment.

G   Scotland.

●   The Agency provides resources to the Student Loans Co Ltd (qv) and distributes access funds to Scottish universities and colleges.
     The Agency maintains a register of educational endowments.

Student Loans Company   (SLC)

■   100 Bothwell Street, GLASGOW, G2 7JD.
     Tel 0141 306 2000   **Fax** 0141 306 2005   http://www.slc.co.uk
     Chairman: Ed Smith   Chief Executive: Ed Lester

E   Established in 1990 within the policy context set by Government and the legislative framework of the Education (Student Loans) Act 1990, the Education (Student Loans) (Northern Ireland) Order 1990, the Education (Scotland) Act 1980, the Teaching & Higher Education Act 1998 and the Education (Student Support) (Northern Ireland) Order 1998. SLC functions as an Executive NDPB of the Government. The Board comprises 14 members including the Chairman and two asessors.

R   To deliver financial support to eligible students pursuing higher education.
     To pay to higher education institutions the public contribution towards tuition fees (England, Wales and Northern Ireland only).
     To supply information to HM Revenue & Customs to ensure repayments are collected under the Income Contingent Repayment Loan Scheme.
     To manage the direct collection of repayments for loans granted under the former Mortgage Style Loan Scheme.

G   United Kingdom.

●   SLC also has offices in Colwyn Bay and Darlington.

Sudley House   See **National Museums Liverpool**.

© CBD Research Ltd · Beckenham · Kent BR3 5JS · Tel 020 8650 7745 · Fax 020 8650 0768 · E-mail cbd@cbdresearch.com · www.cbdresearch.com

Suffolk ACRE   (RCCE)

- Brightspace, 160 Hadleigh Road, IPSWICH, Suffolk, IP2 0HH.
  Tel 01473 354300   Fax 01473 345330   http://www.suffolkacre.org.uk
  Chairman: David Wheeler   Chief Executive: Dr Wil Gibson
- E Established in 1937. Suffolk ACRE functions as a registered charity and company limited by guarantee.
- R To tackle the economic, social and environmental needs of communities in Suffolk by forging effective partnerships between communities and agencies and promoting communal self-help.
- G Suffolk.
- ✍ Suffolk ACRE is one of the 38 Rural Community Councils, represented at the national level by **Action with Communities in Rural England** (qv) and at the regional level by Rural Action East.

Suffolk Police Authority

- Martlesham Heath, IPSWICH, Suffolk, IP5 3QS.
  Tel 01473 782773   http://www.suffolk.police.uk/PoliceAuthority/
  Chairman: Colin Spence
- E Established in April 1995, the Authority is an independent body charged with ensuring that Suffolk Constabulary provides an effective and efficient police service. It is made up of nine county councillors and eight independent members.
- G Suffolk.
- ✍ For further information see **Police Authorities**.

SummitSkills

- Vega House, Opal Drive, Fox Milne, MILTON KEYNES, Bucks, MK15 0DF.
  Tel 01908 303960   Fax 01908 303989   http://www.summitskills.org.uk
  Chairman: Ian Livsey   Chief Executive: Keith Marshall
- E Established on 1 December 2003. It is the recognised Sector Skills Council for the building services engineering sector. The board comprises 14 members including the Chairman.
- G United Kingdom.
- ✍ One of the 25 SSCs within the Skills for Business Network run by the **UK Commission for Employment & Skills**.

Sunderland arc
- ✍ Established in 2002, Sunderland Area Regeneration Company Ltd ceased operations in 2010.

Surrey Community Action

- Astolat, Coniers Way, New Inn Lane, Burpham, GUILDFORD, GU4 7HL.
  Tel 01483 566072   Fax 01483 440508   http://www.surreyca.org.uk
  Chairman: Tim Prideaux, JP, DL   Chief Executive: Jean Roberts-Jones
- E Established in 1950. Surrey Community Action functions as a registered charity and company limited by guarantee. The Board comprises eleven members including the Chairman.
- R To work with communities to enhance the quality of life for people in Surrey by promoting, supporting and strengthening voluntary action.
- G Surrey.
- ✍ Surrey Community Action is one of the 38 Rural Community Councils, represented at the national level by **Action with Communities in Rural England** (qv) and at the regional level by South East Rural Community Councils.

Surrey Police Authority

- PO Box 412, GUILDFORD, Surrey, GU3 1BR.
  Tel 01483 630200   Fax 01483 634502   http://www.surreypa.gov.uk
  Chairman: Peter Williams
- E Established in April 1995, the Authority is an independent body charged with ensuring that Surrey Police provide an effective and efficient police service. It is made up of nine councillor members and eight independent members.
- G Surrey.
- ✍ For further information see **Police Authorities**.

Surrey & Sussex Probation Trust

- 185 Dyke Road, HOVE, E Sussex, BN3 1TL.
  Tel 01273 227979   Fax 01273 227972   http://www.surreysussexprobation.gov.uk
  Chairman: John Steele   Chief Officer: Sonia Crozier

E   Established on 1 April 2010 under the Offender Management Act 2007, merging two area boards (Surrey and Sussex) which had been set up on 1 April 2001 under the Criminal Justice & Court Service Act 2000. The Board comprises eight members including the Chairman.

G   Surrey, East and West Sussex including Brighton & Hove.

✍   For further information see **Probation Trusts**.

Surrey & Sussex Strategic Health Authority

✍   On 1 July 2006 merged with the Kent & Medway Strategic Health Authority to form **NHS South East Coast**.

Surveillance Commissioners   See the **Office of Surveillance Commissioners**.

Surveyors Ombudsman Service

✍   Renamed in April 2010 **Ombudsman Services: Property**.

Sussex Downs Conservation Board

✍   In 2005 merged with the East Hampshire AONB Joint Advisory Committee to form the South Downs Joint Committee which in 2010 was superceded by the Shadow Authority which became the **South Downs National Park Authority** on 1 April 2011.

Sussex Police Authority

■   Sackville House, Brooks Close, LEWES, E Sussex, BN7 2FZ.
     Tel 01273 481561   http://www.sussexpa.gov.uk
     Chairman: Dr Laurie Bush   Chief Executive: Dr John Godfrey

E   Established in April 1995, the Authority is an independent body charged with ensuring that Sussex Police provide an effective and efficient police service. It is made up of four West Sussex County Councillors, three East Sussex County Councillors, two Brighton & Hove City Councillors and eight independent members.

G   East and West Sussex including Brighton & Hove.

✍   For further information see **Police Authorities**.

Sustainable Development Commission   (SDC)

■   Room 101, 55 Whitehall, c/o 3-8 Whitehall Place, LONDON, SW1A 2HH.
     Tel 0300 068 6305   **Fax** 0300 068 6306   http://www.sd-commission.org.uk
     Chairman: Will Day   Chief Executive: Andrew Lee

E   Established on 1 July 2000, in 2006 the Commission was expanded to take on a watchdog role. SDC functions as an Executive NDPB established as a company limited by guarantee, incorporated on 1 February 2009, jointly owned by the Government and the devolved administrations. The Board comprises ten commissioners including the Chairman.

R   To produce evidence-based public reports on contentious environmental, social and economic issues, such as nuclear power.
     To draw on expert opinion to advise key Ministers, policy-makers and stakeholders across Government.
     To respond openly to Government policy initiatives.
     To invite debates on controversial subjects.
     To undertake watchdog appraisals of Government's progress.

G   United Kingdom.

●   The Commission's work is divided into ten policy areas: climate change, consumption, economics, education, energy, engagement, health, housing, regional & local government, and transport.

✍   The future of the Commission is currently being considered in the light of the Department for Environment, Food & Rural Affairs' decision to withdraw its funding at the end of 2010/11, which was announced on 22 July 2010.

Sustainable Development Commission Northern Ireland   (SCD NI)

■   Room E5/11, Castle Buildings, Stormont Estate, BELFAST, BT4 3SR.
     Tel 028 9052 0196email sd-commission.org.uk/northern_ireland.php
     Northern Ireland Commissioner: Jim Kitchen

G   Northern Ireland.

© CBD Research Ltd · Beckenham · Kent BR3 5JS · Tel 020 8650 7745 · Fax 020 8650 0768 · E-mail cbd@cbdresearch.com · www.cbdresearch.com

Sustainable Development Commission Scotland (SDC Scotland)

■ Osborne House, 1 Osborne Terrace, EDINBURGH, EH12 5HG.
   Tel 0131 625 1880 **Fax** 0131 625 1881
   email sd-commission.org.uk/scotland.php
   Scotland Commissioner: Prof Jan Bebbington
G   Scotland.

Sustainable Development Commission Wales (SDC Wales)

■ Room 1, University Registry, King Edward VII Avenue, CARDIFF, CF10 3NS.
   Tel 029 2037 6956   http://www.sd-commission.org.uk/wales.php
   Wales Commissioner: Peter Davies, OBE
G   Wales.

Swansea Local Health Board
✍ Merged on 1 October 2009 with the Bridgend and Neath Port Talbot Local Health Boards to form **Abertawe Bro Morgannwg University Health Board**.

Swyddfa Archwilio Cymru   See **Wales Audit Office**.

T

TACADE

■ Old Exchange Buildings, 6 St Ann's Passage, MANCHESTER, M2 6AD.
   Tel 0161 836 6850   **Fax** 0161 836 6859   http://www.tacade.com
   Chairman: Roger Daw   Chief Executive: Martin Buczkiewicz
E   Established in 1968 as the Teacher's Advisory Council on Alcohol & Drug Education. TACADE functions as a national and international agency with not-for-profit charitable status. The Board of Trustees comprises nine members including the Chairman.
R   To promote the health and well-being of children and young people locally, nationally and internationally including alcohol, drugs, gambling, homophobia, sexual health and smoking.
G   United Kingdom.

Takeover Panel   See **Panel on Takeovers & Mergers**.

Tarbert Harbour Authority

■ Harbour Master's Office, Garval Road, TARBERT, Argyll, PA29 6TR.
   Tel 01880 820344   http://www.tarbertlochfyne.com
   Chairman: Alan Macdonald
G   Tarbert, Loch Fyne.
✍ For further information see **Port & Harbour Authorities**.

TATE

■ Millbank, LONDON, SW1P 4RG.
   Tel 020 7887 8000   http://www.tate.org.uk
   Chairman: Lord Browne of Madingley   Director: Sir Nicholas Serota
E   The Tate Gallery opened in 1897; the current authority of the Board of Trustees is derived from the Museums & Galleries Act 1992. It functions as an Executive NDPB of the Department for Culture, Media & Sport. The Board comprises 14 members including the Chairman.
R   To promote public knowledge, understanding and enjoyment of British, modern and contemporary art by facilitating extraordinary experiences between people and art through the Collection and an inspiring programme in and well beyond the four galleries.
G   United Kingdom.
● TATE is a family of four galleries: Tate Britain and Tate Modern in London, Tate Liverpool and Tate St Ives.

Tax Law Review Committee   (TLRC)

- 3rd Floor, 7 Ridgmount Street, LONDON, WC1E 7AE.
  Tel 020 7291 4800   Fax 020 7323 4780   http://www.ifs.org.uk
  President: Lord Howe of Aberavon, CH, QC   Chairman: Sir Alan Budd, DPhil
- E   Established by the Institute for Fiscal Studies in 1994. Its members represent a broad cross-section of informed
      opinion from industry and commerce, the judiciary, academia, the professions, political and public life.
- R   To keep under review the state and operation of tax law in the UK.
- G   United Kingdom.
- ●   The Committee keeps under review the state and operation of tax law in the UK by selecting particular topics for
      study.

Tay Foundation   See **Rivers & Fisheries Trusts of Scotland**.

Tayside & Central Scotland Transport Partnership   (TACTRAN)

- Bordeaux House, 31 Kinnoull Street, PERTH, PH1 5EN.
  Tel 01738 475775   Fax 01738 639705   http://www.tactran.gov.uk
  Chairman: Cllr Will Dawson   Director: Eric Guthrie
- E   Established on 1 December 2005. The Partnership Board comprises ten Councillor members and four appointed
      members.
- G   Angus, Dundee, Perth & Kinross and Stirling.
- ✍   For further information see **Regional Transport Partnerships**.

Tayside Joint Police Board

- West Bell Street, DUNDEE, DD1 9JU.
  Tel 01382 596007   http://www.tayside.police.uk/jointboard.php
  Convenor: Cllr Ian Mackintosh, JP   Office Manager: Theresa Noble
- E   The Authority is an independent body responsible for Tayside Police's budget and the management of its
      resources.
      The Board is made up of seven councillors from Dundee City, six from Perth & Kinross and five from Angus.
      councils in the Force's area.
- G   Angus, City of Dundee, Perth & Kinross.
- ✍   For further information see **Police Authorities**.

Tayside Local Enterprise Company
- ✍   Now functions as the Dundee office of **Scottish Enterprise**.

Tayside NHS Board

- Kings Cross, Clepington Road, DUNDEE, DD3 8EA.
  Tel 01382 818479   Fax 01382 424003   http://www.nhstayside.scot.nhs.uk
  Chairman: Sandy Watson, OBE, DL   Chief Executive: Prof Tony Wells
- G   Angus, City of Dundee, Perth & Kinross.
- ✍   For further information see **NHS Scotland - Boards**.

Tea Council   See the **United Kingdom Tea Council**.

Teacher Training Agency
- ✍   Closed in August 2005, its functions transferred to the **Training & Development Agency for Schools**.

Teachers TV
- ✍   The Department for Education's contract with Teachers TV came to an end in April 2011.

Technical Advisory Board   (TAB)

- PO Box 38542, LONDON, SW1H 9YE.
  Chairman: Peter Walker
- E   Established in May 2002 under the Regulation of Investigatory Powers Act 2000 (RIPA). TAB functions as an
      Advisory NDPB of the Home Office. The Board comprises six members from the communications industry, six
      from the intercepting agencies and a neutral Chairman.

R   To advise the Home Secretary on the reasonableness of obligations imposed upon communications service providers (CSPs) in order to ensure that they maintain a capability to intercept communications.

G   United Kingdom.

✍   Also known as the RIPA Technical Advisory Board.

Technology Strategy Board
■   North Star House, North Star Avenue, SWINDON, Wilts, SN2 1UE.
      Tel 01793 442700   http://www.innovateuk.org
      Chairman: Dr Graham Spittle

E   Established on 1 July 2007. TSB functions as an Executive NDPB of the Department for Business, Innovation & Skills. The Board comprises twelve members including the Chairman.

R   To drive forward the Government's technology strategy which is to encourage and enable the continuing restructuring of the UK economy in favour high value, knowledge-based design, manufacturing and services.

G   United Kingdom.

Teenage Pregnancy Independent Advisory Group
✍   Established in 2000 to advise Government on the Teenage Pregnancy Strategy which aimed to halve the rate of conceptions among under-18s by 2010, TPIAG was disbanded at the end of its remit in December 2010.

Tees Valley Regeneration
✍   Established in 2002, TVR was an Urban Regeneration Company. It closed in March 2010 with responsibility for regeneration handed over to the local councils.

Tees Valley Rural Community Council   (TVRCC)
■   Unit 2A, Cadcam Centre, High Force Road, Riverside Park, MIDDLESBROUGH, TS2 1RH.
      Tel 01642 213852   **Fax** 01642 253289   http://www.teesvalleyrcc.org.uk
      Chief Officer: Ms Doff Pollard

E   TVRCC functions as a registered charity and company limited by guarantee.

R   To work with local people to enable them to identify and respond to local need.
      To provide accurate and appropriate advice, information and support to voluntary and community groups.

G   Darlington, Hartlepool, Middlesbrough, Redcar & Cleveland, Stockton-on-Tees.

✍   TVRCC is one of the 38 Rural Community Councils, represented at the national level by **Action with Communities in Rural England** (qv) and at the regional level by North East Rural Community Councils.

Teesside International Airport Consultative Committee
✍   See **Durham Tees Valley Airport Consultative Committee**.

Teignmouth Harbour Commission   (THC)
■   Old Quay House, Old Quay, TEIGNMOUTH, Devon, TQ14 8ES.
      Tel 01626 773165   **Fax** 01626 778937   http://www.teignmouth-harbour.com
      Chairman: Jeremy Grammer   Chief Executive: Commander David Vaughan

E   Established in 1924 under the Teignmouth Harbour Act, 1924.

R   To be responsible for navigation & pilotage into the Harbour.

G   Teignmouth.

✍   For further information see **Port & Harbour Authorities**.

Telecommunications Ombudsman   See **Office of the Telecommunications Ombudsman**.

Tenant Services Authority   (TSA)
■   Maple House, 149 Tottenham Court Road, LONDON, W1T 7BN.
      Tel 0845 230 7000   http://www.tenantservicesauthority.org
      4th Floor, One Piccadilly Gardens, MANCHESTER, M1 1RG.
      Chairman: Anthony Mayer   Chief Executive: Claer Lloyd Jones

E   Established on 1 December 2008 under the Housing & Regeneration Act 2008, assuming the regulatory functions of the former Housing Corporation. TSA functions as an Executive NDPB of the Department for Communities & Local Government. The Board comprises twelve members including the Chairman.

R   To improve standards of service delivery for tenants.
      To support decent homes and neighbourhoods.
      To promote effective tenant involvement and empowerment.

To ensure providers are well run and deliver value for money.
To promote and protect public and private investment.
To encourage and support a supply of well-managed social housing.

G   England.

✍   TSA is being abolished and its regulatory functions transferred to the Homes & Communities Agency (qv). Independent economic regulation will be safeguarded and consumer regulation slimmed down.

Tendring Regeneration Ltd

■   Thorpe Road, Weeley, CLACTON-ON-SEA, Essex, CO16 9JH.
Tel 01255 686181   http://www.tdrl.co.uk
Managing Director: Matthew Hill

E   Established on 4 April 2008 by Tendring District Council to be the regeneration vehicle for the area. It traded as INTend until 2010/11. It functions as a non-profit distributing company limited by guarantee.

R   To assist, promote, encourage, develop and secure the regeneration in the social, physical and economic environment of Tendring District.

G   Tendring.

✍   For more information see **Urban Regeneration Companies**.

Textiles Industry Advisory Committee   (TEXIAC)

■   1st Floor, City Gate West, Toll House Hill, NOTTINGHAM, NG1 5AT.
Tel 0845 345 0055
Chairman: Huw Jones

E   Established in 1994 by the Health & Safety Executive (qv). The Committee comprises 13 members including the Chairman.

R   To advise the HSE on the protection of people at work and others from hazards to health and safety arising within the textile and clothing industry.

G   United Kingdom.

Thames Valley Police Authority   (TVPA)

■   The Farmhouse, Oxford Road, KIDLINGTON, Oxon, OX5 2NX.
Tel 01865 846780   http://www.tvpa.police.uk
Chairman: Khan Juna

E   Established in April 1995, the Authority is an independent body charged with ensuring that Thames Valley Police provide an effective and efficient police service. It is made up of ten councillor members (two from Oxfordshire County Council, one from Buckinghamshire County Council and one from each of the seven unitary authorities of Milton Keynes, Bracknell Forest, Slough, West Berkshire, Reading, Wokingham and Windsor & Maidenhead) and nine independent members.

G   Berkshire, Buckinghamshire and Oxfordshire.

✍   For further information see **Police Authorities**.

Thames Valley Probation Trust

■   Kingsclere Road, BICESTER, Oxon, OX26 2QD.
Tel 01869 255300   Fax 01869 255355   http://www.thamesvalleyprobation.gov.uk
Chairman: Malcolm Fearn   Chief Officer: Gerry Marshall

E   Established on 1 April 2001 under the Criminal Justice & Court Service Act 2000 as the Thames Valley Probation Area Board. It became a trust on 1 April 2010 under the Offender Management Act 2007. The Board comprises 13 members including the Chairman.

G   Berkshire, Buckinghamshire and Oxfordshire.

✍   For further information see **Probation Trusts**.

Thames Valley Strategic Health Authority

✍   On 1 July 2006 merged with the Hampshire & Isle of Wight Strategic Health Authority to form the **South Central Strategic Health Authority**.

Theatre Dance Council International   (TDCI)

■   10 Glenfield Road, Heaton Chapel, STOCKPORT, Cheshire, SK4 2QP.
Tel 0161 442 0164   http://www.tdci.org.uk
President: Glenys McGill   Secretary: Derek Young

E   Established on 28 April 1958. TDCI functions as a non-profit organisation.

R   To develop and promote theatre dance disciplines for the benefit of dance teachers and their students.

G   United Kingdom.

- Member associations: Allied Dancing Association (Merseyside and the north west); Associated Board of Dance (midlands); British Association of Teachers of Dancing (national); International Dance Teachers Association; Northern Counties Dance Teachers Association (Northern England).

Theatres Trust

■ 22 Charing Cross Road, LONDON, WC2H 0QL.
Tel 020 7836 8591   Fax 020 7836 3302   http://www.theatrestrust.org.uk
Chairman: Rob Dickens, CBE   Director: Mhora Samuel

E Established in July 1976 under the Theatres Trust Act 1976. The Trust functions as an Advisory NDPB of the Department for Culture, Media & Sport. The Board of Trustees comprises 15 members including the Chairman.

R To work with commercial, public, subsidised and voluntary sectors to secure a sustainable future for theatre buildings.

G United Kingdom.

✍ The Government announced on 14 October 2010 that the Trust will cease to function as a NDPB but continue as a charity.

Thurrock Thames Gateway Development Corporation

■ Gateway House, Stonehouse Lane, PURFLEET, Essex, RM19 1NX.
Tel 01708 895400   Fax 01708 895447   http://www.thurrocktgdc.org.uk
Chairman: Will McKee, CBE

E Established in 2005. It was set up as an Urban Development Corporation (qv) for the Borough of Thurrock.

R To drive economic growth in Thurrock, create homes, jobs and opportunities and make Thurrock a place where people want to live and work.

G Thurrock.

✍ On 14 October 2010 the Government announced that it would abolish the corporation (as an Urban Develompment Corporation) and devolve its functions to Thurrock Council.

Torfaen Local Health Board

✍ Merged on 1 October with the Blaenau Gwent, Caerphilly, Monmouthshire and Newport Local Health Boards to form **Aneurin Bevan Health Board**.

The Tote   See **Horserace Totalisator Board**.

Tourism Ireland

■ Beresford House, 2 Beresford Road, COLERAINE, BT52 1GE.
Tel 028 7035 9200   Fax 028 7035 9212   http://www.tourismireland.com
5th Floor, Bishop's Square, Redmond's Hill, DUBLIN 2, Republic of Ireland.
Tel +353 (0)1 476 3400   Fax +353 (0)1 476 3666

E Established under the framework of the Belfast/Good Friday Agreement 1998. Tourism Ireland functions as a company limited by guarantee registered in the Republic and operates under the auspices of the North South Ministerial Council (qv).

R To promote the island of Ireland overseas as a tourist destination, to which end it employs 160 people in key source markets around the world.

G Northern Ireland, Republic of Ireland.

● Tourism Ireland works in partnership with Fáilte Ireland and the Northern Ireland Tourist Board (qqv) which are responsible for product and enterprise development and marketing to tourism consumers within the island of Ireland.

✍ For further information see the **North South Ministerial Council**.

Tourism South East

■ 40 Chamberlayne Road, EASTLEIGH, Hants, PO50 5JH.
Tel 023 8062 5400   Fax 023 8062 0010   http://www.visitsoutheastengland.com
Chairman: John Williams   Chief Executive: Mike Bedingfield

E Established in 2003 by the South East England Development Agency (qv), replacing the former Southern & South East England Tourist Board. Members include local authorities and representatives of commercial tourist interests in the region.

R To create the conditions for tourism in the region to allow the industry to be successful, develop and grow by providing high quality support to its members, to lead regional marketing campaigns, encourage the highest levels of skills and customer service, support regeneration projects, lobby on behalf of South East tourism businesses, and set up strategic partnership projects of all kinds.

G   Berkshire, Buckinghamshire, Hampshire, Isle of Wight, Kent, Oxfordshire, Surrey, and Sussex.

✍   Also trades as The **Beautiful South**.

Tourism Training Trust

✍   Established in 1994, TTT was one of Northern Ireland's Sector Training Councils.

Tourism West Midlands

■   3 Priestley Wharf, Holt Street, Aston Science Park, BIRMINGHAM, B7 4BN.
    Tel 0121 380 3500   **Fax** 0121 380 3501   http://www.visittheheart.co.uk

E   Established in 2004 by Advantage West Midlands (qv) to replace the former Heart of England Tourist Board. It markets itself as **Visit the Heart of England**, or simply **Visit the Heart**.

G   Herefordshire, Shropshire, Staffordshire, Warwickshire, Worcestershire, West Midlands.

✍   For further information see **English Regional Tourist Boards.**

Tower Hamlets Housing Action Trust

✍   Wound up in 2005 upon completion of its programme.

Trade & Business Development Body

■   Old Gasworks Business Park, Kilmorey Street, NEWRY, Co Down, BT34 2DE.
    Tel 028 3083 4100   **Fax** 028 3083 4155   http://www.intertradeireland.com
    Chairman: Dr David Dobbin, CBE   Chief Executive: Liam Nellis

E   Set up in 1999, one of the six North/South Implementation Bodies established under the British-Irish Agreement of 8 March 1999. Operating under the name of **InterTradeIreland**, it is responsible to the North South Ministerial Council (qv), the Department Culture, Art & Leisure Northern Ireland and the Irish Government. The board comprises twelve members including the Chairman.

R   To enhance the global competitiveness of the all-island economy to the mutual benefit Northern Ireland and the Irish Republic.

G   Northern Ireland, Republic of Ireland.

✍   For further information see **North South Ministerial Council**.

Trade & Investment   See **United Kingdom Trade & Investment**.

TRAFFIC COMMISSIONERS
Senior Traffic Commissioner: Philip Brown

E   Seven Traffic Commissioners are appointed by the Secretary of State for Transport to champion safe, fair and reliable passenger and goods transport in their areas.

R   They are responsible for:
    The licencing of the operators of Heavy Goods Vehicles (HGVs) and of buses and coaches (Public Service Vehicles / PSVs)
    The registration of local bus services
    Granting vocational licences and taking action against drivers of HGVs and PSVs.
    The Scottish Traffic Commissioner is responsible, in addition, for dealing with appeals against:
    Decisions by Scottish local authorities on taxi fares
    Charging and removing improperly parked vehicles in Edinburgh and Glasgow.

G   England, Wales, Scotland.

●   Eastern Traffic Commissioner: Richard Turfitt
       City House, 126-130 Hills Road, CAMBRIDGE, CB2 1NP.
    North Eastern Traffic Commissioner: Tom Macartney
       Hillcrest House, 386 Harehills Lane, LEEDS, LS9 6NF.
    North Western Traffic Commissioner: Beverley Bell
       Suite 4, Stone Cross Place, Golborne, WARRINGTON, WA3 2SH.
    Scottish Traffic Commissioner: Joan Aitken
       Level 6, The Stamp Office, 10 Waterloo Place, EDINBURGH, EH1 3EG.
    South Eastern & Metropolitan Traffic Commissioner: Philip Brown
       Ivy House, 3 Ivy Terrace, EASTBOURNE, BN21 4QT.
    West Midlands & Welsh Traffic Commissioner: Nick Jones
       38 George Road, Edgbaston, BIRMINGHAM, B15 1PL.
    Western Traffic Commissioner: Sarah Bell
       2 Rivergate, Temple Quay, BRISTOL, BS1 6EH.

Traffic Committee for London
✍ See **London Councils Transport & Environment Committee**.

Training & Development Agency for Schools   (TDA)
■ Piccadilly Gate, Store Street, MANCHESTER, M1 2WD.
   Tel 0870 496 0123   http://www.tda.gov.uk
   Chairman: Christopher Baker, MBE   Chief Executive: Graham Holley
E Established on 1 September 2005, taking on the functions of the former Teacher Training Agency and National
   Remodelling Team. TDA functions as an Executive NDPB of the Department for Education (DfE) and works
   closely with the Department for Business, Innovation & Skills. The Agency's Chief Executive is supported by an
   18-strong strategic leadership team.
R To secure an effective school workforce that improves children's life chances.
G United Kingdom.
✍ On 24 November 2010 the Secretary of State for Education announced his intention to transfer the functions of
   TDA to an executive agency of DfE.

Transforming Telford
✍ An urban regeneration company established on 26 July 2007, its functions were transferred to Telford & Wrekin
   Council in April 2010 and there branded as One Telford.

Translink   See **Northern Ireland Transport Holding Company**.

Transport for London Authority   (TfL)
■ Windsor House, 42-50 Victoria Street, LONDON, SW1H 0NL.
   Tel 020 7222 5600   http://www.tfl.gov.uk
   Chairman: Boris Johnson
   Transport Commissioner for London: Peter Hendy, CBE
E Established on 3 July 2000 following the formation of the Greater London Authority (qv). TfL is directly responsible
   to the Mayor of London at the GLA.
R To be responsible for the capital's transport system and, as such, to put the Mayor of London's Transport
   Strategy into action and manage transport services across London.
G London.
✍ Part of the GLA Group - see **Greater London Authority** for more details.

Transport Scotland
■ Buchanan House, 58 Port Dundas Road, GLASGOW, G4 0HF.
   Tel 0141 272 7100   http://www.transportscotland.gov.uk
   Chief Executive: David Middleton
E Launched in January 2006. Scottish Transport is an Agency of the Scottish Executive Enterprise, Transport &
   Lifelong Learning Department. The management board comprises nine persons including the Chief Executive.
R To ensure that Scotland's trunk road and railway systems are managed efficiently, effectively and economically.
   To establish and run national concessionary travel schemes.
   To deliver the Scottish Government's committed programme of enhancements to Scotland's rail and trunk road
   infrastructure.
   To help to build Scotland's National Transport Strategy by advising Ministers on investment priorities for
   tomorrow's rail and trunk road networks.
G Scotland.

Transport Training Services   (TTS)
■ 15 Dundrod Road, Nutts Corner, CRUMLIN, Co Antrim, BT29 4SS.
   Tel 028 9082 5653   **Fax** 028 9082 5689   http://www.transport-training.co.uk
E Established in 1992.
R To promote and provide training for individuals and companies involved in the motor vehicle, road haulage and
   passenger transport industries.
G Northern Ireland.

Transport Tribunal
✍ Since September 2009 **First-tier Tribunal (Transport)**.

Treasure Valuation Committee   (TVC)

■ Department for Portable Antiquities, British Museum, Great Russell Street, LONDON, WC1B 3DG.
   Tel 020 7323 8243
   Chairman: Prof Norman Palmer, CBE, QC
E Established in September 1997 under the Treasure Act 1996. TVC functions as an Advisory NDPB of the
   Department for Culture, Media & Sport, resposible to the British Museum since March 2007. The Committee
   comprises eight members including the Chairman.
R To provide independent advice to government on the fair market value of declared treasure finds which museums
   wish to acquire from the Crown.
G England, Wales, Northern Ireland.

Treasury Solicitor's Department   (TSol)

■ One Kemble Street, LONDON, WC2B 4TS.
   Tel 020 7210 3000   http://www.tsol.gov.uk
   Chief Executive: Paul Jenkins, QC
E Established on 1 April 1996. TSol functions as an Executive Agency acting under the remit of the Attorney
   General. The Chief Executive is formally titled Her Majesty's Procurator General & Treasury Solicitor.
R To provide legal advice and litigation services to Government departments and publicly funded bodies in England
   and Wales, and to deal with Bona Vacantia (property with no known owner).
G England, Wales.

The Tree Council

■ 71 Newcomen Street, London, SE1 1YT.
   Tel 020 7407 9992   Fax 020 7407 9908   http://www.treecouncil.org.uk
   Director-General: Pauline Buchanan Black
E Established in 1974 with Government backing. The Council is an umbrella body and functions as a registered
   charity. Members range from voluntary and community organisations and NDPBs to local authorities and key
   government departments, all concerned with trees, biodiversity and the environment in general.
R To develop channels for dialogue and cooperation between professionals within the wide membership, to
   mobilise the sector to develop and influence policy, to enhance performance within the tree sector, and to
   improve communications between organisations to prevent isolation and maximise impact.
G United Kingdom.

Trent Strategic Health Authority
✍ On 1 July 2006 merged with the Leicestershire, Northamptonshire & Rutland Strategic Health Authority to form
   the **East Midlands Strategic Health Authority**.

Tribiwnlys Prisio Cymru   See **Valuation Tribunal for Wales**.

Tribunal Procedure Committee

■ Area 2/38, 2nd Floor, 102 Petty France, LONDON, SW1H 9AJ.
   Tel 020 3334 6556   Fax 020 3334 6578   http://www.tribunals.gov.uk
   Chairman: Mr Justice Paul Walker
E Established on 19 May 2008 under the Tribunals, Courts & Enforcement Act 2007. It functions as an Advisory
   NDPB of the Ministry of Justice. The Committee comprises eleven members including the Chairman.
R To make rules governing practice and procedure in both tiers of tribunals in HM Courts & Tribunals Service (qv).
G England, Wales, Scotland.

Tribunals Service
R The Tribunals, Courts & Enforcement Act 2007 created a new two-tier Tribunal system, First-tier and Upper, both
   of which are organised into Chambers.
   Each Chamber comprises similar jurisdictions or jurisdictions which bring together similar types of experts to hear
   appeals.
   The Upper Tribunal primarily, but not exclusively, reviews and decides appeals arising from a First-tier Tribunal.
   There are 27 hearing venues in England, four in Scotland and one in Wales.
   There are six administrative centres in England and one each in Scotland and Wales.
● **First-tier Tribunal** (qv)
      General Regulatory Chamber
         First-tier Tribunal (Charity)
         First-tier Tribunal (Claims Management Services)
         First-tier Tribunal (Consumer Credit)

© CBD Research Ltd · Beckenham · Kent BR3 5JS · Tel 020 8650 7745 · Fax 020 8650 0768 · E-mail cbd@cbdresearch.com · www.cbdresearch.com

First-tier Tribunal (Environment)
First-tier Tribunal (Estate Agents)
First-tier Tribunal (Gambling)
First-tier Tribunal (Immigration Services)
First-tier Tribunal (Information Rights)
First-tier Tribunal (Local Government Standards in England)
First-tier Tribunal (Transport)
Health, Education & Social Care Chamber
First-tier Tribunal (Care Standards)
First-tier Tribunal (Mental Health)
First-tier Tribunal (Special Educational Needs & Disability)
First-tier Tribunal (Primary Health Lists)
Immigration & Asylum Chamber
First-tier Tribunal (Immigration & Asylum Chamber)
Social Entitlement Chamber
First-tier Tribunal (Asylum Support)
First-tier Tribunal (Social Security & Child Support)
First-tier Tribunal (Criminal Injuries Compensation)
Tax Chamber
First-tier Tribunal (Tax)
War Pensions & Armed Forces Compensation Chamber
First-tier Tribunal (War Pensions & Armed Forces Compensation)
Upper Tribunal (qv)
Upper Tribunal (Immigration & Asylum Chamber)
corresponding First-tier Tribunal: Immigration & Asylum Chamber
Upper Tribunal (Tax & Chancery)
corresponding First-tier Tribunals: Charity, Tax
Upper Tribunal (Administrative Appeals)
corresponding First-tier Tribunals: all except the above
Upper Tribunal (Lands Chamber).
✎ On 1 April 2011, this and HM Courts Service became a single, unified organisation, **HM Courts & Tribunals Service**.

Trinity House   See **Corporation of Trinity House Deptford Strond**.

Tweed Foundation   See **Rivers & Fisheries Trusts of Scotland**.

Tyne & Wear Integrated Transport Authority   (ITA)
■   Civic Centre, NEWCASTLE UPON TYNE, NE99 2BN.
Tel 0191 232 8520   http://www.twita.gov.uk
Chairman: Cllr David Wood
E   Established in 1986 under the Local Government Act 1985 and known as the Tyne & Wear Passenger Transport Authority until renamed on 9 February 2009 under the Local Transport Act 2008. The Authority comprises 16 Councillors who are appointed by the five Metropolitan District Councils that make up Tyne & Wear.
G   Tyne & Wear.
✎   For further information see **Passenger Transport Executives & Integrated Transport Authorities**.

Tyne & Wear Passenger Transport Executive   Operates under the brand name **Nexus**.

U

Ufi Ltd
■   Dearing House, 1 Young Street, SHEFFIELD, S Yorks, S1 4UP.
Tel 0114 291 5000   Fax 0114 291 5001   http://www.ufi.com
Chairman: John Weston   Chief Executive: Sarah Jones

E　　Established in 1998 in response to the New Labour concept of a University for Industry. The Board comprises twelve members including the Chairman.
R　　To use new technology to transform the delivery of learning and skills.
　　　In 2000 Ufi launched **learndirect** which has become the UK's leading online learning provider.
G　　England, Wales, Northern Ireland.
●　　Ufi operates in Wales, Northern Ireland and all nine England regions.

Ughdarras nan Croitearan　　See **Crofters' Commission**.

Uiscebhealaí Éireann　　See **Waterways Ireland**.

UK. . .
✍　　See **United Kingdom** - all bodies whose names begin with UK or United Kingdom are printed and filed as United Kingdom to avoid any confusion generated by two separate sequences.

Ulster American Folk Park　　See **National Museums Northern Ireland**.

Ulster Folk & Transport Museum　　See **National Museums Northern Ireland**.

Ulster Museum　　See **National Museums Northern Ireland**.

Ulster-Scots Agency
■　　68-72 Great Victoria Street, BELFAST, BT2 7BB.
　　　Tel 028 9023 1113　**Fax** 028 9023 1898　http://www.ulsterscotsagency.com
　　　Chairman: Tom Scott, OBE　Interim Chief Executive: Hazel Campbell
E　　Established on 2 December 1999. The Agency is responsible to the North/South Language Body (qv). The board comprises seven members including the Chairman.
R　　To promote the study, conservation, development and use of Ulster-Scots as a living language, within the island of Ireland and beyond.
　　　To encourage and develop the full range of its attendant culture.
　　　To promote an understanding of the history of the Ulster-Scots.
G　　Northern Ireland, Republic of Ireland.
✍　　For further information see the **North/South Language Body**.
=　　Tha Boord o Ulstèr-Scotch

Ulster Supported Employment Ltd　　(USEL)
■　　182-188 Cambrai Street, BELFAST, BT13 3JH.
　　　Tel 028 9035 6600　**Fax** 028 9035 6611　http://www.usel.co.uk
　　　Chairman: Patrick Bogues　Chief Executive: Sam Humphries
E　　Established on 16 March 1962. USEL is a registered charity and functions as an Executive NDPB of the Department for Employment & Learning Northern Ireland. The Board comprises five persons including the Chairman.
R　　To provide supported paid employment for disabled people.
G　　Northern Ireland.

Union Modernisation Fund
✍　　UMF's Supervisory Board was abolished in July 2010 following the announcement that no further rounds of the UMF (established in 2004) would be held.

United Kingdom Accreditation Service　　(UKAS)
■　　21-47 High Street, FELTHAM, Middx, TW13 4UN.
　　　Tel 020 8917 8400　**Fax** 020 8917 8500　http://www.ukas.com
　　　Chairman: Lord Lindsay　Chief Executive: Paul Stennett, MBE

E   Established in August 1995 by the merger of the National Accreditation Council for Certification Bodies and the National Measurement Accreditation Service. UKAS functions as a non-profit distributing private company limited by guarantee, it is appointed as the national accreditation body by the Accreditation Regulations 2009, and operates under a Memorandum of Understanding with the Government through the Secretary of State for Business, Innovation & Skills. The Board comprises nine members including the Chairman.

R   To assess, against internationally agreed standards, organisations that provide certification, testing, inspection and calibration services. Certification by UKAS demonstrates the competence, impartiality and performance capability of these evaluators.

G   United Kingdom.

United Kingdom Advisory Panel for healthcare workers infected with bloodborne viruses   (UKAP)

■   61 Colindale Avenue, LONDON, NW9 5EQ.
Tel 020 8327 6074
Chairman: Mrs Isabel Boyer

E   Established in December 1991. UKAP functions as a Scientific Advisory Committee and is accountable to Department of Health through the Health Protection Agency (qv). The Panel comprises 22 members including the Chairman.

R   To establish, and update as necessary, criteria on which local advice on modifying working practices may be based.

To provide supplementary specialist occupational advice to physicians of healthcare workers infected with bloodborne viruses, occupational physicians and professional bodies.

To advise individual healthcare workers or their advocates on how to obtain guidance on working practices.

G   United Kingdom.

●   The Panel liaises closely with the Advisory Group on Hepatitis and the Expert Advisory Group on AIDS (qqv).

✍   For further information see **Scientific Advisory Committees**.

United Kingdom Airprox Board   (UKAB)

■   RAF Northolt, West End Road, RUISLIP, Middx, HA4 6NG.
Tel 020 8842 9051   Fax 020 8842 6056   http://www.airproxboard.org.uk

E   Established on 1 January 1999 by the Ministry of Defence and the Civil Aviation Authority (qv). The Board comprises 15 members including representatives from eight civiliam and six military disciplines.

R   To provide impartial, professional and timely assessments to the highest standards on cause and risk for all Airprox reported in UK airspace.

To make safety recommendations when appropriate, aimed at reducing the liklihood of a recurrence of any given Airprox event.

To identify, analyse and alert the CAA and the MoD to the prime causal factors of Airprox.

G   United Kingdom.

United Kingdom Anti-Doping Ltd

■   Oceanic House, 1a Cockspur Street, LONDON, SW1Y 5BG.
Tel 020 7766 7350   Fax 020 7766 7351   http://www.ukad.org.uk
Chairman: David Kenworthy, QPM, DL   Chief Executive: Andy Parkinson

E   Established in 2007. Trading as **UK Anti-Doping**, it functions as company limited by guarantee and an Executive NDPB of the Department for Culture, Media & Sport. The Board comprises seven members including the Chairman.

R   To implement and manage the UK's anti-doping policy.

G   United Kingdom.

United Kingdom Atomic Energy Authority

■   Culham Science Centre, ABINGDON, Oxon, OX14 3DB.
Tel 01235 528822   http://www.uk-atomic-energy.org.uk
Chairman: Prof Roger Cashmore   Chief Executive: Prof Steven Cowley
Shareholder Executive contact: Richard Ramsay

E   Established in July 1954 under the Atomic Energy Authority Act 1954 (as amended by the Atomic Energy Authority Acts 1959 & 1971), the functions of the Authority were extended by the Science & Technology Act 1965. The Authority functions as an Executive NDPB of the Department for Business, Innovation & Skills. The board comprises twelve members including the Chairman.

R   To carry out research into fusion power.

G   United Kingdom.

✍   One of the businesses managed by the **Shareholder Executive**.

Since the sale of UKAEA Ltd to Babcock International in October 2009, the Authority no longer carries out decommissioning or consulting in other nuclear areas.

United Kingdom Automatic Control Council   (UKACC)

- Michael Faraday House, Six Hills Way, STEVENAGE, Herts, SG1 2AY.
  Tel 01438 767295   Fax 01438 767305   http://www.ukacc.group.shef.ac.uk
  Chairman: Prof Sarah Spurgeon   Hon Secretary: Janine Mitchell
- E UKACC is the UK's national member organisation of the International Federation of Automatic Control. The Executive Committee comprises 21 members including the Chairman.
- R To act as an effectiive link between the UK and the international automatic control communities.
- G United Kingdom.

United Kingdom Biodiversity Partnership Standing Committee

- Defra, Nobel House, 17 Smith Square, LONDON, SW1P 3JR.
  Tel 020 7238 6000   http://www.ukbap.org.uk
- E Established in 2002. The Committee functions as an informal stakeholder group of the Department for Environment, Food & Rural Affairs.
- R To guide and support the UK Biodiversity Partnership in implementing the UK Biodiversity Action Plan:
  to develop and enforce a national strategy and associated action plan to identify, conserve and protect existing biological diversity and to enhance it wherever possible.
- G United Kingdom.

United Kingdom Border Agency

- Lunar House, 40 Wellesley Road, CROYDON, Surrey, CR9 2BY.
  Tel 0870 606 7766   http://www.bia.homeoffice.gov.uk
  Chief Executive: Lin Homer, CB
- E The Agency was established in April 2008. It brings together the work previously carried out by the Border & Immigration Agency, customs detection work carried out at the border by from HM Revenue & Customs and UK Visa Services fro the Foreign & Commonwealth Office. The Agency's board comprises 14 members including the Chief Executive.
- R To improve the United Kingdom's security through stronger border protection while welcoming legitimate travellers and trade.
- G United Kingdom.

United Kingdom Bridges Board   (UKBB)

- 119 Britannia Walk, LONDON, N1 7JE.
  Tel 020 7336 1584   Fax 020 7336 1556   http://www.ukroadliaisongroup.org/bridges/
  Chairman: Greg Perks
- E Established in 2001. UKBB functions as an Advisory NDPB of the Department for Transport. The Board comprises 19 members including the Chairman.
- R To bring together national and local government from across the UK to consider engineering matters regarding bridges and other highway structures.
- G United Kingdom.
- ✍ The Board reports to the United Kingdom Roads Liaison Group (qv).

United Kingdom Business Incubation   (UKBI)

- Faraday Wharf, Holt Street, Birmingham Science Park Aston, BIRMINGHAM, B7 4BB.
  Tel 0121 250 3538   Fax 0121 250 3542   http://www.ukbi.co.uk
  Chairman: Graham Ross Russell   Chief Executive: Malcolm Buckler
- E Established in 1998. UKBI functions as an Advisory NDPB of the Department for Business, Innovation & Skills. The Board of Directors comprises 17 mmbers including the Chairman.
- R To provide a nurturing, instructive and supportive environment for entrepreneurs during the critical stages of starting a new business.
- G United Kingdom.

United Kingdom Central Authority   (UKCA)

- 5th Floor, Fry Building, 2 Marsham Street, LONDON, SW1P 4DF.
  Tel 020 7035 4040   Fax 020 7035 6985
- E Established in 1991 when Part 1 of the Criminal Justice (International Cooperation) Act 1990 came into force. UKCA is part of the Home Office.
- R To handle Mutual Legal Assistance (MLA) casework and review MLA legislation and policy.
- G United Kingdom.
- ✍ Mutual Legal Assistance (MLA) is the formal way in which countries request and provide assistance in obtaining evidence located in one country to assist in criminal investigations or proceedings in another.

United Kingdom Central Council for Nursing, Midwifery & Health Visiting
✍ See the **Nursing & Midwifery Council**.

United Kingdom Certification Authority for Reinforcing Steels   (CARES)
■   Pembroke House, 21 Pembroke Road, SEVENOAKS, Kent, TN13 1XR.
    Tel 01732 450000   **Fax** 01732 455917   http://www.ukcares.com
    Chairman: Prof Les Clark
E   Established in 1983. CARES functions as an independent, not for profit certification body accredited by the UK
    Accreditation Service (qv). Members of the board of management are nominated by the members of the
    Authority.
R   To offer certification schemes for companies that produce materials, components, or offer services, primarily in
    the reinforced concrete industry.
G   United Kingdom.
●   Members: Association of Consulting Engineers, BAA plc, British Association Reinforcement, the Civil Engineering
    Contractors Association, CONSTRUCT, Construction Confederation, Highways Agency (qv), Institution of
    Structural Engineers, Post-tensioning Association, Southern Water, and UK Steel Association.

United Kingdom Chemicals Stakeholder Forum   (CSF)
■   Area 2A, Nobel House, 17 Smith Square, LONDON, SW1P 3JR.
    Tel 020 7238 1579
    Chairman: Christopher Hughes
E   Set up in September 2000 following the development of the UK Chemical Strategy in December 1999. CSF
    functions as a stakeholder group of the Department for Environment, Food Rural Affairs. The Forum has 21
    members drawn from industry and various organisations.
R   To advise the Government on how industry should reduce the risks from hazardous chemicals to the environment
    and to human health through the environment.
G   United Kingdom.   The work of the Forum does not cover the chemicals found in pesticides - for these see the
    Pesticides Forum.

United Kingdom Commission for Employment & Skills   (UKCES)
■   28-30 Grosvenor Gardens, LONDON, SW1W 0TT.
    Tel 020 7881 8900   **Fax** 020 7881 8999   http://www.ukces.org.uk
    3 Callflex Business Park, Golden Smithies Lane, WATH-UPON-DEARNE, S Yorks, S63 7ER.**Tel** 01709
    774800   **Fax** 01709 774801
    Chairman: Charlie Mayfield   Interim Chief Executive: Michael Davis
E   Established on 1 April 2008 on the recommendation of Lord Leitch's 2006 Review of Skills, it replaced the
    merged Sector Skills Development Agency and National Employment Panel. UKCES functions as an Executive
    NDPB of the Department for Business, Innovation & Skills, Department for Work & Pensions, HM Treasury,
    Department for Education, and the devolved administrations. The Commission comprises 20 members
    including the Chairman.
R   To assess annually UK progress towards becoming a world-class leader in employment and skills by 2020,
    consistent of the aims and priorities of the four nations.
    To advise the highest levels of Government on policies and delivery that will contribute to increased jobs, skills
    and productivity.
    To monitor the contribution and challenge the performance of each part of the UK employment and skills systems
    in meeting the needs of employers and individuals, and recommend improvements in policy, delivery and
    innovation.
    To promote greater employer engagement, influence and investment in workforce development.
    To fund and manage the performance of the Sector Skills Councils as key industry leaders in skills and
    employment.
G   United Kingdom.
●   The Commission oversees the Investment in People and the Sector Skills Councils (qqv) networks.

United Kingdom Council on Deafness
■   Westwood Park, London Road, Little Horkesley, COLCHESTER, Essex, CO6 4BS.
    Tel 01206 274075   **Fax** 01206 274077   http://www.deafcouncil.org.uk
    Chairman: Susan Daniels
E   Established on 25 April 1994. The Council is a membership organisation restricted to charities and organisations
    working in the field of deafness; it functions as a registered charity and company limited by guarantee. The
    Board comprises nine members including the Chairman.
R   To work with and for deaf organisations in the UK by providing information, advice and support and by
    representing the views of the sector to government and policy makers.
G   United Kingdom.

United Kingdom Council for International Student Affairs   (UKCISA)
- 9-17 St Albans Place, LONDON, N1 0NX.
  Tel 020 7288 4330   **Fax** 020 7288 4360   http://www.ukcisa.org.uk
  Chairman: Prof Christine Hallett
- E   Established in 1968 as the UK Council for Overseas Student Affairs; it merged in 1994 with the Council for International Education. UKCISA is a registered charity and company limited by guarantee; it is partly funded by the Department for Business, Innovation & Skills. The Board of Trustees comprises 15 members including the Chairman.
- R   To promote and facilitate international student mobility to and from the UK; to help students and others involved in international education develop a global perspective; and to contribute to human development, political stability, economic prosperity and greater intercultural understanding.
- G   United Kingdom.

United Kingdom Council for Psychotherapy   (UKCP)
- 2nd Floor, Edward House, 2 Wakley Street, LONDON, EC1V 7LT.
  Tel 020 7014 9955   **Fax** 020 7014 9977   http://www.psychotherapy.org.uk
  Chairman: Andrew Samuels
- E   Established in January 1993. UKCP is a registered charity. The Executive Committee comprises nine members including the Chairman.
- R   To promote and maintain the profession of psychotherapy and high standards in the practice of psychotherapy for the benefit of the public.
- G   United Kingdom.

United Kingdom Debt Management Office   (DMO)
- Eastcheap Court, 11 Philpot Lane, LONDON, EC3M 8UD.
  Tel 0845 357 6500   **Fax** 0845 357 6509   http://www.dmo.gov.uk
  Chief Executive: Robert Stheeman
- E   Established on 5 April 1998. DMO functions as an Executive Agency of the Treasury.
- R   To carry out the Government's debt management policy of minimising its financing costs over the long term, taking account of risk, and to minimise the cost of offsetting the Government's net cash flow over time, while operating in a risk appetite approved by Ministers in both cases.
- G   United Kingdom.
- ●   The DMO receives assistance in its day-to-day operations from the Public Works Loan Board (qv).

United Kingdom Disabled People's Council   (UKDPC)
- Stratford Advice Arcade, 107-109 The Grove, LONDON, E15 1HP.
  Tel 020 8522 7433   http://www.ukdpc.net
  Acting Chairman: Julie Newman   Chief Executive: Jaspal Dhani
- E   Established on 7 November 1981 by six groups of disabled people and known as the British Council (of Organisations) for Disabled People until a recent change of name. The UKDPC is the UK umbrella of disabled people's organisations and functions as a registered charity. The Board of Trustees comprises nine members including the Chairman.
- R   To campaign for equal rights and justice for disabled people.
- G   United Kingdom.

United Kingdom Film Council
- ✍   On 1 April 2011, UKFC's responsibilities for ensuring that the economic, cultural and educational aspects of film are effectively represented at home and abroad transferred to the **British Film Institute**, which took on the role of Lottery distributor for film funding, and**Film London**.

United Kingdom Flight Safety Committee   (UKFSC)
- Graham Suite, Fairoaks Airport, CHOBHAM, Surrey, GU24 8HX.
  Tel 01276 855193   **Fax** 01276 855195   http://www.ukfsc.co.uk
  Chairman: Captain Tony Wride   Chief Executive: Air Cdre Rich Jones, CBE
- E   Established in July 1959 by the then Minister of Aviation. UKFSC functions as an independent body. The Committee comprises the Chairman and 50 other members who represent aircraft operators, manufacturers, insurers, aviation authorities and professional associations in the aviation field.
- R   To improve commercial aviation safety.
- G   United Kingdom.

United Kingdom-wide Food Hygiene Ratings Steering Group
- ■ Aviation House, 125 Kingsway, LONDON, WC2B 6NH.
  Tel 020 7276 8000   Fax 020 7276 8004
  Chairman: Steven Esom
- E Established following a meeting of the board of the Food Standards Agency (qv) held on 10 December 2008. It functions as an Advisory NDPB of the FSA. The Group comprises thirteen members including the Chairman.
- R To provide advice and guidance to the FSA on the implementation and operation of the national Food Hygiene Rating Scheme (FHRS) for England, Wales and Northern Ireland and the Food Hygiene Information Scheme (FHIS) being rolled out in Scotland, with a view to shared learning and communality of approach as far as possible.
- G United Kingdom.
- ● Local Authority enforcement officers are responsible for inspecting food businesses to ensure that they meet the legal requirements on food hygiene. Under SotD schemes, each food outlet is given a hygiene rating or score that reflects the inspection findings.

United Kingdom Government Decontamination Service
- ✍ Established on 1 October 2005, GDS became part of the **Food & Environment Research Agency** on 1 April 2009. Also known as the Government Decontamination Service.

United Kingdom Hydrographic Office   (UKHO)
- ■ Admiralty Way, TAUNTON, Somerset, TA1 2DN.
  Tel 01823 337900   Fax 01823 284077   http://www.ukho.gov.uk
  Chairman: Sandra Rogers   Chief Executive: Mike Robinson   Shareholder Executive contact: Peter Shortt
- E Established on 6 April 1990. UKHO functions as an Executive Agency of the Ministry of Defence.
- R To produce charts and navigational publications for the Royal Navy, and for commercial and private customers.
- G United Kingdom.
- ✍ One of the businesses managed by the **Shareholder Executive**.
  Also known as the Hydrographic Office.

United Kingdom-India Round Table   (UKIRT)
- ■ Foreign & Commonwealth Office, King Charles Street, LONDON, SW1A 2AH.
  Co-Chairmen: Lord Patten of Barnes and Nitin Desai
- E Established in April 2000 by the British and Indian Foreign Ministers. It functions as an Advisory NDPB of the Foreign & Commonwealth Office. The Round Table comprises about 30 senior people, drawn equally from both countries, and meets annually, alternating between UK and India.
- R To discuss issues that may affect the the bilateral relationship and to reflect on ways in which it can be strengthened.
- G United Kingdom, India.
- ✍ The Foreign & Commonwealth Office announced on 14 October 2010 that the future of UKIRT was under consideration.

United Kingdom Lighting Board   (UKLB)
- ■ 119 Britannia Walk, LONDON, N1 7JE.
  Tel 020 7336 1584   Fax 020 7336 1556   http://www.ukroadliaisongroup.org/lighting/
  Chairman: Dana Skelley
- E Established in 2001. UKLB functions as an Advisory NDPB of the Department for Transport. The Board comprises 15 members including the Chairman.
- R To bring together national and local government from across the UK to consider street lighting matters.
- G United Kingdom.
- ✍ The Board reports to the United Kingdom Roads Liaison Group (qv).

United Kingdom National Influenza Pandemic Committee   (UKNIPC)
- ■ Richmond House, 79 Whitehall, LONDON, SW1A 2NS.
  Tel 020 7210 4850
  Chairman: Prof Dame Sally Davies
- E Established in 2005. UKNIPC functions as an Advisory NDPB of the Department of Health. The Committee is chaired by the Chief Medical Officer and has 26 members.
- R To provide specialist advice to the UK Health Departments on the health response during an influenza pandemic.
- G United Kingdom.
- ✍ The Committee met on four occasions in 2005/6.

United Kingdom National Screening Committee   (NSC)

■ Centre Block G, Imperial College Mint Wing, South Wharf Road, LONDON, W2 1NY.
   Tel 020 7717 6000   http://www.nsc.nhs.uk
   Chairman: Dr Harry Burns
E Established in 1996. NSC functions as an Advisory NDPB of the Department for Health. The Committee
      comprises 21 members including the Chairman.
R To advise Ministers, the devolved national assemblies and the Scottish Parliament on the care for implementing
      new population screening programmes not presently purchased by the NHS within each of the countries of the
      UK.
G United Kingdom.
✍ Also known as the National Screening Committee.

United Kingdom Network Management Board   (NMB)

■ 119 Britannia Walk, LONDON, N1 7JE.
   Tel 020 7336 1584   **Fax** 020 7336 1556   http://www.ukroadliaisongroup.org/traffic/
   Chairman: Derek Turner
E Established in 2002. NMB functions as an Advisory NDPB of the Department for Transport. The Board comprises
      16 members including the Chairman.
R To bring together national and local government from across the UK to provide oversight for the implementation
      of transport policy relating to the UK road network.
   To promote safe and efficient network management, seeking a better understanding of congestion and the effect
      of interventions on the network, and by enouraging innovation, adoption of good practice, coordination between
      stakeholders and information exchange.
G United Kingdom.
✍ The Board reports to the United Kingdom Roads Liaison Group (qv).

UNITED KINGDOM PARLIAMENT: Committees

E The many committees that sit within the UK Parliament may be defined in five broad categories:
   1. Commons Select Committees:
   There is a Select Committee for each Government Department, including the Northern Ireland, Scotland and
      Wales Offices, to examine its administration, expenditure and policy.
   Eight Regional Committees, one for each of England's administrative regions outside London, were established
      on 1 January 2009 to examine regional strategies and the work of regional bodies.
   The remaining 18 Select Committees examine:
   Administration; The Armed Forces Bill; Arms Export Controls; Environmental Audit; European Scrutiny; Finance &
      Services; Liaison; Members' Allowances; Modernisation of the House of Commons; Privilege (Police Searches
      on the Parliamentary Estate); Procedure; Public Accounts; Public Administration; Reform of the House of
      Commons; Regulatory Reform; Science & Technology; Standards & Privileges; and Statutory Instruments.
   2. Lords Select Committees:
   The EU Select Committee considers European Union documents and other matters relating to the EU; it has
      seven sub-committees: Economic & Financial Affairs & International Trade (Sub-Committee A); Internal Market
      (B); Foreign Affairs, Defence & Development Policy (C); Environment & Agriculture (D); Law & Institutions (E);
      Home Affairs (F); and Social Policy & Consumer Affairs (G).
   A further 15 Select Committees consider:
   Administration & Works; Communications; Constitution; Delegated Powers & Regulatory Reform; Economic
      Affairs (with a Finance Bill Sub-Committee); House; Hybrid Instruments; Information; Liaison; Merits of Statutory
      Instruments; Privileges; Procedure; Refreshment; Science & Technology; and Selection.
R **3. Joint Committees**:
   Currently five in number, they are the Joint Committees on the Draft Bribery Bill, on Consolidation &c Bills, on
      Human Rights, on Statutory Instruments, and on Tax Law Rewrite Bills.
G **4. General Committees**:
   These comprise
   Public Bill Committees (conduct detailed examination of Bills before Parliament)
   Delegated Legislation Committees (consider Statutory Instruments)
   European Committees (examine EU documents and matters remitted to them by the House)
   Grand Committees (focus of regional issues)
   Second Reading Committees (a formal alternative to a second reading on the Floor of the House).
● **5: Other Committees**:
   Administration Estimate Audit Committee, Advisory Committee on Works of Art, Chairmen's Panel, Court of
      Referees, Ecclesiastical Committee, House of Lords Audit Committee, House of Lords Leader's Group, Joint
      Committee on Security, Members Estimate Committee (and its Audit Committee), Public Accounts Commission,
      Speaker's Committee on the Electoral Commission, Speaker's Committee for the Independent Parliamentary
      Standards Authority, Speaker's Conference (on Parliamentary Representation), and Standing Orders Committee.
✍ See also Introduction.

United Kingdom Passport Service
✍ Since 1 April 2006 the **Identity & Passport Service**.

United Kingdom Roads Board
■ 119 Britannia Walk, LONDON, N1 7JE.
  Tel 020 7336 1584   Fax 020 7336 1556   http://www.ukroadliaisongroup.org/roads/
  Chairman: Matthew Lugg
E Established in 2001. It functions as an Advisory NDPB of the Department for Transport. The Board comprises 14 members including the Chairman.
R To bring together national and local government from across the UK to consider carriageway and footway engineering matters.
G United Kingdom.
● The Board has three sub-groups: the Asset Management Group, the Footway & Cycle Track Management Group and the Pavement Condition Management Group.
✍ The Board reports to the United Kingdom Roads Liaison Group (qv).

United Kingdom Roads Liaison Group   (UKRLG)
■ 119 Britannia Walk, LONDON, N1 7JE.
  Tel 020 7336 1584   Fax 020 7336 1556   http://www.ukroadliaisongroup.org
  Chairman: John Dowie
E Established in 2001. UKRLG functions as an Advisory NDPB of the Department for Transport. The Group comprises eleven members including the Chairman who is head of the DfT's Regional & Local Transport Delivery Directorate.
R To provide all national and local governments across the UK with comment, guidance and advice on strategic policy and management of highways, addressing issues of safety, accessibility, congestion, environment, economy and efficiency.
G United Kingdom.
● UKRLG is the umbrella body for:
  UK Bridges Board
  UK Lighting Board
  UK Network Management Board and
  UK Roads Board (qqv).

United Kingdom Scientific Diving Supervisory Committee   See **Scientific Diving Supervisory Committee**.

United Kingdom Security & Resilience Industry Suppliers' Community   (RISC)
■ Salamanca Square, 9 Albert Embankment, LONDON, SE1 7SP.
  Tel 020 7091 4517   Fax 020 7091 4545   http://www.riscuk.org
  Chairman: appointed annually   Secretary: Derek Marshall
E Established in 2006. RISC is an alliance of industry, trade associations and think tanks.
R To help Government and the Critical National Infrastructure deliver a more secure and safe environment for UK citizens.
G United Kingdom.

United Kingdom Skills
■ 3rd Floor, 36 Queen Street, LONDON, EC4R 1BN.
  Tel 020 7429 2800   http://www.ukskills.org.uk
  Chairman: Chris Humphries, CBE   Chief Executive: Geoff Russell
E Established in 1990, in 2010 it became part of the Skills Funding Agency (qv). UK Skills functions as a company limited by guarantee and a registered charity. The board comprises ten members including the Chairman.
R To oversee WorldSkills UK, the UK's premier skills competitions.
  To manage the UK team entry to EuroSkills and WorldSkills, the world's biggest skills competition.
  To manage the National Training Awards which celebrate exemplary training in the workplace.
  To raise the performance of education and skills in the UK.
  To develop a portfolio of qualifications to complement the competitions.
G United Kingdom.

United Kingdom Space Agency
■ Polaris House, North Star Avenue, SWINDON, Wilts, SN2 1SZ.
  Tel 020 7215 5000   http://www.bis.gov.uk/ukspaceagency/
  Chief Executive: Dr David Williams

E   Established on 1 April 2010. It functions as an Executive Agency of the Department for Business, Innovation & Skills. The Space Leadership Council (qv) provides strategic advice.

R   To coordinate UK civil space activity, support academic research, nurture the UK space industry, raise the profile of UK space activities at home and abroad, increase understanding of space science and its practical benefits, and inspire the next generation of scientists and engineers.

G   United Kingdom.

United Kingdom Sport

■   40 Bernard Street, LONDON, WC1N 1ST.
       Tel 020 7211 5100   **Fax** 020 7211 5246   http://www.uksport.gov.uk
       Chairman: Baroness Sue Campbell, CBE   Chief Executive: Liz Nicholl, OBE

E   Established on 1 January 1997 by Royal Charter. UK Sport functions as an Executive NDPB of the Department for Culture, Media & Sport. The Board comprises ten members including the Chairman.

R   To work in partnership with the home country sports councils and other agencies to lead sport in the UK to world class success.

G   United Kingdom.

✍   It was confirmed by the Government on 14 October 2010 that UK Sport will merge with **Sport England** (qv) after 2012.

United Kingdom Statistics Authority   (UKAS)

■   Statistics House, Tredegar Park, NEWPORT, Gwent, NP10 8XG.
       Tel 0845 604 1857   **Fax** 01633 456179   http://www.statistics.gov.uk
       Chairman: Sir Michael Scholar, KCB   Chief Executive: Jil Matheson

E   Established on 1 April 2008 under the Statistics & Registration Service Act 2007, replacing the former Statistics Commission. The Authority functions as a non-ministerial department directly accountable to Parliament. The Board comprises twelve members including the Chairman.

R   To promote and safeguard the production and publication of official statistics that serve the public good.
       To promote and safeguard the quality and comprehensiveness of official statistics, and ensure good practice in relation to official statistics.

G   United Kingdom.

●   The Authority has oversight of the Office for National Statistics, its executive office, which, as the UK Government's main survey organisation, is its main producer of official statistics. ONS is also the central coordinating agency for the wider Government Statistical Service.

United Kingdom Tea Council

■   9 The Courtyard, Gowan Avenue, LONDON, SW6 6RH.
       Tel 020 7371 7787   **Fax** 020 7371 7958   http://www.tea.co.uk

E   Established in August 1965 under the aegis and by the joint initiative of the major tea producing countries and the UK tea trade. The Council is an independent body and incorporated as a company limited by guarantee.

R   To promote tea and its unique story for the benefit of those who produce, sell and enjoy tea the world over.

G   United Kingdom.

United Kingdom Trade & Investment   (UKTI)

■   Kingsgate House, 66-74 Victoria Street, LONDON, SW1E 6SW.
       Tel 020 7215 8000   http://www.ukti.gov.uk
       Europa Building, 450 Argyle Street, GLASGOW, G2 8LH.
       Acting Chief Executive: Susan Haird, CB

E   Established in 1977 and known as Trade Partners UK & Invest UK, both part of British Trade International, and also as the Invest in Britain Bureau, before changing to its current name in October 2003. The board comprises twelve members including the Chief Executive.

R   To deliver measurable improvement in the business performance of UKTI's international trade customers, with emphasis on innovative and R&D active firms.
       To increase the contribution of foreign direct investment to knowledge intensive economic activity in the UK, including R&D.
       To deliver a measurable improvement in the reputation of the UK in leading overseas markets as the international business partner of choice.

G   United Kingdom.

United Kingdom Transplant

✍   Since October 2005 the transplant service has been part of **NHS Blood & Transplant**.

United Kingdom Xenotranplantation Interim Regulatory Authority
✍ The Authority ceased to exist on 12 December 2006.

United States - United Kingdom Educational Commission

■ Battersea Power Station, 188 Kirtling Street, LONDON, SW8 5BN.　**Fax** 020 7498
4023　http://www.fulbright.co.uk
Chairman: Sandra Kaiser　Executive Director: Penny Egan
E Established on 22 September 1948 and also known as the **US-UK Fulbright Commission**. The Commission's
seven British members are appointed by the Secretary of for Business, Innovation & Skills and the seven
American members by the American Ambassador to the Court of St James.
R To administer the programme of Fulbright awards between the UK and the USA and to provide information about
education, particularly at the higher level, in the latter.
G United Kingdom, United States.
● The Awards Programme offers opportunities for US and UK citizens to study, lecture or pursue research in any
academic field.
For UK citizens, Fulbright offers a variety of grants and places on special programmes in the US.
The Commission is the first port of call for US citizens coming to the UK on a Fulbright exchange.

Universities' Council for the Education of Teachers　(UCET)

■ Institute of Education, 20 Bedford Way, LONDON, WC1H 0AL.
Tel 020 7580 8000　**Fax** 020 7323 0577　http://www.ucet.ac.uk
Chairman: Prof Roger Woods, BSc, PGCE, DipEd, MA　Executive Director: James Noble Rogers, MA, FRSA
E Established in 1967. UCET is a membership organisation comprising universities and further education
institutions. The Committee comprises a representative from each of the member institutions.
R To represent the UK's higher education based professional educators providing research-informed and formally
accredited education, training and development opportunities.
To promote high standards in the education and professional development of teachers.
G United Kingdom.

University Council of Modern Languages　(UCML)

■ LLAS Subject Centre, University of Southampton, Highfield, SOUTHAMPTON, SO17 1BJ.
Tel 023 8059 4814　http://www.ucml.org.uk
Chairman: Pam Moores
E Established in 1993. UCML is a membership body comprising over 50 educational institutions and other
organisations with an interest in modern languages. The General Council comprises one delegate from each
member organisation. The Executive Committee comprises 20 members including the Chairman.
R To represent the views and opinions of scholars and professionals in modern languages to Government, the
funding councils and other bodies at national level.
G United Kingdom.
✍ In July 2008 the Standing Conference of Heads of Modern Languages in Universities (SCHML) amalgamated with
UCML.

Unlinked Anonymous Surveys Steering Group　(UASSG)

■ 61 Colindale Avenue, LONDON, NW9 5EQ.
Tel 020 8200 4400　**Fax** 020 8200 7868
Chairman: Prof Anne M Johnson
E Established in 1990. UASSG functions as an Advisory NDPB of the Department of Health. The Group comprises
11 members including the Chairman.
R To advise on the Unlinked Anonymous Prevalence Monitoring Programme (which aims to measure the distribution
of infection, in particular HIV, in accessible groups of the adult population).
G United Kingdom.

Unrelated Live Transplant Regulatory Authority
✍ On 1 September 2006 the functions of ULTRA were transferred to the **Human Tissue Authority**.

Upland Forum

■ Cathays Park, CARDIFF, CF10 3NQ.
Tel 0300 060 3300　http://www.wales.gov.uk
Chairman: Derek Morgan

E   Established in January 2005, replacing the former Hill Farming Advisory Sub-Committee for Wales. The Forum
     functions as a non-statutory advisory body of the National Assembly for Wales. It comprises 13 members
     including the Chairman.
R   To advise on the wider countryside issues associated with farming in the hill and upland areas of Wales.
G   Wales.

Uplands Land Management Advisory Panel   (ULMAP)
■   Area 4D, Ergon House, Horseferry Road, LONDON, SW1P 2AL.
     Tel 020 7238 6340   **Fax** 020 7238 6414
     Chairman: Marian Jenner
E   Established in November 2002 replacing the former Hill Farming Advisory Committee. ULMAP functions as an
     informal stakeholder group for the Department for Environment, Food & Rural Affairs. The Panel comprises
     around 30 members including the Chairman.
R   To advise Defra on policy issues relating to farming, land management and upland communities in the English
     Uplands within the Less Favoured Areas.
G   England.

UPPER TRIBUNAL

E   The Tribunals, Courts & Enforcement Act 2007 created a new two-tier Tribunal system, First-tier and Upper, both
     of which are organised into Chambers. Each Chamber comprises similar jurisdictions or jurisdictions which
     bring together similar types of experts to hear appeals. The Upper Tribunal primarily, but not exclusively,
     reviews and decides appeals arising from a First-tier Tribunal.
●   The Chambers of the Upper Tribunal are:
        Administrative Appeals
        Immigration & Asylum
        Lands Chamber
        Tax & Chancery.

Upper Tribunal (Administrative Appeals)
■   5th Floor, Chichester Rents, 81 Chancery Lane, LONDON, WC2A 1DD.
     Tel 020 7911 7085   **Fax** 020 7911 7093
E   The Upper Tribunal and its Chambers were established in 2008 under the Tribunals, Courts & Enforcement Act
     2007. The Administrative Appeals Chamber is Superior Court of Record whose decisions are binding on the
     First-tier Tribunals and public authorities below.
R   To assist those wishing to appeal against, or involved in, decisions of the
        General Regulatory Chamber (except Charity),
        Health, Education & Social Care Chamber,
        Social Entitlement Chamber, and
        War Pensions & Armed Forces Compensation Chamber
     of the First-tier Tribunal (qqv).
     To hear first appeals about decisions of the Independent Safeguarding Authority (qv) about safeguarding
     vulnerable groups.
     To hear first appeals about decisions of the Traffic Commissioners (qv).
G   United Kingdom.
✍   For further information see **HM Courts & Tribunals Service**.

Upper Tribunal (Immigration & Asylum)   (UTIAC)
■   PO Box 6987, LEICESTER, LE1 6ZX.
     Tel 0300 123 1711   **Fax** 0116 249 4130
     President: The Hon Mr Justice Blake
E   Immigration & Asylum Chambers were established in both tiers of the Tribunals Service on 15 February 2010
     under the Tribunals, Courts & Enforcement Act 2007. The new chambers replaced the former Asylum &
     Immigration Tribunal.
R   To hear and decide appeals against decisions made by the First-tier Tribunal in matters of immigration, asylum
     and nationality.
G   United Kingdom.
●   Appeals are heard in a number of hearing centres across the United Kingdom.
✍   For further information see **HM Courts & Tribunals Service**.

© CBD Research Ltd · Beckenham · Kent BR3 5JS · Tel 020 8650 7745 · Fax 020 8650 0768 · E-mail cbd@cbdresearch.com · www.cbdresearch.com

Upper Tribunal (Lands Chamber)

- ■ 45 Bedford Square, LONDON, WC1B 3DN
  Tel 020 7612 9710 **Fax** 020 7612 9723
  President: George Bartlett, QC
- E Established on 1 January 1950 under the Lands Tribunal Act 1949. Also known by its former name, the **Lands Tribunal**, it transferred on 1 June 2009 to the Upper Tribunal of the Tribunals Service. It functions as a Tribunal NDPB of the Ministry of Justice. The Tribunal comprises six judges including the President and 3 lay members.
- R To determine disputed compensation in compulsory purchase and certain other types of land compensation cases.
  To hear appeals fron Valuation Tribunals, Leasehold Valuation Tribunals and Residential Property Tribunals.
  To consider applications to discharge or modify restrictions on the use of land and deal with a range of other cases.
- G England, Wales.
- ✍ For further information see **HM Courts & Tribunals Service**.

Upper Tribunal (Tax & Chancery)

- ■ 45 Bedford Square, LONDON, WC1B 3DN.
  Tel 020 7612 9700
  President: Sir Nicholas Warren
- E The Upper Tribunal was established in 2008 under the Tribunals, Courts & Enforcement Act 2007. The Tax & Chancery Chamber comprises eleven judges including the President, 26 deputy judges and 16 lay members
- R To assist those wishing to appeal against, or involved in, decisions of the Tax and Charity Chambers of the First-tier Tribunal and in matters relating to certain decisions of the Financial Services Authority and the Pensions Regulator (qqv).
- G United Kingdom.
- ✍ For further information see **HM Courts & Tribunals Service**.

URBAN DEVELOPMENT CORPORATIONS   (UDCs)

- E Urban Development Corporations were established under the Local Government, Planning & Land Act 1980, the first set up at London Docklands in 1981. They were limited life projects tasked with securing the regeneration of their designated areas. Most were wound up on 31 March 1998, with Cardiff Bay continuing until 2000 and Belfast Laganside until 2007.
  After the Government's Sustainable Communities Plan was published in 2003, UDCs were set up in Thurrock and West Northamptonshire, both of which are now to be devolved to local government. A similarly constituted Urban Development Area has been established in Milton Keynes.
- G England.

Urban Regeneration Agency
- ✍ In 1999 merged with the Commission for the New Towns as English Partnerships, which became part of the **Homes & Communities Agency** in 2008.

URBAN REGENERATION COMPANIES   (URCs)

- E Established in response to Lord Rogers' Urban Task Force Report, the first URC was set up in early 1999 in Liverpool. They are independent companies established by the relevant Local Authority and Regional Development Agency (RDA). The RDAs are set to close by 2012 and the URCs with them.
- R To engage the private sector in a sustainable regeneration strategy, working within the context of a wider Strategic Regeneration Framework or masterplan which takes full account of the problems and opportunities of the whole area.
- G England.
- ● Only two URCs remain in England (Gloucester Heritage and New East Manchester). Others have closed, become Economic Development Companies (qv) or are in the process of becoming Local Enterprise Partnerships (qv).
  Newport Unlimited in Wales, Ilex in Northern Ireland and, in England, North Northamptonshire Development Company, Nottingham Regeneration and Tendring Regeneration are similarly constituted regeneration vehicles.

URENCO

- ■ 18 Oxford Street, MARLOW, Bucks, SL7 2NL.
  Tel 01628 486941 **Fax** 01628 475867 http://www.urenco.com
  Chairman: Chris Clark   Chief Executive: Helmut Engelbrecht   Shareholder Executive: Richard Nourse

E Established in 1971 following the Treaty of Almelo. URENCO is a UK private limited company in which the UK and Dutch Governments each hold a one third share, the remaining one third share is held by the German utilities RWE AG and E.On AG.
R To provide value added services and technology to the nuclear generation industry worldwide.

Utility Regulator See **Northern Ireland Authority for Utility Regulation**.

V

Vale of Glamorgan Local Health Board
✍ Merged on 1 October 2009 with the Cardiff Local Health Board to form **Cardiff & Vale University Health Board**.

Valuation & Lands Agency
✍ Since 1 April 2007 part of the **Land & Property Services** agency.

Valuation Office Agency   (VOA)
■ Wingate House, 93/107 Shaftesbury Avenue, LONDON, W1D 5BU.
  Tel 020 7506 1901 Fax 020 7506 1990 http://www.voa.gov.uk
  Chief Executive: Penny Ciniewicz
E Established on 30 September 1991; It assumed the functions of The Rent Service on 1 April 2009. VOA functions as an Executive Agency of HM Revenue & Customs.
R To compile and maintain the business rating and council tax valuation lists for England and Wales.
  To value property in England, Wales and Scotland for the purposes of taxes administered by HMRC.
  To provide statutory and non-statutory property valuation services in England, Wales and Scotland.
  To provide a rental valuation service to local authorities in England, supplying them with a range of valuations to assist them in settling claims for housing benefit.
  To give policy advice to Ministers on property valuation matters.
G England, Wales, Scotland.

Valuation Tribunal for England   (VTE)
■ Second Floor, Black Lion House, 45 Whitechapel Road, LONDON, E1 1DU.
  Tel 020 7426 3900 Fax 020 7247 6598 http://www.valuationtribunal.gov.uk
  President: Prof Graham Zellick, CBE
E Established on 1 October 2009 under the Local Government & Public Involvement in Health Act 2007, replacing the 56 valuation tribunals that previously existed in England. VTE functions as a Tribunal NDPB of the Department for Communities & Local Government. It is supported in its work by the Valuation Tribunal Service (qv). The President and four Vice-Presidents are appointed by the Lord Chancellor. The panel of chairmen and members are all volunteers and normally three will hear an appeal.
R To handle appeals against council tax, non-domestic rates and drainage rates.
G England.
✍ VTE, together with the Valuation Tribunal Service, is to be abolished and its functions transferred to HM Courts & Tribunals Service (qv).

Valuation Tribunal Service   (VTS)
■ Second Floor, Black Lion House, 45 Whitechapel Road, LONDON, E1 1DU.
  Tel 020 7426 3900 Fax 020 7247 6598 http://www.valuationtribunal.gov.uk
  Chairman: Anne Galbraith, CBE   Chief Executive: Antonio Masella
E Established on 1 April 2004 under the Local Government Act 2003. VTS functions as an Executive NDPB of the Department for Communities & Local Government. The Board comprises seven members including the Chairman.
R To provide and/or arrange the services required for the operation of the Valuation Tribunal for England (qv), including accommodation, staff (including clerks to tribunals), information technology, equipment, training for members, and provision of general advice about procedures relating to proceedings before the Tribunal.

© CBD Research Ltd · Beckenham · Kent BR3 5JS · Tel 020 8650 7745 · Fax 020 8650 0768 · E-mail cbd@cbdresearch.com · www.cbdresearch.com

G   England.
✍   VTS, together with the Valuation Tribunal for England, is to be abolished and its functions transferred to HM
       Courts & Tribunals Service (qv).

Valuation Tribunal for Wales   (VTW)
■   22 Gold Tops, NEWPORT, Gwent, NP20 4PG.
      Tel 01633 266367   Fax 01633 253270   http://www.valuaton-tribunals-wales.org.uk
      Chief Executive: Simon Hill
R   To handle appeals against non-domestic rates and council tax.
G   Wales.
●   The Chief Executive is based at the East Wales VT office. South Wales VT is at the same address. North and
       West Wales VT offices are situated in Colwyn Bay and Caernarfon, respectively.
=   Tribiwnlys Prisio Cymru

VAT & Duties Tribunals
✍   Merged with others on 1 April 2009 to be replaced by the **First-tier Tribunal (Tax)**.

Vehicle Certification Agency   (VCA)
■   No 1 The Eastgate Office Centre, Eastgate Road, BRISTOL, BS5 6XX.
      Tel 0117 951 5151   Fax 0117 952 4103   http://www.vca.gov.uk
      Chief Executive: Paul Markwick
E   Established on 2 April 1990. VCA functions as an Executive Agency of the Department for Transport.
R   To support industry by providing internationally recognised testing and certification for new road vehicles,
       agricultural tractors, off-road vehicles and vehicle parts.
G   United Kingdom.
✍   VCA is part of the DfT's Motoring & Freight Services Group, along with the Driving Standards Agency, the Driver
       & Vehicle Licensing Agency, the Government Car & Despatch Agency and the Vehicle & Operator Services
       Agency (qqv).

Vehicle Inspectorate
✍   Merged on 1 April 2003 with the Traffic Area Network division of the Department for Transport to become the
       Vehicle & Operator Services Agency.

Vehicle & Operator Services Agency   (VOSA)
■   Berkeley House, Croydon Street, BRISTOL, BS5 0DA.
      Tel 0300 123 9000   Fax 0117 954 3212   http://www.dft.gov.uk/vosa/
      Chief Executive: Alastair Peoples
E   Established on 1 April 2003 following the merger of the Vehicle Inspectorate and the Traffic Area Network division
       of the Department for Transport. VOSA functions as an Executive Agency of the DfT. The board comprises the
       Chief Executive, five executive members and three non-executive members.
R   To supervise the MOT scheme to ensure that over 20,200 garages authorised to carry out MOT tests are doing so
       the the correct standards.
      To provide administrative support to the Traffic Commissioners (qv) in considering and processing applications
        for licences to operate commercial vehicles and allow them to carry out their independent regulatory function.
      To conduct statutory annual testing for commercial vehicles and certain private vehicles.
      To conduct routine and targeted checks on vehicles, drivers and operators to ensure compliance with road safety
        legislation.
      To provide a range of educational and advisory activities at the roadside and at operators' premises to promote
        road safety.
      To conduct post-collision investigations and monitor products on the market for manufacturing or design defects,
        to highlight safety concerns and to monitor safety recalls.
G   England, Scotland, Wales
✍   VOSA is part of the DfT's Motoring & Freight Services Group, along with the Driving Standards Agency, the Driver
       & Vehicle Licensing Agency, the Government Car & Despatch Agency and the Vehicle Certification Agency
       (qqv).

Vehicle Systems Installation Board
✍   VSIB went into administration in May 2009.

VETERANS ADVISORY & PENSIONS COMMITTEES (VAPCs)

E   First established in 1921 in the wake of World War I to assist the Ministry of Pensions and known as War Pensions Committees until a recent change of name, VAPCs are statutory bodies constituted under the Social Security Act 1989.

There are 13 UK Committees, each operating in a specific region, with separate committees in the Isle of Man and the Republic of Ireland. They are independent of the Ministry of Defence and the Service Personnel & Veterans Agency (SPVA), qv.

R   To act as advocates for implementing improved cross-Government support, including the services outlined in the Service Personnel Command Paper and the Armed Forces 'Welfare Pathway''.

To raise awareness in their regions of the support available to veterans and the Armed Forces community, including compensation and pension schemes for those injured, disabled or bereaved through Service, advice centres and the work of the MOD's Veretan Welfare Service.

To assist serving personnel, their families and veterans in accessing such services and other local support.

G   United Kingdom, Republic of Ireland, Isle of Man.

✍   Individual VAPCs can be contacted via the Veterans-UK Helpline 0800 169 2277 or the SPVA.

See also the **Central Advisory Committee on Pensions & Compensation**.

Veterans Agency

✍   On 1 April 2007 the Agency merged with the Armed Forces Personnel Administration Agency to form the **Service Personnel & Veterans Agency**.

Veterinary Laboratories Agency

✍   VLA merged on 1 April 2011 with Animal Health to form the **Animal Health & Veterinary Laboratories Agency**.

Veterinary Medicines Directorate (VMD)

■   Woodham Lane, New Haw, ADDLESTONE, Surrey, KT15 3LS.
Tel 01932 336911   **Fax** 01932 336618   http://www.vmd.gov.uk
Chief Executive: Prof Steve Dean

E   Established on 7 June 2001. VMD functions as an Executive Agency of the Department for Environment, Food & Rural Affairs.

R   To protect public health, animal health and the environment and promote animal welfare by assuring the safety, quality and efficacy of veterinary medicines.

G   United Kingdom.

Veterinary Products Committee (VPC)

■   Woodham Lane, New Haw, ADDLESTONE, Surrey, KT15 3LS.
Tel 01932 336911   **Fax** 01932 336618   http://www.vmd.gov.uk/vpc/
Chairman: David Skilton, BVSc, MRCVS

E   Established in 1970 under the Medicines Act 1968. On 30 October 2005 the 1968 Act was disallowed to veterinary medicines by the Veterinary Medicines Regulations 2005, though the statutory requirement for VPC was retained. VPC is part of the Veterinary Medicines Directorate (qv) and functions as a Scientific Advisory Committee and an Advisory NDPB of the Department for Environment, Food & Rural Affairs. The Committee comprises 28 members including the Chairman.

R   To provide the Secretary of State with scientific advice on any aspect of veterinary medicinal products and specified feed additives.

To hear representations on decisions relating to the granting, refusal, variation, suspension or revocation of a marketing authorisation for a veterinary medicinal product or an animal test certificate.

To promote the collection of information relating to suspected adverse reactions for the purpose of enabling such advice to be given.

G   United Kingdom.

✍   For further information see **Scientific Advisory Committees**.

Veterinary Residues Committee (VRC)

■   Woodham Lane, New Haw, ADDLESTONE, Surrey, KT15 3LS.
Tel 01932 338322   **Fax** 01932 336618   http://www.vmd.gov.uk/vrc/
Chairman: Mrs Dorothy Craig, MBE

E   Established in January 2001. VRC is part of the Veterinary Medicines Directorate (qv) and functions as a Scientific Advisory Committee and an Advisory NDPB of the Department for Environment, Food & Rural Affairs (Defra). The Committee comprises 14 members including the Chairman.

R   To provide high quality, independent, expert advice to the Veterinary Medicines Directorate and the Food Standards Agency (qqv).

© CBD Research Ltd · Beckenham · Kent BR3 5JS · Tel 020 8650 7745 · Fax 020 8650 0768 · E-mail cbd@cbdresearch.com · www.cbdresearch.com

To oversee the residue surveillance programmes and surveys to ensure that they are concentrated on issues of possible concern and are well conducted.

To encourage regular dialogue with stakeholders in the promotion of good practices.

To take other initiatives where relevant to attain the Committee's mandate.

G   United Kingdom.

✍   For further information see **Scientific Advisory Committees**.

The Government announced on 14 October 2010 that VRC will be abolished as a NDPB and be reconstituted as a committee of experts, with Defra's Chief Scientific Adviser having more of an oversight of its activities.

Victims' Advisory Panel

✍   Two three-year Panels met, 2003-06 (March) and 2006-09 (July). It was announced by the Government on 14 October 2010 that the body and its functions are to be abolished.

Victims' Commissioner   See **Commission for Victims & Witnesses**.

Victoria & Albert Museum   (V&A)

■   Cromwell Road, LONDON, SW7 2RL.
    Tel 020 7942 2000   http://www.vam.ac.uk
    Chairman: Paul Ruddock   Director: Mark Jones

E   Established in 1857. The Museum functions as an Executive NDPB of the Department for Culture, Media & Sport. The Board comprises 14 Trustees including the Chairman.

R   To enable everyone to enjoy the Museum's collections and explore the cultures that created them, and to inspire those who shape contemporary design.

G   United Kingdom.

Video Appeals Committee   (VAC)

■   3 Soho Square, LONDON, W1V 6HD.
    Tel 020 7440 1570   **Fax** 020 7287 0141
    President: John Wood, CB

E   Established in 1985 under the Video Recordings Act 1984 as an independent body. The Committee comprises 16 members including the President.

R   To hear appeals from submitting companies against any decisions of the British Board for Film Classification (qv) they consider stricter than warranted.

G   United Kingdom.

Video Packaging Review Committee   (VPRC)

■   3 Soho Square, LONDON, W1D 3HD.
    Tel 020 7440 1570   **Fax** 020 7287 0141
    Chairman: David Cooke

E   Established in 1987 by the British Board of Film Classification (BBFC), qv, and the British Video Association. The Committee comprises nine members and is chaired by the Director of the BBFC.

R   To prevent offence to members of the public caused by explicitly violent or sexual imagery on the covers of DVDs and videos.

G   United Kingdom.

Video Standards Council   (VSC)

■   Kinetic Business Centre, Theobald Street, BOREHAMWOOD, Herts, WD6 4PJ.
    Tel 020 8387 4020   **Fax** 020 8387 4004   http://www.videostandards.org.uk
    Chairman: Baroness Shephard   Director General: Laurie Hall

E   Established in 1989. VSC functions as a standards body for the video industry.

R   To ensure compliance with the law and proper trading standards.

G   United Kingdom.

Vision+Media

■   100 Broadway, SALFORD QUAYS, M50 2UW.
    Tel 0844 395 0385   http://www.northwestvision.co.uk
    Chairman: Steve Morrison   Chief Executive: Paul Taylor

E   Established in 2002 as North West Vision, in May 2007 it merged with Media Training Northwest and adopted its current name.

G   Cheshire, Cumbria, Greater Manchester, Lancashire, Merseyside.

✍   For further information see **Creative England** and **Regional Screen Agencies**.

Visit Britain   (VisitBritain)

■   1 Palace Street, LONDON, SW1E 5HE.
    Tel 020 7578 1000   http://www.visitbritain.org
    Chairman: Christopher Rodrigues, CBE   Chief Executive: Sandie Dawe

E   Established on 1 April 2003 when the former English Tourist Council merged with the British Tourist Authority. VisitBritain functions as an Executive NDPB of the Department for Culture, Media & Sport. The Board comprises eleven members including the Chairman.

R   To promote Britain as a tourist destination in 35 key overseas markets, working in partnership with the industry, nations and regions.
    To advise the government on tourism policy and raise awareness of the significance of tourism to the UK economy.

G   United Kingdom.

●   VisitBritain promotes British tourism abroad. Domestic tourism is promoted by:
        Northern Ireland Tourist Board
        VisitEngland
        Visit London
        VisitScotland, and
        Visit Wales (qqv).

✍   VisitBritain is legally constituted as the British Tourist Authority.

Visit Chester & Cheshire

■   Chester Railway Station, 1st Floor West Wing Offices, Station Road, CHESTER,
    CH1 3NT.   http://www.visitchesterandcheshire.co.uk
    Chairman: Edward Pysden   Chief Executive: Chris Brown

E   Established in April 2004 as the tourism board for Chester and Cheshire. It functions as a company limited by guarantee, under the control of the three local authorities and is funded and supported by the Northwest Regional Development Agency (qv). The Board comprises nine members including the Chairman.

R   To build the tourism industry to generate economic return for all, through positive action and effective partnership working.

G   Cheshire, including Chester and Warrington.

✍   One of the five tourist boards supported by the Northwest Regional Development Board (qv).

Visit England   (VisitEngland)

■   Thames Tower, Black's Road, LONDON, W6 9EL.
    Tel 020 8846 9000   http://www.visitengland.com
    Chairman: Penelope, Viscountess Cobham   Chief Executive: James Berresford

E   Established in April 2009 as successor to the England Marketing Advisory Board. VisitEngland functions as an Advisory NDPB of the Department for Culture, Media & Sport. The Board comprises eleven members including the Chairman.

R   To support England's tourism industry in increasing the propensity for domestic and international visitors to take breaks, holidays and day trips in England, resulting in increased consumer spending.

G   England.

●   EnjoyEngland is the consumer-facing brand used in domestic market campaigns.

✍   English tourism is marketed internationally by VisitBritain (qv).

Visit Guernsey

■   PO Box 23, ST PETER PORT, Guernsey, GY1 3AN.
    Tel 01481 723552   http://www.visitguernsey.com

E   Established on 28 August 1948 under the States of Guernsey Tourist Law 1948.

R   To promote the tourist industry of Guernsey, Alderney, Sark and Herm.

G   Bailiwick of Guernsey.

Visit the Heart of England

✍   See **Tourism West Midlands**.

Visit London

■ 2 More London Riverside, LONDON, SE1 2RR.
   Tel 020 7234 5800   **Fax** 020 7378 6525   http://www.visitlondon.com
   Chairman: Tamara Ingram   Chief Executive: Sally Chatterjee
E Established on 6 May 1963 and known as the London Tourist Board until it changed its name in September 2003.
   It functions as a company limited by guarantee and receives public funding from the London Development
   Agency (qv) and London Councils. The Board comprises twelve members including the Chairman.
R To promote London worldwide as a tourist and conference destination.
   To provide a complete service for event organisers.
G London.
✍ London tourism is marketed internationally by VisitBritain (qv).

Visit Manchester

■ Carver's Warehouse, 77 Dale Street, MANCHESTER, M1 2HG.
   Tel 0161 237 1010   http://www.themanchestertouristboard.com
   Chief Executive: Andrew Stokes
E Established in April 2004 as the tourist board for Greater Manchester; since January 2008 it operates as a division
   of Marketing Manchester.
R To provide strategic leadership to the tourism industry within the city-region.
   To promote Manchester as a leading leisure, learning and business tourism destination.
G Greater Manchester.
✍ One of the five tourist boards supported by the Northwest Regional Development Agency (qv).

Visit Scotland   (VisitScotland)

■ Ocean Point One, 94 Ocean Drive, EDINBURGH, EH6 6JH.
   Tel 0131 472 2222   **Fax** 0131 472 2250   http://www.visitscotland.org
   Chairman: Dr Mike Cantlay   Chief Executive: Malcolm Roughead, OBE
E Established under the Development of Tourism Act 1969 as the Scottish Tourist Board, adopting its current name
   in 2001.
   It functions as a Executive NDPB of the Scottish Executive Development Department.
   The Board comprises seven members including the Chairman.
R To help deliver sustainable economic growth by maximising the economic benefits of tourism to Scotland.
G Scotland.
● VisitScotland has 14 area offices which each functions as a single point of contact for tourism businesses,
   complemented by local tourism action plans: these replace the former regional Tourist Boards which were
   abolished on 31 March 2005.
✍ Scottish tourism is marketed internationally by VisitBritain (qv).

Visit Wales

■ Brunel House, 2 Fitzalan Road, CARDIFF, CF24 0UY.
   Tel 0845 010 3300   **Fax** 029 2048 5031   http://www.visitwales.com
E Established on 1 April 2006 replacing the former Wales Tourist Board. Visit Wales functions as an Executive
   NDPB of the National Assembly for Wales.
R To maximise tourism's contribution to the economic, social and cultural prosperity of Wales.
G Wales.
✍ Welsh tourism is marketed internationally by VisitBritain (qv).
= Croeso Cymro

---

visiteastofengland.com   See **East of England Tourist Board**.

Visiting Committees
✍ See **Independent Monitoring Boards**.

Vocational Training Charitable Trust   (VTCT)

■ 3rd Floor, Eastleigh House, Upper Market Street, EASTLEIGH, Hants, SO50 9FD.
   Tel 023 8068 4500   **Fax** 023 8065 1493   http://www.vtct.org.uk
   Chief Executive: Stephen Vickers
E Established in 1966. VTCT is an awarding body for courses and qualifications in the hairdressing and beauty
   sector, including complementary therapies, sports and active leisure and business skills.

G   United Kingdom.

✍   For more information on awarding bodies see the **Federation of Awarding Bodies**.

Volunteering Development Scotland   (VDS)

■   Jubilee House, Forthside Way, STIRLING, FK8 1QZ.
    Tel 01786 479593   **Fax** 01786 849767   http://www.vds.org.uk
    Chairman: Bill Howat   Chief Executive: George Thomson

E   Established in 1984. The Board comprises nine members including the Chairman.

R   To provide a leadership role to enable strategic partners to identify ways in which volunteering can contribute to their desired outcomes.
    To enhance the quality of the volunteering experience by improving the practice of volunteers management.

G   Scotland.

✍   VDS is a member of the UK Volunteering Forum which brings together the national volunteer development agencies of the four countries of the UK.

Volunteering England

■   Regent's Wharf, 8 All Saints Street, LONDON, N1 9RL.
    Tel 0845 305 6979   **Fax** 020 7520 8910   http://www.volunteering.org.uk
    Chairman: Sukhvinder Kaur-Stubbs   Chief Executive: Dr Justin Davis Smith

E   Established in April 2004 following the merger of the Consortium on Opportunities for Volunteering, the National Centre for Volunteering and Volunteer Development England. In 1 July 2007 Student Volunteering England also merged. Formally known as England Volunteering Development Council (EVDC) it is the integrated national volunteer development organisation for England and functions as a registered charity. The Board of Trustees comprises 13 members including the Chairman.

R   To secure and support an England-wide network of quality volunteer development agencies, promoting and enabling volunteering and community involvement.
    To keep volunteering high on the policy agenda, working with Government to provide opportunities for, and remove institutional barriers to, volunteering.

G   England.

✍   Volunteering England is a member of the UK Volunteering Forum which brings together the national volunteer development agencies of the four countries the UK.

W

W5   (whowhatwhenwherewhy) See **National Museums Northern Ireland**.

Wales Audit Office   (WAO)

■   24 Cathedral Road, CARDIFF, CF11 9LJ.
    Tel 029 2032 0500   **Fax** 029 2032 0600   http://www.wao.gov.uk
    Auditor General for Wales: Gillian Body

E   Established on 1 April 2005 under the Public Audit (Wales) Act 2004. WAO functions as a Public Corporation accountable to the National Assembly for Wales.

R   To promote improvement, so that people in Wales benefit from accountable, well-managed public services that offer the best value for money.

G   Wales.

=   Swyddfa Archwilio Cymru

Wales Centre for Health

✍   See **Public Health Wales**.

Wales Council for the Blind   (WCB)

■   2nd Floor, Hallinans House, 22 Newport Road, CARDIFF, CF24 0TD.
    Tel 029 2047 3954   **Fax** 029 2043 0777   http://www.wcb-ccd.org.uk
    Chairman: Cllr Peter Curtis

© CBD Research Ltd · Beckenham · Kent BR3 5JS · Tel 020 8650 7745 · Fax 020 8650 0768 · E-mail cbd@cbdresearch.com · www.cbdresearch.com

E   Established in 1938. WCB is a registered charity, a company limited by guarantee and a membership based organisation. The Board of Trustees comprises eight persons including the Chairman.
R   To promote the welfare of blind and partially sighted people in Wales.
G   Wales.
=   Cyngor Cymru i'r Deillion

Wales Council for Deaf People
■   Glenview House, Courthouse Street, PONTYPRIDD, Glamorgan, CF37 1JY.
    Tel 01443 485687   Fax 01443 408555   http://www.wcdeaf.org.uk
E   Established in 1950. The Council is an umbrella organisation of associations, both statutory and voluntary, working in the field of hearing loss.
R   To support all activities of benefit to people with hearing loss in Wales with the object of enabling these people to lead fuller and more independent lives.
G   Wales.
●   The Council's Communication Support Agency provides British Sign Language (BSL) interpreters, lipspeakers and speech-to-text operatives to facilitate language support for deaf and hard of hearing people.
    The Council offers training courses which can be tailored to suit the needs of individual organisations, for example deaf awareness training.
=   Cyngor Cymru i Bobl Fyddar

Wales Council for Voluntary Action   (WCVA)
■   Baltic House, Mount Stuart Square, Cardiff Bay, CARDIFF, CF10 5FH.
    Tel 029 2043 1700   Fax 029 2043 1701   http://www.wcva.org.uk
    Chairman: Win Griffiths   Chief Executive: Graham Benfield
E   Established in 1934. WCVA is a membership based organisation. There are 35 board members including the Chairman.
R   To represent and campaign for voluntary organisations, volunteers and communities.
G   Wales.
✍   WCVA is a member of the UK Volunteering Forum which brings together the national volunteer development agencies of the four countries of the UK.
=   Cyngor Gweithredu Gwirfoddol Cymru

Wales Management Council   (WMC)
■   PO Box 4284, CARDIFF, CF14 8GP.
    Tel 0845 371 0691   http://www.crc-wmc.org.uk
    Chairman: Ian Rees   Chief Executive: Christopher Ward
E   An employer-led body established to provide leadership towards the goal of first class management. The Council comprises seven members including the Chairman.
R   To champion the case for better management and leadership performance across all sectors in Wales.
G   Wales.
=   Cyngor Rheolaeth Cymru

Wales Probation Trust
■   Cwmbran House, Mamhilad Park Estate, PONTYPOOL, Gwent, NP4 0XD.
    Tel 01495 762462   Fax 01495 762461   http://www.walesprobationtrust.gov.uk
    Tremains Business Park, Tremains Road, BRIDGEND, CF31 1TZ.
    Tel 01656 674747   Fax 01656 674799
    Chairman: Susan Fox   Chief Executive: Sarah Payne
E   Established on 1 April 2010 under the Offender Management Act 2007, merging the four area boards (Dyfed Powys, Gwent, North Wales and South Wales) which had been set up on 1 April 2001 under the Criminal Justice & Court Service Act 2000. The Board comprises twelve members including the Chairman.
G   Wales.
✍   For further information see **Probation Trusts**.
=   Ymddiriedolaeth Prawf Cymru

Wales Rent Assessment Panel
✍   See **Residential Property Tribunal for Wales**.

Wales Tourist Board
✍   Replaced on 1 April 2006 by **Visit Wales**.

Wales Youth Agency
✍ The Agency ceased operations on 2 December and closed 31 December 2005, many of its responsibilities being transferred to the Youth & Pupil Participation Division of the Welsh Government.

Walker Art Gallery   See **National Museums Liverpool**.

The Wallace Collection
■ Hertford House, Manchester Square, LONDON, W1U 3BN.
  Tel 020 7563 9500   **Fax** 020 7224 2155   http://www.wallacecollection.org
  Chairman: Sir John Ritblat   Director: Dame Rosalind Savill
E The museum opened to the public on 22 June 1900. The Collection now functions as an Executive NDPB of the Department for Culture, Media & Sport. The Board of Trustees comprises twelve members including the Chairman.
R To preserve the Collection and Hertford House for future generations to enjoy.
G United Kingdom.
● The Collection displays the works of art collected in the 18th and 19th centuries by the first four Marquesses of Hertford and Sir Richard Wallace, illegitimate son of the fourth Marquess.

Walsall Regeneration Company
✍ WRC closed on 30 September 2010.

Waltham Forest Housing Action Trust
✍ Closed on 31 March 2002 under the Waltham Forest Housing Action Trust (Dissolution) Order 2002.

War Pensions Committees
✍ WPCs have been renamed **Veterans Advisory & Pensions Committees**.

Warkworth Harbour Commissioners
■ Harbour Office, Quayside, Amble, MORPETH, Northumberland, NE65 0AP.
  Tel 01665 710306   **Fax** 01665 710306
G Warkworth, Amble.
✍ For further information see **Port & Harbour Authorities**.

Warrenpoint Harbour Authority   (WHA)
■ The Docks, WARRENPOINT, Co Down, BT34 3JR.
  Tel 028 4177 3381   **Fax** 028 4175 2875   http://www.warrenpointharbour.co.uk
  Chairman: James Stewart, CBE   Chief Executive: Peter Conway
E Established in 1971 under the Warrenpoint Harbour Authority Order 1971. The Authority comprises eleven members including the Chairman.
G Warrenpoint.
✍ For further information see **Port & Harbour Authorities**.

Warship Support Agency
✍ On 1 April 2005 WSA became part of the Defence Logistics Organisation which on 1 April 2007 became **Defence Equipment & Support**.

Warwickshire Police Authority
■ 3 Northgate Street, WARWICK, CV34 4SP.
  Tel 01926 412322   **Fax** 01926 412502   http://www.warwickshirepa.gov.uk
  Chairman: Ian Francis   Chief Executive: Oliver Winters
E Established in April 1995, the Authority is an independent body charged with ensuring that Warwickshire Police provide an effective and efficient police service. It is made up of nine County Council members and eight independent members.
G Warwickshire.
✍ For further information see **Police Authorities**.

Warwickshire Probation Trust

- 2 Swan Street, WARWICK, CV34 4BJ.
  Tel 01926 405843   http://www.warwickshireprobation.org.uk
  Chairman: Robin Verso   Chief Executive: Liz Stafford
- E Established on 1 April 2001 under the Criminal Justice & Court Service Act 2000 as the Warwickshire Probation Area Board. It became a trust on 1 April 2010 under the Offender Management Act 2007. The Board comprises ten members including the Chairman.
- G Warwickshire.
- ✍ For further information see **Probation Trusts**.

Warwickshire Rural Community Council   (WRCC)

- 25 Stoneleigh Deer Park Business Centre, Abbey Park, Stareton, KENILWORTH, Warwickshire, CV8 2LY.
  Tel 024 7630 3232   **Fax** 024 7641 9959   http://www.ruralwarwickshire.org.uk
  Chairman: Brian Douthwaite   Chief Officer: Kay Wilson
- E Established in 1937. WRCC functions as a registered charity and company limited by guarantee. The Board comprises twelve Trustees including the Chairman.
- R To enable the development of sustainable and self-reliant rural communities by being approachable, supportive, professional and in touch.
- G Warwickshire.
- ✍ WRCC is one of the 38 Rural Community Councils, represented at the national level by **Action with Communities in Rural England** (qv) and at the regional level by West Midlands Rural Community Action Network.

Waste Management Advisory Board

- ✍ WMAB (Northern Ireland) published its report on 28 June 2004.

Waste Management Industry Training & Advisory Board   (WAMITAB)

- Peterbridge House, 3 The Lakes, NORTHAMPTON, NN4 7HE.
  Tel 01604 231950   **Fax** 01604 232457   http://www.wamitab.org.uk
  Director General: Dr Lawrence Strong
- E Established in 1989. WAMITAB is the awarding body for courses and qualifications in the waste management industry.
- G United Kingdom.
- ✍ For more information on awarding bodies see the **Federation of Awarding Bodies**.

Water Appeals Commission   (WAC)

- Park House, 87-91 Great Victoria Street, BELFAST, BT2 7AG.
  Tel 028 9024 4710   **Fax** 028 9031 2536   http://www.pacni.gov.uk
  Chief Commissioner: Maire Campbell
- E Established on 1 October 1973 under the Water & Sewerage Services (Northern Ireland) Order 1973, as amended. WAC is part of the Planning Appeals Commission (qv) and functions as a Tribunal NDPB of the Office of the First Minister & Deputy First Minister in Northern Ireland.
- R To make decisions on all appeals against Departmmental decisions on a wide range of planning and environmental matters involving water and sewerage.
- G Northern Ireland.

Water Industry Commission for Scotland   (WICS)

- Ochil House, Springkerse Business Park, STIRLING, FK7 7XE.
  Tel 01786 430200   **Fax** 01786 462018   http://www.watercommissioner.co.uk
  Chairman: Sir Ian Byatt   Chief Executive: Alan Sutherland
- E Established under the Water Industry (Scotland) Act 2002 as amended by the Water Services (Scotland) Act 2005. The Commission functions as an Executive NDPB of the Scottish Executive Rural Affairs Department. The Commission comprises five members including the Chairman.
- R To promote the interests of persons whose premises are connected to the public water supply system and/or the public sewerage system relating to the provision to them of water and sewerage services.
  To determine maximum charges and approve charges schemes.
  To establish a licensing framework for retailing water and sewerage services to non-household customers.
- G Scotland.

Water Regulations Advisory Committee
- ✍ WRAC served from 1996 to 2003 to provide technical expertise to Government on preventing the waste, misuse, undue consumption and contamination of water supplies.

Water Service
- ✍ Now **Northern Ireland Water**, a Government owned company established in April 2007.

Water Services Regulation Authority
- ■ Centre City Tower, 7 Hill Street, BIRMINGHAM, B5 4UA.
  Tel 0121 644 7500 **Fax** 0121 644 7699 http://www.ofwat.gov.uk
  Chairman: Philip Fletcher Chief Executive: Regina Finn
- E Established on 1 September 1989 under the Water Act 1989. **Ofwat** functions as the non-ministerial economic regulator of the water industry in England & Wales. The Board comprises nine members including the Chairman.
- R To set limits on what companies can charge.
  To ensure companies are able to carry out their responsibilities under the Water Industry Act 1991 as updated under the Water Act 2003.
  To protect standards of service, help encourage competition and meet the principles of sustainable development.
- G England, Wales.

WaterVoice Council
- ✍ Replaced 1 October 2005 by the **Consumer Council for Water**.

Waterways Ireland
- ■ 2 Sligo Road, ENNISKILLEN, Co Fermanagh, BT74 7JY.
  Tel 028 6632 3004 **Fax** 028 6634 6257 http://www.waterwaysireland.org
  Chief Executive: John Martin
- E Established on 2 December 1999, Waterways Ireland as one of the North/South Implementation Bodies set up under the British-Irish Agreement of 8 March 1999. It is responsible to the North South Ministerial Council (qv), the Department of Culture, Arts & Leisure Northern Ireland and to the Irish Government.
- R To manage, maintain, develop and restore the inland navigable waterways in its care, principally for recreational purposes.
- G Northern Ireland, Republic of Ireland.
- ● The waterways under the remit of the body are the Barrow Navigation, Erne System, Grand Canal, Lower Bann, Royal, Shannon-Erne Waterway and the Shannon Navigation.
- ✍ For further information see the**North South Ministerial Council**.
- = Uiscebhealaí Éireann= Watterweys Airlann

Waterways Ombudsman Committee
- ■ PO Box 35, YORK, YO60 6WW.
  Tel 01347 879075 http://www.waterways-ombudsman.org
  Chairman: Prof Jeffrey Jowell, QC Waterways Ombudsman: Ms Hilary Bainbridge
- E Established in 2005. The Committee comprises eight members including the Chairman.
- R To appoint, or remove from office, the Ombudsman.
  To keep the operation of the scheme under review.
- G United Kingdom.
- ● The Ombudsman investigates complaints about British Waterways and its subsidiaries.

Watterweys Airiann See **Waterways Ireland**.

WEEE Advisory Body
- ✍ Established in 2008 to review the recycling of waste electric and electronic equipment (WEEE), WAB was abolished on 30 September 2010 and its functions transferred to the Department for Business, Innovation & Skills where five working groups have been set up to allow stakeholders a say in the UK's WEEE policy.

Welcome to Yorkshire
- ■ Dry Sand Foundry, Foundry Square, Holbeck, LEEDS, W Yorks, LS11 5WH.
  Tel 0113 322 3500 http://www.yorkshire.com
  Chief Executive: Gary Verity

E   Established on 1 July 1971 as the Yorkshire Tourist Board. In 2004, following a government decision that the
    Regional Development Agencies should take responsibility for tourism, it became an agency of Yorkshire
    Forward (qv) and adopted its present name.
R   To represent and help generate sustainable business for the region's tourism industry.
G   Yorkshire (North, South, East and West), Lincolnshire (North and North East).

Wellcome Trust
■   Gibbs Building, 215 Euston Road, LONDON, NW1 2BE.
    Tel 020 7611 8888   Fax 020 7611 8545   http://www.wellcome.ac.uk
    Chairman: Sir William Castell, LVO   Chief Executive: Mark Walport
E   Established on the death of Sir Henry Wellcome, whose will decreed that the share capital of the pharmaceutical
    company, the Wellcome Foundation, be vested in trustees to support research of a non-commercial nature. The
    Foundation as floated in 1992, acquired by Glaxo in 1995, and now functions as the world's largest charity. The
    board comprises nine trustees including the Chairman.
R   To foster and promote biomedical research with the aim of improving human and animal health.
G   United Kingdom.

Wells Harbour Commission
■   Harbour Office, West Quay, WELLS-NEXT-THE-SEA, Norfolk, NR23 1AT.
    Tel 01328 711646   Fax 01328 710623   http://www.wellsharbour.co.uk
    Chairman: Charles Ebrill
E   Established in 1663 by Act of Parliament. There are nine Commissioners including the Chairman.
G   Wells-next-the-Sea.
✍   For further information see **Port & Harbour Authorities**.

Welsh Administration Ombudsman
✍   Replaced on 1 April 2006 by the **Public Services Ombudsman for Wales**.

Welsh Advisory Committee on Telecommunications
✍   Superceded in 2003 by the Ofcom **Advisory Committee for Wales**.

Welsh Ambulance Services NHS Trust
■   H M Stanley Hospital, ST ASAPH, Denbighshire, LL17 0RS.
    Tel 01745 532900   Fax 01745 532901   http://www.ambulance.wales.nhs.uk
    Chairman: Stuart Fletcher   Chief Executive: Elwyn Price-Morris
E   Established on 1 April 1998 under the Welsh Ambulance Services National Health Service (Establishment) Order
    1998. The Board comprises 13 members including the Chairman.
G   Wales.
✍   On 1 April 2007 NHS Direct Wales (qv) transferred to become an integral part of the Welsh Ambulance Service.
=   Ymddiriedolaeth GIG Gwasanaethau Ambiwlans Cymru

Welsh Archives Council   See **Archives & Records Council Wales**.

WELSH GOVERNMENT: Committees

E   There are three types of committee established by the Assembly:
    Scrutiny Committees:
    These examine the Government's policies, actions and spending in their particular fields. Currently four in
    number, they are:
        Communities & Culture Committee
        Enterprise & Learning Committee
        Health, Wellbeing & Local Government Committee
        Sustainability Committee (with Rural Developmemt Sub-Committee)
    Legislation Committees (currently five):
    These committees consider any items of legislation referred to them by the Business Committee, which also sets
    the timetable for them to complete their work.
    Other Committees (currently nine):
    These committees, which oversee the work of the National Assembly and of the Welsh Government, are currently:
        Business Committee
        Children & Young People Committee

Equality of Opportunity Committee
European & External Affairs Committee
Finance Committee
Petitions Committee
Public Accounts Committee
Scrutiny of First Minister
Committee on Standards of Conduct.

✍ Note:
The Welsh Government consists of the First Minister and his Deputy, seven Ministers, four Deputy Ministers and the Counsel General.
The National Assembly for Wales consists of all 60 elected Assembly Members.
See also Introduction.

Welsh Blood Service   (WBS)

■ Ely Valley Road, Talbot Green, PONTYCLUN, CF72 9WB.
Tel 01443 622000   **Fax** 01443 622199   http://www.welsh-blood.org.uk
Director: Geoff Poole, MSc, FIBMS, CSci
E WBS is part of the Velindre NHS Trust and is responsible to the Welsh Government.
R To supply blood and blood products and related clinical services to hospitals and other clinical units in Wales.
G South and West Wales.
● The Welsh Transplantation & Immunogenetics Laboratory is based within the WBS and provides services to support local kidney, pancreas and blood stem cell transplants. It also operates the Welsh Bone Marrow Donor Registry.
= Gwasanaeth Gwaed Cymru

Welsh Books Council   (WBC)

■ Castell Brychan, ABERYSTWYTH, Ceredigion, SY23 2JB.
Tel 01970 624151   **Fax** 01970 625385   http://www.cllc.org.uk
Chairman: Prof M Wynn Thomas
E Established in 1961. WBC functions as an Advisory NDPB of the National Assembly for Wales. Membership comprises the Chairman, chief librarians and representatives of various professional bodies and of the Welsh local authorities.
R To promote all aspects of publishing in Wales in both languages.
To promote, encourage and increase the appreciation and interest of the public in literature.
G Wales.
= Cyngor Llyfrau Cymru

Welsh Committee for Professional Development of Pharmacy   (WCPDP)

■ Cathays Park, CARDIFF, CF10 3NQ.
Tel 0845 010 3300
E Established in 1984 as the Welsh Committee for Postgraduate Pharmaceutical Education, it adopted its current name on 1 April 1998. WCPDP functions as a Scientific Advisory Committee and an Advisory NDPB of the National Assembly for Wales.
R To provide advice on the continuing professional development of pharmacists and their support staff in Wales, and to commission programmes of education and development activities to meet identified needs.
G Wales.
✍ For further information see **Scientific Advisory Committees**.

Welsh Consumer Council

✍ On 1 October 2008 the Welsh Consumer Council (Cyngor Defnyddwyr Cymru), with others, was replaced by **Consumer Focus**.

Welsh Dental Committee   (WDC)

■ PHPD3, Cathays Park, CARDIFF, CF10 3NQ.
Tel 029 2082 3777   **Fax** 029 2082 3430
Chairman: Dr Karl Bishop
E Established in April 1974 under the National Health Service Reorganisation Act 1973. WDC functions as a Scientific Advisory Committee and an Advisory NDPB of the National Assembly for Wales. The Committee comprises 15 members including the Chairman.
R To advise the Assembly on professional dental issues in Wales.
G Wales.
✍ For further information see **Scientific Advisory Committees**.

Welsh Development Agency
✍ WDA, established in 1976, was abolished in April 2006 and its functions absorbed into the Welsh Government's Department of Economy & Transport.

Welsh European Funding Office
✍ WEFO is part of the Welsh Government and manages the delivery of the EU Structural Funds programmes in Wales.

Welsh Food Advisory Committee   (WFAC)
■ 11th Floor, Southgate House, Wood Street, CARDIFF, CF10 1EW.
  Tel 029 2067 8999
  Chairman: John Spence
E Established in 2000. WFAC functions as an Advisory NDPB of the Food Standards Agency Wales (qv). There are currently nine members including the Chairman.
R To provide advice and information to the agency on a range of issues.
G Wales.

Welsh Fourth Channel   See **S4C Authority**.

Welsh Grand Committee   See **United Kingdom Parliament: Committees**

Welsh Health Specialised Services Committee   (WHSSC)
■ Unit 3a, Caerphilly Business Park, CAERPHILLY, Glamorgan, CF83 3ED.
  Tel 01143 443443
  Chairmen: Prof Mike Harmer
E Established on 1 April 2010, following the closure of Health Commission Wales. The Committee comprises 15 members including the Chairman.
R To commission tertiary and other highly specialised services which need a population base greater than any individual NHS Trust.
  To have commissioning responsibility for a range of designated services provided on a national basis, including blood and screening services and Wales.
G Wales.

Welsh Industrial Development Advisory Board   (WIDAB)
■ National Assembly for Wales, Cathays Park, CARDIFF, CF10 3NQ.
  Tel 029 2082 3626   **Fax** 029 2082 5214
  Chairman: Valerie Barrett
E Established in 1975 under the Welsh Development Agency Act 1975. WIDAB functions as an Advisory NDPB of the National Assembly for Wales. The Board comprises seven members including the Chairman.
R To advise on applications for Regional Selective Assistance (RSA) in excess of £500,000.
G Wales.
✍ For further information see **Industrial Development Boards** (Regional).

Welsh Joint Education Committee   Now known simply as **WJEC**.

Welsh Language Board   (WLB)
■ Market Chambers, 5-7 St Mary Street, CARDIFF, CF10 2AT.
  Tel 029 2087 8000   **Fax** 029 2087 8001   http://www.byig-wlb.org.uk
  Chairman: Meri Huws   Chief Executive: Meirion Prys Jones
E Established in 1993 under the Welsh Language Act 1993. WLB functions as an Executive NDPB of the National Assembly for Wales. The Board comprises eleven members including the Chairman.
R To promote and facilitate the use of the Welsh language.
G Wales.
= Bwrdd yr Iaith Gymraeg

Welsh Medical Committee   (WMC)

■   PHPD3, Cathays Park, CARDIFF, CF10 3NQ.
       Tel 029 2082 5038   **Fax** 029 2082 3430
       Chairman: Dr Ed Wilkins
E   Established in April 1974 under the National Health Service Reorganisation Act 1973. WMC functions as a
       Scientific Advisory Committee and an Advisory NDPB of the National Assembly for Wales. The Committee
       comprises 21 members including the Chairman.
R   To advise the Assembly on professional medical issues in Wales.
G   Wales.
✍   For further information see **Scientific Advisory Committees**.

Welsh National Board for Nursing, Midwifery & Health Visiting
✍   See the **Nursing & Midwifery Council**.

Welsh Nursing & Midwifery Committee   (WNMC)

■   PHPD3, Cathays Park, CARDIFF, CF10 3NQ.
       Tel 029 2082 3777   **Fax** 029 2082 3430
       Chairman: Jill Paterson
E   Established in July 1974 under the NHS Reorganisation Act 1973. WNMC functions as a Scientific Advisory
       Committee and an Advisory NDPB of the National Assembly for Wales. The Committee comprises 15 members
       including the Chairman.
R   To advise the Assembly for Wales on professional nursing and midwifery issues in Wales.
G   Wales.
✍   For further information see **Scientific Advisory Committees**.

Welsh Optometric Committee   (WOC)

■   PHPD3, Cathays Park, CARDIFF, CF10 3NQ.
       Tel 029 2082 1453   **Fax** 029 2082 3430
       Chairman: Ian Jones
E   Established in April 1974 under the National Health Service Reorganisation Act 1973. WOC functions as a
       Scientific Advisory Committee and an Advisory NDPB of the National Assembly for Wales. The committee has
       eleven members including the Chairman.
R   To advise the Assembly for Wales on professional optical health issues in Wales.
G   Wales.
✍   For further information see **Scientific Advisory Committees**.

Welsh Pharmaceutical Committee   (WPHC)

■   PHPD3, Cathays Park, CARDIFF, CF10 3NQ.
       Tel 029 2082 3777   **Fax** 029 2082 3430
       Chairman: Berwyn Owen
E   Established in 1977 under the National Health Service Act 1977. WPC functions as a Scientific Advisory
       Committee and an Advisory NDPB of the National Assembly for Wales. The Committee comprises 19 members.
R   To advise the Assembly on professional pharmaceutical issues in Wales.
G   Wales.
✍   For further information see **Scientific Advisory Committees**.

Welsh Refugee Council   (WRC)

■   Phoenix House, 389 Newport Road, CARDIFF, CF24 1TP.
       Tel 029 2048 9800   **Fax** 029 2043 2980   http://www.welshrefugeecouncil.org
       Chairman: Aled Eirug   Chief Executive: Mike Lewis
E   Established in 1990. The Council is a registered charity.
R   To deliver high quality, direct services to meet the needs of refugees and asylum seekers.
G   Wales.
=   Cyngor Ffoaduriaid Cymru

Welsh Scientific Advisory Committee   (WSAC)

■   PHPD3, Cathays Park, CARDIFF, CF10 3NQ.
       Tel 029 2082 5417   **Fax** 029 2082 3430
       Chairman: Dr Keith D Griffiths
E   Established in May 1976. WSAC functions as a Scientific Advisory Committee and an Advisory NDPB of the
       National Assembly for Wales. The Committee comprises 20 members including the Chairman.

R To advise the Assembly for Wales on professional scientific health issues in Wales.
G Wales.
✍ For further information see **Scientific Advisory Committees**.

Welsh Therapies Advisory Committee   (WTAC)
■ PHPD3, Cathays Park, CARDIFF, CF10 3NQ.
Tel 029 2082 5417   **Fax** 029 2082 3430
Chairman: Sandra Morgan
E Established in 2001. WTAC functions as a Scientific Advisory Committee and an Advisory NDPB of the Natinal
Assembly for Wales. The Committee comprises 16 members including the Chairman.
R To advise the Assembly on professional therapeutic health issues in Wales.
G Wales.
✍ For further information see **Scientific Advisory Committees**.

Wessex Regional Flood Defence Committee   See **Environment Agency** [South West Region].

West Country Tourist Board
✍ See **South West Tourism**.

West Lakes Renaissance
✍ A former trading name of Furness West Cumbria New Vision Urban Regeneration Company which was wound up
in April 2011.

West Mercia Police Authority
■ PO Box 487, SHREWSBURY, Salop, SY2 6WB.
Tel 01743 264690   **Fax** 01743 264699   http://www.westmerciapoliceauthority.gov.uk
Chairman: Cllr Sheila Blagg
E Established in April 1995, the Authority is an independent body charged with ensuring that West Mercia Police
provide an effective and efficient police service. It is made up of seven councillor members appointed by the
lead local authorities in West Mercia and eight independent members.
G Herefordshire, Shropshire (incl Telford & Wrekin) and Worcestershire.
✍ For further information see **Police Authorities**.

West Mercia Probation Trust
■ Stourbank House, 90 Mill Street, KIDDERMINSTER, Worcs, DY11 6XA.
Tel 01562 748375   **Fax** 01562 748407   http://www.westmerciaprobation.org.uk
Chairman: James Kelly   Chief Executive: David Chantler
E Established on 1 April 2001 under the Criminal Justice & Court Service Act 2000 as the West Mercia Probation
Area Board. It became a trust on 1 April 2008 under the Offender Management Act 2007. The Board comprises
16 members including the Chairman.
G Herefordshire, Shropshire (incl Telford & Wrekin) and Worcestershire.
✍ For further information see **Probation Trusts**.

West Midlands Councils   (WMC)
■ Albert House, Quay Place, Edward Street, BIRMINGHAM, B1 2RA.
Tel 0121 678 1010   **Fax** 0121 678 1049   http://www.wmleadersboard.gov.uk
Chairman: Cllr Philip Atkins   Chief Executive: Mark Barrow
E Established 1 April 2010 following abolition of the West Midlands Regional Assembly, WMC is an independent
membership organisation of the 33 local authorities in the region, represented by the 33 council leaders. The
Chairman, his three vice chairmen and the Chief Exceutive comprise the Management Committee.
R To be responsible, in conjunction with Advantage West Midlands (qv), for regional strategic planning and
economic development.
G Herefordshire, Shropshire, Staffordshire, Warwickshire, West Midlands (Birmingham, Coventry, Dudley, Sandwell,
Solihull, Walsall, Wolverhampton), Worcestershire.

West Midlands Industrial Development Board
✍ See note under **Industrial Development Boards**.

West Midlands Integrated Transport Authority
- Centro House, 16 Summer Lane, BIRMINGHAM, B19 3SD.
  Tel 0121 200 2787   http://www.centro.org.uk
  Chairman: Cllr Angus Adams
- E Established in 1986 under the Local Government Act 2005 and known as the West Midlands Passenger Authority until renamed on 9 February 2009 under the Transport Act 2008. The Authority comprises 27 Councillors who are appointed by the seven Metropolitan District Councils that make up the West Midlands.
- G West Midlands.
- ✍ For further information see **Passenger Transport Executives & Integrated Transport Authorities**.

West Midlands Passenger Transport Executive   Operates under the brand name **Centro**.

West Midlands Police Authority   (WMPA)
- Lloyd House, Colmore Circus Queensway, BIRMINGHAM, B4 6NQ.
  Tel 0121 626 5143   Fax 0121 626 5003   http://www.west-midlands-pa.gov.uk
  Chairman: Bishop Dr Derek Webly, MBE
- E Established in April 1995, the Authority is an independent body charged with ensuring that West Midlands Police provide an effective and efficient police service. It is made up of nine councillor members and eight independent members.
- G The metropolitan boroughs of Birmingham, Coventry, Dudley, Sandwell, Solihull, Walsall and Wolverhampton.
- ✍ For further information see **Police Authorities**.

West Midlands Regional Assembly
- ✍ Abolished on 31 March 2010 (see Regional Assemblies). The region's local authority leaders cooperate as **West Midlands Councils**.

West Midlands Regional Observatory   See **Regional Observatories**.

West Midlands Regional Select Committee and West Midlands Grand Committee   See **United Kingdom Parliament: Committees**.

West Midlands Rural Community Action Network   WMRCAN represents **Community Council for Shropshire**, **Community Council for Staffordshire**, **Community First in Herefordshire & Worcestershire and** Warwickshire Rural Community Council; it operates under the umbrella of **Action with Communities in Rural England**.

West Midlands South Strategic Health Authority
- ✍ On 1 July 2006 merged with the Shropshire & Staffordshire anf the Birmingham & the Black Country Strategic Health Authorities to form the **West Midlands Strategic Health Authority**.

West Midlands Strategic Health Authority
- St Chads Court, 213 Hagley Road, Edgbaston, BIRMINGHAM, B16 9RG.
  Tel 0845 695 2222   Fax 0121 695 2233   http://www.westmidlands.nhs.uk
  Chairman: Elisabeth Buggins, CBE, DL   Chief Executive: Ian Cumming, OBE
- E Established on 1 July 2006 replacing three former Strategic Health Authorities: the Birmingham & the Black Country, the Shropshire & Staffordshire and the West Midlands South.
  The board comprises five non-executive directors including the Chairman, and eleven executive directors including the Chief Executive.
- R To relay and explain national policy, set direction and support and develop NHS Trust bodies (Primary Care Trusts and NHS Trusts providing acute, mental health and ambulance services).
  To ensure that local health systems operate effectively and efficiently, and that national standards and priorities are met.
- G Herefordshire, Shropshire, Staffordshire, Warwickshire, West Midlands (Birmingham, Coventry, Dudley, Sandwell, Solihull, Walsall, Wolverhampton), Worcestershire.
- ✍ One of the ten regional Strategic Health Authorities of England - see **NHS - England** in the Subject Index.For further information see **NHS - England.**

© CBD Research Ltd · Beckenham · Kent BR3 5JS · Tel 020 8650 7745 · Fax 020 8650 0768 · E-mail cbd@cbdresearch.com · www.cbdresearch.com

West Midlands & Welsh Traffic Commissioner   See **Traffic Commissioners**.

West Northamptonshire Development Corporation   (WNDC)
■   PO Box 355, Franklin's Gardens, NORTHAMPTON, NN5 5WU.
  Tel 01604 586600   **Fax** 01604 586648   http://www.wndc.org.uk
  Chairman: John Markham, OBE   Chief Executive: Peter Mawson
E   Established in December 2004. WNDC was set up as an Urban Development Corporation (qv) for Northampton,
    Daventry and Towcester.
R   To promote and deliver sustainable housing growth and regeneration in Northampton, Daventry and Towcester.
G   West Northamptonshire.
✍   On 14 October 2010 the Government announced that it would abolish WNDC as an Urban Development
    Corporation and devolve its functions to local government.

West Sutherland Fisheries Trust   See **Rivers & Fisheries Trusts of Scotland**.

West Yorkshire Integrated Transport Authority   (WYITA)
■   Wellington House, 40-50 Wellington Street, LEEDS, W Yorks, LS1 2DE.
  Tel 0113 251 7218   **Fax** 0113 251 7373   http://www.wypta.gov.uk
  Chairman: Cllr Chris Greaves
E   Established in 1986 under the Local Government Act 1986 and known as the West Yorkshire Passenger
    Transport Authority until renamed on 9 February 2009 under the Transport Act 2008.
    The Authority comprises 22 Councillors who are appointed by the five Metropolitan District Councils that make up
    West Yorkshire.
G   West Yorkshire.
✍   For further information see **Passenger Transport Executives & Integrated Transport Authorities**.

West Yorkshire Passenger Transport Executive   Operates under the brand name **Metro**.

West Yorkshire Police Authority   (WYPA)
■   Ploughland House, 62 George Road, WAKEFIELD, W Yorks, WF1 1DL.
  Tel 01924 294000   **Fax** 01924 294008   http://www.wypa.org
  Chairman: Cllr Mark Burns-Williamson   Chief Executive: Fraser Simpson
E   Established in April 1995, the Authority is an independent body charged with ensuring that West Yorkshire Police
    provide an effective and efficient police service. It is made up of nine councillor members and eight
    independent members.
G   West Yorkshire.
✍   For further information see **Police Authorities**.

West Yorkshire Probation Trust
■   20-30 Lawefield Lane, WAKEFIELD, W Yorks, WF2 8SP.
  Tel 01942 361156   **Fax** 01942 291178   http://www.westyorksprobation.org.uk
  Chairman: Stan Hardy   Chief Officer: Sue Hall
E   Established on 1 April 2001 under the Criminal Justice & Court Service Act 2000 as the West Yorkshire Probation
    Area Board. It became a trust on 1 April 2010 under the Offender Management Act 2007. The Board comprises
    14 members including the Chairman.
G   West Yorkshire.
✍   For further information see **Probation Trusts**.

West Yorkshire Strategic Health Authority
✍   On 1 July 2006 merged with the North & East Yorkshire & Northern Lincolnshire and the South Yorkshire Strategic
    Health Authorities to form **Yorkshire & the Humber Strategic Health Authority**.

Wester Ross Fisheries Trust   See **Rivers & Fisheries Trusts of Scotland**.

Western Agricultural Land Tribunal
■   Defra Building, Electra Way, CREWE, Cheshire, CW1 6GJ.
  Tel 01270 754156   **Fax** 01270 754260
  Secretary: Mr M Baker

E Established under the Agriculture Act 1947 (Section 73).
G Cheshire, Greater Manchester, Lancashire, Merseyside, Shropshire, Staffordshire.
✍ For further information see **Agricultural Land Tribunals**.

Western Education & Library Board   (WELB)
■ 1 Hospital Road, OMAGH, Co Tyrone, BT79 0AW.
   Tel 028 8241 1411   **Fax** 028 8241 1400   http://www.welbni.org
   Chairman: Peter Duffy   Chief Executive: Barry Mulholland
E Established in 1973. WELB functions as an Executive NDPB of the Department of Education Northern Ireland.
G Local Government Districts Derry, Fermanagh, Omagh, Limavady and Strabane.
✍ The ELBs and other legacy organisations will be dissolved when the Education & Skills Authority (qv) becomes
   fully operational.
   For further information see **Education & Library Boards (Northern Ireland)**.

Western Health & Social Care Trust
■ MDCEC Building, Altnagelvin Area Hospital Site, Glenshane Road, LONDONDERRY, BT47 6SB.
   Tel 028 7134 5171   http://www.westerntrust.hscni.net
   Chairman: Gerard Guckian   Chief Executive: Mrs Elaine Way
E Established on 1 April 2007, the Trust brings together the former Altnagelvin, Foyle and Sperrin Lakeland Health &
   Social Services Trusts.
G Derry, Limavady, Strabane, Omagh and Fermanagh.
✍ For further information see **Health & Social Care**.

Western Health & Social Services Board
✍ On 1 April 2009 the four regional boards were replaced by a single **Health & Social Care Board** for Northern
   Ireland.

Western Health & Social Services Council
✍ On 1 April 2009 the four regional councils were replaced by a single **Patient & Client Council** for Northern
   Ireland.

Western Isles Enterprise
✍ WIE is now the Stornoway office of **Highlands & Islands Enterprise**.

Western Isles NHS Board
■ 37 South Beach Street, STORNOWAY, Isle of Lewis, HS1 2BB.
   Tel 01851 702997   http://www.wihb.scot.nhs.uk
   Chairman: John MacKay, OBE   Chief Executive: Gordon Jamieson
G Western Isles.
✍ For further information see **NHS Scotland - Boards**.
= Bord Slainte Nan Eilean Siar

Western Isles Tourist Board
✍ Since 1 April 2005 an area office of **VisitScotland**.

Western Traffic Commissioner   See **Traffic Commissioners**.

Westminster Foundation for Democracy   (WFD)
■ Artillery House, 11-19 Artillery Row, LONDON, SW1P 1RT.
   Tel 020 7799 1311   **Fax** 020 7799 1312   http://www.wfd.org
   Chairman: Gary Streeter, MP   Chief Executive: Linda Duffield
E Established in March 1992. WFD is registered as a company limited by guarantee and functions as an Executive
   NDPB of the Foreign & Commonwealth Office. The Foundation's Board of Governors comprises 14 members
   including the Chairman.
R To achieve sustainable political change in emerging democracies, in priority countries in Africa, Eastern Europe
   and the Middle East.
G United Kingdom.

Whitehaven Harbour Commissioners

- ■ 27 Lowther Street, WHITEHAVEN, Cumbria, CA28 7DN.
  Tel 01946 590515 Fax 01946 590595 http://www.whitehavenhc.org.uk
  Chairman: Gordon Thomson
- E Established under the Whitehaven Town & Harbour Acts & Orders 1708 to 2007.
- G Whitehaven.
- ✍ For further information see **Port & Harbour Authorities**.

Wholesale & Retail Training Council

- ✍ Established in 1992, WRTC was one of Northern Ireland's Sector Training Councils. It closed for business in April 2007.

whowhatwherewhenwhy (W5)   See **National Museums Northern Ireland**.

Wick Harbour Authority   (WHA)

- ■ Harbour Office, WICK, Caithness, KW1 5HA.
  Tel 01955 602030 Fax 01955 605936 http://www.wickharbour.co.uk
  Chairman: Willie Watt
- E Established in 1879 as Wick Harbour Trust, since 1 July 2005 under the Wick Harbour Revision (Constitution) Order 2005 as Wick Harbour Authority. The board comprises six members including the Chairman, plus the Harbour Master.
- G Wick.
- ✍ For further information see **Port & Harbour Authorities**.

Wider Health Working Group

- ✍ The Group has not met since 1997.

Wilton Park

- ■ Wiston House, STEYNING, W Sussex, BN44 3DZ.
  Tel 01903 815020 http://www.wiltonpark.org.uk
  Chairman: Iain Ferguson, CBE   Chief Executive: Richard Burge
- E Originally established in 1946 at Wilton Park near Beaconsfield, it moved to Wiston House in 1951 and became an Executive Agency of the Foreign & Commonwealth Office on 1 September 1991. The Board comprises ten members including the Chairman.
- R To organise internationsl conferences, at Wiston House and elsewhere, at which leading opinion formers discuss the best ways to deal with key political, security and economic issues confronting the world.
- G United Kingdom.

Wilton Park Advisory Council   (WPAC)

- ■ King Charles Street, LONDON, SW1A 2AH.
  Tel 020 7008 6518 Fax 020 7008 1613 http://www.wiltonpark.org.uk/wpac/
  Chairman: Iain Ferguson, CBE
- E WPAC functions as an Advisory NDPB of the Foreign & Commonwealth Office. The Council comprises 16 members including the Chairman.
- R To oversee the conference programme of Wilton Park (qv) and safeguard its academic independence.
- G United Kingdom

Wiltshire Police Authority

- ■ PO Box 847, London Road, DEVIZES, Wilts, SN10 2DN.
  Tel 01380 734022 http://www.wiltshire-pa.gov.uk
  Chairman: Mr Chris Hoare
- E Established in April 1995, the Authority is an independent body charged with ensuring that Wiltshire Police provide an effective and efficient police service. It is made up of nine councillor members from Wiltshire County and Swindon Borough Councils and eight independent members.
- G Wiltshire.
- ✍ For further information see **Police Authorities**.

Wiltshire Probation Trust

■   Rothemere, Bythesea Road, TROWBRIDGE, Wilts, BA14 8JQ.
    Tel 01225 781960   **Fax** 01225 781969   http://www.wiltshireprobation.org.uk
    Chairman: Paul Aviss   Chief Officer: Diana Fulbrook

E   Established on 1 April 2001 under the Criminal Justice & Court Service Act 2000 as the Wiltshire Probation Area Board. It became a trust on 1 April 2010 under the Offender Management Act 2007. The Board comprises twelve members including the Chairman.

G   Wiltshire.

✍   For further information see **Probation Trusts**.

Wine & Spirit Education Trust   (WSET)

■   39-45 Bermondsey Street, LONDON, SE1 3XF.
    Tel 020 7089 3800   **Fax** 020 7089 3847   http://www.wsetglobal.com
    Chief Executive: Ian Harris, AIWS

E   Established in 1969. The Trust is governed by a Board of eight Trustees.

R   To provide high quality education and training in wines and spirits.

G   United Kingdom.

✍   For more information on awarding bodies see the **Federation of Awarding Bodies**.

Wine Standards Board of the Vintners' Company

✍   WSB's functions were transferred on 1 July 2006 to the **Food Standards Agency**.

WJEC

■   245 Western Avenue, CARDIFF, CF5 2YX.
    Tel 029 2026 5000   http://www.wjec.co.uk
    Chairman: Cllr Anthony Hampton   Chief Executive: Gareth Pierce

E   Established on 9 July 1948 as the Welsh Joint Education Committee under the provisions of the Education Act 1944. As WJEC it is now a registered charity and company limited by guarantee, owned by the 22 local authorities in Wales. The Board comprises 22 members including the Chairman.

R   To provide examinations, assessment, professional development, educational resources, and support for adults who wish to learn Welsh.
    To manage the National Youth Orchestra of Wales and the National Youth Theatre of Wales.

G   Wales.

✍   A member of the **Joint Council for Qualifications** and the **Federation of Awarding Bodies** (qqv).

=   CBAC (formerly Cyd-Bwyllgor Addysg Cymru)

Wolverhampton Development Company

✍   Established in 2007 as an Urban Regeneration Company (qv), WDC ceased operations in 2010.

Women's National Commission

✍   Established in July 1969 to advise government on wonen's issues, WNC was closed on 31 December 2010, its core functions transferred to the Government Equalities Office.

Wood Action Group

✍   WAG has become the **Wood Safety Group**.

Wood Safety Group   (WSG)

■   Marshalls Mill, Marshall Street, LEEDS, W Yorks, LS11 9YJ.
    Tel 0845 345 0055   **Fax** 0845 408 9566
    Chairman: Tim Small

E   Established in 2005 and known as the Wood Action Group until 2010. The Group functions as an advisory committee of the Health & Safety Executive (qv). It comprises 18 members including the Chairman.

R   To advise the HSE on health and safety issues relating to workers in the wood and allied industries.

G   United Kingdom.

Workforce Involvement Group   A subgroup of the **Offshore Industry Advisory Committee**.

Working Group on Action to Control Chemicals   (WATCH)

■ Floor FS1, Redgrave Court, Merton Road, BOOTLE, Merseyside, L20 7HS..
   Chairman: Steve Fairhurst
E Established as the scientific and technical sub-committee of the Advisory Committee on Toxic Chemicals (qv).
   WATCH functions as a Scientific Advisory Committee. The Group comprises twelve core members.
R To advise ACTS on scientific and technical issues relating to the assessment and control of health risks from
   chemicals.
✍ For further information see **Scientific Advisory Committees**.

Working Group on COSHH Essentials   A sub-committee of the Health & Safety Executive's **Advisory Committee on Toxic Substances**.

Working Group on European Exposure Limits   A sub-committee of the Health & Safety Executive's **Advisory Committee on Toxic Substances**.

Working Links Ltd

■ Garden House, 57-59 Long Acre, Covent Garden, LONDON, WC2E 9JL.
   Tel 020 7010 7830   http://www.workinglinks.co.uk
   Chairman: Keith Faulkner, CBE   Managing Director: Breege Burke
   Shareholder Executive contact: Michael Harrison
E Established in 2000.
   Working Links functions as a public-private partnership of the Department for Work & Pwnsions.
   The Stakeholder Board comprises eight members including the Chairman.
R To address the challenges faced by the long-term unemployed and help them back into sustainable work.
G United Kingdom.
✍ One of the businesses managed by the **Shareholder Executive**.

Working Party on Food Additives

■ Room 515B, Aviation House, 125 Kingsway, LONDON, WC2B 6NH.
   Tel 020 7276 8000   **Fax** 020 7276 8004
E The Working Party functions as an Advisory NDPB of the Food Standards Agency (qv). It comprises nineteen
   members including the Chairman.
R To provide guidance and information to the FSA on aspects of food additives and flavourings.
G United Kingdom.

Working Party on Materials & Articles in Contact with Food or Drink   (WPFCM)

■ Room 4B, Aviation House, 125 Kingsway, LONDON, WC2B 6NH.
   Tel 020 7276 8550
E Established in 1984. WPFCM functions as an Advisory NDPB of the Food Standards Agency (qv). The Working
   Party comprises 21 members.
R To advise the FSA on cost-effective research on materials and articles in contact with food to ensure that UK
   customers are effectively protected from chemical migration from such materials and articles into food.
G United Kingdom.

Working Ventures UK
✍ Set up in 2006 by the former National Employment Panel to support a network of employer coalitions, it closed in
   2009.

Working Well Together Steering Group   A working group of the Health & Safety Executive's **Construction Industry Advisory Committee**.

World Museum   See **National Museums Liverpool**.

Wrexham Local Health Board
✍ Merged on 1 October 2009 with the Anglesey, Conwy, Denbighshire, Flintshire and Gwynedd Local Health
   Boards to form **Betsi Cadwaladr University Health Board**.

Yarmouth Harbour Commissioners
- The Quay, YARMOUTH, Isle of Wight, PO41 0NT.
  Tel 01983 760321   http://www.yarmouth-harbour.co.uk
  Chairman: Sylvia Mence
E   Established in 1931 under the Yarmouth (Isle of Wight) Pier & Harbour Act 1931 and the Yarmouth Docks, Piers & Ferries Harbour Revision Order 1980.
G   Yarmouth.
✍   For further information see **Port & Harbour Authorities**.

Ymddiriedoaleth GIG Gwasanaethau Ambiwlans Cymru   See **Welsh Ambulance Services NHS Trust**.

Ymddiriedolaeth Prawf Cymru   See **Wales Probation Trust**.

Ymgyrch y Parciau Cenedlaethol   See **Campaign for National Parks**.

York & North Yorkshire Probation Trust
- Thurstan House, 6 Standard Way, NORTHALLERTON, N Yorks, DL6 2XQ.
  Tel 01609 778644   Fax 01609 778321   http://www.nyprobation.org.uk
  Chairman: Ken Bellamy, CBE   Chief Officer: Pete Brown
E   Established on 1 April 2001 under the Criminal Justice & Court Service Act 2000 as the North Yorkshire Probation Area Board. It became a trust on 1 April 2010 under the Offender Management Act 2007. The Board comprises ten members including the Chairman.
G   North Yorkshire.
✍   For further information see **Probation Trusts**.

Yorkshire Culture
✍   One of the eight Regional Cultural Consortiums established for England in 1999, it closed on 31 March 2009, its functions returned to the Department for Culture, Media & Sport.

Yorkshire Dales National Park Authority   (YDNPA)
- Yoredale, Bainbridge, LEYBURN, N Yorks, DL8 3EL.
  Tel 0300 456 0030   Fax 01969 652399   http://www.yorkshiredales.org.uk
  Colvend, Grassington, SKIPTON, N Yorks, BD23 5LB.
  Chairman: Cllr Carl Lis   Chief Executive: David Butterworth
E   The Yorkshire Dales were designated a National Park in 1954. The present Authority was established on 1 April 1997 under the Environment Act 1995. It consists of 22 members including the Chairman.
R   To help anyone who visits, works or lives in the area to protect and maintain the National Park.
    To help people to understand and enjoy the landscape, wildlife and local history of the Yorkshire Dales.
G   Yorkshire Dales.
✍   For further details see **National Park Authorities**.

Yorkshire Forward
- Victoria House, 2 Victoria Place, LEEDS, W Yorks, LS11 5AE.
  Tel 0113 394 9600   Fax 0113 243 1088   http://www.yorkshire-forward.com
  Chairman: Julie Kenny, CBE, DL   Chief Executive: Thea Stein
E   Established on 1 April 1999, one of the nine English Regional Development Agencies.
    Yorkshire Forward functions as an Executive NDPB of the Department for Business, Innovation & Skills.
    The board comprises 15 members including the Chairman.
G   Yorkshire (North, South, East and West), Lincolnshire (North and North East).
✍   The Comprehensive Spending Review in October 2010 confirmed the Government's intention to abolish the RDAs and support the creation of Local Enterprise Partnerships (qv), to be in place by March 2012.

Yorkshire Futures   See **Regional Observatories**.

       © CBD Research Ltd · Beckenham · Kent BR3 5JS · Tel 020 8650 7745 · Fax 020 8650 0768 · E-mail cbd@cbdresearch.com · www.cbdresearch.com

Yorkshire & Humber Assembly
- ✍ Abolished in March 2009 (see Regional Assemblies). The region's local authority leaders cooperate as **Local Government Yorkshire & Humber**.

Yorkshire & the Humber & East Midlands Industrial Development Board
- ✍ See note under **Industrial Development Boards**.

Yorkshire & the Humber Regional Select Committee and Yorkshire & the Humber Grand Committee   See **United Kingdom Parliament: Committees**.

Yorkshire & the Humber Rural Community Action Network   Y&HRCAN represents the **Humber & the Wolds Rural Community Council** and **Rural Action Yorkshire**; it operates under the umbrella of **Action with Communities in Rural England**.

Yorkshire & the Humber Strategic Health Authority
- ■ Blenheim House, Duncombe Street, LEEDS, W Yorks, LS1 4PL.
  Tel 0113 295 2000   **Fax** 0113 295 2222   http://www.yorksandhumber.nhs.uk
  Chairman: Kathryn Riddle   Chief Executive: Bill McCarthy
- E Established on 1 July 2006 replacing three former Strategic Health Authorities: the North & East Yorkshire & Northern Lincolnshire, the South Yorkshire and the West Yorkshire. The board comprises five non-executive directors including the Chairman. and nine executive directors including the Chief Executive.
- R To relay and explain national policy, set direction and support and develop NHS Trust bodies (Primary Care Trusts and NHS Trusts providing acute, mental health and ambulance services).
  To ensure that local health systems operate effectively and efficiently, and that national standards and priorities are met.
- G Yorkshire (North, South, East & West), Lincolnshire (North & North East).
- ✍ One of the ten regional Strategic Health Authorities of England - see **NHS - England** in the Subject Index.

Yorkshire & Humberside Agricultural Land Tribunal
- ■ Defra Building, Electra Way, CREWE, Cheshire, CW1 6GJ.
  Tel 01270 754156   **Fax** 01270 754260
  Secretary: Mr M Baker
- E Established under the Agriculture Act 1947 (Section 73).
- G Lincolnshire (North & North East), Yorkshire (East, North, South & West).
- ✍ For further information see **Agricultural Land Tribunals**.

Yorkshire & Humberside Pollution Advisory Council   (YAHPAC)
- ■ Environmental Protection Division, Town Hall, Kirkgate, SHIPLEY, W Yorks, BD18 3EJ.
  Tel 01274 437003   http://www.yahpac.org
  Coordinator: Ann Barker
- E Established in 1974 by voluntary agreement between local authorities. Membership comprises 30 local authorities in Yorkshire, North Lincolnshire and the surrounding area, and other bodies such as the Environment Agency (qv).
- R To consider all matters relating to environmental pollution and control.
- G Yorkshire, North Lincolnshire.

Yorkshire Regional Flood Defence Committee   See **Environment Agency** [North East Region].

Yorkshire Tourist Board
- ✍ Following a government decision in 2004 that the Regional Development Agencies should take over responsibility for tourism, YTB became an agency of Yorkshire Forward and was rebranded **Welcome to Yorkshire**.

Young Muslims' Advisory Group   (YMAG)
- ■ Eland House, Bressenden Place, LONDON, SW1E 5DU.
  Tel 030 3444 1356   http://www.ymag.opm.co.uk
  Chairman: Abdullah Saif

E   Established on 7 October 2008, to be active until summer 2010. YMAG functions as an advisory NDPB of the Department for Communities & Local Government and the Department for Education. The Group comprises 23 members including the Chairman.

R   To work directly with Government to deepen engagement with Muslim youth on issues such as discrimination, increasing levels of employment, preventing extremism and raising civic participation.

G   England.

Young People's Learning Agency   (YPLA)

■   Cheylesmore House, Quinton Road, COVENTRY, CV1 2WT.
Tel 0845 337 2000   http://www.ypla.gov.uk
Chairman: Les Walton   Chief Executive: Peter Lauener

E   Established in April 2010 under the Apprenticeships, Skills, Children & Learning Act 2009. YPLA functions as an Executive NDPB of the Department for Education. The Board comprises eleven members including the Chairman.

R   To champion education and training for young people by providing financial support for young learners, by funding academies for all their provision and by supporting local authorities to commission suitable education and training opportunities for all 16-19 year olds.

G   England.

✍   The Department for Education announced on 14 October 2010 that the future of YPLA was under consideration, subject to education structural reforms.

Youth Council for Northern Ireland   (YCNI)

■   Forestview, Purdy's Lane, BELFAST, BT8 7AR.
Tel 028 9064 3882   Fax 028 9064 3874   http://www.ycni.org
Chairman: Mrs Máire Young   Chief Executive: David Guilfoyle

E   Established on 1 April 1990 under the Youth Service (Northern Ireland) Order 1989.
The Council functions as an Executive NDPB of the Department of Education Northern Ireland.
The Board comprises ten persons including the Chairman.

R   To support, encourage & enable young people to realise their full potential.

G   Northern Ireland.

✍   The YCNI and other legacy organisations will be dissolved in 2010 when the **Education & Skills Authority**, established on 1 April 2009, becomes fully operational.

Youth Justice Agency of Northern Ireland   (YJA)

■   41-43 Waring Street, BELFAST, BT1 2DY.
Tel 028 9031 6400   Fax 028 9031 6402   http://www.youthjusticeagencyni.gov.uk
Chief Executive: Paula Jack

E   Established on 1 April 2003 as recommended in the Criminal Justice Review 2000. It functions as an Executive Agency of the Department of Justice Northern Ireland. The Management Board comprises five persons.

R   To reduce youth crime and build confidence in the youth justice system.

G   Northern Ireland.

●   The Agency works with children aged 11-17 years who have offended or are at serious risk of offending.

Youth Justice Board for England & Wales   (YJB)

■   1 Drummond Gate, LONDON, SW1V 2QZ.
Tel 020 3372 8000   Fax 020 3372 8002   http://www.yjb.gov.uk
Chairman: Frances Done

E   Established on 30 September 1998 under the Crime & Disorder Act 1998. YJB functions as an Executive NDPB of the Ministry of Justice. The Board comprises twelve members including the Chairman.

R   To advise the Secretary of State on the operation of, and standards for the youth justice system.
To monitor the performance of the youth justice system.
To purchase places for, and place, children and young people remanded or sentenced to custody.
To identify and promote best practice.
To make grants to local authorities and other bodies to support the development of best practice.
To commission research and publish information.

G   England, Wales.

✍   It was announced by the Government on 14 October 2010 that this body is to be abolished and its functions to be transferred into the Ministry of Justice.

YouthNet

- 5th Floor, Premier Business Centre, 20 Adelaide Street, BELFAST, BT2 8GD.
  Tel 028 9033 1880   **Fax** 028 9033 1977   http://www.youthnetni.org.uk
  Chairman: Michael Wardlow   Director: Denis Palmer
- E Established during the 1940s as the Standing Conference of Youth Organisations, it adopted its present title and structure in 1991.
  YouthNet is a membership body and functions as a registered charity and company limited by guarantee. The Executive Committee comprises 15 members including the Chairman.
- R To provide support to member organisations which in turn advance the emotional, intellectual, physical, spiritual and political development of children and young people.
  To provide information, training and guidance, which enhance the effectiveness of member organisations in promoting educational, social and leisure activities for the benefit of young people.
  To provide a grant giving function.
- G Northern Ireland.

Z

ZetTrans   See **Shetland Transport Partnership**.

Zoos Forum

- Zone 1/11, Temple Quay House, 2 The Square, Temple Quay, BRISTOL, BS1 6EB.
  Tel 0117 372 8385
  Chairman: Dr James Kirkwood
- E Established on 29 March 1999. The Forum functions as a Scientific Advisory Committee and an Advisory NDPB of the Department for the Environment, Food & Rural Affairs. It comprises 13 members including the Chairman.
- R To encourage the role of zoos in conservation, education and scientific research.
  To keep under review the operation and implementation of the zoo licensing system and advise or make recommendations to Ministers of any legislative or other changes that may be necessary,
- G United Kingdom.
- ✍ For further information see **Scientific Advisory Committees**.
  The Government announced on 14 October 2010 that the Forum would cease to function as a NDPB and be reconsituted as a committee of experts.

ABBREVIATIONS INDEX

Prepositions, articles and conjunctions are ignored in the alphabetisation of the directory
and have been similarly omitted from the names of organisations in this index.
See inside back cover for the key to the abbreviations used here.

Numerical

4NW	North West Regional Leaders Bd

A

A+DS	Architecture & Design Scotland
AACC	Aberdeen Airport Conslt C'ee
AADB	Accountancy & Actuarial Discipline Bd
AALA	Adventure Activities Licensing Authority
AAMWG	Additives & Authenticity Methodology Working Gp
ABBE	Awarding Body Built Envt
ABM	Abertawe Bro Morgannwg Univ Health Bd
ABRSM	Associated Bd Royal Schools Music
ACAF	Advy C'ee Animal Feedingstuffs
ACAHP	Central Advy C'ee Allied Health Professions
ACAS	Advy Conciliation & Arbitration Service
ACBS	Advy C'ee Borderline Substances
ACC	Anglican Conslt Coun
ACCEA	Advy C'ee Clinical Excellence Awards
ACCO	Advy C'ee Conscientious Objectors
ACDP	Advy C'ee Dangerous Pathogens
ACE	Arts Coun England
	Audience Coun England
ACERT	Advy Coun Educ Romany & Other Travellers
ACHS	Advy C'ee Hazardous Substances
ACHWS	Advy C'ee Historic Wreck Sites
ACMD	Advy Coun Misuse Drugs
ACME	Advy C'ee Mathematics Education
ACMSF	Advy C'ee Microbiological Safety Food
ACN	Audience Coun NI
ACNFP	Advy C'ee Novel Foods & Processes
ACNHS	Advy C'ee Nat Historic Ships
ACNI	Arts Coun NI
ACNRA	Advy Coun Nat Records & Archives
ACoBA	Advy C'ee Business Appointments
ACOD	Advy C'ee Older & Disabled People
ACOPS	Advy C'ee Protection Sea
ACP	Advy C'ee Packaging
	Advy C'ee Pesticides
ACR	Advy C'ee Roofsafety
ACRE	Action Communities Rural England
	Advy C'ee Releases Envt
ACRIB	Air Conditioning & Refrigeration Ind Bd
ACS	Audience Coun Scotland
ACT	Action Communities Cumbria

ACTS	Action Churches Together Scotland
	Advy C'ee Toxic Substances
ACW	Arts Coun Wales
	Audience Coun Wales
AERC	Alcohol Educ & Res Coun
AFBI	Agri Food & Biosciences Inst
AFC	Armed Forces C'ee
AFCLAA	Armed Forces Criminal Legal Aid Auth
AFLELG	Animal Feed Law Enforcement Liaison Gp
AFPRB	Armed Forces Pay Review Body
AGH	Advy Gp Hepatitis
AGNSS	Advy Gp Nat Specialised Services
AGOMM	Advy Gp Military Medicine
AHDB	Agriculture & Horticulture Devt Bd
AHMLR	Adjudicator HM Land Registry
AHRC	Arts & Humanities Res Coun
AHVLA	Animal Health & Veterinary Laboratories Agency
AIAC	Agriculture Ind Advy C'ee
AiB	Accountant Bankruptcy
AJTC	Administrative Justice & Tribunals Coun
ALG	Asbestos Liaison Gp
ALT	Agricl Land Tribunal Wales
AMAB	Ancient Monuments Advy Bd
AMTRA	Animal Medicines Trg Regulatory Auth
ANEC	Assn North East Couns
ANMAC	Aircraft Noise Monitoring Advy C'ee
APA	Asset Protection Agency
APB	Auditing Practices Bd
APC	Animal Procedures C'ee
APCI	Advy Panel Country Information
APJD	Advy Panel Judicial Diversity
APoSM	Advy Panel Substance Misuse
APPSI	Advy Panel Public Sector Information
AQA	Assessment & Qualifications Alliance
AQEG	Air Quality Expert Gp
ARB	Architects Registration Bd
ARCW	Archives & Records Coun Wales
ARHAI	Advy C'ee Antimicrobial Resistance...
ARSAC	Administration Radioactive Substances Advy C'ee
AS	First Tier Tribunal Asylum Support
ASA	Advertising Standards Auth
ASB	Accounting Standards Bd
Asbof	Advertising Standards Bd Finance
ASCB	Army Sport Control Bd
ASDAN	Award Scheme Development & Accreditation Network
ASNTS	Additional Support Needs Tribunals Scotland
ATC	Advocacy Training Council
ATIPAC	Air Travel Insolvency Protection C'ee
AWB	Agricl Wages Bd England & Wales

AWB(NI)	Agricl Wages Bd NI
AWM	Advantage West Midlands
AWMSG	All Wales Medicines Strategy Gp
AWPAG	All Wales Prescribing Advy Gp

B

BAAB	British Acupuncture Accreditation Bd
BABT	British Approvals Bd Telecoms
BAC	British Accreditation Coun Indep. . . Educ
BACC	Bournemouth Airport Conslt C'ee
BAcC	British Acupuncture Coun
BAFE	British Approvals Fire Eqpt
BAS	Bd Actuarial Standards
Basbof	Broadcast Advertising Standards Bd Finance
BASIC	British American Security Inf Coun
BBA	British Bd Agrément
BBBofC	British Boxing Bd Control
BBC	British Broadcasting Corpn
BBFC	British Bd Film Classification
BBNPA	Brecon Beacons Nat Park Auth
BBSRC	Biotechnology & Biological Sciences Res Coun
BC	British Coun
BCAG	Burial & Cemeteries Advy Gp
BCB	British Cheese Bd
BCC	Biocides Conslt C'ee
	British Copyright Coun
BCE	Boundary Cmsn England
BCNI	Boundary Cmsn NI
BCOS	Bishops Conference Scotland
BCPB	British Coun Prevention Blindness
BCPC	British Crop Protection Coun
BCRPM	British C'ee Reunification Parthenon Marbles
BCS	Boundary Cmsn Scotland
BCW	Boundary Cmsn Wales
BDC	British Dance Coun
BEC	British Electrotechnical C'ee
BEFS	Built Environment Forum Scotland
BEIC	British Egg Ind Coun
BELB	Belfast Educ & Library Bd
BFC	British Fashion Coun
BFI	British Film Institute
BFPO	British Forces Post Office
BFRC	British Fenestration Rating Coun
BHA	British Horseracing Auth
BHC	Belfast Harbour Cmsnrs
	British Hallmarking Coun
BIACC	Birmingham Intl Airport Conslt C'ee
BIC	British-Irish Coun
BJC	British Judo Coun
BMC	Bookmakers' C'ee
BNAC	British-North American C'ee
BOE	Church England Bd Educ
BoS	Bd Science
BPC	British Pharmacopoeia Cmsn
BPEX	British Pig Exec
BRAC	Bldg Regulations Advy C'ee
BRAG	Better Regulation Advy Gp
BRCC	Bedfordshire Rural Communities Charity
BSAC	British Screen Advy Coun
BSO	Business Services Org

BSSC	British Shooting Sports Coun
BTDC	British Tourism Devt C'ee
BTPA	British Transport Police Auth
BVEAG	Biologicals & Vaccines Expert Advy Gp
BWMB	British Wool Marketing Bd
BYC	British Youth Coun

C

C&G	City & Guilds
C4C	Channel Four Television Corpn
CA	Compensation Agency
CAA	Civil Aviation Auth
CAABU	Coun Advancement Arab British Understanding
CAAN	Countryside Access & Activities Network
CABE	Cmsn Architecture & Built Envt
CAC	Central Advy C'ee Pensions & Compensation
	Central Arbitration C'ee
	Charities Advy C'ee
CACHE	Coun Awards Care Health & Educ
Cafcass	Children & Family Court Advy Support Service
CAH	Community Action Hampshire
CAJ	C'ee Administration Justice
CAMIP	C'ee Accreditation Medical Illustration. . .
CAN	Community Action Northumberland
CAP	C'ee Advertising Practice
CARA	Coun Assisting Refugee Academics
CARES	UK Certification Auth Reinforcing Steels
CAT	Competition Appeal Tribunal
CAVOG	Cardiff & Vale Glamorgan Community Health Coun
CBBC	China Britain Business Coun
CBC	Church Buildings Coun
CBCEW	Catholic Bishops Conf England & Wales
CC	Consumer Coun NI
CCA	Cheshire Community Action
CCAB	Conslt C'ee Accountancy Bodies
CCB	Community Coun Berkshire
CCC	C'ee Climate Change
	Continuing Care Conf
CCCIS	Conslt C'ee Construction Ind Statistics
CCD	Community Coun Devon
CCEA	Coun Curriculum, Examinations & Assessment
CCJ	Coun Christians & Jews
CCJCS	Central Coun Jewish Community Services
CCMCC	Central Coun Magistrates Courts C'ees
CCMS	Coun Catholic Maintained Schools
CCNI	Charity Cmsn NI
CCRC	Criminal Cases Review Cmsn
	Criminal Courts Rules Coun
CCS	Community Coun Shropshire
	Community Coun Staffordshire
CCSC	Central Consultants & Specialists C'ee

CCU	Coun Christian Unity
CCW	Care Coun Wales
	Countryside Coun Wales
CCWater	Consumer Coun Water
CDA	Community Devt Agency Hertfordshire
CDC	Coun Disabled Children
CDF	Community Devt Foundation
CDOIF	Chemical & Downstream Oil Inds Forum
CDP	City Disputes Panel
CDS	Conf Drama Schools
CDX	Community Devt Exchange
CEC	C'wealth Engineers Coun
	Catholic Educ Cmsn
	Coun Educ C'wealth
Cefas	Centre Envt, Fisheries & Aquaculture Science
CEMB	Coun Ex Muslims Britain
CEMVO	Coun Ethnic Minority Voluntary Sector Orgs
CEPB	Church England Pensions Bd
CEWC Cymru	Coun Educ World Citizenship Cymru
CfA	Coun Administration
CFCE	Cathedrals Fabric Cmsn England
CFEB	Consumer Financial Educ Body
CfEL	Capital Enterprise
CFMC	Stakeholder Gp Current & Future Meat Controls
CFO	Court Funds Office
CFPA	Cromarty Firth Port Auth
CFRA	Chief Fire & Rescue Adviser
CGCE	C'wealth Games Coun England
CGCNI	C'wealth Games Coun NI
CGCS	C'wealth Games Coun Scotland
CGCW	C'wealth Games Coun Wales
CGMA	Covent Garden Market Auth
CHC	Cowes Harbour Cmsn
CHME	Coun Hospitality Management Educ
CHNI	Coun Homeless NI
CHRE	Coun Healthcare Regulatory Excellence
CHULS	C'ee Heads Univ Law Schools
CIC	Construction Ind Coun
CICA	Criminal Injuries Compensation Auth
CICAPNI	Criminal Injuries Compensation Appeals Panel NI
CIE-UK	Nat Illumination C'ee GB
CIFC	NI Central Investment Fund Charities Advy C'ee
CIHE	Coun Ind & Higher Educ
CILT	CILT Nat Centre Languages
CiNI	Children NI
CITB	CITB Construction Skills NI
CJC	Civil Justice Coun
CJI	Criminal Justice Inspection NI
CLA	Copyright Licensing Agency
CLAS	Churches Legislation Advy Service
CLC	Coun Licensed Conveyancers
CLD	Standards Coun Community Learning & Devt
CLOtC	Coun Learning Outside Classroom
CMACE	Centre Maternal & Child Enquiries
CMAL	Caledonian Maritime Assets
CMEC	Child Maintenance & Enforcement Cmsn
CNAC	Central Nursing Advy C'ee

CnaG	Comhairle Gaelscolaíochta
CNC	Crown Nominations Cmsn
CNCC	Coun Nature Conservation & Countryside
CNHC	Complementary & Natural Health Coun
CNP	Campaign Nat Parks
CNPA	Cairngorms Nat Park Auth
	Civil Nuclear Police Auth
COBRIG	Coun Brit Geography
COC	C'ee Carcinogenicity Chemicals Food...
CoCJ	Coun HM Circuit Judges
COGPED	C'ee Gen Practice Educ Directors
COI	Central Office Inf
COIC	Coun Inns Court
CoLRiC	Coun Learning Resources Colleges
COM	C'ee Mutagenicity Chemicals Food...
COMARE	C'ee Med Aspects Radiation Envt
COMEAP	C'ee Med Effects Air Pollutants
CONIAC	Construction Ind Advy C'ee
COPDEND	C'ee Postgraduate Dental Deans & Directors
COPMeD	Conf Postgraduate Med Deans
CoRWM	C'ee Radioactive Waste Management
COT	C'ee Toxicity Chemicals Food Consumer Products...
CPA	Cleveland Police Auth
CPAC	Central Pharmaceutical Advy C'ee
CPCAB	Counselling & Psychotherapy Central Awarding Body
CPIC	Construction Project Inf C'ee
CPMA	Consumer Protection & Markets Auth
CPNA	Coun Photographic News Agencies
CPRC	Civil Procedure Rule C'ee
	Criminal Procedure Rule C'ee
CPS	Crown Prosecution Service
CPSC	Civil & Public Services C'ee
CPSEAG	Chemistry Pharmacy & Standards Expert Advy Gp
CPSSAC	Central Personal Social Services Advy C'ee
CPW	Community Pharmacy Wales
CRB	Criminal Records Bureau
CRC	Cmsn Rural Communities
	Community Relations Coun
CRCC	Cornwall Rural Community Coun
CRD	Chemicals Regulation Directorate
CRF	Coal Research Forum
CRN	Countryside Recreation Network
CSAB	Civil Service Appeal Bd
CSAP	Correctional Services Accreditation Panel
CSC	C'wealth Scholarship Cmsn UK
CSCB	C'ee Scottish Clearing Bankers
CSCNI	Civil Service Cmsnrs NI
CSD	C'ee Safety Devices
CSF	UK Chemicals Stakeholder Forum
CSPL	C'ee Standards Public Life
CST	Coun Science & Technology
CT	Care Tribunal
CTBI	Churches Together Britain & Ireland
CTE	Churches Together England
CTSA	Channel Tunnel Safety Auth
CVU	Coun Validating Universities

CWDC	Children's Workforce Development Coun
CWGC	C'wealth War Graves Cmsn
CYEC	C'wealth Youth Exchange Coun

D

DASA	Defence Analytical Services & Advice
DCfW	Design Comsn Wales
DCNI	Drainage Coun NI
DDRB	Review Body Doctors & Dentists Remuneration
DE	Defence Estates
DE&S	Defence Equipment & Support
DEC	Darwin Expert C'ee
	Disasters Emergency C'ee
DHNA	Dart Harbour & Navigation Auth
DIC	Defence Inds Coun
DLAAB	Disability Living Allowance Advy Bd
	Disability Living Allowance Advy Bd NI
DMO	UK Debt Mgt Office
DMSAC	Distinction & Meritorious Service Awards C'ee
DNPA	Dartmoor Nat Park Auth
DNSC	Defence Nuclear Safety C'ee
DOR	Directly Operated Railways
DPA	Dorset Police Auth
DPBAC	Defence Press & Broadcasting Advy C'ee
DPTAC	Disabled Persons Transport Advy C'ee
DRCC	Durham Rural Community Coun
DSA	Disposal Services Agency
	Driving Standards Agency
DSAB	Diplomatic Service Appeal Bd
DSAC	Defence Scientific Advy Coun
DSC	Dental Schools Coun
DSDA	Defence Storage & Distribution Agency
DSG	Dartmoor Steering Gp
	Defence Support Gp
Dstl	Defence Science & Technology Laboratory
DTVACC	Durham Tees Valley Airport Conslt C'ee
DVA	Defence Vetting Agency
	Driver & Vehicle Agency
DVLA	Driver & Vehicle Licensing Agency
DWI	Drinking Water Inspectorate E&W
DWQR	Drinking Water Quality Regulator Scotland

E

EAB	Examinations Appeals Bd
EACC	Edinburgh Airport Conslt C'ee
EAGA	Expert Advy Gp AIDS
EAL	EMTA Awards
EAS	Energy Action Scotland
EAT	Employment Appeal Tribunal
EBLEX	English Beef & Lamb Exec
ECB	England & Wales Cricket Bd

ECGD	Export Credits Guarantee Department
ECITB	Engg Construction Ind Trg Bd
ECNI	Equality Cmsn NI
ECO	Export Control Org
EDC	Equality & Diversity C'ee
EEDA	East England Devt Agency
EESTC	Electrical & Electronics Servicing Trg Coun
EETB	East England Tourist Bd
EGAC	Export Guarantees Advy Coun
EHRC	Equality & Human Rights Cmsn
EIA	Envtl Investigation Agency
ELG	Enforcement Liaison Gp
EMAS	Employment Medical Advy Service
EMC	East Midlands Counties
EMDA	East Midlands Devt Agency
ENPA	Exmoor Nat Park Auth
ENSG	Energy Networks Strategy Gp
EOLG	Employers Org Local Govt
EPSRC	Engg & Physical Sciences Res Coun
ERAP	Eastern Rent Assessment Panel
ERC	Economic Res Coun
ERINI	Economic Res Institute NI
ESA	Educ & Skills Auth
ESB	English Speaking Bd
ESRC	Economic & Social Res Coun
ETC NI	Engg Trg Coun NI
ETI	Educ & Training Inspectorate
ETT	Electrical Trg Trust

F

FAB	Federation Awarding Bodies
FAWC	Farm Animal Welfare Coun
FCC	Foreign Compensation Cmsn
FCCC	Faith Communities Consultative Coun
FCILC	Foyle Carlingford & Irish Lights Cmsn
FDSS	Food & Drink Sector Skills
FEC	Food Ethics Coun
FERA	Food & Envt Res Agency
FHI	Fish Health Inspectorate
FHSAA	First Tier Tribunal Primary Health Lists
FIAC	Foundries Ind Advy C'ee
FJC	Family Justice Coun
FLA	Football Licensing Auth
FMC	Forensic Medicine C'ee
FOS	Financial Ombudsman Service
FPA	Funeral Planning Auth
FPAG	Fuel Poverty Advy Gp
FPRC	Family Procedure Rule C'ee
FRAB	Financial Reporting Advy Bd
FRC	Financial Reporting Coun
FRRP	Financial Reporting Review Panel
FRSB	Fundraising Standards Bd
FSA	Financial Services Auth
	Food Standards Agency
	Food Standards Agency NI
	Food Standards Agency Scotland
	Food Standards Agency Wales
FSAC	Forensic Science Advy Coun
FSC	Financial Supervision Cmsn
FSNI	Forensic Science NI
FSPB	Food Safety Promotion Bd

FSS	Forensic Science Service
FSSC	Financial Services Skills Coun
FTTIAC	First Tier Tribunal Immigration & Asylum
FWAG	Farming & Wildlife Advy Gp

G

GAAC	Gen Aviation Awareness Coun
GAC	Advy C'ee Government Art Collection
GACC	Glasgow Airport Conslt C'ee
GACR	Gen Advy C'ee Science
GAD	Government Actuary's Department
GAIC	Genetics & Insurance C'ee
GASCo	Gen Aviation Safety Coun
GATCOM	Gatwick Airport Conslt C'ee
GBBCA Forum	George Best Belfast City Airport Forum
GBCC	GB China Centre
GBGB	Greyhound Bd GB
GCC	Gen Chiropractic Coun
GCDA	Government Car & Despatch Agency
GDC	Gen Dental Coun
GEMA	Gas & Electricity Markets Auth
GFSC	Guernsey Financial Services Cmsn
GHSC	Gen Hypnotherapy Standards Coun
GHT	Gloucester Harbour Trustees
GHURC	Gloucester Heritage
GLA	Gangmasters Licensing Auth
	Greater London Auth
GMC	Gen Med Coun
GMITA	Greater Manchester Integrated Transport Auth
GMPA	Greater Manchester Police Auth
GMPTE	Greater Manchester Passenger Transport Exec
GOC	Gen Optical Coun
GOsC	Gen Osteopathic Coun
GPA	Gwent Police Auth
GPACC	Glasgow Prestwick Airport Conslt C'ee
GPCC	Gen Practitioners C'ee
GPhC	Gen Pharmaceutical Coun
GQA	Glass Qualifications Auth
GRCC	Gloucestershire Rural Community Coun
GRCCT	General Regulatory Coun Complementary Therapies
GRP	Gender Recognition Panel
GSCC	Gen Social Care Coun
GTAC	Gene Therapy Advy C'ee
GTCE	Gen Teaching Coun England
GTCNI	Gen Teaching Coun NI
GTCS	Gen Teaching Coun Scotland
GTCW	Gen Teaching Coun Wales

H

HAB	Hospitality Awarding Body
HACC	Heathrow Airport Conslt C'ee
HBAC	Historic Bldgs Advy Coun Wales
HBC	Historic Bldgs Coun
HBLB	Horserace Betting Levy Bd

HCA	Helideck Certification Agency
	Homes & Communities Agency
HCC	Hospital Chaplaincies Coun
	Meat Promotion Wales
HDC	Horticultural Devt Company
HEFCE	Higher Educ Funding Coun England
HEFCW	Higher Educ Funding Coun Wales
HELA	Health & Safety Exec Local Auth Enforcement Liaison C'ee
HESA	Higher Educ Statistics Agency
HFA	Halal Food Auth
HFEA	Human Fertilisation & Embryology Auth
HGC	Human Genetics Cmsn
HGCA	Home Grown Cereals Auth
HHA	Harwich Haven Auth
HHIC	Heating & Hotwater Ind Coun
HIA	Highlands & Islands Airports
HIE	Highlands & Islands Enterprise
HIFEAC	Higher & Further Educ Advy C'ee
HISC	Healthcare Associated Infection... Centre
HITRANS	Highlands & Islands Transport Partnership
HIW	Healthcare Inspectorate Wales
HMC	Historic Monuments Coun
HMCPSI	HM Crown Prosecution Service Inspectorate
HMCS	HM Courts Service >HMC4(11)
HMCTS	HM Courts & Tribunals Service
HMI Prisons	HM Inspectorate Prisons
HMI Probation	HM Inspectorate Probation
HMIC	HM Inspectorate Constabulary
HMICS	HM Inspectorate Constabulary Scotland
HMIE	HM Inspectorate Educ
HMIM	HM Inspectorate Mines
HMIP	HM Inspectorate Prisons Scotland
HMRC	HM Revenue & Customs
HoLAC	House Lords Appointments Cmsn
HOS	Housing Ombudsman Service
HPA	Health Protection Agency
	Humberside Police Auth
HPC	Health Professions Coun
HRP	Historic Royal Palaces
HSAC	Health Services Advy C'ee
HSC	Health & Social Care Bd
HSE	Health & Safety Exec
HSENI	Health & Safety Exec NI
HSL	Health & Safety Laboratory
HTA	Harris Tweed Auth
	Human Tissue Auth
HWRCC	Humber & Wolds Rural Community Coun

I

IAAC	Inf Assurance Advy Coun
IACC	Inverness Airport Conslt C'ee
IAG	Indep Advy Gp Sexual Health & HIV
IAP	Indep Advy Panel Deaths Custody
IAS	Immigration Advy Service
IBAS	Indep Betting Adjudication Service
IC	NHS Inf Centre
ICAA	Intl Curriculum & Assessment Agency
ICC	Irish Coun Churches

ICLR	Incorporated Coun Law Reporting E&W
ICO	Inf Cmsnrs Office
ICS	Institute Customer Service
IDAB	Indl Devt Advy Bd
IFS	IFS School Finance
IIAC	Indl Injuries Advy Coun
IIP	Investors People
ILF	Indep Living Fund
IMBs	Indep Monitoring Bds E&W
	Indep Monitoring Bds NI
IMI	Institute Motor Industry
INI	Invest NI
IPA	Insurance & Pensions Auth
IPC	Infrastructure Planning Cmsn
IPCC	Indep Police Complaints Cmsn
IPO	Intellectual Property Office
IPReg	Intellectual Property Regulation Bd
IPRI	Indl Pollution & Radiochemical Inspectorate
IPS	Identity & Passport Service
	ILEX Professional Standards
IPSA	Indep Parliamentary Standards Auth
IPT	Investigatory Powers Tribunal
IRC	Insolvency Rules C'ee
IRHSF	Ionising Radiation Health & Safety Forum
IRP	Indep Reconfiguration Panel
IRS	Indep Review Service Social Fund
ISA	Indep Safeguarding Auth
ISAC	Indep Scientific Advy C'ee MHRA Database Res
ISC	Indep Schools Coun
	Institutional Shareholders C'ee
	Intelligence & Security C'ee
ISCD	Indep Scientific C'ee Drugs
ISEB	Indep Schools Examinations Bd
	Inf Systems Examinations Bd
ISI	Indep Schools Inspectorate
ITA	Tyne & Wear Integrated Transport Auth
IVDAC	In Vitro Diagnostic Advy C'ee
IWAC	Inland Waterways Advy Coun
IWM	Imperial War Museum
IWRCC	Isle Wight Rural Community Coun

J

JAC	Judicial Appointments Cmsn
JCMBPS	Jt C'ee Mobility Blind & Partially Sighted People
JCMD	Jt C'ee Mobility Disabled People
JCPC	Judicial C'ee Privy Coun
JCQ	Jt Coun Qualifications
JCVI	Jt C'ee Vaccination & Immunisation
JCWI	Jt Coun Welfare Immigrants
JDC	Junior Doctors C'ee
JFSC	Jersey Financial Services Cmsn
JIBECI	Jt Ind Bd Electrical Contracting Ind
JIBPMES	Jt Ind Bd Plumbing Mechanical Engg Services
JIC	Jt Intelligence C'ee
JISC	Jt Inf Systems C'ee
JLIB	Jersey Legal Inf Bd

JMC	Jt Mathematical Coun UK
	Jt Med Command
JNCC	Jt Nature Conservation C'ee
JO	Judicial Office E&W
JSB	Judicial Studies Bd
JSBNI	Judicial Studies Bd NI
JSC	Judicial Studies C'ee
JSIC	Jt Security Ind Coun
JUC	Jt University Coun

L

LAF	Local Authority Forum
LAPT	London Academy Professional Trg
LARAC	Local Auth Recycling Advy C'ee
LBRO	Local Better Regulation Office
LCACC	London City Airport Conslt C'ee
LCOS	London Conf Overseas Students
LCR	London & Continental Railways
LCSG	London Cultural Strategy Gp
LDA	London Devt Agency
LDAP	Legal Deposit Advy Panel
LDNPA	Lake District Nat Park Auth
LEASE	Leasehold Advy Service
LESLP	London Emergency Services Liaison Panel
LFEPA	London Fire & Emergency Planning Auth
LGBCE	Local Government Boundary Cmsn England
LGBCS	Local Government Boundary Cmsn Scotland
LGBCW	Local Government Boundary Cmsn Wales
LGSC	Local Government Staff Cmsn NI
LGYH	Local Government Yorkshire & Humber
LISC	Library & Inf Services Coun NI
LJLACC	Liverpool John Lennon Airport Conslt C'ee
LLACC	London Luton Airport Conslt C'ee
LLTNPA	Loch Lomond & Trossachs Nat Park Auth
LLUK	Lifelong Learning UK
LMC	Livestock & Meat Cmsn NI
LOCOG	London Organising C'ee Olympic & Paralympic Games
LPA	Lerwick Port Auth
LPC	Low Pay Cmsn
LPFA	London Pensions Fund Auth
LPHC	Londonderry Port & Harbour Cmsnrs
LPS	Land & Property Services
LRA	Labour Relations Agency
LRAP	London Rent Assessment Panel
LRRC	Land Registration Rule C'ee
LSB	Legal Services Bd
	Lending Standards Bd
LSC	Legal Services Cmsn
	NI Legal Services Cmsn
LSDANI	Learning & Skills Devt Agency NI
LSIS	Learning & Skills Improvement Service
LSN	Learning & Skills Network
LTNI	Lands Tribunal NI

LTS	Lands Tribunal Scotland
	Learning & Teaching Scotland
LTUC	London Transport Users C'ee
LVRPA	Lee Valley Regional Park Auth
LVSC	London Voluntary Service Coun
LWARB	London Waste & Recycling Bd

M

MAA	Military Aviation Auth
MAC	Microbiology Advy C'ee
	Migration Advy C'ee
MACC	Manchester Airport Conslt C'ee
MACS	Mobility & Access C'ee Scotland
MADeC	Martial Arts Devt Cmsn
MAG	Ministerial Advy Gp
MASC	Med Academic Staff C'ee
MCA	Maritime & Coastguard Agency
	Med Coun Alcohol
MCB	Muslim Coun Britain
MCS	Military Court Service
MDPGA	Ministry Defence Police & Guarding Agency
MEA	Manx Electricity Auth
MEC	Med Ethics C'ee
MEE	Med Educ England
MEI	Mathematics Educ & Ind
MEUC	Major Energy Users' Coun
MGS	Museums Galleries Scotland
MHPF	Meat Hygiene Policy Forum
MHRA	Medicines & Healthcare Products Regulatory Agency
MHRT	Mental Health Review Tribunal NI
	Mental Health Review Tribunal Wales
MHTR	Mobile Telecomms & Health Res Programme C'ee
MHTS	Mental Health Tribunal Scotland
MIC	Mining Ind C'ee
MITA	Merseyside Integrated Transport Auth
MKPC	Milton Keynes Partnership C'ee
MLA	Museums Libraries & Archives Coun
MLC	Medico Legal C'ee
MLT	Mountain Leader Trg
MMO	Marine Mgt Org
MNH	Manx Nat Heritage
MNTB	Merchant Navy Trg Bd
MNWB	Merchant Navy Welfare Bd
MOSI	Museum Science & Industry
MPA	Merseyside Police Auth
	Metropolitan Police Auth
MPC	Bank England Monetary Policy C'ee
MPQC	Mineral Products Qualifications Coun
MQB	Mining Qualifications Bd
MRAP	Midlands Rent Assessment Panel
MRC	Med Res Coun
MRI	Moredun Res Inst
MSC	Marine Stewardship Coun
	Med Schools Coun
	Med Students C'ee
MTC	Meat Trg Coun
MVR	Motor Vehicle Repair Health & Safety Forum
MWC	Mental Welfare Cmsn Scotland

N

NAAC	Chemical Weapons Convention Nat Auth Advy C'ee
NAAFI	Navy Army & Air Force Institutes
NACT	Newcastle Airport Conslt C'ee
NAM	Nat Army Museum
NAO	Nat Audit Office
NAS	Nat Advy Gp Professional Devt Children's Workforce Schools
	Nat Apprenticeship Service
	Nat Archives Scotland
NATMAC	Nat Air Traffic Mgt Advy C'ee
NCA	Nat Coun Archives
	Nursing Coun Alcohol
NCAB	Nat Commissioning Advy Bd
NCB	Nat Children's Bureau
NCDT	Nat Coun Drama Trg
NCEPOD	Nat Confidential Enquiry Patient Outcome...
NCF	Nat Community Forum
NCH	Nat Coun Hypnotherapy
NCISH	Nat Confidential Inquiry Suicide... Mental Illness
NCMD	Nat Coun Metal Detecting
NCOR	Nat Coun Osteopathic Res
NCPC	Nat Coun Palliative Care
NCSC	Nat Coun Social Concern
NCTJ	Nat Coun Trg Journalists
NCVO	Nat Coun Voluntary Orgs
NCVYS	Nat Coun Voluntary Youth Services
NCW	Nat Coun Women GB
NDA	Nuclear Decommissioning Auth
NDIC	Nat Defence Inds Coun
NEA	Nat Energy Action
NEAB	Nat Employer Advy Bd
NEBDN	Nat Examining Bd Dental Nurses
NEBOSH	Nat Examination Bd Occupational Safety & Health
NEELB	North Eastern Educ & Library Bd
NEP	Nat Equality Panel
NEPNEI	Nat Expert Panel New & Emerging Infections
NERC	Natural Envt Res Coun
NES	NHS Educ Scotland
NESTA	Nat Endowment Science Technology & Arts
NFA	Nat Fraud Auth
NFC	Nat Forest Company
NFER	Nat Foundation Educl Res E&W
NFNPA	New Forest Nat Park Auth
NHBC	Nat House Building Coun
NHMB	New Homes Marketing Bd
NHMF	Nat Heritage Memorial Fund
NHS QIS	NHS Quality Improvement Scotland
NHSBSA	NHS Business Services Auth
NHSBY	NHS Blood & Transplant
NHSIII	NHS Institute Innovation & Improvement
NHSLA	NHS Litigation Auth
NHSPRB	NHS Pay Review Body
NIAS	NI Ambulance Service HSC Trust
NIAUR	NI Auth Utility Regulation
NIBRAC	NI Bldg Regulations Advy C'ee
NIBTS	NI Blood Transfusion Service
NICCY	NI Cmsnr Children & Young People

NICE	Nat Institute Health & Clinical Excellence
NICEAC	NI Clinical Excellence Awards C'ee
NICEIC	Nat Inspection Coun Electrical Installation ...
NICEM	NI Coun Ethnic Minorities
NICIE	NI Coun Integrated Educ
NICSAB	Civil Service Appeal Bd NI
NICTS	NI Courts & Tribunals Service
NICVA	NI Coun Voluntary Action
NIEA	NI Envt Agency
NIFAC	NI Food Advy C'ee
NIFHA	NI Fishery Harbour Auth
NIFRS	NI Fire & Rescue Service
NIGALA	NI Guardian Ad Litem Agency
NIGB	Nat Inf Governance Bd Health & Social Care
NIHB	NI Horse Bd
NIHC	Housing Coun
NIHE	NI Housing Exec
NIHEC	NI Higher Educ Coun
NIHRC	NI Human Rights Cmsn
NIJAC	NI Judicial Appointments Cmsn
NIJAO	NI Judicial Appointments Ombudsman
NILA	NI Library Auth
NILC	NI Law Cmsn
NILGOSC	NI Local Government Officers Superannuation C'ee
NIMC	NI Museums Coun
NIMDTA	NI Med & Dental Trg Agency
NIPA	NI Polymers Assn
NIPB	NI Policing Bd
NIPEC	NI Practice & Educ Coun Nursing & Midwifery
NISCC	NI Social Care Coun
NISRA	NI Statistics & Res Agency
NITB	NI Tourist Bd
NITC	NI Teachers Coun
NITHC	NI Transport Holding Company
NLA	Newspaper Licensing Agency
NLB	Northern Lighthouse Bd
NLC	Nat Lottery Cmsn
NLF	Nuclear Liabilities Fund
NLW	Nat Library Wales Bd Trustees
NMB	UK Metwork Mgt Bd
NMC	Nursing & Midwifery Coun
NMNI	Nat Museums NI
NMO	Nat Measurement Office
NMRN	Nat Museum Royal Navy
NMS	Nat Museums Scotland
NMSI	Nat Museum Science & Industry
NMWAG	Nat Muslim Women's Advy Gp
NNDC	North Northants Devt Company
NNPA	Northumberland Nat Park Auth
NOCN	Nat Open College Network
NOMS	Nat Offender Mgt Service
NPG	Nat Portrait Gallery
NPHC	Nat Park Homes Coun
NPIA	Nat Policing Improvement Agency
NPSA	Nat Patient Safety Agency
NPTC	Nat Proficiency Tests Coun
NRAC	Nuclear Res Advy Coun
NRAP	Northern Rent Assessment Panel
NRCC	Norfolk Rural Community Coun
NRL	Nottingham Regeneration
NS&I	Nat Savings & Investments

NSC	Nat Security Coun UK Nat Screening C'ee
NSC FAnGR	Nat Stdg C'ee Farm Animal Genetic Resources
NSCG	Nat Specialised Commissioning Gp
NSD	Nat Services Division
NSI	Nat Security Inspectorate
NSMC	North South Ministerial Coun
NSS	NHS Nat Services Scotland
NTA	Nat Treatment Agency Substance Misuse
NTC	Nat Toy Coun
NTIPDU	Nat Trg Inspectorate Professional Dog Users
NWDA	Northwest Regional Devt Agency
NWIS	NHS Wales Informatics Service
NWSF	Nat Water Safety Forum
NYA	Nat Youth Agency
NYMNPA	North York Moors Nat Park Auth
NYPA	North Yorkshire Police Auth

O

OBR	Office Budget Responsibility
OCPA	Office Cmsnr Public Appointments E&W
OCPANI	Office Cmsnr Public Appointments NI
OCR	Oxford Cambridge & RSA Examinations
ODA	Olympic Delivery Auth
ODLQC	Open & Distance Learning Quality Coun
OFFA	Office Fair Access
Ofsted	Office Standards Educ
OFT	Office Fair Trading
OIAC	Offshore Ind Advy C'ee
OISC	Office Immigration Services Cmsnr
OJAG	Office Judge Advocate General
OJC	Office Judicial Complaints
OLC	Office Legal Complaints
OLD	Olympic Lottery Distributor
OMC	Occupational Medicine C'ee
OME	Office Manpower Economics
ONE	One North East
OPA	Oil & Pipelines Agency
ORCC	Oxfordshire Rural Community Coun
ORR	Office Rail Regulation
OS	Ordnance Survey
OSAB	Ofcom Spectrum Advy Bd
OSC	Office Surveillance Cmsnrs
OSCR	Office Scottish Charity Regulator
OSHA	Office Strategic Health Auths
OSS	Office Social Services
Otelo	Office Telecommunications Ombudsman
OTS	Office Tax Simplification

P

P&SC	Parliamentary & Scientific C'ee
PABEW	Police Advy Bd E&W
PABIAC	Paper & Board Ind Advy C'ee
PABS	Police Advy Bd Scotland

PAC	Pet Advy C'ee
	Planning Appeals Cmsn
PACTS	Parliamentary Advy Coun Transport Safety
PAT	Pensions Appeal Tribunals Scotland
	Police Arbitration Tribunal
PAW	Partnership Action Wildlife Crime
PBNI	Probation Bd NI
PC	Parades Cmsn
PCC	Patient & Client Coun
	Press Complaints Cmsn
PCCS	Police Complaints Cmsnr Scotland
PCNPA	Pembrokeshire Coast Nat Park Auth
PDCS	Pension Disability & Carers Service
PFC	Professional Fees C'ee
PfS	Partnerships Schools
PHC	Padstow Harbour Cmsnrs
	Pet Health Coun
	Poole Harbour Cmsnrs
PHMC	Public Health Medicine C'ee
PHSO	Parliamentary & Health Service Ombudsman
PIAC	Printing Ind Advy C'ee
PIC	Population Investigation C'ee
PLA	Port London Auth
PLAB	Professional & Linguisitic Assessments Bd
PLR	Public Lending Right
PMCPA	Prescription Medicines Code Practice Auth
PNB	Police Negotiating Bd
POAC	Proscribed Orgs Appeals Cmsn
POB	Professional Oversight Bd
PPC	Private Practice C'ee
PPF	Pension Protection Fund
PPO	Prisons & Probation Ombudsman E&W
PPPA	People Pay & Pensions Agency
PRA	Prudential Regulatory Auth
PRC	Pesticide Residues C'ee
PressBof	Press Standards Bd Finance
PRHP	Private Rented Housing Panel
PRONI	Public Record Office NI
PSC	Public Services Cmsn
PSNC	Pharmaceutical Services Negotiating C'ee
PSNI	Pharmaceutical Society NI
PSPRB	Prison Service Pay Review Body
PTEG	Passenger Transport Executive Gp
PTUCS	Public Transport Users C'ee Scotland
PvEAG	Pharmacovigilance Expert Advy Gp
PWLB	Public Works Loan Bd
PWTAG	Pool Water Treatment Advy Gp

Q

QAA	Quality Assurance Agency Higher Educ
QCDA	Qualifications & Curriculum Devt Auth
QEIICC	Queen Elizabeth II Conference Centre
QMS	Quality Meat Scotland
QNJAC	Quarries Nat Jt Advy C'ee
QVS	Queen Victoria School

R

RAB	Renewables Advy Bd
	Restraint Accreditation Bd
RACCDC	Regional Advy C'ee Communicable Disease Control
RAD	Rural Action Derbyshire
RAFSB	Royal Air Force Sports Bd
RAFTS	Rivers & Fisheries Trusts Scotland
RAP	Rent Assessment Panel NI
RBG	Royal Botanic Gardens Kew
RBGE	Royal Botanic Garden Edinburgh
RCAHMS	Royal Cmsn Ancient & Historical Monuments Scotland
RCAHMW	Royal Cmsn Ancient & Historical Monuments Wales
RCAN	Rural Community Action Nottinghamshire
RCC	Rural Community Coun Leics & Rutland
RCCE	Rural Community Coun Essex Suffolk ACRE
RCCF	Rural Climate Change Forum
RCCM	Res Coun Complementary Medicine
RCCP	Registration Coun Clinical Physiologists
RCEWA	Reviewing C'ee Export Works Art
RCUK	Res Couns UK
RDC	Rural Devt Coun
REC	Religious Educ Coun E&W
RFA	Renewable Fuels Agency
RFAT	Reserve Forces Appeal Tribunals ><(05)
RHAG	Rural Housing Advy Gp
RHC	Railway Heritage C'ee
RIAC	Railway Ind Advy C'ee
RINH	Rowett Institute Nutrition & Health
RISC	UK Security & Resilience Ind Suppliers Community
RM	Royal Mint
RMA	Risk Mgt Auth
RMAC	Royal Mint Advy C'ee
ROSCO	Road Operators Safety Coun
RPA	Rural Payments Agency
RPSGB	Royal Pharmaceutical Society GB
RPTS	Residential Property Tribunal Service
RQIA	Regulation & Quality Improvement Auth
RSAP	Road Safety Advy Panel
RSCNI	Road Safety Coun NI
RSSB	Rail Safety & Standards Bd
RUBIAC	Rubber Ind Advy C'ee

S

SAAS	Student Awards Agency Scotland
SaBTO	Advy C'ee Safety Blood Tissues & Organs
SAC	Science Advy Coun
	Stamp Advy C'ee
	Statistics Advy C'ee
SACC	Southampton Airport Conslt C'ee
SACCA	Scottish Advy C'ee Credit & Access

SACDA	Scottish Advy C'ee Distinction Awards	**SEAC**	Schools Educ Advy C'ee
SACDM	Scottish Advy C'ee Drug Misuse		Spongiform Encephalopathy Advy C'ee
SACGM(CU)	Scientific Advy C'ee Genetic Modification	**SEEC**	South East England Couns
SACMILL	Scientific Advy C'ee Medical Implications Less Lethal Weapons	**SEEDA**	South East England Devt Agency
		SEELB	South Eastern Educ & Library Bd
		SELB	Southern Educ & Library Bd
SACN	Scientific Advy C'ee Nutrition	**SENTW**	Special Educl Needs Tribunal Wales
SACTRA	Stdg Advy C'ee Trunk Road Assessment	**SEPA**	Scottish Envt Protection Agency
		SEStran	South East Scotland Transport Partnership
SAP	Spoliation Advy Panel		
SAPC	Scottish Accident Prevention Coun	**SEUPB**	Special EU Programmes Body
SAS	Scottish Ambulance Service	**SFAC**	Scottish Food Advy C'ee
SASA	Science & Advice Scottish Agriculture	**SFC**	Scottish Further & Higher Educ Funding Coun
SASC	Staff & Associate Specialists C'ee	**SfC&D**	Skills Care & Development
SAWB	Scottish Agricl Wages Bd	**SfE**	Standards England
SBATC	Scottish Bldg Apprenticeship & Educ Coun	**SFELC**	Scottish Food Enforcement Liaison C'ee
SBCC	Scottish Bldg Contract C'ee	**SFRAU**	Scottish Fire & Rescue Advy Unit
SBTAF	Small Business Trade Association Forum	**SFT**	School Food Trust
			Scottish Futures Trust
SCAM	Stdg Conf Archives & Museums	**SHC**	Scottish Health Coun
SCAP	Scottish Charity Appeals Panel	**ShEx**	Shareholder Executive
	Stdg Conf Academic Practice	**SHIFC**	Scottish Highlands & Islands Film Cmsn
SCAR	Scientific C'ee Antarctic Res		
SCCRC	Scottish Criminal Cases Review Cmsn	**SHR**	Scottish Housing Regulator
		SIA	Security Ind Auth
SCCYP	Scotland's Cmsnr Children & Young People	**SIAC**	Special Immigration Appeals Cmsn
		SIB	Strategic Investment Bd
SCD NI	Sustainable Devt Cmsn NI	**SIFC**	Scottish Inter Faith Coun
SCDEA	Scottish Crime & Drug Enforcement Agency	**SJCRME**	Scottish Jt C'ee Religious & Moral Educ
SCDI	Scottish Coun Devt & Ind	**SLAB**	Scottish Legal Aid Bd
SCE	Service Children's Educ	**SLARC**	Scottish Local Auths Remuneration C'ee
SCELB	Staff Cmsn Educ & Library Bds		
SCHES	Stdg Conf Heads European Studies	**SLC**	Scottish Law Cmsn
SCIA	Scottish Coun Intl Arbitration		Student Loans Company
SCIS	Scottish Coun Indep Schools	**SLCC**	Scottish Legal Complaints C'ee
SCLR	Scottish Coun Law Reporting	**SLIC**	Scottish Library Inf Coun
SCNP	Scottish Coun Nat Parks	**SLMAC**	Strangford Lough Mgt Advy C'ee
SCO	Scottish C'ee Optometrists	**SMACAP**	Scottish Ministerial Advy C'ee Alcohol Problems
SCOLMA	Stdg Conf Library Materials Africa		
SCOPAC	Stdg Conf Problems Associated Coastline	**SMC**	Scottish Medicines Consortium
		SNBTS	Scottish Nat Blood Transfusion Service
SCOSS	Stdg C'ee Structural Safety		
SCOTH	Scientific C'ee Tobacco & Health	**SNH**	Scottish Natural Heritage
SCPA	Scottish Cmsn Public Audit	**SNWM**	Scottish Nat War Memorial
SCPP	Stdg Conf Physics Profs	**SOBHD**	Scottish Official Bd Highland Dancing
SCRA	Scottish Children's Reporter Administration		
		SOCA	Serious Organised Crime Agency
SCRC	Scottish Cmsn Regulation Care	**SPA**	Service Prosecuting Auth
	Sheriff Court Rules Coun	**SPCC**	Scottish Prison Complaints Cmsn
SCS	Scottish Court Service	**SPI**	Scientific Pandemic Influenza Advy C'ee
SCSC	Stdg Coun Scottish Chiefs		
SCSH	Scottish Coun Single Homeless	**SPPA**	Scottish Public Pensions Agency
SCUDD	Stdg Conf Univ Drama Departments	**SPPC**	Scottish Partnership Palliative Care
SCUTREA	Stdg Conf Univ Teaching & Research...	**SPRC**	Scottish Pre Retirement Coun
		SPS	Scottish Prison Service
SCVO	Scottish Coun Voluntary Orgs	**SPSA**	Scottish Police Services Auth
SDC	Sustainable Devt Cmsn	**SPSO**	Scottish Public Services Ombudsman
SDC Scotland	Sustainable Devt Cmsn Scotland		
SDC Wales	Sustainable Devt Cmsn Wales	**SPT**	Strathclyde Partnership Transport
SDPB	Scottish Dental Practice Bd	**SPTC**	Scottish Parent Teacher Coun
SDS	Skills Devt Scotland	**SPVA**	Service Personnel & Veterans Agency
SDSC	Scientific Diving Supervisory C'ee		
SE	Scottish Enterprise	**SQA**	Scottish Qualifications Auth

© CBD Research Ltd · Beckenham · Kent BR3 5JS · Tel 020 8650 7745 · Fax 020 8650 0768 · E-mail cbd@cbdresearch.com · www.cbdresearch.com

SRA	Solicitors Regulation Auth
SRAP	Southern Rent Assessment Panel
SRC	Scottish Refugee Coun
SSA	Social Security Agency
SSAC	Scottish Science Advy Coun
	Social Security Advy C'ee
SSAIB	Security Systems & Alarms Inspection Bd
SSCS	First Tier Tribunal Social Security & Child Support
SSDT	Scottish Solicitors Discipline Tribunal
SSRB	Senior Salaries Review Body
SSRC	Social Science Res C'ee
SSSC	Scottish Social Services Coun
SSSNB	School Support Staff Negotiating Body
STACC	Stansted Airport Conslt C'ee
STFC	Science & Technology Facilities Coun
STRB	School Teachers Review Body
SVAP	Security Vetting Appeals Panel
SVUK	Standards Verification UK
SWC	South West Couns
SWestrans	South West Scotland Transport Partnership
SWIA	Social Work Inspection Agency
SYPTE	South Yorkshire Passenger Transport Exec

T

TAB	Technical Advy Bd
TACTRAN	Tayside & Central Scotland Transport Partnership
TAS(NI)	Appeals Service NI
TCCT	Churches Conservation Trust
TDA	Trg & Devt Agency Schools
TDCI	Theatre Dance Coun Intl
TEC	Envt Coun
	London Couns Transport & Envt C'ee
TEXIAC	Textiles Ind Advy C'ee
TfL	Transport London Auth
THB	Powys Teaching Health Bd
THC	Teignmouth Harbour Cmsn
TLRC	Tax Law Review C'ee
TMP	Merseyside Partnership
tOSI	Ombudsman Services
TPAS	Pensions Advy Service
TPO	Property Ombudsman
TSA	Tenant Services Auth
TSol	Treasury Solicitors Department
TTS	Transport Trg Services
TVC	Treasure Valuation C'ee
TVPA	Thames Valley Police Auth
TVRCC	Tees Valley Rural Community Coun

U

UASSG	Unlinked Anonymous Surveys Steering Gp
UCET	Univs Coun Educ Teachers
UCML	Univ Coun Modern Languages
UKAB	UK Airprox Bd
UKACC	UK Automatic Control Coun

UKAP	UK Advy Panel Healthcare Workers Infected Bloodborne Viruses
UKAS	UK Accreditation Service
	UK Statistics Auth
UKBB	UK Bridges Bd
UKBI	UK Business Incubation
UKCA	UK Central Auth
UKCES	UK Cmsn Employment & Skills
UKCISA	UK Coun Intl Student Affairs
UKCP	UK Coun Psychotherapy
UKDPC	UK Disabled Peoples Coun
UKFSC	UK Flight Safety C'ee
UKHO	UK Hydrographic Office
UKIRT	UK India Round Table
UKLB	UK Lighting Bd
UKNIPC	UK Nat Influenza Pandemic C'ee
UKRLG	UK Roads Liaison Gp
UKTI	UK Tr & Investment
ULMAP	Uplands Land Mgt Advy Panel
USEL	Ulster Supported Employment
UTIAC	Upper Tribunal Immigration & Asylum

V

V&A	Victoria & Albert Museum
VAC	Video Appeals C'ee
VCA	Vehicle Certification Agency
VDS	Volunteering Devt Scotland
VMD	Veterinary Medicines Directorate
VOA	Valuation Office Agency
VOSA	Vehicle & Operator Services Agency
VPC	Veterinary Products C'ee
VPRC	Video Packaging Review C'ee
VRC	Veterinary Residues C'ee
VSC	Video Standards Coun
VTCT	Vocational Trg Charitable Trust
VTE	Valuation Tribunal England
VTS	Valuation Tribunal Service
VTW	Valuation Tribunal Wales

W

WAC	Water Appeals Cmsn
WAMITAB	Waste Mgt Ind Trg & Advy Bd
WAO	Wales Audit Office
WATCH	Working Gp Action Control Chemicals
WBC	Welsh Books Coun
WBS	Welsh Blood Service
WCB	Wales Coun Blind
WCPDP	Welsh C'ee Professional Devt Pharmacy
WCVA	Wales Coun Voluntary Action
WDC	Welsh Dental C'ee
WELB	Western Educ & Library Bd
WFAC	Welsh Food Advy C'ee
WFD	Westminster Foundation Democracy
WHA	Warrenpoint Harbour Auth
	Wick Harbour Auth
WHSSC	Welsh Health Specialised Services C'ee
WICS	Water Ind Cmsn Scotland
WIDAB	Welsh Indl Devt Advy Bd
WLB	Welsh Language Bd

WMC	Wales Mgt Coun
	Welsh Med C'ee
	West Midlands Couns
WMPA	West Midlands Police Auth
WNDC	West Northamptonshire Development Corporation
WNMC	Welsh Nursing & Midwifery C'ee
WOC	Welsh Optometric C'ee
WPAC	Wilton Park Advy Coun
WPAFC	First Tier Tribunal War Pensions & Armed Forces Compensation
WPFCM	Working Party Materials. . . Contact Food
WPHC	Welsh Pharmaceutical C'ee
WRC	Welsh Refugee Coun
WRCC	Warwickshire Rural Community Coun
WSAC	Welsh Scientific Advy C'ee
WSET	Wine & Spirit Educ Trust

WSG	Wood Safety Gp
WTAC	Welsh Therapies Advy C'ee
WYITA	West Yorkshire Integrated Transport Auth
WYPA	West Yorkshire Police Auth

Y

YAHPAC	Yorkshire & Humberside Pollution Advy Coun
YCNI	Youth Coun NI
YDNPA	Yorkshire Dales Nat Park Auth
YJA	Youth Justice Agency NI
YJB	Youth Justice Bd E&W
YMAG	Young Muslims Advy Gp
YPLA	Young People's Learning Agency

© CBD Research Ltd · Beckenham · Kent BR3 5JS · Tel 020 8650 7745 · Fax 020 8650 0768 · E-mail cbd@cbdresearch.com · www.cbdresearch.com

INDEX of NAMES
Chairmen, Chief Executives, etc

Prepositions, articles and conjunctions are ignored in the alphabetisation of the directory
and have been similarly omitted from the names of organisations in this index.
See inside back cover for the key to the abbreviations used here.

A

Abbott, Perry (Commander)
Stdg Coun Baronetage

Abbott, Peter (Admiral Sir)
Nat Museum Royal Navy

Abbott, Steve
Screen Yorkshire

Abraham, Ann
Parliamentary & Health Service Ombudsman

Abraham, David
Channel Four Television Corpn

Abramsky, Jenny (Dame)
Nat Heritage Memorial Fund

Acheson, Arthur
Ministerial Advy Gp

Ackroyd, Richard K
Scottish Water

Adair, Desmond (Dr)
London Academy Professional Trg

Adair, Roy
Belfast Harbour Cmsnrs

Adams, Angus
West Midlands Integrated Transport Auth

Adams, Sheenagh
Registers Scotland

Adamson, Andreana
State Hospitals Bd Scotland

Adgey, Jennifer (Prof)
Indep Scientific Advy C'ee MHRA Database Res

Adshead, John
London City Airport Conslt C'ee

Agius, Marcus
Royal Botanic Gardens Kew

Agnew, Rosemary
Scottish Legal Complaints C'ee

Ahern, Brian
Radon Coun

Ainsworth, John
Open & Distance Learning Quality Coun

Aitchison, Tom
Lothian & Borders Police Bd

Aitken, Joan
Traffic Cmsnrs

Aitken, John (Judge)
First Tier Tribunal Primary Health Lists

Akhter, Saria
Scottish Charity Appeals Panel

Akker, John
Coun Assisting Refugee Academics

Alderson, Matti
Removals Ind Ombudsman Scheme

Aldridge, Robert
Scottish Coun Single Homeless

Alexander, Helen
Port London Auth

Alexander, Pam
South East England Devt Agency

Allan, Alex
Jt Intelligence C'ee

Allan, Stuart
Public Standards Cmsnr Scotland

Allden, Alison
Higher Educ Statistics Agency

Allen, Bryan
British Dance Coun

Allister, Geoff
Roads Service

Allisy-Roberts, Penny (Dr)
Ionising Radiation Health & Safety Forum

Alty, John
Intellectual Property Office

Amy, Ron
Review Body Doctors & Dentists Remuneration

Anderson, Derick
Loughs Agency

Anderson, Karen
Architecture & Design Scotland

Anderson, Michael (Prof)
Nat Library Scotland

Anderson, Timo (Air Marshal)
Military Aviation Auth

Anderson-Evans, David
London Conf Overseas Students

Anderton, Julian
Energy Ombudsman

Andrews, Ian (Sir)
Serious Organised Crime Agency

Andrews, Margaret
NI Fishery Harbour Auth

Angel, John (Prof)
First Tier Tribunal Environment
First Tier Tribunal Inf Rights

Anne (The Princess Royal)
Corporation of Trinity House of Deptford Strond

Antrobus, Derek
Envt Agency - North West Region

Appleby, Louis (Prof)
Nat Confidential Inquiry Suicide... Mental Illness

Appleby, Sarah
Enforcement Liaison Gp

Appleton, Mike
Blackpool Fylde & Wyre EDC

Arbuthnot, Ivan
Gen Teaching Coun NI

Archer, John
Crouch Harbour Auth

Archer, Lesley
Gloucestershire Rural Community Coun

Archer, Mary
Essex Probation Trust

Archer, Paul
NI Ambulance Service HSC Trust

Arculus, David (Sir)
British Library Advy C'ee

Armitage, Mary (Dr)
Medicines Women's Health Expert Advy Gp

Armitt, John
Engg & Physical Sciences Res Coun
Olympic Delivery Auth

Armour, Robert
Scottish Coun Devt & Ind

Armstrong, Katherine
Community Coun Somerset

Armstrong, Lynda
British Safety Coun

Arnott, James M
Scottish Coun Intl Arbitration

Arthur, Michael (Prof)
Advy Gp Nat Specialised Services

Arthur, Peter
Cardiff & Vale Glamorgan Community Health Coun

Ashley, Derrick
Lee Valley Regional Park Auth

Ashmore, Philip
School Support Staff Negotiating Body

Ashton, Wendy
Disability Wales

Ashurst, Stewart
Stansted Airport Conslt C'ee

Aspden, John
Financial Supervision Cmsn

Astling, Viv
Birmingham Intl Airport Conslt C'ee

Aston, Terry
Rubber Ind Advy C'ee

Atkins, Philip
West Midlands Couns

Atkins, Susan (Dr)
Service Complaints Cmnsr Armed Forces

Atkinson, Maggie
Children's Cmsnr England

Austin, Trevor
Nat Coun Metal Detecting

Aviss, Paul
Wiltshire Probation Trust

Ayling, Bob
HM Courts & Tribunals Service

Aylward, Mansel (Prof Sir)
Public Health Wales

Ayres, Jon (Prof)
Advy C'ee Pesticides
C'ee Med Effects Air Pollutants

B

Bacon, Pat
Lifelong Learning UK

Bailey, Andrew
Prudential Regulatory Auth

Bailey, Mark (Prof)
Armagh Planetarium & Observatory

Bailey, Susan (Prof)
Restraint Accreditation Bd

Baillie, John (Prof)
Accounts Cmsn [Scotland]

Baillie, Tam
Scotland's Cmsnr Children & Young People

Bainbridge, Andrew
Major Energy Users' Coun

Bainbridge, Hilary
Waterways Ombudsman C'ee

Bainbridge, Janet (Prof)
Scientific Advy C'ee Genetic Modification

Baird, Ken (Dr)
Food Safety Promotion Bd

Bajaria, Narendra
Peak District Nat Park Auth

Baker, Christopher
Trg & Devt Agency Schools

Baker, David
Community Coun Devon

Baker, M
Midlands Agricl Land Tribunal
Northern Agricl Land Tribunal
Western Agricl Land Tribunal
Yorkshire & Humberside Agricl Land Tribunal

Balcombe, Tony
Southampton Airport Conslt C'ee

Balcon, Tim
Energy & Utility Skills

Balfour of Burleigh (Lady)
Nuclear Liabilities Fund

Ballantyne, Fiona
Museums Galleries Scotland

Balmer, Anne
Southern Health & Social Care Trust

 © CBD Research Ltd · Beckenham · Kent BR3 5JS · Tel 020 8650 7745 · Fax 020 8650 0768 · E-mail cbd@cbdresearch.com · www.cbdresearch.com

Banerjee, Millie
British Transport Police Auth

Bannister, Barbara (Dr)
Anti Infectives HIV & Hepatology Expert Advy Gp

Barbour, James (Prof)
Lothian NHS Bd

Bari, Muhammad Abdul (Dr)
Muslim Coun Britain

Barker, Ann
Yorkshire & Humberside Pollution Advy Coun

Barker, Arthur
Envt Agency - North East Region

Barker, John (Dr)
Foreign Compensation Cmsn

Barling (Justice)
Competition Appeal Tribunal

Barlow, Peter
Conf Drama Schools

Barnecutt, Jeremy
Solicitors Disciplinary Tribunal E&W

Barnes, Alison
New Forest Nat Park Auth

Barnes, Ann
Kent Police Auth

Barnes, Kathy
Service Personnel & Veterans Agency

Baron, Julia
Community Coun Shropshire

Barrett, Peter (Dr)
Indep Reconfiguration Panel

Barrett, Valerie
Welsh Indl Devt Advy Bd

Barrett, Vaughan
Scottish Prison Complaints Cmsn

Barrow, Mark
West Midlands Couns

Bartlett, George
Upper Tribunal Lands Chamber

Bartley, Keith
Gen Teaching Coun England

Bassett, Claire
Criminal Cases Review Cmsn

Bastock, Tony (Dr)
Chemical Weapons Convention Nat Auth Advy
C'ee

Batchelor, Paul
Crown Agents Oversea Govts & Administrations

Bate, Simon
Derbyshire Police Auth
New East Manchester

Bateman, Mike (Dr)
Envt Agency - South East Region

Batey, Peter
GB China Centre

Batho, Mark
Scottish Further & Higher Educ Funding Coun

Bayley, Mark
London & Continental Railways

Beacham, John (Dr)
Cogent

Beacom, Brian
Scottish Health Coun

Beamish, Richard
Asset Skills

Beath, John (Prof)
Economic Res Institute NI

Beaumont, Martin
Skillsmart Retail

Beaumont, Trevor
Horserace Totalisator Bd

Bebbington, Jan (Prof)
Sustainable Devt Cmsn Scotland

Beddington, John (Prof Sir)
Coun Science & Technology

Beddoe, Gwyneth
Food Standards Sampling Coordination Working
Gp

Bedingfield, Mike
Tourism South East

Beer, Gareth
Newport Unlimited

Belinis, Kate
Community Devt Agency Hertfordshire

Bell, Beverley
Traffic Cmsnrs

Bell, Sarah
Traffic Cmsnrs

Bellamy, Ken
York & North Yorkshire Probation Trust

Bellars, Wendy
Queen Victoria School

Belton, Adrian
Food & Envt Res Agency

Benfield, Graham
Wales Coun Voluntary Action

Benjamin, Jon
Bd Deputies Brit Jews

Bennett, David (Dr)
Monitor

Bennett, Jeremy
Gender Recognition Panel

Bennett, Kirsten
Cambridgeshire ACRE

Bennett, Simon
Forensic Science Service

Bennett, Tim
DairyCo

Benson, David
Milford Haven Port Auth

Benson, Graham
Screen South

Bensted, John
Gloucestershire Probation Trust

Beringer, Guy
Export Credits Guarantee Department

Berresford, James
Visit England

Bessant, Lesley
Northumbria Probation Trust

Best (Lord)
Property Ombudsman

Bett, Stephen
Norfolk Police Auth

Bettison, Paul
Local Government Regulation

Bezant, Richard
Envt Agency - South East Region

Bichard (Lord)
Design Coun

Biggar, Donald
Quality Meat Scotland

Biles, Mike (Dr)
Housing Ombudsman Service

Billiald, Sarah
Kent Probation Trust

Billingham, Patricia
Betsi Cadwaladr Community Health Coun

Bird, Viv
Booktrust

Birss (Judge)
Copyright Tribunal

Birt, Michael
Jersey Legal Inf Bd

Bishop, Chas
East Midlands Tourism

Bishop, Karl (Dr)
Welsh Dental C'ee

Bishop, Kevin (Dr)
Dartmoor Nat Park Auth
Dartmoor Steering Gp

Bishop, Roger
Awarding Body Built Envt

Black, Robert
Audit Scotland

Blackburne (Justice)
Land Registration Rule C'ee

Blacke, Fiona
Nat Youth Agency

Blackmore, Stephen (Prof)
Royal Botanic Garden Edinburgh

Blackstone (Baroness)
British Library

Blagg, Sheila
West Mercia Police Auth

Blain, Peter (Prof)
Advy Gp Military Medicine

Blair, Dorothy
Companies House

Blakemore, Colin (Prof)
Gen Advy C'ee Science

Blazwick, Iwona
London Cultural Strategy Gp

Blelloch, John (Sir)
Sentence Review Cmsnrs

Blizzard, Joy
Local Auth Recycling Advy C'ee

Bloomfield, Linda
Merseyside Probation Trust

Blundell, Tom (Prof Sir)
Biotechnology & Biological Sciences Res Coun

Board, Douglas
Refugee Coun

Board, Kate
CILT Nat Centre Languages

Boddington, Caroline
Crown Nominations Cmsn

Body, Gillian
Wales Audit Office

Boggis-Rolfe, Richard
Nat Employer Advy Bd

Bogues, Patrick
Ulster Supported Employment

Bosson, Shelley
Gwent Police Auth

Bowe, Collette
Office Communications

Bowen, Ann
Pharmaceutical Society NI

Bower, Cynthia
Care Quality Cmsn

Bowles, Hugh (Captain)
Mevagissey Harbour

Bowman, Clive (Dr)
Continuing Care Conf

Boyd, Gavin
Coun Curriculum, Examinations & Assessment
Educ & Skills Auth

Boyer, Isabel
UK Advy Panel Healthcare Workers Infected
Bloodborne Viruses

Boyle, Mark
Horserace Totalisator Bd

Boyle, Patrick
Indep Living Fund

Boyle, Paul
Financial Services Skills Coun

Boyle, Paul (Prof)
Economic & Social Res Coun

Bracewell, Stephen
Harwich Haven Auth

Brack, Ian
Olympic Lottery Distributor

Bradley, Anna
Communications Consumer Panel
Coun Licensed Conveyancers
Gen Optical Coun

Bradley, Lachlan
Scottish Jt C'ee Religious & Moral Educ

Bragg, Neil
Horticultural Devt Company

Brand, Chris
British Horseracing Auth

Brearley, Jonathan
Energy Networks Strategy Gp

Brechin, George
Fife NHS Bd

Breckinridge, Alasdair (Prof)
Medicines & Healthcare Products Regulatory
Agency

Brennan, Ursula
Defence Bd
Defence Press & Broadcasting Advy C'ee

Brewer, David
CPR Regeneration

Brewer, David (Sir)
China Britain Business Coun

Brewer, Richard
Ancient Monuments Advy Bd

Bridge, John
Agriculture & Horticulture Devt Bd
Opportunity Peterborough

Bridges, Andrew
HM Inspectorate Probation

Bridgewater, Peter (Dr)
Jt Nature Conservation C'ee

Bright, Roger
Crown Estate

Brigstocke, John (Sir)
East Midlands Strategic Health Auth
Judicial Appointments & Conduct Ombudsman

Brindley, Lynne (Dame)
British Library

Brodie (Lord)
Judicial Studies C'ee

Brook, Roger
Rivers & Fisheries Trusts Scotland

Brookes, Rodney (Sir)
Quality Assurance Agency Higher Educ

Brooks, Alan
Jt C'ee Mobility Blind & Partially Sighted People

Brooks, Paul
Skills Logistics

Broom, William
Gen Hypnotherapy Standards Coun

Brown, Andrew
C'ee Advertising Practice

Brown, Bill
Engg Trg Coun NI

Brown, Catherine
Animal Health & Veterinary Laboratories Agency

Brown, Chris
Visit Chester & Cheshire

Brown, David
South Yorkshire Passenger Transport Exec

Brown, David (Sir)
Ofcom Spectrum Advy Bd

Brown, Ed
Momentum

Brown, Ian (Dr)
Advy C'ee Animal Feedingstuffs
Envt Agency - North East Region
Pesticide Residues C'ee

Brown, Janet (Dr)
Scottish Qualifications Auth

Brown, John (Canon)
Rural Community Coun Essex

Brown, Keith
East England Tourist Bd

Brown, Malcolm
Mission & Public Affairs

Brown, Penny
Humber & Wolds Rural Community Coun

Brown, Pete
York & North Yorkshire Probation Trust

Brown, Philip
Traffic Cmsnrs

Brown, Roz
South Yorkshire Probation Trust

Brown, Stan
Forensic Science NI

Brown, Sylvia
Action Communities Rural England

Brown, Tim
Postcomm

Brown, W Michael B
Rules Golf C'ee

Browne of Madingley (Lord)
TATE

Browning, Helen
Food Ethics Coun

Brownlee, Graham
Nat Community Forum

Bruce, Peter
Fraserburgh Harbour Cmsnrs

Bruce, Russell
Durham Tees Valley Probation Trust

Brunstrom, Richard
Partnership Action Wildlife Crime

Bryans, Judith (Dr)
Dairy Coun

Brydon, Donald
Royal Mail Gp

Buchanan, Alistair
Gas & Electricity Markets Auth

Buchanan Black, Pauline
Tree Coun

Buckland, Yve (Dame)
Consumer Coun Water
NHS Institute Innovation & Improvement

Buckler, Malcolm
UK Business Incubation

Buckman, Laurence (Dr)
Gen Practitioners C'ee

Buczkiewicz, Martin
TACADE

Budd, Alan (Sir)
Tax Law Review C'ee

Budd, John
Cambridgeshire & Peterborough Probation Trust

Budworth, Teresa
Nat Examination Bd Occupational Safety & Health

Buggins, Elisabeth
West Midlands Strategic Health Authority

Bull, Mike
Devon & Cornwall Police Auth

Bullock, Steve (Sir)
Employers Org Local Govt

Bullpitt, Michael
Isle Wight Rural Community Coun

Bunch, James T
Rules Golf C'ee

Bunker, Richard
CILT Nat Centre Languages
Nat Foundation Educl Res E&W

Bunting, Frank
NI Teachers Coun

Bunting, Mary
North South Ministerial Coun

Burge, Anne
Registration Coun Clinical Physiologists

Burge, Richard
Wilton Park

Burgess, Stuart (Dr)
Cmsn Rural Communities

Burke, Breege
Working Links

Burley, Lindsay (Dr)
NHS Educ Scotland

Burley, Robin
Built Environment Forum Scotland

Burns (Lord)
Channel Four Television Corpn

Burns, Harry (Dr)
NHS>
UK Nat Screening C'ee

Burns, Jessica
Additional Support Needs Tribunals Scotland

Burns, John
Dumfries & Galloway NHS Bd

Burns, Margaret
NHS Health Scotland

Burns-Williamson, Mark
West Yorkshire Police Auth

Burrows, Mary
Burslem, Sandra (Dame)
Office Qualifications & Examinations Regulator

Burt, Pauline
Film Agency Wales

Burton, Edmund (Sir)
Inf Assurance Advy Coun

Burton, Michael (Sir)
Central Arbitration C'ee

Buscombe (Baroness)
Press Complaints Cmsn

Bush, Laurie (Dr)
Sussex Police Auth

Butcher, Joanne
Nat Coun Trg Journalists

Butler, Bill
Security Ind Auth

Butler, Norman (Brigadier)
Isle Man War Pensions C'ee

Butler, Paul
London Voluntary Service Coun

Butterworth, David
Yorkshire Dales Nat Park Auth

Byatt, Ian (Sir)
Water Ind Cmsn Scotland

Byles, Tim
Partnerships Schools

C

Cadman, Deborah
East England Devt Agency

Caine, Dinah
Skillset

Caithness (Earl)
Stdg Coun Scottish Chiefs

Calam, Derek H (Prof)
Chemistry Pharmacy & Standards Expert Advy Gp

Calder, William
Scrabster Harbour Trust

Calderwood, Richard
Greater Glasgow & Clyde NHS Bd

Callaghan, Bill (Sir)
Legal Services Cmsn

Callaghan, Paul
One North East

Calland, Anthony (Dr)
Caller, Max
Local Government Boundary Cmsn England

Calman, Kenneth (Sir)
Bd Science

Calvert, Janice
Pool Water Treatment Advy Gp

Cameron, David (Dr)
Grampian NHS Bd

Cameron, Dugald (Prof)
Glasgow Prestwick Airport Conslt C'ee

Cameron, Lorna
Scottish C'ee Optometrists

Cameron, Michael
Scottish Housing Regulator

Cameron, Sandy (Prof)
Parole Bd Scotland

© CBD Research Ltd · Beckenham · Kent BR3 5JS · Tel 020 8650 7745 · Fax 020 8650 0768 · E-mail cbd@cbdresearch.com · www.cbdresearch.com

Camley, Mark
  Royal Parks
Campbell, Bridget
  Scottish Advy C'ee Drug Misuse
Campbell, Calum
  Borders NHS Bd
Campbell, Donald
  MG ALBA
Campbell, Gerard
  NI Cmsnr Children & Young People
Campbell, Hazel
  Ulster Scots Agency
Campbell, Henrietta (Dr)
  NI Food Advy C'ee
Campbell, Maire
  Planning Appeals Cmsn
  Water Appeals Cmsn
Campbell, Noreen
  NI Coun Integrated Educ
Campbell, Sue (Baroness)
  UK Sport
Cannadine, David (Prof Sir)
  Nat Portrait Gallery
Canning, John (Dr)
  Professional Fees C'ee
Canterbury (Archbishop of)
  Archbishops' Coun Church of England
Cantlay, Mike (Dr)
  Loch Lomond & Trossachs Nat Park Auth
  Visit Scotland
Capaldi, Nick
  Arts Coun Wales
Capstick, Martin
  Aircraft Noise Monitoring Advy C'ee
Carey, Richard
  Grampian NHS Bd
Cargo, David
  Belfast Educ & Library Bd
Carlton, Karen
  Public Appointments Cmsnr Scotland
Carnall, Ruth
  London Strategic Health Auth
  Nat Specialised Commissioning Gp
Carnell, Jack
  Energy & Utility Skills
Carr, Alison
  Architects Registration Bd
Carr, Peter (Sir)
  North East Strategic Health Auth
Carruthers, Ian (Sir)
  South West Strategic Health Authority
Carruthers, Jonathan
  Humberside Probation Trust
Carruthers-Watt, Miranda
  Lancashire Police Auth
Carson, Ian (Dr)
  Regulation & Quality Improvement Auth

Carson, Trevor
  Learning & Skills Devt Agency NI
Carter, John (Sir)
  Nat House Building Coun
Carter, Nick
  Prospect Leicestershire
Carter, Paul
  South East England Couns
Carvill, Pat
  NI Clinical Excellence Awards C'ee
Casement, Patrick
  Coun Nature Conservation & Countryside
Casey, Louise
  Cmsn Victims & Witnesses
Cashmore, Roger (Prof)
  UK Atomic Energy Auth
Cassidy, Michael
  Museum London
Castell, William (Sir)
  Wellcome Trust
Castello, Antonia
  Mental Health Review Tribunal Wales
Cathcart, James
  British Youth Coun
Caudwell, Robert
  Envt Agency - Anglian Region
Causon, Jo
  Institute Customer Service
Cavanagh, Colm
  NI Coun Integrated Educ
Cavanagh, Michael
  C'wealth Games Coun Scotland
Caven, Norman (Dr)
  NI Statistics & Res Agency
Cayton, Harry
  Coun Healthcare Regulatory Excellence
  Nat Inf Governance Bd Health & Social Care
Cearns, Kathryn
  Financial Reporting Advy Bd
Ceeney, Natalie
  Financial Ombudsman Service
Chakrabarti, Shami
  Nat Coun Civil Liberties
Chamberlain, Paul
  Community Action Hampshire
Chambers, N M (Judge)
  Incorporated Coun Law Reporting E&W
Chambers, Robert
  Essex Police Auth
Chantler, David
  West Mercia Probation Trust
Chapman, John (Prof)
  Stdg Conf Physics Profs
Chapman, Mary
  Institute Customer Service
Chapman, Nick
  NHS Direct

Chatterjee, Sally
Visit London

Chaudhry, Farkhanda
Scottish Inter Faith Coun

Chilton, Robert (Dr)
Standards England

Chisholm, John (Sir)
Med Res Coun
Nat Endowment Science Technology & Arts

Chote, Robert
Office Budget Responsibility

Christensen, Poul
Natural England

Churchill, Lawrence
NEST Corpn

Churchill, Sophie
Nat Forest Company

Churton, Steve
Royal Pharmaceutical Society GB

Ciniewicz, Penny
Valuation Office Agency

Clare, Roy
Museums Libraries & Archives Coun

Clark, Chris
URENCO

Clark, Frank (Prof)
Scottish Cmsn Regulation Care

Clark, Judith
Envt Agency - North West Region

Clark, Les (Prof)
UK Certification Auth Reinforcing Steels

Clark, Rod
Nat School Government

Clarke, Alan
NI Tourist Bd
One North East

Clarke, Giles
England & Wales Cricket Bd

Clarke, James
Pesticides Forum

Clarke, John
Nottinghamshire Police Auth
Rivers Agency

Clarke, Tim
Harwich Haven Auth

Clarke-Hackston, Fiona
British Screen Advy Coun

Clasper, Mike
HM Revenue & Customs

Cleaver, Anthony (Sir)
Engineering UK

Cleland, Ronnie
Audit Scotland

Clements, Ian (Dr)
Health & Social Care Bd

Clements, Judy
Adjudicator's Office

Clemo, Jon
Norfolk Rural Community Coun

Cleverly, James
London Waste & Recycling Bd

Clowes, Elaine
Skills Active

Clowes, Mike
Hawk Bd

Coare, Pam
Stdg Conf Univ Teaching & Research. . .

Coats, Margaret
Gen Chiropractic Coun

Cobham, Penelope (Viscountess)
Cochrane, Claire
Stdg Conf Univ Drama Departments

Cochrane, John
Engg Trg Coun NI

Cockburn, A M
Scottish Solicitors Discipline Tribunal

Cockburn, Bill
Senior Salaries Review Body

Cockburn, David
Certification Office Trade Unions. . .

Cockburn, James
Fisheries Electricity C'ee

Coe (Lord)
London Organising C'ee Olympic & Paralympic
Games

Coe, Anthony
Envt Agency - Anglian Region

Cogbill, Alan
Local Government Boundary Cmsn England

Coggon, David (Prof)
C'ee Toxicity Chemicals Food Consumer
Products. . .
Mobile Telecomms & Health Res Programme C'ee

Coghlin (Justice)
Lands Tribunal NI

Cohen, Bronwen (Dr)
Children Scotland

Cohen, Malcolm (Dr)
Central Coun Magistrates Courts C'ees

Coker, Beverley
Nat Examining Bd Dental Nurses

Colbourne, Jeni (Prof)
Drinking Water Inspectorate E&W

Cole, John
NI Health & Social Services Estates Agency

Cole, Ray
Cumbria Police Auth

Coleman, Brian
London Fire & Emergency Planning Auth

Colgan, Pat
Special EU Programmes Body

Collett, Steve
Cheshire Probation Trust

Collier, David
England & Wales Cricket Bd

© CBD Research Ltd · Beckenham · Kent BR3 5JS · Tel 020 8650 7745 · Fax 020 8650 0768 · E-mail cbd@cbdresearch.com · www.cbdresearch.com

Collins, Bob
Equality Cmsn NI

Collins, Brian
Indep Monitoring Bds NI
South West Scotland Transport Partnership

Collins, Evelyn
Equality Cmsn NI

Collins, Ken (Dr)
Scientific Diving Supervisory C'ee

Collins, Philip
Office Fair Trading

Collins, Tony
Eastern Agricl Land Tribunal
South Eastern Agricl Land Tribunal
South Western Agricl Land Tribunal

Collis, Kim
Archives & Records Coun Wales

Colton, Adrian
Gen Coun Bar NI

Compton, John
Health & Social Care Bd

Compton, Steve
Opportunity Peterborough

Congdon, Richard
Centre Maternal & Child Enquiries

Connell, Jo
Advy C'ee Older & Disabled People

Connett, Alan
South West Couns

Conniff, Peter
Bedfordshire Police Auth

Conroy, Paul M (Revd)
Bishops Conference Scotland

Constance, Angela
Scottish Cmsn Public Audit

Conway, Peter
Warrenpoint Harbour Auth

Cook, Allan
Semta

Cook, Christopher
Lincolnshire Probation Trust

Cook, Elaine
Community Coun Berkshire

Cook, John
Brecon Beacons Nat Park Auth

Cook, Lesley
English Speaking Bd

Cook, Stuart
Energy Networks Strategy Gp

Cooke, David
British Bd Film Classification
Video Packaging Review C'ee

Cooke, Janet
London Transport Users C'ee

Cooke, Tim
Nat Museums NI

Cooksey, David (Sir)
London & Continental Railways

Cooksey, Len
Robin Hood Airport Conslt C'ee

Cooney, Gabriel (Prof)
Historic Monuments Coun

Cooper, David
Betsi Cadwaladr Community Health Coun

Cooper, Greg
British Bd Agrément

Cooper, Tony
Humber & Wolds Rural Community Coun

Cope, Jerry
Prison Service Pay Review Body

Corden, Richard
Cmsn Compact

Cormack, Arthur
Bord Gaidhlig

Cornick, David
Churches Together England

Corsar, Ken
Lanarkshire NHS Bd

Cosgrove, David
Durham Tees Valley Airport Conslt C'ee

Cottom, Andrew
Powys Teaching Health Bd

Coupal, Shahriar
C'ee Advertising Practice

Couper, Jean
Scottish Criminal Cases Review Cmsn

Cousins, Edward
Adjudicator HM Land Registry

Coutts, Garry
Highland NHS Bd
Scottish Social Services Coun

Covey, Donna
Refugee Coun

Cowan, Cathie
Orkney NHS Bd

Cowan, Ian
Community Pharmacy Wales

Cowley, Steven (Prof)
UK Atomic Energy Auth

Cox, Geoff
Paper & Board Ind Advy C'ee
Printing Ind Advy C'ee
Quarries Nat Jt Advy C'ee

Cox, John
Air Travel Insolvency Protection C'ee

Cox, Sebert
Durham Tees Valley Probation Trust

Cox, Tim
British Accreditation Coun Indep... Educ

Coyne, Gerard
Regen WM

Cracknell, Chris
Asset Skills

Craggs, Vic
C'wealth Youth Exchange Coun

Craig, Dorothy
Veterinary Residues C'ee

Craig, Gordon
State Hospitals Bd Scotland

Craig, Peter
NI Fire & Rescue Service

Crawford, Catherine
Metropolitan Police Auth

Crawford, Gerald
Drainage Coun NI

Crawford, Patrick
Export Credits Guarantee Department

Crawforth, John
Greater Manchester Probation Trust

Cresswell, Richard
Envt Agency - South West Region

Crichton, Ian
NHS Nat Services Scotland

Crick, Colin P
Newport Harbour Cmsnrs

Croisdale-Appleby, David (Prof)
Skills Care
Skills Care & Development

Crombie, Sandy (Sir)
Creative Scotland

Crook, Barrie
Hampshire Probation Trust

Cross, Bill
Rural Action Yorkshire

Cross, James
Marine Mgt Org

Cross, John
English Beef & Lamb Exec

Cross, Martin
Edexcel

Crothers, Terry
C'wealth Games Coun NI

Crouch, Anthony (Dr)
Counselling & Psychotherapy Central Awarding
Body

Crowder, Robert
Rural Community Action Nottinghamshire

Crowe, E Alan
Isle Man Post Office

Crozier, Sonia
Surrey & Sussex Probation Trust

Crump, Bernard (Prof)
NHS Institute Innovation & Improvement

Cubie, Andrew (Sir)
Northern Lighthouse Bd

Cullen, Bernard (Prof)
Staff Cmsn Educ & Library Bds

Cumming, Ian
West Midlands Strategic Health Authority

Cunningham, Paul (Commodore)
Disposal Services Agency

Curran, Stephen
Strathclyde Police Auth

Currie, Jim
NI Guardian Ad Litem Agency

Currin, Brian
Sentence Review Cmsnrs

Curtis, Peter
Wales Coun Blind

Curtis, Reg
Navy Army & Air Force Institutes

D

Dalton, Graham
Highways Agency

Dalton, Ian
North East Strategic Health Auth

Dangerfield, Peter (Dr)
Med Academic Staff C'ee

Daniels, Susan
UK Coun Deafness

Dardis, John
Food Safety Promotion Bd

Dare, Peter
Coun Photographic News Agencies

Darling, Paul
Football Licensing Auth

Dart, Geoff
Office Manpower Economics

Dasgupta, Partha
Pensions Advy Service

Datta, Shreelata (Dr)
Junior Doctors C'ee

Davey, Alan
Arts Coun England

Davidson, Howard
Envt Agency - South East Region

Davidson, Martin
British Coun

Davidson, Robin (Prof)
Alcohol Educ & Res Coun

Davidson, Tony (Revd)
Irish Coun Churches

Davies, C A
Agricl Land Tribunal Wales

Davies, Carole-Anne
Design Comsn Wales

Davies, Cilla
Gwent Police Auth

Davies, Dai
Meat Promotion Wales

Davies, David (Sir)
Nuclear Res Advy Coun

Davies, Delcie
Brecknock & Radnor Community Health Coun

© CBD Research Ltd · Beckenham · Kent BR3 5JS · Tel 020 8650 7745 · Fax 020 8650 0768 · E-mail cbd@cbdresearch.com · www.cbdresearch.com

Davies, John H
Civil Service Appeal Bd

Davies, Lesley
Durham Police Auth

Davies, Marcia
Agriculture Ind Advy C'ee

Davies, Mike
Royal Mint

Davies, Peter
Sustainable Devt Cmsn Wales

Davies, Rhian
Disability Wales

Davies, Sally (Prof Dame)
NHS
UK Nat Influenza Pandemic C'ee

Davies, Tony (Prof)
Advy C'ee Wales (Ofcom)

Davies, Vanessa
Bar Standards Bd

Davis, Bryan
Social Security Agency

Davis, Michael
UK Cmsn Employment & Skills

Davis, Sue
Stdg Conf Heads European Studies

Davis Smith, Justin (Dr)
Volunteering England

Davison, Tim
Lanarkshire NHS Bd

Daw, Roger
TACADE

Dawe, Mark
Oxford Cambridge & RSA Examinations

Dawe, Sandie
Visit Britain

Dawson, Shaun
Lee Valley Regional Park Auth

Dawson, Will
Tayside & Central Scotland Transport Partnership

Day, John (Air Chief Marshal Sir)
Royal Air Force Museum

Day, Michael
Historic Royal Palaces

Day, Will
Sustainable Devt Cmsn

Deakin, Nick
Med Students C'ee

Deakin, Richard
NATS

Dean of Thornton-le-Fylde (Baroness)
Covent Garden Market Auth

Dean, Steve (Prof)
Veterinary Medicines Directorate

Dean, Tony
Envt Agency - North West Region

Deech, Ruth (Baroness)
Bar Standards Bd

Deighton, Paul
London Organising C'ee Olympic & Paralympic Games

Delany, Sarah
Construction Project Inf C'ee

de Laszlo, Damon
Economic Res Coun

Delay, Tom
Carbon Trust

Delpy, David (Prof)
Engg & Physical Sciences Res Coun

Dent, Julie
London Probation Trust

Dervaird (Lord)
Scottish Coun Intl Arbitration

Desai, Nitin
UK India Round Table

De Trafford, John
Pension Disability & Carers Service

Devaney, John
NATS

Devanny, Aileen
Private Rented Housing Panel

Deverell, Jack (General Sir)
Nat Army Museum

Devine, Joseph (Bishop)
Catholic Educ Cmsn

Dewing, David
Geffrye Museum

Dhanda, Parmjit
Faith Communities Consultative Coun

Dhani, Jaspal
UK Disabled Peoples Coun

Dhanowa, Charles
Competition Appeal Tribunal

Dickens, Rob
Theatres Trust

Dickson, Niall
Gen Med Coun

Dillon, Andrew
Nat Institute Health & Clinical Excellence

di Mambro, Louise
Judicial C'ee Privy Coun

Dingwall, Tom
Blyth Harbour Cmsn

Dixon, Andrew
Creative Scotland

Dixon, Jim
Peak District Nat Park Auth

Dixon, Michael (Dr)
Natural History Museum

Dixon, Peter
Gen Chiropractic Coun

Dobbin, David (Dr)
Strategic Investment Bd
Trade & Business Devt Body

Dobbyn, Francis
Oil & Pipelines Agency

Docherty, David (Dr)
Coun Ind & Higher Educ

Dogget, Barry (Air Commodore)
Royal Air Force Sports Bd

Doherty, Malcolm
Lancashire Police Auth

Donaghy, Colm
Southern Health & Social Care Trust

Donaghy, Michael J (Dr)
Neurology Pain & Psychiatry Expert Advy Gp

Donaldson, Liam (Sir)
Nat Patient Safety Agency

Done, Frances
Youth Justice Bd E&W

Donnelly, Martin (Dr)
Disability Living Allowance Advy Bd NI

Doran, Alan
Human Fertilisation & Embryology Auth

Doran, Tony
CITB Construction Skills NI

Dorman, Edmund
Gloucester Harbour Trustees

Dorrance, Richard C (Dr)
Coun Awards Care Health & Educ

Dougal, Andrew
Warwickshire Rural Community Coun

Douglas, Anthony
Children & Family Court Advy Support Service

Douglas, Neil
Scottish Food Enforcement Liaison C'ee

Douglas, Rob
South East England Devt Agency

Douglas-Todd, Jennifer
Hampshire Police Auth

Dovey, Sue
Community Action Hampshire

Dow, Frances (Dr)
Marshall Aid Commemoration Cmsn

Dowd, Mark
Merseyside Integrated Transport Auth

Dowie, John
UK Roads Liaison Gp

Downs, Carolyn
Legal Services Cmsn

Doyle, Chris
Coun Advancement Arab British Understanding

Drever, David
Gen Teaching Coun Scotland

Drummond Young (Lord)
Scottish Law Cmsn

Duckworth, Simon D'Olier
City London Police Auth

Duff, Gordon W (Prof Sir)
Cmsn Human Medicines
Scientific Pandemic Influenza Advy C'ee

Duffield, Linda
Westminster Foundation Democracy

Duffy, Peter
Western Educ & Library Bd

Duncan, Stanley
Driver & Vehicle Agency

Dunion, Kevin
Scottish Inf Cmsnr

Dunleavy, Pauline
Employment Appeal Tribunal

Dunn, Maggie
Complementary & Natural Health Coun

Dunstone, Charles
Princes Trust Coun

Dutton, Sue
Lifelong Learning UK

Dutton, William (Prof)
Advy C'ee England (Ofcom)

Dyke, Greg
British Film Institute

Dyke, John
Exmoor Nat Park Auth

E

Earle, Michael
Irish Coun Churches

Earley, Rory
Capital Enterprise

Earnshaw, Adrian
Communications Cmsn

Earwicker, Martin J
Nat Museum Science & Industry

Eaton, Sheila
Nat Coun Women GB

Ebrill, Charles
Wells Harbour Cmsn

Eddleston, Adrian (Prof)
Gen Osteopathic Coun

Edge, Susan
Standards Verification UK

Edinburgh (HRH Duke of)
City & Guilds

Edmonds, David
Legal Services Bd

Edward, David (Prof Sir)
Scottish Coun Indep Schools

Edwards, Aled (Revd)
Cytun

Edwards, Christopher (Prof Sir)
Med Educ England

Edwards, David
Engg Construction Ind Trg Bd

Edwards, Jim
Signature

© CBD Research Ltd · Beckenham · Kent BR3 5JS · Tel 020 8650 7745 · Fax 020 8650 0768 · E-mail cbd@cbdresearch.com · www.cbdresearch.com

Edwards, Peter
Film Agency Wales

Egan, Penny
Geffrye Museum
US-UK Educl Cmsn

Eirug, Aled
Welsh Refugee Coun

Elkins, Roger
Stdg Conf Problems Associated Coastline

Elliot, Alison (Dr)
Scottish Coun Voluntary Orgs

Elliot, Frances (Dr)
NHS Quality Improvement Scotland

Elliott, Alex (Prof)
C'ee Med Aspects Radiation Envt

Elliott, C H (Major General)
Army Sport Control Bd

Elliott, David (Dr)
NI Library Auth

Ellis, David
Falmouth Harbour Cmsnrs

Ellis, Kevin
Cambridgeshire & Peterborough Probation Trust

Ellis, Vernon (Sir)
British Coun

Elson, Susan
Solicitors Disciplinary Tribunal E&W

Elton, Les (Sir)
Northern Film & Media

Elvidge, John (Sir)
Government Skills

Emberson, Eleanor
Scottish Court Service

Emery, Bill
Office Rail Regulation

Emery, Vic
Scottish Police Services Auth

Engelbrecht, Helmut
URENCO

England, Barrie
Foreign Compensation Cmsn

Ennals, Paul (Sir)
Children's Workforce Development Coun
Nat Children's Bureau

Epton, James
Community Lincs

Erskine-Crum, Douglas
Horserace Betting Levy Bd

Eshun, Ekow
Fourth Plinth Cmsning Gp

Esom, Steven
UK Wide Food Hygiene Ratings Steering Gp

Essien, Anthony
Leasehold Advy Service

Etherington, Stuart
Nat Coun Voluntary Orgs

Evans, Deirdre
Nat Services Division

Evans, Derek
Agricl Wages Bd England & Wales

Evans, Jean-Louis
British Approvals Bd Telecoms

Evans, Norma
Northern Health & Social Care Trust

Evans, Robin
British Waterways

Evans, Simon
North Northants Devt Company

Everitt, Richard
Port London Auth

Ewart, Wallace (Prof)
Advy C'ee NI (Ofcom)

F

Fairhurst, David
People First

Fairhurst, Steve
Working Gp Action Control Chemicals

Falconer, Charles (Lord)
One NG

Farmer, Peter B (Prof)
C'ee Mutagenicity Chemicals Food...

Farnham, Lyndon
Jersey Tourist Bd

Farnish, Christine
Consumer Focus

Farookhi, Imtiaz
Nat House Building Coun

Farr, Tim
Envt Agency - Midlands Region

Farrar, Mark
CITB Construction Skills

Farrar, Mike
North West Strategic Health Auth

Faulkner, Barry
Greyhound Bd GB

Faulkner, Keith
Working Links

Fearn, Malcolm
Thames Valley Probation Trust

Fender, Brian (Sir)
Nat Coun Drama Trg

Ferguson, Iain
Wilton Park
Wilton Park Advy Coun

Fergusson, Iain
Scottish Bldg Contract C'ee

Fernie, George (Dr)
Forensic Medicine C'ee

Ferris, Caro-lynne (Dr)
Countryside Access & Activities Network

Fewster, Kevin
Nat Maritime Museum

Fidler, Kel (Prof)
Engg Coun

Field, Frank
Cathedrals Fabric Cmsn England

Field, Sam
Dorset Community Action

Fielding, Mary
Dorset Probation Trust

Fieldsend, Tristan
Stdg Conf Problems Associated Coastline

Figgures, Andrew
British Transport Police Auth

Finch, Janet (Prof Dame)
Coun Science & Technology
Ombudsman Services
Ombudsman Services PRS Music

Finch, Paul
Cmsn Architecture & Built Envt

Finch, Roger (Prof)
Advy C'ee Antimicrobial Resistance...

Findlay, Jonathan
Strathclyde Partnership Transport

Fingleton, John
Office Fair Trading

Finn, Anthony
Gen Teaching Coun Scotland

Finn, Michael D
Bldg Regulations Advy C'ee

Finn, Regina
Water Services Regulation Auth

Firth, Paul
Creative Sheffield

Fisher, Mike
Hampshire Probation Trust

Fisher, Paul (Dr)
IFS School Finance

FitzGerald, Niall
British Museum

Fitzpatrick, Barry
Indl Court

Fitzpatrick, Julie (Prof)
Moredun Res Inst

FitzSimons, Tony
Gloucestershire Probation Trust

Fleck, Richard
Auditing Practices Bd

Fleming, David
Nat Museums Liverpool

Fleming, Gillian
Ombudsman Services Property

Fletcher, John
North York Moors Nat Park Auth

Fletcher, Kim
Nat Coun Trg Journalists

Fletcher, Philip
Water Services Regulation Auth

Fletcher, Stuart
Welsh Ambulance Services NHS Trust

Fleurot, Magali
Countryside Recreation Network

Florence, Nigel
ABC Awards

Flynn, Jenny
Durham Rural Community Coun

Fogle, Ben
Campaign Nat Parks

Foley, Tom
Med Students C'ee

Folwell, Keith
Conslt C'ee Construction Ind Statistics

Forbes, Bobby
Scientific Diving Supervisory C'ee

Forbes, Graham (Very Revd Dr)
Mental Welfare Cmsn Scotland

Forfar, J Colin (Dr)
Cardiovascular Diabetes Renal ... Expert Advy Gp

Forgan, Liz (Dame)
Arts Coun England

Forsythe, John
Advy C'ee Safety Blood Tissues & Organs

Foster, Andrew (Sir)
C'wealth Games Coun England

Foster, Joanna
Crafts Coun

Foster, Richard
Criminal Cases Review Cmsn

Foulkes, Tom
C'wealth Engineers Coun

Fountain, Tony
Nuclear Decommissioning Auth

Fowlie, Anna
Scottish Social Services Coun

Fox, Chris (Sir)
Civil Nuclear Police Auth

Fox, Liam (Dr)
C'wealth War Graves Cmsn
Defence Coun

Fox, Susan
Wales Probation Trust

Foxall, Colin
Passenger Focus

Fraenkel, Beatrice
Architects Registration Bd

France, Elizabeth
Office Legal Complaints

Francis, Alan
Design Comsn Wales

Francis, David
Cardiff & Vale Univ Health Bd
Community Action Northumberland

© CBD Research Ltd · Beckenham · Kent BR3 5JS · Tel 020 8650 7745 · Fax 020 8650 0768 · E-mail cbd@cbdresearch.com · www.cbdresearch.com

Francis, Ian
Warwickshire Police Auth

Frank, Marius
Award Scheme Development & Accreditation Network

Frankel, Mark
Public Works Loan Bd

Franklin, Chris (Prof)
C'ee Postgraduate Dental Deans & Directors

Fraser, Brian
Scottish Fire & Rescue Advy Unit

Fraser, David
Scottish Refugee Coun

Frawley, Tom
NI Ombudsman

Frayling, Christopher (Prof Sir)
Royal Mint Advy C'ee

Freeman, Jeane
NHS National Waiting Times Centre Bd

Freeman, Peter
Competition Cmsn

Friend, James (Prof)
Scientific C'ee Tobacco & Health

Fripp, Eric
Jt Coun Welfare Immigrants

Fuge, Bernadette (Dr)
Age Cymru

Fulbrook, Diana
Wiltshire Probation Trust

Fullagar, Bill
NHS Blood & Transplant

Fuller, Michael
HM Crown Prosecution Service Inspectorate

Furniss, Jane
Indep Police Complaints Cmsn

Fyffe, Bob (Revd Canon)
Churches Together Britain & Ireland

G

Gailey, Yvonne
Risk Mgt Auth

Galbraith, Anne
Valuation Tribunal Service

Gallagher, Ed (Prof)
Renewable Fuels Agency

Gallagher, Gerry
Housing Coun

Galloway, Ian (Revd)
Church & Society Coun

Galvin, Bill
Pensions Regulator

Garbutt, David
Scottish Ambulance Service

Gardner, Beth
Coun Learning Outside Classroom

Gargan, Nick
Nat Policing Improvement Agency

Garner, Bernard
Nexus

Garnham, Diana
Science Coun

Garnham, Rob
Gloucestershire Police Auth

Garrett, Doug
Blackpool Fylde & Wyre EDC

Gaskell, Chris (Prof)
Science Advy Coun

Gates, Brian (Prof)
Religious Educ Coun E&W

Gates, Terry
Channel Tunnel Safety Auth

Gates, Tony
Northumberland Nat Park Auth

Gazzard, Brian (Prof)
Expert Advy Gp AIDS

Gelling, Donald
Insurance & Pensions Auth

Gemmell, Campbell (Dr)
Scottish Envt Protection Agency

George, Charles
Faculty Office

Geraghty, Jane
Nottinghamshire Probation Trust

Geraghty, Stephen
Child Maintenance & Enforcement Cmsn

Gerhold, Dorian
House of Commons Cmsn
Public Accounts Cmsn

Getty, Mark
Nat Gallery

Gibb, Andrew
Scottish Coun Law Reporting

Gibson, Peter (Sir)
Intelligence Services Cmsnr

Gibson, Wil (Dr)
Suffolk ACRE

Gifford, David
Coun Christians & Jews

Gilbert, Bob
Intellectual Property Office

Gilbert, Christine
Office Standards Educ

Giles, Charles
British Boxing Bd Control

Gillespie, Alan (Dr)
Economic & Social Res Coun

Gillies, Crawford
Scottish Enterprise

Gilligan, Barry
NI Policing Bd

Gilliland, John
Rural Climate Change Forum

Gillingwater, Richard
CDC Gp

Gilvarry, Evlynne
Gen Dental Coun

Glackin, Rose Mary
Central Scotland Jt Police Bd

Glentoran (Lord)
British Shooting Sports Coun

Glover, Anne (Prof)
Scottish Science Advy Coun

Goddard, Jim
Jt University Coun

Godfrey, John (Dr)
Gatwick Airport Conslt C'ee
Sussex Police Auth

Goldfield, Bob (Dr)
Dover Harbour Bd

Goldring, Judena
NI Law Cmsn

Goldsmith, Louise
Chichester Harbour Conservancy

Goldstein, Jeffrey (Prof)
Nat Toy Coun

Goldstraw, Christine
Nottinghamshire Probation Trust

Goodall, Andrew (Dr)
Aneurin Bevan Health Bd

Goodman, John (Prof)
Police Arbitration Tribunal

Goodman, Michael
Leeds Bradford Intl Airport Conslt C'ee

Goodway, Russell
Community Pharmacy Wales

Gordon, Helen
Royal Pharmaceutical Society GB

Gordon, Iain (Prof)
James Hutton Institute

Gordon, Ian
Standards Commission Scotland

Gordon, Robert
East England Local Government Assn

Gore, Martin (Prof)
Gene Therapy Advy C'ee

Gorringe, Edward
NI Judicial Appointments Cmsn

Goudie, Stanley J
Educ & Training Inspectorate

Gould, Joyce (Baroness)
Indep Advy Gp Sexual Health & HIV

Gouldstone, Simon
Central Arbitration C'ee

Grabiner, Michael
Partnerships Schools

Grace, Clive
Local Better Regulation Office

Graf, Philip
Press Standards Bd Finance

Graham, Alistair (Sir)
Phonepay Plus

Graham, Andrew (Lt Gen)
Defence Academy Mgt Bd

Graham, Christopher
Inf Cmsnrs Office

Graham, Martin
Norfolk & Suffolk Probation Trust

Grammer, Jeremy
Teignmouth Harbour Cmsn

Grant, Sharon
London Transport Users C'ee

Gray, Bernard
Defence Equipment & Support

Gray, Martin
Nat Savings & Investments

Greaves, Chris
Metro
West Yorkshire Integrated Transport Auth

Grebliuniate, Ina
Coun Hospitality Management Educ

Green, Andrew
Nat Library Wales Bd Trustees

Green, Andy
Space Leadership Coun

Green, Ann
Royal Armouries

Green, David
Cairngorms Nat Park Auth

Green, Martin
Community Pharmacy Scotland

Green, Nicholas
Gen Coun Bar

Green, Sylvia
Rural Action Derbyshire

Greene, Moya
Royal Mail Gp

Greenhalgh, Richard
Coun Ind & Higher Educ

Greenland, Sheridan
Office Judicial Complaints

Greenlees, Rosy
Crafts Coun

Greenwood, Amanda
Community Devt Exchange

Gregory, Peter (Prof)
Advy C'ee Novel Foods & Processes

Gregson, Dorothy
Cambridgeshire Police Auth

Greig, Martin (Cllr)
Grampian Jt Police Bd

Griffin, Barry
Road Safety Coun NI

Griffin, George E (Prof)
Advy C'ee Dangerous Pathogens

Griffith, Maureen
NI Practice & Educ Coun Nursing & Midwifery

 © CBD Research Ltd · Beckenham · Kent BR3 5JS · Tel 020 8650 7745 · Fax 020 8650 0768 · E-mail cbd@cbdresearch.com · www.cbdresearch.com

Griffiths, Andrew
NHS Wales Informatics Service

Griffiths, Bill
Forensic Science Service

Griffiths, David
Correctional Services Accreditation Panel

Griffiths, Keith D (Dr)
Welsh Scientific Advy C'ee

Griffiths, Oliver
Export Credits Guarantee Department

Griffiths, Peter
Lymington Harbour Cmsnrs

Griffiths, Richard
Sir John Soane's Museum

Griffiths, Win
Abertawe Bro Morgannwg Univ Health Bd
Wales Coun Voluntary Action

Grimshaw, Mark
Rural Payments Agency

Grossart, Angus (Sir)
Nat Museums Scotland
Scottish Futures Trust

Grossman, Loyd
Churches Conservation Trust

Grundy, Ken
Nottingham Regeneration

Guckian, Gerard
Western Health & Social Care Trust

Guilfoyle, David
Youth Coun NI

Gummett, Philip (Prof)
Higher Educ Funding Coun Wales

Guthrie, Eric
Tayside & Central Scotland Transport Partnership

Gwyther, David
British Hallmarking Coun

H

Hackemer, Gerald
Gen Aviation Safety Coun

Hackitt, Judith
Health & Safety Exec

Haddon-Cave, Charles
Advocacy Training Council

Haddrill, Stephen
Financial Reporting Coun

Haines, Andrew
Civil Aviation Auth

Haird, Susan
UK Tr & Investment

Hakin, Barbara (Dame)
East Midlands Strategic Health Auth

Hales, Tony
British Waterways

Hall, Andrew
Assessment & Qualifications Alliance

Hall, Andrew (Prof)
Jt C'ee Vaccination & Immunisation

Hall, Laurie
Video Standards Coun

Hall, Sue
West Yorkshire Probation Trust

Hallett (Lady Justice)
Judicial Studies Bd

Hallett, Christine (Prof)
UK Coun Intl Student Affairs

Hamer, Christopher J
Property Ombudsman

Hamilton (Lord)
Court Session Rules Coun
Criminal Courts Rules Coun

Hamilton, Alastair
Invest NI

Hamlyn, Lynda
NHS Blood & Transplant

Hammond, Gill
Government Skills

Hampson, Stuart (Sir)
Crown Estate

Hampton, Anthony
WJEC

Handcock, Peter
HM Courts & Tribunals Service

Handyside, Alistair
South West Tourism

Hanna, Brian
Local Government Staff Cmsn NI

Hannah, Chris
Skills Health

Hanney, Tom
North South Ministerial Coun

Harbage, William
Prescription Medicines Code Practice Auth

Harbison, Jeremy (Dr)
NI Social Care Coun

Harding, Chris
Norfolk Police Auth

Hardwick, Nick
HM Inspectorate Prisons

Hardy, Stan
West Yorkshire Probation Trust

Harland, Stuart
Funeral Planning Auth

Harmer, Mike (Prof)
Welsh Health Specialised Services C'ee

Harper, Digby
British Bd Agrément

Harris, Charles
Coun HM Circuit Judges

Harris, Geoffrey (Dr)
South Central Strategic Health Auth

Harris, Graeme (Dr)
Envt Agency - Wales

Harris, Ian
Wine & Spirit Educ Trust

Harris, John
Jersey Financial Services Cmsn

Harris, Mark
Nat Lottery Cmsn

Harris, Martin (Sir)
Office Fair Access

Harris, Stewart
Sport Scotland

Harris, Toby (Lord)
Indep Advy Panel Deaths Custody

Harris, Tricia
London Luton Airport Conslt C'ee

Harrison, Alan (Dr)
Staffordshire & West Midlands Probation Trust

Harrison, David J (Prof)
Scottish Hospital Endowments Res Trust

Harrison, Michael
Working Links

Harrop, Gordon
Cwm Taf Community Health Coun

Hartley, Ian
British Wool Marketing Bd

Hartshorne, Anthea
East Midlands Airport Indep Conslt C'ee

Harvey, Dan
Nat Museums NI

Harvey, Tom
Northern Film & Media

Harwood, Peter
Guernsey Financial Services Cmsn

Hassall, Tom
Advy C'ee Historic Wreck Sites

Hastings, Alison
Audience Coun England

Hastings, Howard
NI Tourist Bd

Hatton, Wai-yin (Dr)
Ayrshire & Arran NHS Bd

Havercroft, Carole
Heathrow Airport Conslt C'ee

Havlin, Sarah
Agricl Wages Bd NI

Hawkes, Philippa
Community Coun Somerset

Hayden, Pat
Inverness Airport Conslt C'ee

Hayes, Elaine
Envt Agency - South West Region

Hayes, Paul
Nat Treatment Agency Substance Misuse

Haywood, Jane
Children's Workforce Development Coun

Hazell, Tony (Prof)
Nursing & Midwifery Coun

Hazelwood, John
Gloucestershire Rural Community Coun

Head, Chris
Community Action

Heap, Michael
Intellectual Property Regulation Bd

Heffer, Peter (Dr)
Avon & Somerset Police Auth

Heffernan, Adrian
Bedfordshire Probation Trust

Heighton, Martyn
Advy C'ee Nat Historic Ships

Hemming, Steve
Humberside Probation Trust

Hemsted, Stephen
Advertising Standards Bd Finance
Broadcast Advertising Standards Bd Finance

Henderson, Bill
Isle Man Office Fair Trading

Henderson, Jane
South West Regional Devt Agency

Henderson, John
Scotland's Colleges

Henderson, Richard
Administrative Justice & Tribunals Coun

Hendy, Peter
Transport London Auth

Henig, Ruth (Baroness)
Security Ind Auth

Hennessy, Annette
Cumbria Probation Trust

Hennessy, Joe
Jt C'ee Mobility Disabled People

Hennigan, Linda
Bedfordshire Probation Trust

Henning, Ian
Advy C'ee Roofsafety

Henry, Charles
Gen Aviation Awareness Coun

Henry, Mick
Northumbria Police Auth

Henshaw, David (Sir)
North West Strategic Health Auth

Henwood, Stephen
Nuclear Decommissioning Auth

Herdan, Bernard (Dr)
Nat Fraud Auth

Herron, Margaret
Drinking Water Inspectorate NI

Heskett, Robert
Queen Elizabeth II Conference Centre

Hewell, Jenny
Coun Administration

Heymann, David (Dr)
Health Protection Agency

Hickson, Philip
Derbyshire Police Auth

Higgins (Lord Justice)
Judicial Studies Bd NI

Higgins, Chris (Prof)
Spongiform Encephalopathy Advy C'ee

Higgins, David
Olympic Delivery Auth

Higgins, Joan (Prof Dame)
NHS Litigation Auth

Higgins, Julia (Dame)
Advy C'ee Mathematics Education

Higgins, Martin
Food Safety Promotion Bd

Higson, Peter
Healthcare Inspectorate Wales

Hill, Christopher (Rt Revd)
Coun Christian Unity

Hill, Matthew
Tendring Regeneration

Hill, Rick
Consumer Coun NI
NI Screen

Hill, Simon
Valuation Tribunal Wales

Hill, Tony
Museum Science & Industry

Hill-Tout, Paul
Forestry Cmsn England

Hillan, Lynne
London Couns Grants C'ee

Hills, David (Colonel)
Coun Inns Court

Hills, John (Prof)
Nat Equality Panel

Hinett, Graham
British Fenestration Rating Coun

Hinnigan, Lin
Qualifications & Curriculum Devt Auth

Hirst, David (Sir)
Spoliation Advy Panel

Hirst, John
Met Office

Hirst, Larry
E Skills UK

Hitchins, Bill
Dartmoor Nat Park Auth

Hoare, Chris
Wiltshire Police Auth

Hobart, David
Gen Coun Bar

Hobman, Tony
Consumer Financial Educ Body

Hockaday, Neil
Dart Harbour & Navigation Auth

Hodge, Simon
Forestry Enterprise Scotland

Hodges, Christopher (Dr)
Pharmaceutical Services Negotiating C'ee

Hodgson, Geoff
Northeast Tourism Advy Bd

Hodgson, Isabell (Prof)
Coun Hospitality Management Educ

Hogan, Seán
Agri Food & Biosciences Inst
Educ & Skills Auth

Hogbin, Ann
C'wealth Games Coun England

Hogg (Baroness)
Financial Reporting Coun

Holgate, Stephen (Prof)
Advy C'ee Hazardous Substances

Holland, Chris
Office Telecommunications Ombudsman

Holland, Peter
Nat Policing Improvement Agency

Holland, Sean
Office Social Services

Holley, Graham
Nat Advy Gp Professional Devt Children's
   Workforce Schools
Trg & Devt Agency Schools

Holt, Elaine
Directly Operated Railways

Holt, Mary
Advy C'ee Clinical Excellence Awards

Homer, Lin
UK Border Agency

Hope, Jane
Cairngorms Nat Park Auth

Hopkins, Tony
NI Higher Educ Coun

Hopper, Stephen D (Prof)
Royal Botanic Gardens Kew

Horner, Sue
Booktrust

Hornsby, Timothy
Horniman Public Museum & Public Park Trust

Horrocks, Peter
BBC World Service

Horsfall, Sarndrah
Nat Patient Safety Agency

Hough, Robert
Northwest Regional Devt Agency

Houghton, John
Civil Service Cmsn

Houlden, Abigail
Leeds Bradford Intl Airport Conslt C'ee

Houlden, Bryony
South West Couns

Houlder, Bruce
Service Prosecuting Auth

Houlihan, Michael
Nat Museum Wales

Houston, Glenn
Regulation & Quality Improvement Auth

Houston, Graham
Scottish Qualifications Auth

Houston, Linda
Library & Inf Services Coun NI

Houston, Stewart
British Pig Exec

Howard, Jacqui
Registration Coun Clinical Physiologists

Howard, John
Montgomery Community Health Coun

Howarth of Breckland (Baroness)
Children & Family Court Advy Support Service

Howat, Bill
Volunteering Devt Scotland

Howe of Aberavon (Lord)
Tax Law Review C'ee

Howell, Michael
City & Guilds

Howells, Gwyn
Meat Promotion Wales

Howells, Richard
Pembrokeshire Coast Nat Park Auth

Howes, Rupert
Marine Stewardship Coun

Howeson, Charles
South West Strategic Health Authority

Howie, Pauline
Scottish Ambulance Service

Howl, Sue
Devon & Cornwall Police Auth

Hudson, Bob
Public Health Wales

Hughes, Archie
Defence Support Gp

Hughes, Chris
Learning & Skills Network
NCFE

Hughes, Christopher
Coun Educ C'wealth
UK Chemicals Stakeholder Forum

Hughes, David
Prospect Leicestershire

Hughes, Geoff
Countryside Recreation Network

Hughes, Mark
Northwest Regional Devt Agency

Hughes, Phil
Nat Examining Bd Dental Nurses

Hully, Maeve
Patient & Client Coun

Hume, John R (Prof)
Royal Cmsn Ancient & Historical Monuments
Scotland

Humfryes, Delyth
Dyfed-Powys Police Auth

Humphreys, Steve
Judicial Office Scotland

Humphries, Chris
UK Skills

Humphries, Sam
Ulster Supported Employment

Hunt of Chesterton (Lord)
Advy C'ee Protection Sea

Hunt, Michael
Buckinghamshire Community Action

Hunter, D
First Tier Tribunal Immigration Services

Hunter, Kenneth
NI Bldg Regulations Advy C'ee

Hunter, Noel
Nat Measurement Office

Huston, Felicity
Office Cmsnr Public Appointments NI

Hutchinson, Al
Police Ombudsman NI

Hutchinson, Mark
People Pay & Pensions Agency

Hutton, Deirdre (Dame)
Civil Aviation Auth

Huws, Meri
Welsh Language Bd

Hyams, Edward
Energy Saving Trust

Hyde, Ruth
East Midlands Tourism

Hyman, Saul
Conf Drama Schools

Hynes, Alice
Guild H E

I

Ibbotson, Janet
British Copyright Coun

Imrie, Russell
South East Scotland Transport Partnership

Inglewood (Lord)
Reviewing C'ee Export Works Art

Ingram, Paul
British American Security Inf Coun

Ingram, Tamara
Visit London

Innes, Stuart
London City Airport Conslt C'ee

Inskip, Geoff
Centro

Irvine, Jane
Pensions Ombudsman
Scottish Legal Complaints C'ee

Irving, Will (Prof)
Advy Gp Hepatitis

© CBD Research Ltd · Beckenham · Kent BR3 5JS · Tel 020 8650 7745 · Fax 020 8650 0768 · E-mail cbd@cbdresearch.com · www.cbdresearch.com

Iverson, Les (Prof)
Advy Coun Misuse Drugs

Jack, Michael
Office Tax Simplification

Jack, Paula
Youth Justice Agency NI

Jack, Stephen
Indep Living Fund

Jackson, Bryan (Dr)
East Midlands Devt Agency

Jackson, Helen
Campaign Nat Parks

Jackson, Len
Indep Police Complaints Cmsn

Jackson, Neville (Prof)
Low Carbon Vehicle Partnership

Jackson, Paul
Engineering UK

Jackson, Peter (Prof)
Social Science Res C'ee

Jadeja, Kanchan
Nat Coun Voluntary Youth Services

Jagger, Terence
Crown Agents Oversea Govts & Administrations

James, Jeff
Cardiff Airport Conslt C'ee

James, Ralph
Aneurin Bevan Community Health Coun

Jameson, Mick
South Yorkshire Integrated Transport Auth

Jamieson, Gordon
Western Isles NHS Bd

Jardine, Angela
Gen Teaching Coun Wales

Jardine, Ian
Scottish Natural Heritage

Jardine, Lisa (Prof)
Human Fertilisation & Embryology Auth

Jarvis, Richard
Civil Service Cmsn

Jarvis, Richard (Dr)
Public Health Medicine C'ee

Jay of Ewelme (Lord)
House Lords Appointments Cmsn

Jay, Alexis
Social Work Inspection Agency

Jay, Jeffrey (Dr)
British Coun Prevention Blindness

Jeavons, Richard
Indep Reconfiguration Panel

Jefferies, Liz
Rural Community Action Nottinghamshire

Jefferson, Peter
Cornwall Rural Community Coun

Jefferson, William
Lake District Nat Park Auth

Jeffrey, Dianne
Age UK

Jeffrey, John
Moredun Res Inst

Jenkins, Chris
C'wealth Games Coun Wales

Jenkins, David
Aneurin Bevan Health Bd

Jenkins, Paul
Treasury Solicitors Department

Jenner, Marian
Uplands Land Mgt Advy Panel

Jermey, Bill
Meat Trg Coun

Jessiman, Ian
Aberdeen Harbour Bd

Jewell, Tony (Dr)
NHS

Jobling, Marc
Institutional Shareholders C'ee

John, Gareth
C'wealth Games Coun Wales

John, Martin
Office Public Guardian E&W

Johns, David (Prof)
Genetics & Insurance C'ee

Johnson, Anne M (Prof)
Unlinked Anonymous Surveys Steering Gp

Johnson, Boris
Greater London Auth
Transport London Auth

Johnson, Julian
New Forest Nat Park Auth

Johnson, Stephen (Dr)
Broads Auth

Johnston, Brendan
NI Social Care Coun

Johnston, Grenville
Caledonian Maritime Assets
Highlands & Islands Airports

Johnston, Peter
Risk Mgt Auth

Johnston, Rotha
Audience Coun NI

Jones, Alun Ffred
CyMAL

Jones, Chris (Dr)
Cwm Taf Health Bd

Jones, Clive
Jersey Financial Services Cmsn
Skillset

Jones, Gareth
Companies House

Jones, Huw
Textiles Ind Advy C'ee

Jones, Huw (Dr)
Sports Coun Wales

Jones, Ian
Welsh Optometric C'ee

Jones, Jon Owen
Forestry Cmsn Wales

Jones, Maggie
Children England

Jones, Maggie (Baroness)
Ombudsman Services Property

Jones, Mark
Victoria & Albert Museum

Jones, Meirion Prys
Welsh Language Bd

Jones, Merfyn (Prof)
Betsi Cadwaladr Univ Health Bd

Jones, Mike A
Liverpool John Lennon Airport Conslt C'ee

Jones, Nick
Traffic Cmsnrs

Jones, Rich (Air Cdre)
UK Flight Safety C'ee

Jones, Richard
Caernarfon Harbour Trust

Jones, Ron (Prof)
Farriers Registration Coun

Jones, Sam
Heathrow Airport Conslt C'ee

Jones, Sarah
Ufi

Jones, Simon
Investors People

Jones, Tegryn
Pembrokeshire Coast Nat Park Auth

Jordan, Joanna
Advy Panel Substance Misuse

Jowell, Jeffrey (Prof)
Waterways Ombudsman C'ee

Joynson, Sally
Screen Yorkshire

Judge (Lord)
Criminal Procedure Rule C'ee

Judge, Barbara (Lady)
Pension Protection Fund

Judge, Richard (Dr)
Centre Envt, Fisheries & Aquaculture Science

Juna, Khan
Thames Valley Police Auth

K

Kaiser, Sandra
US-UK Educl Cmsn

Kaur, Gurvir
Adjudicator HM Land Registry

Kaur, Pramila
Scottish Inter Faith Coun

Kaur-Stubbs, Sukhvinder
Volunteering England

Keane, Ann
HM Inspectorate Educ & Trg Wales

Keanie, John
Patient & Client Coun

Kearon, Kenneth (Revd Canon)
Anglican Conslt Coun

Kebede, Zelalem (Dr)
Coun Ethnic Minority Voluntary Sector Orgs

Keeble, Sally
Coun Educ C'wealth

Keegan, Brian
Scotland's Colleges

Keen, Richard
Historic Bldgs Advy Coun Wales

Keggans, Michael
Dumfries & Galloway NHS Bd

Kell, Douglas (Prof)
Biotechnology & Biological Sciences Res Coun

Kellaway, Richard
C'wealth War Graves Cmsn

Kelly, Christopher (Sir)
C'ee Standards Public Life
Financial Ombudsman Service

Kelly, James
West Mercia Probation Trust

Kelly, Mike
Isle Man Post Office

Kelly, Rosemary
Arts Coun NI

Kelsall, Greg
Coal Research Forum

Kennecutt, Mahlon C (Prof)
Scientific C'ee Antarctic Res

Kennedy, David
C'ee Climate Change

Kennedy, Ian (Sir)
Indep Parliamentary Standards Auth

Kennedy, Paul (Sir)
Interception Communications Cmsnr

Kennedy, Seamus (Dr)
Agri Food & Biosciences Inst

Kennedy, Sue
C'ee Carcinogenicity Chemicals Food...
C'ee Med Effects Air Pollutants
C'ee Mutagenicity Chemicals Food...

Kenny, Bernadette
Church England Pensions Bd

Kenny, Chris
Legal Services Bd

Kenny, Julie
Yorkshire Forward

© CBD Research Ltd · Beckenham · Kent BR3 5JS · Tel 020 8650 7745 · Fax 020 8650 0768 · E-mail cbd@cbdresearch.com · www.cbdresearch.com

Kenworthy, David
UK Anti Doping

Kenyon, Jane
North Yorkshire Police Auth

Kerr, Adrian E
Local Government Staff Cmsn NI

Kerr, Norman
Energy Action Scotland

Kerr, Philip (Rt Revd)
Action Churches Together Scotland

Kershaw, Alan
ILEX Professional Standards

Kester, David
Design Coun

Keyes, Jim
Health & Safety Exec NI

Khawaja, Masood
Halal Food Auth

Kidney, John
Cmsnrs Irish Lights

King, Ian
Defence Inds Coun

King, James
Public Transport Users C'ee Scotland

King, Mervyn
Bank England
Bank England Monetary Policy C'ee

King, Tony
Pensions Ombudsman

Kingon, Stephen
Invest NI

Kinniburgh, Ian
Shetland NHS Bd

Kirkland, John (Dr)
C'wealth Scholarship Cmsn UK
Marshall Aid Commemoration Cmsn

Kirkwood, James (Dr)
Zoos Forum

Kitchin, Jim
Sustainable Devt Cmsn NI

Klee, Chris
Envt Agency - South West Region

Knight, Alex
Helideck Certification Agency

Knight, Bill
Financial Reporting Review Panel

Knight, David
Nat Open College Network

Knight, Ken (Sir)
Chief Fire & Rescue Adviser

Knowles, Denis
Liverpool John Lennon Airport Conslt C'ee

Knox, Irene
NI Library Auth

Knox, Tim
Sir John Soane's Museum

Koser, Khalid (Dr)
Advy Panel Country Information

Kuipers, Joe
Avon & Somerset Probation Trust

L

Lacey, Christine
Scottish Official Bd Highland Dancing

Lacey, Peter
Bristol Intl Airport Conslt C'ee

Lacey, Richard
Poole Harbour Cmsnrs

Ladyman, Stephen
Road Safety Advy Panel

Laing, Richard
CDC Gp

Lakhani, Mayur (Prof)
Nat Coun Palliative Care

Lamb, Tim
Sport & Recreation Alliance

Lammy, David
Coun Educ C'wealth

Lampard, Kate
South East Coast Strategic Health Authority

Lamyman-Jones, Carol
Bd Community Health Couns Wales

Lang of Monkton (Lord)
Advy C'ee Business Appointments

Lang, Ruth
All Wales Medicines Strategy Gp

Langlands, Alan (Sir)
Higher Educ Funding Coun England

Langley, Gordon (Sir)
Panel Takeovers & Mergers

Langrish, Frank
British Wool Marketing Bd

Langrish, Michael (Rt Revd)
Churches Legislation Advy Service

Langslow, Derek (Dr)
East England Tourist Bd
Marine Mgt Org

Lanning, Jill
Federation Awarding Bodies

Large, Catherine
Creative & Cultural Skills

Large, Terry
Hawk Bd

Latham, David (Sir)
Parole Bd England & Wales

Latham, Michael (Sir)
Jt Ind Bd Electrical Contracting Ind

Lauener, Peter
Young People's Learning Agency

Laurenson, Sandra
Lerwick Port Auth
Shetland NHS Bd

Laverick, Jo
Durham Rural Community Coun

Laverty, Mick
Advantage West Midlands

Lavery, David A
NI Courts & Tribunals Service

Lawrence (Judge)
Advy C'ee Conscientious Objectors

Lawrence, Mike
Nat Nuclear Laboratory

Lawrence, Philip
Coal Auth

Lawrence, Vanessa
Ordnance Survey

Laws, Melanie
Assn North East Couns

Lawson, Duncan (Prof)
Jt Mathematical Coun UK

Lazenby, Terry
Engg Construction Ind Trg Bd

Leafe, Richard
Lake District Nat Park Auth

Leather, David
Greater Manchester Passenger Transport Exec

Leather, Suzi (Dame)
Charity Cmsn

Lechler, Robert (Prof)
Clinical Trials Expert Advy Gp

Lee, Andrew
Sustainable Devt Cmsn

Lee, Graham
British Bd Film Classification

Lee, Katie
GB China Centre

Lee, Paul
Horserace Betting Levy Bd

Lees, Diane
Imperial War Museum

Leese, Richard (Sir)
Morth West Regional Leaders Bd

Leeson, Pauline
Children NI

Leggett, Jeremy
Action Rural Sussex

Leigh, Bertie
Nat Confidential Enquiry Patient Outcome...

Leighton, John
Nat Galleries Scotland

Leinster, Paul
Envt Agency

Lemos, Gerard
Consumer Financial Educ Body
Lending Standards Bd

Lenehan, Christine
Coun Disabled Children

Lennon, Jim
NI Blood Transfusion Service

Lennon, Linda
Parole Bd England & Wales

Leslie, Neil
Scottish C'ee Optometrists

Lester, Craig
Nuclear Decommissioning Auth

Lester, Ed
Student Loans Company

Levenson (Lord Justice)
Sentencing Coun

Levitt, Tom
Community Devt Foundation

Lewis, Ashton
Manx Electricity Auth

Lewis, Dan
Economic Res Coun

Lewis, Gill
Norfolk & Suffolk Probation Trust

Lewis, Mike
Welsh Refugee Coun

Lewis, Patricia
Mental Health Tribunal Scotland

Lewis, Peter
Crown Prosecution Service
London Voluntary Service Coun

Lewis, Richard
Sport England

Lewis, Rita
British Acupuncture Accreditation Bd

Lewis, Sally
Avon & Somerset Probation Trust

Lewis, Tessa (Dr)
All Wales Prescribing Advy Gp

Lewsley, Patricia
NI Cmsnr Children & Young People

Liaquat, Ziggy
Edexcel

Lickorish, Derek
Fuel Poverty Advy Gp

Likierman, Andrew (Sir)
Nat Audit Office

Limb, Ann (Dr)
Legal Deposit Advy Panel
Milton Keynes Partnership C'ee

Lindsay (Lord)
UK Accreditation Service

Lis, Carl
Yorkshire Dales Nat Park Auth

Lisney, Robert
Advy C'ee Packaging

Livingstone, Ian
Scottish Local Auths Remuneration C'ee

© CBD Research Ltd · Beckenham · Kent BR3 5JS · Tel 020 8650 7745 · Fax 020 8650 0768 · E-mail cbd@cbdresearch.com · www.cbdresearch.com

Livsey, Ian
Summit Skills

Llanwarne, Trevor
Government Actuary's Department

Llewelyn, Ivor
Envt Agency - South East Region

Lloyd, Annabel
Parliamentary & Scientific C'ee

Lloyd, Colin
Fundraising Standards Bd

Lloyd, Jan
Covent Garden Market Auth

Lloyd, Lesley
Lancashire & Blackpool Tourist Bd

Lloyd, Linda
Rural Action Yorkshire

Lloyd, Neil
NHS Professionals

Lloyd Jones (Justice)
Boundary Cmsn Wales

Lloyd Jones, Claer
Tenant Services Auth

Lockwood, Roger
Northern Lighthouse Bd

Lockyer, Alison
Gen Dental Coun

Lodge, Trevor
Judicial Appointments Bd Scotland

Logan, Fiona
Loch Lomond & Trossachs Nat Park Auth

Lohman, Jack (Prof)
Museum London

Long, Steve
Criminal Records Bureau
Mountain Leader Trg

Loughran, Oliver
Criminal Injuries Compensation Appeals Panel NI

Love, Robin
Cattewater Harbour Cmsnrs

Love, Steve
Ministry Defence Police & Guarding Agency

Lovegrove, Stephen
Shareholder Executive

Loveluck, Paul
Nat Museum Wales

Lowe, Roger
CDC Gp
NATS

Lowey, Eddie
Manx Electricity Auth

Lowson, Ian (Sir)
Stdg Coun Baronetage

Lucas, Henry
Farming & Wildlife Advy Gp

Lugg, Matthew
UK Roads Bd

Lund, Mark
Central Office Inf

Lunn, Rodney
Shoreham Port Auth

Lyon, Inglis
Highlands & Islands Airports

Lyon, John
Parliamentary Cmsnr Standards

Lyons, Michael (Sir)
BBC Trust

Lyscom, David
Indep Schools Coun

M

McAleavey, Seamus
NI Coun Voluntary Action

McAllister, Ian (Sir)
Carbon Trust

McAllister, James
Indep Monitoring Bds NI

McAllister, Laura (Prof)
Sports Coun Wales

McAllister, Maureen
South West Tourism

Mac an Fhailigh, Ferdie
Foras Gaeilge

McAreavey, John (Most Revd)
Coun Catholic Maintained Schools

McArthur, Neil
Cromarty Firth Port Auth

Macartney, Tom
Traffic Cmsnrs

McBriar, Jim
Strangford Lough Mgt Advy C'ee

McBride, Michael (Dr)NHS

McCabe, Pauline
Prisoner Ombudsman NI

McCabe, Tom
Scottish Ministerial Advy C'ee Alcohol Problems

McCaffrey, David (Dr)
Coal Research Forum

McCandless, Frances
Charity Cmsn NI

McCann, Lucy
Stdg Conf Library Materials Africa

McCartan, Eamonn
Sports Coun NI

McCartan, Pat
Belfast Health & Social Care Trust

McCarthy, Bill
Yorkshire & Humber Strategic Health Auth

McCarthy, Suzanne
Office Immigration Services Cmsnr

McCaughey, Brian
Probation Bd NI

McCaughey, Hugh
South Eastern Health & Social Care Trust

McCaw, Tom
Community First

McClaran, Anthony
Quality Assurance Agency Higher Educ

McClean, Jimmy
Indep Monitoring Bds NI

McClean, Mark
Care Tribunal

McClelland, John
Scottish Further & Higher Educ Funding Coun

McClintock, Aileen
Public Record Office NI

McClintock, Bill
Property Ombudsman

McCloskey, (Justice)
NI Law Cmsn

McConnell, Colin
NI Prison Service

McCormack, Brendan (Prof)
Age NI

McCracken, Justin
Health Protection Agency

McCrisken, Trevor (Dr)
British American Security Inf Coun

McCulloch, Lyn
Statute Law C'ee NI

McCulloch, Nigel (Rt Revd)
Coun Christians & Jews

McCurdy, Gerry
Food Standards Agency NI

McCurdy, Shane
North Eastern Educ & Library Bd

McCusker, Jim
Labour Relations Agency

McCusker, Tony
Community Relations Coun

Macdonald, Alan
Tarbert Harbour Auth

McDonald, Andrew
Indep Parliamentary Standards Auth

Macdonald, David (Prof)
Darwin Expert C'ee

Macdonald, Ian
Greater Manchester Integrated Transport Auth

MacDonald, Jim
Architecture & Design Scotland

McDonald, Martin
Rural Devt Coun

McDonald, Sandra
Office Public Guardian Scotland

MacDonald, Sandy
Funeral Planning Auth

McDonough, Roisín
Arts Coun NI

McDougall, Lynn
Immigration Advy Service

McDowell, Sid
Public Services Cmsn

McEachran, Colin M
Pensions Appeal Tribunals Scotland

MacEachran, Jane
Grampian Jt Police Bd

McGhie (Lord)
Lands Tribunal Scotland
Scottish Land Court

McGill, Glenys
Theatre Dance Coun Intl

McGill, Maria
Scottish Partnership Palliative Care

McGinley, Aideen
Ilex (Londonderry)

McGlone, Gordon (Dr)
Lantra

McGoldrick, James (Prof)
Fife NHS Bd

McGrath, Brian
Londonderry Port & Harbour Cmsnrs

McGrath, Harvey
London Devt Agency

McGrath, Thomas
Charity Cmsn NI

Machin, Derek
Private Practice C'ee

McIlvenny, Gerard
Healthcare Associated Infection... Centre

McInroy, Stuart
Bookmakers' C'ee

McIntosh, Bob (Dr)
Forestry Cmsn Scotland

McIntosh, Stuart
Cowes Harbour Cmsn

MacIntyre, Duncan
Highlands & Islands Transport Partnership

McIntyre, Jim
One NG

McIntyre, Paddy
NI Housing Exec

Maciver, Jane
Stornoway Port Auth

MacIver, Netta
Scottish Children's Reporter Administration

McIvor, Liam
NI Ambulance Service HSC Trust

Mackay, Charles
Historic Royal Palaces

MacKay, John
Western Isles NHS Bd

McKay, Neil (Sir)
East England Strategic Health Auth

Mackay, Neville
Scottish Public Pensions Agency

© CBD Research Ltd · Beckenham · Kent BR3 5JS · Tel 020 8650 7745 · Fax 020 8650 0768 · E-mail cbd@cbdresearch.com · www.cbdresearch.com

Mackay, Peter
Local Government Boundary Cmsn Scotland

McKeating, Brendan (Dr)
Armed Forces C'ee

McKee, Joe (Dr)
NI Fire & Rescue Service

McKee, Will
Thurrock Thames Gateway Devt Corpn

McKee, William
Belfast Health & Social Care Trust

McKellar, Keith
Hannah Res Institute

McKenna, Alison
First Tier Tribunal Charity

McKenna, Colm
South Eastern Health & Social Care Trust

Mackenzie, Fiona (Prof)
Forth Valley NHS Bd

MacKenzie, George
Nat Archives Scotland

MacKenzie, Laurence
NI Water

McKeown, Antoinette
Consumer Coun NI

McKeown, Helena (Dr)
C'ee Community Care

McKie, Peter (Prof)
Health & Safety Exec NI

McKillop, Tom (Sir)
Science Coun

Mackintosh, Ian
Accounting Standards Bd
Tayside Jt Police Bd

McKnight, Marcella
Compensation Agency

McLaren, Colin
Drinking Water Quality Regulator Scotland

McLaughlin (Justice)
Boundary Cmsn NI

McLaughlin, Brenda
Civil Service Cmsnrs NI

McLaughlin, Carmel (Dr)
Communications Cmsn

McLaughlin, Gerald
NHS Health Scotland

MacLauren, Winsome
Envt Coun

Maclay, Michael
Citizenship Foundation

McLean, Alistair
Fundraising Standards Bd

MacLean, Anne
Mobility & Access C'ee Scotland

Macleod, Hamish
Forestry Cmsn Scotland

Macleod, Iain A
Stornoway Port Auth

Macleod, Norman
Northern Jt Police Bd

McLuckie, Dave
Cleveland Police Auth

McMahon, Malcolm
Catholic Bishops Conf England & Wales

McMahon, Mary
Public Health Agency

McMillan, Malcolm
Scottish Law Cmsn

McMillen, John
NI Envt Agency

McMurray, Frances
NI Practice & Educ Coun Nursing & Midwifery

McMurray, Terry (Dr)
NI Med & Dental Trg Agency

McNamara, John
Alliance Sector Skills Couns

McNaught, Ian (Capt)
Corporation of Trinity House of Deptford Strond

McNeill, John
Police Complaints Cmsnr Scotland

McNicol, Donald B (Dr)
Scottish Dental Practice Bd

McNulty, Roy (Sir)
Advantage West Midlands
Ilex (Londonderry)

McQuillan, Harry
Community Pharmacy Scotland

McVeigh, Angela
Central Nursing Advy C'ee

McVeigh, Robert
C'wealth Games Coun NI

McWilliams, Monica (Prof)
NI Human Rights Cmsn

Maguire, Michael (Dr)
Criminal Justice Inspection NI

Maguire, Tom
Stdg Conf Univ Drama Departments

Maiden, Mike
Staffordshire & West Midlands Probation Trust

Mair, Ranald
Scottish Care

Major, Frank
Envt Agency - North East Region

Male, Roy
Lancashire Probation Trust

Malthouse, Kit
Metropolitan Police Auth

Maltin, Charlotte
Audit Advy C'ee Scotland

Manion, David
Age Scotland

Manley, Andrew
Defence Estates

Mann, Chris
Powys Teaching Health Bd

Mannings, Keith
Strathclyde Police Auth

Mantell, Mary
Community Coun Shropshire

Margetts, Rob (Sir)
Ordnance Survey

Markham, John
West Northamptonshire Development Corporation

Markwick, Paul
Government Car & Despatch Agency
Vehicle Certification Agency

Marlow, Francis
Partnership Action Wildlife Crime

Marsden, Christopher
Stdg Conf Archives & Museums

Marshall, Derek
UK Security & Resilience Ind Suppliers Community

Marshall, Gerry
Thames Valley Probation Trust

Marshall, Gordon (Prof)
Higher Educ Statistics Agency

Marshall, Keith
Summit Skills

Martin (Judge)
Office Social Security & Child Spt Cmsnrs NI

Martin, Chris
Hywel Dda Health Bd

Martin, David (Dr)
Jt Mathematical Coun UK

Martin, Donald
Harris Tweed Auth

Martin, Jane
Cmsn Local Administration England

Martin, Jim
Scottish Public Services Ombudsman

Martin, Louise
Sport Scotland

Martin, Peter
Lantra

Martin, Richard
NHS Professionals

Martin, Tim
NI Water
Royal Mint
Scottish Water

Martin, Will
Marine Stewardship Coun

Masella, Antonio
Valuation Tribunal Service

Mason, Catherine
NI Transport Holding Company

Mason, Graeme
Newcastle Airport Conslt C'ee

Mason, Keith (Prof)
Science & Technology Facilities Coun

Mason, Lee
Langstone Harbour Bd

Mason, Marisa (Dr)
Nat Confidential Enquiry Patient Outcome...

Mason, Peter
Nat Measurement Office

Mason, Tom (Dr)
Armagh Planetarium & Observatory

Massey of Darwen (Baroness)
Nat Treatment Agency Substance Misuse

Massey, Alan
Maritime & Coastguard Agency

Massie, Bert (Sir)
Cmsn Compact

Masterton, Gordon
Construction Ind Coun
Stdg C'ee Structural Safety

Matchett, George
Central Scotland Jt Police Bd

Mathers, Bob
Lancashire Probation Trust

Matheson, Jil
UK Statistics Auth

Mathewson, George (Sir)
Royal Botanic Garden Edinburgh

Matthews, Bill
Audience Coun Scotland
NHS Nat Services Scotland

Matthews, Chris
Humberside Police Auth

Matthews, Jack
Improve

Matthews, Peter (Prof)
NI Auth Utility Regulation

Matthews, Tim
Remploy

Matthews, Trevor
Financial Services Skills Coun

Maude, Francis
Public Sector Transparency Bd

Maund, Robert G
Scottish Coun Nat Parks

Mawson, Peter
West Northamptonshire Development Corporation

Maxwell, Bill (Dr)
HM Inspectorate Educ

May, Christine
Scottish Library Inf Coun

Mayer, Anthony
London Pensions Fund Auth
Tenant Services Auth

Mayfield, Charlie
UK Cmsn Employment & Skills

Mayhew Jonas, Judith (Dame)
Indep Schools Coun

Mc... see Mac...
Mead, Elaine
Highland NHS Bd

Mee, Laurence (Prof)
Advy C'ee Protection Sea

 © CBD Research Ltd · Beckenham · Kent BR3 5JS · Tel 020 8650 7745 · Fax 020 8650 0768 · E-mail cbd@cbdresearch.com · www.cbdresearch.com

Meek, Kip
South West Screen

Meldrum, Gordon (Dep Chf Constable)
Scottish Crime & Drug Enforcement Agency

Mellor, Chris
NI Water

Melmoth, Graham (Sir)
Nat Coun Voluntary Orgs

Melville-Ross, Tim
Higher Educ Funding Coun England

Menary, Rob
Devon & Cornwall Probation Trust

Mence, Sylvia
Yarmouth Harbour Cmsnrs

Menzies, John
Scottish Agricl Wages Bd

Mercer, Ronnie
Scottish Water

Metcalf, David (Prof)
Migration Advy C'ee

Middleton, David
Transport Scotland

Middleton, Peter (Sir)
Creative Sheffield

Milanovic, Michael (Dr)
Cambridge ESOL

Milburn, Martina
Princes Trust Coun

Millar, Graeme (Prof)
Scottish Food Advy C'ee

Millar, Keith
Animal Feed Law Enforcement Liaison Gp

Millar, Stanley
Disability Living Allowance Advy Bd NI

Miller, Patrick
Gen Advy C'ee Science

Mills, Barbara (Dame)
Professional Oversight Bd

Mills, Chris
Envt Agency - Wales

Mills, Sian
Special Educl Needs Tribunal Wales

Milne, Charles (Prof)
Food Standards Agency Scotland

Milne, Claire
Gambling Supervision Cmsn

Milner, Susan (Dr)
Stdg Conf Heads European Studies

Mitchell, Arthur
Rural Devt Coun

Mitchell, Janine
UK Automatic Control Coun

Mitchell, Nick
GoSkills

Mitchell, Paul
British Copyright Coun

Mitchell, Peter
Mathematics Educ & Ind

Mitchell, Sarah
Resuscitation Coun UK

Moffat, Andrew
Port Tyne Auth

Mogg (Lord)
Gas & Electricity Markets Auth

Moir, David
Northamptonshire Probation Trust

Monks, Paul (Prof)
Air Quality Expert Gp

Montgomery, Jonathan (Prof)
Advy C'ee Clinical Excellence Awards
Human Genetics Cmsn

Montgomery, Lindsay
Scottish Legal Aid Bd

Moore, Ann (Prof)
Nat Coun Osteopathic Res

Moore, David
Envt Agency - Anglian Region

Moore, Jeff
Cwm Taf Community Health Coun
East Midlands Devt Agency

Moore, Michael
Buckinghamshire Community Action

Moores, Pam
Univ Coun Modern Languages

Moran, Terry
Pension Disability & Carers Service

Morgan, Declan (Sir)
NI Judicial Appointments Cmsn

Morgan, Derek
Upland Forum

Morgan, Peter (Prof)
Rowett Institute Nutrition & Health

Morgan, Sally (Baroness)
Office Standards Educ

Morgan, Sandra
Welsh Therapies Advy C'ee

Morland, Eddie
Health & Safety Laboratory

Morley, David (Dr)
Open & Distance Learning Quality Coun

Morley, Oliver
Nat Archives

Morrell, Dave
Montgomery Community Health Coun

Morris, Candy
South East Coast Strategic Health Authority

Morris, David
Nat Examination Bd Occupational Safety & Health

Morris, Gillian (Prof)
NHS Pay Review Body
Police Advy Bd E&W
Police Negotiating Bd

Morris, K (Dr)
NI Blood Transfusion Service

Morrish, James
Envt Agency - South West Region

Morrison, Alasdair
MG ALBA

Morrison, Steve
Vision & Media

Morrow, Duncan
Community Relations Coun

Morrow, Joe (Dr)
Mental Health Tribunal Scotland

Morse, Amyas
Nat Audit Office

Mortimer, Gail
Gen Teaching Coun England

Morton, Uel
Quality Meat Scotland

Motion, Andrew (Sir)
Museums Libraries & Archives Coun

Mottram, Richard (Sir)
Defence Science & Technology Laboratory

Mounsey, Helen (Dr)
Coal Auth

Mountford, Roger
Dover Harbour Bd

Muir, Craig
Human Tissue Auth

Mulholland, Barry
Western Educ & Library Bd

Mullen, Ian
Forth Valley NHS Bd

Mummery (Lord Justice)
Clergy Discipline Comsn
Investigatory Powers Tribunal

Munby (Lord Justice)
Law Cmsn

Munby, Steve
Nat College Leadership & Childrens Services

Munro, Hugh (Brigadier)
HM Inspectorate Prisons Scotland

Munson, Andrew
Newlyn Pier & Harbour Cmsnrs

Murphy, Paul
Greater Manchester Police Auth

Murphy, Tony
Southern Educ & Library Bd

Murray, Allan
Glass Qualifications Auth

Murray, Diana
Royal Cmsn Ancient & Historical Monuments
Scotland

Murray, Janice
Nat Army Museum

Murray, John (Prof)
Scottish Coun Intl Arbitration

Murray, Tom
British Hallmarking Coun

Myers, Kevin
Health & Safety Exec Local Auth Enforcement
Liaison C'ee

Mytton, Elizabeth (Dr)
C'ee Heads Univ Law Schools

N

Nagler, Stuart
Hertfordshire Police Auth

Nairne, Sandy
Nat Portrait Gallery

Namazie, Maryam
Coun Ex Muslims Britain

Napier, Robert
Homes & Communities Agency
Met Office

Nathan, Sara
Animal Procedures C'ee

Nayler, Jeremy
C'ee Accreditation Medical Illustration...

Naylor, John
Office Scottish Charity Regulator

Nellis, Liam
Trade & Business Devt Body

Nelson, Peter
Distilling Ind Trg C'ee

Nerney, Julie
British Safety Coun

Neuberger of Abbotsbury (Lord)
Advy Coun Nat Records & Archives
Civil Justice Coun

Neuberger, Julia (Dame)
Advy Panel Judicial Diversity

Nevill, Amanda
British Film Institute

Newbigin, John
Creative England

Newham, Deirdre
Northamptonshire Police Auth

Newman, George (Sir)
Security Vetting Appeals Panel

Newman, Julie
UK Disabled Peoples Coun

Nichol, Duncan (Sir)
Skills Justice

Nicholl, Liz
UK Sport

Nicholls, Bob
Gen Pharmaceutical Coun

Nicholls, Graham
Lincolnshire Probation Trust

Nicholls, Tony
Oil & Pipelines Agency

Nichols, Dinah
Nat Forest Company

© CBD Research Ltd · Beckenham · Kent BR3 5JS · Tel 020 8650 7745 · Fax 020 8650 0768 · E-mail cbd@cbdresearch.com · www.cbdresearch.com

Nicholson, Paul
Occupational Medicine C'ee

Nickell, Stephen (Prof)
Advy C'ee Civil Costs

Nickolds, Geoff
Envt Agency - Midlands Region

Nisbet, Isabel
Office Qualifications & Examinations Regulator

Nobbs, Amanda
Envt Agency - South East Region

Noble, Theresa
Tayside Jt Police Bd

Nolan, Caroline
Strangford Lough Mgt Advy C'ee

Nolan, Jo
Screen South

Norbury, Caroline
South West Screen

Norgrove, David
Family Justice Review Panel
Low Pay Cmsn

Norman, Derek
Envt Agency - North West Region

Normington, David (Sir)
Civil Service Cmsn
Office Cmsnr Public Appointments E&W

Norton, Suzie
Screen WM

Nourse, Richard
URENCO

Nutt, David (Prof)
Indep Scientific C'ee Drugs

O

Oates, Ann
Eastern Rent Assessment Panel

Oatway, Carole
Criminal Injuries Compensation Auth

O'Brien, Keith Patrick (Cardinal)
Bishops Conference Scotland

O'Brien, Sarah (Prof)
Advy C'ee Microbiological Safety Food

O'Connor, Denis (Sir)
HM Inspectorate Constabulary

O'Connor, Mike
Consumer Focus

O Crosain, Tarlach
Foyle Carlingford & Irish Lights Cmsn

Odell, Sandra
Jt University Coun

O'Doherty, Garvan
Londonderry Port & Harbour Cmsnrs

O'Donoghue, Mike
Gen Aviation Safety Coun

O'Donoghue, Richmond
Failte Ireland

Ogilvy, Graeme
Learning & Teaching Scotland

O'Hagan, Leonard J P
Belfast Harbour Cmsnrs

O'Higgins, John
Audit Cmsn Local Auths & NHS England

O'Higgins, Michael
Pensions Regulator

O'Keeffe, Chris
Indep Betting Adjudication Service

Oldershaw, Chris
Gloucester Heritage

Oliver, Stephen (Sir)
First Tier Tribunal Claims Mgt Services

Ollerenshaw, Margaret
Cheshire Police Auth

Olowe, Victor
Communications Consumer Panel

Ó Maoilmhichil, Liam
Foras Gaeilge
North South Language Body

O'Neil, Alastair
Edinburgh Airport Conslt C'ee

Ó Peatáin, Caoimhin
Comhairle Gaelscolaíochta

Opie, Lisa
EM Media

Oppenheimer, David
Nat Endowment Science Technology & Arts

O'Reilly, Anne
Age NI

Ormerod, Mark
Farming & Wildlife Advy Gp
Law Cmsn

Ormiston, Andy
O'Rourke, John
Consumers C'ee GB

O'Rourke, Pat
Livestock & Meat Cmsn NI

Orr, Joanne
Museums Galleries Scotland

Osborn, Ruth
Bournemouth Airport Conslt C'ee

Osborne, Iain
NI Auth Utility Regulation

Osborne, Peter
Parades Cmsn

O'Shea, Timothy (Prof Sir)
Jt Inf Systems C'ee

O'Sullivan, Catherine
Aneurin Bevan Community Health Coun

Otani, Robin
British Judo Coun

Outram, Christine
Med Educ England

Outram, Frances
Small Business Trade Association Forum

Ovenstone, Peter
Railway Heritage C'ee

Owen, Arwel Ellis
Care Coun Wales
S4C Auth

Owen, Berwyn
Welsh Pharmaceutical C'ee

Owen, Trefor
Forestry Cmsn Wales

Owen, Valerie
Envt Agency - South East Region

Owens, Lynn (Dr)
Nursing Coun Alcohol

P

Pahl, Nick
British Acupuncture Coun

Palmer, Denis
YouthNet

Palmer, Keith (Prof)
Indl Injuries Advy Coun

Palmer, Nigel (Captain)
Merchant Navy Trg Bd

Palmer, Norman (Prof)
Treasure Valuation C'ee

Palmer, Veronica
NI Transport Holding Company

Paraskeva, Janet (Dame)
Child Maintenance & Enforcement Cmsn
Olympic Lottery Distributor

Paren, Margaret
South Downs Nat Park Auth

Parfitt, David
Film London

Parker, Colin
Aberdeen Harbour Bd

Parker, Gavin (Prof)
Community Coun Berkshire

Parker, Guy
Advertising Standards Auth

Parker, Jim
Public Lending Right

Parker, Mike
Liverpool Vision

Parkes, John
Public Works Loan Bd

Parkin, Paul
Cornwall Rural Community Coun

Parkinson, Andy
UK Anti Doping

Parry, Morgan
Countryside Coun Wales

Parsons, David
East Midlands Counties
Merchant Navy Welfare Bd

Parsons, Ruth
Historic Scotland

Partington, Denise
Community Futures

Passmore, Adrian
Regen WM

Paterson, Alex
Highlands & Islands Enterprise

Paterson, Jill
Welsh Nursing & Midwifery C'ee

Paterson, John M
Montrose Port Auth

Paterson, Kenneth R (Prof)
Scottish Medicines Consortium

Patrick, John (Prof)
Coal Research Forum

Patten of Barnes (Lord)
UK India Round Table

Patterson, Bill
Labour Relations Agency

Patterson, Trevor
Pharmaceutical Society NI

Payne, Sarah
Wales Probation Trust

Pead, Diane V
Radon Coun

Pearce, Trevor
Serious Organised Crime Agency

Pearsall, David
Staffordshire Police Auth

Pearson, Keith
East England Strategic Health Auth

Peggie, Margaret
Sports Leaders UK

Pemberton, Max
Fowey Harbour Cmsnrs

Penhaligon, Jeff (Capt)
Looe Harbour Commissioners

Penn, David
British Shooting Sports Coun

Penn, Rosemary
Financial Supervision Cmsn

Penny, Nicholas
Nat Gallery

Peoples, Alastair
Vehicle & Operator Services Agency

Perham, Michael (Rt Revd)
Hospital Chaplaincies Coun

Perks, Greg
UK Bridges Bd

Perman, Ray
James Hutton Institute

Perricone, Guy
Associated Bd Royal Schools Music

Perrins, John (Dr)
C'ee Safety Devices

Perry, Sarah
Advocacy Training Council

Perryman, Charles
South Yorkshire Police Auth

Peters, Samantha
Gen Optical Coun

Phillips, Aneurin
Snowdonia Nat Park Auth

Phillips, David H (Prof)
C'ee Carcinogenicity Chemicals Food...

Phillips, Hayden (Sir)
Royal Nat Theatre

Phillips, Helen (Dr)
Natural England

Phillips, Marta
Pensions Advy Service

Phillips, Stephen
China Britain Business Coun

Phillips, Trevor
Equality & Human Rights Cmsn

Pick, Geoff
Nat Coun Archives

Pickard, Robert (Prof)
C'ee Radioactive Waste Management

Pickup, Ron
Community Futures

Pierce, Gareth
WJEC

Pierleoni, Marco
Land Registry

Pike, Jamie
Defence Support Gp

Piper, Ian
Forward Swindon

Pirmohamed, Munir (Prof)
Pharmacovigilance Expert Advy Gp

Pitkeathley (Baroness)
Coun Healthcare Regulatory Excellence

Pitt, Michael (Sir)
Infrastructure Planning Cmsn

Place, Steve
Dorset Community Action

Plant, Charles
Solicitors Regulation Auth

Platt, Jane
Nat Savings & Investments

Platten, Guy
Caledonian Maritime Assets

Podger, Geoffrey
Health & Safety Exec

Poll, Ian (Prof)
Defence Scientific Advy Coun

Pollard, Doff
Tees Valley Rural Community Coun

Pollard, Nigel
Nat Illumination C'ee GB

Pollock, Christopher (Prof)
Advy C'ee Releases Envt

Pollock, Sam
Police Ombudsman NI

Pomeroy, Brian
Gambling Cmsn

Pomfret, Chris
Better Regulation Advy Gp

Poole, Geoff
Welsh Blood Service

Pope, Will
East England Devt Agency

Porkess, Roger
Mathematics Educ & Ind

Porter, Kirby
Library & Inf Services Coun NI

Porter, Len
Rail Safety & Standards Bd

Porter, Mark (Dr)
Central Consultants & Specialists C'ee

Poupard, Chris
Envt Agency - South East Region

Powell, Chris (Sir)
Advertising Standards Bd Finance
Broadcast Advertising Standards Bd Finance

Powell, Dai
Disabled Persons Transport Advy C'ee

Powell, Michael
Gen Aviation Awareness Coun

Prentice, Ann (Dr)
Scientific Advy C'ee Nutrition

Prescott, Jeremy
Rural Community Coun Leics & Rutland

Preston, Jeremy
Cowes Harbour Cmsn

Preston, Kieran
Metro

Preston, Liam
British Youth Coun

Pretswell, Willie
Scottish Prison Service

Pretty, David
New Homes Marketing Bd

Price, Gareth
Coun Educ World Citizenship Cymru

Price, Jennie
Sport England

Price, John
Review Bd Govt Contracts

Price, Karen
E Skills UK

Price, Richard
EDI

Price-Morris, Elwyn
Welsh Ambulance Services NHS Trust

Prichard, Jon
Engg Coun

Prideaux, Tim
Surrey Community Action

Priest, Richard
Isle Wight Rural Community Coun

Pritchard, John (Rt Rev)
Church England Bd Educ

Pritchard, Tom (Prof)
Envt Agency - Wales

Prosser, Ian
Railway Ind Advy C'ee

Prosser, Ian (Sir)
Navy Army & Air Force Institutes

Pryor, Louise
Bd Actuarial Standards

Puddicombe, Bill
Essex Probation Trust

Pugh, David
Newspaper Licensing Agency

Pugh, Gillian (Dame)
Nat Children's Bureau

Purt, Trevor
Hywel Dda Health Bd

Pyper, Susan
Envt Agency - South East Region

Pysden, Edward
Visit Chester & Cheshire

Q

Quallington, Richard
Community First Herefordshire & Worcestershire

Quayle, David
Northamptonshire ACRE

Quinn, Andrea
Scottish Police Services Auth

Quysner, David
Capital Enterprise

R

Raeburn, Jim
Press Standards Bd Finance

Rahman, Habib
Jt Coun Welfare Immigrants

Ralston, Stuart (Prof)
Gastrointestinal Rheumatology Immunology . . .
Expert Advy Gp

Ramsay of Cartvale (Baroness)
Atlantic Coun UK

Ramsay, Richard
Nat Nuclear Laboratory
UK Atomic Energy Auth

Ramsden, Mike
NHS Inf Centre

Randall, Ann
PAA VQ SET

Randall, John
Police Advy Bd E&W
Police Negotiating Bd

Rapson, Sarah
Identity & Passport Service

Ratter, Drew
Crofters Cmsn

Rauprich, Susanne
Nat Coun Voluntary Youth Services

Rawlins, Michael (Prof Sir)
Nat Institute Health & Clinical Excellence

Rayment, Jacqui
Hampshire Police Auth

Read, Philippa
Community First

Redgwell, Graham
Stansted Airport Conslt C'ee

Redmond, Liz
Stakeholder Gp Current & Future Meat Controls

Redmond, Phil (Prof)
Nat Museums Liverpool

Reed (Lord)
Children Scotland

Rees, Ian
Wales Mgt Coun

Rees, John (Dr)
Administration Radioactive Substances Advy C'ee

Rees, Michael (Prof)
Med Academic Staff C'ee

Rees, Rob
School Food Trust

Reeves, Keith B
Dyfed-Powys Police Auth

Regan, Tony
Civil Nuclear Police Auth

Reid, Keith (Dr)
Public Health Medicine C'ee

Reiter, Nick
Crofters Cmsn

Remnant, Philip
Shareholder Executive

Rennison, Andrew
Forensic Science Advy Coun

Reynolds, David
North Northants Devt Company

Rhind, David (Prof)
Advy Panel Public Sector Information

Rhodes, Richard
Cumbria Probation Trust

Rich, Paul
NHS Business Services Auth

Richards (Justice)
Insolvency Rules C'ee

 © CBD Research Ltd · Beckenham · Kent BR3 5JS · Tel 020 8650 7745 · Fax 020 8650 0768 · E-mail cbd@cbdresearch.com · www.cbdresearch.com

Richards, Ed
Office Communications

Richardson, Eve
Nat Coun Palliative Care

Richmond, John
Glasgow Airport Conslt C'ee

Riddle, John
Northumberland Nat Park Auth

Riddle, Kathryn
Yorkshire & Humber Strategic Health Auth

Ridge, Janet
Bedfordshire Rural Communities Charity

Ridley, Jacky
Defence Vetting Agency

Rifkind, Malcolm (Sir)
Intelligence & Security C'ee

Riley, Jonathon (Lieutenant-General)
Royal Armouries

Rintoul, Gordon (Dr)
Nat Museums Scotland

Ritblat, John (Sir)
Wallace Collection

Ritchie, Ian
Scottish Science Advy Coun

Ritchie, Mike
C'ee Administration Justice

Ritchie, Pat
Homes & Communities Agency

Robathan, Andrew
Central Advy C'ee Pensions & Compensation

Roberts, Caerwyn
Snowdonia Nat Park Auth

Roberts, Dave
Alcohol Educ & Res Coun

Roberts, Ian
North Wales Police Auth

Roberts, Jacquie
Scottish Cmsn Regulation Care

Roberts, Kevin
Agriculture & Horticulture Devt Bd

Roberts, Roger
Action Communities Cumbria

Roberts, Russell
South Wales Police Auth

Roberts-Jones, Jean
Surrey Community Action

Robertson, Andrew
Greater Glasgow & Clyde NHS Bd

Robertson, Archie
David MacBrayne

Robertson, Iain
Scottish Legal Aid Bd

Robertson, Roger
Brightlingsea Harbour Cmsnrs

Robins, Mick
Indep Monitoring Bds E&W

Robinson, Anne
Campaign Nat Parks

Robinson, Frank
Historic Bldgs Coun

Robinson, Judy
Bedfordshire Rural Communities Charity

Robinson, Kim
Fire Service College

Robinson, Leslie
Cheshire Probation Trust

Robinson, Mike
UK Hydrographic Office

Robinson, Nicola (Prof)
Res Coun Complementary Medicine

Robinson, Sarah
C'ee Gen Practice Educ Directors

Robson, Eric
Cumbria Tourism

Rodrigues, Christopher
Visit Britain

Roe, William
Highlands & Islands Enterprise
Skills Devt Scotland

Rogers, James Noble
Univs Coun Educ Teachers

Rogers, John
Skills Health

Rogers, Paul
Ofcom Spectrum Advy Bd

Rogers, Peter
London Devt Agency

Rogers, Ruth
Cambridgeshire Police Auth

Rogers, Sandra
UK Hydrographic Office

Rollinson, Tim
Forestry Cmsn

Rooker, Jeff
Food Standards Agency

Rooney, Eddie (Dr)
Public Health Agency

Roper, Angela (Dr)
Coun Hospitality Management Educ

Rosborough, Linda
Marine Scotland

Rose, Christopher (Sir)
Office Surveillance Cmsnrs

Roseff, Will
Bookmakers' C'ee

Ross, Hugh
NI Polymers Assn

Rossiter, Sue
Nat Foundation Educl Res E&W

Rough, Ian
Scottish C'ee Optometrists

Roughead, Malcolm
Visit Scotland

Routledge, Martin
London Luton Airport Conslt C'ee

Routledge, Philip (Prof)
All Wales Medicines Strategy Gp

Rowe, Andrea
Skills Care

Rowledge, Ricky
Coun Homeless NI

Rowntree, Brian
NI Housing Exec

Roy, Paul
British Horseracing Auth

Roylance-White, Alison
Cheshire Community Action

Rubenstein, Alan
Pension Protection Fund

Rubin, Peter (Prof Sir)
Gen Med Coun

Ruddock, Paul
Victoria & Albert Museum

Rudge, Alan (Sir)
Royal Cmsn Exhibition 1851

Ruscoe, Colin (Dr)
British Crop Protection Coun

Russell, Geoff
Skills Funding Agency
UK Skills

Russell, Gerald
Conslt C'ee Accountancy Bodies

Russell, Graham
Local Better Regulation Office

Russell, Graham Ross
UK Business Incubation

Russell, Ian
Remploy

Russell, Mark
Actis Capital

Russell, Muir (Sir)
Judicial Appointments Bd Scotland

Rutledge, David
Livestock & Meat Cmsn NI

Ruttle, Stuart (Dr)
Cmsnrs Irish Lights

Ryder, Jane
Office Scottish Charity Regulator

Rylance, Rick (Prof)
Arts & Humanities Res Coun

S

Sagar, Deep
Envt Agency - Wales
Leasehold Advy Service

Saif, Abdullah
Young Muslims Advy Gp

Salmon, Trevor
NI Local Government Officers Superannuation C'ee

Salter, David (Dr)
Nat Commissioning Advy Bd

Sampson, Adam
Office Legal Complaints

Samuel, Mhora
Theatres Trust

Samuels, Andrew
UK Coun Psychotherapy

Sandhu, Bhupinder (Prof)
Equality & Diversity C'ee

Sandiford, Delbert
Hertfordshire Probation Trust

Sangster, Ted
Milford Haven Port Auth

Sansom, Mark (Captain)
Falmouth Harbour Cmsnrs

Sants, Hector
Financial Services Auth
Prudential Regulatory Auth

Saunders, David
Competition Cmsn

Saunders, Frances (Dr)
Defence Science & Technology Laboratory

Saunders, Jenny
Nat Energy Action

Saunders, John
Infrastructure Planning Cmsn

Saunders, William P (Prof)
Dental Schools Coun

Savill, Rosalind (Dame)
Wallace Collection

Sawers, Lesley (Dr)
Scottish Coun Devt & Ind

Saxon, Ian
Brecon Beacons Nat Park Auth

Scales, Neil
Merseytravel
Passenger Transport Executive Gp

Scampion, John
Immigration Advy Service

Scard, Dennis
Shoreham Port Auth

Schlesinger, Philip (Prof)
Advy C'ee Scotland (Ofcom)

Scholar, Michael (Sir)
UK Statistics Auth

Scholte, Nick
NHS Business Services Auth

Scott, Alan (Dr)
Indl Court

Scott, George
Community Action Northumberland

Scott, John
C'wealth Games Coun Scotland

© CBD Research Ltd · Beckenham · Kent BR3 5JS · Tel 020 8650 7745 · Fax 020 8650 0768 · E-mail cbd@cbdresearch.com · www.cbdresearch.com

Scott, John Ross
Orkney NHS Bd

Scott, Lexie
NI Museums Coun

Scott, Nicola
Coun Learning Resources Colleges

Scott, Tom
North South Language Body
Ulster Scots Agency

Seabrooke, Alison
Community Devt Foundation

Seaman, Anne
Skillsmart Retail

Seex, Anne
Cmsn Local Administration England

Selby, Peter (Dr)
Indep Monitoring Bds E&W

Seligman, Mark
Indl Devt Advy Bd

Sellwood, Philip
Energy Saving Trust

Serota, Nicholas (Sir)
TATE

Shah, Samir (Dr)
Screen WM

Shanahan, Patrick
Action Rural Sussex

Shanbhag, Radhakrishna (Dr)
Staff & Associate Specialists C'ee

Shand Smith, Lewis
Ombudsman Services
Ombudsman Services PRS Music

Shanmugalingam, Jo
Royal Mail Gp

Sharp, Alison
Aberdeen Airport Conslt C'ee

Sharp, John (Dr)
Oxfordshire Rural Community Coun

Sharp, Kevin
Humberside Police Auth

Sharpe, Sue
Pharmaceutical Services Negotiating C'ee

Shaw, Joanne
NHS Direct

Shaw, Richard
South Downs Nat Park Auth

Shaw, Ruth
Football Licensing Auth

Shaw, Sue
Action Communities Rural England
Community Devt Exchange

Shayer, Ron (Dr)
Scientific C'ee Tobacco & Health

Sheerman, Barry
Parliamentary Advy Coun Transport Safety

Shennan, Andrew (Prof)
C'ee Blood Pressure Monitoring. . .

Shephard (Baroness)
Video Standards Coun

Shepherd, Anne
Population Investigation C'ee

Shepherd, Ian (Lt Colonel)
Scottish Nat War Memorial

Sherling, Clive
Football Foundation

Shiner, Janice
Nat Youth Agency

Shipp, Peter
Road Operators Safety Coun

Shooter, Mike (Dr)
Children Wales

Shortt, Peter
British Waterways
Covent Garden Market Auth
Defence Science & Technology Laboratory
Defence Support Gp
Met Office
UK Hydrographic Office

Shreeve, Gavin
IFS School Finance

Shuttleworth, Nick
Rural Community Coun Essex

Sigsworth, David (Prof)
Scottish Envt Protection Agency

Sills, Richard (Dr)
Energy Ombudsman

Silver, Ruth (Dame)
Learning & Skills Improvement Service

Sime, Martin
Scottish Coun Voluntary Orgs

Simmonds, Brigid
Sport & Recreation Alliance

Simmonds, Heather
Prescription Medicines Code Practice Auth

Simmons, Richard
Cmsn Architecture & Built Envt

Simms, Neville (Sir)
BRE Trust

Simons, Justine
Fourth Plinth Cmsning Gp

Simpson, Fraser
West Yorkshire Police Auth

Sinclair, Gerard
Scottish Criminal Cases Review Cmsn

Sinclair, Jim (Dr)
Jt Coun Qualifications

Singer, Adam
British Screen Advy Coun

Singh, Dara
Jobcentre Plus

Singh, Karamjit
Indep Review Service Social Fund
NI Judicial Appointments Ombudsman

Sischy, Judith
Scottish Coun Indep Schools

Sissling, David
  Abertawe Bro Morgannwg Univ Health Bd

Sitton-Kent, Mark
  Envt Agency - Midlands Region

Skeffington, Joan
  Central Advy C'ee Allied Health Professions

Skelley, Dana
  UK Lighting Bd

Skelly, Bill
  HM Inspectorate Constabulary Scotland

Skilton, David
  Veterinary Products C'ee

Skinner, Robert
  Lending Standards Bd

Slaven, Tracey
  Student Awards Agency Scotland

Sloan, Stanton
  South Eastern Educ & Library Bd

Sloman, Anne
  Church Buildings Coun

Sloyan, Mick
  British Pig Exec

Small, David
  Forest Service

Small, Tim
  Wood Safety Gp

Smart, Peter (Dr)
  Aberdeen Airport Conslt C'ee

Smith (Lady Justice)
  Coun Inns Court

Smith, Alasdair (Prof)
  Armed Forces Pay Review Body

Smith, Anthony
  Passenger Focus

Smith, Chris (Lord Smith of Finsbury)
  Advertising Standards Auth
  Envt Agency

Smith, Cynthia
  Planning Service

Smith, Dai (Prof)
  Arts Coun Wales

Smith, David
  Scottish Bldg Apprenticeship & Educ Coun

Smith, Ed
  Student Loans Company

Smith, Eddie
  New East Manchester

Smith, Greg
  Gloucester Heritage

Smith, Ian
  Microbiology Advy C'ee

Smith, Mike
  Horserace Totalisator Bd

Smith, Peter (JP)
  South Yorkshire Probation Trust

Smith, Peter (QC)
  Parole Cmsnrs NI

Smith, Philip
  ENTRUST

Smith, Robert
  British Boxing Bd Control

Smith, Tim
  Food Standards Agency

Smith, Tony
  Consumer Coun Water

Smitham, Peter
  Actis Capital

Smyth, Edward (Dr)
  Healthcare Associated Infection... Centre

Smyth, John F (Prof)
  Oncology & Haematology Expert Advy Gp

Smyth, Rosalind (Prof)
  Paediatric Medicines Expert Advy Gp

Smyth, Stephen (Br)
  Action Churches Together Scotland

Sneddon, Jasmine
  Scottish Bldg Contract C'ee

Snodgrass, Anthony (Prof)
  British C'ee Reunification Parthenon Marbles

Snook, Nigel
  EDI

Soar, Jasmeet (Dr)
  Resuscitation Coun UK

Sofat, Janardan
  Kent Probation Trust

Somerville, Julia
  Advy C'ee Government Art Collection

Somerville, Patrick J
  Jt Security Ind Coun

Soulsby of Swaffham Prior (Lord)
  Pet Advy C'ee

Souter, Carole
  Nat Heritage Memorial Fund

Southall, Anna
  Big Lottery Fund

Spaight, Anne
  Disability Living Allowance Advy Bd

Sparrow, Mike (Dr)
  Scientific C'ee Antarctic Res

Speaker of the House of Commons
  Boundary Cmsn England
  Boundary Cmsn NI
  Boundary Cmsn Scotland
  Boundary Cmsn Wales

Speed, Stephen
  Insolvency Service

Speirs, Jim
  Nat Inspection Coun Electrical Installation ...

Spence, Colin
  Suffolk Police Auth

Spence, John
  Welsh Food Advy C'ee

Spence, Ronnie
  NI Legal Services Cmsn
  Probation Bd NI

© CBD Research Ltd · Beckenham · Kent BR3 5JS · Tel 020 8650 7745 · Fax 020 8650 0768 · E-mail cbd@cbdresearch.com · www.cbdresearch.com

Spencer, Jonathan
Church England Pensions Bd

Spina, Barbara
Stdg Conf Library Materials Africa

Spittle, Graham (Dr)
Technology Strategy Bd

Sporle, Katrine
Planning Inspectorate

Spurgeon, Sarah (Prof)
UK Automatic Control Coun

Spurr, Michael
Nat Offender Mgt Service

Spyer, Mike (Prof)
London Strategic Health Auth

Squire, Peter (Air Chief Marshal Sir)
Imperial War Museum

Stafford, Andrew
Royal Mint

Stafford, John
Merseyside Probation Trust

Stafford, Liz
Warwickshire Probation Trust

Stapleton, Nigel
Postcomm

Steele, John
Surrey & Sussex Probation Trust

Stein, Thea
Yorkshire Forward

Steinberg, Max
Liverpool Vision

Stennett, Paul
UK Accreditation Service

Stephens, Elan Closs
Audience Coun Wales

Stephens, Ian
Cumbria Tourism

Sterling of Plaistow (Lord)
Nat Maritime Museum

Sterling, Michael (Prof)
Science & Technology Facilities Coun

Stevely, Bill (Prof)
Ayrshire & Arran NHS Bd

Stevenson, Allan
Potato Coun

Stevenson, Bob
Animal Medicines Trg Regulatory Auth

Stevenson, Lee
Birmingham Intl Airport Conslt C'ee

Stevenson, Mich
Nottingham Regeneration

Stewart, David
Envt Agency - North East Region

Stewart, James
Warrenpoint Harbour Auth

Stewart, Jim
Northern Health & Social Care Trust
Poole Harbour Cmsnrs

Stewart, Kevin
Nestrans

Stheeman, Robert
UK Debt Mgt Office

Stimpson, Antony
Forensic Science Service

Stocken, Oliver
Natural History Museum

Stokell, Neil
GoSkills

Stokes, Andrew
Visit Manchester

Stollard, Paul (Dr)
Asbestos Liaison Gp

Stone, John
Learning & Skills Network

Stone, Nigel (Dr)
Exmoor Nat Park Auth

Stone, Roger
Local Government Yorkshire & Humber

Strathie, Lesley
HM Revenue & Customs

Straughan, Tim
NHS Inf Centre

Street, Paula
Gatwick Airport Conslt C'ee

Streeter, Gary
Westminster Foundation Democracy

Stringer, Patricia
Public Services Cmsn

Strong, Hilary
Nat Coun Drama Trg

Strong, Lawrence (Dr)
Waste Mgt Ind Trg & Advy Bd

Stronge, Bob
NI Coun Voluntary Action

Studholme, Harry (Sir)
South West Regional Devt Agency

Stunell, Andrew
Pet Advy C'ee

Sullivan, Eugene
Audit Cmsn Local Auths & NHS England

Summers, Andrew
Companies House

Sunderland, John (Sir)
Corporate Governance C'ee

Sutcliffe, Andrea
Appointments Cmsn

Sutcliffe, Isabel
Federation Awarding Bodies

Sutcliffe, Jim
Bd Actuarial Standards

Sutherland of Houndwood (Lord)
Associated Bd Royal Schools Music

Sutherland, Alan
Water Ind Cmsn Scotland

Sutherland, Mike (Captain)
Fowey Harbour Cmsnrs

Swan, Mark
Nat Air Traffic Mgt Advy C'ee

Sweeney, Ed
Advy Conciliation & Arbitration Service

Swinson, Margaret
Churches Together Britain & Ireland
Local Government Improvement & Devt

Symons, Tom
British-North American C'ee

T

Tainsh, Neil
Lands Tribunal Scotland

Talbot, Jay
Community Coun Devon

Tambling, Pauline
Creative & Cultural Skills

Tapster, Caroline
East England Local Government Assn

Tate, Geoff
Security Systems & Alarms Inspection Bd

Taylor, Ian
Parliamentary & Scientific C'ee

Taylor, John
Advy Conciliation & Arbitration Service

Taylor, Michael
Dorset Police Auth

Taylor, Mike
London Pensions Fund Auth
Nottingham Regeneration

Taylor, Paul
Vision & Media

Teasdale, Graham (Prof Sir)
NHS Quality Improvement Scotland

Tengatenga, James (Rt Revd)
Anglican Conslt Coun

Thew, Rosemary
Driving Standards Agency

Thewlis, Sarah
Nursing & Midwifery Coun

Thin, Andrew
Scottish Natural Heritage

Thomas, Angela E (Dr)
Biologicals & Vaccines Expert Advy Gp

Thomas, Anthony
Coun Learning Outside Classroom

Thomas, M Wynn (Prof)
Welsh Books Coun

Thomas, Paul (Rear Admiral)
Rail Safety & Standards Bd

Thomas, Quentin (Sir)
British Bd Film Classification

Thomas, Richard
Administrative Justice & Tribunals Coun
Martial Arts Devt Cmsn

Thomas, Roger
Countryside Coun Wales
Higher Educ Funding Coun Wales

Thompson, Beverley
Northamptonshire Probation Trust

Thompson, Derek
Electrical Trg Trust

Thompson, Jeff (Prof)
Examinations Appeals Bd

Thompson, Keith
Scottish Nat Blood Transfusion Service

Thompson, Mark
British Broadcasting Corpn

Thompson, Penny
Gen Social Care Coun

Thompson, Peter
Durham Police Auth

Thompson, Ruth
Nat Energy Action

Thomson, Ben
Nat Galleries Scotland

Thomson, George
Volunteering Devt Scotland

Thomson, Gordon
Whitehaven Harbour Cmsnrs

Thomson, Kenneth
Scottish Advy C'ee Distinction Awards

Thornhill, Michael
Habia

Thornton, Andy
Citizenship Foundation

Thornton, Margaret
Bristol Intl Airport Conslt C'ee

Thorogood, Paul
Football Foundation

Thorpe, Alan (Prof)
Natural Envt Res Coun
Res Couns UK

Thurley, Simon (Dr)
English Heritage

Tillman, Harold
British Fashion Coun

Tilsley, Stephen
EMTA Awards

Tilt, Richard (Sir)
Social Security Advy C'ee

Timms, Peter
David MacBrayne

Tipple, Nigel
CPR Regeneration

Todd, Chris
British Crop Protection Coun

Todd, Ian
Police Complaints Cmsnr Scotland

© CBD Research Ltd · Beckenham · Kent BR3 5JS · Tel 020 8650 7745 · Fax 020 8650 0768 · E-mail cbd@cbdresearch.com · www.cbdresearch.com

Todd, Rosemary
Community Action

Tolhurst, Alan
Robin Hood Airport Conslt C'ee

Tombs, Chris
Community Devt Agency Hertfordshire

Tomos, Rheon
S4C Auth

Tooke, John (Prof Sir)
Med Schools Coun

Topping, Brian
Scottish Accident Prevention Coun

Toulson (Lord Justice)
Judicial Appointments Cmsn

Towers, Mark
Defence Analytical Services & Advice

Towler, Keith
Children's Cmsnr Wales

Townsend, Antony
Solicitors Regulation Auth

Traves, George
Bridlington Harbour Cmsnrs

Treves, Vanni
Nat College Leadership & Childrens Services

Trinick, Christopher
Qualifications & Curriculum Devt Auth

Truman, Crispin
Churches Conservation Trust

Tse, Simon
Driver & Vehicle Licensing Agency

Tucker, Hilary
Greater Manchester Probation Trust

Richard Turfitt
Traffic Cmsnrs

Turner, Adair (Lord)
C'ee Climate Change
Financial Services Auth

Turner, Derek
UK Metwork Mgt Bd

Turner, John
Envt Agency - Midlands Region
NHS 24

Turner, Juan
Isle Man Arts Coun

Tyler, Andrew (Dr)
Defence Equipment & Support

Tyler, Graham
Littlehampton Harbour Bd

Tyndall, Peter
Public Services Ombudsman Wales

Unsworth, Paul
Health & Safety Exec Local Auth Enforcement
Liaison C'ee

Unwin, Tim (Prof)
C'wealth Scholarship Cmsn UK

V

van der Gaag, Anna (Dr)
Health Professions Coun

van Leuven, Nik
Guernsey Financial Services Cmsn

Varley, Rosie
Gen Social Care Coun
Office Public Guardian E&W

Vaughan, Graham (Cdr)
Teignmouth Harbour Cmsn

Verity, Gary
Welcome Yorkshire

Verso, Robin
Warwickshire Probation Trust

Vick, David
Insurance & Pensions Auth

Vickers, Stephen
Vocational Trg Charitable Trust

Vincent, Ernest
Queen Elizabeth II Conference Centre

Vine, John
Indep Chief Inspector UK Border Agency

Vitmayer, Janet
Horniman Public Museum & Public Park Trust

Vlasto, Michael
Nat Water Safety Forum

von Bertele, Mike (Maj Gen)
Jt Med Command

W

Wade, Martyn
Nat Library Scotland

Wakelin, Peter
Royal Cmsn Ancient & Historical Monuments
Wales

Waldegrave of North Hill (Lord)
Nat Museum Science & Industry

Walker, Andrew
Office Telecommunications Ombudsman

Walker, Anna
Office Rail Regulation

Walker, James (Prof)
Centre Maternal & Child Enquiries

Walker, Paul (Justice)
Tribunal Procedure C'ee

Walker, Peter
Technical Advy Bd

U

Underhill (Justice)
Employment Appeal Tribunal

Walker, Rhiannon Ellis
Special Educl Needs Tribunal Wales

Walker, Stephen
NHS Litigation Auth

Walker, Steve
Offshore Ind Advy C'ee

Walker, Tim
Gen Osteopathic Coun

Walker, Timothy
Accountancy & Actuarial Discipline Bd

Wall, Nicholas (Sir)
Family Justice Coun
Family Procedure Rule C'ee

Wall, Patrick (Prof)
Advy Body Delivery Official Controls

Wallace, Andrew
Rivers & Fisheries Trusts Scotland

Wallace, John
Peterhead Port Auth

Wallace, Maggy
Complementary & Natural Health Coun

Wallace, Nigel
Glasgow Prestwick Airport Conslt C'ee

Wallace, Philip
Insolvency Service

Wallis, Alan
Staffordshire Police Auth

Wallis, Edmund
Natural Envt Res Coun

Walmsley, Maureen
Cheshire Community Action

Walport, Mark
Wellcome Trust

Walsh, Dominic
Sports Coun NI

Walsh, Mike
Disasters Emergency C'ee

Walsh-Heron, John
Adventure Activities Licensing Authority

Walton, Les
Young People's Learning Agency

Wanless, Peter
Big Lottery Fund

Ward, Christopher
Wales Mgt Coun

Ward, Emma
Channel Four Television Corpn
Ordnance Survey

Ward, Jack
Nat Proficiency Tests Coun

Ward, Rees
Defence Inds Coun

Ward, Roger
King's Lynn Conservancy Bd

Wardle, Peter
Electoral Cmsn

Wardlow, Michael
YouthNet

Warhurst, Pamela
Forestry Cmsn

Warlow, Ashley
Hywel Dda Community Health Coun

Warnock, Chris
NI Fishery Harbour Auth

Warren, Nicholas (Sir)
Upper Tribunal Tax & Chancery

Warren, Nicholas John
First Tier Tribunal Gambling

Warwick, Diana (Baroness)
Human Tissue Auth

Wates, James
CITB Construction Skills

Wathes, Christopher (Prof)
Farm Animal Welfare Coun

Watkins, Maurice
Greyhound Bd GB

Watson, Allan
NHS 24

Watson, Brian
Berwick-upon-Tweed Harbour Cmsn

Watson, Grant
Newport Unlimited

Watson, Hazel (Prof)
Nursing Coun Alcohol

Watson, Ian
ILEX Professional Standards

Watson, Jenny
Electoral Cmsn

Watson, Linda
Oxfordshire Rural Community Coun

Watson, Mike (Dr)
Conf Postgraduate Med Deans

Watson, Paul
Assn North East Couns

Watson, Sandy
Tayside NHS Bd

Watt, Willie
Wick Harbour Auth

Watts, Anne
Appointments Cmsn

Watts, Graham
Construction Ind Coun

Watts, Terry
Proskills UK

Waugh, Simon
Nat Apprenticeship Service

Way, Elaine
Western Health & Social Care Trust

Weale, Albert (Prof)
Nuffield Coun Bioethics

Wearne, Steve
Food Standards Agency Wales

Webb, Adrian (Prof Sir)
Administrative Justice & Tribunals Coun

Webb, Jane
Prisons & Probation Ombudsman E&W

Webb, Tessa
Hertfordshire Probation Trust

Webley, Derek (Bishop Dr)
West Midlands Police Auth

Webster, Duncan
Central Coun Magistrates Courts C'ees

Weightman, Bill
Merseyside Police Auth

Weir, Patricia
Gingerbread
Staff Cmsn Educ & Library Bds

Welch, Chris
Community Coun Staffordshire

Welford, Christopher
ENTRUST

Wells, Tony (Prof)
Tayside NHS Bd

West, Catherine
London Couns Transport & Envt C'ee

West, Helen
Leicestershire & Rutland Probation Trust

Weston, John
Ufi

Wheatley, Martin
Consumer Protection & Markets Auth

Wheatley, Stephen
Envt Agency - Anglian Region

Wheeler, David
Suffolk ACRE

White, Andrew
Hertfordshire Police Auth

White, Barry
Scottish Futures Trust

White, Denise
Derbyshire Probation Trust

White, Fiona
Community Lincs

White, Ian R (Dr)
Advy C'ee Borderline Substances

White, Nigel
British Cheese Bd

White, Paul
Nat Coun Hypnotherapy

White, Philip
Construction Ind Advy C'ee

Whitehead, John
Sea Fish Ind Auth

Whitehouse, Paul
Gangmasters Licensing Auth

Whiteing, Paul
Phonepay Plus

Whiteman, Rob
Local Government Improvement & Devt

Whiting, John
Office Tax Simplification

Whitty, Christopher (Prof)
Nat Expert Panel New & Emerging Infections

Whyman, Barrie
East Midlands Airport Indep Conslt C'ee

Wigley, Dafydd
Nat Library Wales Bd Trustees

Wilcke, Stephan
Asset Protection Agency

Wiliam, Eurwyn
Royal Cmsn Ancient & Historical Monuments
Wales

Wilkes, John
Scottish Refugee Coun

Wilkie, Sandy
Dairy Coun

Wilkins, Ed (Dr)
Welsh Med C'ee

Wilkinson, Carole
Scottish Children's Reporter Administration

Wilkinson, John
Land & Property Services

Wilkinson, Mike
Lancashire & Blackpool Tourist Bd

Wilkinson, Paul
Improve

Wilkinson, Phil
Ascentis

Willegers, Ryan
Lymington Harbour Cmsnrs

Willetts, David
Space Leadership Coun

Williams, Allison
Cwm Taf Health Bd

Williams, Bryn
Brecknock & Radnor Community Health Coun

Williams, Catriona
Children Wales

Williams, David (Dr)
UK Space Agency

Williams, Debbie
EM Media

Williams, Jan
Cardiff & Vale Univ Health Bd

Williams, Jennie
Indep Schools Examinations Bd

Williams, Jenny
Gambling Cmsn

Williams, Jo
Care Quality Cmsn

Williams, John
Tourism South East

Williams, Mark
British Egg Ind Coun

Williams, Paul
Sea Fish Ind Auth

Williams, Peter
Surrey Police Auth

Williams, Phillip
Cardiff & Vale Glamorgan Community Health Coun

Williams, Rhian Huws
Care Coun Wales

Williams, Richard
NI Screen

Williamson, Gavin
Coun Educ C'wealth

Williamson, Pauline
Northumbria Probation Trust

Williamson, Ronnie
NI Guardian Ad Litem Agency

Willison, Toby
Envt Agency - North East Region

Wilmot, Gillian
Derbyshire Probation Trust

Wilsenach, André
Alderney Gambling Control Commission

Wilson, Alan (Prof Sir)
Arts & Humanities Res Coun

Wilson, Andy
North York Moors Nat Park Auth

Wilson, Jane
Leicestershire & Rutland Probation Trust

Wilson, Kay
Warwickshire Rural Community Coun

Wilson, Kerr (Dr)
Chemicals Regulation Directorate

Wilson, Lena C
Scottish Enterprise

Wilson, Mary
Borders NHS Bd

Wilson, Paul
London Probation Trust

Windfuhr, Kirsten
Nat Confidential Inquiry Suicide… Mental Illness

Wineman, Vivian
Bd Deputies Brit Jews

Winfield, Steve
Greyhound Bd GB

Winstanley, Charles (Dr)
Lothian NHS Bd

Winter-Scott, Rosemary
Accountant Bankruptcy

Winters, Oliver
Warwickshire Police Auth

Wisdom, Brian
People First

Wise, Jan (Dr)
Medico Legal C'ee

Wiseman, Andrew
Export Guarantees Advy Coun

Wiseman, John
Dorset Probation Trust

Wishart, Allan
Shetland Transport Partnership

Wishart, Rob
ScotStat

Wolfson, Bob
Award Scheme Development & Accreditation Network

Wood, David
Tyne & Wear Integrated Transport Auth

Wood, John
Video Appeals C'ee

Wood, Paul
Local Government Boundary Cmsn Wales

Woodcock, Paul
Envt Agency - Anglian Region

Wooderson, Alan
Devon & Cornwall Probation Trust

Woods, Alan
Envt Agency - Anglian Region
Skills Justice

Woods, Roger (Prof)
Univs Coun Educ Teachers

Woolf, Joanna
Cogent

Woolfson, David (Prof)
British Pharmacopoeia Cmsn

Woolgar, Peter
Motor Vehicle Repair Health & Safety Forum

Woolman (Lord)
Boundary Cmsn Scotland

Wootton, Adrian
Film London

Worthington, David
Creative & Cultural Skills

Wride, Tony
UK Flight Safety C'ee

Wrigglesworth, Ian (Sir)
Port Tyne Auth

Wright, Anne (Dr)
Nat Lottery Cmsn
School Teachers Review Body

Wright, Christopher
Bridlington Harbour Cmsnrs

Wright, James
Age Scotland

Wright, Jane
Civil Procedure Rule C'ee

Wright, John (Judge)
First Tier Tribunal Mental Health

Wright, Keith
Civil Service Appeal Bd

Wright, Malcolm
NHS Educ Scotland

Wright, Tom
Age UK
British Tourism Devt C'ee
Edinburgh Airport Conslt C'ee

© CBD Research Ltd · Beckenham · Kent BR3 5JS · Tel 020 8650 7745 · Fax 020 8650 0768 · E-mail cbd@cbdresearch.com · www.cbdresearch.com

Wulwik, Peter (Judge)
First Tier Tribunal Consumer Credit
First Tier Tribunal Estate Agents

Wye, Rob
Learning & Skills Improvement Service

Y

Yates, John
Cambridgeshire ACRE

Yeates, Damien
Skills Devt Scotland

Yeo, Marcus
Jt Nature Conservation C'ee

York (Archbishop of)
Archbishops' Coun Church of England

Young, Andrea
South Central Strategic Health Auth

Young, Andrew
Coun Administration

Young, Barry
Lincolnshire Police Auth

Young, Derek
Theatre Dance Coun Intl

Young, Dominic
Newspaper Licensing Agency

Young, Geoff
British Electrotechnical C'ee

Young, Jill
NHS National Waiting Times Centre Bd

Young, Máire
Youth Coun NI

Younger, Sam
Charity Cmsn

Yu, Patrick
NI Coun Ethnic Minorities

Z

Zellick, Graham (Prof)
Valuation Tribunal England

Lists & Labels

CBD Research Ltd has details of over 7,000 associations, societies, federations and Chambers of Commerce in the UK and Ireland.

The complete collection is available as the Directory of British Associations, either in book or CD Rom format.

However, you may not want details of over 7,000 associations. You might just be looking for associations who hold conferences… or print journals… or have over 100 members… or are celebrating an anniversary next year.

We can provide customised printed lists or mailing labels to fit your criteria. All lists & labels are taken straight from our constantly updated collection.

We can search by:

- **Year of formation**
- **Location** (postcode or county)
- **Type of organisation** (e.g. trade, medical, sports)
- **Legal status** (e.g. registered charity)

- **Activities** (e.g. conferences)
- **Membership numbers** (individual or corporate)
- **Publications**

For more details & a no-obligation free quote, call us on 020 8650 7745, fax 020 8650 0768 or email cbd@cbdresearch.com.

Selected lists are not available in electronic format.

Price List	
(All prices are plus VAT.)	
Quantity	**Price**
Up to 400	£65.00 (minimum)
400 – 999	£0.160 each
1000 - 1499	£0.155 each
1500 - 1999	£0.150 each
2000 - 2999	£0.140 each
3000 - 3999	£0.130 each
4000 - 4999	£0.120 each
5000 - 5999	£0.110 each
6000 - 6999	£0.100 each
7000 up	£0.090 each

SUBJECT INDEX

Prepositions, articles and conjunctions are ignored in the alphabetisation of the directory
and have been similarly omitted from the names of organisations in this index.
See inside back cover for the key to the abbreviations used here.

A

Abattoirs
Advy Body Delivery Official Controls
Livestock & Meat Cmsn NI

Accident prevention
Scottish Accident Prevention Coun
>+ Water: accident prevention

Accountancy & financial reporting
Accountancy & Actuarial Discipline Bd
Accounting Standards Bd
Auditing Practices Bd
Conslt C'ee Accountancy Bodies
Financial Reporting Advy Bd
Financial Reporting Coun
Financial Reporting Review Panel
Nat Audit Office
Professional Oversight Bd
Wales Audit Office

Accreditation
UK Accreditation Service

Activity holidays
Adventure Activities Licensing Authority

Actuaries
Accountancy & Actuarial Discipline Bd
Bd Actuarial Standards
Government Actuary's Department

Acupuncture
British Acupuncture Accreditation Bd
British Acupuncture Coun
>+ Complementary medicine

Addiction > **Alcohol & alcoholism;   Drugs: misuse**

Additives (food) > **Food: safety**

Administration training
Coun Administration

Adoption > **Children: law**

Adult & continuing education
Open & Distance Learning Quality Coun
Stdg Conf Univ Teaching & Research...
>+ Further & higher education;   Universities

Adventure activities
Adventure Activities Licensing Authority

Advertising
Advertising Standards Auth
Advertising Standards Bd Finance
Broadcast Advertising Standards Bd Finance
C'ee Advertising Practice
Creative & Cultural Skills

Advocacy > **The Bar**

Aerospace > **Aviation**

Africa
Stdg Conf Library Materials Africa

Aged people > **Old people: welfare**

Agrément
British Bd Agrément

Agriculture
Agriculture & Horticulture Devt Bd
Consumers C'ee GB
Coun Food Policy Advisors
Farming & Wildlife Advy Gp
Food Ethics Coun
Upland Forum
Uplands Land Mgt Advy Panel

Agriculture: chemicals
Advy C'ee Pesticides
British Crop Protection Coun
C'ee Mutagenicity Chemicals Food...
C'ee Toxicity Chemicals Food Consumer
    Products...
Chemicals Regulation Directorate
Food & Envt Res Agency
Pesticide Residues C'ee
Pesticides Forum

Agriculture: education & training
Lantra
Nat Proficiency Tests Coun

Agriculture: health & safety
Agriculture Ind Advy C'ee

Agriculture: land disputes
Agricl Land Tribunal Wales
Eastern Agricl Land Tribunal
Midlands Agricl Land Tribunal
Northern Agricl Land Tribunal
Scottish Land Court
South Eastern Agricl Land Tribunal
South Western Agricl Land Tribunal
Western Agricl Land Tribunal
Yorkshire & Humberside Agricl Land Tribunal

Agriculture: machinery
Vehicle Certification Agency

Agriculture: payments
Indep Agricl Appeals Panel
Rural Payments Agency

Agriculture: research
Agri Food & Biosciences Inst
>+ Crop protection & research

Agriculture: wages
Agricl Wages Bd England & Wales
Agricl Wages Bd NI
Scottish Agricl Wages Bd

**AIDS Acquired Immune Deficiency Syndrome >
HIV & AIDS**

Air conditioning
Air Conditioning & Refrigeration Ind Bd
Summit Skills

Air defence > Royal Air Force; Armed forces

Air freight > Logistics

Air pollution
Air Quality Expert Gp
C'ee Med Effects Air Pollutants

Air traffic control > Aviation: safety & control

Air transport safety > Aviation: safety & control

Air travellers > Aviation: consumer interests

Airmisses
UK Airprox Bd
>+ Aviation: safety & control

Airport
Highlands & Islands Airports

Airport consultative committees
Aberdeen Airport Conslt C'ee
Birmingham Intl Airport Conslt C'ee
Bournemouth Airport Conslt C'ee
Bristol Intl Airport Conslt C'ee
Cardiff Airport Conslt C'ee
Durham Tees Valley Airport Conslt C'ee
East Midlands Airport Indep Conslt C'ee
Edinburgh Airport Conslt C'ee
Gatwick Airport Conslt C'ee
George Best Belfast City Airport Forum
Glasgow Airport Conslt C'ee
Glasgow Prestwick Airport Conslt C'ee
Heathrow Airport Conslt C'ee
Inverness Airport Conslt C'ee
Leeds Bradford Intl Airport Conslt C'ee
Liverpool John Lennon Airport Conslt C'ee
London City Airport Conslt C'ee
London Luton Airport Conslt C'ee
Manchester Airport Conslt C'ee
Newcastle Airport Conslt C'ee
Robin Hood Airport Conslt C'ee
Southampton Airport Conslt C'ee
Stansted Airport Conslt C'ee

Airworthiness > Aviation: safety & control

Alcohol & alcoholism
Alcohol Educ & Res Coun
Med Coun Alcohol
Nat Coun Social Concern
Nursing Coun Alcohol
Scottish Ministerial Advy C'ee Alcohol Problems
TACADE
>+ Drugs: misuse

Allergies
Cardiovascular Diabetes Renal ... Expert Advy Gp

Alternative medicine > Complementary medicine

Amateur theatre > Theatre

Ambulance services
NI Ambulance Service HSC Trust
Scottish Ambulance Service
Welsh Ambulance Services NHS Trust
>+ Health, NHS Headings

America (North)
British American Security Inf Coun
>+ Canada;   USA

**Ancient monuments > Historic buildings &
monuments**

Anglican church > Church of England

Animals: disease control
Animal Health & Veterinary Laboratories Agency

Animals: feedstuffs
Advy C'ee Animal Feedingstuffs
Animal Feed Law Enforcement Liaison Gp

Animals: medicines > Veterinary products

Animals: protection & research
Animal Health & Veterinary Laboratories Agency
Animal Procedures C'ee
Envtl Investigation Agency
Partnership Action Wildlife Crime
Veterinary Medicines Directorate
>+ specific animals

Animals: welfare
Animal Health & Veterinary Laboratories Agency
Farm Animal Welfare Coun
Partnership Action Wildlife Crime

Antarctica
Antarctic Act Tribunal
Scientific C'ee Antarctic Res

Anti-doping
UK Anti Doping

Antiques > Art & antiques headings

Apprenticeship
Nat Apprenticeship Service
Young People's Learning Agency

Aquaculture > Fisheries headings

Arab–British understanding
Coun Advancement Arab British Understanding

Arbitration & conciliation
Advy Conciliation & Arbitration Service
Central Arbitration C'ee
City Disputes Panel
Scottish Coun Intl Arbitration

Arboriculture > Forestry

Architecture
Architects Registration Bd
Architecture & Design Scotland
BRE Trust
Built Environment Forum Scotland
Cmsn Architecture & Built Envt
Design Comsn Wales
Ministerial Advy Gp
Sir John Soane's Museum
>+ Historic buildings & monuments

Archives
Advy Coun Nat Records & Archives
Archives & Records Coun Wales
CyMAL
Lifelong Learning UK
Manx Nat Heritage
Museums Libraries & Archives Coun
Nat Archives
Nat Archives Scotland
Nat Coun Archives

© CBD Research Ltd · Beckenham · Kent BR3 5JS · Tel 020 8650 7745 · Fax 020 8650 0768 · E-mail cbd@cbdresearch.com · www.cbdresearch.com

Public Record Office NI
Stdg Conf Archives & Museums

Armed forces
Advy C'ee Conscientious Objectors
Defence Academy Mgt Bd
Defence Coun
Defence Science & Technology Laboratory
Government Skills
Imperial War Museum
Indep Monitoring Bd MCTC
Nat Army Museum
Nat Museum Royal Navy
>+ Army; Royal Air Force; Royal Navy; Defence
   headings

Armed forces: children's education
Queen Victoria School
Service Children's Educ

Armed forces: communications
British Forces Post Office
Defence Equipment & Support

Armed forces: courts >**Courts: military**

Armed forces: health
Advy Gp Military Medicine
Armed Forces C'ee
Jt Med Command
Scientific Advy C'ee Medical Implications Less
   Lethal Weapons

Armed forces: housing
Defence Estates

Armed forces: land
Dartmoor Steering Gp
Defence Estates

Armed forces: logistics
Defence Equipment & Support
Defence Storage & Distribution Agency
Defence Support Gp

Armed forces: pay & pensions
Armed Forces Pay Review Body
Isle Man War Pensions C'ee
Senior Salaries Review Body
Service Personnel & Veterans Agency

Armed forces: recruitment & training
Defence Vetting Agency

Armed forces: reservists
Reserve Forces Appeal Tribunals >**Armed forces:**
   supplies
Defence Equipment & Support
Defence Scientific Advy Coun
Disposal Services Agency

Armed forces: welfare
First Tier Tribunal War Pensions & Armed Forces
   Compensation
Navy Army & Air Force Institutes
Royal Hospital Chelsea
Service Complaints Cmnsr Armed Forces
Service Personnel & Veterans Agency

Arms & armour
Royal Armouries

Arms control
Export Control Org

Army
Army Sport Control Bd
>+ Armed forces

Art & antiques: exports
Reviewing C'ee Export Works Art

Art & antiques: theft
Spoliation Advy Panel

Art collections
Advy C'ee Government Art Collection

Art galleries
Museums Galleries Scotland
Nat Galleries Scotland
Nat Gallery
Nat Museums Liverpool
Nat Museums NI
Nat Portrait Gallery
TATE
Wallace Collection
>+ Museums

Arthritis & rheumatism
Gastrointestinal Rheumatology Immunology . . .
   Expert Advy Gp

Arts in general
Arts Coun England
Arts Coun NI
Arts Coun Wales
Creative & Cultural Skills
Creative Scotland
Fourth Plinth Cmsning Gp
Isle Man Arts Coun
>+ specific arts

Arts therapy
Central Advy C'ee Allied Health Professions
Health Professions Coun
Welsh Therapies Advy C'ee

Asbestos
Asbestos Liaison Gp

Assay
British Hallmarking Coun
Jt C'ee Assay Offices GB

Assemblies: Wales & Northern Ireland >
   Parliaments & Assemblies

Astronomy
Armagh Planetarium & Observatory

Asylum > **Immigration**

Atomic energy > **Nuclear industry**

Audience research
Audience Coun England
Audience Coun NI
Audience Coun Scotland
Audience Coun Wales

Auditing > **Accountancy & financial reporting,**
   Public sector auditing

Automation & control
UK Automatic Control Coun

Aviation
Civil Aviation Auth
>+ Airport & Airport consultative committees

Aviation: consumer interests
Air Travel Insolvency Protection C'ee

Aviation: safety & control
Gen Aviation Awareness Coun
Gen Aviation Safety Coun
Military Aviation Auth
Nat Air Traffic Mgt Advy C'ee
NATS
UK Airprox Bd
UK Flight Safety C'ee

Awarding bodies
1st 4 Sport Qualifications
ABC Awards
Ascentis
Assessment & Qualifications Alliance
Award Scheme Development & Accreditation
   Network
Awarding Body Built Envt
British Safety Coun
Cambridge ESOL
CITB Construction Skills
City & Guilds
Coun Awards Care Health & Educ
Coun Curriculum, Examinations & Assessment
Counselling & Psychotherapy Central Awarding
   Body
Edexcel
EDI
EMTA Awards
Engg Construction Ind Trg Bd
English Speaking Bd
Federation Awarding Bodies
Future Awards & Qualifications
Glass Qualifications Auth
Hospitality Awarding Body
IFS School Finance
Institute Motor Industry
Intl Curriculum & Assessment Agency
Lantra
London Academy Professional Trg
Meat Trg Coun
Nat Examination Bd Occupational Safety & Health
Nat Open College Network
Nat Proficiency Tests Coun
NCFE
Oxford Cambridge & RSA Examinations
PAA VQ SET
Scottish Qualifications Auth
Signature
Sports Leaders UK
Vocational Trg Charitable Trust
Waste Mgt Ind Trg & Advy Bd
Wine & Spirit Educ Trust
WJEC
>+ Education: examinations/assessment

B

Bankruptcy > Insolvency

Banks & banking
Asset Protection Agency
Bank England
C'ee Scottish Clearing Bankers
Consumer Protection & Markets Auth
Financial Ombudsman Service
Financial Services Auth

Financial Supervision Cmsn
First Tier Tribunal Consumer Credit
Lending Standards Bd
Prudential Regulatory Auth

The Bar
Advocacy Training Council
Coun Inns Court
Exec Coun Inn Court NI
Gen Coun Bar
Gen Coun Bar NI

Baronets
Stdg Coun Baronetage

Barristers > The Bar

Beauty industry
Habia

Benefit > specific form

Betting > Bookmaking;   Gambling

Bingo > Gambling

Biocides
Biocides Conslt C'ee

Biodiversity
Darwin Expert C'ee
Nat Stdg C'ee Farm Animal Genetic Resources

Bioethics
Nuffield Coun Bioethics

Biology & biotechnology
Biotechnology & Biological Sciences Res Coun
Natural History Museum

Birth registration > Population registration

Bishops: appointments
Crown Nominations Cmsn

Blindness
British Coun Prevention Blindness
Jt C'ee Mobility Blind & Partially Sighted People
Wales Coun Blind

Blood services
Advy C'ee Safety Blood Tissues & Organs
C'ee Blood Pressure Monitoring. . .
NHS Blood & Transplant
NI Blood Transfusion Service
Scottish Nat Blood Transfusion Service
Welsh Blood Service

Board industry
Paper & Board Ind Advy C'ee

Bookmaking
Bookmakers' C'ee
Horserace Betting Levy Appeal Tribunal E&W
>+ Gambling

Books
Booktrust
Skillset

Botanic gardens
Royal Botanic Garden Edinburgh
Royal Botanic Gardens Kew

© CBD Research Ltd · Beckenham · Kent BR3 5JS · Tel 020 8650 7745 · Fax 020 8650 0768 · E-mail cbd@cbdresearch.com · www.cbdresearch.com

Boundaries > **Local government:**
   boundaries;   Parliamentary boundaries

Bovine Spongiform Encephalopathy > **Spongiform Encephalopathy**

Boxing
   British Boxing Bd Control

Britain
   British Coun
   British-North American C'ee

Broadcasting
   BBC Trust
   BBC World Service
   British Broadcasting Corpn
   Communications Cmsn
   Office Communications
   Skillset
   >+ Audience research;   Television

Broadcasting: spectrum > **Radio spectrum**

BSE > **Spongiform encephalopathy**

Budget responsibility
   Office Budget Responsibility

Building & construction
   Advy C'ee Roofsafety
   Conslt C'ee Construction Ind Statistics
   Construction Ind Advy C'ee
   Construction Ind Coun
   Construction Project Inf C'ee
   >+ Housing

Building & construction: training
   CITB Construction Skills
   CITB Construction Skills NI
   Engg Construction Ind Trg Bd
   Scottish Bldg Apprenticeship & Educ Coun

Building contracts
   Scottish Bldg Contract C'ee

Building materials
   Proskills UK

Building materials: certification
   British Bd Agrément
   UK Certification Auth Reinforcing Steels

Building regulations
   Bldg Regulations Advy C'ee
   NI Bldg Regulations Advy C'ee

Building societies
   Financial Services Auth
   Financial Supervision Cmsn

Buildings: subsidence
   Coal Auth

Built environment > **Architecture**

Bureaucracy
   Local Better Regulation Office

Burial
   Burial & Cemeteries Advy Gp

Buses > **Passenger transport**

Business appointments
   Advy C'ee Business Appointments

Business: development & support > **Industrial & economic development**

Business: education > **Management**

Business skills
   Coun Administration

Business: SMEs > **Small & medium size enterprises**

C

Canada
   British-North American C'ee

Canals & inland waterways
   British Waterways
   Broads Auth
   Inland Waterways Advy Coun
   Waterways Ireland
   Waterways Ombudsman C'ee

Cancer
   C'ee Carcinogenicity Chemicals Food...
   Oncology & Haematology Expert Advy Gp

Caravans
   Skills Active

Carbon abatement technologies
   Carbon Trust
   Low Carbon Vehicle Partnership
   Renewable Fuels Agency

Carcinogenic chemicals
   C'ee Carcinogenicity Chemicals Food...

Cardiology
   Cardiovascular Diabetes Renal ... Expert Advy Gp

Care > **type of care eg Social services**

Care homes
   Scottish Care

Careers guidance
   Lifelong Learning UK

Cars > **Motor vehicles**

Cartography > **Maps & mapping**

Casinos > **Gambling**

Catering
   Coun Hospitality Management Educ
   Hospitality Awarding Body

Cathedrals
   Cathedrals Fabric Cmsn England

Catholic > **Roman Catholic**

Cemeteries
   Burial & Cemeteries Advy Gp

Ceramics industry
   C3HARGE

Cereals
   Home Grown Cereals Auth

Certification
   UK Accreditation Service

Channel Tunnel
Channel Tunnel Safety Auth
London & Continental Railways

Chaplains
Hospital Chaplaincies Coun
Mission & Public Affairs

Charities
Big Lottery Fund
Charities Advy C'ee
Charity Cmsn
Charity Cmsn NI
Disasters Emergency C'ee
First Tier Tribunal Charity
Fundraising Standards Bd
NI Central Investment Fund Charities Advy C'ee
Office Scottish Charity Regulator
Scottish Charity Appeals Panel

Cheese
British Cheese Bd
>+ Dairy

Chemical weapons
Chemical Weapons Convention Nat Auth Advy
    C'ee

Chemicals: hazardous
Advy C'ee Hazardous Substances
Advy C'ee Toxic Substances
Chemical & Downstream Oil Inds Forum
UK Chemicals Stakeholder Forum
Working Gp Action Control Chemicals

Chemicals: industry training
Cogent

Chemists: pharmaceutical > Pharmacy

Child Support
Appeals Service NI
Child Maintenance & Enforcement Cmsn
First Tier Tribunal Social Security & Child Support
Office Social Security & Child Spt Cmsnrs NI
>+ Social security benefits

Childbirth
Centre Maternal & Child Enquiries

Children: abused
Criminal Records Bureau

Children: disabled
Coun Disabled Children
First Tier Tribunal Special Educl Needs & Disability

Children: law
Children & Family Court Advy Support Service
Children's Panels
Family Justice Coun
NI Guardian Ad Litem Agency
Scottish Children's Reporter Administration

Children: welfare
C'ee Community Care
Care Tribunal
Children's Cmsnr England
Children's Cmsnr Wales
Children England
Children NI
Children Scotland
Children Wales
Children's Workforce Development Coun
Coun Awards Care Health & Educ

Indep Safeguarding Auth
Nat Children's Bureau
Nat College Leadership & Childrens Services
NI Cmsnr Children & Young People
Scotland's Cmsnr Children & Young People
Skills Care & Development
TACADE
Upper Tribunal Administrative Appeals

China
China Britain Business Coun
GB China Centre

Chiropody
Central Advy C'ee Allied Health Professions
Health Professions Coun
Welsh Therapies Advy C'ee

Chiropractic
Gen Chiropractic Coun
>+ Complementary medicine

Christian unity
Action Churches Together Scotland
Churches Together Britain & Ireland
Churches Together England
Coun Christian Unity
Cytun
Irish Coun Churches

Church of England
Anglican Conslt Coun
Archbishops' Coun Church of England
Church England Bd Educ
Clergy Discipline Comsn
Mission & Public Affairs
Nat Coun Social Concern

Church of England: appointments
Church Cmsnrs
Crown Nominations Cmsn

Church of England: buildings
Cathedrals Fabric Cmsn England
Church Buildings Coun
Church Cmsnrs
Churches Conservation Trust

Church of England: pensions
Church Cmsnrs
Church England Pensions Bd

Church of Scotland
Church & Society Coun

Church: unity > Christian unity

Circuit judges
Coun HM Circuit Judges

Citizenship
Citizenship Foundation
Coun Educ World Citizenship Cymru

Civil aviation > Aviation headings

Civil defence
London Emergency Services Liaison Panel

Civil engineering
Construction Ind Advy C'ee
Engg Construction Ind Trg Bd
Stdg C'ee Structural Safety
UK Bridges Bd

Civil law
Civil Justice Coun

© CBD Research Ltd · Beckenham · Kent BR3 5JS · Tel 020 8650 7745 · Fax 020 8650 0768 · E-mail cbd@cbdresearch.com · www.cbdresearch.com

Civil liberties & human rights
C'ee Administration Justice
Investigatory Powers Tribunal
Nat Coun Civil Liberties
NI Human Rights Cmsn

Civil Service
Civil & Public Services C'ee
Civil Service Appeal Bd
Civil Service Appeal Bd NI
Civil Service Cmsn
Civil Service Cmsn
Civil Service Cmsnrs NI
Government Skills
Nat School Government

Civil Service: business appointments
Advy C'ee Business Appointments

Civil Service: pay
Senior Salaries Review Body

Clans
Stdg Coun Scottish Chiefs

Climate
Met Office

Climate change
C'ee Climate Change
Energy Networks Strategy Gp
Envt Agency
James Hutton Institute
Rural Climate Change Forum

Clinical research > Medical research

Clinical scientists
Health Professions Coun

Clinical trials
Clinical Trials Expert Advy Gp

Clostridium difficile > Infection control

Clothing & textile industry
British Fashion Coun
Harris Tweed Auth
Skillset
Textiles Ind Advy C'ee

Coal & coal mining
Coal Auth
Coal Research Forum
>+ Mining

Coastal environment
Advy C'ee Protection Sea
Stdg Conf Problems Associated Coastline

Coastguards
Maritime & Coastguard Agency

Coins & medals
Royal Mint
Royal Mint Advy C'ee

Common Agricultural Policy
Rural Payments Agency

The Commonwealth
C'wealth Engineers Coun
C'wealth Youth Exchange Coun
Coun Educ C'wealth
Judicial C'ee Privy Coun

Commonwealth Games
C'wealth Games Coun England
C'wealth Games Coun NI

C'wealth Games Coun Scotland
C'wealth Games Coun Wales

Commonwealth: scholarships
C'wealth Scholarship Cmsn UK
>+ Education: grants

Communications interception
Interception Communications Cmsnr
Investigatory Powers Tribunal
Technical Advy Bd

Community care & regeneration
Princes Trust Coun

Community Health Councils
Abertawe Bro Morgannwg Community Health Coun
Aneurin Bevan Community Health Coun
Betsi Cadwaladr Community Health Coun
Brecknock & Radnor Community Health Coun
Cardiff & Vale Glamorgan Community Health Coun
Cwm Taf Community Health Coun
Hywel Dda Community Health Coun
Montgomery Community Health Coun

Community justice
Civil Justice Coun

Community relations
Community Devt Exchange
Community Devt Foundation
Community Relations Coun
Nat Community Forum

Companies: governance
Corporate Governance C'ee

Companies: registration
Companies House

Compensation (foreign)
Foreign Compensation Cmsn
>+ other types of compensation eg Criminal injuries

Competition
Competition Appeal Tribunal
Competition Cmsn

Complaints > Consumer interests; also specific subjects

Complementary medicine
Complementary & Natural Health Coun
Medicines & Healthcare Products Regulatory Agency
Res Coun Complementary Medicine
>+ specific type

Computing & computers > Information technology;   specific applications

Conciliation services > Arbitration & conciliation

Conferences centres
Queen Elizabeth II Conference Centre
Wilton Park
Wilton Park Advy Coun

Conscientious objectors
Advy C'ee Conscientious Objectors

Conservation > **Countryside, Environment**

Construction > **Building & construction;   Civil engineering**

Consultants (medical) > **Medical practice**

Consumer interests
Consumer Coun NI
Consumer Coun Water
Consumer Focus
Consumers C'ee GB
Isle Man Office Fair Trading
NI Auth Utility Regulation
Office Fair Trading
Water Services Regulation Auth

Continuing education > **Adult & continuing education**

Control engineering
UK Automatic Control Coun

Conveyancing
Coun Licensed Conveyancers

Copyright & intellectual property
Advy Panel Public Sector Information
British Copyright Coun
Copyright Tribunal
Intellectual Property Office
Newspaper Licensing Agency
Ombudsman Services PRS Music
Public Lending Right

Corporate governance
Corporate Governance C'ee

Corporation tax > **Taxation**

Costumes
Nat Museums Scotland
Victoria & Albert Museum

Council tax
Valuation Tribunal England
Valuation Tribunal Service
Valuation Tribunal Wales

Counselling > **Psychotherapy**

Country information
Advy Panel Country Information

Countryside: conservation
Coun Nature Conservation & Countryside
Countryside Coun Wales
Jt Nature Conservation C'ee
Manx Nat Heritage
Natural England
Strangford Lough Mgt Advy C'ee

Countryside: recreation
Countryside Access & Activities Network
Countryside Recreation Network
>+ National parks

Court of Appeal
Civil Procedure Rule C'ee
Judicial C'ee Privy Coun

Court of Session
Court Session Rules Coun

Courts: administration
HM Courts & Tribunals Service
Judicial Office E&W
Judicial Office Scotland
Military Court Service

NI Courts & Tribunals Service
Scottish Court Service
Skills Justice

Courts: funds
Court Funds Office
Office Official Solicitor & Public Trustee

Courts: military
Military Court Service
Office Judge Advocate General
Service Prosecuting Auth

Courts: procedures > **Rules of Court**

Covent Garden Market
Covent Garden Market Auth

Covert surveillance > **Surveillance**

Crafts
Crafts Coun
Victoria & Albert Museum

Cricket
England & Wales Cricket Bd

Crime & crime prevention
Nat Fraud Auth
Risk Mgt Auth
Scottish Crime & Drug Enforcement Agency
Serious Organised Crime Agency
>+ Police headings

Crime victims > **Victims of crime**

Criminal injuries compensation
Compensation Agency
Criminal Injuries Compensation Appeals Panel NI
Criminal Injuries Compensation Auth
First Tier Tribunal Criminal Injuries Compensation

Criminal records
Criminal Records Bureau

Crofters
Crofters Cmsn

Crop protection & research
British Crop Protection Coun
James Hutton Institute
Science & Advice Scottish Agriculture
>+ Agriculture headings

Crown Agents
Crown Agents Oversea Govts & Administrations

Curriculum
Coun Curriculum, Examinations & Assessment
Educ & Skills Auth
Qualifications & Curriculum Devt Auth

Customer service
Institute Customer Service

Customs & Excise
Adjudicator's Office
First Tier Tribunal Tax
HM Revenue & Customs
Nat Museums Liverpool

Cycling
Cycling England
UK Roads Bd

D

DA-Notices
Defence Press & Broadcasting Advy C'ee

Dairy
Dairy Coun
DairyCo
>+ Cheese

Dance
British Dance Coun
Scottish Official Bd Highland Dancing
Theatre Dance Coun Intl

Data protection
First Tier Tribunal Inf Rights
Inf Cmsnrs Office
Nat Inf Governance Bd Health & Social Care
>+ Freedom of information

Databases > Information systems & services

Deafness
Signature
UK Coun Deafness
Wales Coun Deaf People
>+ Hearing aids

Death in custody
Indep Advy Panel Deaths Custody

Death registration > Population registration

Defence
Chiefs Staff C'ee
Defence Bd
Defence Coun
Defence Inds Coun
Defence Science & Technology Laboratory
Jt Intelligence C'ee
Ministry Defence Police & Guarding Agency
Nat Defence Inds Coun
>+ Armed forces headings

Defence Advisory Notices
Defence Press & Broadcasting Advy C'ee

Defence: education
Defence Academy Mgt Bd

Defence: logistics > Armed forces: logistics

Defence: ministry personnel
Defence Vetting Agency
People Pay & Pensions Agency

Defence: research & evaluation
Defence Scientific Advy Coun

Defence: statistics
Defence Analytical Services & Advice

Defence: storage > Armed forces: logistics

Democracy
Westminster Foundation Democracy

Demography
Population Investigation C'ee

Dental education
C'ee Postgraduate Dental Deans & Directors
Dental Schools Coun
Gen Dental Coun

Med Educ England
Nat Examining Bd Dental Nurses
NI Med & Dental Trg Agency

Dental practice
Gen Dental Coun
Scottish Dental Practice Bd
Welsh Dental C'ee

Dentists' distinction awards > Distinction awards (NHS)

Dentists' remuneration
NHS Business Services Auth
Review Body Doctors & Dentists Remuneration
Scottish Dental Practice Bd

Deportation > Immigration

Dermatological products
Advy C'ee Borderline Substances
Gastrointestinal Rheumatology Immunology ...
   Expert Advy Gp

Design
Creative & Cultural Skills
Design Coun
Victoria & Albert Museum

Development > Urban development / renewal; & other areas of development

Diabetes
Cardiovascular Diabetes Renal ... Expert Advy Gp

Dietetics
Central Advy C'ee Allied Health Professions
Health Professions Coun
Nutrition Forum
Welsh Therapies Advy C'ee

Diplomatic service
Diplomatic Service Appeal Bd

Disabled persons: employment
Equality 2025
Equality Cmsn NI
Remploy
Ulster Supported Employment

Disabled persons: health & welfare
Advy C'ee Older & Disabled People
Assist UK
Disability Living Allowance Advy Bd
Disability Living Allowance Advy Bd NI
Disability Wales
Indep Living Fund
Jt C'ee Mobility Disabled People
Pension Disability & Carers Service
UK Disabled Peoples Coun
>+ Children: disabled; & specific disability eg
   Deafness

Disabled persons: transport
Disabled Persons Transport Advy C'ee
Mobility & Access C'ee Scotland

Disaster relief
Disasters Emergency C'ee

Disease control: animal
Animal Health & Veterinary Laboratories Agency

Disease control: human
Regional Advy C'ee Communicable Disease
   Control

Diseases: rare >**Health: rare diseases & disorders**

Distance learning
Open & Distance Learning Quality Coun
>+ Adult & continuing education

Distilling
Distilling Ind Trg C'ee

Distinction awards (NHS)
Advy C'ee Clinical Excellence Awards
Distinction & Meritorious Service Awards C'ee
NI Clinical Excellence Awards C'ee
Scottish Advy C'ee Distinction Awards

Distribution > **Logistics**

Diving
Scientific Diving Supervisory C'ee

DNA Database (National)
Nat DNA Database Ethics C'ee
>+ Genetics

Docks > **Ports & harbours** headings

Doctors > **Medical practice**

Dogs
Nat Trg Inspectorate Professional Dog Users

Domestic appliances
Electrical & Electronics Servicing Trg Coun

Domestic heating
Fuel Poverty Advy Gp
Heating & Hotwater Ind Coun
Summit Skills

Drainage > **Land drainage**

Drama > **Theatre**

Drinks industry
Food & Drink Sector Skills
Improve

Driver & vehicle licensing
Driver & Vehicle Agency
Driver & Vehicle Licensing Agency

Driving & medical conditions

Driving tuition, tests & standards
Driving Standards Agency
First Tier Tribunal Transport
Transport Trg Services

Drowning accidents > **Water: accident prevention**

Drugs: medicinal > **Pharmaceuticals**

Drugs: misuse
Advy Coun Misuse Drugs
Advy Panel Substance Misuse
Indep Scientific C'ee Drugs
Nat Coun Social Concern
Nat Treatment Agency Substance Misuse
Scottish Advy C'ee Drug Misuse
Scottish Crime & Drug Enforcement Agency
TACADE
>+ Alcohol & alcoholism

Duty (tax) > **Customs & Excise**

E

Ecology > **Environment**

Economic development > **Industrial & economic development**

Economic Development Companies
Blackpool Fylde & Wyre EDC
CPR Regeneration
Creative Sheffield
Forward Swindon
Liverpool Vision
One NG
Opportunity Peterborough
Prospect Leicestershire

Economic research
Economic Res Coun
Economic Res Institute NI
Economic & Social Res Coun
Office Budget Responsibility

Ecumenicalism > **Christian unity**

Education
Bd Science
Belfast Educ & Library Bd
Comhairle Gaelscolaíochta
Coun Educ C'wealth
Educ & Skills Auth
Learning & Teaching Scotland
NI Coun Integrated Educ
North Eastern Educ & Library Bd
Royal Cmsn Exhibition 1851
South Eastern Educ & Library Bd
Southern Educ & Library Bd
Staff Cmsn Educ & Library Bds
Western Educ & Library Bd
>+ specific fields of education

Education: adult > **Adult & continuing education; Further & higher education**

Education: examinations/assessment
Coun Curriculum, Examinations & Assessment
Educ & Skills Auth
Examinations Appeals Bd
Indep Schools Examinations Bd
Inf Systems Examinations Bd
Jt Coun Qualifications
Mathematics Educ & Ind
Office Qualifications & Examinations Regulator
Qualifications & Curriculum Devt Auth
>+ Awarding bodies

Education: grants
C'wealth Scholarship Cmsn UK
Hannah Res Institute
Marshall Aid Commemoration Cmsn
Student Awards Agency Scotland
US-UK Educl Cmsn

Education: health & safety
Higher & Further Educ Advy C'ee
Schools Educ Advy C'ee

Education: independent
Indep Schools Coun
Indep Schools Examinations Bd
Indep Schools Inspectorate
Scottish Coun Indep Schools

Education: personal development
Award Scheme Development & Accreditation Network

Education: religious > **Religious education**

Education: research
Nat Foundation Educl Res E&W

Education: school trips
Coun Learning Outside Classroom

Education: service children > **Armed forces: children's education**

Education: special
Additional Support Needs Tribunals Scotland
First Tier Tribunal Special Educl Needs & Disability
Special Educl Needs Tribunal Wales

Education: standards
Educ & Training Inspectorate
HM Inspectorate Educ
HM Inspectorate Educ & Trg Wales
Indep Schools Inspectorate
Office Standards Educ
Standards Verification UK

Eggs
British Egg Ind Coun

1851 Exhibition
Royal Cmsn Exhibition 1851

Elderly people > **Old people: welfare**

Elections
Electoral Cmsn

Electrical industry
British Electrotechnical C'ee
Electrical Trg Trust
Jt Ind Bd Electrical Contracting Ind
Nat Inspection Coun Electrical Installation . . .

Electricians
Summit Skills

Electricity
British Electrotechnical C'ee
Energy Networks Strategy Gp
Energy Ombudsman
Energy & Utility Skills
Fisheries Electricity C'ee
Gas & Electricity Markets Auth
Manx Electricity Auth
NI Auth Utility Regulation

Electronics
Electrical & Electronics Servicing Trg Coun

Embryology
Human Fertilisation & Embryology Auth

Emergency planning & services
London Emergency Services Liaison Panel

Employers' associations
Certification Office Trade Unions. . .
Nat Employer Advy Bd

Employment
Gangmasters Licensing Auth
Investors People
Jobcentre Plus
Nat Apprenticeship Service
Public Services Cmsn
Remploy
Working Links

Employment tribunals
Employment Appeal Tribunal
Employment Tribunals
Indl Tribunals & Fair Employment Tribunal

Energy
Energy Saving Trust
Major Energy Users' Coun
Renewable Fuels Agency
Renewables Advy Bd
>+ specific forms of energy eg Gas

Energy efficiency
Awarding Body Built Envt

Engineering
C'wealth Engineers Coun
Coun Science & Technology
Engg Coun
Engineering UK

Engineering: research
Engg & Physical Sciences Res Coun

Engineering: training
Engg Trg Coun NI
Semta

English
British Coun
Cambridge ESOL
English Speaking Bd
Professional & Linguisitic Assessments Bd

Environment
Advy C'ee Protection Sea
Centre Envt, Fisheries & Aquaculture Science
Coun Nature Conservation & Countryside
Energy Saving Trust
Envt Agency
Envt Agency - Anglian Region
Envt Agency - Midlands Region
Envt Agency - North East Region
Envt Agency - North West Region
Envt Agency - South East Region
Envt Agency - South West Region
Envt Agency - Wales
Envt Coun
Envtl Investigation Agency
Farming & Wildlife Advy Gp
First Tier Tribunal Environment
Food & Envt Res Agency
Lantra
London Couns Transport & Envt C'ee
Manx Nat Heritage
Marine Stewardship Coun
Natural Envt Res Coun
NI Envt Agency
Princes Trust Coun
Rural Climate Change Forum
Scottish Envt Protection Agency
Scottish Natural Heritage
Sustainable Devt Cmsn
Sustainable Devt Cmsn NI
Sustainable Devt Cmsn Scotland
Sustainable Devt Cmsn Wales
UK Biodiversity Partnership Stdg C'ee
Yorkshire & Humberside Pollution Advy Coun
>+ Countryside: conservation

Equal opportunity
Equality Cmsn NI

Equality & Diversity C'ee
Equality & Human Rights Cmsn
Nat Coun Women GB
Nat Equality Panel

Estate agents: complaints
First Tier Tribunal Estate Agents
Ombudsman Services Property
Property Ombudsman

Ethnic minorities
Advy Panel Judicial Diversity
Coun Ethnic Minority Voluntary Sector Orgs
NI Coun Ethnic Minorities

European funding
Special EU Programmes Body

European studies
Stdg Conf Heads European Studies

Examinations > Education: examinations/ assessment

Excise > Customs & Excise

Experiments (animals) > Animals: protection & research

Explosives
Explosives Inspectorate

Exports
Export Control Org
Export Credits Guarantee Department
Export Guarantees Advy Coun
UK Tr & Investment

Extractive industries > specific type eg Mining

F

Facilities management
Asset Skills

Fair trading > Consumer interests

Faith: multi- & inter-faith bodies
Churches Legislation Advy Service
Coun Christians & Jews
Faith Communities Consultative Coun
Religious Educ Coun E&W
Scottish Inter Faith Coun

Faith: schools > Religious education

Families: one parent
Gingerbread

Family law
Children & Family Court Advy Support Service
Family Justice Coun
Family Justice Review Panel
Family Procedure Rule C'ee

Farming > Agriculture

Farriers
Farriers Registration Coun

Fashion > Clothing & textile industry

Ferry services
Caledonian Maritime Assets
David MacBrayne
>+ Passenger transport

Fertilisers > Agriculture: chemicals

Fertility
Human Fertilisation & Embryology Auth
Medicines Women's Health Expert Advy Gp

Film & video
British Film Institute
British Screen Advy Coun
Creative Scotland
EM Media
Film Agency Wales
NI Screen
Skillset
Video Standards Coun

Film & video: areas
Creative England
Film London
Isle Man Film
Northern Film & Media
Scottish Highlands & Islands Film Cmsn
Screen South
Screen WM
Screen Yorkshire
South West Screen
Vision & Media

Film & video: classification
British Bd Film Classification
Video Appeals C'ee

Film & video: packaging
Video Packaging Review C'ee

Finance
Financial Ombudsman Service
Financial Policy C'ee
Financial Services Auth
Financial Services Skills Coun
Financial Supervision Cmsn
Guernsey Financial Services Cmsn
IFS School Finance
Jersey Financial Services Cmsn
>+ Personal finance

Financial reporting > Accountancy & financial reporting

Fire prevention & protection
British Approvals Fire Eqpt
Nat Security Inspectorate
Scottish Fire & Rescue Advy Unit
Security Systems & Alarms Inspection Bd

Fire services
Chief Fire & Rescue Adviser
Fire Service College
London Fire & Emergency Planning Auth
NI Fire & Rescue Service

First aid & resuscitation
Resuscitation Coun UK

Fisheries
Envt Agency
Envt Agency - Anglian Region
Envt Agency - Midlands Region
Envt Agency - North East Region
Envt Agency - North West Region
Envt Agency - South East Region
Envt Agency - South West Region
Envt Agency - Wales
Fish Health Inspectorate

© CBD Research Ltd · Beckenham · Kent BR3 5JS · Tel 020 8650 7745 · Fax 020 8650 0768 · E-mail cbd@cbdresearch.com · www.cbdresearch.com

Fisheries Electricity C'ee
Foyle Carlingford & Irish Lights Cmsn
Loughs Agency
Marine Mgt Org
Marine Scotland
Marine Stewardship Coun
Rivers & Fisheries Trusts Scotland
Sea Fish Ind Auth

Fisheries research
Centre Envt, Fisheries & Aquaculture Science
Marine Scotland

Flight safety > Aviation: safety & control

Flight: history
Nat Museum Royal Navy
Nat Museums Scotland
Royal Air Force Museum

Flood defence
Drainage Coun NI
Envt Agency
Envt Agency - Anglian Region
Envt Agency - Midlands Region
Envt Agency - North East Region
Envt Agency - North West Region
Envt Agency - South East Region
Envt Agency - South West Region
Envt Agency - Wales
Rivers Agency
Water Appeals Cmsn

Flu > Influenza

Food: genetically modified > Genetically modified organisms

Food: industry
Coun Food Policy Advisors
Food Cmsn
Food & Drink Sector Skills
Food Ethics Coun
Improve

Food: research
Food Standards Agency
Gen Advy C'ee Science
Hannah Res Institute

Food: safety
Additives & Authenticity Methodology Working Gp
Advy C'ee Microbiological Safety Food
Advy C'ee Novel Foods & Processes
Advy C'ee Pesticides
Audit Advy C'ee Scotland
Better Regulation Advy Gp
C'ee Carcinogenicity Chemicals Food...
C'ee Mutagenicity Chemicals Food...
C'ee Toxicity Chemicals Food Consumer
    Products...
Consumers C'ee GB
Enforcement Liaison Gp
Food & Envt Res Agency
Food Incidents Task Force
Food Safety Promotion Bd
Food Standards Agency
Food Standards Agency NI
Food Standards Agency Scotland
Food Standards Agency Wales
Food Standards Sampling Coordination Working
    Gp
NI Food Advy C'ee

Pesticide Residues C'ee
Scottish Food Advy C'ee
Scottish Food Enforcement Liaison C'ee
Spongiform Encephalopathy Advy C'ee
UK Wide Food Hygiene Ratings Steering Gp
Veterinary Residues C'ee
Welsh Food Advy C'ee
Working Party Food Additives
Working Party Materials... Contact Food

Food: school
School Food Trust

Food: specially formulated
Advy C'ee Borderline Substances

Football
Football Foundation
Football Licensing Auth

Forces > Armed forces

Forensic science & medicine
Forensic Medicine C'ee
Forensic Science Advy Coun
Forensic Science NI
Forensic Science Service
Scottish Police Services Auth
Skills Justice

Forestry
Forest Res
Forest Service
Forestry Cmsn
Forestry Cmsn England
Forestry Cmsn Scotland
Forestry Cmsn Wales
Forestry Enterprise Scotland
Nat Forest Company

Foundation trusts
Monitor

Foundries
Foundries Ind Advy C'ee

Freedom > Civil liberties & human rights

Freedom of information
First Tier Tribunal Inf Rights
Inf Cmsnrs Office
Scottish Inf Cmsnr
>+ Data protection

Fuel poverty
Energy Action Scotland
Fuel Poverty Advy Gp
Nat Energy Action

Fulbright scholarships
US-UK Educl Cmsn

Funerals
Funeral Planning Auth

Further & higher education
British Accreditation Coun Indep... Educ
Coun Ind & Higher Educ
Coun Learning Resources Colleges
Coun Validating Universities
Guild H E
Higher Educ Funding Coun England
Higher Educ Funding Coun Wales
Higher Educ Statistics Agency
Jt Inf Systems C'ee
Learning & Skills Devt Agency NI

Learning & Skills Improvement Service
Learning & Skills Network
Lifelong Learning UK
NCFE
NI Higher Educ Coun
Office Fair Access
Quality Assurance Agency Higher Educ
Scotland's Colleges
Scottish Advy C'ee Credit & Access
Scottish Further & Higher Educ Funding Coun
Skills Funding Agency
Standards Verification UK
Stdg Conf Academic Practice
Stdg Conf Univ Teaching & Research...
Ufi
UK Coun Intl Student Affairs
Young People's Learning Agency
>+ specific branches of education

G

Gaelic
Bord Gaidhlig
MG ALBA

Galleries > Art galleries

Gambling
Alderney Gambling Control Commission
First Tier Tribunal Gambling
Gambling Cmsn
Gambling Supervision Cmsn
Indep Betting Adjudication Service
Nat Coun Social Concern
>+ Horseracing

Gangmasters
Gangmasters Licensing Auth

Gardens > Botanic gardens

Gas
Cogent
Energy Ombudsman
Energy & Utility Skills
Gas & Electricity Markets Auth
NI Auth Utility Regulation

Gastroenterology
Gastrointestinal Rheumatology Immunology ...
Expert Advy Gp

General practitioners > Medical practice

Genetically modified organisms
Advy C'ee Novel Foods & Processes
Advy C'ee Releases Envt
Food Standards Agency
GM Inspectorate E&W
GM Inspectorate Scotland
Scientific Advy C'ee Genetic Modification

Genetics
Gene Therapy Advy C'ee
Genetics & Insurance C'ee
Human Genetics Cmsn
Nat DNA Database Ethics C'ee
Scottish Hospital Endowments Res Trust

Geography
Coun Brit Geography

Glass
C3HARGE
Glass Qualifications Auth
Proskills UK

GMO > Genetically modified organisms

Golf
Rules Golf C'ee

Government advertising
Central Office Inf

Government art collection
Advy C'ee Government Art Collection

Government contracts
Buying Solutions
Review Bd Govt Contracts

Government statistics > Statistics

Government transport
Government Car & Despatch Agency

Greyhound racing
Greyhound Bd GB

Gypsies > Travellers

H

Haematology
Oncology & Haematology Expert Advy Gp

Hairdressing
Habia
Hairdressing Coun

Halal food
Halal Food Auth

Hallmarking > Assay

Harbours > Ports & harbours headings

Harris Tweed
Harris Tweed Auth

Haulage > Logistics

Hawks
Hawk Bd

Hazardous substances > Chemicals: hazardous

Head teachers
Nat College Leadership & Childrens Services

Health: education
Nat Institute Health & Clinical Excellence
NHS Health Scotland

Health: improvement of
Med Res Coun
NHS Institute Innovation & Improvement
NI Health & Social Services Estates Agency
Public Health Agency
Public Health Wales
UK Nat Screening C'ee

Health: information
NHS 24
NHS Direct
NHS Direct Wales
NHS Inf Centre
Patient Information Expert Advy Gp

© CBD Research Ltd · Beckenham · Kent BR3 5JS · Tel 020 8650 7745 · Fax 020 8650 0768 · E-mail cbd@cbdresearch.com · www.cbdresearch.com

Health: professionals & personnel
Health Professions Coun
Skills Health
>+ NHS: staff

Health: rare diseases & disorders
Advy Gp Nat Specialised Services
Nat Services Division
Nat Specialised Commissioning Gp
NHS Specialised Services
Welsh Health Specialised Services C'ee

Health research > Medical research

Health & safety
Advy C'ee Dangerous Pathogens
Advy C'ee Hazardous Substances
Advy C'ee Toxic Substances
C3HARGE
Chemical & Downstream Oil Inds Forum
Construction Ind Advy C'ee
Employment Medical Advy Service
Foundries Ind Advy C'ee
Health & Safety Exec
Health & Safety Exec Local Auth Enforcement
    Liaison C'ee
Health & Safety Exec NI
Health & Safety Laboratory
Health Services Advy C'ee
Higher & Further Educ Advy C'ee
HM Inspectorate Mines
Local Authority Forum
Offshore Ind Advy C'ee
Paper & Board Ind Advy C'ee
Printing Ind Advy C'ee
Quarries Nat Jt Advy C'ee
Rubber Ind Advy C'ee
Schools Educ Advy C'ee
Small Business Trade Association Forum
Textiles Ind Advy C'ee
>+ specific industries

Health & safety: qualifications
British Safety Coun
Nat Examination Bd Occupational Safety & Health

Health service > NHS headings; & specific services

Health & Social Care > NHS Northern Ireland

Healthcare
Business Services Org
Care Quality Cmsn
Healthcare Inspectorate Wales
NHS National Waiting Times Centre Bd
NHS Quality Improvement Scotland
Public Health Agency
Southern Health & Social Care Trust

Healthcare associated infections > Infection control

Healthcare regulation
Coun Healthcare Regulatory Excellence
Regulation & Quality Improvement Auth

Hearing aids
Health Professions Coun
>+ Deafness

Heart
Cardiovascular Diabetes Renal ... Expert Advy Gp

Heating > Domestic heating

Heavy goods vehicles > Logistics

Helicopter landing sites
Helideck Certification Agency

Hepatitis
Advy Gp Hepatitis
Anti Infectives HIV & Hepatology Expert Advy Gp
Unlinked Anonymous Surveys Steering Gp

Herbal medicine
Pharmacovigilance Expert Advy Gp
>+ Complementary medicine

Higher education > Further & higher education;   Universities

Highland dance
Scottish Official Bd Highland Dancing

Hill farming
Upland Forum
Uplands Land Mgt Advy Panel

Historic buildings & monuments
Advy C'ee Historic Wreck Sites
Ancient Monuments Advy Bd
Cadw
English Heritage
Historic Bldgs Advy Coun Wales
Historic Bldgs Coun
Historic Monuments Coun
Historic Royal Palaces
Historic Scotland
Manx Nat Heritage
Nat Heritage Memorial Fund
NI Envt Agency
Royal Cmsn Ancient & Historical Monuments
    Scotland
Royal Cmsn Ancient & Historical Monuments
    Wales
Theatres Trust

Historic ships
Advy C'ee Nat Historic Ships

Historical manuscripts > Archives

HIV & AIDS
Anti Infectives HIV & Hepatology Expert Advy Gp
Expert Advy Gp AIDS
Indep Advy Gp Sexual Health & HIV
Unlinked Anonymous Surveys Steering Gp

Homeless
Coun Homeless NI
Scottish Coun Single Homeless

Horseracing
Bookmakers' C'ee
British Horseracing Auth
Horserace Betting Levy Bd
Horserace Totalisator Bd

Horses: breeding & welfare
British Horseracing Auth
NI Horse Bd

Horses: shoeing > Farriers

Horticulture
Agriculture & Horticulture Devt Bd
Covent Garden Market Auth

Horticultural Devt Company
Science & Advice Scottish Agriculture
>+ **Botanic gardens**

Horticulture: education & training
Lantra
Nat Proficiency Tests Coun

Hospices > **Palliative care**

Hospitals
Scottish Hospital Endowments Res Trust
State Hospitals Bd Scotland
>+ NHS headings

Hospitals: chaplains
Hospital Chaplaincies Coun
Mission & Public Affairs

Hospitals: staff > **NHS: staff**

Hotels & restaurants
Coun Hospitality Management Educ
Hospitality Awarding Body
People First

House of Commons > **Members of Parliament; Parliaments & assemblies**

House of Commons: staff
House of Commons Cmsn

House of Lords > **Lords; Parliaments & assemblies**

Housing
Asset Skills
Homes & Communities Agency
Housing Coun
Nat House Building Coun
New Homes Marketing Bd
NI Housing Exec
Rural Housing Advy Gp
Scottish Housing Regulator
Tenant Services Auth

Housing: complaints
Housing Ombudsman Service
Private Rented Housing Panel
Public Services Ombudsman Wales

Human fertilisation & embryology
Human Fertilisation & Embryology Auth

Human rights > **Civil liberties & human rights**

Human tissue
Human Tissue Auth

Humanities
Arts & Humanities Res Coun

Hydroelectric power
Fisheries Electricity C'ee
>+ Electricity; Energy

Hydrography
UK Hydrographic Office

Hypnotherapy
Gen Hypnotherapy Standards Coun
Nat Coun Hypnotherapy

I

Immigration
First Tier Tribunal Asylum Support

First Tier Tribunal Immigration & Asylum
First Tier Tribunal Immigration Services
HM Inspectorate Prisons
Immigration Advy Service
Indep Chief Inspector UK Border Agency
Indep Monitoring Bds E&W
Jt Coun Welfare Immigrants
Migration Advy C'ee
Office Immigration Services Cmsnr
Refugee Coun
Special Immigration Appeals Cmsn
UK Border Agency
Upper Tribunal Immigration & Asylum

Immunisation > **Vaccination & immunisation**

Immunology
Gastrointestinal Rheumatology Immunology . . .
Expert Advy Gp

In vitro diagnostic devices
In Vitro Diagnostic Advy C'ee

Income tax > **Taxation**

Independent schools > **Education: independent**

India
UK India Round Table

Industrial design
Design Coun

Industrial & economic development
Highlands & Islands Enterprise
Indl Devt Advy Bd
Invest NI
Scottish Coun Devt & Ind
Scottish Enterprise
Trade & Business Devt Body
Welsh Indl Devt Advy Bd
>+ Regional planning & development

Industrial health & safety > **Health & safety**

Industrial injuries
Indl Injuries Advy Coun
>+ Health & safety

Industrial relations
Labour Relations Agency

Industrial tribunals > **Employment tribunals**

Industry: development > **Industrial & economic development**

Industry & higher education
Coun Ind & Higher Educ

Infection control
Advy C'ee Antimicrobial Resistance. . .
Healthcare Associated Infection. . . Centre

Infectious diseases
Nat Expert Panel New & Emerging Infections
Unlinked Anonymous Surveys Steering Gp

Infertility > **Fertility**

Influenza
Scientific Pandemic Influenza Advy C'ee
UK Nat Influenza Pandemic C'ee

Information security
Inf Assurance Advy Coun

Information systems & services
Jt Inf Systems C'ee
Library & Inf Services Coun NI

© CBD Research Ltd · Beckenham · Kent BR3 5JS · Tel 020 8650 7745 · Fax 020 8650 0768 · E-mail cbd@cbdresearch.com · www.cbdresearch.com

Lifelong Learning UK
NHS Wales Informatics Service
Scottish Library Inf Coun
>+ specific locations ie Libraries

Information technology
E Skills UK
Inf Systems Examinations Bd
Inf Technology Working Party
Momentum

Infrastructure
Infrastructure Planning Cmsn
Scottish Futures Trust

Inland revenue > Taxation

Inland waterways > Canals & inland waterways

Inns of Court
Coun Inns Court

Insecticides > Agriculture: chemicals

Insolvency
Accountant Bankruptcy
Air Travel Insolvency Protection C'ee
Insolvency Practitioners Tribunal
Insolvency Rules C'ee
Insolvency Service
Insolvency Service NI

Institutional shareholders
Institutional Shareholders C'ee

Insurance
Financial Services Auth
Financial Services Skills Coun
First Tier Tribunal Claims Mgt Services
Genetics & Insurance C'ee
Insurance & Pensions Auth

Intellectual property > Copyright & intellectual property

Intelligence services
Intelligence & Security C'ee
Intelligence Services Cmsnr

Interception of communications > Communications interception

International information
Advy Panel Country Information

International understanding
British-North American C'ee
Coun Educ World Citizenship Cymru
Wilton Park
Wilton Park Advy Coun

Investment
Actis Capital
Capital Enterprise
CDC Gp
Charities Advy C'ee
Financial Services Auth
Financial Supervision Cmsn
Institutional Shareholders C'ee
Nat Savings & Investments
NI Central Investment Fund Charities Advy C'ee
Shareholder Executive
Strategic Investment Bd
UK Tr & Investment

Ireland
North South Ministerial Coun

Trade & Business Devt Body

Irish
Comhairle Gaelscolaíochta
Foras Gaeilge
North South Language Body

Irradiation of food
Advy C'ee Novel Foods & Processes
>+ Food: safety

J

Jews
Bd Deputies Brit Jews
Central Coun Jewish Community Services

Journalism
Nat Coun Trg Journalists
Press Complaints Cmsn
Skillset
>+ Newspapers & periodicals

Judiciary: appointments
Advy Panel Judicial Diversity
Judicial Appointments Bd Scotland
Judicial Appointments Cmsn
Judicial Appointments & Conduct Ombudsman
NI Judicial Appointments Cmsn

Judiciary: circuit judges
Coun HM Circuit Judges

Judiciary: complaints
Office Judicial Complaints

Judiciary: salaries
Senior Salaries Review Body

Judiciary: training
Judicial Studies Bd
Judicial Studies Bd NI
Judicial Studies C'ee

Judo > Martial arts

Junior doctors
Junior Doctors C'ee
>+ Medical practice

Justice > specific forms eg Civil law

Justices of the Peace
Advy C'ees Justices Peace
Justices Peace Advy C'ees
NI Judicial Appointments Ombudsman
>+ Magistrates

L

Laboratories
Health & Safety Laboratory
Science & Technology Facilities Coun
UK Accreditation Service

Land drainage
Agricl Land Tribunal Wales
Drainage Coun NI
Eastern Agricl Land Tribunal
Midlands Agricl Land Tribunal
Northern Agricl Land Tribunal

Rivers Agency
South Eastern Agricl Land Tribunal
South Western Agricl Land Tribunal
Valuation Tribunal England
Water Appeals Cmsn
Western Agricl Land Tribunal
Yorkshire & Humberside Agricl Land Tribunal

Land registration
Adjudicator HM Land Registry
Land & Property Services
Land Registration Rule C'ee
Land Registry
Registers Scotland

Land use
James Hutton Institute

Land valuation
Land & Property Services
Lands Tribunal NI
Lands Tribunal Scotland
Upper Tribunal Lands Chamber
Valuation Office Agency

Landfill
ENTRUST

Landlords > Housing; Rents

Language therapy
Central Advy C'ee Allied Health Professions
Health Professions Coun

Languages > Modern languages; specific language

Law
Bar Standards Bd
Churches Legislation Advy Service
Coun Inns Court
Faculty Office
Gen Coun Bar
Gen Coun Bar NI
ILEX Professional Standards
Jersey Legal Inf Bd
Legal Services Bd
Solicitors Regulation Auth

Law: case review
Criminal Cases Review Cmsn
Scottish Criminal Cases Review Cmsn

Law: education
C'ee Heads Univ Law Schools

Law: health
Medico Legal C'ee
NHS Litigation Auth

Law: reform & revision
Civil Justice Coun
Law Cmsn
NI Law Cmsn
Scottish Law Cmsn
Statute Law C'ee NI

Law: reporting
Incorporated Coun Law Reporting E&W
Scottish Coun Law Reporting

Law: sentencing
Sentencing Coun

Leasehold property
Leasehold Advy Service
>+ Land valuation

Legal aid & services
Armed Forces Criminal Legal Aid Auth
Legal Aid Advy C'ee
Legal Services Cmsn
NI Legal Services Cmsn
Office Legal Complaints
Scottish Legal Aid Bd
Scottish Legal Complaints C'ee
Scottish Solicitors Discipline Tribunal
Solicitors Disciplinary Tribunal E&W
Treasury Solicitors Department

Legal costs
Advy C'ee Civil Costs

Legal education > Law: education

Legionella
Legionella C'ee

Libraries
Belfast Educ & Library Bd
British Library
British Library Advy C'ee
Coun Learning Resources Colleges
CyMAL
Educ & Skills Auth
Legal Deposit Advy Panel
Legal Deposit Advy Panel
Library & Inf Services Coun NI
Lifelong Learning UK
Museums Libraries & Archives Coun
Nat Library Scotland
Nat Library Wales Bd Trustees
NI Library Auth
North Eastern Educ & Library Bd
Public Lending Right
Scottish Library Inf Coun
South Eastern Educ & Library Bd
Southern Educ & Library Bd
Staff Cmsn Educ & Library Bds
Stdg Conf Library Materials Africa
Western Educ & Library Bd

Lifesaving
Nat Water Safety Forum

Lighthouses
Cmsnrs Irish Lights
Corporation of Trinity House of Deptford Strond
Northern Lighthouse Bd

Lighting
Nat Illumination C'ee GB
>+ Street lighting

Literacy > Adult & continuing education

Local government
Enforcement Liaison Gp
First Tier Tribunal Local Government Standards England
Greater London Auth
Local Authority Forum
Local Government Improvement & Devt
Local Government Regulation
Standards Commission Scotland
Standards England

Local government: administration
Cmsn Local Administration England
Public Services Ombudsman Wales
Scottish Public Services Ombudsman

© CBD Research Ltd · Beckenham · Kent BR3 5JS · Tel 020 8650 7745 · Fax 020 8650 0768 · E-mail cbd@cbdresearch.com · www.cbdresearch.com

Local government: boundaries
Electoral Cmsn
Local Government Boundary Cmsn England
Local Government Boundary Cmsn Scotland
Local Government Boundary Cmsn Wales

Local government: finance
Public Works Loan Bd
Scottish Local Auths Remuneration C'ee

Local government: staff
Employers Org Local Govt
Local Government Staff Cmsn NI
NI Local Government Officers Superannuation
C'ee
Staff Cmsn Educ & Library Bds

Logistics
NHS Business Services Auth
Skills Logistics
>+ Armed forces: logistics

London
Fourth Plinth Cmsning Gp
Greater London Auth
London Couns Grants C'ee
London Cultural Strategy Gp
London Devt Agency
London Pensions Fund Auth
London Transport Users C'ee
London Voluntary Service Coun
Museum London
Royal Parks
Transport London Auth
Visit London

London 2012 > Olympic Games

Lords
House Lords Appointments Cmsn

Lotteries
Gambling Cmsn
Nat Lottery Cmsn

Lottery funding
Big Lottery Fund
Nat Heritage Memorial Fund
Olympic Lottery Distributor

Low pay
Low Pay Cmsn

M

Magistrates
Central Coun Magistrates Courts C'ees
Judicial Studies Bd
NI Judicial Appointments Ombudsman
>+ Justices of the Peace

Management
Nat School Government
Wales Mgt Coun

Manufacturing technologies
Semta

Manuscripts > **Archives**

Maps & mapping
Land & Property Services

Ordnance Survey
>+ Hydrography

Marches > **Parades**

Marine environment
Advy C'ee Protection Sea
Marine Mgt Org

Marine pollution
Maritime & Coastguard Agency

Marine safety
Maritime & Coastguard Agency

Marketing > **specific product**

Marriage registration > **Population registration**

Martial arts
British Judo Coun
Martial Arts Devt Cmsn

Mathematics
Advy C'ee Mathematics Education
Jt Mathematical Coun UK
Mathematics Educ & Ind

Measurement
Nat Measurement Office
UK Accreditation Service

Meat
Advy Body Delivery Official Controls
British Pig Exec
English Beef & Lamb Exec
Livestock & Meat Cmsn NI
Meat Hygiene Policy Forum
Meat Promotion Wales
Meat Trg Coun
Quality Meat Scotland
Stakeholder Gp Current & Future Meat Controls

Medals > **Coins & medals**

Medical auxiliaries > **NHS: staff**

Medical awards > **Distinction awards (NHS)**

Medical conditions & driving

Medical education
C'ee Gen Practice Educ Directors
Conf Postgraduate Med Deans
Gen Med Coun
Med Educ England
Med Schools Coun
Med Students C'ee
NHS Educ Scotland
NI Med & Dental Trg Agency

Medical equipment
C'ee Blood Pressure Monitoring...
C'ee Safety Devices
In Vitro Diagnostic Advy C'ee
Medicines & Healthcare Products Regulatory
Agency
Microbiology Advy C'ee

Medical ethics
Med Ethics C'ee
Nuffield Coun Bioethics

Medical illustration
C'ee Accreditation Medical Illustration...

Medical practice
Gen Med Coun
Nat Confidential Enquiry Patient Outcome...

Private Practice C'ee
Professional & Linguisitic Assessments Bd
Welsh Med C'ee

Medical practice: remuneration
Armed Forces C'ee
Central Consultants & Specialists C'ee
Gen Practitioners C'ee
Junior Doctors C'ee
Professional Fees C'ee
Review Body Doctors & Dentists Remuneration
Staff & Associate Specialists C'ee

Medical research
Med Academic Staff C'ee
Med Res Coun
Nat Commissioning Advy Bd
Nuffield Coun Bioethics
Wellcome Trust
>+ Clinical scientists

Medicine: complementary > Complementary medicine

Medicine: occupational
Occupational Medicine C'ee

Medicine: herbal > Complementary medicine

Medicines > Pharmaceuticals

Members of Parliament
Indep Parliamentary Standards Auth
Parliamentary Cmsnr Standards

Menopause
Medicines Women's Health Expert Advy Gp

Mental health
C'ee Community Care
First Tier Tribunal Mental Health
Mental Health Review Tribunal NI
Mental Health Review Tribunal Wales
Mental Health Tribunal Scotland
Mental Welfare Cmsn Scotland
Nat Confidential Inquiry Suicide... Mental Illness
Office Public Guardian E&W
Office Public Guardian Scotland
Regulation & Quality Improvement Auth
State Hospitals Bd Scotland

Merchant Navy
Merchant Navy Trg Bd
Merchant Navy Welfare Bd

Mercury sphygmomanometers
C'ee Blood Pressure Monitoring...

Mergers & take-overs
Panel Takeovers & Mergers

Metal detecting
Nat Coun Metal Detecting

Meteorology > Climate

Midwives
Healthcare Inspectorate Wales
NI Practice & Educ Coun Nursing & Midwifery
Nursing & Midwifery Coun
Welsh Nursing & Midwifery C'ee

Military > Armed forces headings

Milk > Dairy

Mineral supplements > Nutrition

Minerals
Mineral Products Qualifications Coun
Proskills UK

Minimum wage
Low Pay Cmsn

Mining
HM Inspectorate Mines
Mineral Products Qualifications Coun
Mining Ind C'ee
Mining Qualifications Bd

Mobile telecommunications
Mobile Telecomms & Health Res Programme C'ee

Modern languages
CILT Nat Centre Languages
Stdg Conf Heads European Studies
Univ Coun Modern Languages

Monetary policy
Bank England Monetary Policy C'ee

Monopolies & mergers
Panel Takeovers & Mergers
>+ Competition

Motor vehicles
Driver & Vehicle Agency
Institute Motor Industry
Low Carbon Vehicle Partnership
Motor Vehicle Repair Health & Safety Forum
Vehicle Certification Agency
Vehicle & Operator Services Agency

Motorways > Roads

Mountaineering
Mountain Leader Trg

MRSA > Infection control

Museums
British Museum
CyMAL
Horniman Public Museum & Public Park Trust
Manx Nat Heritage
Museums Galleries Scotland
Museums Libraries & Archives Coun
Nat Museum Wales
Nat Museums Liverpool
Nat Museums NI
Nat Museums Scotland
NI Museums Coun
Stdg Conf Archives & Museums
Victoria & Albert Museum

Museums: specialised
Geffrye Museum
Imperial War Museum
Museum London
Museum Science & Industry
Nat Army Museum
Nat Maritime Museum
Nat Museum Royal Navy
Nat Museum Science & Industry
Natural History Museum
Royal Air Force Museum
Royal Armouries

© CBD Research Ltd · Beckenham · Kent BR3 5JS · Tel 020 8650 7745 · Fax 020 8650 0768 · E-mail cbd@cbdresearch.com · www.cbdresearch.com

Sir John Soane's Museum
Wallace Collection

Music
Associated Bd Royal Schools Music
Ombudsman Services PRS Music

Music: therapy
Health Professions Coun

Muslims
Coun Ex Muslims Britain
Halal Food Auth
Muslim Coun Britain
Nat Muslim Women's Advy Gp
Young Muslims Advy Gp

Mutual Legal Assistance
UK Central Auth

N

National curriculum > Curriculum

National Debt
Nat Savings & Investments
UK Debt Mgt Office

National Health Service > NHS headings

National Insurance
Adjudicator's Office
First Tier Tribunal Tax

National Lottery > Lotteries

National parks
Campaign Nat Parks
Dartmoor Steering Gp
Lee Valley Regional Park Auth
Scottish Coun Nat Parks

National parks: authorities
Brecon Beacons Nat Park Auth
Broads Auth
Cairngorms Nat Park Auth
Dartmoor Nat Park Auth
Exmoor Nat Park Auth
Lake District Nat Park Auth
Loch Lomond & Trossachs Nat Park Auth
New Forest Nat Park Auth
North York Moors Nat Park Auth
Northumberland Nat Park Auth
Peak District Nat Park Auth
Pembrokeshire Coast Nat Park Auth
Snowdonia Nat Park Auth
South Downs Nat Park Auth
Yorkshire Dales Nat Park Auth

National security
British American Security Inf Coun
Defence Press & Broadcasting Advy C'ee
Intelligence & Security C'ee
Investigatory Powers Tribunal
Jt Intelligence C'ee
Nat Security Coun
Security Vetting Appeals Panel
UK Security & Resilience Ind Suppliers Community
>+ Defence

National Theatre
Royal Nat Theatre
>+ Theatre

Natural history
Natural History Museum

Nature conservation >Countryside: conservation; Environment

Navigation
Corporation of Trinity House of Deptford Strond
Envt Agency
Envt Agency - Anglian Region
Envt Agency - Midlands Region
Envt Agency - North East Region
Envt Agency - North West Region
Envt Agency - South East Region
Envt Agency - South West Region
Envt Agency - Wales
>+ Hydrography

Navy > Royal Navy; Merchant Navy

Neurology
Neurology Pain & Psychiatry Expert Advy Gp

New Covent Garden Market
Covent Garden Market Auth

News agencies
Coun Photographic News Agencies

Newspapers & periodicals
Newspaper Licensing Agency
Press Complaints Cmsn
Press Standards Bd Finance

NHS
Indep Reconfiguration Panel
NHS Institute Innovation & Improvement

NHS - England (national)
Nat Specialised Commissioning Gp
NHS Direct
NHS Specialised Services

NHS - England (regional)
East England Strategic Health Auth
East Midlands Strategic Health Auth
London Strategic Health Auth
North East Strategic Health Auth
North West Strategic Health Auth
Office Strategic Health Auths
South Central Strategic Health Auth
South East Coast Strategic Health Authority
South West Strategic Health Authority
West Midlands Strategic Health Authority
Yorkshire & Humber Strategic Health Auth

NHS - Northern Ireland (national)
Health & Social Care Bd
NI Ambulance Service HSC Trust

NHS - Northern Ireland (regional)
Belfast Health & Social Care Trust
Northern Health & Social Care Trust
South Eastern Health & Social Care Trust
Western Health & Social Care Trust

NHS - Scotland (national)
Nat Services Division
NHS 24
NHS Educ Scotland
NHS Health Scotland
NHS National Waiting Times Centre Bd
NHS Quality Improvement Scotland
Scottish Health Coun

NHS - Scotland (regional)
Ayrshire & Arran NHS Bd
Borders NHS Bd
Dumfries & Galloway NHS Bd
Fife NHS Bd
Forth Valley NHS Bd
Grampian NHS Bd
Greater Glasgow & Clyde NHS Bd
Highland NHS Bd
Lanarkshire NHS Bd
Lothian NHS Bd
Orkney NHS Bd
Shetland NHS Bd
Tayside NHS Bd
Western Isles NHS Bd

NHS - Wales (national)
Bd Community Health Couns Wales
NHS Direct Wales
NHS Wales Informatics Service
Public Health Wales
Welsh Ambulance Services NHS Trust
Welsh Health Specialised Services C'ee

NHS - Wales (regional)
Abertawe Bro Morgannwg Univ Health Bd
Aneurin Bevan Health Bd
Betsi Cadwaladr Univ Health Bd
Cardiff & Vale Univ Health Bd
Cwm Taf Health Bd
Hywel Dda Health Bd
Powys Teaching Health Bd

NHS: complaints
First Tier Tribunal Primary Health Lists
NHS Litigation Auth
Parliamentary & Health Service Ombudsman
Public Services Ombudsman Wales

NHS: foundation trusts
Monitor

NHS: fraud & corruption > NHS: security

NHS: funding & accountancy
Audit Cmsn Local Auths & NHS England
Audit Scotland
NHS Business Services Auth

NHS: pensions
NHS Business Services Auth

NHS: security
NHS Business Services Auth

NHS: staff
Health Services Advy C'ee
NHS Pay Review Body
NHS Professionals
UK Advy Panel Healthcare Workers Infected
Bloodborne Viruses

NHS: supplies
Buying Solutions
NHS Nat Services Scotland
NHS Supply Chain
NHS Wales Informatics Service

Noise pollution
Aircraft Noise Monitoring Advy C'ee

North Atlantic Treaty Alliance
Atlantic Coun UK

Northern Ireland Assembly > Parliaments & Assemblies

Northern Ireland: discrimination
NI Human Rights Cmsn

Nuclear decommissioning
Nuclear Decommissioning Auth
Nuclear Liabilities Fund

Nuclear disarmament
British American Security Inf Coun

Nuclear fusion
UK Atomic Energy Auth

Nuclear industry
Cogent
Nat Nuclear Laboratory
Nuclear Res Advy Coun
URENCO

Nuclear safety
Defence Nuclear Safety C'ee

Nuclear waste
C'ee Radioactive Waste Management
Nat Nuclear Laboratory

Nuclear weapons
Defence Nuclear Safety C'ee

Nurses & nursing services
Central Nursing Advy C'ee
NI Practice & Educ Coun Nursing & Midwifery
Nursing & Midwifery Coun
Welsh Nursing & Midwifery C'ee

Nutrition
Food Cmsn
Nutrition Forum
Rowett Institute Nutrition & Health
Scientific Advy C'ee Nutrition

O

Observatories
Armagh Planetarium & Observatory

Occupational health & safety > Health & safety

Occupational medicine > Medicine: occupational

Occupational therapy
Central Advy C'ee Allied Health Professions
Health Professions Coun
Welsh Therapies Advy C'ee

Official secrets > National security

Offshore industry

Oil industry
Chemical & Downstream Oil Inds Forum
Cogent
Offshore Ind Advy C'ee

Oil storage
Oil & Pipelines Agency

Oilseeds
Home Grown Cereals Auth

Old people: welfare
Advy C'ee Older & Disabled People
Age Cymru
Age NI

Age Scotland
Age UK
C'ee Community Care
Continuing Care Conf
Older People's Cmsnr NI

Olympic Games (London 2012)
London Organising C'ee Olympic &
Paralympic Games
Olympic Delivery Auth
Olympic Lottery Distributor

Ombudsmen > + specific subject eg Banks & banking

One-parent families
Gingerbread

Open government
Public Sector Transparency Bd

Ophthalmology
Ophthalmic Gp C'ee

Optical practice
Gen Optical Coun
Scottish C'ee Optometrists
Welsh Optometric C'ee

Organ transplantation
Advy C'ee Safety Blood Tissues & Organs
Human Tissue Auth
NHS Blood & Transplant

Orthodontics > Dental headings

Orthoptics
Central Advy C'ee Allied Health Professions
Health Professions Coun
Welsh Therapies Advy C'ee

Orthotics
Central Advy C'ee Allied Health Professions
Health Professions Coun

Osteopathy
Gen Osteopathic Coun
Nat Coun Osteopathic Res
>+ Complementary medicine

P

Packaging
Advy C'ee Packaging
Working Party Materials... Contact Food

Paediatrics
Paediatric Medicines Expert Adyvy Gp

Paedophiles
Criminal Records Bureau

Pain relief
Neurology Pain & Psychiatry Expert Advy Gp

Palaces
Historic Royal Palaces

Palliative care
Nat Coun Palliative Care
Scottish Partnership Palliative Care

Paper & board industry
Paper & Board Ind Advy C'ee

Parades
Parades Cmsn

Paramedics
Health Professions Coun

Parent teacher relations
Scottish Parent Teacher Coun

Park homes
Nat Park Homes Coun
> + Caravans

Parks > National parks; Royal parks

Parliamentary boundaries
Boundary Cmsn England
Boundary Cmsn NI
Boundary Cmsn Scotland
Boundary Cmsn Wales

Parole system
Parole Bd England & Wales
Parole Bd Scotland
Parole Cmsnrs NI

Parthenon Marbles
British C'ee Reunification Parthenon Marbles

Passenger transport
Centro
First Tier Tribunal Transport
GoSkills
Greater Manchester Integrated Transport
Auth
Greater Manchester Passenger Transport
Exec
Highlands & Islands Transport Partnership
London Transport Users C'ee
Merseyside Integrated Transport Auth
Merseytravel
Metro
Nestrans
Nexus
Passenger Focus
Passenger Transport Executive Gp
Public Transport Users C'ee Scotland
Shetland Transport Partnership
South East Scotland Transport Partnership
South West Scotland Transport Partnership
South Yorkshire Integrated Transport Auth
South Yorkshire Passenger Transport Exec
Strathclyde Partnership Transport
Tayside & Central Scotland Transport
Partnership
Transport London Auth
Transport Scotland
Tyne & Wear Integrated Transport Auth
Upper Tribunal Administrative Appeals
Vehicle & Operator Services Agency
West Midlands Integrated Transport Auth
West Yorkshire Integrated Transport Auth
>+ Railways;   Transport

Passports
Identity & Passport Services

Patents & trade marks
Intellectual Property Office
Intellectual Property Regulation Bd

Pathogens
Advy C'ee Dangerous Pathogens

Patients (care of)
Care Quality Cmsn
Nat Confidential Enquiry Patient Outcome...

Nat Patient Safety Agency
Patient & Client Coun

Patients (records)
Nat Inf Governance Bd Health & Social Care

Pavements
UK Roads Bd

Pay > Minimum wage; Salaries (public sector); &
individual profession

Pensions
Central Advy C'ee Pensions & Compensation
Insurance & Pensions Auth
Isle Man War Pensions C'ee
NEST Corpn
Pension Disability & Carers Service
Pension Protection Fund
Pensions Advy Service
Pensions Ombudsman
Pensions Regulator

Pensions: individual schemes
Church England Pensions Bd
London Pensions Fund Auth
NHS Business Services Auth
NI Local Government Officers Superannuation
C'ee
Pensions C'ee
Scottish Public Pensions Agency

Periodicals > Newspapers & periodicals

Personal development
Award Scheme Development & Accreditation
Network

Personal finance
Consumer Financial Educ Body
Financial Ombudsman Service
>+ Investment; Pensions

Pesticides > Agriculture: chemicals

Petroleum > Oil industry

Pets
Pet Advy C'ee
Pet Health Coun

Pharmaceuticals
All Wales Medicines Strategy Gp
All Wales Prescribing Advy Gp
Biologicals & Vaccines Expert Advy Gp
British Pharmacopoeia Cmsn
C'ee Mutagenicity Chemicals Food...
Central Pharmaceutical Advy C'ee
Chemical & Downstream Oil Inds Forum
Chemistry Pharmacy & Standards Expert Advy Gp
Cmsn Human Medicines
Indep Scientific Advy C'ee MHRA Database Res
Medicines & Healthcare Products Regulatory
Agency
Nat Institute Health & Clinical Excellence
Pharmacovigilance Expert Advy Gp
Prescription Medicines Code Practice Auth
Scottish Medicines Consortium
Welsh Pharmaceutical C'ee
>+ Clinical trials

Pharmacy
Community Pharmacy Scotland
Community Pharmacy Wales
Gen Pharmaceutical Coun

Pharmaceutical Services Negotiating C'ee
Pharmaceutical Society NI
Royal Pharmaceutical Society GB
>+ Pharmaceuticals

Pharmacy: training
Med Educ England
Pharmaceutical Society NI
Royal Pharmaceutical Society GB
Welsh C'ee Professional Devt Pharmacy

Photography
Coun Photographic News Agencies
Skillset

Physical recreation > Sport & physical recreation

Physics
Stdg Conf Physics Profs

Physiology
Registration Coun Clinical Physiologists

Physiotherapy
Central Advy C'ee Allied Health Professions
Health Professions Coun
Welsh Therapies Advy C'ee

Pigs
British Pig Exec

Pipelines (oil)
Oil & Pipelines Agency

Planetariums
Armagh Planetarium & Observatory

Planning > Regional planning & development;
Town & country planning

Plant science
Plant Varieties & Seeds Tribunal
Royal Botanic Garden Edinburgh
Royal Botanic Gardens Kew

Plastics & polymers
Cogent
NI Polymers Assn

Plumbing
Jt Ind Bd Plumbing Mechanical Engg Services
Summit Skills

Podiatry > Chiropody

Poisons > Toxic substances

Police
Criminal Justice Inspection NI
HM Inspectorate Constabulary
HM Inspectorate Constabulary Scotland
Ministry Defence Police & Guarding Agency
Nat Policing Improvement Agency
Police Advy Bd E&W
Police Advy Bd Scotland
Police Arbitration Tribunal
Police Discipline Appeals Tribunal
Scottish Police Services Auth
Skills Justice

Police: authorities
Avon & Somerset Police Auth
Bedfordshire Police Auth
British Transport Police Auth
Cambridgeshire Police Auth
Central Scotland Jt Police Bd
Cheshire Police Auth
City London Police Auth

© CBD Research Ltd · Beckenham · Kent BR3 5JS · Tel 020 8650 7745 · Fax 020 8650 0768 · E-mail cbd@cbdresearch.com · www.cbdresearch.com

Civil Nuclear Police Auth
Cleveland Police Auth
Cumbria Police Auth
Derbyshire Police Auth
Devon & Cornwall Police Auth
Dorset Police Auth
Durham Police Auth
Dyfed-Powys Police Auth
Essex Police Auth
Gloucestershire Police Auth
Grampian Jt Police Bd
Greater Manchester Police Auth
Gwent Police Auth
Hampshire Police Auth
Hertfordshire Police Auth
Humberside Police Auth
Kent Police Auth
Lancashire Police Auth
Leicestershire Police Auth
Lincolnshire Police Auth
Lothian & Borders Police Bd
Merseyside Police Auth
Metropolitan Police Auth
NI Policing Bd
Norfolk Police Auth
North Wales Police Auth
North Yorkshire Police Auth
Northamptonshire Police Auth
Northern Jt Police Bd
Northumbria Police Auth
Nottinghamshire Police Auth
South Wales Police Auth
South Yorkshire Police Auth
Staffordshire Police Auth
Strathclyde Police Auth
Suffolk Police Auth
Surrey Police Auth
Sussex Police Auth
Tayside Jt Police Bd
Thames Valley Police Auth
Warwickshire Police Auth
West Mercia Police Auth
West Midlands Police Auth
West Yorkshire Police Auth
Wiltshire Police Auth

Police: complaints
Indep Police Complaints Cmsn
Police Complaints Cmsnr Scotland
Police Ombudsman NI
Public Services Ombudsman Wales

Police: international cooperation
UK Central Auth

Police: pay & conditions
Police Negotiating Bd

Police: undercover officers > Surveillance

Pollution > Environment; specific forms of pollution

Polymers > Plastics & polymers

Population registration
Identity & Passport Service
NI Statistics & Res Agency
ScotStat

Population studies
Population Investigation C'ee

Portraits
Nat Portrait Gallery

Ports & harbours: England
Berwick-upon-Tweed Harbour Cmsn
Blyth Harbour Cmsn
Bridlington Harbour Cmsnrs
Brightlingsea Harbour Cmsnrs
Cattewater Harbour Cmsnrs
Chichester Harbour Conservancy
Cowes Harbour Cmsn
Crouch Harbour Auth
Dart Harbour & Navigation Auth
Dover Harbour Bd
Falmouth Harbour Cmsnrs
Fowey Harbour Cmsnrs
Gloucester Harbour Trustees
Harwich Haven Auth
King's Lynn Conservancy Bd
Lancaster Port Cmsn
Langstone Harbour Bd
Littlehampton Harbour Bd
Looe Harbour Commissioners
Lymington Harbour Cmsnrs
Mevagissey Harbour
Newlyn Pier & Harbour Cmsnrs
Padstow Harbour Cmsnrs
Poole Harbour Cmsnrs
Port London Auth
Port Tyne Auth
Sandwich Port & Haven Cmsnrs
Shoreham Port Auth
Teignmouth Harbour Cmsn
Warkworth Harbour Cmsnrs
Wells Harbour Cmsn
Whitehaven Harbour Cmsnrs
Yarmouth Harbour Cmsnrs

Ports & harbours: Northern Ireland
Belfast Harbour Cmsnrs
Coleraine Harbour Cmsnrs
Londonderry Port & Harbour Cmsnrs
NI Fishery Harbour Auth
Warrenpoint Harbour Auth

Ports & harbours: Scotland
Aberdeen Harbour Bd
Caledonian Maritime Assets
Cromarty Firth Port Auth
Fraserburgh Harbour Cmsnrs
Lerwick Port Auth
Mallaig Harbour Auth
Montrose Port Auth
Peterhead Port Auth
Scrabster Harbour Trust
Stornoway Port Auth
Tarbert Harbour Auth
Wick Harbour Auth

Ports & harbours: Wales
Caernarfon Harbour Trust
Milford Haven Port Auth
Neath Harbour Cmsnrs
Newport Harbour Cmsnrs

Postage stamps
Stamp Advy C'ee

Postal services
British Forces Post Office
First Tier Tribunal Transport

Government Car & Despatch Agency
Isle Man Post Office
Postcomm
Royal Mail Gp

Postal services: interception > Communications interception

Postgraduate study & awards
Arts & Humanities Res Coun
>+ specific subject

Potatoes
Potato Coun

Pottery
C3HARGE

Power generation > Electricity; Energy; Nuclear industry

Premium rate telephone services
Phonepay Plus
>+ Telecommunications

Press > Newspapers & periodicals

Printing industry
Printing Ind Advy C'ee
Proskills UK

Prisons & prisoner welfare
Correctional Services Accreditation Panel
Criminal Justice Inspection NI
HM Inspectorate Prisons
HM Inspectorate Prisons Scotland
Indep Monitoring Bds E&W
Indep Monitoring Bds NI
Nat Offender Mgt Service
NI Prison Service
Scottish Prison Service
Sentence Review Cmsnrs
>+ Parole system; Probation

Prisons: complaints
Prisoner Ombudsman NI
Prisons & Probation Ombudsman E&W
Scottish Prison Complaints Cmsn

Prisons: medical staff
Civil & Public Services C'ee

Prisons: staff
Prison Service Pay Review Body
Skills Justice

Probation
Correctional Services Accreditation Panel
Criminal Justice Inspection NI
HM Inspectorate Probation
Nat Offender Mgt Service
Prisons & Probation Ombudsman E&W
Probation Bd NI

Probation: trusts
Avon & Somerset Probation Trust
Bedfordshire Probation Trust
Cambridgeshire & Peterborough Probation Trust
Cheshire Probation Trust
Cumbria Probation Trust
Derbyshire Probation Trust
Devon & Cornwall Probation Trust
Dorset Probation Trust
Durham Tees Valley Probation Trust
Essex Probation Trust
Gloucestershire Probation Trust

Greater Manchester Probation Trust
Hampshire Probation Trust
Hertfordshire Probation Trust
Humberside Probation Trust
Kent Probation Trust
Lancashire Probation Trust
Leicestershire & Rutland Probation Trust
Lincolnshire Probation Trust
London Probation Trust
Merseyside Probation Trust
Norfolk & Suffolk Probation Trust
Northamptonshire Probation Trust
Northumbria Probation Trust
Nottinghamshire Probation Trust
South Yorkshire Probation Trust
Staffordshire & West Midlands Probation Trust
Surrey & Sussex Probation Trust
Thames Valley Probation Trust
Wales Probation Trust
Warwickshire Probation Trust
West Mercia Probation Trust
West Yorkshire Probation Trust
Wiltshire Probation Trust
York & North Yorkshire Probation Trust

Property development & services > Building headings

Property disputes > Land registration

Property (ownerless)
Treasury Solicitors Department

Prosecution services
Crown Prosecution Service
HM Crown Prosecution Service Inspectorate
Service Prosecuting Auth

Prosthetics
Central Advy C'ee Allied Health Professions
Health Professions Coun

Psychiatric medicine
Neurology Pain & Psychiatry Expert Advy Gp

Psychotherapy
Counselling & Psychotherapy Central Awarding Body
Health Professions Coun
UK Coun Psychotherapy

Public administration
Jt University Coun
Nat Audit Office
NI Ombudsman
Parliamentary & Health Service Ombudsman
Scottish Public Services Ombudsman

Public appointments
Appointments Cmsn
House Lords Appointments Cmsn
Office Cmsnr Public Appointments E&W
Office Cmsnr Public Appointments NI
Public Appointments Cmsnr Scotland

Public companies
Actis Capital
British Waterways
CDC Gp
Channel Four Television Corpn
Covent Garden Market Auth
Defence Science & Technology Laboratory
Defence Support Gp

Export Credits Guarantee Department
Fire Service College
Forensic Science Service
Horserace Totalisator Bd
Met Office
Nat Nuclear Laboratory
NATS
Navy Army & Air Force Institutes
NI Water
Nuclear Decommissioning Auth
Ordnance Survey
Queen Elizabeth II Conference Centre
Royal Mail Gp
Royal Mint
Scottish Water
UK Atomic Energy Auth
UK Hydrographic Office
URENCO
Working Links

Public health
Bd Science
Health Protection Agency
Public Health Medicine C'ee
Public Health Wales
>+ NHS headings

Public Lending Right
Public Lending Right
>+ Copyright & intellectual property

Public life (standards in)
C'ee Standards Public Life
Standards Commission Scotland
Standards England

Public records > Archives

Public sector auditing
Accounts Cmsn [Scotland]
Audit Cmsn Local Auths & NHS England
Audit Scotland
Public Accounts Cmsn
Scottish Cmsn Public Audit
>+ Local government: finance

Publishing
Booktrust
Welsh Books Coun
>+ Books; Newspapers & periodicals

Q

Qualifications > Curriculum; Education: examinations/assessment

Quality control & certification
UK Accreditation Service

Quarrying
Mineral Products Qualifications Coun
Quarries Nat Jt Advy C'ee

R

Racing > Greyhound racing; Horseracing

Radiation
C'ee Med Aspects Radiation Envt

Ionising Radiation Health & Safety Forum
>+ Radiography & radiology

Radio > Broadcasting

Radio spectrum
Ofcom Spectrum Advy Bd
Office Communications

Radioactive substances
Administration Radioactive Substances Advy C'ee
Indl Pollution & Radiochemical Inspectorate
>+ Nuclear waste

Radiography & radiology
Central Advy C'ee Allied Health Professions
Health Professions Coun

Radon
Radon Coun

Railways
BRB Residuary
Directly Operated Railways
London & Continental Railways
Office Rail Regulation
Railway Heritage C'ee
Transport London Auth
>+ Passenger transport

Railways: health & safety
Rail Safety & Standards Bd
Railway Ind Advy C'ee
Transport Scotland

Rare diseases & disorders > Health: rare diseases & disorders

Rates
Land & Property Services
Valuation Tribunal England
Valuation Tribunal Wales
>+ Taxation

Reclamation > Recycling & reclamation

Records > Archives

Recreation > Sport & physical recreation

Recycling & reclamation
Advy C'ee Packaging
Local Auth Recycling Advy C'ee
London Waste & Recycling Bd

Red tape
Local Better Regulation Office

Refractories
C3HARGE
>+ Building products

Refrigeration
Air Conditioning & Refrigeration Ind Bd

Refugees
Coun Assisting Refugee Academics
Refugee Coun
Scottish Refugee Coun
Welsh Refugee Coun

Regional health bodies > NHS headings

Regional planning & development
Advantage West Midlands
Assn North East Couns
East England Devt Agency
East England Local Government Assn
East Midlands Counties

East Midlands Devt Agency
Indl Devt Advy Bd
Infrastructure Planning Cmsn
Local Government Yorkshire & Humber
London Devt Agency
North West Regional Leaders Bd
Northwest Regional Devt Agency
One North East
Planning Appeals Cmsn
Planning Inspectorate
South East England Couns
South East England Devt Agency
South West Couns
South West Regional Devt Agency
Welsh Indl Devt Advy Bd
West Midlands Couns
Yorkshire Forward
>+ Town & country planning

Regulation
Local Better Regulation Office

Regulators > specific industry eg Gas

Reinsurance > Insurance

Religion > Faith, specific faiths

Religious education
Catholic Educ Cmsn
Church England Bd Educ
Church & Society Coun
Coun Catholic Maintained Schools
Religious Educ Coun E&W
Scottish Jt C'ee Religious & Moral Educ

Removals
Removals Ind Ombudsman Scheme

Renal disease
Cardiovascular Diabetes Renal... Expert Advy Gp

Rents
Eastern Rent Assessment Panel
London Rent Assessment Panel
Midlands Rent Assessment Panel
Northern Rent Assessment Panel
Private Rented Housing Panel
Rent Assessment Panel NI
Residential Property Tribunal Service
Residential Property Tribunal Wales
Southern Rent Assessment Panel
Valuation Office Agency

Research & development > individual area of research

Respiratory diseases
Cardiovascular Diabetes Renal... Expert Advy Gp

Restaurants > Hotels & restaurants

Restraint techniques
Restraint Accreditation Bd

Resuscitation
Resuscitation Coun UK

Retail trade
Skillsmart Retail

Retirement
Scottish Pre Retirement Coun

Rheumatism > Arthritis & rheumatism

Rivers
Drainage Coun NI

Rivers Agency
Rivers & Fisheries Trusts Scotland

Road haulage > Logistics

Road safety
Parliamentary Advy Coun Transport Safety
Road Operators Safety Coun
Road Safety Advy Panel
Road Safety Coun NI

Roads
Highways Agency
Roads Service
Stdg Advy C'ee Trunk Road Assessment
Transport Scotland
UK Network Mgt Bd
UK Roads Bd
UK Roads Liaison Gp
>+ Street lighting

Roman Catholic organisations
Bishops Conference Scotland
Catholic Bishops Conf England & Wales
Catholic Educ Cmsn
Coun Catholic Maintained Schools

Romanies > Travellers

Roofing
Advy C'ee Roofsafety

Royal Air Force
Royal Air Force Museum
Royal Air Force Sports Bd

Royal estates
Crown Estate
Historic Royal Palaces
Royal Parks

Royal Marines > Armed forces

Royal Navy
Defence Nuclear Safety C'ee
Nat Maritime Museum
Nat Museum Royal Navy
>+ Armed forces

Rubber
Rubber Ind Advy C'ee

Rules of Court
Civil Procedure Rule C'ee
Court Session Rules Coun
Criminal Courts Rules Coun
Criminal Procedure Rule C'ee
Family Procedure Rule C'ee
Sheriff Court Rules Coun

Rural development
Action Communities Cumbria
Action Communities Rural Kent
Action Rural Sussex
Bedfordshire Rural Communities Charity
Buckinghamshire Community Action
Cambridgeshire ACRE
Cheshire Community Action
Cmsn Rural Communities
Community Action
Community Action Hampshire
Community Action Northumberland
Community Coun Berkshire

Community Coun Devon
Community Coun Shropshire
Community Coun Somerset
Community Coun Staffordshire
Community Devt Agency Hertfordshire
Community First
Community First Herefordshire & Worcestershire
Community Futures
Community Lincs
Cornwall Rural Community Coun
Dorset Community Action
Durham Rural Community Coun
Gloucestershire Rural Community Coun
Humber & Wolds Rural Community Coun
Isle Wight Rural Community Coun
Norfolk Rural Community Coun
Northamptonshire ACRE
Oxfordshire Rural Community Coun
Rural Action Derbyshire
Rural Action Yorkshire
Rural Community Action Nottinghamshire
Rural Community Coun Essex
Rural Community Coun Leics & Rutland
Rural Devt Coun
Rural Housing Advy Gp
Suffolk ACRE
Surrey Community Action
Tees Valley Rural Community Gp
Warwickshire Rural Community Coun

S

Safeguarding > **Children: welfare**

Safety in the workplace > **Health & safety**

Salaries (public sector)
Armed Forces Pay Review Body
NHS Pay Review Body
Office Manpower Economics
Police Negotiating Bd
Prison Service Pay Review Body
Review Body Doctors & Dentists Remuneration
School Support Staff Negotiating Body
School Teachers Review Body
Senior Salaries Review Body
>+ specific industry or occupation

Salmon
District Salmon Fishery Bds

Scholarships > **Commonwealth: scholarships;
Education: grants**

School curriculum > **Curriculum**

School food
School Food Trust

School rebuilding
Partnerships Schools

School support staff
Nat Advy Gp Professional Devt Children's Workforce
Schools
School Support Staff Negotiating Body
Trg & Devt Agency Schools

School trips
Coun Learning Outside Classroom

Schools > **Curricula for schools;   Education:
examinations / assessment**

Schools' inspection > **Education: standards**

Science
Bd Science
Coun Science & Technology
Defence Science & Technology Laboratory
Defence Scientific Advy Coun
Engg & Physical Sciences Res Coun
Nat Endowment Science Technology & Arts
Nat Museum Science & Industry
Parliamentary & Scientific C'ee
Res Couns UK
Science Advy Coun
Science Coun
Science & Technology Facilities Coun
Scottish Science Advy Coun
Semta
Welsh Scientific Advy C'ee
>+ Technology, & specific scientific applications

Scientific Advisory Committees
Administration Radioactive Substances C'ee
Advy C'ee Animal Feedingstuffs
Advy C'ee Antimicrobial Resistance
Advy C'ee Borderline Substances
Advy C'ee Dangerous Pathogens
Advy C'ee Hazardous Substances
Advy C'ee Microbiological Safety Food
Advy C'ee Novel Foods & Processes
Advy C'ee Pesticides
Advy C'ee Releases Envt
Advy C'ee Safety Blood Tissues & Organs
Advy Coun Misuse Drugs
Advy Gp Hepatitis
Air Quality Expert Gp
Animal Procedures C'ee
Bldg Regulations Advy C'ee
C'ee Carcinogenicity Chemicals Food...
C'ee Med Aspects Radiation Envt
C'ee Med Effects Air Pollutants
C'ee Mutagenicity Chemicals Food...
C'ee Radioactive Waste Management
C'ee Safety Devices
C'ee Toxicity Chemicals Food Consumer
Products...
Cmsn Human Medicines
Coun Science & Technology
Defence Nuclear Safety C'ee
Defence Scientific Advy Coun
Disabled Persons Transport Advy C'ee
Expert Advy Gp AIDS
Farm Animal Welfare Coun
Gen Advy C'ee Science
Gene Therapy Advy C'ee
Genetics & Insurance C'ee
Human Genetics Cmsn
Indl Injuries Advy Coun
Jt C'ee Vaccination & Immunisation
Nat Expert Panel New & Emerging Infections
Nuclear Res Advy Coun
Pesticide Residues C'ee
Regional Advy C'ee Communicable Disease
Control
Science Advy Coun
Scientific Advy C'ee Genetic Modification
Scientific Advy C'ee Nutrition

Scientific Pandemic Influenza Advy C'ee
Social Science Res C'ee
Spongiform Encephalopathy Advy C'ee
UK Advy Panel Healthcare Workers Infected
    Bloodborne Viruses
Veterinary Products C'ee
Veterinary Residues C'ee
Welsh C'ee Professional Devt Pharmacy
Welsh Dental C'ee
Welsh Med C'ee
Welsh Nursing & Midwifery C'ee
Welsh Optometric C'ee
Welsh Pharmaceutical C'ee
Welsh Scientific Advy C'ee
Welsh Therapies Advy C'ee
Working Gp Action Control Chemicals
Zoos Forum

Scottish Parliament > **Parliaments & assemblies**

Sea fisheries > **Fisheries**

Security industry
Jt Security Ind Coun
Nat Security Inspectorate
Nat Trg Inspectorate Professional Dog Users
Security Ind Auth
Security Systems & Alarms Inspection Bd

Security: national > **National security**

Security vetting
Defence Vetting Agency
Security Vetting Appeals Panel

Sentencing
Sentencing Coun

Service children's education > **Armed forces: children's education**

Sewerage > **Water: treatment & supply**

Sex equality > **Equal opportunity**

Sexually transmitted infections
Indep Advy Gp Sexual Health & HIV

Shareholders > **Institutional shareholders; Investment**

Sheriff courts (Scotland)
Sheriff Court Rules Coun

Ships: historic
Advy C'ee Nat Historic Ships

Shipwrecks
Advy C'ee Historic Wreck Sites
Corporation of Trinity House of Deptford Strond
Royal Cmsn Ancient & Historical Monuments
    Wales

Shooting
British Shooting Sports Coun

Single-parent families
Gingerbread

Skills
Alliance Sector Skills Couns
Asset Skills
CITB Construction Skills
Cogent
Creative & Cultural Skills
E Skills UK
Energy & Utility Skills
Financial Services Skills Coun

GoSkills
Government Skills
Improve
Institute Motor Industry
Lantra
Learning & Skills Devt Agency NI
Learning & Skills Improvement Service
Learning & Skills Network
Lifelong Learning UK
Momentum
Nat Apprenticeship Service
People First
Proskills UK
Semta
Skills Active
Skills Care & Development
Skills Devt Scotland
Skills Funding Agency
Skills Health
Skills Justice
Skills Logistics
Skillset
Standards Verification UK
Summit Skills
Ufi
UK Cmsn Employment & Skills
UK Skills

Skin treatments > **Dermatological products**

Small & medium size enterprises
Capital Enterprise
Small Business Trade Association Forum
UK Business Incubation

Smoking
Scientific C'ee Tobacco & Health

Social science research
Economic & Social Res Coun
Jt University Coun
Social Science Res C'ee

Social security benefits
Appeals Service NI
First Tier Tribunal Social Security & Child Support
Indep Review Service Social Fund
Office Social Security & Child Spt Cmsnrs NI
Social Security Advy C'ee
Social Security Agency

Social work & services
Belfast Health & Social Care Trust
Business Services Org
Care Coun Wales
Care Quality Cmsn
Care Tribunal
Central Personal Social Services Advy C'ee
First Tier Tribunal Care Standards
Gen Social Care Coun
Health & Social Care Bd
Jt University Coun
NHS Inf Centre
NI Health & Social Services Estates Agency
NI Social Care Coun
Northern Health & Social Care Trust
Office Social Services
Patient & Client Coun
Regulation & Quality Improvement Auth
Scottish Cmsn Regulation Care
Scottish Social Services Coun

Skills Care
Skills Care & Development
Social Work Inspection Agency
South Eastern Health & Social Care Trust
Southern Health & Social Care Trust
Western Health & Social Care Trust
>+ Voluntary service

Software > **Information technology**

Solicitors > **Law**

Space science & technology
Space Leadership Coun
UK Space Agency

Special education > **Children:
welfare; Education: special**

Spectrum > **Radio spectrum**

Speech therapy
Central Advy C'ee Allied Health Professions
Health Professions Coun
Welsh Therapies Advy C'ee

Spongiform Encephalopathy
Spongiform Encephalopathy Advy C'ee
Stakeholder Gp Current & Future Meat Controls

Sport & physical recreation
1st 4 Sport Qualifications
Army Sport Control Bd
Royal Air Force Sports Bd
Skills Active
Sport England
Sport & Recreation Alliance
Sport Scotland
Sports Coun NI
Sports Coun Wales
Sports Leaders UK
UK Anti Doping
UK Sport
>+ specific sport

Spying > **Communications interception;
Surveillance**

Stamps
Stamp Advy C'ee

Standards in public life
First Tier Tribunal Local Government Standards
England
Office Judicial Complaints
Parliamentary Cmsnr Standards
Public Standards Cmsnr Scotland

Statistics
NI Statistics & Res Agency
ScotStat
Statistics Advy C'ee
UK Statistics Auth

Steel
UK Certification Auth Reinforcing Steels

Street lighting
UK Lighting Bd

Strikes
Advy Conciliation & Arbitration Service
Central Arbitration C'ee
Indl Court

Structural safety
Stdg C'ee Structural Safety
>+ Building & construction; Civil engineering
Students: welfare
London Conf Overseas Students
Student Loans Company
UK Coun Intl Student Affairs

Submarines > **Royal Navy**

Subsidence
Coal Auth

Substance misuse > **Drugs: misuse**

Suicide
Nat Confidential Inquiry Suicide. . . Mental Illness

Surveillance
Office Surveillance Cmsnrs

Surveying
Land & Property Services
Ombudsman Services Property

Sustainable development > **Environment; Land
use**

Swimming pools
Pool Water Treatment Advy Gp

T

Take-overs
Panel Takeovers & Mergers

Taxation
Adjudicator's Office
Appeals Service NI
First Tier Tribunal Tax
HM Revenue & Customs
Office Tax Simplification
Tax Law Review C'ee
Upper Tribunal Tax & Chancery
>+ Customs & Excise

Tea
UK Tea Coun

Teachers
Gen Teaching Coun England
Gen Teaching Coun NI
Gen Teaching Coun Scotland
Gen Teaching Coun Wales
NI Teachers Coun
>+ **School support staff**

Teachers: heads
Nat College Leadership & Childrens Services

Teachers: pay & conditions of service
School Teachers Review Body

Teachers: training
Higher Educ Funding Coun Wales
Nat Advy Gp Professional Devt Children's
Workforce Schools
Office Standards Educ
Trg & Devt Agency Schools
Univs Coun Educ Teachers

Technology
Coun Science & Technology
Defence Science & Technology Laboratory

Defence Scientific Advy Coun
    Nat Endowment Science, Technology & Arts
    Parliamentary & Scientific C'ee
    Science Coun
    Science & Technology Facilities Coun
    > + Science

Telecommunications
    Advy C'ee England (Ofcom)
    Advy C'ee NI (Ofcom)
    Advy C'ee Scotland (Ofcom)
    Advy C'ee Wales (Ofcom)
    Communications Cmsn
    Communications Consumer Panel
    E Skills UK
    Major Energy Users' Coun
    Momentum
    Office Communications
    Office Telecommunications Ombudsman
    >+ Mobile telecommunications

Telecommunications equipment
    British Approvals Bd Telecoms

Telecommunications interception > Communications interception

Telephone services
    Phonepay Plus

Television
    British Broadcasting Corpn
    Channel Four Television Corpn
    Creative Scotland
    Office Communications
    S4C Auth
    Skillset

Television audiences > Audience research

Television (regional)
    Audience Coun England
    Audience Coun NI
    Audience Coun Scotland
    Audience Coun Wales
    Isle Man Film
    MG ALBA
    Scottish Highlands & Islands Film Cmsn

Tenants > Housing;   Rents

Territorial Army > Armed forces: reservists

Terrorist organisations
    Proscribed Orgs Appeals Cmsn

Textile industry > Clothing & textile industry

Theatre
    Conf Drama Schools
    Nat Coun Drama Trg
    Royal Nat Theatre
    Stdg Conf Drama Departments
    Theatres Trust

Third sector > Charities; Voluntary service

Timber > Wood

Tobacco > Smoking
Totalisator
    Horserace Totalisator Bd
Tourism
    British Tourism Devt C'ee
    Cumbria Tourism
    East England Tourist Bd
    East Midlands Tourism
    Failte Ireland
    Isle Man Tourist Bd
    Isles Scilly Tourist Bd
    Jersey Tourist Bd
    Lancashire & Blackpool Tourist Bd
    Merseyside Partnership
    NI Tourist Bd
    Northeast Tourism Advy Bd
    People First
    South West Tourism
    Tourism Ireland
    Tourism South East
    Tourism West Midlands
    Visit Britain
    Visit Chester & Cheshire
    Visit England
    Visit London
    Visit Manchester
    Visit Scotland
    Visit Wales
    Welcome Yorkshire
Town & country planning
    Architecture & Design Scotland
    BRE Trust
    Built Environment Forum Scotland
    Cmsn Architecture & Built Envt
    Design Cmsn Wales
    Ministerial Advy Gp
    Planning Appeals Cmsn
    Planning Inspectorate
    Planning Service
    >+ Regional planning & development
Toxic substances
    Advy C'ee Toxic Substances
Toys
    Nat Toy Coun
Trade > Exports
Trade marks > Patents & trade marks
Trade unions
    Certification Office Trade Unions...
    Indl Court
Trading standards
    First Tier Tribunal Consumer Credit
    Isle Man Office Fair Trading
    Office Fair Trading
Training > Employment; Skills
Transparency
    Public Sector Transparency Bd
Transplants > Organ transplantation
Transport
    London Couns Transport & Envt C'ee
    NI Transport Holding Company
    Parliamentary Advy Coun Transport Safety
    Road Operators Safety Coun

© CBD Research Ltd . Beckenham . Kent BR3 5JS . Tel 020 8650 6645 . Fax 020 8650 0768 . E-mail cbd@cbdresearch,com . www.cbdresearch.com

Transport Trg Services
>+ individual type of transport

Transsexuals
Gender Recognition Panel

Travellers
Advy Coun Educ Romany & Other Travellers

Treasure
Treasure Valuation C'ee

Trees
Tree Coun
>+ Forestry

Tribunals
Administrative Justice & Tribunals Coun
Appeals Service NI
First Tier Tribunal Claims Mgt Services
HM Courts & Tribunals Service
Insolvency Practitioners Tribunal
NI Courts & Tribunals Service
Tribunal Procedure C'ee
Upper Tribunal Administrative Appeals
>+ specific subjects eg Industrial tribunals

Tweed
Harris Tweed Auth

U

Ullans > **Ulster Scots**

Ulster Scots
North South Language Body
Ulster Scots Agency

Universities
C'ee Heads Univ Law Schools
Coun Validating Universities
Higher Educ Funding Coun England
Higher Educ Funding Coun Wales
Office Fair Access
Quality Assurance Agency Higher Educ
Scottish Advy C'ee Credit & Access

Urban regeneration
BRE Trust
Community Coun Berkshire
Gloucester Heritage
Homes & Communities Agency
Ilex (Londonderry)
Milton Keynes Partnership C'ee
New East Manchester
Newport Unlimited
North Northants Devt Company
Nottingham Regeneration
Regen WM
Tendring Regeneration
Thurrock Thames Gateway Devt Corpn
West Northamptonshire Development Corporation

Urban Regeneration Companies
Gloucester Heritage
New East Manchester

USA
British-North American C'ee
Marshall Aid Commemoration Cmsn
US-UK Educl Cmsn

V

Vacant property
Treasury Solicitors Department

Vaccination & immunisation
Biologicals & Vaccines Expert Advy Gp
First Tier Tribunal Social Security & Child Support
Jt C'ee Vaccination & Immunisation

Valuation > **Land valuation; Rates**

Value Added Tax (VAT) > **Customs & Excise**

Vehicle licensing > **Driver & vehicle licensing**

Vehicles > **Motor vehicles**

Ventilation > **Air conditioning**

Veterinary products
Animal Medicines Trg Regulatory Auth
Veterinary Medicines Directorate
Veterinary Products C'ee

Veterinary science
Animal Health & Veterinary Laboratories Agency
C'ee Mutagenicity Chemicals Food...
Moredun Res Inst
Veterinary Residues C'ee

Victims of crime
Cmsn Victims & Witnesses

Video > **Film & video**

Vitamins > **Nutrition**

Vocational education & training > **Further & higher education**

Voluntary service
Cmsn Compact
London Couns Grants C'ee
London Voluntary Service Coun
Nat Coun Voluntary Orgs
NI Coun Voluntary Action
Scottish Coun Voluntary Orgs
Volunteering Devt Scotland
Volunteering England
Wales Coun Voluntary Action
>+ Social work & services

Volunteer reserve forces
Nat Employer Advy Bd
>+ Armed forces

W

War graves & memorials
C'wealth War Graves Cmsn
Scottish Nat War Memorial

War museums
Imperial War Museum
Nat Museums Scotland

War pensions
Central Advy C'ee Pensions & Compensation
First Tier Tribunal War Pensions & Armed Forces
Compensation
Pensions Appeal Tribunals Scotland
Service Personnel & Veterans Agency

Warehousing > Logistics

Waste management
    C'ee Radioactive Waste Management
    Energy & Utility Skills
    London Waste & Recycling Bd
    Waste Mgt Ind Trg & Advy Bd

Water: accident prevention
    Nat Water Safety Forum

Water: treatment & supply
    Consumer Coun Water
    Drinking Water Inspectorate E & W
    Drinking Water Inspectorate NI
    Drinking Water Quality Regulator Scotland
    Energy & Utility Skills
    Major Energy Users' Coun
    NI Auth Utility Regulation
    NI Water
    Scottish Water
    Water Appeals Cmsn
    Water Ind Cmsn Scotland
    Water Services Regulation Auth

Waterways > Canals; Rivers

Weather > Climate

Weighing > Measurement

Welfare services > Social work & services

Welsh
    S4C Auth
    Welsh Books Coun
    Welsh Language Bd
    WJEC

Welsh Assembly Government > Parliaments & assemblies

Windows (energy efficiency)
    British Fenestration Rating Coun
    >+ Energy efficiency

Wine
    Wine & Spirit Educ Trust

Women
    Medicines Women's Health Expert Advy Gp
    Nat Coun Women GB

Woodland > Forestry

Wool
    British Wool Marketing Bd

X

X-rays > Radiography & radiology

Y

Youth justice
    Youth Justice Agency NI
    Youth Justice Agency E & W

Youth organisations
    British Youth Coun
    C'wealth Youth Exchange Coun
    Nat Coun Voluntary Youth Services
    Nat Youth Agency
    Youth Coun NI
    YouthNet

Z

Zoology
    Zoos Forum

© CBD Research Ltd . Beckenham . Kent BR3 5JS . Tel 020 8650 7745 . Fax 020 8650 0768 . E-mail cbd@cbdresearch.com . www.cbdresearch.com